# TRACES ON THE RHODIAN SHORE

It is said of the Socratic philosopher, Aristippus, so Vitruvius wrote in the preface to the sixth book of his *De architectura*, that being shipwrecked and cast on the shore of Rhodes and seeing there geometrical figures on the sand, he cried out to his companions, "Let us be of good hope, for indeed I see the traces of men." After making his observation, Aristippus departed for the city of Rhodes (another unique creation of man) and there in its gymnasium talked philosophy.

Frontispiece of David Gregory's edition of Euclid's *Opera* (Oxford, 1703) illustrating the shipwreck of Aristippus as related by Vitruvius in the Preface to Book VI of his *De architectura*.

CLARENCE J. GLACKEN

# Traces on the Rhodian Shore

NATURE AND CULTURE IN WESTERN THOUGHT
FROM ANCIENT TIMES TO THE END OF
THE EIGHTEENTH CENTURY

UNIVERSITY OF CALIFORNIA PRESS
Berkeley, Los Angeles, London

University of California Press
Berkeley and Los Angeles, California
University of California Press, Ltd.
London, England
Copyright © 1967, by
The Regents of the University of California
ISBN: 0-520-02367-6 (cloth)
ISBN: 0-520-03216-0 (paper)
Library of Congress Catalog Card Number: 72-95298
Printed in the United States of America

7   8   9   10

The paper used in this publication meets the minimum
requirements of American National Standard for
Information Sciences—Permanence of Paper for Printed
Library Materials, ANSI Z39.48-1984. ∞

*To my wife, Mildred, and my children, Karen and Michael*

# Preface

In the history of Western thought, men have persistently asked three questions concerning the habitable earth and their relationships to it. Is the earth, which is obviously a fit environment for man and other organic life, a purposefully made creation? Have its climates, its relief, the configuration of its continents influenced the moral and social nature of individuals, and have they had an influence in molding the character and nature of human culture? In his long tenure of the earth, in what manner has man changed it from its hypothetical pristine condition?

From the time of the Greeks to our own, answers to these questions have been and are being given so frequently and so continually that we may restate them in the form of general ideas: the idea of a designed earth; the idea of environmental influence; and the idea of man as a geographic agent. These ideas have come from the general thought and experience of men, but the first owes much to mythology, theology, and philosophy; the second, to pharmaceutical lore, medicine, and weather observation; the third, to the plans, activities, and skills of everyday life such as cultivation, carpentry, and weaving. The first two ideas were expressed frequently in antiquity, the third less so, although it was implicit in many discussions which recognized the obvious fact that men through their arts, sciences, and techniques had changed the physical environment about them.

In the first idea, it is assumed that the planet is designed for man alone, as the highest being of the creation, or for the hierarchy of life with man at the apex. The conception presupposes the earth or certain known parts of it to be a fit environment not only for life but for high civilization.

The second idea originated in medical theory. In essence, conclusions were drawn by comparing various environmental factors such as atmospheric conditions (most often temperature), waters, and geographical situation with the different individuals and peoples characteristic of these environments, the comparisons taking the form of correlations between environments and individual and cultural characteristics. Strictly speaking, it is incorrect to refer to these early speculations as theories of climatic influence, for there was no well-developed theory of weather and climate; it would be more correct to refer to them as theories of airs, waters, and places in the sense in which these terms are used in the Hippocratic corpus. Although environmentalistic ideas arose independently of the argument of divine design, they have been used frequently as part of the design argument in the sense that all life is seen as adapting itself to the purposefully created harmonious conditions.

The third idea was less well formulated in antiquity than were the other two; in fact, its full implications were not realized until Buffon wrote of them, and they were not explored in detail until Marsh published *Man and Nature* in 1864. Like the environmental theory, it could be accommodated within the design argument, for man through his arts and inventions was seen as a partner of God, improving upon and cultivating an earth created for him. Although the idea of environmental influences and that of man as a geographic agent may not be contradictory—many geographers in modern times have tried to work out theories of reciprocal influences—the adoption by thinkers of one of these ideas to the exclusion of the other has been characteristic of both ancient and modern times; it was not perceived, however, until the nineteenth century that the adoption of one in preference to the other led to entirely different emphases. One finds therefore in ancient writers, and in modern ones as well, ideas both of geographic influence and of man's agency in widely scattered parts of their work without any attempt at reconciling them; since Greek times the two ideas have had a curious history, sometimes meeting, sometimes being far apart.

The main theme of this work is that, in Western thought until the end of the eighteenth century, concepts of the relationship of human culture to the natural environment were dominated—but not exclusively so—by these three ideas, sometimes by only one of them, sometimes by two or even the three in combination: Man, for example, lives on a divinely created earth harmoniously devised for his needs; his physical qualities such as skin and hair, his physical activity and mental stimulation are determined by climate; and he fulfills his God-given mission of finishing the creation, bringing order into nature, which God, in giving him mind, the eye, and the hand, had intended that he do. This group of ideas and certain subsidiary ideas which gathered around them were part of the matrix from which in modern times the social sciences have emerged; the latter of course have deep roots as well in the history of theology, ethics, political and social theory, and philosophy. In Western civilization these three ideas have played an important role in the attempt to understand man, his culture, and the natural environment in which he lives. From the questions they have posed have come the modern study of the geography of man.

One does not easily isolate ideas for study out of that mass of facts, lore, musings, and speculations which we call the thought of an age or of a cultural tradition; one literally tears and wrenches them out. There is nothing disembodied about them, and the cut is not clean. They are living small parts of complex wholes; they are given prominence by the attention of the student.

These simple truths introduce a more difficult problem. Where and when does one stop? Let me give some examples. Everyone recognizes that a striking shift in the attitude toward nature occurred in the Latin Middle Ages during the twelfth and thirteenth centuries. The designed world of that era was more complex than was that of the early Church Fathers, and it bore a lighter load of symbolism. More attention was given to everyday matters and to secondary causes. But in exploring this theme one quickly becomes involved in realism versus nominalism, in modern ideas concerning the origins of science, in changes in religious art such as the portrayal of the Crucifixion, the Ascension, and the Virgin and Child, in the role of the Franciscan order in nature study, in the implications of Etienne Tempier's condemnation of 1277, and in the more realistic approaches to the study of botany—and indeed of the human form. These subjects comprise another work; yet they are suggested by themes in this one.

Galileo—to take a second illustration—pushed aside secondary qualities in his methodology. It proved to be the correct way to make discoveries in theoretical science. This procedure, which could have cleared the way for a purposive control over nature through applied science, contributed less to the development of natural history, whose students found it hard to simplify the variety and individuality of life which were clearly apparent to the senses. Smells and colors were important. In the eighteenth century Buffon in his criticism of Descartes realized the limitations of abstract thought. Natural history requires description, study of detail, of color, smell, environmental changes, of the influence of man whether his acts are or are not purposive. Modern ecology and conservation also need this kind of examination, for many of their roots lie in the old natural history. So we have another book contrasting the history of methodology in physics with that of natural history and biology, noting the obvious fact that teleology continued as a working scientific principle far longer in the latter than it did in physics. We should contrast also the purposive control over nature through applied science with the unlooked for, perhaps unconscious and unperceived, changes that men perpetually make in their surroundings.

Large related bodies of thought thus appear, at first like distant riders stirring up modest dust clouds, who, when they arrive, reproach one for his slowness in recognizing their numbers, strength, and vitality. One thinks of the history of ideas concerned with gardens, sacred landscapes, and nature symbolism.

Only rarely can one look at a landscape modified in some way by man and say with assurance that what one sees embodies and illustrates an attitude toward nature and man's place in it. Landscape painting presents similar difficulties. What indeed are we to make of Pieter Bruegel the Elder's *Fall of Icarus*? An exception, in my opinion, is the history of the garden, whether it is English, Chinese, or Italian. In gardens, one can almost see the embodiment of ideas in landscapes. Is art imitating nature, or is nature opposed to art? Is the garden like a lesson in geometry, are its lawns well raked, or does it suggest soft rolling meadows? And what does it say about the attitudes men should have not only to their surroundings but to themselves? But this theme would require yet another book; one can see the possibilities in the writings of Siren and in Clifford's *A History of Garden Design*.

In the world as a whole, there are few more inviting themes for the historian of attitudes toward the earth than the role of the sacred. Today the best illustrations come from non-Western cultures, but the history of Western civilization is rich in them too. One thinks of Scully's study of Greek sacred architecture and its landscapes, the possible origins of Roman centuriation in cosmic speculation, the celestial city and the heavenly Jerusalem, cathedral siting in the Middle Ages, sacred groves, and nature symbolism. Indeed, gardens, sacred landscapes, religious and esthetic attitudes toward environmental change by man, entice one into studies with profound human meaning which are not easily exhausted.

There are many illustrations in this work of that separation between man and nature which occurs so frequently in Western thought, and conversely of the union of the two as parts of live and indivisible wholes. The dichotomy has plagued the history of geographical thought (for example, the distinction, which many would now abandon, between the natural and the cultural landscape) and contemporary ecological discussions concerned with man's disturbance of the balance of nature. Essays confidently begin with assertions that man is part of nature—how could he be otherwise?—but their argument makes sense and gains cogency only when human cultures are set off from the rest of natural phenomena. I cannot claim to have clarified this difficult subject. In Western thought, it is too involved in other histories of ideas—in the philosophy of man, in theology, in the problem of physical and moral evil.

Did the distinction between man and nature begin in primordial times when man saw himself, so clearly like the animals in many respects, but able nevertheless to assert his will over some of them? Was it enshrined in Western thought by the Jewish teaching that man, sinful and wicked as he is, is part of the creation but distinct from it too because he is the one living being created in the image of God? Was it in the ancient consciousness of artisanship that men felt themselves superior to other living and nonliving matter? Prometheus was considered to be a supreme craftsman and was worshipped as such, particularly in Attica.

Is another phase of the problem the distinction between the ways in which men have lived their lives, some in the country, some in the town or the city, the former closely identified with what is natural, the latter with the artificial, the creation of man? Did not Varro say that "divine nature made the country, but man's skill the towns," illustrating the old distinction between nature and art? Did this deep-lying conviction gain added strength and incontrovertible proof through the theoretical accomplishments of seventeenth century science and the practical mastery to which they led, awarenesses so vividly expressed in the writings of Leibniz? What the Arab scientists, the medieval alchemists, Bacon, Paracelsus, Descartes, Leibniz himself had hoped for was now being realized: man had reached the point at which he could be confident of his progressive ability to control nature.

My first awareness of the existence and importance of the history of ideas came to me as a young Berkeley undergraduate when, over thirty years ago, I took Professor Teggart's course on the Idea of Progress. Today I still remember these lectures vividly and possess the classroom notes. Frederick J. Teggart was a man of enormous learning and a superlative lecturer. The *Prolegomena to History*, the *Processes of History*, the *Theory of History*, his review of Spengler's *Decline of the West*, opened up fields of scholarship I scarcely knew existed.

To the reader it must seem that the present work is exclusively a product of the library. Actually, the early stimulus to study these ideas came also from personal experience and from observations which pointed to the role of ideas and values in understanding the relationships of culture to the environment. During the depression years, as I worked with resident and transient families on relief, with migratory farm workers who had come from the Dust Bowl, I became aware—as did countless thousands of others—of the interrelationships existing between the Depression, soil erosion, and the vast migration to California.

In 1937 I spent eleven months traveling in many parts of the world. The yellow dust clouds high over Peking, the dredging of pond mud along the Yangtze, the monkeys swinging from tree to tree at Angkor Vat, a primitive water-lifting apparatus near Cairo, the Mediterranean promenade, the goat curd and the carob of Cyprus, the site of Athens and the dryness of Greece, the shrubs, the coves, the hamlets, and the deforestation of the Eastern Mediterranean, the shepherds of the Caucasus, the swinging swords of Central Asians in the markets of Ordzhonikidze, the quiet farms of Swedish Skåne— these and many other observations made me realize as part of my being the commonplace truth that there is a great diversity both of human cultures and of the physical environments in which they live. It is the difference between knowing about the midnight sun and spending a summer night on the Arctic circle. One is continually asking questions about the circumstances which stimulate human creativity, about the effect of religious belief, about the custom and tradition which men have soaked into their soils. And although I have used abstract words like "man" and "nature" as a convenience, it is really human culture, natural history, the relief of the land that I mean. Phrases like "man and nature" are useful as titles, as a shorthand to express far more complex sets of ideas.

In 1951, living in three small Okinawan villages and studying their way of life, I could see the profound importance of the Chinese family system, altered of course by the Japanese and the Okinawans themselves, and the influence of the system of inheritance on the use and the appearance of the land. In such circumstances, it seems natural to see differences in traditions concerning culture and the environment, to see the ideas developed in Western civilization merely as a few of many possibilities.

Finally during a year spent in Norway in 1957, visiting its old towns, especially those of the Gudbrandsdal, its farms, an occasional *seter*, and reading about the history of its forests, I saw more clearly and vividly how deep is the European interest in the history of landscapes, the Norwegian interest in the history of farms, the *seter*, place names—in all aspects of rural life. The water-driven saws from the eighteenth century at the open-air museums at Bygdøy in Oslo and at Elverum on the Glomma made me read the literature on environmental change in the Middle Ages with new attentiveness because this important invention was first illustrated in the *Album* of Villard de Honnecourt in the thirteenth century.

In many places one can see evidences of a relationship between religious attitudes toward the earth and the appearance of a landscape, of limitations imposed by a local environment, of the historical depth of changes made in the physical environment by human culture.

When I started on this work in the mid-1950's, I had merely intended to write an introduction to a work based on a doctoral thesis, "The Ideas of the Habitable World," which covered the period from the eighteenth century to the present. Later I decided to give fuller consideration to classical antiquity and to the Middle Ages. Finally, what was originally intended to be a short sally became a major expedition because I became convinced that the origins and earlier histories of these ideas were important and made modern attitudes toward the earth more meaningful; they could also suggest possible comparative studies with Indian, Chinese, and Muslim thought.

I had intended, moreover, to bring the history down to the present, feeling there was a great advantage in showing the sweep of these ideas over two millennia. It was a bitter disappointment, therefore, to make the decision about two years ago to stop at the end of the eighteenth century. The task I felt was now beyond my individual powers. The thought of the nineteenth and twentieth centuries requires a different kind of treatment and properly should be a separate work. The volume of material is too great, but more than volume is involved. The materials are more complex, they are more specialized, and they are widely scattered through many disciplines. In another work I hope to write on certain nineteenth and twentieth century themes in a way consistent with the capacity of a single individual, for despite the indispensability of symposia and other types of cooperative scholarship I still feel there is a place for individual interpretation of broad trends in the history of thought.

Furthermore, I was convinced—allowing for the artificiality of dividing thought by centuries or periods—that in the time span from classical antiquity roughly to the end of the eighteenth century there was a coherent body of thought gathered about these ideas. Buffon, Kant, or Montesquieu, I think, would have found the classical world strange, but the gulf between their times and classical times would have been less than that between 1800 and 1900.

A historian of ideas must go where his nose leads him, and it often leads him into chilly but not inhospitable regions whose borders are patrolled by men who know every square foot of it. Although I can lay no claim to being a specialist in a particular century or in the classical or medieval periods, my own specialization in the history of geographic thought has forced me to study many periods because their contributions are so great they cannot be ignored. Problems like this must be faced by anyone who wishes to go beyond the narrowest limits. A historian of geographic ideas (especially in the earlier periods) who stays within the limits of his discipline sips a thin gruel because these ideas almost invariably are derived from broader inquiries like the origin and nature of life, the nature of man, the physical and biological characteristics of the earth. Of necessity they are spread widely over many areas of thought.

Whenever possible I have read the original sources, and only in exceptional cases have I referred to the huge volume of secondary literature. I intend here no condescension to these secondary sources, because we often owe newer insights to their scholarship. My general rule has been to cite those to which I am indebted and others which are of interest to, but somewhat peripheral to, my themes. For the most part, therefore, I have made my own interpretations; in some cases the aid of expert knowledge of the text, expositions of the meaning of certain words at a particular time, and the *Quellenuntersuchungen* of the classical period are indispensable; examples are Reinhardt on Posidonius and Panaetius, Lovejoy and Armstrong on Plotinus, Klauk on the geography of Albert the Great. In some cases, especially in chapter 7, I have quoted documents published in secondary works mainly because the originals—often in French or German town and provincial archives, in rare books, or in charters —were unavailable to me.

Because of the great number of thinkers who have discussed the ideas whose history I am concerned with here, a few words should be said about the problem of selection. My general rule has been to select those works which made an important contribution to the idea in question and those which, while showing little or no originality, introduced the idea into other fields or revealed either continuity in thought or the continuing importance of the idea. The *Airs, Waters, Places* of the Hippocratic corpus makes an original contribution to environmental theory; Aristotle does not, but he used environmental ideas in political and social theory. Failure to make a selection would have made my work tedious beyond endurance, for in these fields there are many repetitious scrolls written with different quills. I have also given generous space to a significant thinker at the expense of lesser contemporaries. In the Middle Ages the problem of selection in discussing the idea of design is particularly difficult because it is mentioned by virtually all thinkers; I am convinced that my emphasis on St. Basil, Origen, St. Augustine, Albert the Great, St. Thomas, and Raymond Sibiude is reasonable. In the Renaissance, Bodin's handling of environmental theories is far more thorough than that of any of his contemporaries; in fact, he is often their source. In the eighteenth century Buffon speaks with greatest authority on the agency of man in changing nature, Hume and Kant on teleology in nature, Montesquieu on environmental questions.

This work is concerned only with the development of these ideas in Western civilization; it is thus parochial in the sense that this civilization has furnished unique molds for them. There is no ecumenical thought, although the literature on the scientific method may be an exception. Various great traditions—Indian, Chinese, Muslim among them—have flourished, often in isolation, often interacting with and influencing one another. The Western tradition—its science, technology, critical scholarship, its deep-seated interest in theology, philosophy, political and social theory, and geography—is the most varied and cosmopolitan, partly because it has received and absorbed so much from the others.

A few remarks are in order concerning the frequent use of certain words. "Nature," "physical environment," "design," "final causes," "climate," and other words and expressions which appear in this work have a long history, accumulating different and often vague meanings in the course of time. In the literature, therefore, one cannot find precision where it is not. Often the meaning of words is assumed as being obvious and needing no explanation.

The word "nature," as everyone knows, has many meanings in Greek and Latin and in modern languages. With all of its failings it is a grand old word. When Huxley wrote *Evidence as to Man's Place in Nature* (1863), he discussed man's place in the evolutionary scale of being. When Marsh wrote *Man and Nature* in 1864 he described the earth as modified by human action. Sometimes the word is synonymous with the physical or natural environment; sometimes it has a more philosophic, religious, theological aura than these more matter-of-fact terms express. Occasionally it attains grandeur as in Buffon's reference to it as "le trône extérieur de la magnificence Divine."

In the literature, the words "natural" and "physical" environment have often been used interchangeably. They correspond to *Umwelt* and *milieu*, their use being confined to physical and biological phenomena. They are general terms for the organic and inorganic realms of earth including those changed by man. They are never used in the sense social scientists often use the word "environment," that is, the cultural milieu (upper-class quarter, slums, neighborhoods).

In general "man" is used as a convenient word meaning "mankind"; "culture," "society," however, are the more exact terms. "Man" is so abstract that it conceals the complexities and intricacies which the other words suggest.

For long periods, "climate," "clime," were used in the original Greek sense as a translation of κλίμα; Montesquieu in the *Spirit of Laws* uses it in this sense. In his work on the climate and soil of the United States (English translation, 1804), Count Volney remarks upon the shift in meaning of "climate" which was then taking place. The literal meaning, he said somewhat inaccurately, is a degree of latitude. Since, however, generally speaking, countries are hot or cold according to latitude, the second idea became intimately associated with the first, and "the term climate is now synonymous with the habitual temperature of the air."

Many terms lose precision because of long usage. Generally speaking, "argument from design" has been used interchangeably with a theologically based teleology and with the "doctrine of final causes," although such usages are hard to defend. It has frequently been pointed out that the word "causes" in "final causes" means something entirely different from the usual meaning of "cause" as in "efficient cause." Similarly, physico-theology and natural theology have often been used synonymously with the theologically based teleological view of nature; both terms have also served to distinguish their subject matter and concepts from those of revealed religion. Still others have distinguished between physico-theology and natural theology, including in the latter more discussion of man, leaving to the former illustrations of design in the physical and biological world. William Derham, however, contrasted physico-theology with astro-theology, the former being concerned with proofs of the divine wisdom based on earthly processes, and the latter, from the cosmic order. Historically these expressions are closely related to formulations of proofs for the existence of God by St. Thomas Aquinas, Kant, and others.

It must be admitted that there is no escape from these terms; the confusion exists in the literature. Over eighty years ago L. E. Hicks marched bravely into the swamps; he disapproved of using the terms "argument from design" and the "teleological view of nature" synonymously, because teleology was not the only possible course open to the Creator; he could also establish an order by design. Hicks did not claim that the older teleological view of nature declined *pari passu* with the expansion of the newer scientific view, but he did identify teleology with the older theology, and order with science. The distinction here is one between teleology with emphasis on purpose (not only of every entity in nature but of nature itself) and an order based on natural law without considering the question of purpose. For the latter concept, he proposed the term eutaxiology after the Greek word εὐταξία, meaning good order and discipline. The teleological view led to an emphasis on end or purpose, adaptation of means to ends; the eutaxiological, on order and plan. So far as I know eutaxiology died in infancy for lack of care.

The expressions "web of life" and "balance" or "equilibrium in nature" have often been used interchangeably. They are metaphors suggesting the existence of intricate interrelationships in nature and delicate adjustment among its constituent parts. One sees likenesses with the spinners of webs, the other is derived from classical physics. Perhaps the "web" calls attention to interrelationships more than does "balance" or "equilibrium," which places the emphasis on delicacy of adjustment, but I have never seen such distinctions expressed.

Finally, I should like to say a word about the introduction to Part I, which may seem disproportionately long. It is intended to serve two purposes: to provide the immediate background for the parallel histories of the three ideas in the classical period and to make more intelligible the thought of later periods which, with all the changes enforced by new conditions and circumstances, still rests solidly, at least in part, on classical foundations.

# Acknowledgments

I wish to express my deep appreciation to the Institute of Social Sciences, University of California, Berkeley, for its long support of this work and to acknowledge with particular gratitude the many kindnesses of its director, Professor Herbert Blumer.

It has been my good fortune to be a member of a department during the tenure of three chairmen, Carl Sauer, John Leighly, and James Parsons, whose own commitments to and sympathies for humanistic studies have been a continuing encouragement to me; these remarks also apply to my colleague, Paul Wheatley, who in addition has read parts of the manuscript and generously helped me in the interpretation and translation of several passages from classical and medieval Latin. Professor Lesley Simpson's translation of the Laws of Burgos opened up new vistas to me; his deep knowledge of the writings of the Conquest period made me realize how important many of the ideas discussed in this work were in the post-Columbian New World, even if these themes are too vast for exploration here. Since I first took undergraduate courses from her over thirty years ago, I have enjoyed the warm friendship of Margaret Hodgen; her incisiveness and her sensitivity to the history of ideas are once more in evidence in her *Early Anthropology in the Sixteenth and Seventeenth Centuries*, a masterly exposition of early modern conceptions of man and his culture. Her courageous scholarly career has been an inspiration to many of her students.

I am most grateful to my colleagues at the University, Professor John K. Anderson of the Classics Department for reading and criticizing the draft chapters on the classical period; Professor Bryce Lyon, formerly of the Department of History at Berkeley and now at Brown University, for the medieval period; Professor Kenneth Bock, Department of Sociology, for the modern period; and also to Mr. John Elston for the medieval period. The errors which remain are my own. The interest which Professor Clarence E. Palmer, Institute of Geophysics and Planetary Physics, University of California at Los Angeles, showed in this work was a source of great encouragement to me. I wish to acknowledge the helpful advice of Grace Buzaljko, of the University of California Press, and the suggestions by Gladys Castor in her careful copyediting of the text. For several years I have had the valuable assistance of Florence Myer; I cannot speak too highly of the conscientiousness, skill, and patience she has shown in typing the drafts and final copy of a long and difficult manuscript. My wife Mildred through the years has helped me in innumerable ways and has assisted in preparing the manuscript for the Press.

Furthermore, I wish to express my appreciation to Mr. Steve Johnson for doing the line drawings and for his skill and patience in suggesting through pictorial representation the abstract ideas with which the book is concerned. The reader may also be interested in learning that many of the drawings are broad adaptations of or have been suggested by the works of others. The drawing for chap. 1 was suggested by Isabelle's reconstruction of the interior of the Pantheon and reproduced in Rodenwaldt's *Die Kunst der Antike*; chap. 3, by Zeno Diemer's pictorial reconstruction of the intersection of five aqueducts southeast of Rome; chap. 4, by a miniature from the Geroevangelistary, Darmstadt Landesbibliotek, from Max Hauttmann, *Die Kunst des frühen Mittelalters*; for the introduction to Part II, by the view of the minster of Ste-Foy in Conques (Aveyron) from the same work; chap. 5, by a reproduction, "God as architect of the universe," from a Bible moralisée, Vienna, in von Simson, *The Gothic Cathedral*; chap. 6, by a figure in a pen drawing *ca.* 1200, depicting the air as an element of cosmic harmony, reproduced in the same work; chap. 7, by a drawing of a Benedictine, from R. P. Helyot, *Histoire des ordres religieux et militaires* (1792), Vol. 5; for the right panel of the drawing for the introduction to Part III, a detail from Theodor de Bry, *Americae pars quarta*, 1594, reproduced in Albert Bettex's *The Discovery of the World*, 131–132; chap. 8, by Joseph Anton Koch's painting, *Waterfalls near Subiaco*, Nationalgalerie, Berlin, reproduced in Marcel Brion, *Romantic Art*; chap. 9, from a diagram showing relationships of the four elements to the four qualities (source unknown to me); for the introduction to Part IV, by an engraving showing Bernard de Jussieu returning from a voyage to England in 1734 and bringing back two cedars of Lebanon in his tri-cornered hat, from Cap, *Le Muséum d'histoire naturelle*; chap. 11, by illustrations of microscopes and telescopes in Singer's *A History of Technology*, Vol. 3, pp. 634–635; chap. 12, by a frequently reproduced portrait of Montesquieu; chap. 14, by a page from the original edition of Buffon's *Des Époques de la Nature*, 1778; conclusion, by a detail from the frontispiece.

Books and articles relating to specific periods are cited in the notes of the appropriate chapter. I wish to acknowledge here, however, my indebtedness to certain works which cover longer time periods. Zöckler's two-volume *Geschichte der Beziehungen zwischen Theologie und Naturwissenschaft mit besondrer Rücksicht auf Schöpfungsgeschichte* (1877–1879) is a monumental study. Sympathetic himself to theologico-teleology, Zöckler's indefatigable thoroughness places all students of this general field in his debt. Hicks's little known and peppery work *A Critique of Design-Arguments* (with many quotations from original sources) reveals how lively, even in the eighties of the last century, were the advocates and critics of design. Franklin Thomas's *Environmental Basis of Society* (1925) I read many years ago, gaining from it my first insight into the sweep of environmental ideas from the classical period to the early twenties of this century. A great deal of work has been done in this century on the history of population theory, but it is largely confined to specific periods. Stangeland's work, "Pre-Malthusian Doctrines of Population" (1904), is still stimulating; he had many insights into the relationships between population theory and political and social theory, theology, and other disciplines. Lovejoy's *Great Chain of Being* (1948) has made an important segment of Western thought intelligible; especially valuable to me, *inter alia*, are his discussions of a hierarchy in nature, interpretations of man's place in it, and most of all, the principle of plenitude.

Lastly, I wish to express my appreciation to the following publishers who have granted permission to quote from works published by them. I am particularly grateful to the Harvard University Press and William Heinemann, Ltd., for their generosity in permitting extensive quotation from authors whose works are published in the Loeb Classical Library: Apollonius Rhodius, *Argonautica*; Aristotle, *Parts of Animals*; Cicero, *Academica, De fato, De oratore, De natura deorum, De republica*; Columella, *De re rustica*; Diodorus of Sicily; Galen, *On the Natural Faculties*; Greek Bucolic Poets; Hesiod, *The Homeric Hymns and Homerica*; Hippocrates, Vol. I, *Airs, Waters, Places* and *Ancient Medicine*, Vol. IV, *Nature of Man*; Horace, *The Odes and Epodes, Satires and Epistles*; Philo, *On the Creation*; Plato, *Timaeus, Critias*; Pliny, *Natural History*; Plutarch, *Moralia*, Vol. 4, "On the Fortune or the Virtue of Alexander," and Vol. 12, "Concerning the Face Which Appears in the Orb of the Moon"; Ptolemy, *Tetrabiblos*; Seneca, *Epistolae Morales*; Theophrastus, *Enquiry into Plants*; Tibullus, in *Catullus, Tibullus, and Pervigilium Veneris*; Xenophon, *Memorabilia* and *Oeconomicus*.

Selections from Arthur O. Lovejoy, *The Great Chain of Being*, copyright 1936 and 1964 by the President and Fellows of Harvard College, and from Arthur O. Lovejoy and George Boas, *Primitivism and Related Ideas in Antiquity*, are reprinted by permission of Harvard University Press, Cambridge, Mass.

Selections from *Émile; or, Education* by Jean Jacques Rousseau, translated by Barbara Foxley, Everyman's Library, E. P. Dutton & Co., New York, and Dent & Sons, Ltd., London, are reprinted with permission of the publishers.

Passages from *The Critique of Judgment* by Immanual Kant, translated from the German by James Creed Meredith, and from Lucretius, *De rerum natura libri sex*, translated from the Latin by Cyril Bailey, are reprinted with permission of the publishers, Clarendon Press, Oxford.

Selections from D. Winton Thomas, editor, *Documents from Old Testament Times*, Harper Torchbooks, The Cloister Library, New York, Harper and Brothers, 1961, and originally published by Thomas Nelson and Sons, Ltd., London, 1958, are reprinted with permission of the publishers.

Selections are reprinted with permission from the publishers from *Saint*

*Benedict* by Abbot Justin McCann, O.S.B., © 1958 Sheed & Ward, Inc., New York.

Lines from *Mediaeval Latin Lyrics* translated by Helen Waddell, Penguin Classics, Penguin Books, 1962, are reprinted by permission of Constable Publishers, London.

Quotations from Étienne Gilson, *History of Christian Philosophy in the Middle Ages*, © 1955 by Étienne Gilson, are reprinted with permission of Random House, Inc., New York.

Lines from Leibniz, *Selections*, edited by Philip P. Wiener, 1951, are reprinted with permission of Charles Scribner's Sons, New York.

Selections from *The Romance of the Rose* by Guillaume de Lorris and Jean de Meun, translated by Harry W. Robbins, copyright, ©, 1962, by Florence L. Robbins, are reprinted by permission of E. P. Dutton & Co., Inc.

The Scripture quotations in this publication are from the Revised Standard Version of the Bible, copyrighted 1946 and 1952, and from the Apocrypha, copyrighted 1957, by the Division of Christian Education of the National Council of Churches, and are used by permission.

CLARENCE J. GLACKEN

*Berkeley, California, 1966*

# Contents

PREFACE                                                                  vii

ACKNOWLEDGMENTS                                                          xvii

ABBREVIATIONS                                                            xxv


## PART ONE
## The Ancient World

INTRODUCTORY ESSAY                                                          3
    1. General Ideas, *3*  2. The Hellenistic Age and Its Characteristic Attitudes Toward Nature, *18*

I    ORDER AND PURPOSE IN THE COSMOS AND ON EARTH                 35
    1. Theology and Geography, *35*  2. Beginnings of the Teleological View of Nature, *39*  3. Xenophon on Design, *42*  4. The Artisanship of God and of Nature, *44*  5. Aristotle's Teleology of Nature, *46*  6. Misgivings of Theophrastus, *49*  7. Stoic Views of Nature, *51*  8. On the Nature of of the Gods, *54*  9. The Development of Antiteleological Ideas in the Epicurean Philosophy, *62*  10. Plutarch, the Hermetical Writings, and Plotinus, *74*

2    AIRS, WATERS, PLACES                                            80
    1. Greek Sources of the Environmental Theory, *80*  2. The Hippocratic Treatise "Airs, Waters, Places," *82*  3. Herodotus' Interest in Custom and Environment, *88*  4. Location Theories and Hippocratic Influences, *91*  5. The Problem of Cultural Diversity, *95*  6. Ethnology and Environment in Selected Roman Writings, *100*  7. Strabo's Eclecticism, *103*  8. Vitruvius on Architecture, *106*  9. Critiques of Philo and Josephus, *110*  10. Environmental and Astrological Ethnology, *111*  11. Servius on Virgil, *114*

3    CREATING A SECOND NATURE                                        116
    1. On Artisanship and Nature, *116*  2. Antigone and Critias, *119*  3. Environmental Change in the Hellenistic Period, *122*  4. General Descriptions of Environmental Change, *127*  5. Theophrastus on Domestication and Climatic Change, *129*  6. Rural Life and the Golden Age, *130*  7. Is the Earth Mortal?, *134*  8. Interpreting Environmental Changes Within a Broader Philosophy of Civilization, *138*  9. Conclusion, *147*

4    GOD, MAN, AND NATURE IN JUDEO-CHRISTIAN
    THEOLOGY                                                        150
    1. Introduction, *150*  2. The Creation, Sin, and Dominion, *151*  3. Man in the Order of Nature, *154*  4. Earthly Environment, *155*  5. Attitudes

Toward Nature and the Wisdom Literature, *157*   6. Romans 1:20, *161*
7. Contemptus Mundi, *162*   8. Key Ideas and the Nature of Their Influence, *163*

# PART TWO
# The Christian Middle Ages

INTRODUCTORY ESSAY                                                         171

5   THE EARTH AS A PLANNED ABODE FOR MAN                                  176
1. The Early Patristic Period, *176*   2. Origen, *183*   3. Philo and the Hexaemeral Literature, *187*   4. St. Basil and the Hexaemeral Literature, *189*
5. St. Augustine, *196*   6. The Legacy of the Early Exegetical Writings,
*202*   7. Continuities from Boethius to the Theophany of John the Scot,
*208*   8. St. Bernard, St. Francis, and Alan of Lille, *213*   9. Ferments from
the Mediterranean, *218*   10. Averroes and Maimonides, *220*   11. Frederick II on Falcons, *224*   12. Albert the Great, *227*   13. St. Thomas Aquinas, *229*   14. St. Bonaventura and Ramon Sibiude, *237*   15. Secular Views
of Nature, *240*   16. The Condemnations of 1277, *248*   17. Conclusion, *250*

6   ENVIRONMENTAL INFLUENCES WITHIN A DIVINELY
    CREATED WORLD                                                        254
1. Introduction, *254*   2. Classical Echoes, *257*   3. Remarks Introducing a
More Systematic Thought, *262*   4. Albert the Great, *265*   5. The Encyclopedist, Bartholomew of England, *271*   6. St. Thomas to the King of
Cyprus, *273*   7. East and West: Otto of Freising and Giraldus Cambrensis,
*276*   8. Roger Bacon: Geography and Astrological Ethnology, *282*
9. Gunther of Pairis, *285*   10. Conclusion, *286*

7   INTERPRETING PIETY AND ACTIVITY, AND THEIR
    EFFECTS ON NATURE                                                    288
1. Introduction, *288*   2. The Christian Religion and the Modification of
Nature, *293*   3. Interpreting Man's Dominion Over Nature, *295*   4. Philosophies of Work, *302*   5. Animals—Wild and Domestic, *309*   6. Purposeful Change, *311*   7. An Earth to Change, *313*   8. Forest Clearance in
Northwest Europe, *318*   9. The Uses of the Forest, *320*   10. Custom and
Use, *322*   11. The Great Age of Forest Clearance, *330*   12. Alpine Valleys, *341*   13. Soils, *345*   14. Hunting, *346*   15. Lesser Themes of Environmental Change, *347*   16. Conclusion, *348*

# PART THREE
# Early Modern Times

INTRODUCTORY ESSAY                                                         355
1. Introduction, *355*   2. The Age of Discovery, *357*   3. Sebastian Münster,
*363*   4. José de Acosta, *366*   5. Giovanni Botero, *368*

8   PHYSICO-THEOLOGY: DEEPER UNDERSTANDINGS OF
    THE EARTH AS A HABITABLE PLANET                            375
    1. Introduction, *375*   2. Final Causes and Their Critics, *376*   3. Deteriora-
    tion and Senescence in Nature, *379*   4. George Hakewill's *Apologie*, *382*
    5. Quarrels Over the Ancients and Moderns and the Mechanical View of
    Nature, *389*   6. The Cambridge Platonists, *392*   7. Design and the Mul-
    tiplication and Dispersion of Mankind, *398*   8. Fantasy, Cosmology, and
    Geology and What They Led To, *406*   9. Ray and Derham on the Wis-
    dom of God, *415*   10. Conclusion, *426*

9   ENVIRONMENTAL THEORIES OF EARLY MODERN TIMES           429
    1. Introduction, *429*   2. On Leon Battista Alberti, *430*   3. General Ques-
    tions Regarding Climate and Culture, *432*   4. On Jean Bodin in General,
    *434*   5. His Divisions of the Earth, *436*   6. Bodin's Use of the Humors,
    *438*   7. Other Problems, *441*   8. Further Applications of Environmental
    Theories, *447*   9. On National Character, *451*   10. On Melancholy, *456*
    11. Conclusion, *458*

10  GROWING CONSCIOUSNESS OF THE CONTROL OF NATURE          461
    1. Introduction, *461*   2. Renaissance Philosophies of Technology, *462*
    3. Francis Bacon, *471*   4. Optimism of Seventeenth Century Writings,
    *475*   5. Silva and Fumifugium, *484*   6. The French Forest Ordinance of
    1669, *491*   7. Conclusion, *494*

PART FOUR

# Culture and Environment in the Eighteenth Century

INTRODUCTORY ESSAY                                            501

11  FINAL STRENGTHS AND WEAKNESSES OF
    PHYSICO-THEOLOGY                                          504
    1. Introduction, *504*   2. On Leibniz, *505*   3. Natural History, *508*   4.
    Population and Geography in the Divine Order, *512*   5. On Final Causes
    in Nature, *517*   6. Tout Est Bien, *521*   7. Hume, *524*   8. Kant and Goethe,
    *530*   9. Herder, *537*   10. Humboldt, *543*   11. Conclusion, *548*

12  CLIMATE, THE MOEURS, RELIGION, AND GOVERNMENT           551
    1. Introduction, *551*   2. Fontenelle, Chardin, and Du Bos, *552*   3. Ar-
    buthnot on the Effects of Air, *562*   4. On Montesquieu in General, *565*
    5. Climatic Theory in the *Esprit des Lois*, *568*   6. Another Side of Mon-
    tesquieu, *576*   7. Critics of Climatic Theory, *581*   8. Climate and Na-
    tural History, *587*   9. Building on the Foundations of Montesquieu,
    Buffon, and Hume, *592*   10. On William Falconer, *601*   11. New Culti-
    vations: Robertson and America, *605*   12. New Cultivations: The For-
    sters and the South Seas, *610*   13. Conclusion, *620*

13  ENVIRONMENT, POPULATION, AND THE
    PERFECTIBILITY OF MAN                                     623
    1. Introduction, *623*   2. On the Populousness of Ancient and Modern Na-
    tions, *625*   3. Progress and the Limitations of the Environment, *632*

4. On the Malthusian Principle of Population in General, *637*   5. Conceptions of Progress, Theology, and the Nature of Man in the Malthusian Doctrine, *644*   7. Conclusion, *653*

14   THE EPOCH OF MAN IN THE HISTORY OF NATURE                    655
1. Introduction, *655*   2. Opportunities for Comparison, *656*   3. Climatic Change and the Industry of Man, *658*   4. Count Buffon: On Nature, Man, and the History of Nature, *663*   5. Count Buffon: On Forests and Soils, *668*   6. Count Buffon: On Domestications, *672*   7. Count Buffon: On Natural and Cultural Landscapes, *679*   8. The American Pandora's Box, *681*   9. "In a Sort, They Began the World a New," *685*   10. Nature and Reason Harmonized, *693*   11. The Torrents of the Var, *698*   12. The Society Islands: A Union of Nature and Art, *702*   13. Conclusion, *704*

CONCLUSION                                                        706
BIBLIOGRAPHY                                                      715
INDEX                                                             749

# Abbreviations

| | |
|---|---|
| *AAAG* | *Annals of the Association of American Geographers* |
| *Act. SS. O. B.* | Iohannes Mabillon, ed., *Acta sanctorum Ordinis s. Benedicti in saeculorum classes distributa.* NA |
| *Aen.* | Virgil, *Aeneid* |
| *Agr.* | Tacitus, *Agricola* |
| *AHR* | *American Historical Review* |
| *Alsat. dipl.* | Schoepflin, *Alsatia diplomatica.* NA |
| *AMA* | Grand et Delatouche, *L'Agriculture au Moyen Âge* |
| *ANF* | The Ante-Nicene Fathers. *Translations of the Writings of the Fathers down to* A.D. *325* |
| *Ann.* | Tacitus, *Annals* |
| *Ant.* | Sophocles, *Antigone* |
| *Anth.* | Stobaeus, *Anthrologion* |
| Arist. | Aristotle |
| Ath. | Athenaeus, *The Deipnosophists* |
| *BDK* | *Bibliothek der Kirchenväter* |
| *Ben.* | Seneca, *On Benefits* |
| Beuchot | *Oeuvres Complètes de Voltaire*, ed. Beuchot |
| *Bus.* | Isocrates, *Busiris* |
| *Cassiod.* | Cassiodorus |
| *CEHE* | *Cambridge Economic History of Europe* |
| Cic. | Cicero |
| *Comm. in Verg. Aen.* | *Servii Grammatici Qui Feruntur in Vergilii Carmina Commentarii* |
| *Conf.* | St. Augustine, *Confessions* |
| *Cons. of Phil.* | Boethius, *Consolation of Philosophy* |
| *Contr. Cels.* | Origen, *Contra Celsum* |
| *Cyr..* | Xenophon, *Cyropaedia* |
| *De civ. dei* | St. Augustine, *De civitate dei*; *The City of God* |
| *De div. nat.* | John the Scot, *De divisione naturae* |
| De Maulde | *Étude sur la Condition Forestière de l'Orléanais au Moyen Âge et à la Renaissance* |
| *De oper. monach.* | St. Augustine, *De opere monachorum*; *Of the Work of Monks* |
| *De Princ.* | Origen, *De Principiis* |
| *De prop. rerum* | Bartholomew of England, *De proprietatibus rerum* |
| *De Trin.* | St. Augustine, *De Trinitate*; *On the Holy Trinity* |

| | |
|---|---|
| *DNL* | Albert the Great, *De natura locorum* |
| *Doc. Hist.* | Lovejoy and Boas, *Primitivism and Related Ideas in Antiquity. A Documentary History of Primitivism and Related Ideas* |
| *DPE* | Albert the Great, *De causis proprietatum elementorum liber primus* |
| Du Cange | Du Cange, *Glossarium mediae et infimae latinitatis* |
| *EB* | *Encyclopaedia Britannica* |
| *EL* | Montesquieu, *Esprit des Lois*; *Esprit des Loix*; *Spirit of Laws* |
| *EN* | Buffon, "Des Époques de la Nature" |
| *Enn.* | Plotinus, *Enneads* |
| *Ep. mor.* | Seneca, *Epistolae morales* |
| *Etym.* | Isidore of Seville, *Etymologiarum libri xx* |
| *FGrH* | Jacoby, *Die Fragmente der Griechischen Historiker* |
| Fr. | Fragment |
| *Fragm. phil. Graec.* | Mullach, *Fragmenta philosophorum graecorum* |
| *GAE* | Bailey, *The Greek Atomists and Epicurus* |
| Geo. Lore | Wright, *The Geographical Lore of the Time of the Crusades* |
| *Germ.* | Tacitus, *Germania* |
| *GR* | *Geographical Review* |
| *HCPMA* | Etienne Gilson, *History of Christian Philosophy in the Middle Ages* |
| Hdt. | Herodotus |
| Hes. | Hesiod |
| *Hex. Lit.* | Frank E. Robbins, *The Hexaemeral Literature* |
| Hippoc. | Hippocrates |
| *Hist. Lang.* | Paul the Deacon, *History of the Langobards*; *De Gestis Langobardorum* |
| *HN* | Buffon, *Histoire Naturelle, Générale et Particulière*, 15 vols., 1749–1767 |
| *HNM* | Buffon, *Historie Naturelle des Minéraux* 5 vols., in-4°, 1783–1788 |
| *HNO* | Histoire *Naturelle des Oiseaux* 9 vols., 1770–1783 |
| *HNS* | Buffon, *Supplements à l'Histoire Naturelle*, 7 vols., 1774–1789 |
| *HT* | Singer *et al.*, *A History of Technology* |
| Huffel | *Economie Forestière* |
| *HW* | Rostovtzeff, *The Social and Economic History of the Hellenistic World* |
| Isoc. | Isocrates |
| *JHI* | *Journal of the History of Ideas* |

| | |
|---|---|
| *JWH* | *Journal of World History* |
| *Lex. Man* | Maigne D'Arnis, *Lexicon Manuale ad Scriptores, Mediae et Infimae Latinitatis* |
| *LP* | Montesquieu, *Lettres Persanes*; *Persian Letters* |
| Lucr. | Lucretius, *De natura rerum* |
| *Mem.* | Xenophon, *Memorabilia* |
| *Met.* | Ovid, *Metamorphoses* |
| *Metaph.* | Aristotle, *Metaphysics* |
| *Mon. Ger. Hist.* | *Monumenta Germaniae Historica* |
| *Mon. Ger. Hist.:* | *Monumenta Germaniae Historica: Capitularia* |
| *Capit. Reg. Franc.* | *Regum Francorum* |
| *Mon. Germ. Dip.* | Pertz, ed., *Monumenta Germaniae Historica Diplomatum Imperii* |
| Montal. | Montalembert, *The Monks of the West, from St. Benedict to St. Bernard* |
| *MR* | William L. Thomas, ed., *Man's Role in Changing the Face of the Earth* |
| NA | Cited but not available to the writer |
| *Nat. D* | Cicero, *De natura deorum* |
| *Nat. Fac.* | Galen, *On the Natural Faculties* |
| *NH* | Pliny, *Natural History* |
| *NPN* | *A Select Library of Nicene and Post-Nicene Fathers of the Christian Church* |
| *Obs.* | Johann Reinhold Forster, *Observations Made During a Voyage Round the World* |
| *OCD* | *The Oxford Classical Dictionary* (Oxford: Clarendon Press, 1957 [1949]) |
| *OCSA* | *Oeuvres Complètes de St. Augustin* (Latin and French) |
| *Oct.* | *The Octavius of Minucius Felix* |
| *Oec.* | Xenophon, *Oeconomicus* |
| *Oes. W.* | *Oesterreichische Weisthümer* |
| *P. Cairo Zen.* | Edgar, *Zenon Papyri* |
| *PAPS* | *Proceedings of the American Philosophical Society* |
| *PG* | Migne, *Patrologiae cursus completus, Series graeca* |
| *Phys.* | *Physics* |
| *PL* | Migne, *Patrologiae cursus completus, Series latina* |
| *PMLA* | *Publications of the Modern Language Association* |
| Przy. | Przywara, *An Augustine Synthesis* |
| *PSP* | Kirk and Raven, *The Presocratic Philosophers* |
| *PW* | *Paulys Real-Encyclopädie der classischen Altertumswissenschaft* |
| *Rep.* | Cicero, *Republic* |

| | |
|---|---|
| *RSV* | *Revised Standard Version of the Bible* |
| *SCG* | Thomas Aquinas, *On the Truth of the Catholic Faith. Summa Contra Gentiles* |
| Schwappach | *Handbuch der Forst- und Jagdgeschichte Deutschlands* |
| Sen. | Seneca |
| Soph. | Sophocles |
| SS | Forster, *Sämmtliche Schriften* |
| *ST* | Thomas Aquinas, *Summa Theologica* |
| *TAPS* | *Transactions of the American Philosophical Society* |
| *Tetrabib.* | Ptolemy, *Tetrabiblos* |
| Theophr. | Theophrastus |
| Thuc. | Thucydides |
| *Tim.* | Plato, *Timaeus* |
| USDA | U. S. Dept. of Agriculture |
| Vitr. | Vitruvius, *De architectura*; *The Ten Books on Architecture* |
| *Vorsokr.* | Diels, *Die Fragmente der Vorsokratiker* |
| *VRW* | Forster, *A Voyage Round the World* |
| Xen. | Xenophon |

O Lord, how manifold are thy works!
In wisdom hast thou made them all;
the earth is full of thy creatures.

*Psalm 104:24*

I hold that Asia [Minor] differs very widely from Europe in the nature of all its inhabitants and all of its vegetation. For everything in Asia grows to far greater beauty and size; the one region is less wild than the other, the character of the inhabitants is milder and more gentle. The cause of this is the temperate climate, because it lies towards the east midway between the risings of the sun, and farther away than is Europe from the cold.

HIPPOCRATES,
*Airs, Waters, Places*, xii

We enjoy the fruits of the plains and of the mountains, the rivers and the lakes are ours, we sow corn, we plant trees, we fertilize the soil by irrigation, we confine the rivers and straighten or divert their courses. In fine, by means of our hands we essay to create as it were a second world within the world of nature.

CICERO,
*De Natura Deorum*, II, 60

# PART ONE

# The Ancient World

# Introductory Essay

### 1. General Ideas

What is most striking in conceptions of nature, even mythological ones, is the yearning for purpose and order; perhaps these notions of order are, basically, analogies derived from the orderliness and purposiveness in many outward manifestations of human activity: order and purpose in the roads, in the grid of village streets and even winding lanes, in a garden or a pasture, in the plan of a dwelling and its relation to another.

The Sumerian theologian, for example, assumed an order in the cosmos, created and since maintained by a pantheon of "living beings, manlike in form but superhuman and immortal," who, invisible to human eyes, govern the cosmos according to law. Each of these superhuman living beings was thought to be in charge of a particular component of the cosmos (heaven, the sun, the sea, a star, and so forth). On earth these beings performed similar duties for "natural entities such as river, mountain, and plain; cultural entities such as city and state, dike and ditch, field and farm; even implements such as the pickax, brickmold, and plow." This theology apparently was based on the analogy of human society. Men had created cities, palaces, temples; without their continuing care, they would fall in decay, and cultivated lands would become like deserts. Therefore the cosmos must also be controlled by living beings, but they are stronger and more effective because their tasks are far more complex.[1]

Such an outlook may be in the background of the idea of a divinely designed earth, that divine power is inseparable from an order of nature. Aristotle said that our ancestors had handed down in mythical form traditions that the celestial bodies are gods "and that the divine encompasses the whole of nature."[2] The earth may be created for man alone, or for all life, even if (as for Job) the purpose is neither apparent nor discoverable by him.

The idea that there is a continuous interaction between man and his environment—man changing it and being influenced by it—also has its mythological antecedents, but its full development belongs basically, I think, to rational thought, because such a conception requires a sense of history. The Sumerian thought the civilization of which he was a part—its institutions, cities, towns, farms, and so on—had been more or less the same from the beginning,

> from the moment the gods had planned and decreed it to be so, following the creation of the universe. That Sumer had once been desolate marshland with but few scattered settlements, and had only gradually come to be what it was after many generations of struggle and toil, marked by human will and determination, man-laid plans and experiment and diverse fortunate discoveries and inventions—such thoughts probably never occurred even to the most learned of the Sumerian sages.[3]

In such myths the gods often are doing what humans do. In the myths of Sumer there is activity, change, creativity. Enki brings order to the earth and arranges for its cultivation; he pours water into the beds of the Tigris and the Euphrates; he stocks them with fish, setting up laws for the sea (the Persian Gulf) and the wind; he creates cereals, he opens "the holy furrows," he entrusts the plow and yoke to the god of canals and ditches, the pickax and the brickmold to Kabta, the god of bricks; he lays foundations of houses, stables, sheepfolds, fills the valley with animals. Of this myth emphasizing the agricultural character of the region and its dependence on water, Moscati says "it is dominated by the specific conception of order as inseparably bound up with existence, so that 'create' and 'set in order' are synonymous."[4]

This passage concerned with origins includes a description of a creative act largely in terms of a sensible husbandman, describes natural phenomena which

---

[1] Based on Kramer, *History Begins at Sumer*, p. 78.

[2] *Metaph.*, Bk. Lambda, 8, 1074b.

[3] Kramer, "Sumerian Historiography," *Israel Exploration J.* 3 (1953), pp. 217–232, ref. on p. 217.

[4] Kramer, *History Begins at Sumer*, pp. 97–98, including quotations and analysis; Moscati, *Face of the Ancient Orient*, p. 34.

influence life, and the primordial ordering of the environment to make it useful. Enki's acts suggest the theme of God's care for the world so dramatically expressed in the Hymn to the Sun and in the 104th Psalm.

In the myths of many peoples environmental and natural forces affect men; they are personified as are Enlil and Enki. These notions of order and purpose, of divine activity in creating habitable places with their fields and canals for man are the mythical antecedents, I think, from which there emerged in historical time rational speculation about the relation of man to his environment, just as Hippocratic medicine emerged from and was a rejection of an older medicine based on the cult of Aesculapius, whose lore, derived from observation and experience, however, was a rich prelude to the Hippocratic practice of medicine.[5]

These three ideas—of a designed earth, of the influence of the environment on man, and of man as a modifier of the environment—were, however, often modified and enriched by other theories relating to culture growth and to the nature of the earth. The most important of them were the principle of plenitude, interpretations of cultural history, ideas regarding the effects of human institutions (such as religion and government), and the organic analogy applied both to the growth and decline of nations and peoples and to the earth itself. Let us examine each of these briefly.

The origin of the principle of plenitude—the term is Lovejoy's—has been traced by him to the *Timaeus* of Plato. If one asks "*How many* kinds of temporal and imperfect beings must this world contain?" the answer is "*all* possible kinds. The 'best soul' could begrudge existence to nothing that could conceivably possess it, and 'desired that all things should be as like himself as they could be.'" Even if Plato in the *Timaeus* is speaking only of living things or of animals, "with respect to these, at least, he insists upon the necessarily complete translation of all the ideal possibilities into actuality." Plato's "Demiurgus acted literally upon the principle . . . that it takes all kinds to make a world." In stating the principle, Lovejoy says he makes

a wider range of inferences from premises identical with Plato's than he himself draws; i.e., not only the thesis that the universe is a *plenum formarum* in which the range of conceivable diversity of *kinds* of living things is exhaustively exemplified, but also any other deductions from the assumption that no genuine potentiality of being can remain unfulfilled, that the extent and abundance of the creation must be as great as the possibility of existence and commensurate with the productive capacity of a "perfect" and inexhaustible Source, and that the world is the better, the more things it contains.[6]

[5] Sarton, *A History of Science. Ancient Science through the Golden Age of Greece,* pp. 331–333, and the references there cited. Sarton discusses lustral bathing, incubation and its accompanying dreams in the cult of Aesculapius, and the important role of the herb collectors and the diggers.

[6] Lovejoy, *The Great Chain of Being,* pp. 50–52.

The principle of plenitude thus presupposes a richness, an expansiveness of life, a tendency to fill up, so to speak, the empty niches of nature; implicit in it is the recognition of the great variety of life and perhaps its tendency to multiply. When the principle of plenitude was fused with the Aristotelian idea of continuity, this richness and fecundity of all life was seen as manifesting itself in a scale of being from the lowest to the highest forms, and revealing itself in a visible order of nature.[7]

In the course of this work, we shall frequently see evidence that this richness, diversity, and fullness of life was recognized as an important principle in the interpretation of nature. In natural history, the principle reached its perfection in Count Buffon's work; it is implicit—with concepts of balance and harmony in nature—in early ecological theory. It seems to be fundamental to Malthus' theory of population and his emphasis on fertility. It is significant also that—from premises remote indeed from Plato's or from those Lovejoy derived from him—modern ecologists in stating the scientific case for conservation have said that the more rich and varied life is, the more stable is the ecosystem.[8]

Even in antiquity some thinkers viewed cultural development in terms of a series of stages from a presumed remote origin to the present, a view that implied that cultures could be understood with only casual references to the physical environment; the chief emphasis was on man, his mind, his senses, his techniques, his inventiveness, which, in the acquisition of the arts and sciences, led him from one stage to the next. Although the idea that all cultures go through an ideal series of stages experienced its greatest development after the age of discovery, one finds suggestive hints of the comparative or historical method in Thucydides, Plato's *Laws*, Dicaearchus, Varro, and Vitruvius. Proofs were adduced from observations of contemporary or historical peoples representing various stages of development. In his βίος Ἑλλάδος, Dicaearchus, the pupil of Aristotle, had (according to Varro) first suggested the idea of a cultural development from a pastoral to an agricultural stage.[9] The theory was unhistorical because stages were substituted for events; in postulating a conjectural history of the stages through which a people or an institution

[7] Lovejoy, *op. cit.*, pp. 52–62, points out that Aristotle rejected the principle but that the Aristotelian idea of continuity later was fused with it, that the principle becomes coherent and organized with Neoplatonism. See the index *sub nomine* for the subsequent history of the principle.

[8] See Elton, *The Ecology of Invasions by Animals and Plants*, pp. 143–153, 155; Fosberg, "The Island Ecosystem," Fosberg, ed., *Man's Place in the Island Ecosystem*, pp. 3–5; Bates, *The Forest and the Sea*, p. 201.

[9] Bock, *The Acceptance of Histories*, has a brief discussion of the idea in classical times, pp. 43–55. See also, Teggart, *Theory of History*, pp. 87–93 and *passim*. Varro, *On Farming*, II, i, 3–5. See also, Martini, "Dikaiarchos, 3," *PW*, Vol. 5, cols. 546–563, and Warmington, "Dicaearchus," *OCD*, p. 275. For further discussion of D, see chap. 3, sec. 7.

evolved, it neglected the changes in the physical environment made by specific people at specific times, and ignored the fact that different peoples have lived in different physical environments.

In addition to these theories of culture growth, there were the all-embracing theories of cyclical change and degeneration from a golden age. The idea of a cyclical growth in the life of nations and states, following the analogy of the life cycle of an organism, as well as the idea of eternal recurrence, was common in antiquity.[10] The organic analogy becomes important to our theme when it is applied, as Lucretius applied it, to the earth itself: it would grow weary with age and would die like any other mortal. The constancy of nature throughout time was denied, and a decline in the fertility and bounty of nature was to be expected as a matter of course. Echoes of this idea, and rebuttals of it, are found well into the eighteenth century. The notion of a degeneration from a golden age also had implications insofar as the earth as a habitable environment was concerned, for one characteristic of the golden age was the fertility of its soils, which provided ample food spontaneously and without human intervention—in sharp contrast with the toil required to glean a living from the soils of the contemporary age.

Occasionally in the writings of the Greek and Roman thinkers, statements were made regarding the effects of place and situation in forming the character of a people, ideas which were partly environmentalistic, partly cultural in their emphasis: the effect of physical isolation in producing the bravery and hardiness of rude and uncultivated peoples distant from the influences of civilization; the harmful influences of a maritime location with the ease of entry of undesirable foreign customs; the effects of government, of religion, of law, and of social institutions.

The questions which the Greeks asked concerning man and the earth were not isolated nor were they divorced from the problems of everyday life. They were asked because they were related to inquiries ranging from abstract theories regarding the origins of the earth and of man to the practical techniques of farming. Greek theories of medicine and ethnology (itself a product of

---

[10] The best source is Lovejoy and Boas, *Primitivism and Related Ideas in Antiquity*. The work, with pertinent excerpts and translations from the classical writings, includes a masterly analysis by Lovejoy on ideas of primitivism, social change, the golden age, etc., in antiquity. The literature dealing with the idea of cycles in antiquity is extensive; the following works will acquaint the reader with the leading advocates of these theories: Apelt, *Die Ansichten der griechischen Philosophen über den Anfang der Cultur*; Billeter, *Griechische Anschauungen über die Ursprünge der Kultur*; Gilbert, *Die meteorologischen Theorien des griechischen Altertums*; Seeliger, "Weltalter," in Roscher, ed., *Ausführliches Lexikon der griechischen und römischen Mythologie.* VI, cols. 375–430, and "Weltschöpfung," *ibid.*, cols. 430–505. Apelt deals primarily with the cyclical theory. Billeter's is an excellent short analysis with many references to the sources and to the older literature. Seeliger's articles are fundamental.

travel and exploration) found their earliest extensive exposition in the writings
of the Hippocratic school of medicine and in the histories of Herodotus. The
medical tradition, self-consciously shedding earlier beliefs in the divine origin
of disease, sought rational explanations for the existence of both health and
disease, explanations which called for consideration, among other factors, of
the nature and direction of winds, the effects of swamps and damp places,
the relation of sunlight and of the sun's position in the heavens to the proper
siting of houses and villages, and which, by extension, encompassed investigation of the effects of "airs, waters, and places" on national character.[11] Early
Greek literature—both the works which have survived and those which have
been lost except for fragments—reveals a deep interest in the customs and
characteristics of peoples: the Greek dramatists, like Aeschylus and Aristophanes, the histories of Herodotus, and even the Hippocratic corpus. Travel
and exploration, the early attempt by Anaximander to map the inhabited
world, the gathering of lore about behavior, food habits, cultural preferences
(so conspicuous in Herodotus)—these were the sources of knowledge and
observation from which abstract generalizations were derived.[12] The classic
comparisons between the Egyptians living in a desert fertilized by the Nile,
the nomadic Scythians on the bleak plains of southern Russia, and the mainland Greeks and those of Ionia in the temperate climate of summer drought
and winter rain of the Mediterranean shore, lent credence to the belief that
racial and cultural differences were caused by climate.[13]

The speculations of the Ionian philosophers regarding the basic composition
of matter, the manner in which the present order of the cosmos had come into
being, the doctrine of the four elements and the humors also prepared the
way for wide-ranging speculations regarding the earth and man's relation to
it. An important step was taken by Anaximander (born *ca.* 610 or 609 B.C.),
who rejected the single-element theories (that fire, air, or water was the basic
element), postulating instead an eternal and unchanging substance, the
ἄπειρον, "the boundless," or in Kahn's words, "a huge, inexhaustible mass,

[11] On Greek medicine and the Hippocratic corpus, see Sarton, *op. cit.*, (see n. 5,
above), pp. 331–383. These chapters contain exhaustive references to the classical sources
and to the modern literature on the subject.
[12] On the map: Agathemerus I, i, and Strabo, Bk. I, chap. I, 11; Herodotus IV, 36. In
Kirk and Raven, *PSP*, pp. 103–104 and discussion. See the chapters on traders and
craftsmen, citizens and foreigners, and slaves, in Ehrenberg, *The People of Aristophanes*,
pp. 113–191.
[13] On Greek ethnology, cultural theories and similar matters, see Cary, *The Geographic Background of Greek and Roman History* (some references to theories in addition to geographical reconstruction); Glover, *Herodotus* (much more attention to
other writers than the title implies); Myres, "Herodotus and Anthropology," in R. R.
Marett, ed., *Anthropology and the Classics*; Sikes, *The Anthropology of the Greeks*
(still a wise and impressive work); Trüdinger, *Studien zur Geschichte der griechisch-
römischen Ethnographie* (short but excellent and with many references to the sources).

stretching away endlessly in every direction."[14] It was not identified with any one of the commonly recognized elemental forms.[15] It had no origin, it was indestructible, its motion was eternal. "A consequence of this motion is the 'separation' of particular substances."[16] Order is characterized by a struggle of the opposites: "out of those things whence is the generation for existing things, into these again does their destruction take place, according to what must needs be; for they make amends and give reparation to one another for their offense, according to the ordinance of time."[17] The interaction of opposites—the coldness of air or mist and the heat of fire, the dryness of earth and the wetness of water—"provides the clue to the process whereby an ordered world comes into being out of the boundless unity."[18] Anaximander's philosophy is an early attempt to understand the nature of—and to account as well for—the diversity of substances of which the sensible world clearly is composed.[19] Anaximander's cosmology represents the structure of the universe as being an order, a κόσμος, a universe governed by law; it does not appear, however, to be a teleological conception.[20]

The formulation of the doctrine of the four elements by Empedocles (*ca.* 492–432 B.C.) of Acragas (Agrigentum) in Sicily was of decisive importance in many disciplines. The doctrine of the four roots (the word *element* being of later usage) is one of the most influential physical theories ever formulated.[21] With some revisions (like Aristotle's addition of aether to make a fifth), it

[14] Kahn, *Anaximander and the Origins of Greek Cosmology*, p. 233. The true sense of ἄπειρος is "what cannot be passed over or traversed from end to end," p. 232.

[15] Kahn, *op. cit.*, p. 163, comments that it is an anachronism to apply the doctrine of the four elements to Anaximander's times.

[16] Zeller, *Outlines of the History of Greek Philosophy*, p. 44.

[17] Simplicius *Phys.* 24, 13 = Diels Vorsokr. 12 A 9. See text and translation of the fragment, Kahn, p. 166; another version in Kirk and Raven, *PSP*, p. 105; cf. 117.

[18] Cornford, *Principium sapientiae*, p. 163.

[19] See Cornford, *op. cit.*, on Anaximander's system, pp. 159–186. Cornford says the older historians of philosophy thought the Ionians were interested only in finding the one substance of which all things consist. "But if we look at the systems themselves, the question they answer is different: How did a manifold and ordered world arise out of the primitive state of things?" p. 159. See also his discussion of Aristotle on Anaximander (*Phys.* 204 b 27), p. 162. It should not be thought that the elements fire, water, air, earth were discoveries of the philosophers; as Gilbert says, awareness of them was deeply imbedded in folk belief. (*Die meteorologischen Theorien des griechischen Altertums*, p. 17.) The question for the philosophers was the manner in which the existence of these supposed elements could be reconciled with theories of the composition of the universe and the order in it.

[20] On the philosophical significance of the opposites in Greek thought, see Kahn, *op. cit.* (see n. 14 above), pp. 126–133; on their origins in Greek thought, pp. 159–163.

[21] Sarton, *op. cit.* (see n. 5 above), p. 247; on his medical influence, p. 249. See also Gilbert, *op. cit.* (see n. 10 above), pp. 105–124, and on his biology, pp. 336–346. For another side of E. see Cornford, *op. cit.*, pp. 121–124. See Kirk and Raven, *PSP*, esp. Fr. 6 (where Zeus stands for fire, Hera for earth, Hades for air, Nestis for water), p. 323, and fragment 17, pp. 326–327. Empedocles calls them ῥιζώματα. See also discussion pp. 327–331.

was the basis of much of Greek science and of medieval interpretations of nature (for example, St. Francis' *Canticle of Brother Sun*); in an applied form it dominated much of the thinking in chemistry, soil theory, practical agriculture, and physical theory well into the eighteenth century.[22]

Empedocles names four elements—earth, air, water, and fire—as the basic substances upon which two other existences—love the unifying, hate the divisive—react, conceiving of these, like the elements themselves, as being corporeal.[23] Every element of which the world is composed has its counterpart in the human body. This is a hint of the theory of humors and of the doctrine of correspondences between the elements of physical nature and those of the human body, a doctrine later expanded in the enormous literature concerned with the relation of the macrocosm of the universe to the microcosm of man.

Implicit in the doctrine of the elements was the idea of opposites (powers like hot, cold, wet, dry, by which one element acted on another). In a Mediterranean climate, it would be natural to associate hot with dry and cold with moist. In fact, to Aristotle the opposites were the true elements.[24] The elements were eternal and imperishable, change occurring from their mixing and separation. Although the idea that the universe is composed of elements is a very ancient one and had been much discussed in Miletus, Empedocles' accomplishment was not that he discovered the four elements nor that he replaced single-element theories with them, but that he confined the number to four; his decisive role was "to crystallize attention on the four primary forms, and thus to replace a fuller Milesian series by the canonical tetrad."[25] The Greek theory of elements, with the ideas of opposites, may well have been based on observation: conflicts in daily life, the vigor of life, and the dynamic interplay of conflicting forces.[26]

Since the human body is composed of the same elements as are all other natural phenomena, the substances of which it is composed would be analogous to water, air, fire, and earth, although obviously they, in the form of humors, did not exist in the human body in their external forms. The humors of the

---

[22] Sarton, *op. cit.* (see n. 5 above), p. 247.

[23] Sambursky, *The Physical World of the Greeks*, pp. 31–33; see also Bailey, *GAE*, pp. 28–31.

[24] *Metaph.* IV, 1. On Aristotle and the elements, Kahn, *op. cit.* (see n. 14 above), p. 129; Kirk and Raven, *PSP*, pp. 330–331; Ross, *Aristotle*, pp. 105–107. Kahn's work is of great interest to the history of geography, especially physical geography. The doxography, bringing together many early theories of physical causation, is an illuminating background to Aristotle's *Meteorologica*. Among many topics discussed by Kahn are the classic doctrine of the four elements, pp. 121–126; the history of the idea of the elements, pp. 134–159, with illuminating histories of the Greek words ἀήρ and αἰθήρ, particularly in the period roughly from Homer and Hesiod to the flowering of the Milesian school; the history of the word ἄπειρον and Anaximander's concept of it. Of equal interest is Sambursky's *Physical World of the Greeks*.

[25] Kahn, *op. cit.* (see n. 14 above), p. 150; see also p. 155.

[26] See Kahn, *op. cit.* (see n. 14 above), p. 133.

body correspond to the elements of which the macrocosm is composed: air, consisting of the qualities of hot and moist, is represented in the body by the blood; fire, a mixture of hot and dry, by bile; water, cold and moist, by phlegm; and earth, a mixture of cold and dry, by black bile or melancholy. The commonest complaints of the Greeks, chest troubles and malaria, gave evidences of these humors: phlegm, blood (hemorrhaging in fevers), yellow bile, and black bile (the vomiting in remittent malaria).[27]

The origin of the doctrine of the humors is unknown; perhaps it comes from the theory of the four elements or has an independent origin in the history of Egyptian medicine.[28] Bodily counterparts of the elements are suggested by Empedocles, the humors are described in the Hippocratic writings, and Galen later restated them in more sophisticated form as the correspondences.

The theory of health as a harmonious blending and balancing of powers, held by Alcmaeon of Croton (*ca.* 500 B.C.) and the Hippocratic thinkers, made possible a theoretical development which could bridge the gulf between abstract physiological theory and the variety of human cultures.

> Alcmaeon maintains that the bond of health is the "equal balance" of the powers, moist and dry, cold and hot, bitter and sweet, and the rest, while the "supremacy" of one of them is the cause of disease; for the supremacy of either is destructive. Illness comes about directly through excess of heat or cold, indirectly through surfeit or deficiency of nourishment; and its centre is either the blood or the marrow or the brain. It sometimes arises in these centres from external causes, moisture of some sort or environment or exhaustion or hardship or similar causes. Health on the other hand is the proportionate admixture of the qualities.[29]

The doctrine of the humors is clearly stated in the Hippocratic writings. "The body of man has in itself blood, phlegm, yellow bile and black bile; these make up the nature of his body, and through these he feels pain or enjoys health. Now he enjoys the most perfect health when these elements are duly proportioned to one another in respect of compounding, power and bulk, and when they are perfectly mingled." This statement is preceded by criticisms of former theories; an appeal is made for direct observation of bodily processes, avoiding any analogy derived from the four elements in nature.[30]

[27] See Jones's discussion in the general introduction to his translation of *Hippocrates* (Loeb Classical Library), Vol. I, p. xlviii.

[28] See Allbutt, *Greek Medicine in Rome*, p. 133, who suggests that Ionia had active trade relations with Egypt, seeing in Herodotus IV, 187 evidence already of the existence of the humoral pathology. See also Jones, *ibid.*, pp. xlvi–li; and Sarton, *op. cit.* (see n. 5 above), pp. 338–339, and *idem*, "Remarks on the Theory of Temperaments," *Isis*, 34 (1943), pp. 205–208.

[29] Aetius, V. 30, 1. Kirk and Raven, *PSP*, p. 234. In this quotation, equal balance translates ἰσονομία (the same word is used in *Airs, Waters, Places*); supremacy, μοναρχία, and environment, χώρα.

[30] *Nature of Man*, IV; and the criticism of other ideas I–III; on the authorship of the treatise, p. xxvi. *Hippocrates* (Loeb Classical Library), Vol. IV. See Cornford's remarks, *op. cit.* (see n. 18 above), pp. 36–37, which have suggested my own.

Since good health consisted in a proper proportioning of the humors, some aspect of the physical environment—most often temperature—was regarded as bringing about the dominance of one humor over another; this dominance would vary with different regional climates or within the seasons of a single climate. The influence affected individuals and whole peoples, a fallacy finally exposed by Herder in the eighteenth century in the course of criticizing Montesquieu's *Spirit of Laws*.

It is far from my purpose to discuss the elements and the humors themselves; this long story, with all its confusions, belongs to physical and medical history. The important point is that the humoral doctrine also had a long and exciting life lasting well into the late eighteenth century and that it was the theoretical basis of the older theories of climatic influence. The doctrine of the four elements strongly influenced the history of soil theory, chemistry, and agriculture—hence ideas of the nature of the physical environment as a whole—and the doctrine of the humors influenced theories of psychology and physiology, making prominent the supposed changes brought about in both the mind and the body by climate as a whole, sudden temperature change, and the seasons.

Ideas concerning the relation of man to nature could not develop without a feeling for and an interpretation of nature. Since the path-breaking historical chapters of Alexander von Humboldt's *Cosmos*, an extensive literature on this subject has shown the depth and range of feeling toward nature, among both the Greeks and the Romans, in poetry, art, landscape painting, and philosophy, a strong feeling for nature being conspicuous in the writings of the Stoic philosophers, Panaetius and Posidonius.[31] One has the impression in reading Greek and Roman descriptions of nature that their writers are thinking of a domesticated nature, a pleasant commingling of nature and art: the villages on the Mediterranean shore; the beauties of cultivated fields; vines or olive groves on hillsides, sometimes close to streams, or near a forest.

The importance of nature and of natural surroundings in the history of Greek civilization has recently been emphasized by Vincent Scully. If his interpretation is accepted by students of Greek architecture, the Greek landscape will be seen in an entirely new light.

All Greek sacred architecture explores and praises the character of a god or a group of gods in a specific place. That place is itself holy and, before the temple was built upon it, embodied the whole of the deity as a recognized natural force.

[31] Soutar, *Nature in Greek Poetry, passim*, and the works of Helbig and Woermann cited in note 65 of this intro. Humboldt had mixed feelings about the Greek and Roman feeling for nature. *Cosmos*, Vol. II, pp. 19–38. See also Biese, *Die Entwicklung des Naturgefühls bei den Griechen und Römern*. Biese refers also to pioneering investigations which revised earlier opinions regarding the lack of a feeling for nature among the ancients; on Panaetius and Posidonius, see Pohlenz, *Der Hellenische Mensch*, pp. 279–299.

With the coming of the temple, housing its image within it and itself developed as a sculptural embodiment of the god's presence and character, the meaning becomes double, both of the deity as in nature and the god as imagined by men. Therefore, the formal elements of any Greek sanctuary are, first, the specifically sacred landscape in which it is set and, second, the buildings that are placed within it.

The landscape and the temples together form the architectural whole, were intended by the Greeks to do so, and must therefore be seen in relation to each other.[32]

The single most important generalization to be made about the attitudes toward nature held by the peoples of the classical world is that these varied greatly throughout the long span of ancient history. Earlier writers tended either to minimize their existence or to content themselves with generalizations about the period as a whole, citations in support of a thesis being taken from writers who lived as much as a thousand years apart. Even Ruskin in his discussion of classical landscape thought it quite in order to confine himself to Homer, whom he regarded as being representative of the whole period. Surely Ruskin was wrong. Homer can stand as the example for the ancient world only if Theocritus, Virgil, Lucretius, and Horace never lived. One should not expect such cultural unity in the classical world with any more assurance than one would for the medieval or the modern period; the time span from the Homeric poems to Ausonius' *Mosella* is well over a millennium.

There is reason to believe, however, that the ideas of nature and the attitudes toward it that matured mainly in the Hellenistic period are different from those of the pre-Hellenistic era and indeed are important for an understanding of all subsequent ideas about the subject. For this reason, the question is discussed in the second part of this introduction.

There was, however, more than appreciation of nature; there were curiosity and inquiry manifest in an interest in mining, in the way peoples obtained their food, in canals, in agricultural techniques. The Greek and Roman treatises on agriculture, from the *Oeconomicus* of Xenophon, with his praises of Persian agriculture, to the *Natural History* of Pliny, have the strong flavor of nature study, of watching and observing nature to learn the arts of sowing, tilling, and plant breeding, while the writers of the Roman period, like Varro, Columella, and Pliny, were deeply interested in the improvement of soils, methods of plowing, irrigation, drainage, removal of stones, clearing away of thickets, winning of new lands for cultivation, manuring, and insect control.

Neither should one forget the echoes of the primordial Mediterranean world: its age-old veneration of Mother Earth, who acts literally like a mother, an earth that must be inseminated. In myth and in rite, there is a preoccupation with fertility—of man, of the earth. Agriculture, keeping cattle, herding goats

---

[32] Vincent Scully, *The Earth, The Temple, and the Gods. Greek Sacred Architecture*, pp. 1–2. See chapter 1, "Landscape and Sanctuary," although the entire book is devoted to exploring this theme.

and sheep—these kept men close to the tilled and untilled soil alike, reminding them of the land's fertility. From their beliefs there gradually came rational ideas of soil fertility, techniques of planting, and animal feeding.[33]

Philo the Jew, living in the rich mixtures of Hellenistic Alexandria at the beginning of the Christian Era, saw this already old conception clearly and believed in it.

> Nature has bestowed on every mother as a most essential endowment teeming breasts, thus preparing in advance food for the child that is to be born. The earth also, as we all know, is a mother, for which reason the earliest men thought fit to call her "Demeter," combining the name of "mother" with that of "earth"; for, as Plato [*Menexenus* 238 A] says, earth does not imitate woman, but woman earth. Poets quite rightly are in the habit of calling earth "All-mother," and "Fruit-bearer" and "Pandora" or "Give-all," inasmuch as she is the originating cause of existence and continuance in existence to all animals and plants alike. Fitly therefore on earth also, most ancient and most fertile of mothers, did Nature bestow, by way of breasts, streams of rivers and springs, to the end that both the plants might be watered and all animals might have abundance to drink.[34]

Finally there was the search for evidence of purpose in human life and in the universe. This sense of purpose, this feeling that the earth and human life existing on it were not without meaning and plan is particularly evident in Plato and Aristotle, although neither was the first to introduce it. The belief that there was a purpose, an end in nature and in natural processes, rested on two main arguments: the unity and harmony of the cosmos and the artisan analogy, the belief that a creator acts like an individual craftsman—a carpenter building a house—who has the end product he desires well in mind at the start; the work ($\check{\epsilon}\rho\gamma o\nu$) of creation is like the art ($\tau\acute{\epsilon}\chi\nu\eta$) of an artisan.

Although it would require a separate work to trace adequately the idea of unity in nature, we may at least hint at some of the elements which entered into this belief. If there was a unity of the cosmos, it could be assumed for its component parts, and thus for the earth, the life existent upon it, and for mankind despite the diversity of peoples.

What were thought to be the evidences of this unity and harmony? First there is regularity in the phenomena of the heavens, with the exception of comets or showers of falling stars, which could be interpreted as manifestations of divine interference with the natural order. Then, there are the phases of the moon and their periodicity, the revolution of the sun and seasonal change, the movements of the planets, the twenty-four-hour period of day and night. Possibly, as Cumont has suggested, Babylonian astronomers were more interested in the moon than in the sun. Her phases measured time before

---

[33] See Guthrie, *The Greeks and Their Gods*, p. 59. Eliade, *Patterns in Comparative Religion*, pp. 239–240.
[34] Philo, *On the Creation*, 133.

the duration of the year was known, and the sacred calendars which regulated religious and civil life were based on her course. Portents were seen in her eclipses, and to this divinity were ascribed many mysterious influences, including effects on plants and the health of women.[35]

The movements of the apparently eternal heavenly bodies in time led to astrology, which also fostered a sense of unity in the cosmos. Cumont and other scholars think it appeared rather late, the former dating the beginnings of astral religion with the Chaldeans in the sixth century B.C. The rising and setting of the sun brought with them not only heat and cold but light and darkness. In Mediterranean lands especially, seasonal change could be associated with certain appearances in the sky. It could be concluded that the stars had a connection with the natural phenomena on earth and with the course of human life. "Everything in sky and earth alike is incessantly changing, and it was thought that there existed a correspondence between the movements of the gods above and the alterations which occurred here below."[36] Astrology thus could become the science of cosmic environmentalism as we see it carefully worked out in the *Tetrabiblos* of Ptolemy: The stars influence all life on earth, while the natural environment on earth can account for differences within fundamental similarities. In the later development of astral religion in the Roman Empire, astrology became an all-embracing philosophy bestowing a unity and harmony on the universe.

> Astrological paganism deified the active principles which move all celestial and terrestrial bodies. Water, fire, earth, the sea, and the blast of the winds, but above all the luminous heavens of the fixed stars and planets revealed the boundless power of the God who filled all nature. But this pantheism no longer naively regarded this nature as peopled by capicious spirits and unregulated powers. Having become scientific, it conceived the gods as cosmic energies, the providential action of which is ordered in a harmonious system.[37]

It would indeed be hard to exaggerate the importance of astrology in the history of human thought, but it is equally hard to grasp its significance. It appears and reappears constantly in the books which are the sources of the ideas we are concerned with. Somehow astrology has been pushed aside by many general students of thought almost as an embarrassment or a thicket to go around rather than to penetrate. It consistently appears in a role far more exalted than its character of influencing the lives of an individual, the nativities. Its historic role, however, has been much more profound than this. It was a great unifying principle of nature, a cosmic environmentalism. Lynn Thorn-

---

[35] Cumont, *Astrology and Religion Among the Greeks and Romans,* p. 70. Cumont maintained that in hot countries the sun is an enemy; the moon, gently illumining the landscape, is friendly.

[36] *Ibid.,* pp. 11–12, 16.

[37] *Ibid.,* pp. 68–69.

dike has gone so far as to compare it with the Newtonian discoveries of the principles of natural law.

> The stars were not themselves affected by their movement and light, since they were eternal and incorruptible. But their motion and rays had to have some effect, and an outlet for this vast store of energy was found in our elemental world, whose changes and fluctuations and variations paralleled the shifting pattern of the eternal heavens and the varying projection of rays of light and influence thence. Furthermore, the earth was thought of as the center and bottom of the universe, and it was fitting that inferiors should be ruled and governed by superiors—the heavenly bodies.

The *Principia* of Newton eliminated the distinction between superiors and inferiors, but "during the long period of scientific development before Sir Isaac Newton promulgated the universal law of gravitation, there had been generally recognized and accepted another and different universal natural law, which his supplanted. And that universal natural law was astrological."[38]

Thorndike's interpretation illumines the thought of men such as Posidonius, Ptolemy, Albert the Great, Thomas Aquinas, and Jean Bodin, in whose thought astrology of the natural law type was a basic assumption.

These evidences were the strongest and perhaps they were the oldest. Analogies drawn from human affairs are also very ancient. The Sumerian theologians took "their cue from human society," and the divine pantheon composed of living beings, in manlike form but superhuman and immortal, superintended the universe according to established rules and regulations. The *me*'s (divine laws, rules, and regulations governing the universe) also were derived from cultural elements.[39] The history of the Greek word κόσμος suggests that observation of order in human affairs may have inspired its wider application to the organic world and then to the universe. In Homer and in other early literature the word and words derived from it "denote in general any arrangement or disposition of parts which is appropriate, well-disposed, and effective. The primary idea is of something physically neat and trim rather than morally or socially 'correct.' " The word then came to mean "finery, rich adornment." It also referred to the order of an assembled army and to the goatherds separating flocks which had mingled in pasture. The term denoted "a concrete arrangement of beauty or utility, as well as the more abstract idea of moral and social 'order.' " Its "social overtones were particularly important, and it may be that from the beginning, κόσμος was applied to the world of nature by conscious analogy with the good order of society." To the Ionian philosophers, the cosmos meant an arrangement of all things in which every natural power has its function and its limits assigned. As in any

---

[38] Thorndike, "The True Place of Astrology in the History of Science," *Isis*, 46 (1955), pp. 273–278. The first quotation is on p. 274, the second on p. 273.
[39] Kramer, *History Begins at Sumer*, pp. 78–79, 99–100.

good arrangement, the term implies a systematic unity in which diverse elements are combined or composed.[40] By the fifth century, the word not only meant universal order; it was also applied to the structure, form, and functioning of the human body. The unity of the microcosm, the human body with all its diversity, may well have inspired the idea of an all-embracing unity in the macrocosm.[41]

There was also the theory of the Pythagoreans, the harmonic analogy, the connection between planetary movements, which were like vibrations, and angular velocities, which were like harmonic ratios producing the music of the spheres. In this conception, the universe is pervaded (says Kahn) by geometric principles of harmony and equilibrium.[42]

The biological analogy also had great force, the unity amidst diversity being characteristic of life; in it were strong inducements toward a teleology. From Anaximander to Plato "the origin of the universe is compared to the formation and birth of a living being. This ancient pairing of cosmogony and embryology explains why the elemental bodies are referred to by Anaxagoras and Empedocles as the 'seeds' or 'roots' of all things."[43] Lucretius, as we shall see later, applied the biological analogy to the earth.

It was ideas like these, I think, that made men believe that diversity was not an illusion, nor unity imaginary.[44] The idea that there is a unity and a harmony in nature is probably the most important idea, in its effect on geographical thought, that we have received from the Greeks, even if among them there was no unanimity regarding the nature of this unity and harmony.

The idea of terrestrial unity of which human beings were a part called attention to the fitness of the earth itself as an environment for human beings and for the sustenance of all other forms of life; to the inequality of environments and the differences among them; and, by implication, to the unequal distribution of peoples and to the boundaries that might divide off a densely inhabited from a desolate region. The Greek concept of the οἰκουμένη is part of this tradition; in antiquity it had at least six different meanings, but the most common was the "inhabited world," the world known to be peopled and to be capable of supporting life. The concept of the οἰκουμένη was a concrete one, and back of it was the realization that peoples lived in different environments, sometimes similar, more often differing from one another, and

[40] Kahn, *Anaximander and the Origins of Greek Cosmology*, pp. 220–230; quotations on pp. 220, 223.
[41] "Nat. Hom." 7, *Works of Hippocrates* (Loeb Classical Library), Vol. IV. Cited by Kahn, *op. cit.*, p. 189.
[42] See Sambursky, *The Physical World of the Greeks*, pp. 53–55; Kahn, *op. cit.*, p. 206, and Spitzer, "Classical and Christian Ideas of World Harmony," *Traditio*, 2 (1944), pp. 414–421.
[43] Kahn, *op. cit.*, p. 213.
[44] See Sambursky, *op. cit.*, p. 129.

if the two are considered together—the peoples and the environments—the relationship might be a purely circumstantial one, or a theoretical one carrying a heavy burden of dogmatism and deduction.[45]

## 2. The Hellenistic Age and Its Characteristic Attitudes Toward Nature

It is difficult in a few paragraphs to say anything meaningful about such a long and complex period as the Hellenistic age; yet an attempt should be made to show how crucial it was to the history of ideas being considered in this work. In fact, it is more crucial than the times of Herodotus or even of Plato and Aristotle, and one can sympathize with Tarn's statement that "so far as modern civilisation is based on Greek it is primarily on Hellenism that it is based."[46] There is agreement in general but not in detail in defining the age. Droysen coined the term "Hellenistic," and the Hellenistic centuries are usually defined as the period from the death of Alexander in 323 B.C. to the founding of the Roman Empire by Augustus in 30 B.C.

Since this discussion is confined to those aspects of the age which throw light on the ideas being studied, it does not demand the precision in defining it which an independent work would demand. I will keep to the accepted definition without, however, feeling the need to apologize for including materials outside the inclusive dates. It seems obvious, for example, that the nature descriptions and bucolic poetry of Virgil, Tibullus, and Horace have much in common with those of Theocritus, Moschus, and Bion. Plutarch, who spans the first and second centuries, seems at home in the culture of the Hellenistic age (he is an important source of its history), while Varro and Columella, one an Italian, the other a Spaniard, write about plant introductions, plant and animal breeding, and reactions to rural life, which were characteristic of the Mediterranean world after Alexander's time.

The Hellenistic age is of unusual interest to a student of cultural geography. I will resist the temptation to compare it with the Renaissance or the age of discovery[47] (the similarities are superficial, the differences profound), but it is clearly one of those periods of extraordinary culture contact in the history of Western civilization in which men became aware of new and different environments and of the people living in them. Impressive as are the examples in Herodotus, they cannot campare in this regard with the compilations of Strabo, and the gulf would be greater if more works from the Hellenistic period had survived.

---

[45] On ancient concepts of the οἰκουμένη, See Gisinger, "Oikumene," in *PW*, Vol. 17:2, cols. 2123–2174; Kaerst, *Die antike Idee der Oikumene*; and Partsch, "Die Grenzen der Menschheit. I Teil: Die antike Oikumene," *Berichte über die Verhandlungen der Königl. Sächsisch. Ges. d. Wiss. zu Leipzig, Phil.-hist. kl.*, 68 (1916), pp. 1–62.

[46] Tarn, *Hellenistic Civilization*, 3rd ed., rev. by Tarn and Griffith, p. 1.

[47] For a discussion of this point, see *HW*, Vol. 1, pp. 127–129.

One should not, however, dwell on differences alone. Comparisons were important too. Much of what the Greeks participating in Alexander's conquests saw was indeed new; even the old or familiar appeared in a new light. From long acquaintance with Egypt they knew well the contrast between the fertility of the Nile Valley and the harsh, barren Libyan desert bordering it. The plant life of Persia, known from the March of the Ten Thousand, was not too strange. The flora of Anatolia resembled that of the Mediterranean; the sun-drenched plains of Mesopotamia were reminders of African wastelands, and the Greeks had long been at home on the Pontus. The campaign in India brought out striking parallels: in the west, the Nile; in the east, the Punjab, partly in an evergreen tropical zone with its rich and abundant vegetation. In the west on journeys to the oasis of Siwa in the Libyan desert they had seen the luxurious vegetation of the great oasis of Ammon. But in the east they traversed, in an excruciating campaign, the bare sea of sands of Baluchistan. Entirely new, however, were the rich, forested, cool slopes of the Himalaya and the mangrove forests of the northwest coast of the Arabian Sea which reached from the Indus delta far into the Persian Gulf.[48] Theophrastus' *Enquiry into Plants* is a product of this increased knowledge of the world's vegetation. Who can read the fourth book, "Of the Trees and Plants Special to Particular Districts and Positions," without being aware that such knowledge was based on gatherings from the Mediterranean and Egypt to the Indus? Theophrastus writes as if he had been on the islands near the mouth of the Indus where the great mangrove trees, big as planes or the tallest poplars, stood in the water; when the tide came in, all was covered but the projecting branches of the tallest trees and to them were fastened the ships' cables, as they were to the roots at ebb tide. Theophrastus has heard that, on the east side of the island of Tylos in the Persian Gulf, the trees are so numerous that they make a regular fence when the tide goes out, and that the island also produces the wool-bearing tree (cotton) in abundance. One can agree with Bretzl that plant geography starts with Theophrastus. And Theophrastus starts with Alexander; he has before him observations of the scientific travelers on the campaign reporting new ethnographic, geographic, geologic, and botanical facts.[49]

There were not only the Himalayas and the mangroves; the Greeks of the period had a far more thorough knowledge of the Mediterranean world than had their forbears. The Near East, as Rostovtzeff has pointed out, appears in the sixteenth and seventeenth books of Strabo's *Geography* as a well-known and well-trodden land.[50] The campaigns of Alexander carried Hellenic culture to the Indus and to Chinese Turkestan. Ptolemaic monarchs by the third century B.C. had occupied Zanzibar, parts of the coasts of East Africa, and the

---

[48] Based on Bretzl, *Botanische Forschungen des Alexanderzuges*, pp. 1–3.
[49] Theophrastus, *Enquiry into Plants*, IV, vii, 4–7; Bretzl, *op. cit.*, pp. 4–5.
[50] *HW*, Vol. 2, p. 1040.

Sudan. That the tropics were habitable was probably known long before Eratosthenes said so, for Dalion had gone south beyond Meroë. Eratosthenes himself is an admirable exemplar of the period. In his work are the beginnings of scientific geography. He includes not only the theories of his predecessors but recent accumulations of knowledge as well. Strabo says of him that he wished to revise the map of the earth (II, 1, 2). Although he is most famous for his brilliance in devising a method for measuring the circumference of the earth with astonishing accuracy (if a certain value for the *stade* be accepted), he was also keenly interested in the contrast between the inhabited world (οἰκουμένη) and the terrestrial, wishing to set the former accurately within the latter. In his cultural geography, he was capable, judging by a passage on the deforestation of Cyprus, of seeing clearly the relation of governmental policy to changes in the land.[51] (See chap. 3, sec. 4.)

The discovery of the seaway to India (117–116 B.C.), the Roman conquest and colonization of Spain, North Africa, the Balkan peninsula, and Gaul enlarged immeasurably the awareness of peoples and environments. A central region of refined civilization (from Babylonia to Italy and Sicily), says Heichelheim, "was surrounded by a larger, outer zone (from the Ganges to the Atlantic) of assimilated barbarian kingdoms, Greek colonial states, and Roman outer provinces and subject allies, in which there were islands of *polis* economy or Roman municipal settlements"; from them native villagers gradually appropriated Hellenistic and Roman agricultural skills. In this Greco-Roman development, over such a large area of the earth's surface, planned colonization, economic planning, capital formation, transfer and investment, bills of exchange, and world currencies made possible "a changed appearance of the cities and even more of the countryside from Spain and Gaul to India and Turkestan."[52]

Fully as remarkable was the enlarged knowledge of primitive peoples. What wonders the members of Alexander's party saw, who sailed from the mouth of the Indus to the Shatt-al-Arab along the shores of Gedrosia and Carmania (that is, along the shares of Baluchistan to the Persian shores of the Gulf of Oman)! They and later observers as well were in the lands of the fish eaters. According to Diodorus on the authority of Agatharchides of Cnidos, the third

---

[51] Tarn, "The Date of Iambulus: a Note," *Classical Quarterly*, Vol. 33 (1939), pp. 192–193. On the habitability of the zones between the tropics, see Tittel, "Geminos, 1," *PW*, Vol. 7:1, col. 1034; Gisinger, "Geographie (Eratosthenes)," *PW Supp. Bd.*, 4, cols. 606-607. On E.'s measurements, see Sarton, *Hellenistic Science and Culture in the Last Three Centuries B.C.*, pp. 103–106; Bunbury, Vol. I, chap. 16; Thomson, *History of Ancient Geography*, pp. 158–166.

[52] Heichelheim, "Effects of Classical Antiquity on the Land," *MR*, pp. 168–169. This is an admirable short statement on the Hellenistic period (upon which these remarks are based), pp. 168–172. See also his article, "Monopole (hellenistisch)," *PW*, 16:1, esp. cols. 157–192. I am indebted to Professor Heichelheim for stimulating discussions and the suggestions he gave me at the Wenner-Gren symposium in 1955.

Ptolemy, Euergetes I, who reigned from 246–221 B.C., sent one of his friends, Simmias, to spy out the land, and he made an investigation of the peoples along the Red Sea and presumably to the shores of Baluchistan [III, 18, 4]. Indeed the third book of Diodorus, which contains only ethnological fragments, mostly from Agatharchides (early second century B.C.), has some of the most interesting descriptive ethnography ever written. Not the least interesting is the account [III, 2–10] in part from Agatharchides, in part from other sources, in which the confident Ethiopians are depicted as believing themselves to be the first men, their civilization to be unique and creative, and the Egyptian, in part at least, being derived from their own. The themes of the food quest, habitation, death and burial customs, and cultural isolation appear frequently in these remarkable passages. It is clear that the Greeks who studied them were much impressed by food as a criterion of culture, for most of the people are named according to the dominant item of their diet: the ichthyophagi (the fish eaters), the chelonophagi (turtle eaters), the rhizophagi (root eaters), the hyolophagi (wood eaters), the spermatophagi (the seed eaters), and so on in the descriptions of peoples bordering on the Red Sea and the Indian Ocean and the interior lands of Ethiopia.

There are absorbing antiphonal themes—the persistence of the old native cultures even with Hellenization, and the extension of Greek culture under the aegis of new rulers in sympathy with it, with the help too of the new common language, the κοινή, the language of the Septuagint and of the Greek New Testament. These themes are so complex that they would require a long monograph reinterpreting the ethnology of the ancient world. I must content myself with mentioning these facts, with an illustration or two, because they show that alternatives other than environmental explanations were available to account for cultural differences.[53] The pattern is not one of deep and broad Hellenization of the cultures comprising this world, but is one in which non-Greek cultures persist, possibly with some Greek penetration, while the Greek enclaves, epitomes of that culture, all bear the stamp of the typical Greek settlement. Students of the age thus have emphasized both the unity of the Hellenistic world and the respect of its rulers for the customs and religion of native peoples. The Ptolemies were "chary of modifying the immemorial customs of the temples." They "were loathe to abandon the existing traditions, to break with the deeply rooted habits and customs of the country." A votive stele of Anubis of Attic type was found at Philadelphia in the Fayûm, an eloquent illustration of Greek respect for Egyptian religion.[54]

In a letter to Zenon (employed by the finance minister Apollonius, a pow-

---

[53] For materials of great interest to Hellenistic cultural geography, see *HW*, Vol. 2, pp. 1053–1134, and Partsch, "Die Grenzen der Menschheit. I Teil: Die antike Oikumene," *Berichte über die Verhandl. der Königl. Sächsischen Ges. d. Wiss. zu Leipzig. Phil.-hist. kl.*, Vol. 68 (1916), 2 Heft.

[54] *HW*, Vol. 1, p. 281, 291; the votive stele is shown in Plate 39, Vol. 1, facing p. 319.

erful Greek estate-holder in the Egyptian Fayûm) from the third century
B.C., two feeders of cats, who were attached to the cult of Boubastis in the
village of Sophthis, state that the king and Apollonius had ordered that persons
of their profession be exempted from compulsory labor throughout the
country. However, Leontiskos, the chief policeman, sent them to work at the
harvest; they complied with the order, not wishing to trouble Zenon. Leontiskos then sent them off to make bricks, leaving in peace for their own ends
two professional brickmakers in the same village. The cat feeders appeal to
Zenon to conform to the order of the king and of the chief financial official
($\delta\iota o\iota\kappa\eta\tau\eta\varsigma$).[55]

Among the decrees of Euergetes II (B.C. 118) is one defining the jurisdiction of courts; disputes involving contracts written in Greek between Greeks
and Egyptians go before the Greek judges ($\chi\rho\eta\mu\alpha\tau\iota\sigma\tau\alpha\iota$); those written in
Egyptian between Greeks and Egyptians go before native courts in accor-
dance with national laws, as do those between Egyptians.[56]

On the other hand, the study of areas of Greek colonization such as the
Fayûm and of Zenon's archives gives the impression, as we shall see in Chapter
3, of innovation, of dynamic Greek enclaves in a traditional Egyptian setting.
"But the Greek superstructure of Egypt, important as it was, was no more
than a superstructure."[57] The Greeks in Egypt were newcomers in a land of
ancient culture with long experience in living and religious feeling.

The apparent persistence and unchanging nature of life in the Near East
probably also struck the Greeks because it was in such contrast with the
movement and change of their own. A particularly striking passage in Diodorus throws some light on this contrast. He is discussing the antiquity of the
Chaldeans of Babylon. Since they are assigned to the service of the gods, their
lives are spent in study, "their greatest renown being in the field of astrology."
Using various methods, they are also occupied with soothsaying and divination. Their training is quite unlike that of Greeks engaged in the same en-
deavors. Among the Chaldeans the study goes from father (who is relieved
of all other duties to the state) to son. The parents are ungrudging teachers,
their sons trusting pupils, and training from early childhood allows them to
attain great skill. Among the Greeks, the student who takes up a large number
of subjects without preparation turns quite late to these higher studies; he
labors on them, gives them up, distracted by the need to earn a livelihood.
Only a few go on to the higher studies and continue in them to make profits
and they "are always trying to make innovations in connection with the most
important doctrines instead of following in the path of their predecessors."
The barbarians, "by sticking to the same things always, keep a firm hold on

---

[55] *P. Cairo Zen.*, 59451. Apollonius' concern for religious cults, both Greek and
Egyptian, is frequently met up with in the Zenon papyri. No date is given.
[56] *The Tebtunis Papyri*, 5, 207–220 = Vol. 1, pp. 54–55.
[57] *HW*, Vol. 1, pp. 265–266, quotation on p. 205; cf. p. 55.

every detail," while the profit-seeking Greeks "keep founding new schools and, wrangling with each other over the most important matters of speculation, bring it about that their pupils hold conflicting views, and that their minds, vacillating throughout their lives and able to believe anything at all with firm conviction, simply wander in confusion."[58]

The early Seleucids, like the Ptolemies, were careful not to offend the religious feelings of their subjects. Although there is considerable evidence for this, one example will suffice: Uruk-Warka, the holy city of Babylonia, became once more "in the times of the Seleucids an important centre of Babylonian religion, learning, and science."[59]

These illustrations show a cultural diversity which even the simplest observer could see owed something to history and to tradition. This observation can be stated in a different way: in the Hellenistic age there was a notable broadening of the concept of the οἰκουμένη. In earlier times "the inhabited world" was predominantly a geographic concept; in the Hellenistic world it assumed also a cultural connotation.

Plutarch praises Alexander's accomplishments in educating other peoples and on occasion in changing their customs. When Alexander was civilizing Asia, "Homer was commonly read, and the children of the Persians, of the Susianians, and of the Gedrosians learned to chant the tragedies of Sophocles and Euripedes." Socrates, tried on a charge of introducing foreign deities, fell victim to Athenian informers, while "through Alexander Bactria and the Caucasus learned to revere the gods of the Greeks." Plutarch emphasizes more than modern scholars would the uncivilized and brutish in the lands Alexander conquered, and he ignores the long urban tradition of the Near East: Alexander "established more than seventy cities among savage tribes and sowed all Asia with Grecian magistracies, and thus overcame its uncivilized and brutish manner of living. Although few of us read Plato's *Laws*, yet hundreds of thousands have made use of Alexander's laws, and continue to use them." It was better to have been vanquished by Alexander than to have escaped him, for the vanquished could become civilized: "Egypt would not have its Alexandria, nor Mesopotamia its Seleuceia, nor Sogdiana its Prophthasia, nor India its Bucephalia, nor the Caucasus a Greek city hard by. . . ."[60] This broadened concept is related to the effects of Alexander's conquests, to the κοινή, to the Hellenization of this part of the world, and to Stoicism.

Plutarch paraphrases approvingly the thoughts expressed by Zeno, the founder of the Stoic philosophy, whose main principle was "that all the inhabitants of this world of ours should not live differentiated by their respective rules of justice into separate cities and communities, but that we should

---

[58] Diodorus, II, 29, 3–6. See also Kaerst, *Gesch. d. Hellenismus*, Vol. 2, pp. 149–150, to whom I owe the reference.

[59] *HW*, Vol. 1, p. 435.

[60] Plutarch, *On the Fortune or the Virtue of Alexander*, I 328D, 328D–E, 329A.

consider all men to be of one community and one polity, and that we should
have a common life and an order common to us all, even as a herd that feeds
together and shares the pasturage of a common field." According to Plutarch,
Alexander sought always to bring men together, "uniting and mixing in one
great loving-cup as it were, men's lives, their characters, their marriages, their
very habits of life." Plutarch says he felt no envy in not having had the opportunity of seeing Alexander on the throne of Darius, but "methinks I would
gladly have been a witness of that fair and holy marriage-rite, when he brought
together in one golden-canopied tent an hundred Persian brides and an hundred
Macedonian and Greek bridegrooms, united at a common hearth and board."
Alexander desired that all men be subject to "one law of reason, and one form
of government and to reveal all men as one people, and to this purpose he
made himself conform." The deity recalled his soul too soon, else this unity
would have come about.[61] Stoicism too, with its emphasis on universal sympathy, and on the interrelation of man and nature as part of a design, on God's
care for the world, and on the universal participation of men in the divine,
encouraged a cosmopolitanism in outlook already foreshadowed in the hopes
of Alexander.[62] There may indeed, therefore, have been a wide diffusion of
the idea of a cultural as well as a geographic οἰκουμένη, although admittedly
the documentation is not thorough. Poseidippus in the third century B.C. said,
"There are many cities, but they are one Hellas."[63] Plutarch's remarks about
Alexander and his times, and his ideas about a man's home being the world,
which are expressed in *On Exile*, communicate some of this feeling as well—
in an age notable also for misery, slavery, cruelty in war.[64]

   There was not only a sharper awareness of the natural and the cultural
environment in the Hellenistic period, but, despite the scanty evidence for
such a long time, it would seem that there was a transformation as well in
esthetic, philosophical, poetic, and artistic attitudes toward nature. The feeling for nature in the ancient world—nature imagery, comparisons between
natural phenomena and human emotions, appreciation of individual aspects
of nature such as a flower or a breeze or of the ensemble of the individual components that manifests itself in a landscape—needs reexamination in the light
of modern knowledge. It is not that the basic sources have changed much nor
that we are lacking in studies; it is doubtful whether additional epigraphic and
numismatic materials, paintings on vases, and the like would seriously undermine the main trends apparent in the surviving written sources and the modern
monographic literature. To my knowledge, however, there is no thorough

---

[61] *Ibid.* The quotations are from I, 329A–B, 329C, 329D–E, and 330D.
[62] Kaerst, *Die antike Idee der Oikumene*, p. 13; Tarn, *Hellenistic Civiliz.*, pp. 79–81.
[63] Kock, ed., *Comicorum Atticorum Fragmenta*, Fr. 28, vol. 3, p. 345; quoted by Tarn,
*op. cit.*, p. 86.
[64] Plutarch, *On the Fortune or the Virtue of Alexander*, I 329A–D, *On Exile*, 600D–
602D. On human misery during this period see esp. *HW*, chaps. 4, 6; Tarn, *op. cit.*,
chap. 3.

recent study of the subject; the most detailed ones were written in the nine-teenth century, mainly by historians of literature and of art.

Bearing in mind, then, this need for reexamination of the sources and that it is beyond the scope of this work to undertake it, there are substantial reasons for believing that the roots of modern attitudes toward nature are to be found in the Hellenistic age rather than in earlier periods. Admittedly these are dif-ficult to substantiate both for the reasons already cited and because so much has been lost. More so than in the past, the subject becomes widely diffused in different fields: poetry, belles lettres, philosophy, religion, landscape paint-ing, agricultural writing. Tentatively one might say that realistic and vivid nature description is distinct from religious themes and certainly from the polytheism of Homer. If it is religious it is likely to be nature description in service of the design argument, as in the Stoic writings. The Epicurean philos-ophy—its world was also a unity whose creator was not God but nature—could inspire the vivid nature writings of Lucretius. The awareness of the oriental garden in the Hellenistic period, the tree-lined promenade, the interest in creating natural enclaves in cities, inspirations from cultures farther east, played their role in making a feeling for nature far more prominent than it had been in the earlier Greek world. No earlier period in the history of West-ern civilization revealed such strong, self-consciously expressed contrasts be-tween the urban and rural as did the Hellenistic, probably a result of unique conditions of urban life of the age not only in city building but in the increased size of cities. None of these observations are new; similar ones were made in 1871 by Karl Woermann in his work on nature-feeling of the Greeks and Romans and in 1873 by Wolfgang Helbig in his researches into the early his-tory of landscaping painting.[65] Helbig argued that before the Hellenistic age nature was an ever-present good—and never far removed. The alienation of man from nature he attributed to the rise of the great Hellenistic cities. So strong is man's dependence on nature, he further argued, that any artificial divorcement from it leads to attempts to reestablish the communion, and then to self-conscious sentiments about nature and a distinct method of artistic ex-pression. Both Helbig and Woermann stressed the influence of the Oriental garden when it became known; the growth in the size and splendor of cities (culture becomes concentrated in them) created an awareness of the contrast between city and country, engendering a literature on nature in this and in the immediately following Roman period. Stimulating and vigorous as these works still are, their confident conclusions are only interesting possibilities, for the ideas in question probably apply only to the most self-conscious and

[65] Woermann, *Ueber den landschaftlichen Natursinn der Griechen und Römer*, pp. 65–66; see also his *Die Landschaft in der Kunst der alten Völker*, esp. pp. 201–215; Helbig, "Beiträge zur Erklärung der campanischen Wandbilder, II," *Rheinisches Museum*, N. F., Vol. 24 (1869), pp. 497–523, esp. p. 514, and his *Untersuchungen über die Campanische Wandmalerei*, chap. 23. I am greatly indebted to these stimulating works; they are es-pecially helpful in providing copious citations to the sources.

articulate inhabitants; one may doubt that they are part of popular belief. The scanty evidence can scarcely suggest any generalization. An idyll ascribed to Theocritus, a few lines from Bion, cannot sum up a centuries-long period any more than Homer can. Regardless, however, of the problem of representativeness, I would like to quote a few passages from the familiar Hellenistic and Roman writers in order to show that significant attitudes toward nature found expression at that time. In general, these were realistic even when dealing with mythological subjects or with the activities of gods; they were more sustained than short epithets or similes; they had verisimilitude, bearing the marks of observation, of country walks, of conversations with shepherds.

The first of these works, *The Argonautica* of Apollonius Rhodius (third century B.C.) is a version of one of the oldest Greek sagas, the voyage on the "Argo" of Jason and his companions to Colchis in search of the Golden Fleece. We are concerned here not with the tale but with the incidental descriptions of nature which appear from time to time during the progress of the voyage.

(1) Running past the Tisaean headland, the son of Oeagrus, touching his lyre, "sang in rhythmical song of Artemis," and as he sang, "the fishes came darting through the deep sea, great mixed with small, and followed gambolling along the watery paths. And as when in the track of the shepherd, their master, countless sheep follow to the fold that have fed to the full of grass, and he goes before gaily piping a shepherd's strain on his shrill reed; so these fishes followed; and a chasing breeze ever bore the ship onward" [I, 570–579].

(2) Jason, with the spear given him by Atalanta, "went on his way to the city like to a bright star, which maidens, pent up in new-built chambers, behold as it rises above their homes, and through the dark air it charms their eyes with its fair red gleam and the maid rejoices, love-sick for the youth who is far away amid strangers, for whom her parents are keeping her to be his bride; like to that star the hero trod the way to the city" [I, 775–781].

(3) In the passage between Scylla and Charybdis, they have the assistance of the Nereids (who circle the ships like dolphins) and of Thetis (who guides the ship's course). "And the ship was raised aloft as the current smote her, and all around the furious wave mounting up broke over the rocks, which at one time touched the sky like towering crags, at another, down in the depths, were fixed fast at the bottom of the sea and the fierce waves poured over them in floods" [IV, 920–979; quotation is in lines 943–947].

(4) There are sensitive delineations of light, especially that of morning, which enhance the beauty and add to the total impression of the landscape. "Now . . . gleaming dawn with bright eyes beheld the lofty peaks of Pelion, and the calm headlands were . . . drenched as the sea was ruffled by the winds . . ." [I, 519–521]. "But when the sun rising from far lands lighted up the dewy hills and wakened the shepherds," they loosed their hawsers, put on board their spoil, "and with a favouring wind they steered through the eddying Bosporus" [II, 164–168].

(5) Hera and Athena visit Cypris, Eros' mother, to urge the boy to pierce Medea, daughter of Aetes, with his arrow so that she might love Jason; they act without delay and successfully. Eros then "fared forth through the fruitful orchard of the palace of Zeus," he passed through the gates of Olympus high in air, then in a downward path from heaven he turned toward earth. "And beneath him there appeared now the life-giving earth and cities of men and sacred streams of rivers, and now in turn mountain peaks and the ocean all around, as he swept through the vast expanse of air" [III, 164–166].

(6) "Now dawn returning with her beams divine scattered the gloomy night through the sky; and the island beaches laughed out and the paths over the plains far off, drenched with dew, and there was a din in the streets; the people were astir throughout the city, and far away the Colchians were astir at the bounds of the isle of Maeris" [IV, 1170–1175].

(7) There are also comparisons between a state of mind and the appearance of nature. Medea, in love with Jason and kept wakeful by her cares, dreads his fate before the strength of the bulls. "And fast did her heart throb within her breast, as a sunbeam quivers upon the walls of a house when flung up from water, which is just poured forth in a caldron or a pail may be; and hither and thither on the swift eddy does it dart and dance along; even so the maiden's heart quivered in her breast" [III, 755–759].

In this period the most familiar examples of the feeling for nature are in the writings of Theocritus, Bion, and Moschus (or from those writings conventionally attributed to them). In this bucolic poetry, especially that of Theocritus, there are charming allusions to the details of Mediterranean rural life: to goatherd's sticks, to bees, to grazing meadows. This freshness of description is also evident in urban scenes, as in *The Women at the Adonis Festival*, which is set in Alexandria. Gorgo makes a morning call on Praxinoa asking her to the festival of Adonis, which is being held at the Palace of Ptolemy II. Going with difficulty through the crowded streets of Alexandria— "How we're to get through this awful crush," says Gorgo on the way, "and how long it's going to take us, I can't imagine. Talk of an antheap!"—they arrive at the palace, where Gorgo insists that Praxinoa admire the delicate and tasteful embroideries. Praxinoa replies "Huswife Athena!" Gorgo marvels that the weavers and embroiderers are capable of such detailed work. "How realistically the things all stand and move about in it! They're living! It *is* wonderful what people can do." And the Holy Boy, Adonis, "how perfectly beautiful he looks lying on his silver couch with the down of manhood just showing on his cheeks . . . !" [Theocritus, Idyll XV, 78–86].

The wonderment has its rural parallels, set in country sounds and scenes. "Something sweet is the whisper of the pine," says Thyrsis, "that makes her music by yonder springs, and sweet no less, master Goatherd, the melody of your pipe" [Id. I, 1–3]. Intimate touches sketch the life of the herdsman. "I go a-courting of Amaryllis, and my goats they go browsing on along the hill with Tityrus to drive them on. My well-beloved Tityrus, pray feed me my goats; pray lead them to watering, good Tityrus, and beware or the buckgoat, the yellow Libyan yonder, will be butting you" [Id. III, 1–5]. The goatherd tells Thyrsis he is no apprentice at the art of country music. "So let's come and sit yonder beneath the elm, this way, over against Priapus and the fountain-goddesses, where that shepherd's seat is and those oak-trees" [I, 19–23]. In the fifth idyll, Lacon tells Comatas, "You'll sing better sitting under the wild olive and this coppice. There's cool water falling yonder, and here's grass and a greenbed, and the locusts at their prattling" [V, 31–34]; but Comatas's tastes in natural surroundings are different: "Thither I will never come. Here I have oaks and bedstraw, and bees humming bravely at the hives, here's two springs of cool water to thy one, and birds, not locusts, a-babbling upon the tree, and, for shade, thine's not half so good; and what's more the pine overhead is casting her nuts" [V, 45–49].

In *The Harvest-Home*, the poet and his companions set out from Cos to the country to participate in the harvest festival. On the way they overtake the goatherd, Lycidas of Cydonia, "which indeed any that saw him must have known him for, seeing liker could not be. For upon his shoulders there hung, rank of new rennet, a shag-haired buck-goat's tawny fleece, across his breast a broad belt did gird an ancient shirt, and in's hand he held a crook of wild olive" [VII, 10–20]. They left the goatherd to take another road; the three of them,

> Eucritus and I and pretty little Amyntas turned in at Phrasidamus's and in deep greenbeds of fragrant reeds and fresh-cut vine-strippings laid us rejoicing down. / Many an aspen, many an elm bowed and rustled overhead, and hard by, the hallowed water welled purling forth of a cave of the Nymphs, while the brown cricket chirped busily amid the shady leafage, and the tree-frog murmured aloof in the dense thornbrake. Lark and goldfinch sang and turtle moaned, and about the spring the bees hummed and hovered to and fro. All nature smelt of the opulent summer-time, smelt of the season of fruit. Pears lay at our feet, apples on either side, rolling abundantly, and the young branches lay splayed upon the ground because of the weight of their damsons [VII, 128–146].

In Theocritus' hymn to Castor and Polydeuces, the men of Jason's ship went down the ladders, Castor and Polydeuces wandering away from the rest to see "the wild woodland of all manner of trees among the hills." Beneath a slabby rock they found a freshet ever brimming with pure clear water. The pebbles at the bottom were like silver and crystal, and there grew beside it long and tall firs, poplars, planes, and spiry cypresses, "as all fragrant flowers which abound in the meadows of outgoing spring to be loved and laboured of the shag bee" [XXII, 34–43].

Both in Bion and in Moschus there are passages implying a communion of man with nature, a sympathy within nature for the misfortunes of men, suggesting the pathetic fallacy that Ruskin found so distasteful (*Modern Painters*, Part IV, chap. 12). In Bion's *Lament for Adonis* (30–39), not only do the

Nymphs and Aphrodite mourn but so also do the elements of nature—for him and for Cypris, beautiful while Adonis lived, whose loveliness has now died with him.

> With all the hills 'tis *Woe for Cypris* and with the vales 'tis *Woe for Adonis*; the rivers weep the sorrows of Aphrodite, the wells of the mountains shed tears for Adonis; the flowerets flush red for grief, and Cythera's isle over every foothill and every glen of it sings pitifully *Woe for Cytherea, the beauteous Adonis is dead*, and Echo ever cries her back again, *The beauteous Adonis is dead*.

Similarly, in *The Lament for Bion* (usually published in the works of Moschus and probably the work of a pupil of Bion), the same sympathy comes forth from nature.

> Cry me waly upon him, you glades of the woods, and waly, sweet Dorian water; you rivers, weep I pray you for the lovely and delightful Bion. Lament you now, good orchards; gently groves, make you your moan; be your breathing clusters, ye flowers, dishevelled for grief. Pray roses, now be your redness sorrow, and yours sorrow, windflowers; speak now thy writing, dear flower-de-luce, loud let thy blossoms babble ay; the beautiful musician is dead.[66]

In a fragment attributed to Moschus, a fisherman muses about the elements and how they affect him.

> When the wind strikes gently upon a sea that is blue, this craven heart is roused within me, and my love of the land leads to the desire of the great waters. But when the deep waxes grey and loud, and the sea begins to swell and to foam and the waves run long and wild, then look I unto the shore and its trees and depart from the brine, then welcome is the land to me and pleasant the shady greenwood, where, be the wind never so high, the pine-tree sings her song.

The fisherman prefers life on shore, to sleep beneath the plane "and the sound hard by of a bubbling spring such as delights and not disturbs the rustic ear" [Fr. 4].

Among the Roman writers who were strongly influenced by Hellenistic tastes, descriptions, details of rural life, themes of communion with nature, and comparisons between city and country were also expressed, often with vigor and beauty or, as Columella did, with bitterness. One need only recall the nature imagery of Lucretius.

(1) To Venus, the life-giver (*alma Venus*), mother of Aeneas and thus of the Roman people, and the goddess of love, he says in the opening lines, "Thou, goddess, thou dost turn to flight the winds and the clouds of heaven, thou at thy coming; for thee earth, the quaint artificer (*suava daedala tellus*) puts forth her sweet-scented flowers; for thee the levels of ocean smile, and the sky, its anger past, gleams with spreading light." With spring and the coming of the strong west wind, "first the birds in high heaven herald thee, goddess,

---

[66] *The Lament for Bion*, 1–7. Bion's fragments 9 on the evening star and 12 on Galatea's lover combine sentiments of communion with nature with love and unrequited love.

and thine approach, their hearts thrilled with thy might. Then the tame beasts grow wild and bound over the fat pastures, and swim the racing rivers; so surely enchained by thy charm each follows thee in hot desire whither thou goest before to lead him on." For Venus alone is "pilot to the nature of things, and nothing without thine aid comes forth into the bright coasts of light, nor waxes glad or lovely. I long that thou shouldest be my helper in writing these verses. . . ."[67]

(2) The body has modest needs—only that which gives delight and takes away pain. Nature does not need banquets in palaces, nor golden images of youths about halls grasping fiery torches; nor need fretted and gilded rafters reecho to the lute; men can "lie in friendly groups on the soft grass near some stream of water under the branches of a tall tree, and at no great cost delightfully refresh their bodies, above all when the weather smiles on them, and the season of the year bestrews the green grass with flowers" [II, 20–33].

(3) "For often the fleecy flocks cropping the glad pasture on a hill creep on whither each is called and tempted by the grass bejewelled with fresh dew, and the lambs fed full gambol and butt playfully; yet all this seems blurred to us from afar, and to lie like a white mass on a green hill" [II, 317–322].

(4) "For often before the sculptured shrines of the gods a calf has fallen, slaughtered hard by the altars smoking with incense, breathing out from its breast the hot tide of blood. But the mother bereft wanders over the green glades and seeks on the ground for the footprints marked by those cloven hoofs, scanning every spot with her eyes, if only she might anywhere catch sight of her lost young, and stopping fills the leafy grove with her lament. . . ." [II, 351–360.]

A practical and utilitarian attitude toward nature so conspicuous in Virgil's *Georgics* might be counterbalanced by a lyrical and esthetic interpretation of landscape so congenial to the *Eclogues*. Here, says Tityrus, after hearing Melibaeus' complaints about the evils which have befallen him and his estate, you can rest tonight with me on the verdant leaves. There are ripe apples, soft chestnuts, and plenty of pressed cheese for us. Now the distant housetops are smoking and the longer shadows fall from the high mountains [*Ec.* I, 80 *ad fin*]. Mossy fountains, grass softer than sleep, green arbutus covering you with its thin shade, keep off the noon heat from the flock; already the burning summer approaches and now the buds are swelling on the fruitful vine [*Ec.* VII, 45–48]. Virgil expresses a desire for communion with nature, assuming, no doubt, that a deeper understanding of life comes with divorcement from the world of men. Let Pallas live, he says, in the cities she has built; the woods above all please us [*Ec.* II, 62].

[67] Lucr. I, 1–25. On the invocation to Venus and its possible inconsistency with Epicurean doctrine, see Bailey's ed. of Lucr. Vol. 2, pp. 588–591. See also Latham's very graceful trans. of this passage in the Penquin Classics ed.

Of the writers of antiquity whose writings have come down to us, however, none has shown a preference for rural life so clearly as has Horace. The joys of the country are associated with the carefree existence of a pristine race of mortals, free of anxiety in money matters, of war-making, of sailing on the angry sea, of life in the Forum and the "proud thresholds of more peaceful citizens." The rural dweller may "wed his lofty poplar-trees to well-grown vines"; look out upon "the ranging herds of lowing cattle"; prune away the useless branches and graft on fruitful ones, store his honey, shear his sheep. The modest wife and mother (in addition to her usual duties) piles high "the sacred hearth with seasoned firewood," pens "the frisking flocks in wattled fold," and milks the cows. Beloved are the scenes of homeward-coming sheep, weary oxen dragging along "the upturned ploughshare on their tired necks" [*Epode* 2]. Horace, "a lover of the country," sends greetings to Fuscus, "lover of the city." "You keep the nest; I praise the lovely country's brooks, its grove and moss-grown rocks." The contrast is really one between art and nature. Like the slave in the priest's household who was fed to satiety with so many sacrificial cakes that he ran away in order to get plain food, he prefers bread to honeyed cake. He follows Stoic teaching when he asks, if it is our duty to live agreeable to nature, what is to be preferred to the country? City advantages are unfavorably compared with country simplicities and even in the city nature is not avoided. "Why, amid your varied columns you are nursing trees, and you praise the mansion which looks out on distant fields. You may drive out Nature with a pitchfork, yet she will ever hurry back, and ere you know it, will burst through your foolish contempt in triumph." "Is the grass poorer in fragrance or beauty than Libyan mosaics?" Is the water in the leaden pipes of the city purer than the water which "dances and purls down the sloping brook?" [*Epistles*, Bk. 1, 10]. Similar themes appear in Tibullus, a contemporary of Virgil and of Horace; his poetry, as does Horace's, contrasts the urban with the rural, the life devoted to wealth, position, or warfare with that associated with humility, desire for a modest fortune, quiet, physical activity, and simplicity [I, i, 1–30]. "When the time is ripe, let me plant the tender vines and the stout orchard trees with my own deft hands, a countryman indeed" [I, i, 7]. Like Varro, he regards the country as the primordial teacher of man. "I sing the country and the country's gods" [II, i, 37]. "They were the guides when man first ceased to chase his hunger with the acorns from the oak." They taught him to build, to train bulls to be his slaves, and to use the wheel. These savage activities were replaced by the planting of fruit trees and gardens, and the "golden grapes gave up their juices to the trampling feet, and sober water was mixed with cheering wine. From the country comes our harvest, when in heaven's glowing heat the earth is yearly shorn of her shock of yellow hair" [II, i, 37–50]. The toils of country life are realistically described [II, iii]; ". . . nor think it shame to grasp the hoe at times or chide the laggard oxen with the goad, nor a trouble to carry homewards in my arms a ewe lamb or youngling goat forgotten by its dam and left alone" [I, i].

Among the agricultural prose writers, Varro and Columella were more philosophical and stern; their belief in primordial rural strength only hardened them in their conviction that the city was an unnatural creation. To Varro the farming life was more ancient than that of the town by an astounding number of years, "and small wonder, for divine nature made the country, but man's skill the towns, and all the arts were discovered in Greece, 'tis said, within the space of a thousand years, but there was never a time when there were in the world no fields which could be cultivated."[68] Columella was perhaps the most bitter commentator in the ancient world about city and country. He lamented the abandonment "with shameful unanimity" of rural virtues and rural discipline, recalling that the Roman heroes and statesmen of old defended their country in need, returning to the plow with peace. Echoing complaints made by Varro "in the days of our grandfathers," Columella says that heads of families have quit the sickle and the plow, have crept within city walls; "we ply our hands [i.e., applaud] in the circuses and theatres rather than in the grainfields and vineyards; and we gaze in astonished admiration at the posturings of effeminate males, because they counterfeit with their womanish motions a sex which nature has denied to men. . . ." The city is a place of excess, of gluttony and drunkenness, debauching the young into premature ill health. In contrast is the life of the country, which is presumed to be closer to ways which are most natural to man because they were gifts originally given mankind by the gods.[69]

The nature imagery of Homer is vivid, but it is closely related to the activities of the gods; in the Hellenistic age, the tendency was to see the aspects of nature as they really were. The fuller knowledge of geography, the experiences of trade, travel, and exploration are manifest in such literature, for landscapes could be compared.[70] The nature poetry and landscape description of the Hellenistic age cannot be matched in any previous period in the classical world, and they may be compared with passages from Ausonius, St. Augustine, the *Romance of the Rose*, and with such writings in modern times.

The interest in nature, emboldened and intensified by inspirations from the East (such as the garden), combined with the enlargement of urban life, brought about a sharpening of the distinction, if one can trust the evidence from men like Horace, Varro, and Columella, between nature and art. This generalization admittedly is difficult to establish, but there does seem ground for belief in the emergence of a self-conscious awareness of the sharp contrast

---

[68] Intro. to Bk. III; cf. intro. pref. to Bk. II.

[69] Columella, *On Agriculture*, Bk. I, pref. 13–21; see also Varro, Bk. II, pref. 3, which is the passage to which C. refers.

[70] Helbig, *Untersuchungen*, pp. 204–209.

between rural and urban life.[71] Indeed, it is probably one of the periods in Western civilization in which the contrast between natural and cultural landscapes has been sharpest. This phenomenon does not first appear with the age of forest clearance in the Middle Ages, the eighteenth century ordering of nature, or the Industrial Revolution. The enlarged size of many Hellenistic cities may well have increased awareness of this distinction, the presence of gardens and tree-lined promenades suggesting a desire to create a small realm of nature within the city.

This discussion brings us to the last point about the Hellenistic period: its importance in the history of Western urbanism. Notwithstanding the deprecating remarks often made about the city, it is hard to deny the existence of a strong urban tradition, an affection for the city as a superior creation of man which existed in the Mediterranean world, and a sharing of this tradition by the peoples of the Hellenistic world. It is hard to believe that Aristotle could think the city an artificial rather than a natural creation; with his strong conviction that man is a social animal, life in the *polis* would be a natural existence for man. For the present it is enough to say that urbanization in this period was of a special nature: it took place most conspicuously in Asia Minor and for the most part in areas which had been urbanized since very ancient times, and Alexandria became one of the greatest, most interesting, and cosmopolitan cities of history.

In chapter 3 there will be more to say about the Hellenistic city because it obviously engenders environmental change.

[71] *Ibid.*, pp. 270 ff.

# Chapter 1

# Order and Purpose in the Cosmos and on Earth

## 1. THEOLOGY AND GEOGRAPHY

In ancient and modern times alike, theology and geography have often been closely related studies because they meet at crucial points of human curiosity. If we seek after the nature of God, we must consider the nature of man and the earth, and if we look at the earth, questions of divine purpose in its creation and of the role of mankind on it inevitably arise. The conception of a designed world, in both classical and in Christian thought, has transcended personal piety. In Western thought the idea of a deity and the idea of nature often have had a parallel history; in Stoic pantheism they were one, and in Christian theology they have supplemented and reinforced one another. Whether a God or the gods had a share in the life of men spent in their beautiful, earthly home, or whether, as the Epicureans believed, the order of nature was not to be ascribed to divine causes, the interpretations which arose out of these arguments have had a dominant place in molding the conception of the earth as a suitable environment for the support of life.

Living nature has been one of the important proofs used to demonstrate the existence of a creator and of a purposeful creation; in the pursuit of this proof there has been an intensification, a quickening, and a concentration of interest in the processes of nature itself. Proof of the existence of divine purpose involved consideration of the assumed orderliness of nature, and if this orderliness were granted, the way was open for a conception of nature as a balance and harmony to which all life was adapted.

The conception of the earth as an orderly harmonious whole, fashioned either for man himself or, less anthropocentrically, for the sake of all life, must be a very ancient one; probably we must seek its ultimate origin in earlier beliefs in the direct personal intervention of the gods in human affairs or in the personification of natural processes in the naming of gods of the crops, and in the old myth of the earth-mother so widespread in the ancient Mediterranean world. There are hints that this conception was established long before the Greeks.

Explaining the way in which knowledge of the Gods has been imparted to men, Plutarch says men accepted heaven as the father, earth as the mother, the father pouring forth spermlke water, the earth-mother receiving it and producing [*De placitis philosophorum* I, vi, 11]. Diodorus says the Chaldeans thought the world was eternal, its disposition and orderly arrangement the work of divine providence, its basis astrology [II, 30, 1–3]. Plutarch elsewhere speaks of a widely held belief of Greeks and barbarians alike that the universe is not of itself suspended aloft without sense or reason or guidance. Wilson has called attention to an old Egyptian text, "interesting and unusual in making the purposes of creation the interests of humans; normally the myth recounts the steps of creation without indication of purpose." The gods take care of men created in their image.

> Well tended are men, the cattle of God. He made heaven and earth according to their desire, and he repelled the water monster (at creation). He made the breath (of) life (for) their nostrils. They are his images that have issued from his body. He arises in heaven according to their desire. He made for them plants and animals, fowl and fish in order to nourish them. He slew his enemies and destroyed (even) his (own) children when they plotted rebellion (against him).[1]

In the Memphite theology, whose original text belongs to the early Old Kingdom, Wilson notes the emergence of the idea of a rational principle in nature which appeared two millennia before the Greeks and Hebrews. Ptah, the god of Memphis, was the heart (that is, the mind, will, and emotion) and the tongue (the organ of expression and command) of the gods. "There was an articulate intelligence behind the creation. Through the thought of the heart and the expression of the tongue, Atum himself and all the other gods

---

[1] Plutarch, *Isis and Osiris*, 369C. John A. Wilson in Henri Frankfort, *et al.*, *Before Philosophy*, p. 64.

came into being." This, Wilson believes, was the closest the Egyptians ever came to the Logos doctrine; the search for a first principle "was inquisitive and exploratory beyond the normal Egyptian placidity with the universe as created."[2]

And in the hymn to Amun (written in the time of Amenhotep II, *ca.* 1436–1411 B.C.), the god Amon-Re creates pasture for beasts, fruit trees for man, that on which the fish and the birds, gnats, worms, flies, may live, giving breath to what is in the egg, sustaining the son of the slug. The concern of the primeval creator-god Aten, here identified with Atum, is for all mankind regardless of race or color:

> Atum, who made the common folk,
> Who varied their natures and made their life,
> Who diversified their hues, one from the other.[3]

Even more striking is the famous hymn of Akh-en-Aton (1369–1353 B.C.) to Aten, the sun god, a hymn which owes its fame to its beauty, to its place in the history of monotheistic ideas, and to the speculation it has aroused because of the striking similarities between it and the 104th Psalm. One passage from this hymn reveals the antiquity of the idea of the glory of the creator being manifested in his works:

> How manifold is that which thou hast made, hidden from view!
> Thou sole god, there is no other like thee!
> Thou didst create the earth according to thy will, being alone:
> Mankind, cattle, all flocks,
> Everything on earth which walks with (its) feet,
> And what are on high, flying with their wings.[4]

---

[2] Wilson, *The Culture of Ancient Egypt*, pp. 59–60; an excerpt relating to this question is translated on p. 60. Wilson dates the period of the Old Kingdom from 2700 to 2200 B.C. After remarking that this search for a first principle was only an approach to abstract thinking, Wilson continues, "But we must remember that the Memphite Theology lies two thousand years before the Greeks or Hebrews. Its insistence that there was a creative and controlling intelligence, which fashioned the phenomena of nature and which provided, from the beginning, rule and rationale, was a high peak of pre-Greek thinking, a peak which was not surpassed in later Egyptian history." See also the extracts from "The Theology of Memphis," trans. by John A. Wilson in James B. Pritchard, ed., *Ancient Near Eastern Texts*, 2nd ed., pp. 4–6. For another discussion, Rudolf Anthes, "Mythology in Ancient Egypt," in Samuel Noah Kramer, ed., *Mythologies of the Ancient World*, pp. 61–64; see also his discussion of the so-called "Credo of a Highpriest of Thebes," p. 47. Anthes says "The Theology of Memphis" is a badly preserved inscription on a monolith erected about 700 B.C. copied on King Shabaka's orders from an old papyrus roll. A dating of 2500 B.C. appears possible and has been generally accepted for the time being, p. 61; the hymn to Osiris was engraved on a tombstone of Amenmose, *ca.* 1550 B.C., pp. 82–85.

[3] Quoted in Williams, "The Hymn to Aten," in D. Winton Thomas, ed., *Documents from Old Testament Times*, p. 150. On the hymn to Amun, see pp. 149–150.

[4] Strophe VI, lines 52–57, *ibid.*, p. 147.

Like the hymn to Amun, that to Aten recognizes that there are differences among peoples, and praises a creator who cares for all:

> The foreign lands of Hurru and Nubia, the land of Egypt—
> Thou dost set each man in his place and supply his needs;
> Each one has his food, and his lifetime is reckoned.
> Their tongues are diverse in speech and their natures likewise;
> Their skins are varied, for thou dost vary the foreigners.[5]

This creator does not hesitate to make different environments for different kinds of men. Long before Herodotus and Plato talked of the distinctive sources of Egyptian water, the Hymn to Aten distinguishes between the Egyptian Nile and the Nile of other countries. The creator makes a life for foreign peoples, but they have been given their Nile in the sky that it may, like the sea, flow down the sides of their mountains, watering "their fields amongst their towns."

> The Nile in the sky is for the foreign peoples,
> For the flocks of every foreign land that walk with (their) feet,
> While the (true) Nile comes forth from the underworld for Egypt.

It is perhaps the earliest mention of the distinction between a land owing its water solely to an exotic stream and a land dependent upon rainfall.[6]

---

[5] Strophe VII, lines 58–62, *ibid.*, p. 147.

[6] Strophe VIII, lines 69–77. See also Deuteronomy 11:10–12. According to Williams, the evidence indicates that the cult of Aten had developed "probably as early as the reign of Thutmose IV (*ca.* 1411–1397 B.C.)" p. 142; the evidence also is inconclusive that Akh-en-Aton is the world's first monotheist, pp. 143–144. Of the often-noted parallel between Psalm 104 and the hymn, he says that while Egyptian literary work influenced Hebrew literature, "we may wonder how a Hebrew poet, more than half a millennium later, could have become acquainted with the central document of a religion which later ages execrated and sought to obliterate from their memory. Despite the complete eclipse of Atenism after the death of Akhenaten, however, its influence remained in art and literature, and many of the ideas contained in the Aten Hymn, itself dependent on earlier models . . . found expression in later religious works. From sources such as these the Psalmist may well have obtained his inspiration." *Ibid.*, p. 149.

Wilson, *The Culture of Ancient Egypt*, pp. 225–229, also discusses the similarities between this hymn and Psalm 104. See the earlier discussions of Breasted, *A History of Egypt*, pp. 371–374 ff., and *The Dawn of Conscience*, pp. 367–370, to which Wilson refers. Breasted, *Dawn of Conscience*, p. 368, quotes Hugo Gressman's conclusion that the mythological motif of the creation of the world probably originated in Babylonia and that "The *motif* of the divine care of the world was a later idea, which made its way into Palestinian Psalmody under the influence of Egypt." See also translations on pp. 282–284. Wilson concludes that there is no direct relationship. "Hymns of this kind were current long after the fall of Akh-en-Aton, so that when Hebrew religion had reached a point where it needed a certain mode of expression it could find in another literature phrases and thoughts which would meet the need." Of the positive qualities of the hymn, he writes ". . . it expressed beautifully the concept of a god who was creative, nurturing, and kindly and who gave his gifts to all mankind and to all living things everywhere and not to the Egyptians alone," p. 229.

## 2. BEGINNINGS OF THE TELEOLOGICAL VIEW OF NATURE

If the notion of God's care for the world existed—as apparently it did from very ancient times—it could gradually be joined with the conception of a unity and harmony in the universe, the two becoming the components of the idea of purposefulness in the creation—that it was the result of intelligent, planned, and well-thought-out acts of a creator. When, in fact, does the idea of a teleology in nature emerge, one abstract and broad enough to be applied to the life of an individual, to the earth as a planet, and to the cosmos? Anaximander espoused the principle of a universe governed by law, but it fell short of teleology.

In Anaxagoras, Diogenes of Apollonia, and Herodotus, however, there are hints which ultimately lead to the teleology of Plato and Aristotle.

To Anaxagoras, Mind "is infinite and self-ruled, and is mixed with nothing but is all alone by itself." It is "the finest of all things and the purest, it has all knowledge about everything and the greatest power; and Mind controls all things, both the greater and the smaller, that have life." Mind controls the rotation and its beginning; it knows when things are "mingled and separated and divided off. . . ." Mind arranges the "rotation in which are now rotating the stars, the sun and moon, the air and the aither that are being separated off." "And the dense is separated off from the rare, the hot from the cold, the bright from the dark and the dry from the moist"; and "nothing is altogether separated off nor divided one from the other except Mind" which is all alike. The argument for intelligent management is based largely on celestial phenomena, on the existence of mixtures and of opposites.[7] If one agrees with Socrates that Anaxagoras was "a man who made no use at all of Mind, nor invoked any other real causes to arrange the world, but explained things by airs and aithers and waters and many other absurdities,"[8] one can see a more active and a more spiritual principle at work in the thought of Diogenes of Apollonia who, it has been said, is the first to have expressed an authentic teleological view of nature.[9]

Intelligence is required, he said, for the underlying substance "so to be divided up that it has measures of all things—of winter and summer and night and day and rains and winds and fair weather" [Fr. 3]. The argument is based on the weather and seasonal and diurnal change. May it not come also from observing the characteristics of the Mediterranean climate with its rainy winters and arid summers with bright cloudless skies, its famous winds blowing from many directions?

[7] Fr. 12, Simplicius *Phys.* 164, 24 and 156, 13. In Kirk and Raven, *PSP*, pp. 372–373.
[8] Plato *Phaedo*, 98 B 7, text and translation being in Kirk and Raven, *PSP*, p. 384.
[9] See Theiler, *Zur Geschichte der teleologischen Naturbetrachtung bis auf Aristoteles*, p. 19.

Men and other living things breathe air and live by it; for them it is "both soul and intelligence" [Fr. 4]. Air is that which men call intelligence; "all men are steered by this and . . . it has power over all things." It is divine, it reaches everywhere, it disposes all things, it is in everything. Everything has some of it, the amounts however varying. It is "many-fashioned, being hotter and colder and drier and moister and more stationary and more swiftly mobile and many other differentiations are in it both of taste and of colour, unlimited in number" [Fr. 5]. All living things have the same soul; this air is warmer than that outside, cooler than that near the sun. The bodily heat of all men is not the same, but neither are the differences so great that they become unlike. Differentiation thus is possible within a broader and basic similarity. "Because, then, the differentiation is many-fashioned, living creatures are many-fashioned and many in number, resembling each other neither in form nor in way of life nor in intelligence, because of the number of differentiations. Nevertheless they all live and see and hear by the same thing, and have the rest of their intelligence from the same thing" [Fr. 5]. In this conception, it is the meteorological and biological elements in the teleology which are most prominent.[10]

According to Aetius, Diogenes and Anaxagoras thought the world (κόσμος) "out of its own propensity" made an inclination to the south, and that living creatures then emerged. The inclination may have been owing to a wise Providence so that thereby some parts of the world may be habitable, others not, depending upon the rigorous cold, scorching heat, or temperate climate of various regions.[11]

And of the sense of purpose in the acts of creator-deities, Herodotus wrote: "Of a truth, Divine Providence does appear to be, as indeed one might expect beforehand, a wise contriver. For timid animals which are a prey to others are all made to produce young abundantly, that so the species may not be entirely eaten up and lost; while savage and noxious creatures are made very unfruitful."[12]

[10] Fr. 3 = Simplicius *Phys.* 152, 13; Fr. 4 = *ibid.*, 152, 18; Fr. 5 = *ibid.*, 152, 22; in Kirk and Raven, *PSP*, pp. 433-435.

[11] Fr. 67, Diels, *Vorsokr.* (6th ed., Berlin, 1952), Vol. II, p. 22. The source is Aetius II, 8. 1.

[12] Hdt. III, 108. Herodotus has been talking about vast numbers of winged serpents guarding trees bearing frankincense; the Arabians said the whole world would swarm with them if their numbers were not kept in check. Herodotus then describes reasons for the high fertility of hares, low fertility of lions, and the natural checks to viper and winged serpent multiplication. It is all fabulous, but the idea of differential rates in increase of animal populations is certainly there (III, 107-109). For commentaries on this passage, see Nestle, *Herodots Verhältnis zur Philosophie und Sophistik*, pp. 16-18 and How and Wells, *A Commentary on Herodotus*, Vol. I, pp. 290-291, cf. Plato, *Protagoras*, 321 B. Nestle thinks that Hdt. III, 108, and Plato, *Protagoras*, 321 B, have a common source in Protagoras' περὶ τῆς ἐν ἀρχῇ καταστάσεως. See Diogenes Laertius, IX, 55.

In this passage the purposeful creation is confined to the fertility of animals, but it reveals the antiquity of the observation that there is a differential fertility among animals, depending upon whether they prey or are preyed upon, and that nature has great reproductive power.

In the myth which Plato has the Sophist Protagoras tell his audience, themes of creation, fertility, adaptation, are woven in with the doctrine of the elements and the idea of design. The gods, already in existence before mankind, fashioned living creatures out of earth and fire, and various mixtures of both, and when they were on the verge of being created, Epimetheus and Prometheus were ordered by the gods "to equip them, and to distribute to them severally their proper qualities." Epimetheus said to Prometheus, "Let me distribute and do you inspect." In distributing attributes to animals, Epimetheus was guided by the principle of preventing the extinction of any one kind. Each animal found a niche and a refuge depending on its nature, like the birds flying in the sky, or animals burrowing in the earth. After being provided with the means of protecting themselves against other animals, they were then given protection against the elements: hair, thick skins, hoofs, hard, callous skins under the feet. Their sources of food were also different: some got herbs, fruit, roots; others, animals—a hint that there is a relationship between animal life and the kinds of plant life in a planned world. Predators had few young, but those who were preyed upon avoided extinction by being prolific.

When he came to inspect, Prometheus, noticing that Epimetheus had distributed all the qualities he had to the animals, saw in his perplexity that other endowments must be bestowed on man when he appeared; Prometheus stole the mechanical arts of Hephaestus and Athena, and fire, without which they could not practice these arts. With these gifts, for which Prometheus paid such a heavy penalty, man "had the wisdom necessary to support life," though he lacked political wisdom. Man thus possessed qualities and skills derived from the gods; with them he invented language and names, learned construction and the handicrafts and how to get food from the soil. The arts of man take the place of the natural protections and defenses granted the animals. Can one interpret this myth to mean that man can survive and perpetuate himself only by applying his arts, his tools, and his inventions to nature, to manipulate and fashion it to his own ends? While being alert to the danger of reading this passage with modern eyes, one can still discern the biological idea of a natural control of animal populations through predation and environmental conditions, contrasted with a social idea of the arts which are to man what protective devices, dexterities, and adaptations are to the animals. This myth may represent an early attempt to explain how man, a part of nature, has a position with relation to it far different from that of other forms of life. Although the order of nature and human art are of divine origin, man and animals, both part of the same creation, have endowments of an entirely different order.[13]

### 3. XENOPHON ON DESIGN

In a famous passage Xenophon puts arguments into the mouth of Socrates which were used by virtually every writer sympathetic to the design argument through the middle of the nineteenth century, elaborated and illustrated, to be sure, by the incomparably richer body of scientific knowledge of modern times.

Three kinds of proof are used in demonstrating the existence of a divine providence: the proof of physiology, of the cosmic order, and of the earth as a fit environment. Socrates, anticipating Paley's *Natural Theology* and the famous *Bridgewater Treatises* of the nineteenth century, points out that the creator seems to have given men eyes, ears, nostrils, and the tongue for some useful purpose; of what use would smells be, he asks, without nostrils? The eyelids are compared to doors, opening for seeing, closing with sleep; other illustrations from the human anatomy are given to the same purpose. The gods have given erect carriage to man alone; he can see above him, ahead of him, and he is less exposed to injury; and in addition man has been given a soul. In this long history of the physiological argument, the eye—followed closely by the hand—has been a classic proof of design.[14]

From the hands came the arts; from the eyes, the ability to see the divine creation; from the erect carriage, the ability to look upward to the stars, instead of bending like the animals toward the earth. The old astronomers, says Cumont, "marvelled at the power of the eye, and the ancients expressed their astonishment at the range of vision which reached the remotest constellations. They give it the preeminence over all the other senses, for the eyes are to them the intermediaries between the sidereal gods and human reason."[15]

The second, the argument based on cosmic order—the forerunner of the astro-theology of the eighteenth century and a basic argument of all natural theologies—may be passed over to consider the third, which is of chief interest—the evidence of design apparent on the earth itself. Socrates asks Euthydemus whether he has ever considered how carefully the gods have provided for the requirements of man, and, when Euthydemus replies that he has not, he

---

[13] Plato, *Protagoras*, 320 d–322 d (trans. by Jowett). This famous myth has been interpreted in many ways, perhaps most often as an idealized account of the development of civilization. Guthrie sees Protagoras (the Sophist, not the Platonic dialogue) as the first thinker who advanced a kind of social-contract theory of the origin of law, *The Greeks and Their Gods*, pp. 340–341. For an interpretation by a modern authority on the Sophists, see Untersteiner, Mario, *The Sophists* (trans. by Kathleen Freeman), pp. 58–64, and for references to the literature on the myth, pp. 72–73, esp. fn. 24.

[14] Xen., *Mem.* I. iv. 4–15; see 8–9 on the elements, the mind, and chance.

[15] Cumont, *Astrology and Religion Among the Greeks and Romans*, p. 57.

and Socrates together point out in detail the nature of divine foresight: light is provided for man, but night is also necessary for a period of rest, and if some tasks, like sailing, must be done at night, there are the stars to guide us while the moon marks off the divisions of the night and of the month. The gods have made the earth yield food and they have devised the seasons. Water, aiding earth and the seasons, is supplied in great abundance; and fire, another evidence of divine foresight, not only protects man from the cold and dark, but is needed in everything of any importance which men prepare for their use. After the winter solstice, the sun approaches to mature some crops and to dry up others already matured. Even its northward turning is gradual and gentle—here the design fits in admirably with the temperate climates—for it does not retreat far enough to freeze man and it returns to be again in that part of the heavens of most advantage to us. Euthydemus then says, "I begin to doubt whether after all the gods are occupied in any other work than the service of man. The one difficulty I feel is that the lower animals also enjoy these blessings." Socrates replies that the animals are produced and nourished for the sake of man, who gains more advantages from the animals than from the fruits of the earth. ". . . A large portion of mankind," he adds, with eyes clearly on the sheep and goats of the eastern Mediterranean, "does not use the products of the earth for food, but lives on the milk and cheese and flesh they get from live stock. Moreover, all men tame and domesticate the useful kinds of animals, and make them their fellow-workers in war and many other undertakings." They are stronger than man, but he can put them to whatever use he chooses. The gods gave man his senses in order that he might take advantage of the innumerable beautiful and useful objects in the world. "Yes, and you," says Socrates, "will realise the truth of what I say if, instead of waiting for the gods to appear to you in bodily presence, you are content to praise and worship them because you see their works."[16] This statement in the *Memorabilia*, along with the arguments of the Stoic Balbus in Cicero's *De natura deorum* became the prototype of all subsequent writings. No basically new idea, despite its use over two millennia, was ever added to it, although the illustrations became more sophisticated and more plentiful.

Xenophon's *Memorabilia*[17] was much admired by the early Stoics, and his works and Cicero's were influential in the seventeenth century attempt to interpret the earth and the living nature on it as evidence of purpose. The characteristics of the arguments presented by Socrates and Euthydemus in the *Memorabilia* are as important as the ideas themselves. These characteristics have reappeared countless times in the modern literature of natural theology, biology, geography, and demography, and therefore should be recapitulated here. There is the strong sense of wonderment at the works of nature, a won-

---

[16] Xen., *Mem.* IV. iii. 2–14.
[17] For the sources of Xenophon's ideas, see Theiler, *Zur Gesch. d. teleolog. Naturbetrachtung bis auf Aristoteles*, pp. 19–54.

derment heightened in modern times under the influence of Christianity. It often replaces curiosity, for in it there is little exhortation to study and to investigate nature, although this objection is not true of the late seventeenth and early eighteenth century students of natural history. It is as if the two men are looking out over the pleasing landscape of the Mediterranean shore with its blue skies, its vines, and its cultivated fields, and are seeing there living proofs of a reasoned and purposive creation. Natural theology never lost this wonderment, nor a feeling for the wholeness and the unity of all nature.

The strong utilitarian and practical bias of the ideas is equally striking, whether all manifestations of nature are considered as creations for the welfare and comfort of man alone, or whether—in modern restatements—the design is viewed less anthropocentrically and becomes the means of interpreting and explaining the existence of all life. The emphasis on favorable conditions for food production, for navigation, for human comfort, for the discovery and application of the arts and sciences—all made possible by divine arrangements —so strongly expressed in these passages, has characterized the vast majority of conceptions of the earth written from this point of view. Finally, the order and beauty of nature described here, including the advantages of seasonal change, can be argued more persuasively for the temperate zones.

### 4.  THE ARTISANSHIP OF GOD AND OF NATURE

Even more important in the history of these ideas is the concept of the artisan deity which Plato advanced in the *Timaeus*. This concept is the sophisticated expression of earlier mythological themes of God as a needleworker, a potter, a weaver, a smith. "Almost everywhere the primordial creation is burdened with the earthly weight of a lowly handicraft, with the tool of physical demiurgy." The world-creator of the *Timaeus* "is a sublimation of the mythical artisan-god."

In his exposition Timaeus makes a distinction between the ideal and the eternal (that which is *existent* always and has no *becoming*) and the real and the transitory (that which is *becoming* always and is never *existent*); the first is apprehended by thought aided by reasoning, the second is merely the object of opinion aided by unreasoning sensation. Anything, like the cosmos, which has a becoming must have a cause of this becoming. If the divine artisan uses the eternal as his model, his creation will be beautiful, but if he takes the created model (or the becoming) as his own model, his creation will not be beautiful. The whole cosmos has been created: it is visible, tangible, and has a body, and thus is a becoming apprehended by belief and sensation. Upon which model did the architect-creator make the cosmos? Timaeus answers that it was made in the model of the eternal, for it is too beautiful not to have been so modeled, and it would be impious to suppose it to be patterned on a created model. "But it is clear to everyone that his gaze was on the Eternal;

for the Cosmos is the fairest of all that has come into existence, and He is the best of all the Causes." The creator "was good, and in him that is good no envy ariseth ever concerning anything; and being devoid of envy He desired that all should be, so far as possible, like unto Himself," desiring that "so far as possible, all things should be good and nothing evil." God finding everything "in a state of discordant and disorderly motion" brought it to a state of order. The cosmos was intentionally made the most beautiful and the best; it has come into being through God's providence. Since it is made after the eternal model, one can assume that only one such has been created, that it is a living creature with soul and reason. The cosmos, as a living creature, contains within it "all of the living creatures which are by nature akin to itself." In the beginning God made this body of the universe of fire and earth, later inserting water and air between them. All of the elements were used up in order to make it perfect and whole; since they were used up, another such living body could not be made. The living whole, made in the shape of a sphere, was secure from both old age and disease;[18] the creator-artisan not only acts for the best but he acts like a human artisan in having in his mind's eye the model or plan of the kind of universe he is creating.

Plato was not the first to advance teleological ideas regarding the creation of the cosmos but he seems to be the first to see it as the work of an intelligent, good, reasoning, and divine artisan.[19] It was this idea—especially the short passages from 27D to 30D—which influenced the theology of the early Church fathers; Plato's God, however, is clearly not the Christian God, though many attempts have been made to find strong similarities between them.[20]

The soul is the cause of individual life, and purposefully ordered life reveals itself in regular movements. By analogy the world soul is the first and oldest creation of the Demiurgus; it is the principle of order and of orderly movement in the skies. In the cosmos, the four elements are bound together by friendship, associations ordained by God.[21]

The Platonic artisan is mind imposing itself on reluctant matter. "Plato

---

[18] This discussion is based on Plato's *Timaeus* (Loeb Classical Library), 27–33C. The argument is summarized in 69B, ff., followed by a detailed description of the creation of the various parts of the body from the teleological point of view. See also R. G. Bury's comments, in the intro. to his trans. of *Timaeus* in the Loeb Classical Library, pp. 14–15, and Bluck, *Plato's Life and Thought*, pp. 137–140. The first quotation on the nature of the artisan-god is from Robert Eisler, *Weltenmantel und Himmelszelt*, p. 235 as translated in Ernst R. Curtius, *European Literature and the Latin Middle Ages*, pp. 545–546. After mentioning that the Timaeus is a sublimation of the mythical artisan-god, Curtius continues, "Both elements then fuse with the potter, weaver, and smith god of the Old Testament in the medieval topos of the Deus artifex," p. 546.

[19] Theiler, *op. cit.*, has made a thorough study of this idea, including exhaustive references to the teleological principle in the writings of Plato and Aristotle.

[20] Bultmann, *Primitive Christianity*, pp. 15–18, discusses this point.

[21] Spitzer, "Classical and Christian Ideas of World Harmony," *Traditio*, Vol. 2 (1944), pp. 417–419.

bases his physical doctrine on the principle that Reason [ νοῦς] and Life [ψυχή] are prior in nature to Body [ σῶμα ] and to blind physical causation [ ἀνάγκη ]."[22]

What is most revealing in Plato's conception, from the point of view of our history, is the relationship of artisanship to art, the δημιουργός to τέχνη. The Greeks' respect for the artisan and for the beauty and order produced by intelligence and manual skill lies deep in their history. "Even in the distant age of bronze the inhabitants of Greece and the islands held the skilled worker in metal in very high regard. His art was both a mystery and a delight, and he was thought to owe his gifts to supernatural beings around whom many legends grew." Hephaestus is a divine artificer because he is so great an artist in metal and ivory and precious stones. "The mortal smith worked, as he thought his god worked, with his delicate moulds engraved by his own hand, and employed drills, chisels, punches, and flats. There is no lack of evidence from the prehistoric bronze age of the fineness of such work."[23] In a period which lacked precision measurements and instruments, high skill was achieved in carving, chasing, and engraving on gold, silver, bronze, ivory, and gems and in the construction of monuments and buildings which required plans. The respect for artisanship could lead to two general ideas: (1) the creator as artisan, and (2) man as a being who can create order and beauty out of brute material, or more broadly, who can control natural phenomena with a combination of intelligence and skill.

In the *Timaeus*, the idea is expressed that we live in a world full of the richness, fullness, and variety of life owing to the non-envying nature of the divine artisan. (See the discussion of the "principle of plenitude," pp. 5–6.)

Over two thousand years before Voltaire was making fun of Pope and Leibniz, Plato had declared that this was the best of all possible worlds, that the arrangements observable in the cosmos and on the earth itself were a result of the work of a generous and unstinting divine artisan, and that the fullness and variety of life was inherent in the very making of the cosmos as a living being. These ideas, together with those derived from Christian thought, go far toward explaining attitudes toward the earth which persisted until the publication of the *Origin of Species*.

## 5. ARISTOTLE'S TELEOLOGY OF NATURE

Unlike Plato, Aristotle apparently had no need for an artisan deity, but the evidence is inconsistent and uncertain whether he believed the structure and history of the cosmos to be the fulfillment of divine planning, to be due to

---

[22] *Laws* 899b. 9; the quote is from Kahn, *Anaximander and the Origins of Greek Cosmology*, p. 206; see also pp. 206–207. On the artisan, see also Sambursky, *The Physical World of the Greeks*, p. 67.
[23] Seltman, *Approach to Greek Art*, pp. 12–13.

individual beings consciously working toward ends, or that nature itself unconsciously strives toward ends. Ross believes it is the third "which prevails in Aristotle's mind."

Aristotle's doctrine of the four causes and his belief that nature does nothing in vain gave further support to the teleological argument in philosophy and biology and its application to the earth. The final cause is the rational end implicit in the formative process, the final cause being responsible for the character of the course which the Logos follows. The final cause is the crucial one; it is "the *logos* of the thing—its rational ground, and the logos is always the beginning for products of nature as well as for those of Art." The works of nature can be understood on the analogy of processes observed in the making of machines and contrivances by man, for it is impossible to conceive of such a machine or such a contrivance being made without a preconceived pattern existing in the mind of the artificer. In his healing the physician thinks of health, and in his construction the builder thinks of a completed house, and once they have these goals in mind, "each of them can tell you the causes and rational grounds for everything he does, and why it must be done as he does it."[24] Aristotle explains that this purposeful activity, so clear in the plans of the doctor or the builder, is even more true of nature, but "the final cause, or the Good, is more fully present in the works of Nature than in the works of Art." Nature, like man, is a craftsman, but an infinitely more powerful one.

In applying his method to the study of animals, Aristotle says that we should investigate all of them, even those that are mean and insignificant, for when we study animals we know that "in not one of them is Nature or Beauty lacking. I add 'Beauty,' because in the works of Nature purpose and not accident is predominant; and the purpose or end for the sake of which those works have been constructed or formed has its place among what is beautiful." It is the figure and form, not merely the bricks, mortar, and timber, that concerns us in a house; "so in Natural science, it is the composite thing, the thing as a whole, which primarily concerns us, not the materials of it, which are not found apart from the thing itself whose materials they are."[25]

In the *Politics* Aristotle expresses clearly but in disappointingly crude fashion the idea of purpose in nature, including the relation of plants and animals to the needs of man. Variety in the kinds of animals corresponds to that in the kinds of food, for food habits make differences in their ways of life. Nature has determined their habits in order that they can obtain their choice of foods with greater ease. Plants must be intended for the use of animals; animals, we can infer, exist for man; the tame for use and food, the wild—

---

[24] Arist., *Parts of Animals* (Loeb Classical Library), I. i. (639b 15–22). See W. D. Ross, *Aristotle*, on alternative interpretations of teleology and the role of God, pp. 181–182.
[25] *Ibid.*, I. v. (645a 24–37).

if not all—for food, clothing, and various instruments. "Now if Nature makes nothing incomplete, and nothing in vain, the inference must be that she has made all animals for the sake of man."[26] In this anthropocentric conception of interrelationships in nature, the distribution of plants and animals is directly related to the needs and uses of man; the idea has been repeated countlessly in modern times, although many writers on natural theology in the seventeenth and eighteenth centuries protested against it as being incompatible with the Christian religion, maintaining that it was but another example of man's pride. No doubt man owed his existence to such providential arrangements in nature, but these did not exist for him alone.

Aristotle says that if men, living luxuriously in well-planned houses under the earth—and who had heard by rumor of the existence of deities or divine powers—should suddenly behold, if the jaws of the earth were opened up, the earth, the seas, the sky, the clouds, the winds, the sun, moon, and stars and the heavenly bodies fixed in their eternal courses, "surely they would think that the gods exist and that these mighty marvels are their handiwork."[27]

What, then, are the general characteristics of Aristotle's teleology of which these illustrations are a part? Everything is done for an end; the cosmos, although eternal, is the result of planning. Recurrences in the cosmic order are evidences of plan and purpose—and thus of artisanship, for one studies nature as one studies an object made by a man: What is it made of? How is it made and by what techniques? What are the functions of each constituent part? What is its purpose?[28]

Aristotle often describes nature anthropomorphically as if it were a tidy and frugal householder, so well-ordered is it. Not everything, however, can be explained by final causes; for some phenomena material and efficient causes are sufficient: the eye as a whole may be explained by final causes, but not its color, for that serves no useful purpose.[29]

Of particular interest is Aristotle's application of teleological ideas to biology, because of his contributions to that field. It is an immanent teleology. "The end of each species is internal to the species; its end is simply to be that kind of thing, or, more definitely, to grow and reproduce its kind, to have sensation, and to move, as freely and efficiently as the conditions of its existence—its habitat, for instance—allow." A characteristic of one species is not designed for another; nature gives an organ only to an animal that can make use of it.

For whose ends does this purposiveness exist in nature? Aristotle does not suggest that the individual animal acts out his life purposefully. "It is generally

[26] Arist., *Politica*, I. 8. (1256ᵃ 18–30, 1256ᵇ 10–25.)
[27] In Cic., *Nat. D.* (Loeb Classical Library ), II, 37. 94–95. See Hume, *Dialogues Concerning Natural Religion*, Part XI.
[28] On Aristotle's teleology in physics, see Sambursky, *The Physical World of the Greeks*, pp. 103–112.
[29] W. D. Ross, *Aristotle*, pp. 81–82.

nature that is described as acting for a purpose, but nature is not a conscious agent; it is the vital force present in all living things." ". . . Aristotle appears to rest content, as many thinkers have done since, with the surely unsatisfactorý notion of purpose which is not the purpose of any mind."[30] If the purpose is an unconscious one, how can it be a purpose? "But Aristotle's language suggests that he (like many modern thinkers) did not feel this difficulty, and that, for the most part, he was content to work with the notion of an unconscious purpose in nature itself."[31]

If Aristotle's teleology of nature is unsatisfactory, if there is uncertainty regarding purpose and the role of mind, these flaws did not affect its adoption with necessary changes by Christian thinkers whose Christian God could supply purpose and the design in full measure.

### 6. MISGIVINGS OF THEOPHRASTUS

By the death of Aristotle in 322 B.C., several important ideas concerning the relationship of man to the earth had already been well established: the hidden divine force could be discerned in the works of the creation; a creator-artisan, a demiurge, had, like a craftsman, made order out of the disorderly matter of the universe; there was a purpose or a final cause inherent in natural processes; there was a fullness and richness of life in nature; and plants existed for animals and animals for man.

Could all of these ideas have been inspired by such commonplace observations as the variety and richness of plant life, the role of the plan in crafts like the carpenter's, the heavy reliance of man on domestic animals and they on man, the necessity of plant life to the survival of these animals? In these earlier writings, however, references to the terrestrial order were not elaborated upon although it was conceived of as a balanced and harmonious creation of which man was a part; it is in this conception that we should seek the origins of the modern idea of a balance in nature, so important in the history of biology and ecology, with the significant difference that in the modern idea human activities have often been regarded as interferences—often destructive—in this balance.

Theophrastus (372/369–288/285 B.C.), Aristotle's pupil who took over the school when Aristotle left Athens, saw difficulties in the teleological view

---

[30] *Ibid.*, p. 125.

[31] *Ibid.*, p. 182. Ross cites a possible exception to Aristotle's denial that a characteristic of one species may be designed for the benefit of another: "Sharks have their mouth on their under surface in order that, while they turn to bite, their prey may escape—but also to save them from over-eating!" p. 125. This discussion is based on Ross, pp. 125, 181–182; on teleology applied to the state, see p. 230. On Aristotle's teleology see also Zeller, *Outlines of the History of Greek Philosophy*, pp. 197–198. For full documentation, see Zeller's *Die Philosophie der Griechen in ihrer geschichtlichen Entwicklung*, II Tl., II Abt., 4th Aufl., pp. 421–428; see also Theiler, *op. cit.* (see n. 17 above), 83–101.

of nature so forcefully expressed by both Plato and Aristotle, pointing out the shortcomings of final causes and the shakiness of the assumption of planfulness and purposiveness in nature. His examples are taken from cosmic and terrestrial phenomena and from the plant and animal kingdoms. It is difficult, he says, to find plans in each class of things, to link them up with a final cause, difficult "both in animals and in plants and in the very bubble." This linking may be possible "by reason of the order and change of *other* things," such as seasonal change "on which depends the generation both of animals and of plants and fruits, the sun being, as it were, the begetter." Theophrastus obviously thinks teleological explanations are rough approximations, to be used with caution; difficulties in them call for an inquiry to determine the "extent to which order prevails, and an account of the reason why more of it is impossible or the change it would produce would be for the worse."[32]

The finding of ends in nature, he says, is not so easy as is claimed. In a sentence suggesting an objection Kant later made in his illustration of the pine tree growing on the sand (see below, p. 530), Theophrastus asks, "Where should we begin and with what sort of things should we finish?" Is this directed against the fault which Ross noted in Aristotle's teleology that his notion of purpose was unsatisfactory because it was not the purpose of any mind? Many things occur, he adds, not for the sake of an end but by coincidence or necessity; celestial and terrestrial phenomena are in this category. "For to what end are the incursions and refluxes of the sea, or droughts and humidities, and, in general, changes, now in this direction and now in that, and ceasings-to-be and comings-to-be, and not a few other things, too, that are like these?"[33] Theophrastus finds similar failures of teleological explanation in animals possessing useless parts, in the nutrition and in the birth of animals, phases of which are owing to necessity and coincidence. He warns against assuming uncritically "that nature in all things should desire the best and when it is possible give things a share in the eternal and orderly. . . ."[34] His attitude differs from that later expressed by Lucretius: Theophrastus, speaking primarily from a biological point of view, advocates a skepticism regarding the validity of final causes in interpreting the nature of nature; Lucretius condemns them entirely, although he has his own private teleology. Theophrastus points out that what does *not* obey or receive the good greatly predominates, the animate being a small part, the inanimate infinite in the universe, "and of animate things themselves there is only a minute part whose existence is actually better than its non-existence would be." Again in calling attention to the narrow range of applicability of the doctrine of final causes, Theophrastus questions its validity as a satisfactory explanation for whatever order may exist. Obviously Theophrastus thinks that there is physical dis-

---

[32] *Metaphysics*, IV, 15.
[33] *Metaphysics*, IX, 29.
[34] *Metaphysics*, IX, 31.

order in nature, that order must be proved, not assumed: ". . . We must try to find a certain limit, both in nature and in the reality of the universe, both to final causation and to the impulse to the better. For this is the beginning of the inquiry about the universe, i.e. of the effort to determine the conditions on which real things depend and the relations in which they stand to one another."[35]

In the *De natura deorum*, Velleius, the Epicurean spokesman, has nothing complimentary to say of either Theophrastus or his pupil Strato. Theophrastus is "intolerably inconsistent; at one moment he assigns divine pre-eminence to mind, at another to the heavens, and then again to the constellations and stars in the heavens." Nor is Strato, surnamed the natural philosopher, worthy of attention: "In his view the sole repository of divine power is nature, which contains in itself the causes of birth, growth and decay, but is entirely devoid of sensation and of form." Cicero himself says Strato wants to exempt the deity from exertion on any extensive scale: "He declares that he does not make use of divine activity for constructing the world." All existing phenomena have been produced by natural causes—he has no patience with Democritus' atomic theory—teaching that "whatever is or comes into being is or has been caused by natural forces of gravitation and motion."[36]

## 7. STOIC VIEWS OF NATURE

Although the idea that the earth is a designed and fit environment for life was formulated in all its essentials by the fourth century B.C., it was further cultivated and enriched by the Stoics, a crucial change in emphasis apparently being taken by Panaetius and his pupil Posidonius.

Panaetius, a Rhodian born about 185 B.C., had traveled widely throughout the Mediterranean world, including Egypt and Syria; at Athens he studied under the Stoic Diogenes of Babylon,[37] himself a pupil of Chrysippus. Panaetius lived in Rome where Polybius inspired him with interests in history, especially that of Rome's triumphal and inexorable march to world power, interests which made him fully conscious of the importance of historical development to a deeper understanding of the present.[38] Panaetius gave a deeper meaning to the old Stoic belief that the beauty and purposefulness of the world is to be ascribed to a creative primeval force, less by new ideas than through appreciation of the visible aspects of nature. Through him the feeling for nature in Hellenistic poesy and painting was brought to bear on a philosophical world view: not only is there a splendor in the cosmic

---

[35] *Metaphysics*, IX, 32, 34.
[36] Velleius' speech is in *Nat. D.*, I, 13, 35, Cicero's in *Academica*, II, 38, 121.
[37] W. D. Ross, "Diogenes (3)," *OCD*, p. 285.
[38] This discussion of Panaetius is based on Pohlenz, "Panaitios, 5," *PW*, 18:3, col. 421, and on his *Die Stoa*, Vol. I, pp. 191–207.

order, but there is joy in the beauty of the earth—of the Greek landscape
with its alternation of land and sea, its innumerable islands, its contrasts between the lovely shores and the steep mountains and the rough cliffs, and
the variety of plant and animal life existing in this landscape. It not only has
beauty; it also has a perfection. Do we not recognize the work of a purposefully creative nature as the Nile and the Euphrates fertilize the fields, in the
winds, in day and night, summer and winter everywhere, for these make life
and growth possible? The most wonderful fact of all is that nature not only
has created its beings once but has provided for their perpetuation. The apex
of the creation is man, his erect carriage being his decisively differentiating
characteristic. He need not, like the animals, look at the ground in searching
for food, but can see the creation as one viewing a panorama from an eminence,
seeing there the external world which he can make use of with the help of his
intelligence. Panaetius however does not share the old Stoic anthropocentric
belief that the earth has been created for human needs alone; man is here
and he makes use of its beauties and resources.

These ideas, many of which reappear in Cicero's *De natura deorum*, show
the early fusion of esthetic and utilitarian attitudes toward the earth. It is
beautiful and it is useful; these two simple characterizations of the earth explain
much of the subsequent history of attitudes toward it: it is beautiful to look
upon and its beauty should be preserved; it is useful because it possesses the
materials for the exercise of the mind of man, whose creations, tools, and
machines change and improve it to meet his ever-recurring and increasing
demands.[39] Panaetius also made one of the earliest attempts to use ideas of
environmental influence within a framework of the design argument. Rejecting Stoic beliefs in astrology, he accepts Hippocratic ideas, finding in
man a distinctive characteristic—that he belongs to a community whose character is determined by climate and landscape.[40]

One senses in Posidonius' thought—which has come down to us only in
the works of others—a profound sense of the importance of geography and
of the biological interrelationships existing in the terrestrial harmony.[41] Both
Panaetius and Posidonius seem to be set apart from the pre-Socratic philos-

[39] Pohlenz, *Die Stoa*, Vol. I, pp. 195–197. This paragraph is based on Pohlenz's analysis
of Panaetius and the characteristics which distinguished him from the older Stoics. See
also Cic., *Nat. D.* II, 52–53, and Pohlenz, Vol. II, pp. 98–99. His sources, says Pohlenz,
were mostly Xenophon, Aristotle, and the teleological physiology of Erasistratus. "Aber
ihm selbst [Panaetius] gehört die Grundstimmung, die überall in der Welt das Wirken
eines zweckbewusst schaffenden Logos spürt, und die 'natürliche Theologie'; die in
diesem die Gottheit erkennt." Vol. I, p. 197. See also p. 193.

[40] Pohlenz, *Die Stoa*, Vol. I, p. 218.

[41] Because of the extraordinary difficulty of Posidonian scholarship (largely a question
of *Quellenuntersuchungen*) and because of the controversial nature of many of the interpretations, I have used the following secondary sources: Reinhardt, K., "Poseidonios
von Apameia," *PW*, 22:1, cols. 558–826 (an article giving impressive evidence of the
depth of Posidonian scholarship, its controversies, and its difficulties) and the same
author's *Poseidonios*, and Pohlenz's discussion as already cited.

ophers, from Plato, Aristotle, and the earlier Stoics, in their greater use of ethnological, geographical, and biological materials. The emphasis shifts from the cosmos as a whole, from physical theory such as the doctrine of the elements, from theories of origins and of cosmogony, to an investigation of visible phenomena on earth. With the inspiration of Panaetius, Posidonius found in the Stoic teleological teachings a way of unifying—and then of understanding—separate fields of knowledge; Posidonius has been called the greatest scientific traveler of antiquity.[42] One has the impression of a profoundly curious man traveling throughout Gaul, Italy, Spain—where he studied the tides at Gades—in order to observe the diversity of peoples and of environments in which they lived.[43] Posidonius had a sense of the significance of history; both writers were impressed with the theme of Polybius who set down the events which in a period of fifty years had led Rome from a position as a peninsular power to world hegemony.[44] The sense of history, the sense of life and growth in nature, of natural phenomena such as the tides, gave his thinking a dynamic force which the older Stoic conceptions lacked, for to them the unity and harmony of nature seems to be more like a fixed and hard-set mosaic. What lay behind his belief that the world is perfect, that its processes are based on purpose, that being and life belong together, that life permeates the entire cosmos, that it is a vital force found everywhere? Posidonius accepted astrology; his teacher Panaetius had rejected it. But it clearly is the astrology of which Thorndike wrote, the great cosmic influences exerted as a natural law on the sublunary world.

To Posidonius, Panaetius' theories of environmental causality were not carrying things back far enough. Climate and landscape themselves were determined by the position of the sun under the influence of the other stars. This way of thinking led him to postulate the direct influences of the stars on a people, and the indirect influences on the characteristics of individuals. All parts of the cosmos are bound together by sympathy: the moon and the tides, the sun and vegetation, the influence of the stars on individuals and on a people. The influence of the sun and the moon on earthly life are plain enough. Could one not go beyond this and speak of the influences of the farther planets and constellations? One must go beyond the climatic theories of Panaetius, for climate and landscape were the result of the position of the sun and the influence of other stars.[45]

Man is very much a part of nature; he grows in his environment and is affected by it—here theories of environmental influence, such as the preem-

---

[42] Pohlenz, *Die Stoa*, Vol. I, p. 209.

[43] *Ibid.*, Vol. I, pp. 209–210: on his personal experiences with the Celts, his study in Spain, the influence of the sea on coastal formations, of mining, inventions, his revulsion at the inhuman treatment of slaves in the mines, and his school in Rhodes in which Cicero was a student.

[44] *Ibid.*, Vol. I, pp. 211–212.

[45] *Ibid.*, I, p. 218.

inent qualities of temperate climates, are introduced. These relationships, however, can only be understood by conceding the existence of harmonies in the whole cosmos. The sun, an example of divine foresight, is created for the benefit of all life; it makes possible the existence of plants and animals, the alternation of day and night, the climate, the pigmentation of man; it makes the earth wet or dry, fruitful or barren. Human arts are imitations of nature, for only human thought could invent the ship's rudder by observing a fish's tail, the invention being possible because the same Logos, the same rational plan, is at work in human thinking as is manifest in nature. Human art, as distinguished from that of the animals, is manifested in its manifold inventions devoted not only to the satisfaction of needs but to the making of a more beautiful life. It is the creativity of the Logos, and not necessity, which has brought about the development of human culture; man with his intelligence, his innumerable accomplishments and his inventions, is part of nature, and his powers, derived from nature, enable him to succeed in a wide variety of undertakings, powers, and abilities which are denied the plants and the animals. The earth is created by the gods not only for their own sakes but for man and the lower orders of plant and animal life.[46] The central thought of Posidonius' philosophy, Reinhardt has said, is that of development reaching its goal through differentiation. How is one to explain multiplicity from unity, the complex from the simple? From the poets and from history he gathered his materials to show the original unity of all the highest human activities and their gradual development into the now dominant complexity.[47]

Posidonius' thought is derived from ideas in biology, history, astronomy, geography, and ethnology. It seems ecological too, and the emphasis on esthetics and the beauties of nature as convincing evidence of a purposefully made earth and cosmos makes one understand both the reverence in which he was held in antiquity and his influence, through writers like Cicero, Seneca, Strabo, and Vitruvius, on the thought of modern times, an influence which is all the greater if it is true, as has been suggested, that the second book of Cicero's *De natura deorum* is derived in large part from Posidonius.[48]

## 8. On the Nature of the Gods

Cicero's dialogue, *De natura deorum*, with its contrasting views of the Epicureans, the Academics, and the Stoics, became an important repository of religious ideas, including the design argument; it became—with similar writ-

---

[46] *Ibid.*, pp. 222–224; 227–228.

[47] Reinhardt, *Poseidonios*, p. 75.

[48] Posidonius will be discussed later with relation to environmental theories. His ideas of nature were closely tied up with old Stoic ideas that fire was the most vigorous and most active element and therefore would gradually get the upper hand. (Pohlenz, *Die Stoa*, I, p. 219.) On his ideas of sympathy and the cosmos as an organic whole, see *idem*, *Kosmos und Sympathie*, pp. 117–119. On the earth as a home for men, *idem*, "Poseidonios von Apamea," *PW*, 22:1, cols. 809–810.

ings of Seneca and the *Timaeus* of Plato—a vehicle for the reintroduction of the classical design argument in the Renaissance and in the influential natural theologies of the seventeenth and eighteenth centuries.[49]

The four interlocutors of the dialogue are Balbus, a Stoic, Velleius, an Epicurean, and Cotta and Cicero, Academics and disciples of Plato. Cicero introduces the dialogue by reviewing the principal attitudes which are held concerning the nature of the gods: the view that the gods take no cognizance of human affairs, which Cicero impatiently dismisses; the view of those men "of eminence and note," meaning the Stoics, who conceive of the world as directed by divine intelligence and reason, the products of the earth, and atmospheric and seasonal changes being their gifts to man. Even Carneades' sharp criticism of this point of view is done "in such a manner as to arouse in persons of active mind a keen desire to discover the truth."[50]

Velleius, the representative of Epicureanism, ridicules both Plato's artisan-deity, who does not create but who makes order out of chaos, and the Stoic idea of providence.

> I am not going to expound to you doctrines that are mere baseless figments of the imagination, such as the artisan deity and world-builder of Plato's *Timaeus*, or that old hag of a fortune-teller, the *Pronoia* (which we may render "Providence") of the Stoics; nor yet a world endowed with a mind and senses of its own, a spherical, rotary god of burning fire; these are the marvels and monstrosities of philosophers who do not reason but dream. What power of mental vision enabled your master Plato to descry the vast and elaborate architectural process which, as he makes out, the deity adopted in building the structure of the universe? What method of engineering was employed? What tools and levers and derricks? What agents carried out so vast an undertaking? And how were air, fire, water and earth enabled to obey and execute the will of the architect?[51]

It is noteworthy that this criticism employs technological figures of speech, but with Plato the analogy of the human artisan supports, while with Velleius it denies, the planned creation.

Later Balbus retorts that Velleius has a very limited understanding of the Stoic vocabulary; he and others of like belief are too enamored of their own ideas to inform themselves of others'. *Pronoia* is not a hag, not a special kind of deity. Velleius apparently does not understand ellipsis: if the words understood and therefore omitted are supplied, the meaning of pronoia is not an

---

[49] The literature on the sources of Cicero's *Nat. D.* is enormous. Book II has been especially studied for the influence of Panaetius and Posidonius. See the magistral study of Arthur Stanley Pease, *M. Tulli Ciceronis de natura deorum*, 2 vols., Vol. 1 being a commentary on Bk. I of *Nat. D.*; Vol. 2, on Bks. II and III. This work includes the text of *Nat. D.* and an illuminating introduction.

[50] Cic., *Nat. D.*, I, 1–2. On Carneades, see Pohlenz, *Die Stoa*, Vol. I, p. 176. Carneades objected to the Stoic belief in the divinity of the world: the purposefulness of nature could be explained by natural causes without assuming a purposively creating intelligence. Animals could not be created for man alone; every being had in itself a naturally directed end or purpose.

[51] Cic., *Nat. D.*, I, 8, 18–20.

"old hag" but a world "governed by the providence of the Gods" (*providentia deorum mundi administrari*) [*Nat. D.*, II, 29, 73–74].

Although Cotta rebuts at length the Epicurean view, he is reluctant to advance any of his own, and the main burden of refutation is left to Balbus, who says that the Stoics consider the question of the immortal gods from four points of view: proof of their existence, their nature, their governance of the universe, and their concern with human affairs.[52] Balbus cites approvingly the reasons the old Stoic Cleanthes gave for the formation in the minds of men of ideas of the existence of gods: foreknowledge of future events through divination; "the magnitude of the benefits which we derive from our temperate climate, from the earth's fertility, and from a vast abundance of other blessings"; the awe instilled into the mind by the violence in nature, such as storms, earthquakes, pestilence, and blazing meteors; and the strongest of all, the observed regularity and order in the heavens.[53]

Like human creations, the cosmos is presumed to have a builder. An environmental explanation is then introduced in a position subordinate to the main idea: man lives on earth, the lowest region of the cosmos and therefore of the densest air. What one observes of certain cities and districts whose inhabitants are more dull-witted than average, owing to the dense air, is true of all men because they live on earth, but even human intelligence may infer the existence of a mind of surpassing ability and divine in the universe.[54] The earth however, is but a part of the cosmic harmony, the richness of vegetation followed by barrenness, the changes of the sun's course at the solstices, the rising and setting of the moon, and a musical harmony maintained by a divine spirit.[55]

Balbus argues that nature "progresses on a certain path of her own to her goal of full development" (as in the life cycle of vines and cattle) unless she is interfered with. Painting, architecture, the arts and crafts, have within them an ideal of perfect workmanship; this tendency is even greater in nature. There might be interferences with individual natures but nothing "can frustrate nature as a whole, since she embraces and contains within herself all modes of being."[56] This use of human art and the planfulness of human technical undertakings to explain the processes of nature, followed then by a disparagement of human compared with the divine artisanship, is common to the design arguments of both ancient and modern times. In fact a similar argument was used by Darwin in the *Origin of Species* when he wrote that the power of man through artificial selection to affect plant and animal life was dwarfed by the power of natural selection in the world of nature.[57]

Balbus quotes the Stoic Chrysippus as saying that "just as a shield-case is

[52] Cic., *Nat. D.*, II, 1, 3–4. For Cotta's statement, see I. 21–44, 57–124.
[53] *Ibid.*, 5, 13–15.
[54] *Ibid.*, 6, 17–18.
[55] *Ibid.*, 7, 19–20.
[56] *Ibid.*, 13, 35.
[57] Darwin, *The Origin of Species*, Modern Library ed., pp. 29, 52, 65–66.

made for the sake of a shield and a sheath for the sake of a sword, so everything else except the world was created for the sake of some other thing. . . ." The grain and fruits produced by the earth were made for animals, and animals for man, for he rides the horse, plows with the ox, hunts with the dog. And man with all his imperfections was made to contemplate and imitate the world. It has been said that Chrysippus was the "great champion" if not the originator of this idea. The basic assumption is that of a hierarchy of being in which, typically, plants exist for the sake of animals, animals for man, and man in order to contemplate God [*Nat. D.*, II, 14, 37–39]. Man's intelligence must lead us to infer the existence of a divine mind of surpassing ability in the universe [*Nat. D.*, II, 6, 18]. The Stoic idea of sympathy is at work here; there are interconnections and affinities among things in the whole creation, strong bonds between the macrocosm and the microcosm that is man. If we grant man's unique position as a reasoning and intelligent being, see him as part, albeit a small one, of the great mind of the universe, then it is reasonable to say that all things in this world which man uses have been created and provided for him, that the world was created for both gods and man, that the things in it are for the enjoyment of man [*Nat. D.*, II, 61–62, 154].

This kind of thinking has spawned comparisons of the world (*mundus*) with a house or a city, even with Athens and Sparta. The revolutions of the sun and moon are spectacles for man. An earth producing for wild beasts alone would be meaningless. Things are made for the sake of those who can use them. The utilitarian argument for domestication, especially of the dog, sheep, and oxen, fits in nicely with this thinking. The neck of the ox is "born to the yoke," his back unsuited for burdens; with their aid the earth was brought under tillage [II, 63, 159]. The birds give "so much pleasure that our Stoic Providence appears to have been at times a disciple of Epicurus" [II, 64, 160]. From such arguments emerges the idea of divine care for humanity, not only as a whole but for subgroups of men and for individuals [II, 65, 164].

> Here somebody will ask, for whose sake was all this vast system contrived? For the sake of the trees and plants, for these, though without sensation have their sustenance from nature? But this at any rate is absurd. Then for the sake of the animals? It is no more likely that the gods took all this trouble for the sake of dumb, irrational creatures. For whose sake then shall one pronounce the world to have been created? Doubtless for the sake of those living beings which have the use of reason; these are the gods and mankind, who assuredly surpass all other things in excellence, since the most excellent of all things is reason [*ratio*]. Thus we are led to believe that the world and all the things that it contains were made for the sake of gods and men [II, 53, 133].

In such a world the beasts may be cast in the role of thieves.[58] This argument, obviously like Xenophon's, has had exceedingly important consequences in the history of thought regarding nature and natural history:

[58] On Chrysippus' anthropocentric views, De Lacy, "Lucretius and the History of Epicureanism," *Trans. and Proc. of the Amer. Philolog. Assn.* 79 (1948), p. 16, basing

it gave a strong utilitarian bias in interpreting the meaning of all natural phenomena, a bias that persisted in natural theologies until the middle of the
nineteenth century, even if they rejected the idea that all nature existed for
man alone. Even with this rejection, however, the products of nature were
studied and interpreted in the light of their usefulness to man. An equally important corollary of the utilitarian interpretation is the attitude toward domesticated plants and animals: domestications are a result of the order of
nature, not interferences with it. Domesticated plants and animals are the expected consequences of man's activities on an earth designed for him, his arts
and inventions and techniques arising not out of necessity but out of the
opportunities offered by a rich, full, fertile nature. It is in the design argument
that we should seek early theories of plant and animal domestication; the
historical reasons for domestication were confused with the observed contemporary uses of domesticated plants and animals. It was not until Eduard
Hahn's time that the age-old conception of animal domestication as a result
of utility was broken down, for Hahn emphasized the nonutilitarian and ceremonial origins of domestication. In the Stoic conception, represented here by
Chrysippus, the dominant idea, later diffused far out of the range of Stoicism,
is that the horse is made for transport, the ox for ploughing, and the dog for
hunting and protection.

According to Balbus, all life owes its existence to its inherent heat, and this
element "possesses in itself a vital force that pervades the whole world." The
heat principle is closely related to generation and fertility; all parts of the world
are and have been sustained by heat, for the hot and fiery principle diffused
throughout nature has within it the power of generation: "the necessary cause
of both the birth and the growth of all living creatures, whether animals or
those whose roots are planted in the earth."[59] It is not animated nature alone
but the whole universe that possesses this generative principle and hence an
organic character. Balbus quotes Zeno, the founder of the Stoic school, who
defined nature as "a craftsmanlike fire, proceeding methodically to the work
of generation"; the craftsmanlike fire of nature, which, like the hand of a
human artisan but with much greater skill, teaches other arts and with foresight plans out its work in detail. Universal nature is the creator of individual
nature; it is the world-mind, correctly called prudence or providence, chiefly
concentrated upon securing for the world, "first the structure best suited for

---

his opinion on the fragments of C. in von Arnim, *Stoicorum veterum fragmenta*, Vol. 2,
pp. 332–334. On comparisons of the world with a house or city, see Pease's comments
under *domus aut urbs utrorumque*, *Nat. D.*, Vol. 2, pp. 950–951, with many citations
from other writers. On the position of beasts, *ibid.*, under *mutarum* Vol. 2, p. 895, *Nat.
D.*, II, 63, 157–158. The idea that the purpose of one life form was to serve another
[*Nat. D.*, II, 14, 37] was not held as we have seen by Aristotle; on the immanent teleology of Aristotle, see Ross, *Aristotle*, p. 125, but see also notes 26 and 31 above.
[59] Cic., *Nat. D.*, II, 9, 24; 10, 28.

survival; next, absolute completeness; but chiefly, consummate beauty and embellishment of every kind."[60]

This theory of the purposiveness of universal nature is combined with the theory of the four elements to explain visible nature. The art of universal nature, through the four elements, nourishes the earth and impregnates it with seeds, the earth in turn not only nourishing the plants but through its exhalations sustaining the air, the ether, and the heavenly bodies. The four elements in various combinations and supervised by an intelligent and designing nature are the components of an ordered universe. Nature, responsible for the growth and continuity of plant life, by extension governs the whole universe, and since she does nothing in a faulty way she has produced the best possible effect from the materials at her disposal; she has produced, like the artisan-creator of the *Timaeus*, the best of all possible worlds. "Now the government of the world contains nothing that could possibly be censured; given the existing elements, the best that could be produced from them has been produced. Let some one therefore prove that it could have been better."[61]

In his exposition of the proofs for the existence of gods, Balbus, following possibly the biological, esthetic, and geographic tradition of Panaetius and Posidonius, calls attention to the convincing proofs afforded by earthly scenes. Situated in the middle of the universe, the earth is clothed with flowers, grass, trees, and grain, "forms of vegetation all of them incredibly numerous and inexhaustively varied and diverse." Intermingling qualities which are both natural and the product of human art, Balbus speaks of the springs, rivers, the verdure of the river valleys, the caverns, caves, crags, mountains and plains, the veins of gold and silver and marble.

> Think of all the various species of animals, both tame and wild! think of the flights and songs of birds! of the pastures filled with cattle, and the teeming life of the woodlands! Then why need I speak of the race of men? who are as it were the appointed tillers of the soil, and who suffer it not to become a savage haunt of monstrous beasts of prey nor a barren waste of thickets and brambles, and whose industry diversifies and adorns the lands and islands and coasts with houses and cities. Could we but behold these things with our eyes as we can picture them in our minds, no one taking in the whole earth at one view could doubt divine reason.[62]

On the surface this passage seems little more than a poetic description of everyday scenes of Mediterranean life. Actually it is an important statement of the position that man's changes of the earth are consistent with the teleological view of nature. Man becomes a kind of caretaker of the earth; his cultivation combats disease, and his struggles with the wild animals exercise a

---

[60] *Ibid.*, 22, 57–58.
[61] *Ibid.*, 23. The quotation is from 34, 86–87. "World," as usual, translates *mundus*, the cosmos.
[62] *Ibid.*, 39, 98–99.

control over excesses which might occur without his superintendence. His own creations have unmistakably added to the beauty; even his dispersion on the islands scattered throughout the seas or along the coasts has contributed to this beauty.

In this glowing appreciation, there is no distinction between domesticated and pristine nature. The thought expressed in this passage has inspired many similar statements in modern times, for the *De natura deorum* was widely read and highly prized by thinkers of the Renaissance and of the seventeenth and eighteenth centuries.

Evidences of an intelligent and divine nature are apparent on earth. The air by the sea, different by day and night, rises upward, condenses into clouds whose rain enriches the earth. The agitations of the air produce winds and seasonal change; the air is the medium of the flight of birds, and it nourishes men and animals when it is inhaled.[63] Vegetation draws nourishing moisture from the earth, the stocks providing stability and transport for the nourishing sap. Like the animals, the plants have protective covering to resist heat and cold. Animals, provided with appetite and sense to distinguish between palatable and poisonous foods, divide up and create boundaries for themselves in nature, so to speak, in the way they get their food: by walking, crawling, flying, swimming, by seizing with their mouths and teeth or their claws and beaks, or by sucking, bolting the food whole, or chewing; some are adapted to getting food on the ground, while others with long necks have a wider range. The predatory beasts are strong or swift; others, like the spider, possess artifice and cunning, and among others there is a symbiotic relationship.[64]

The correlation of animals with their habitats is worked in with other ideas of natural history: Nature takes care in providing for the propagation of plants and animals, creating in the aggregate the beauty one sees on the earth, even though certain types of plants and animals must depend on man for their preservation and improvement.[65] And it is absurd to think that this mighty fabric of nature—the abundance and variety of food, the winds moderating the intemperate heat, the utility of rivers, tides, forested mountains, salt beds, and medicines and the diurnal change from day to night—was designed for plants and animals; it is more credible that the universe, including the earth, was made for the gods and man.[66] Unlike the rest of the creation, man has been given a mind to understand, his senses to observe and feel, and a hand to do things; he is part of nature but his endowments allow him more freedom in his physical environment, a more wide-ranging experience, and greater opportunities to assist in the improvement of nature and to profit by its use.

[63] *Ibid.*, 39, 101.
[64] *Ibid.*, 47–48, 120–124. See comment on the mussel or *pina* and its symbiotic relationship with the tiny shrimp, II, 48, 123.
[65] *Ibid.*, 52, 130.
[66] *Ibid.*, 53, 133.

The human hand—as a manipulator of tools and as an instrument in its own right—becomes the great agency of human art and change, an observation countlessly repeated in modern times, for with his hands man made possible agriculture, fishing, animal domestication, mining, forest clearing, carpentry, navigation, irrigation, and river diversion; with them man had changed the earth, making it more responsive to his own ends.[67]

The importance of the Stoic portion of this dialogue lies in the range of its ideas, in the clear exposition of the conception of harmony in the creation as a whole, and a harmonious ordering of physical and biological phenomena on earth, including the recognition of man as a modifier of the natural environment (to be discussed more fully later).

The Stoic statement also is the best exposition in classical antiquity of the application of the design argument to the earth as a habitable planet. Few noteworthy additions were made to it by later writers in antiquity. The geographer, Strabo, a Stoic, says that the region around the modern city of Toulouse is so harmoniously arranged and its people are so industriously engaged in their various ways of life that one might well credit the workings of a Providence, "such a disposition of these regions not resulting from chance, but from the thought of some [intelligence]."[68] Providence is a "broiderer and an artificer of countless works" who has created all life for the gods and for man. Providence has given the heavens to the gods, earth to man, fashioning it for his use.[69] Seneca, also a Stoic, argued that Providence supplied men not only with necessities but with the luxuries of nature: so pampered are we by the products of the earth that even the slothful can find sustenance in the chance produce of the earth. The birds, fish, the land animals, all pay tribute to man. The utilitarian view of nature shows itself in the praise of rivers which encircle the meadows, make navigation possible, and provide even in their flooding water for the parched earth. Seneca was probably the first thinker to apply the design argument to mining and the distribution of minerals, a favorite theme of some nineteenth century English geologists who saw a divine planning in the faulting of strata, thus making the English coal measures more accessible. The mines are deep in the earth; though silver, copper, and iron have been concealed from him, man has been endowed with the ability to discover them. Seneca also believes that transhumance is an evidence of divine care: God furnishes food for flocks wherever they are, and he "has ordained the alternation of summer

[67] *Ibid.*, 60, 150–152. Balbus's argument in II, 52–53 is an admirable summary of the arguments for a designed earth based on its beauty and utility, its design for the uses of man, and the characteristics of man which enable him to take advantage of these opportunities.
[68] Strabo, IV, i. 14.
[69] Strabo, XVII, i. 36. Strabo continues that man is a land animal; that Providence provided cavities for the water which encompasses the earth, and eminences for man's habitation (including the necessary waters for his use), and that the relationship between land and sea is constantly changing.

and winter pasturage"; man cannot even take credit for his inventions, for God has given us the power through our intellects to make them.[70] Like Xenophon and Cicero, Seneca became an important authority in the modern history of the design argument; these three names occur frequently in support of Christian interpretations of the nature of the earth, especially in the sixteenth and seventeenth centuries.[71]

## 9.  The Development of Antiteleological Ideas in the Epicurean Philosophy

By the beginning of the Hellenistic period, teleological arguments still had the weight of great authority behind them. Plato had postulated an artisan-deity who planned with care and attention, personally seeing to it that the cosmos would never decay; it was eternal and divine. There was the concord of the elements within, and none on the outside, for they had all been used up. [Tim. 31B4–32C4]. Aristotle's teleology also was strong, especially in biology, although there were demurrers, as we have seen, from Theophrastus and his pupil Strato.

The Hellenistic period is notable both for an intense and continuing interest in teleological explanation especially among the Stoics and for a dogged resistance to it by Epicurus and his disciples, as is amply clear in the poem of Lucretius. Both points of view (especially in the second and first centuries B.C.) have in common a broadened concept of the unity and harmony of nature. They are often based on observations of natural processes, such as the hydrologic cycle, interrelationships and regularities in nature as seen among plants and animals, and of physical geography, reflecting probably the direct or indirect inspiration of Aristotle's biology and his *Meteorologica*. This emphasis on process moreover is congenial to both sides: in one case nature is creatrix, in the other divine planning has been at work.

Since we have already discussed the early history of teleological ideas, let us now do the same for the opposing ones, beginning with the pre-Epicurean times, continuing on to Epicurus, then to the Epicurean spokesman, Velleius, in *De natura deorum*, and finally to Lucretius, and try to suggest what was distinctly Roman about the poet that went into his interpretations and illustrations and set him apart from Epicurus.

The preludes leading up to the philosophy of Epicurus (342/1–271/70 B.C.) may be summarized around the following themes: (1) the consequences

---

[70] Sen., *Ben.*, IV, 5–6.

[71] This was particularly true of the "great Tully." For a good example, see the tribute to and criticism of Cicero from this point of view in Francesco Petrarca, "On His Own Ignorance and That of Many Others," in *The Renaissance Philosophy of Man*, Cassirer, Kristeller, and Randall, eds., pp. 79–90, 97–100. The passage from Aristotle in *Nat. D.*, II, 37, 95, is also quoted, p. 83.

of the failure of Parmenides' monism, (2) interest in efficient causes, (3) opportunities offered by Empedocles' theory of the four elements, (4) Leucippus' contribution to atomic theory, followed by that of Democritus. It will be necessary in this exposition, however, to discuss broader questions bearing on cosmology as a whole in order to place the ideas applicable to the earth in their proper setting.

Let us begin, then, with Parmenides' belief that a conception of the world (κόσμος) cannot be attained by the evidence of the senses but only by way of the mind. He believed the world to be a "solid body, pure matter, a corporeal *plenum.*" It is "a finite, eternal, indivisible, immovable, spherical, corporeal mass: motion, change, variety, birth, and death, all that we know by the experiences of our senses are mere delusions." The way of truth is reached only by the mind, not by the senses, for Parmenides "expelled the senses from the way of Truth." "The strict following out of this principle," says Bailey, "could only lead to a view of Unity, which was wholly divorced from experience, and seemed to be entirely devoid of fruitful results." Bailey further argues that Parmenides' theory was "the death-blow of Monism." The expedients of the later Ionians to preserve the unchangeable One and to reconcile it with the ever-changing many failed because they involved the abandonment of the principle of unity.[72]

Since Parmenides' theory "had made it impossible any longer to maintain the single homogeneous substance as the primary basis of the world," and since such a theory could not account for variety and complexity, there was opportunity for a thinker to be "a mediator between the system of Parmenides and the evidence of the senses." Empedocles seemed to regard himself as being philosophically equipped for this role.[73] The four elements certainly were plain enough to the senses. The concept of an element implies a unity, a homogeneity of the matter making up the particle, while combinations of elements can account for variety and complexity. The concept also suggests the impossibility of further breakdown or divisibility beyond the element, while the variety and complexity of what is apprehended by the senses suggest opportunities in combinations of a finite number of elements. The four-element theory with accompanying love and strife (which were equally corporeal) was therefore of great importance to the atomic theory because each element is "absolutely homogeneous with itself, indestructible, unchangeable."[74] The way is now open for the atomists who see unity—not in a single ultimate homogeneous "nature," "but by postulating an absolute homogeneity

---

[72] In preparing this section, I am indebted (as can readily be seen) to Bailey's *The Greek Atomists and Epicurus* (henceforth *GAE*), to his great ed. of Lucretius, and to Pease's equally impressive ed. of Cicero's *Nat. D.* Bailey, *GAE*, pp. 25, 26; Parmenides, *Vorsokr* A 22, Vol. I, p. 221.

[73] *GAE*, pp. 27–28.

[74] *Ibid.*, pp. 29–31, 50–51, quotation on p. 29; *Vorsokr* B 17, lines 19–20, Vol. I, p. 316.

of substance in the infinite particles and referring variety to difference in shape and combinations."[75]

Such attempts to explain unity and observed diversities encourage inquiry into the mechanisms by which such diversities occur; that is, they encourage looking into efficient causes, which then attain a dignity denied them when they play ancillary roles in doctrines of final causes. Historically the latter have had a close affinity with religious ideas and religious interpretations of nature; the quest for causes within the phenomena themselves, without supernatural interventions, leads into concepts of natural law and, if these are not in turn tied in with doctrines of final causes, into a concept of nature and the natural order in which the unity and harmony which is postulated comes about because nature herself is a creatrix.[76]

The four-element theory of Empedocles, as well as the atomic theory which came later, called attention to the importance of division, for, said Leucippus, ultimately a point is reached at which further division is impossible; ultimate particles of matter are thus indivisible and are atoms.[77] The importance of division and of the ultimate indivisible particle lies in the concept of a "least possible for existence," the atom being the stopping point for destruction, the starting point for creation, as, for example, in the disintegration of an organic substance on death, and the subsequent growth of new life from a new beginning. "Thus a discrete infinity is reconciled with permanence: there are infinite particles, but thanks to their very essential character, the world can never be frittered away into nothingness."[78] "Necessity" is the cause of atomic motion, the term probably signifying that everything is in motion for a reason, probably also, as with Democritus, that "atoms in moving obeyed the law of their own being."[79] Thus Leucippus strove for a concept of all-pervading natural law. Our world is not unique—it is only one of an infinite number. The concept of a plurality of worlds is very clearly stated by Leucippus; whether Anaximander had the idea before him is a matter of controversy.[80] Leucippus is probably the originator of the atomist theory which later became such a powerful support to the antiteleological and antitheological philosophy of Epicurus and his followers.[81]

Democritus (*fl.* 420 B.C.) made further contributions to the atomic theory, among them the idea that "nothing is created out of the non-existent or is de-

---

[75] *GAE*, p. 43.

[76] For an illuminating discussion of the efficient cause, see *GAE*, pp. 46–52.

[77] *Ibid.*, p. 73.

[78] *Ibid.*, p. 74.

[79] *Ibid.*, p. 85, cf. p. 93.

[80] On infinite worlds, see the doxography in Kahn, *Anaximander and the Origins of Greek Cosmology* and the discussion of Zeller's, Cornford's, and Burnet's views, pp. 46–53. Kahn believes "there is no good evidence of such a doctrine for any other thinker earlier than Leucippus," p. 50.

[81] *GAE*, p. 93; on Leucippus as founder of atomism, pp. 106–108.

stroyed into the non-existent."[82] Later Lucretius used the same idea to combat irrational fear, and to argue against the existence of capricious behavior and arbitrary creation by divine beings on earth and in the sky—"nullam rem e nilo gigni divinitus umquam."[83] More boldly than Leucippus, Democritus postulates wider applicability of the idea of necessity in order to be rid of mysterious semireligious forces like love and strife and mind, and of the religious tradition and its dependence on ideas of a final cause. The universe is not ruled by design or purpose. To Democritus "creation is the undesigned result of inevitable natural processes." His was more than a physical theory, for he had "an eye from the first for the metaphysical implications of the new conception of the universe."[84] Atoms did not form themselves into a whirl so that a cosmos would be created; there is no design within nor by an external power, but while they fall into the whirl "accidentally," once it is formed "the result by a process of strict necessity is a world." One of Democritus' purposes in asserting the claims of "necessity" as a kind of natural law was apparently to combat teleological explanation.[85]

In view of its subsequent importance, and of its prominence in Lucretius' poem, a word should be said here about the senescence of nature, an idea which is adumbrated in Democritus. There are stages of growth in the worlds, which are infinite in number and which are in varying stages of completion, some increasing, others decaying. The idea that a world might be growing in one part, decaying in another "is a little difficult to understand on atomic principles," but it is a striking way of sorting out differences among worlds in an infinity of them. "A world grows towards its prime until it can no longer take in any addition from without."[86]

In the physical world Democritus asserts the supremacy of "necessity" in order to establish natural law, to eliminate theological conceptions of the world, and the idea of chance, but the idea of "necessity" is not extended to the moral sphere, the precepts here being naïve; it is assumed that man acts with a free will.[87]

We are now in a position to discuss the antiteleological ideas in the Epicurean philosophy whose key assumption is that gods have no part in the government of the world.[88] The creation has its marvels, the heavenly bodies

---

[82] *Ibid.*, pp. 119–120; *Vorsokr* A 1, Vol. 1, p. 81, a doctrine enunciated before by Melissus, *Vorsokr* Fr. B 1, Vol. 2, p. 268; Epicurus, *Epistle* 1, 38 (to Herodotus).

[83] *GAE*, p. 120; Lucr. I, 150.

[84] *Ibid.*, pp. 122, 123.

[85] *Ibid.*, p. 141; *Nat. D.*, I, 24, 66; Lucr. I, 1021–28.

[86] *GAE*, p. 147. Democritus, *Vorsokr* A 40, Vol. 2, p. 94. See Lucr. II, 1105 *ad fin.* The passage from D. is quoted by Bailey on p. 146, who suggests that the general idea may have been inspired by the stages in Empedocles' world caused by the interaction of strife and love, p. 147.

[87] *GAE*, pp. 186–188.

[88] *Prin. Doctrines*, 1, Bailey ed. of Epicurus, p. 95.

their majesty, and there is order in their movement, but these observations do not constitute evidence that the heavenly bodies are divine beings. In Epicurus, at least in the fragments that have come down to us, the argument seems based mostly on the orderliness of the cosmos rather than on an order of nature on earth.[89] Neither are the heavenly bodies evidence of the creation and the government of the world by the will of gods nor are such conceptions of creation derived from sensation.[90]

Apparently Epicurus is combatting two other ideas, the artisan-deity or δημιουργός of Plato's *Timaeus*, and the *Pronoia* of the Stoics, that is, the conception of continuing divine care for the progress of events in the world.[91] Epicurus not only wishes to exclude the gods from the world "but even any notion of the unconscious forethought of Nature itself, which might seem to give colour to a theological view of phenomena."[92]

What are some of the ramifications of the antiteleological ideas of the Epicurean philosophy as they appear, chiefly in Cicero's *De natura deorum* and Lucretius' *De natura rerum*? Although it is an argument *ex silentio* (because so many of Epicurus' writings have been lost), it might be that later Epicureanism, as represented by Gaius Velleius, the Epicurean protagonist in *De natura deorum*, and by Lucretius' *De natura rerum*, is much less concerned with the cosmos, much more with natural processes observable on earth. The same observation applies to their Stoic opponents of the Hellenistic period, probably to Panaetius (if more were known of his nature philosophy), Posidonius, Balbus, the Stoic protagonist in *De natura deorum*, to the Stoic geographer Strabo, and indeed also to Cicero. The interest in nature, discussed in the Introductory Essay, lends credence to this speculation.

Cicero thinks the principal question in the dispute about the nature of the gods is whether or not they take an active part in the governance of the world; similar questions also arise about their activities in the creation. Velleius is cast in the role of a cocksure partisan who is in easy communication with the assembly of the gods in Epicurus' intermundane spaces, but Cotta, the Academic, nevertheless praises his qualifications as an expert.[93] Velleius attacks, as we have seen, Plato's artisan-deity, using the deprecating words *opifex* and *aedificator* (*non opificem aedificatoremque mundi, Platonis de Timaeo deum*). *Opifex* was used chiefly of the banaustic occupations, bearing somewhat the same relation to *artifex* as *artisan* or *mechanic* does to *artist*.[94] He also attacks, as we have seen, "that old hag of a fortune teller, the *Pronoia* of the Stoics."

To Velleius, the Stoic God is overworked, having none of the repose essential for godhood. "If the world [*cosmos*] itself is god [*deus*] what can be

---

[89] *Epistle* 1 (*to Herodotus*), 76–77; 2 (*to Pyth.*), 97; Lucr. V, 114–145.

[90] Lucr. V, 122–125; *Epistle* 3 (*to Menoecus*), 124; *GAE*, p. 441.

[91] *GAE*, p. 474; Lucr. V, 165–186.

[92] *GAE*, p. 476.

[93] *Nat. D.*, I, 1, 2; I, 8, 18; I, 21, 57–60.

[94] Pease's ed. of *Nat. D.*, Vol. 1, p. 175, under *opificem*.

less restful than to revolve at incredible speed round the axis of the heavens [*circum axem caeli*] without a single moment of respite? but repose is an essential condition of happiness."[95] In opposition to the Stoic idea of an artificer and of the divine nature of the creative act, Velleius says that the act is "so easy, that nature will create, is creating and has created worlds without number."[96] The concept of nature as continually creating has curious resemblances to the Christian idea of the *creatio continua*, but in the latter conception God is continually creating as evidence of his care for the world.

Velleius sketched a conception of the earth that was opposed to the teleology of the Stoics, the idea of a divine artisan, and to the "world-builder of Plato's *Timaeus*." Velleius asks how it can be that the world was created for men when so many are fools, so few wise; certainly the beauties of the earth were not made for a god's own pleasure. He ridicules the idea that since the earth is part of the universe it is also part of god: are the uninhabitable deserts, either hot or cold, to be regarded as the limbs of god suffering the extremes of temperature? [*Nat. D.*, I, 9–10, 21–25]. There is no more illuminating comparison to be made regarding man's place in nature as seen in the Epicurean and the Stoic philosophies than by setting this thought against the speech of Balbus in which precisely the opposite argument is used. To Velleius there is not enough human intelligence and wisdom in the world to make the creation worthwhile; to Balbus, a creation for the sake of plants or dumb animals without a reasoning being like man to behold it is unthinkable [*Nat. D.*, II, 53, 133].

What now of the Lucretian aspects of Epicureanism?[97] All students of Lucretius have taken it for granted that the attacks on final causes, on design, on conceptions of the gods as participating in the governance of the cosmos are expositions of the fundamental ideas of Epicurus, the assumption being that Lucretius showed a scrupulous faithfulness to his teachings. Lucretius, however, is also interested in concrete illustration: "He is never happy without the visible demonstration of the parallel from the world of sense."[98] He is familiar with many aspects of nature. Seashore and inland scenes as well attract him, and his observations on husbandry show perhaps a greater interest in rural than in urban life. "One great charm of the work is that it breathes of the open air more than of the library." Any reader of the poem, especially one interested in physical and cultural geography, rural life, and natural history, would agree with Sellar's observation.[99]

[95] *Nat D.*, I, 20, 52; see Pease's commentary, *Nat. D.*, Vol. 1, pp. 331–332 on this and the strong Epicurean emphasis on repose as a necessary condition of godhood.

[96] *Nat. D.*, I, 20, 53 and Pease's note under *effectura*, *Nat. D.*, Vol. 1, p. 334.

[97] See De Lacy, "Lucretius and the History of Epicureanism," *Trans. and Proc. of the Amer. Philog. Assoc.*, Vol. 79 (1948), pp. 12–23, which sums up the scholarly activity in this field since the publication of Bailey's *The Greek Atomists and Epicurus* in 1928.

[98] Bailey's ed. and commentary on Lucr. Vol. 1, pp. 15–16.

[99] Sellar, *The Roman Poets of the Republic*, pp. 292–294; quotation is on p. 294.

The Epicurean doctrines are there but the illustrations are earthy ones. There are the processes of nature observable on earth; there are also the subjective attitudes toward nature. These characteristics set him apart from the older Epicurean thinkers (bearing in mind of course that much of what they wrote has not survived), and the ideas of beauty in nature, of city-country contrasts, of communion with nature, are shared with other poets of the Hellenistic period. (See the discussion of attitudes toward nature in the Hellenistic period in the Introduction.)

In this antiteleological view with its nature imagery, what becomes of nature as a concept? It acquires an unwonted independence; nature is "quit of her proud rulers, doing all things of her own accord alone, without control of gods." She is a creatrix, she is likened to a helmsman, the earth to a quaint artificer.[100] Figures of speech often come from the language of tillage; all things coming from seeds require care, and tilled lands are better for them than are the untilled. The necessity of toil in order to survive proves the falsity of the notion that something can come from nothing. The truth of the corollary, also from Epicurus, that nothing can be annihilated is based primarily on biology, in essence a description of the cycle of life in its environment, each element playing its role: the sky, the rain from the sky, the earth, the crops, the green branches, the fruit-bearing trees for food, the glad towns with their children, the woods with their birds, the cattle browsing over glad pastures, yielding their milk, and new forthcoming broods [I, 250–264]. Frequently Lucretius expresses an interest in processes, in natural sequences, interrelationships between the physical and the cultural world, as that between the heavens and the rains, and the fields and the glad cities.

What are his criticisms of the design argument? In the first place it cannot explain origins [I, 1021; V, 419–32]. Neither can it explain the uses of the various body organs; with a gusto that, had they read him, must have dismayed the authors of the nineteenth century Bridgewater treatises, to say nothing of William Paley, Lucretius says, "Nothing at all was born in the body that we might be able to use it, but what is born creates its own use" [IV, 834–835]. Skillfully he shows the fallacy of comparing these organs (like the hand, the eye, the nose) with human inventions (like darts, beds, cups). Such artifacts which satisfy the needs of life may well have been discovered for the purpose of using them [IV, 851–854]. Artifacts come out of the human world; their purposes are not to be confused with parts of the body which have developed specialized skills. Long before Voltaire ridiculed believers in final causes who thought that noses were designed for spectacles, Lucretius saw the pitfalls in having an artisan-deity behave as if necessity were the mother of invention. Neither can the design argument explain the existence of heavenly bodies, for here too nature is not a product of design,

---

[100] Lucr. II, 1090–92; *natura creatrix*, I, 629; II, 1117; V, 1362; as artificer (*suavis daedala tellus*), I, 7. See Bailey's commentary on Lucr. 7, *adventumque tuum*, Vol. 2, p. 593.

but a helmsman, *natura gubernans*, steering with her own power "the courses of the sun and the wanderings of the moon" [V, 76–81]. Lucretius quickly makes it clear that it is not necessary to use his theory of the atoms to rebut the belief that the earth is arranged by divine plan, that the sun and moon rotate according to the same plan or for the purpose of promoting the growth of crops or of animals; one need only point to the imperfections of the cosmos and of the earth, the role of beasts in relation to man, the weakness and help-lessness of the infant compared with the self-reliance of the young of animals.

It is physical evil, the imperfections of the earth, seen in terms of its fitness as an environment for man, that Lucretius considers evidences against the design argument: large parts of the earth are either useless or hostile to man, an inconceivable arrangement were it the product of design. There are too many flaws. Too much area is taken up by mountains, the forests with their wild beasts, rocks, waste pools, and by the sea "which holds apart the shores of the lands." This attitude toward the seas is in marked contrast with that of the teleologists, to whom the seas are purposefully made highways for trade, navigation, and intercourse among peoples. Almost two-thirds of the earth's area, Lucretius says, is taken up by places with burning heat or ceaseless frost. Even the small amount of arable land is available to man only after his inces-sant struggle to keep it free from the natural vegetation which covers it. The soil of the earth in its present condition (Lucretius recounts elsewhere the theme of the spontaneous fertility of soils of the golden age) is little suited to man, who must work it hard, condition it, watch over it. It is man's way "ever wont for his livelihood to groan over the strong mattock and to furrow the earth with the deep-pressed plough. But that by turning the fertile clods with the share, and subduing the soil of the earth we summon them to birth, of their own accord the crops could not spring up into the liquid air." Man must remake the earth to his own needs and purposes in a constant struggle against weeds, inclement weather, and plant disease. Even if he has succeeded in tilling the small amount of arable soil, when his crops mature they may be ruined by heat, rain, frost, or wind, while the changing seasons bring disease and pestilence with them. Lucretius finds no place in the design argument for the beasts, for they are menaces to the human race. Furthermore, there are unforeseen changes in weather, and each seasonal change brings with it its own diseases. Human life is uncertain. Nature may be a creator, but to Lucre-tius, when she created, her eye obviously was not on man. This enumeration of the flaws of the earth as evidence of lack of design is based on more general ideas. The imperfection of the earth as a fit environment for human life, and the principle of plenitude, are assumed; the combination of the two ideas is the basis for believing in the struggle for existence. Organic matter can quickly fill up even an imperfect earth. Since agriculture was the dominant way of life and the chief source of production in the ancient world, the struggle understandably is described in terms of the difficulties of making the soil yield a living. It would seem that to Lucretius the earth is a fitter environment for plant and animal life (as in the ease with which young animals adapt to their environment) than for humans. Lucretius' interpretation of life as a laborious fight against nature obviously is not in the tradition of the golden age when men were happy and comfortable with untilled soils; indeed they did not have to till them, for nature abounded in untilled riches. But is he also thinking of the Italy of his own day, of the bare rocks, the eroded mountains, the swamps, the poverty?[101]

Although Lucretius is an enemy of design arguments, of the idea of an artisan-deity, and doctrines of final causes, he himself is not free of teleological assumptions.[102] Furthermore, the idea of senescence in nature is obviously teleological. This teleology, however, is of a lower order of metaphysical importance; it operates within the general concept of the chance creation of an infinity of worlds and is used to explain differences among them. The idea of senescence in nature which Lucretius puts so forcefully is apparently an elaboration of the original idea of Democritus. It is applied to conditions on earth and literally to the earth itself; as a teleological process independent of human agency, it also becomes an explanation (false, as Columella saw) of environmental change. If the earth no longer yields so much as it did in yesteryear, its failures could be due to old age.

In Lucretius, the application of the idea of senescence to the earth is of special interest because of its importance as a geographical concept. The general idea is also in Epicurus, who applies it to worlds (κόσμοι), but the process with him seems to be of a physical rather than a biological nature.[103] It cannot be said that the demonstration is successful even by the presuppositions of ancient science, although it is interesting to see what Lucretius regards as evidence and how he used it. Today it would largely be stated in the vocabulary of geomorphology, such as physical weathering, erosion, and deposition. Although Lucretius did not accept the four-element theory, he nevertheless wrote of these mighty members and parts of the world (*maxima mundi membra*) in a popular sense to illustrate his argument. Only those well disposed to the idea that the earth is mortal would be won over by Lucretius' evidence, though it is far better than that offered in modern times and against which George Hakewill in the seventeenth century inveighed so tirelessly and eloquently.[104]

Lucretius' argument element by element is as follows: The earth [V, 247–

---

[101] Lucr. V, 155–165, 195–234; on primitive man, V, 925–987. Bailey, *Lucr.*, Vol. 3, pp. 1350–1351. Of these arguments (V, 195–234) along popular rather than philosophical lines, Giussani says L. "ceases to be Epicurus and becomes Lucretius." Quoted in Bailey *Lucr.*, Vol. 3, p. 1350.

[102] See Patin, *Études sur la poésie latine*, ch. vii, "l'antilucrèce." See V, 1204–17 and Bailey's comments *Lucr.* Vol. 1, p. 17.

[103] *Epistle* 1 (*to Herodotus*), 73.

[104] See chap. 8, sect. 4. See also Bailey's comment on V, 237 citing Giussani on L.'s popular use of the four-element theory, *Lucr.* Vol. 3, p. 1356.

260] is carried off as dust by the winds, into swamps by the rain, and by stream erosion; in other words, it is moved by processes of physical weathering.[105] What is described is not so much a tale of mortality as a cycle: the earth causes plant and animal life to grow, but on their passing away, what remains is restored to the earth as dust in proportion to what the earth has given [V, 257–260]. It is like a parent and like a tomb.[106]

Neither is the case for water [V, 261–272] convincing, but here too the argument is interesting because it is based on processes of physical geography. It is the cycle of water running downhill ultimately reaching the sea, and water in the atmosphere evaporated mostly from the sea by the sun and wind. What is shown, however, is not mortality but circulation, metamorphosis of forms of water and a constancy in the bulk of the earth's water, else the seas would grow larger and larger.[107]

The case for air [V, 273–280], like that for earth and water, is based on the observation that it, notably in the form of wind, does not permanently retain its gains. Here again Lucretius seems to prove convincingly that the elements, despite their transformations and circulation, remain about the same in quantity, that one does not gain at the expense of another. If the air retained these gains, everything would be dissolved in it; since observation does not confirm this condition, the air is in equilibrium. Air is created by an efflux from things, renewing them, however, by ultimately surrendering its acquisitions. Is this argument, I wonder, based on anything more complex than the experience of seeing a gust of wind picking up dust from one place and depositing it in another, or the sporting of a breeze with a dried leaf?

The fourth element in Lucretius' discussion is light [V, 281–305], not fire as one would expect. Since light, however, is composed of fire particles, what is true of it can be extended to apply to all forms of fire. Here the conception is not cyclical, because light is not involved with other elements. Consistent with the atomic theory, "it is not a continuous stream, but a succession of discrete particles," whose flow any obstacle, like a cloud, can cut off, but if the flow is unobstructed "the particles succeed each other so quickly that the light appears to be continuous." These flowing particles of light in fact do perish, but there are constant renewals from the sun's ceaseless flooding of the sky with fresh brightness [V, 281–283].

Lucretius finds further evidences of senescence in everyday observation. Stones are vanquished by time, high towers fall in ruins, rocks crumble away. Natural objects and artifacts betray evidences of mortality. He shrewdly deprecates "shrines and images of the gods grown weary and worn, while the

---

[105] Bailey points out that in V, 251–256 the earth (*terra*) means soil, and in the last four lines it has a wider meaning, *Lucr.* Vol. 3, p. 1357, comment under V, 247.

[106] For a discussion of the elements in the senescence argument, see Bailey, *Lucr.* Vol. 3, pp. 1357–1366.

[107] *Lucr.* VI, 608–638 on a form of the hydrologic cycle.

sacred presence cannot prolong the boundaries of fate nor struggle against the laws of nature." The monuments of men fall into bits, and stones rushing headlong would not have fallen had they resisted time and "held out against all the siege of age without breaking."[108]

Another evidence of mortality is the apparent infancy of civilization; certain arts are being perfected and are growing, the improvement of ships and the newness of music being illustrations. If past catastrophes have obliterated the traces of men, their civilizations and cities, then they show how close the world can be brought to destruction. If you believe in these, "all the more must you be vanquished and confess that there will come to pass a perishing of earth and sky as well" [V, 324–344].

Earth history tells a similar story. The birth of plant life, described sensuously and subjectively as "bright verdure," "flowering fields" gleaming "in their green hue," was followed by living creatures, the earth producing animals formed by rain and sun.[109] Possibly there were more and larger animals in the earth's youth. Life is associated with heat and moisture, earth with food, warmth with raiment, grass as a couch for young animals. This periodization of earth history is also associated with climatic change, in the early period there being no extremes of heat.

The earth is a mother and like a mother will with age no longer be able to bear children: the life-giving earth fluids are compared with a mother's milk. This interpretation of earth history explains declining soil fertility and, indirectly, poverty and the hardness of life [V, 782–836].

I have considered at some length this conception of senescence in nature as it appears in Lucretius, even though it is a subsidiary theme; it is important because it postulates a form of environmental change, teleological in character, which proceeds independent of the agency of man and which has influenced subsequent conceptions of civilization and of the nature of life. If we can credit Columella's sweeping statement, the conception was strong among the "leading men of our state" at the time he was writing, probably around A.D. 60.[110]

Lucretius expresses a philosophy of the "niggardliness of nature," to use a favorite expression of eighteenth century population theorists like Robert Wallace and Thomas Malthus. There is between the Stoics and Lucretius an ancient counterpart of the modern cleavage between the natural theologians, who conceive of nature as benevolent because it is a product of beneficent and all-knowing design, and the Malthusians and the Darwinians, who emphasize the contrast between the reproductive power in nature and the lim-

---

[108] Lucr. V, 308–309, 315–317.

[109] Cf. II, 1150–74 where the world is considered old; there L. seems to have nature in mind, here civilization. Bailey, *Lucr.* Vol. 3, p. 1370.

[110] Columella, *On Agriculture*, Bk. I, Pref. 1. See chap. 3, sec. 7.

ited ability of the earth to support life. Lucretius thus attacks the design argument, not on scientific grounds but on the basis of observations that might be made by a farmer or a parent. To him the earth is a being subject to the same processes as is the organic matter growing upon it; it will grow, mature, die.

Pliny expressed both the Stoic and Epicurean viewpoints. Of the four elements, earth is kindest to man; hence we have called her Mother Earth, for she belongs to man as the sky belongs to God. It is a beneficent earth, in life and in the shelter of death. Earth, kind and indulgent, produces for man, either voluntarily or under compulsion, a great profusion of natural products. She is fertile for the sake of man, her herbs provide his medicines, and even the poisons she produces enable man to escape life when it is too hard to bear. The beauty and bounty of earth are set against the imperfections of man, who is constantly abusing her, but this criticism is not that of the conservationist but of the moralist. Earth is thrown into the sea, excavated to make channels, disturbed with water, iron, wood, fire, stone, and in tillage. Her insides are probed for metals and stones. Pliny wonders if wild animals, so hostile to man, were not intended to be the guardians of the earth, protecting her from his sacrilegious hands.[111]

Seemingly, nature has created all things for man "though she asks a cruel price for all her generous gifts, making it hardly possible to judge whether she has been more a kind parent to man or more a harsh stepmother." Like Lucretius, Pliny makes an unfavorable comparison between the animals—with all their protective endowments which allow them self-reliance from the beginning—and the helplessness of human infancy. However, he is no believer in the senescence of the earth and, in a passage reminiscent of Columella, he says that the earth does not grow old as does a mortal; its fertility can be maintained by care and good husbandry.[112]

It is possible now to reach some conclusions about the teleological and anti-teleological thinking in the Hellenistic period. Both show a feeling for nature —its beauties and utilities. Passages in the *De natura deorum* (some possibly based on Panaetius and Posidonius) and from Lucretius illustrate this truth. Both recognize the harmony and interconnectedness of things, the Stoics for obvious reasons, the Epicurean school because nature has the role of creatrix, of gubernans. In both the activity of man is important, as is his power to control or change the environment. The Stoics recognize it because man participates in divine reason, a participation which enables him to use the earth's resources, created in large part for him, to his advantage. Lucretius recognizes it because it is a consequence of human development from primitive life to civilization; men's achievements are the product of necessity and

---

[111] Pliny, *NH*, II, 63.
[112] Pliny, *NH*, VII, 1; XVII, 3, 35–36.

imitation. Through discovery and invention (see chap. 3, sec. 7), especially the discovery of metallurgy, man has been able to create the countrysides which Lucretius describes with vigor and affection.

### 10. PLUTARCH, THE HERMETICAL WRITINGS, AND PLOTINUS

That teleological explanation was still current in the latter part of the first century A.D. is clear from the writings of Plutarch. In the dialogue, *Concerning the Face Which Appears in the Orb of the Moon* (according to Cherniss, the dramatic date of the dialogue is later than A.D. 75), Theon, the literary authority among the interlocutors, raises the question of teleological explanation in connection with the possibility that the moon can support life. If life is not possible there, then the assertion that the moon is an earth is absurd, there being no apparent purpose in its existence—it neither brings forth fruit nor provides "for men of some kind an origin, an abode, and a means of life, the purposes for which this earth of ours came into being, as we say with Plato, 'our nurse, strict guardian and artificer of day and night' " (937D). Theon then introduces difficulties (largely environmental, like excessive heat or aridity) standing in the way of life existing on the moon (938A–B).

In a lengthy reply, Lamprias asks if it is necessary to say that the moon is made in vain if men cannot live there; this proposition he denies (938D). If the moon is not inhabited by men, and thus exists in vain and without purpose, the same objection could be made of the earth (here are reminders of Lucretius), for only a small part of it is productive in animal and plant life, large parts being wasteland with winter storms or summer droughts, or under the sea.

The implication is that such characterizations and divisions of the earth's surface are false. The uninhabited or uninhabitable parts of the earth are indispensable to the well-being of the inhabited world, for "it is by no means for nothing that these parts come to be." "The sea gives off gentle exhalations, and the most pleasant winds when summer is at its height are released and dispersed from the uninhabited and frozen region by the snows that are gradually melting there."[113] This argument resembles that used by Ray, Keill, and Halley in the seventeenth century as part of the justification for wastelands and the vast expanse of sea. It is the kind of argument which a defender of design must be prepared to make.

Even though the moon may be destitute of life, it still performs useful functions such as providing reflections from the light diffused about it, or being a point of confluence for the rays of the stars, or digesting exhalations from the earth (928C), and tempering excessive heat and harshness of the sun. Citing

---

[113] Plutarch, *Concerning the Face Which Appears in the Orb of the Moon*, 938D–E. Cherniss (Loeb ed.) calls attention here to Theophrastus' *De ventis*, ii, § 11, and Aristotle's *Meteorology*, 364 a 5–13; on the date of the dialogue see p. 12. Reinhardt, *Kosmos und Sympathie*, finds here strong influences of Poseidonian cosmology (p. 171).

ancient belief, he says the moon was held to be Artemis, a virgin and sterile, and helpful to females (938F). Pointing to plant life on earth that requires little rain or snow and which is adapted to summer and rarefied air, he asks whether similarly adapted plants might grow on the moon. In these extremely interesting lines about the characteristics of plants and their adaptability to differing environmental conditions (especially of aridity), Plutarch is making use of the knowledge which came from Alexander's conquests and which is enshrined in the works of Theophrastus.[114]

Furthermore, environments can be deceptive in appearance. Who would guess the richness and diversity of life in the sea from looking at it? Living beings on the moon need not have the same characteristics they possess on earth for purposes of generation, nourishment, livelihood. Such ideas ignore the diversities of nature (940B). Life on earth need not be the model for life in the cosmos. If men exist on the moon, they might be light in body, "capable of being nourished by whatever comes their way"; they might well be amazed at the earth, continuing here the theme of deceptive appearances, "when they look out at the sediment and dregs of the universe, as it were, obscurely visible in moisture, mists, and clouds, as a lightless, low, and motionless spot, to think that it engenders and nourishes animate beings which partake of motion, breath, and warmth."[115]

The ideas of Xenophon, Plato, and Aristotle, elaborated upon and enriched by Panaetius and Posidonius, thoroughly explored in turn by Cicero, and commented upon by Plutarch, reappear in a group of writings, the *Hermetica* (associated more frequently with astrology as a religious conception of the world), ascribed to Hermes Trismegistus and probably written in the third century A.D., according to their most recent English editor and translator. Men were created in order to contemplate heaven; God bade them to increase and multiply and to "have dominion over all things under heaven, and that they might come to know God's power, and witness nature's workings, and that they might mark what things are good, and discern the diverse natures of things good and bad, and invent all manner of cunning arts."[116]

It is God's glory that he makes all things "and the making of things is, so to

---

[114] 939C–F. See Bretzl, *Botanische Forschungen des Alexanderzuges, passim* and the Cherniss ed. in the Loeb Library where references to Theophrastus are given.

[115] See also Lamprias' discussion of providence and Zeus and the meaning of a natural condition or a natural position, 927D–928C; Sulla's myth, esp. the relation of body, soul, and mind to earth, moon, and sun; the purpose of the moon in the cosmos and its role in the life cycle of souls, 940F *ad fin.*, and Cherniss' remarks, pp. 20–26. In "Whether Fire or Water is More Useful," 956F–957A, the sea is extolled, the water providing from its own self a fifth element; the sea is given great credit for human progress, plant interchanges, etc., because it encourages commerce, cooperation, and friendship; the piece, however, is not now regarded as a genuine work of P. See Cherniss' intro. in the Loeb ed. of the *Moralia*, Vol. 12, pp. 288–289.

[116] *Hermetica*, Lib. III 3b. The workings of the cosmos are likened to the activities of a good husbandman, Lib. ix, 6–8, and to a father who has received his supply of good from God. Lib. x, 3.

speak, God's very being."[117] Nothing is to be considered evil in relation to the maker himself; evil and fullness are by-products, accidents of the creation, and they are compared to rust on metal, to dirt on the body. In this idea the principle of the fullness of nature is explained, and the nature of evil is accounted for: It is not God that creates evil, but the "lasting on" of things causes "evil to break out on them"; hence God inspired change in the world to purge it of its evil.[118]

Often believers in an all-embracing and interrelated nature were embarrassed, as many modern natural theologians have been, by the existence—and the utility—of insects and other lower forms of life. How did they fit into the web of existence that this harmonious order of nature demanded? A feeble answer given by one of the Hermetic writers was that some organisms, like flies and worms, are produced only to be destroyed. Or, the insects are part of the order of nature even if man does not know their uses. Even in the theologies of modern times the insects and other smaller kinds of creatures were designed to annoy man, to keep his pride within reason, and to remind him of his fall from grace; like the modern manufacturers of insecticides, these thinkers capitalized on the obviously great powers of insects as annoyances to the human race, and they concluded that insects must be considered somewhat differently, since like other arrangements of nature, they did not have clear and demonstrable utility.

Finally, we must consider the vivid, often dramatic, conceptions of Plotinus. Although the earth is but a part of the cosmos permeated with life, it is itself replete with every possible gradation of living matter; it is a colorful earth of struggle and conflict with its own peculiar and striking beauties. The cosmos—including the earth within it—is eternal but it is neither a product of chance nor of the motions of the atoms nor of an artisan working according to a preconceived plan.[119]

Of the three Plotinian hypostases, the highest, the transcendent first principle, the One or the Good, is beyond human comprehension, "He is a very positive Reality, of infinite power and content and superabundant excellence." The One is formless because it is infinite but it is "not a God 'outside' the world," for all gradations of being have some of it within them.[120] The *Nous* is an emanation of this first principle, while the universal soul, an emanation of Nous, is good and divine, and forms and rules the material universe. There are two levels of soul, a higher level "where it acts as a transcendent principle of form, order, and intelligent direction, and the lower where it operates as an

---

[117] *Hermetica*, Lib. xiv, 7.
[118] *Ibid.*
[119] Plotinus, *Enn.*, III, 2, 1. Plotinus also discusses the question of the existence of an evil creator and the possibility that there is no creator at all. For Plotinus I am indebted to Armstrong, *Plotinus*, pp. 11–42, and Lovejoy, *The Great Chain of Being*, pp. 63–66.
[120] Armstrong, *Plotinus*, pp. 31, 32.

immanent principle of life and growth." This lower form of the soul is called nature. The universe is an organic whole, full of life, and all gradations of being. To Plotinus, the material universe is "a living organic whole, the best possible image of the living unity-in-diversity of the World of Forms in *Nous*."[121] The great fullness and diversity of life is derived ultimately from the transcendent first principle: it is perfect, and being so, it cannot endure to remain in itself; it generates and produces some other thing—and this is true of beings with and without the power of choice and even of inanimate things: thus "fire warms, snow chills, drugs have their own outgoing efficacy."[122] It is not possible for the Perfect Being to remain unto itself—as if jealous or impotent— something must be begotten of it. "And this generation of the Many from the One cannot come to an end so long as any possible variety of being in the descending series is left unrealized."[123]

Such a philosophy, with its emphasis on life, its fullness and diversity, produces a vivid and rich view of the earth. In reading Plotinus, moreover, one feels that strong personal predilections and appreciations are interwoven with the abstract ideas: an appreciation of nature, an interest in the theatre, in warfare, in practical everyday affairs. It is true, he says, that there is constant warfare in nature: the animals devour one another, men attack one another; but to him animals that prey and those that are preyed upon are equally necessary to the diversity and abundance of life characteristic of the whole cosmos. The struggle is subordinated to a higher concept, for life returns in another form; it is like the murder of actors in a play. They are not really killed but change their makeup and assume a new role. Life goes on even if there is individual suffering and death; there would be a "bleak quenching of life" were this not so, for "as the plan holds, life is poured copiously throughout a Universe, engendering the universal things and weaving variety into their being, never at rest from producing an endless sequence of comeliness and shapeliness, a living pastime."[124] All life, no matter how lowly, "is an activity and not a blind activity like that of a flame"; it aims like "the pantomimic dancer with his set movements" at a pattern. Strongly asserting the human feeling for beauty and nature, Plotinus criticizes the view that the soul made the creation after a decline in its powers; this it could not do, for the creative act of the soul is proof that it has not lost its connection with the divine. The soul could not, like a sculptor on earth, have been planning for its own glory; it created out of the need of its own nature and it cannot be held that it has repented of its work; the soul "must be already accustomed to the world, must be growing more tender toward it with the passing of time." There is no war-

---

121 *Ibid.*, the two quotations being on pp. 37 and 39, respectively.
122 Plotinus, *Enn.*, V, 4, 1. Quoted in Lovejoy, *op. cit.*, p. 62. See also V, 1, 6 and V, 2, 1.
123 Lovejoy, *The Great Chain of Being*, p. 62.
124 *Enn.*, III, 2, 15.

rant for believing this world to be of unhappy origin because there are many disturbing things in it, for to so believe would be to think the world to be the same with the intelligible realm and not merely its reflection. And even though it is only a reflection, what a marvelous one it is!

> And yet—what reflection of that world could be conceived more beautiful than this of ours? What fire could be a nobler reflection of the fire there than the fire we know here? Or what other earth than this could have been modelled after that earth? And what globe more minutely perfect than this, or more admirably ordered in its course, could have been conceived in the image of the self-centered circling of the World of Intelligibles?[125]

The order of the universe is compared to the work of a general who plans the campaigns and provisioning of his troops, working out beforehand his complex plans to insure success. The earthly general must plan without the knowledge of his opponent, but where there is the mighty general of Providence "whose power extends over all that is, what can pass unordered, what can fail to fit into the plan?"[126] Our earth takes part in this nobility of the universe. "This earth of ours is full of varied life-forms and of immortal beings; to the very heavens it is crowded."[127]

Even if there is no divine artisan here, the ordered cosmos, and within it the ordered earth, is a product, an emanation of the nature of perfection which must be active, the emanation from one to the other taking place without any diminution of its essence.[128]

There is not only beauty but reasonableness in the ordering of all natural phenomena, including those observable on earth. Not only this, but the earth is full and rich with all varieties of life; one feels that in its very profusion life is becoming dense almost to the point of overcrowding. The cosmos as a whole and the earth within it, made after a perfect model, is the best of all possible worlds.[129]

Plotinus' ideas were one of the inspirations of the Cambridge Platonists whose concept of plastic nature[130] was influential in providing the philosophical background for probably the best physico-theology written in the western world, John Ray's *Wisdom of God Manifested in the Works of the Creation,*

[125] *Ibid.,* 2, 16; II, 9, 4.
[126] *Ibid.,* III, 3, 2.
[127] *Ibid.,* II, 9, 8.
[128] On the praise of beauty and order in the visible world see (in addition to II, 9, 8) II, 16–17; III, 2, 3. ("The world, we must reflect, is a product of Necessity, not of deliberate purpose: it is due to a higher Kind engendering in its own likeness by a natural process.") See also Pohlenz, *Die Stoa,* Vol. I, pp. 390–393. "Ganz in der Tonart der Stoa preist darum Plotin die Schönheit und Ordnung der sichtbaren Welt, die selbst in den kleinsten Lebewesen und in der Blumenpracht der Pflanzenwelt zutage tritt," p. 393.
[129] Lovejoy, *The Great Chain of Being,* pp. 64–65.
[130] See for example Raven's discussion of Ralph Cudworth, *Science and Religion,* pp. 114–119.

a book which will be discussed in greater detail in a subsequent chapter. The principle of plenitude, outlined by Plato and developed here by Plotinus, shows the striking preoccupation of Western thinkers with the fertility of nature, so easily observed in the multiplication of plant life, insects, and the smaller animals. The principle of plenitude later could provide a basis for pessimistic conclusions regarding the ability of the earth to support an indefinite multiplication of life, an observation which introduced ideas of natural or artificial checks to natural fertility, such as war, infanticide, disease, and plague. Its optimistic side is revealed in the exaltation with which the richness, variety, and fullness of the life principle is asserted as a manifestation of cosmic order.

The speculations of the ancient thinkers regarding the nature of the cosmos and of the earth as part of it, the role of a demiurge, gods, or of Providence—however the guiding principle or agent was defined—produced a conception of the earth, based on philosophical speculation and everyday observation, which had lasting effects on Western geographic thought. Whether the earth was conceived of as a product of a divine artisan with a plan, or, as with Plotinus, as an emanation from Nous, itself an emanation of the One, the principle of balance, harmony, and order in nature was not only acknowledged but enshrined, even before the reinforcements of Judeo-Christian theology, as one of the great interpretations of the role of the earth in human destiny.

# Chapter 2

# Airs, Waters, Places

## 1. GREEK SOURCES OF THE ENVIRONMENTAL THEORY

The sources of the environmental theory are both in the philosophical and scientific theory of the Greeks and in conclusions drawn from practical life and common observation. There is some evidence for the belief that the Greeks ascribed to the climate—or perhaps to temperature—the distinctive characteristics of their civilization. From early times there have been two types of environmental theory, one based on physiology (such as the theory of the humors) and one on geographical position; both are in the Hippocratic corpus. In general, the environmental theories based on physiology have evolved from the notion of health and disease as indicating a balance or imbalance respectively of the humors,[1] and from empirical observations such as the advantages

---

[1] Hippoc., *Nature of Man*. He criticizes the single-element theory of the composition of the human body. I–II. "The body of man has in itself blood, phlegm, yellow bile and black bile; these make up the nature of his body, and through these he feels pain or enjoys health. Now he enjoys the most perfect health when these elements are duly

of certain town or house sites, situation with relation to altitude (possibly because high places were above malarial swamps) or nearness to water, and to certain prevailing winds. Since Greek times, these theories have shown the effects of their origin; to very recent times they have been based on a psycho-physiological theory (the mental and physical stimulation of invigorating climate) or on geographical position, the latter types often being associated with the literature of political and economic theory.

The history of environmental theories is distinct from that of the idea of design because the main stimulus of the former came originally from medicine, although it is true that adaptation of life to the physical environment is implicit in the idea of an orderly and harmonious nature. Theories based on a physiological doctrine were the dominant ones in antiquity and in modern times to about the time of Carl Ritter, although both Montesquieu and Herder had broader views. The humor theory made possible a greater degree of generalization than did ideas of influence of situation, relief, or the quality of soils, because these influences were applied to local situations (as Thucydides applied them in his discussion of the effects of the poor soils on the history and civilization of Attica). Later the siting of the city of Rome was a favorite illustration.

The importance of the humor theory from a geographic point of view, as we have seen, was that the dominance of one or another humor in the human body might be ascribed to environmental conditions. Attention was thus called to the problem of mixtures of the humors in their effects both on the body and on peoples as a whole. This of course is an important theme in the Hippocratic writings and in many of the questions posed in the *Problems* of Aristotle, a work thoroughly Hippocratic in tone, which, if not that of Aristotle, is believed to contain materials derived from him.

The humor theory also presupposes a sympathy between body and mind, the good or bad humors of the body working on the mind, the passions and disturbances of the mind influencing the body. The humors—with the mind-body relationships—in combination with the influences of airs, waters, and places, thus could explain not only physical and mental health, but the physical and cultural characteristics of peoples as a whole.

Virtually all the familiar assertions of modern times, even if we charitably stop with Montesquieu, are found in a cruder form in antiquity: warm climates produce passionate natures; cold, bodily strength and endurance; temperate climates, intellectual superiority; and among the nonphysiological theories, a fertile soil produces soft people, a barren one makes them brave.

Although the second part of the Hippocratic *Airs, Waters, Places* (chaps.

---

proportioned to one another in respect of compounding, power and bulk, and when they are perfectly mingled" (IV). See also Hippoc., *Ancient Medicine*, xix.

12–24) is the earliest systematic treatise concerned with environmental influences on human culture, fragments of the writings of Heraclitus and Diogenes of Apollonia reveal the antiquity of the belief that moisture is unfavorable to thinking, a belief possibly suggested by the state of drunkenness. "A dry soul is wisest and best," says Heraclitus (*fl. ca.* 500 B.C.) and, "A man when he is drunk is led by an unfledged boy, stumbling and not knowing where he goes, having his soul moist."[2]

According to Theophrastus, Diogenes (*fl.* 440–430 B.C.) attributed thinking, the senses, and life to air. Thought is caused by pure dry air; "for a moist emanation inhibits the intelligence; for this reason thought is diminished in sleep, drunkenness and surfeit." Other living creatures have inferior intellects because they breathe moisture-laden air from the earth; birds breathe pure air, but owing to their constitution, like that of fishes, air permeates the body only around the abdomen; plants lack intelligence; they are not hollow and receive no air within.[3]

## 2. The Hippocratic Treatise "Airs, Waters, Places"

Throughout this work I have used the name of Hippocrates as if it were self-evident that he is the author of *Ancient Medicine* and *Airs, Waters, Places*, but there is little but custom to warrant such a practice. Through the eighteenth century there was general agreement that the works traditionally ascribed to him were indeed his; only in the nineteenth century was this view challenged, were the problems of authenticity examined, but no agreed-upon solution was found. No one knows if Hippocrates is the author of any of these works. *Ancient Medicine* may date from the end of the fifth century, possibly being composed by an early disciple of Hippocrates. *Airs, Waters, Places* apparently is genuine in the sense that with very few demurrers it has been included in the ancient so-called Hippocratic corpus. Editors of Hippocrates' works have included both in the corpus, a practice followed by Littré and Jones. It is reasonable to suppose that the essay was composed early enough to influence men like Aristotle, and some have seen its influence in the concluding chapter of Herodotus' histories. These uncertainties regarding dating and authenticity should not obscure the fact that rightly or wrongly Hippocrates through the ages has been regarded as a very real physician, as the author of the work, and that *Airs, Waters, Places* has been one of the most popular of his treatises.[4]

[2] Kirk and Raven, *PSP*, #233, 234, p. 205. The first is Fr. 118, Stobaeus, *Anth.* III, 5, 8; the second Fr. 117, *ibid.*, III, 5, 7. These authors think Heraclitus' main philosophical activity ended by 480, p. 183. The *floruit* follows the OCD.

[3] Kirk and Raven, *PSP*, #615, p. 441. Source: Theophr. *de sensu* 39–44 = Diels, *Vorsokr.* 6th ed., 64 A 19, Vol. 2, pp. 55–56.

[4] For a discussion of the Hippocratic corpus, see W. H. S. Jones's "General Introduction" in Vol. 1 of the Loeb ed. of Hippocrates, and Sarton, *Ancient Science Through the Golden Age of Greece*, chaps. 13–14.

The reader of *Airs, Waters, Places*, however, quickly notices that it lacks unity, that in fact there are two different essays, one medical, the other ethnographical and geographical. In 1889, Fredrich pointed out this fact, arguing that it had two different and independent parts, chapters 1–11, and 12–24. Subsequent textual study confirmed Fredrich's views, without, however, achieving agreement concerning the relationship between the two parts and the authorship.[5]

In his very interesting reexamination of the question, Edelstein argues that the purpose of the first eleven chapters is to provide a physician coming to a strange city with the opportunity of acquainting himself, without having to inquire of anyone, with all important factors likely to be involved in treatment before he starts it. It is intended to be a prognostic book acquainting the physician with environmental conditions, the usual diseases, and the seasonal occurrence of various diseases.[6]

In the second part on Europe and Asia and the differences among their peoples, some of the difficulties are owing to lacunae in the text, such as the loss of the descriptions of Egypt and Libya. Edelstein is of the opinion that the transmission of the two parts as if they constituted a unified work, even though they have no relation to one another, occurred because someone had a personal interest in the two different fields and preserved the work as a unit. In this way one can account for the inclusion of chapters 12–24 in a medical corpus because they could just as well have been written by a geographer.[7]

Edelstein also proposed a new hypothesis regarding the origin of the Hippocratic corpus; one of its most interesting aspects is the history of opinion regarding it and its authorship.[8] If one relies on the earlier sources, one cannot go beyond the claim that Hippocrates in his own time was regarded as a distinguished and famous physician; he was not *the* physician, nor was he a demigod. An important turning point in attitudes toward him occurred when Celsus made greater claims for him, describing him as the first of all physicians worthy of being remembered ("primus ex omnibus memoria dignis").[9]

To Celsus, Hippocrates, unlike later physicians, is active in all fields of medicine, and he is a figure of heroic dimensions; to Erotian, he is a writer who ranks with Homer; to Galen, he is the ideal doctor. The history of Hippocratic glossology and commentary shows that the so-called works as a whole were gathered late, the earliest that can be established dating from the time of Hadrian.[10] All known sources, however, are silent on the authenticity

---

[5] For a short history of this criticism, see Edelstein, *Peri aerōn und die Sammlung der Hippokratischen Schriften*, pp. 1–4 in which the contributions of Fredrich, Wilamowitz, Jacoby, Heiberg, and Trüdinger are briefly discussed.

[6] *Ibid.*, pp. 5–6, 8, 31–32.

[7] *Ibid.*, p. 59; see chap. 1 for a detailed review of the textual problems.

[8] *Ibid.*, chap. 4, "Die Hippokratische Frage."

[9] The reference is to Celsus, *De Medicina*, I, 18, 12–13. Edelstein, pp. 126–127.

[10] *Ibid.*, pp. 128–129, on Celsus, Erotian (compiler of a glossary to H., prob. *fl.* in the times of Nero), Galen; on early commentaries, p. 150.

of the writings. Edelstein's admittedly hypothetical conclusion is that the works of Hippocrates did not come to Alexandria (at least their presence cannot be proved), but that a body of ancient and anonymous medical writings did. The opinion of history had so enhanced the reputation of Hippocrates even though no works of his had survived, that men were interested in him and wanted to read him. The corpus of anonymous literature, possibly from his period, deposited in the Alexandrian library posed for grammarians or doctors the question whether among them there might be the works of Hippocrates. At first the attributions were few, gradually increasing because of the high regard in which his memory was held. Finally the dominant view emerged. The fifth century physician had obliterated by his fame the work of lesser men, the great name had attracted to it the entire corpus of anonymous authorship. Traditionally, *Airs, Waters, Places* is among the Hippocratic writings, but Edelstein thinks the author is one of the old physicians whose name was forgotten, whose work with many other anonymous writings had been brought to Alexandria.[11]

To the end of the eighteenth century, however, Hippocrates was a real man, and *Airs, Waters, Places* one of his authentic masterpieces. Perhaps with Jones one can think of Hippocrates, not as a physician, but as the spirit of medical trends in the late fifth century B.C.

So much has been written on Hippocrates' essay that it is almost impossible to say anything fresh about it; its value to our theme is that it reveals how closely interrelated are the early histories of medicine, geography, and anthropology.

The fundamental philosophy of the second part of the essay is derived from a comparison of three physical environments, one of extreme cold, another of extreme heat, the third temperate and intermediate between the extremes. The first, the northern region of extreme cold, is inhabited by the Scythians and the Longheads ($\mu\alpha\kappa\rho\omicron\kappa\acute{\epsilon}\phi\alpha\lambda\omicron\iota$) (in Eastern Europe roughly equivalent to the southern half of the Ukrainian S.S.R.) and the people of the Phasis River region (the Phasis, famous for its association with the expedition of the Argonauts, is the modern Rioni flowing through western Georgia into the eastern shore of the Black Sea); the environment of the southern hot extreme is represented by Egypt and Libya (this part is lost), and the temperate by Ionia. The contrast of Asia with Europe, with which the essay is also concerned, is of a different character; the division is an east-west instead of a north-south one (hence longitudinal rather than latitudinal), but the Scythians are the only example of a European people given.

In *Airs, Waters, Places*, Hippocrates discusses several important themes, among them the proper siting of houses with relation to the sun, the good and bad qualities of waters, the seasonal distribution of disease, and—of greatest

[11] Edelstein, *op. cit.*, pp. 179–181.

interest, because it concerns peoples, not individuals—comparisons between Europe and Asia "to show how they differ in every respect, and how the nations of the one differ entirely in physique from those of the other."[12]

The temperate climate of Asia—meaning in this passage the Mediterranean climate of the coast of Asia Minor—is responsible for the greater beauty and size of both its inhabitants and its vegetation. "Growth and freedom from wildness are most fostered when nothing is forcibly predominant, but equality in every respect prevails."[13] Another region in Asia—with its woods, its rain and spring water, with the bountiful plant life enabling man to domesticate the wild plants, and with its desirable breeds of cattle—produces tall men of fine physique, differing little from one another. The climate of the region is likened to spring, but one must not expect of these people courage, endurance, industry, or high spirits whether they are native born or immigrants.

Hippocrates says he is not concerned with peoples ($\check{\epsilon}\theta\nu o\acute{\iota}$) that are similar but with those that differ, either through nature or custom from one another. This matter-of-fact statement may reveal the reason for the interest in differing physical environments in antiquity. Although Hippocrates was interested in differences, not similarities, among peoples, his was basically a medical, not an ethnographic, interest. Climatic variations, seasonal change, different types of landscapes, could explain at least in part—for Hippocrates is not a strict determinist—the reasons for these differences. If Hippocrates had shown an interest in accounting for similarities rather than differences, the history of environmental theories would have been entirely different.

In his first example, differences are explained by cultural reasons. The Longheads ($\mu\alpha\kappa\rho o\kappa\acute{\epsilon}\phi\alpha\lambda o\iota$), whose ethnic affiliation and provenance are not made clear, are an example of the inheritance of acquired characteristics, for through their custom of elongating the head from earliest infancy, the process becomes natural with continuous practice through the generations. Cultural contact, however, had caused some decline in the practice. "At the present time longheadedness is less common than it was, for owing to intercourse with other men the custom is less prevalent."[14] Custom, the inheritance of acquired characteristics, and cultural contact, not climate, account for the present condition of these people.

Asia, however, is not uniform nor are all people of Asia like those of its Mediterranean shore, for those dwelling on the Phasis in Colchis live in hot, wooded marshes with heavy year-round rains. The water, including that of

---

[12] Hippoc., *Airs, Waters, Places*, xii.

[13] *Ibid.*, xii. Hippocrates continues (xiii) to make correlations between physical types, types of land, and seasonal change. The greatest climatic variation is correlated with wild and uneven land, while small seasonal variation is correlated with level land. Types of human physiques are correlated also with wooded, well-watered mountains, light dry land, marshy meadows, and plains of bare, parched earth. The correlations made in this passage are physical, not mental.

[14] *Ibid.*, xiv.

the Phasis, is stagnant. Excess of water and fog inhibits growth; the inhabitants, tall and gross, have yellowish complexions, and deep voices because they breathe moist and turbid air.[15]

The asiatics lack spirit and courage and are less warlike than the Europeans because they are subject neither to mental shocks nor to violent physical change, "which are more likely to steel the temper and impart to it a fierce passion than is a monotonous sameness." Hippocrates, however, recognizes that the institutions of the Asiatic peoples also contribute to their character: despotism and forced military service to further the ends of rulers rather than their own (their rewards being danger and death) might even succeed in changing naturally brave and spirited men. Here the contrast is between the people of Asia who live under despots and those—whether Greek or non-Greek—who do not and who consequently live independently, work for their own advantage, and exhibit greater bravery and belligerance.[16]

Both climatic and cultural causes are given for the behavior of the Scythians, a homogeneous people who represent the cold extreme as the Egyptians represent the hot and who are as affected by the monotony of the cold as the latter are by the heat. The lack of violent seasonal change induces in them a similarity in mental and physical qualities. The people, however, are noted for the sterility of the men, a condition which is explained by climatic effects acting on the human body, and by their riding, the affliction being characteristic of the rich Scythians, for those too poor to ride horses are less susceptible to becoming sterile. Using this example, Hippocrates argues that disease is not a divine visitation, but a natural outcome of specific conditions and activities.

Equally illuminating is the discussion of sterility in women, caused, says Hippocrates, by the fatness and moistness of their flesh which prevents the womb from absorbing the seed, by menstrual difficulties, and by the closing with fat of the mouth of the womb. As proof Hippocrates contrasts the fat and lazy Scythian women with the Scythian slave girls. "These, because of their activity and leanness of body, no sooner go to a man than they are with child." Here also is the famous description of the Anaries, the Scythian men who because of their sterility became effeminate, dressing and acting like women and doing women's work.[17]

Speaking of the Europeans, Hippocrates attempts several correlations between the characteristics of the people and those of the environment, such as humidity, altitude, and terrain. Peoples living in mountainous regions—rugged, high, and watered, and with sharp seasonal changes—will be likely

---

[15] *Ibid.*, xv.

[16] *Ibid.*, xvi.

[17] *Ibid.*, xxi–xxii. See also Herodotus, I, 105; IV, 67, who calls them *Enarees*. Sarton thinks this name might be the Scythian word for androgyne or homosexual. *Hist. of Science. Ancient Science Through the Golden Age of Greece*, p. 369, fn. 65.

to have large physiques, possess endurance and courage, and tend to wildness and ferocity. Peoples living in meadow-like stifling hollows where hot winds prevail more than cold will be "inclined to be broad, fleshy, dark haired; they themselves are dark rather than fair, less subject to phlegm than to bile. Similar bravery and endurance are not by nature part of their character, but the imposition of law (νόμος) can produce them artificially." Again, Hippocrates qualifies the determinism by noting the force of social institutions. Peoples living on high level land, windy and watered, will be tall, will resemble one another, but will be "rather unmanly and tame in character." Those living on thin, dry and bare soil, with sharp seasonal contrasts, will be hard, fair, stubborn, and independent. And peoples living in rich, soft, well-watered lands and where the water is near the surface (becoming hot in summer, cold in winter) with favorable seasonal change are

> fleshy, ill-articulated, moist, lazy, and generally cowardly in character. Slackness and sleepiness can be observed in them, and as far as the arts are concerned they are thick-witted, and neither subtle nor sharp. But where the land is bare, waterless, rough, oppressed by winter's storms and burnt by the sun, there you will see men who are hard, lean, well-articulated, well-braced, and hairy; such natures will be found energetic, vigilant, stubborn and independent in character and in temper, wild rather than tame, of more than average sharpness and intelligence in the arts, and in war of more than average courage.[18]

These contrasts between hard and soft environments have often been compared with the celebrated passage with which Herodotus ends his histories. (See below, pp. 90–91.) Indeed, it would be difficult to overestimate the amount of speculation about the influence of mountains, valleys, swamps, hard and soft environments that this essay has inspired.

Although *Airs, Waters, Places* has several leading ideas (the close relationship between culture and environment, the inheritance of acquired characteristics, the prevalence of occupational disease, the influences of institutions such as government), it owes its influence to the first of these, the effects of airs, waters, and places. The essay presents the first formulation of the environmental idea, but in its ethnological part there is a far more eclectic approach to the study of culture than would appear from the more dogmatic statements, although these were the ones that were copied by succeeding generations.

It is significant too that only the *Airs, Waters, Places* has been referred to by humanistic thinkers interested in the history of cultural anthropology and geography. *Ancient Medicine* is based on entirely different presuppositions regarding human culture: man, spurred on by necessity and his dissatisfactions, conquers his environment; through the domestication of plants and animals and the invention of cooking, he has attained his present high stan-

[18] Hippoc., *op. cit.*, xxiv.

dards of civilization. Necessity drove men to the study of medicine, because sick men did not profit by the same way of living and the same regimen as did healthy men. Present foods would not have been discovered had man been satisfied with "the same food and drink as satisfy an ox, a horse, and every animal save man . . . ," for in the beginning they had similar nourishment. Even the men of antiquity suffered from crude foods; the majority died because their constitutions were too weak. "For this reason the ancients too seem to me to have sought for nourishment that harmonised [*sic*] with their constitution, and to have discovered that which we use now." Bread was produced from wheat, cake from barley; they experimented with boiled and baked foods, mixing them in various combinations to suit the human constitution. This experimentation is in essence medicine, for it was carried on for the purpose of insuring good health and providing nourishment; it is a study that constantly goes on, for students of gymnastics and exercises are continually discovering foods and drinks that are easily assimilated and which make a man grow stronger.[19]

Since, however, it was *Airs, Waters, Places* that influenced subsequent theorists in history, ethnology, and geography, it is the nature of its legacy that is of most interest. It is responsible for the fallacy that, if environmental influences on the physical and mental qualities of individuals can be shown, they can by extension be applied to whole peoples. If Hippocrates had made it clear that environment, medicine, and ethnology are three different studies, that the influence of climate on the individual was a proper study of medicine and that ethnology required other methods—as indeed his own descriptions prove—the rigorous correlations derived from Hippocrates would not have been pressed so ardently over a period lasting at least 2,300 years, nor would it have been necessary for Arnold Toynbee in our own day to have refuted Hippocrates' ideas in his discussion of the genesis of civilizations.[20]

### 3.  Herodotus' Interest in Custom and Environment

The contrasts in the cultural and environmental materials used by Herodotus and Hippocrates (or an unknown author) show the different worlds in which the two men lived, the latter being mainly interested in medicine and its related fields, the former in history, travel, customs, and differing environments. The ideas of Herodotus must to some degree be interpreted by the reader; they are seldom stated by the historian. Among them, there seems to be a general pessimistic attitude toward the life both of individuals and of cities; chance plays a strong role; there are reversals of power and neither

[19] Hippoc., *Ancient Medicine*, iii.
[20] Toynbee, *A Study of History*, Vol. I, pp. 249–271, more compactly in the Somervell abridgement of Vols. I–VI, pp. 55–59. Toynbee himself translated parts of *Airs, Waters, Places* in *Greek Historical Thought*, pp. 143–146 (Mentor Books).

weakness nor happiness is long in one place; the power of custom and the resistance to cultural change are characteristic emphases, but there is also a lively interest in cultural borrowings.

Herodotus is sensitive to contrasts in physical environments, and occasionally, as in the famous passage (IX, 122) discussed below, reminiscent of the *Airs, Waters, Places,* and in his descriptions of Scythia he attempts to make correlations between environment and culture.[21]

The combination of their way of life and the nature of the land, he says, makes the Scythians virtually unconquerable, even unassailable. Attackers of the Scythians invite their own destruction, for these nomadic peoples carry their dwellings with them, shoot from horseback, live on their cattle and in their wagons. The nature of the country and its rivers help them greatly in resisting attacks. "For the land is level, well watered, and abounding in pasture; while the rivers which traverse it are almost equal in number to the canals of Egypt."[22]

But for the most part environments are simply described. The air and climate of the Ionian cities are depicted as being the most beautiful in the world; other countries are cold or damp, or hot and subject to drought.[23] The Egyptians, except the Libyans, on the other hand, he believes to be the healthiest people of the world because their climate has no sudden changes.[24]

The Greeks, as both Herodotus and Plato make amply clear, were interested in the uniqueness of the Egyptian environment (as well as in its culture and history) and in environmental contrasts between the two countries, an interest observable in the history of Herodotus and in the *Critias,* the *Laws,* and the *Timaeus* of Plato, reverberations of which appear in the writings of Josephus in the first century A.D. The fundamental contrast is in the water sources of the two countries, the Egyptians obtaining theirs from the river, the Greeks from rain. (We have already seen that a distinction is made in the eighth strophe of *The Hymn to Aten* [fourteenth century B.C.] by the Egyptians between themselves, who have the true Nile which comes forth from the underworld, and the foreign peoples whose Nile is in the sky. See p. 38.)

The Egyptians had to do little work, with so much ready water, while the Greeks, dependent on rainfall, could expect both drought and inundations.

---

[21] For a discussion of this relationship, see Heinimann, *Nomos und Physis,* pp. 172–180. The traditional view is that Herodotus and Hippocrates had a common source in Hecataeus; Pohlenz thought Herodotus to be the source of the Hippocratic writing, Nestle, that Herodotus derived it from Hippocrates. Heinimann concludes that both medicine and ethnography had a considerable prior development and that there are no direct connections between the two which can lead to any firm dating of *Airs, Waters, Places.*

[22] Hdt. IV, 46–47. Quotation in chap. 47.

[23] *Ibid.,* I, 142.

[24] *Ibid.,* II, 77.

Great floods, apparently from periodic torrential rainfall, play an important role in the supposed history of Greek civilization before Atlantis was destroyed by submergence. In his conversations with the Egyptian priests, Herodotus theorizes that continual deposition of the waters of the Nile is building up lands so rapidly that in the future it may no longer perform its old role. The priests told him, "When Moeris was king, the Nile overflowed all Egypt below Memphis, as soon as it rose so little as eight cubits"; now it requires at the very least fifteen cubits before the land is flooded. "It seems to me, therefore, that if the land goes on rising and growing at this rate, the Egyptians who dwell below Lake Moeris, in the Delta (as it is called) and elsewhere, will one day, by the stoppage of the inundations, suffer permanently the fate which they told me they expected would some time or other befall the Greeks." On hearing that the only source of water for the Greeks was rain, the priests said, "Some day the Greeks will be disappointed of their grand hope, and then they will be wretchedly hungry."[25]

The Egyptians living on flooded lands need not break the ground with the plough or the hoe; where farmers elsewhere have to work hard, the husbandman in Egypt "waits till the river has of its own accord spread itself over the fields and withdrawn again to its bed, and then sows his plot of ground, and after sowing turns his swine into it—the swine tread in the corn—after which he has only to await the harvest."[26]

Herodotus also distinguishes between the grain and the marsh lands of Egypt: the marsh peoples have the same customs as the rest of the Egyptians, but they differ in resources available to them, for they make use of the lotus, a roselike lily, the byblus (papyrus), and some of them live entirely on fish.[27] Herodotus reveals throughout his work, as Glover and Myres have pointed out, a keen interest in the location of mines, minerals, and food sources and in questions of environment, economics, and social institutions, although he does interpret cultures as combinations of these elements.[28]

The only instance of environmental theory in Herodotus is at the end of the work where the speech of Cyrus resembles Hippocratic teachings. Cyrus is urged by his countrymen to assent to living in the newly conquered regions where life is easier than in the remote harsh regions in which the Persians dwell. Cyrus replies that it would be far preferable to live in the harsh environment in which they now dwell as free men, than to live in luxury as slaves in the fertile captured valleys. It has been suggested that Herodotus may have inserted this passage as a warning that the Persian threat still existed and that

[25] *Ibid.,* 13.
[26] *Ibid.,* 14.
[27] *Ibid.,* 92.
[28] Glover, *Herodotus*, pp. 115–119; Myres, "Herodotus and Anthropology," in Marett, *Anthro. and the Classics*, pp. 152–157, 160–163.

the Greeks might learn the lesson of Cyrus, whose famous speech has interesting affinities with Toynbee's ideas of the stimulus of a hard environment in the genesis of civilizations. A similar thought is expressed by Xenophon, who describes the Chaldeans as a most warlike and poor people, serving for hire, who live in mountain country, little of which is either fertile or productive.[29]

## 4. LOCATION THEORIES AND HIPPOCRATIC INFLUENCES

Thucydides continued a type of geographical explanation already discernible in Hippocrates, although the theory of balance in health and the humors are the cornerstones of the latter's thinking. Geographical factors such as soil, location, siting, isolation, or maritime location, however, need not be based on medical theory. Thus, Thucydides describes early Hellas as a place in which migrations were very frequent, the peoples, under pressure of overpopulation, moving from one place to another; these migrations affected the fertile areas of Hellas most, such as Thessaly, Boeotia, large parts of the Peloponnesus, excepting its rugged central portion, Arcadia, because they encouraged covetousness and invasion. Attica, on the other hand, enjoyed stability; its inhabitants remained the same, for the soils were so infertile that they offered little inducement to an invader. The stability of the Athenian cultural tradition permitted the growth of Attica, which prospered not only because of its own people but because of the number of refugees entering the region until the Athenian population grew to the point that colonies had to be sent to Ionia. The Greek colonization of Asia Minor became an indirect consequence of Attica's infertile soils, providing the necessary conditions of peace and stability that led to population growth and colonization.[30]

Even more perceptive of the complex cultural, economic, and environmental elements making up a civilization is a short pamphlet, dating perhaps from the early Peloponnesian War and preserved in the works of Xenophon, commenting on land-sea relationships and the significance of the geographical distribution of resources. The subject peoples of a land power are more likely than those of a sea power to unite in a war of liberation, for the latter is able to control its peoples, divided by the seas, who cannot live on their own resources, but must depend on exports and imports. Athens owes her prosperity to her ability to draw upon the resources of various lands through her control of the sea, and owes her civilization to the mixture of ideas coming about through trade: "The Athenians rejoice in a cosmopolitan civilization for which the entire Hellenic and non-Hellenic worlds have been laid under contribution...." Control of the sea is important because the geographical distribution

[29] Hdt., IX, 122. See How and Wells, *Commentary on Herod.*, under this passage, and Xen., *Cyr.* III, ii, 7.
[30] Thuc., I, 1–2.

of resources has enforced an interdependence among peoples. Neither timber nor flax is produced, nor are copper and iron found in the same country, "nor any other two or three materials in a single country, but always one here and the other there." A country which controls the sea prospers by using the resources of land-based countries, dependent on one or two favorable resources, which, however, are insufficient for their prosperity.[31]

Isolated comments in the dialogues of Plato reveal that ideas concerning the influence of the natural environment were current in his time also. Two passages, one in the *Phaedo*, the other in the *Timaeus*, are free of environmental determinism. In the former, Socrates makes his famous remark about the vastness of the earth, saying that we who dwell in the region extending from the river Phasis to the Pillars of Hercules (i.e., the limits of the inhabited world), along the borders of the sea, are just like ants or frogs by a pond and inhabit only a small portion of it, and that many others dwell elsewhere in many similar places.[32] There is a related idea in the *Timaeus* that "in every place where there is no excessive heat or cold to prevent it there always exists some human stock, now more, now less in number."[33] Later the Egyptian priest says that the goddess Athena had given first to the Greeks, then to the Egyptians, an order on earth based on the cosmic order and "she established your State, choosing the spot wherein you [Solon] were born since she perceived therein a climate duly blended, and how that it would bring forth men of supreme wisdom. So it was that the Goddess, being herself both a lover of war and a lover of wisdom, chose the spot which was likely to bring forth men most like unto herself, and this first she established."[34] In the *Laws*, Plato saw a relationship between virtue and geographical location—similar ideas appeared later in Cicero and Caesar—the dangers to morals being greatest with a maritime location and its opportunities for foreign influences;[35] but his is really an attack on the evils of culture contact, the maritime situation merely offering more convenient opportunities for this to occur. Ideas in the Hippocratic tradition also appear here. Districts are well or poorly endowed because of characteristics such as climate, waters, and soils. The best district has a heavenly breeze and portions of its land are under the care of daemons. The lawgiver should examine these physical characteristics of districts as best he can in order to frame his laws accordingly and he should pursue the same policy in colonizing a country.[36]

[31] Pseudo-Xenophon, *Athenian Institutions*, ed. by E. Kalinka, 1913. Teubner edition, 2. 2–8, 11–16. Trans. in Toynbee, *Greek Historical Thought*, pp. 162–164, under the title, "The Influence of Sea Power on History."

[32] Plat, *Phaedo*, 109b.

[33] Plat, *Tim.* 22E–23A. This is part of the speech of the old Egyptian priest to Solon regarding the youth of Greek civilization and the physical causes of the destruction of civilization.

[34] *Ibid.*, 24 C–D.

[35] Plato, *Laws*, IV, 704D–705D.

[36] *Ibid.*, V, 747D–E.

This theme that the ruler should know his own land thoroughly in order to frame just laws was repeated by St. Thomas Aquinas, Jean Bodin, Giovanni Botero, and by Montesquieu.

There is no profit in attempting to reconcile these views with one another or with Plato's idea of the divine artisan in the *Timaeus*, for there is no systematic body of theory here. The most that can be said is that the *Timaeus* outlines an all-embracing conception of creation and its creator and that these ideas relating to terrestrial environments gathered from observation, common belief, and directly or indirectly from the Hippocratic writings (with no thought of reconciling one with the other) describes influences of a lower order working within the grand harmony of the whole. Plato's remarks, however, like those of Hippocrates, Herodotus, and Aristotle, do give substance to the assertion made by some modern scholars that the Greeks thought they owed a great deal of their civilization to the advantages of a temperate Mediterranean climate. Aristotle's theory is, for example, a simplified version of Hippocrates' with a political interpretation. The peoples of the cold regions, including those living in Europe, are spirited but deficient in skill and intelligence. They preserve their liberty but they lack political organization and are incapable of governing others. The peoples of Asia are the opposite; they are intelligent and inventive, but lack spirit and are in subjection and servitude. The Greeks, living in a region intermediate between these extremes of hot and cold, enjoy the advantages of both; they are high-spirited and intelligent. Only the lack of unity among the Greeks prevented the formation of a universal empire which their climate would have made possible.[37] Like Hippocrates, Aristotle falls short of a strict determinism, for to him the Greek failure is human and its causes are not to be sought in the physical environment.

To Aristotle the golden-mean position of Greece had the captivating quality of being a combination of the best, not the worst, of the two extremes. With him, the correlation between climate and peoples is direct, without any intermediary physiological explanation; the golden mean applies to both the environment and the culture. This has been one of the most influential statements ever made regarding the relation of climate to peoples, not because of its originality—it could make little claim to this—but because of the prestige of Aristotle and his writings. To my knowledge, it has been quoted more widely than any other statement by a classical writer on this subject, excepting possibly *Airs, Waters, Places*, and the speech of Cyrus in Herodotus. Its historical importance is that it carried the environmental theory over from medicine to political and social thought, diffusing the self-flattering conclusion that the most advanced nations are in the temperate climates.

Of more technical interest than this short variant of the Hippocratic doctrine in the *Politics* are the materials in the *Problems* of Aristotle, compiled

[37] Arist., *Politics*, IV, 7, 1327[b].

possibly not earlier than the fifth or sixth century A.D. "The *Problems*, though resting in the main on Aristotelian presuppositions, show considerable traces of a materialism which was characteristic of the later Peripatetic school." The work apparently was compiled from the Theophrastean corpus, from the writings of the Hippocratic school, and in a few cases from the extant works of Aristotle. "It affords interesting evidence of the variety of the studies to which Aristotle stimulated his pupils."[38]

The approach to the problems related to medicine (Book I) and to those relating to the effect of locality on temperament (Book XIV) is similar, and the work demonstrates the strong and continuous influence of the Hippocratic corpus on medical, ethnological, and geographical thinking. These problems, often stated in the form of questions, contain within them assertions which in modern scientific inquiry would be considered the subjects for investigation. The dominant idea in both books is that excesses of any kind produce aberrations and distortions, and that the proper blending of qualities produces the temperate, the mean between the extremes; like the Hippocratic treatises to which they undoubtedly owe their inspiration, they stress the influence of seasonal change, prevailing wind, rain, dampness, excesses of heat and cold, and the ill effects of marshes, owing no doubt to the prevalence of malaria. Why do those living in hollows or marshes age quickly? Why do we become drowsier in marshy districts? Why do people on shipboard, even though on the water, have a healthier color than those living in marshes?[39]

> Why are those who live under conditions of excessive cold or heat brutish in character and aspect? Is the cause the same in both cases? For the best mixture of conditions benefits the mind as well as the body, but excesses of all kinds cause disturbance, and, as they distort the body, so do they pervert the mental temperament.[40]
>
> Why are the inhabitants of warm regions cowardly, and those who dwell in cold districts courageous? Is it because there is a natural tendency which counteracts the effects of locality and season, since if both had the same effect mankind would inevitably be soon destroyed by heat or cold? Now those who are hot by nature are courageous, and those who are cold are cowardly. But the effect of hot regions upon those who dwell in them is that they are cooled, while cold regions engender a natural state of heat in their inhabitants.
>
> Why are those who live in warm regions wiser than those who dwell in cold districts? Is it for the same reason as that for which the old are wiser than the young? For those who live in cold regions are much hotter, because their nature recoils owing to the coldness of the region in which they live, so that they are very like the drunken and are not of an inquisitive turn of mind, but are courageous and sanguine; but those who live in hot regions are sober because they are cool. Now everywhere those who feel fear make more attempt to inquire into things than do the self-confident, and therefore they discover more. Or is

---

[38] Ross, *Aristotle*, 19.
[39] Arist., *Problemata*, XIV, 7, 909$^b$ 1–3; 11, 909$^b$ 38–40; 12, 910$^a$ 1–3.
[40] *Ibid.*, 1, 909$^a$ 13–17.

it because the race of those who live in warm regions is more ancient, the inhabitants of the cold regions having perished in the Flood, so that the latter stand in the same relation to the former as do the young to the old?[41]

The *Problems* are probably representative of the types of questions which were asked and which interested men for centuries—not only the medical practitioners but those who used these medical speculations as a means of understanding peoples and their environments.

## 5. THE PROBLEM OF CULTURAL DIVERSITY

Polybius made a more original contribution to the environmental theory than Aristotle had made; to him the cultural milieu also exists. Hippocrates had said that institutions could alter qualities induced by the physical environment. Polybius carries this thought much further, describing in detail a striking example from his native Arcadia to illustrate the force of environmental and cultural influences. The Greek historian, a hostage of the Romans and the chronicler of Rome's rapid rise to world dominion from the fall of Greece to the fall of Carthage, described the differences, in Arcadia in the Peloponnesus (he was born in Megalopolis), between the Cynaetheans, who had a reputation for cruelty, lawlessness, and savagery, and the other Arcadians who had "a certain reputation among all the Greeks for virtue, not only because of their friendliness to strangers and kindliness in life and deeds but above all because of their religious piety. . . ." The Cynaetheans owed their unpleasant qualities and their misfortunes at the hands of the Aetolians to their abandonment of institutions created by the Arcadians in accordance with nature. These institutions were centered around music, for it lay at the very core of their existence as a people. The children sang the hymns and paeans glorifying the gods and heroes of the country; they competed with one another in flute festivals, in games, or, in their youth, in manly competitions. The musical education, starting with infancy, never left them throughout life: military marches, elaborate dances, theatricals, continued the early emphasis on the value of music to the people. The Arcadians of old did not introduce music out of frivolity but out of necessity: life was hard in Arcadia, the austere manners of whose people were a consequence of the chilly and gloomy climate. "To our climate all of us become adapted by necessity." Character, form, complexions, and customs owe their nature to climate. The Arcadians, in order to alleviate the strictures of a hard climate, introduced music, common assemblies, choruses of boys and girls together, and "in short devised all manner of measures to tame and soften the hardness of the soul through education." The Cynaetheans, most in need of the softening because of the special rigors of their climate, did nothing, engaging merely in warfare and internecine strife.

[41] *Ibid.*, 8, 909$^b$ 8–25; 15, 910$^a$ 26–35.

Polybius asks his readers to bear in mind that the Arcadians do not practice music for the sake of luxury, and in an apostrophe, he expresses the hope that God may allow the Cynaetheans to civilize themselves by education, especially by music, and free themselves from their savagery.[42]

This is the first full exposition known to me of the idea that an environment produces a certain kind of ethnic character, which by conscious, purposive, and hard work, can be counteracted by cultural institutions (such as music) which are all-pervasive. Here the transition from a primordial state (probably of barbarism, induced by the environment) to civilization is made by the conscious decision of a body of culture-heroes or elders. The conception is similar to a dominant idea in modern historiography that the history of civilization is the story of man from a time when nature controlled him until he controlled nature, the difference between the two being that in modern histories the divorcement from environmental control is ascribed, not to conscious efforts of culture-heroes, but to the increase of knowledge, technical skill, and invention.

It might be well at this point to introduce two passages from Diodorus, both of which may be fragments of a work on the Red Sea by Agatharchides, who about 116 B.C. became guardian to a young Ptolemy. They reflect contemporary interest in the ethnology of Africa and of the shores of the Red Sea. The first, which may come, however, from several sources, is concerned with the origin of the human race. According to Diodorus' account, historians say the Ethiopians were the first of all men. They were not immigrants but were autochthonous, and the physical environment there favored the generation of men. Men dwelling beneath the noonday sun were generated first by the earth because the sun's heat at the generation of the universe "dried up the earth when it was still wet and impregnated it with life" [III, 2, 1]. Alas! time and the Leakeys have dealt harshly with Diodorus, the Ethiopians, and the historians. Olduvai gorge is far to the south where the noonday sun is also high in the heavens, but it now seems certain they were right in claiming Africa to be the homeland of man.

The second, which is ascribed to Agatharchides, is an interesting variant of the usual correlations; like Polybius, he emphasizes the hold of custom on a people. Agatharchides contrasts countries of climatic extremes, cold Scythia and hot upper Egypt and the troglodytic country. The inhabitants of each of these inhospitable countries love their own so much that they would sacrifice their lives to avoid being taken from it, for countries hold a spell over men who have become accustomed to them, and the time spent from infancy allows them to overcome the hardships caused by the climate. In twenty-four days, he says, one could go from the coldest north to the warmest part of the inhabited earth in the south; with such marked climatic differences "it is

[42] Polybius, IV, 20. This selection is also translated in Lovejoy and Boas, *Primitivism and Related Ideas in Antiquity*, pp. 345–347.

nothing surprising that both the fare and the manner of life as well as the bodies of the inhabitants should be very different from such as prevail among us" [III, 34, 8].

We have already mentioned Posidonius' contributions to the idea of a designed world and his conception of the earth—influenced by the sun, the stars, and the moon—as a habitat of the human race.

The problem of the diversity of peoples on earth, however, remained as a perennial puzzle: the unity of the human race living in its earthly environment, the diversity of its peoples, differing from one another, and living in widely varying environments. Posidonius seems (we cannot be sure) to have been one of the earliest thinkers to have considered these two aspects of the problem of unity and diversity. Earlier writers like Plato and Aristotle were concerned with teleology and design and climatic influence, but their ideas were too casual; they did not relate environmental ideas closely to the idea of design. It is by no means certain that Posidonius did either, but it is likely. Posidonius borrowed ideas from the Hippocratic treatise *Airs, Waters, Places*, and seems to have been one of the intermediaries who kept the Hippocratic ideas alive for later thinkers.[43] Too little is known in detail about Posidonius' writings as a coherent whole, but he apparently had more to say on environmental questions relating to human beings than any writer before him, perhaps including Hippocrates and Aristotle. Posidonius was also deeply involved in the meaning of history and in the ethnology of primitive peoples. He continued the histories of Polybius, inspired by his predecessor's theme: "The providence of God had imposed on Rome the task of building an empire, and this empire was actually working out to the material and moral benefit of its subjects." To Posidonius "apparently, the commonwealth of God was reflected in the world-wide Roman republic, and the unity of history was realized in the unity of the Roman Empire."[44] Posidonius was also a student of the ethnology of the Gauls and the Germans, whom he probably "did not distinguish from the Celts," and he has a place in the history of the comparative method because of his belief that primitive peoples now existing represent early conditions in the history of mankind.[45]

Only fragments of Posidonius' works have survived, but these show clearly his intense interest in ethnology and justify the belief that he was profoundly interested in studying cultures and that he made many firsthand investigations of their customs, especially in Gaul and Spain. (Caesar used Posidonius as a source for his description of the Celts.)

The works of Strabo and Athenaeus are notably rich in illustrations of this

[43] Berger, *Gesch. d. wiss. Erdkunde der Griechen*, p. 545.
[44] Piero Treves, "Historiography, Greek," in *OCD*, p. 433.
[45] Piero Treves, "Posidonius (2)," in OCD, p. 722. In my opinion, this short article is the best statement of Posidonius' leading ideas, the most objective assessment of his significance; it is refreshing to read it after the long, speculative, and polemical writings of the Germans.

interest.[46] Most of their citations of Posidonius, however, are to customs, economic activities, techniques (such as the mining operations of Spain), straightforward descriptions without causal explanation. Posidonius is a source of facts; one can see this in Strabo's dependence on him for much of the Spanish and Celtic materials. It is known too from the works of Strabo, Galen, and Vitruvius, that Posidonius was very interested in the causal relationship between environment and culture, perhaps pursuing this interest even more intensely than is suggested in the surviving fragments. Strabo has criticized his fellow Stoic for being "much too fond of imitating Aristotle's propensity for diving into *causes*, a subject which we [Stoics] scrupulously avoid, simply because of the extreme darkness  in which all *causes* are enveloped."[47]

Posidonius divided the earth regionally in two distinct ways: into the *klimata* and into zones. (These caused much confusion in later commentaries.) The klimata have nothing to do with modern concepts of climate. In antiquity the seven klimata were divisions of the habitable earth extending from the parallel at the mouth of the Borysthenes (the Dnieper) in the north to that of the Meroë in the south. The klimata were marked off, one from the other, by half-hour differences in the length of the longest day; they were not climatic zones, but regions of significant latitudinal differences.[48]

Posidonius apparently was one of the first to investigate more closely the influence of solar radiation on temperature in each of the klimata; he did not, however, make correlations between the klimata and the characteristics of peoples, but between the latter and the five zones.[49] Two of them, the Arctic and the Equatorial regions, being too cold or too hot, could be excluded as uninhabitable, leaving three in the temperate part of the earth. The zones were not set off by imaginary lines, as is the Arctic circle; their boundaries varied with the country. The northern part of this temperate zone bordered on the cold Arctic, the southern, on the hot equatorial regions. Since only the northern hemisphere was inhabited, these three zones in the temperate regions of the earth were of concern to peoples of the habitable world.

Posidonius made a further division of zones (for which Strabo also criticized him) which had nothing to do with the latitude. These were narrow bands, bordering on each tropic, which were divided into east and west zones, probably acknowledging here that differences among peoples could not be explained by latitude alone; there might be differences among peoples living in the eastern and western portions of the same zone. This division possibly owes its existence to the known contrast between the Indians and the

---

[46] Ninck, *Die Entdeckung von Europa durch die Griechen*, pp. 8, 193–200, 241–245. There are many passing references to Posidonius in Athenaeus, but see especially *Deipnosophistae* IV, 151$^e$–153$^d$, 154$^a$ for quotations from Posidonius on the Celts and the Parthians. These are straight ethnological accounts. For further interesting descriptions see IV, 210$^{e-f}$.

[47] Strabo, II, iii, 8. Hamilton trans.

[48] Honigman, *Die Sieben Klimata*, pp. 4–9, 25–30.

[49] Strabo, II, iii, 7. Honigman, *op. cit.*, p. 25.

Ethiopians, both of whom, if we follow Eratosthenes, were supposed to dwell in about the same latitude, the Indians, however, being more hardy and less dried out by the sun's heat than the Ethiopians.[50]

Like Hippocrates, Posidonius regarded the climate as an important cause affecting the nature of a people. According to Galen, Posidonius thought that mixtures of airs influenced the activity of the body, which in turn excited the activity of the mind, and that the environmental conditions could explain why men were cowardly or courageous and why they loved pleasure or worked hard.[51] There is similar evidence from Strabo, whose indignation at Posidonius for carrying these correlations too far prompted the famous passage, to be discussed shortly, in which he criticizes the determinism of environmental theories.

Indeed, Strabo has preserved an interesting discussion of the problems of mental, linguistic, and cultural causation in ethnology and history. He approves of Posidonius' method in looking for the etymology of names "in nations of one stock and community; thus between the Armenians, Syrians, and Arabians, there is a strong affinity both in regard to dialect, mode of life, peculiarities of physical conformation, and above all in the contiguity of the countries. Mesopotamia, which is a motley of the three nations, is a proof of this; for the similarity amongst these three is very remarkable." Strabo adds—and it is not certain here whether he is expressing his own views or those of Posidonius—that although the same characteristics are dominant in all, there may be differences owing to latitude between the Armenians of the north, the Arabs of the south, and the Syrians between them.[52]

Strabo also quotes Posidonius' ideas regarding life in two narrow zones, lying beneath the tropics and divided in two by them, which have the sun directly overhead for about half a month each year. The wastes of the hot and arid and sandy regions are proof of the power of the burning sun. Silphium and parched grains resembling wheat are the only plants that can grow there. There are no mountains to attract the clouds, and no rivers. "The consequence is that the various species are born with woolly hair, crumpled horns, protruding lips, and wide nostrils; their extremities being as it were gnarled. Within these zones also dwell the Ichthyophagi [the fish eaters]."[53] This passage apparently groups both human and animal qualities together.

It is a great loss that the thought of Posidonius as a coherent whole must be

---

[50] See Strabo, II, iii, 7–8.

[51] For the fragments of Posidonius, see Jacoby, *FGrH*, IIA, pp. 222–317, and commentary IIC, pp. 154–220. On differences among peoples, Fragment 28 (= Strabo II, 2, 1–3, 8); Fr. 80 (= Strabo XVII 3, 10); Fr. 102 (= Galen, *de plac. Hipp. et Plat.* 5); Fr. 120 (= Manilius IV, 715ff); Fr. 121 (= Vitruvius VI, 1); Fr. 122 (= Pliny, *NH* II, 80 [189–190]). The ethnography of Posidonius, with references, is reviewed thoroughly by Trüdinger, *Studien zur Gesch. der griechisch-römischen Ethnogr.*, pp. 80–126, who objects to the identification of the passage in Manilius with Posidonius' writings.

[52] See Strabo I, ii, 34.

[53] Strabo, II, ii, 3.

derived from the work of others. Strabo's geography has survived almost intact; reinforcing his fame is the added prestige of survival, but despite the painstaking researches of modern times and the impressive works of Reinhardt, Posidonius is still a controversial figure. It is not known precisely and to what degree, for example, his environmental ideas are related to astrological ethnology. Posidonius believed in the unity of the cosmos and in the reality of cosmic influences on the earth. Reinhardt thinks his astrology and astrological ethnology to be rational, free of the later excesses of astrology in the Roman Empire; these ideas are rational because they involve the study of the influence of the sun on terrestrial life, of the moon on the tides, and thus interpret the earth as part of the cosmos under the influence of cosmic forces. Boll, on the other hand, believes Posidonius to be the chief means by which astrology entered the Roman Republic. It is known that he was different in this respect from his teacher, Panaetius, who had no patience with astrology. Boll's view, moreover, has been disputed by Trüdinger.[54]

It may be that Posidonius' fundamental position was that the heavenly bodies, reflecting the sympathy which, like law, rules the cosmos, determine the general influences affecting life on this planet, and the influences having local and specific application might be sought for in the environmental conditions existing on earth, although astrology could also be used for such details as well. There seems to be little doubt (as Cicero's protests, to be discussed shortly, reveal) that astrology had a strong hold on thought regarding man's place in the cosmos, that theories of environmental influence were more subject to criticism, analysis, revision, and qualification owing to evidences from everyday observation than were general theories about the influence of the heavenly bodies. One distinguishes also between cosmic sympathy and the crude nativities of popular astrology. Galen, in the second century A.D., a believer in teleology and in a designed world, a worshipper of Hippocrates and a believer in environmental ideas in the tradition of both Hippocrates and Posidonius, was hounded by a Roman populace dominated by the crudest forms of astrology.

### 6.  ETHNOLOGY AND ENVIRONMENT IN SELECTED ROMAN WRITINGS

No doubt the ancient theories of environmental causation cluster around Hippocrates and Posidonius. In the secondary literature, however, especially the German, Posidonius is everywhere, writing and thinking everything, and

---

[54] On Posidonius and astrology see Boll-Bezold, *Sternglaube und Sterndeutung*, p. 23, "Im Anfang des I. Jahrhunderts v. Chr. aber steht in Poseidonios, dem grossen Stoiker, die Astrologie auf der Höhe der damaligen griechischen Wissenschaft"), p. 23. See also pp. 26, 99–100. Cumont, *Astrology and Religion Among the Greeks and Romans*, pp. 40, 46–48. See, however, Trüdinger, *op. cit.*, pp. 117, 119–126, where the more environmental ideas of Posidonius are stressed, together with the importance of the sun and the klimata. He was not a "*Stubenethnograph*" like Timaeus or Agatharchides, p. 119.

everyone is copying from him. A considerable literature tries to identify his work in the work of others; Cicero, Vitruvius, Ptolemy, and Caesar immediately come to mind. I have preferred, however, to discuss many of these passages as they appear in each work, even though it may be true that many of the ideas are derived from Posidonius.

Neither is there any doubt that the effects of climate are in the minds of many Roman writers. We need not list them all for they have corroboratory, not theoretical, significance. Choerilus of Issus, in Horace's opinion a wretched poet but a favorite bard of Alexander the Great, was paid in Philip's royal coin "for his uncouth and ill-formed verses." Alexander, whose taste in painters and brass molders was good, had so little in poetry that Horace says one would think him born in the heavy air of Boeotia.

Both Seneca and Florus later mention the harshness and severity of the frozen north, both believing the men living there possess characters as savage as their climate. Athenaeus (*fl.* about A.D. 200), following Polybius, also sees a correlation between the hardness and austerity of a people and a cold and gloomy climate.

Furthermore, Lucretius closes his poem on the theme of environmental biology. Epidemics of external origin come in like clouds and mists or they arise from an earth rotted by drenching rain or by the pelting of sunbeams. He is impressed by the effect on people of climates to which they are not accustomed, with the difficulties of acclimatization, noting climatic contrasts between England and Egypt, the climate of the Crimea, of Cadiz southward toward places where men with black skins live. These four regions are distinguished by the four winds and quarters of the sky, and their inhabitants differ in complexion, features, and susceptibility to disease. Lucretius is only incidentally concerned with psychological and cultural effects, but he is very interested in the distribution and etiology of disease. He notes the incidence of elephantiasis in Egypt, gout of the feet in Attica, eye diseases in Achaia. Differences in the air make other regions unfit for other bodily members or organs. With these remarks, Lucretius introduces the long description of the plague at Athens with which the poem ends. The air creeps in like a mist or cloud, it contaminates a region, settling on the grain or on other human or animal plant food, or men inhale the suspended elements. The same deadly results are achieved if men move to bad air or if the bad air moves to them. Accordingly, Lucretius traces the course of the Athenian plague from the heart of Egypt—where he thinks it originated—and the poem ends with a description of its miseries.[55]

Cicero had learned much from his teacher Posidonius and had used many of the latter's writings as a basis for his own works, but he lacks Posidonius'

[55] Horace, *Epistles* II, 1, 244. Seneca, *De ira*, II, 15, *De consolatione ad Helviam*, 7; Florus III, 3; Ath. XIV, 626. Lucr., *De rerum natura*, VI, 1138–1286 (based on the Latham translation). See also Bailey's commentary *Lucr.*, Vol. 3, pp. 1723–1744.

interest in geographical matters and subjects. The distrust of a maritime site for cities, already manifest in Plato, reappears in the writings of Cicero. If port cities participate in the advantages of international trade, they also import foreign ideas, which contribute to an unsettling of life, drawing people away from their ancient customs and traditions. A maritime location causes men's minds to go wandering; they have hopes, dreams, temptations, desires for luxury, incited by the commerce of the sea. Fear of culture contact was a recurring theme in ancient writings; it appears among writers so widely spaced in time as Herodotus, Plato, Cicero, and Strabo. Cicero blamed the overthrow of Carthage and Corinth (and indeed of all Greece) on these disadvantages peculiar to maritime cities.

How could Romulus have acted "with a wisdom more divine" in selecting a river site for Rome near the sea, which had none of the drawbacks of a maritime location? He must have had a "divine intimation that the city would one day be the seat and hearthstone of a mighty empire; for scarcely could a city placed upon any other site in Italy have more easily maintained our present widespread dominion." Though in the midst of a pestilential region [i.e., the Pontine Marshes] Rome is healthful, for it has its springs and its hills "which not only enjoy the breezes but at the same time give shade to the valleys below."[56] Similar sentiments were expressed later by Strabo.

In an arresting passage, Cicero shows his awareness of environmental theories based on the humors, and his impatience with an exaggerated application of them to particular situations, his criticism, however, showing even greater impatience with the fatalism and astrology of the Stoics Chrysippus and Posidonius. The passage also reveals the hardiness of the idea that moistness is associated with lack of mental vigor.

> We see the wide difference between the natural characters of different localities: we notice that some are healthy, others unhealthy, that the inhabitants of some are phlegmatic and as it were overcharged with moisture, those of others parched and dried up; and there are a number of other very wide differences between one place and another. Athens has a rarefied climate, which is thought also to cause sharpness of wit above the average in the population; at Thebes the climate is dense, and so the Thebans are stout and sturdy. All the same the rarefied air of Athens will not enable a student to choose between the lectures of Zeno, Arcesilas and Theophrastus, and the dense air of Thebes will not make a man try to win a race at Nemea rather than at Corinth. Carry the distinction further: tell me, can the nature of the locality cause us to take our walk in Pompey's Porch rather than in the Campus? in your company sooner than in someone else's? on the 15th of the month rather than on the 1st?

It is not environmental but astrological theory that Cicero is ridiculing here; if these environmental influences cannot be used to explain individual decisions and personal predilections, neither can astrological influences be used

[56] Cic., *Rep.* II, 4–6.

for like purposes. The condition of the heavenly bodies "may influence some things, but it certainly will not influence everything."[57]

One must not, however, give the impression that classical ethnology was always concerned with finding or criticizing causal explanations of a physical nature. Much of it was descriptive. In Caesar's ethnology, for example (some of which is thought to be derived from Posidonius), sharp contrasts are made among such peoples as the Gauls, the Romans, and the Helvetii, but the explanations of these differences are cultural, not environmental: the isolation and lack of contact of the Belgae insure continuing qualities of bravery and hardness among them; cultural contact, as has happened with the contemporary Gauls compared to those of former days, brings about a softness and a diminution in the old hardness and belligerency. Caesar shows also a marked distrust of a maritime life and maritime situation in degrading and softening a people through the adoption of foreign customs.

Tacitus' ethnology is like Caesar's: in general it is straightforward description without theoretical emphasis. In *Agricola*, however, Tacitus discusses possible resemblances between the original inhabitants of Britain and those of the continent, especially resemblances of the people of southeastern England to the Gauls. Did they share a common origin (*durante originis vi*)? Was it the similar climates (*positio caeli*) of the two lands, Gaul and England, which extend outward in opposite directions? Tacitus rejects the climatic hypothesis, finding more credible the idea that the Gauls themselves occupied the neighboring island of England.

But there is neither philosophy nor bias here, for elsewhere Tacitus says that the Mattiaci closely resemble the Batavi, but differ from them in that their spirit is invigorated by the soil and air of their country.[58]

## 7. STRABO'S ECLECTICISM

Strabo was a more eclectic thinker on cultural geography than his predecessors. The earth he seems to regard somewhat as a stage, its relief being the background and setting in which historical events take place. Adopting the Greek idea of the οἰκουμένη, Strabo says that the geographer should concern himself only with the inhabited earth; his is an early and vigorous claim for the consideration of cultural and human geography and for the study of those parts of the earth where human beings live and use their environment.[59] In a famous passage on the habitability of Europe, Strabo says that good management can make wintry and mountainous areas habitable, the Greeks owing

---

[57] Cic., *De fato*, IV, 7–8.
[58] Caesar, *The Gallic Wars*, Bk. I; Bk. VI, 11–20. In S. A. Handford's translation, *The Conquest of Gaul* (Penguin Classics), the ethnological materials from Books I and VI are placed at the beginning of the work. Tac., *Agr.*, XI, 2; *Germ.*, 29.
[59] Strabo, II, v, 34.

their success in this to economy in government, their arts, and their techniques. The Romans also had taught commerce to many who were in total ignorance of it.

There are echoes of Hippocrates and of Herodotus in his discussion of a hard environment. "Where the climate is equable and mild, nature herself does much towards the production of these advantages. As in such favoured regions everything inclines to peace, so those which are sterile generate bravery and a disposition to war."[60] Strabo, however, did not apply the idea without qualification to all cases. Speaking of the tribes in northern Spain, he says that their rough and savage manners are the result of their wars and their isolation, but these characteristics have been softened because they are at peace and because of their contact with the Romans. "Wherever these [influences] are not so much experienced people are harsher and more savage. It is probable that this ruggedness of character is increased by the barrenness of the mountains and some of the places which they inhabit."[61] Augustus had put a stop to their wars and Tiberius had introduced among them a cultural polity. The combination of environmental and cultural influences is reminiscent of Hippocrates and Polybius, but Strabo applied these explanations to wider vistas and to different cultural situations.

Strabo discusses at some length the environmental conditions of Italy and their influence on Roman ascendancy: it is island-like with its seas and its northern frontier mountains; its harbors, while few, are good; its situation enables it "to possess many advantages of atmosphere and temperature of climate, in which both animals and plants, and in fact all things available for sustaining life, may be accommodated with every variety both of mild and severe temperature. . . ." Owing to the Apennines the whole land is provided with "the advantages of the best productions both of hill and plain." "Italy, likewise, being situated in the very midst of the greatest nations, I allude to Greece and the best provinces of Asia, is naturally in a position to gain the ascendancy, since she excels the circumjacent countries both in the valour of her population and in extent of territory, and by being in proximity to them seems to have been ordained to bring them into subjection without difficulty."[62]

Like Posidonius, Strabo was a Stoic and there were hints of this influence in his writings, but he resisted what to him were the dogmatic correlations of Posidonius. In one of the most famous of the ancient theoretical statements about culture and the environment, Strabo criticizes the idea of design and causal relationships between peoples and their environment:

> In fact, the various arrangements [of a country] are not the result of premeditation, any more than the diversities of nations or languages; they all depend on circumstances and chance. Arts, forms of government, and modes of life,

[60] Strabo, II, v, 26.
[61] Strabo, III, iii, 8.
[62] Strabo, VI, iv, 1.

arising from certain [internal] springs, flourish under whatever climate they may be situated; climate, however, has its influence, and therefore while some peculiarities are due to the nature of the country, others are the result of institutions and education. It is not owing to the nature of the country, but rather to their education, that the Athenians cultivate eloquence, while the Lacedaemonians do not; nor yet the Thebans, who are nearer still. Neither are the Babylonians and Egyptians philosophers by nature, but by reason of their institutions and education. In like manner, the excellence of horses, oxen, and other animals, results not alone from the places where they dwell, but also from their breeding. Posidonius confounds all these distinctions.[63]

Strabo was born in Amasia, the capital of the Pontic kingdom (southwest of the modern port of Samsun in Turkey) about 64 B.C. and he died about A.D. 24; his mature years were spent in the reigns of Augustus and of Tiberius. His geography was written purposely as a contribution to government and administration, at a time when Augustus was encouraging the trade of the Empire.[64] The descriptions of peoples in his geography are the culmination of fact gathering which had gone on for four hundred years and was to continue, after Strabo's death, in less impressive form, notably in the works of Pliny. Something happened to Strabo which must have also happened as an aftermath of Alexander's invasions and discoveries and certainly happened after the age of discovery and at the end of the nineteenth century: the accumulation of knowledge regarding the world's peoples and their remarkable diversity put great strains on simpler causal explanations that had been satisfactory in the past. That is the reason for the wavering—and even the inconsistency—of Strabo. Some of the ideas are traditional, some are based on contemporary observation. Causal explanations had to be more eclectic than they had been before, as differences in language and ways of life became apparent on a vaster scale, just as geographers at the end of the nineteenth century, with all its discoveries, became impatient with the explanations of their immediate predecessors. Strabo's geography is the high point of classical cultural-geographical theory; after it there is little, either in Pliny, in Ptolemy, or in Vitruvius which is as satisfactory or as stimulating. In his pages, so full of human activity, exploration, and techniques, dogmatic explanations have an uneasy tenure, and there is a solid reason (even with the confusion of his sources) for the admiration of Strabo by modern geographers.[65]

---

[63] Strabo, II, iii, 7.

[64] On Augustus' encouragement of empire trade, see Charlesworth, *Trade-Routes and Commerce of the Roman Empire*, pp. 9–13; see also Charlesworth's appreciation of Strabo, pp. xiv–xv, 13.

[65] See Bunbury's fine chapters on Strabo in Vol. II of *A History of Ancient Geography*. On Strabo's neglect of Latin writers in his geography, see Vol. II, p. 216. The neglect itself teaches a lesson in the consequences of physical or other barriers to the interchange of knowledge and ideas. "But we cannot wonder if Strabo, writing at Amasia, was ignorant of literary works that were well known at Rome, when we find that his own great work, notwithstanding its importance and its great merits, remained for a long period comparatively unknown, and is not even once cited by Pliny in the vast array of authorities which he has brought together."

## 8. Vitruvius on Architecture

In Vitruvius' work on architecture there is the most extensive discussion of culture and environment since the time of Hippocrates with the possible exceptions of Posidonius and Strabo. Modern scholars have emphasized, however, that the environmental theories and the theory of cultural development of Vitruvius are derived from Posidonius. Nevertheless, let us discuss them as they appear in Vitruvius for they are pertinent to his tasks as well. Four ideas are of interest. The first three are well developed, the last is mentioned incidentally: the relation of climate (1) to the problems of architecture and (2) to the nature of peoples; the development of the house; and the effects of cultural contact.

Vitruvius' discussion of climate and architecture reminds one of the similar discussion in the first part of *Airs, Waters, Places*: fortified towns should be located on a high site, without mist or frost, and in a temperate climate away from marshes; summer heat has a weakening effect on both healthful and unhealthful places, while in winter even unhealthful districts are much more healthful. Hot winds should be avoided, for bodies are composed of the four elements and if one of them, like heat, predominates "it destroys and dissolves all the others with violence." The human constitution is much better adapted to cold than to heat, for those removed from cold to heat waste away, while those going from a hot to a cold climate of the north even become more healthy. A temperate climate is best for balance and healthfulness, a conclusion drawn from the theory of the mixing of the humors.

Marshes and heat—malaria and hot weather—seem to have been the main fears of the ancient physicians and architects. The emphasis on heat (that is, fire), if those who stress Vitruvius' dependence on Posidonius are correct, follows from the significance of fire in the Stoic philosophy.[66]

Later Vitruvius makes correlations between zones and cultural and biological types. This portion of Vitruvius' work presumably has been derived entirely from Posidonius; certainly Vitruvius has forgotten the refinements of zonation just as Strabo claims Posidonius forgot them, in the sweeping contrasts between the north and the south.

His reasons, however, for discussing these questions are the practical ones of the architect: houses should be adapted to climatic conditions so that "we may amend by art what nature, if left to herself, would mar." The moist atmosphere of the extreme northern cold does not draw out moisture from the

---

[66] On Vitruvius' dependence on Posidonius, see Pohlenz, *Die Stoa*, Vol. I, p. 360, and Reinhardt, *Poseidonios*, pp. 43, 79–83, 402. Vitr., I, iv, 1, 4–6, 8. The element theory is used to explain the adaptability of birds, fishes, and land animals to their environment, I, iv, 7. Vitruvius also discusses pasturage and food of cattle as indicators of healthful qualities, I, iv, 10; like Hippocrates, he is very sensitive to the dangers of marshes, I, iv, 11–12. Earlier Vitruvius stresses the necessity of the architect's studying medicine because of the κλίματα, air, healthful siting, and waters. I, 1, 10.

body, and the people have a large blood supply, which accounts for their bravery in war. The tall, fair people with straight red hair, the Germans or the Gauls, are helpless before fever. The cold damp air also gives a heavy pitch to the voice, and the body and the mind, chilled by a dense, moist atmosphere, are sluggish, as is proved by observing the activity of snakes in warm and in cold weather. The peoples of the north are courageous, but they are likely to lose the advantage of this quality through lack of judgment.

Contrary conditions exist in the south, whose peoples are exposed to the direct rays of the sun; there too much water is drawn out from the bodies, leaving little blood, and although they endure fever and heat easily, they are timid in battle because they lack the strong blood of the northern peoples. The southern peoples are short and swarthy, their hair is curly, their eyes black, their legs strong. Their voices, unlike those of the northern peoples, are shrill, a combination of the warm and dry elements, and the heat and rarity of the atmosphere do not oppress the body nor the mind as the dense atmosphere of the north does, and they are keenly intelligent, although they lack courage because it is sucked out of them by the heat of the sun. Possibly Vitruvius is drawing here on personal knowledge of the ethnology of North Africa, for he was in the African war of 47–46 B.C., landing with Caesar at Hadrumentum, the modern Sousse in Tunisia, and it is the desert peoples of these regions he seems to be describing; the observations of the Germanic tribes were probably derived from Posidonius. His explanation of the contrast between the people of the warm desert and those of the colder regions of northwestern Europe is the familiar physiological explanation based on the theory of the humors.[67] Like Aristotle on the Greeks, Vitruvius, with becoming modesty, declares "the truly perfect territory," located between the extremes, "is that which is occupied by the Roman people." Combining an idea of providential design with the environmental theory and adding a pinch of astrology, Vitruvius concludes that Italy by her preeminence breaks "the courageous onsets of the barbarians, and by her strength of hand thwarts the desires of the southerners. Hence, it was the divine intelligence that set the city of the Roman people in a peerless and temperate country, in order that it might acquire the right to command the whole world." With this avowal, so modern in its identification of divine purpose with national policy, Vitruvius returns to the task at hand: to make houses "suitable in plan to the peculiarities of nations and races, since we have the expert guidance of nature herself to our hand."[68]

One sees however an entirely different side of Vitruvius in the theory of cultural development derived from the theory of the origin and development of the house. This too, it has been said, comes from Posidonius. All mankind lived like beasts in a simple state of savagery until the accidental discovery of

[67] Vitr. VI, i, 2–9.
[68] *Ibid.*, 10–12.

fire made possible the establishment of society; the sounds made by individuals around the fire led to speech and language, later to the deliberative assembly and to social intercourse, and these conditions were favorable to the construction of shelters. Improvements in shelters were made through imitation and the application of intelligence and industry, leading to further advances in carpenters' skills, later to other arts and techniques, making possible the transition from a rude culture to a civilization. The simple huts of olden times had developed into houses with symmetry, built on foundations. In the contemporary thatched or oak-shingled roofs of the houses of Gaul, Spain, Lusitania, Aquitania, the Caucasus, Colchis (between the Black Sea and the Caucasus), regions where carpenters could draw on a plentiful supply of trees, and even in the Phrygian houses (in Asia Minor) where wood was scarce, Vitruvius notes house types which reveal both the steps in the development of the house and regional adaptations and inventions owing to ingenuity in using available local materials. Nature had given men senses, as she had the beasts, but she also gave them the power of thought and understanding, through which they had conquered the animals and advanced from building to other arts and sciences, passing in this way "from a rude and barbarous mode of life to cultivation and refinement."[69] It was a theory of independent invention. The theoretical history is similar to the developmental theories of modern times, using the comparative or the historical method, in which the psychic unity of man is assumed, similar inventions taking place at various unrelated places throughout time, in response to environmental conditions which, granting similar intellectual endowment among all peoples, call forth similar answers to similar problems. In these two divergent approaches of Vitruvius, there is moreover, a suggestion of the differences in approach, already described, between the *Airs, Waters, Places* and the *Ancient Medicine* of Hippocrates.

Vitruvius says of a spring at the hill summit of Halicarnassus, that it had an evil reputation for inducing an unnatural lewdness among those who drank its waters; but the waters were not at fault, for a Greek colonist had set up a shop near the spring and the water attracted the barbarians (whom the colonists previously had driven off to the mountains), who in their meetings with the Greeks gave up their own customs. "Hence this water acquired its peculiar reputation, not because it really induced unchastity, but because those barbarians were softened by the charm of civilization."[70]

Two ideas of Vitruvius, the influence of climate, and cultural development through a series of stages, reveal the antiquity of two different approaches which have strongly influenced much of the modern study of culture itself and of culture in relation to environment. Each has different presuppositions, and consequently different kinds of results are to be expected of them.

[69] Vitr. II, i, 1–7; quotation in par. 6.
[70] *Ibid.*, viii, 11–12; quotation in par. 12.

Historically, the environmental theory has been essentially a static theory. Peoples and cultures are as they are because of environmental conditions, although it is true that these can be modified by human institutions. The culture is often considered to be a response to the environment, reinforcing or counteracting its influences, but in actual fact neither cultures nor environments are studied as a whole. Neither does the environmental theory fit in well with cultural change that is not caused by environmental change, and it is inhospitable to the consequences of cultural contact.

In ancient and modern times, the history of the influence of the environmental theory has been disappointing; the correlations so slavishly copied replaced study and independent thought. The old theory served a useful purpose in calling attention to the diversity of peoples and environments; but the next step, the study of the spread of human cultures over different environments and the consequent differences among them in the way they made use of their resources was not taken. But this point of view, engulfed by the tediously repeated influences, was not clearly and systematically formulated until the nineteenth century.

In the idea of the development of a culture through an ideal series of stages, the physical environment plays only a generalized role; it is the inventiveness and the psychic unity of man that count, for men spurred on by environments remote from one another will arrive at the same or similar techniques, arts, inventions. Once this initial environmental stimulus is acknowledged, the subsequent emphasis is on the cultural evolution and the stages which characterize it; the universal phenomenon is the development itself, although there may be minor deviations owing to local environmental differences. The changes which a culture makes in its environment are almost completely ignored in both approaches; since ancient times the environmental changes made by man, and environmental influences on him, have had an independent history, they were never reconciled with one another, and their different presuppositions were not examined until the nineteenth century.

Pliny's environmental theory is of interest chiefly because it shows the continuing influence of Hippocratic ideas, and perhaps also of Posidonius (who is one of the authorities listed generally by Pliny in the second book of his *Natural History*), and because Pliny applies the climatic theory to the origin of racial differences. He contrasts the Ethiopians "burnt by the heat of the heavenly body near them" and the peoples of the cold north with their white skins and straight, blond hair: "The latter are fierce owing to the rigidity of their climate but the former wise because of the mobility of theirs." Men are tall in both regions owing to the "pressure of the fires" in the one and to "the nourishing effect of the damp" in the other. The middle part of the earth, a blending of extremes, has "tracts that are fertile for all sorts of produce," men are of medium height, are also a blending even in complexion; "customs are gentle, senses clear, intellects fertile and able to grasp the whole of nature; and they also have governments, which the outer races never have possessed, any more than they have ever been subject to the central races, being quite detached and solitary on account of the savagery of the nature that broods over those regions."[71] This passage also shows the tenacity of the idea that temperate climates are suited for civilization and that nature in the temperate regions lacks the wildness and the savagery of the extremes; it also illustrates how climatic explanations were used to account for differences among peoples which might have been explained by racial or cultural intermixture.

### 9.  CRITIQUES OF PHILO AND JOSEPHUS

Critiques of the role of environmental influence in Greek civilization were made both by Philo the Jew (30 B.C.–A.D. 45) and by Josephus (born A.D. 37/38). Philo compares the cosmos to a great city (*megalopolis*) with one constitution and one law, "the law (*logos*) of nature, commanding what should be done and forbidding what should not be done." Cities on earth, variously located and unlimited in number, have different constitutions and laws, "for individually they have invented and added new customs and laws. The cause of this is the unwillingness not only of Greeks to mingle and associate with barbarians, and of barbarians with Greeks, but also that of each race in regard to its own stock." Philo criticizes the Greek explanations of this variety in constitutions and laws; environmental explanations, "unfavorable seasons, sterility, poor soil, the site, that it is maritime or inland or insular or on the mainland or suchlike things," are not the true causes, which are covetousness and mistrust of one another. It is thus the cultural milieu; covetousness and mistrust make them dissatisfied with the decrees of nature; "they call laws the things which seem to communities of like-thinking people to have general utility." Individual constitutions are an addition to the natural constitution, particular laws, additions to the natural.[72]

And Josephus' defense of the Jews against various slanders leveled at them by Apion becomes in fact a criticism of the methods of the Greek historians: he adroitly argues that past natural catastrophes have affected Greek ideas about themselves; like Philo, he sees the importance of culture and tradition (for example in the meticulously accurate record-keeping) in molding a people's history. Josephus is astonished that the Greek historians have dealt so little with Jewish history; he criticizes them for their ignorance, their inaccuracies, their failure to agree among themselves, and their arrogant atti-

---

[71] Pliny, *NH*, II, 80. This passage has been identified with a fragment of Posidonius. Note 51, *supra*.

[72] *De Josepho*, VI, 28–31, in Boas, *Primitivism and Related Ideas in the Middle Ages*, p. 8; see also Boas' discussion of Stoic ideas in this passage, pp. 7–8, and the discussion of Philo, pp. 1–14.

tudes toward non-Hellenic historians. Hellenic civilization is recent, but not only do the older civilizations of Egypt, Chaldea, and Phoenicia have historical records, but the records were preserved; these nations are located in places which have not suffered catastrophes that have destroyed the records of the past. The Greeks' territory has suffered countless natural catastrophes that have wiped out the memory of the past; their records have been destroyed, and their people have had to begin life over and in this renewal have falsely thought that each new beginning for them was a new beginning of everything. The Greeks therefore are mere pretenders as experts in history, and unlike other nations, including the Jews, they neglected to keep public registries and to record events; hence their inaccuracy, their false sense of the antiquity of their way of life.[73]

10. ENVIRONMENTAL AND ASTROLOGICAL ETHNOLOGY

There is little of substance to record of environmental theories in the early Roman Empire after the time of Strabo, Diodorus, Vitruvius, and Pliny. If many of their ideas were scattered and fragmentary, repetitious, and often dogmatic, theirs nevertheless was an age of enlightment compared with what was to come. In the second century Galen, repeating the ideas of Hippocrates, was a voice in a wilderness of Roman medical charlatanry; more typical was the *Tetrabiblos* of Ptolemy, an incredible melange indicative of the force and widespread acceptance of astrology. From these times well into the sixteenth century a cosmic environmentalism, an "astrological ethnology," competed with and often displaced much of the older thought.

In his short historical essay on the genesis of the humors, Galen said little could be added to what the ancients (among whom he named Hippocrates, Aristotle, Praxagoras, Philotimus) had contributed: "Of occupations also, localities and seasons, and above all, of natures themselves [living organisms], the colder are more phlegmatic, and the warmer more bilious." In Galen, medical theory is bound up with teleology, for there is art and design in the parts of the body as there is in nature.[74]

We are in another world, however, in the second-century work of Claudius Ptolemy. Elements of familiar environmental theory and astrological ethnology are both present, although one can detect an independent treatment of each in comparing *Tetrabiblos* II, 2, with II, 3; the two represent different historic traditions, one environmental, the other astrological. The work is important in showing linkages between environmental and astrological theories.

[73] Josephus, *Against Apion*, Bk. I, 1–59, esp. 6–14. A selection also in Toynbee, *Greek Historical Thought*, pp. 63–69.
[74] Gal. *Nat. Fac.* II, viii (117–118). Other typical passages showing this teleological idea in nature: I, xiv (46); II, iii (87–88); II, iv (88–89). The argument is developed in even more detail in *De usu partium*, I, 1–4; III, 10; XI, 14.

Ptolemy's method can only be outlined, for his argument is so involved and his correlations so intricate and numerous that the reader must be referred to the text itself.[75]

Ptolemy divides astronomical prognostication into two great parts: the universal and general relating to whole races, countries, and cities, and the individual and specific relating to individuals. General inquiries are further subdivided into countries, cities, and "greater and more periodic conditions" (wars, famines, pestilences, earthquakes, deluges, etc.) and the "lesser and more occasional" (seasonal changes in temperature, variations in the intensity of storms, heat, winds, crop production).

Ptolemy then describes the characteristics of the inhabitants of the klimata, dividing peoples into a southerly, a northerly, and an intermediate region; these discussions are reminiscent of Vitruvius and Pliny. The Ethiopians living in the region from the equator to the summer tropic, like the plants and animals, are burned by the overhead sun; they "have black skins and thick, woolly hair, are contracted in form and shrunken in nature, are sanguine of nature, and in habits are for the most part savage because their homes are continually oppressed by the heat."

The Scythians, removed from the sun and the zodiac (i.e., in more northern latitudes), are cooled, but they are nourished by more moisture and are not exhausted by the heat; their complexions are white, they are straight-haired, "tall and well-nourished, and somewhat cold by nature; these too are savage in their habits because their dwelling places are continually cold."

The peoples dwelling between these two extremes share in the equable temperature of the air which varies "but has no violent changes from heat to cold. They are therefore medium in colouring, of moderate stature, in nature equable, live close together, and are civilized in their habits."[76]

Ptolemy recognizes that within these general divisions finer distinctions can be made, that special local characteristics because of "situation, height, lowness, or adjacency" may modify the general ones: "And again, as some peoples are more inclined to horsemanship because theirs is a plain country, or to seamanship because they live close to the sea, or to civilization because of the richness of their soil, so also would one discover special traits in each arising from the natural familiarity of their particular climes [i.e., the klimata] with the stars in the zodiac."[77]

At this point Ptolemy elaborates a purer form of astrological ethnology. Briefly the method is this: the inhabited world (οἰκουμένη) is divided into

[75] Ptolemy, *Tetrabiblos*, II, 1–3 (53–75).

[76] *Ibid.*, 2 (56–58). Robbins, the translator of the *Tetrabiblos* (see also his references) believes the astrological ethnology is derived from Posidonius. See also Berger, *Gesch. der wiss. Erdkunde der Griechen*, pp. 556–558. For a strong dissent see Trüdinger, *Studien zur Gesch. der griechisch-römischen Ethnogr.*, pp. 81–89.

[77] Ptolemy, *Tetrabiblos*, II, 2 (58).

four quarters which are correlated with the four triangles recognized in the zodiac: a northwestern (Aries, Leo, Sagittarius, governed by the occidental aspect of Jupiter and Mars), a southeastern (Taurus, Virgo, Capricornus, and the co-rulers Venus, Saturn, and Mercury), a northeastern (Gemini, Libra, Aquarius; governed by Saturn and Jupiter in oriental aspect), and a southwestern (Cancer, Scorpio, Pisces, ruled by Mars and Venus in oriental aspect). With these main divisions, and with further refinements (e.g., the northwest is chiefly dominated by Jupiter on account of the north wind, but Mars assists because of the southwest wind) it is possible to divide up the inhabited world, showing the astrological influences, not only in broad regions, but on individual peoples living within them. These influences Ptolemy correlates with the characteristics of peoples as they were known in his day. They make interesting and often racy reading. This is not the place, however, to follow this important and depressing literature any further; it is astonishing to see the breadth and detail of the ethnological materials which are correlated with so much precision, assurance, and finality.[78]

If one can judge by the later criticisms of Plotinus, a subtle blending of astrological and environmental ideas took place. Plant growth and distribution are under the control of the sun; there is a large body of lore concerning the effect of the moon, especially on sowing; and it is but a step further to seek similar influences in the stars. Human behavior could also be brought within their purview. The sun affects men because of seasonal change and climatic differences among regions; astral influences are superimposed on the solar influences. Plotinus considers these theories and rejects them: their advocates "have merely devised another shift to immolate to the heavenly bodies all that is ours, our acts of will and our states, all the evil in us, our entire personality; nothing is allowed to us; we are left to be stones set rolling, not men, not beings whose nature implies a task." Although these eloquent sentences are directed at astrology and divination, he clearly meant the criticism to apply to theories of the influence of the physical environment which are mentioned along with the astrological ideas. "Place and climate, no doubt, produce constitutions warmer or colder; and the parents tell on the offspring, as is seen in the resemblance between them. . . . None the less, in spite of physical resemblance and similar environment, we observe the greatest difference in temperament and in ideas: this side of the human being, then, derives from some quite other Prin-

---

[78] *Ibid.*, 3 (59–74). For the extension of the argument to explain certain alleged sexual practices, see translator's note 4, p. 135, and the literature there referred to. On astrology in Ptolemy's time, see also translator's intro., pp. ix–x. On astrological ethnology see Trüdinger, in footnote 76, *supra*, and Boll's footnote to Gisinger's article, "Geographie," in *PW*, Supp. Vol. 4, col. 656. According to Boll, Manilius (IV, 744ff.) and the *Tetrabiblos* are our main sources indicating its importance in the ancient world. Boll cites modern studies indicating the probability that Manilius IV, 711–743, and *Tetrabib.*, II, 2, are derived from Posidonius. See the literature cited by Boll.

ciple (than any external causation or destiny)." The principle of which Plotinus is speaking and which causes him to reject these determinisms is based on a central idea in his philosophy: "That to what is primarily ours, our personal holding, there is added some influx from the All. . . ."[79]

## 11. SERVIUS ON VIRGIL

Over eight hundred years after the early Greek speculations on the elements, humors, and the effects of airs, waters, and places, Servius the Grammarian, in the fourth century A.D., wrote his famous commentaries on the works of Virgil; his commentary on the *Aeneid* VI, 724, brings together theology, physical theory, and a theory of environmental influence into a consistent whole that explains the unity and the diversity of life. Servius' commentary is on the opening lines of the speech of Anchises, father of Aeneas: "The sky and the lands, the watery plains, the moon's gleaming face, the Titanic Sun and the stars are all strengthened by Spirit working within them, and by Mind, which is blended into all the vast universe and pervades every part of it, enlivening the whole mass."[80]

On this, Servius says that what in Greek is the all, τό πᾶν, consists of the four elements and God. God who brought forth the universe is a kind of divine spirit permeating the elements. Since all things come from God and the elements, they have one origin; they partake of the same nature. What is it in us that is from God, what from the four elements? Our soul is from God, our body from the elements. In our body earth, moisture, vapor, heat are perceptible as are the elements. Like them, too, the body is not capable of understanding; like God, the soul is. The elements change as does the body which derives its being from them. On the other hand, God does not pass away and neither does the soul. A part always shares the characteristics of its class.

But if it be objected that imperishable beings do exist and have a single origin, why do we not perceive all living creatures in a like manner? Dissimilarities are not in the soul; they have their origin in the body. A lively or sluggish body produces a vivacious or sluggish spirit. This can be shown in one and the same body; in a healthy body there is a corresponding liveliness of spirit, in sickness a sluggishness; in very severe cases, there may be a deprivation of reason as in delirium. When the spirit has entered thus far into the body, it does not express its own nature, but changes in quality. We observe that the Africans are crafty, the Greeks capricious, the Gauls of a more sluggish disposition; these characteristics are caused, as Ptolemy saw, by the nature of the region. (Presumably each region creates its own influences through the

[79] Plotinus, *Enneads*, III, 1.5. The rest of this passage is devoted to an incisive and devastating criticism of astrology. Plotinus may also be criticizing astrological ideas which are frequently expressed in the ideas of the Hermetical thinkers.

[80] Virgil, *Aeneid*, VI, 724. Trans. by W. J. Jackson Knight (Penguin Classics).

humors on the bodily, and consequently the mental, state.) Ptolemy also realized that if a person goes from one region to another his nature will change to a degree but not entirely, because he receives from the beginning a bodily predisposition which subsequent environmental changes cannot completely alter.

The sentence on national character, "Inde Afros versipelles, Graecos leves, Gallos pigrioris videmus ingenii: quod natura climatum facit, sicut Ptolomaeus deprendit . . ." was copied by Isidore of Seville, and found its way into the geography of Bartholomaeus Anglicus in the thirteenth century, the theory now being removed from its more profound context of theology and physical and medical theory.[81]

These Greek and Roman notions of environmental influence—hardy Mediterranean perennials they were and gnarled like the olive—proved their power and vitality in the medieval and modern world. Themes with so many variations could constantly be readapted by new composers to new situations. Thinkers of the Middle Ages built on them, and the reports of the voyages and travels following the age of discovery often even reinforced them. What was a frugal and industrious European, living in his horrid, filthy cities, to think when he beheld the easy, apparently carefree and happy life of the peoples of the warm tropics? or of the tropical island paradises? The new pages might be exotic, exciting, and baffling, but the spectacles of those who read them were already old with fond and constant use.

[81] *Servii Grammatici Qui Feruntur in Vergilii Carmina Commentarii*, ed. by Thilo, Vol. 2 (Books VI–XI of the *Aeneid*), VI, 724. The sentence continues, "qui dicit translatum ad aliud clima hominem naturam ex parte mutare; de toto enim non potest, quia in principio accepit sortem corporis sui" (pp. 99–101).

# Chapter 3

# Creating a Second Nature

### 1.  ON ARTISANSHIP AND NATURE

If the apparent unity and order of nature led men to a belief that behind it was a plan, a purpose in which human beings were deeply involved, if differences among peoples were perceived as a matter of everyday observation in the Eastern Mediterranean, and if these were ascribed to custom (νόμος) or to nature (φύσις), there was also an awareness of the novelty that men could create in nature, of differences brought about by art and by the power derived from the control over domestic animals. Man was a creator of order, an agent of control, a possessor of the unique skill of the artisan. Long before the Greeks there was impressive evidence of these skills in the metallurgy, mining, and building of the older civilizations, especially of Egypt. It has been said by many that Greek science, unlike modern science, did not lead to the control of nature[1] but the occupations, crafts and the skills of everyday life were evidences that changes were possible that either brought order, or more anthropocentrically, produced more orderly accessibility to things men

[1] Among them Sambursky, in *Physical World of the Greeks*, p. 17.

needed. If by control over nature one means its modern sense, the application of theoretical science to applied science and technology (granting that they cannot be thus neatly separated), there was no such control in the ancient world. Conscious change of the environment need not, however, rest on complex theoretical science, as we well know from Roman centuriation. The power of mind was acknowledged in the analogy of the creator-artisan and in its potentials for rearrangement of natural phenomena, such as in the establishment of a village, the discipline of animals by men, the indirect control over wildlife with weapons, snares, and the like.

Finally there is the mythology of the celestial archetypes of territories and temples, of which their worldly counterparts are copies. The world "in which the presence and the work of man are felt—the mountains that he climbs, populated and cultivated regions, navigable rivers, cities, sanctuaries—all these have an extraterrestrial archetype, be it conceived as a plan, as a form, or purely and simply as a 'double' existing on a higher cosmic level." Desert regions, uncultivated lands, unknown seas, and similar areas strange to human occupation lack a prototype of this kind; they "do not share with the city of Babylon, or the Egyptian nome, the privilege of a differentiated prototype. They correspond to a mythical model, but of another nature: all these wild, uncultivated regions and the like are assimilated to chaos; they still participate in the undifferentiated, formless modality of pre-Creation. This is why, when possession is taken of a territory—that is, when its exploitation begins—rites are performed that symbolically repeat the act of Creation: the uncultivated zone is first 'cosmicized,' then inhabited." Thus, "Settlement in a new, unknown, uncultivated country is equivalent to an act of Creation."[2]

Myths of this kind strongly suggest that man is an orderer of nature. In the literature interpreting the changes that men make in their environment, in the attempts to bestow meaning on these changes, there are, as we shall see, recurrent themes of man as a finisher of the creation, of man bringing order into nature, and after the age of discovery, of European man discovering new lands, which despite the presence of primitive peoples, are considered to be unchanged since the creation and awaiting his transforming hand. Did men become aware of themselves as modifiers of nature, as creators of a new environment because of the distinctions they made between themselves and the animals—mainly, higher intelligence and upright carriage—because they had a sense of creating a κόσμος, an order, because their artisanship enabled them to bring about this cosmos, and because through their power over plants and animals they were able to maintain and perpetuate it? Early Greek writings on the subject, few as they are, suggest that these awarenesses did exist.

In reading the comments of the ancient authors regarding the changes which man has made in the physical environment, one has two impressions:

---

[2] Eliade, *Cosmos and History*, pp. 9–10.

there was a recognition of man as an active, working, achieving being, despite the seeming stability that might be implied from the dominance of environmental influences (a contradiction arising, I think, out of the failure of systematic study, thus leaving the way open for isolated remarks with no attempt at reconcilations), and that the living nature that these men observed—and often loved—was, as we now know, a nature already greatly altered by man.

In the ancient world, there was a lively interest in natural resources and how man could exploit them: in mining, in ways of obtaining food, in agricultural methods, in canals, in maintaining soil fertility, in drainage and grazing and many other economic activities which—even if they produced only a partial philosophy of man as a part of nature which he was engaged in changing—are eloquent proof of his busyness, his incessant restlessness in changing the earth about him. The preoccupation with technology is clear in the literature related to primitivism, whether the individual thinkers looked back to a happier, less complicated period or approved of the amenities of their own civilization. The golden age of the past was often an age of simplicity and one in which the soil required no cultivation but supported life spontaneously rather than by tillage and ordered plantings; if there had been a moral decline to the hard realities of the contemporary iron age, it owed much to the advances of the arts and sciences and to applied technology. In Seneca's famous criticism of Posidonius, to use but one example, he chides the Greek thinker for saying that it was the wise men, the philosophers, who built cities and dwellings, who made fish preserves, who invented tools, weaving, farming, and the potter's wheel. "Was it philosophy," he asked, "that erected all these towering tenements, so dangerous to the persons who dwell in them?" Seneca speaks here with understandable feeling against city life, against builders whose multistoried apartment houses were eternally falling down because they were too carelessly thrown together and because their base was not substantial enough for their height. No, these were products not of man's wisdom but of his ingenuity: they were the work of practical men, artisans, men intent on the everyday affairs of life, not of philosophers, for wisdom trains minds, not hands, and the wise man in following nature had no need for the craftsman. In this sharp disparagement of the artisan, there was ample suggestion of his power and effectiveness, for it was his works—of no interest to the philosopher or at least to a philosopher like Seneca—which had brought about changes in nature.[3] Seneca's eloquent praise of the wise men who had nothing to do with the inventions, improvements, and gadgets of the day describes vividly in sharp and indignant words the evils of a civilization too dependent on its machines, its laborsaving devices, and its creature comforts. Seneca does not

---

[3] Sen., *Ep. mor.*, 90, 7–13. On the flimsy apartment houses (*insulae*), the unscrupulous and avaricious builders, and the dangers of falling buildings, see Jérôme Carcopino, *Daily Life in Ancient Rome* (New Haven: Yale University Press, 1960 [1940], pp. 23–33.

even have patience with those whose sartorial tastes are more refined than those of the Scythians. His primitivism could not have been shared by many, considering the enthusiasm with which his artisans go about doing things.

Although many of these thinkers had traveled widely, the environment they knew best and about which they wrote with greatest affection was that of the Mediterranean basin. In the fifth century B.C., it was known that the history of its settlement was already a long one. Hippocrates had said that the present ways of living, unlike those—and the crude foods—of an earlier age, had been discovered and elaborated over a long period of time.[4] They were accustomed to surroundings full of evidences of change and of human activity. It is an irony that environmental theories should have had their origin in a region with such a long record of human changes. It was not like von Humboldt traveling in the tropics, which overwhelmed him with the lushness of their vegetation and in which so little of man was to be seen, nor was it like the young Darwin who saw in the luxuriant forests of Brazil the grand scale of natural wonders compared with the insignificance of man and his doings.

One feels that to these writers—Greek and Roman alike—the vineyards, the olive orchards, the irrigation ditches, the grazing goats on the rocky summits, the villages, and the villas were inseparable from the landscape of the dry parched hills of the Mediterranean summer, the winds for which there were so many local names, the deep blueness of the sea, and the bright Mediterranean skies. It was an altered landscape upon which they gazed and whose beauties they loved.

## 2. ANTIGONE AND CRITIAS

The observations, made in antiquity, concerning human modifications of the earth may be roughly divided into three different types: (1) general descriptions which by their very nature indicate an awareness that throughout history man does make changes in the physical geography of a locality, (2) more specific but scattered comments which appear in the writings concerned with plants, agriculture, estate management, stock raising, and grazing, and (3) statements which are part of a broader body of belief such as the Epicurean and the Stoic philosophies.

Two passages, however, one from Sophocles' *Antigone*, the other from Plato's *Critias*, are in a class by themselves. In the famous lines of the chorus in *Antigone*, one is reminded of the exuberant twenty-fourth chapter of the twenty-second book of St. Augustine's *City of God*, the enthusiastic praise of science in the eighteenth century, and of contemporary enthusiasms about man's control over nature. Man's power to navigate the seas and to use the

[4] Hippoc., *Ancient Medicine*, III.

plow, his success in hunting, in plant and animal domestication, in architecture, and the protection his arts have given him have succeeded beyond all his dreams, for he has conquered all but death.

> Wonders are many, but none there be
> So strange, so fell, as the Child of Man.

His navigation has mastered the seas, and the earth has felt his touch:

> Oh, Earth is patient, and Earth is old,
> And a mother of Gods, but he breaketh her,
> To-ing, froing, with the plough-teams going,
> Tearing the soil of her, year by year.

The birds, the wild animals of the woods, and the fish have not escaped him:

> The nets of his weaving are cast afar,
> And his Thought, in the midst of them circleth full.

He has forced the horse and the mountain bull to serve him. He has been able through his speech, thought, and arts to build and protect himself from cold and rain.

> All-armèd he: unarmèd never
> To meet new peril he journeyth;
> Yea, his craft assuageth each pest that rageth,
> And help he hath gotten against all save Death.

The chorus ends on the thought that "the craft of his engines has passed his dream, / In haste to the good or the evil goal," contrasting the man who holds law and the oath of God supreme with the blindness of him who lacks these qualities. The exaltation in the presence of man's works, the appreciation of his tricks in hunting and fishing, of his skills in the domestication of animals and in agriculture, are contrasted with the realization that man is his own enemy, that his accomplishments are nothing without justice and righteousness.[5]

The passage in the *Critias* concerns the legendary war between the peoples of Atlantis and those, led by the people of Athens, living within the Pillars of Hercules. In this former time, now existent in dim memory only, most men were artisans, farmers, or warriors. Plato says of Attica that its soil surpassed all others, and that it could at that time maintain large numbers exempt from

[5] Soph., *Ant.*, lines 332–375. Trans. by Gilbert Murray, in Toynbee, *Greek Historical Thought*, pp. 128–129. On Sophocles' pessimism see Kitto, *Greek Tragedy*, pp. 122, 151, 154–155, and J. C. Opstelten, *Sophocles and Greek Pessimism*, pp. 143–145. In O.'s opinion, this choric song was inspired in part by the mood of the whole play, in part by Aeschylus' *Choëphoroi* (vv 583–596). The song describes two sides of man's δεινότης, his inventiveness and his shortcomings, especially in understanding; ". . . according to the poet, man has little or no reason to pride himself on the potentialities contained in the achievements of his inventive mind" (p. 145).

the tasks of husbandry. The proof of this is in the remnant of Athenian soils —"What is now left of our soil rivals any other in being all-productive and abundant in crops and rich in pasturage for all kinds of cattle; and at that period, in addition to their fine quality it produced these things in vast quantity." Why, Plato asks, should we call this present land a remnant of the land of the past? Because the land is a promontory jutting out into the sea, and the soil, in this 9,000-year period, has been washed down and deposited in the depths of the sea. "And, just as happens in small islands, what now remains compared with what then existed is like the skeleton of a sick man, all the fat and soft earth having wasted away, and only the bare framework of the land being left." Plato then describes the former arable hills, fertile valleys, and forested mountains "of which there are visible signs even to this day. . . ." Mountains which today have food only for bees could, not so long ago, grow trees fit for the largest buildings, whose rafters are still sound. Cultivated trees provided pasturage for flocks, and the soil was well watered and the rain was "not lost to it, as now, by flowing from the bare land into the sea." Evidences of tree growth, of the moisture-retentiveness of the soils, Plato finds in the conditions around the sanctuaries of his day. In those old days the district owed its excellence to its soils, the techniques of skilled husbandry, the generous water supply, and the temperate seasons.

It is evident that Plato is writing of a period so far in the past that his account can be accepted neither as factual nor as evidence of the deterioration of the Mediterranean landscape owing to natural and man-made catastrophes from the remote past to Plato's time. There is, however, clear evidence here of the recognition by Plato that natural erosion and human activities—such as deforestation—may in their cumulative effects change a landscape throughout time. Deforestation, in this case, seems to have assisted the normal erosional processes of streams carrying soil in suspension from the mountaintops to the sea.[6]

To my knowledge, this important passage had little influence on later thought concerning culture and environment except for occasional quotations during the eighteenth and nineteenth centuries; it has been frequently referred to, however, in twentieth century conservation literature. The *Laws* and the *Timaeus* were far more influential in outlining a theory of cultural development, the latter, furthermore, in introducing the notion of a demiurge who creates an orderly universe. If Plato in the *Laws* had noted that men change their environments through long settlement and that soil erosion and deforestation are parts of cultural history, he could have introduced at an early time these vital ideas into cultural history and changed the course of speculation regarding both man and environment.

[6] Plato, *Critias*, 110C–111D.

## 3. Environmental Change in the Hellenistic Period

Although the notices from pre-Hellenistic times reveal an awareness of environmental change, they are isolated. In the ancient world as a whole, there is no lack of evidence regarding change, but interpretations of it are few. One learns of grafting, fertilizing, the laying-out of towns, but for the most part the facts are stated, and that is all. Occasionally it is possible to infer an attitude from the spirit of the writing or the spirit behind the activities described. Excellent illustrations come from Ptolemaic Egypt, such as *The Tebtunis Papyri*, the correspondence of Apollonius and Zenon, the reclamation work of Cleon and Theodorus in the Fayûm (i.e., Lake Moeris about fifty miles southwest of Cairo). All of them suggest the fervor with which the Greek colonists went about their tasks in Egypt, implying a philosophy of activity, optimism and desire for land improvement.

When Hieron of Syracuse engages in shipbuilding and Archimedes superintends it, and boats are launched with the windlass he constructed [Ath. 206-d, 207-b], one receives as he does in the rest of Callixenus's famous description of Ptolemaic times, which Athenaeus has preserved, the impression that men consciously seek to change their environment, whether by building cities or ships or by introducing plants for their own purposes.

On February 16, 256 B.C., Apollonius, the minister and landholder, approves of an order which Zenon had given that olive and laurel shoots should be planted in the park at Philadelphia where Zenon had now gone or was going to reside as superintendent of Apollonius's property.[7] In a letter dated December 27, 256 B.C., Zenon is ordered to take from Apollonius's own garden and from the palace grounds in Memphis pear shoots and young plants—as many as possible—and to get some sweet-apple trees from Hermaphilos; all are to be planted in orchards at Philadelphia. In another letter of the same date, Apollonius orders Zenon to plant at least three hundred fir trees all over the park and around the vineyard and the olive trees. "For the tree has a striking appearance and will be of service to the king"; it will provide him timber for his ships and be an ornament to his estate.[8] On January 7, 255 B.C., Apollonius reminded Zenon that it was time to plant vines, olives, and the other shoots;

---

[7] P. Cairo Zen., 59125; see also *HW*, Vol. 1, pp. 287–289. In the preparation of this section on environmental change in the Hellenistic world, I am greatly indebted to Rostovtzeff's great work; there is scarcely a reference which does not come from him. It is impossible to consider in a work of this kind all the evidence he has brought to bear on the problem; a summary of his findings alone would fill many pages. Particularly important are his pages on the development of resources by the Hellenistic monarchs, on the analysis of Hellenization, and on urbanization. I have tried here to give examples which might make understandable the rich additions of this period to the ideas I am discussing. I have profited also from the works of Heichelheim, Kaerst, Tarn, and Pohlenz. On the Zenon papyri see Rostovtzeff, *A Large Estate in Egypt in the Third Century B. C.*, and Préaux, *Les Grecs en Égypte d'après les Archives de Zénon.*

[8] P. Cairo Zen., 59156, 59157.

Zenon should send to Memphis for them and give orders to begin planting. Apollonius promises to send from the Alexandria district more vine shoots and whatever other kinds of fruit trees may be useful.[9] On October 8, 255 B.C., Apollonius orders Zenon to take at least three thousand olive shoots from his park and from the gardens at Memphis. Before the fruit is gathered, he is to mark each tree from which he intends to take shoots. And he is to choose above all the wild olive and the laurel, for the Egyptian olive is suitable only for parks and not for olive groves.[10]

In one of the most famous documents in *The Tebtunis Papyri*, the instructions of a *dioecetes* to a subordinate, which dates from the late third century B.C., the latter is responsible for inspecting the water-conduits to see if water intakes have the prescribed depth and if there is sufficient room for them, and it is the duty of an *oeconomus* of a nome to supervise the irrigation system (29–40). He inspects the sowing, he obtains accurate impressions by observing the crops sprouting, easily noticing lands which are sown badly or not at all (49–57). One indispensable duty is to see that the nome is sown with the kinds of crops prescribed by the sowing schedule (57–60). (This instruction apparently applies to royal land.) He should plant mature local trees at the right season: willows, mulberries, acacias, and tamarisks about the month of Choiak. The *oeconomi* had general control over planting, guarding, and cutting trees and bushes. The trees were planted in nurseries; when they were old enough they were transplanted to the royal embankments, the special contractors being responsible for guarding them against sheep or other dangers.[11]

Again, the Hellenistic period is crucial; the most sweeping ideas, descriptions, and interpretations come, with few exceptions, out of this three-century-long period or from others inspired by it. The striking statements (discussed below) of Eratosthenes, Theophrastus, the Stoic spokesman in *De natura deorum*, of Lucretius in the Hellenized Roman period, and of those who, like the Hermetic writers, come later but clearly have close affiliations with the Hellenistic thinkers, make one wonder what would be revealed had so much not been lost in transmission.

The prevailing mood of the Eastern Greeks in early Hellenistic times, says Rostovtzeff, was one of buoyant optimism; they had confidence and faith, supported by the leading philosophical schools, "in the unlimited capabilities of man and his reason."[12] This observation would certainly apply to many of the Stoics and, judging by Lucretius, to the Epicureans too. Agriculture and related occupations such as cattle-breeding were the most important sources of wealth in the ancient world. Intensification of such economic activity is favorable to landscape changes visible to the eye. Canals appear, swamps van-

[9] *Ibid.*, 59159.
[10] *Ibid.*, 59184.
[11] *The Tebtunis Papyri* 703 = Vol. 3, pp. 66–102.
[12] *HW*, Vol. 2, p. 1095.

ish, river courses change. If, as seems probable from reading the classical writers on agriculture, the judging of soils empirically was a primordial skill, the good soils had long since been known and further improvement could come only from the acquisition of new land. Land reclamation during this period was based on the science of mechanics, and on practical experience with canal-digging, irrigation, and swamp drainage. The purpose of one famous scheme, the drainage of Lake Copais in Boeotia under the supervision of Crates, a mining engineer in Alexander's army, apparently was to increase the cultivated area of Greece.[13] Similar projects were undertaken in the Eastern Hellenistic monarchies and in Egypt.[14]

The economic system of the Ptolemies, says Rostovtzeff, "was inspired by one motive, the organization of production, with the main purpose of making the State, in other words, the king, rich and powerful."[15] In the conscious development of the natural resources of Ptolemaic Egypt, about which far more is known than of the other large areas of the Hellenistic world, the purpose was to make the country self-sufficient, and to create in modern terminology a favorable balance of trade. Here, and in the quotation from Eratosthenes below, environmental change is a product of conscious government policy.[16] In carrying out this policy, the solicitude of the Ptolemies for the Greek settlers led to visible changes in the appearance of the land, an apt illustration of the influence of national tastes and diet which are exported to another land. The Egyptian drink was beer, but the Greeks liked wine, and soon there were extensive vine plantings in Ptolemaic Egypt. It was the same with the indispensable olive. So vineyards and olive groves became witnesses of the Greek presence as did the fruit trees and the sheep. (It was not that such plantings were unknown in Egypt before, but they were few and not very successful.)

A history of attempts at plant acclimatization, especially in Egypt, would have in it a chapter on Greek taste in food and clothes. Experiments were not confined to Egypt, for Harpalus attempted to acclimatize pines in Mesopotamia. Theophrastus says Harpalus tried repeatedly to plant ivy in the gardens of Babylon and failed.[17] The Greeks liked wool for their clothing, and sheep in Ptolemaic Egypt became important. Foreign sheep were imported and efforts made to acclimatize them. In the great procession of Ptolemy Philadelphus, there were Arabian, Ethiopian, and Euboean sheep [Ath. V 201c]. Plant and animal introductions and acclimatizations, however, were not unique to the Hellenistic period; since Xenophon's time at least, the introduction and

---

[13] Strabo IX, ii, 18, does not say this was the purpose; Crates in a letter to Alexander said many places had already been drained.

[14] See *HW*, Vol. 1, pp. 351–380, for an extensive discussion of Egypt.

[15] *Ibid.*, p. 316.

[16] *Ibid.*, pp. 351, 353.

[17] On Harpalus' attempts at acclimatization see Bretzl, *Botanische Forschungen des Alexanderzuges*, pp. 234–236. Theophr., *Enquiry into Plants*, IV, iv, 1.

acclimatization of plants when necessary were familiar in the Greek world.[18] After the Hellenistic period, similar activities seem to prosper, as one can see from Columella. Certain places are famous for certain kinds of vines, grains, or animal breeds, and he even provides a list of common Greek and Latin names for dogs.

If one could have taken a series of photographs of Ptolemaic Egypt at suitable intervals, one could probably see, at least through the earlier period, the different crops, the new devices, and the introductions that created a more variegated landscape.[19]

It is tantalizing to speculate on the policy of the Hellenistic monarchs toward deforestation, because this practice probably more than any other in a preindustrial society changes the ecosystem and the appearance of the land. The rulers of Egypt had given careful attention to tree planting and to cutting, but it is not known if they were interested in conservation.[20]

During the Hellenistic period, brilliant successes in the exact sciences contributed to the improvement of methods of production and exchange by the invention of new technical devices.[21] Rostovtzeff has emphasized the special place of architects and engineers because of the immense amount of building, especially in the principal islands and the great commercial cities along the coasts of Asia Minor, the Straits, and the Propontis: remodeling harbors, replanning and rebuilding of such cities as Miletus, Ephesus, Smyrna, and lesser cities of Asia Minor. New cities and new temples were built, and others already in existence were rebuilt to make life within them easier, through drainage and the construction of aqueducts. Building obviously was also closely related to the exploitation of mines, quarries, and forests where they existed. War and military construction played a vital part too. Rostovtzeff is also of the opinion that Vitruvius in *De architectura* depicted not the ideal architect but the conception of an architect he inherited from the Hellenistic period, as shown by his insistence on a "harmonious co-operation" in the exercise of the architect's functions, between science and learning on the one hand and his practical craft on the other. If this is true, a comparison between the ideals of an architect expressed by Vitruvius and by Alberti in the fifteenth century (chap. IX, sec. 2) would seem a fruitful one; both were interested in harmonies, philosophy, the relation of any building, whether a home or a city, to its surroundings in the broad sense of the word.[22] There seemed to be

[18] See *HW*, Vol. 2, p. 1162.

[19] *Ibid.*, Vol. 2, pp. 1167–1168.

[20] *Ibid.*, Vol. 2, pp. 1169–1170; note 113, pp. 1612–1613, and *The Tebtunis Papyri* 703, 191–211, already discussed, and 5, 200. On forest policy, Heichelheim, "Monopole," *PW*, Vol. 16:1, col. 188; *HW*, Vol. 1, pp. 298–299.

[21] *HW*, Vol. 2, p. 1180; Heichelheim, "Effects of Classical Antiquity on the Land," *MR*, p. 169, and Sarton, *Hellenistic Science, passim.*

[22] *HW*, Vol. 2, p. 1234. In the light of Rostovtzeff's words, see the illuminating discussion by Vitruvius in Bk. I, ch. 1, and Bk. VII, Pref.

closer alliance between building construction and military engineering, and science and art, than between practice and theory in agriculture, in the absence of scientifically conducted agricultural experiments. The technical innovation that occurred was not revolutionary; it was based partly on scientific discoveries, partly on the interchange of long-established methods among the constituent nations of the Hellenistic world.[23]

A city too is a physical environment; it is characterized by an extremely dense concentration of products of human purpose, perhaps including suggestions of a natural landscape in trees, promenades, gardens, parks. It may be all houses and streets with an occasional tree; it may be full of gardens, promenades, and parks which, even though suggesting artificiality, are in contrast to the concentrations of wood, stone, and other symmetrically arranged materials surrounding them. In the Hellenistic period there is reason, as we have seen, to believe that there was a sharpening of the contrast between the city and the country, but the evidence is most spotty. The descriptions of the charms of the countryside are set off against a long urban tradition which was not born in the Mediterranean world but was well nourished there.

Alexander created in the Near East a few large settlements of the Greek urban type. Alexandria was the outstanding example. He refounded some, like Gaza in Palestine, perhaps Tyre in Phoenicia, after he had destroyed them. One should speak of the Hellenistic period more in terms of the variety of urban life which flourished then and the activities nourishing it rather than as a period of city-building, because so many of the cities already were there. Established old cities were enlarged, new ones on the extended pattern were established. Some of the cities kept their native names, others, like Ptolemais-Ake, received new dynastic names. Some were recent foundations, others were pre-Ptolemaic. During the Hellenistic period new life was infused into Greek centers of export trade. Greek-Phoenician cities like Sidon and the harbor of Al-Mina were the most notable of the revived semi-Greek emporia.[24]

Scores of Greek poleis were located in the oriental parts of the Asian empire "at the points of the great and strategic commercial roads which from time immemorial had connected with each other the most civilized and progressive parts of the Oriental world."

Most of the Greek poleis created by Alexander thus were not brand-new cities, nor transformations of small villages. The former in most cases already had been commercial centers. Neither were roads his creation, nor did he connect great centers of caravan trade with the sea. "The new and momentous feature of it [his colonization] was the transformation of the Oriental marts into business centers of a type hitherto unknown to the east."[25] One might

---

[23] *HW*, Vol. 2, pp. 1230–1238, 1302.
[24] *HW*, Vol. 1, pp. 130–131.
[25] *HW*, Vol. 1, pp. 132–133.

thus accept Rostovtzeff's distinction between urbanization of the Hellenistic and that of the later Roman world. The Romans introduced urban life and the urban mentality of Greco-Italian type, he says, into areas of almost purely tribal and village life; the Seleucids built Greek cities for many purposes— first and foremost was colonization for military and political purposes—but real urbanization had been achieved in Syria, Babylon, and Mesopotamia long before Alexander.[26]

In the preceding discussions, the Hellenistic period has been described as an active era, characterized by a broad philosophical outlook toward man and his environment, including the nature of man, his place in the universe, and what distinguishes him from other forms of life, and also by a practical outlook toward resources embodied in the economic and political aspirations of the Hellenistic monarchs. Most of the important passages, moreover, date from this period or from writings inspired by it; there are a few from earlier times—Hesiod, Herodotus, Isocrates, Xenophon—but they too, like Plato and Sophocles, seem isolated examples.

4. GENERAL DESCRIPTIONS OF ENVIRONMENTAL CHANGE

Occasionally there is an awareness of changes in the environment through time without, however, any interpretation of their significance. One of the most commonly quoted sayings of Herodotus is that Egypt is "an acquired country, the gift of the river." But Herodotus knows this is only a half truth. Egyptian civilization is more than the gift of the Nile, for the Egyptian people themselves had changed their land. The mythical Sesostris built canals, and the face of the countryside had been changed by forced labor: an Egypt whose countryside had been suitable for horses and carriages was now unsuited to either because canals had replaced them and changed the road network.[27]

Isocrates wrote of another mythical Egyptian king, Busiris, the son of Poseidon and of Libya, who thought the country of his mother's birth unworthy of him and had therefore subjugated Egypt. Unlike those places which lacked the favorable climate and situation for all kinds of crops—they were inundated by rain or devastated by the heat—Egypt, that is the delta of the Nile, placed in the most beautiful part of the world, could produce the most abundant and varied products, defended by the eternal rampart of the river. The Nile had made it possible for the Egyptians to act like gods in

[26] *HW*, Vol. 3, note 262, p. 1436. See also V. Tscherikower, "Die hellenistischen Städtegründungen von Alexander dem Grossen bis auf die Römerzeit," *Philologus* Supp. Bd. 19, Heft I (1927), vii + 216 pp. See also *HW*, Vol. 3, note 5, p. 1091, Tarn's discussion in *Hellen. Civiliz.*, ch. 3, and Heichelheim, "Effects of Classical Antiquity on the Land," *MR*, pp. 168–169.
[27] Hdt., II, 5, 108; Kees, "Sesostris," *PW*, 2A:2, col. 1873.

making their lands produce. Zeus distributed the rains and the droughts to other peoples, but the individual Egyptian was like Zeus himself in controlling these.[28] (These contrasts between the water sources of the Egyptians and those of other countries, as we have already seen, go back at least to the *Hymn to Aten*; they are mentioned also in Herodotus and in Plato.)

Later in the Hellenistic period, Theocritus admires not only Ptolemy, but Egypt, the Nile, and human skill as well. Ten thousand lands and ten thousand nations cultivate their lands with the help of rain from Zeus; but no country is so fruitful as the low country of Egypt where the Nile brings the water, soaking and breaking the soil, "nor no country, neither, possessed of so many cities of men learned in labour. The cities builded therein are three hundreds and three thousands and three tens of thousands, and threes twain and nines three, and in them the lord and master of all is proud Ptolemy."[29]

There is extant a beautiful floor mosaic from a bath at Antioch (fourth century B.C.). The scene in Egypt illustrates three personifications of its richness: fertile earth, careful cultivation, the Nile. Nor is the combination difficult to understand. Technology is a connecting link between inventive man and nature.[30]

Strabo also comments on the environmental changes which the Egyptians have brought about in their own country, incidentally explaining the details of their control of water and drought. To the Greeks, the Egyptian environment must have been as fascinating as was their civilization.

> The attention and care bestowed upon the Nile is so great as to cause industry to triumph over nature. The ground by nature, and still more by being supplied with water, produces a great abundance of fruits. By nature also a greater rise of the river irrigates a larger tract of land; but industry has completely succeeded in rectifying the deficiency of nature, so that in seasons when the rise of the river has been less than usual, as large a portion of the country is irrigated by means of canals and embankments, as in seasons when the rise of the river has been greater.[31]

Among the geographers of the Hellenistic period, Eratosthenes shows a striking awareness of the complex cultural and historical factors involved in environmental change. The plains of Cyprus in past times, he says, had been covered with forests; clearings were made to provide fuel for smelting copper and silver, and timber with which to build ships "as the sea was now navigated with security and by a large naval force." Cuttings for these purposes were insufficient to "check the growth of timber in the forests," and the people

---

[28] Isoc., *Bus.*, 10–14. On the legend, see Hiller v. Gaetringen, "Busiris, 5," *PW*, 3, cols. 1074–1077.

[29] Idyll XVII, 77–85.

[30] *Nat. D.*, II, 60, 150–152; *de fin.* V, 74; Lucr. I, 159–214. For the plate, see *HW*, Vol. 1, facing p. 352.

[31] Strabo, XVII, i, 3.

were allowed to cut down trees and "to hold the land thus cleared as their own property, free from all payments." Eratosthenes thus relates the changes in the landscape to mining, navigation, and to governmental land policy.[32]

## 5. THEOPHRASTUS ON DOMESTICATION AND CLIMATIC CHANGE

Historically, students of plant and animal life and of land forms have been sensitive to the influence of human activities on these phenomena. Botanists, for example, have been interested in the nature of domestication and in plant successions due to human agency. In the ancient world, Theophrastus was such a student, asking two questions which have become of surpassing interest in modern times. In what ways does a domesticated plant differ from a wild one? Is it possible for man to change the climate? Both answers reveal, as Plato's discussion of erosion reveals, a curiosity regarding man's ability to change plants and to bring about environmental conditions which may favor or inhibit plant growth.

Theophrastus' distinctions between wild and domesticated plants are disappointing, being little more than recastings of common observations. He rejects Hippon's idea that each plant has a wild and a domestic form and recognizes that human care is related to domestication, and that some wild plants cannot live under cultivation. Certain trees, however, which degenerate from a parent tree which grows from seeds, may be improved by cultivation and special attention. The pomegranate changes character if it receives plenty of river water and pig manure, the almond if its gum is allowed to exude by inserting a plug in the tree and if it is given various other kinds of care.[33] Domesticated plants are likened to the tamed animals which live in close association with man. Possibly Theophrastus has cosseting in mind. The following passage suggests that artificial selection of desirable qualities is the chief distinction between a wild and a domesticated tree, although he seems to be talking about a formerly domesticated tree now living ferally. "Any tree which runs wild deteriorates in its fruits, and itself becomes dwarfed in leaves, branches, bark and appearance generally; for under cultivation these parts, as well as the whole growth of the tree, become closer, more compact and harder; which indicates that the difference between cultivated and wild is chiefly shown in these respects.[34]

His discussion of climatic change owing to human agency, however, is more significant to our theme because it is the beginning of the long history of speculation concerning this subject. Theophrastus says that there are dis-

---

[32] Strabo, XIV, vi, 5.

[33] Theophr., *An Enquiry into Plants*; on Hippon, I, iii, 5, and III, ii, 2; I, iii, 6; II, ii, 6, 11.

[34] Theophr., *An Enquiry into Plants*, III, ii, 3. In IV, iv, one has a glimpse into the botanical results of Alexander's conquests. On this subject see Bretzl, *Botanische Forschungen des Alexanderzuges*.

tricts, like that around Larissa in Thessaly, where in former times the trees did not freeze, the air was denser and the district warmer; the entire district, moreover, had the appearance of a large marsh. When, however, the water was drained off and was prevented from accumulating again, the district became cold and the freezings increased. The evidence for this local change of climate, he says, is that the olive trees, even those in the city itself, which were formerly large and beautiful, have disappeared, and the vines are often attacked by the cold as they never were before. In another example, Aenos on the Hebrus (Maritza) became warmer when the river's waters were made to flow nearer to it. On the other hand, in the vicinity of Philippi, it formerly froze more than now: the fields were drained. The greater part of the district was dried up and put into cultivation. In this case the uncultivated area is the colder and it has denser air; the forest cover prevents the penetration of the sun's rays or the breezes even if there are stagnant accumulations of water within the woods.

In the Larissa example, drainage leads to greater extremes of cold, while the presence of water has a moderating effect, and in the Philippi example, the clearing of the woodlands has opened up the land, exposing it to the sun and bringing about a warmer climate. Similar statements in Pliny are clearly derived from Theophrastus.[35]

Theophrastus' examples of climatic change due to human agency were of very small areas, but to him there was clearly a universal principle at work, as is apparent from the theory on which the explanation is based. This inquiry, which starts so modestly with Theophrastus, the pupil of Aristotle, became the theme of countless writers in modern times, especially in the eighteenth and nineteenth centuries.

It would be incorrect, however, to say that these particular ideas stimulated later investigations, for they seem to have occurred independently to many men in different periods. The effects of clearings on climate were discussed by Albert the Great in the Middle Ages; after the age of discovery, discussions multiplied because so many travelers, especially in North America, observed, or thought they observed, or believed the reminiscences of the old, that the climate became warmer when the woods of the newly discovered lands were cleared.


## 6.   Rural Life and the Golden Age

Among the ancient authors, modifications in the environment made by man are most frequently mentioned in the treatises on agriculture. Some writers,

---

[35] Theophr., *De causis plant.* V, 14, 2–4, 5 (= *Opera, quae supersunt omnia* p. 284). I am indebted to Capelle, "Meteorologie," *PW*, Supp. vol. 6, col. 354, for the reference to this passage. See also *De ventis*, 13, *Opera* p. 379, on the changing climate of Crete, for which, however, no reason is given. See also Pliny, *NH*, XVII, iii, 30.

like Xenophon and Cato, were concerned with the practical details of the art; others linked the agriculture of their day with the fertility of the golden age, contrasting the fruitfulness of the soil then with the exacting work of contemporary tillage (Hesiod, Lucretius, and Virgil are good examples); still others, like Varro, Columella, and Pliny, linked agriculture with wider questions of cultural history and philosophy.

In his *Oeconomicus*, Xenophon describes the moral values of an agricultural life; Socrates, the chief spokesman, praises the Persian king for an interest in agriculture, and for his encouragement of what the Persians call "paradises" which are "full of all the good and beautiful things that the soil will produce. . . ." (According to an inscription engraved about A.D. 100–150, Darius praised Gadatas, apparently the satrap of the Ionian province, for cultivating in western Asia fruit trees brought from beyond the Euphrates, that is, west of the river, perhaps from Syria.)[36] The earth yields to men both the necessities and luxuries of life, and the art of stockbreeding is "closely linked with husbandry"; but to gain these things men must work for them.[37] Farmers are exhorted to keep the soil permanently fertile; everyone knows the value of manure and that nature produces it, but despite its abundance, some men collect it, others neglect to do so. Nature sends the rain, and if the vegetation that must be cleared from the fields before sowing is thrown into water "time of itself will make what the soil likes"; every kind of vegetation or soil turns into manure in stagnant water. Men too must learn how to drain land properly and to remove excessive salts. "For the slothful cannot plead ignorance, as in other arts: land, as all men know, responds to good treatment. Husbandry is the clear accuser of the recreant soul."[38]

Similar advice on maintaining soil fertility through proper care and manuring is common also in the agricultural treatises of Cato, Columella, and Pliny. Cato, sharing with Xenophon an esteem for agricultural ways, has said in often-quoted lines: "What is good cultivation? Good ploughing. What next? Ploughing. What third? Manuring."[39] Pliny also discusses the advantages of hillside ploughing, the causes of soil fertility, and the prevention of soil exhaustion.[40]

The agricultural writings were also related to the myth of a golden age as described by Hesiod and many succeeding writers: not only did the people of the golden age possess physical and moral superiority but the fertility of their soil was so great that it supplied men with food without the need of

---

[36] "Letter of Darius, 521–485 B.C.," in Tod, *Greek Historical Inscriptions* (2d ed., Oxford, 1951), No. 10, pp. 12–13. The authenticity of the text has been challenged. On Gadatas, see Xen., *Cyr.* V, iii, 10. See also Xen., *Oec.* IV, 8.

[37] Xen., *Oec.* IV, 13; V. 2–3. In *Oec.* V, there is a long discussion of the beauties and the moral and economic advantages of farming; the quotation is in V, 3.

[38] Xen., *Oec.* XX, 10–15.

[39] Cato, *On Agriculture*, LXI, quoted by Pliny, *NH*, XVIII, 174.

[40] Pliny, *NH*, XVIII, 2.

tillage. The theme, originating with Hesiod and repeated (or copied) by many later writers like Seneca, Ovid, Varro, and Virgil, is that the present age requires the active toil and the careful management of land to secure from it a living which in the golden age was spontaneously bestowed by the earth.[41]

Hesiod, whose poem is a combination of conjectural history and moral and agricultural precepts, believed that the gods hid the means of life from man; if they did not, man would lay aside his tasks and his fields would not be cultivated.[42] Environmental change comes about under the goad of necessity.

Hesiod thought there were five stages in the cultural history of man: the golden, the silver, and the bronze ages, followed by a race of demigods, then the contemporary or the iron age. The people living in the golden age experienced no sorrow ("remote and free from toil and grief"), never suffered old age, and had all good things of life, "for the fruitful earth unforced bare them fruit abundantly and without stint. They dwelt in ease and peace upon their lands with many good things, rich in flocks and loved by the blessed gods."[43] The golden age was characterized by happy shepherding and innate soil fertility. An important element of this myth is the notion that the soil is most fertile when it is least interfered with by human art. Whether the meaning is that the present age represents a decline of soil fertility corresponding to cultural decline of the iron age (an improbable interpretation), or whether it simply meant that in the golden age there prevailed a condition opposite to that observed in the iron age—in which a living was hard to get from the soil—is difficult to say, but the role of hard work in preparing the land for cultivation and keeping it in good condition, through plowing and fallowing, is certainly striking. "Plough in the spring; but fallow broken up in the summer will not belie your hopes. Sow fallow land when the soil is still getting light: fallow land is a defender from harm and a soother of children."[44]

The idea of soil fertility of the golden age persisted in antiquity as a theme in culture history from the time of Hesiod to that of Seneca, roughly a period of seven centuries, to say nothing of countless later repetitions. Perhaps the soil fertility of the golden age was but one aspect of the blissfulness of life in

---

[41] This theme recurs constantly in classical literature; see, for example, Lovejoy, *Primitivism and Rel. Ideas in Antiquity*, the passages from Ovid (*Met.*, I, 76–215), with comment pp. 43–49; *Amoros*, III, viii, 35–36, p. 63), Virgil (*Georgics*, I, 125–155, p. 370); Dicaearchus, in Porphyry, *De abstinentia*, IV, 1, 2, p. 94. See also the remarks on cultural primitivism, pp. 7–11, and the funny parodies of the golden age by the Greek comic poets, pp. 38–41.

[42] Hes., *Works and Days*, lines 42–45.

[43] *Ibid.*, lines 110–120. On the historical significance of this passage, see Lovejoy, *op. cit.*, pp. 27–28.

[44] *Ibid.*, see lines 460–464.

that remote period which was set against a less bountiful nature of the iron age; the idea, however, was repeated so often and over so long a period that it may have become a literary convention without special meaning. "The very soil," says Seneca of the heroic age, "was more productive when untilled, and yielded more than enough for peoples who refrained from despoiling one another."[45] Ovid too describes the golden age as one in which man had made little change in the primeval environment. "Not yet had the pine-tree, felled on its native mountains, descended thence into the watery plain to visit other lands; men knew no shores except their own. . . . The earth herself, without compulsion, untouched by hoe or ploughshare, of herself gave all things needful." Men gathered food that was about them, like the arbutus, berries, and acorns. The spontaneous crops of the earth were like the domesticated plants of human art. "Anon, the earth untilled, brought forth her stores of grain, and the fields, though unfallowed, grew white with the heavy, bearded wheat. Streams of milk and streams of sweet nectar flowed, and yellow honey was distilled from the verdant oak."[46] Varro, citing Dicaearchus, agrees that the remotest stage of human life must have been the state of nature "when man lived on those things which the virgin earth produced spontaneously."[47]

Regardless of the interpretation one places on these ideas of soil fertility of the golden age—whether the soil fertility is but one aspect of an idyllic existence all of whose parts are harmonious with one another, whether these ideas are part of the whole sympathy with primitivism and its supposed graces compared with the hard realities of contemporary life—it is reasonable, I think, to conclude that in a less idyllic later age, the soils required the active cooperation of man, who wrested a living from nature through the arts and techniques of tillage, soil replenishment, and soil care. In the contrasts between the spontaneities of the golden age and the purposeful toil of the present, it was recognized that the existence of human society, wicked as it is, requires the alteration of the primitive landscape.

Hesiod's descriptions of the golden age probably were in sharp contrast with the harsh realities of his own time (perhaps, the eighth century B.C.). In Aristophanes' time (fifth to fourth centuries B.C.) conditions were also harsh. The Attic farmer, almost naked, worked soils which "to a large extent [were] poor, stony and often still uncultivated." Despite deforestation, charcoal-burning was still practiced and important. "Swelling land which could be graphically described as 'the buttocks of the field' was rare, in spite of the famous phrase of 'rich Athens', or the beautiful patriotic outburst of

---

[45] Sen., *Ep. mor.*, 90, 40.
[46] Ovid., *Met.*, I, vv. 95–112.
[47] Varro, *On Farming*, Bk. II, chap. I, 3–4. See also *Fragment I, Vita Graeciae*, Porphyry, *De abstinentia*, IV, I, 2, text and translation in Lovejoy and Boas, *Doc. Hist.*, pp. 94–96.

Aristophanes: 'O beloved city of Kekrops, native-born Attica, hail, thou rich soil, udder of the good land!' . . . [and] it was only in the dreamland of fairy-tale that ample crops would grow without hard labour."[48]

## 7. Is the Earth Mortal?

Theories of soil exhaustion were also related to the idea of senescence in nature, an application of the organic analogy to the earth itself. The theory is ably expressed and refuted by Columella, who lived, probably, in the first century A.D.; although he does not mention Lucretius by name, it is his doctrine which Columella is attacking.

This idea of the senescence of the earth survived through the Middle Ages and into modern times; it was one consideration in the quarrel between the ancients and the moderns. Men like George Hakewill, Jon Jonston, John Evelyn, discuss it; and Montesquieu, arguing in the *Persian Letters* that the populations of modern times are less than those of ancient times, asks, through a letter his Persian Rhedi wrote from Venice to Usbek in Paris in 1718: "How can the world be so sparsely populated in comparison with what it once was? How can nature have lost that prodigious fertility of primitive times? Could she be already in her old age, and will she fall into her dotage?"[49]

Lucretius believes, as we have seen, that the earth is a mortal body; it will grow old gradually, and ultimately it will die. Nor is it sacrosanct. It is non-sense, he says, to think that "the glorious nature of the world" has been fashioned by the gods according to a divine plan for the sake of man; it is foolish to think of a divine artisan who has created an eternal and immortal abode for him. He ridicules the idea that it is a "sin ever to stir from its seats by any force what was established for the races of men for all time by the ancient wisdom of the gods, or to assail it with argument, and to overthrow it from top to bottom. . . ."[50] Here to digress a moment, he may be referring to attitudes which have been commonplace in modern times: the sinfulness of interfering with divine arrangements through human art. In modern times the point of view has been urged against the diversion of rivers, the digging of canals, and of course in medicine, the administration of anesthesia being an outstanding example. If the Lord had intended these things, they would have been created by Him in the beginning. Perhaps Lucretius is criticizing popular belief, similar to that mentioned by Tacitus in the next century. In an arresting passage, Tacitus calls attention to the effect of religious belief in preserving the natural order, mentioning popular objections to diversions of rivers on the ground that nature herself had made the best provision for their

[48] Ehrenberg, *The People of Aristophanes*, pp. 75–76.
[49] Montesquieu, *The Persian Letters*, Letter 112, trans. by Loy.
[50] *Lucr.*, V, 156–164.

sources, their courses, and their mouths. A discussion began in the Senate, he says, whether the inundations of the Tiber should be checked by changing the courses of its tributary rivers and lakes. Various deputations from municipalities and colonies were heard. The Florentines pleaded that if the course of the Chiana [Clanis] were deflected into the Arno, they would be ruined. If this scheme caused the Nar [Nera] to overflow after the stream had split into rivulets, the most productive fields of Italy would be doomed. The Reatines (of Reate, modern Rieti) protested against damming the Veline Lake (Lago di Piè-di-Lugo) at its outlet into the Nar. "Nature," they said, "had made the best provision for the interests of humanity, when she assigned to rivers their proper mouths—their proper courses—their limits as well as their origins. Consideration, too, should be paid to the faith of their fathers, who had hallowed rituals and groves and altars to their country streams. Besides, they were reluctant that Tiber himself, bereft of his tributary streams, should flow with diminished majesty." On this Tacitus comments, "Whatever the deciding factor—the prayers of the colonies, the difficulty of the work, or superstition—the motion of Piso, 'that nothing be changed,' was agreed to."[51] (The effects of such beliefs have been great, indeed, in the history of human settlement. The influence of religious beliefs in preserving natural landscapes could be illustrated by examples from many parts of the world and from many periods of history. Sacred groves around sanctuaries, to use but one example, are often indicators of former landscapes which have now disappeared. The desirability of preserving trees, and rude notions of the evils of indiscriminate deforestation, often seem mixed in with the beliefs in the gods of the sacred grove.)

No, Lucretius continues, the universe is too full of imperfections, the earth too full of land which cannot be used, to admit the possibility of its creation for man by divine power. (See chap. I, sec. 9.) Furthermore, the earth is older than it was. The greater fertility of the golden age is ascribed to the youth of the earth. The strength of man and his oxen is worn down; the plow can scarcely turn the soil of the grudging fields. The ploughman compares his ill fortune with the blessings of his fathers, who won a living from the soils so much more easily. "So too gloomily the planter of the worn-out, wrinkled vine rails at the trend of the times, and curses the age, and grumbles to think how the generations of old, rich in piety, easily supported life on a narrow plot, since aforetime the limit of land was far less to each man. Nor does he grasp that all things waste away little by little and pass to the grave fordone by age and the lapse of life."[52]

Columella attacks a similar idea, apparently widely accepted among the administrators of the state; in fact, he begins his work with the attack, later

[51] Tac., *Ann.*, I, 79. See also I, 76.
[52] *Lucr.*, II, 1157–1174.

reemphasizing his objections. Leading men of the state complain about the lack of soil fertility and bad climatic years as being responsible for poor crops, basing their complaints "as if on well-founded reasoning, on the ground that, in their opinion, the soil was worn out and exhausted by the over-production of earlier days and can no longer furnish sustenance to mortals with its old-time benevolence." Speaking more plainly, Columella continues:

> For it is a sin to suppose that Nature, endowed with perennial fertility by the creator of the universe, is affected with barrenness as though with some disease; and it is unbecoming to a man of good judgment to believe that Earth, to whose lot was assigned a divine and everlasting youth, and who is called the common mother of all things—because she has always brought forth all things and is destined to bring them forth continuously—has grown old in mortal fashion.

Columella does not mean that the soils cannot be exhausted, that they are everlastingly productive, but that their failures may have a human cause.[53]

The comparison of Mother Earth with a human mother, he says, is a false one. After a certain age, even a woman can no longer bear children; her fertility once lost cannot be restored, but this analogy does not apply to soil which has been abandoned, for when cultivation is resumed "it repays the farmer with heavy interest for its periods of idleness." Soil exhaustion is not related to the age of the earth but to agricultural practices. Columella cites Tremelius, apparently an older respected writer on soils: "Virginal and wooded areas, when they are first cultivated, yield abundantly, but soon thereafter are not so responsive to the toil of those who work them." His observation is correct, says Columella, but the interpretation is wrong. Such land is fruitful not because it has lain fallow longer and is younger, but because of the accumulated nourishment of the leaf fall and herbage of years. When clearing takes place and the axe and the plow break up plant roots, the soil's source of food is cut off; the soil, formerly rich, now grows infertile through deprivation of its former source of food. It is not because of old age or senescence of the earth "but manifestly because of our own lack of energy that our cultivated lands yield us a less generous return. For we may reap greater harvests if the earth is quickened again by frequent, timely, and moderate manuring."[54]

Manures—green and animal—are considered at length.[55] Seemingly trivial influences on the soil should be observed, such as studying moisture in the soil before allowing it to be trampled by cattle. In a passage which reminds one of Thorp's discussion of migrant fertility in China, Columella says that in about the middle of February elevated slopes should get manure with hay

[53] Columella, *De re rustica*, Pref., 1–3.
[54] *Ibid.*, II, 1, 1–7.
[55] *Ibid.*, II, xiv–xv; see also index, Vol. III, of the Loeb edition.

seed, "for the more elevated slope supplies nourishment to the land that lies below when a pouring rain or a hand-conducted rivulet carries the liquid manure along with its own waters to the part below. And it is for this reason that wise farmers, even in ploughed land, manure a hillside more heavily than a valley, because . . . the rains are forever carrying all the richer matter down to the lowland."[56]

Columella believes in an "equable law of fertility for all green things, even as for human beings and other living creatures." Nature has distributed her gifts to all regions. He points to the natural endowments of Italy, which "is most responsive to care bestowed by mankind, in that she has learned to produce the fruits of almost the entire world when her husbandmen have applied themselves to the task. Therefore our doubts should be lessened as to that fruit which is a native, as it were, belonging to and born of our soil." Like Victor Hehn in the nineteenth century, he thinks that Italy has many plants which were domesticated on other shores and brought there by human beings.[57]

Similar thoughts, probably derived from Columella, are expressed by Pliny, for he cites among his many authorities on agriculture the lost work of Mago the Carthaginian, Columella, and Varro. Pliny is aware of the significance of domestication; he distinguishes between trees growing wild and spontaneously and orchard trees which owe their formation, if not their actual birth, to the art and ingenuity of man. There is some of Columella's common sense in his discussion of soils, for they should not be regarded as old in a mortal sense; soils will last with care, and it is unnecessary to denude hillsides if the plowing is done skillfully. In hillside plowing the farmer should avoid plowing up and down the hillside. It is "ploughed only across the slope of the hill, but with the share pointing now up hill and now down."[58] Pliny also preserved ideas of climatic change owing to human agency, following the observations on this subject made by Theophrastus.

In the agricultural writings from Xenophon to Virgil, one can detect a widening realization of man's ability to change the natural order. The confidence is grounded in observation and empirical knowledge. With few exceptions, however, the main emphasis is on the fertility of arable land. This general emphasis on arable land, even if the problems of grazing were occasionally considered, is characteristic of modern agricultural chemistry through the time of Liebig. The detailed study of changes in the non-arable environments, like the grazing lands and the forests, is a modern interest although there are hints in medieval writings that changes were taking place there too and that they were significant (see pp. 330–341).

[56] *Ibid.*, II, xvii, 6–7; Thorp, *Geog. of the Soils of China*, pp. 433–436.
[57] Columella, *De re rustica*, III, viii, 1, 5. Victor Hehn, *Kulturpflanzen und Hausthiere in ihrem Übergang aus Asien nach Griechenland und Italien sowie in das Übrige Europa.*
[58] Pliny, *NH*, XVII, i, 1; 3, 29–30; quotation is in XVIII, 49, 178.

## 8. Interpreting Environmental Changes
### Within a Broader Philosophy of Civilization

Among the works of writers whose interpretations of environmental change are part of a broader philosophy, those of Cicero, the Hermetic writers (who probably derive their ideas on this matter from the Stoics), Lucretius, Varro, and Virgil are the most instructive. Despite differences in approach, each of them either implicitly or explicitly assumes that cultural history has at least in part been the history of environmental change and that the development of the arts and sciences has brought about changes in the physical environment.

In the Stoic philosophy, man's technological achievements, his inventions, the changes he brings about in nature, are combinations of the skill of the hand, the discoveries of the mind, observations of the senses; he has his share of the artisanry and reason which permeates the world, the earth being particularly suited to him, as witness the arrangements of external nature like the Nile, the Euphrates, and the Indus, that exist for his preservation and care.[59]

Environmental change by man, the creation of a "second nature" within the world of nature, is explained in essence by the basic qualitative difference between human and animal art. Man is a reasoning creature, whose cumulative experience through time permits innovation and invention; he participates in the creative life and spirit pervading the whole world.[60]

The naturalistic view of Lucretius presents an alternative interpretation without benefit of the artisan analogy and the argument from design. Men by their struggles add to what is already provided by nature. Tilled lands are better than untilled ones; they produce more. Earning a livelihood is en-meshed in a physical and human cycle: rain from the skies ultimately brings food to the towns; later the water of the streams returns to the ocean to be lifted again to the sky.[61] Lucretius is deeply aware of the physical difficulty men have in maintaining the environments they create; with failure, careless-ness, or laziness, the thorns, coppice, and weeds will again invade the tilled field.

One of the most arresting of Lucretius' discussions of man's interferences in the world of nature, however, is in his conception of animal domestication. It has a surprising teleological character, surprising too in the assumption of self-conscious choice by the animals. Animal domestication is a "commenda-tion"; the animals are entrusted to human tutelage, but Lucretius does not say who commended or entrusted them to our tutelage, nor does he explain the purpose of this puzzling pupil-teacher relationship. The animals are cast in the role of self-conscious determiners of their own fate. Domestication has

[59] *Nat. D.*, II, 52, 130; *de fin.* 5, 39.
[60] Pohlenz, *Die Stoa*, Vol. 1, pp. 227–228; see also Kaerst, *Gesch. d. Hellenismus*, Vol. 2, pp. 124–125.
[61] Lucr. I, 208–214, 250–264, 782–788.

survival value for certain kinds of animals who flee from the hard life of nature. Lucretius implies that there is self-conscious and purposive action by animals who weigh alternatives and that domestication is semicontractual on the part of the animals but is undertaken by men for utilitarian, not humanitarian, purposes. (The utilitarian explanation of animal domestication can be harmonized with either the Epicurean or the Stoic philosophy; in the latter it is in accordance with the design, especially if it is assumed that the resources of the world useful to man are in fact created for him). In the Lucretian philosophy (is this true of Epicurus too?) animal extinctions may be explained in two ways: the animals in nature either fail to survive in the struggle for existence, or fail to find human protection. The passages in Lucretius on natural selection and struggle for existence, however, have little resemblance to Darwinian evolutionary theory; the fixity of species is assumed, the role of man is decisive for several species of the more docile animals, and human interferences in the animal world are assumed to be of ancient age. Man is interfering very early in the order of nature, singling out certain species whose survival and multiplication are no longer dependent on the natural environment alone but on him.[62] The idea expressed here by Lucretius reappears in the discussions of animal domestication in the *Histoire Naturelle* of Buffon, the most impressive natural history written during the eighteenth century. Buffon was an ardent admirer of Lucretius' writings.

Men in the past, though hardier than those of today, did not spend their energies at the plow, for they knew nothing of plowing, planting, or pruning. Like people of the golden age, they accepted freely the spontaneous gifts of the earth. The invention of fire was a great step forward in the conquest of nature; lightning, or possibly the friction of tree branches with one another, first made it available.[63] Then, in lessons from the sun and its effects on earthly substances, men learned how to cook. With the invention of fire, the next step was the discovery of metallurgy.

Lucretius' theory of the origin of metallurgy reveals how conscious he was of the activities of man: the discovery of the metals (copper, gold, iron, silver, lead) he ascribes to great forest fires which may have been started by lightning, by warring men who started fires against one another, or by those who desired to increase their arable lands and pastures at the expense of forests or who wished to kill off wild beasts. "For hunting with pit and fire arose first before fencing the grove with nets and scaring the beasts with dogs."[64] The forest fire, whatever its cause, burned so fiercely that the melted streams of silver, gold, copper, and lead flowed into the hollows of the earth's surface, and men, attracted by the luster and polish of the metals, could see from their odd shapes that they could be molded. They could now make tools to clear forests and

---

[62] Lucr., V, 855–877.
[63] *Ibid.*, V, 925–987, 1091–1104.
[64] *Ibid.*, V, 1241–1296. The quotation is of V, 1250–1251.

work up lumber, and to till the fields, first with copper tools and later with the iron plow.

Taught by the model of nature and in imitation of her, men planted and grafted plants, and experimented with various types of cultivation. With gentle care, they brought the wild fruits under human protection and cultivation, and following the suggestions of nature, they widened areas of change, substituting a domesticated environment for the pristine.

> And day by day they would constrain the woods more and more to retire up the mountains, and to give up the land beneath to tilth, that on hills and plains they might have meadows, pools, streams, crops, and glad vineyards, and the grey belt of olives might run between with its clear line, spreading over hillocks and hollows and plains; even as now you see all the land clear marked with diverse beauties, where men make it bright by planting it here and there with sweet fruit-trees, and fence it by planting it all round with fruitful shrubs.[65]

Lucretius' poem has now been discussed in three different contexts: his rebuttal of the basic ideas which supported the argument from design, his conception of the organic, and therefore the mortal, nature of the earth, and his ideas of environmental change as a part of culture history. These latter ideas seem more historical in character, less theoretical, and are set apart from the other two. In the passages just quoted, he is clearly describing, in poetical language and without any suggestion of decay or death, the manner in which a people transforms the landscape.

Man's progress in the arts has its effects on his environments as well; he has learned by imitation, by using his mind, and he has increased his knowledge by practice and experience; he has saved many animal species; he has domesticated plants, has cleared and drained land, and the landscape about him is, at least in part, a result of his own creativity.

Varro's work on farming is significant to our theme because it is an attempt —very influential in modern times—to describe the historical sequence in the use of land, investigations inspired by the peripatetic philosopher and student of Aristotle, Dicaearchus, whose life of Greece ($\beta\iota\circ\varsigma$ $\text{E}\lambda\lambda\acute{\alpha}\delta\circ\varsigma$) had influenced many writers, Posidonius among them. Dicaearchus, according to Varro, thought that men originally lived in a state of nature, using the products which the earth voluntarily afforded. For them it was a happy state, a golden age. According to Porphyry, Dicaearchus thought of the golden age as a happy condition not because men were physically, mentally, or morally superior to later generations, but because they did not desire amenities which could only be obtained by hard physical effort; since they had no higher aspirations, they had few cares and sorrows. There was less sickness because the food was simpler, and there was less strain; there were no wars, for there was no object in strife. From this state of nature men descended to a less desirable condition, the pastoral stage, nourishing themselves on wild-growing acorns, ar-

[65] *Ibid.*, V, 1370–1378.

butus berries, mulberries and other fruits, and on animals which were captured, confined, and tamed for food. Sheep probably came first, being useful, tractable, and adaptable to man, bringing him milk, cheese, wool, and skin. The pastoral stage was followed by the agricultural, which retained much of the former two states, lasting a long time before the present era. Several species of wild animals survive: the sheep of Phrygia, goats of Samothrace, and the wild goats of Italy; it is the same with swine, and there are many quite wild cattle in Dardania, Maedica and Thrace, wild asses in Phrygia and Lycaonia, and wild horses in Hither Spain. To Dicaearchus the existence of these animals in the present proves his theory that domestication grew out of taming and that present-day livestock-raising is a survival of the pastoral stage.[66]

Varro agrees with this, and it is no surprise that the author of *De lingua latina* carries the argument a step further and tries to prove the antiquity of animal domestication, especially that of the sheep, on philological grounds. The Greek and Latin tongues reveal that the most famous ancients were shepherds. Goats and sheep were esteemed by the ancients, and astrologers named constellations after them. Many place-names could be traced to the names of animals. The Roman people themselves sprang from shepherds.[67]

What is the historical significance of this theory? In the first place, it turned attention away from the environment itself to the sequences of stages which characterized cultural history. Varro's method is similar to the modern comparative or historical method in which cultures are assumed to pass through an ideal series of stages, the early stages in the sequence being recognized either from survivals existing in antiquity or among peoples in various stages of development existing in the contemporary world. The stage theory has been severely criticized in the twentieth century (now, however, it is being revived in a much more sophisticated form), from the ethnological and historical point of view, for its neglect of historical materials in favor of abstract formulations; but of equal importance is the fact that such a theory at the outset discourages any attempt to study the history of an environment or the manner in which a culture has changed it. Varro was far less dogmatic about his theory than many of his later imitators, for he accused the Romans themselves (like Cicero, his contemporary, he was alarmed that so much of the arable land of the small holders was being turned into grazing lands for the large landowners) of deserting the countryside for the cities, of importing grain and wine from abroad, of reversing the historic process by reverting from an agricultural to a pastoral life.

"And so in that country where the city's founders were shepherds and

---

[66] Varro, *On Farming*, I, 2, 15–16; II, 1, 3–4. See Fragment I of Dicaearchus' *Vita Graeciae* (n. 47 above). Cf. *Doc. Hist.*, n. 159, p. 95, in which the authors comment on the proverb "Enough of the oak-tree," meaning satiety with eating acorns and a desire for a better diet and life. See also *PW*, "Dikaiarchos," and Wehrli, *Die Schule des Aristoteles. Texte und Kommentar. Heft. I. Dikaiarchos*, pp. 56–59.

[67] Varro, *op. cit.*, II, 1, 3–9.

taught agriculture to their descendants, these descendants have reversed the process, and, through covetousness and in despite of laws, have turned corn-land into meadow, not knowing the difference between agriculture and grazing."[68]

It is true that Varro recognizes that modifications of the natural order are part of cultural and economic history; different kinds of cultures, based on economic systems, use their environments in different ways, but the concreteness, the rich historical and geographical material, is lost in reducing the process to stages.

The idea that in the economic development of mankind the pastoral stage preceded the agricultural has been effectively challenged only in modern times. The stage theory, or variants of it, has appeared in many twentieth century economics textbooks, although Lord Kames in the eighteenth century and Alexander von Humboldt in the nineteenth pointed out that a pastoral or nomadic stage could not be observed in the New World. Modern research, moreover, has stressed the late appearance of nomadism.[69]

In other passages Varro makes interesting comments on agriculture and grazing: he distinguishes between the productiveness of agriculture and the removal of the vegetation by grazing animals; it is best therefore for both agriculture and pasture-farming to be practiced together so that, in addition to other advantages, the farmer can profit from the manure in helping to further plant growth.

Varro also describes transhumance in southern Italy: ". . . Flocks of mine used to winter in Apulia which spent the summer on the mountains about Reate, though the pastures were far from each other and connected between these two places by public tracks like a pair of baskets by their yoke."[70] Unlike modern discussions of transhumance, there is no mention of overgrazing or of deforestation in order to increase the grazing lands.

Varro also has unkind words for the goat. Fundanius, Varro's father-in-law, disparaged agriculture because, as Dicaearchus had shown, pastoral life had preceded it. To this Agrius, "a Roman eques of the Socratic school," replies by quoting the laws for settlers: "On land planted with young trees let not the settler pasture the offspring of the she-goat—creatures which even astronomy has removed to a place in the sky not far from the bull." Fundanius replies that the law applies to "certain cattle," for certain animals, like the she-goat, "are hostile to cultivation and poisonous to plants for by nibbling at them they ruin all young plants, and not the least, vines and olive trees."[71]

---

[68] *Ibid.*, II, Intro., 4.

[69] The earliest criticism of the universality of this stage theory, as far as I know, is that of Henry Home (Lord Kames); see *Sketches of the History of Man*, Vol. II, pp. 82–84. Lord Kames thought the puzzle could be solved with more knowledge.

[70] Varro, *On Farming*, II, Intro., 4–5; quotation on transhumance is in II, 2, 9, and see also II, 1, 16–17, and II, 10, 1–3, on the qualifications of shepherds.

[71] *Ibid.*, I, 2, 1, 15–18; Fundanius continues, 19–20.

To Father Liber, the discoverer of the vine, he-goats were sacrificed because of their misdeeds; no such sacrifice was made to Minerva because the goat bruised the olive tree and his saliva was poisonous to vegetation. At Athens goats could enter the Acropolis only once a year for the sacrifice "lest the olive tree, which they say first sprang up there, be touched by a she-goat." In a later chapter on the breeding and selection of goats, Varro says that they are happier in woodland glades than in meadows, that they like wild shrubs and the small branches in cultivated areas, and that a tenant generally is forbidden by contract to allow them to graze on a farm he has rented.[72]

Varro's remarks are interesting because they reveal an awareness of the power of this domesticated animal (an extension of human activity because it is under man's control) as a destroyer of the vegetation of the farm or the mountain wilderness. The loud complaints about the destructive grazing habits of the goat—as the cause of widespread environmental deterioration—that have appeared so frequently since the nineteenth century have to my knowledge no real counterparts in antiquity, perhaps because their habits were not interpreted as part of a broader ecological problem (as modern students of vegetational change have seen them); probably also little was known of the cumulative effects of such environmental change.

The development of civilization, in Virgil's reconstruction, is accompanied by transformations of the land. Employing the myth of the golden age, he saw even before Jove an "Earth, unbidden, which gave the more freely of all her store, in that none asked her bounty." Jove stopped this bounty, fashioning nature as we know it now; he gave the snake its poison, made the wolf a beast of prey, made the ocean swell, "scattered the honey from the leaf, swept the fire away, and stayed the wine that once streamed in every brook . . ." so that man, profiting by experience, might evolve the arts like agriculture and mining. Only after Jove had acted was navigation known on the rivers and on the seas (the "rivers felt the hollowed alder; then the mariner numbered the stars and named them . . .") or was it possible to capture wild beasts, "to cheat the bird with lime, and to circle the vast glades with hounds . . . ," to fish in the streams and on the sea. "Then came the iron's rigour and the blade of the rasping saw: in the old days men cleft their facile timber with the wedge! Then art followed on art." Ceres showed men how to turn the soil; now they had to learn how to combat plant diseases and the animals that preyed on their crops.[73] Virgil calls upon the farmer to cultivate his land, to cosset the plants, "Come, then, ye husbandmen, and learn the tillage that each kind claims for its own, mellow your harsh fruits by culture, nor suffer your fields to lie idle. There is joy in planting Ismarus with the vine, and joy in clothing great Taburnus with the olive." Nature can be subdued; wild trees that are grafted or transplanted in trenches "will resign

---

[72] *Ibid.*, I, 2, 20; II, 3, 7–8.
[73] Virgil, *Georgics*, I, 120–159. On firing, manuring, and fallowing land, I, 71–99.

their wild spirit, and, by dint of constant tilling, assume with readiness whatever character thou wilt have them bear." Know the soils, weave hedges to keep the flocks from your vines, for they are more harmful with their iron teeth and their scarrings of the "deep-gnawed stem" than the snow, the hoarfrost, "or the summer brooding heavy above the thirsty crags."[74]

Virgil thus describes changes in the land, brought about first by Jove, and then by human art: man is an overseer, protecting his crops from wild animals and his own domesticated animals and guarding them from disease, spreading his cultivation—of the olive and the vine—through lands not now given to them; all his activities are a product of that intelligence and that knowledge based on experience with which he has changed his mode of life and the countryside upon which he is dependent.

In my opinion, the most important attempt to reconcile the environmental changes by man with both a philosophy of man and the order of nature was made by the Stoic philosophers and by those who came under their influence, ideas expressed most clearly in those writings of Cicero which include the contributions of Panaetius and Posidonius: Man cooperates with nature and ever improves on its pristine condition; the changes which he has made and is to make are in fact part of the divine purpose in creating the world. This conception is significant, too, because of the immense prestige of Stoicism in the Hellenistic period, including the widespread acceptance of Stoic ideas during the latter period of the republic and the early period of the empire.

> To the Stoics, however, it was the same Logos which was at work both in the Cosmos and within man. It therefore followed naturally that man also carried within him the creative energies which led him on to craftsman-like productive work. To be sure, the old Stoics had no particular interest in the arts and crafts. Panaetius, therefore, had tried all the harder to demonstrate that human beings, endowed with the senses and hands, are well-fitted for craftsmanship, that the Logos has, in fact, developed, with their help, all the possible arts, and that by means of them the earth's entire surface has been transformed to their ends, and that there has been created in nature, as it were, a second nature. Then his pupil, Posidonius, defined exactly what the practical goals of men should be: "to work jointly with nature—and with all their energies—in the actual formation and ordering of the Cosmos."[75]

Rejecting the opinion of Democritus that man had developed his art by imitating nature and the skills of animals, Posidonius, admitting that man might have received some stimulus from these sources, maintained however that by virtue of his own Logos, revealing itself in outstanding individuals, man had created something entirely different, something in accordance with his own being: his arts were not products of instinctive behavior, like the web of the spider or the honeycomb of the bee; human art embraced all realms

[74] *Ibid.*, II, 35–39, 49–53, 371–380.
[75] Translated by the writer from the German of Max Pohlenz, *Der Hellenische Mensch*, pp. 276–277.

of life, unfolding itself in many diverse ways through the creative performance of individual personalities.[76]

Man is thus a part of nature; he shares his creative endowment with the
whole cosmos but his arts are in a different realm of being than are those of
the animals. With his hands, his tools, his intelligence, he has changed the
earth by creating arts and techniques of agriculture, fishing, animal domestication, by mining, clearing, and navigation. Cicero has Balbus the Stoic unite
the design argument that nature has given man opportunities, such as the life-
giving floods of the Nile, the Euphrates, and the Indus, with the idea that
man in turn has not only preserved but improved animals and plants which
would become extinct without his care; that nature has given man hands, a
mind, and senses, the basic endowments of his art: the mind to invent, the
senses to perceive, the hands to execute. By human hands much of nature
has been both controlled and changed. Our foods are a result of labor and
cultivation; wild and domesticated animals are put to many uses; the mining
of iron is indispensable to tillage; clearings are made for fire, cooking, house-
and ship-building.

"We enjoy the fruits of the plains and of the mountains, the rivers and the
lakes are ours, we sow corn, we plant trees, we fertilize the soil by irrigation,
we confine the rivers and straighten or divert their courses. In fine, by means
of our hands we essay to create as it were a second world within the world of
nature."[77] Balbus the Stoic is speaking here, but Cicero has revealed elsewhere
his appraisal of the power of men to change the earth about them.

In short, what advantage and convenience could have been realized from the
brute creation, had not men assisted? Men, undoubtedly were the first who discovered what useful results we might realize from every animal; nor could we
even at this time either feed, tame, preserve, or derive from them advantages
suited to the occasion, without the help of man. And it is by the same that such
as are hurtful are destroyed and such as may be useful are taken. Why should
I enumerate the variety of arts without which life could by no means be sustained?[78]

---

[76] See again, Sen., *Ep. mor.*, 90, 7–13; Pohlenz, *op. cit.*, p. 277. Both Seneca and Posidonius show their awareness of environmental changes by man resulting from mining
and agriculture. Seneca says he differs from Posidonius when the latter "says that wise
men discovered our mines of iron and copper, 'when the earth, scorched by forest fires,
melted the veins of ore which lay near the surface and caused the metal to gush forth' "
(90, 12). Seneca also criticizes Posidonius on his ideas of agricultural improvement. "This
trade also, he declares, is the creation of the wise,—just as if cultivators of the soil were
not even at present day discovering countless new methods of increasing the soil's
fertility!" (90, 21–22).

[77] Cic., *Nat. D.*, II, 60, 151–152. See the whole passage, II, 60, 150–152, which is too
long for quotation here, and the important commentaries on these passages in Pease,
*De natura deorum*, II, pp. 939–945. These mention the sources and the use made of them
by later thinkers, especially the early Church Fathers. Pohlenz argues that *Nat. D.*,
II, 59–60, 147–153, are derived from Panaetius. See note 75 above.

[78] Cic., *De officiis*, II, 4.

With Cicero surely it was not a matter of philosophy alone; it must also have been the observation of past and present Roman technical achievements: mining, commerce, trade, the Cloaca Maxima, the land surveys, and the roads were evidences that the power of man was not only great but of a different order than that of any other kind of life.[79]

Even more explicitly is the role of human agency in changing and improving the designed earth expressed in the Hermetical writings. In the *Asclepius*, the ideas held by the Stoics reach a climax in the conception of the interrelationships existing between God, nature, and man. The creation of man accomplishes two purposes: veneration of heaven and the administration of earthly things in partnership with God. "He raises reverent eyes to heaven above; he tends the earth below." No passages in ancient literature, with the exception of those in Cicero, express so clearly the activity of man in changing the natural environment and in so doing fulfilling a destiny inherent in God's design.

> And when I say "the things of earth," I do not mean merely the two elements, water and earth, which nature has placed in subjection to men; I mean all things that men do on land and water, or make out of earth and water, as for instance tillage and pasture, building, harbour-works and navigation, and intercourse and mutual service, that strong bond by which members of the human race are linked together. [For to man is given the charge] of that part of the universe which consists of earth and water; and this earthly part of the universe is kept in order by means of man's knowledge and application of the arts and sciences. For God willed that the universe should not be complete until man had done his part.

The reason that man can accomplish his role is explained later by the same author: man's knowledge is dependent on his memory and "it is the retentiveness of his memory that has given him dominion over the earth."[80]

If, as the Hermetical writer says, the earthly part of the universe is to be kept in order by man, modern air archaeology has revealed, as has no other study, dramatic examples of this order in ancient landscapes. The photographs show landscapes, not ideas, but in looking at such evidence of change in the central Mediterranean lands, one wonders why *homo artifex* is not in the classical world a more important figure than he is. For what suggests more efficaciously a planned, ordered, geometric landscape than does Roman centuriation? This method of partition of newly occupied lands—its uncertain origins possibly being in the third century B.C.—by which the land was divided up into squares of 20 *actus* on the side (776 x 776 yards) still appear strikingly in the air photos of the Po Valley and of Apulia, less clearly in many other Mediterranean areas. "The forceful imprint of the elaborate gridded road-systems which betoken it can still be traced across some thousands of square

---

[79] See also Cic., *De senectute*, XV, 53; *De oratore* III, xlv.
[80] Hermetica, *Asclepius* I, 6a; 8; III, 32b. See also I, 11b.

miles on both sides of the central Mediterranean." Centuriation, Bradford continues, well displayed "the arbitrary but methodical qualities" in Roman administration. "With an absolute self-assurance and great technical competence, the same formal topographical framework of land-division was superimposed on the well-watered alluvium of the Po Valley and the near-desert of Tunisia, in a nicely balanced blend of the doctrinaire and opportunist." Such parceling of land made large-scale gardening easier; in arid Tunisia, centuriation made intensive dry-farming easier, the many field-boundary banks and ditches impeding surface erosion. Its milieu was the lowlands but there were interlockings with the pastures, the woods, the hills, and the mountains. It was a field system redolent of frontier conditions, of new settlement and colonization. Centuriation was a striking recreation of the natural landscape, one that rivals, probably even excels, the geometric order of the formal garden of France, such as the intricate designs of the parterres at Versailles.[81]

## 9. CONCLUSION

The thinkers of antiquity developed conceptions of the earth as a fit environment for human life and human cultures whose force was still felt in the nineteenth century. The conception of a designed earth was strongest among the Academic and the Stoic philosophers, but even among the Epicureans there could exist a harmony between man and nature, orderly even if not a product of design. Geographically, it was a most important idea: if there were harmonious relationships in nature (granting the necessary but subordinate role of struggle and evil) of which man was a part, the spatial distribution of plants, animals, and man conformed to and gave evidence of this plan; there was a place for everything and everything was in its place. It assumed the adaptation of all forms of life to the arrangements of nature found on the earth.

Furthermore, this conception was hospitable to our two divergent if not contradictory ideas: the influence of the environment on man, and man's ability to change it to his own uses. The first could be accommodated by pointing to evidence of design in the different climates of the earth and the peoples, plants, and animals living in them and adapted to them. So could the second. Man, as the highest being of creation, changes nature—even improves it—through art and invention; his habitats, in Strabo's words, show that art is in partnership with nature. His environments may be those of art— the towns and cities, centuriation, clearings, irrigation works, farming and viticulture—but they are really products of his divinely endowed intelligence; his inventions, tools, and techniques spring from a higher creative source as he improves and brings the pristine earth to a finished state.

[81] John Bradford, *Ancient Landscapes*, pp. 145, 149; on the origins of centuriation, p. 166.

Equally important was the utilitarian bias of these speculations, especially in those thinkers who saw the creation as serving the uses of man, and who, interpreting the past by observation of the present, saw in the usefulness of the grains, of beasts of burden, of the dog, the sheep, and the goat the reasons for their creation. These domestications took place in the past for purposes illustrated by the uses to which they are put in the present. And lastly, if one may speak of ancient thought in modern language, the idea of design was antidiffusionist in character; the idea of a design with all parts well in place and adapted to one another in an all-embracing harmony implied stability and permanence; nature and the human activity within it were a great mosaic, full of life and vigor, conflict and beauty, its harmony persisting among the myriads of individual permutations, an underlying stability.

Since classical times, this conception of a designed earth has been but a part of a wider teleology and a philosophy of final causes, but one should not forget that it is the beauty, the utility, the productivity of nature on earth that, with proper selectivity and avoidance of the harsh and unproductive, provided convincing evidence of purpose in the creation, and in turn a traditional proof for the existence of God. The conception of the earth developed by the classical thinkers and the moderns who followed them was no abstract natural law. It could be enriched with lovely, often poetic, descriptions of nature itself. It owes its force and its influence to its all-embracing character; all ideas could be fitted into it and this hospitality was the reason for its failure: anything that existed, any relationship could be explained as part of the design, if one ignored (as Lucretius refused to do) certain characteristics of the earth as a habitable planet that were hard to explain as products of purpose and design. The Stoic-Epicurean disagreement was strikingly similar to the nineteenth century arguments of the natural theologians such as Paley, Chambers, and many others, with Lyell, Darwin, and their sympathizers.

In the classical period, the history of environmental theories based on physiology and the humors is basically a commentary on the *Airs, Waters, Places* of the Hippocratic corpus. The history of theories based on situation is derived from multiple sources, a result both of the diversity of Mediterranean life and of relief and site in the Mediterranean basin and in less-known peripheral areas. Generalizations emerged from the role of the sea in Greek history, the rise of Rome to become the cosmopolitan capital of an empire, and of the effects of Greek and Roman civilization on the barbarian peoples living adjacent to them. It is noteworthy that in antiquity the criticisms of environmental theories came from those who were impressed by the force of custom and tradition and cultural contact; there were no critics who stressed, as an alternate view, the role of man in changing the environment.

In antiquity, Panaetius, Posidonius, Cicero, and the Hermetical writers came closest to giving philosophical significance to the environmental changes made by man. If the earth was divinely ordered for life, man's mission on earth was to improve it. Such an interpretation found room for triumphs in irrigation, drainage, mining, agriculture, plant breeding. If this interpretation of man serving as a partner of God in overseeing the earth were correct, understanding man's place in nature was not difficult. When, however, unmistakable evidences that undesirable changes in nature were made by man began to accumulate in great volume in the eighteenth and nineteenth centuries, the philosophical and theological underpinnings of the classical, and later of the Christian, idea of stewardship were threatened. For if man cleared forests too rapidly, if he relentlessly killed off wildlife, if torrents and soil erosion followed his clearings, it seemed as if the lord of creation was failing in his appointed task, that he was going a way of his own, capriciously and selfishly defiant of the will of God and of Nature's plan; but castigations of this kind do not appear until the eighteenth and nineteenth centuries, reaching their culmination in Marsh's *Man and Nature*.

The influence of these classical ideas was exerted in part through Christian theology and the writings of the early Church Fathers. Judeo-Christian ideas of the earth, however, must also be considered, for the modern fusion of the two traditions produced concepts of the earth as a habitable planet which served men well into the nineteenth century. The physico-theologists of the seventeenth, eighteenth, and nineteenth centuries looked with respect on the Platonic and Stoic thinkers, but they had a Christian God and their synthesis had the headier ingredients of classical thought, Christian theology, and modern science.

There is a sharp contrast between ancient and modern literature on the modifications of the earth by human agency. If the surviving works from the ancient world are representative, the contrast is a measure not only of the vast increase in the amount and rate of change in modern times, but also of an awareness of change, accumulating in the Middle Ages, advancing rapidly in the seventeenth, eighteenth, and nineteenth centuries, rising to a crescendo in our own times, and for which we are still seeking explanations that rise above description, technical solutions, and naïve faith in science.

# Chapter 4

# God, Man, and Nature
# in Judeo-Christian Theology

### 1. Introduction

Christian thought, like any other which brings into focus numerous ideas from many sources (the ideas of God, of freedom, of nature, and of progress are examples), is not a unified body of thought; it is more like a series of texts which have accumulated numerous exegeses which comment not only on the texts but on other exegeses as well. Attitudes toward man, nature, God, the world (whether we mean the cosmos, the physical earth, or the social milieu) are in this category. Contradictory ideas may grow up; balancings and reconciliations of ideas may be both subtle and fragile. Examples are the problems of physical and moral evil (that is, the tragic consequences to human beings of a catastrophic storm or of cruelty inflicted by one person or another). God is good; he loves the world and his creations. He also saw fit to destroy them. The beauties of the earth are of his making, but man must walk warily among them, for his destiny lies not in this world but in the next world. Nevertheless, God saw to man's creation and to his multiplication, willing that he have dominion over all life on earth.

Man is a created being. So is the earth in which he lives. Much of Christian thought, in so far as it is related to our themes, is concerned with establishing connections between these two creations. The outstanding attempt (antedating Judeo-Christian thought, as we have seen) is the theme of God's care for the world—care for man, his fellow beings, the plants and the animals, the physical earth. God's care for the world can thus be a unifying theme. In this and the following chapters illustrations of this truth will appear.[1]

Apart from its religious importance, perhaps the most significant observation to be made about the account of the creation in Genesis I is that it is brief. Words are used so sparingly in describing the successive acts in the creation of the cosmos that, with the growth of Christianity and the continuing strength of Judaism, an enormous exegetical literature was inevitable. The acts of creation are basically concerned with physical and biological matters, and the ensuing exegesis, whether it is Philo's around the beginning of the Christian Era or a nineteenth century attempt to reconcile scripture with religion, of necessity used materials currently available from botany, zoology, physics, astronomy, sacred and profane history, and even ethnology. There are strong incentives also in this theology toward the love of nature and even toward its study. The intense otherworldliness and rejection of the beauties of nature because they turn men away from the contemplation of God are elaborated upon far more in theological writings than in the Bible itself.

God is the Creator of heaven and earth. Unlike Greek speculation, Genesis I is unconcerned with their origins. Neither is God the artisan-deity of Plato's *Timaeus*, bringing order out of recalcitrant materials. The creation is evidence of the existence of God, but it must not be confused with him. The beauties and the glories of the creation are not to be loved for themselves: they are of God but God is not in them; they may be teachers of mankind, leading it, with the help of the words of God, to the life that is to come after death. God has bestowed strong powers on man, notwithstanding his propensity to evil; man has a divine mission to control the whole creation. To achieve this, it is God's intention that mankind multiply itself, spread out over the earth, make its dominion over the creation secure.

## 2. The Creation, Sin, and Dominion

"In the beginning God created the heavens and the earth. The earth was without form and void, and darkness was upon the face of the deep; and the Spirit of God was moving over the face of the waters."[2]

---

[1] See generally, Rudolf Bultmann, *Primitive Christianity in its Contemporary Setting*, pp. 15–34.

[2] Clarke, *Concise Bible Commentary*: "Hebrew history for the O.T. writers begins with Abraham, the stories in Gen. 1–11 belonging rather to world history as then conceived" (p. 10). See also p. 336: "Yahweh [beginning Gen. 2:4] is a figure very far

In the first chapter of Genesis, "the organization of human life within the pattern *of the week*, the last day of which is a holy day, is . . . presented as purposely ordained by God and reflects the world's first week in which the creative work was accomplished."[3]

Light was created before the sun during the first day, that is, from evening to evening in the Hebrew manner. In the second, He created the firmament, or the heavens, separating the waters above from those below. On the third day, two works were accomplished: the waters were confined and dry land appeared, with its varieties of vegetation. The fourth day saw the creation of the lights of the firmament, one for night, and one for day, to indicate the march of the seasons and the passage of the years. On the fifth day, He created the creatures of the sea and the birds. Finally, on the last day, there were also two works: the creation of the animals and the creation of man.

The living things which God created—sea monsters, fish, birds—were blessed by God. "Be fruitful and multiply, and fill the waters in the seas, and let birds multiply on the earth" (Gen. 1:22). God said to man also, "Be fruitful and multiply, and fill the earth and subdue it; and have dominion over the fish of the sea and over the birds of the air and over every living thing that moves upon the earth" (Gen. 1:28). Seed-yielding plants and fruit trees were provided for animals and for men, since they were vegetarians.

Man, unique and in the center of the creation, is set apart from all other forms of life and matter because God has willed this role for him; he is "the climax of God's work, set here as a steward, responsible to his Creator for all he does with the world over which he is given dominion."[4]

The idea of stewardship has played an interesting role in the history of Christian thought toward other forms of life and even of inanimate nature; in recent years it has often been invoked in pleas for conservation and nature protection, Christian stewardship being closely linked with the responsibility that a temporary sojourner on earth has toward posterity.

Man is made in the image of God (Gen. 1:27) in the sense that "the total being of man bears a likeness to the total being of God. Man alone on this earth has this likeness; the animals do not possess it (though in paganism they did)."[5]

The cosmos and every element in it are continually dependent on God's care

---

removed from the majestic Deity of Gen. 1. Like a potter using clay he makes man out of the dust of the earth." In many of his actions, he "behaves like a magnified man." See also Clarke's commentaries under Gen. 1 to 8, and Frazer, *Folk-lore in the Old Testament*, Vol. I, pp. 3–6, 45–52. See also Bultmann's discussion of the doctrine of creation, *op. cit.*, pp. 15–22.

[3] Wright and Fuller, *The Book of the Acts of God*, p. 50.

[4] *Ibid.*, p. 49.

[5] *Ibid.*, p. 54.

for their survival. "Without God's constant concern, the order of nature would be wiped out in a moment and would revert to the original chaos."[6] It is this belief in God's continuing care which, I believe, is the basis of the famous idea of the *creatio continua*, common in the Middle Ages and in modern times as well, as we see in John Ray's preface to *The Wisdom of God Manifested in the Works of the Creation*. The creation is a continuing process requiring the constant care, activity, and solicitude of God.

Since He is a transcendent creator, evidences of His work are in the creation; it is however limited in what it can reveal because it is only a creation. Much but not all can be known about God through it. "God is the ultimate mystery beyond all things knowable; he is known only because, and in the manner that, he has revealed himself."[7]

In the second creation myth, man's relation to the earth is entirely different. The earth, already in existence, lacks vegetation because there is no rain. The order of creation begins with man (created from dust and made to live by God's breathing in his nostrils), followed by plants (by divine planting in the Garden of Eden), animals (produced out of the earth by God) and woman (from the rib of Adam). Adam was placed in the Garden of Eden "to till it and keep it" (Gen. 2:15). Is there not here a hint that man is a caretaker of nature, that nature may be man's garden? The vocabulary of the myth is that of a peasant farmer; the plants are domesticated and the gardener of Eden tends them, perhaps removing the weeds, but he is a caretaker, not a farmer.[8] The animals are created as helpers of man—the Lord brings them to Adam for naming[9] but they are wanting; Adam must have a helper fit for him alone.

When Eve yielded to the persuasions of the serpent, with irrevocable effects on Adam, Eve, and the serpent, the Lord said to Adam, "cursed is the ground because of you" (Gen. 3:17); henceforth toil will be needed for holding on to life. The story of the Fall became important to the Christian idea of nature because it is the source of the belief, widely held through the seventeenth century, that the fall of man has caused disorder in nature and a decline

[6] *Ibid.*, p. 51.

[7] *Ibid.*, p. 53.

[8] Clarke, *Concise Bible Comm.*, "The story supposes that fruit and edible plants already exist. All man need do is to tend the garden and keep it safe; the toil of the cultivator lies in the future. Truly a peasant's paradise" (p. 342). "Der Mensch soll den Garten bearbeiten und bewachen; zu Grunde liegt diesem Zuge nicht etwa der modern-protestantische Gedanke vom Wert des Berufes und der Arbeit; sondern es ist das naive Ideal eines antiken Bauern, dass die ersten Menschen Gärtner gewesen seien: der Baum trägt seine Früchte, Jahr für Jahr, fast ohne Arbeit des Menschen; der Acker aber muss alljährlich mühsam bestellent werden 3 17ff.; so ist das Ideal des Bauern, Gärtner zu sein und von Baumfrüchten mühelos zu leben; und nun gar Gärtner im Paradiese!" Hermann Gunkel, *Genesis*, p. 10.

[9] "By naming the animals Adam gives them their essential nature." Clarke, *op. cit.*, p. 342. See also Gunkel, *Genesis*, p. 11.

in its powers, an idea clearly distinct from the classical idea of senescence in nature based on the organic analogy.[10] The passage is also important historically because it introduced the idea of toil as a consequence of sin. Many Christian exegetes, however, have held that agriculture was a pleasing activity and not to be associated with sin.

Life becomes hard. Adam and Eve are driven from the garden. In succeeding generations, God regrets the creation of man and is determined to eradicate him, the beasts, and the birds (Gen. 6:7). God spared Noah and the animals which accompanied him, and God told him as they left the ark, "that they may breed abundantly on the earth, and be fruitful and multiply upon the earth" (Gen. 8:17).

### 3. Man in the Order of Nature

When Noah built the altar and made offerings, the Lord said in his heart, "I will never again curse the ground because of man, for the imagination of man's heart is evil from his youth; neither will I ever again destroy every living creature as I have done. While the earth remains, seedtime and harvest, cold and heat, summer and winter, day and night shall not cease" (Gen. 8:21–22). God blesses Noah and his sons, telling them again to be fruitful and to multiply, to fill the earth, that they are to have dominion over all living things. "Every moving thing that lives shall be food for you; and as I gave you the green plants, I give you everything" (Gen. 9:3). God makes a covenant with Noah and his sons, their descendants, and with the creatures that were on the ark. There will be no more floods to destroy the earth (Gen. 9:11). Henceforth mankind and his creatures can expect, despite the evil of the world, an ordered universe without further worldwide catastrophe; man can count on order, regularity, and permanence in nature, and can be assured that the earth will remain the permanent abode of man (Gen. 9:8–17). According to the apocryphal book of Enoch[11] (composed over a period of a century, 165–63 B.C.) the elements of nature actually took the oath of the covenant.

The order of the cosmos and man's place in nature are reaffirmed elsewhere in the Old Testament. "Yahweh is the God of an ordered universe; . . ."[12] he cares for the world which he created for human habitation. "For thus says the Lord, who created the heavens (he is God!), who formed the earth and made it (he established it; he did not create it a chaos, he formed it to be inhabited!). . . ." (Isa. 45:18.)

---

[10] This theme is considered in more detail in the discussion of the Middle Ages. See George Boas, *Essays on Primitivism and Related Ideas in the Middle Ages.*

[11] Robinson, *Inspir. and Rev. in the OT*, p. 10; *I Enoch* lxix, 16ff. See chap. 4, p. 247, note 11, of the Charles trans. On *I Enoch*, see Wright and Fuller, *The Book of the Acts of God*, pp. 234–235.

[12] Stanley Cook, *An Introduction to the Bible*, p. 129.

The theme may be compared to that of Psalm 8 where man, despite his insignificance in a cosmos encompassing the moon and the stars ("What is man that thou art mindful of him, and the son of man that thou dost care for him?") plays an exalted role as an expression and an evidence of God's purpose. "Yet thou hast made him little less than God, and dost crown him with glory and honor. Thou hast given him dominion over the works of thy hands. . . ." (Ps. 8:5, 6.) "The heavens are the Lord's heavens, but the earth he has given to the sons of men" (Ps. 115:16). The theme that man, sinful though he be, occupies a position on earth comparable to that of God in the universe, as a personal possession, a realm of stewardship, has been one of the key ideas in the religious and philosophical thought of Western civilization regarding man's place in nature.

## 4. Earthly Environment

God's power is infinite: "He binds up the waters in his thick clouds. . . . He covers the face of the moon, and spreads over it his cloud. . . . The pillars of heaven tremble, and are astounded at his rebuke. By his power he stilled the sea. . . . By his wind the heavens were made fair. . . ." (Job 26:8–13.) The environmental conditions on earth are God's handiwork. God is an omnipotent weatherman particularly interested in heat, rain, and wind. "Hear this, O Job; stop and consider the wondrous works of God": the "balancings of the clouds," the heat and stillness created by the south wind, and the skies spread out "hard as a molten mirror" (Job 37:14–18; see also 36:24–33). The Lord silences Job in the language of the carpenter and the mason: "Where were you when I laid the foundation of the earth? Tell me, if you have understanding. Who determined its measurements—surely you know! Or who stretched the line upon it? On what were its bases sunk, or who laid its cornerstone? . . ." (Job 38:4–6.) Who set bounds for the sea and said to it, "Thus far shall you come, and no farther, and here shall your proud waves be stayed"? (Job 38:11.) (The attention given to water and to the confinement of the seas—probably owing to arid climates and to the Mediterranean—is very noticeable both in the Bible and in the patristic literature.) The Lord queries Job on his understanding of the order of nature; to really understand, he would have had to witness its planning. ("Have you commanded the morning since your days began, and caused the dawn to know its place? . . .") (Job 38:12.) Does Job comprehend the depths of the sea, the expanse of the earth, the dwelling place of light and of darkness, the storehouses of snow and hail? "Who can number the clouds by wisdom? or [in the language of the desert] who can tilt the waterskins of the heavens, when the dust runs into a mass and the clods cleave fast together?" (Job 38:37–38.)

The Lord asks Job questions about the habits of the mountain goat, why the wild ass ("to whom I have given the steppe for his home, and the salt land for his dwelling place") goes free (Job 39:6), about the faithfulness of the wild ox to man, the habits of the ostrich, the power and usefulness of the horse, the soaring of the hawk, and the nest of the eagle in the rocky crag (Job 39). Further illustrations are given Job of man's weak powers of understanding the creation with descriptions of the life habits of the behemoth and the leviathan.[13]

By this questioning, the Lord instructs Job in the workings of an ordered world in which so many relationships unsuspected by him must be considered. He is speaking of various physical environments: deserts, streams, and mountains, and mountain pastures and the animals which inhabit them, and their breeding habits and means of self-preservation which enable them to continue as a species, despite their preying on one another. The purpose, the forethought, and the wisdom shown in the order of nature on earth transcend the insights of even the most pious, patient, and understanding heart. The Lord explains that nature serves man—even limits him—but nature is not for him alone and its significance does not depend on human wants. "Who has cleft a channel for the torrents of rain, and a way for the thunderbolt, to bring rain on a land where no man is, on the desert in which there is no man; to satisfy the waste and desolate land, and to make the ground put forth grass?" (Job 38:25–27.)[14]

The book of Job shows that the processes of nature may be beyond the comprehension of man; but they are mysteries only to him, for they are the product of a divine and rational purpose. There are similar ideas in Psalm 104, but the message is more cheering and exultant. The cosmos is ordered and beautiful; it is created by God though he is not part of it. "Man is indeed central in the picture, though at first sight he seems to take so small a place."[15] He is central because the "culmination of the Psalm in the praise of God by man" is made by "the one earthy creature in which praise can be articulate."[16]

---

[13] Clarke, *Concise Bible Comm.*, says that the anticlimactic speech of Yahweh in Job 40, 41 may be due to the fact that the second speech of Yahweh may be derived from an Egyptian wisdom book, p. 473; see also p. 474.

[14] "Perhaps the lesson most needed today is that of 38, 26 ["to bring rain on a land where no man is, on the desert in which there is no man"]—while Nature has its influence on man's destiny, this does not exhaust its meaning for God." *Ibid.*, p. 474.

[15] Robinson, *Inspir. and Rev. in the OT*, p. 8. "If the first speech of Yahweh in the Book of Job gives us the fullest Old Testament review of Nature's mysterious details, the best picture of Nature as a going concern is to be gained from Psalm civ. even though this is partly borrowed from the Egyptian 'Hymn to the Sun.' " [On this point, see chap. I, note 6.] "The point of view is here a different one from that of 'Job.' It is not the incomprehensible mystery of these items in the catalogue of Nature that attracts the eye of the psalmist, but the harmonious order which rules them all, through the moon and the sun, so that the night is made for the wild creatures and the day for man." *Ibid.*, pp. 8–9.

[16] "The psalm really illustrates the thought of Isa. xlv:18, which says that God formed the earth that it might be inhabited, and the thought of Psalm viii, which sets man in the supreme place amongst the creatures of God" *Ibid.*, p. 9, footnote 1.

The Lord in his wisdom has created the varied relief of the earth, confined the seas, and has made water easily obtainable for all life. God is a generous, compassionate, and continuous overseer of the natural processes on earth; "the earth is satisfied with the fruit of thy work" (Ps. 104:13). He has seen to it that there are wild plants for the animals, cultivated plants for man, that the birds and the land animals have proper habitats ("the high mountains are for the wild goats; the rocks are a refuge for the badgers" Ps. 104:18), that even the predatory beasts have their prey. "O Lord, how manifold are thy works! In wisdom hast thou made them all" (Ps. 104:24).[17]

It is not to be wondered at that Psalm 104 has been quoted so often by thinkers sympathetic to the design argument and the physico-theological proof for the existence of God. The life, beauty, activity, order, and reasonableness in nature are described without mysteries, joyously—even triumphantly. God is separate from nature but he may be understood in part from it. In the late seventeenth century, John Ray prefaced his famous work, *The Wisdom of God Manifested in the Works of the Creation* with the twenty-fourth verse of Psalm 104; with him and thinkers of similar belief, the praise of God by the discovery of wisdom in his works becomes a bridge between science and religion: praise and love the Lord, and show this love by study and learning, for in this way one obtains knowledge of nature and a deeper understanding of the works of God.

Elsewhere the theme of the majesty of the Lord and his care for man is reiterated, "O Lord, our Lord, how majestic is thy name in all the earth!" (Ps. 8:1.) The Creator has also been solicitous of man, whom He has made little less than God. "Thou hast given him dominion over the works of thy hands; thou hast put all things under his feet . . ." (Ps. 8:6): sheep, oxen, the beasts of the field, the birds, and the life in the sea. This is the most important idea in Christian theology relating to one of our themes, the idea of man as a controller and modifier of his environment. God, the maker of heaven and earth, has given the earth to man to rule over it. His dominion over the animals is exerted in two ways: through domestication and through man's ability to extinguish animal life in order to obtain food or for other purposes.

## 5. ATTITUDES TOWARD NATURE AND THE WISDOM LITERATURE

"The heavens are telling the glory of God; and the firmament proclaims his handiwork" (Ps. 19:1). God is "the hope of all the ends of the earth, and of the farthest seas" (Ps. 65:5): he has created the earth with water, and blessed the growth of plants on the soil. "Thou crownest the year with thy bounty; the tracks of thy chariot drip with fatness. The pastures of the wilderness drip, the hills gird themselves with joy, the meadows clothe themselves with flocks,

---

[17] Compare Ps. 148.

the valleys deck themselves with grain, they shout and sing together for joy" (Ps. 65:11–13). This sublime passage, one of many descriptions of the beauties of nature in the Old Testament and especially in the Psalms, is matched, in its mingling of landscapes made beautiful by nature and by man, only by the beauty of Psalm 104.

Further evidence of a love for and delight in nature and of a belief that it is manifestation of God's handiwork comes from the conception of *wisdom* developed particularly in Proverbs of the Old Testament and in the Wisdom of Solomon and Ecclesiasticus of the apocryphal writings. In this literature, "Wisdom is regarded as a Being dependent on God but in some sense separate from Him."[18] "Wisdom" is human and divine; Yahweh creates wisdom before the creation itself; "Wisdom comes to be a personification, almost a person; it is the artificer of all things."[19] Wisdom is conceived of as a "mediating and quasi-personalized entity."[20] Most writers have seen Hellenistic influences in the wisdom literature; it clearly is not a doctrine of immanence nor is it the Stoic Logos. The most lucid expression of the conception is Wisdom's speech in Proverbs (8:22–31).

> The Lord created me at the beginning of his work, the first of his acts of old. Ages ago I was set up, at the first, before the beginning of the earth. When there were no depths I was brought forth, when there were no springs abounding with water. Before the mountains had been shaped, before the hills, I was brought forth; before he had made the earth with its fields, or the first of the dust of the world. When he established the heavens, I was there, when he drew a circle on the face of the deep, when he made firm the skies above, when he established the fountains of the deep when he assigned to the sea its limit, so that the waters might not transgress his command, when he marked out the foundations of the earth, then I was beside him, like a master workman; and I was daily his delight, rejoicing before him always, rejoicing in his inhabited world and delighting in the sons of men.[21]

In this passage the joy in nature, the joy in human life, the joy in doing things that one does superlatively well, are in startling contrast with the sombre themes of another exemplar of the wisdom literature, the book of Job.

[18] Rankin, *Israel's Wisdom Literature.* For a detailed list of this literature, see pp. 1–2, footnote 1. See especially pp. 1–15; 35–52; 198–210; and chap. IX on "The Figure of Wisdom"; these are the most important discussions for our theme. Quotation is on p. 224.

[19] Cook, *Intro. to the Bible*, p. 68. On Wisdom's being replaced by the Logos in Philo, see *ibid.*; on Hellenistic influence on *The Wisdom of Solomon*, see p. 67. See also Robinson, *op. cit.*, pp. 10–11, and Bultmann, *Primitive Christianity*, pp. 96–97.

[20] Robinson, *Inspir. and Rev. in the OT*, p. 10. "The precise origin of the figure of Wisdom in Hebrew usage is obscure and disputable. Here it must be sufficient to say that its appearance suggests outside influence, possibly Iranian. [Follows Rankin, *Israel's Wisdom Literature*, pp. 228–254.] Its unifying function in regard to Nature is obvious. The world becomes a revelation of the divine wisdom, and Nature is a unity in the sense that it exhibits the wisdom of its divine Creator and Upholder" (p. 11).

[21] This is but part of the hymn to wisdom. See Proverbs 8–9:6. In 9:1–6 Wisdom becomes virtually an omnipotent housewife.

Neither Wisdom nor the Creator is the artisan-deity of Plato, but the Lord here seems like a surveyor and to a lesser extent an architect, Wisdom the highly competent journeyman who sees at a glance what must be done and how to do it. One can almost see the two of them, the master and the respected servant, walking on an equal footing through the fields discussing where to mark the boundaries, where to plant the grains, where to build the houses.

In the Wisdom of Solomon,[22] which may be regarded as an extension of the teachings of Proverbs 8, the Spirit of God fills the world[23] and death is not of God's making; his creation meant that all things should have being. "For he created all things that they might exist, and the generative forces of the world are wholesome. . . ." (1:14.) These verses elaborate the thought of Genesis 1:31, that the creation is good and that the Lord is satisfied with it.[24] Man's knowledge comes from God: our being and words, our understanding, our prudence, our skills, knowledge of the order of the world, the structure of the world and the activity of the elements (7:16–18), the course of the months, of the seasons, the sun, the cycles of the year, the constellations (19–20): "I learned both what is secret and what is manifest, for wisdom, the fashioner of all things, taught me" (7:21–22); she is not only a teacher, she is "a breath of the power of God. . . ." (7:25). "She reaches mightily from one end of the earth to the other, and she orders all things well" (8:1). She is compared to a young love, a bride, she lives with God who loves her and she participates in his craftsmanship (8:2–5). God made the world with his word, and has created man to rule the creation "in holiness and righteousness. . . ." (9:3.) But wisdom is his helpmate. "With thee is wisdom, who knows thy works and was present when thou didst make the world, and who understands what is pleasing in thy sight and what is right according to thy commandments" (9:9). Wisdom watched over Adam and gave him dominion over all else (10:1). God's love of his creation is emphasized (11:25–26). But why cannot man see and know God? Men "were unable from the good things that are seen to know him who exists, nor did they recognize the craftsman while paying heed to his works. . . ." (13:1.)[25] Instead they made gods of fire, wind, stars, turbulent water, the sun, and the moon. Perhaps, delighted with their beauty,

---

[22] According to Clarke, *Concise Bible Comm.*, the text of the Wisdom of Solomon (= the Vulgate Book of Wisdom) points to multiple authorship because it lacks unity; it is based on the teaching of Proverbs 8. Its author has "a considerable, if second-hand, knowledge of Greek philosophy, especially Plato and the Stoics" (p. 646). On this book's influence on New Testament writings, especially Paul's The Epistle to the Romans, p. 647.

[23] Clarke, *op. cit.*, points out the similarity between this idea and the Stoic conception of "the soul of the world" (p. 647).

[24] Clarke's commentary on Wisdom of Solomon, 1:13–16, *op. cit.*, p. 647.

[25] This passage occurs in the long discussion of idolatry. "The heathen failed to appreciate the argument from design, or to deduce from beauty the Author of beauty; the treatment of the subject is thoroughly Greek. Note that 9 contradicts 1." Clarke, commentary on Wis. of Sol., 13:1–9, *ibid.*, pp. 649–650.

men mistook them for gods? (13:2–3.) "For from the greatness and beauty of created things comes a corresponding perception of their Creator" (13:5).

Similar themes, often suggesting Proverbs 8, are also in Ecclesiasticus, or the Wisdom of Jesus the Son of Sirach.[26] The power of man over the whole creation is reasserted as a divine plan for the birth, life-span, and death of man (17:1–3). Wisdom is like a mistress, or perhaps she is only a servant-girl. "Wisdom will praise herself, and will glory in the midst of her people. In the assembly of the Most High she will open her mouth, and in the presence of his host she will glory: 'I came forth from the mouth of the Most High, and covered the earth like a mist' " (24:1–3). Wisdom describes herself and the Lord's care for his creation in the nature imagery of daily life. "I grew tall like a cedar in Lebanon, and like a cypress on the heights of Hermon," or tall as the palm, the rose, the olive, the plane tree. "Like a vine I caused loveliness to bud, and my blossoms became glorious and abundant fruit" (24:13–17). In the imagery of trees, honey, wine, fruit, the harvest, and streams, the beauty and the honor and the riches of wisdom are set forth. Sometimes the metaphors describing the Lord's wisdom in fashioning the geography of the earth as he did are strikingly beautiful, even if the symbol is a commonplace possession of a Mediterranean people: "At his word the waters stood in a heap, and the reservoirs of water at the word of his mouth" (39:17).

The ways of God as a continuing creator, who interferes in the orderly and expected routines of nature and with the physical arrangements on earth when he sees fit to do so, are a boon to the good, a curse to the sinner (39:27). "Fire and hail and famine and pestilence, all these have been created for vengeance; the teeth of wild beasts, the scorpions and vipers, and the sword that punishes the ungodly with destruction. . . ." (39:29–30.)

The theme of natural catastrophes, of purposeful and violent changes in the physical nature of the earth as a punishment for sin—often collective sin—has been a strong one in Christian theology, reaching its climax in the Lisbon earthquake of November 1, 1755, an event which shook this and other Christian beliefs to their foundations.[27]

Anthropocentric interpretations, reminiscent of Xenophon and like those the early Church Fathers will make, explain the courses of the sun and the gentler moon whose changes give man a calendar in the sky (43:1–8); the stars, "a gleaming array in the heights of the Lord" (43:9). All natural phenomena—the winds, snow, frost—are of his doing. "Many things greater than these lie hidden, for we have seen but few of his works" (43:32). Admirable as the creation is, God is not immanent in it; he is a transcendent being. "Who has seen him and can describe him? Or who can extol him as he is?" (43:31.)

---

[26] Ecclesiasticus (Vulgate) is Ecclesiasticus, or The Wisdom of Jesus the Son of Sirach; it was probably written between 200 and 180 B.C. Clarke, p. 651.

[27] This will be discussed in chap. XI. See T. D. Kendrick, *The Lisbon Earthquake*, pp. 113–169.

## 6. ROMANS 1:20

In the New Testament, the interrelationships of God, man, and earth are not always clear; perhaps this lack of clarity is because of the syncretism of the religion.[28] The most important ideas are in Paul's writings, one a *theologia naturalis* in miniature, the other an expression of a vanity and corruption which reached even the creation; both have had a deep influence on the Christian attitude toward nature and, by extension, on the study of natural history.

Paul attributes the sin of man to his failure to see in nature the works of God.[29] "Ever since the creation of the world his invisible nature, namely, his eternal power and deity, has been clearly perceived in the things that have been made" (Rom. 1:20). With some change, this could have been written by a Stoic philosopher; it is also a complement to Psalm 104. Men have no excuse for not knowing or for not honoring God. Neither is there any excuse for idolatry. "Claiming to be wise, they became fools, and exchanged the glory of the immortal God for images resembling mortal man or birds or animals or reptiles" (Rom 1:22–23). It is a theme repeated often in Christian theology: worship the Creator, not the creature. The works of God can be discerned in the creation, but God is transcendent, the creation is by him but not of him, and it is only a partial teacher. One can see His ways in it, but worship is for the Creator alone. There is a parallel thought in the Acts. Paul and Barnabas interfere with the priest of the temple of Zeus who is about to make a sacrifice; they tell the people to turn to the living God, the Creator, adding, "In past generations he allowed all the nations to walk in their own ways; yet he did not leave himself without witness, for he did good and gave you from heaven rains and fruitful seasons, satisfying your hearts with food and gladness" (Acts 14:16–17).[30]

The creativeness of God is contrasted with the lesser talents of man. "For 'the earth is the Lord's, and everything in it' " (I Cor. 10:26). "What then is Apollos? What is Paul? Servants through whom you believed, as the Lord assigned to each. I planted, Apollos watered, but God gave the growth"

---

[28] See Bultmann's chapter, "Primitive Christianity as a Syncretistic Phenomenon," in *Primitive Christianity*, pp. 175–179. "Christian missionary preaching was not only the proclamation of Christ, but, when addressed to a Gentile audience, a preaching of monotheism as well. For this, not only arguments derived from the Old Testament, but the natural theology of Stoicism was pressed into service" (p. 177). See also illustrations, in part discussed here, of syncretism, in the New Testament, pp. 178–179.

[29] Paul prefaces these remarks by acknowledging his obligations to Greeks and barbarians (1:14–15), by asserting the power of the Gospel "to the Jew first and also to the Greek" (1:16), continuing that it is not difficult to know about God: "For what can be known about God is plain to them, because God has shown it to them" (1:19).

[30] A similar thought is in Acts 17:24–25. God does not live in shrines made by man; he is not served by human hands. He is responsible for nations, for their boundaries, "Yet he is not far from each one of us, for 'In him we live and move and have our being' " (17:27–28).

(I Cor. 3:5–6). "For we are fellow workmen for God; you are God's field, God's building" (I Cor. 3:9; cf. 16). "For everything created by God is good, and nothing is to be rejected if it is received with thanksgiving. . . ." (I Tim. 4:4.) God cares for the world and loves it (John 3:16).

Romans 1:20, like Psalm 104, has been an important support not only for the argument from design (the wisdom of God as manifested in the creation) but also in keeping Christian theology on an even keel, avoiding excessive otherworldliness, rejection of this world, and complete estrangement from human society. St. Augustine uses it for this purpose. St. Bonaventura finds the reflection of God in his traces in the sensible world, ending his discussion with the quotation of Romans 1:20, and St. Thomas Aquinas, as we shall see, has a vital interest in showing the goodness, not the corruption, of nature.[31]

### 7.   CONTEMPTUS MUNDI

These are the affirmations of the closeness of the relationship between God, man and nature; they are also, I believe, the dominant ones in the Old and the New Testaments. Nevertheless it is undeniable that there has been in Christian theology, especially in the exegetical literature, a *contemptus mundi*, a rejection literally of the earth as the dwelling place of man, a distaste for, and disinterest in, nature, opposition to a *theologia naturalis*, the belief that one can find in the creation the handiwork of a reasonable, loving, and beneficent creator. Romans 1:20 (quoted with such approval and piety by the scientists of the seventeenth century) was an invitation to a deeper understanding of God and of nature; opposed to it was Romans 5:12–14, which is concerned directly with the condition of man. One man, Adam, brought death into the world through sin; death came to all men because they too sinned. Sin existed before the law, "but sin is not counted where there is no law. Yet death reigned from Adam to Moses, even those whose sins were not like the transgression of Adam, who was a type of the one who was to come" (Rom. 5:13–14). This passage, containing the essence of the doctrine of original sin, is essentially a commentary on Genesis 3:17–18, the other important passage leading to a pessimistic view of man and of nature, in which the Lord addresses the serpent and Eve and Adam, giving punishment to each. The punishments, however, are more than personal; they mark an alteration in nature: "Cursed is the ground because of you" (Gen. 3:17), the Lord says to Adam; now it will exact its toll of him and he will labor against the thorns and the thistles; a product of the earth, he will return to it when he dies.[32]

---

[31] St. Augustine, *On Christian Doctrine*, Bk. I. chap. 4; St. Bonaventura, *The Mind's Road to God*, chap. 2, 11–12; see also *St. Thomas Aquinas. Philosophical Texts*, chap. V, on "Creation."

[32] See Isa. 24:4–6. "The earth mourns and withers"; "it lies polluted"; "a curse devours the earth and its inhabitants suffer for their guilt." In Isa. 11:6 conditions existent in the Garden of Eden are restored.

According to one contemporary view, "the doctrine of the Fall with its sequel, the infection and total corruption of nature," has had a "far-reaching effect in estranging Christendom from an interest in science."[33] Paul's purpose was to demonstrate the greatness of Jesus' coming, because it was a symbol of life and redemption in contrast with sin and death which followed the first Adam. In Romans 5:12–14 "it is by no means certain that the Apostle's language enforces the belief that Adam's sin tainted his posterity." Thus in subsequent theological doctrine, elements that were subordinate and incidental in the writings of St. Paul became of crucial importance in Christianity. Romans 8:18–39 is far more representative of Paul's thinking and of the tradition: the creation "waits with eager longing for the revealing of the sons of God" (Romans 8:19). The fertility of the creation is owing to the will of God. The creation itself may look forward to a glorious millennium free from decay. The creation, "groaning in travail," and man are groping to a higher order and fulfillment. The imperfections, the "groaning," are not because of man's sin: these too are part of God's purpose and interaction. "St. Paul is far too good a theist, far too close a student of the Old Testament, to believe that the imperfection of creation is due to any act of devil or man: only God is in control of His World. Nor because still imperfect is that world deprived of the power to strive and agonize and yearn for that which is to come. With the active assistance of God's indwelling Spirit the creation gropes its way forward in hope."[34]

According to another, the Fall symbolizes man's problem as being one of rebellion against his Creator. "He has used the freedom that God has given him for the purpose of ruling over the earthly creation in order to assert his independence of God and to become like God." He refuses to accept his status as a creature dependent on God, he seeks independence from Him, and equality with Him—and in so doing loses communion between himself and God. "His assertion of independence is actually his separation from the source of all life and all blessing."[35]

## 8. KEY IDEAS AND THE NATURE OF THEIR INFLUENCE

The first chapter of Genesis inspired the hexaemeral literature, brought into being by the bare listing of acts in the six days of the creation. It was started by Philo, cultivated with charm by St. Basil, disseminated by the Latin prose of St. Ambrose, who borrowed much from Basil. Since Genesis 1 left so many questions unanswered, the hexaemeral writings, whether apologetics, exegesis, or homiletics, thus made use of knowledge for religious ends. (The hexaemeral literature continues through the Middle Ages, reaches magnificent expression

---

[33] Raven, *Science and Religion*, p. 34.
[34] *Ibid.*, pp. 35–36.
[35] Wright and Fuller, *The Book of the Acts of God*, pp. 56–57.

in Milton's *Paradise Lost*, and degenerates badly in the nineteenth century reconciliations between Genesis and geological theory, brought to a head by the controversies over historical geology and evolution.) The more literally the writers of hexaemerons interpreted the sequences of the creation, the more the need for evidence from physics and biology. Christian piety, natural curiosity, the desire for reliable exegesis made a more detailed embroidering of the account inevitable; the materials, many physical, biological, and geographical, were organized around the account of the six-day creation, becoming of the highest significance to revealed religion. The hexaemeral literature can be regarded as a vast curiosity and irrelevancy; it is closer to the truth, I think, to see it as a body of commentary which, however faulty, kept alive and before men's minds the idea that the history of the cosmos and thus of the earth had been an eventful one, and that the observation of nature was closely related to an understanding of the creation.

In the somber account of Genesis 1 no value judgments are made of man; his sin, his fall, and the consequences are part of the other story. The first chapter, moreover, gave a Christian setting to the argument of design; the subsequent history of that argument in medieval and modern times shows clearly the components coming from Biblical sources and those from the classical world.

The second chapter of Genesis (apart from its great religious significance) has had an enormous influence on the history of Western man's conception of mankind and of ethnological thought because it introduced questions concerning the nature of Adam as a man, thus inviting comparisons between him and the types of men who were born after the Fall. These comparisons introduced questions—which were widely discussed in the Middle Ages—concerning the nature of cultural primitivism, just as Greek and Roman thought, for different reasons and from different sources, had produced a similar literature. In inspiring the Garden of Eden literature, especially the attempts to locate and describe the Garden, Genesis 2 both influenced geographical speculation and encouraged idealized descriptions of nature—often they are descriptions of Mediterranean-type environments—and some which even point indirectly to environmental influences on man.

The idea, derived from Genesis 3, that the fall of man had also caused a deterioration in nature influenced conceptions of the nature of the earth, at least until the end of the seventeenth century. This deterioration and the toil required after the Fall to induce productivity in the soil were the counterpart in the physical world of evil in the moral world.

This deterioration is not an organic change; it is not a decline in the powers of nature. It is a curse, for to the Hebrews not only persons but objects could be cursed. The curse is not in forcing man henceforth to work—he is created for work—but in forcing him to toil among the thorns and thistles of stubborn and ungenerous fields.[36] Even though there might be imperfections and a niggardliness in nature well suited to the evil propensities of man, this idea conflicted with another: it is God and not human evil that is responsible for the condition of the earth.

Questions concerning the constancy of nature are important and we will meet them again; they are important for the same reason that Lucretius' organic analogy and Columella's objections to it were important, for if the powers of nature are not constant, but decay as an organism decays, men can do little but resign themselves to geographical conditions which, with the passage of time, will only worsen and will inevitably lead to decay and death. The application of the organic analogy to the earth, however, is not characteristic of Judeo-Christian thought, although the idea of senescence in nature appears in II Esdras in which a comparison is made between the young, born from the womb of a young mother, with those of lesser stature when the mother is old. The stature of each succeeding generation will be smaller because each is "born of a creation which already is aging and passing the strength of youth." (II Esdras 5:55. See also 14:10–18.) This passage and the ideas of Lucretius were frequently cited in modern discussions of the constancy of nature.

The writings in the Old and New Testaments and in the Apocrypha are often notable for the beauty and richness of their nature imagery. The similes and other figures of speech might be in the language of the shepherd, the peasant, the artisan, or the farmer doing simple tasks. "I went forth," says Wisdom, "like a canal from a river and like a water channel into a garden. I said, 'I will water my orchard and drench my garden plot'; and lo, my canal became a river, and my river became a sea" (Sirach, 24:30–31).

These descriptions of nature, conspicuous in the Psalms, Job, and Sirach suggest daily life in a rural setting, the highland pasture and the grain field, the orchard, the olive grove, or the irrigation ditch. The Psalms dwell on the beauty of nature, the need to love it as a work of the Creator and to seek him in it. It is not God however that one sees in nature; it is only his works. Subsequent Christian theology is replete with these warnings of the danger of absorption in, contemplation and worship of, His works. The thought is well expressed in the Wisdom of Solomon (in the Apocrypha). Men ignorant of God, witnesses of earthly beauty, do not "recognize the craftsman while paying heed to his works" (13:1). No matter how fervid the natural theology, no matter how deep is the realization of earthly and celestial beauty, there must never be any confusion between the maker and his works. This distinction has been decisive in the Christian attitude toward the earth as a living place for man; too fervid praise for the works of the creation might lead to

---

[36] Gunkel, *Genesis*, p. 22.

neglect of the revealed word or, as in the case of deism, to outright rejection
of Christianity.

Most striking, for our themes, is the idea of the dominion of man as expressed in Genesis, and repeatedly expressed in other writings, notably Psalm
8. But one must not read these passages with modern spectacles, which is easy
to do in an age like ours when "man's control over nature" is a phrase that
comes as easily as a morning greeting. Is this idea of dominion anything more
than a distillation of everyday observation of the techniques involved in the
care of plants—gardening and oasis agriculture, grain growing, horticulture—
the ability to kill the wild and subjugate domestic animals—putting the latter
to work in the tasks of agriculture, herding or transport, or using their bodies
for food or clothing? Is there not here also an assertion of the dignity of man
who, made in the image of God, on His sufferance exercises dominion over
living things on earth comparable in a small way with God's control of the
universe? This power, moreover, is not achieved by, nor is it because of his
abilities; he is lord of the creation because his superior place has been given
him by God. Man's power as a vice-regent of God on earth is part of the
design of the creation and there is in this fully elaborated conception far less
room for arrogance and pride than the bare reading of the words would
suggest.

> Thou hast given him dominion over
> the works of thy hands;
> thou hast put all things under his feet,
> all sheep and oxen,
> and also the beasts of the field,
> the birds of the air, and the fish of the sea,
> whatever passes along the paths of the sea.
>                                     Psalm 8:6–8

The power, though great, is derivative; it is thrust upon man; he has not earned
it.[37]

Genesis also posed important historical questions: how had the world's
population grown; how had the distribution of men throughout the habitable
world taken place and how had conspicuous changes among them occurred?
Noah's three sons, Shem, Ham, Japheth, accompany him off the ark. The
world owes its peopling to them (Gen. 9:18). Then follow the genealogy of
the sons of Noah, the lands they occupied, their occupations and skills; from

---

[37] "According to v. 7, man's power over creation is a kind of ethico-juridical power
from God, perhaps in imitation of God's power over the universe and man. The terminology of the verse reflects clearly the terminology for such a concept, and the context implies that man has this power over all kinds of beings, even those apparently
beyond his control. Especially in Gen. 1 and 2 it is clear that man has the right to use
all things for his own purposes. Man may not be able to enforce this right at all times,
but fundamentally he has it, thanks to God's establishment of man as lord of the earth."
Conrad Louis, *The Theology of Psalm VIII*, p. 93.

these lands "the nations spread abroad on the earth after the flood" (Gen. 10:32). (The uncertainties regarding the aborigines of the New World in the fifteenth century stopped with a papal bull pronouncing these peoples to be human, thus reconciling their presence with the Christian belief in the unity of the human race and its subsequent diffusion.) The biblical tradition is friendly to ideas of cultural diffusion, as the literature on the ten tribes of Israel attests; in modern times, the idea of independent invention based on the psychic unity of mankind has in part been a reaction to the extravagances based on an uncritical acceptance of biblical sources.

The Lord, seeing the city and the tower of Babel, scattered the people over the face of the earth with little thought of furthering intellectual communication. The world before the dispersion had "one language and few words." The story thus explains differences in language and habitat of contemporary peoples.[38] Was this the only plausible means of explaining the cultural diversity of their world, with its many languages and dialects, a world which according to scripture had originally been alike and unified?

Genesis also presented the problem of accounting for the growth in world population from the times of Noah and his sons to the contemporary era. In a typical chronology of sacred history, which was still being published in the nineteenth century, the creation occurred *anno mundi* 1; the birth of Noah in 1056; God's resolve upon the flood and his command to Noah to build the ark in 1535; the embarkation of Noah, his wife, their three sons and their wives, and the animals in 1656, Noah being then 600 years old; the disembarkation in 1657; the construction of the tower of Babel in 1757; the birth of Christ in 4004.[39]

There is nothing in this literature to compare with the classical speculations on the influences of the physical environment. There is the suggestion, however, that man is adapted to nature, dependent upon it, capable also of using it. "Eliphaz promises to an upright Job a covenant with the stones of the field, i.e., the removal of their threat to its fertility, whilst the beasts of the field will be at peace with him."[40] Plowing, harrowing, sowing, threshing, are done properly because the farmer is correctly instructed: "His God teaches him" (Isa. 28:26). The farmer thus carries out the purposes of Yahweh.

The influence of religion thus spreads far beyond ethics, philosophy, and theology; gathering evidence of the existence of God from observing the natural order, it brings geography and ethnology within its purview, often determining the framework within which the great themes of cultural history and human geography have been studied.

---

[38] See also Gunkel, *Genesis*, p. 93.
[39] See *Lavoisne's Complete Genealogical, Historical, Chronological, and Geographical Atlas* (London: 1822), Chronological Maps No. 2 and 7. See also Map 6, *Division of the Earth Among the Posterity of Noah.*
[40] Robinson, *Inspir. and Rev. in the OT*, p. 10; Job 5:23.

The Judeo-Christian conceptions of God and of the order of nature were often combined by the early Church Fathers with both the classical argument of design and the idea of an artisan-deity or demiurge, creating a conception of the habitable world of such force, persuasiveness, and resiliency that it could endure as an acceptable interpretation of life, nature, and the earth to the vast majority of the peoples of the Western world until the sixth decade of the nineteenth century.

In one aspect, at least, that which glorified man and nature rather than denied them, the Judeo-Christian idea of man's dominion over nature emphasized his creativity, his activity, his technical advancement, because these qualities were not of his making but had been placed there by God. He not only had these godlike qualities, he was also close to God. Men were in an equivocal position with regard to the rest of the creation. God had brought it into being but He was not a part of it. Man was made in God's image. He too was not a part of nature in the way that plants and animals were; he was more a steward of God, and if he partook of the lowliness of nature, he also partook of the Godhead from which his stewardship came.

Christianity and the ideas which lay behind it is a religion and a philosophy of creation. It is preoccupied with the Creator, with the things he created and their relationships to him and among themselves. What is more usual than to find among the Church Fathers of the patristic period and the later scholastics long expositions of the nature of the Creator and his creation? This preoccupation inexorably built up its exegesis, great in volume if not in originality, but in so doing, different conceptions of life and of nature were fashioned in the incipient Western civilization. They were not Greek and Roman ideas in Christian dress; on the contrary, except for the environmental theories, the classical ideas now were ancillary to the new synthesis. The new foundations were built on this religion in northwestern Europe, less enmeshed in tradition than was the age-old Mediterranean civilization, in an environment calling for practicality and experiment.

# PART TWO

# The Christian Middle Ages

# Introductory Essay

The Bible was the most studied book of the Middle Ages.[1] Men's views of the nature of the earth as a fit environment were molded by it and by appropriate chapters in classical physics, biology, and theology (much of it in the exegetical literature) which, remaining subordinate to the Bible, could support and strengthen it in those parts where it needed illustration and supplementation. Naturally, the idea of the earth as a habitat planned and designed by God dominated the other two ideas, which, however, were related to it but in a subordinate position—because they were on a lower level of philosophical and theological generalization.

The words "Christian Middle Ages" are used here in a broad sense and as a convenience in characterizing the thought from the patristic period (the first through the sixth centuries) through the Middle Ages to 1500; perhaps this use is permissible despite the acknowledged artificiality of such periodization, especially when different ideas are involved whose course is not the same

[1] Smalley, *The Study of the Bible in the Middle Ages, passim.*

either in strength or in continuity. We are not concerned here with the rich cosmopolitan thought of Muslim, Jew, and Christian in the Muslim Mediterranean world, except when it forced revisions either in knowledge or in method among Christian thinkers, or for occasional excursions such as the discussions of Frederick II's *Art of Falconry*, or Maimonides' *The Guide for the Perplexed*.

The thought of this period, at least with relation to our theme, consists of much more than passive continuities and linkages from the ancient to the modern world, although they are there. In the patristic period and in the so-called Dark Ages, we are in formative periods of Western civilization, which, it need scarcely be said, does not have classical foundations with Christian facades.² The patristic period was particularly vital, for the formulation of new doctrine, exegesis, and the defense of the religion against its classical detractors required thought and energy. Positions had to be taken on the relation of sin to nature and to man, reexaminations had to be made of the problem of evil in nature as well as in man. A new chronology and a new annalistic history were needed, as were a Christian ethnology and a theory on the unity and dispersion of the human race. How revealing in these respects, among others, are the anonymous *Letter to Diognetus*, *The Divine Institutes* of Lactantius, the *Contra Celsum* of Origen, and *The City of God* of St. Augustine!

Later, can one not see revealing episodes in the lives of the Anglo-Saxon missionaries to Germany in the life and correspondence of St. Boniface and in *The Life of St. Sturm* by Eigil, Abbot of Fulda, both dating from the eighth century? An emboldened Christianity growing in strength enforced new views of living nature, of the earth, of man himself, largely but not entirely inspired by Genesis, the Psalms, Job, and Paul's writings. In its very nature Christianity focused on the creator, the created, and that which bound them together.

Interesting additions were made to the idea of man as a modifier of his environment, the result of the slow accumulation of observations, over a wide area of western Europe and for a long period of time, of changes, often embodied in traditions, rights, and usages. There was thus the continuing problem of interpreting nature, of showing its essential goodness, and yet divorcing it from God, even if it was not investigated in a modern sense. The least originality was shown with the environmental ideas, although the applications are not lacking in interest.

These conclusions are not surprising when we consider revisions in the interpretation of the Middle Ages brought about by modern scholarship.

Assaults have been made on the notion of the Dark Ages. Western monasticism has been more closely studied with relation to economic growth. The

---

² See Bark's criticisms of Pirenne's treatment of Boethius and the fathers of the patristic period, *Origins of the Medieval World*, pp. 29–30.

vast field of medieval technology is beginning to be explored. Wider recognition has been given to the area and scope of environmental change whether it be the quarrying of millions of tons of stone for the three-hundred-year period of cathedral building in western Europe or the clearing of tracts of forests and woodland for the village, the arable, the vine. The Middle Ages thus are no longer regarded as an unhappy and sleepy interlude in the millennial march of mankind. Recent discussions concerning the nature of the Renaissance and the origins of modern science have also pointed to the dangers of periodization; there have even been complaints that things have now gone too far the other way, that the creativity of the Middle Ages is being exaggerated at the expense of real breaks with the past which occurred later.[3] One obstacle in the way of an understanding of this period, as far as our themes are concerned, has been the widely held belief, despite learned articles and monographs dating back to the nineteenth century, that the peoples of classical antiquity and of the Middle Ages had neither interest in nor capacity for appreciating nature. Even as late as 1943, it was necessary for Lynn Thorndike—quoting Émile Mâle with approval, "The Middle Ages, so often said to have little love of nature, in point of fact gazed at every blade of grass with reverence"—to say that the notion that the thinkers of the Italian Renaissance introduced the appreciation of natural beauty into modern Europe must be abandoned.[4] Many writers of the late nineteenth and the twentieth centuries had tried to correct the erroneous notion that the love and appreciation of nature in itself and in its relationships to mankind have been discoveries of modern times. In geography, the tendency, in considering the relation of culture to

[3] On revisions of the idea of the Dark Ages, see Bark, *op. cit.*; on monasticism and economics, Raftis, "Western Monasticism and Economic Organization," *Comparative Studies in Society and History*, 3 (1961), pp. 452–469. On the study of medieval technology, White, "Technology and Invention in the Middle Ages," *Speculum*, 15 (1940), pp. 141–159; *Idem*, *Medieval Technology and Social Change*; Singer, *et al.*, eds., *A History of Technology*, Vol. II: Thomson, "The Medieval Artisan," pp. 383–396 and Gille, "Machines," pp. 629–658. On cathedrals see von Simson, *The Gothic Cathedral*, and Gimpel, *The Cathedral Builders*; Bloch, *Les Caractères Originaux de l'Histoire Rurale Française*, new edition with Supplement by Dauvergne, 2 vols. On revisions in attitudes toward the Renaissance and the Middle Ages, see Walter Ferguson, *The Renaissance in Historical Thought*, and latterly, the articles of Durand, Baron, Cassirer, Johnson, Kristeller, Lockwood, and Thorndike in the Symposium on the Renaissance, *JHI* 4, (1943), pp. 1–74. See this bibliography *sub nomine* for the titles of the articles. On the origin of science, see Alexander Koyré, "The Origins of Modern Science: A New Interpretation," *Diogenes*, No. 16 (Winter, 1956), pp. 1–22. Koyré's paper discusses issues raised by A. C. Crombie's study of Robert Grosseteste. See also this author's *Medieval and Early Modern Science*, 2 vols. All of these works have extensive bibliographic references to older literature, Bark's being particularly pertinent to the general statements made here.

[4] Mâle, *Religious Art in France of the Thirteenth Century* (= *The Gothic Image*, Harper Torchbooks, Cathedral Library), p. 53; quoted by Thorndike, *Hist. of Magic and Exp. Sci.*, Vol. 2, pp. 536–537, and in "Renaissance or Prenaissance," *JHI*, 4 (1943), p. 71.

environment, to skip from antiquity to modern times, with cursory consideration for the Middle Ages, left similar gaps in medieval contributions and continuities and minimized the strong influence of theology on geographic theory.

The hexaemeral literature which gave painstaking study to the order of the
creation of animate and inanimate nature was of great importance in the early
period, although hexaemera were written throughout the Middle Ages up
until the nineteenth century. The hexaemeron of St. Basil was the most impressive, that of St. Ambrose, who relied heavily on Basil, the most influential
because he wrote in Latin.

The hexaemeral literature naturally was hospitable to the design argument;
the creation had proceeded in a sequence which brought about an ordered
world. The artisan analogy of the Platonic and Stoic philosophers could be
introduced and reconciled with Christian thought: God's creative acts were
like works of art—not a strange simile to Church Fathers, who had been pagans
themselves, many with a broad knowledge of classical thought. To the Greek,
the universe, like a work of art, had form and matter; Israel, however, "Never
developed its mythology along the lines of the Greek *arché*. The world was
never conceived after the analogy of a work ($\xi\rho\gamma o\nu$ ) or a product of craftsmanship ($\tau\xi\chi\nu\eta$)." The Old Testament "never speculates about the purpose ($\tau\xi\lambda o s$) of creation, or inquires into the rational intelligibility of the
universe."[5] The analogy of the universe with the earth contained in it as a work
of art thus became a Christian acquisition as well; Philo, the Hellenized Jew of
Alexandria, may have introduced this modified conception of the creation into
Judeo-Christian thought.

Neither were ideas of environmental influence lacking in the Middle Ages,
although they seem to have been crowded out by a greater interest in astrology
and astrological ethnology; sometimes, as in Albertus Magnus, there is interest in both. Environmental ideas might be nothing more than straight borrowing from classical thought, or they might be reconciled with Christian theology
as St. Thomas Aquinas reconciled them when he says, in his work on government written for the king of Cyprus, that a ruler in founding a city must consider the value of the site, just as God did in planning for the creation of the
world.

The geographical tradition also was continued in the Middle Ages by many
descriptive but relatively nontheoretical writings, the *de natura locorum* literature, illustrated by the compendium of Isidore of Seville of the eighth century
and by Albert the Great, Vincent of Beauvais, Bernard Silvestre, and Bartholomaeus Anglicus of the thirteenth, and by lay and religious travels, which
kept alive—albeit often in obsolete and crude form—notions of contrasting
environments and the fabulous accounts of little-known places. The *de natura
locorum* literature was almost completely of the compendium type, a gazetteer

---

[5] Bultmann, *Primitive Christianity*, p. 128; quotations on pp. 16, 17. Cf. p. 96.

using as source materials contemporary observations and the geographical accounts of the ancients which were known to the authors.

Lastly, the Middle Ages was a period of extensive environmental change: forest clearance, land drainage, the transformation of primeval-appearing environments by monastic orders such as the Cistercians, and often the reverse process of the return of once-cultivated lands to a wild state. There is a considerable literature on environmental change in the Middle Ages from Merovingian and Carolingian times until the fifteenth century; but the contemporary interpretations of its significance in my experience are few. Those which we have may be prompted by the establishment of settlements and of the replacement of forests with domesticated plants like the vine; they may reflect religious feelings, the gospel of work, or man assisting God, nature, and himself, an outlook characteristic of the monastic orders, at least in the West. Later they hint of the need to control undesirable practices: the heavy pig- and cattle-feeding in the forest, excessive demands of charcoal makers, undesirable grazing habits of domestic animals.

Human activities in classical times and in the Middle Ages, unlike those since the Industrial Revolution, made less dramatic and certainly less striking changes in the physical environment. If a dominant idea existed, it was that man, blessed with the faculty of work, assisted God and himself in the improvement of an earthly home even if the earth were, in Christian theology, only a sojourners' way station.

The most compelling reason for the observation and study of nature, however, was that it led to a greater understanding of God. It was part—but only part—of the proof of the existence of God, of God's plan for a designed world, and of the truth of the Christian religion.

One must be careful, however, in generalizing about such a long and varied period. The early Church Fathers, including St. Augustine, did not, in the apologetics and in their attempts to ward off the pagan attacks, neglect the evidences from nature in order to prove the superiority of the Christian over the pagan religion and the living reality of God's design, just as later thinkers like Albertus Magnus, in their studies of nature and their defenses of Christianity, did not neglect the original works, the commentaries, and the translations of the Muslim civilization. The early Church Fathers, including St. Augustine, eagerly grasped at any evidence of God's plan to be found in the order of nature on earth. Their use of this evidence constituted no superfluous ornamentation and illustration for a doctrine already proven. In the later Middle Ages, however, as Thorndike has pointed out, although nature study was still a part of the general study of God's design, it had achieved also a certain independence and was carried on more for its own sake.

# Chapter 5

# The Earth as a Planned Abode for Man

### 1. The Early Patristic Period

Probably every religious writer of the Middle Ages had something to say regarding the earth as an abode for man because it was so fundamental a topic and because it constantly came up in exegesis, especially of Genesis, the Psalms, and some of the Pauline writings.

During the patristic period, the Church Fathers accepted, with necessary revisions, many ideas concerning the earth which had been held by the classical philosophers. The cosmological, physiological, and physico-theological arguments of the Greek and Roman thinkers used in support of the design argument were adopted by them; these arguments were in fact absorbed by Christian theology.

The *Octavius* of Minucius Felix (*ca.* second century A.D.) is one of the most revealing of these transition documents. He is a Christian who often refers to the pagans as "our ancestors." Classical astronomy and geography, Greek cosmogony beginning with Thales, are put to Christian uses. Epicureanism is rebutted, but there is sympathy for Plato's Timaeus, and the Christian God is cast in the role of a divine artificer.[1] Many Church Fathers accepted the artisan analogy, making here, too, a necessary change by identifying the artisan with the Christian God—a Creator planning his creation with the finished product in mind before his plan is executed. There was, however, a great difference between the everyday artisan using materials which he did not create and the divine artisan who created matter and fashioned it according to his plan. Although the term *physico-theology* is a modern one, this was what these men were creating; they were building up proofs and gathering illustrations of the existence of God from the world of nature observable on earth. The physico-theology of the pre-Augustinian period surpassed in comprehensiveness anything produced in antiquity and was unexcelled until early modern inventions such as the microscope permitted a more thoroughgoing investigation into the evidences of this divine planning even in the hitherto imperceptible aspects of nature. This view did not go unchallenged, however; St. Augustine objected to the literal comparison of God's creativity with man's artisanship. God does not, like an artisan, create with his hands; "working invisibly, [he] effects visible results."[2]

The hexaemeron of St. Basil and the letters of St. Jerome are the most impressive of these works, especially Basil's, which for charm, comprehensiveness, and understanding has not been excelled in its genre, even evoking a tribute from Alexander von Humboldt, who was not overly friendly to pietistic literature.[3] The hexaemeral literature, so widely cultivated in the early part of the Christian Era, linked the short, cryptic sentences of Genesis 1 with the easily observed complexities of the visible creation; the accomplishments of the Creator performed in definite sequence on each of the six days had produced a finished and orderly product—and a permanent one, until the final conflagration should destroy it. Both the order and the permanence of nature in a finite world were established to their satisfaction; for the living creation would last as long as the earth because its permanence was part of the Lord's covenant (Gen. 8:21; esp. 9:8–11). We may illustrate these remarks with examples—not with any pretense at completeness—to show the existence of these attitudes toward the earth, despite the strength of an otherworldly scorn

---

[1] "After his conversion, Tertullian seems to have completely forgotten what reasons he had once had to be a pagan. This is something which Minucius Felix has never forgotten. Among all the Apologists of the second and third centuries, Minucius Felix is the only one who has shown us the two sides of the question." Gilson, *HCPMA*, p. 46. On classical ideas in Christian teleology, see Pease, "Caeli enarrant," *Harvard Theolog. Rev.*, 34 (1941), pp. 103–200.

[2] *City of God*, XII, 23.

[3] Von Humboldt, *Cosmos*, trans, by Otté. Vol. 2, pp. 39–42. Humboldt also tells of his pleasure in reading Minucius Felix and "the delineation (chap. 1) of his twilight rambles on the shore near Ostia . . ." (p. 39.)

for nature. Extensive discussion had already taken place before St. Augustine, in whose works they are brought into sharp focus with a richness of detail.

In the early period, as one would expect, the ties with classical ideas were still close. The early Christian writings were not all vituperative; often in the writings of Tertullian, Lactantius, and Minucius Felix there are friendly comparisons of Christian with classical thought, especially with the works of Plato and of the Stoic philosophers.[4] The design argument, adopted freely from antiquity, was recast in a Christian mold, the beauties of the earth being evidence of a divine harmony and of God's grace.

The transition can be observed in a letter, written about A.D. 96, from the church of Rome to the church of Corinth; its author is believed to be a certain Clement, third Bishop of Rome, according to the episcopal lists of Irenaeus. It was "so highly esteemed in Christian antiquity that for a while it was even reckoned as part of the canon in Egypt and Syria," and Clement of Alexandria cited it as scripture.

"The earth, flowering at His bidding in due seasons, brings forth abundant food for men and beasts and all the living things on its surface, without reluctance and without altering any of His arrangements." The seasons peacefully give way to one another, the winds—without hindrance—perform their functions, and the smallest of living beings live, as the Lord wishes, in peace and harmony—an arrangement that benefits all men, "and more than superabundantly to us who have found refuge in His mercies through our Lord Jesus Christ."[5] The theme that the earth serves all men well but is especially bountiful and instructive to those who have absorbed the teachings of Christ and made them their own is a recurrent one in the history of Christian attitudes toward man and the earth.

In Minucius Felix' dialogue, *Octavius*, reminiscent of Cicero's *De natura deorum*, we see Christian apologists defending themselves against the accusations of the pagans even while attacking their beliefs. The pagan interlocutor, Caecilius, an Epicurean, repeats the Lucretian arguments of a cosmos built up of atoms without divine assistance; these are answered by the Christian Octavius with the familiar replies about the order in the heavens and the erect carriage which enables man to look to heaven. In the oft-performed marriage of theology and utility, darkness and light provide periods for rest and labor, and the order of the heavens assists navigation and tells men when plowing times have come. The sequence of the seasons would be disturbed if it were

[4] *E.g.*, Min. Fel., *Oct.*, 19, 20.
[5] "The Letter of St. Clement to the Corinthians," trans. by Glimm, chap. 20, *The Fathers of the Church. The Apostolic Fathers*, pp. 26–27. The quotation is from Cyril Richardson's intro. to the same epistle in *Early Christian Fathers*, p. 33. Elaborating on Job 38:11, Clement says the sea is gathered into basins, that laws restrain it from overrunning its barriers. The impassable ocean and worlds beyond it are regulated by the same divine law. See also chap. 33. On this extremely interesting and important letter, see Glimm's and Richardson's introductions, and Lietzmann, *The Founding of the Church Universal*, p. 61.

not guided by the highest intelligence. Geographical information, possibly derived from Posidonius, illustrates God's care for the world.

"Neither does God have care alone for the universe as a whole, but also for its parts. Britain is deficient in sunshine, but it is refreshed by the warmth of the sea that flows around it. The river Nile tempers the dryness of Egypt; the Euphrates cultivates Mesopotamia; the river Indus makes up for the want of rains, and is said both to sow and to water the East" (*Oct.* 18).

The utilitarian argument is applied to small portions of the earth's surface; no explanation is given of the need of having bad winters. Perhaps they set off the advantages of spring! Everyday observation of nature and superficial knowledge of a favored environment become the supports of proof. It does not matter if the argument is circular. Nature is assumed to be the result of God's plan; it is also an important proof of it.

Opposite in argument, similar in purpose, is Arnobius' arresting work *The Case Against the Pagans* (*Adversus nationes*). Apparently a new convert, he had little knowledge of the Old or of the New Testaments; he taught that the soul is not necessarily immortal; and he ridiculed in the manner of Lucretius— whom he had clearly read assiduously—the concept of an artisan-deity and the anthropocentric view of the world. No wonder his latest English translator and editor has said that *The Case Against The Pagans* "is in many ways the most remarkable patristic document now extant. . . ." It is thought that he lived during the reign of Diocletian, writing his book shortly before or after A.D. 300. Possibly Lactantius was his pupil, but he does not mention Arnobius in his writings. Nor does St. Augustine, despite his deep interest in the same subject, the refutation of pagan accusations against Christianity; only Jerome tells us anything of him.

Arnobius neither appeals to the authority of the prophets, nor quotes from the New Testament, possibly because he did not know them well, or because his purpose was to impress the pagans with their guilt, not to convert them. A sizeable controversial and inconclusive literature is concerned with Lucretius's influence on him, but there is no doubt that he used many Epicurean arguments even if he was not one himself.

Arnobius rebuts (as did St. Augustine and Hakewill, quoting Arnobius at length, in the seventeenth century) the claim that Christianity is responsible for natural calamities and catastrophic environmental change. The rebuttal appeals to natural law and to the arrangements inherent in nature. There is no reason to believe that Christianity brought about changes in the earth, the sun, the stars, the seasons, the winds, plants, animals, and man—including his reproductive processes—as the pagans alleged. Christians have not altered and could not alter the primordial laws of nature. Nor are Christians responsible for diseases, plagues, crop failures, wars. These have a long history; their occurrence and recurrence can be documented in periods before the times of Christ.

The sustained attack on the anthropocentric interpretation of nature, reminiscent of Lucretius, argues that if the tides, the stars, and natural catastrophes injure human beings, they cannot be regarded as evils. It is the same criticism that Herder made of Voltaire's poem on the Lisbon disaster. [See p. 524.] Such events are in another realm; they are apart from human existence and human values. They are part of nature's plan. A tranquil sky is not wicked because it prevents merchants from sailing the seas [I, 9]. The knowledge of origins and final causes is concealed from man [I, 11].

Sharply critical of the famous argument that because he possesses reason man, creator of the arts and sciences, is superior to the animals, Arnobius replies that the arts are earthly phenomena, not god-given, "These are not the blessings of knowledge but the inventions of paupers—necessity" [II, 17–18]. Like the Epicureans, he is an enemy of artisan-deities. The pagan gods are not artisans or deliverers. Apollo does not bring rain. The pagan gods are latecomers on an earth created by God, who set natural processes in being long before they were born [I, 30]. He ridicules Timaeus; the origins and diversity of things do not come from his mixing in the Platonic bowl. Here it is Timaeus, not the Creator, who does the mixing [II, 52]. Nor are the gods skilled mechanics. Why should they be? [III, 20–21.] He challenges his opponents to explain the causes of hail, raindrops, and other natural phenomena; their previous attempts have all been failures.

Arnobius can use Epicurean arguments against typical ancient conceptions of nature, purpose, artisanry, especially those inspired by the Stoic and Platonic philosophies, because his own philosophy is based on absolute faith in the meaning of Christ's life, and Lucretius can therefore be used to telling effect because it is faith, not knowledge, that is fundamental.[6]

Whether or not he was a pupil of Arnobius, Lactantius (probably late third and early fourth century, for he lived during Diocletian's persecution of the Christians) certainly does not pursue this line of attack. His ideas are like those of Minucius Felix; they are congenial to the Stoic philosophy. Although the luckless Lactantius is most often remembered for the dogged assurance with which he denied the possibility of people living in the antipodes, his writings in fact are marked by a broad humanity, culture, and extensive knowledge of classical thought. With him also the typical utilitarian arguments of antiquity become items in God's plan to outfit man with the abundant productions of the earth.

Lactantius agrees that the Stoics were right in saying that the creation was for man, for man does enjoy the products of the earth, but they failed to ex-

---

[6] I am indebted to McCracken's notes and translation of this work for the discussion of Arnobius. On his date, see pp. 7–12; on A. and Lactantius, pp. 12–15; on A. and Lucretius, pp. 29–30, 37–38; on his knowledge of scripture, pp. 25–26; on Timaeus, note 297, Vol. 1, p. 331. St. Jerome's testimonies on Arnobius are quoted, facing p. 3. See also Gilson, *HCPMA*, pp. 47–49, who says A. "remains an interesting witness to the remarkable progress achieved by the opponents of Christianity in their criticism of the new religion" (p. 47).

plain the reason for God's creating man or the use that Divine Providence would make of him. Lactantius replies that the world was created for man so that he could recognize God in order to honor him. Who but man looks up to heaven, to the sun, the stars, and the whole creation of God? This pagan argument leads to the important conclusion that man's works, his changes in nature, are part of these providential arrangements and that man, through his inventiveness, is making use of the raw materials furnished by God. The utilitarian arguments presuppose that the changes in the earth made by man represent the completion of a task set by God who purposely left his creation unfinished. In his simple thoughts about the utility of fire, heat, trees, springs, rivers, plains, and mountains, no distinction is made between areas which man has changed by using them for agriculture, and wild mountain regions which supply his wood and fuel. The earth is more beautiful than it was at creation: it is a nature, improved by the art of man with divine approval and intention.

Perhaps these attitudes—which one often finds in antiquity, the Middle Ages, and early modern times—arose because of a less firm distinction than there was in the late nineteenth and the twentieth centuries between urban and rural life. In this modern literature the rebellion against civilization does not seem to be directed against its rural enclaves in the countryside but against massive displacements of both by the city. In these earlier centuries—perhaps well into the early Industrial Revolution—nature seems to be what man sees about him, an intermingling of the natural and the cultural.

Lactantius repeats the time-honored praise of the sea for its fish and its trading opportunities, of the moisture-bearing Mediterranean winter, of the final ripening of the fruits in the dry warmth of summer, of the phases of the moon which like a natural calendar tell off the times for summer journeying, campaigns, and field work (quotes Virgil, *Georgics* I.289).

In adopting classical ideas of the utility of the earth to man, Lacantius thus assumed that human art and technology are part of the creation and that changes made by man in the earth are extensions of God's foresight; there is a continuity from the creative act of God to the art of man. Although the opposing tradition that man should not interfere with nature has also been strong (if God had wanted it different he would have done it that way at once), the tradition that man helps the Creator in improving nature also dates from the earliest days of Christian apologetics.[7]

What of the ascetic, otherworldly, and nature-rejecting attitudes of the early Church Fathers? In my opinion, they had two different outlooks, one on the nature of the earthly habitat, another on the nature of the city of God. Each had its own place, although there was no question of the superiority of one to the other. This distinction applies whether the world is thought of symbolically as life, as a vale of tears, as the social environment, or literally as

---

[7] "The Epitome of the Divine Institutes," chaps. 68–69; "A Treatise on the Anger of God," chap. 13. On the antipodes, "The Divine Institutes," Bk. 3, chap. 24, *ANF*, Vol. 7.

the planet whose plants and animals and whose orderly arrangement support human existence.

The anonymous author of the *Letter to Diognetus* spoke of the Christians as dwelling on earth, their homeland being in heaven (Phil. 3:20). Although this text expresses the otherworldliness of Christian society, it also embraces attitudes toward the physical earth; it is man's temporary habitat during life and he cannot be indifferent to it even if his permanent home is in heaven, and even if it is a creation of a lower order.

There are few statements in the early literature to match the acuteness of the following observations from this letter. They seem especially striking to a twentieth century mind sensitive to ideologies and aspirations of minorities. Even if there is a suggestion of self-righteousness, there is also an awareness of the social milieu which makes men alike in one way, different in another. Uniformities of dress, speech, behavior are there; so are the deep, less conspicuous differences.

> For Christians cannot be distinguished from the rest of the human race by country or language or customs. They do not live in cities of their own; they do not use a peculiar form of speech; they do not follow an eccentric manner of life. . . . This doctrine of theirs has not been discovered by the ingenuity or deep thought of inquisitive men, nor do they put forward a merely human teaching, as some people do. Yet, although they live in Greek and barbarian cities alike, as each man's lot has been cast, and follow the customs of the country in clothing and food and other matters of daily living, at the same time they give proof of the remarkable and admittedly extraordinary constitution of their own commonwealth. They live in their own countries, but only as aliens. They have a share in everything as citizens, and endure everything as foreigners. Every foreign land is their fatherland, and yet for them every fatherland is a foreign land. They marry, like everyone else, and they beget children, but they do not cast out their offspring. They share their board with each other, but not their marriage bed. It is true that they are "in the flesh," but they do not live "according to the flesh." They busy themselves on earth, but their citizenship is in heaven.[8]

In his defense of Christianity against accusations that it embraced atheism, cannibalism, and incest, Athenagoras (second century A.D.) says that God, like an artist or a potter, gives beauty and form to matter. We praise the art of the Creator, not the beauty and order He has created; we admire the beauty and splendor of a royal residence but pay homage to the emperor. Emperors, however, make and adorn their palaces for themselves, but God did not make the world as if he were in need of it. The world is like an instrument in tune, but still we worship the creator of the harmony. "I will not beg of matter what it cannot give; I will not pass God by to worship the elements, which can do no more than they are bidden. For even if they are beautiful to behold

---

[8] "Letter to Diognetus," *The Library of Christian Classics. Vol. 1, Early Christian Fathers*, 5–6. On this passage, see Gilson, *HCPMA*, pp. 10–11.

as the work of their maker, yet are they by the nature of matter corruptible." (Quotes Plato, *Politics*, 269D.)[9]

These arguments, reminiscent of Plato and Plotinus, are intended, as is the *Timaeus*, to demonstrate that the creation is a work of love, and not an act performed by God for his own satisfaction. Belief in the unselfishness of God underlies the idea of a beneficent nature, good and motherly toward men, a belief which served them well until they were overawed by the harsh austerities of natural selection and the struggle for existence.

Tatian (born *ca.* A.D. 120), taking his cue from the famed Pauline text, Romans 1:20, writes in a similar spirit. "I refuse to adore that workmanship which He has made for our sakes. The sun and the moon were made for us: how, then can I adore my own servants?"[10]

In these pre-Augustinian writings—and more could be quoted to the same purpose—admiration for the earth (and its beauties) as the habitat of man is restrained, often reluctant; the divinely conceived earth is still *only a creation* and we owe our allegiance to the Creator and not to it.

On the other hand, Irenaeus (born *ca.* A.D. 126) in his attack on Gnosticism forcefully argued for a position which could only lead to neglect of the study of the earth; we cannot even solve the mysteries of nature, let alone those of God. We are ignorant of the Nile's sources, of the tides, of meteorological phenomena like the cause of rain, lightning, and thunder; of the phases of the moon and the homing places of migratory birds. If we know so little about nature, how is it possible to know God? If scriptural explanations are lacking, the phenomena of nature and the knowledge of God will always be imperfectly understood mysteries. Even if we cannot really understand God, said Irenaeus, we know from scripture that the creation was a generous act; God bestowed harmony on all things, assigning them at their creation their proper stations.[11]

## 2. ORIGEN

Few of the early Christian teachers have written as interestingly concerning man, his environment, and Providence as has Origen (185–*ca.* 254). In the *Contra Celsum*, Celsus is a Platonist type of thinker (Origen constantly refers to him as an Epicurean but drops the epithet in the fifth book) who uses pagan arguments to criticize Christian claims and beliefs while Origen replies,

[9] "A Plea Regarding Christians," *The Library of Christian Classics. Vol. 1, Early Christian Fathers*, chaps. 15–16. Quote in chap. 16.

[10] "Address of Tatian to the Greeks," chap. 4, *ANF*, Vol. 2, p. 66.

[11] "Against Heresies," Bk. 2, chap. 2, 4, *ANF*, Vol. 1, p. 361. "Obviously, the immediate purpose of Irenaeus was to destroy the very notion of a *Gnosis* conceived as the integral rationalization of the Christian mysteries, but his insistence on the deficiency of natural knowledge introduced, if not for the first time, at least with a force which was then new, what will remain, up to the time of Montaigne's *Apology for Raymond Sebond*, the favorite theme of a certain type of Christian apologetics." Gilson, *HCPMA*, p. 22.

sometimes strongly, sometimes lamely. To a modern reader the areas of agreement are surprisingly numerous. In this work two of our ideas—of the designed earth and of man as a modifier of his environment—are discussed in a clear and profound manner. Origen was an eloquent advocate of the doctrine of the identity of Providence, the creative spirit of man, and the Logos, a doctrine often smothered in the castigation of sinful man that has been such a dreary and unattractive part of Christian thought.

It is true that Origen expresses this viewpoint too. St. Augustine and St. Thomas Aquinas criticized him for ascribing the diversity of nature to the fall of life from the primeval unity and harmony in which God created it. Judging by the care with which St. Augustine examines it and the incisiveness with which he attacks it, this teaching that the whole creation is in some way a product of a primeval fall was considered—as St. Thomas in the thirteenth century considered it—a threat to fundamental Christian doctrine.[12] Origen's *Peri Archon* (*De Principiis*), however, does not give so uniformly a pessimistic view of nature as St. Thomas implies.[13] What other cause, says Origen,

> are we to imagine for so great a diversity in the world, save the diversity and variety in the movements and declensions of those who fell from the primeval unity and harmony in which they were at first created by God, and who, being driven from that state of goodness, and drawn in various directions by the harassing influence of different motives and desires, have changed, according to their different tendencies, the single and undivided goodness of their nature into minds of various sorts?[14]

The tone of *Contra Celsum* is entirely different. God, Origen says, did not create a wicked nature; men have become evil because of upbringing, perversion, and environment (presumably the social milieu).[15] God can do nothing wrong, the power of wrongdoing contradicting "His divinity and all His divine power."[16] God is an artificer, constructing various forms of life for the benefit of the whole, Origen says, in opposition to Celsus' view that even if the soul is God's work the body is not.[17] Long before St. Augustine rejected the idea of eternal recurrence, Origen wrote that ideas of this kind were incompatible with the belief that the universe is cared for by God "in accordance with the conditions of the free will of each man, and that as far as possible it

---

[12] *City of God*, XI, 23; Aquinas, *ST*, Pt. I, Q. 65, Art. 2.

[13] *De Princ.* Bk. 2, chap. 9, 2 = *ANF*, Vol 4, p. 290; on the meanings of *mundus* and *kosmos*, Bk. 2, chap. 3, 6, p. 273. See also Gilson, *HCPMA*, p. 37, 41–42.

[14] *De Princ.*, Bk. 2, chap. 1, 1, p. 268. Gilson comments that Origen implies that "even beasts have become diversified on account of a primitive 'apostasy,' or voluntary desertion from the divine One," (*HCPMA*, p. 573, note 39).

[15] *Contr. Cels.*, III, 69. On Celsus' philosophy and Origen's attitude toward him, see Chadwick's intro., pp. xxv–xxvi.

[16] *Ibid.*, III, 70.

[17] *Ibid.*, IV, 54.

is always being led on to be better. . . ." The determinism of eternal recurrence denied both free will and improvement.[18]

Celsus said the Christians believe God made all things for man, and Origen replies that

> Celsus, being muddle-headed, did not see that he is also criticizing the Stoic school of philosophers. They quite rightly put man and the rational nature in general above all irrational beings, and say that providence has made everything primarily for the sake of rational nature. Rational beings which are the primary things have the value of children who are born; whereas irrational and inanimate things have that of the afterbirth which is created with the child.[19]

Celsus, "at last displaying his Epicurean views more clearly," says that thunder, lightning, and rain are not made by God (and even if they were, they were not created for the nourishment of man any more than they were for plants, trees, grass, and thorns). Origen replies—traditionally—that the nature we see cannot be explained by mere chance; God has intentionally provided a home for mankind.[20]

The earth and nature do not exist for men for a narrow anthropocentric reason, but because God favors the rational over the irrational. Man obtains these favors and possesses an earthly home because he is rational.

Origen pursues this important theme more vigorously in objecting to Celsus' notions of the providential care of man and wild animals. Celsus, obviously with Lucretius in mind, says, "Though we struggle and persevere we sustain ourselves only with difficulty and toil, whereas for them [i.e., the animals] 'everything grows without sowing and tillage.'" Origen's answer is the classical answer adapted to Christian needs: necessity is the mother of invention; God made rational creatures purposely more needy than the irrational animals to compel men to use their minds and to discover the arts. The answer is really part of a traditional concept of man as being a helper of God, completing and improving the creation.

If obvious criticisms may be made of this conception, at least it preserved the dignity of man; it saw religious value in his mind, his industry, his skills, his inventiveness. It did not deny the world or the importance of man's activities in it.

Celsus asks why we should regard human beings as rulers of the irrational animals. Why could one not argue that men were made for the wild animals to hunt and to eat? Nature has given them weapons to destroy men, who are weaker and who must devise nets and weapons and obtain the cooperation of other men and of dogs to protect themselves. Origen praises human intel-

---

[18] *Ibid.*, V, 21; see also IV, 67.
[19] *Ibid.*, IV, 74.
[20] *Ibid.*, IV, 75.

ligence; it is superior to the strength and physical endowments of the animals. By our intelligence we tame and domesticate animals; we can protect ourselves against those which we do not domesticate and we can use them—as we use the domestic animals—for food. Origen seems to follow Stoic doctrine here.

> The Creator, then, has made everything to serve the rational being and his natural intelligence. And for some purposes we need dogs, for example for guarding flocks or herds of cattle or goats, or as house-dogs; for others we use beasts to carry burdens or baggage. Similarly the species of lions and bears, leopards and boars, and animals of this sort, are said to have been given to us in order to exercise the seeds of courage in us.[21]

Although this passage repeats the trite utilitarian ideas of nature, the existence of the domestic animals is proof of human intelligence and skill and that rational creatures, cooperating with God, give meaning to the creation.

"In reply to what you say [says Celsus], that God gave us the ability to catch the wild beasts and to make use of them, we will say that it is likely that before the existence of cities and arts and the formation of societies of this kind, and before there were weapons and nets, men were captured and eaten by wild beasts and that it was very rare for beasts to be caught by men."[22] To this interpretation that man's rule over the rest of the creation has been contingent upon the development of culture, that it is historical in character and did not exist from the beginning, Origen can think of nothing better to say than to grant for the sake of argument the truth of the thesis and then to add that in the beginning there was more solicitous care for the human race; there were divine voices, oracles, visions of angels.

> And it is probable that at the beginning of the world human nature received more help until men had progressed in intelligence and the other virtues, and in the discovery of the arts, and were able to live independently, not needing those beings who minister to God's will always to be looking after them and caring for them with some miraculous appearance. It follows from this that it is untrue that at the beginning *men were carried off and eaten by wild beasts and that it was very rare for beasts to be caught by men.*[23]

This weak answer, however, does express the interesting idea that the human race had attained its mastery over life with maturity; in the beginning, like an infant in a nursery, it had to be protected until it had developed its powers. Then, like a grown child, not only could it hold its own but later it could achieve the striven-for suzerainty. The child abandoned in the wilds is at the mercy of the wolf; the growing youth, the vigorous man, can kill him easily with a snare or a bow and arrow.

[21] *Ibid.*, IV, 78; see Lucr., V, 218; Chadwick's remarks *Contr. Cels.*, pp. x–xi; and chap. I, secs. 7–8, and chap. III, sec. 7, on Stoic views.
[22] *Ibid.*, IV, 79.
[23] *Ibid.*, IV, 80.

### 3. Philo and the Hexaemeral Literature

The hexaemeral literature, the literature of comment and exegesis on the six-day creation, was an admirable vehicle for bringing the biological, geographical, and physical writings of the pagan world to bear on a central theme in Christian theology, the order of creation of plants, animals, birds, fish, and man.[24] Why was the creation a sequence and not a single act? Was creation in sequence a manifestation of divine orderliness? The answers to the first question were varied but one important answer was that the sequence in creation demonstrated to man at each step the existence of God. The answer to the second was a uniformly affirmative one: the account in Genesis was a description of the activities of an orderly God.

Philo's *On the Creation* is an early—perhaps the earliest—example of such an hexaemeron; in it one can see classical and Hebrew ideas of man and nature being combined almost before one's eyes.[25] Philo emphasizes the need of recognizing God's power as a father and a maker (δυνάμευς ὡς ποιητοῦ καὶ πατρὸς) "and not to assign to the world [κόσμος] a disproportionate majesty." Furthermore, a father and a maker cares for what he has brought into being.[26]

Philo says that God made all things in preparation for man "as for a living being dearest and closest to Himself. . . ." It was God's will that man on coming into the world should live and live well, that he should "find both a banquet and a most sacred display" (συμπόσιον καί θέατρον ἱερώτατον)—the banquet meaning the fruits of the earth for his sustenance, use, and enjoyment, the display meaning the orderly heavens, all sorts of spectacles "circling with most wondrous movements, in an order fitly determined always in accordance with the proportion of numbers and harmony of revolutions."[27]

Man's existence on earth is characterized by a dominion over nature of far-reaching proportions that can be seen in everyday life. (See chap. VII, Sec. 3.) The Creator has so made man that he is at home in all the elements: he lives and moves on land; he can dive, swim, sail, fish; "merchants and ship-masters and fishers for purplefish and oyster-dredgers and fishermen generally are the clearest evidence of what I have said." His erect body allows him to move through the air; and he is heavenly because with the gift of sight he draws near the sun, the moon, the planets, and the fixed stars. Man being composed of the four elements is at one physically with the world, but divine

---

[24] Generally, Robbins, *The Hexaemeral Literature. A Study of the Greek and Latin Commentaries on Genesis*. Robbins shows the strength of this tradition to the time of Milton (see *Paradise Lost*); actually the hexaemeral literature was very much alive in the nineteenth century, when, as Darwin and Lyell discovered, many thinkers were still following in "the footsteps of the Creator day by day."

[25] See Robbins, *op. cit.*, pp. 24–35, in which other Jewish hexaemeral writings are also discussed.

[26] *On the Creation*, 7–10.

[27] *Ibid.*, 77–78.

reason grants him kinship with the first father ("Every man, in respect of his mind, is allied to the divine Reason, having come into being as a copy or fragment or ray of that blessed nature. . . .")[28]

Although the world was created in six days, the Creator did not require this time, for He could do all things simultaneously. "Six days are mentioned because for the things coming into existence there was need of order." Order involves number, and of the numbers six is the most favorable to productivity: it is the first perfect number after one since it is equal to the product of its factors (one, two, three) and their sum; half of it is three, a third, two, a sixth, one. In its nature it is both male and female "and is a result of the distinctive power of either." Male may be considered odd, female even; three is the starting point of the odd numbers and two of the even, their product being six. Since the world is the most perfect of things which have come into existence, it should be constituted in accordance with a perfect number, six; and as the world was "to have in itself beings that sprang from a coupling together, [it] should receive the impress of a mixed number, namely the first in which odd and even were combined, one that should contain the essential principle both of the male that sows and of the female that receives the seed."[29] St. Augustine repeats the same thought: God did not require a protracted time for creation; because six is a perfect number it signifies also the perfection of his works. "And therefore we must not despise the science of numbers, which, in many passages of holy Scripture, is found to be of eminent service to the careful interpreter."[30]

Although we will not follow Philo through every day of the creation, a few examples of his exegesis show the kinds of questions considered by one infatuated with the properties of numbers.

In these creative acts of God, each day receives its share of the whole. The initial acts of the creation are not counted as a "first" day but as "one day" to avoid counting it with the others. What Philo means can be understood from Genesis 1:5: "And there was evening and there was morning, one day." Following the lore of the properties of numbers, "one day" has the nature of a unit. The Creator conceives the models of its parts, then the ideas, then the sensible world.[31]

On the third day it was necessary to control the briny water so that the land would not be barren for crops of trees; dry land is separated from the sea; the earth is put in order and clothed. All plants at the creation are perfect, the fruit ripe, ready for immediate consumption.[32]

Heaven is created on the fourth day. Four is a perfect number; much evi-

---

[28] *Ibid.*, 147, 145–146.
[29] *Ibid.*, 13–14.
[30] *City of God*, XI, 30.
[31] *On the Creation*, 15, 19. (Follows *Timaeus* 29E.)
[32] *Ibid.*, 38–41.

dence is adduced to prove this, the simplest being that it is the base and source of ten the complete number. What ten is actually, four is potentially. If the numbers from one to four are added together, the sum is ten. Further evidences of its importance are the four elements, the four seasons, and that "it was made the starting-point of the creation of heaven and the world." Since this numeral is "deemed worthy of such high privilege in nature" it comes as no surprise that light was created on this day; then man's glances turned upward to the heavens, and man started toward the birth of philosophy.[33]

It is only natural for the animals to be created on the fifth day, there being no kinship so close to animals as this number, as one can see in the five senses.[34]

Man's place in nature is explained by his order in the creation, the most inferior, the fishes, coming first, the most superior, man, being last, those between the two extremes coming in the middle. What is it that sets man off then from the rest of the living creation? It is that man is created after the image and likeness of God; nothing earth-born is more like God than is man; it is in mind, the sovereign element of the soul, not in body, for mind was molded after the archetype, the Mind of the Universe. To an individual, his mind is like a god to him; "for the human mind evidently occupies a position in men precisely answering to that which the great Ruler occupies in all the world."[35] This comes about as close as one can come to finding man's place within Old Testament nature and also to finding his apartness. It is mind which brings about the apartness and it is mind which also brings about the control over other forms of life.

#### 4.  ST. BASIL AND THE HEXAEMERAL LITERATURE

In the following centuries, the important contributions to the development of these ideas were made by St. Basil, St. Ambrose, and St. Augustine. Basil's hexaemeron, written in Greek, was a source for the hexaemeron of Ambrose, which, composed in Latin, was more widely understood in the West. Augustine as a young man was greatly inspired by Ambrose, then Bishop of Milan, and he had also used Basil's hexaemeron in Latin translation.[36] The works of these men reveal some interest in interpreting living nature; if their eyes were on Heaven, there was at least an occasional glance at the earth below. It is not surprising that there should be an intense interest in nature, because any hexaemeron, or any commentary on Genesis, which took the

---

[33] *Ibid.*, 47–53.

[34] *Ibid.*, 62.

[35] *Ibid.*, 69.

[36] Works and bibliography in Gilson, *HCPMA*, pp. 581–582, 589–591. On the literature of the Latin translation of Basil's hexaemeron, p. 582; on Ambrose's interest in moral lessons rather than abstract speculations, p. 589; on Augustine's learning from St. Ambrose, the " 'spiritual meaning' hidden behind the letter of the scripture," p. 590.

six-day creation story literally (Augustine, however, did not)[37] of necessity had to document it with facts and observations taken from plant and animal life and from the general configuration of the land and of the sea.[38]

One must remember also the outlook of educated Christian thinkers of the fourth century A.D. Pagan thought and literature were known to them; many had been converts to Christianity; they bolstered their own religion with whatever could be salvaged from the science, philosophy, and even the religion of the pagans.[39] If in the later Middle Ages it was necessary for Christian theologians to meet the challenge of Muslim thought and the translations, by studying and incorporating the new and the acceptable wherever possible, there was in this early period a similar necessity for the Christian thinkers to show the quality of their thought and to use known facts or supposed facts to demonstrate the superiority of their religion to the best that pagan philosophy and theology could offer.

St. Basil's (*ca.* 331–379) is the most comprehensive of the early hexaemera. His exegesis is expressed in the famous homilies which he prepared for his simple and untutored congregation; they are unencumbered with technical details or abstruse hairsplitting. Their intent is to show the wisdom of the Creator, a wisdom evident in the balance and harmony of nature, in the adaptation of all life—including the special adaptations of man, the highest manifestation of life on earth—to terrestrial conditions.

Like the natural theologies of modern times, the early hexaemera had striking characteristics in common, among them an appalling lack of originality, but the better ones did attempt a synthesis, relying heavily on the biology of Aristotle, the philosophy of Plato, and the nature imagery of Virgil, which would make the creation sequence understandable and believable.[40]

The charm of Basil's hexaemeron is due to the clarity and simplicity of its form: it is a popular, not a technical, treatise, and Basil obviously felt that his congregation would understand his meaning best through the simple, homely, moralizing illustrations which he used.

Basil begins by noting "the good order which reigns in visible things," questioning then the conclusions of Greek science and philosophy, particularly the idea that because bodies are impelled by a circular force they have

[37] *E.g.*, see conveniently his allegorical interpretation of Gen. 1, in *Conf.*, Bk. xiii.

[38] See *inter alia*, the following works in *The Catholic University of America Patristic Studies*: Vol. 1, Jacks, *St. Basil and Greek Literature*; Vol. 29, Diederich, *Vergil in the Works of St. Ambrose*; Vol. 30, Springer, *Nature-Imagery in the Works of St. Ambrose*.

[39] See, for example, Jacks' remarks on the education of St. Basil, *op. cit.*, pp 18–26, and pp. 7–17 on Christian and pagan learning.

[40] On the influence of the *Timaeus* on the hexaemeral literature, see Robbins, *Hex. Lit.*, pp. 2–11. "Plato is accorded respectful treatment, in general, by the Hexaemeral writers. There were, however, certain Platonic assumptions that the church could not accept, especially the theory of the eternity of matter, the doctrine of metempsychosis, which Origen was accused of holding, and the theory that the ideal pattern of creation is independent of God" (p. 11).

no beginning, a clear protest against cyclical ideas applied to broader fields and derived from the analogy of circular motion. The world had a beginning and it will have an end.[41]

The world is not eternal, as the Greeks thought; it has been created. Before this creation an order of things existed, the Creator-demiurge could work in an atmosphere favorable to the exercise of his supernatural powers, permitting him to perfect his works.[42] To this world it was necessary to add a new one, the present world, "both a school and training place where the souls of men should be taught at a home for beings destined to be born and to die." It is in this present world too that the passage of time was created, "for ever pressing on and passing away and never stopping in its course." Mortal creatures are adapted to the nature of time; they grow, or perish "without rest and without certain stability." Existence is compared to being in a current whose motion carries a plant or an animal from life to death. Creatures live in surroundings "whose nature is in accord with beings subject to change." Time and life are transitory, for in time "the past is no more, the future does not exist, and the present escapes before being recognized." The pregnant idea of a time-dominated world being a school for man, later secularized and expanded, suggests the modern theme of the earth as a nursery and as a school for mankind, prominent in the writings of Herder in the eighteenth century, repeated in the geography of Carl Ritter in the early nineteenth, and introduced into America through the lectures of Ritter's Swiss-born pupil, Arnold Guyot, at Princeton in 1849.[43] It is one of the key ideas in the Christian attitude toward the earth before the Darwinian theory of natural selection made nature more brutal than the nature, described by earlier writers, designed for man by a beneficent Creator. Thus, ours is not a chance creation nor is it created without reason, for it has a useful purpose: "since it is really the school where reasonable souls exercise themselves, the training ground where they learn to know God; since by the sight of visible and sensible things, the mind is led, by a hand to the contemplation of invisible things."[44] (Quotes Rom. 1:20.)

The artisan analogy serves the ends of Christian theology too, for creative arts survive the creative act. Basil contrasts them with dancing and music which stop with the end of the performance; but our admiration must be greater for the artisan—the architect, the wood worker, the weaver, the worker in brass—than for his creation. Similarly the world is a work of art from which one learns to know God: it is like a building proclaiming the fame of the architect. The earth is good, useful, beautiful; if the thought here is

---

[41] *Hex.*, Hom. 1, 1–3 (NPN, Vol. 8, pp. 52–53).

[42] Basil follows apparently Origen, *De Princ.*, II, 1, 3. See also Robbins, *Hex. Lit.*, on Basil's use of Plato, Aristotle, Origen, and Philo, pp. 42–44.

[43] *Hex.*, Hom. 1, 5, (NPN, Vol. 8, p. 54). Guyot, *Earth and Man*, pp. 30, 34–35.

[44] *Ibid.*, Hom. 1, 6, p. 55.

not derived directly from the *Timaeus*, it at least owes much indirectly to it. "Being good, He made it a useful work. Being wise, He made it everything that was most useful. Being powerful, He made it very great."[45] The beneficent Christian God has fashioned, not out of caprice or personal necessity but out of His goodness, the powerful, useful, beauteous world of nature we behold.

At its creation the earth was still in need of finishing. Everything was under water; God had yet to adorn his work with the beauties of plant life. Basil compares the unfinished with a finished earth, "for the proper and natural adornment of the earth is its completion: corn waving in the valleys—meadows green with grass and rich with many colored flowers—fertile glades and hilltops shaded by forests."[46]

In the third homily, which is concerned with cosmology and the elements, Basil speaks of the importance of air and water. There are vast quantities of water in the earth because it is necessary to preserve the earth against fire until the final conflagration. In the meantime, fire is necessary to support life with the arts like weaving, shoemaking, architecture, agriculture; heat, a milder form of fire, is continuously needed for the reproduction and survival of animals and fish and for the ripening of fruit. Water and fire thus balance one another; both are indispensable. These ideas are based on the classical doctrine of the four elements. Basil sees the divine plan as he surveys the habitable parts of the earth linked together by the encircling seas: "and irrigated by countless perennial rivers, thanks to the ineffable wisdom of Him Who ordered all to prevent this rival element to fire from being entirely destroyed." Eventually, however, fire will triumph. (Quotes Isa. 44:27.)[47]

Basil has proofs of the fitness of the environment: the changes in the sun's position in the heavens during the year (the solstices are especially noticed) mean that there is no excessive heat in one place, but a temperate climate throughout the habitable world.[48] The thinkers of the pre-Columbian era living in northwest Europe or in the Mediterranean had less difficulty in showing favorable climates to be part of the design than did those following the age of discovery who were confronted with sharper extremes.

Basil, like Ambrose who followed him in this, had a sensitive appreciation of the beauties of the sea. The sea was also useful, because it was the source of the earth's moisture through subterranean conduits or through evaporation of its waters. According to a widely held theory, refuted decisively by Bernard Palissy in the sixteenth century, water from the sea reached subterranean canals and caves and was blown by the wind up through channels

[45] *Ibid.*, Hom. 1, 7, p. 56.

[46] *Ibid.*, Hom. 2, 3, p. 60.

[47] *Ibid.*, Hom. 3, 4–6, pp. 67–69. On ancient science and Basil's and other hexaemera, see Karl Gronau, *Poseidonios und die Jüdisch-Christliche Genesisexegese*. See pp. 77–78 for the classical background of the discussion of water and fire.

[48] *Ibid.*, Hom. 3, 7, pp. 69–70.

in the soil, being purified in the process.[49] The other source of the earth's water suggests a rough form of the hydrologic cycle. The sea receives the waters of the land without overflowing its shores because the sun evaporates the water, the moisture-laden air ultimately returning to land to release its waters to enrich the earth.

Basil, born in Caesarea, had traveled to Constantinople, Athens, and Egypt, and probably knew and loved the Mediterranean and its islands. The island-encircling sea has both beauty and utility.

Commenting on Genesis 1:10 ("And God saw that it was good") Basil says it was not merely its pleasant aspect that God saw; the Creator contemplated his works, not with his eyes but in his ineffable wisdom. "A fair sight is the sea all bright in a settled calm; fair too, when, ruffled by a light breeze of wind, its surface shows tints of purple and azure,—when, instead of lashing with violence the neighboring shores, it seems to kiss them with peaceful caresses." According to Scripture, God does not find the goodness and charm of the sea in its beauty, but in its purposes, for it is the source of moisture, it encircles the islands "forming for them the rampart and the beauty, because it brings together the most distant parts of the earth, and facilitates the inter-communication of mariners."[50] There is none of the distrust of a maritime location as a destroyer of indigenous cultural values expressed, as we have seen, by Cicero and Caesar.

To Basil, the very existence of organic life is one of the best proofs of the essential nature of the earth and of God. The grasses serve both animals and man, but those who worship the sun as the cause of vegetation err, for plant life existed before the creation of the sun.[51] In rejecting pagan belief in the sun as a source of plant growth, Basil denied not only pagan science but the evidences of the senses. The beauty and harmony of nature, as evidenced in plant life, are related to the creative act of God, and it was necessary, as Basil, and later Ambrose, thought, to insist, following Genesis, that plants were growing before the sun was created. The sun is not a creator of the becoming: God's benevolence opens up the earth's bosom, his grace allows it to bring forth its fruits; the sun is younger than the green [Ambrose].[52]

[49] The theory was held in variant forms even to the Renaissance. See Bernard Palissy, *Admirable Discourses* (1580), for the refutation of the idea and evidence that the waters of the earth are derived from rain. Leonardo was far more conventional in this respect.

[50] *Hex.*, Hom. 4, 6, p. 75.

[51] On this interesting and curious subject see Gronau, *op. cit.*, pp. 100–106. Gronau believes Basil used some type of compendium of natural history based on Aristotle or Theophrastus rather than the work of any specific classical writer.

[52] Jacks, *St. Basil and Greek Literature*, pp. 108–109. Plutarch (*De Plac. Philosophorum* V, 910 C) credits Empedocles with the theory that trees, the first living things, existed before the sun and the creation of day and night. Basil says of this: "If they are sure that the earth was adorned before the genesis of the sun, they ought to withdraw their vast admiration for the sun, because they believe most plants and grasses vegetated before it rose" (Jacks' trans.). See *Hex.*, Hom. 5, 1.

*The Earth as a Planned Abode*

There is a strong sense of the partnership of man and nature in Basil's eulogy of the trees which supply food, roofs, ships' timber, and fuel. Even a succession initiated by man is commented upon: "It has been observed that pines cut down, or even submitted to the action of fire, are changed into a forest of oaks." Furthermore, man can remedy (through artificial selection) natural defects of fruits by his own devices, and gardeners have learned to know the sex of the palm and the fig.[53]

Both Basil and Ambrose were interested in animal life; they saw great significance in the ability of animals to live together and in the protective devices they possess which are useful for their survival; each species has its own habitat. In the sea, the smaller fish are the prey of the larger—an opportunity now to moralize on the human propensity to oppress inferiors. Each kind of fish, nevertheless, has its home in the sea assigned to it with equality and justice. How do fish migrate from gulf to gulf toward the North Sea, and how do they know they can cross the Propontis into the Euxine? "Who puts them in marching array? Where is the prince's order?"[54]

In a notable passage, Basil reveals how intense is his interest in finding in nature evidences of the divine. "I want creation to penetrate you with so much admiration that everywhere, wherever you may be, the least plant may bring to you the clear remembrance of the Creator."[55]

It is true that the early Church Fathers, including St. Basil, added little if anything to the store of knowledge regarding the earth; their biology, their geography, their natural history came entirely from pagan sources. Basil's hexaemeron is a compendium of classical science and natural history organized around a Christian principle; it is, in fact, a rich storehouse of ancient science, now in the service of the Christian religion.[56] Basil's physico-theology is the best of its kind until the works of Ray and Derham in the late seventeenth and early eighteenth centuries; these men had, however, the benefits of the heady discoveries which Galileo, Descartes, Newton, and others had heaped upon the student of nature and the servants of God alike.

St. Ambrose shares with St. Basil, from whom he borrowed so much, this strong desire to interpret and appreciate the physical world of nature about him, but his work is more allegorical, and has more moralizing in it. Ambrose also uses the classical writings, especially those of Virgil. His classical education, his early interest in nature, stimulated by the impressions of a trip he made as a boy from Trèves (Trier) on the Moselle to Milan, probably were the sources of this intense love of nature that appears not only in his hexaemeron

---

[53] *Hex.*, Hom. 5, 7. Cf. Ambrose, *Hex.* 3, 13, 53–57, *PL*, Vol. 14, cols. 191–194. For the classical references to caprification, see Gronau, *op. cit.* (n. 47 above), p. 102.

[54] *Hex.*, Hom. 7, 4, p. 92. See also Hom. 7, 1–3.

[55] *Ibid.*, Hom. 3, 2, p. 76.

[56] On Basil's reading and his sources, see Jacks, *op. cit.*, p. 19, and Karl Gronau's exhaustive commentary on Basil's hexaemeron, pp. 7–112.

but in his letters and the hymns.[57] Although nature is described not for its own sake but for its uses in moral and religious teaching, his pleasure is unconcealed, and the pious phrases are suffused with the color, fragrance, and beauty of nature.

In his hexaemeron, Ambrose borrowed so much from Basil that it seems in reading Ambrose one is reading Basil again. Elaborating on the twenty-fourth verse of Psalm 104, Ambrose says the world (*mundus*) is a sign (*specimen*) of divine creation the sight of which leads us to praise the Maker (*operator*). If we interpret "in the beginning" in terms of number (i.e., sequence), heaven and earth were created and then the earth, with its hills, lowlands, and habitable regions, was finished in detail.[58] Like his Christian and classical predecessors, he cannot explain why only certain parts of the earth should be habitable. The actual becomes the ideal; what is desirable to the eye is the mirror of the design.

Ambrose, like Basil (both were influenced by Philo), feels called upon to justify the time taken for the creation when God could have made everything instantaneously. God, however, wishes to bury classical theories once and for all. The creation was spread over six days in order that there would be no mistaken belief that the world is eternal and uncreated and so that by this example man could be induced to imitate Him. In unabashed analogies from the daily life of the artisan, Ambrose says God would have us imitate him, that we first create a thing and then we finish and adorn it, for, had we ideas of doing both at once, we could complete neither. The embroidery comes after the weaving. God created the world first; then he adorned it so that we may know that He who created it was also responsible for its adornment and furnishing. We would not think the creation and the adornment were the work of different hands: one is believed in through the other. This is also the general argument of St. Basil.[59]

Like some of the classical and biblical writers and those of the Old and New Testaments, Ambrose was fascinated with water, his praise of the sea (following Basil) being one of the most frequently quoted of his nature passages. It is benevolent (III, 5, 22): It gives rain to the land; and it is the lodging place of rivers (*hospitium fluviorum*), the source of rain (*fons imbrium*). It is a wall against the dangers of war, a barrier against the barbarian fury. Along its shores are the alluvial soils, deposited by the rivers flowing into it. It is a

[57] On Ambrose's use of classical writers (especially Virgil) whose writings were important in the education of fourth century youth, and his dependence on Plato and Origen in biblical exegesis, see Diederich, *Vergil in the Works of St. Ambrose*, pp. 1–6, a large part of which is devoted to a painstaking comparison of passages in the works of Ambrose with corresponding ones in Virgil. These are mostly from the *Georgics* and the *Aeneid*, less from the *Eclogues*. See also Joh. Niederhuber's introduction to his German translation of the Hexaemeron, *BDK*, Vol. 17.

[58] Ambrose, *Hexaemeron*, 1, 5, 17; 1, 4, 12, in: *PL*, Vol. 14, cols. 139, 141–142.

[59] *Ibid.*, 1, 7, 27, *PL*, cols. 148–149.

source of taxes and a means of livelihood at harvest failure through trade and commerce, and in other ways. In his practical theology, each wave has its use in this transparently utilitarian view of nature.[60]

Ambrose's hexaemeron is less intellectual than is Basil's; there is much more allegory and spiritual interpretation in it, an emphasis which had a marked influence on Augustine, but Ambrose also kept alive and passed on the conception of man as a partner of God in improving the earth. (See pp. 298–299.)[61]

## 5.  St. Augustine

Viewed against the background of these predecessors, Augustine follows along well-trodden paths. What is distinctive in him is the wealth of ideas and the imagination with which they are explored.

His ideas regarding the natural order on earth are not so intimately related to the sequence of creation as were the hexaemeral treatises of St. Basil and St. Ambrose, for Augustine's own hexaemeron *De Genesi ad litteram libri duodecim* is not a literal one and therefore puts less stress on natural phenomena associated with the creation than does St. Basil.[62] Broadly speaking, Augustine's contributions to the conception of nature as observed here on earth are derived from Greek biology and philosophy (especially Plato) and from the Bible and biblical exegesis.

St. Augustine's conception of the relation of God, the Creator, to the creation observable on earth and to man may be summarized as follows: It is God, the Creator, whose workmanship in creating heaven and earth we must constantly adore. The earth and earthly things are to be spurned when we compare them with the greater glories of the City of God, but neither are life on earth and the beauties of nature to be despised because they are on a lower order in the scale of being or because they represent an order inferior to the Divine Order. The earth, life on earth, the beauties of nature, are also creations of God. Man full of sin and prone to sinning is nevertheless a glorious product of God's greatness: man's arts and skills are proof of this, but this greatness does not come from an innate worth in man—it is no occasion for pride—but from the goodness of God who created him. Let us now illustrate these general ideas from the works of St. Augustine.

In the Judeo-Christian doctrine, the distinction between the Creator and the created (even though proofs of the Creator's existence may, to some extent, be obtained from observing the creation) is unequivocal, as it must be: there can never be any question of the inferiority of the natural order, lovely

---

[60] *Ibid.*, 3, 5, 22, *PL*, cols. 177–178. In his German translation of Ambrose's *Hex.*, Niederhuber says the philosopher Secundus replied to Hadrian's question what the ocean was by saying the sea was a "hospitium fluviorum" and a "fons imbrium." (Mullach, *Fragm. phil. Graec.*, I, 518.) *BDK*, Vol. 17, p. 89 note.

[61] Gilson, *HCPMA*, p. 589, note 11. See also p. 55, and Augustine, *Conf.* VI, 4.

[62] Robbins, *Hex. Lit.*, pp. 64–65. See also Augustine, *Conf.* XIII.

as it is, to God. It is a distinction that lies at the root of Christian belief and in the Christian attitude toward nature: one should never become so entranced with the beauties of nature that he mistakes them for anything other than creations like himself. Augustine emphasizes this distinction many places in his work.[63] The distinction does not mean the rejection of natural theology. Augustine in fact has made good use of Romans 1:20.[64] Although one can find in the creation evidences of the creator, they must be correctly interpreted. The strength and the dangers of natural theology are well brought out in his commentary on Psalm 39: "Learn in the creature to love the Creator, and in the work Him who made it. Let not that which was made by Him take hold of thee, so that thou lose Him by Whom thou also wert thyself made."[65] In one of his sermons, he distinguishes between evil in the world of men and the goodness inherent in the order of nature. Evil even plays an important and positive role in teaching man where his interests lie.

> Evils abound in the world in order that the world may not engage our love. Those who have despised the world with all its superficial attractions were great men, faithful saints; we are not able to despise it foul as it is. The world is evil, yea, it is evil, and yet it is loved as though it were good. But what is this evil world? For the sky and the earth and the waters and the things that are in them, the fishes and the birds and the trees are not evil. All these are good; it is evil men who make this evil world.[66]

Augustine is thinking, too, of the pagan religions, of the personification of nature and of the earth. The distinction between the creator and the created rests on the belief that there is one God, and that the phenomena of nature, despite their great variety, are the work of a single artisan, not of many.[67]

In a long exposition and criticism of the lost work of Varro, *Antiquitatum rerum humanarum et divinarum libri XLI* (the last sixteen books dealing with *res divinae*), Augustine protests that the pagan ideas of the gods start with the conception of the earth as the mother of the gods. The earth is no mother; it itself is a work of God.[68] Augustine expresses contempt of and disgust with the effeminate and the emasculated men consecrated to the worship of the Great Mother Earth.[69] All the great works observable on earth—the gift of a

---

[63] I am greatly indebted to Przywara's *An Augustine Synthesis* (cited as Przy.) for many of the references to Augustine. For examples of Augustine's distinction, see "Contra Julianum," IV, 3, 33, *OCSA*, Vol. 31, p. 286, Przy. p. 346; "De Trin.," IX, 7–8, 13, *NPN* 1st Ser. Vol. 3, pp. 130–131, Przy. p. 346; *ibid.*, XV, 4, 6, *NPN*, as cited, p. 202, Przy. pp. 74–75; "Sermones ad Populum," 1st Ser., 158, 7, 7, *OCSA*, Vol. 17, pp. 487–488, Przy. pp. 367–368; "Enarrationes in Psalmos," 39, 7, 8, *OCSA*, Vol. 12, p. 273, Przy. p. 410.

[64] *City of God*, VIII, 10, and *De Trin.* VI, 10, 12, Przy. pp. 141–142.

[65] "Enarrationes in Psalmos," 39, 8, *OCSA*, Vol. 12, p. 273, Przy. p. 410.

[66] "Sermones ad Populum," 1st Ser., 80, 8, *OCSA*, Vol. 16, p. 573, Przy. p. 434.

[67] City of God, VI, 8; VII, 23, 30.

[68] *Ibid.*, VI, 8.

[69] *Ibid.*, VII, 26. Several chapters of the *City of God* are concerned with Varro's lost work: IV, 31; VI, 2–6; VII, 6, 22–26.

rational mind, the ability to reproduce, the course of the moon, to mention only a few of Augustine's examples—are not, as Varro thinks, creations to be distributed among the gods; they are creations of one God. Heaven and earth are filled with His power.

The Creator, whom St. Augustine compares with a shepherd or a husbandman ("ille summus pastor, ille versus agricola")[70] is infinitely superior to what he has made.[71] Following the guidance of Plato and the *Timaeus*, the Creator is also an artificer of infinite skill who is pleased to create, and what He creates is a world of order[72] and it is created out of His goodness, for He is pleased to create. He upbraids Origen for not seeing this and for missing the significance of Genesis 1:31 ("And God saw everything that he had made, and behold, it was very good").[73]

In an important passage, St. Augustine distinguishes between the actual order of nature and the standards of value which human beings place upon it. Living things rank above the lifeless, and among the living, sentient beings like the animals are above the trees, those of the sentient beings that are intelligent, like man, are in turn superior to cattle. And among the intelligent the immortal angels rank above mortal man. These gradations in the order of nature may not be pleasing to men who may prefer forms without sensation to sentient beings.

> And so strong is this preference, that, had we the power, we would abolish the latter from nature altogether, whether in ignorance of the place they hold in nature, or, though we know, sacrificing them to our own convenience. Who, *e.g.*, would not rather have bread in his house than mice, gold than fleas? But there is little to wonder at in this, seeing that even when valued by men themselves (whose nature is certainly of the highest dignity), more is often given for a horse than for a slave, for a jewel than for a maid. Thus the reason of one contemplating nature prompts very different judgments from those dictated by the necessity of the needy, or the desire of the voluptuous; for the former considers what value a thing in itself has in the scale of creation, while necessity considers how it meets its need; reason looks for what the mental light will judge to be true, while pleasure looks for what pleasantly titillates the bodily sense.[74]

In distinguishing between the order in nature and human evaluations of it, Augustine departs from the familiar utilitarian view of nature. In another passage, he is even more forthright in exposing the narrowness of the utilitarian view of nature. The phenomena of nature are to be judged by their own, not by human, standards. "Therefore, it is not with respect to our convenience or discomfort, but with respect to their own nature, that the creatures are glorify-

---

[70] "Sermones ad Populum," 1st Ser., 46, 8, 18, *OSCA* Vol. 16, pp. 264–265, Przy. p. 273.
[71] *De Trin.*, XV, 4, 6; *City of God*, XI, 4.
[72] *City of God*, XI, 4.
[73] See the discussion of Origen, p. 185. *City of God*, XI, 23. On the goodness on earth being the result of the goodness of God, see *De Trin.*, VIII, 3, 4–5, Przy. p. 134.
[74] *City of God*, XI, 16.

ing to their Artificer."[75] Augustine here upholds a tradition that is teleological in character but which is centered upon the excellence and purposiveness of individual creations for their own sakes without regard to their usefulness to man. It is reminiscent of Aristotle's conception of the end of a species being internal to it; a characteristic of one species is not designed for another.[76]

Augustine's distinction between Jerusalem and Babylon, symbolizing the love of God and the love of the world, is helpful in understanding his attitude toward nature. These two cities are separate, but not completely isolated from one another. Neither is Babylon completely useless.[77]

The earth is most certainly not lacking in beauty. In fact, familiarity with its wonders may blunt our perceptions. "But in all the varied movements of the creature what work of God's is not wonderful? And yet these daily wonders have by familiarity become small in our esteem. Nay, how many common objects are trodden underfoot which, if carefully examined, amaze us!"[78] This strong urge to see in the creation the works of the Creator is tempered with the thought that we must see its limitations as a means of understanding God even if its beauties proclaim His existence. And although it is dangerous to quote in support of a thesis scattered passages from a prolific author written at different times in his life and for different purposes, I think we will make no mistake in quoting passages from various sources regarding Augustine's view of nature; the emphasis may vary, but he never lets himself stray far from the idea that nature and the earth are creations of God, that they have beauty, grace, usefulness, that one should never lose oneself in them, worshipping them, and forgetting the Creator and the City of God. "Let us not seek in this (earthly) beauty that which it has not received, for because it has not received that which we seek it is on that account in the lowest place. But for that which it has received let us praise God, since even to this that is lowest He has given also the great good of outward fairness."[79]

Augustine warns that men's love should be directed to God, as if pantheism and the worship of the creation were a constant danger. He himself had come too late to the love of God; he had gone astray by looking at the fairness of the creation. God was with him, he was not with God and the creation had impeded the understanding: "And there made I search for Thee, and in a deformed manner I cast myself upon the things of Thy creation, which yet thou hadst made fair. . . . Those things withheld me from Thee, which yet, if they had not their being in Thee would not be at all."[80]

[75] *Ibid.,* XII, 4; see also chap. 5.
[76] See p. 48 and Ross, *Aristotle,* p. 125.
[77] See *City of God,* XIV, 28, and "Enarrationes in Psalmos," 44, 2; 136, 2, *OCSA,* Vol. 13, pp. 92–94; Vol. 15, pp. 244–245, Przy. p. 267.
[78] "Epistola," 137, 3, 10, *OCSA,* Vol. 5, p. 166, Przy. pp. 50–51.
[79] "Contra Epistolam Manichaei quam vocant Fundamenti liber unus," chap. 41, par. 48, *OCSA,* Vol. 25, p. 476, Przy. p. 1.
[80] *Conf.* X, 27, Przy. p. 75.

The cosmological and physico-theological arguments are used in a variety of moods, some of passionate lyrical beauty, to show how men arrive at a knowledge of God by observing the order and beauty of the visible creation.

> Ask the loveliness of the earth, ask the loveliness of the sea, ask the loveliness of the wide airy spaces, ask the loveliness of the sky, ask the order of the stars, ask the sun making the day light with its beams, ask the moon tempering the darkness of the night that follows, ask the living things which move in the waters, which tarry on the land, which fly in the air; ask the souls that are hidden, the bodies that are perceptive; the visible things which must be governed, the invisible things which govern—ask all these things, and they will all answer thee, Lo, see we are lovely. Their loveliness is their confession. And these lovely but mutable things, who has made them, save Beauty immutable?[81]

Man's place in this creation is consistent with its harmony and order, consistent too with the scale of being, of creatures high and low, that fill up all nature. God determined upon a single parent for man as a warning that with the propagation of the human race, the unity of its growing multitudes should be preserved. The creation of woman from Adam's side signifies how close the ties of man and wife should be: "These works of God do certainly seem extraordinary, because they are the first works." Man's sin and fall did not deprive him of the ability to propagate but his fecundity is now infected with lust. Before the Fall, our parents could obey the injunction to increase and multiply without lust. Lust began after sin. Having children is "part of the glory of marriage, and not of the punishment of sin."[82] St. Augustine attempts, by a rudimentary population theory whose premises are in the Scriptures, to account for the growth of the world's population and for the retention of certain blessings bestowed on the human race despite the miseries it has endured.

It is a creation having the continuing governance of God; if His creations were deprived of His strength they would perish. The actual work of the six days refers only to the creation of natures, not to controlling them; God continues in his governance of the universe.[83]

The most important idea concerning man's relation to the Creator and to the rest of the creation is that men become gods, not by themselves, but "by participation in that one God who is the true God." ("Non enim existendo sunt homines dii, sed fiunt participando illius unius, qui verus est Deus.")[84] Even in the arts and the sciences (like agriculture), divine power governs; man merely helps. "God, who while man plants and waters, Himself giveth the increase."[85] Man is a miracle existing in a visible world that is also a mighty

---

[81] "Sermones ad Populum," 2d series, No. 241, chap. 2, par. 2, *OCSA*, Vol. 18, p. 238, Przy. p. 116.

[82] *City of God*, XII, 27; XIV, 21.

[83] "Epistola," 205, 3, 17, *OCSA*, Vol. 6, pp. 117–118, Przy. pp. 117–118; "De Genesi ad litteram," IV, 12, 22–23, *OCSA*, Vol. 7, pp. 121–122, Przy. pp. 117–118.

[84] "Enarratio in Psalmos," 16th Disc. on Ps. 118, par. 1, *OCSA*, Vol. 14, p. 585, Przy. p. 306.

[85] *De Trin.* III, 5, 11, Przy. pp. 43–44. Cites I Cor. 3:7.

miracle.[86] Man's nature was created as a mean between the angelic and the bestial and in such a way that if he had subjected himself to the Creator, he could have become an angel and achieved immortality without the intervention of death, but if he offended the Creator by the proud use of his free will, he became subject to death and to living as the animals.[87] It is man's mind, not his body, which is in the image of the Creator.[88] There is much evil in man, says Augustine, but his condition "would be lowered if God had not wished to have men supply His word to men."[89] It is man, not nature, that is evil.[90]

Man, a creation of God, is assisted by Him, and often assists Him. It is this relationship which makes St. Augustine so hostile to astrology—which he rejects as being absurd on the face of it and incompatible with man's relation to God. Many of the earlier Church Fathers, seeing in the pagan gods and in astrology a threat to Christian doctrine, were far more critical of astrology than were the thinkers of the late Middle Ages.[91]

The place of man as an active power in nature will be discussed later (see chap. VII). It is sufficient now to mention that his discussion of the miseries and misfortunes inherent in human life is followed by most enthusiastic praise of man and his skills, praise of man as an inventor, a creator, a discoverer, whose talents range widely over the arts, agriculture, the hunt, and navigation. Man still has dignity and greatness, and they have not been engulfed by his sin.[92]

With St. Augustine, the design argument, the scale of being, and the principle of plenitude achieve greater stature than contributions to the hexaemeral and exegetical literature; they constitute a Christian synthesis, a philosophical view of man and nature.

The synthesis grew in importance because the Christian religion grew in importance. It is a parochial, delicate, and audacious synthesis whose polarities offer hard choices: one is the way of physico-theology and of nature study, of appreciation of man and his creative abilities; the other is the way of ascetic otherworldliness, the contempt for nature, the condemnation of man, themes also profoundly affecting the Christian outlook on man and nature in the Middle Ages and in modern times as well.

Augustine did not invent these extremes. They were implied in the Scriptures. They can be seen, however, as plainly in him as in any important early Christian thinker. Who does not feel the other extreme in reading the first few

[86] See *City of God*, X, 12.
[87] *Ibid.*, XII, 21.
[88] "In Joannis Evangelium," Tr. 23, par. 10, *OCSA*, Vol. 9, p. 521, Przy. p. 18.
[89] *On Christ. Doct.*, Prol. 6.
[90] "Sermones ad Populum," 1st ser., No. 80, par. 8, *OCSA*, Vol. 16, p. 573, Przy. p. 434.
[91] St. Augustine, *On Christ. Doct.*, II, 21–22; on the Church Fathers and astrological fatalism, see also Eliade, *Cosmos and History*, pp. 132–133, and the references there cited, and Grant, *Miracle and Natural Law in Graeco-Roman and Early Christian Thought*, pp. 119, 265–266.
[92] *City of God*, XXII.

books of the *Confessions?* Who can resist sympathizing with his father when Augustine writes of him,

> The brambles of lust grew high above my head and there was no one to root them out, certainly not my father. One day at the public baths he saw the signs of active virility coming to life in me and this was enough to make him relish the thought of having grandchildren. He was happy to tell my mother about it, for his happiness was due to the intoxication which causes the world to forget you, its Creator, and to love the things you have created instead of loving you, because the world is drunk with the invisible wine of its own perverted, earthbound will.[93]

There is, I must confess, a difficult problem in selection and quotation. In tracing the history of the idea of a designed earth, pertinent passages emphasizing the importance of nature in Christian theology and illustrating a love of and aesthetic appreciation of it may be quoted or cited more frequently than is warranted by their significance in the literature. Through selection of materials, the thought of some Church Fathers can be presented so that they appear more ascetic and less tolerant, having less love of life, nature, and learning, so that their thought becomes "incompatible with any high valuation of nature."[94] Many expressed both viewpoints; one cannot assume consistency or that contradictions or differences in emphasis will be reconciled.

The idea of a divinely designed earth—beautiful, lovely, and useful because of its order and harmony, made by a benevolent Creator for man endowed with the intelligence and skill to use it—prospered, despite this early obsession with sex, the dreary emphasis on sin, miracles, and marvels, and painful allegorizing, because it had strong support in Scripture, the fundamental passage being Genesis 1:31, and because the Christian religion needed, as the frequent quotation of Romans 1:20 shows, what later was known as the physico-theological proof of the existence of God.

Religious thinkers are the main sources for the thought of this age; they are excellent on theology, but it is less certain that they mirror the true feelings of less literate and articulate people. Newer studies of industry, techniques, and agriculture in the Middle Ages often point to enthusiastic activity and to the survival, perhaps improvement, of many industrial techniques in the so-called Dark Ages.[95]

## 6. THE LEGACY OF THE EARLY EXEGETICAL WRITINGS

Three ideas concerning the earth and nature emerged from the exegesis of the patristic period; they were widely disseminated in the later Middle Ages and important through the seventeenth century. They were rooted in the idea of

---

[93] *Conf.* II, 3, trans. by Pine-Coffin.
[94] On this subject see Raven, *Science and Religion*, pp. 48–49.
[95] See also Bark, *Origins of the Medieval World*, pp. 148, 153. Salin and France-Lanord, *Rhin et Orient, Vol. 2, Le Fer à l'Époque Mérovingienne*, especially pp. 3–5, 235–243.

God as a maker, an artisan, *deus artifex,* and of God being manifest in his works; many times their inspiration was Romans 1:20.

There is a book of Nature which when read along with the book of God, allows men to know and to understand Him and his creation; not only man but nature suffered from the curse after the Fall; one may admire and love the natural beauty of the earth if this love and admiration are associated with the love of God. This idea is similar to the first but it lacks the contrast with revealed religion and the strong dependence on the artisan analogy. It is the view which leads to St. Francis' "The Canticle of Brother Sun."

## Nature as a Book

God is revealed in the Scripture; his works are also visible in the world. The book of nature is contrasted with the Bible, the book of revelation, the former, however, being of a lower order than the latter because God is revealed in His word but only partly so in His works because he is a transcendent God. The book of nature becomes a commentary, further substantiation of the truth of the revealed word. Athanasius, for example, praises the book of creation whose creatures are like letters (ὥσπερ γράμμασί) proclaiming in loud voices to their divine master and creator the harmony and order of things.

Nature conceived of as a book thus often supplemented revelation as a means of knowing God and his creation; but the conception could, as it did with Lull and Sibiude, get out of hand, assuming a strong, independent existence. How early this notion appeared in Christian theology I do not know, but it is already well developed by John Chrysostom (died 407), whose clear, simple, repetitious homilies resemble St. Basil's. Does his ingenious argument arise out of his historical sense, the cultural and lingual diversity, and the economic well-being of the peoples he knows? If God instructs by books, he says, such teaching puts a premium on literacy and wealth. The literate man can read, the wealthy can buy his Bible. What can the poor and illiterate do if they do not have the book of nature? The book also puts a premium on knowledge of the language in which it is written; "but the Scythian, and the Barbarian, and the Indian, and the Egyptian, and all those who were excluded from that language, would have gone away without receiving any instruction." Such things cannot be said of the heavens; all men can read here, at least all men who can see. From this volume in the skies the wise, the unlearned, the poor, the rich, all can learn the same. Quoting Psalms 19:3, he speaks of the universal appeal of the creation "which utters this voice so as to be intelligible to barbarians, and to Greeks, and to all mankind without exception." The same learning can come from contemplating the alternation of day and night, the order of the seasons which "like some virgins dancing in a circle succeed one another with the happiest harmony," the relation of land to the sea, and the balancing of the powers of nature. The sandy shores break up and throw back upon the sea its powerful waves; hot and cold, dry and moist, fire and water, earth and air, are at strife but they do not consume one another; and a similar balancing of the humors takes place in the body. Man was not present at the creation; even if he were he could not have understood. Thus the mode of creation has become the best teacher of man. In early Christianity these arguments would have a powerful appeal to the untutored and to converts of diverse cultural backgrounds, for like Basil's, the homilies have charm and are sprinkled with allusions to the experiences of everyday life.[96] St. Augustine also expresses the idea fully and vigorously: "Some people, in order to discover God, read books. But there is a great book: the very appearance of created things. Look above you! Look below you! Note it; read it. God, whom you want to discover, never wrote that book with ink; instead He set before your eyes the things that He had made. Can you ask for a louder voice than that? Why, heaven and earth shout to you: 'God made me!' "[97]

And in his discourse on Psalm 45, Augustine says that Divine Scripture is the book in which one learns, the universe (*orbis terrarum*) the book in which one sees. No one can read the pages of a book if he does not know the letters, but in the world even the most unlettered can read (*in toto mundo legat et idiota*).[98]

The metaphor is constantly used in subsequent writings. Alan of Lille (twelfth century), author of the *Complaint of Nature*, wrote,

> Omnis mundi creatura
> Quasi liber et pictura
> Nobis est et speculum[99]

The idea of the world or nature as a book "originated in pulpit eloquence, was then adopted by medieval mystico-philosophical speculation, and finally passed into common usage." The metaphor suggests the thought of Paul in Romans 1:20, the text being especially conspicuous in John Chrysostom's homilies; it also suggests that what one sees in nature is a reflection of something else. The expression, as Curtius says, frequently was secularized and was common in the Renaissance and later, but by this time, I think, the mood and the meaning had changed; one read the book of nature not to find out about

[96] Athanasius, "Oratio contra Gentes," 34, *PG*, Vol. 25, 68B–69A. John Chrysostom, "The Homilies on the Statues, or to the People of Antioch," IX, 5–9, *A Library of the Fathers of the Holy Catholic Church*, Vol. 9, pp. 162–170. See also "The Homilies on the Epistle of St. Paul the Apostle to the Romans," III, Ver. 20, *op. cit.*, Vol. 7, p. 36. On his natural theology, see *op. cit.*, Vol. 9, Hom. X, 3–10, pp. 175–185; Hom. XI, 5–13, pp. 192–199. See von Campenhausen, *The Fathers of the Greek Church*; for the background of Chrysostom's famous sermons on the statues, delivered in 387, see the essay on him in this work.

[97] I quote this because of its interest without being able to give the source. Hugh Pope, *St. Augustine of Hippo*, quotes it on p. 227, but the citation of *De Civ. Dei*, Bk. XVI. viii, 1, is not correct.

[98] "In Psalmum 45," *OCSA*, Vol. 12, p. 389.

[99] *PL*, Vol. 210, 579A.

something else but to learn about nature itself.[100] The idea of nature as a book prepared the way for bolder formulations by Ramon Lull and Ramon Sibiude (Raymundus de Sabunde, Raymond Sebond) who saw flaws in the revealed word and its exegesis, laying the groundwork for a natural theology in the later Middle Ages. (See sec. 14.)

## The Effect of Man's Sin and Fall on Nature

The sin and fall of man posed another question: Was there a deterioration in nature corresponding to and coincident with the sin of man? We have already met up with the difficulties the classical authors had in explaining physical evil (predators, earthquakes, and everyday annoyances such as insects, despite the fact that bees and to some extent ants were often much admired). The activities of bees and ants, however—especially the bees—provided rich material for moralizing, for proving God's design even with the most humble beings, and for reading some strict lectures to the human race. If it was hard to find a place for them in the biological order, they were at least respectable and often more reliable, industrious, and dependable than man. They were representatives of a social order inferior to but still comparable with human society. Learn, says John Chrysostom, from irrational animals as we in our families learn from thoughtful children. He applauds the prudence and industry of the ant. The bee's service to man carries its own moral for him because the bee labors for others; less enthusiasm, however, is shown for the self-centered spider. Similar morals are drawn from observations on the habits of the asp, the dog, and the fox.

The thinkers of the Middle Ages, too, had their store of stock answers to explain physical annoyances and evil. Among the most popular were that man in his ignorance does not know the uses of insects, an answer combining humility with irresponsibility; that they were designed to stimulate a more sincere study of the wisdom of God, to inculcate in man moral lessons and virtues; that they were nuisances reminding him of his sinfulness and weaknesses and thus teaching him humility; that the order of nature serves man but is not entirely subject to him, an answer which permitted humility and was less anthropocentric; and that there had been a change in nature corresponding to the new state of human affairs following the fall of man whose existence, though continuing, would be plagued by lust, sin, toil, and evil—and annoyances of insects.

In his commentary on Genesis, Bede asks why God, after the creation but before the Fall, had put the fish, birds, and other animals under man's dominion, for God at first had clearly intended that man would have food derived only from plants. Bede answers that God, foreseeing man's fall, had taken the pre-

---

[100] Curtius, *European Literature and the Latin Middle Ages*, p. 321; see his discussion of the book of nature, pp. 319–326, quoting the passage from Alan of Lille, p. 319.

caution of providing him with his later needs in future sin. Birds and even vicious and poisonous animals had obeyed God's holy servants in the wilderness without harming them.[101]

One of the most interesting examples comes from the early thirteenth century. Alexander Neckam compares the contemporary with the original condition of man, explaining the extent of man's dominion over nature and his partial successes in animal domestication. Both achievements are explained historically.

Contemporary life may be a reminder of the state of man before the Fall. "The very herds and flocks serve to remind him of the glory of his primitive dignity, which he had before the Fall." Man lost his domain over the whole animal creation because he presumptuously insisted on divine prerogatives; this pride and this usurpation were the causes of his being deprived of control over large portions of nature; the Lord, however, in his pity allowed man as a consolation the use of certain animals. The insects—and the poisonous plants— were allowed by the Lord to continue living, in order to remind man of his pride and his deceit. Thus the earth is governed by moral, not biological, causes.

These attempts to explain changes in nature and the earth from its antediluvian condition—which were made all through the Middle Ages and into modern times as well—were essentially attempts to account for obvious disharmonies in nature. On the earth, still beautiful though spoiled by the Fall, the natural order had been brought into harmony with the imperfect moral stature of man. There were on this beautiful earth barren wastes, wild beasts preying upon man and the gentler animals, poisonous snakes and herbs, and annoying insects. The obvious struggles in nature were reconciled with the facts of a revealed religion. One could explain, too, the survival of man despite his sin and fall; he continued to live and to reproduce himself, but under less favorable circumstances than existed before the Fall. Despite the hardships which nature had put in man's way, the human race had multiplied—even prospered to a degree—and had retained sufficient moral stature to comprehend and even haltingly and sinfully to obey the commands of God. And lastly, was it not a way of explaining the enormous cultural significance of animal domestication? God had not deprived man of all control. The gentler animals still were his servants.[102]

[101] John Chrysostom, "The Homilies on the Statues, or to the People of Antioch," XII, 5–6, *A Library of the Fathers of the Holy Catholic Church*, Vol. 9, pp. 204–206. On Bede's hexaemeron, see Robbins, *Hex. Lit.*, pp. 77–83, and Werner, *Beda der Ehrwürdige*, pp. 152–161. According to Bede, before the Fall the earth had no poisonous plants nor anything unhealthful; there was no unfruitful vegetation, no wolf stalking before the sheepfold, no snake had eaten the dust; all animals lived harmoniously, feeding on herbs and tree-fruits. *Hexaemeron*, Bk. 1, PL 91, 32 A–C.

[102] Alexander Neckam, *De naturis rerum*, Bk. 2, ch. 156. (Ed. Th. Wright, London, 1863). Translated in Boas, *Essays on Primitivism and Related Ideas in the Middle Ages*,

## Nature and the Love of God

The consciousness of nature, if not the love of natural beauty for its own sake, finds support in the Bible, in biblical exegesis, particularly in the hexaemeral and the Eden literature during the Middle Ages. What is the meaning of this consciousness of nature? There is a constant striving to see correspondences between natural beauty and biblical texts, and for symbolism, as in the selection of a cloister site shaped like the Greek capital *delta*, Δ, because it symbolized the trinity, to describe paradise as an ideal landscape. It would be wrong to say that such appreciation of nature leads inevitably to science, to an investigation of nature, especially to the interrelationships of biology and human society; it could just as well lead to mysticism, to the nature poetry of the troubadors, to allegory, to the poetic imagery of Dante, to natural religion, magic, and esoteric lore.[103] This literature, ranging from description to allegory, finding both moral lessons and a glorification of life in nature and its relation to the Creator, however, kept alive the notion of the earth as the home of man, even if it were little more than an anteroom to the next world. These nature sentiments—concrete and passionately felt—often are found in the literature on the founding and siting of cloisters. Although many were placed on uninviting land such as swamps and dense forests, sites were often chosen for their beauty: the cloister gardens in the beautifully sited places were considered miniature pictures of the glories of creation.[104] Possibly too the site of the monastery on Mt. Athos (Hagion Oros, ἅγιον ὄρος), on the easternmost arm of the Chalcidice peninsula, inspired the literature on site selection of monasteries.[105] It is true that there was little nature study; rather it was nature observation with a purpose, nature appreciation which became the material for edification, for homilies, moralizing, allegories, and for the praise of God. There are hints, however, of individual tastes, illustrated by the oft-quoted verses,

> Bernardus valles, montes Benedictus amabat
> Oppida Franciscus, claras Ignatius urbes.[106]

---

pp. 83–85. The theme was also thoroughly explored in the seventeenth century. See chap. 8, and Victor Harris, *All Coherence Gone.*

[103] See the wise remarks of Olschki, *Die Literatur der Technik and der angewandten Wissenschaften vom Mittelalter bis zur Renaissance* (Vol. I of *Gesch. d. neusprachlichen wissenschaftlichen Literatur*), esp. footnote 1, pp. 13–15.

[104] See Zöckler, *op. cit.*, Vol. I, pp. 313–315, for an interesting discussion on natural beauty and the founding of cloisters; see also Ganzenmüller, *Das Naturgefühl im Mittelalter*, pp. 98, 149, and the symbolism of the Trinity in selecting cloister sites shaped like the Greek letter *delta*, p. 98. Ganzenmüller and others point out that sites were not intentionally chosen because they were poor or unhealthful.

[105] See Hussey, *The Byzantine World*, pp. 127–128.

[106] Quoted from Wimmer, *Historische Landschaftskunde*, p. 154, footnote 1. I do not know their origin.

There was no need to prove Christ's divinity by contemplating the wonders of the creation—he was revealed in the Scripture—but on the other hand, evidences of God from the order of the heavens and of nature on earth were stronger than human conceptions. The strongest religious personalities of the Middle Ages, Anselm of Canterbury, Petrus Damiani, Bernard of Clairvaux, St. Francis of Assisi, St. Bonaventura, embraced nature not only as a creation of God but as the image of the Eternal.[107]

### 7. CONTINUITIES FROM BOETHIUS TO THE THEOPHANY OF JOHN THE SCOT

With these remarks on the legacy of the exegetical literature, we may now return to our principal theme and show by examples continuities and variations in these ideas from Boethius to John the Scot.

Boethius' (*ca.* 450–524/25) ideas are traditional but they appear in the *Consolation of Philosophy,* an extremely influential literary and philosophical work; in it also is an epitome in twenty-eight verses of the *Timaeus,* as annotated by Chalcidius, who flourished probably at the end of the third or the beginning of the fourth century.[108] Boethius comments on the smallness of the habitable parts of the earth and the vanity of seeking fame when one is confined "to this insignificant area on a tiny earth." Lessons in the need of humility and on the insignificance of man in the cosmos were common in Christian theology long before the Copernican revolution allegedly made man feel alone and lost in the universe.[109] The artisan analogy is there; so is the significance of man's erect carriage and other typical arguments of the physico-theological proof, although Boethius leans to the cosmological.[110]

John the Damascene belongs to the Greek patristic age, but he is well known to the Latin scholastics. Writing in the seventh century, he is cited by St. Thomas Aquinas in the thirteenth. The divine being is incomprehensible to us, he says, but God has not left us in complete ignorance, for nature has implanted the idea of God in us. The order of nature, assumed from theology and the doctrine of the four elements, teaches us that there is a God in control of the opposing forces of fire and water, of earth and air; He has forced them together, and he is responsible for their continuing to operate together amicably.[111]

The most important transmitter of these ideas in the Latin West however, is Isidore of Seville, whose major work, the *Etymologiae,* and the lesser *De*

---

[107] On this point see Ganzenmüller, *op. cit.,* pp. 291–292.

[108] *Cons. of Phil.,* Bk. 3, Poem 9. For summary with references to the literature on Chalcidius, see Gilson, *HCPMA,* pp. 586–587.

[109] *Ibid.,* Bk. 2, Prose and Poem 7.

[110] *Ibid.,* Bk. 4, Prose 6; Bk. 5, Poem 5; Bk. 3, Prose 12.

[111] *Expositio accurata fidei orthodoxae,* I, 1; in II, 11, John describes the temperate climate of paradise. On general ideas see Gilson, *HCPMA,* pp. 91–92, 600.

*rerum natura* were influential sources for those portions of the great encyclopedic works of the later Middle Ages dealing with the properties of things (*de proprietatibus rerum*) by such writers as Alexander Neckam, Robert Grosseteste, Albertus Magnus, Alexander of Hales, Thomas de Cantimpré, Vincent Beauvais, and Bartholomew of England.[112]

Historians of many disciplines have emphasized the role of Isidore of Seville in transmitting classical knowledge to the Latin West in encyclopedic form, Gilson likening the *Etymologiae* in the Middle Ages to the Encyclopaedia Britannica or Larousse in modern times.[113] In both of Isidore's works, one can recognize the doctrine of the elements, the humors, and the threadbare geographical description and theory.

Isidore mentions many times the Christian belief in the beauty of God being manifest in His creation.[114] A chapter in one of his manuals on theology is entitled, "Quod ex creaturae pulchritudine agnoscatur creator." In simple Latin, he instructs his readers in the terminology of classical physics, cosmology, and geography: he tells them that the Greek *kosmos* is the Latin *mundus*, he defines microscosm and the *klimata*; in his discussion of the four elements he mentions that the Greek στοιχεῖα are the equivalents of *elementa*.[115] The *Etymologiae* contain much more: a bestiary; an elaboration of the four-element theory and a discussion of the στοιχεῖα; a gazetteer type of geography, including an interesting chapter on the Mediterranean Sea, with notes on cities, buildings, arable land; Varro's system of land classification and a digest of agricultural practice, with references to Hesiod, Democritus, Mago the Carthaginian, Cato, and Varro. Isidore also copies part of the remarks of Servius the Grammarian, about national characteristics of the Romans, Greeks, Africans, and Gauls, thus incorporating in his influential work ideas of environmental influence which were repeated by other encyclopedists later in the Middle Ages.[116]

The Irish-born John the Scot or Johannes Scotus Erigena (*Eriu, Hibernia, Scottia* were the main ancient names for Ireland), a learned man—possibly a clerk, possibly a monk—at the court of Charles the Bald, was acquainted, unlike most Western scholars, with Greek literature and could read the Greek language; it is now believed, however, that these were continental acquisitions, and that he arrived in Gaul from Ireland with only a rudimentary knowledge of Greek.

His *De divisione naturae* is of interest to us because it is preoccupied with the idea of nature and with the related concepts of creator and creature. The

---

[112] On this literature, see Delisle, "Traités Divers sur les Propriétés des Choses," *Hist. Litt. de la France*, Vol. 30, pp. 354–365.

[113] Gilson, *HCPMA*, p. 107.

[114] E.g., *Sententiarum libri tres.*, Bk. I, chap. 4.

[115] *De natura rerum*, chap. 9.

[116] Isidore, "Etym.," *PL*, Vol. 82. Bestiary, Bk. XII; the elements, Bk. XIII, chap. 3, 2; geography, Bk. XIV; Varro, Bk XV, chap. 13, 6; Servius, Bk. IX, 2.

key to the meaning of the sensible world he finds in the Greek word *theo-phania*. By the divine being, he says, we do not mean God alone, for Holy Scripture often designates as God what is really his manner of being, which in turn is revealed to thinking and rational creatures in proportion to their power of grasping it. This way of being the Greeks call a theophany, an apparition of God (*dei apparitio*). Take as an example, he says, the expression, "I saw God sitting" (*Vidi Dominum sedentem*); by this one does not mean that he has seen the being of God Himself, but something created by Him (*cum non ipsius essentiam, sed aliquid ab eo factum viderit*).[117] God even creates Himself in the sense that he reveals himself, that his work is a theophany.

*De divisione naturae* is presented as a dialogue between teacher and pupil, and the latter is always accommodatingly moving the furniture around for the next scene. The universe, like the Holy Scripture, is a revelation. The teacher asks the pupil to consider whether spatial and temporal recurrences observable in parts of the sensible world are without their secrets or not (*vacant quodam mysterio, necne*). The cooperative pupil replies that he will not lightly assert they are so bereft, for there is nothing in the visible phenomena of the corporeal world which does not also signify something incorporeal and spiritual. The pupil then asks the master for a short discussion of these recurrences, and as always happens in such dialogues, the well-prepared master readily replies.

His illustrations reveal the strong impression which cyclical processes have made on him. To those who contemplate the nature of things with both spiritual insight and the judgment of the senses (*animi conceptione et corporalis sensus judicio*), it is clearer than light itself that this recurrence takes place in the heavens, the continually moving spheres returning always in their courses to their point of origin. The sun and moon are examples; none need be given of other planets, for such knowledge is known to all who know astronomy (*astrologia*).

The cyclical nature of things, their periodic return to former positions or states, is also revealed in terrestrial phenomena. What of air? Does it not at definite times return to the same states of cold, heat, and the temperate? (Possibly he means here diurnal or seasonal march of temperature.) What of the sea? Does it not absolutely follow the course of the moon? What of animals of the land and sea? What of plants and grasses? Do they not also have their times for bursting forth into buds, flowers, leaves, fruits? This growth too is cyclical, the end of the movement is the beginning, the beginning the end. Thus cyclical regularities in the heavens and the organic cycle on earth, so frequently used as analogies in Greek thought, are adduced as evidence of law, harmony, order, and divine revelation in nature.[118]

---

[117] Cappuyns, *Jean Scot Érigène*, pp. 7–8, 13–14, 28; on his profession, pp. 66–67; on God creating himself, p. 346. *De div. nat.*, I, 7, *PL*, Vol. 122, 446D.
[118] *De div. nat.*, V, 3, 866A–D. See Burch, *Early Med. Philos.*, p. 9.

In describing God as the cause of goodness, he again resorts to cyclical or supposed cyclical phenomena. Let us take, he says, our examples from nature. This goodness is compared to a river which, rising at its source, flows in its bed ever downward uninterruptedly to the sea. In the same way divine goodness, being, life, wisdom—everything which is in the primordial source of all— flows downward like a stream, first into the primordial causes, bringing them into being. Next, continuing downward through these primordial causes, ineffable in their workings, but still in harmony with them, they flow from higher to lower, finally reaching the lowest ranks of the All. The return flow is through the most secret pores of nature by a most concealed path to the source.

The highest, the supreme good, thus bestows existence on the first order of being, which in turn shares it with the next lower one, the division of being continuing downward by this sharing (*participatio*) to the lowest order of being. *Participatio*, he says, is nothing other than the derivation of existence by one order from the one next higher in the scale. In this hierarchy of being all orders do not have life in themselves, nor are they life; they derive it from above.[119] The metaphor of the flowing river is clearly suggested by the ancient idea of the natural cycling of water from mountain to sea and return. The water rises in a spring of the mountaintop, it grows to be a river, descending in its course to the sea, and returning to land by submarine channels. Then it reaches to the top, often by some kind of natural alembic, since it was not known that springs in the mountains owed their existence to rainfall.

The emphasis on theophany, on God being revealed in the creation, implies that God knows himself through his creative acts, "for whatever He knows He creates, and what He creates derives from Himself. Accordingly, the whole creation is a process of divine revelation, with each being an aspect, finite and limited, of God's own nature."[120]

It is this idea which relieves the philosophy of the charge of pantheism, so often made by earlier students of John the Scot. In a certain sense, God and the creature are one and the same. We ought not to think, he says, of God and creature as two and different from one another but as one and the same. (*Proinde non duo a seipsis distantia debemus intelligere Deum et creaturam, sed unum et id ipsum.*) The creature exists in God while God himself in a wonderful and ineffable way is created in the creature.[121]

Two of his celebrated four species or divisions of nature are concerned with God, two with the creation. "We comprehend nature by reason because nature is itself rational." If we do not know God or his nature, we can infer from the order of the sensible and intelligible world that he exists and that he

---

[119] *De div. nat.*, III, 3–4, 628C–632C.
[120] Leff, *Med. Thought*, p. 68.
[121] *De div. nat.*, III, 17, 678C–D.

is the cause of all things. The first species, the nature which creates but is not created (*creat et non creatur*), is God as the principle of all things; the second, the nature which is created and creates (*creatur et creat*), represents archetypal ideas or primordial causes; the third, the nature which is created and does not create (*creatur et non creat*), is the sensible world, the world of appearances, the creation as we see it; and the fourth, the nature which neither creates nor is created (*nec creat neque creatur*), represents God the creator after he has attained his goal, being now at rest and having ceased to create. The four species of nature are composed of two sets of opposites: the first and the third, the second and the fourth. Such a division of nature accounts for the origin of creation, the forms or ideas of which the visible creation is a reflection, the visible creation and its clear purposiveness, the cessation of creative acts on the sixth day despite God's continuing governance of the world. It also accounts for the diversity of life. "The division of nature signifies that act by which God expresses himself and makes himself known in a hierarchy of beings which are other than, and inferior to him."[122]

Individual life partakes of an all-pervading universal life. There is no life form which in some way is not governed by life force (*vitae virtute non regitur*). It is called the world soul (*universalissima anima*) by the wise of the world because it binds together the whole cosmos. In truth, inquirers into divine wisdom call it a common life (*communem vitam appellant*).[123]

In John the Scot's philosophy, man's relation to nature was changed by the Fall. The diversity of human life and the differences among people are *post peccatum*. Paradise symbolizes original human nature and Adam's sleep a turning away from the spiritual road to desire for earthly things, a lust for sexual intercourse. The sleep which Adam fell into willingly really means a turning of the spirit from the eternal to the temporal, from God to creature. The consequences are the world as we know it, the two sexes, and reproduction in the manner of cattle.[124]

Essentially however it is an optimistic philosophy of man in his relation to nature even if it is burdened with an anthropocentrism that sees in human wickedness a power sufficient to alter the processes of nature. A theophany assumes an optimistic attitude toward the creation. "Because all creatures both derive from God as principle, and move towards Him as end, the whole of nature is a movement powered by love of God."[125]

---

[122] *Ibid.*, I, 1–2, 441B–443A; II, 2, 527B. The quotation on the rationality of nature is from Burch, *Early Med. Philos.*, p. 9; that on hierarchy, from Gilson, *HCPMA*, p. 117.

[123] *De div. nat.*, III, 36, 728D–729A.

[124] *Ibid.*, IV, 20, 835C–836B. See also Burch's discussion, *op. cit.*, pp. 20–24, on the fall of man.

[125] Leff, *Med. Thought*, p. 69. (John the Scot discusses at length the four elements in connection with his hexaemeron, physical geography, and Eratosthenes' measurement of the earth's circumference), *De div. nat.*, III, 32–33.

## 8. St. Bernard, St. Francis, and Alan of Lille

The love of nature and of God, manifested in perceptions of the creation as a book, as visible evidence of God's care for the world, as a theophany, reappear in various forms in St. Bernard, St. Francis, and Alan of Lille.

In the writings of St. Bernard (1091–1153), there are attitudes toward nature which date back to St. Augustine and before; they do more than glorify religion. The beauties and attractions of nature are accepted as long as they are associated with God and his works. One could learn about Him from the earth, from the trees, from the grains, the flowers, and the grass. In his oft-quoted letter to Heinrich Murdach, St. Bernard writes, "Believe me, I have discovered that you will find far more in the forests than in the books; trees and stones will teach you what no teacher permits you to hear."[126]

In St. Bernard's description of the cloister at Clairvaux, the landscape is changed from a wilderness and given meaning because human beings impose an order upon it; when men change nature they can make it more useful—perhaps, even, more charming and more beautiful.

The abbey is situated at the foot of two mountains separated by a valley: on the sides of one the grain is growing, the vineyards are on the other, and "each of them offers to the eye a beautiful sight, and supplies a needful support for the inmates." On the summits of the mountains, the monks collect dry branches, "grub up the brushwood which disfigures the ground," dig the soil "to scatter (as I may say after Solomon 'the bastard slips' [= Vulgate, Wisdom V, 3]) which choke the roots, entangle the boughs of the rising trees" so that there will be no hindrance to the growth of the oak, the lime, or the beech.

Within the wall that encloses the valley in which the cloister is situated fruit trees have been planted, and here the sick monks find solace and pleasure; it is a place suitable for healing. "See how, in order to cure one's sickness, the goodness of God multiplies remedies, causes the clear air to shine in serenity, the earth to breathe forth fruitfulness, and the sick man himself to inhale through eyes, and ears, and nostrils, the delights of colours, of songs, and of odours."

St. Bernard is pleased with the ways in which the monks have diverted the river Aube to their own uses so that water now in many ways performs the labor of men. The river's sinuous bed "which the labour of the brethren, and not Nature, has made" divides the valley in two. The water is controlled to check inundations; it runs great mills and farther on it fills the boiler for the brewer, and the fullers use it to operate heavy pestles or mallets or wooden foot-shaped blocks relieving them of heavy labor; the water then passes to

---

[126] See Jean Leclercq, *The Love of Learning and the Desire for God*, pp. 135–136; P. Sinz, "Die Naturbetrachtung des hl. Bernhard," *Anima* I (1953), pp. 30–51, and E. Gilson, "Sub umbris arborum," *Mediaeval Studies* (1952), pp. 149–151.

weavers' workshops. The tiny streams diverted from the Aube "wander in careless curves through the meadows, irrigating the fields before returning to the main stream."[127]

"That spot has much charm, it greatly soothes weary minds, relieves anxieties and cares, helps souls who seek the Lord greatly to devotion, and recalls to them the thought of the heavenly sweetness to which they aspire. The smiling countenance of the earth is painted with varying colours, the blooming verdure of spring satisfies the eyes, and its sweet odour salutes the nostrils." The beauty reminds him of the fragrance of the clothing of the Patriarch Job, of the purple robe of Solomon, which could not equal the beauty he beheld. "In this way, while I am charmed without by the sweet influence of the beauty of the country, I have not less delight within in reflecting on the mysteries which are hidden beneath it."[128]

This passage is one of the few known to me in the writings of the Middle Ages which combine a strong religious view of nature with an appreciation of natural beauty and with a frank, exultant admiration for the way the monks, through their skill, their techniques, their water mills, can complete what nature has given them. Implicit in it is the idea of man as a partner of God, sharing in, changing, and improving the creation to his own best uses because these accomplishments are for the greater glory of God. It would seem the monks thought their labor had re-created paradise, in the transformation of a chaotic and disordered wilderness.

We shall return to this theme in chapter VII. The Clairvaux description is that of an ideal landscape of the Cistercian order inspired by the Benedictine Rule, at a time when the monks did much of the work themselves or closely supervised it, when worldliness had not intervened between religious ideas and landscape change. Here is also the fervent activity that later brought about forest clearance; the arable; the dissemination of seeds, stocks, roots; construction work to use the countryside to better advantage; skill in animal husbandry.

With St. Francis (1182–1226) the emphasis is on communion with nature, the humanization of nonhuman life, the joys of poverty in the religious life of the countryside. In *The Canticle of Brother Sun* written by St. Francis during the illnesses of his last two years of life, the saint has praise for the Lord and all his creatures: for Sir Brother Sun, a symbol of the Lord, for Sister Moon and the stars ("In the sky You formed them bright and lovely and fair"), for Brother Wind ("And for the Air and cloudy and clear and all Weather, / By which You give sustenance to Your creatures!"), for Sister Water (useful, humble, lovely, chaste), for Brother Fire (beautiful, merry, mighty, and strong), for our Sister Mother Earth ("Who sustains and governs us, / And produces fruits with colorful flowers and leaves!").[129]

[127] *Works*, Vol. 2, pp. 461, 464.
[128] *Ibid.*, Vol. 2, pp. 464–465.
[129] "The Canticle of Brother Sun," in *The Little Flowers of St. Francis* (and other

St. Francis followed rapturously and most literally the exhortation of Romans 1:20. "Who could tell," Brother Thomas of Celano says of him, "the sweetness which he enjoyed in contemplating in His creatures the wisdom, power and goodness of the Creator?" He called all creatures by the name of brother; toward the worms, he glowed with exceeding love; in winter he had honey and the best wine provided for the bees; when he came upon an abundance of flowers, he would preach to them and "invite them to praise the Lord, just as if they had been gifted with reason. So also cornfields and vineyards, stones, woods, and all the beauties of the field, fountains of waters, all the verdure of gardens, earth and fire, air and wind would he with sincerest purity exhort to the love and willing service of God."[130]

If Ugolino de Monte Santa Maria's *The Little Flowers of Saint Francis* is not folklore but the product of an oral tradition lasting about a century after the saint's death, then we behold in St. Francis a man who speaks to other creatures as if they were human, scolding them when they need to be scolded, telling them their duties toward God and what they should do to observe His commands. He make covenants, as he did with the wolf of Gubbio; indeed nonhuman life has its own dignity, existing for its own purposes and in its own right. This thought, as we have seen, was expressed by St. Augustine as well; the scale of nature, divinely ordained, is a scale with man at the apex, but this does not mean that all life exists for him and is at his disposal.

At Cannara, he orders the swallows to stop twittering until his preaching is over, and they obey.[131] In his sermon to the birds, he addresses them as humans, reminding them of their debt to God, of the freedom God has given them, of their wondrous clothing, of the food they need not work for. God preserved them in the ark, and provided many nesting places in remote refuges for them. "Therefore, my little bird sisters, be careful not to be ungrateful, but strive always to praise God." The birds acknowledge the words and bow their heads, and St. Francis marvels at their variety, attention, familiarity, and affection. He therefore "devoutedly praised the wonderful Creator in them and gently urged them to praise the Creator."[132]

When the boy of Siena surrenders to St. Francis the doves he is taking to market, the saint praises him and then explains to the doves, "I want to rescue you from death and make nests for you where you can lay your eggs and fulfill the Creator's commandment to multiply."[133]

---

works), trans. by Raphael Brown, p. 317. On the canticle, see note 1 to chap. 19, p. 336, and note 20, p. 350, on the meaning of *per*, here translated *for*. On the substance of St. Francis' sermon to the birds, *The Little Flowers of St. Francis*, pp. 76–77; on the visitations and consolations of God and St. Francis' seeing the Creator in all created things, p. 164; on the surrounding of St. Francis by the birds, pp. 177–178.

[130] Brother Thomas of Celano, *The First Life of S. Francis of Assisi*, trans. by A. G. Ferrers Howell, chap. 29 (80–81). On the birds, the leveret, and the fish, chap. 21 (58–61).

[131] *Little Flowers*, p. 75.

[132] *Ibid.*, pp. 76–77; quotations on p. 77.

[133] *Ibid.*, p. 92.

At Gubbio, the ravenous wolf who had devoured both man and beast is no match for St. Francis' holiness, which God now wished to call to the attention of the people. St. Francis went to meet the fierce wolf, the fearful peasants warning him of the dangers. The saint made the sign of the cross and the power of God checked the wolf. "Come to me, Brother Wolf. In the name of Christ, I order you not to hurt me or anyone." Scolding him for his depredations, for destroying animals, and for brazenly killing men who are made in God's image, he tells the wolf he deserves death, but he wishes to make peace. The wolf agrees and St. Francis promises him food every day because the evil in him has come from hunger. In return, the wolf promises he will hurt neither man nor beast. "And as St. Francis held out his hand to receive the pledge, the wolf also raised its front paw and meekly and gently put it in St. Francis' hand as a sign that it was giving its pledge." In the name of the Lord Jesus Christ, St. Francis ordered the wolf to enter the town, where the pact negotiated between him and the wolf was ratified by the people, St. Francis acting as bondsman. Neither side ever broke the covenant.[134]

The scene has been brought to life by Stefano di Giovanni Sassetta, one of the great Sienese painters of the fifteenth century. The saint, serene among his admiring townsmen at the gate, grasps the friendly paw of the handsome wolf, which looks like a playful dog. The gay and lighthearted group is the center of interest, diverting attention from the bloody and mangled corpse near the wolf. And in harmony with St. Francis' associations with them, the birds above are in ordered flight.

Many students have found in the Franciscan a deeper understanding of nature than in any other order. To St. Francis living things might be symbols, but they were placed on earth for God's own purposes (not for man's), and they, like man, praise God. In preaching to birds and flowers and in his pact with the wolf he imputes a moral philosophy to them (and a contractual responsibility on the wolf's part) that is virtually human, coming here close to heresy. Absent is the crude identification of divine with human purpose; living nature attains a dignity and holiness far removed from the crude utilitarian conceptions of the believers in design. White, for example, sees in St. Francis' thought a revolutionary change in outlook toward nature in the Middle Ages, the saint rebelling in his humility against the egotistic anthropocentrism of the earlier theology; he sees in him the greatest revolutionary in history because he first taught Europe that nature is interesting and important in and of itself, and because he forced man to abdicate his monarchy over creation, instituting a democracy of all of God's creatures.[135]

To Alan of Lille (1128–1202), Nature is active and efficacious; personified

---

[134] *Ibid.*, pp. 89–91; quotations on pp. 89, 90.

[135] Lynn White, Jr., "Natural Science and Naturalistic Art in the Middle Ages," *AHR*, 52 (1947), pp. 432–433. White adds that this attitude was implied, for example, in Psalm 148. On Franciscan observation of the natural world, see also George Boas's intro. to his trans. of St. Bonaventura's *The Mind's Road to God*, p. xix.

and a creature herself of God, she is aware of the reasonableness and holiness of her laws. *The Complaint of Nature* (*De planctu naturae*) is an excellent illustration of a traditional Christian conception of nature, with reminders of Plotinus, Boethius, and John the Scot, before it became necessary to meet the full force of alternate religious beliefs from the south, and to meet the challenge of a revived and much commented-upon classical cosmology. Alan (especially in the last third of the twelfth century) lived at a time when Jewish and Muslim thought was beginning to intrude upon Christian belief; in his work on the Catholic faith, for example, he showed the new fears in the attack on the Albigenses, the Waldenses, the Jews, and the pagans. The *De planctu naturae*

> expresses the Christian idea of nature common to practically all mediaeval theologians, except, of course, the extreme representatives of strict other-worldliness (*contemptus saeculi*). Just as in Boethius and in Bernardus Silvestris, Nature represents here the inexhaustible fecundity from which springs the pullulation of beings. It is the source of universal life, and not only the cause of beings but their rule, their law, their order, their beauty and their end. Nature could not be too highly praised in her works, which are, through her, the works of God.[136]

The most important idea of the poem, from our point of view, is that nature's power is small compared with that of God, great compared to that of man. Nature, removed as in Neoplatonism from the One or from God and described variously as a mother and as a chain of being, is apostrophized as a creation of God. She is the reflection of God's works; she is God's deputy whose pen is guided by the hand of God. Venus is an underdeputy of Nature, who with Hymen and Cupid keeps all life, especially human life, going. Ideas of the maintenance of population through time, of the natural order on earth, of a chain of being, are only slightly concealed by the allegory. Nature regularizes the acts of God. Like *The Romance of the Rose*, which owes so much to *De planctu naturae*, Alan's castigation of mankind is a moral one; it laments the willful separateness of man from nature owing to the evil within him. Of all beings, man alone in his depravity and with his unnatural vices fails to observe the laws of nature. Among other aberrations, he severely indicts male homosexuality because it is a departure from nature's principle of love. There is obedience in the firmament, in the stars, in the winds, in the friendship of land and sea—for they all keep to their own stations—in the fish, and in the marriage in an imperial embrace of rains to the earth. The harmonies observable everywhere in nature are not observable in man.[137]

---

[136] Gilson, *HCPMA*, pp. 172; quote on p. 176. The work is modeled on Boethius' *Consolation of Philosophy*, p. 175. For a detailed study, see de Lage, *Alain de Lille. Poète du XIIe Siècle. De planctu naturae* illustrates the importance of the principle of plenitude in medieval thought. See Lovejoy, *The Great Chain of Being*, pp. 67–98, for the medieval period, although he does not discuss Alan of Lille.

[137] On Alan's sources, see de Lage, *op. cit.*, pp. 67–75.

God achieves harmony by governing the four elements. The four elements of the macrocosm correspond with the four humors in man, the microcosm. Nature is God's vicar, an intermediary between man and God. The power of God is superlative; of Nature, comparative; of man, positive. Alan develops the personification of Nature through long apostrophes to her by the interlocutors and her replies to them.[138]

God himself has created in Nature a network of secondary causes, defining and directing their areas of influence. Once having created the system, the Creator respects its autonomy and normally does not interfere in its functioning.[139] The governance of the universe is compared to that of a great city, God in his heavenly citadel commanding, the angels in the air (as in the middle of a city) administering, and man "like one foreign-born dwelling in a suburb of the universe," serving.

Nature is a real handmaiden of God:

> For I, as I work, am not able to press my step in the footprints of God as He works, but I contemplate Him in His activity from a long way off, as it were with longing. His operation is simple, mine is multiform; His work is faultless, mine is defective; His is marvelous, mine is transient; He is incapable of being born, I was born; He is the maker, I am the made; He is the Creator of my work, I am the work of the Creator; He works from nothing, I beg work from another; He works by His own divine will, I work under His name.

## 9. FERMENTS FROM THE MEDITERRANEAN

Peter the Venerable, Abbot of Cluny, in 1143 visited the monasteries of the Cluniac order in Spain and there arranged for a Latin translation of the Koran (made by Robert of Ketene, or Ketton) in order that its heresies might be more easily exposed, a work in which he assisted in his own right by composing his *Libri II adversus nefariam sectam saracenorum*.[140] "From that time on, Christianity found itself confronted with two living religions, that is, with something quite different from doctrinal divergencies between individual Christians."[141] The Christian world, itself threatened with heresy and schism, now had to meet the challenge of an exceedingly cosmopolitan civilization; it was also confronted with the original work and the translations which were

---

[138] "Tres potestatis gradus possumus invenire, ut Dei potentia superlativa, Naturae comparativa, hominis postiva dicatur," *PL*, Vol. 210, 446B. See also de Lage, *op. cit.*, pp. 64–65.

[139] *Ibid.*, p. 67. On nature description, see Metre 1–3, Prose 1–2; nature as a viceregent of God, Prose 3; governance of the universe, Prose 3; God and nature compared, Prose 3; the three powers, Prose 3; sexual aberrations, Prose 4, lines 100–150, 179–191, and *passim*; Nature, Venus, Hymen, and Cupid, Prose IV, lines 375–385. Prose IX reviews the general argument. See also Chenu, "Découverte de la Nature et Philosophie de l'Homme à l'École de Chartres au XII<sup>e</sup> Siècle," *JWH*, Vol. 2 (1954), pp. 313–325.

[140] Gilson, *HCPMA*, pp. 635–636.

[141] *Ibid.*, p. 172; see also pp. 238, 240, 275.

being produced by scholars in the Arab world. The more forward-looking of these men saw that this knowledge should be used in support of the faith; the *Summae* against the gentiles, the reawakening of interest in nature, in mathematics, and in Greek literature, especially in Aristotle, are all parts of this movement. The exposition of Aristotelian ideas (first the Aristotle translated from the Arabic that contained Neoplatonism and Arab thought, then a purer Aristotle from the Greek original) closely associated with the names of Albertus Magnus and his pupils, Thomas of Cantimpré and St. Thomas Aquinas, intensified interest in the teleological view of nature which is so positively set forth in the philosophy of Aristotle.[142]

Already in the twelfth century there was a growing interest in natural processes and in secondary causes, a realization that little was accomplished merely by saying that the most trivial and the most fundamental aspects of the creation alike were owing to God's wisdom. Thorndike has given two excellent illustrations of this. The nephew of Adelard of Bath (twelfth century), seeking the reason for the growth of herbs from the earth, asks, "To what else can you attribute this save to the marvellous effect of the marvellous divine will?" Adelard agrees that it is the creator's will, but there are natural reasons at work too. When the nephew ascribes all causes indifferently to God, Adelard replies that, without detracting from God, nature "is not confused and without system" and "human science should be given a hearing upon these points which it has covered."[143] His contemporary, William of Conches in Normandy, exasperated by those who say, "We do not know how this is, but we know that God can do it," replies, "You poor fools, God can make a cow out of a tree, but has He ever done so? Therefore show some reason why a thing is so, or cease to hold that it is so."[144]

The cosmopolitan character of Mediterranean civilization, both Christian and Muslim, provided a new ferment. With the Norman conquest of Sicily (1060–1091), a Christian-Islamic culture flourished under Roger I with Muslims in positions of authority; the great Arab geographer al-Idrisi was in the court of Roger II, and under Frederick II, the grandson of Roger II, translations of Aristotle's and Averroes' works became part of the curriculum of the newly founded University of Naples (1224) which St. Thomas Aquinas attended. Frederick's kingdom in Sicily had a Greek element using Greek, a Muslim element speaking Arabic, and scholars who knew Latin.[145]

Even St. Thomas Aquinas "was no child of the Gothic North, like Albert

[142] Leff, *Medieval Thought*, p. 171. See also Gilson's discussion of the Aristotles of Avicenna, Averroes, and St. Thomas, *HCPMA*, pp. 387–388.
[143] Quoted in Thorndike, Vol. 2, p. 28. In *Quaestiones Naturales*, chap. 4. See Chenu, *op. cit., passim.*
[144] Quoted in Thorndike, Vol. 2, p. 58. In *De philosophia mundi* = PL 90, pp. 1127–1178; or 172, pp. 39–102. On the organization of *De philosophia mundi*, Gilson, *HCPMA*, p. 623. See Chenu, *op. cit., passim.*
[145] Hitti, *The Arabs. A Short History*, pp. 206–211.

or Abelard, but a native of that strange borderland [Naples] of Western civilization where feudal Europe mingled with the Greek and Saracen worlds."[146]

The Muslim world had a common law, language, and religion, but it too was in part a product of an ancient and deep-seated Mediterranean culture, its cosmopolitanism coming not only from Muslim, but also from Jewish and Christian scholarship. Thomas Aquinas uses Maimonides and Averroes and "employs a manner of argumentation familiar from Muslim scholasticism."[147]

These southern breezes stimulated interest in geography, in environmental influences, in the earth's nature, in the properties of things. There was no relaxation in embracing the notion of a divinely designed earth with its harmonious adaptations, but the teleology, enforced by Aristotle's writings, opened up areas of interpretation (as for example the doctrine of the eternity of the world) more removed from biblical exegesis than had been the case when men depended on the Bible and the *Timaeus* for their cosmogony. Circumstances had changed; a few went along old paths paying little attention to the new learning, but this course had its dangers. "A few others, led by a deep-seated fear of seeing Christian theology outdistanced by pagans and infidels in the main fields of secular learning, considered it their duty to catch up with the 'philosophers' and to put the Christians on a footing of equality with their opponents." Men like Robert Grosseteste, Roger Bacon, and Albert the Great "were also convinced that, ultimately, the acquisition of secular learning would help to spread the Christian truth, but their writings bear witness to a properly scientific interest."[148] This partial union of Christian theology with Aristotelian teleology, of the divine word as revealed in the Scriptures with the closer observation of the natural surroundings, strengthened the cosmological and physico-theological proof of the existence of God.

### 10.   Averroes and Maimonides

Let us examine briefly two examples, Averroes and Maimonides, from this civilization of the south. Averroes' ideas of design and teleology are Aristotelian; they are Muslim counterparts of Christian thinking. The religion of Mohammed is also a revealed religion, monotheistic with a transcendent God who creates and acts in the manner of the Judeo-Christian God. In Sûrah 16 of the Koran, *The Bee*, God shows his concern for his creation; he is especially mindful of man. The lower orders of the creation exist for Him and are subject to his dominion much as they are in the Old Testament.

[146] Christopher Dawson, *Medieval Essays*, p. 133.

[147] von Grunebaum, *Medieval Islam*, p. 342. See also Christopher Dawson's two essays "The Moslem West and the Oriental Background of Later Medieval Culture," and "The Scientific Development of Medieval Culture," in his *Medieval Essays*; especially p. 111, on the cultural unity of Islam.

[148] Gilson, *HCPMA*, p. 275.

Like Christian thinkers fond of classical analogies which cluster around words like *art, nature,* and *work,* Averroes sees in the artisan analogy a fundamental way of understanding the creation. In the study of beings we first must recognize the art in them, then the work of art, then the artisan. Similarly, we recognize in the cosmos the work of an artisan; the more perfect the recognition of the art which it reveals, the more perfect becomes the recognition of the artist.[149]

Divine law invites one to a profound and rational study of the universe. (Quotes Sûrah 59:2.) Mahomet had said of those who denied his revelations, "Have they not considered the dominion of the heavens and the earth, and what things Allah hath created? . . . (Sûrah 7:185.) Averroes adds that divine law makes it an obligation to apply rational speculation to one's reflections on the universe. Such speculation takes its most perfect form in the rational syllogism called demonstration. One thus must know the differences among various kinds of syllogisms, the demonstrative, the dialectic, the oratorical, the sophistical.

Syllogisms however are constructed by men of different natures, habits, tastes, and training; interpretations of religious law will therefore differ. Thus, the three-fold classification of such interpreters is fundamental to his philosophy. Since the Koran is a divine book, it appeals to all three.

Men of the first class are innocent of interpretation of any kind; they are accessible only to oratorical argument and exhortation. All men belong in some degree to this class; no sound man of spirit is a stranger to it, but primarily this is the class of the common people who believe without examination in mysteries and in miracles.

The second class is more restricted in membership than the first; in it are men who like dialectical disputation, who are dialectical by nature or by nature and long habit combined. They are Averroes' villains, for they are the theologians who see contradictions and difficulties but lack the ability either to find or to comprehend a demonstrative solution, even if their reasonings may have some semblance of truth. The divergent interpretations they pass on to the vulgar, who comprehend them poorly and in diverse senses; hence, the hostile sects, the persecution, sedition, and religious wars of Islam. Religious peace would be reestablished if the sects disappeared, if governments permitted the two upper classes to communicate to the lower class only those interpretations proper for it, for the lower class would then be neither burdened with the impossible task of understanding the philosophers nor contaminated by theologians.

Men of the third and least numerous class give assent only by apodictic

---

[149] Ibn Rochd (Averroès), *Traité Décisif sur l'Accord de la Religion et de la Philosophie.* Arab text with French trans., notes and intro. by Léon Gauthier. 3d ed., pp. 1–2, 4–5. Analysis based on Fr. trans.

demonstration, admitting neither miracles nor mysteries. They become such men by nature or art—the art of philosophy. These philosophers perceive the difficulties and resolve them in a single and unique way.

The common man and the philosopher are both sound in their own way; they, unlike the dialectical theologians, do religion no harm, establish no sects. A profound understanding of the creation and the great philosophical ideas, however, is for the trained and disciplined few. Only harm can come from the irresponsible diffusion of interpretations to these incompetent to receive them. Real exegesis is highly specialized; there is and should be a gulf between the ideas of nature of the philosopher and those of the common people.[150]

In Muslim thought exegesis has probably been carried on even more subtly and more voluminously than in Christian. When they came to the Latin West, Averroes' ideas added to the questionings which Christian exegesis itself had already raised. Both reveal the stimulus to inquiry which exegesis inevitably provides. Like Basil's, it could be literal and full of facts from classical botany, zoology, geography, astronomy, and other sciences; or it could be symbolic like the hexaemeral writings of Ambrose, Augustine, and John the Scot. It could be, as Averroes taught, on different levels, like the exterior and symbolic sense of the common man and the interior and hidden sense of the philosopher. Different historical circumstances demanded different remedies, as Thomas Aquinas saw in combatting heresy, for one way might be required with a Jew who knew the Old Testament, another with a heretic versed in the New, another with an early Church Father who could deal with the pagan world because he had been a pagan himself, another with a Muslim who cares nothing for the Christian Scripture. Some exegesis might require more emphasis on nature, some on revelation, as Chrysostom, Augustine, Aquinas, Lull, and Sibiude realized.

At this time exegesis becomes a kind of sociology of knowledge, a probing particularly effective in analyzing nature both as it is seen in the everyday world and in its symbolism. It suggests that interpretation may be cultural and psychological, that while it is not opposed to piety, it has a validity of its own independent of piety.

Maimonides is of special interest because of the common Jewish and Christian concern with Old Testament exegesis. In Maimonides' exegesis, Genesis is not taken literally; it is interpreted according to the theory of the four elements.[151] Living long before the days of the higher criticism, he assumes the two creation stories are one and that they may be reconciled with one another. In the first account, male and female are created (Gen. 1:27) and the creation is now finished (Gen. 2:1). But the second account then describes the further creations of Eve, the trees of life and knowledge, the serpent, as if these events occurred after Adam was placed in the Garden of Eden. All our sages agree, he says, that these creations took place on the sixth day, for noth-

---

[150] *Ibid.*, pp. 8, 23–26, 29–31. See also Gauthier's remarks, pp. xi–xiv.
[151] *The Guide for the Perplexed*, Pt. II, chap. 30, pp. 213–214.

ing new was created after the end of that day. "None of the things mentioned above is therefore impossible, because the laws of Nature were then not yet permanently fixed."[152] Observance of the Sabbath has two purposes: to confirm the true theory of creation, and to remind us of God's kindness in freeing us from the burdens of the Egyptians. The Sabbath "gives us correct notions, and also promotes the well-being of our bodies." It also allows man to pass one seventh of his life in rest and comfort.[153] The genealogies of nations are set down in order to supply information concerning the multiplication and dispersal of the human race; lacking them, people might doubt the truth.[154]

In his discussion of the macrocosm and the microcosm, Maimonides says all forms of life are not vital to the order of nature. Some species are an integral part of the system because they have the power of generation; others, like insects generated in dunghills, animals in rotten fruit or in fetid liquids, and worms in the intestines, have no purpose; the power of generation is denied them. "You will, therefore, find that these things do not follow a fixed law, although their entire absence is just as impossible as the absence of different complexions and of different kinds of hair amongst human beings."[155] Nature also creates an economy for man, making what is necessary cheap, what is a luxury dear. Air, the most necessary, is more plentiful than water, which in turn is more necessary and cheaper than food, to say nothing of staple and luxurious foods.[156] Such a crude utilitarian natural theology is not typical of Maimonides, however.

Design in nature implies purpose. But whose purpose? Aristotle, he says, repeatedly points out that nature does nothing in vain. Plants exist for animals; the parts of animals have design and purpose. This we may grant. "All this refers only to the immediate purpose of a thing; but the existence of an ultimate purpose in every species, which is considered as absolutely necessary by every one who investigates into the nature of things, is very difficult to discover: and still more difficult is it to find the purpose of the whole Universe."[157]

One cannot infer that the universe is created for man. Man should know his station; the universe does not exist for him, but because the Creator wills it. Man should see himself as a being in a hierarchy, below the spheres and the stars and inferior to the angels, but still the highest being composed of the four elements. "Man's existence is nevertheless a great boon to him, and his distinction and perfection is a divine gift."[158]

How does Providence work in the design and plan of nature? Maimonides examines previous theories at length, following then with his own. Aristotle,

---

[152] *Ibid.*, Pt. II, chap. 30, p. 216.
[153] *Ibid.*, Pt. II, chap. 31, p. 219, Pt. III, chap. 43, p. 352.
[154] *Ibid.*, Pt. III, chap. 50, p. 381.
[155] *Ibid.*, Pt. I, chap. 72, p. 116.
[156] *Ibid.*, Pt. III, chap. 12, p. 271.
[157] *Ibid.*, chap. 13, p. 273.
[158] *Ibid.*, chap. 12, p. 268.

he says, argued that incidents in the existence of individual beings in each species, whether rational or irrational, are due to chance, not to management. A storm causes the leaves of a tree to drop, and stirs up the sea, causing the ship and its passengers to go down; an ox annihilates ants with his excrement; worshippers are killed when the foundations of the house give way. Are such incidents due to chance or to design?[159]

Maimonides agrees with Aristotle that Divine Providence does not extend to the individual members of a species, but he makes an exception in the case of man.

> For I do not believe that it is through the interference of Divine Providence that a certain leaf drops [from a tree], nor do I hold that when a certain spider catches a certain fly, that this is the direct result of a special decree and will of God in that moment; it is not by a particular Divine decree that the spittle of a certain person moved, fell on a certain gnat in a certain place, and killed it; nor is it by the direct will of God that a certain fish catches and swallows a certain worm on the surface of the water.

If, however, men go down with the ship or are killed when a roof falls in on them, these deaths are not by chance but by the will of God. He accepts this theory because he has not "met in any of the prophetical books with a description of God's Providence otherwise than in relation to human beings."[160]

## 11. Frederick II on Falcons

Let us remain a little longer in the south of Europe. If many have seen in the dignity which St. Francis accorded to all life the creation of an atmosphere favorable to the study of nature, others (notably Charles Haskins) have seen in *The Art of Falconry of Frederick II of Hohenstaufen* (1194–1250) an exemplar of what could be accomplished in natural history by observation in the Middle Ages.[161] So much has been written about this work as a contribution to the scientific study of natural history, particularly to ornithology, that a few general remarks will be enough to show why it has achieved such fame. Most students of the "Emperor of the Romans, King of Jerusalem and of Sicily" stress the stimulus of his intellectual milieu, the Sicilian court that knew the Muslim, the Christian, and the Jew. "For his investigations of falcons, Frederick had at his disposal the whole machinery of his bureaucratic admin-

[159] *Ibid.*, chap. 17, p. 283.

[160] *Ibid.*, pp. 286–287. The theory that God had providence over man both as a species and as an individual and over the rest of life only as a species was listed as an error by Giles of Rome. In his *Errores Philosophorum*, Giles compiled the errors of Aristotle, Averroes, Avicenna, Algazel, Alkindi, and Maimonides as a "stern warning and admonition to read the new philosophical literature critically, and not to forget the teachings of the faith." Josef Koch's introduction to the *Errores Philosophorum*, trans. by Riedl. For Giles' text, XII Maimonides, 9, pp. 63–65.

[161] *The Art of Falconry Being the De Arte Venandi cum Avibus of Frederick II of Hohenstaufen.* Translated and edited by Casey A. Wood and F. Marjorie Fyfe. The translator's introduction is largely based on Haskins; the book has many beautiful plates

istration," the emperor carrying on an extensive correspondence on falcons with people living in various parts of the empire.[162] This information from many different localities made him aware of the broader aspects of bird study such as the relation of climate to nesting, migration, food habits, and so forth.

Most exhilarating is the casual treatment of Aristotle, who to him is an authority, fallible as is anyone else; he can take him or leave him, and when his own observation or the testimony of his friends or other experts in falconry conflict with Aristotle, it does not take him long to make up his mind whose to accept. He notices, for example, how the black pupils of the hawk are enlarged when its eyes are fixed on an object, diminished when not staring at something engaging its attention.[163]

This discourse on man's ancient interference with the world of the bird of prey is suffused with deep knowledge and affection. Few passages in the literature of natural history, in my opinion, surpass the discussion of the shirker and the coward among the birds of prey and how they are to be treated (IV, 27–28).

> Shirkers are those falcons that can perform better than they do but dissemble and and give a poor account of themselves. Cowards are those that have been wounded by cranes and are therefore afraid, or unwilling, to attack or capture the quarry. Hence the difference between them is that the one cloaks her true character and the other is really afraid. The shirker, if slipped at a weak or injured crane, will take it; but the coward will not touch any prey, injured or uninjured, weak or strong, so long as her fear lasts.[164]

To Frederick, this kind of hunting was an art which he approached out of love; he despised those who hunted with pits, nets, and animals. In his prologue, he said bird life was one of the "attractive manifestations of nature," its study a way of understanding nature. Although many oriental books on falconry were known to him, it is generally believed that Frederick's depended very

---

of birds, and of buildings associated with Frederick's reign, especially those in Apulia. On the work, see Charles H. Haskins "The 'De Arte Venandi cum Avibus' of the Emperor Frederick II," *Eng. Hist. Rev.*, Vol. 36 (1921), pp. 334–355; *idem.*, *Studies in the History of Mediaeval Science*, pp. 299–326, a revision of the *Eng. Hist. Rev.* article; *idem*, "The Latin Literature of Sport," *Speculum*, 2 (1927), 235–252. See also Ernst Kantorowicz, *Kaiser Friedrich der Zweite, Ergänzungsband*, pp. 155–157, for extensive references.

[162] Haskins, *op. cit.*, *Eng. Hist. Rev.*, Vol 36 (1921), p. 353; and for examples, pp. 354–355.

[163] See the general prologue of the work for criticism of Aristotle. "Nowhere does Frederick's emancipation from tradition and authority stand out more clearly than in his attitude toward Aristotle." Haskins, *op. cit.*, *Eng. Hist. Rev.*, Vol. 36 (1921), p. 346. For a restrained view both of Muslim and Frederick's experimentation, see von Grunebaum, *Medieval Islam*, pp. 334–336. On the Sicilian-Arab line of monarchs beginning with Roger I, see Philip K. Hitti, *The Arabs. A Short History*, pp. 208–211. Roger II and Frederick II were called "the two baptized sultans of Sicily." In Hitti's opinion (pp. 210–211) Frederick's greatest single contribution was the founding of the University of Naples in 1224. On the hawk's pupils, *Art of Falconry*, Bk. I, chap. 24, p. 60.

[164] *Art of Falconry*, Bk. IV, chaps. 27–28. The quotation is from chap. 27, pp. 303–304.

little upon them, that his work is a fresh start with little reliance on predecessors, including Aristotle, who is cited mainly when the author disagrees with him.[165]

From a broader geographical point of view, the work adopts the ancient doctrine of the seven *klimata* as given by al-Idrisi, discusses those which various birds choose for their eyries, those within which migrations take place, districts suited to crane hawking. The book shows acquaintance with the northern latitudes and the kinds of birds and the bird migrations taking place there.[166] Perhaps the geographical tradition was still strong at his court, for al-Idrisi (*ca.* 1099–1154), the Arab geographer and cartographer, had been attached to the court of Frederick's grandfather, Roger II (1101–1154), at Palermo for twenty-five years.

What are some of the general ideas of this detailed and technical treatise? An Aristotelian type of teleology explains the nature of organs, but there are no religious overtones. Every organ of a bird, he says, is made of material suited to its function and this organ has a functional purpose. Thus if Nature formed organs to fulfill their appropriate functions, it might be predicated that she would make one bird in order that it might destroy another, that is, that "Nature has created one species for the annihilation of another, and according to this axiom, Nature is not only benevolent in one species and malevolent in another but, what is more important, exhibits her two opposite aspects at the same time, for each species finds in another what is harmful to it."[167] Training birds involves making them do things unnatural to them. The size of cranes, he says, exceeds that of falcons and it is thus unnatural for falcons to capture such large birds of their own free will; they must be taught and helped by man.[168]

The important point is not that falconry was so well understood at this time, or that there was such close observation of birds over a thirty-year period and such skill in training them, but that these matters were studied by a learned man and emperor and by other experts associated with him and were then written down. Kantorowicz has wisely said that observation had not been lost and then rediscovered by Frederick, for the peasant or the hunter of the Middle Ages saw as sharply as did peasants and hunters of past times. But those articulate enough to have given literary expression to their observations seldom had an eye for the world of the senses.[169] The emperor had the sharp eye of the peasant and the hunter, an interest in the natural world, and the trained intelligence to set down in writing what he saw. This is the lesson of Frederick II.

[165] See Haskins, *op. cit.*, *Eng. Hist. Rev.*, Vol. 36 (1921), p. 346.
[166] *Art of Falconry*, Bk. II, chaps. 4–5; on bird migrations, Bk. I, chaps. 22–23.
[167] *Ibid.*, Bk. I, chap. 23–I, p. 57.
[168] *Ibid.*, Bk. IV, chap. 27, p. 303.
[169] Kantorowicz, *Kaiser Friedrich der Zweite*, p. 336.

## 12.  ALBERT THE GREAT

Although he cannot be compared with Frederick, Albert the Great (1193–1280) in the north was also sympathetic to the rational and independent study of nature. Indeed, he contributed to all the ideas whose history we are considering. The idea of a divinely designed earth recurs repeatedly in his writings; it is an expected and important part of his theology. He commented exhaustively on Aristotle's philosophy of nature, adding fresh, if modest, observations of his own.[170] He wrote on geography, following apparently the model of Isidore of Seville's compendium of place-names and place descriptions. (Isidore of Seville in turn may be compared with Pliny in this respect.) To description he adds, however, a sustained discussion of theories of environmental influence. (See chap. 6, sec. 4.) Less sustained is his recognition of environmental change occurring through human agency, but he tries to understand domestication, the advantage of manuring, the effect the clearing of trees had on the land. (See chap. 7, sec. 7.)

In the early period, the Christian view of the earth was influenced by the ideas of Plato, of the Neoplatonists, and finally of Augustine: the earth represented the finished product of artisanship, the natural order resembling a mosaic where everything was in its place and the design of the Creator was clear. In Albert's writings, in the combination of the biblical account of the creation (rejecting the Aristotelian idea of the eternity of the cosmos) with Aristotelian thought, the older view of the earth does not disappear, but there is a subtle shift in emphasis. There is not only a purposefulness in each living organism—even within its component parts—but also a purposefulness of the whole. A vigorous revival of that most subtle of all teleological ideas of nature, that it does nothing in vain, takes place.

In considering Albert's contribution, one must avoid the two extremes: the disparagement that emphasizes his aping of the past, and the extravagant praise of Albert as an innovator, ignoring the fables, the lore of the bestiary, the demonology, and the astrology which are there.

With Albertus Magnus a new value is placed on contemporary natural surroundings and their proper observation. Albert was a monk of the mendicant Dominican order; according to the Dominican Jammy, who edited and published his works in the middle of the seventeenth century, Albert journeyed from cloister to cloister on foot, begging for his food. It is quite likely that his extensive foot-journeys had a close relationship to his observation; he had traveled widely in Germany, Italy, and France, these travels becoming more extensive with his appointment as Provincial for Germany in 1254. From 1254

---

[170] For a well considered appraisal, see Raven, *Science and Religion*, pp. 66–73. Raven also makes clear the rationalistic and hagiological pitfalls in the study of Albert as a natural historian (p. 71).

to 1259 he visited the Dominican monasteries and south and north Germany as far as Lübeck on the North Sea.[171]

In the journeys from cloister to cloister, he had walked through Austria, Bavaria, Swabia, Alsace, the Rhine and Moselle valleys to Brabant, to Holland, to Westphalia, Holstein, Saxony, Meissen, Thuringia.[172] Albert was thus well acquainted personally with some of the most dramatically contrasted landscapes of Europe: the Alps, the valleys of the Rhine and its tributaries (Cologne was his favorite residence), the central uplands of Germany, and the landscapes of the North European plain.

Albert aspires to a natural theology that is based on learning. Human knowledge is incomplete, and as long as it is incomplete, we are that much poorer in our knowledge of God and his works; investigation and observation are compatible with Christianity, they are necessary for the true knowledge of the created and the Creator. To Albert the beauties of the earth are more than symbols, its apparent order more than a simple illustration of design.[173] In discussing the nature of floods, for example, he includes with historical illustration, universal floods, floods somewhat less than universal, and purely local ones. There are some, he says, who ascribe all these to divine disposition, who assert that it is unnecessary for us to seek any further than the will of God for their cause. We agree with that in part, Albert says: "This world governed by the will of God, is made also for the punishment of evil men. We say however that God does this by natural causes whose prime mover, God himself, is able to give movement to everything else. Moreover we do not ask concerning the causes of his willing, but concerning natural causes which are like instruments effecting his wishes in such matters."[174]

The earth was an environment suited to the perfect man before the Fall; it remained a fit environment for man after it, even if nature no longer possessed its previous perfection; thistles and poisonous earth for example, had first

---

[171] Jammy, intro. to Vol. I of Albert's works, Jessen, *Botanik der Gegenwart und Vorzeit*, p. 145. Meyer began, and his friend Jessen finished, an edition of Albert's *De Vegetabilibus*, published in Berlin in 1867. On his travels, see also Wimmer, *Deutsches Pflanzenleben nach Albertus Magnus* (1908), pp. 8–9.

[172] Jessen, *op. cit.*, pp. 145–146.

[173] *Ibid.*, p. 152. Because of the forbidding volume of Albert's writing, his thought is still imperfectly studied in detail. Among the works concerned with his natural history, I have found the following to be the most helpful: Ernst Meyer, "Albertus Magnus," *Linnaea*, 10 [1836], pp. 641–741, 11 [1837], pp. 545–595. This article shows how late, and how full of error has been the study of Albert as a natural historian; see Vol. 10, pp. 642–652, for Meyer's critique of former students of the subject. These articles are summarized in Meyer's famous work, *Geschichte der Botanik*, Vol. 4, pp. 9–84. Meyer shows that Albert's ideas of agriculture and plants appeared later in the work of Pietro Crescenzi (Petrus Crescentiis), the famous Italian agricultural writer, 1230?–?1310. Meyer discusses the importance of Albert's foot travels in his nature study. J. Wimmer's *Deutsches Pflanzenleben nach Albertus Magnus* is a fundamental work on Albert's natural history.

[174] *DPE*, Tr. 2, Caput 9, Jammy, Vol. 5, p. 311.

come into being after the Fall.[175] Although nature might be imperfect, its study takes us into a realm of knowledge worth knowing for its own sake and because it is useful knowledge.

To learn through nature study is not only a pleasurable experience, it is also useful for life and the welfare of a country. Granted that nature is the sole principle underlying all natural phenomena, nevertheless everything which is susceptible to change can be changed, for better or for worse, through art and cultivation. Men can effect great changes in plants, converting them from the wild to the domestic state by manuring, working the soil, sowing, and grafting. Let us talk, he continues, of the cultivation of the fields, of gardens, meadows, orchards, and of other activities by which plants are taken from the wild to the domestic state.[176]

Unlike the abstract formulations of his pupil, St. Thomas Aquinas, Albert's range is from the mightier questions with which St. Thomas concerned himself to the familiar smells of the barnyard. The agricultural portions of the work, often derived from the Roman writers and Palladius, have a live, contemporary ring to them in their discussion of manuring, the working of soils, grafting. He is interested in land classification,[177] in fields first brought into cultivation, in the problem of the roots of felled trees robbing the new crops of their food, of hillside slopes whose soil is carried by the waters to the valleys below.[178]

The designed earth of St. Albert is more than an abstraction or a conventional illustration of the physico-theological proof of the existence of God. It is holy, it is a creation, but it can also be talked about in the language of the vineyardist, the gardener, the farmer, the horticulturist.

### 13. St. Thomas Aquinas

In the *Summa Theologiae*, St. Thomas Aquinas lists and discusses five arguments proving the existence of God, the fifth being derived from the evidence of the governance of the world. The order and regularity observed in the behavior of natural bodies which lack the intelligence to act purposefully presuppose the direction of a being with knowledge and intelligence "as the arrow is shot to its mark by the archer." There is thus an intelligent being directing all natural things to their end, "and this being we call God."[179]

---

[175] *Summa Theologiae*, Pt. 2, Tr. 11, Q. 44, p. 279; Q. 46, Mem. 3, p. 314. Cites Bede, Augustine, Gen. 3, Jammy, Vol. 18.

[176] *De veget. et plantis*, Bk. 7, Tr. 1, chap. 1, Jammy, Vol. 5, p. 488.

[177] *Ibid.*, Bk. 7, Tr. 1, chap. 5, Jammy, Vol. 5, pp. 492–493.

[178] On newly cultivated lands and tree felling, chap. 8; hillside slopes, chap. 7, Jammy, Vol. 5, pp. 492–496.

[179] The five proofs are in *ST*, Pt. I, Q. 2, Art. 3, pp. 13–14. See also *SCG*, Bk. 1, chap. 13, par. 5, where St. Thomas discusses John the Damascene and Averroes.

The artisan analogy is useful also in explaining the variety and the multiplicity of the creation.

> Since every agent intends to introduce its likeness into its effect, in the measure that its effect can receive it, the agent does this more perfectly as it is the more perfect itself; obviously, the hotter a thing is, the hotter its effect, and the better the craftsman, the most perfectly does he put into matter the form of his art. Now, God is the most perfect agent. It was His prerogative, therefore, to induce His likeness into created beings most perfectly, to a degree consonant with the nature of created being.

No one species can attain to this likeness of God. No single creature can express in full manner the likeness of God, it cannot be equal to God. "The presence of multiplicity and variety among created things was therefore necessary that a perfect likeness to God be found in them according to their manner of being."[180]

The hierarchy of, and continuity in, nature—its observed variety, richness, multiplicity, fullness—are therefore necessary to obtain a perfect representation of God.[181] The greater the variety, the greater the multiplicity of things, the more closely is perfection approached. This argument is consistent with St. Thomas's fourth proof of the existence of God, the proof from the "gradation to be found in things."

Furthermore, it is better to have a multiplicity of species than a multiplicity of individuals of one species. St. Thomas comes close to a concept of balance and harmony in nature: despite characteristics that produce conflict (the lion cannot be blamed for having characteristics harmful to the lamb) there is an order in their manner of living. In nature no one species, left to itself, will multiply to the point of dominance. The diversity and inequality of the creation are necessary to order, which, it would seem, means the orderly working together of many creatures differing among themselves in gradation of intellect, in form, and in species.[182]

God's intellect is the principle involved in the creation of living beings; the greatest perfection of the universe would therefore require some creatures who can share His intellectual nature. Since God creates out of his goodness and in a wish to communicate a likeness of Himself to his creatures, this likeness in the living creation would consist in more than mere existing but also in knowing. In this way is man set apart from the rest of the creation.[183]

St. Thomas comments on the language of the Psalms (on God's works, on

---

[180] *SCG*, Bk. 1, chap. 45, par. 2.

[181] *Ibid.*, Bk. 2, chap. 45, par. 3–4. See also Lovejoy, *Great Chain of Being*, pp. 73–80.

[182] *SCG*, Bk. 2, chap. 45, par. 6–8. Here is St. Thomas's summary: "The diversity and inequality in created things are not the result of chance, nor of a diversity of matter, nor of the intervention of certain causes or merits, but of the intention of God Himself, who wills to give the creature such perfection as it is possible for it to have." *SCG*, Bk. 2, chap. 45, par. 9. In par. 10, he continues the same theme with comments on Gen. 1:31.

[183] *SCG*, Bk. 2, chaps. 23–24; 46, par. 2, 5–7.

"the works of Thy hands"), adding that "we understand heaven and earth, and all that is brought into being by God, as the handicraft produced by a craftsman."[184] "This sort of meditation on the divine works is indeed necessary for instruction of faith in God." We can admire and reflect on His wisdom (quotes Psalm 103:24 = 104:24 in RSV). In this appeal for knowledge in support of faith through contemplation of God's works, it is the great passages on the beauty of nature and of the creation in the Bible and the Apocrypha that are cited: Ecclesiasticus, the Psalms, Paul to the Romans and to the Corinthians.[185] These are the passages which have inspired much of the natural theology of modern times as well.

The art and handicraft of God, like those of the human artisan, require order, wisdom, and intellect. Using Aristotelian sources, the Psalms, and Proverbs, St. Thomas argues the case for reason in the activity of God, criticizing "the error of those who said that all things depend on the simple will of God, without any reason."[186] St. Thomas relies again on the wisdom argument and the artisan analogy: "All ordering, therefore, is necessarily effected by means of the wisdom of a being endowed with intelligence. Even so, in the world of the mechanical arts, the planners of buildings are called the wise men of their craft."[187]

St. Thomas, and other schoolmen, made a clear distinction between natural and revealed theology, and if the former was inferior to the latter, it was at least a valuable aid in the interpretation of nature and the understanding of God. The dangers to the faith of an undue interest in natural theology were not yet apparent, nor were the dangers to revealed religion in the reading of the book of nature. These became apparent later in the writings of Ramon Lull and Ramon Sibiude (Raymond Sebond) and, in modern times, in the attachment of the deists to natural theology, although these ideas were not confined to them, being shared by many pious and orthodox men.

In St. Thomas, the idea of order, planning, and design were joined with thoughts on the beauty of the creation, described in the Scriptures to produce a rigorous natural theology.[188] In the *Summa Contra Gentiles*, he composed the most important and cogent discussion of natural theology which appeared in the Middle Ages. He distilled—with generous acknowledgment—the ideas

---

[184] *SCG*, Bk. 2, chap. 1, par. 6; chap. 2, par. 1; see also chap. 24, 4–6, in which Psalm 104 (103):24 is again quoted; and chap. 26, 6.

[185] *Ecclesiasticus, or the Wisdom of Jesus the Son of Sirach*, 1:9, 42:15; Ps. 139:6, 11, 14; *Wisdom of Solomon*, 13:4; Pss. 104:24; 92:4; Rom. 1:20; II Cor. 3:18, and others. These citations to the RSV of the Bible and the Apocrypha differ from the references to the Vulgate given as footnotes or in the text to *SCG*, Bk. 2, chap. 2 of the Image Book edition.

[186] *SCG*, Bk. 2, chap. 24, par. 7; par. 4 and 6 citing Aristotle, *Metaph*. I, 2, *Eth. Nic*. VI, 4; and par. 6, Ps. 104:24 and Prov. 3:19 in the RSV.

[187] *SCG*, Bk. 2, chap. 24, par. 4.

[188] See Webb, *Studies in the History of Natural Theology*, pp. 235–236.

of the early Church Fathers with their reliance on the beauties of nature and natural history in support of the Christian religion in meeting pagan criticism. In his natural theology, St. Thomas recognizes two themes (already mentioned) running through much of the literature on nature in the Middle Ages: the existence of God in a revealed religion requires no other proof than the Word, but evidences from the natural order add supplementary support, open up new paths to learning the ways of God. It is, again, the distinction between the book of God and the book of nature.

Aristotle's teleology and his concept that nature does nothing in vain supported this natural theology. Aristotle, however, did not engulf St. Thomas, who in fact transformed Aristotle and made him speak on behalf of the Christian God.[189]

It is, however, idle to speak of nature, man, and the earth separately, for they make up a broader problem: the status of Christianity as a religion, and its ability to combat supposed error, either from within or without, and to achieve intellectual quality and dignity. The problem in St. Thomas's time is similar to that of the early Church Fathers who used evidences from the world of nature and from classical science in support of their ideas of God, the creation, and the order of nature. St. Thomas saw the problem with great clarity:

> To proceed against individual errors, however, is a difficult business, and this for two reasons. In the first place, it is difficult because the sacrilegious remarks of individual men who have erred are not so well known to us so that we may use what they say as the basis of proceeding to a refutation of their errors. This is, indeed, the method that the ancient Doctors of the Church used in the refutation of the errors of the Gentiles. For they could know the positions taken by the Gentiles since they themselves had been Gentiles, or at least had lived among the Gentiles and had been instructed in their teaching. In the second place, it is difficult because some of them, such as the Mohammedans and the pagans, do not agree with us in accepting the authority of any Scripture, by which they may be convinced of their error. Thus, against the Jews we are able to argue by means of the Old Testament, while against heretics we are able to argue by means of the New Testament. But the Mohammedans and the pagans accept neither the one nor the other. We must, therefore, have recourse to the natural reason, to which all men are forced to give their assent. However, it is true, in divine matters the natural reason has its failings.[190]

Furthermore, there was the question of goodness or the evil in nature, a recurrent and confusing theme in Christian theology, since it was complicated by the ideas both of a curse on nature after the fall of man and of the physical and moral inferiority of the sensible world to the City of God. We do not see in St. Thomas the same interest in observing nature as we see in Albert the Great's *Summa de creaturis*; neither do we see the almost mystical and lyrical attachment to nature and living things so typical of St. Francis of Assisi. There

---

[189] See Gilson, *HCPMA*, p. 365.
[190] *SCG*, Bk. 1, chap. 2, par. 3.

is no mistaking, however, his awareness of nature and of its philosophical and theological significance. There is a constant effort to show its beauty and goodness; he combats an extreme otherworldliness, including contempt for the earth as man's home and for the problems of life.

Thomas is never tired of demonstrating the goodness of nature. And here it is important to appreciate the circumstances under which he wrote. In attacking the assumption that nature is evil, he is not merely criticizing a perverse theory. He is concerned with the greatest danger that ever assailed the Medieval Church. The thirteenth century saw a widespread revival of Manichaean beliefs, against which . . . Augustine had strenuously fought. The most notorious example of this rigid Puritan creed was the Albigensian heresy, on which the Church had exacted such terrible punishment. But the heresy had been almost as general as the Catholic Faith. The doctrines of this movement were based upon a dualism of spirit and matter, and it was believed that all forms of matter were evil. Nature, including the bodies of animals and men, was indiscriminatingly condemned. The Albigenses rejected the fundamental doctrines of orthodox Christianity and advocated social practices which threatened the continuance of the human race.[191]

St. Thomas' criticism is illustrated by his comment on Origen who, he said, believed that "corporeal creatures were not made according to God's original purpose, but in punishment of the sin of spiritual creatures." Origen's opinion is false, Thomas replies, because the universe must be looked upon as an organic whole, each one of whose parts exists for its own particular end. Some are less noble than others, but they form a hierarchy of life within the organic unity of the universe from the least noble to God himself. Nature is not a reflection of sin; the cosmos, a creation of God, reflects his glory and proves his goodness. It is doctrine consistent with Genesis 1:31 and with Psalms 8 and 104.[192]

This criticism of Origen is of interest, because the latter in *Contra Celsum*, as we have seen, expresses ideas similar to those of St. Thomas: God favors the rational over the irrational, hence the favored position of man in nature, and the subordination of much of the irrational life to him.[193]

Since St. Thomas accepts the teleological view of nature, no existence can be divorced from the ends for which it was created. Teleological ideas historically have always depended a great deal on the world of nature for their confirmation, especially the biological world where the apparent confirmation is so ready at hand. Even a man like St. Thomas, so interested in abstract— almost legalistic—formulations, is forced to the sensible world and especially to the biological realm.[194] St. Thomas had adopted the Aristotelian view of nature with its emphasis on final causes, and he, like Aristotle, had to consider

---

[191] Carré, *Realists and Nominalists*, p. 97.
[192] *ST*, Pt. 1, Q. 65, Art. 2. See also Carré, *op. cit.*, pp. 97–98.
[193] See *Contra Celsum*, IV, 75, 78.
[194] See also Carré, *op. cit.*, pp. 70, 73.

the secondary causes, subordinate to the final cause which brings about the desired end. Secondary causes redound to the greater glory of the creator, his greatness is not diminished because he fails to do everything personally, because he acts through subsidiary and intermediate causes. Furthermore, it is secondary causes, and not the Creator, which are responsible for the existence of evil in the world and the imperfections of nature. It is not the Divine intention to deprive lower agents of their causality; a child is born from the semen of a man, an object becomes hot because it is near a hot object. The direct intervention of God is not manifested here. Lower agents must have powers as part of the ends for which they were created, without calling in the agency of God to perform every act of a physical or reproductive nature, such as warming up with fire, or reproduction in the organic world. Since Divine Guidance does not exclude the working of secondary causes, we can understand how evil and imperfection can arise out of their working; here St. Thomas uses homely examples from daily life. An artisan may be very skilled but his product may be imperfect because of an imperfection in his instrument; a man may limp, not because of any defect in the mobile power of his body but because of a twist in his leg bone. "So, it is possible, in the case of things made and governed by God, for some defect and evil to be found, because of a defect of the secondary agents, even though there be no defect in God Himself."[195]

God's adornment of the world is part of His creative act. In the beginning, the earth, invisible, void, shapeless, empty, is "without the comeliness which it owes to the plants that clothe it, as it were, with a garment."[196]

The work of creation therefore is divided into three phases: the creation of heaven and earth without form; the work of distinction, the perfection of heaven and earth "either by adding substantial form to formless matter (cites Augustine, *Gen. ad. litt.* II, 11) or by giving them the order and beauty due them as other holy writers suppose"; and the work of adornment which itself is accomplished in phases. On the first day of the adornment, the fourth in the creation, the lights are created "to adorn the heavens by their movements"; on the second day, the fifth of the creation, birds and fishes are created "to make beautiful the intermediate element, for they move in air and water which are here taken as one"; and on the third day of the adornment, or the sixth of creation, the animals are created "to move upon the earth and adorn it."[197] On the seventh day a further ordering of nature was accomplished; God acted on this day, not by further creation "but by directing and moving His creatures to the work proper to them, and thus He made some beginning of the *second* perfection."[198]

[195] *SCG*, Bk. 3, chap. 69, par. 12; chap. 71, par. 2; and the important discussion of Bk. 3, chaps. 69–71.
[196] *ST*, Pt. 1, Q. 69, Art. 2, = pp. 344–345.
[197] Pt. 1, Q. 70, Art. 1, = p. 346.
[198] Pt. 1, Q. 73, Art. 1, Obj. 2, and Reply to Obj. 2, = p. 353.

What men can learn from the order in nature is limited: they can observe it and conclude from it that an artisan exists, but they are unable to discern the nature of the creative being or whether there is one or many.[199] Consistent with his teleological position, St. Thomas says that the Creator has only the good in mind in devising the orderly processes of nature. Leaves, for example, are so arranged that they protect the fruit of the plant, and various natural protective devices perform a like purpose in animals. They are not products of chance. "Therefore, the natural agent tends toward what is better, and it is much more evident that the intelligent agent does so. Hence, every agent intends the good when it acts."[200] The synthesis now expresses the goodness, the order, and the beauty of nature.

St. Thomas's description of the Garden of Eden throws an interesting light on his conception of the most desirable physical environment. Eden is an idyllic place, but not for lazy idlers, for work here is not wearing, as it became after the Fall. Paradise has a temperate climate; he agrees with Isidore (*Etym.* xiv, 3) that it is most fittingly in the east, "the most excellent part of the earth," because the east "is the right hand on the heavens." Since the right is nobler than the left, "it was fitting that God should place the earthly paradise in the east." (Cites Aristotle, *De Caelo*, II, 2.)[201] To the objection that men have explored the entire habitable world and have not yet found paradise, St. Thomas replies that it is shut off by mountains, or seas, or torrid regions which cannot be crossed, so that people who have written about topography make no mention of it; he discusses the possible location of paradise on the equator, but is more inclined to agree with Aristotle (*Meteor*, II, 5) that the equatorial regions are uninhabitable. This idea, too, was elaborated on at length by Bodin in the sixteenth century.[202]

St. Thomas asks if man was placed in paradise to dress it and to keep it, and then answers, following Augustine, that cultivation in paradise would be pleasant "on account of man's practical knowledge of the powers of nature." To St. Thomas, tilling the earth in a quiet rural setting in a temperate climate seems to have been an idyllic existence worthy of man even before the Fall.[203]

---

[199] *SCG*, Bk. 3, Pt. 1, chap. 38, 1.

[200] *SCG*, Bk. 3, chap. 3, par. 9.

[201] This idea of the right and left of the heavens reappears frequently in the Renaissance, as for example, in the *Methodus* of Bodin. *ST*, Pt. 1, Q. 102, Art. 1, p. 499.

[202] *ST*, Pt. 1, Q. 102, Art. 2. Reply Obj. 4, p. 501. On ideas of the habitability of the equatorial regions held in the Middle Ages, see Wright, *The Geographical Lore of the Time of the Crusades*, pp. 162–165. "The study of Moslem astronomy," says Wright (p. 162), "brought to Europe the opinion that the equatorial zone itself was not only habitable but actually inhabited." Wright also refers to the long passage in Peter Alphonsi [1106?] on the temperate climate of Arin (Aren) on the equator. *Dialogi*, = *PL* 157, col. 547. Albert the Great believed the tropics habitable if one could take shelter in caves when the sun is perpendicular overhead. *De natura locorum*, Bk. I, 6, Jammy, Vol. 5, p. 270. Gallois, *Les Géographes Allemands de la Renaissance*, believes Albert was almost alone in this belief, p. 137.

[203] *ST*, Pt. 1, Q. 102, Art. 3, p. 501.

St. Thomas also considers the effect of the sin of man on the order of nature. One consequence of the Fall was that those creatures which obeyed man in his state of innocence no longer obeyed him in sin; his control over animal life—he is referring to domestication—was only partial after the Fall. Man's power in his state of innocence is related to his place in the order of perfection. Citing Aristotle (*Pol.* I, 5) on the role of plants in feeding the animals and of the animals in serving man, St. Thomas says, "It is in keeping with the order of nature, that man should be master over animals."[204]

Man "in a certain sense contains all things." Reason makes him like the angels, sensitive powers, like the animals, natural forces, like the plants, and his body is like inanimate things. Before the Fall, man's mastery over plant and animal life "consisted not in commanding or in changing them, but in making use of them without hindrance."[205] St. Thomas thus reconciles man's obvious though partial control over animal life by domestication with the fall from grace and with his retention—despite the Fall—of enough attributes of the Divine to make him worthy of a continuing control over nature. The relation of man to plant and especially to animal domestication must always have been a question to excite curiosity; St. Thomas's explanation was consistent with Christian theology. (See p. 206 on Alexander Neckam.)

Man's place in nature and his partial control over it are consequences of his place in the hierarchy of being; because of this, he also makes use of the natural environment, adapting what it affords to his own needs.[206] His dominion over nature is but an expression of the rational plan of Divine Providence, that rational creatures rule over others. Since man shares at least to some extent in the intellectual light, the animals, which do not participate in understanding, are subject to man by order of Divine Providence.[207]

Perhaps the most significant observation to be made concerning St. Thomas's ideas of God, man, and man's place in the natural world, is that they have a cosmopolitan character. The guiding ideas, it is true, do not differ from the great Christian texts of the past, but the discussions and the amplifications are the result of intrusions from the south and from the past. Viewed in this light, St. Thomas' *Summa Contra Gentiles* is one of the most interesting books ever written.

It would seem that the basic assumption in his philosophy of man and nature is that man rules over the hierarchies of being lower than he is, simultaneously adapting benign nature to his manifold uses, not as a right nor because of power and intellect which he has created by and for himself, but because of the rational and the divine within him, placed there by God. Man's position in nature, despite his power and control, is therefore a derivative one, calling for humility on his part.

[204] *ST*, Pt. 1, Q. 96, Art. 1, p. 486.
[205] *ST*, Pt. 1, Q. 96, Art. 2, p. 487.
[206] *SCG*, Bk. 3, Pt. 1, chap. 22, par. 8.
[207] *Ibid.*, chap. 78, par. 1; 81, par. 1. Quotes Gen. 1:26 in part.

## 14. St. Bonaventura and Ramon Sibiude

In the first chapter of *The Mind's Road to God*, St. Bonaventura speaks of God's traces in the sensible world, the text being inspired by Romans 1:20. Statements like this can be found among all theologians of the Middle Ages, including St. Bonaventura's great rivals the Thomists. Different interpretations of nature, however, can emerge from commentaries on Romans 1:20. St. Bonaventura's has been called exemplarism,[208] a word that encompasses many ideas we have already discussed. Everything in nature is a sign of God. We have seen this exemplarism in the notion of nature as a book; it is implicit in the theophany of John the Scot, in Alan of Lille's mirror, in the nature reverence of St. Francis, and later in the thought of Ramon of Sibiude. It follows, in this Augustinian tradition, that creatures are important because they provide the traces of God. They have no significance of their own. The emphasis is not on the study of nature per se; creatures confirm the work of God.

Quoting Proverbs 16:4 and Psalms 16:2, St. Bonaventura says God created things not because they were useful to Him nor because of His need, nor to increase His glory, but to display it and impart it ("non, inquam, propter gloriam augendam, sed propter gloriam manifestandam, et propter gloriam suam communicandam"), in the display and imparting of which the highest usefulness of the creature is attained, that is, His glorification and His felicity.[209]

It is this exemplarism that contrasts with interpretations of nature by men like Albertus Magnus and to a lesser degree Thomas of Cantimpré, who represent "the tendency of the period to interest itself in the realities, as well as in the symbolisms, of the natural world."[210] One should not speak in polarities but in trends—the trend toward interest in realities versus that toward "the fulfillment of a religious obligation"[211]—in nature study, for one can find exemplarism in most of these writers, including St. Thomas Aquinas.

In the early period at least, the Franciscans emphasized the simple preaching of the Bible, recruited members of the lower classes, and identified themselves essentially with rural life; these circumstances may have caused the order as a rule "to put more emphasis upon the observation of the natural world than its great rival, Thomism, did."[212]

St. Bonaventura became the seventh general of the Franciscan order in 1257, consciously trying to follow in the footsteps of St. Francis. In the thirty-third year after the saint's death, Bonaventura ascended Mount Alverna to

---

[208] Leff, *Medieval Thought*, p. 200.
[209] "In quatuor libros sententiarum," Lib. 2, Dist. 1, pars 2, art. 2, quaest. 1, concl. (*Opera omnia*, Vol. 2, p. 265.)
[210] Taylor, *The Medieval Mind*, Vol. 2, p. 429.
[211] See George Boas' introd., *Mind's Road to God*, p. xix.
[212] *Ibid.*, Leff, *op. cit.*, p. 181.

meditate "on the ascent of the mind to God." There, as did St. Francis, he saw the vision "of the winged Seraph in the likeness of the Crucified."[213]

In *The Mind's Road to God*, St. Bonaventura describes the six stages in the ascent to God, the first and lowest of which is the reflection of God in his traces (*vestigia*) in the sensible world, the word meaning, says Boas, the art which reveals the artist, the handiwork which reveals the traces of workmanship. The saint "seems haunted by the basic metaphor of the universe's being a sort of mirror (*speculum*) in which God is to be seen." We must mount Jacob's ladder, placing "the first rung of the ascension in the depths, putting the whole sensible world before us as a mirror; by which ladder we shall mount up to God...."[214]

All creatures of this world lead the mind to the contemplation of God because they are "shadows, echoes, and pictures, the traces, simulacra, and reflections of that First Principle most powerful, wisest, and best; of that light and plenitude; of that art productive, exemplifying, and ordering, given to us for looking upon God." They are exemplifications "set before our yet untrained minds" to guide them to the intelligences that they do not see.

Every creature is a sort of picture, a likeness of eternal wisdom; "Those who are unwilling to give heed to them and to know God in them all, to bless Him and to love Him, are inexcusable while they are unwilling to be carried forth from the shadows into the wonderful light of God."[215]

A more interesting work of this genre is the *Theologia Naturalis* of Ramon Sibiude (Raymond Sebond); he wrote it in 1436, and it was published about 1484, but apparently it had little influence. His name probably would now be forgotten were it not for Montaigne's famous—and longest—essay which contains little about either Ramon Sibiude or his thought. His work, however, is a landmark in the history of natural theology and of Christian apologetics associated with the propagation of the faith.

Sibiude's work is regarded largely as a continuation of ideas already expressed by Ramon Lull. In Lull's natural theology—and in this Sibiude followed him—God revealed himself in two books, the book of nature, and the Bible.

Scotus Erigena's 'theophanic' universe, the *liber creaturarum* of William of Auvergne and Saint Bonaventure, in fact the whole symbolism of the Lapidaries and the Bestiaries, without forgetting the symbolism that decorated the porches of mediaeval cathedrals or shone in their windows, were so many testimonials of a general confidence in the translucency of a universe in which the least of all beings was a living token of the presence of God. If, as is commonly believed, he was associated with the Franciscan Order, Lull had not far to look to make acquaintance with this universe. Saint Francis of Assisi and Saint Bonaventure had lived in no other one (Gilson).

[213] *The Mind's Road to God*, Prologue, 2.
[214] Boas, *op. cit.*, p. 7, note 1; *Mind's Road to God*, chap. 1, 9.
[215] *Mind's Road to God*, chap. 2, 11-13.

Two great reservoirs of knowledge are available to man, says Sibiude, the book of creatures and the book of scriptures. If his doctrine of the all-sufficiency of the book of nature were followed, however, the evidences of scripture would be subordinated to those seen in the visible creation, a point of view calling for the vigorous study of nature, not for experimentation and observation for its own sake but, in Webb's striking phrase, with an "attentive sense," a characteristic true of both ancient and modern natural theology. Sibiude says that of the two books which have been given to him, man has possessed the book of nature from the beginning. A book is composed of letters and man is rational, but he had no knowledge at the creation and had to acquire it. He could do this only with a book, for knowledge is impossible without a book in which it is set down. A creature is a letter written by the finger of God, and many creatures, like many letters, make up a book. The book of nature, however, is superior to the book of scripture: it cannot be falsified, destroyed, or misinterpreted; it will not induce heresy, and heretics cannot misunderstand it.[216]

This doctrine, however, is not so heretical as it might at first appear. It emerges naturally from biblical exegesis. Holy Writ contains the truth, men's opinions are always open to error. No doctrine has a firmer grounding in Christian theology than this. Not all commentaries on Holy Writ have equal merit. St. Augustine had explained this in the "Contra Faustum Manichaeum." If we encounter an absurdity in the authentic canon of the Old or the New Testament, he says, we cannot say the author is in error; it is due to the faultiness of the manuscript, the translator has been deceived, or we have not grasped the author's meaning. The authority of later writers, below canonical rank, is lower. They may contain truth, but it is far from being the same as the canon.[217] Obviously exegesis had within it the seeds of disputation and controversy; and it could be carried to the point that Sibiude carried it in regarding the written word as inferior to the book of nature.

The physico-theological proof of the existence of God therefore has unusual weight in Sibiude's work. The creation is the work of an artisan, God having determined the correct proportions of things, limited them, and arranged them. In the hierarchy of nature, there are devices for keeping the numbers of each kind of creature in balance (one does not increase to the point of crowding out all else), and the natural array is a harmonious one.

[216] On the publication of *Theologia Naturalis*, Gilson, *HCPMA*, pp. 701–702, note 61. Lull was born in Palma de Mallorca in 1235; on his place in Christian apologetics, especially in exposing the errors of the Averroists and the Muslims, pp. 350–351. Quotation is on p. 353.
Webb has argued that Sibiude's book was placed on the Index because of Sibiude's "doctrine of the all-sufficiency of the book of Nature." Quotations on pp. 296, 297. Sibiude's *Theologia Naturalis* was translated into French by Michel Montaigne; it is not to be confused with his apology for Raymond Sebond. See the preface to the *TN*, chap. 3.
[217] "Contra Faustum Manichaeum," XI, chap. 5, *OCSA*, Vol. 25, pp. 538–539; *NPN*, Vol. 4, p. 180.

Man is exalted over the organic and inorganic world, but his superior station, like the inferior stations of the plants and animals, is not of his making. The ways of obtaining subsistence correspond with the hierarchy of life: trees take their nourishment directly from the earth with their roots, animals use their mouths, and man lives more nobly than either. These arrangements of nature rest, of course, on the assumptions of the fixity of species and of an order on earth established at the creation. Sibiude's questions answer themselves: Who sees that each creature remains in its proper rank, station, and order? Who made these gradations permanent? Who keeps the land and the sea within bounds?[218]

Neither Lull nor Sibiude relied on scripture or on authority. Lull argued, and Sibiude followed him in this, about the articles of faith and tried to show the logical value of Catholic truths without appeal either to the Scriptures or to the doctors of the church.[219] Sibiude regarded man as the most important of creatures after the angels; in the hierarchy, all things ranking below him find their end in him, as man finds his end in God. For this reason, man appears as a connecting link between the sensible world of nature and the divine.[220]

Not since St. Basil's time had there been such thorough use of the world of nature in the service of theology. Sibiude's thought is not a daring departure, but a one-sided extension—almost an exaggeration—of the traditional belief. The creation is reliable evidence of God's presence and his handiwork; it is a book not subject to the error of misinterpretation, schism, conflicting doctrine. This is an attitude which comes close to the natural religion of the seventeenth and the eighteenth centuries.

## 15. SECULAR VIEWS OF NATURE

Not all of this thought about man, nature, and the earth served religious purposes. If religious men like Albertus Magnus were also interested in natural history, plants, and agriculture as practical matters, this preoccupation had its counterpart in secular writings and in art. An excellent example in poetry is *The Romance of the Rose* (1237, 1277), one of the most widely read and enjoyed poems of the Middle Ages. Chaucer has translated part of it into English. Lorris's part has beautiful passages of nature description; de Meun's, of equal beauty, is broadly based on scholastic learning and is controversial. Guillaume de Lorris's poetry in the *Romance* "won an immediate following," while de Meun's "created a furore."

In his apology (chap. 70) De Meun defends himself against a charge of bawdiness of speech by saying that his language is necessary for his tale. Of his supposed misogyny, he says he writes for instruction's sake to depict human

---

[218] *Theologia Naturalis.* Sibiude gives the main outline of his argument in his preface.
[219] Probst, *Le Lullisme de Raymond de Sebonde (Ramon de Sibiude)*, p. 18.
[220] *Ibid.*, p. 16. On Sibiude's natural theology, see also Webb, *Studies in the Hist. of Nat. Theology*, pp. 292–312.

life as it is, that there is early authority for women's behavior. He has no intention of making personal attacks on those who follow the Holy Church or who lead a devoted religious life, but he will seek out hypocrisy and has proof of his accusations.

> If Holy Church can find a single word
> Which she may foolish deem, I ready stand
> To make amends, if they will satisfy
> Whenever she may deign to fix a fitting time.[221]

De Meun was a man of learning and of historical sense; he translated Vegetius' *De re militari*, Boethius' *Consolation of Philosophy*, the *Life and Letters of Peter Abélard and Heloïse*, and Giraldus Cambrensis' *Topography of Ireland*. Because of its popularity and preeminence, and the breadth of the conception, especialy de Meun's, the poem is a sensitive expression of many ideas current in his age.[222] It is full of interest to anyone studying the history of ideas of nature, and one is immediately struck by the influence of Alan of Lille's *De planctu naturae*. In Guillaume de Lorris's part, including the last seventy-eight lines of an anonymouts poet (lines 1–4058), there are many charming passages full of life, sparkle, and appreciation of natural beauty, but they are simple, personal, with little pretense of philosophic depth or significance. In Jean de Meun's part (lines 4059–21780) the conceptions of nature, the Creator, the earth, and man are expressed as Alan expressed them, by a personified "Nature" and by "Genius." Discussions of sexuality, written in bold metaphorical language (the hammer and the anvil also come from Alan), are really strong affirmations of life, fecundity, and plenitude in nature. Man's behavior is castigated when it departs from the norm characteristic of the rest of nature.

The Platonic artisan-deity creates an earth of beauty and loveliness; this generous creator has a plan and purpose, and like the God of the Jews, creates *ex nihilo*. In the beginning God ordained chaos, a mass of confusion and disorder; then he separated out the elements "which never since have been anatomized," numbered them, and stationed each element in its proper place.

> The lighter rose aloft; the heavy sank
> Down to the center—medials between.
> In time and space He rightly each ordained.[223]

When, according to His design God "has thus His other creatures all disposed," He established "Nature" to serve him, appointing her his chamberlain, his constable, his steward, and his vicar-general.

> God honors me so much that in my ward
> He leaves the lovely golden chain that binds
> The elements, which bow before my face.[224]

---

[221] *The Romance of the Rose*, chap. 70, 124–127.
[222] See Charles Dunn's introduction to *The Romance of the Rose*, trans. by Robbins, esp. pp. xvi–xviii; on its fame, pp. xxv–xxvii.
[223] *Ibid.*, chap. 81, lines 46–48; on the creation, lines 18–31.
[224] *Ibid.*, chap. 81, lines 64–66, and lines 49–63.

It is God's will that all obey Nature, observing her rules, forgetting none of her laws. Of all the creation only man fails to observe these regulations with care. Man however has freedom of the will; he can bring reason to his relationship with the cosmos; the influence of the stars may be great but reason can withstand it.

> Each wise man knows
> That Reason is not subject to the stars;
> For 'neath their power she was not brought to birth.[225]

Man owes to his understanding the power over the dumb, destitute beasts that cannot speak or understand one another.

> But, if they were endowed with speech and sense
> To understand each other and themselves,
> It would go hard with man.[226]

Maned coursers would neither permit the bit nor let knights mount them; no ox would submit to the yoke; no ass or mule would carry a burden for a despised master; no elephant would bear a castle high on his back; no cat or dog would serve man, for they could well support themselves. There would be war if animals had the endowments of man; his plots to conquer them would be met by similar artifices. The animals would fight a dramatic war to the finish with the human race, from the apes and monkeys to the bugs, nits, and flesh worms who even now are bold.[227]

> So boldly that a man must leave his work
> To beat them down and drive the pests away.[228]

The moral is that men must avoid wickedness and vices which dull the senses and intoxicate. Man can use free will and follow reason; if he does not, he can plead no mitigation.

Men should see that violent storms of thunder and lightning ("The trumpets, kettledrums, and tambourines of the celestial orchestra") have natural causes.

> For nothing but the tempest and the wind
> Are needed to explain the havoc wrought.[229]

Men now have books to study about nature. Aristotle has observed more of nature than any man since the times of Tubal-cain, and Alhazen's book on optics "none but fools neglect."[230]

In the remarkable chapter 87, again reminiscent of Alan of Lille, partly

---

[225] *Ibid.*, chap. 82, lines 43–45; on nature's laws, chap. 81, lines 53–74.
[226] *Ibid.*, chap. 82, lines 543–545.
[227] *Ibid.*, lines 545–580.
[228] *Ibid.*, lines 581–582.
[229] *Ibid.*, chap. 83, lines 11–12, 28–29.
[230] *Ibid.*, lines 119–123. On Tubal-cain see Gen. 4:22.

moralizing, partly didactic, de Meun commends the whole creation, the heavens, the elements, plants, birds, animals, and insects, all except man. The heavenly bodies on their courses fulfill their duty; the elements behave; plants are attentive to nature's laws. Good scholars are the fish and fowl:

> They breed according to their several wonts,
> And thus do honor to their lineage.
> Great comfort 'tis to see how each of them
> Strives to prevent his race from dying out.[231]

The animals are given a clean bill of health too; they couple well and graciously:

> No bargaining
> Delays their union when they're in accord.[232]

The insects—the flies, the ants, and the butterflies—the worms "that breed in rottenness," adders and snakes like good scholastics "are studious to do my work."[233]

Man is a companion of creatures everywhere, shares the blessings which they have, but he alone fails. Like the stones, he has being; like the herbs, life; like the beasts, feeling; like the angels, thinking. (See above on St. Thomas, p. 236.) Of him, Nature complains,

> He has whatever humans can conceive;
> He is a microcosm in himself—
> Yet worse than any wolf cub uses me.

Man, however, is out of Nature's jurisdiction; she did not provide him with his understanding.

> I'm neither wise nor powerful enough
> To make a creature so intelligent.[234]

Jesus came to save sinful man; but Nature says she does not know how he became mortal without her aid except that in His omnipotence God could create him. She expresses amazement that he was born of the Virgin Mary, "since it could never be / By Nature that a virgin could give birth." In the exhortation to fecundity, Genius speaking on behalf of Nature makes a plea for human sexual activity compatible with the divine plan.[235]

The plea for a natural sex life and the attack on the sexual abstinence of the clergy (sympathetic with the seculars, he was particularly bitter toward the Dominicans) are cast in striking metaphorical language, often of the farmer and the smithy. He sees no merit in the argument that God in his omnipotence

---

[231] *Ibid.*, chap. 87, lines 37–40. See this chapter entire.
[232] *Ibid.*, lines 48–49.
[233] *Ibid.*, lines 54–57.
[234] *Ibid.*, chap. 88, lines 27–29, 33–34.
[235] *Ibid.*, lines 110–112. On Plato's thought, lines 37–73.

has removed desire from some men, for He would want all men to have an equal share of his grace. If all men shared this lack of sexual desire mankind would be extinct.

> I believe
> That 'tis His will that all—not just a few—
> Pursue the road that best will lead to Him.
> If 'tis His will that some lead virgin lives,
> The better to follow Him, then why not all?[236]

Although he challenges the divines to refute him, he has little hope of success; they will discuss "but never will conclude." Like Alan of Lille, he opposes aberrant sexual behavior and for the same reason: sexual activity and reproduction are parts of the divine plan of nature; perversions and permanent continence divorce man from the rest of the law-abiding creation and bring about disharmony.

> But those who with their stylets scorn to write
> Upon the precious tablets delicate
> By means of which all mortals come to life,
> Which Nature never lent us for disuse. . . .[237]

And again, using the ancient identification of woman with the plowed earth,

> And those who are so blinded by their sins
> Or by the pride by which they are deranged
> That they despise the furrow, fair and straight
> Amidst the blooming and luxuriant field,
> And to the proper roadway never keep
> But go like wretches to the desert wastes
> Where they misuse their plows and lose their seed. . . .[238]

The stress is on the force and power of life, the richness and fecundity of nature, and on nature as an instrumentality of God. The sexual act as part of the divine intent should be conducted in accordance with its high purpose; de Meun's is not a philosophy of license and excess.

> Be active in your functions natural—
> More active than the squirrel, and more deft
> And lively than the birds or than the breeze.
> Provided only you work manfully,
> I pardon all your sins; lose not that boon!
> Exert yourselves gaily to leap and dance,
> And rest not, lest your members grow lukewarm.
> All your utensils in the task employ;
> He who works well by work will warm himself.

[236] *Ibid.*, chap. 91, lines 90–94. On de Meun's attitude toward the mendicants, see intro. pp. xxii–xxiv.

[237] *Ibid.*, chap. 91, lines 100, 101–104.

[238] *Ibid.*, lines 111–117. On woman and furrow, see Eliade, *Patterns in Comparative Religion*, pp. 259–260.

Plow, barons, plow—your lineage repair;
For if you do not there'll be nothing left
To build upon.[239]

Indeed, in the twelfth and thirteenth centuries, conceptions of the earth and the living and nonliving nature upon it progress beyond wonderment, simple piety, and commentaries on theology. There is less interest in miracles, more in regularities and in natural law. More is made of the distinction between divine works and nature's works. There is much interest in the observation of nature in the twelfth and thirteenth centuries[240] and, as we have learned from Emile Mâle, in its faithful representation in religious art.

The whole medieval world, according to Mâle, is regarded as a symbol, and the artists carrying out their work on the churches under supervision express the religious thought of their day. But once this all-embracing symbolic interpretation has been complied with in the conception, subordinate decoration may proceed at will. The symbolism is like a canopy, the realism within reflecting often the interests, joys, and aspirations of the untutored and unsophisticated artisan and craftsman who do not hide their light under a bushel. "At Chartres and Bourges . . . in the windows given by the guilds, the lower part shows the donors with the badges of their trade—trowel, hammer, woolcarding comb, baker's shovel and butcher's knife. In those days no incongruity was felt in placing these pictures of daily life side by side with scenes from the legends of the saints."[241]

Jean Gimpel also has written of this commingling of the sacred and the earthly. Of the Cathedral of Chartres he writes,

> Examining the church closely, it becomes evident that the guilds obtained the best possible placement for their windows. They were installed along the side aisles or in the ambulatory nearest the public, while glass donated by bishops and lords was relegated to the clerestory windows of the nave and choir. The cloth merchant, the stonecutter, the wheelwright, and the carpenter each had himself depicted in a medallion in the lower part of the window donated by his guild, as close as possible, as it were, to future clients.[242]

It is an error, Mâle continues, to find symbolism in everything the sculptor of these times did.

> The impartial student of the decorative fauna and flora of the thirteenth century finds it purely a work of art, the expression of a deep and tender love of nature. Left to himself the medieval sculptor did not trouble about symbols, but was simply one of the people, looking at the world with the wondering eyes of a child. Watch him creating the magnificent flora that came to life under his hand. He does not try to read the mystery of the Fall or the Redemption

---

[239] *Ibid.*, chap. 91, lines 151–162.
[240] See Crombie's discussion of thirteenth century biology in *Medieval and Early Modern Science*, Vol. I, pp. 139–161.
[241] Mâle, *The Gothic Image*, pp. 1–5, 29; quotation on pp. 64–65.
[242] Gimpel, *The Cathedral Builders*, p. 47.

into the budding flowers of April. On the first day of spring he goes into some forest of the île-de-France, where humble plants are beginning to push through the earth. The fern tightly rolled like a powerful spring still has its downy covering, but by the side of the streams the arum is almost ready to open.[243]

There is much more that must be left to the reader of Mâle himself and to the authorities like Violett-le-Duc to whom he refers. There are the evolutions in the sculptoring of blossoms, the bas-reliefs devoted to realistic descriptions of the activities of each month, often differing from place to place because of differences in the times of seasonal change.

There are no strong contrasts between town and country, and the rural inspiration is evident in the bas-reliefs of the church. Every detail in the thirteenth century bas-relief was

the outcome of the artist's direct experience of life and nature. At the very gates of the little walled towns of the Middle Ages lay the country with its ploughed land and meadows and the rhythmical sequence of pastoral toil. The towers of Chartres rose above the fields of La Beauce, the cathedral of Reims dominated the vineyards of Champagne and the apse of Notre Dame at Paris the surrounding woods and meadows. And so the sculptors drew inspiration from immediate reality for their scenes of rural life.[244]

And again,

In the small medallions which cover the basement of the cathedral porch at Lyons a number of creatures of the fields and woods are to be seen. Two chickens scratch themselves, a claw hidden under their feathers, a squirrel leaps from branch to branch of a tree clustered with nuts, a crow settles on a dead rabbit, a bird flies off with an eel in his beak, a snail crawls among leaves, and a pig's head shows between the branches of an oak-tree. These animals have been carefully observed, and their characteristic movements are given.

To these sculptors, the great church seemed an epitome of the world and "a place in which all God's creatures may find a home." In a Book of Hours (end of the thirteenth century), "A monkey disguised as a monk walks on stilts, or a musician gives a concert by scraping together the jawbones of an ass."[245]

The sketchbook of Villard de Honnecourt, so often discussed in histories of art, has a place also in the history of nature description. A pelican tears its breast, a magpie perched on a slab holds a cross in its beak. A lord seated with his lady holds a falcon on his right hand. A mounting rider is poised with one foot in the stirrup. A snail with five antennae emerges from its shell, two lifelike parrots grasp their perch with their claws, a frequently reproduced sketch. A minstrel, with his dancing dog, plays the viol; a parrot is perched on the

[243] Mâle, *op. cit.*, p. 51.

[244] *Ibid.*, p. 67. Of great interest but peripheral to our theme is chapter 2, on the method used in medieval iconography, in which Mâle organizes his work around the *Speculum Majus* of Beauvais, the thirteenth century encyclopedist. (For an analysis of this remarkable work, see J. B. Bourgeat, *Études sur Vincent de Beauvais*.)

[245] *Ibid.*, pp. 54, 63, 61.

arm of a graceful woman, her dog jumping beside her. A wild hare and a wild boar are sketched above two crouching figures who are possibly shooting dice. A lion trainer, he says, beats his two hounds when he wishes the growling lion to obey him; the puzzled lion, seeing the beating, has his own spirits dampened and obeys. Villard prides himself on having drawn the lion from real life. He sketches a porcupine, a bear, a jaguar, a grasshopper, a cat, a fly, a dragonfly, a crustacean, a curled dog, grazing sheep, two ostriches, their long necks intersecting to form a rough V, a man with a scythe, a hooded falconer in a triangle, four stonemasons revolving around a broken cross, and the earliest known representation of the water-driven saw.[246]

Although medieval art, church architecture, decorative art, and poetry, are far beyond my modest scope and would carry us into broader fields concerned with the relation of nature to art, of romantic love to nature, of symbolism to nature, and a vast number of other topics, we may very briefly take note of inquiries which give evidence either of a secular view of nature or of a more realistic portrayal of human beings and natural phenomena.

Iconographical representation in the thirteenth century of the Ascension, of the Virgin and the Child, and of the Crucifixion is faithful to human feeling. Christ is shown contorted by pain, with blood flowing from his wounds.[247]

In the iconography of the six-day creation, the early period (roughly fifth and sixth centuries) favored the early days of the creation, the cosmological episodes, while the period of efflorescence of this art (from the middle of the twelfth to about the middle of the thirteenth century) stressed the later acts of creation, that is, what had happened on earth.[248]

Nature poetry, some of it ordered about the march of the seasons (like the church bas-reliefs of which Mâle speaks), is closely associated with love of life, abandonment of study in youth, and romantic love. In the famous anthology of medieval lyrics, the manuscript of Benedictbeuern, there are these lines:

> The earth lies open-breasted
> In gentleness of spring,
> Who lay so close and frozen
> In winter's blustering,
> The northern winds are quiet,
> The west wind winnowing,
> In all this sweet renewing
> How shall a man not sing?[249]

---

[246] *The Sketchbook of Villard de Honnecourt*, edited by Theodore Bowie. See descriptions of the plates, pp. 7–14, and Mâle's remarks on Villard, pp. 54–55.

[247] White, "Natural Science and Naturalistic Art in the Middle Ages," *AHR*, Vol. 52 (1947), pp. 425–426, and footnote 9. White sees the beginning of an age deeply concerned with the investigation of nature around 1140. On the representation of the crucifixion, see also pp. 432–433, and Mâle, p. ix.

[248] See Schmidt, *Die Darstellungen des Sechstagewerkes von Ihren Anfängen bis zum Ende des 15 Jahrhunderts*, pp. 90–92, cited by White, *op. cit.*, p. 430.

[249] *Medieval Latin Lyrics*, trans. by Helen Waddell, p. 219.

Such lyrics of the age from 1150–1250, says Helen Waddell, owe much to Celtic, to Arabic, and especially to pagan sources. The famous manuscript of Benedictbeuern is an impressive example. The drinking song shows no patience for the restrained or the timid drinker. The lyric praises the sweet folly of youth, who must realize that time passes as do the opportunities for such folly. Youth and spring go together, but the beauty of nature, the delicious wandering among trees and the picking of flowers, are no match for loving a young girl. Summer too is for love, and unrequited love is winter. The love themes often borrow generously from classical mythology. In nature, summer must yield to winter, but there is no such cooling of the fire of real love.[250]

## 16.   THE CONDEMNATIONS OF 1277

Other ferments appear in the 219 theses held by Étienne Tempier, Bishop of Paris, to be errors and condemned by him in 1277. The errors, reminiscent of those previously condemned by the same bishop in 1270, are taken from the writings of Averroes, Avicenna, Andrew Capellanus (the treatise *Liber de Amore*), St. Thomas Aquinas, and from unknown authors. Some may have been sayings never put in writing. They affect the ideas under discussion only indirectly; they are more relevant to the history of physics, cosmology, theology, and philosophy. The condemnation, however, showed a natural hostility to the Aristotelian doctrine of the eternity of the world, staunchly opposing anticreationist ideas. Consistent with this position was the rejection of the so-called doctrine of the double truth, according to which a proposition could be considered false from the point of view of reason, true from the point of view of faith. Philosophy and theology thus could be and should be kept apart.[251] Bishop Tempier complained that such men acted as if there were two contrary truths, one based on philosophy, the other on the Catholic faith. ("Dicunt enim ea esse vera secundum philosophiam, sed non secundum fidem catholicam, quasi sint due contrarie veritates, et quasi contra veritatem sacre scripture sit veritas in dictis gentilium dampnatorum, de quibus scriptum est: 'Perdam sapientam sapientium,' quia vera sapientia perdit falsam sapientiam.")[252] Broadly viewed, however, the Bishop's condemnation was an attack on the possibility of a separate existence for a non-Christian philosophy rather than a narrower attack on Averroes and his Christian sympathizers.[253] The interpretation that there was no conflict between the two truths because revelation was a higher form of truth than that derived from natural law was also

---

[250] *Ibid.*, pp. 7, 340–342.
[251] On the condemnation as a whole, see Gilson, *HCPMA*, Pt. 9; condemned works, p. 406; condemnation of 1270, p. 404; double truth, pp. 387–388, 406; Leff, *Med. Thought*, pp. 224–23:.
[252] *Chartularium Universitatis Parisiensis*, Vol. I, p. 543.
[253] Leff, *Med. Thought*, pp. 226–229.

vulnerable to the charge of insincerity and of paying lip service to revelation.[254]

The condemnation rejected the theses that the world is eternal to the extent that all species are eternal (87), and that there never has been a first man and there never will be a last man—that the generation of man from man has always taken place in the past and will always take place in the future (9). Both theses conflicted with the Christian belief in the creation as an historical event. De Meun's characters in the *Romance of the Rose* had already espoused some of the condemned errors, among them that continence is not in itself a virtue (168), total abstinence from the activity of the flesh corrupts virtue and the species, and simple fornication as is natural between an unattached man and an unattached woman is not a sin (183). Other condemned theses were also critical of the virtue of chastity and abstinence (172, 181, cf. 166).

Broadly speaking again, these condemned theses stated the case for the naturalness of normal human sexual relations. Others were critical of Christianity, maintaining that there are falsehoods and errors in the Christian as in other religions (174); the Christian law hampers education (175); one has his happiness in this life, not in another (176); the discourse of the theologian is based on myth (152). All of these theses suggested possibilities of learning outside the immediate supervision of Church dogma.[255] Astrology and black magic (206) were also condemned.

Étienne Tempier's condemnation of the 219 errors was aimed at preserving theology as the all-embracing discipline and the Christianity that existed before the coming of the new knowledge from the Mediterranean Muslim world. The main targets were Siger of Brabant, Roger Bacon, Boethius of Dacia (Sweden), and Thomas Aquinas. Both Gregory IX and Urban IV, however, had favored the reception of Aristotle's writings "in a manner that would insure a maximum of benefit to Christianity as well as a minimum of harm." The Papacy did not confirm the condemnation, recognizing the importance of the new learning, and approving "St. Thomas's ideal of a reconciliation between Aristotelian science and the Christian faith."[256]

The episode itself is an interesting subject in the history of ideas. To Thorndike, the condemnation is an intrusion of theology into the province of natural science, comparable to Rome forbidding the teaching of Copernican theory

---

[254] Hooykaas, "Science and Theology in the Middle Ages," *Free University Quarterly*, Vol. 3 (1954), pp. 90–91.

[255] This is the enumeration of *Chartularium Universitatis Parisiensis*, Vol. I, pp. 543–555. Many modern writers use Mandonnet's rearrangement of the theses (*Siger de Brabant*, Vol. 2, 2d ed., pp. 175–181) instead of the *CUP* where they are listed in haphazard order. See also Dunn's intro. to *The Romance of The Rose*, pp. xxv–xxvi.

[256] Pegis' intro. to *SCG*, Bk. I, p. 15; Dawson, *Medieval Essays*, pp. 132–133. See also Gilson, *HCPMA*, pp. 402–410 and the accompanying notes. Many of the condemned propositions with notes on their derivation are cited on pp. 727–729. Other interesting observations in Leff, *Med. Thought*, pp. 229–231. See also Pierre Duhem, *Le Système du Monde*, Vol. 6, chap. 1, and Alexander Koyré, "Le Vide et l'Espace Infini au XIVᵉ Siècle," *Archives d'Histoire Doctrinale et Littéraire du Moyen Âge*, 24 (1949), 45–91, esp. pp. 45–51.

as the truth and to the silencing of Galileo, a comparison rejected by Hooykaas. In a famous passage, Pierre Duhem says the birth of modern science may well date from this time. The condemnations were a blow at the determinism of Aristotle and Averroes. The Bishop, says Duhem, solemnly proclaimed the possibility of a plurality of worlds and that the ensemble of the celestial spheres could, without contradiction, be activated by rectilinear movement. The idea here apparently is that no Greek determinisms control God; He can create and govern as He wishes. There are no limits set by natural law to His activity.

Gilson claims less but thinks it is the date on which the birth of modern cosmologies became possible in a Christian environment.

Leff sees in it the beginning of a change in thought "from synthesis to separation. There was the progressive attempt to disengage what belonged to faith from what could be known by reason. . . . Never again, after 1277, shall we see quite the same confidence in reason's ability to know that which was a matter of belief."

Christopher Dawson considers it a transitory affair, impeding for a time the inevitable attempt to reconcile Aristotelian science with Christian thought, and Hooykaas thinks that in the denial of the eternity of the species, the way was unintentionally cleared for developmental theories. Finally, Crombie says that "with the condemnation of the Averroïst view that Aristotle had said the last word on metaphysics and natural science, the bishops in 1277 left the way open for criticism which would, in turn, undermine his system." Natural philosophers had another alternative; they already had Aristotle's philosophy of nature; now they could begin to form their own hypotheses, "to develop the empirical habit of mind working within a rational framework, and to extend scientific discovery."[257]

## 17. Conclusion

In these concluding remarks, I wish to make a few general points pertinent to our theme but which if elaborated upon will carry us too far afield into the history of philosophy, theology, logic, and science. It is true that we can expect more unity of thought in the Middle Ages than in other periods because of the unique and commanding position of Christian theology. In no age, however, does one idea dominate all others. Alternatives arise out of agreed-upon unities. No age is so monolithic or so intellectually disciplined that it loses the capacity for cherishing old ideas or for entertaining new ones. The intellectual possessions of an age have a museum-like quality as do the works of prolific

[257] Thorndike, *A Hist. of Magic and Exper. Sci.*, Vol. 3, p. 470; Hooykaas, "Science and Theology in the Middle Ages," *Free Univ. Quarterly*, Vol. 3 (1954), pp. 101–102, 103–105; Duhem, *Études sur Léonard de Vinci*, Vol. 2, p. 411; Gilson, *La Philosophie au Moyen Âge*, 2d ed., p. 460, and *HCPMA*, p. 408; Dawson, *Medieval Essays*, pp. 132–133; Leff, *Medieval Thought*, pp. 230–231; Crombie, *Medieval and Early Modern Science*, Vol. 1, p. 64.

authors who live a long time. Knowledge and opinion accumulate, often with no greater order than exists in a small county museum piled high with the furniture, trinkets, and daguerrotypes of its pioneer residents and their heirs. Different and often conflicting ideas persist, and one does not necessarily displace another.

In his *Medieval Thought*, Leff sees a distinct break with the past occurring in the fourteenth century, characterizing the thirteenth as an age of synthesis, the fourteenth as one of separation. In his opinion, attempts to show continuities between the two are misguided. From the viewpoint of our study, the attempt to abandon reason as a tool of theology was probably the most important development. Reason no longer supports theology; revelation becomes a matter of faith; the theologian and the philosopher are no longer the same. "Beyond expressing God's will to create," says Leff of Duns Scotus, who represents this trend, "this world could offer no explanation of His ways; it certainly could not specify the way in which God worked. Consequently, there is a discontinuity between the divine and the created which is absent from the much more precise order of St. Thomas."[258] In the new thought, therefore, reason is confined to the study and interpretation of natural phenomena.

It has also been suggested that nominalism, beginning with the teaching of Roscelinus (Roscelin of Compiègne, 1050–*ca.*1125), and continuing with his critical pupil, Peter Abelard (1079–1142), "opened the great dispute over universals which led men to take a greater interest in the individual material object as such and not, as St. Augustine had done, to regard it as simply the shadow of an eternal idea."[259] Of William of Ockham's (1300?–1349) extreme nominalism it has been said that he departs both from an earlier "unspeculative piety" and the typical attitude, *Fides quaerens intellectum*, of Augustine, Anselm, and Thomas Aquinas, that it is reason's task to clarify "in logical terms, as far as possible, the deliverances of revelation." "Since there are no universal principles in things, principles are generalizations from particulars. His preference for sensible realities over metaphysical entities governs his contributions to physics."[260]

If William of Ockham restricted reality to individuals and knowledge to experience, it was possible to reject many concepts as purely mental constructs; everything except individuals and knowledge from experience exists in the intellect, and the explanation of universals is therefore psychological.[261] With Ockham too, reason cannot prove revealed faith; consequently, the same methods are unsuited to theology and to natural science.

[258] Leff, *Med. Thought*, p. 267.
[259] Crombie, *Medieval and Early Modern Science*, Vol. 1, p. 25. Hooykaas, *op. cit.*, pp. 120–135, and Carré's discussion of St. Augustine's realism, the nominalism of Roscelinus and Abelard and the intermediate position of St. Thomas, *Realists and Nominalists*, esp. pp. 30–31, 40–42, 58–61, 99–100.
[260] Carré, *op. cit.*, quotations on pp. 121, 120.
[261] Leff, p. 281.

In the following two chapters, we will be less concerned with religion and theology; in them we shall see evidence of the value placed on practical experience and of interest in technology, trends which also could undermine a thoroughgoing religious interpretation of nature and encourage a clear distinction between natural and supernatural knowledge. Furthermore, if proofs and verifications are taken from experience, the material and the efficient causes could lead a more independent existence, with less weight being given to final and the formal causes.[262] These considerations, however, lead us into discussions of the origin of science. The history of the idea of a designed earth, however, is not subsumed under the history of the scientific method; it is a continuing part of philosophy and theology as well, with closer affinities to biology than to physics, because the former has been more hospitable than has the latter to teleology, design, and final causes.[263]

At the end of our period, there are several alternatives. Interpretations of design based on Augustine, "the book of nature" literature, the theophanies, persist into the fifteenth century in the work of Sibiude. Schooling in Aristotelian ways of thinking, especially in the period from 1240 on, when the works of Aristotle were translated from the Greek without accretions, established the Greek philosopher's teleological view of nature, as is plain especially in St. Thomas's fifth proof of the existence of God. Independent observation and study of nature as in the work of Albertus Magnus could be conducted within the framework of this teleology. The natural philosophy both of Albert the Great and of St. Thomas offered encouragement in the study of nature. Albert especially liked to study the concrete in nature even if he felt called upon in so doing to apologize for adapting himself to "rustic intelligences."[264]

What then is the next development in this history? It comes, I think, in Renaissance thought, with the rediscovery of Cicero and the natural theology of *De natura deorum*, which contains, as we have seen, clear expositions of the idea of a designed earth. Further contributions then come from the Cambridge Platonists whose thought helped in the construction of the great natural

---

[262] *Ibid.*, p. 296.

[263] See Lynn White, "Natural Science and Naturalistic Art in the Middle Ages," *AHR* (52) 1947, pp. 421–435. White stresses that scientists of the later thirteenth and fourteenth centuries differed with Aristotle, once they understood him. See also the cogent remarks on the Aristotelian tradition by Kristeller, *Renaissance Thought*, pp. 29–34, who emphasizes the strength of the tradition and the pitfalls in commonly accepted generalizations regarding the displacement of Aristotelianism by Platonism in the Renaissance. For modern research on the origin of science, see the several essays (which, with the exception of Crombie's, originally appeared in the *Journal of the History of Ideas*) in Wiener and Noland, eds., *Roots of Scientific Thought*, especially Crombie, "From Rationalism to Experimentalism," pp. 125–138; Randall, Jr., "Scientific Method in the School of Padua," pp. 139–146; Koyré, "Galileo and Plato," pp. 147–175; Moody, "Galileo and Avempace: Dynamics of the Leaning Tower Experiment," pp. 176–206; Randall, Jr., "The Place of Leonardo Da Vinci in the Emergence of Modern Science," pp. 207–218; and Zilsel, "The Genesis of the Concept of Scientific Progress," pp. 251–275.

[264] Quoted in Thorndike, *op. cit.*, Vol. 2, p. 536.

theologies of Ray and Derham in the latter half of the seventeenth and the early part of the eighteenth centuries.

Thus the idea seems to be growing that even if this earth is only a temporary abode, much can be learned about it that is useful and instructive to the Christian. There are divine works, like the creation and miracles, and the works of nature; both are ultimately the work of God, but the works of nature are accomplished through laws which can be studied.[265]

When I first started reading in the medieval period, I felt that one could describe its contributions in bold strokes, that it was a period in which certain easily recognizable changes had taken place in the attitude toward the earth. I realize now that this feeling was an error, that this complex period was creative because fundamental developments regarding man's relation to nature took place then.

What might one say, then, of the significance of the period as a whole? From this bewildering mass of material, most of which is centered around the Bible or is seldom far from it, roads lead in many directions, to theology, to mysticism, to the lyric, to a secular study of nature tolerant of secondary causes, to exegesis, controversy, and disputation.

To me, its outstanding characteristic is its preoccupation with creation. The sun, the moon, the constellations, are formidable in their glory, but the continuously visible creation on earth, as one constantly sees in the naturalistic, symbolic, and allegorical writings, is the evidence men know best. This long discussion of creation and its meaning in the formative period of Western civilization intensified interest in unity and harmony in nature, in physical and moral evil, in intermediate agencies between God and the world of daily life, be they secondary causes or the nature personifications of Alan of Lille and Jean de Meun. If I were to single out a second word, I would say *exegesis*, the means by which creator and creature were examined, including the hexaemeral literature, the *Summae*, the homilies. From exegesis came the alternative views of nature—mystical, sacred, symbolic, secular. What happened resembled Mâle's description of medieval religious art: the world remained a symbol all right, but within it the humble artisans decorated the church with branches and blossoms realistically portrayed and did not neglect self-advertisement. If the symbolic world was indeed like a great hemispheric tent, within it were also busyness, practicality, interest in the immediate, truths I became convinced of in collecting materials for chapter VII.

If this interpretation is correct, a reworking of Western ideas of man and nature took place in the Middle Ages. These became the ideas which modern man had to reckon with, and their reverberations are still with us.

[265] On this general theme, see Chenu, "Découverie de la Nature et Philosophie de l'Homme a l'École de Chartres au XII⁰ Siècle," *Journ. of World Hist.*, Vol. 2 (1954), pp. 313–325. Ref. on p. 318.

# Chapter 6

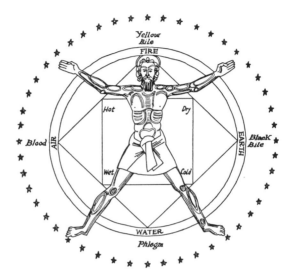

# Environmental Influences Within a Divinely Created World

### 1. INTRODUCTION

In the sixth century, Cassiodorus said that monks should know about cosmography in order to recognize the location of places mentioned in sacred books.[1] It is a good text with which to begin a discussion of geographic ideas in the Middle Ages.

The idea of a close relationship existing between God, the earth, and man, dominant throughout the Middle Ages, did not mean that ideas of environmental influence would gradually die out as being inconsistent with an all-pervasive theology. Classical antiquity had offered choices in considering the relation of humanity to nature and to the divine. In the Middle Ages, there was only one choice, but Christian theology was not hostile to ideas of environmental influence, nor indeed in the high and late Middle Ages, to ideas of astrological influences, even though the early Church Fathers had castigated

[1] Cassiod., *Intro. to Divine and Human Readings*, Bk. I, chap. 25.

astrology. Aristotle's *Metaphysics* and *De Caelo* and Arab commentaries on them inspired among Christian thinkers after the twelfth century a veneration of the heavenly bodies far greater than had existed in the period prior to the recovery of these works.[2]

After all, environmental theories are often simple theories of adaptation. The elements of the creation, existing in order and harmony, limited and controlled by God, are adapted to one another, even on an earth which may have suffered a disarrangement after the fall of man. Throughout its history, the design argument has been friendly to philosophies of environmental adaptation, playing a role in its time comparable to nineteenth century theories of the inheritance of acquired characteristics or of natural selection, which also assumed varying degrees of environmental adaptation.

To my knowledge, no exhaustive examination has ever been made of theories of geographical influence in the Middle Ages; such a study would not be rewarding since it would only tediously and repetitiously accumulate examples of a few basic ideas.[3] Theories of the four elements, of mixtures, and of the

---

[2] Webb, *Studies in the History of Natural Theology*, pp. 153–155.

[3] See Kretschmer, *Die Physische Erdkunde in Christlichen Mittelalter*; Wright, *The Geographical Lore of the Time of the* Crusades; and Kimble, *Geography in the Middle Ages*, pp. 176–180. On travel and voyaging, Beazley, *The Dawn of Modern Geography*, 3 vols. (the work, however, deals very little with theoretical questions); and Wright's *Geographical Lore* is very valuable for its discussion of ideas; so is Kimble's work, which includes chapters on classical and Muslim geography. See also Delisle, "Traités Divers sur les Propriétés des Choses," *Hist. Litt. de la France*, Vol. 30 (1888), pp. 334–388. Mollat, "Le Moyen Âge," in Nougier, Beaujeu, and Mollat, *Histoire Universelle des Explorations*, Vol. 1, pp. 254–408; and Olschki, *Marco Polo's Precursors*.

I have reluctantly omitted discussion of Ibn Khaldūn. His ideas belong to Arab thought and not to the West, least of all in this period. They were not well known in the West until de Slane published his translation of the prolegomena, 1863–1868. Ibn Khaldūn's thought is of great interest, however, because it contains environmental ideas from classical sources; it uses the concept of the seven klimata together with ideas coming from his interpretation of Arab history. It is an exciting example (Vitruvius comes to mind here also) of two traditions meeting but with no reconciliation. See *The Muqaddimah*, translated by Rosenthal, especially Bk. I, chap. 1, third Prefatory Discussion. Von Grunebaum points out that the Mu'tazilite, al-Naẓẓâm, in the ninth century accounted for differences in body build and intelligence on climatic grounds, and that his disciple al-Jâḥiẓ (died 869)

> adduces climatic considerations to explain why Zoroaster threatened his followers with eternal cold rather than with eternal fire. He goes on to argue that, since this threat would be effective only among the inhabitants of the mountainous region where Zoroaster actually began to preach his religion, this very doctrine would prove the local limitations of his mission and his message. In contrast to the merely provincial validity of Zoroastrianism, the Koranic hell-fire, whose terror is not based on local apprehensions—considering that the Arabs were exposed to both heat and cold—gives evidence of the universal character of Mohammed's mission and message (an interpretation which, incidentally, Jâḥiẓ finds it useful to corroborate from Revelation itself).

Von Grunebaum, "The Problem: Unity in Diversity," in von Grunebaum, ed., *Unity and Variety in Muslim Civilization*, pp. 17–37. Reference on pp. 19–20. See also pp. 22, 24–25. Climate plays a role in cultural relativism and in casting doubts on the universality and validity of religions in modern times in the West, as we shall see, from Bodin to Montesquieu and Voltaire. See also Levy, *The Social Structure of Islam*, pp. 482–484.

humors were accepted in the Middle Ages; consequently, environmental theories in this period are either copies or variations of Greek and Roman ideas. Many of the encyclopedic writers used classical sources or epitomes derived from them. In the seventh century, Isidore of Seville used Servius the Grammarian; in doing so, he probably made indirect use of Hippocrates, Aristotle, Posidonius; in the thirteenth century Bartholomew of England, one of the most comprehensive of the later encyclopedists in his exposition of geographical theory, often depended on Isidore for the traditional materials, but showed refreshing vigor in recording contemporary life.[4]

Environmental and astrological theories continue to explain racial and cultural differences. They also continue, as they did in antiquity, their relationship with political theory: Thomas Aquinas is close to the ancients like Hippocrates, Plato, Aristotle, and Vitruvius, close also to Dante, to moderns like Bodin, Botero, Machiavelli, Burton, and even to Montesquieu. Environmental theories have been important to political theorists because, following Plato's example, they are considered indispensable to proper government: to be just and efficacious, law must conform to the nature of the people, and their nature is often determined by their environment. The environment—climate, soils, relief, and the like—was studied little for its own sake; men accepted it as given and applied traditional generalizations as a matter of course to contemporary affairs.

Since theories of environmental influence in the Middle Ages were derived from classical speculations, there is the same division into physiological theory, based on the Hippocratic tradition and the humoral psychology and physiology, and the theories of location and of position. There were also other borrowings from classical sources, such as the idea that cultural isolation was the result of physical isolation, of being away from the kaleidoscopic world of trade, navigation, and the intermingling of peoples.

In the twelfth and thirteenth centuries especially, more sophisticated environmental theories appear among the encyclopedic writers, the most impressive discussions being those of Giraldus Cambrensis (1146?–1220), Albert the Great (1196? or 1206?–1280), St. Thomas Aquinas (1225?–1274), and Bartholomaeus Anglicus (*fl.* 1230–1250). Although the ideas of these writers—particularly those dealing with places remote in time or place and outside their own vision—are derived from the classical writers, occasionally there is novelty in their application, in their adaptation to Christian theology, and in their observation of contemporary conditions.

The most significant writings appeared either early, in the wake of classical civilization, or after the partial rediscovery of classical thought from the Muslim world and enlivened by travel and the gathering of observations which

---

[4] Philipp, "Die historisch-geographischen Quellen in den etymologiae des Isidorus v. Sevilla," *Quellen und Forschungen zur alten Geschichte and Geographie*, Heft 25, Pt. 1, 1912; Pt. 2, 1913.

it inspired. The connecting link between the two periods is the work of Isidore of Seville, whose gazetteer-like compendium is a simple account of places and of rude economics, as well as geographical description.

## 2.  CLASSICAL ECHOES

Even before Isidore, one feels the reverberations of far-off Greek thought in the sentences of Orosius and of Cassiodorus, the statesman who left the court of King Theodoric to enter the monastery of Vivarium about A.D. 540. The Teutones and the Cimbri, says Orosius, endured Alpine snows, invading, with forces intact, the plains of Italy; there they became effeminate under the influence of a mild climate, abundant drink, food, and baths. The letters of Cassiodorus, full of interest for the light they throw on civilized society during the period of the migrations, include a few revealing sentences which show that in different localities and at different times the Greek ideas of climatic influence had not been lost in the millennial span from the time of Hippocrates to his own.

Cassiodorus was born about 477 in Scyllacium on the Gulf of Squillace, whose site is believed to be at or near the modern Roccella, or La Roccelleta del Vescovo di Squillace.[5] In his praise of the city—his style is at times charming, at times overly ornate and bombastic—he mentions its natural qualities to illustrate the effect of nature on man. Its airs, temperate throughout the whole year, allow men to live without sorrow and fear of violent seasons. "Hence, too, man himself is here freer of soul than elsewhere, for this temperateness of the climate[6] prevails in all things." Variations of familiar correlations are here: a hot country makes people sharp and fickle; a cold country makes them slow and sly; and the temperate country "composes the characters of men by its own moderation." Then follows an interesting statement, the earliest one on this subject known to me, that seems to confirm an opinion already expressed in the first part of this work, that the Greeks themselves ascribed their greatness to physical causes:

> Hence was it that the ancients pronounced Athens to be the seat of sages, because, enriched with an air of the greatest purity, it prepared with glad liberality the lucid intellects of its sons for the contemplative part of life. Assuredly for the body to imbibe muddy waters is a different thing from sucking in the transparency of a sweet fountain. Even so the vigour of the mind is repressed when it is clogged by a heavy atmosphere. Nature herself hath made us subject to these influences. Clouds make us feel sad; and again a bright sky fills us with

[5] Orosius, *Seven Books Against the Pagans*, Bk. V, 16; Hodgkin, *The Letters of Cassiodorus*, pp. 68–72, with map; Philipp, "Scylletium," *PW*, 2A: 1, cols. 920–923.

[6] Hodgkin, *The Letters of Cassiodorus*, Bk. XII, letter 15. Translating "hinc et homo sensu liberior est quia temperies cuncta moderatur." "Variarum Libri Duodecim," *Variae* XII, 15, 3, In *Mon. Ger. Hist., Auctores Antiquissimi*, Vol. 12, 1894, ed. Mommsen, p. 372.

joy, because the heavenly substance of the soul delights in everything that is unstained and pure.[7]

The comparison between muddy waters for the body and heavy air for the mind suggests the humoral psychology, the reference to the heavy atmosphere is reminiscent of Cicero's *De fato* and of Heraclitus' association of moisture with dullness, while the Platonic overtones of the last lines suggest the compatibility of these theories with Christian theology.

These ideas persisted in works like those of Cassiodorus—and his is only an example—for better reasons than the unimaginative patience of tireless copying and the force of inertia. They continued because they were serviceable in accounting for cultural, and especially for racial, differences. Pliny, the most influential of the classical writers on natural history during the Middle Ages, made, as we have seen, a correlation between race and climate. (See chap. II, sect. 8.) It seemed clear enough that the Negro peoples who lived in the hottest climates received the strongest and most direct solar heat, that the Mediterranean peoples were in an intermediate position, and that the northerners were at the other extreme. The climatic explanation could also be applied to other differences. Equally important has been the hold on men's minds of the idea of latitudinal differences, the crudeness of this correlation concealing not only the errors of the generalization but also the longitudinal problem, that peoples living along different meridians in the same latitude might also differ from one another.

Although it is true, as Kimble has pointed out, that most discussions of environmental influence appeared late in the Middle Ages when there were far greater opportunities for travel, classical ideas of environmental influences were transmitted into Christian thought quite early, and the man responsible for their transmission was Isidore of Seville.[8]

---

[7] Hodgkin, *The Letters of Cassiodorus*, Book XII, Letter 15, pp. 503–504. In the letters, there are interesting passages on the care and maintenance of channels and aqueducts; see Book V, Letter 38, p. 286, on clearing shrubs from the aqueduct of Ravenna. "Vegetation is the peaceable overturner of buildings, the battering-ram which brings them to the ground, though the trumpets never sound for siege." The theme of aqueducts, their advantages and maintenance, is pursued very interestingly in Book VII, Formula 6 (Formula of the Count of the Aqueducts), pp. 324–326. On Cassiodorus, see Leslie Jones's introduction to *An Introduction to Divine and Human Readings*, pp 3–64. This work has extensive references to modern scholarly studies on Cassiodorus.

[8] Kimble, *Geography in the Middle Ages*, p. 176. "The cloistered life of the early Fathers provided few opportunities for the contemplation of the cultural landscape. It was not until men began to travel as they did in the Crusading epoch that they began to perceive the varying relationships existing between landscape and life." Monks in certain monastic orders, however, were very much aware of their environment and of their ability to change it even if they did not depart from the environs of the monastery. It is true that there was not the opportunity for comparison or for observing differences in the cultural landscape that the Crusader had but there was the difference between the woods and the clearing, the vine-covered and the forested hill, the agricultural field and the drained swamp, etc.

Isidore thought he had discovered in the etymologies of the names of things the key to their essential nature. Ethiopia, he says, was so named because of the color of its people, the name being derived from the Greek words for *burn* and *face*. Their color is caused by their nearness to the sun and from the influence of the heavenly bodies; they live in a region of continual summer, for all of it is in the south.[9] The thought is also probably derived indirectly from Pliny. Isidore says that just as there is diversity in the heavens so are there differences in human faces, in coloring, in bodily development, and in the nature of peoples. Following Servius the Grammarian, he says the seriousness of the Romans, the lightheartedness of the Greeks, the cunning of the Africans, the fierce and courageous nature of the Gauls—all have environmental causes.[10]

A second environmental idea came out of the experience of the barbarian migrations; it was advanced by Paul the Deacon (eighth century) in his *History of the Langobards*, and has been influential even in modern times. Paul, a Benedictine monk, is believed to have entered the monastery of Monte Cassino before 782, where he lived the quiet studious life of a religious man;[11] he had served the emperor Charlemagne intermittently in the latter's efforts to encourage and promote learning. Paul was one of the many men, from the fourth to the eighth century, who were concerned with the history and the migrations of the barbarian peoples, and who—if only incidentally—were interested in the causes of the invasions of the Latin West.

Theories of overpopulation and consequent land hunger as causes of migration were common in classical times.[12] In the late fourth and early fifth centuries, the ecclesiastical historian Socrates, as well as Sozomen, had advanced similar theories to explain the migrations of the Goths and the Huns. Cassiodorus had himself prepared a history of the Goths, now lost, which was used by Jordanes in his work.[13] The unique feature of Paul's theory was that

---

[9] According to Webster's New International Dictionary, 2d ed. unabridged, definition of "Ethiope," the Greek word *Aithiops* apparently is derived from *aithein*, to burn, and *ōps*, face, or it may originate from a native African name. Isidore, *Etymologiae*, Bk. XIV, chap. 5, 14, *PL*, Vol. 82, 511C. See Philipp, *op. cit.*, Pt. 2, p. 128, for sources. Is the ultimate source through intermediaries Pliny, *NH*, II, 80? See also Sarton, *Appreciation of Ancient and Medieval Science During the Renaissance*, pp. 78–80.

[10] See Servius' *Comm. in Verg. Aen.*, VI, 724, and pp. 114–115 above. Isidore, *Etym.*, Bk. IX, chap. 2, 105, *PL*, Vol. 82, 338C. See also Philipp, *op. cit.*, Pt. 2, pp. 32–33. Repeated in essence by Bartholomew of England, *De proprietatibus rerum* (13th Century), Book XV, chap. 66, 2. Servius used *climatum*, undoubtedly a translation of the Greek *klima*; it does not mean climate, but like klima suggests a latitudinal zone, or perhaps in medieval and early modern times a region, as in the English word "clime." See also H. C. Darby, "The Geographical Ideas of the Venerable Bede," *Scott. Geog. Mag.* Vol. 51 (1935), pp. 84–89.

[11] McCann, *Saint Benedict*, revised ed. (Image Books), pp. 205–208.

[12] For a summary and discussion of these theories, see Teggart, *Rome and China*, pp. 225–235.

[13] One wonders if this theory originated with Cassiodorus, whose history of the Goths is lost. Jones says its purpose was to show the nobility of the modern nations and there-

it offered a climatic explanation for overpopulation. He believed that the north (perhaps meaning southern Scandinavia and northern Germany) had been a hive of nations (*officina gentium*): the northlands were the source of many barbarian migrations, the climate being the cause of the fecundity of the people, who multiplied in sufficient number to force emigration. "The region of the north, in proportion as it is removed from the heat of the sun and is chilled with snow and frost," Paul says in the opening sentences of his work, "is so much the more healthful to the bodies of man and fitted for the propagation of nations, just as, on the other hand, every southern region, the nearer it is to the heat of the sun, the more it abounds in diseases and is less fitted for the bringing up of the human race."[14]

The indefatigable Isidore had, in the *Etymologiae*, derived the name Germany from *germinare*, "to sprout or bud," a derivation adopted by Paul, who thought that the whole region from the Tanais (Don) to the west (not further defined) "is not improperly called by the name of Germany."

Its inability to feed the people it is capable of producing accounts for the invasions of Europe and Asia. "Everywhere ruined cities throughout all Illyria and Gaul testify to this, but most of all in unhappy Italy which has felt the cruel rage of nearly all these nations." Paul, however, mentions that reasons (which he does not specify) other than overpopulation have been alleged for the emigration of people living in Scandinavia who, dividing themselves into three groups, "determined by lot which part of them had to forsake their country and seek new abodes." It has been suggested that a sibyl may have told them to go forth in order to attain salvation from on high.[15]

This simple, straightforward account, with its combination of climatic theory and the idea of a northern womb of nations, had momentous consequences in the history of environmentalistic theories, for it initiated the speculations, lasting well into the nineteenth century, regarding Scandinavia as an overpopulated homeland of barbarian peoples.

Jordanes' *Gothic History* (written A.D. 551)—possibly relying heavily on Cassiodorus' lost *Gothic History*, even if we find it hard to believe that the latter's steward loaned it to him for only three days—started the notion that "Scandza" was a womb or a hive of nations, whose migrating peoples were likened to a swarm of bees, without, however, any reason being given for the likeness.[16] Paul's assignment of an environmental cause started a train of

---

by to bring about a "reconciliation of the decadent Latin race with that of the more vigorous Goths," p. 12. Such a theme might well have involved an argument like Paul's, but this is the merest guess. See Jones's trans. of *An Introduction to Divine and Human Readings*, pp. 12–14; Jordanes' abstract, p. 14.

[14] Paul the Deacon, *Hist. of the Langobards*, Bk. I, chap. 1.

[15] Isidore, *Etym.*, Bk. XIV, 4, 4, *PL*, Vol. 82, 504B–C. Paul the Deacon, *Hist. Lang.*, Bk. I, chap. 1–2, and Foulke's note 4, p. 3.

[16] See Jones's introduction to Cassiodorus, *An Introduction to Divine and Human Readings*, pp. 12–14. For a discussion of Cassiodorus and Jordanes, see also Mierow's

thought which ultimately correlated climate with the liberty-loving Gothic peoples of the north, contrasting them with the weak and effete southerners.[17]

The sentences with which this Benedictine monk begins a history of the people from whom he himself had descended illustrate how important it is in the history of ideas to note the repetitions coming about when the ignorant copy from one another. The joining of the old classical tradition of climatic influences with the desire to find a cause for the turmoil, suffering, and devastation of the period of the barbarian migrations (so clear in Paul the Deacon's history) initiated a train of thought which lasted at least a thousand years.[18]

Since Paul's theory was an attempt to explain a series of historical events, it was not directly concerned with theology. One might expect, however, that sooner or later, environmental theory would be linked directly with the creation of man and his subsequent cultural differentiation. Such a linking occurred in the writings of John the Scot, who, as we have seen, was well acquainted with Greek thought.

To devoted believers, the Christian religion posed extremely difficult questions about the origin and present condition of mankind. The creation of man, in a manner entirely different from that of the animals, introduced questions concerning the reasons for taking one particular part of Adam's body for creating Eve. The obvious present racial and cultural diversity of man raised questions concerning the original unity of the human race and the role of sin or other influences after the Fall in bringing about cultural and racial differences.

These questions were to be considered at great length by the cosmographers of the sixteenth and seventeenth centuries. The voyages of discovery and the knowledge derived from them enormously complicated the explanations of the change from uniformity to diversity in the human race and of the mechanisms of its dispersion.

If the first man had not sinned, said John the Scot, he would not have experienced a division of his nature into two sexes: he would have remained

---

edition and translation, *The Gothic History of Jordanes,* esp. pp. 13–16, 19, 23–29, and Jordanes' own words in his preface, which have been received with some skepticism; he says he read the books a second time on a steward's loan of three days. The famous sentence is, "Ex hac igitur Scandza insula quasi officina gentium aut certe velut vagina nationum cum rege suo nomine Berig Gothi quondam memorantur egressi. . . ." *De origine actibusque Getarum,* IV, 25, ed. Mommsen, p. 60.

[17] Kliger, *The Goths in England,* p. 1. "The analysis of Gothic character found in these early texts [Tacitus, St. Augustine, Salvian, Jordanes, Paul the Deacon] described the Goths as a Teutonic folk to whom political liberty was dear" (p. 2). Proponents seized on the theory of Paul the Deacon, although he had made no correlation between climate and love of liberty. See also pp. 10–15, and the discussion, "Climate and Liberty," tracing the idea of the environmental influence on the love of freedom, especially from the Renaissance to the eighteenth century, pp. 241–252.

[18] On the subsequent attempts of the Uppsala scholars (Redbeck, Joannes and Olaus Magnus and other Swedish writers) to show that Sweden was really the *vagina gentium,* see Kliger, p. 12, and the works to which he refers.

unchangeable in the primordial condition in which he was created in the image of God. Overcome by the sense of guilt at his sinning, he suffered a division of his nature into masculine and feminine. Because he did not wish to obey the divine law concerning his reproduction, his existence was, as just punishment, reduced to that of an animallike and transitory multitude of masculine and feminine beings. In Christ, there was a beginning of a new unity like the primordial one, and a likeness of the future resurrection.[19] Since the Fall, there have been distinctions more numerous than those of sex; there has also been a variety of departures in qualities, size, and in other ways from the original single form. Changes in individual characteristics (like stature) do not have their origin in nature (i.e., in the primordial form of man) but arise from the sin and the Fall and from spatial and temporal differences owing to the land, water, air, food, and similar circumstances. It is known to all, he says, that differences in customs and in ways of thinking came into being after the sin and the Fall.[20]

To my knowledge, John the Scot was the first to use an environmental explanation to illumine puzzling uncertainties in the Christian concept of early man. It seems, however, to be an isolated idea without influence on either the thinkers of the Middle Ages or those of modern times. It was not one of his major teachings and it may have been lost in the text of a very long book.

### 3.  REMARKS INTRODUCING A MORE SYSTEMATIC THOUGHT

In the eleventh, twelfth, and thirteenth centuries, changes were occurring in the nature of geographical description. They were not revolutionary, nor were they divorced from the past. The solid anchors of geographical description were the works of the classical geographers—and the inspirations of biblical geography. Such was the geography of Isidore of Seville whose descriptions of places had often come through key transmitters like Servius the Grammarian or St. Ambrose. Isidore's was a compendium; the works of the encyclopedists of the twelfth and thirteenth centuries—Albert the Great, Bartholomew of England, Vincent of Beauvais, and others—were also compendia. Was there any difference between the earlier and the later compendia as far as geographical knowledge is concerned? There was; Bartholomew of England—who certainly relied heavily on earlier writers, as his many descriptions of places ending with the phrase, as Herodotus says, or as Isidore says in book XV—gives the clue. Bartholomew says he started out merely to describe biblical

---

[19] *De div. nat.*, II, 6, *PL* 122, 532A–533A.

[20] "Siquidem diversitas hominum a seipsis, qua uniuscujusque species ab aliis discernitur, et staturae modus variatur, non ex natura provenit, sed ex vitio, et diversitate locorum et temporum terrarum, aquarum, aërum, escarum, ceterarumque similium, in quibus nascunter et nutriuntur. De diversitate morum cogitationumque superfluum est dicere, cum omnibus manifestum sit, ex divisione Naturae post peccatum, initium sumpsisse." *Ibid.*, II, 7, 533B.

places; he ends with many others, biblical, clerical, and modern, that are strongly based on his own or his contemporaries' personal travel and observation. Bartholomew's *De proprietatibus rerum* was written perhaps in the middle of the thirteenth century; but there are remarkably fresh breezes already in the twelfth in William of Tyre's chronicle, *A History of Deeds Done Beyond the Sea*, in which descriptions of places—there are no theories of environmental influence—are vivid, detailed, and exciting. Hovering over the places and their history like an angry cloud is the all-pervading misery of the human race. The breezes are equally fresh—at least on occasion—in Otto of Freising's *The Deeds of Frederick Barbarossa* and in Adam of Bremen's (died 1076?) *History of the Archbishops of Hamburg-Bremen*. These books are, partially at least, independent of the bookish learning based on the classical geographies; there are also simple contemporary observations about food, the location of a place, the nature of trade, of which the author, however, makes little theoretical use.

Subtle changes were made in the old theories based on Hippocrates, Aristotle, or Galen. The timeworn examples of the classical authors were not merely repeated; they were handy now in illuminating situations of which these men were aware. The adaptation of an old tradition to new conditions was much more subdued than that which took place after the age of discovery, and which is particularly noticeable in the writings of Bodin, Botero, and Montesquieu.

In addition to the classical inspiration, certain other interests in the high Middle Ages encouraged the emergence of environmental theories. There was the continuing and perennial interest in places because of their religious interest and importance or because of their historical and economic significance. There was also an interest in national character with or without causal explanations of it. Making generalizations about the characteristics of one's neighbors seems to be an old human occupation. Bartholomew of England, to use but one example, discusses the fine bodies, the strength, the courage, the handsome faces of the Hollanders, their honesty, their devotion to God, their trustworthy and peaceable nature, their lesser inclination to pillage and robbery than that which exists among other German peoples.[21] No reasons are given for these admirable characteristics, but when writers did try to explain national characteristics or cultural differences, they relied heavily on environmental explanations.

The encyclopedias of the Middle Ages included an important body of knowledge dealing with the nature of places (*de natura locorum*) and the properties of things (*de proprietatibus rerum*), a literature which generally included a compendium on geography and sections on the four elements, the humors, mixtures, and qualities, all of which were pertinent to cosmography

---

[21] Bartholomew of England, *De proprietatibus rerum*, Bk. XV, chap. 110, 5. *De Ollandia*.

as it was envisaged in the Middle Ages. Albert the Great, discussing the properties of the elements in relation to places in the *De causis proprietatum elementorum*, refers the reader to his essay on the nature of places for more detailed discussions of the effects of different places, such as coasts, mountains, and seas.[22] Writings on the nature of places and of the properties of things thus were closely linked together. The doctrine of the four elements, the idea that complex compounds were mixtures of them, introducing—as in classical times—ideas of mixture and proportion, called attention to the influence of a given place in bringing about various combinations of the elements and thus creating differences.

There were many such discussions among writers like Gervase of Tilbury, Alexander Neckam, Thomas Cantimpré, his teacher, Albertus Magnus, Albert's more famous pupil, St. Thomas Aquinas, Bartholomaeus Anglicus, and Robert Grosseteste. I have selected from this literature four works which seem to illustrate well—and in some detail—ways in which environmental theories were involved in the general thought of that age: the *De natura locorum* of Albertus Magnus, *On Kingship* of St. Thomas, the geographical sections of Bartholomew of England's *De proprietatibus rerum*, and the historical works of Giraldus Cambrensis, *The Topography of Ireland*, *The History of the Conquest of Ireland*, and the *Itinerary of Archbishop Baldwin Through Wales*, introducing the latter with a discussion of Otto of Freising. In addition I have added some notes on Roger Bacon's ideas of sacred geography and astrological ethnology. Each of these works illustrates in a different way the reforming of old ideas in the face of new situations, and in one case at least—that of St. Thomas—a reconciliation of environmental theories with the most exalted theological doctrine. Some of these ideas had come directly from classical sources through Isidore; others were made known through the rediscovery of Vitruvius, Vegetius, and Aristotle's *Politics*. Some probably came from the Arabs, among them Avicenna (980–1037), whose writings show his knowledge of classical medical theory. In his didactic poem (*Canticum de Medicina*) written for novices as an introduction to the study of medicine, Avicenna restates many of the medical aphorisms of the classical world relating to mixtures, humors, airs, foods, and drink.[23] The mixtures (warm and cold, dry and moist) and the corresponding humors are seasonally dominant: phlegm in winter, blood in spring, yellow bile in summer, black bile in the fall; similar correlations are made with the ages of man, children and the young being warm, older people, especially the very old, cold. Skin, hair, and eye color are caused fundamentally by mixtures determined by climate.

[22] Albert the Great, *De causis proprietatum elementorum liber primus* (hereafter *DPE*), Tr. I, chap. 5 (Jammy, Vol. 5, p. 297).

[23] Avicenna, "Das Lehrgedicht über die Heilkunde (Canticum de Medicina)," trans. from the Arabic into German by Karl Opitz, in *Quellen und Studien zur Geschichte der Naturwissenschaften und der Medizin*, Vol. 7, Heft 2/3, 1939, pp. 150–220. See verses 12–80, 116–146, pp. 160–163, 165–166.

The mixtures in the seven klimata can be recognized by differences in skin color. The aphorisms on the air, the effects of the sun's heat, mountain and valley climates, wind directions, swamps, are concerned primarily with effects on physical health, for he is interested in medical problems, not cultural questions.

### 4. ALBERT THE GREAT

There is an interesting conjunction of ideas in Albert the Great's celebrated treatise on the nature of places (*Liber de natura locorum*).[24] If we merely recite his ideas concerning the influence of the environment, we will see that indeed he had much to say about these matters but that it would be more profitable to read Hippocrates, Galen, the Posidonian fragments in Strabo, Pliny, and Vitruvius, and Ptolemy, because these are clearly the sources, either direct or indirect, of his theories.

If, however, one tries to discover the part they played in his thought—and perhaps in the age as a whole—something more exciting and living emerges. Environmental theories have a definite, if modest, part in his theory of causality. A study of them enables one to perceive how it is possible to consider these geographical matters (and the encyclopedists of the Middle Ages were intimately concerned with geography as a field of study because of the importance of biblical and classical place-names) as part of a larger body of knowledge and theory concerned with a divinely created unity. Awareness of this unity leads one to God, to an understanding of the creation and the relationship of peoples to their environments. What were the general relationships among these areas of thought? First, the Christian belief in God's creation of the earth did not conflict with theories of the constituents of matter—the four elements or the four humors or combinations of them—because God in his omnipotence could have created any number of each or any combination of them. Second, following ancient theory, the four elements were related to theories of place or location because it was believed that the latter would influence the combination, one preponderating over the other, depending on the spot it occupied on the earth's surface.[25] Any place which an entity—man, plant, or animal—occupied on the earth's surface differed in some way from every other place for two main reasons: the influence of the stars and the influence of physical conditions on earth.

Although this is not the place to discuss the history of astrology, it is nec-

[24] In this analysis I am greatly indebted to Klauck's "Albertus Magnus und die Erdkunde," *Studia Albertina*, pp. 234-248. Klauck discusses earlier contributions on Albert's cosmological and geographical writings; his own, however, is far superior to any of them in its explication of the principles of geography as seen by Albert. Here, of course, we are only concerned with a small part of Albert's geographical theory.

[25] See, for example, the beginning lines of *DPE*, Bk. I, Tr. I, chap. 5 (Jammy, p. 297 recto).

essary to add that astrological theories and theories of environmental influence are not necessarily competing ideas, that acceptance of one does not mean rejection of another. They might supplement one another. The use of both types of idea systems to create a consistent causal explanation of the great variety of life and matter elsewhere in nature is prominent among thirteenth century writers like Albert the Great who, unlike earlier thinkers, had become familiar with the physical works of Aristotle. Ptolemy, as we have seen, had not achieved such a synthesis, considering them as if they were two unrelated aspects of knowledge. Albert the Great combines them. One of the significant differences between a thinker of the thirteenth century like Albert the Great or Roger Bacon and the earlier Church Fathers is in their different attitudes toward astrology. Denunciations of astrology, as we have been, are commonplace among the early fathers. To Augustine, it was the equivalent of worshipping false gods, and it implied a denial of the freedom of the will.[26] Astrology stood in the way of a belief in God and in Christ, and its false teachings led many away from the truth of the Christian teaching. To Albert, however—such is the resilience of the design argument—stellar influences are but another example of the creativity of God. God is the Creator of all; citing Hermes Trismegistus, Albert says that the formative energy influencing the sublunary sphere is in the stars. The astrological influences are often the more general ones; local influences, including nearness of mountains and of seas, supplement them or further differentiate within an area of general similarity caused by cosmic influences. Men who are well versed in the lore of the stars can, by their knowledge and art, either further or ward off stellar influence.[27]

Albert's insistence on the need to know the nature of places in detail is also noteworthy; it is part of an interest in nature, natural history, and geography, which the recovery of the Greek and Latin works through the Arabs had stimulated. The interest which Albert shows in the theories of environmental influence is part of a vaster conception which includes theology, astrology, geography, and nature study.

In the broadest sense, Albert's contributions to human geography lay in his revival of the *De natura locorum* literature of the classical writers and the early Christian encyclopedists like Isidore, a revival convincingly shown in the dreary third tractate on cosmography,[28] and his systematic presentation

---

[26] See St. Augustine's cogent criticism, *The City of God*, V, 1, *On Christian Doctrine*, II, chaps. 21–22; and above, chap. 5, note 91.

[27] *DNL*, Tr. I, chap. 5 (Jammy, Vol. 5, p. 268, misprinted as p. 277). The reference to Hermes is to the *De virtibus universalibus*. See also Tooley, "Bodin and the Medieval Theory of Climate," *Speculum*, Vol. 28 (1953), p. 67, and footnotes 23, 24.

[28] *DNL*, Tr. I, chap. 1 (Jammy, Vol. 5, p. 263). The cosmography of *DNL* is taken up with gazetteer-like geography, a recitation of the rivers, cities great and small, lakes, etc., relieved occasionally by a personal remark regarding a place or its historical significance.

with contemporary additions and illustrations of ideas of environmental influence. Presumably from Arab sources (he cites Avicenna and Ptolemy), his writings called attention to important questions of the habitability of many parts of the earth, including the equatorial regions and those of the southern hemisphere.[29]

Albert's interest in places and their nature rests on a solid foundation: without a detailed knowledge of the variety of places and of the causes of this variety one cannot have a natural science, and those who fail to seek such knowledge err. General observation is insufficient, for attention must be directed at the specific and particular, as Plato and Aristotle had directed theirs.[30]

Albert's treatment of geographical materials is confused because he inherited from the classical writings two different ways of dividing the habitable world into regions and does not try to reconcile one with the other. At first glance, most reliance seems to be placed on the seven klimata, and he speaks of their value in classifying the character and nature of places (". . . deinde etiam tangemus terminos latitudinum septem lineis notabilibus, quae climata discernant, ut ex illis natura et proprietas loci cuiuslibet ostendatur").[31] Then he abandons this commitment in favor of a description of the habitable world, dividing it into east, west, north, and south quarters. There are indications elsewhere, moreover, of the use of the three zones which had nothing to do with the klimata,[32] that is, the frigid, torrid, and temperate zones and the correlations with race, color, personal qualities, and physical characteristics accompanying them.

Albert accepts the traditional classification of the seven klimata: one and seven, the tropical and the boreal, are the extremes; two and six are less extreme, two resembling one, and six, seven; four and five are more benign and temperate. Following classical custom, the klimata apply only to the inhabited parts of the earth (oikoumenē), and there was a difference of one half-hour in the length of the longest day from one *klima* to the next, ranging from thirteen hours at Meroë, the first and southernmost klima, to sixteen at the Borys-

[29] *DNL*, Tr. I, chap. 6 (refers to Ptolemy and Avicenna), and chap. 7 (Jammy, Vol. 5, pp. 268–272). See also Kretschmer, *Die Phy. Erdkunde im Christ. Mittelalter*, p. 140, and Klauck, *op. cit.*, pp. 239–240.

[30] Ex omnibus his igitur satis liquet, quod oportet scire naturam loci, nec sufficit tractatus qui in physicis habitus est de ipso, eò quod ille non nisi universaliter certificat de ipso: sed oportet nos scire diuersitates locorum in particulari, & causas diuersitatis ipsorum, & accidentia diuersorum locorum: tunc enim perfectè sciemus ea quae generantur et corrumpuntur in locis. *DNL*, Tr. I, chap. 1 (Jammy, p. 263 top recto). The references to Plato and Aristotle are made after elaborating upon these themes.

[31] *Ibid.*, Tr. III, chap. 1 (Jammy, Vol. 5, p. 283 bottom recto). One becomes hopelessly confused in reading the classical and medieval sources (and some of the modern discussions as well) on the seven klimata. The only guide out of this swamp known to me is Honigmann's *Die sieben Klimata.* . . .

[32] Honigmann, *op. cit.*, pp. 17–19, 26–27; the use of the klimata and the zones in Posidonius is probably the source of much later confusion, especially if it is true that Vitruvius (whom Albert mentions in this connection) based his discussion on Posidonius.

thenes (the Dnieper) in the seventh and northernmost.[33] Albert subdivides each of the seven klimata into three regions. He makes no attempt, however, to correlate cultural or physical characteristics of human beings with each of these twenty-one divisions. Instead he emphasizes the importance of seasonal variations in heat and seminal moisture, selecting these because they are indispensable to all life.[34] Varying mixtures, determined by the place, account for the characteristics of living things.

The important klimata from the point of view of contrasts and comparisons are the first and the seventh extremes and the intermediate fourth and fifth. The first klima is a region of excessive heat and dryness, cold and moisture being diminished there. The semen, generated from hot foods and ripening in great heat in the body, falls into the womb, where it is boiled away. (It is a wonder any pregnancy at all takes place!) The sun's heat is also responsible for the black skin and the curly hair.[35]

In a more detailed discussion in the *De natura locorum*, the people born in the hottest places are very hot themselves—wrinkled like pepper seeds from too much dryness. The black skin color (the Ethiopians are the examples) is explained as follows: The hot and dry womb receives hot semen; in the heat the thinner liquid of the semen boils away, and the heavy and the earthy which remains creates the blackness of the skin. (Albert is most obscure regarding the earthy parts of the body like bones and teeth, which are white.) Their dry bodies, surrounded by very hot air, are continually losing water. These people are light and agile; they have little fear of fever. The heat takes all the moisture from them, so that their private parts are weak and sterile. The spirit of life escapes with the moisture and they live only to thirty years. Although women (for obvious reasons) conceive with difficulty owing to the dryness and the debility, they deliver easily—the womb is lax and soft. Natives leaving the first for the fourth or fifth klima would undergo a change in their color from black to white.

Those people who, like the Indians, live in the first klima in areas of moving heat (the monsoon?) are quick-witted in invention and outstanding in philosophy and magic—but here astral influences seem to dominate.

The peoples—and their physiological processes—in the seventh klima are in great contrast to those of the first. On the border of the seventh klima—and even beyond it—are the Dacians and the Goths in the West, the Slavs in the East. They are white because of the cold which constricts the blood and may even press it out. The women of the north menstruate rarely, he

[33] Honigmann, *Die sieben Klimata*, p. 9. See also his discussions of the seven klimata and the Arabs.
[34] "Propter quod si sciuerimus ex loco varietatem calidi & humidi, sciemus universaliter (secundum quod competit huic scientiae) naturas corporum generatorum quas habent ex locis." *DNL*, Tr. II, chap. 2 (Jammy, Vol. 5, p. 280).
[35] *DPE*, Bk. I, Tr. I, chap. 5 (Jammy, Vol. 5, pp. 297–298).

says, citing Aristotle, but they may bleed through the nose. Because their bodies are not porous, much heat remains in them causing them to be fleshy and full of phlegm.[36] Women conceive rarely and when they do they have difficult deliveries. These women Albert compares with German women who readily become pregnant—almost more so than any others—but they, too, have very difficult deliveries. The coldness, constricting their bodies, hinders the drying-out of their life spirit and the body fluids and they remain energetic. There is always an abundance of warmth in their blood and in their dispositions.[37] Thus they greatly dread fevers (there is so much heat and moisture within them), but fear wounds much less because they have so much blood. The inhabitants of the seventh klima do not excel in physical labor, because their bodies are heavy. They are dull-witted and untutored but they could be aroused to better things by study. The Dacians and the Slavs, unlike the people of Milan, do not bother themselves with the study of law, humanistic inquiry, and the arts.[38]

The qualities in the fourth klima and the fifth near it are really means of the desirable qualities of extremes, a conclusion consistent with classical opinion. Their peoples live to old age, their works, as natural as they are spirited, are most praiseworthy, and they have good customs. The customs of the peoples of the north are brutish (literally wolflike) because of the heat in their hearts. The southerners are extremely lighthearted. The temperate peoples live easily among themselves, practice justice, keep their word, respect peace and the society of men. Albert paraphrases approvingly Vitruvius' comment that the success of the Roman Empire was due to its temperate environment between the extremes.[39] Here he is obviously concerned with a simpler classification than the klimata: merely the very cold, the very hot, and the temperate climates.

But Albert has other environmental theories as well, such as contrasts between the mountains and the sea, or the woods and the marshes; they are supervening causes (*accidentia*) which bring about differences owing to purely local physical conditions. These remind one of Hippocrates' discussions.

Men born in stony, flat, cold, dry places are extremely strong and bony; their joints are plainly visible; they are of great stature, skilled in war and

---

[36] "Et hoc [i.e., the heat kept within the body] augt corpora eorum et facit ea carnosa et phlegmatica. . . ." *DNL*, Tr. II, chap. 3 (Jammy, Vol. 5, p. 282).

[37] ". . . quia frigus loci et constrictio corporum eorum impedit evaporationem spirituum & humoris: propter quod virtus earum fortis semper manet, & illa facit eas concipere multum: & quando non perfecte sunt emundatae a menstruis. Et haec etiam causa est, quare corpora earum calida sunt vehementer: et ideo sunt audaces: quia calor semper abundat sanguine et spiritu." *Ibid.*, p. 282, Tr. II, chap. 3 (Jammy, Vol. 5, p. 282 bottom verso).

[38] *DNL*, Tr. II, chap. 3 (Jammy, Vol. 5, p. 282).

[39] The reference is to Vitr., *On Arch.*, Bk. VI, chap. 1, 10–11. *DNL*, Tr. II, chap. 3, *ad fin* (Jammy, Vol. 5, p. 282 recto).

handy in waging it, and they have bony limbs. Their customs are wild and they are like men of stone. Peoples, however, of moist and cold places, have beautiful and smooth faces, their joints are well covered over, they are fleshy and fat, not very tall, and their bellies are extended. They are daring because they have such fiery hearts, but they slacken quickly at their work. They lack zeal in war. Their faces are white or yellow. People living in mountains frequently have knotty and strumous necks and throats (goiter?) because the water is such that too much phlegm is generated in them.[40]

On the other hand, Albert's thought illustrates how old and persistent is the belief that men are not helpless in the face of a harsh or unfriendly environment. Often they can change it. Areas near or in the middle of a forest have stifling and dense air ("habent aërem suffocatum et spissum"); many are cloudy and have whirlwinds. The floor of the forest is moist; the vapor, in contact with the trees, becomes confined and dense. For that reason the wise men of the past improved their localities by cutting down trees and woods. The walnut and the oak and other trees are harmful because they either poison the air with their bitterness or confine it because of their height, thus preventing it from escaping and from being purified. Environmental influences thus are not necessarily permanent, for they can be changed by human agency. The passage is reminiscent of the statement of Theophrastus, repeated by Pliny, that the cutting of trees can change the climate of a place.[41]

Albertus Magnus's *De natura locorum* is the most important and the most elaborate discussion of geographical theory with relation to human culture since the Hippocratic *Airs, Waters, Places*. The lack of originality of the treatise should not obscure its significance as a landmark in the continuity of ideas. Diversity of places meant diversity among the phenomena situated on them; a place was also important for astrological reasons. And both environmental and astrological influences were aspects of that unity and harmony imposed on the elements by divine will. Albert also perpetuated the old error of extrapolating to entire peoples environmental influences that presumably caused mental or physical differences among individuals. As it was with the ancients, so it was with Albert: the environmental theory became a handy explanation for racial differences—especially skin color and type of hair—and for physiological and cultural differences.

Albert achieved a well-ordered system of thought on man and nature. This is a created, not an eternal, world, and the cosmos shows evidence of

---

[40] *DNL*, Tr. II, chap. 4 (Jammy, Vol. 5, pp. 282–283). The chapter continues in the manner of Vitruvius with a discussion of the proper siting of houses, clothing, and medicine and their relation to various places. What applies to men applies also to animals, plants, and stones.

[41] *DNL*, Tr. I, chap. 13, *ad fin* (Jammy, Vol. 5, p. 278).

the order and the beauty intended by God. The heavenly bodies have their spheres of influence on earth and they are supplemented by local physical conditions on earth; moreover, he does not forget the study of nature as a whole, for climate, habitat, and local conditions were as necessary in understanding natural history as they were in understanding peoples.[42]

## 5. The Encyclopedist, Bartholomew of England

The encyclopedists of the twelfth and thirteenth centuries, like Isidore of Seville in the sixth and seventh, from whom they copied so much, normally included a treatise on geography or cosmography; usually it was a compendium-like collection of place-names, provinces, and quotations from the ancients. Works of this kind were written by Albertus Magnus, Alexander of Hales, Thomas de Cantimpré, Vincent Beauvais, and Bartholomew of England —the latter's discussion of geography in the *De proprietatibus rerum* being the most impressive of these discussions. These attempts to summarize geographical knowledge generally leaned heavily on Pliny, Isidore, Orosius, St. Augustine, St. Basil, and St. Ambrose.

Although little is known of his life, Bartholomew presumably was born in England; he lived in France and apparently traveled widely in—or heard direct reports of—the lowlands, France, and Germany. The *De proprietatibus rerum*, believed to have been published around the middle of the thirteenth century, had circulated in England before the end of the thirteenth century; it was translated into Italian, French, and English, the French translation of Jean Corbechon being especially popular. It was still widely read and influential at the beginning of the sixteenth century.[43] Bartholomew was a student of Robert Grosseteste, who himself had written a short essay on the nature of places, which, however, is of little interest to our present theme.[44]

[42] See, for example, "De animalibus," Bk. XII, Tr. I, chap. 4, 59, in *Beiträge zur Geschichte der Philosophie des Mittelalters*, Vol. 15 (1916), p. 820.

[43] Delisle, "Traités Divers sur les Propriétés des Choses," *Hist. Litt. de la France*, Vol. 30, pp. 363–365. Delisle tries to make a case for the French birth of Bartholomew. I am indebted to William J. Humphries' unpublished doctoral dissertation (Berkeley, 1955) which summarizes the main sources on his life; the dissertation consists of the edited Latin text and the French translation of 1372 by Jean Corbechon of Book XV on geography. The *De prop. rerum* treats the following subjects in the order shown: God, the angels, the soul, the elements and the humors; parts of the body; life, family, and society; melodies; the celestial world, movement and time, matter and the elements, atmospheric phenomena, birds, water and fish, earth and mountains, provinces, minerals, plants, animals, and special properties of matter.

[44] The Bartholomew-Grosseteste relationship is mentioned here because of the important place of the latter in the history of experimental science. On Grosseteste (d. 1253) see A. C. Crombie's *Robert Grosseteste and the Origins of Experimental Science, 1100–1700*, and a summary discussion in his *Medieval and Early Modern Science*, Vol. 2, pp. 11–23. See also Anton E. Schönbach, "Des Bartholomaeus Anglicus Beschreibung

Bartholomew's ideas are also derived from the physiological theories of the ancients.[45] The cool, drying north wind closes the pores and bodily heat is retained; hence the tallness and fairness of the northerners. Those influenced by the hot and moist south wind lack the boldness, wrath, and anger of men of the north.[46] These and other environmental explanations are used when he is borrowing from others, but when he is speaking of places he knows of in contemporary life, it is likely that either there will be no explanations for the conditions or the explanations will not be environmental ones. A theme which could profitably be explored in the history of geographical thought is that ideas of environmental influence have been more convincing and acceptable when applied to far-off days—or places—than when applied to times and situations well known to the observer. There are too many obvious factors to be observed in everyday life to permit of one explanation. Moreover, Bartholomew's failure to confine himself to his stated purpose—to write about sacred places—is symptomatic of his wider interests (as many of the articles show) in the commercial importance of places and in the national characteristics of peoples.

In his discussion of Europe, Bartholomew says he follows Pliny in contrasting the white and the black peoples. Adopting Isidore's etymology of Ethiopia, he gives a climatic explanation of racial color.[47] The entry on Gaul shows knowledge of Isidore's generalization, derived from Servius the Grammarian's commentary on the Aeneid, about the klimata being responsible for the gravity of the Romans, the lightheartedness of the Greeks, the malice of the Africans, and the courage of the Gauls; the thought is repeated in the entry on Poitou.[48]

These borrowings, however, if quoted alone, give a wrong impression. The pattern of the more general entries is to give brief characterizations of the land and of the people: whether the land is fertile and grows grains or vines or other crops, whether it has marshes, woods, and wild animals; whether the people are brave, good, crafty, or cruel. In the discussions of Flanders and of

---

Deutschlands gegen 1240," *Mitt. des Insts. für österreichische Geschichtsforschung*, Vol. 27 (1906), pp. 54–90; and H. C. Darby, "Geography in a Medieval Text-Book," *Scott. Geog. Mag.*, Vol. 49 (1933), pp. 323–331.

[45] See *De prop. rerum*, Book IV, chap. 2, on race, skin coloring, and climate. References are to Aristotle *De caelo et mundo*, chap. 6, with references to Galen. All of Book IV is concerned with the elements and the humors.

[46] *De prop. rerum*, Bk. XI, chap. 3. See Kimble, *Geog. in the Middle Ages*, p. 178, where there is an interesting example of the conflict between environmental theory (represented by the above citation from Bartholomew) and astrological theory drawn from the *Liber Canonum Astrologiae of John Calderia*, a physician of Venice (fifteenth century).

[47] Pliny, *NH*, II, 80. *De prop. rerum*, Bk. XV, "De Europa," 7. A very threadbare theme by now; Albert the Great had worn it thin. Bk. XV, 52, "De Ethiopia," 1.

[48] *Ibid.*, Bk. XV, 66, 2, "De Gallia," and "De Pictavia," 122, 5, where Isidore is again referred to. See Isidore, *Etym.*, Book IX, chap. 2.

Holland, the shopworn wares of Pliny and Isidore are forgotten. The people of Flanders, by digging turf from their bogs, make up for their deficiency in wood; the vigorous fire has a disagreeable odor and the ashes are useless.[49] His complimentary description of Holland has already been mentioned. Dissimilarities among peoples of the same nation living under similar climatic conditions are recognized but without causal explanation. France possesses fine quarries and excellent building materials, and the soils of Paris are remarkable for their gypsum, which the Parisians call "plaster." Bartholomew has generous praise for Paris as a city.[50] He recognizes the fact that cultural characteristics may be the result of the mixing of peoples. The people of Poitou mixed in with the French and learned their language and customs; they owe their beautiful bodies and their physical strength to the Picts from whom they have descended. He cites Isidore then on environmental influences on build, color, and spirit. Mixing with the English has changed Scottish manners; the Scots are no longer like their primitive forefathers, who lived like the people of Ireland, in forests, and who were jealous of, and gloried in, their ancient customs. There are similarities among the peoples of Slavia, the differences among them, however, being religious, for there are pagans and those of Greek and of Latin worship.[51]

One could write an interesting essay on conceptions of the physical environment of the Garden of Eden held by writers of the Middle Ages, because their descriptions often reveal what they considered to be ideal living conditions. Bartholomew, quoting Isidore on the derivation of the word "paradise," agrees with him that because of its great height the Flood failed to reach it. Paradise is neither cold nor hot; it has eternally temperate air, with flowering plants and pleasant scenes. It is a place worthy of one made in the image of God; following Strabus and Bede, he says that paradise was suited to man in a state of innocence. It is high; as Bede and Isidore say, it touches the circle of the moon, and with its quiet, pure air it is a region of eternal life. The pictures of the Garden of Eden are idealized earthly environments, conspicuous for health, fertility, lushness of vegetation, and a temperate climate. Stagnant and disease-bearing swamps obviously were not part of the environment of paradise, whose beauty and habitability were commensurate with the nature of man before the Fall.[52]

### 6. St. Thomas to the King of Cyprus

St. Thomas Aquinas's *On Kingship, To the King of Cyprus* is concerned in part with the relationship of the physical environment to the governing of

---

[49] *Ibid.*, 58, 5, "De Flandria."
[50] *Ibid.*, 57, "De Francia"; on Paris, 6–9.
[51] *Ibid.*, 122, "De Pictavia"; 152, 4–5, "De Scotia"; 140, 1, "De Sclavia."
[52] *Ibid.*, 112, "De Paradiso." One of the longest articles in the work.

a state, an important theme in the history of both political theory and geographic thought.

St. Thomas, who follows the celebrated passage from Aristotle closely in this matter, says that man cannot live alone, that he is a political animal, that he must have government, and that a monarchy (relying on the analogy of God as a ruler of the universe) is the best form of government, though the monarch should not be a tyrant. In founding a city, or in governing one after its establishment, a king must take many things into consideration, including site selection, the nature of the atmosphere, and the food supply.

This work may have been written as an "offering to Hugh II of Cyprus, a Lusignan king whose house had been friendly with the Dominican activity, or to one of his family for the churches they built, or as a reminder to the Christian princes that their services were needed after the fall of Jerusalem in 1244 and the unsuccessful crusade of St. Louis of France," for "an increased activity of the Dominicans is noticeable to rally princes and peoples to the precarious cause of the Holy Land." These are conjectures, but the age of the Crusades did offer many opportunities for comparing different environments. Medieval accounts of Cyprus describe a variety of conditions from the temperate and healthful to the hot and marshy; such variety demonstrated the need to consider the climate in establishing settlement. "It is perhaps on account of similar reports that St. Thomas thought it advisable to remind the king of the ancient teaching on the relation between civil life and climate and on the importance of medicine for politics. . . ."[53] His guides in this endeavor are Aristotle (especially the *Politics* and the *Physics*), Vitruvius, and Vegetius.[54]

In comparing civil authority with divine works, St. Thomas says that the founder of a city, or a kingdom, must try, as best as his human powers will allow him, to have as his model the example of God's creation of the world, seen in the production of things and in "the orderly distinction of the parts of the world." We observe certain kinds of distributions: stars in the heavens, birds in the air, fish in the water, animals on land. "We notice further that, for each species, the things it needs are abundantly provided by the Divine Power."[55] (Illustrates the point by recapitulating Genesis 1.)

The founder of a city or kingdom can never be a creator in this sense, for he cannot create men, places for them to live in, or other necessities. He must, through his arts and techniques, make use of things already existing in nature, as the smith uses iron, and the builder, wood or stone. "Therefore the founder of a city and kingdom must first choose a suitable place which will preserve the inhabitants by its healthfulness, provide the necessities of life

[53] *On Kingship*. Translator's introd., pp. xxxi, xxiii–xxiv.
[54] Aristotle, *Pol.*, VII, 7; *Physics*, VII, 3, 246b; *On Length and Shortness of Life*, I, 465a, 7–10; Vegetius, *De re militari*, I, 2; Vitr., *On Arch.*, Bk. I, chap. 4. See also translator's notes pp. 68–80.
[55] *On Kingship*, 99.

by its fruitfulness, please them with its beauty, and render them safe from their enemies by its natural protection."[56] The parallel between the divine plan and the civil plan is clearly drawn; the work accomplished in founding a city is a kind of creativity—of a far lower order than God's—in which kings and their subjects can participate. The geographic portion of the treatise, therefore, is largely concerned with matters of earthly planning helped by the practical traditions of antiquity and by the example of divine planning. Some parts of a kingdom may be suitable for establishing cities, others, for villages or hamlets; sites can be chosen for military camps, places of learning, markets, churches, law courts, the trades, providing the necessities for all persons according to their position and station in life.

The Aristotelian golden mean (representing in its physiological aspect a harmonious balancing of the humors) is the keystone in the planning arch. "A temperate region should be chosen, for the inhabitants derive many advantages from a temperate climate. In the first place, it ensures them health of body and length of life; for, since good health consists of the right temperature of the vital fluids (i.e., humors),[57] it follows that health will be best preserved in a temperate clime, because like is preserved by like." Extremes are therefore bad; like Albert, he cites the supposed thirty-year life-span of men in the very hot parts of Ethiopia because the moisture which, with the heat, is necessary to maintain life is dried up.[58]

"Then, too, a temperate climate is most conducive to fitness for war, by which human society is kept in security." (Quotes to this point, Vegetius, *De re militari*, I, 2, on climatic influences affecting military recruits.) A temperate climate also "is of no little value for political life" (cites Aristotle's *Politics*, VII, 7, 1327b, 23–32).

The healthfulness of a site should be considered; marshy places should be avoided, and it should have the proper exposure (cites Vitr., I, 4). The healthfulness of a place can be judged by the condition of the food which it produces. "The ancients were wont to explore this condition by examining the animals raised on the spot." Next in importance to good air is good water. The appearance of the people also reveals the healthfulness of its climate. A place should be healthful and fertile, and of the two means of obtaining food, by growing crops or by trading, the former is to be preferred because men become more self-sufficient. Echoing the classical belief in the harmfulness to morals of trade, St. Thomas says that intercourse with foreigners (following Aristotle, *Pol.*, V, 3, 1303a 27; VII, 6, 1327a 13–15) "is particularly harmful to civic customs. Foreigners with their different customs cannot be expected to act like citizens, who, however, may be led from their own ways

---

[56] *Ibid.*, 100.
[57] *Ibid.*, 124. On the classical sources, see notes to 124–127.
[58] *Ibid.*, 125.

by the example of the strangers."[59] This is an astonishing statement in view of the vast efforts made in city-founding in the twelfth and thirteenth centuries; St. Thomas stays so close to the classical model and to religious ideas concerning profit that he apparently ignores his best contemporary examples —the new cities and the complexities generated by them.

The site of a city "must claim the inhabitants by its beauty": it should have broad meadows, abundant forests, mountains, groves, plenty of water; but as befits a believer in the golden mean, neither should it be too beautiful, for its beauty will tempt men too much to pleasure, thus dulling and impairing the judgment of the senses (follows Aristotle, *Eth. Nic.*, VI, 5; *Eth.*, VI, 4.)

St. Thomas's essay on kingship is more than a restatement, in the thirteenth century, of ideas derived from the writings of Aristotle, Vegetius, and Vitruvius; he seems also to be concerned with contemporary situations to whose solution the ideas of the ancients were apposite. The classical ideas were the best available; Albert the Great had said that the subject of climate, medicine, and civil society had interested kings since ancient times. The reasons for this interest in St. Thomas's time were substantially the same as they were in the classical world: there was clearly a relationship between the physical environment and health. And the thinkers of the Middle Ages were willing to follow their classical mentors in believing the relation extended to mental, racial, and cultural differences, too. The important thought in this essay, however, is the comparison of kingly rule on earth with divine rule of the universe. The king, like God in his creations in the higher sphere, plans and establishes cities and kingdoms rationally, as a man of reason and intelligence should, applying human arts and inventions, and studying thoroughly the airs, waters, and places before beginning the onerous and responsible tasks of creating a kingdom.

### 7. EAST AND WEST: OTTO OF FREISING AND GIRALDUS CAMBRENSIS

In *The Geographical Lore of the Time of the Crusades*, John K. Wright noted the emergence during the Crusades, when men of the Latin West were becoming acquainted with the peoples of the eastern Mediterranean, of a philosophy of history which assumed a geographical march in the course of civilization. This conception grew out of world history as it was then known and out of the knowledge—from biblical and classical sources—of the greater antiquity of the lands to the east (*ex oriente lux*). It was therefore believed that throughout history centers of civilization had moved from east to west.

---

[59] *Ibid.*, 126, 128–129. The ancients, according to Vitr., *On Arch.*, Bk. I, chap. 4, 9, examined the livers of cattle. St. Thomas was also hostile to trade on religious grounds because it provoked greed; it was softening and unfavorable to military activity; it also concentrated people too much within city walls, leading to dissension and sedition. Trade could not be avoided altogether, but it should be carried on in moderation.

But there was no comfort in the doctrine. "For it was felt that mankind would meet its final doom when the movement had reached the uttermost limits of the Occident."[60] In the fourth century, Severian of Gabala said that God with an eye to the future placed man in the Garden of the East "in order to cause him to understand that, just as the light of heaven moves toward the West, so the human race hastens towards death."[61] As we have seen, there was also the tradition of the southward migration of civilization owing to the distinctive characteristic of the northlands as an *officina gentium*.

The theme of the geographic march of history has been a recurring one in the history of Western thought. It enjoyed some popularity in the nineteenth century, being found in Hegel's philosophy of history, in Ritter's geographical thought, and in that of his pupil and disciple, Arnold Guyot. Carl Ritter, the most dedicated teleological and pietistic theorist of nineteenth century geography, used the analogy with far happier consequences than those foreseen by the gloomy Severian. Asia is literally the land of morning and the source of civilization, and Europe is the land of evening, the seat of advanced civilization; Africa is a nondescript and undistinguished midday, and the north polar regions, night. The discovery of the New World, however, created a new Orient for Europe; the land of evening.[62] In the twentieth century, the idea of the northward advance of civilization has enjoyed some popularity, resting, however, on partial views, the most obvious an overemphasis on the significance of the history of western Europe in the history of civilization.

Anticipations of this theme, like Severian's, appeared before the Crusades. Marcus Justinus (third century A.D.?) wrote an epitome of Pompeius Trogus's *Historiae Philippicae*, in which Justin saw a progression of the sites of world empire from the east (Assyria, Media, Persia) to the West (Macedonia and Rome). "Justin represents the power (*imperium*) or authority which rules the world as being handed over by a failing world empire to its successor. This idea (under the name of *translatio imperii*) plays an important part in the historical views of the Middle Ages. . . ." Christian writers adopted the idea, Jerome mentioning the Assyrian-Babylonian, the Medo-Persian, Macedonian and Roman sequence. Orosius substituted Carthage for Persia, the four empires corresponding to the cardinal directions.[63] The conception was elaborated upon by Otto of Freising (1114?–1158). In a wise passage of *The Two Cities*, Otto says that we are trained "by the passage of time and the resultant experience in life, yes, trained the more quickly the more advanced the age of the world is in which we are set," and that we devise new things after mastering what has been achieved before. The "lapse of time and the course

---

[60] Von Grunebaum, *Medieval Islam*, p. 62.
[61] Quoted by von Grunebaum from Wright, *Geo. Lore*, p. 234.
[62] *Geographical Studies*, trans. by Gage, p. 73.
[63] See Mierow's discussion in the introduction to his translation of Otto, Bishop of Freising's *The Two Cities*, p. 29, to which I am indebted for this material. Orosius, 2, 1, 5.

of events" reveal things to men, things which could not be seen by their ancestors from whom the future was hidden. "And so all now see to what the Roman Empire came—that Empire which, because of its preëminence, was thought by the pagans to be eternal and even by our people to be almost divine."

Human power or wisdom originating in the East "began to reach its limits in the West," passing from the Babylonians to the Medes, Persians, Macedonians, to the Romans, to the Greeks under the Roman name, and from them to the Franks and then—such is the mutability of human affairs—to the Germans.[64] This westward flow has been true also of the history of religion, as is evidenced by the flourishing state of Western monastic life—monks, formerly most numerous in Egypt, now are found in greatest numbers "in the regions of Gaul and Germany, so that one need not wonder at the transfer of power or of wisdom from the East to the West, since it is evident that the same transfer has been effected in matters of religion."[65] There is in *The Two Cities*, however, such an atmosphere of sorrow, of the all-pervading misery of the human race, that it may be questioned whether his idea of the geographical march of civilization has any roots in environmental determinism. Rather the influence of the church is the dominant theme; the fall of the Roman Empire and the rise of the Catholic Church are key events in human history. The Church, exalted and enriched by the state and the favor of rulers like Constantine, could not have so deeply humiliated the state until it, enfeebled by its own priesthood, was destroyed by its own material sword and the spiritual sword of the Church. By Roman times civilization had so advanced that men would accept Christianity, and Christ with his new laws could come to a world bowed before Roman power and molded by the wisdom of philosophers. The temporal had failed; the spiritual, with its inevitable contempt for the world, had advanced. Men of the world grow more unclean, while the monastic and secular clergy as God's citizens attain through His grace a fullness of virtues, recognizing that the Church too has its grain and its chaff. Otto had joined the Cistercian order; he was sympathetic with its mysticism and its asceticism. The state no longer represented the city of Earth, even the Church no longer represented the city of God. He frankly wonders about the present earthly exaltation of the Church. His Cistercian asceticism turns him away from the transitoriness and impermanence of life, the mutability and uncertainty of earthly fortune, of *civitas mundi*, to the abiding nature of the eternal *civitas dei*.[66]

[64] *The Two Cities*, Bk. V, prologue, p. 322. See Mierow's remarks, p. 30. *The Two Cities*, Bk. VI, chap. 24, pp. 384–386; on the transitoriness of the supposedly permanent abiding place of power with the Franks, see Bk. V, chap. 36, pp. 357–359.

[65] *The Two Cities*, Bk. VII, chap. 35, Mierow trans., p. 448.

[66] *Ibid.*, Bk. III, prologue, p. 220; Bk. VII, prologue, pp. 404–405; and chaps. 9, p. 415; 24, pp. 433–434; 34, p. 445. On Otto's times and the gloominess of his views of the world and the more cheerful atmosphere of his *The Deeds of Frederick Barbarossa*, see Mierow's intro., pp. 57–61; on his philosophy of history, pp. 61–72.

In the work of Giraldus Cambrensis (*ca.* 1146–*ca.* 1220), however, the contrasts between East and West are of a geographical, not a historical, character. His descriptions suggest a knowledge of conditions in the eastern Mediterranean in the sharply contrasting pictures of the healthful West (represented by Ireland) and the disease-ridden East.

This Welsh historian expressed in *The Topography of Ireland* (completed in 1187), with all its marvels, fables, and vanities, ideas which differed, as had Bartholomew's, from the usual classical borrowings. Some seem to have come from personal observation of Irish conditions, some from reports of the Crusades.

Giraldus arranges all phenomena on earth in an ascending hierarchy: inorganic nature, followed by plants, animals, man, and the angels. God, like the potter who is superior to the clay he molds, transcends all created being. These thoughts inspire in Giraldus a humility which, like the divine hierarchy, is a familiar stage piece of the Middle Ages. ". . . O man, with what face, with what temerity thou presumest to scrutinize and trace out those mysteries, to the investigation of which the very angels esteem themselves wholly incompetent."[67] We need not take this humility too seriously, for Giraldus is curious about everything; no eye-lowered shyness prevents him from giving himself full credit for his many abilities.

To Giraldus, "Ireland is the most temperate of all countries"; there is green grass for the cattle in summer and winter, and there is no need for cutting hay, no need for stalls. The air is healthful—"no clouds bring infection, and there are no pestilent vapours, or tainted breezes." Strangers, however, are subject to only one disorder, dysentery. This interpretation of idyllic temperate Ireland is spoiled by his belief in the senescence of nature, from which, however, Giraldus lets the Irish off lightly. ". . . As the world grows older, and is falling as it were into the decrepitude of old age, and draws to an end, the nature of almost all things is corrupted and deteriorated." Floods, dense clouds, and fogs apparently are the signs of old age, but Giraldus seems impatient with his theme, ending on a happier but inconclusive note. "Notwithstanding, no disturbance of the atmosphere, no seasonableness of the weather, either troubles those who are in health and spirits, or affects the nerves of delicate persons." The senescence of nature is forgotten; the Irish are in no imminent danger.

The East has its silk, precious metals, gems, and aromatic shrubs, but unlike the West with its temperate and healthful climates, it has bad air. In a passage,

---

[67] *Topography of Ireland*, Dist. I, chap. 9, Wright ed., p. 31. Although he had been sent in 1188 to Wales with Primate Baldwin to preach the Third Crusade, Giraldus never was in the Holy Land. He accompanied Henry II to France—the news of Saladin's capture of Jerusalem was received in late 1187—and on Henry's death the new king, Richard I, sent him back to Wales because of his hold on the Welsh, relieving him of his vow. See Wright's introduction to *The Historical Works of Giraldus Cambrensis*, and the article on him in the 11th edition of the *Encyclopaedia Britannica*.

possibly a distillation of many reports of hardship, disease, and death in the eastern lands, Giraldus says, "In those countries all the elements, though created for the use of man, threaten wretched mortals with death, undermine health, and bring life to an end." There is death in contact with the earth and the rocks, in the drinking water, the air, the thunder and lightning, the blazing sun; there is death from overeating and from drinking wine undiluted with water. People poison one another. There is danger from wild animals and snakes. The East with its venom and poison thus is no match for the Irish climate whose golden moderation offsets the advantages of oriental pomp and circumstance. God has been particularly generous to the Irish land. There is no fear of the open air or of the rocks; life is better despite the poorer soils and their lower yields. "The nearer, indeed, we go to the regions of the East, and warmer climates, the greater is the fertility of the soil, and the more plentifully does the earth pour forth her fruits. . . . The people also, thanks to a brighter atmosphere, although slender in person, are of a more subtle intellect." They attain their ends more by poison than by violence, more by their arts than by their arms. The western parts of the world have a more sterile soil, but the air is more healthful and the people though less acute are more robust; "for where the atmosphere is heavy, the fields are less fertile than the wits." Giraldus adds a touch of astrological ethnology to emphasize the point about environmental distinctions.

> Bacchus and Ceres, therefore, rule in the East, with their attendant Venus, who, deprived of them, is chilled; Minerva, also, who was always nursed and attracted by a purer sky. Here [in the West] reigns [*sic*] Mars, Mercury, and the Arcadian god. In the East is accumulated a superabundance of wealth; here we have a modest and honorable competence. There the atmosphre is serene, here it is salubrious. There the natives are fine witted; here, their understandings are robust. There they arm themselves with poisons, here with manly vigour. There, they are crafty, here bold in war. There men cultivate wisdom, here eloquence. There Apollo rules, Mercury here; there Minerva, here Pallas and Diana.

It all sounds like Ptolemy's *Tetrabiblos*. In an elaborate summation, combining geographical contrasts with the humoral psychology and physiology and analogies drawn from the ages of man, Giraldus concludes that the advantages lie with the West.

> As much then as ease of mind is more desirable than anxiety, as preservation is better than cure, and as it is better to enjoy constant health than, after much suffering, to seek for remedies, so in the same degree, the advantages of the West are to be preferred to those of the East; and so far nature has cast a more favourable eye on the regions fanned by the West, than those swept by East winds. It appears to be very probable that as moisture tempers and softens the morning and evening of day, while noon is scorching, and the earliest and latest years of man are mellowed by a moist temperament, while his middle age is fervid, so while, in respect of the regions on the meridian and its confines, the sun raging

in those parts as if in the prime of youth, infects the air with disease, so a more humid climate renders the boundaries of its rising and setting temperate.[68]

In this extraordinary attempt to explain the differences between the East and the West, Giraldus seems captivated by the magnificence and the richness of the Eastern potentates (there is no mention of the poor), and he shows a wistful, almost reluctant, preference for the quieter and less flamboyant life in the West. Climate and disease seem to be the real bases for these cultural distinctions. These ideas, peppered with mythological allusions, astral effects, environmental influences, and correlations with the ages of man (a frequent topic discussed by the encyclopedic writers of the Middle Ages) are far less remarkable than his theory of stages of economic development; it might well be the theory of Dicaearchus adapted by Giraldus to Irish history.

> The Irish are a rude people, subsisting on the produce of their cattle only, and living themselves like beasts—a people that has not yet departed from the primitive habits of pastoral life. In the common course of things, mankind progresses from the forest to the field, from the field to the town, and to the social condition of citizens; but this nation, holding agricultural labour in contempt, and little coveting the wealth of towns, as well as being exceedingly averse to civil institutions—lead the same life their fathers did in the woods and open pastures, neither willing to abandon their old habits or learn anything new. They, therefore, only make patches of tillage; their pastures are short of herbage; cultivation is very rare, and there is scarcely any land sown. This want of tilled fields arises from the neglect of those who should cultivate them; for there are large tracts which are naturally fertile and productive. The whole habits of the people are contrary to agricultural pursuits, so that the rich glebe is barren for want of husbandmen, the fields demanding labour which is not forthcoming.[69]

There are few kinds of fruit trees—not because they could not be imported and, once imported, cultivated, but because "the lazy husbandman does not take the trouble to plant the foreign sorts which would grow very well here." There are metals but they are not mined; neither is there interest in manufacturing linen or wool or in the trades and mechanical arts. The slothful people like only the exemption from toil and their freedom. Their dress, the custom of allowing the hair and beard to grow long, are further evidences of their barbarism.

> But habits are formed by mutual intercourse; and as this people inhabit a country so remote from the rest of the world, and lying at its furthest extremity, forming, as it were, another world, and are thus secluded from civilized nations, they learn nothing, and practise nothing but the barbarism in which they are born and bred, and which sticks to them like a second nature. Whatever natural gifts they possess are excellent, in whatever requires industry they are worthless.[70]

[68] *Topog. of Ireland*, Dist. I, chap. 25, pp. 51–52; chap. 26, p. 52; chap. 27, pp. 54–55; chap. 28, p. 56.
[69] *Ibid.*, Dist. III, chap. 10, p. 124.
[70] *Ibid.*, pp. 125–126.

This passage can stand comparison with writings on cultural history and with theories of economic evolution of the nineteenth century. In Giraldus' theory, the forest takes the place of the pastoral stage—the Mediterranean grazing lands of the ancients—probably because the forests had a comparable significance in the grazing of animals. There is no sentimentalizing about primitive life, but it is described with understanding and objectivity. Most striking is the idea that men do not necessarily make use of resources which nature makes available to them, and that an advantageous physical environment will have little meaning in understanding a people if one does not also know their habits and predilections. Equally striking is the use Giraldus makes of the role of isolation and its relation to cultural inertia. People, one can almost hear him say, are changed less by their environment than by the other peoples whom they chance to meet. These passages, bearing the stamp of observation and experience, have little of the fancifulness of his other speculations.

His discussions of culture and environment have the inconsistencies that come from blending the borrowings from others with facts known from personal knowledge. To him the East could best be understood through its climate, its luxury, and the prevalence of disease. Climate plays its part in understanding the West, too, but cultural isolation is the key to understanding the Irish, so great is the contrast between them—living so long in their cherished isolation—and those who have known agriculture and the village life of civilization.

## 8. ROGER BACON: GEOGRAPHY AND ASTROLOGICAL ETHNOLOGY

In his discourse on mathematics, Roger Bacon explored extensively the interrelationships of theology, astronomy, and geography, but his fundamental interest was in astrology because he saw in the heavens the great cosmic forces influencing the sublunary world. Although most of what he has to say is more appropriate to an essay on astrological ethnology, it would be a mistake to ignore him in this work, because of the blending of astrology with geography, and the importance of *place* in his thought.

The aim of philosophy, he says, is to know the creator through the creature. The theophany, however, must include the whole cosmos because of the vast magnitude of celestial things. Celestial and earthly phenomena lead us to praise and reverence the creator, but the two are not comparable with regard to their end, the latter being insignificant in comparison with the former. This is the basic conception: celestial things, creations of God, are vaster than anything on earth, and their influence is therefore greater.[71]

Bacon repeatedly insists upon the importance of accurate knowledge of

[71] *Opus Majus*, Pt. II, chap. 7, Vol. I, p. 49; Pt. IV, pp. 200–201.

places and the task of astronomy in determining their exact location. Precise determinations are indispensable for the proper interpretation of theology and the sacred texts. The thought goes far beyond insistence on an accurate sacred geography so that men may know the exact locations of places mentioned in the Scriptures. Such knowledge is indispensable for comprehending the spiritual meaning of places; it also becomes the way toward understanding the earthly theophany and the spiritual message of landscapes, or individual mountains, rivers, or cities.

Let us outline the argument and summarize Roger Bacon's illustration. Nothing of importance can be known about things unless the places where they are, are also known. The sciences of astrology and astronomy must delimit the habitable and the uninhabitable parts of the world, and further divide the former into proper regions. History without geography precludes literal and spiritual knowledge. For men ignorant of places "the rind of history frequently has no taste because of the infinite number of places, and especially owing to the manifold falsity of the new Bibles; and as a consequence he will be impeded in rising to the spiritual meanings and only imperfectly will be able to explain them." But the man who knows about places, the man who has "learned their location, distance, height, length, width, and depth, and has tested their diversity in heat and dryness, cold and humidity, color, savor, odor and beauty, ugliness, pleasantness, fertility, sterility, and other conditions, will be pleased very greatly by the literal history, and will be able easily and admirably to gain an understanding of the spiritual meanings." Corporeal roads signify spiritual roads, and corporeal places, the ends of spiritual roads.

Such thinking shows his sympathy with allegorical exegesis. Bacon quotes Jerome approvingly: "He will have a clearer insight into the sacred Scriptures, who has viewed Judea with his own eyes, and has learned the memorials of the ancient cities and the names either the same or changed of the places." But the argument is not that through such knowledge one's impressions of biblical scenes and landscapes become more exact, vivid, colorful. It is that exact literal geography leads to precise symbolic interpretation. He praises the ecclesiastics, Jerome, Orosius, Isidore, Cassiodorus, Eusebius of Caesarea, who saw the need for sacred geography. These men accomplished in essence the task as Jerome had seen it: "We made it our care to undertake this labor [his commentary in the second book of Chronicles] along with the most learned of the Jews, that we might traverse the province of which all the Churches of Christ speak."[72]

How does exact literal geography lead to confident symbolic interpretation? Let us take Bacon's illustration. The south-flowing Jordan lies east of Jerusalem. Between the river and the city are Jericho and its plain, the Mount

[72] *Ibid.*, Vol. I, pp. 203–205.

of Olives (to the east of Jerusalem), the Valley of Jehoshaphat (i.e., NT Kedron), lying between the Mount of Olives and Jerusalem, and finally the holy city itself. What is the spiritual meaning of this literal geography?

The river Jordan represents the world for many reasons: it empties into the Dead Sea which symbolizes Hades. Jericho signifies the flesh, the Mount of Olives, "the excellence of the spiritual life, owing to the excellence of the mountain." The Valley of Jehoshaphat signifies humility, Jerusalem, "the vision of peace, and morally it is the sacred soul that possesses peace of heart; allegorically it signifies the Church militant; analogically the Church triumphant."

One who wishes to approach life's end with peace of mind, who wishes to be a perfect and faithful member of the Church, who wishes in this life to reach the heavenly Jerusalem, should either leave Jordan (the world) behind him by subjecting it to him or withdraw from Jordan as do the monks of monastic orders. Then he must attack the flesh, a harder task than leaving Jordan. This conquering of the flesh must be done gradually. Thus, the flesh is Jericho with its plain. Bacon here shows his opposition to drastic physical strains exerted on the body by sudden, dramatic asceticism. The task is to be approached as through a plain to Jericho. When Jordan and Jericho are behind him, a man is prepared "to ascend to the excellency of the spiritual life and to the sweetness of devotion." He therefore ascends the Mount of Olives "to reach the summit of perfection and to plunge into the sweetness of prayer and contemplation." Then he must cross the Valley of Jehoshaphat, that is, he must end his life in perfect humility. When he has done so, he is in Jerusalem in a triple sense: in the peace of heart, in the peace of God, in the peace of the Church militant.[73]

Many other spiritual meanings, Bacon says, are to be found in geography. The influence of geographical landscapes on religious allegory is an interesting theme; in Christian theology it appears in the early hexaemera, which do not give literal interpretations. The nature imagery of St. Ambrose is especially rich in allegory taken from geography, nature, and agriculture and viticulture.

Exact knowledge of places, of longitude and latitude, is therefore a means of eliciting divine meanings, "in drawing forth many things from few, great things from small, obscure things from those that are more manifest." To a practiced eye, landscapes assume the character of a theophany.

The key to this understanding is astronomy, for one learns by means of it what planets hold sway over different regions thus creating differences among them.[74] The influence of the stars may be resisted, but the rational soul may be "strongly influenced and aroused, so that it gratuitously desires those things to which the celestial force inclines it, just as we see men, owing to association, advice, fear and love and the like, change greatly their intention,

[73] *Ibid.*, pp. 205–207.
[74] *Ibid.*, p. 208.

and gratuitously wish for those things which they previously did not wish for, although they are under no compulsion, like him who in the hope of safety casts into the sea his most precious wares."[75]

Roger Bacon is aware of the cultural diversity in the various klimata, among the Scythians, Ethiopians, Picards, French, Normans, Flemings, and the English, but the causes of these differences are in the heavens, not on earth or in men. Observation, however, forces him to modify the generalization, because Bacon sees too the cultural influence of a great city on its environs; a province surrounding a famous city assumes its manners and customs because "the city serves as a refuge and a central point for transacting the affairs of life," because cities have power over neighboring districts, and be ause of communication and violence. A similar relationship exists when a pc werful kingdom lies among lesser ones.

When Bacon turns to more practical matters, his plea for geography and a knowledge of places is basically a plea for enlightened knowledge of the world, in the spirit of his plea for learning foreign languages. Things of the world cannot be known except through a knowledge of the places where they are contained, whether these are phenomena of nature, morals, sciences, men's customs, or differing techniques in practicing the arts and sciences. Knowledge of peoples and places is necessary for trade, conversion, understanding of the nonbeliever, for opposing him and the Antichrist. Travelers must know the climates and the characteristics of the foreign lands they visit. They can select temperate places through which to travel. Men have destroyed themselves and the business interests of Christians because they have passed through places too hot in the hot season, too cold in the cold. People who seek to convert need a knowledge of climate, of places, of rites, customs, and conditions of nations.[76]

## 9.  Gunther of Pairis

In the poetry of almost all ages, one finds evidence of the popularity of environmental ideas; their presence is often discernible in nature poetry. Some of the most pleasing descriptions of nature written in the Middle Ages appeared in the epic poem of Gunther of Pairis (in Alsace), written about 1186/1187, and celebrating the early reign years (1152–1160) of Frederick I (Barbarossa).[77] The poem has exquisite descriptions of the scenery of the well-peopled Frankish land—its fields, trees, and noble vines—of the regions of the Rhine and the Moselle; of the route through the Ardennes to Aachen;[78] of the Apennines moderating the summer heat and the hot breath of the south

---

[75] *Ibid.*, p. 271.
[76] *Ibid.*, p. 273; p. 321.
[77] *Der Ligurinus Gunthers von Pairis im Elsass*, intro., p. viii.
[78] *Ibid.*, Bk. I, vss. 385–434.

wind; of the Alps walling out the northern cold; and of the Po, gathering its waters from the Alps and the Apennines, flowing into the Adriatic.[79] These are descriptions with no causal relationships between man and nature. The people living along the Baltic, however, are described as being in a close relationship with their environment. Little is known of their customs—their natural situation protects them—but they are rude, uncultivated, terrible in appearance, and frightful. They are not subject to the control of law, they practice bloodletting, theirs is an unsettled, changing spirit which is foreign to the feeling of devoted Christian emotion.[80]

These reprehensible qualities are caused partly by nature, partly by the harmful influences of neighbors who are still worse. For the Baltic has no island—apparently he thought these lands about the shores of the sea were islands—whose ground is not hardened by eternal cold, and only the mattock can be used to till the miserable land. The people of the Baltic resort to hunting and pillage and in times of hunger even to cannibalism. Under these conditions, the people whom they influence could scarcely be highly cultivated. The passage illustrates a conventional approach to a people known mostly by hearsay in far-off places and whose peculiarities are explained by their remoteness and by their environment.

10. CONCLUSION

Writers of the Middle Ages offered little that was original in the study of geographical influences on man. For as one reads in the theology, philosophy, science, and pseudoscience of the Middle Ages, the geographical theory seems insignificant in comparison with the attention given in the high and late Middle Ages to magic, astrology, and alchemy as bodies of knowledge worthy of study. These gifts in new Muslin clothing promised much: control over nature and over man, a boundless new creativity of breathtaking proportions. The extended consideration of the subject by Albert the Great, however, reassures one that environmental theory was indeed a significant body of thought in the Middle Ages. In avoiding the literature on the fabulous—the oddities of far-off places, the dog-headed men, men with their heads in their chests, one-eyed men—which was conspicuous and respectable in these times, I may have given a misleading impression of a greater reasonableness in geographic theory than was actually the case. But there is another side to the fabulous and the fantastic. William Archbishop of Tyre's descriptions of the Levantine cities visited by the Crusaders, and over which they fought and died, are unsparing. So are the pages of Otto of Freising. Adam of Bremen's descriptions of the Northlands—Jutland, Fyn, Zealand, Scania, Norway, Vin-

[79] *Ibid.*, Bk. II, vss. 56–118.
[80] *Ibid.*, Bk. VI, vss. 25–49.

land, Iceland, and others—are far superior in imaginative description to the gazetteer-like compositions of the past. In these works there are no theories of geographic causation, but their authors have a lively understanding of the nature of an environment and its uses.[81] The theories of geographical influence in the Middle Ages continued the classical tradition of postulating a close relationship between the physical environment and mental and spiritual well-being, deriving a practical art from them useful in the siting of houses and towns, and in finding healthy and avoiding unhealthy places, of using them also as handy explanations of cultural differences, and finally of seeing in them aids to statecraft in devising good laws. These theories thus fit well into the Christian theology and philosophy of the Middle Ages. There need be no conflict if they are regarded as generalizations of regional or local significance elucidating the plan and the design of God. They had the weight of classical science behind them; they were relevant to the problems, trials, and illnesses of the wicked on an earth quite different in moral vigor from the paradise in which the first man lived.

St. Thomas Aquinas came as close as anyone to pointing out the pertinence of the one to the other. God made and planned the cosmos; the king made and planned his kingdom. In his puny way and yet partaking of the divine, the king would consider everything—the advantages of a place, its healthfulness, its influence on its human inhabitants—as a creative and creating mortal, possessed of reason and a sense of order, should.

[81] See William Archbishop of Tyre, *A History of Deeds Done Beyond the Sea*, Bk. I, chap. 7, on the origin and ancestry of the Turkish race; the description and history of Constantinople, Bk. II, chap. 7; the description of Jerusalem and its water supply, Bk. VIII, chaps. 1–4; the description of Caesarea, Bk. X, chap. 15. And also see Otto of Freising, *The Deeds of Frederick Barbarossa*, Bk. II, chap. 13, for descriptions of Po Valley, the Alps—which he called the Pyrennes—and the Apennines. The Lombards, he said, lost their barbaric rudeness; intermarrying with the Romans, their sons inherited "something of the Roman gentleness and keenness from their mother's blood, and from the very quality of the country and climate, retain the refinement of the Latin speech and their elegance of manners." See also the description of the mountain of Freising in connection with his summary of the life of St. Corbinian, in *The Two Cities*, Bk. V, chap. 24, pp. 348–349. Adam of Bremen, *History of the Archbishops of Hamburg-Bremen*, Book IV, on a description of the islands of the north.

# Chapter 7

# Interpreting Piety and Activity,
# and Their Effects on Nature

### 1. INTRODUCTION

The modern study of the Middle Ages has revealed an active, energetic world, and it would be remarkable if in its surviving records there were no interpretations of the significance of the changes made in the physical environment by man.[1]

[1] In the preparation of this chapter I am indebted to many secondary works; although I have consulted the original documents when this was possible, many of the ideas were gleaned from quotations of documents the originals of which, because of bibliographical rarity or inaccessibility, were unavailable to me. The following works were of particular value: Grand and Delatouche, *L'Agriculture au Moyen Âge de la Fin de l'Empire Romain au XVIe Siècle*, cited as *AMA*; Huffel, *Economie Forestière*, cited as Huffel; De Maulde, *Etude sur la Condition Forestière de l'Orléanais au Moyen Âge et à la Renaissance*, cited as De Maulde); and Schwappach, *Handbuch der Forst- und Jagdgeschichte Deutschlands*, cited as Schwappach.

Since this discussion is concerned with attitudes or ideas and not with the actual history of environmental change, the following works—in addition to those cited above

Many historical geographers and historians of medieval times have seen in the widespread environmental changes by human agency of that long period, a close relationship to its social and economic history. Let us name a few of the themes. (1) The contributions of land reclamation in Western Europe in the eleventh and twelfth centuries to "the emancipation of the common man."[2] (2) The antiphonal themes of resistance to and the progress of such change, the role of classes and the growth of organizing ability among them; examples are the maintenance of forests for royal and noble hunters at the expense of the less well-off who were anxious to clear and increase the arable, economic and religious motives in colonization, and the use of contractors and subcontractors in forest clearance.[3] (3) The role of the frontier in medieval times and the comparative study of frontier history, a theme especially attractive to the American historian James Westfall Thompson, who saw parallels between the German expansion from the feudal west to the nonfeudal east and the nineteenth century history of the American frontier. Thompson also saw in Frederick Jackson Turner's frontier hypoth-

---

—may be consulted; they are valuable for their discussions and for their references to other literature. Darby, "The Clearing of the Woodland in Europe," in *MR*, pp. 183–216; *idem*, "The Face of Europe on the Eve of the Discoveries," in *The New Cambridge Modern History*, Vol. 1, pp. 20–49. Darby's writings on the historical geography of Britain, the fens, and the Domesday Book have also been concerned with environmental change. Bloch, *Les Caractères Originaux de l'Histoire Rurale Française*, rev. ed., in two volumes, the supplementary volume being edited by Dauvergne, Vol. 1, pp. 1–20, Vol. 2, pp. 1–30. Vols. 1 and 2 of the *Cambridge Economic History of Europe* (cited as *CEHE*) are also of interest, the following articles being most pertinent to the subject matter of this chapter. Vol. 1: Koebner, "The Settlement and Colonisation of Europe," pp. 1–88; Parain, "The Evolution of Agricultural Technique," pp. 118–168; Ostrogorsky, "Agrarian Conditions in the Byzantine Empire in the Middle Ages," pp. 194–223, and chap. 8, "Medieval Agrarian Society in its Prime," pp. 278–492 (Ganshof on France, the Low Countries, and western Germany; Mickwith on Italy, Smith on Spain; Aubin on the lands east of the Elbe and the German eastward colonization; Rutkowski on Poland, Lithuania, and Hungary; Struve on Russia, Neilson on England, and Bolin on Scandinavia). Vol. 2: Postan, "The Trade of Medieval Europe: the North," pp. 119–256; Nef, "Mining and Metallurgy in Medieval Civilisation, pp. 429–492; Jones, "Building in Stone in Medieval Western Europe," pp. 493–518. The voluminous writings of G. G. Coulton often touch on these themes. For a summary of his views on the Benedictine Rule, monasteries, the peasant, and clearing, see *Medieval Village, Manor, and Monastery*, pp. 212–230. See also his *Five Centuries of Religion*, Vol. 2. As is well known, Coulton is very critical of many modern apologists of the monastic orders, who, he believes, exaggerate their direct participation in the actual work of reclamation. He is quite sympathetic with St. Benedict and the early monks working under the Benedictine Rule. Boissonnade, *Le Travail dans l'Europe Chrétienne au Moyen-Âge* (English trans., *Life and Work in Medieval Europe*). Thompson, *An Economic and Social History of the Middle Ages*. White, *Medieval Technology and Social Change*.

[2] On the history of this idea and for a case study from maritime Flanders, see Lyon, "Medieval Real Estate Developments and Freedom," *AHR*, Vol. 63 (1957), pp. 47–61. See also, Koebner, *CEHE*, Vol. 1, pp. 3, 5, 11.

[3] Darby, "The Clearing of the Woodland in Europe, *MR*, pp. 193–194; Ganshof, *CEHE*, Vol. 1, p. 281; Koebner, *ibid.*, pp. 45–47, 69, 71–72.

esis a suggestive interpretation for earlier periods as well. To me, the differences destroy much of the value in the comparison: one, with a modest technology, was the work of centuries, the other, with the aid of machinery, the work of decades. A more profitable comparative history would be with the Mediterranean or the Chinese cultural landscapes through forest clearance, the driving back of wild animals and the extinction of the larger predators, town building, irrigation, canal building, diking, and the like. The study of this eastern German movement is of anthropological interest also, as the thirteenth century description of the manners of the Prussians reveals; the theme of environmental change here may be associated with culture contact. The eastward expansion of the Germans therefore involved dramatic landscape changes, the creation of new settlements, forest villages (*Waldhufendörfer*), river control, and marsh drainage. Landscapes whose appearance reflected new kinds of densities arising out of human choices replaced the older environment. For these reasons there has been a close association in European scholarship between environmental change and settlement history.[4]

Finally, (4) there is the continuity of peasant competence and the history of peasant ways, for peasants had the hands, used the tools, possessed empiric knowledge of animals and plants.[5]

The age as a whole is marked by the retreat of forest, heath, marsh, and bog, and the creation of new towns and arable, but we must not regard these activities as progressively expanding, as the modern study of deserted villages reminds us. Quarrying, another landscape change, was related to the building demands of feudalism and the Church, mining, to forest use and to the exploration of remote regions thought to have ore deposits, reverberations of traditional activities vividly described later in the early pages of Agricola.

Furthermore, one should emphasize the precarious nature of these environmental changes: they had no necessary permanence; they might be merely small and dispersed clearings in a forest. This precariousness and lack of permanence are revealed in the modern study of the *Wüstungen*, *les vagues*, the deserted places, evidences of the reversion of the Roman arable to brush or forest, or of areas once cleared but no longer occupied. Some of the most intimate descriptions in the hagiography of the Middle Ages suggest the meeting of the monks with feral animals and their joy, in coming upon a deserted field, in recreating a paradise like the Garden of Eden. The *vastinae*,

[4] See note 1. Lyon, *op. cit.*, p. 47. Thompson, *An Economic and Social History of the Middle Ages*, pp. 517–519. Koebner, *ibid.*, pp. 80–81. See also "The German Push to the East," in Ross and McLaughlin, eds., *The Portable Medieval Reader*, pp. 421–429. The valuable *Ordensritter und Kirchenfürsten*, ed. by Bühler, from which the selection is taken and translated, is not readily available in the U.S.

[5] On this theme, see Koebner, *CEHE*, Vol. 1, p. 75; Coulton, *Med. Village, Manor, and Monastery*, pp. 214, 219–221. Pfeiffer, "The Quality of Peasant Living in Central Europe," *MR*, p. 241.

the *solitudines*, the *mansi, eremi loca invia, alsi, non vestiti* were some of the names applied to them.[6]

The clearings, whether made by the monasteries, the large manorial organizations, or by individual men, had little of the permanence and inevitability with which we associate environmental change by human cultures today. In the last hundred years in the areas of the world in which cultural modifications of the landscape have progressed most rapidly, there is little alarm, I think, that barring worldwide destruction, nature again may claim the landscapes of man. The feeling that a clearing once made, a swamp once drained, must be jealously guarded lest the whole area revert to its primitive state is remote; it has been superseded by other worries because of the comparative ease with which the changes of nature and the clearings can be maintained. It is one of the interesting contrasts between these times and a past which lasted perhaps up to the beginning of the nineteenth century: now it is a question not of maintaining the cultural landscapes against the powerful recuperative power of nature but of conserving the natural environment in the face of the expansion of economies, tourism, and mechanistic concepts of aesthetics.

Various historians have written of the great eras in the history of environmental change in the Middle Ages, and these dates, naturally, have varied somewhat. Grand and Delatouche distinguish three principal periods of clearing—and of drainage: (1) the deforestation of the first barbarian kingdoms (the Merovingians), with the earlier stimulus of the Roman example (on the other hand, barbarians were often unfriendly to forest clearance because of their belief that the seats of the gods were in the innermost forest and were therefore holy);[7] (2) the Carolingian period; and (3) the period from the middle of the eleventh through the thirteenth centuries,[8] the *âge des grands défrichements*, a most fascinating period in human history because of its inherent interest as an example of landscape change on a large scale, because of its lasting effects, because of the relationship of Christian theology to a philosophy of change, and because of the glimmerings of understanding—empirical rather than theoretical or experimental—of certain ecological relationships: the forest and agriculture, the effects of grazing animals, shepherds' fires and forest destruction, health, and environmental change—which we will meet with in the following pages. Other periods were far less active,

---

[6] Boissonnade, *op. cit.*, pp. 31–32; *AMA*, pp. 55, 244. For an extensive bibliography on the Wüstungen, see Guyan, "Die mittelalterlichen Wüstlegungen als archäologisches und geographisches Problem dargelegt an einigen Beispielen aus dem Kanton Schaffhausen," *Zeit. für Schweizerische Gesch*, Vol. 26 (1946), pp. 433–478; see especially pp. 476–478 for the bibliography, and pp. 462–65 for the reasons adduced for the existence of deserted places.

[7] Koebner, *CEHE*, Vol. 1, pp. 20, 43–44.

[8] *AMA*, pp. 237–246.

distinguished by plagues, catastrophes, and invasions or anarchy, like that from the middle of the ninth to the middle of the tenth century consequent upon the Viking and Saracen invasions of Europe, the Black Death in the fourteenth century, and the Hundred Years' War (usually dated from 1337 to the middle of the fifteenth century). The periods during which these great changes in the appearance of the landscape took place naturally varied from area to area and from time to time. The emphasis also changed: the early monastic enthusiasms bound up closely with the ideals of St. Benedict and St. Augustine later became more comfortable and worldly, and then corrupt. In the late Middle Ages, the history of landscape change is associated both with individuals and with the great domains, lay and ecclesiastical. It is not—and cannot be—our task to describe the history of these changes themselves; it is necessary, however, to make the general point in order to give substance to the interpretations made of the changes. The most valuable clues are in specialized—and local—histories of forestry, grazing, transhumance, and mining.

Although one cannot divorce the ideas from the circumstances and events which caused them to thrive and gave them meaning, we can distinguish in the Middle Ages three different general ideas of man as a modifier of his environment.

Despite some obvious objections, I have taken my illustrations from different countries and from different times. What I wish to say is that in the Middle Ages, many men, widely scattered in place, living at different times, were conscious of the reality of human modifications of nature by men like themselves, that these changes were local in character and in the very nature of things could not be synthesized into a body of thought represented by the modern conservation literature. Today it is much easier to learn about them than it was at the time. Occasionally, it is true, one meets with a statement applying to a large area and a long time-span. Caesarius of Prüm remarked that "it is known that during this long time [from 893 to 1222], many forests have been cut down (*multas silvas exstirpatas*), many estates have been built (*villas aedificatas*) and that the tithes had increased; in the period mentioned many mills had been erected, vines planted and an immeasurable extent of land had been cultivated."[9]

These three general types of ideas are (1) those clearly inseparable from Christian theology; (2) those without any necessary religious significance or which, at least, are not directly related to theological questions, as for example the effect of drainage on health, of first clearance on climate, of pine plantings on sand dunes; and (3) those which combine the two, like the Benedictine Rule and the early strictness of the Cistercians, the Premonstrants, the Chartrists, in which work was both a duty to God and a practical activity related to

---

[9] Quoted in full in Lamprecht, *Deutsches Wirtschaftsleben im Mittelalter*, Vol. 1:1, p. 402. See also Wimmer, *Geschichte des deutschen Bodens*, p. 56.

the virtues and advantages of clearing, drainage, protection of woods for pasture, or the creation of alps or mountain pastures. Piety was an active ally compatible with these desired changes in nature. Creating a landscape fit for Christian settlement for conversion and colonizing was a reward of piety.

## 2. THE CHRISTIAN RELIGION AND THE MODIFICATION OF NATURE

Christian thinkers, like the classical, asked two fundamental questions. How does man differ from other forms of life, especially the mobile, large land animals, those closest to him in the hierarchy of being? How did man invent arts like house building, weaving, and tillage? Man is intelligent, inventive, skillful in the use of the eye and the hand which enforce the decisions of his mind; the animals, lacking these qualities, have self-reliance from early infancy and are much better endowed with protective covering—hair, fur, thick skins —than is man. Man, with a mind and a soul—but without these natural protections—thus has a certain capacity to create his own environment, and through his own inventiveness to create useful and protective devices which more than make up for his natural weakness. This was the classical answer, the answer that necessity is the mother of invention. The Christian answer was that of Genesis, that man created in God's image has by God's grace dominion over all nature. Many of the Church Fathers combined the two.

Theories of environmental influence had their place in medieval Christian thought, as we have seen, and it was easy to reconcile them with the dominant theology. It was equally easy—except for the extreme ascetic and the other-worldly—to accept man's activities as part of his life on this earth, changes being inevitable in this partnership with God, as he practiced agriculture, used the forests and the domesticated animals and plants. The idea that man lived as God's helper in finishing the creation, in a finite, created, and destructible world, could be easily expressed by rural figures of speech of the Bible; it was more easily understood than the sophisticated Greek ideas of environmental influence. The occupations of town and rural life—tilling, cutting of trees, irrigation, grafting, building stone fences, quarrying—could easily persuade men they were partners of God in improving the creation. "Yet the fundamental ethos of the new religion," Christopher Dawson has said, "was in no way alien to the peasant life. Its first beginning had been amongst the fishermen and peasants of Galilee, and Gospel teaching is full of the imagery of the field and the fold and the vineyard."[10]

The early Christian Fathers were aware of the agricultural philosophy of antiquity, especially as it was expressed by Varro and in Virgil. (The degree to which they applied the organic analogy to the earth is hard to answer

[10] Dawson, *The Making of Europe*, p. 174.

clearly; many of them rejected the idea of a senescence in nature, possibly following Philo: nature as a creation of God was a fertile and abundant gift and was not mortal in a human sense.) The earth owes its fertility to the goodness and the planning of the Creator; human beings can live so long as they till and plant it, prune its trees, or graft them, or introduce them into new places.

It would be remarkable, therefore, if no bridge was built from theology to farming, grazing, and the forest—that is, if no divine purpose was seen in man's ability to sustain himself by using the earth and changing it to meet his desires. The monks of the West could enter on virgin lands or reclaim those once prosperous and fertile under the Romans. In forests, which were more than reserves for royal and noble hunters, men could graze the horses, cattle, swine, sheep, and goats, gather honey for sweetening and wax for the Church candles, and collect dead branches for fuel.

What has been said of the monks could apply to the whole Church. One must live and propagate the faith even in a sinful world that is but a shabby anteroom to the heavenly city to come. The monastic settlements "were forced by necessity to take up the peasant's task, to clear the forest and to till the ground. The lives of the monastic saints of the Merovingian period, whether Gallic or Celtic, are full of references to their agricultural labours— their work of clearing the forest and of bringing back to civilization the lands that had been abandoned during the period of the invasions."[11]

To the very religious, the earth, as the home of man, was a vital link in his partnership with God. There was often a deep feeling among the monks that in their forest retreats, their clearings, their tillage, they were duplicating conditions like those of Paradise before the Fall. Nor should one dismiss lightly the legends of wild animals appearing in the forests, becoming helpers of the monks, as expected excesses of enthusiastic hagiography; distorted in the telling and the repetition, the legends may well be based on actual conditions in which monks reclaimed deserted lands, using feral animals and perhaps redomesticating them. In the early history of the monastic orders, when the religious ideals were still stronger and not yet diluted by prosperity and worldliness, there was a close relationship between the ideals of the contemplative life, the philosophy of work in the Benedictine Rule, and the daily tasks of normal living, whether of monks or of their lay helpers. It was understood how changes in the environment could affect them. Such understanding is apparent in the conflicts over customary rights and usages, often very simply as the shepherds who cause forest fires by fires they light to warm themselves while tending their flocks, in forest legislation, and in the intimate relationship between the forest and the arable land.

[11] *Ibid.*, p. 178.

### 3. Interpreting Man's Dominion Over Nature

It was not uncommon for religious thinkers to adopt a positive attitude toward man's activity on earth, an attitude that recognized his need to change the earth and which often valued technical inventions. Certain writings of Philo the Jew, of Tertullian, Origen, St. Basil of Caesarea, St. Gregory of Nyssa, St. Ambrose, St. Augustine, Theodoret, and Cosmas Indicopleustes illustrate the breadth and scope of ideas which linked religion, technology, and environmental change.

Philo's belief in an artisan-deity who had created the earth by design led him to consider the question of man's dominion over nature, which the Old Testament repeatedly assured men they possessed. In no other early writer known to me is there so vivid a commentary on this dominion which God had granted man; moreover there is reason to believe that men became convinced of the reality of this dominion through their age-old association with domesticated animals in Asia Minor and the eastern Mediterranean.

Man, appearing last and suddenly, Philo says, produced consternation among the animals; the mere sight of man was enough to tame them, the most ferocious of the animals being the first and most easily tamed. Their docility was reserved for man alone, their pugnacity continuing unabated among themselves. All living things on land, water, and in the air were subject to him.

> The clearest proof of man's rule is afforded by what goes on before our eyes. Sometimes vast numbers of cattle are led by one quite ordinary man neither wearing armour nor carrying an iron weapon nor anything with which to defend himself, with nothing but a sheepskin to cover him and staff wherewith to show them which way to go and to lean on should he grow weary on his journeys. See, there is a shepherd, a goatherd, a cowherd leading flocks of sheep and goats, and herds of kine. They are men not even strong and lusty in body, unlikely, so far as healthy vigour goes, to create consternation in those who see them. And all the prowess and strength of all those well-armed animals, who possess the equipment which nature provides and use it in self-defence, cower before him like slaves before a master, and do his bidding.[12]

The everyday handling of the bull at the plow, the shearing of the ram, the mastery over the horse, the most spirited of animals, shows how easily this power is exerted.

Man in his control over nature is compared to a driver and pilot ($\dot{\eta}\nu\acute{\iota}o\chi o\nu$ $\delta\acute{\eta}$ $\tau\iota\nu\alpha$ $\kappa\alpha\grave{\iota}$ $\kappa\nu\beta\epsilon\rho\nu\acute{\eta}\tau\eta\nu$). It would be a mistake to suppose that man lacked power because he was the last to be created, because he followed behind the others. The driver follows the team but holds the reins; and on the acts of the pilot at the stern depends the safety of all.

[12] Philo, *On the Creation*, 84–85.

"So the Creator made man all things, as a sort of driver and pilot, to drive and steer the things on earth, and charged him with the care of animals and plants, like a governor suboroinate to the chief and great King."[13] What a gracious and transparent passage! How quickly it explains man's dominion by his prowess and skill in the control of animals and the domestication of plants.

In a remarkable rebuttal of the doctrine of metempsychosis, Tertullian (*ca.* 160–*ca.* 240) skillfully brings ideas of migration, population increase, and environmental change by human agency to bear on the argument.[14] If the living come from the dead as the dead now do from the living, then the population of the earth should always be the same; there should be the same number of people on earth that started life in the beginning. This is clearly not the case, he says, because people in the past have migrated because of overpopulation. (Tertullian's source is apparently Varro's lost work on divine and human things.) In fact, he continues, there has been a gradual increase in the world's population in various centers of growth, people coming there from a mother city as *aborigines*. Tertullian probably means by this term nomads, exiles, conquerors, or ordinary emigrants,[15] from overpopulated areas. The world now not only has more people in it, but it is also daily becoming more cultivated. Indeed, faith and reason can coexist, for it was Tertullian also who said, "Credo quia ineptum."

"All places are now accessible, all are well known, all open to commerce; most pleasant farms have obliterated all traces of what were once dreary and dangerous wastes; cultivated fields have subdued forests; flocks and herds have expelled wild beasts; sandy deserts are sown; rocks are planted; marshes are drained; and where once were hardly solitary cottages, there are now large cities."[16] The complaint is that the growing numbers of the world's peoples become a burden which the earth's substances cannot sustain. "Our wants grow more and more keen, and our complaints bitter in all mouths, whilst Nature fails in affording us her usual sustenance." Pestilence, famine, earthquakes, have pruned the luxuriance of the human race; but these men have never returned to earth "after their millennial exile," a reference to Plato's term for "the usual time for the purification during the interval between two subsequent incorporations."[17]

---

[13] *Ibid.*, 88.

[14] In what follows I am indebted to J. H. Waszink's edition of *De Anima* (*Quinti Septimi Florentis Tertulliani De Anima*), Latin text, introduction, and commentary. See the commentary on *De Anima*, chap. 30, pp. 370–377.

[15] Tertullian, who knew Greek well, used the term ἀποικία, a colony or settlement, to describe this kind of migration. The word also had the sense of a daughter colony; on *aborigines*, see Waszink, *op. cit.*, pp. 372–373.

[16] "A Treatise on the Soul" (*De Anima*), trans. by Peter Holmes, chap. 30, 3, *ANF*, Vol. 3, p. 210. Tertullian did not really say *credo quia absurdum.* See Gilson, *HCPMA*, p. 45.

[17] Waszink, *op. cit.*, p. 376, under 30, 4: *Mille Annos*, and the references there cited: Plato, *Republic*, 10, 615A; *Phaedrus*, 249A; Virgil, *Aeneid*, 6, 748.

Tertullian had expressed similar ideas in *On the Pallium* (*De pallio*) from which the passages in *De anima* are derived. "How much of the earth has this age transformed! How many of her cities has the triple vigor of our (present) empire produced, increased, or restored!"[18] Tertullian sees a relationship between population growth in scattered centers throughout the world and the transformations of the landscape, but his checks to population growth are not related to environmental change nor is there a suggestion of environmental deterioration as a result of expanding population. But Tertullian was interested in keeping dead souls from coming back to earth, not in environmental change. Although Tertullian said, in his plea to the rulers of the Roman Empire for justice, that Christian truth knows "she is but a sojourner on the earth," he added that the accusation that Christians are "useless in the affairs of life" is false. "We are not Indian Brahmins or Gymnosophists [i.e., the naked Indian philosophers], who dwell in woods and exile themselves from ordinary human life. . . . So we sojourn with you in the world, abjuring neither forum, nor shambles, nor bath, nor booth, nor workshop, nor inn, nor weekly market, nor any other places of commerce."[19]

According to Origen, man changes nature because he needs the arts, for he lacks the necessities of life and the protective covering of the animals. The classical argument of necessity being the mother of invention is compatible with Origen's Christian theology because God had appointed man a partner in nature over which he was to rule as a master. Human understanding is made to be exercised, not to be idle. God made man a needy being to force him to discover arts in order to nourish and to protect himself. It is the human intellect that Origen values. Those having no interest in religion or philosophy should be in need so that they may be spurred on to discover the arts. If these men were prosperous, they would neglect their intellects. Need for the life-giving necessities brought about agriculture, viticulture, gardening, carpentry, blacksmithing, weaving, wool-carding, spinning, building and then architecture, and sailing and navigation because the necessities of life are not found in all places. Providence makes the rational creature more needy than the irrational animals. The sequence is from God to man's intellect to the arts, and from them to the changes made in the landscape. The latter, however, are not stressed; but the cultivation of the mind through the stimulus of need is.[20]

---

[18] "Quantum reformavit orbis saeculum istud! quantum urbium aut produxit aut auxit aut reddidit praesentis imperii triplex virtus!" (*De pallio*, II, 7). The passages immediately preceding this must have been of great interest, but they are too garbled for quotation.

[19] *Apology*, trans. by Thelwall, chap. 1, *ANF*, Vol. 3, p. 17; chap. 42, p. 49. The whole apology is interesting for the information it gives regarding the accusations made by the critics of the Christians and their replies.

[20] Origen, *Contra Celsum*, IV, 76. Chadwick, *Contra Celsum*, p. 245, calls attention to the importance of Plato's *Protagoras*, 321A–B; Cicero's *De natura deorum*, II, 47, 121;

In the second homily on the text, "the earth was invisible and unfinished,"[21] St. Basil says that God created both the essence and the form of the earth, the matter which He created being in harmony with the form He wished it to have. Many details of the creation He passed over in purposeful silence, such as the manner in which water, air, fire, came into being, because it was necessary to train the human intelligence to discover the truth. Contemporary observations that excessive moisture impairs the earth's productivity suggest to Basil the nature of a still incomplete earth whose waters are not yet confined within their proper bounds. Excessive dampness prevents the earth from being seen (because of fog) and from being complete, "for the proper and natural adornment of the earth is its completion: corn waving in the valleys—meadows green with grass and rich with many coloured flowers—fertile glades and hill-tops shaded by forests." The description of the furnishing of the earth—which in Basil's example includes changes made by man—explains, in lieu of direct divine information on the subject, what God did. The landscapes of his own day, by implication, are adornments and completions, like God's furnishings.[22]

Gregory of Nyssa expresses a view which affirms the value of nature and things of this earth even though they must be in a subordinate position to the kingdom of God. Gregory says there is a connection between the actual and the spiritual; God has created both and rules over them. Nothing in the creation should be rejected, nor is anything excluded from the community of God (follows I Tim. 4:4). This union of spiritual and physical is embodied by God in man.[23] Man is a master over nature which helps him on his way to God, nature itself being raised up and exalted in the process. God made an earth full of riches, including the gold, silver, stones, valued by man; he allowed men to appear on earth to witness these wonder works and to assume his role as master of them.[24] Mastery over the lower beings was necessary to satisfy his needs: mastery over the horse because of the slowness and difficulty of human bodily movements; over the sheep because of our nakedness; over the oxen because humans are not grass eaters; over the dog because his jawbone is a living knife for men. His mastery of iron gives him the protection that horns and claws afford the animals.[25]

St. Ambrose (340–397), whose writings contain so much symbolism, so many comparisons between religious acts and the everyday duties of agricul-

---

and Plutarch's *Moralia*, 98D, in the distinction which Origen makes between inventing man and the well-endowed rational man; see also Chadwick's remarks on Stoicism and Origen, pp. x–xi.

[21] Gen. 1:2, trans. in the *RSV*, "The earth was without form and void," etc.

[22] Basil, *Homilies in Hexaemeron*, II, 3.

[23] *The Great Catechism*, chap. 6.

[24] *On the Making of Man*, chap. 2.

[25] *Ibid.*, chap. 7.

ture, gardening, and viticulture (the Church is a field filling the granaries, the bishop, like a farmer, cares for the fields under his charge), thinks of man as a farmer improving the earth in partnership with God.[26] In a letter to Valentinian Augustus in the autumn of 384, he writes that the world was much more beautiful when it was furnished than at the beginning of creation. "Formerly, the earth did not know how to be worked for her fruits. Later when the careful farmer began to rule the fields and to clothe the shapeless soil with vines, she put away her wild dispositions, being softened by domestic cultivation."[27]

These statements of the early Church Fathers set the stage for a famous and rather surprising passage in Augustine's *City of God*, surprising because his name is often associated with an ascetic denial of the world, and because of his tendency to make an almost insuperable gulf—which only the Church is capable of bridging—between sinful man and a perfect God. Augustine, however, generously praises human intelligence, skill, and creativity, granting of course that he owes them to the Creator. These capacities have enabled man to create the arts by which human society has come into being. God has given the soul a mind in which reason and understanding, asleep in infancy, awaken with maturity and attain knowledge: thus the mind is capable of instruction, of understanding the true, and of loving the good. The soul can make war on error and other inborn vices, conquering them "by fixing its desires upon no other object than the supreme and unchangeable Good."

And even though this be not uniformly the result, yet who can competently utter or even conceive the grandeur of this work of the Almighty, and the unspeakable boon He has conferred upon our rational nature, by giving us even the capacity of such attainment? For over and above those arts which are called virtues, and which teach us how we may spend out our life well, and attain to endless happiness—arts which are given to the children of the promise and the kingdom by the sole grace of God which is in Christ—has not the genius of man invented and applied countless astonishing arts, partly the result of necessity, partly the result of exuberant invention, so that this vigour of mind, which is so active in the discovery not merely of superfluous but even of dangerous and destructive things, betokens an inexhaustible wealth in the nature which can invent, learn, or employ such arts? What wonderful—one might say stupefying —advances has human industry made in the arts of weaving and building, of agriculture and navigation! With what endless variety are designs in pottery, painting, and sculpture produced, and with what skill executed! What wonderful spectacles are exhibited in the theatres, which those who have not seen them cannot credit! How skilful the contrivances for catching, killing, or taming wild beasts! And for the injury of men, also, how many kinds of poisons, weapons, engines of destruction, have been invented, while for the preservation or restoration of health the appliances and remedies are infinite! . . . Who could

[26] Springer, *Nature-Imagery in the Works of St. Ambrose*, pp. 77, 82, and *passim*.
[27] St. Ambrose, *Letters*. Letter 8 (53 in the Benedictine enumeration), p. 47; see also Letter 49 (43), pp. 254-264.

tell the thought that has been spent upon nature, even though, despairing of re-counting it in detail, he endeavoured only to give a general view of it? In fine, even the defense of errors and misapprehensions, which has illustrated the genius of heretics and philosophers, cannot be sufficiently declared.[28]

Theodoret, Bishop of Cyrrhus (*ca.* 390–458), in his work on *Providence*, had skillfully adapted the classical finalistic arguments to Christian theology, hoping in this way to win over the intellectuals who still rejected the Church despite its political triumphs.[29] Man is depicted as some classical writers de-picted him, as a triumphant doer and transformer whose hands and arms—their significance and preciousness lay in their being instruments in the ser-vice of intelligence—plow up the land, sow it, dig ditches, cut the vine, reap the harvest, bind the sheaves, and winnow the grain. The arms have enabled the human spirit to embellish the earth with flowery meadows, rich harvests, spacious woods, and a thousand routes over the sea. Wisdom coming from God enabled man to invent the tools of mining and agriculture, the arts bor-rowing from one another what is useful to each. The architect borrows the tools he needs from the blacksmith, the blacksmith gets his shelter from the architect, and both take their nurture from agriculture, but the agriculturalist too needs his horse and his tools. If one gets back to beginnings one sees how God has granted man the use of things he needs: man has thus become a miner, a builder of cities, a sailor joining the land to the sea. It is part of God's care for the world that man not only lives, but lives well.[30]

The most striking early statement of man's stewardship of nature because he is the earthly representative of the divine appears in Cosmas Indicopleustes' *The Christian Topography*, written probably between 535 and 547. He com-pared the creation which took place before the appearance of man with the preparation that goes into furnishing and decorating a house before living in it. God had gathered in this house all His manifold and diversified works. When the preparations were complete, God acted like a king who "when he has founded a city and completed it, places there his own image, tinting and embellishing it with various colours. . . ." The image God placed in His house is that of man, whom He selected to complete and to adorn it. Since man is an image of God, the angels hover around him as guardians, minister-ing to him. For a like reason the whole creation serves him: the familiar uses of the sun, air, fire, and water to man are listed, and the utilitarian view of nature is neatly meshed in with God's and the angels' care for man, who is the "bond uniting all the creation in friendship"; "the dispensation under

---

[28] *City of God*, Bk. XXII, chap. 24.

[29] On the probable reasons for writing this work, see Azéma's introduction to his French translation of Theodoret's *Discours sur la Providence*, pp. 30–32; see also Gil-son's remarks, *HCPMA*, pp. 596–597.

[30] See the fourth discourse entire, 613–616D on the hands and arms; 616A–D on the arts which change nature; 617A on mutual borrowings in the arts; 620A–B, man as a builder; and also Azéma's discussion of the passages, p. 164, note 76.

which he lives is a school for his own instruction, and for that of all rational beings." The notion of the creation as a school for mankind we have already met in St. Basil; in the late eighteenth century Herder uses it in describing the role of the earth in the education of the human race.

In his exalted position, man is "the king of all things on earth and reigns along with the Lord Christ in the heavens, and becomes a fellow-citizen of heavenly beings, and unto whom as the image of God all creation ministers while it is under subjection to God, and preserves its affection and gratitude toward its Creator."[31] We need not press the point further regarding this early Christian concept of man as a modifier of nature, as an agent of God in furnishing and finishing the creation. Most of these expositions appear in the apologetic and homiletic literature—apologetic because it had to meet the still cogent criticisms of the pagans, homiletic because it was devoted to explaining the new faith, sometimes as St. Basil explained it in simple terms, sometimes as Theodoret explained it on a level requiring a deeper knowledge of classical science and philosophy. In defending their new religion, many Christian thinkers felt they could not ignore the charge that it meant a full renunciation of the world, nor could they fail to recognize the industry, activity, and accomplishments of man. One senses that the Christian position is being made with a certain urgency by Tertullian. We are accused of being useless in the affairs of life, he says, but "We sail with you, and fight with you, and till the ground with you; and in like manner we unite with you in your traffickings—even in the various arts we make public property of our works for your benefit."[32]

These ideas were both inheritances from classical thought and fitting supplements to scriptural teaching. The classical inheritance was built on the role of the mind, the eye, the hand in invention, which in turn led to environmental change with the aid often of the domesticated animals, even if in their daily life these thinkers disdained manual work as the occupation of slaves. In the Christian teaching, human activities were in accordance with the biblical injunction "to fill the earth and subdue it." There was no incompatibility between the purposes of God and the workings of man, for man was finishing and furnishing the earth with God's help and encouragement.

The strength of this interpretation is evidenced by its reappearance in the

[31] Cosmas, *The Christian Topography* (trans. J. W. McCrindle), Bk. 3, 169, pp. 104–105, Bk. 5, 210, p. 167. On the date of composition, pp. x–xi; scattered throughout the work are many reminders of classical and early Christian ideas of man, matter, and the earth: the theory of four elements, pp. 10–11, 20–21, 85–86; the antipodes, pp. 14–15, 136–137; the nature of the earth and of paradise, p. 33; conventional ideas of environmental influence, 41; the idea of a scale of being, p. 108; the refinement of human, compared with the grossness of animal, copulation, p. 109; the youth and importance of the arts, the youth of the world, pp. 124–125; the klimata, pp. 244–252; comment on Rom. 1:20, pp. 293–294; and against eternal recurrence, p. 301.
[32] Tertullian, *Apology*, 42, ANF, Vol. 3, p. 48.

writings of St. Thomas. Man is a partner of God, applying his intelligence to his own uses. When God put sinless man in paradise he intended that this first man dress it and keep it as a labor of love; it was not the labor of sin it later became.[33] Dressing and keeping paradise "would have been pleasant on account of man's practical knowledge of the powers of nature."[34] Dressing and tillage are thus kept distinct from sin and the Fall. St. Thomas implies that there is divine approval of man's work and the uses to which he puts the earth even after the Fall.

### 4. PHILOSOPHIES OF WORK

The monks of the Western monasteries, however, had a different outlook from that of the apologists and homilists, and their experiences became the foundation for new interpretations of the changes men make in their environment. Their attitudes were less classical and less bookish than those of the early Church Fathers and St. Thomas. They had their justification in theology and in the dignity of daily tasks. The rule of St. Benedict and earlier writers on monasticism, like St. Basil and St. Augustine (and later St. Thomas Aquinas), had also given this dignity to physical labor in such marked contrast with the classical attitude. Labor was dissociated from the Fall in the sense that there was a pleasure to be had in work; it was not a penalty of sin alone. Almost all students of the Western monastic orders emphasize the strong practical demands which religious, social, economic, and climatic conditions in the Latin West, following the barbarian invasions, imposed on their members, coloring their ideals; the conditions they faced might be remedied in part with meditation and prayer, but also required was the use of the axe, the torch, the hoe, the plow, the dog, and the ox, whether by the monks themselves or others working for them. Although one cannot insist on the hard and fast distinction between the philosophy of the apologists and the homilists and that of the founders and abbots of monastic orders (one man might be both), interpretations of man as a modifier of the environment were far more frequent among the latter than among the former, because their roots were in the practical everyday problems of monastic life.

It is true that the ideals of Western monasticism came from Eastern monasticism, which itself had emphasized manual labor. The stress was on the search for God by the individual, divorcement not only from the life of the world but from the secularity of the church.[35] Their spiritual works have

[33] Cites Gen. 2:15, reading in the *RSV*: "The Lord God took the man and put him in the garden of Eden to till it and keep it."

[34] *Summa Theologica*, Pt. I, Quest. 102, Art. 3, Vol. 1, p. 501.

[35] Workman, *The Evolution of the Monastic Ideal*, pp. 10–13, 154–157, 219–220. Workman emphasizes that the monks rebelled against the secularization of the church as well as fleeing from the world; the systematization of work and the revolution in man's conceptions of the place of toil made by St. Benedict; the greater devotion to and more serious application of the idea of work by monks of the West.

such titles as *On celestial desire, For the contemplation and love of the celestial homeland, which is accessible only to those who despise the world, Praise of the celestial Jerusalem, On the happiness of the celestial homeland.* The irony, as Workman was fond of pointing out, was that the ideal of labor, later manifested in economic undertakings, ultimately brought them back into the world.[36]

To St. Bernard, the monk is a dweller in Jerusalem, which might be anywhere, a place away from the world and from sin, where one comes close to God, angels, and saints. "The monastery is then a Jerusalem in anticipation, a place of waiting and of desire, of preparation for that holy city towards which we look with joy."[37]

> The cloister is a "true paradise," and the surrounding countryside shares in its dignity. Nature "in the raw," unembellished by work or art, inspires the learned man with a sort of horror: the abysses and peaks which we like to gaze at, are to him an occasion of fear. A wild spot, not hallowed by prayer and asceticism and which is not the scene of any spiritual life is, as it were, in the state of original sin. But once it has become fertile and purposeful, it takes on the utmost significance.[38]

If we recall Eliade's words on the cosmic city as a divine archetype for the earthly city, these sentences of Dom Leclercq take on new meaning. When possession is taken of lands, and their exploitation begins, "rites are performed that symbolically repeat the act of Creation: the uncultivated zone is first 'cosmicized,' then inhabited."[39]

In the development of monasticism in the Latin West, monks were often led away from an exaggerated emphasis on solitude to new values called forth by the conditions they faced: the need to expand spiritual care, the activity of conversion, the clearing and the building necessary to accomplish these, the proper setting of the monasteries for water supply and accessibility and often for the appreciation of beauty and scenery.[40]

Even piety has its inexorable practical demands: "a flock of sheep was needed to provide the parchment for copying a book by Seneca or Cicero." Wild animals hunted by permits or in the forests owned by the abbey could supply the leather and skins for the bindings.[41] What began in retreat ended in activity, conversion, clearing, planting, stockbreeding. In the founding of monasteries away from the cities, there was often a consciousness of transforming the landscape for human needs. The poet Mark (thought to be a monk at Monte Cassino under Simplicius, the third abbot, *ca.* 560, or a pilgrim

---

[36] Workman, *op. cit.*, pp. 157, 220–224. On spiritual works, see Jean Leclercq, *The Love of Learning and the Desire for God*, pp. 27, 94–97, 105.

[37] Jean Leclercq, *op. cit.*, pp. 59–60; quote on p. 60.

[38] *Ibid.*, p. 136.

[39] Eliade, *Cosmos and History*, p. 10. See *supra*, pp. 207, 213–214; on God's creation of a celestial Jerusalem before its earthly counterpart was built by man, pp. 8–9.

[40] McCann, *Saint Benedict*, pp. 57–64, pp. 47–48.

[41] Leclercq, *op. cit.*, p. 129.

visiting Monte Cassino in the eighth century) described such a transformation of Monte Cassino with the founding of the Benedictine order, a transformation creating beauty, providing comfort, inspiring piety, and with a moral
teaching.

> Lest men should tire who seek thy high abode
> Winds round its sides a gently-sloping road.
> Yet justly does the mountain honor thee,
> For thou hast made it rich and fair to see.
> Its barren sides by thee are gardens made,
> Its naked rocks with fruitful vineyards laid,
> The crags admire a crop and fruit not theirs,
> The wild wood now a bounteous harvest bears.
> E'en so our barren deeds to fruit thou trainest,
> Upon our arid hearts pure waters rainest.
> Turn now to fruit the evil thorns, I pray,
> That vex the stupid breast of Mark alway.[42]

The influence of the Benedictine Rule is a familiar theme in the history of
Western civilization; manual labor, once despised as the lot of slaves, becomes a guiding principle. Many of the rules are concerned with practical
affairs. The work of God may be performed in the oratory, the monastery,
the garden, or on the road (chap. 7).

The most frequently quoted chapter is the forty-eighth, beginning, "idleness is the enemy of the soul. The brethren, therefore, must be occupied at
stated hours in manual labour, and again at other hours in sacred reading."[43]
The Benedictine Rule, however, was not the first, as we have seen, to prescribe manual labor; such a provision was in the orders of St. Pachomius in
Egypt, whose cenoby was an agricultural and industrial colony, and in the
Basilian rule. St. Augustine, whom St. Benedict had cited on the matter, was
outspoken about the desirability of monks working. Let us examine his reasons.

St. Augustine makes the point over and over that monks should work with
their hands, not symbolically but literally. In the *Retractationes*, which gives
reasons for composing the work, he says that some monks in monasteries being
established at Carthage maintain themselves by the work of their own hands,
while others wish to live "on the oblations of the faithful" (*ex oblationibus
religiosorum vivere volebant*). By doing no work for their maintenance, they

---

[42] Quoted in McCann, *Saint Benedict*, pp. 203–204. Latin text in Migne, *PL*, Vol. 80,
183–186. For other references to the poem, McCann, p. 204, footnote.

[43] "Otiositas inimica est animae; et ideo certis temporibus occupari debent fratres in
labore manum, certis iterum horis in lectione divina" (chap. 48). Manual labor was
liberally defined; it included not only the normal manual labor of the fields and of
general maintenance within the monastery, but such tasks as copying manuscripts. On
the subject of manual work in the rule (*De opera manuum cotidiana*), see McCann,
*Saint Benedict*, pp. 75–76, 140–141. D. Oswald Hunter Blair, *The Rule of St. Benedict*
(Latin and English with notes). On the sacred groves and other pagan survivals in
Monte Cassino (based on St. Gregory), see McCann, p. 70; on the work of God, pp.
77–78. See also chaps. 19 and 20 of the Rule.

thought—and boasted of it—that they were but fulfilling Gospel precepts, relying heavily on Matthew 6:25–34 (and on I Cor. 3:5–10). The Heavenly Father feeds the birds, who neither sow nor reap nor gather food into barns; neither do the lilies toil or spin. Augustine writes primarily to rebut this point of view.[44]

He makes the point so often that it cannot possibly be missed that all this is a false reading, that the appropriate texts are elsewhere, mainly in Paul, the most cited being II Thessalonians 3:10: "If anyone will not work, let him not eat." Paul, he says, wished the servants of God to do manual work whose end is a spiritual reward; they should depend on their own and no other hands for their food and clothing.[45] (See Paul's strong words in II Thess. 3:6–12.)

It is a remarkable document, diffuse and repetitious, sometimes pithy, contemptuous of cant, and based almost entirely on the writings of Paul. In it is the germ of the Benedictine teaching that idleness is the enemy of the soul, and there are strong words for lazy and arrogant monks who fail to set a good example for the newcomer. If they wish to be like the birds, then let them also not store up for the morrow.[46] Nor has he patience with those who ask how one can find time for labor and still preach the gospel; again he points to Paul's life and writings. Can one not sing divine hymns while working, like rowers with their boat songs? Even laborers can continue work while singing their bawdy songs.[47] "What then hinders a servant of God while working with his hands to meditate in the law of the Lord, and sing unto the name of the Lord Most High? provided, of course, that to learn what he may by memory rehearse, he have times set apart."[48]

Augustine sees a pleasure in a period of manual work. In a well-ordered monastery with a rule, a monk can follow his labors with reading, prayer, or work pertaining to divine letters, for the perils of idleness are great. Look at the undisciplined young widows who learn how to be idle, to be busybodies and chatterboxes. (Quotes I Tim. 5:13.)[49]

If the poor, who have worked in the world all their lives, come to monasteries and then lead lazy lives, what of the rich who renounce all to work at humble tasks? The rich should not be "brought low into piety so that the poor may be linked up into pride." He sees no sense in this reversal of roles, the exchanging of daintinesses (*et quo veniunt relictis deliciis suis qui fuerant praediorum domini, ibi sint rustici delicati*).[50] The monk seeking excuses for not working is presumptuous and insincere, and like those who will not shear off their long hair, lacking in humility.[51] He seems to imply that even a

---

[44] *Retractationes*, Bk. II, chap. 21; *De op. monach.* 2, NPN, Vol. 3, p. 504.
[45] *Ibid.*, 3–4, p. 504.
[46] *Ibid.*, 30, p. 518.
[47] *Ibid.*, 20, p. 514; 37, p. 521.
[48] *Ibid.*, 20, p. 514.
[49] *Ibid.*, 26, p. 516.
[50] *Ibid.*, 33, p. 519; text in *OCSA*, Vol. 22, p. 118.
[51] *Ibid.*, 39, pp. 522–523.

monk's life requires variety in prayer, study, and practical activity and that no lessening of piety need be anticipated because of it. It seems clear too that the basic justification for this and for the labor rule comes from Paul.

Benedict put Augustine's teaching, or Paul's, in practice. Work meant orderly daily activity, not miscellaneous tasks done randomly. Work (*opus secundarium*) was subordinate only to the work of God (*opus dei*), that is, the performance of the Divine Office, the daily psalmody and prayer. "Pray and work." According to Herwegen, a recent student of the rule, *otiositas* (idleness) meant rest from public, official activity—inactivity without benefit to the commonalty.[52]

Let us now look at some accounts of the foundings of monasteries and interpretations made of their significance. According to the venerable Bede, Ethelwald, who ruled the province of Deira, offered land to "God's servant Cedd" (d. 659) to found a monastery. Cedd accepted the offer. "In accordance with the king's wishes, Cedd chose a site for the monastery among some high and remote hills, which seemed more suitable for the dens of robbers and haunts of wild beasts than for human habitation. His purpose in this was to fulfill the prophecy of Isaiah: *'in the haunts where dragons once dwelt shall be pasture, with reeds and rushes,'*[53] and he wished the fruit of good works to spring up where formerly lived only wild beasts, or men who lived like the beasts."[54] The desire to choose remote sites which would become little paradises and centers for conversion is well brought out in Eigil's *Life of St. Sturm* (d. 779), the first abbot of Fulda monastery and a student of St. Boniface.[55] Boniface had encouraged Sturm in his desire to become a hermit, giving him assistance and his blessing. "Go to the solitude which is called Bochonia and see if the place is fit for servants of God to dwell in, for even in the desert God is able to prepare a place for His followers."[56] After finding a place with the proper

[52] Herwegen, *Sinn und Geist der Benediktinerregel*, p. 283. See the discussion of chapter 48 (*De opera manuum cotidiana*), pp. 282–293. Herwegen says *otiositas* approximates in meaning the German word *Musse* with the overtones of inactivity and public irresponsibility. On the Benedictine Rule and the need for regularity and variety of occupation, see Eileen Power, *Medieval English Nunneries c. 1275 to 1535*, chap. 7. "It is extremely significant that monasticism broke down directly St. Benedict's careful adjustment of occupations became upset" (p. 288).

[53] In the King James version, Isa. 35:7, "in the habitation of dragons, where each lay, shall be grass with reeds and rushes," and in the *RSV*, "the haunt of jackals shall become a swamp, the grass shall become reeds and rushes." Isa. 35:1 could well have fitted in with monastic aspirations: "The wilderness and the dry land shall be glad, the desert shall rejoice and blossom. . . ." (*RSV*).

[54] Bede, *A History of the English Church and People*, trans. Sherley-Price, Bk. III, chap. 23 (Penguin Classics), p. 177.

[55] See the collection, *The Anglo-Saxon Missionaries in Germany*, trans. and ed. C. H. Talbot (*The Makers of Christendom* series), especially Willibald's *The Life of St. Boniface*, and *The Correspondence of St. Boniface*, for vivid descriptions of missionary activity of the early Christian church in the West. Eigil's *The Life of St. Sturm* is valuable for the light it throws on monastic practical activity.

[56] Eigil's "The Life of St. Sturm," *loc. cit.*, p. 183.

soil and water supply, he returned to Boniface, who, after reflection, advised him to seek another spot because of the dangers of attack by the Saxons. Sturm searched a second time, reporting again to Boniface, who "was very eager to establish monastic life in the wilderness. . . ." Sturm said that no suitable place had been found, to which Boniface replied "that the place predestined by God had not yet been revealed. . . ."[57] After further exploration, the indefatigable, psalm-singing hermit, halting only at nightfall and cutting down trees to make a circular defense to protect his ass, saw a place which he felt was a blessed one, foreordained by God for such holy use.[58]

"As he walked over the ground and saw all the advantages the place possessed, he gave thanks to God; and the more he looked at it from every angle, the more pleased with it he became. So charmed was he with the beauty of the spot that he spent practically a whole day wandering over it, exploring its possibilities. Finally, he blessed it and turned his face towards home."[59] Boniface then went to Carloman, King of the Franks, telling him, "I believe that it would redound to your everlasting reward if, God willing, and with your help, monastic life could be established and a monastery could be founded in the eastern part of your kingdom, a thing that has not been attempted before our time."[60] The king gave the chosen site and on January 12, 744, the founders and the brothers appeared on it. Two months later Boniface visited the site; it was agreed by all that a church should be built. So the bishop

> ordered all the men who had accompanied him to the spot to cut down the woods and clear the undergrowth, whilst he himself climbed the brow of a hill, which is now called *Mons Episcopi*, and spent his time praying to God and meditating on Sacred Scripture. . . . After a week of felling trees and clearing away the brushwood the turf was piled up ready to make lime: then the bishop gave the brethren his blessing, commended the place to God and returned home with the workmen he had brought with him.[61]

The monks in the new monastery followed the Rule of St. Benedict.

These episodes in the life of St. Sturm illustrate a sequence that probably was repeated many times: the acquisition of the site from the temporal power, careful choice of the site with special attention to soil fertility and running water, the felling of the trees, a location in a pleasant but remote place which would permit enclaves for conversion and the life of prayer and meditation. It is noteworthy that aesthetic considerations probably entered into the site selection.[62]

---

[57] *Ibid.*, p. 185.
[58] *Ibid.*, pp. 186–188.
[59] *Ibid.*, p. 188.
[60] *Ibid.*, p. 189.
[61] *Ibid.*, p. 190.
[62] Dimier and Dumontier, "Encore les Emplacements Malsains," *Rev. du Moyen Âge Latin*, Vol. 4 (1948), pp. 60–65 have given many examples, taken from P. Leopoldus Janauschek, *Originum Cisterciensium tomus I, in quo, praemissis congregationum domi-*

How were the monastic ideals, at least in their earlier and more idealistic periods, related to the modification of the landscape? Improvements made in deserted or uninhabited lands became, to the working monks, hearths of spiri-. tual perfection. In fact, the combination of technical skill in agriculture with the ability to provide spiritual care made the monasteries following the Benedictine Rule very powerful in many parts of Europe.[63] Some of the fervor inherent in this combination of landscape change and the spiritual life can be sensed in the life of St. Benedict of Aniane in Aquitaine, the leader of the Carolingian monastic reform, presiding in 817 over the Council of Aachen, one of whose purposes was to secure a more strict observance of the Benedictine Rule. Of him it was said that he guided the plow with the plowman, used the ax with the woodsman, reaped with the reapers.[64]

Of the monastic orders, the Benedictines, the Cistercians, the Premonstratensians, and the Carthusians were the most active in changing the landscape.

In the charter of charity (*Charte de charité*) written in 1119 by the abbot Stephen Harding for Citeaux and its four daughter institutions, Clairvaux, la Ferté, Morimond, and Pontigny, he prescribed work on the soil, like that which God in Genesis had imposed on man. Harvesting was one of the most meritorious works, St. Bernard, the first abbot of Clairvaux, himself directing the hay harvest.[65] Practical and religious ideals were at work; despite the abuses to come, a powerful combination of piety and a philosophy of work brought about lasting landscape changes at an important juncture in the history of Western civilization. (For a long time the legend persisted that the Cistercians had purposefully sought out unhealthy lowlands for their monasteries, al-

---

*ciliis adjectisque tabulis chronologico-genealogicis veterum abbatiarum a monachis habitatarum fundationes . . . descripsit,* of sites well and poorly chosen, most of which date from the twelfth century (this book was unavailable to me). In none, however, was the site purposely chosen for its bad qualities. In many, when it became apparent that the site was poor, or its air unhealthy, it was moved.

Beaupré, founded in 1135 "in pulcherrimo situ" (Janauschek, p. 38); Marienthal, 1143, "in valle amoenissima fontibus et piscinis irrigua" (p. 76). Of poorly sited places, Fountains. diocese of York, 1132, "in loco spinis consito . . . ab antiquis temporibus non habitato . . . ferarum latebris quam humanis usibus magis accomodato" (p. 37). And description of what went on with monastic activity: At Byland, diocese of York, after its attachment to the Cistercian order in 1147, "fratres nemus viriliter exstirparunt, per fossas longas et latas magnas aquas de paludibus extraxerunt, et postquam apparuit terra solida, paraverunt sibi locum latum, idoneum et honestum" (J, p. 104).

[63] See also the long quotation on this general subject of spiritual care and seignorial expansion being combined in the church in Lamprecht, *Deutsches Wirtschaftsleben im Mittelalter,* Vol. 1:1, p. 117.

[64] The life of St. Benedict of Aniane by Ardo in *Act. SS. O. B.,* saec. IV, pars 1, p. 204 (NA). Quoted in Montal., Vol. 5, p. 198, note 2. Reprinted in PL, Vol. 103, cols. 351–390; cf. 368 B.

[65] *AMA,* pp. 149, 250–251. See also the story of Herluin, the founder of the abbey of Bec in 1034, Goyau, "La Normandie Bénédictine et Guillaume le Conquérant," *Revue des Deux-Mondes,* 15 Nov., 1938, pp. 337–355; ref. on p. 339.

though St. Bernard had recommended their establishment in valleys because there one finds grassy and fertile lands ideal for grain growing.)[66]

Its force can be seen from a description of the activities of the Cistercians in the twelfth century in north Germany. The abbot was with the workers when they started to fell the trees for making the arable. In one hand he had a wooden cross, in the other a vessel of holy water. When he arrived in the center of the woods, he planted the cross in the earth, took possession of this untouched piece of earth in the name of Jesus Christ, sprinkled holy water around the area, and finally grasped an axe to cut away some shrubs. The small clearing made by the abbot was the starting point for the monks' work. One work group (*incisores*) cut down the trees, a second (*exstirpatores*) took out the trunks, a third (*incensores*) burnt up the roots, boughs, and the undergrowth.[67] Such scenes however, require qualification. Even in the mid-twelfth century the lay brothers (*conversi*) of the Cistercians and not the monks were doing the hardest work; and towards the end of the thirteenth century, occasionally earlier, abbeys had begun to abandon direct cultivation by granges operated by lay brothers (which played such an important role in the economic development of the monasteries), resorting to tenant farmers to cultivate the land.[68]

## 5. Animals—Wild and Domestic

Hagiography saturated with legend described the miracles of the monks in pagan lands, and their relationships with the wild and domestic animals. They throw additional light on religious motives and religious beliefs directly or

---

[66] Dimier and Dumontier, *op. cit.*, pp. 60–65 and the numerous interesting quotations from original sources there cited.

[67] Winter, *Die Cistercienser des nordöstlichen Deutschlands*, Pt. 2, p. 171. Winter's source is Dubois, *Geschichte von Morimund*, pp. 204, 206, a work unavailable to me.

[68] *AMA*, p. 673. See also Hans Muggenthaler, *Kolonisatorische und wirtschaftliche Tätigkeit eines deutschen Zisterzienserklosters im XII. und XIII. Jahrhundert*. This extremely interesting work decribes the colonizing and economic activity of Waldsassen cloister in the Egerland on the left bank of the Wondreb in an area bordering on Slav culture. Today it is close to the Czech frontier. When the Bishropric was established at Prague in 973, Egerland became a firm frontier against the east. The cloister was founded in 1133. The Cistercians preferred, as expected, a valley for the site and adhered to the Benedictine Rule. The monastery had active granges; it specialized in viticulture and garden agriculture. Although the rule forbade eating of meat, it also specialized in livestock for milk products, hides, and wool. The monks worked in the forest, kept bees, fished. The trades included stonemasonry and goldsmithery, despite an original distaste for magnificent church art. There were the food industries (such as bread making), the costly installations for mills and breweries, clothes making and cloister tailoring (*camera sartoria*). The monks, says Muggenthaler, were shrewd businessmen. The decline occurred in the middle of the thirteenth century owing to the desire for a more comfortable life and for luxuries, to a falling off in discipline, and also to the founding of the mendicant orders, the ensuing competition with them and other orders, and a consequent decline in the Cistercian labor force because the lay elements turned to the mendicant orders.

indirectly related to environmental change. The monks entered the forests, says Montalembert (1819–1870), a passionate defender of the monastic orders, "sometimes axe in hand, at the head of a troup of believers scarcely converted, or of pagans surprised and indignant, to cut down the sacred trees, and thus root out the popular superstition."[69] St. Benedict himself had cut down the sacred grove at Monte Cassino, a survival of pagan worship in a Christian land. St. Sturm "seized every opportunity," says the monk Eigil, his biographer, "to impress on them [the pagans] in his preaching that they should forsake idols and images, accept the Christian faith, destroy the temples of the gods, cut down the groves and build sacred churches in their stead."[70] What a wonderful study could be made, from an anthropological point of view, of the lives of these early saints and of their contacts with the heathen! Montalembert writes with glowing sympathy of St. Columban whose highhanded behavior should have prepared him for trouble. These monastic enclaves in the forest—places of solitude and contemplation, work and agricultural experimentation—apparently became asylums and refuges for wild beasts hunted by royalty: there is much legend concerning the friendship of monks for wild animals, including the deer and the wolf.[71] In the life of St. Sequanus, wolves become laborers helping with the clearing and building.[72] Of course, friendship with animals had long been part of Christian lore; animals and insects often were held up, as we have seen, as models of behavior. St. Anthony Abbot had his centaur; St. Mark and St. Jerome, their lions; St. Euphemia, her lion and her bear; St. Roch, his dog; St. Clement of Rome, his lamb, and so forth. Legends gathered around the buffalo, the hare, and the stag, apparently because it was believed that the monks, so close to the animals of the forest, lived a harmonious life with them. The ancient authors (who record instances of the taming and the devotion of wild animals) "are unanimous in asserting that this supernatural empire of the old monks over the animal creation is explained by the primitive innocence which these heroes of penitence and purity had won back, and which placed them once more on a level with Adam and Eve in the terrestrial Paradise."[73] Animal behavior revealed the recreation of the earth before the Fall. These monks seem to have felt that they regained a dominance over nature which had been denied men since the Fall. Their acceptance of such ideas, their devotion, their industry and fanaticism,

---

[69] Montal., Vol. 2, p. 190; on St. Columbanus, pp. 273–274.

[70] Eigil, "The Life of St. Sturm," in *Anglo-Saxon Missionaries in Germany*, p. 200. On the relation of tree conservation to religious belief, see Maury, *Les Forêts de la Gaule et de l'Ancienne France*, pp. 7–39. Many references to original sources and older secondary accounts; much has been written on this since Maury's book was published (1867), but it is widely scattered.

[71] Montal., Vol. 2, pp. 200–213, of the first Merovingians.

[72] *Ibid.*, p. 200; other legends on pp. 216–217, 222. See also Workman, *Evol. of Monastic Ideal*, pp. 34–37.

[73] Montal., Vol. 2, p. 212.

their extirpation of pagan belief where possible if involuntary, were powerful influences toward change, combining a zeal for conversion with readiness
to make those changes in the natural environment which were required for
the performance of heavenly tasks on earth. Their activity would seem a confirmation of Job 5:23: "For you shall be in league with the stones of the field,
and the beasts of the field shall be at peace with you." The friendliness and
docility of these animals was God's way of showing man how great had been
the obedience of all nature to him before he was banished from the Garden
of Eden, how partial was the control he regained after the Fall.[74]

The Breton hagiographical epic, most of which was written after the tenth
century but which was also indicative of conditions after the time of Charlemagne, abounds in descriptions of the clearing away of undergrowth and wild
forest. St. Armel yokes a doe and a stag to his plow. St. Pol Aurelian and St.
Corentin colonize Léon and Cornwall.[75]

The plungeons had obeyed when St. Martin commanded them to leave the
waters for the desert; a raven carried bread to the hermit Paul.[76] The presence
of animals might indicate the sites of monastic foundations. "Innumerable are
the legends which show these wild animals obedient to the voice of the monks,
reduced to a kind of domestic condition by the men of God, obliged to serve
and follow them."[77] Wolves and stags were especially helpful.[78] La Borderie
suggested that legends of wild animals serving men as domesticated animals
originated in the reversion to a feral state of oxen, horses, and dogs with the
gradual disappearance of the Gallo-Roman population. The monks found
them and used them.[79] "The miracle consisted in restoring to man the empire
and use of the creatures which God had given him for instruments. This re-
domestication of animals which had relapsed into a savage condition is one
of the most interesting episodes in the civilising mission of the ancient ceno-
bites."[80] If this were widely believed by the zealous monks, what an intoxi-
cating experience it must have been to regain a partial dominance over nature
that had been lost since the Fall!

### 6.  Purposeful Change

The power of the monks and their helpers, owing to their discipline and association together, to change a landscape, mostly by deforestation, was of a
magnitude and fervor far removed from the more modest efforts of the laity.

---

[74] *Ibid.*, p. 217.
[75] *AMA*, p. 243. See note 4 for further references to secondary French sources.
[76] Montal., Vol. 2, p. 218.
[77] *Ibid.*, pp. 221–222. Quote on p. 222.
[78] *Ibid.*, pp. 224–226.
[79] *Ibid.*, pp. 226–227.
[80] *Ibid.*, p. 227, based on Arthur la Borderie, *Discours sur le rôle historique des saints de Bretagne*.

Of the Benedictines it has been said that their farms were model farms and that personal energy was increased a hundredfold by mutual association and by discipline.[81]

The Christian themes of man's dominion over nature and of the philosophy of work meshed well with the practical needs of a new civilization, based on wood and water, which was growing up in western Europe. Orderic Vital, giving arguments for the transfer of an abbey to Saint Evrul from Norrei, said it was of first importance that Norrei had no woods, no water in its vicinity: ". . . locus iste . . . habitationi monachorum aptus non est, quia ibidem aqua deest, et nemus longe deest. Certum est quod absque his duobus elementis monachi esse non possunt."[82] Places without woods or water were no places for monks; it was a truth that would apply to virtually all the monasteries of western Europe, a truth that reveals much about the nature of the environment, of the use of resources, of the technology, and of the monastic leadership. The monasteries of the countryside had responded to the practical demands of conversion by creating new enclaves of faith, often becoming training schools for agriculture, gardening, and forest conservation when and where it was needed.[83] And these earthly accomplishments were viewed with pride. "The Church," says Boissonnade of reclamation from the eleventh to the fourteenth centuries, "in particular, held colonization to be a work of piety, which increased both her influence and her fortune." The landowning classes thought of income, the peasants, of bettering their lot by labor. "All the élite of society placed itself at the head of the movement."[84]

A certain exaltation in changing nature shows itself in widely scattered areas and periods. From the Carolingian times comes this paean to human accomplishment. "Quid quondam Corbeia? quid Brema, modo urbes in Saxonia? quid Fritzlaria? quid Herschfeldum, oppidum in Thuringia aut potius in Hassia? quid Salisburgum, Frisinga, Eichstadium, urbes episcopales in Boioaria? quid oppida S. Galli et Campidona apud Helvetios? quid numerosa alia oppida in tota Germania? horridae quondam solitudines ferarum, nunc amoenissima diversoria hominum."[85]

The theme of the last sentence is repeated often in the Middle Ages—what formerly were frightful wastelands suited only for beasts have now become most pleasant abodes for man. In the remotest wildernesses, new creations, human counterparts of God's, could be made; God had endowed men with the zeal and resolution to do these tasks. Indeed, this conquest of the *horridae quondam solitudines ferarum* was frequently likened to the work of a creation

---

[81] See for example Brutails, *Roussillon*, p. 10.

[82] Sauvage, *Troarn*, quoted, p. 270. The original source is *Orderic Vital*, Vol. 2, pp. 16–17. See Guizot's ed., *Histoire de Normandie*, Vol. 2, pp. 14–15, in *Collection des Mémoires Relatifs à l'Histoire de France*, Vol. 26.

[83] See Boissonnade, *Life and Work in Medieval Europe*, p. 65.

[84] *Ibid.*, p. 226.

[85] *Act. SS. O. B.* Sect. 3 (NA), as quoted in Schwappach, p. 37, footnote 3.

itself. Even more lyrical is the well-known description of William of Malmesbury (between 1090 and 1096–1143) of the abbey founded on the isle of Thorney in the English fenlands, combining the religious theme of an earthly paradise and the secular theme of the rivalry of nature and art.

It is the image of paradise (*paradisi simulacrum*) in which is reflected even Heaven itself in its loveliness. In the fenlands too are trees abounding, slender and smooth-barked, struggling toward the stars. A level sea of herbs, pleasing by its greenness, attracts the eye, and there is nothing to stumble on as one hastens through the grassy field. Not even the tiniest part of the land there is left untilled. Here the nourishment of the soil rises to the fruit-bearing trees, there the field is bordered with vines, either spreading upon the ground or lifted high on trellises. Indeed, there is here a rivalry of nature and of art, the one creating what the other has forgotten. What can one say of the elegance of the buildings? How marvelous it is that in the midst of the fens such solid earth supports their firm foundations! A vast solitude is given the monks for their repose so that in that place they might hold fast to Heaven, where they more clearly behold their own mortality.[86]

### 7. An Earth to Change

So far we have emphasized religious ideas, but they in fact are often more concerned with theological questions than with environmental change. Conceptions of the dominion of man over nature, his continuing partial dominion after the Fall, the re-creation of the antediluvian order by the monks in the paradises of their new clearings, are interpretations, fundamentally, of man's relation to God, and only secondarily, to the natural surroundings.

It would be unwise, therefore, to overemphasize the power of these ideas as guides in interpreting the change which took place during the whole period of the Middle Ages, just as it would be equally unwise to ascribe all to the monastic ideal with its gospel of work for monks, founded on the writings of St. Paul, Basil, Augustine, and the Benedictine Rule. These ideas were more characteristic of earlier periods, but later, notably in the *âge des grands défrichements*, all classes, with their own ideas, rights, greeds, aspirations, participated in environmental change. Religious ideals were there, but underlying them were practical problems also. The story therefore becomes less a purely religious, more an economic and social, history even with the continuing importance of ecclesiastical bodies. Ideas correspondingly acquire a more secular character because they emerge from conditions created by technology, by practical knowledge of sowing, grafting, plant breeding, by economic competition, and by social aspirations and the like.

---

[86] William of Malmesbury, *De gestis pontificum anglorum libri quinque*, Lib. IV, §186, pp. 326–327, this passage trans. by C. J. Glacken. Cf. Dawson, *The Making of Europe*, pp. 200–201.

We should bear in mind the tradition of peasant competence and the importance of lay activity. The lay brethren of the Cistercians were more peasants than monks; the peasant pioneers and their landlords had impressive roles in clearing parts of Italy and in canalizing the Po, and deforestation was undertaken by the secular lords of Normandy and the German lay lords.

It would seem therefore that we proceed from a period in which theological ideas of man as a modifier of nature dominate to one in which these ideas are the result of experience, by ecclesiastic and lay alike, in the exploitation of natural resources.

Attitudes of monasteries, for example, might be indistinguishable from those of lay institutions as far as environmental change is concerned. As they became larger and more prosperous, as the network of their economic interests spread beyond the countrysides in which they were established, their attitudes toward change varied with their economic interests. Some might wish to preserve their forests, while others were desirous of clearing; some found themselves at odds with the nobles who resisted forest clearance; some did not wish to drain land, valuing their ponds and swamps for their fish; others might want to dry them up and turn them into arable. The old enthusiasm and devotion, based on the Benedictine rule of daily work, lost its force, and the later history of many monasteries takes on a melancholy character of greed, worldliness, and corruption.

These attitudes emerge from no single body of thought; the theological implications were always in the background, but new points of view, as with Albert the Great in natural history, were born of that vast complex of custom enveloping agriculture, grazing, and forest use. While Albert was a theologian, the discussion which follows shows him to be concerned with the rational use of the natural environment and improvement of it through practice and theory.

In his writings on this subject, practical observations based on his own experience of German farming or on the experience set forth in the writings of the past, notably those of Palladius in the fourth century, replace the general and often rhetorical comments of the earlier period. Even when Albert's materials have been borrowed from earlier writers, he shows an interest in the practical matters without being immediately concerned with their theological implications.[87]

Albert says that nature, the single principle of all natural things, may be improved—or worsened—by art and culture. Manuring, working the soil, sowing, grafting, change it greatly. Comparing the characteristics of wild with

---

[87] On participants in clearings and changes in attitudes by the monks toward manual labor through the centuries, see G. G. Coulton, *Medieval Village, Manor, and Monastery*, pp. 208–222. Coulton warns against exaggerating the amount of field labor done by monks even in the pioneer ages; see pp. 208–213. On Albert's interest in practical affairs, see Wimmer, *Deutsches Pflanzenleben nach Albertus Magnus*, p. 39.

domesticated plants, he says that wild trees are thornier, their bark is rougher, their leaves and fruit are more numerous but smaller. The wild grains and vegetables become larger, softer, and mild tasting when they have been cared for under cultivation.[88] The plow and the hoe (*aratio et fossio*) transform the desert wild to cultivated land. They open up the earth to receive the seed, and the fertilizing forces in the earth become active with the breaking of the soil surface. Through the use of these tools, the energies of the soils are equally distributed, there being also a mixing of the warm and cold, the dry and moist. The plow and the hoe break up the earth into smaller parts, but if this is done in too wet weather, the soil will not spread out well, and if in too dry weather, the hard clods cannot be broken up.[89]

Albert warns of the dangers to soils on slopes; they might become dry and barren because both moisture and the humus tend to work their way down to the valley floor. The slopes can be protected by such practices as plowing across the slope rather than up and down, by not comminuting the earth too finely, or by building a stone wall along the lower edge of the field.[90]

Albert mentions the necessity of safeguarding the agriculture of the north German marshlands by building dikes against the sea and by digging ditches to lead off surplus rainwater.[91] Making simple polders and drainage ditches, already old practices here in Albert's time, apparently were striking examples to observers in the Middle Ages of human efficiency and the productiveness of human labor.

Of unusual interest is Albert's discussion of the *novale* and the *ager novalis*, that is, both the newly cleared and the fallow land. He has a theory—apparently widely held in the Middle Ages—that in clearing a patch of forest for farming, it is necessary to carefully remove all rhizomes of the cutover trees lest they draw all the nourishment of the soils to themselves.[92] Firing of the forest to clear it is mentioned. The time-honored custom of allowing a field to lie fallow, he says, in effect makes new out of old land because its previous energies are restored.[93]

Albert also pointed to the gradual decline in area of natural pastureland (*ager compascuus*) and the increase in the meadow (*prata*), which owed

---

[88] Albert the Great, *De Vegetabilibus*, Bk. VII, Tr. I, chap. 1 (Jammy ed., Vol. 5, pp. 488–489).

[89] *Ibid.*, chap. 4, p. 491. Albert uses *adaequatio* (also meaning the equal division of an inheritance among heirs, *Lex. Man.* p. 72) for the distribution of soil nourishment, and *comminutio* for breaking up the soil into fine particles.

[90] *Ibid.*, chap. 7, pp. 494–495. The sense of Albert's advice seems to be the same or very similar to Pliny's: a farmer should avoid plowing up and down the hillside, but should plow across the slope of the hill "with the share pointing now up hill and now down" (Pliny, *Nat. Hist.*, Bk. XVIII, 49, 179).

[91] *Ibid.*, chap. 6, pp. 493–494. See also Wimmer, *Geschichte des deutschen Bodens*, pp. 103–106.

[92] *Ibid.*, chap. 8, p. 495.

[93] *Ibid.*, chap. 2, p. 490.

much to human care through drainage and irrigation, the canals draining off the surplus water, and the nearby brooks, at least once before the beginning of spring, bringing water to the areas in need of it.[94]

He is acquainted, as we have already seen, with the idea that cutting down trees affects the climate; the statement appears in his discussion of environmental influences and the ability of man to purposefully change unhealthful places into healthful ones.[95] These practical discussions are in strong contrast with the writings of Albert's pupil, St. Thomas, whose ideas of man and nature come from theology and philosophy. Albert's are often mellowed by the observations of a wandering mendicant monk noticing, on the walking tours made necessary by the duties of his office, the changes he saw about him and applying the accumulated agricultural lore of his own and former times to an attempt to understand them.

It is in these centuries of the high and late Middle Ages that one begins to hear murmurings that reach such enormous volume in the modern world: the idea that men can make desirable and undesirable changes in nature.

These changes probably had a corporate or communal, rather than an individual, character in the Middle Ages. Individuals act as members of a community with interlocking rights of use which are based on law and tradition. Legislation, common law, local custom, are inseparable from the realities of environmental change. Legislation of this kind is often, of necessity, practical and secular because it is concerned with resource distribution. Large areas of France in the feudal period were governed by the same written and common law. In the Midi and in Alsace it is Roman law modified by local customs and the common law, which in turn may be a fusion of Roman and Germanic institutions modified by canon law and adapted to French custom. Such general legislation with jurisdiction over a considerable area was known as *consuetudo pagi, mos provinciae, coustume du pays*; but it was supplemented and modified by even more local customs, often peculiar to a domain, a *mansus*, even a forest. These are the *consuetudo loci, lex terrae*. The combination of the general and the particular enables us to envisage a physical environment blanketed by a mesh of law, customs, and traditions of varying and different weave.[96]

---

[94] *Ibid.*, chap. 12, pp. 499–500.

[95] *Ibid.*, chap. 8, p. 495; chap. 12, pp. 499–500. I am indebted for the discussion and for these references to Wimmer, *Deutsches Pflanzenleben nach Albertus Magnus*, pp. 38–43, 47–48. On Albert's interest in manuring and fertilizers, Wimmer says, "Im Düngen sieht er nun das Hauptmittel für die Überführung der Pflanzen 'aus dem Zustand der Wildheit in den der Zahmheit' und spricht über die Notwendigkeit und den Effekt desselben bereits Sätze aus, die fast ein Liebig hätte niederschreiben können, und die jedenfalls die Theorien der landwirtschaftlichen Autoren des 17. und 18. Jahrhunderts vorausnehmen" (pp. 41–42).

[96] On their general importance and specific significance in forestry, see Huffel, Vol. 1:2, p. 100, who quotes an old Basque proverb from Lagrèze, *La Navarre Française* (Paris, 1882): "Chaque pays a sa loi et chaque maison sa coutume" (p. 100).

Modifications of the physical environment by man may be compared with technological advances. They often proceed on their own momentum, with or without a philosophy—or they might create their own. It is in the nature of environmental change that this momentum should exist, if for no other reason than that one thing leads to another, and because of the multiplication of chores and the accumulation of small changes inescapable from practical life. A peasant cuts down a stand of trees, not because it is part of his religion to work or because idleness is a sin, but because he wants to plant his cleared fields. The scattered notices show that during the Middle Ages interpretations of change ranged over a wide field: the Alpine woods, torrents, and inundations; the protective forest; agriculture and forestry; transhumance; selective use of soils; hunting, domestication, and the chase.

In what follows, illustrations are taken from several places and from different periods. Although this procedure is open to the obvious criticism that isolated illustrations have little value in interpreting the nature of change over such a large area over so long a period, they show that certain attitudes did exist. No coherent body of knowledge, however, like a modern book in conservation, came into being.

In the Latin West (and in the British Isles, especially after the Norman Conquest) the basic attitudes are indistinguishable from the vast complex of customs and usages concerned primarily with agriculture, forest use, and grazing. One can see these processes at work, particularly in Marc Bloch's studies, in the writings of men like Robert Dauvergne and Roger Dion, in specialized histories of individual monasteries, and in histories of individual forests. Circumstances obviously varied from time to time and from place to place but the many notices often have a sameness about them in their essentials. Complaints about shepherds' fires, uses of wood for barrel staves, the felling of oaks for swarms of bees, the granting of free pannage for pigs, might not be characteristic of every place but they were characteristic of types of environmental use for centuries. Often the descriptions become enclaves of awareness, even if the writers have refrained from interpretations. They suggest also the nature of the historical process by which men have become aware of their power to change the environment. The surviving materials from the ancient world do not permit this insight—at least to a satisfying degree. In my opinion, those from the Middle Ages do, to some degree. The process begins with the isolated and local awareness one finds, for example, in charters, rules, letters, and lives of the saints; it continues with the partial diffusion of knowledge in the Middle Ages (by encyclopedic works like Albert the Great's and through travel) leading ultimately to the awareness that is characteristic of the modern world, which rests on the opportunity for collection and comparison of instances made possible by the infinitely better dissemination of knowledge that followed the invention of printing.

We may begin with two preliminary observations: there is a striking difference between the physical environment of northwest Europe and that of the Mediterranean; and forest clearance is the central theme about which all other modification of the landscape by human agency revolves.

## 8.    Forest Clearance in Northwest Europe

If monasteries and settlements were to be created, a start in the removal of forest (using fire and the axe or both) and in the drainage of marshes had to be made. The woods of northwest Europe were, of course, infinitely greater in extent, different in species, and finer in quality than those of the Mediterranean, whose trees and scrub, the product of the distinctive Mediterranean climate, had been exposed to destructive activities dating from the immemorial past.

Northwestern Europe in the Middle Ages was a civilization of wood to a far greater degree than the Mediterranean region had been. A substantial part of economic life revolved around the elaborate rights of forest use, with demands on the one hand for clearance to provide the arable, with demands on the other to save the forest in order to protect old rights of usage or to prevent torrents and soil erosion. One cannot read the history of the period without becoming aware of the pivotal importance of the forest and its close ties to town and country life. In western Europe, there was the unique combination of an environment requiring great changes for the continuance of civilization there, and a conscious interest in the tools, techniques, and technology necessary for accomplishing this purpose. "L'Antiquité n'a pas eu l'idée d'un mechanisme général. Il est probable que cette nouvelle conception de la technique est véritablement née au Moyen Âge."[97]

The publication in 1931 of Lefebvre des Nöettes' *L'Attelage et Le Cheval de Selle à Travers les Âges* greatly stimulated interest in invention and its relation to social and environmental change in the Middle Ages. Let us set forth his thesis in broad philosophical terms, omitting the technical discussions and illustrations upon which they rest for proof. In the front rank of man's conquests of nature, he says, is his ability to use animal power; controlling and directing the energies of animals like the horse and oxen, in order to use them as draft animals, has been one of the most difficult problems that man has had to solve in his struggle for existence. There is, he continues, a fundamental difference in the use of draft power in the ancient world and in the age beginning in about the tenth century. Animal power in the ancient world was very inefficiently used, the reason being in the method of harnessing animals. Of key importance is a change in the role of the horse. In ancient times, collars of soft leather were placed around the horses' necks in such a way that they pressed on their windpipes, interfered with their breathing, and severely re-

---

[97] Gille, "Les Développements Technologiques en Europe de 1100 à 1400," *JWH*, Vol. 3 (1956), pp. 63–108. Refs. on pp. 65–66, quote on p. 77.

stricted their efficiency and their ability to pull heavy loads. In about the tenth century (dating is by no means precise) the horse began to replace the ox as a draft animal because of the invention of a new, stiff collar resting on the shoulder. The transition, he thought, took place under the first Capetians; he regarded the invention as an immense boon to humanity because he thought the vastly increased efficiency in the use of draft animals had a direct bearing on the disappearance of slavery. This idea has been the most controversial of his findings.

The invention immensely increased men's ability to modify the landscape, making construction, clearing, cultivation, and the transportation of heavy materials over long distances easier.[98]

It is true that inventions were brought in from elsewhere, but a distinction must also be made between the place where an invention is made and the place where it is applied to greatest effect. Water mills possibly originated in the Mediterranean region despite unfavorable conditions for their year-round use; most of its rivers either are very low or dry up entirely in the summer. The environment of northwestern Europe provided much better conditions for the use of this invention. (The water mills of late Roman times are mentioned in the charming verses of Ausonius [died about 395] on the Moselle.)[99] It was an important addition to a civilization in which wood was an indispensable raw material and source of energy (for heating, cooking, charcoal making, mining, etc.), in which the forest was the locale for such diverse activities as grazing, hunting, beekeeping. Recent studies of medieval technology point, moreover, to the so-called Dark Ages as a period of greater technological competence and activity than had previously been thought.[100] Particularly intriguing is the invention and the dispersion throughout northwestern Europe and Scandinavia of the hydraulic saw. To my knowledge little detail is known of the origin of this great invention which was to become so powerful an agent in changing the environment, especially along riverbanks.[101] Finnish, Swedish, and Norwegian historians have stressed the deci-

---

[98] *L'Attelage et Le Cheval de Selle*, pp. 2–5, 122–124. On its relation to environmental change, *AMA*, p. 446. Discussion of the origin and diffusion of this invention and modern critiques of the slavery thesis (including Marc Bloch's) are outside the scope of this work, but see *AMA*, pp. 444–449, and Bark, *Origins of the Medieval World*, pp. 125–135 and the references there cited.

[99] Bloch, "Avènement et Conquêtes du Moulin à Eau," *Annales d'Histoire Économique et Sociale*, Vol. 7 (1935), p. 541. Ausonius, *Mosella*, V, 362, and now White, *Medieval Technology and Social Change*, pp. 80–84.

[100] See Forbes, "Metallurgy," in Singer, *et al.*, *History of Technology*, Vol. 2, pp. 62–64; Salin and France-Lanord, *Rhin et Orient*, Vol. 2, Le Fer à l'Époque Mèrovingienne (Paris, 1943). Gille, "Notes d'Histoire de la Technique Métallurgique. I. Les Progrès du Moyen-Âge. Le Moulin à Fer et le Haut-Fourneau," *Métaux et Civilisations*, Vol. 1 (1946), p. 89, on the effects of the Norse invasions in bringing in new metallurgical techniques from Scandinavia. See also White, *op. cit.*, pp. 82–83.

[101] Gille, "Le Moulin à Eau," *Techniques et Civilisations*, Vol. 3 (1954), pp. 1–15; ref. on p. 12.

sive changes its introduction brought about in the economic history of their countries. Marc Bloch believed the hydraulic saw went back to the third century A.D. at least,[102] although admittedly the first drawing of the valuable invention is in the album of Villard de Honnecourt (composed about the middle of the thirteenth century); moreover, the first mention of the saw, in Du Cange's dictionary, is later than the date of the album.[103]

Fire, the small tools like saws and axes capable of making rapid changes in a landscape, and the larger installations like the hydraulic saw, the water mills, the use of navigable waterways on a scale unknown to the peoples of antiquity, to say nothing of the artisans and their techniques,[104] were the technological resources with which environmental change, especially in the twelfth century and onwards, was accelerated.

Why must one regard the forests and attitudes toward them as the crucial element in our theme? Because they were involved in both the need for change and the need for stability. Their disappearance might not grieve either the agriculturalist or the Alpine shepherd; their preservation might be the hope of the lowland shepherd, of another farmer, of the royal or noble hunter. But we cannot identify attitudes with occupations; too much depended on local interests. The monks at one place might favor a clearing; at another, they might oppose any clearing or draining, and ferry people over the marshlands whose waters abounded in precious fish.

### 9.  The Uses of the Forest

Attitudes toward forests are derived from the uses—religious, economic, or aesthetic—to which they are put. The old Swedish proverb that the forest is the mantle of the poor suggests its closeness to the life of the ordinary man.

From the Merovingians through the end of the Middle Ages, forests had so many uses that for the moment it is better to consider them in broad categories: as sources of food and household needs; for grazing, hunting, and beekeeping; as the locale of small industries and of charcoal making; as valuable primitive areas in their own right. The intimate relationship is clear in the numerous customs relating to forest use, in the alarms heard in many countries regarding misuse of the forests, and in the forests as places of work.

In the period (roughly from the Merovingian through the Carolingian age), the list of the uses of the forest in the old German economy is already impressive—and worth summarizing in detail. The people gathered acorns and beechnuts. They used the broadleaved trees (like the oak and the aspen) and the conifers (like the Scotch-fir, fir, larch, yew) for building houses; the oak, beech, pine, and fir were used for shingling, the conifers for interior finishing and partitions. All woods were burned for fuel. Benches, tables, chairs, chests,

[102] Bloch, *op. cit.*, p. 543.
[103] Gille, *op. cit.*, p. 12.
[104] Gille, "Des Dév. Technolog. en Europe," *JWH*, 3 (1956), pp. 65–66, 91.

boxes, cupboards, were made out of oak, ash, mountain ash, maple, birch, wild apple; humbler people used fir. Owing to a lack of potter's clay in quantity, dishes and kitchen utensils, baking troughs, vats, barrels, dippers, racks, were made of oak, beech, fir, linden, and the finer products, especially spoons, of common maple. Winnowing and grain shovels, wheel rims (fellies), axles, barrows, flax-breakers, winepresses—later, oil stampers and presses—came from the beech; and from the elm, wagons, axles, hubs, rims, ladders, harrows, paddles for the mill wheels. The birch was used for cart shafts and ladders, the privet for spokes, while the roots and the lower end of the trunk of the red beech were made into the tubs carried on sleds. Hoops and bands around barrels and tubs came from the birch and the willow, rope and cord from the bast of the linden. The light alder furnished flailing sticks; it and the conifers, well borers and the wooden conduits. The alder was also used for this purpose and for piles in the swampy ground. From the forest came the wood for the winepress, the plow, the wagon, the stave, the plow handle, the wooden rim of the wagon wheel, the fence. Twigs of birch, through age-old custom, were the brooms; pine torches and glowing chips served for illumination. Dugouts were made of oak trunks, the boat mast of fir, the rudder of beech. From the ash were made the spear and the shaft of the axe; from the linden, the shield and boilers; from the yew, the bow; from the alder, bows, lances, arrows, and bolts. Drinking vessels came from the rooty wood of the maple and from other trees. Tannin and various dyes were derived from wood bark; the foliage of various trees supplied litter and fertilizer, and ash leaves were used for fodder. One could get a refreshing drink from the trunk of the birch, food from the wild apple and the wild pear. The linden, ash, birch, alder, aspen, and larch furnished charcoal. Resins were in demand for calking household wooden vessels. And the master of the house was laid in his coffin—a hollowed-out tree.

The forest was used for the hunt and the pasturing of cattle and smaller livestock; it was the place for gathering acorns, beechnuts, and berries. When the witty Heriger, Bishop of Mainz (913–927), was told of a false prophet "who with many good reasons had advanced the idea that Hell was completely surrounded by a dense forest," he laughingly replied, "I would like to send my swineherd there with my lean pigs to pasture."[105]

The classification of trees according to their grazing value apparently was an early practice among the barbarian peoples of the Latin West. Trees were classified as productive (*fructiferi*) or nonproductive (*infructosi, steriles*) most likely because of their mast; and the Scotch-fir and the pines were included among the fructiferi in the Law of the Burgundians because their usefulness was equivalent to that of the mast-producing trees.[106]

[105] Examples are taken from Heyne, *Das Deutsche Nahrungswesen*, pp. 148–151. The passage relating to Bishop Heriger is quoted in part, p. 151, footnote 153. The poem has been translated from the Latin into English by Helen Waddell, *Medieval Latin Lyrics*, p. 161.

[106] Schwappach, p. 46.

In the laws of the Visigoths and the Langobards there were detailed regulations about swine grazing in the forests, the German tribes giving less attention to it. There is fuller mention in the *Capitulare de villis et curtis imperialibus* of Charlemagne and in the rules of the cloister of Prüm. During the mast season, the bonded freedmen of that cloister could graze their swine in turn—to each a week at most.[107] In a notice from the ninth century, the number of swine that could be fed with mast in a forest becomes the measure of its size.[108]

Beekeeping was also an ancient tradition. Customary law included provisions for the rights of ownership to a swarm that was discovered, and to a swarm that had flown off and lodged itself in a tree hollow. Beekeeping was important up to the end of the Middle Ages: honey was used as a sweetener and in the preparation of mead, and beeswax was indispensable for illumination, especially in the churches. Barbarian laws mentioned honey and wax before wood among the products of the forest. In France there is a long and interesting relationship between bees and the oak. Swarms of bees were hunted in the forests; the kings of France and the ecclesiastical and lay nobles had officers especially charged with traversing the forest in search of swarms. The desire for bees was so intense that it was necessary to prohibit the cutting of trees, especially of oaks which harbored them. "Au moyen-âge on n'hésitait pas à abattre les plus beaux arbres pour s'emparer des essaims."[109]

The use of fire in clearing and of charcoal in industry are characteristic of all countries and of all periods in the Middle Ages. Firing was a traditional means—often forbidden—of clearing land. Charcoal making was closely related to smelting, to glassmaking. Forests might have, as in the Harz, their tar boilers.[110] Wood or charcoal was used in salt cooking, iron smelting, tar boiling, as in Norway even before the introduction of the water-driven saw.[111]

## 10. CUSTOM AND USE

These uses—the forest histories of individual European countries are full of illustrations similar to those mentioned here—suggest that a parallel historical development also took place in the growth of a body of rights, usages, and customary law which codified and regulated exploitation. This network of rights and usages is the key to an understanding of preindustrial ecologies; in it is the vivid detail which abstract formulations like "man and nature" obscure.

[107] *Ibid.*, p. 48.
[108] *Ibid.*, p. 48, footnote 14.
[109] Huffel, Vol. 1:1, p. 5, footnote 1, and general discussion, pp. 4–7; see also De Maulde, pp. 227–229. On beekeeping, *AMA*, pp. 528–534.
[110] Schwappach, p. 166.
[111] Best survey in A. Bugge, *Den norske Traelasthandels Historie*, Vol. 1, pp. 12–14 and *passim*; on the water-driven saw in Norway, see pp. 5–6. See also Sandmo, *Skogbrukshistorie* (of Norway), pp. 48–73.

These illustrations of forest use presuppose a highly organized society. As one reads the long lists of rights and customary usages, immortalized in words and phrases in which medieval Latin is so rich, one is impressed with the fact that these usages and uses grew because there was no other way that people could exist. If the nobles wrung Magna Carta out of King John, they also extracted a Forest Charter, and more was to come with the concessions in the long forest charter of Henry III. "The Forest Charter took its place beside the Great Charter as part of the foundations on which the English social scene was laid."[112] It is true that rights and usages may have had an ultimate religious foundation, but their immediate reason for existence was the needs and demands of everyday life. These uses are like strands which enmesh individuals, institutions, other usages, until the whole age and its landscape are covered with them. This body of custom and tradition is the medieval counterpart of the modern concept of culture.

It is in this body of custom and tradition—in addition to the inheritance of agricultural lore from the classical period—that one must look for sensitivities to the significance of environmental change. It is not so important to unearth, if this were possible, the earliest laws against deforestation, or for forest protection; it is more important to see that there occurs within this entangling net of custom and usage an awareness of desirable and undesirable changes being made in the natural environment or an insistence on main-~aining unchanged an environment that had been satisfactory in the past. These were essentially lay and empirical observations; the religious ideas of man as a partner of God in remaking the earth were always in the background, but they were too bookish and too abstract and general to be applied to everyday situations.

There are so many thousands of possible illustrations that it might be well to choose an example from one area so that the nature of these usages might be suggested in the briefest possible space. In his study of the forest of Orléans in the Middle Ages and the Renaissance, from which the following illustrations are taken, De Maulde set down a list of about 350 places which enjoyed any right of use or pasture whatever; the listing of such places requires over forty pages.

Aluran mayoralty has the right to dry wood (*bois mort*) in the woods of St. Benedict (1391, 1396); Ambert priory has free pannage for sixty pigs, free pasture for sixteen plow cattle, fourteen mules and their foals, and the right to use wood for general repair, stakes for vines, fence poles, and firewood (1301, 1322, 1403).[113] Auxérre Les Brosses and others have the right to dry

[112] Stenton, *English Society in the Early Middle Ages*, p. 106. See the discussion, pp. 97–119.
[113] There were many classifications of wood, but distinguishing among them is difficult; De Maulde says that usage is confused even in the contemporary documents. Two common types of wood considered useless or harmful were *Mortuus boscus* (= French

oaks—half-dry standing, green lying down—for building and burning (1353, 1440, 1497–1610). Le Bréau, la Rivière, Charency, and others have rights of pasture for animals in exchange for a *mine* of oats per hearth and rights of pannage (1396, 1559, 1361). Buisson-Aiglant, Puteville, Marchais-Creux have pasturage at all times except for goats (1317, 1320); Hôtes de Chalette and Lancy had rights of building and burning (1337). The priory of Chappes, in consideration of three masses per week for the duke, had the right of fattening a hundred pigs and a boar in the forest (1361). The abbey of Cour-Dieu had pasture rights, pannage, use of two or three oaks per year, and of wood to repair plows in the woods of Chérupeau (thirteenth century). The manor of Laleu had rights of use in the forest of St. Benedict (*emprés pied*) for fire-wood and construction timber for houses, mills, and bridges (earliest date 1317). A leprosarium had access to firewood (*bois mort*), free grazing for one hundred pigs for each of its two tenants, and rights of pasture (1311). The administrators of the Hôtel-Dieu, Orléans, had the right to what remained of the firewood above the needs of the Hôtel-Dieu provided they did not reduce the heat of the poor (1327).[114]

What De Maulde has said of the forest of Orléans is a useful guide in con-sidering the role of forests elsewhere in Europe in the Middle Ages. The forest of Orléans furnished raw materials for a large number of small industries, the basis of the wealth of the rural villages. Forests did not impede commerce, nor were they useless for industry. The accusation that they were impenetrable and thus obstacles to civilization was based on misinformation; forest roads helped commerce; if they were poor and impassable, they were no more so than those of other environments.[115] It is a point well taken, for some writers of the Middle Ages and modern students who have copied them give the im-pression that forests and mountains were the enemies of civilization, dreaded places where no one went unless he was forced to, that mountains, unappre-ciated for their beauty, were looked upon as angry barriers to be crossed. They give the impression of complaining townsmen, and neglect the lively local history of forest use and transhumance throughout the whole Middle Ages.

So numerous have these individual rights been that attempts have been made to classify them into broad groups; it has been suggested that they may be based on the three needs they must frequently and urgently meet: to provide food for cattle, firewood, and construction wood.[116] The first and the most

---

*mort-bois*) which meant broadly a non-fruit-bearing tree, and *Boscus mortuus* (= French *bois mort*), which meant dry or dead wood. Du Cange, Art. *Boscus*. In the green forest, wood was classified as *sec estant* (that is still standing) and *sec gisant* (lying around). See De Maulde, pp. 142–146. See also *Lex. Man.*, *Boscus*; and Huffel, 1:2, p. 145, *sub nomine, Bois, Boscus.*

[114] De Maulde, pp. 182, 183, 187, 188, 189, 190, 195, 201, 202, 208.
[115] De Maulde, pp. 236–237.
[116] *AMA*, pp. 424–425.

important of these, *jus ad pascendum*,[117] concerns the rights to feed animals in the forest, that is, with rights of pannage and of pasture; the second,[118] *jus ad calefaciendum, ad comburendum*, or *ad focagium*,[119] is in general the right to firewood; and the third, *jus ad edificandum, ad construendum*, or *marrenagium*, is the right to obtain wood for repair or construction,[120] and including *jus ad sepiendum*, the right to have lumber to build stockades, barriers, and to make vine stakes in grape country.[121]

Forests and woods naturally differed from one another in ownership and types of rights inherent in them. If usages, rights, and common practices are regarded as customs with the force of law, these usages appear in their true light as being decisive influences in the rational or the haphazard exploitation of the forest—or of any other resource which might be dependent on forestry for its energy, such as mining.[122]

[117] See, for example, Du Cange and the *Lex. Man.*, under *Pastio, Glandagium, 1. Pascagium, Pascharium, Pascio*, pertaining to swine feeding.

[118] See *Lex. Man.*, under *Lignaricia*, the definition based on the Irmino Abbey usage: "Jus lignorum exscindendorum in silvis ad annum usum pro quo tenentes certam pensitationem domino exsolvebant. . . ." See also *Lagnagium*, and *Lignarium*.

[119] See *Lex. Man.*, under *Foagium*, 3rd meaning: "Jus capiendi lignum in silvis"; also known by the French words derived from this Latin word, *fouage, affouage*. This right gave each hearth or family group (not an individual) the right to gather dry wood (*bois mort*) without restriction, and also occasionally *mort-bois* (wood from non-fruit-bearing trees) in amounts determined by local usage. *AMA*, p. 424.

[120] *Lex. Man.*, under *Materia, Materiamen*, words designating woods suitable for building purposes.

[121] On the existence of the *silve palarie*, where one obtained *pali* (meaning both vine props and stakes), which often were thickets of chestnut trees, see *AMA*, p. 425.

[122] The word *forest*, which for centuries has had a very general meaning, being applied to the most varied types of wooded areas with the most diverse usage and tenure, originally designated an area of land that need not necessarily be wooded. In the barbarian kingdoms which displaced the Roman holdings in the West, during the fifth, sixth, and the first half of the seventh centuries, the word *forest* in its modern sense probably is best rendered by the Latin word *silva*, an exploited area, also a clearing made in the forest area; *nemus* too was used, but it often referred to an unexploited forest as well. *Forestis* appears, apparently for the first time, in the texts of the middle of the sixth century. In a diploma of Childebert I, dated in 556 (whose authenticity, however, has been suspected), the king designated a fishing reserve on the river, calling it his *forestis*, its general meaning being something set aside or reserved. (*Mon. Germ. Dip.* I, pp. 7, 41 ff. See also Heyne, *Das deutsche Nahrungswesen*, pp. 153–154, note 160; Huffel, 1:1, p. 302, note 3, dates it *ca.* 558 under Childebert II.) It has been suggested that *forestis* (*forestas* or *forastis*) originally designated the waters or the forests or the wooded lands outside the boundaries of villas, often belonging to the king or high dignitaries; this name suggests a derivation from the Latin word *foris*, meaning out of doors or abroad. In France at least the use of *forestis* to designate wooded terrain possibly dates from 648; in a diploma Sigebert II grants a canton of the Ardennes forest (*in foreste nostra nuncupata Arduinna*) to construct there an abbey later called Malmédy-Stavelot (Huffel, 1:1, pp. 302–303).

The *forestis* originally was undeveloped and outside the boundaries of the manor, whose inhabitants were denied use of it (*ibid.*). The inhabitants had rights to the waters and woods within the manor, the king or the lord, sole right to the waters and woods without. "It was his *forastis*, his *forestis dominica*. Often this epithet dominica is added

The reservation of choice forest areas for hunting grounds is a type of forest use that has been mentioned frequently in modern histories of forestry. The argument is that there was unwitting conservation, not because the need for such conservation was understood, but because royal or noble enthusiasm for hunting enforced exclusions of destructive intruders. In France, these policies engendered hatreds against the forests and their royal and noble owners that reached a climax in the French Revolution. Although there is no doubt that forest landscapes were maintained which would otherwise have been destroyed, this emphasis does less than justice to the history of forest use and to the complexities in customary practice and usage, especially in the later Middle Ages.

Three such examples, *gruerie*, *afforestatio*, and *baliveau*, illustrate the influence of law or custom in preserving or changing a landscape. In his study of the forest of Orléans, De Maulde said, "La gruerie est le fondement de tout ce que concerne les bois." The essence of the practice was that an owner was not permitted to exploit a forest at his own pleasure; it was subject to the supervision of the central authority, an officer of the king supervising sales and the operations they involved. The right of gruerie often accompanied the right of *grairie*, that is, the exclusive enjoyment of subsoil rights, of pastures, and of the hunt.

Gruerie is known in the Middle Ages under two names (and their variants): *gruagium* and *danger*; De Maulde found traces of it in the twelfth century, and that it was in full vigor at century's end. Under gruerie, owners could sell their wood only with formal permission of the prince. In November, 1202, Philippe-Auguste permitted the canons of Saint-Liphard de Meung to sell their wood for three years at Bucy; in 1235 a charter of the chapter of Saint-Verain de Jargeau announced the king's permission to sell two hundred arpents of wood, the chapter deciding, entirely voluntarily and as a concession, that the king would receive two-thirds of the sale.[123] The same charter suggests

---

to the word *forestis* in the documents beginning in the seventh century." By the ninth century the *forestis* is the forest belonging to the king or some exalted person, reserved to the chase and where no cultivator (colon) could enter to cut wood or to take game (Huffel, 1:1, p. 304).

In Germany the word has had a similar history. Before the end of the eighteenth century *foresta* (*forestis*, *foreste*) designated the royal forest or one conferred on a noble by the king as contrasted with other wooded lands; later it had the meaning of a wooded area (Bannforst) in which hunting rights were denied to all except the king or those allowed by him to hunt there. Royal forest holdings in which hunting rights were not reserved were usually called *silva* or *nemus* (Schwappach, pp. 56–59, and the references to other literature, footnote 8, p. 56. See also his "Zur Bedeutung und Etymologie des Wortes, 'Forst,' " *Forstwissenschaftliches Centralblatt*, 1884, p. 515).

[123] The two important notices, printed in De Maulde, p. 36, are as follows:

Ego prior de Flotans, et fratres ejusdem loci, notum facimus presentibus et futuris quod dominus rex francorum concessit nobis quod nos venderemus nemus nostrum quod est circa domum nostram ad faciendam ecclesiam nostram; tali conditione quod de cetero non poteri-

that originally gruerie represented the expenses of guarding the forest and were a levy on the woods corresponding to that levied on agricultural produce. The right of the king to grant permission for sales is acknowledged by the prior of Flotin in 1202; with Saint-Verain de Jargeau it has become a tax.[124]

Although he was hostile to it, De Maulde credited gruerie with accomplishing a near miracle with the forest of Orléans, a "masse si homogène, si dense, ait pu se conserver dans tout le moyen âge avec son intégralité aussi complète. . . ."[125]

Under *afforestatio*, certain forested tracts, reserved and forbidden of access, were protected from the waste and improvidence arising out of the continual daily exercise of common rights and usages for the period required for healthy forest production.[126]

The reasons for afforestatio apparently were little different from modern motives; they were related to forest preservation and to economic gain. At the beginning of the Carolingian period, the population was growing, clearings had begun to reduce the areas of the forest, the lords began to regulate and even to prohibit the exercise of certain rights. Rights of use covered only the needs of those entitled to them, and areas sufficient to satisfy these needs were set aside. The rest were prohibited (*defensa*). Many names were used to designate these prohibited areas: *défends, bétal, embannie, haie, plessis.* Such an area was also called a *foresta*[127] and to inclose it was to afforest it.

Early in the history of western Europe, as the Capitulary of Louis the Debonair (818) forbidding the lords from creating new *forestae* makes clear,[128] there was a struggle between those possessing traditional rights of use and desiring to exercise them and those who wanted to limit them or to change

---

mus vendere predictum nemus ullo modo absque mandato domini regis. Actum anno Domini millesimo ducentesimo secundo, mense novembri.

Omnibus presentes litteras inspecturis, Simon decanus, totumque capitulum Jargogilense, salutem in Domino. Noverint universi quod nos de ducentis arpentis nemorum nostrorum de Monlordino que illustris Francorum rex nobis concessit ad vendendum, volumus et concedimus quod de denariis venditiones dominus rex percipiat duas partes, et nos tertiam. Actum anno Domini millesimo ducentesimo tricesimo quinto, mense novembri.

[124] Further discussion in De Maulde, pp. 36–55. The right existed until the revolution; the National Assembly from its earliest days had demanded its suppression, pp. 54–55. On *gruerie* applied to non-navigable streams, see p. 55. De Maulde (p. 33) was no friend of the custom, regarding it as transferring "d'un manière quelque peu socialiste et barbare" rights of proprietors to communal state ownership represented by the ducal administration. See also *Lex. Man.*, article *Dangerium*, whose definition relating to forestry is taken from Du Cange. "In re forestaria, dangerium dicitur jus quod rex habet in forestis et silvis Normanniae, in quibus proprietarii caesionem facere non possunt inconsulto rege, aut illius officialibus, sub commissi poena quam *danger* vocant." De Maulde points out, pp. 32–33, that the practice is not confined to Normandy as Du Cange says. Note also the usage *in forestis et silvis*.

[125] De Maulde, p. 32.

[126] *AMA*, p. 432.

[127] See Huffel, 1:2, pp. 81–82; p. 81, footnote 2.

[128] *Ibid.*, p. 82.

them. Even if these struggles had little to do with forest conservation per se, the theme is a stimulating one. Victories and defeats are reflected in the landscape. The partisans of change won out: it is the contrast between the clearing in the forest at the beginning of the Middle Ages and the spot of forest in the arable at the end.

Reforestation (or afforestation in the modern sense of the word) through natural regeneration was accomplished by leaving behind small trees or saplings often after an area had been cut over. Du Cange defines the term for this practice as *baivarius* (or *bayvellus*), as "arbor ad propagationem sylvae relicta";[129] the word has come down in French in the forms of *baiviaux* and *baliveau*, usually translated as staddle. According to Huffel, baivarius was very ancient in France; in the old texts trees were often called *estallons* (= *étallons, stallions*.) In the French forest ordinance of 1376, the purpose of baliveau is clearly to "repeople" the forest, warnings being given and penalties provided for failures to comply. From eight to ten stallions were required for an arpent (from sixteen to twenty per hectare). Balivage is repeatedly required in the royal forest ordinances during the Middle Ages, the old texts mentioning also the frequent failures to comply with the minimum number of trees to be left. And in the French forest ordinance of 1516 the baliveaux are like studs carrying the seeds needed to repeople the forests; the ordinance expresses the wish that a sufficient number of the beautiful trees be spared for the purpose.[130]

Baliveaux were probably the only effective means of reproduction in a cut-over forest. The practice was important too because rights of pannage ruined the possibility of natural reproduction; if the pigs were gone, the trees left after sale could reseed the clearing.[131]

There are notices from the sixteenth century (possibly representative of earlier abuses too) indicating that neither buyers nor sellers could be relied upon to spare these trees for reseeding or to be conscientious in their choice of the trees to remain; baliveaux were designated by the timber marks of a forestry official—some fleur-de-lis marks were discovered in baliveaux felled in the nineteenth century. [132] The grand master or deputy forester often added

---

[129] Du Cange, *Lex. Man.*, under *Baivarius*. According to Huffel, the origin of the word is unknown. See his discussion, "Les Méthodes de l'Aménagement Forestier en France," *Annales de l'École Nationale des Eaux et Forêts*, Vol. 1, Fascicule 2 (1927), p. 15, note 2.

[130] *Ibid.*, pp. 15–16:

Pour ce qu'au temps passé les maistres, en faisant et vendant ventes de bois, ont par inadvertance ou autrement oublié à faire retenue de baiviaulz ou estallons pour la repueple des forez . . . ordené est que doresnavant en toutes ventes sera entendue la retenue des bayveaulx et estallons, de huit ou dix en l'arpent; et ce seront tenus les maistres de mettre en leurs lettres . . . et s'il n'y est mis, si sera-t-il sou entendu (et si cettee mention est omise elles sera néanmoins sous-entendue). Si lesdits maistres oublient ou délaissent a faire cette retenue . . . ce sera en leur péril et en seront, avec les marchans (meaning here both buyer and seller) chargiez de faire restitution. . . .

Quoted from Vol. 6 of *Recueil des Ordonnances des Rois de France de la 3e Race*.

[131] De Maulde, p. 452.

[132] *Ibid.*, p. 424.

a countermark to that of the master of the guard, and the buyer who cut down such a marked baliveau exposed himself to a serious penalty. De Maulde has listed the names of trees which reached "colossal dimensions." Many of them, especially in the sixteenth century, were famous. Certain regions were named after the trees. Often these great relict trees were in fields far from forests. So great was the respect given them, so remote was the possibility of cutting them down, that they became landmarks for the bounding of inheritances, a custom perpetuated in the Orléans and neighboring *pays*, with equal penalties in the fifteenth century for removing a boundary marker or cutting down a tree used as one.[133] The trees, left for natural reproduction, became objects of beauty in their permanence, becoming living legal documents. In the Middle Ages—as in contemporary life—the multiplicity of rights set bounds to the exploitation of natural resources. One writer has said that attempts to limit these rights seem almost as old as the rights themselves. One senses an uneasy truce throughout the Middle Ages between these two tendencies. Rights of usage were not empty legalisms; they were expressions of the necessity of eating and having access to food on the land. Viewing the Middle Ages as a whole, it seems that the tendency was toward more precise definition and delimitation of these rights with time.[134]

Conflicts of interest involved in the modification or preservation of the landscape[135] necessarily were local in nature. For the most part it was not a question of conservation in the modern sense of the word, although, as will be pointed out in more detail later, the need for a balance between the forests and the arable, and for forest conservation, was recognized. The cultivators in their expansion met up with the opposition of the forest intendants and similar officials who, in defending the woods, defended also their hereditary offices, which existed only because of the forests they supervised. The monks could have been on either side. When they were clearing the woods, they often conflicted with the *forestarii*. The Bollandists' lives of the saints have preserved anecdotes illustrating conflicts with these forestarii. The monks and their helpers, under the Benedictine Rule, cleared perhaps for seven hours a day and their clearings naturally lessened the importance of an area as a wooded land. Vaudrégisile, count of the Palace under Dagobert I, became a monk; he was the first abbot of Fontanelle. He began to deforest lands near the mouths of the Seine, forests given him by Erchinoald, mayor of the Palace, the queen Bathilde, and King Clovis II. One day while Vaudrégisile was supervising the

---

[133] *Ibid.*, pp. 455–456.
[134] These remarks are inspired in part by those in *AMA*:
La multiplicité des droits, l'antiquité et l'imprécision de leur origine, le caractère empirique et infiniment varié de leur détermination sont à l'origine de nombreaux abus, d'empiètements incessants, de contestations sans fin (pp. 430–431). De telles pratiques étaient tellement dommageables à la conservation et à l'exploitation rationnelle des forêts, que les tentatives des propriétaires pour limiter ou réglementer les usages sont presque aussi antiques que ces droits eux-mêmes (p. 432).
[135] See also Darby, "The Clearing of the Woodland in Europe," *MR*, pp. 193–194.

clearings, the *forestarius* of the royal forest approached with the intention of killing him with his lance. At the moment of striking, the arm of the assassin, suddenly paralyzed, is locked immobile in its raised position until the abbot, by a prayer to heaven, returns to the forestarius the use of his limb. This fascinating tableau probably was inspired by many acts of prosaic violence untouched by rescuing miracles. Another anecdote from the same period (the seventh century) reveals, by a pun on the word *foris*, the antagonism between the monks who were clearing the woods and the forest warden (forestarius). The sharpness of the bitter rebuke is owing to one meaning of *foris* ("outside of") and the derivation of the word *forestis* (and, by extension, *forestarius*) from *foris*. "Recte quidem forestarii dicti sunt," said the bishop, "isti quia foris stabunt extra regnum Dei." "Indeed they are correctly called *forestarii* because they will stand outside the Kingdom of God."[136] If God was on the side of the *défricheurs* this time, there were also other times when He was guarding their lands from the axe and the torch.

Even those who liberally gave their lands to the monks might mistrust their zeal for deforestation, restricting rights of future clearance. Jean, the Bishop of Orléans, in 1123 gave woods to the abbey of Cour-Dieu, but only for meadows. In 1171, his successor, Manassès, gave wooded land, with a home, to the abbey at Pre-Cottant, for feeding animals, for an abbey garden, but not for cultivation.[137]

## 11.  THE GREAT AGE OF FOREST CLEARANCE

During the period of the great forest clearance, however (roughly from the eleventh through the thirteenth centuries), the Church encouraged an active Christian life for its adherents; new lands gained from the pagan East could be acquired in their own names and in the name of God. Replacing heathen with Christian customs often indirectly caused changes in the landscape. In a thirteenth century description of the Prussians, which conveys the spirit of an active Christianity, zeal for clearing, and resistance to it, they are described as illiterate, ignorant of God, worshippers of all kinds of creatures. "They also had fields, woods, and waters which were holy to them, so that they neither plowed nor fished nor cut wood in them. . . ."

In an imperial confirmation (1226), Frederick II approves the grant by Conrad, duke of Masovia and Kujavia, to Brother Hermann and his brothers of the Teutonic order of Culm in the land of the Prussians, the emperor taking notice of the active piety of this master (*In Erwägung der tatbereiten Frömmigkeit dieses Meisters*). Not only was the grant approved but they could

---

[136] Based on Huffel, 1:1, p. 332, footnote 2.
[137] The two texts, quoted by De Maulde, pp. 109–110, are as follows: "Quantumcumque nemoris circumadjacentis extirpando in usum pratorum vertere voluerint . . ."; and 1171: "Domum de Prato Constancii . . . ad suorum nutrimentum animalium, ad hortos ibi excolendos, ad prata facienda excepto quod ibi agriculturam non exercebunt."

also with God's grace conquer in Prussia with rights to mountains, plains, rivers, forest, and lake as an ancient imperial right.[138] The ecclesiastical lords had viewpoints differing from both the heathen and the feudal barons. "They were," according to Huffel, "more cultured and they had more refined manners than the rude feudal barons, they were less exclusively preoccupied with following the wild beasts to the depths of the forests. They wanted to construct convents, to erect magnificent churches and cathedrals that we still admire today."[139] *Aedificare* meant not only to erect a building, but also to deforest and to improve land.[140] They accumulated books, objects of art, jewelry, pontifical ornaments. They tried to attract newcomers to their domains and to justify to them the dictum so widespread in the Middle Ages that "one has a good life under the cross."[141]

On the other hand, there might be a good case for not changing a landscape, because of the economic advantages of continuing it either in its natural, or in a relatively unimproved, state. For example, in 1068 Roger de Montgomeri gave the Benedictine monastery of Troarn in the valley of the Auge in Normandy a marshland (*sclusa*) for its own use.[142] In the eleventh and twelfth centuries it apparently was still a wasteland without significant revenues except from fishing and hunting. In 1295 attempts were made to dry up the marsh by constructing dikes and drainage ditches, the monks also constructing dikes near the coast to obtain additional land and to protect it from the sea.[143]

The swampy pastures of the valley of the Auge and the rights to the grass and to fish were highly valued by the monks.[144] In the thirteenth and fourteenth centuries, they acquired more meadows, especially marshy pasturelands from the sea.[145] The value placed on this grass is indicated by the seriousness with which the monks regarded thefts of it. They had exclusive rights to swans, which they valued highly—the swans were also symbols of their lordship of the marsh. The keepers of the swans had the right and duty to follow them to whatever place they had escaped to. In 1314 a certain Simon Legier

[138] See "The German Push to the East," trans. by H. F. Schwarz from Bühler, ed., *Ordensritter und Kirchenfürsten*, pp. 74–75, in Ross and McLaughlin, eds., *The Portable Medieval Reader*, 421–429 (references on p. 427). On Culm, "Kaiserliche Bestätigung der Schenkung des Kulmerlandes an den deutschen orden (1226)," Bühler, pp. 72–73; *Port. Med. Reader*, trans. p. 425.

[139] Huffel, 1:2, p. 137.

[140] *Ibid.*, p. 138, footnote 1. *Lex. Man.* gives these meanings of *aedificare*: to edify, to be of use, and with the reflexive *se*, to choose a domicile, to cultivate a field, to sow.

[141] *Ibid.*, pp. 137, cf. 137–138.

[142] Sauvage, *Troarn*, p. 255. Roger de Montgomeri donna à son abbaye de Troarn, dès 1068, "totam sclusam . . . Troarni a terra usque ad terram." Footnote 3, Preuves, II. "Le mot 'sclusa' nous paraît l'analogue, en ce qui touch les marais, des mots 'foresta,' 'garenna.' "

[143] *Ibid.*, pp. 255–258.

[144] *Ibid.*, p. 258.

[145] *Ibid.*, p. 258.

was fined forty livres for having cut grass "in exclusive Troarno" and for having chased the swans from their reserve.[146]

The monks used many plants of the marsh for forage, for litter, in cooperage, furniture making, house covering; they also extracted turf for fuel.[147] In 1297 turf extraction in the marsh of Terriers was regulated by the monastery; after 1297, it is no longer mentioned in the acts of the monastery, possibly because of its rarity.[148] The abbey exercised its hunting and fishing rights on the marsh —the estuary of the Dive was a nest of wild birds—and had a virtual fishing monopoly.[149] By the end of the thirteenth century the abbey also had seven mills on the arms of the Dive.[150] The abbey had forest holdings to which it owned exclusive rights. Its house gardens flourished and its enclosures, bounded by trees or a hedge, were devoted to crops or to meadow; vines grew on the sunny slopes.[151] With the exception of the gardens, the meadow, and the vines, the economic life of the monastery was based on preserving the environment in its natural state, a policy which met with difficulties in the pre-scriptions of the Duke of Normandy at Caen (in response, in part at least, to the complaints of the inhabitants); the monks appealed to the king, and sub-sequently some of the rights which they had been deprived of were restored.[152]

The conflict between those who wished to preserve primeval landscapes and those who insisted on deforestation was often a conflict over rights; it was not a question of resistance to change or eagerness for change, of the preserva-tion of old beauty or the creation of new. The common welfare might be involved, for deforestation of an area might nullify age-old rights. One example dates back to the ninth century. The residents of the royal fisc of Tectis [Theux] intended to divide up and deforest the forest of Astanedum [Staneux, near Spa?] where they enjoyed rights of use. A diploma of the emperors Louis and Lothaire [829] held that they enjoyed the forest land in common and that they could not deforest.[153] Adjustments might be made

---

[146] *Ibid.*, p. 259.

[147] *Ibid.*, p. 260.

[148] *Ibid.*, p. 261.

[149] *Ibid.*, pp. 262–263.

[150] *Ibid.*, p. 267. Technically the word *flet* here translated as *arm* is "un bras d'eau d'importance quelconque, mais d'écoulement peu rapide" (p. 256, note 5).

[151] *Ibid.*, pp. 274, 276–277.

[152] For the details, *ibid.*, pp. 267–270: In 1295 Guillaume du Grippeel, Viscount of Caen, ordered the destruction of some fisheries, enlarging and cleaning out of the arms of the river, the cleaning of the bridges, the maintenance of landmarks (repères), the reinforcement of dikes, etc. The monks complained to the King, who ordered legal remedies for some of the torts committed against the abbey. Three royal orders, *mandements*, were involved, Philippe le Bel and Louis Hutin, Feb. 24, Oct. 10, 1314, and Jan. 18, 1315 (pp. 267–268).

[153] Huffel, 1:2, p. 79, footnote 1. Huffel's source is the *Cartulaire* of *Stavelot-Malmedy*; this act "est le plus ancien, à notre connaissance, qui consacre par écrit la jouissance en commun d'un droit d'usage forestier par un groupement rural.".

through compromise. In 1219, the archbishop of Rouen met with the opposition of the Lord and the men of Saint-Aubin-Le-Cerf on his plan to deforest a part of the forest of Alihermont and found a new parish there, the complainants holding that their rights of usage would thereby be diminished. The latter consented to the clearing and in exchange the archbishop ceded them a canton of the forest for their exclusive use, plus eighty livres, granting exemption of all duties normally payable for enjoying the rights of usage.[154]

In the Middle Ages the exercise of rights of use was a powerful means of maintaining a landscape or of changing it; but this exercise had little to do directly with evaluating the consequences of human use of the land. There is, however, evidence that such interpretations were often made. Men were aware of their influence on the forest, on wildlife, on the pasturelands and the soils. They recognized their creativity when they built dikes to hold the sea, planted grasses to fix the sand dunes, and planned useful and beautiful gardens.

The antiphonal themes of forest clearance and forest conservation are discernible certainly in the times of Charlemagne; in all likelihood they are much older. Lay and ecclesiastical administrators alike seem to be self-conscious and purposive directors of environmental change.

We further decree, said Charlemagne in his *Admonitio Generalis* to all bishops (789), following that which the Lord has commanded in the law [i.e., Exodus 20:8-10] and which my own father of blessed memory had also ordered, that labor not be performed on the Lord's Day: that men neither do work in the countryside, nor care for the vineyards, nor plow the field, nor mow or gather the hay, nor build a fence, nor stub in the woods, nor fell trees (*nec in silvis stirpare vel arbores caedere*), nor work in stone, nor build houses, nor work in the garden, nor indulge themselves in pleasures, nor go hunting.[155]

In the *Capitulare de Villis* (*Capitulary of Manors and Farms*) there are provisions for the proper pasturing of stallions for the good of both the horse and the pastureland; instructions to the royal officers of each district to have in their jurisdiction a wide variety of artisans, including fishermen, birdcatchers, workmen who know how to make nets for hunting, fishing, and birdsnaring; provisions for the accounting of revenues from all these activities; instructions for the extermination of wolves, including the number taken, the surrender of their pelts, and seeking out the young in May, killing them with

---

[154] The basic source is Delisle, *Études sur la condition de la classe agricole en Normandie en moyen âge*, pp. 156-157, cited in Huffel, 1:2, pp. 140-141, footnote 2, where additional examples are given.

[155] Charlemagne, "No. 22: Admonitio Generalis. 789. m. Martio 23," *Mon. Ger. Hist. Capitularia Regum Francorum*, ed. Boretius, Vol. 1, §81, p. 61. Certain exemptions follow, and there are similar prohibitions for women's work.

powders—probably poisoned—or by capturing them with hooks, or by using pits and dogs; instructions for the proper selection of plants and trees for the gardens.[156]

One of Charlemagne's decrees has often been cited as evidence of willful deforestation: "Whenever there are men competent for the task, let them be given forest to cut down in order to improve our possessions."[157]

The thirty-sixth article of the *Capitulare de Villis*, however, is the most significant from the point of view of our theme: "That our *silva* and *foresta* be well guarded: and where there is a place suitable for clearing have it done, not allowing the woods to increase in the fields."[158]

The chapter sums up an important characteristic of the civilization in a few sentences: the foresta seems primarily to mean an area reserved as a refuge for wild animals; the plan calls for a balance between forest and arable, the protection of game for royal hunting, and income from pannage. The officers of the royal manors and farms are to observe carefully the woods and the reserved forests (*silvae vel forestes*). Those districts suited to agriculture may be deforested, but harmful clearing should not be permitted in districts which ought to remain wooded. Protect the royal game; take care of the falcon and the hawk for the chase; pay what is owed (literally, *censa nostra*) for the enjoyment of forest rights. If the royal officers, the mayors of the palace, or their men take their pigs to the forest for its mast, they should be the first to pay the fee, the *decima*, one-tenth of all pigs taken to the royal forest, thus setting a good example.

Perhaps too much can be read into this famous chapter—and it is all too easy to do so. It has been interpreted as the first conservation measure, and also as one which gave the signal for deforestation and put the stamp of approval on it.[159] Granting its restricted application, as commentators have

---

[156] *Capit. de villis*, art. 13, on pasturing horses (*waraniones*); 69, on wolves; 45, on artisans; 62, on revenues; 70, on plants. See also Du Cange, articles on *waranio*, *admissarius equus*, *emissarius equus*.

[157] "Ubicumque inveniunt utiles homines, datur illis silva ad stirpandum, ut nostrum servitium inmelioretur." 77: "Capitulare Aquisgranense," art. 19, in *Mon. Ger. Hist. Capit. Reg. Franc.* ed. Boretius, Vol. 2, p. 172.

[158] *Capit. de Villis*, 36. Meaume, *Juris. Forest.*, p. 8, par. 21, thinks the C. de V. a domestic regulation applicable only to the villae of the prince and that its importance has been greatly exaggerated. Meaume makes the interesting observation (par. 22) that Pecquet, the famous grand master of waters and forests in the Dept. of Normandy in the reign of Louis XV was the first to invoke the capitularies in support of the opinion that Gaul would have been so overrun by forests in the ninth century that one of the first concerns of Charlemagne would have been to favor clearings and to prohibit new forest plantings. Pecquet's fame rests on his commentary and discussion of the French Forest Ordinance of 1669 (*Les Lois Forestière*, Paris: 1753. NA). Meaume calls him "excellent forestier, mais fort mauvais historien."

[159] For a discussion of this chapter, see Maury, *Les Forêts de la Gaule*, pp. 102–103, who cites Meaume's opinion that it was applicable only to royal holdings and that Charlemagne did not want the forests invading the cultivated areas, a real danger because those enjoying pannage rights were interested in the extension of the forests. Charle-

pointed out, may there not be a groping here for a balance between the forest and agriculture, between grazing and agriculture, because the forests were so vital for grazing pigs? The laws of the barbarian peoples clearly show the role of pigs and other domestic animals in the forest economy. These capitularies —and those of Charlemagne's successors—may well acknowledge that growing populations, the multiple use of forests, and the demand for productive crop-land were interrelated.

The passage is as significant for the interpretation it has evoked as for its intrinsic importance. To some German historians of the nineteenth century, it was evidence that the Carolingian epoch was one of great and wide-ranging colonization and consequent environmental change.[160] Halphen, however, has disputed this view, considering the extent of Carolingian colonization and de-forestation to be exaggerated and only a continuation of trends already set in motion by St. Columban and his disciples from the sixth to the eighth century. The taming of nature, he adds, may have progressed a little more in Carolingian times through the establishment of new ecclesiastical foundations and by conquest.

Interpretations of environmental change appear with increasing frequency in the period from about the end of the tenth to the fourteenth century. I am not interested, however, in compiling, for their own sakes, lists of complaints of harmful practices or exultant notices reporting the conquest of a new en-vironment; it is more important to show by illustrations the beginnings of scattered and unrelated recognitions of the power of human agency in chang-ing the physical environment. This is a period in some ways like the Caro-lingian, an age of colonization and clearance, following one of virtual anarchy. The Scandinavian invasions and the pressure of the Magyars had brought about widespread internal disorder; Europe was surrounded by barbarian peoples and the higher civilization of Islam.

> The acts of the synod of Troslé in 909 give us some idea of the despair of the leaders of the Frankish church at the prospect of the universal ruin of Christian society. "The cities," they wrote, "are depopulated, the monasteries ruined and burned, the country reduced to solitude." "As the first men lived without law or fear of God, abandoned to their passions, so now every man does what seems good in his own eyes, despising laws human and divine and the commands of the Church. The strong oppress the weak; the world is full of violence against the poor and of the plunder of ecclesiastical goods." "Men devour one another like the fishes in the sea."[161]

---

magne's successors apparently continued the policy of prohibiting both the establishment of new forests and the deforestation, without permission, of already forested lands. See also *AMA*, p. 242, on Charlemagne's precursors.

[160] See Louis Halphen's discussion of Inama-Sternegg's *Deutsche Wirtschaftsge-schichte*, Vol. I, pp. 275–280, and Alfons Dopsch's *Die Wirtschaftsentwicklung der Karolingerzeit vornehmlich in Deutschland*, and his comments on *De Villis*, cap. 36, and the *Capitularia*, art. 19, in *Études Critiques sur l'Histoire de Charlemagne*, pp. 240–245.

[161] Dawson, *The Making of Europe*, pp. 225–226. See also *AMA*, pp. 244–245.

In the eleventh century, however, observations of landscape change begin to increase; in my opinion there has been a continuity of such observations from those times to the present. In these matters, however, there is in the Middle Ages not one history but innumerable local histories, as any student who has read monographs of the historical geography of small areas of France, Germany, or Switzerland has observed. The observations appear also in the celebrated *Weisthümer*,[162] and in histories of local forests, like Plinguet's history of the forest of Orléans and the enlightening work of De Maulde on the same subject. In what general work on the Middle Ages do we have a detailed history of an Alpine valley? Yet it is this kind of local history that gives us an appreciation of the nature of environmental change through time.

The theme of forest conservation (or perhaps more correctly, the theme of a balance between agriculture, industry, and forestry) is really an expression of the fact that the history of forestry in the Middle Ages is inextricably intertwined with many other histories, especially of agriculture, grazing, mining, and viticulture. The Carolingian belief in the beneficence of forest clearance (with the exception of the statement that royal forest land unsuited for other uses should be permitted to remain in forest) was superseded in the twelfth and thirteenth centuries by an opposite belief: the clearing, not the forest, had to be justified. The shift in favor of the forests probably had humble beginnings in the careless waste of simple housebuilding and in the deforestation of the most accessible places.[163]

According to Grand and Delatouche, beginning in the twelfth century an imperious need was felt for forest protection, a need associated with increases of the rural population, the growth of new towns, and the establishment of industries which needed wood for fuel and construction, and with the clearing of forests by fire. The tree was the raw material of the cabinetmaker, the joiner, the cooper, the wheelwright, and from its wood were made the agricultural tools, the fences, and the charcoal for the forges and the glassworks. Pleas for conservation arise out of this very sensitive position of the forest. It had to be cleared to make room for the town, the vine, the crop, but if it vanished, the life's blood of the economy vanished too.

I have already mentioned the varied and extensive uses of the forest in the medieval period (and which continue into modern times) that sharply distinguish the forest of those times as a cultural environment from one in our

---

[162] The *Weisthum* was a custom or precedent written down and often having the force of law. See also Pfeifer, "The Quality of Peasant Living in Central Europe," in *MR*, p. 245. There are many such collections. Perhaps the best known of the greater collections are the *Oesterreichische Weisthümer*, collected by the Vienna Royal Academy of Sciences, and Grimm's *Weisthümer*, in 7 volumes, collected by J. Grimm and published by the historical commission of the Academy of Sciences of Munich, at Göttingen, 1840–1878.

[163] On these themes, see Schwappach, p. 154; Heyne, pp. 148–159; *AMA*, p. 433.

own. The most convincing evidence known to me of this delicate balance between the forest, the arable, the town, and industry is in two *Weisthümer* from the city of Erfurt, one of 1289, another of 1332, the last being known also as the *Bibra-Büchlein*.[164] In this *Weisthum*, there is a list of products of the Thüringerwald which are brought into Erfurt. There were brooms made of twigs, or large bundles of twigs bound together for sweeping; various types of containers, tubs, or barrels; well-buckets; hoops, kegs, and various types of wooden measuring vessels for milk, salt, and other uses; the wheelbarrow; various kinds of braided materials, especially from the willow and used for binding grapevines to the stakes; bast; various kinds of mats and roofing materials, perhaps woven from tree bast or bundles of twigs, and so forth; troughs, keys, a specially prepared type of grass or reed girdle made of selected kinds of foliage; wooden drinking vessels; a kind of long-handled dipper; possibly hop poles or vine stakes; kneading troughs; wooden rollers, logwood, maybe bowstrings; crossbows; split wood; poles; spear shafts, ax handles or helves, possibly a sword sheath or a girdle; wood fibers for sieves; harrows, hollowed-out conduits which apparently carried beer in various stages of manufacture from one part of the brewery to the other; wooden siphons; swine-feeding troughs; wooden cribs or possibly stalls; thick wooden wheel disks with holes bored in the center, perhaps for wagons or mill wheels; other wooden wheels; grain measures; chests; sieves; various wooden vessels; wooden pushers to shove bread into the oven; and saddles.

There are also examples of direct governmental encouragement of forests, even to the extent of ordering the changing of land from agricultural to forest uses. The German kings Albert I and Henry VII in the fourteenth century ordered various formerly forested lands which had been converted to agriculture returned to forest; the order of 1304 affected the Hagenauer Forest and the Frankenweide near Annweiler, and in 1309 and 1310,[165] the Nürnberg

---

[164] This discussion is based on the text of *Das Bibra-Büchlein* as edited by Kirchoff in *Die ältesten Weisthümer der Stadt Erfurt*, #2, 14, pp. 42–47. I have followed Kirchoff's notes and discussions of the meanings of the words. On the *Bibra-Büchlein*, pp. vi–vii; the meaning of *kunes*, rendered here as hop poles or vine stakes, is doubtful, pp. 43–44, footnote 36. There is discussion of the *Weisthum* in Schwappach, pp. 164–165.

[165] The texts on which this is based (not available to me) are from J. D. Schoepflin, *Alsatia diplomatica* Vol. 2, No. 829, *Spicilegium tabularum litterarumque veterum Frankf*, 1724, p. 500; and L. C. von Wölkern, *Historia diplomatic Norimbergensis*, p. 224, No. 68, dated 1309. The text from *Alsat. Dipl.*, Vol. 2, No. 829 (about 1304) is as follows:

Mandamus, ut nullus hominum nemus nostrum et imperii dictum Heiligvorst deinceps vastare vel evellere radicitus aut novalia aliqua facere audeat aliqualiter vel presumat. Sed volumus ut de pertinenciis et juribus ipsius nemoris apud antiquiores homines circa metas nemoris residentes diligens inquisitio habeatur, et ea que per inquisicionem habitam inventa fuerint dicto nemori pertinere, sine sint culta vel inculta, nemori predicto attineant et inantea non colantur, sed pro augmento nemoris foveantur.

The text from *Hist. Dipl. Norimb.*, p. 224, No. 68 is especially interesting: "Mandamus, quatenus sylvam nostram et imperii sitam prope Nuremberg ex utraque parte ripae,

royal forest. It has been suggested that natural regeneration and seeding from neighboring stands were the means of restoring the forest, and that environmental conditions (such as forest meadows) unfavorable for the distribution of the seed were discouraged as much as possible. (Artificial planting of stands was a later development.) No new clearings could be made in the Hagenauer Forest; the replacement of the arable by forest lands should be fostered. The Nürnberg ordinance required the restoration to forest of the lands on both shores of the Pegnitz River which had in the past fifty years been cleared and transformed into cultivated fields.

In his history of German forestry, Schwappach finds that the first scattered and localized regulations against deforestation begin in the twelfth century and grow continually more numerous until by the end of the Middle Ages forest protection is the rule, permission to clear, a special exception.[166] The motives behind these laws prohibiting clearance seem to have been the desire to protect the reserved forests (*Bannforst*) possibly because they were royal hunting grounds, to prevent new clearing, to protect sources of mast and pasture.[167] It is difficult to determine if the older prohibitions were in the interest of hunting alone or of other forest uses as well, for hunting was more than a pleasure; it was an important source of food even for royalty. Clearly a balance between the forest—a source of energy, tools, utensils, and of plant and animal food—and cropland yielding food was desired. According to Schwappach, this tendency to encourage a forest economy by prohibiting clearings first appears in a privilege of the Archbishop Eberhard of Salzburg (1237) who, in the interest of salt production, forbade the transformation of cleared-over forest lands into arable fields or meadow, in order that the forest could grow there again.[168] In Albert's ordinance of 1304 prohibiting *novalia* and destructive activities in the Hagenauer Forest and ordering the return of many of these lands to woods, the same author discerns a transition from purely negative prohibitions to positive measures for forest care.[169]

In Henry VII's sharper restatement of King Rudolph's ordinance of 1289 with reference to the protection of the Nürnberg royal forest, it was said that "harm had come to him and to the city of the kingdom in the destruction of the forest of the kingdom and its transformation into cultivated land." In this

---

quae dicitur pegniz, a quinquaginta annis citra per incendium vel alio modo quocunque destructam seu vastatam, ac postmodum in agros a quibuscunque redactam in arbores et in sylvam, sicut solebat esse primitus, auctoritate nostra regis redigatis" (about 1309, repeated in 1310). The texts are in Schwappach, pp. 181–182, footnote 4.

[166] *Ibid.*, p. 154.

[167] *Ibid.*, pp. 154–155.

[168] The source, not available to me, is Hansiz, *Germania sacra*, Vol. 2, p. 339: " . . . illud quoque juris eis concedentes, ut succisis nemoribus patellae ipsorum deputatis sive deputandis nulli liceat fundum eorum nemorum excolere vel pasturae animalium usupare, ut ligna in eisdem fundis possint recrescere" (about 1237, from Schwappach, p. 156, note 31).

[169] *Ibid.*, p. 156.

remarkable document, the transformation of forest to cultivated lands is regarded as a calamity! It reminds one of Evelyn's castigation of agriculture as the enemy of the forest in the seventeenth century. In 1310, the same king ordered all those to whom the provisions of the document applied to swear on All Souls' Day a corporal oath—that is, to be in contact with holy relics—and in the presence of the imperial judge in the town (the *Schultheiss*) who had close relationships with the council, with law enforcement, and with the mayor, to restore the forest to its former condition and to tolerate no acquisition by outsiders through purchase or by any other means of rights of forest use of any description.[170]

In 1331, King Ludwig of Bavaria promulgated more regulations concerning the forest (*Forst*) and the royal forest (*Reichswald*) on both sides of the Pegnitz River in Nürnberg. Once a year all officials, foresters, and beekeepers from both banks of the Pegnitz were to be summoned by the council, to appear before it, and to swear to the Holy One to adhere to decisions resolved upon as being good and useful for the kingdom and the city and to censure any act considered harmful to the forest. Only a forester had the right to authorize removal of wood from the forests. Officials, foresters, and their assistants might permit only those to remove wood from the forest or might sell only to those who had enjoyed such rights from olden times. The highest forestry administrative official was duty bound to reside in Nürnberg, and rights in the forest could not be sold by him or by anyone else because such a sale was harmful to the city or to the kingdom.[171] These regulations bind up the fate of the forest with the people and the city, to make the city and its forested surroundings one. "Am Schluss unserer Periode [that is about the middle of the fourteenth century]," says Ernst Mummenhoff, an historian of Old Nürnberg, "erscheint der Wald als ein Unzertrennliches mit der Stadt verbunden."[172]

This is the most dramatic of all the efforts, known to me, in the Middle Ages to preserve local forests in the environs of an important city; the conditions described here suggest an understanding of the complex interrelationships existing between town and forest.

Even more remarkable—for whatever reason—is the active participation of the clergy in the cause of forest conservation. In 1328, the year in which he was chosen for his office, the Bishop of Bamberg had to swear that he would take the forests of the bishopric under his faithful protection, and that he would not permit the inauguration of new clearings, a ceremony and oath repeated in the choice of a bishop in 1398.[173] Further evidence of the increas-

---

[170] Mummenhoff, *Altnürnberg*, pp. 55–57. On the precise meaning of *Schultheiss* at this time, see pp. 13, 20–21.
[171] *Ibid.*, p. 58.
[172] *Ibid.*, p. 61.
[173] Wimmer, *Geschichte des deutschen Bodens*, p. 133.

ing concern for forests is shown in the 151 forest regulations enacted in various parts of Germany in the period from 1482 to 1700.[174]

Important and delicate relationships also existed between the forest and industry. We may take as an example glassmaking, so important throughout Central Europe in the fourteenth and fifteenth centuries. Large amounts of wood were needed in all stages of manufacture. These glassworks were located in the forests because it was cheaper to build them there than to pay transport costs of such a bulky source of energy. The migration of industry from one cleared part of a forest to the other, as happened in the Black Forest, was common before it became more stabilized. Glassmaking, like mining, highlighted the role of the forest as a source of energy and as the locale of industry.[175]

Similar demands were made where mining and smelting took place. The Catalan forge of the peasant needed charcoal and ore. The smelter required nearby areas rich in wood. Operations of this kind already were going on modestly during the migrations of the barbarians; deforestation for this and other reasons took place in the Carolingian age.[176] Similar migrations in the forests occurred with the setting up of sawmills, which began to multiply rapidly on watercourses at the end of the fifteenth century.[177] Sawmills, first mentioned in the German lands at the end of the fourteenth and the beginning of the fifteenth century, were springing up in the Austrian and Bavarian Alps and in the Black Forest.

Mining, including salt mining, accentuated these overall trends by gradually bringing more remote environments within the economic network. Mining also demanded great quantities of wood. Since there were no modern explosives, rock had to be broken up by heating—the fuel source was wood—followed by dousing with water to split and crack it. According to Schwappach, the Harz and Hallein forest areas were specifically designated for mining and salt mining about 1237. In the German lands miners apparently had generous access to the use of wood.[178]

In this sense, viticulture too was an industry, for it was dependent on the

---

[174] Of interest also is the older work (1802) of Anton, *Geschichte der teutschen Landwirthschaft von den ältesten Zeiten bis zu Ende des fünfzehnten Jahrhunderts,* Vol. 3, pp. 429–489 on forestry, covering the period from 1158–1350.

[175] See Dirscherl, "Das ostbayerische Grenzgebirge als Standraum der Glasindustrie," *Mitt. der Geo. Gesell. in München,* Vol. 31 (1938), pp. 103–104. Note the discussion of the Black Forest, pp. 103–104, the Spessart, Steigerwald, Thüringerwald, the Silesian Bergland, the Fichtelgebirge, east and west Prussia, and Pomerania, pp. 103–108.

[176] Guyan, *Bild und Wesen einer Mittelalterlichen Eisenindustrielandschaft im Kanton Schaffhausen,* p. 64. See also pp. 58–60, 65.

[177] *AMA,* p. 439, citing Ch. Guyot, *Les forêts lorraines avant 1789,* Nancy, 1886.

[178] Schwappach, p. 142. Harz and Hallein from Hansiz, *Germaniae Sacrae,* Vol. 2, p. 330; and T. Wagner, *Corpus Iuris Metallici* (Leipzig 1791), about 1484. See Nef, "Mining and Metallurgy in Medieval Civilisation," *CEHE,* Vol. 2, pp. 436–438; and Gille, "Les Dév. Technolog. en Europe," *JWH,* Vol. 3, pp. 91–92, on the influence of the Germans on mining and mining techniques.

forest for stakes and various plant fibers which bound the vine to the stake. One can in fact discern two different themes, the vine as an enemy of the forest because it displaces the tree, and the forest and viticulture as complementary, with forest areas being set aside (as with mining) for the needs of viticulture.

It is easy to see therefore, from these examples, why the literature of the forest reaches back so far and why reflections on desirable and undesirable changes in the environment accumulated as various types of environments came into use for different purposes.

## 12. ALPINE VALLEYS

An attractive theme in the geography of the Middle Ages is the settlement of the high Alpine valleys because of the liberty and security they afforded; some of the settlers were interested in protective forests, which in modern times, especially in France, have received so much attention in relation to torrent control. (In an Austrian *Weisthümer*, placed at Flaurling in the valley of the Inn in the fifteenth century, cutting down trees in certain districts is prohibited so that no harm will come either to the church or to the neighbors from the stream.)[179]

In the latter part of the nineteenth century, François Arnaud made a study of the valley of the Ubaye, a left-bank tributary of the Durance in the department of Basse Alps; it was included in Demontzey's well-known work on the extinction of the Alpine torrents in France.

The valley of the Ubaye had enjoyed almost complete independence since the thirteenth century; it attracted "comme un eldorado de liberté" refugees from neighboring feudal areas. Its population had become so dense that deforestation and the cultivation of cereals had been pushed to the extreme limits. The local government, moreover, struggled to avoid the disastrous consequences of deforestation and of turf removal (*dégazonnement*).

These settlements in the Middle Ages were organized into communes (*mandements* or *consulats*) which were more populous and greater in area than the contemporary French commune. Each mandement had a council (*capitulum*), composed of the heads of all the families, whose official acts were known as capitulations. A consul or syndic chosen by the council was charged with the strict supervision of these capitulations, being assisted in the tasks by sworn overseers called jurats.[180]

---

[179] Huffel, 1:1, p. 134; *Oesterreichische Weisthümer*, III, p. 26. "Mer, her richter, offen wir, das (iemant) in der lent hinder des pfarrers kabasgarten im poden hinein nach pis a den vodern schroffen weder däxen noch klain holz nicht solt schlachen pei umb, damit der kirchen und den nachpaurn von dem pach kain schad widerfar" (quoted in Schwappach, p. 181, footnote 2).

[180] Huffel, 1:1, pp. 134–135.

The oldest capitulations (reprinted by Arnaud), those of Meyronnes and Larch of August 29, 1414, regulate the pastures and the use of wood in privately owned property.[181] These provisions, examples of which are given here, tell their own story:

Prohibition against cutting wood or having wood cut within the boundaries of the mountain; this applies even to proprietors on their own meadows.

Prohibition against pasturing sheep, or any other animals, at Adrech (above Larch) and at Adrech de Plan above Saint-Ours from St. John's Day to St. Luke's Day (from June 24 to October 18).

Everyone is prohibited from taking out both dry and green wood.

Strangers to the communities of Meyronnes and Le Larch are prohibited from pasturing their livestock on their lands (clearly aimed at eliminating the transhumants).

Residents of the two communities are prohibited from having flocks of sheep of more than six trenteniers (180 beasts) without permission of the consuls.

Pasturing either large or small livestock in new meadows less than ten years old is forbidden.

It is forbidden to have more than six head of cattle per inhabitant without permission of the consuls.

It is forbidden to allow animals to graze in the mountains before St. John's Day (June 24). The capitulations of January 9, 1436, provided for severer penalties including punishment in the pillory and the carcan as examples to others.

These capitulations show that much was understood about the relation of deforestation to torrents, about the dangers of excessive grazing and grazing during the wrong times of the year and in the wrong places, and about the necessity of strictly regulating transhumance.

During the Middle Ages men were aware of the destructiveness of domesticated animals, but this had to be weighed against their indispensability. The goat, an extreme example, often was as important an animal as the pig.[182] Its destructiveness, however, was more dreaded than that of any other domestic animal, and the greatest care was taken to watch it. Du Cange has cited a

---

[181] François Arnaud, "Notice historique sur les Torrents de la Vallée de l'Ubaye," in Demontzey, *L'Extinction des Torrents en France par le Reboisement*, pp. 408–425. This area has been recently restudied by Thérèse Sclafert, *Cultures en Haute-Provence. Déboisements et Pâturages au Moyen Age. Les Hommes et la Terre*, IV (1959). See esp. Part II, chap. 4, "La Protection des Bois et la Lutte contre l'Érosion," pp. 181–212, where many illustrations are given, including those published by Arnaud, pp. 184–185.

[182] "Si elle [the goat] ne fut généralement pas la bête idéale des exploitations agricoles ni l'élément le plus normal des troupeaux, en revanche, son prix modique, sa sobriété, sa rusticité refractaire a la tuberculose, sa fidélité familière, son peu de volume, la qualité et l'abondance relative de sa lactation ont fait de la chèvre, autrefois plus que de nos jours, la providence des petites gens" (*AMA*, p. 505).

Norman text in which goats did not have the right of *bannovium* (literally the time when animals are allowed to graze in the common fields),[183] but must be carefully guarded lest they nibble the young shoots of the trees, the copse, the hedge, and the vine. "Around 1080, persons with rights to use the forest of Lançon, in Anjou, could drive neither sheep nor goats into the woods.[184] There was a similar strictness in the Midi: in 1337, the proprietor of seven goats which were found browsing in the forest of Saint-Parquier, paid the same fine as if he had cut down an oak."[185]

The history of the regulation of forest grazing by custom, usage, or law probably is very old; none is known to me in the Greek and Roman period except that agricultural writers were concerned with the depredations of animals in cultivated fields, but not in mountain pastures or in the forests. There is however a notice in the capitularies of Clotaire II (614 or 615) prohibiting the swineherds of the royal *villas* to graze pigs in ecclesiastical and privately owned forests, but this may have been an economic measure controlled by the supply of acorns.[186]

In the history of German forestry there are examples of the prohibition of sheep and goat grazing dating back to the twelfth century. "What right do goats, sheep, swine have to the Vorholz," one *Weisthum* asks. "They have no right," is the reply, "but pigs are permitted at mast time."[187] In the *Dreieicher Wildbann* (*ca.* 1338), the shepherd could drive his flock into the forest only so far as he could throw his staff. Neither were Austrian Weisthümer silent on goats; they were allowed to graze only in the remote parts of the Alpine forest.[188]

---

[183] In the *Lex. Man.*, "Bannovium: Tempus quo licet pecora pasci per agros communes." See Du Cange, article, *Fraiterius*, and *AMA*, p. 505.

[184] Translated from AMA, p. 505, whose source is the *Cartulaire de Saint Aubin*, Vol. 1, p. 262.

[185] *AMA*, p. 505, whose source is "Comptes de la Sénéchaussée de Toulouse," in *Histoire du Languedoc*, Vol. X, c. 783; Saint-Parquier, cant. de Montech (Tarn-et-Garonne).

[186] Edict of Chlotharii II, *ca.* 614 or 615, chap. 21: "Porcarii fisales in silvas ecclesiarum aut privatorum absque voluntate possessoris in silvas eorum ingredi non praesumant." 23: "Et quandoquidem pastio non fuerit unde porci debeant saginari cellarinsis in publico non exigatur" (*Capitularia*, ed. Boretius). See also Huffel, 1:1, p. 278, note 1.

[187] Refers to Lower Saxony. See Grimm, *Weisthümer*, p. 259, Item 6; Schwappach, p. 169, footnote 47.

[188] An Austrian *Weisthum* from Amt Obdach about 1391 provides, "Es sol auch kainer unser underthanen in dem ganzen ambt Obedach nit gaisz haben bei der straff" (*Oes. W.*, Vol. VI, 274). The same collection, referring to Alpine goat grazing in Altenthan about 1437, says, "Wer gaisz hat, soll sie wie vor alter an die grasze wäld und hölzer, dasz si den hann nit kräen hören und niemand schäden thun treiben" (Vol. 1, 30). The reference to the shepherd is in Grimm's *Weisthümer*, VI, 397, 6: " . . . auch sal ein gemein hirte nicht verrer mit seinen schafen und ziegen in den walt farin, dan he mit sime stabe gewerfen mag, und sal alle zit da vor stên und werinde sin heruz" (*Dreieicher Wildbann* about A.D. 1338). These texts are quoted in part by Schwappach, pp. 169–170.

These and many other similar regulations are evidences of a genuine concern for the well-being of the forest as a habitat of living things. It had to be preserved as a breeding ground for the wild animals needed for the hunt and as pasturage for the domestic animals. According to Maury the provisions in Salic law to protect forests really intended the preservation of the domestic animals; and in protecting grazing lands for pigs, sheep, goats, it guaranteed a suitable environment for birds and bees, protecting the trees against reckless destruction by those with rights of usage.[189] There are indications too that when a forest had been cut over, care was taken with the young regrowth; how widespread this practice was cannot be ascertained. De Maulde, for example, cites an agreement between a Lord Bouchard de Meung and the commanderie of the Hospital de Saint-Jean-de-Jérusalem at Orléans (approved in 1160 by the bishop of Orléans) concerning the clearing of a forest to build a village, further clearings to come with the bishop's consent as the population grew. Peasants had rights of use in these forests for their cattle, but if a clearing was made, those cut-over areas in which the regrowth was taking place were denied to the animals.[190] The same author cites some ancient texts concerning the forest of Orléans in which all animals except goats (*capris tamen exceptis*) are allowed to graze; to the latter, access is persistently denied.[191]

It is possible that man's realization of his power to make radical changes in the environment by means of his influence on the breeding, housing, and wandering of domestic animals comes late, even though grazing at will on open, flat, or mountain lands is a very ancient example of man's ability to make changes in the physical environment through controlled concentrations of animals at selected places. Regulating the multiplication of animals and their densities has vast cumulative effects. These slower ecological processes were less apparent than the immediately visible effects of clearing through purposeful firing or cutting. Of course it is true that the habits of the animals could be readily observed. Goat damage to young trees, to the young shoots of trees, and even to an entire stand of trees was not difficult to discover. Forest fires, moreover, were often started by shepherds, accidentally, or intentionally to secure a finer growth of grass. The shepherd, the domestic animal, and fire thus became a powerful combination.

In many countries, the activities of the woodcutter and the herder have been associated with forest fires. In his history of the forest of Orléans, De Maulde has cited interesting notices from the parishes of Vitry and Courcy,

---

[189] Maury says that in the Salic law the legislation protecting forests really intended to preserve the domestic animals; in protecting grazing lands for pigs, sheep, goats, it also guaranteed a suitable environment for birds and bees, protecting also the trees against reckless destruction by those with rights of usage (Les Forêts de la Gaule, pp. 90–91).

[190] De Maulde, pp. 114–115.

[191] *Ibid.*, p. 149, and footnote 6.

dating from the middle of the fifteenth century. A fine of five sous was levied for lighting a fire in a forest with dry wood, a distinction being made between starting a fire at the base of a dry oak or one still green. A fire started against an oak which is more dry than green increased the fine by five sous regardless of the season. If the oak is more green than dry, the fine is increased to fifteen sous *parisis*.

Forest fires were controlled through custom, those having the right to burn for pasture having also the obligation to fight fires. They were put out by beating with brooms, by backfiring, and by trenching. The dangers of burning were recognized, but so was the role of fire in creating new fertility.

In the same work, De Maulde cites evidence showing an acute realization in the fourteenth century of the tragic effects of indiscriminate deforestation. The cutover areas or *vagues*, were overgrown with broom (*genêt*) and heath following deforestation. Texts of the thirteenth century distinguished between woods and the places where woods should be but were not, between the real forest and the confusion of bramble. In the fifteenth century, the word *alaise* was used to define part of a forest, detached from the rest, sometimes by extensive stretches of vagues, and forming a well-defined region of its own, created not only by neglect but by the animals that nibbled and trampled the sprouting seedlings, preventing regrowth.[192]

## 13. SOILS

The possibility of improving the soils through human agency was recognized in the Middle Ages. Soil theory, based on the doctrine of the four elements, was empirical in nature. The importance of fertilizers was also realized as is shown by the discussions of Albert the Great and Pietro Crescenzi (Petrus de Crescentis [1230–1310], whose *Opus Ruralium Commodorum* had profited from Albert's work). Marling seems to have been one of the chief means of improving soils, animal manures playing a subordinate role (and a lesser part than in modern times) owing to the smaller size of the animals and their frequent grazing in open fields, meadows, and forests.[193]

Of greater interest is a theory mentioned by Sclafert in her study of the deforestation of the southern Alps: in the eyes of the peasant, whose harvests were often so precarious, the trees of the forest—useless vegetation—were his enemies, attracting to themselves all the juices of the soil ("attirait à elle tous les

---

[192] *Ibid.*, pp. 87–91. The notice on young seedlings is from a letter of patent in 1543.

[193] For a discussion of fertilizers during the Middle Ages, especially in France, see *AMA*, pp. 261–269. See also Bertrand Gille, "Les Développements Technologiques en Europe de 1100 à 1400," *JWH*, 3 (1956), p. 96, on differences between the Middle Ages and classical antiquity in agricultural methods, at least as they appear in the Roman writers on agronomy, marling, fallowing, and in the agricultural writers such as Walter of Henley (thirteenth century), Petrus de Crescentis (fourteenth century), and others.

sucs de la terre pour nourrir un végétation inutile").[194] Among the monks, some believed in the theory, while others opposed cutting down forests for this reason. Albert the Great had warned against leaving rhizomes of cut-over trees in the soil. (See p. 315.) In the later Middle Ages, when more land was obtained by draining marshes and from other kinds of reclamation, perhaps the conflict between forest and the arable was less intense.[195]

## 14.  Hunting

Hunting had a varying relationship to agriculture: there are indications in the late Middle Ages of a shift away from an emphasis on the preservation of wildlife (even though there might be no closed season for the privileged few who could hunt) to the preservation of crops and domesticated animals subject to the depredations of the wild animals. Furthermore, hunting is a sensitive subject in the Middle Ages because of its relationship to theology, and the official attitude of the Christian Church was at odds with an apparently widespread and irresistible infatuation with hunting. One could expect of the Church, as with many religions, a counsel of compassion and pity and even friendship with the wild beasts. In Christian doctrine, sparing them, refraining from cruelty to them, was part of the duty of man, and was performed in the name of humanity.[196] Christian hagiography is full of instances of friendship with small animals and even with large predators. Myths and legends woven by later writers around the lives of their favorite saints had them in their forest retreats, striking up friendships with the animals, or as Montalembert has said, retraining feral animals.[197] This Christian hagiography may indeed be a form of protest against heartless killing of wild animals.[198] St. Jerome had said there were numerous examples in the scriptures of holy fishermen, but not a single example of a holy hunter; St. Ambrose, that the just had never been found among the hunters; and Pope Nicholas I had declared that only reprobates are given to the chase. These sentiments were expressed before Saint Hubert, Bishop of Liège, became, in the eleventh century, patron saint of hunters.[199]

Such was the passion for hunting in the Middle Ages that the Church vainly held its clerics from it. In principle, the only hunting actually prohibited was

[194] Sclafert, "A Propos du Déboisement des Alpes du Sud," *Annales de Géographie*, Vol. 42 (1933), pp. 266–277, 350–360, ref. on p. 274.

[195] Anton, *Geschichte der teutschen Landwirtschaft*, Vol. 3 (1802), has given many interesting details from older documents which illustrate this theme, pp. 185–216. See also *AMA*, pp. 260–264.

[196] Dom Leclercq, "Chasse," in *Dict. d'Arch. Chrét. et de Liturgie*, Vol. 3, col. 1087.

[197] Montalembert's discussion is particularly interesting because of his sympathy—amounting to hagiolatry—with the monks. See Vol. 2, pp. 226–231.

[198] For general discussions of hunting and the chase, see *AMA*, pp. 547–618 (*Le gibier et la chasse*) and the pertinent chapters of Schwappach.

[199] Leclercq, "Chasse," *loc. cit.*

the chase with horn, shouting, and dogs, and falconry, because of the luxurious and worldly display they symbolized. Kings and councils reportedly tried to control the ecclesiastical zeal for hunting. In the Council of Agde (506) the clergy was forbidden to hunt with dogs or to possess hawks. In Carolingian and later times there were repeated prohibitions against the use of dogs, hawks, falcons, and various other birds of prey, and of sentinels.[200] The basic objection to hunting and the reasons for trying to control it—among the lay and clergy alike—was that it embodied atavistic instincts which should be kept at bay.[201] The utilitarian argument in favor of hunting apparently was very strong, and this attitude is understandable once it is realized that hunting was more than a pleasurable pastime; it supplied food, even for the highly placed; it controlled species harmful to crops and to domestic animals; it furnished pelts, furs, and hides for gloves and the bindings of monks' books, the latter need often being advanced as a justification for clerical hunting, especially of the chamois. Hunting caused a notable, if temporary, change in the landscape: the large managed forests were crossed by wide roads favorable both to the habitat of the wild life and to the ease of the hunt.[202] Under the circumstances, it is easy to understand recurring opposition to deforestation on the part of the large royal, noble, or ecclesiastical landholders during the Middle Ages. National historians of European forestry have repeatedly stressed the role of hunting in forest conservation.

> *La chasse*, [says Huffel of French forest history] en dehors même du rôle utile du gibier pour l'alimentation, a toujours tenu une grande place en forêt. Nos rois, chacun le sait, étaient restés, comme leurs premiers ancêtres, des chasseurs passionnés. La conservation, àtravers les siècles, d'un immense domaine forestier royal, ducal ou seigneurial s'explique surtout par le soin jaloux avec lequel les souverains ménageaient le terrain de leurs chasses: c'est au culte de nos rois pour le "noble déduit" que nous devons, en grande partie, de posséder dans le domaine national cette partie infiniment précieuse et la plus riche de nos forêts qui provient de l'ancien domaine souverain.[203]

15. LESSER THEMES OF ENVIRONMENTAL CHANGE

These are the main themes concerning environmental changes, but there are also minor ones, some of religious, some of lay origin, that should at least be mentioned. One is the garden. In interpreting its plan and purpose, one should not forget the Christian paradise theme and the monastic cemetery garden.

[200] Quotations from original sources in Schwappach, p. 61. Article 55 of the Council of Agde (Concilium Agathense, 506): "Episcopis, presbyteris, diaconibus canes ad venandum aut accipitres habere non liceat." On the kinds of animals inhabiting the German "Urwald," see Schwappach's chapter, *Jagdausübung*, pp. 64–70.

[201] See the remarks in *AMA*, pp. 554–556, for the many attempts, largely unsuccessful, to control hunting.

[202] *AMA*, p. 569.

[203] Huffel, 1:1, p. 6.

The pleasure garden (not the utilitarian garden cultivated because its plants were medically useful) was often conceived of as a simulation of the Garden of Eden. To cultivate the garden was more than a task for the holy; it was also a reliving of part of the creation. The experience was aesthetic and religious.[204]

One of the truly great landscape changes in modern times has been marsh, bog, marine, and lacustrine drainage. This extensive drainage of marsh and bog lands, however, seems primarily to be a phenomenon of modern times—mostly since the late seventeenth century—although there are many famous examples from earlier periods, such as the reclamation of the marsh lands of the Po (twelfth century on) and the imperially recruited Dutch immigrants' reclamation in an area of modern Berlin. Desire for land and improvement of health were the powerful motives. That an empirical relationship existed between illness and almost still or stagnant water was realized in ancient medicine. In some parts of Europe, health reasons may have been a controlling cause of drainage. In the old French Mediterranean province of Roussillon, the purpose of drainage was to eliminate the stagnant waters and deadly fevers at Bages, Nyles, and other places; most of the canals of Salange and of the suburb of Elne may have been dug for this purpose; subterranean drains may have been used for the same reason. The Count of Roussillon Guinard had a pond dried up northeast of Perpignan. And sales were made to the Templars of Masdeu for drainage purposes.[205]

There are on the other hand instances of the creation of artificial ponds. Temporary ponds were used in the Middle Ages in the Dombes and in La Brenne of France (this latter area, more than the Pays de Dombes, still has its lakes and marshes and bogs), thus combining agriculture with fishing and using at the same time the fertile soil particles carried in suspension. Barrages built at the base of the valley dammed up water from the neighboring hills on the exhausted soil; the newly formed pond was allowed to remain until the soil was well rested and fertilized. Then the barrage was pierced, the water flowed off, and the new earth could be plowed. The advantages of this form of migrant fertility, however, were clearly offset by the health dangers.[206]

### 16.  Conclusion

There were many other activities which involved environmental change, the establishment of towns, villages, and monasteries: the draining of swamps; the making of an occasional polder; and—long before Bremontier and his immediate predecessors—a planting of pine to fix the sand dunes of Leiria, Portugal,

---

[204] See Heyne's discussion, *Das Deutsche Nahrungswesen*, pp. 62–100.
[205] Brutails, *Étude sur la Condition des Populations Rurales du Roussillon au Moyen Âge*, pp. 3–4.
[206] See the Comte de Dienne, *Hist. du Desséchement des Lacs et Marais en France avant 1789*, p. 5. The author gives no exact date for these ponds in the Middle Ages.

in 1325.[207] Indeed, one meets from time to time in medieval literature an unmistakably joyous and lyrical feeling of creating something new. The evidence is spotty and proves little for the Middle Ages as a whole. A few quotations cannot be made to characterize a millennium. Nevertheless they are interesting in themselves; even the Church saw the advantage of improvements in life coming about through changes of the environment. The old saying, already referred to, that one lives well under the cross, had more than a spiritual meaning; it could also mean economic well-being through the activities of the monasteries of the countryside. Men of the Church saw themselves as spiritual leaders in the creation of a new environment; these attitudes appear early in the activities of the fathers in the West, in the shift from the love of solitude and prayer and the desire for release from the cares of the world to a missionary zeal which included everyday tasks of clearing, building, draining. (The later history of course was much less edifying.)

The most general conclusion to be drawn is the conclusion that can also be drawn of the contemporary period: there were many interpretations, and these were based on different religious, economic, and aesthetic values, as are our own.

It is often said that what distinguishes the modern from the medieval and classical periods is the modern sense of triumph in the control over nature in contrast with an earlier and unrelenting dependence. Such contrasts rest on an underevaluation of the extent of environmental change in classical and medieval times, on the belief that an advanced technology and sophisticated theoretical science are required for extensive and permanent change, and on a too sharp contrast between the so-called industrial revolution and the industry and technology of the past. One may wonder at the failure of the thinkers of the Middle Ages to create a theoretical science comparable with that of Galileo and Newton; fail they did, but they lacked neither an empirical knowledge of forestry, agriculture, drainage, nor a technology permitting them to induce sweeping and lasting changes in their environment. In fact, they made some of the most drastic changes in landscapes in human history up to that time.

An ascetic ideal was the original stimulus in evolving a philosophy of man as a creator of new environments. The early saints purposefully retired from the world, and they fancied that by their clearings they were re-creating the earthly paradise, reasserting the complete dominion over all life that existed before the Fall. The attractive force of these retirements, both to other monks and to the laity, and organized efforts at conversion led to Christian activism, in which taming the wild was a part of the religious experience. One of the many great roles St. Bernard played was to increase the Church's potential for landscape change. Under his influence one can see the Cistercian order changing from remoteness and renunciation to a role of active Christianizing of new

[207] Gille, "Les Dév. Technol. en Europe de 1000 à 1400," *JWH*, 3 (1956), pp. 96–97. No source is given.

and old lands alike. The success of such undertakings depended on practical knowledge and sense like that expressed in the *Instituta capituli generalis* of 1134; "victus debet provenire de labore manuum, de cultura terrarum, de nutrimento pecorum."[208]

In the age of the great défrichements, lay ambition and church ambition alike called for activity and change as a part of economic expansion and of conversion. The result was a yearning, to use a modern expression, for control over nature. In the later Middle Ages the interest in technology, in knowledge for its own sake whether to improve thinking or to better the human condition, in clearing, and in drainage and the like betrayed an eagerness to control nature.[209] As in all epochs of human history, modification of the physical environment is linked with ideas, ideals, and practical needs. The period of great cathedral building embodied a religious ideal; it also meant vast quarrying; probably more stone was removed from the earth in this period than in any comparable period of the past. In the three centuries from 1050 to 1350 stone quarried in France built eighty cathedrals, five hundred large churches, and tens of thousands of small churches. The Christian duties of conversion and lay expansion and colonization meant firing, clearing, burning. The grain and the grape have their practical, their cultural, and their religious history.[210]

---

[208] Quoted in Muggenthaler, *Kolonisatorische und wirtschaftliche Tätigkeit eines deutschen Zisterzienserklosters im XII. und XIII. Jahrhundert*, p. 103.

[209] See White, *Medieval Technology and Social Change*, p. 79; and Nef, "Mining and Metallurgy in Medieval Civilisation," *CEHE*, Vol. 2, p. 456.

[210] In 1913, Herbert Workman published *The Evolution of the Monastic Ideal*, in which he advanced the thesis that Eastern monasticism had degenerated into "Gnostic extremes" and "idle self-centeredness," that St. Benedict's contribution was that he added objective remedies for the vices of this earlier Eastern subjectivism. In essence St. Augustine had done this in his treatise on monks written earlier. St. Benedict, Workman continued, did not see the momentous consequences of this fusion of the monastic ideal with a philosophy of work. "Benedict did not see—the deserts in which they lived prevented the early monks from seeing—that the introduction of labour was destined, in the long run, to draw back the monk into the world from which he had fled, or, rather, to draw the world after him to the centres of light and peace which his labours created in the wilderness" (*Evol. of the Monastic Ideal*, p. 157). Important as this development might be for the history of Western civilization (even so unsparing and consistent a critic of monasticism as G. C. Coulton praised St. Benedict and the Benedictine Rule), Workman argued that the combination was fatal to the ideals of monasticism as they were at first envisaged. In fact, he constructs a theoretical history of a monastic order which is cyclical in nature; first, there is the enthusiastic desire for solitude of an original founder who goes to the dark forests, wastes, or deserts; if he gains a reputation, his presence has an attractive force on other monks, the group now attracting more and more, including lay people, so that what had started out as a makeshift hut became an abbey. The tiny enclave became an organized community, and axes and spades cleared the woods and the swamps, and "by the alchemy of industry turned the sands into waving gold, and planted centres of culture in the hearts of forests" (*ibid.*, pp. 219–220). The combination, he claimed, was fatal because of the conflict between renunciation

The life of Albert the Great provides a clue. He shared with his contemporaries and the Christian thinkers of the past a belief in a designed earth, in nature as a book revealing the artisanry of God, in the need to know nature for religious and practical ends; he thought also of the role of the environment in cultural matters, and he saw the force of clearing, of burning, of domestication, of manuring. That is what it was, a chain from theology to manuring.

---

and the wealth which accumulated with toil, leading to worldliness, corruption, decline, with the process again being repeated in another ascetic beginning (*ibid.*, pp. 220–224). Workman was a Methodist minister and a very devout Christian. See also the critical and sympathetic introductory preface to this edition by David Knowles, O.S.B. On the cathedrals, see Gimpel, *The Cathedral Builders*, p. 5.

# PART THREE

# Early Modern Times

# Introductory Essay

## 1. INTRODUCTION

There is considerable justification in this history of ideas for discussing the Renaissance and the age of discovery together. During the Renaissance, interest in classical learning far exceeded that shown by learned men of the Middle Ages: the sources were clearer, they came from the classical world more directly, and there were more of them. The pages of Leon Battista Alberti's (1404–1472) *Ten Books on Architecture* are eloquent witnesses of direct study. How thoroughly he has read most of the authors who even indirectly contribute to his work and with what a critical eye he has studied Vitruvius! Along with this interest in the ideas of the ancient world there was, if we are to judge the writings of men like Le Roy and Sebastian Münster, an awareness that something new had appeared in human history, an awareness increased by the results of the age of discovery.

Furthermore, judging by the memoirs of Aeneas Sylvius Piccolomini, Pope Pius II (1405–1464), in the Renaissance it was possible to combine a love of scenery with historical associations, seeing in the fusion the beauties of landscapes altered and unaltered by man. Let us look at these memoirs a little more closely.

There is wildness in his Italian landscapes, but reminders of human activities—the olive grove, the vineyard, the ruin—are never far away. The pleasure of a scenic view is often experienced as part of a pontifical duty, a signatura, a meeting of cardinals. In "the sweet season of early spring" he follows the Mersa upstream to the baths; the "indescribably lovely" country immediately around Siena, "its gently sloping hills planted with cultivated trees and vines or plowed for grain," overlooks "delightful valleys green with pasture land or sown fields, and watered by never-failing streams." Birds "sing most sweetly" in the thick forests growing naturally or planted by man. Human intrusions—country seats and monasteries—are on every Sienese hill. The party ascends the eel-filled Mersa, progressing from an intensively cultivated entrance "thickly dotted with castles and villas" to the wilder country near the baths. There, about the twenty-second hour, it was his custom to go to the meadows, sitting on the greenest and grassiest parts of the river bank to hear embassies and petitioners, his path to the baths strewn by flowers brought by peasants' wives.

He spends a summer at Tivoli in order to avoid sweltering and unhealthful Rome. On the way, a conversation about the Trojan War continues on to the geography of Asia Minor. Later, at his leisure, he wrote a description of Asia, "quoting from Ptolemy, Strabo, Pliny, Q. Curtius, Julius Solinus, Pomponius Mela, and other ancient authors passages that seemed to him relevant to an understanding of the subject." How revealing is this passage—the classical essay composed in cultivated landscapes dotted with ruins! It is like Alberti.

Ruins are all about in Tivoli; Pius thinks the temple on the cliffs above the Aniene may have belonged to Vesta and he notes traces of a once splendid amphitheatre. A part of the Aniene diverted through the city "serves mills, workshops, and fountains and adds greatly to the beauty of the place." About three miles from the city is the magnificent villa of Hadrian which was built like a big town. "Time has marred everything": ivy now covers walls which once were decorated with embroidered tapestries; briers and brambles grow in the proud places of purple-robed tribunes; queens' chambers are the lairs of serpents. Between the villa and the city are beautiful vineyards, olive groves, trees, including the pomegranates, growing among the vines. The huge and towering masses of aqueducts still stand; even as ruins they attest the costliness of their construction.

On the visit to Subiaco, the man-made landscape—the beauty of the vines, the usefulness of river diversion, achievements such as the new vineyards, "heavy with ruddy grapes which had been quarried out of the rock"—again attracts his attention. There is in Viterbo a commingling of city ("there is hardly a house without its spring or its garden") and countryside. "Almost every day at dawn he would go out into the country to enjoy the sweet air before it grew hot and to gaze on the green crops and the blossoming flax, then most lovely to see with its sky-blue color." Of Mt. Amiata in the Sienese territory he wrote that it is "clothed to the very summit with forests," the upper part, often cloud-capped, is in beech, below the beech are the chestnuts, and below them the oaks and cork trees, the lowest slopes being in vines, cultivated trees, tilled fields and meadows. It reminds one of Lucretius's description which has already been quoted. (V, 1370–1378; see p. 140).

The landscape is redolent of the human past. He visits Lake Nemi via the Appian Way whose pavement is still visible. "The road was in many places more beautiful than at the height of the Roman Empire since it was shaded on the sides and overhead by leafy filbert trees which were at their greenest and most flourishing in that month of May. Nature who is superior to any art has made the road most delightful."

In this work there are hints of what is to come in greater volume in the following centuries: aesthetic appreciation of nature, the evocative power of landscape, historical associations, ruins whose present aspect, far different from that of their efflorescence, assume a role *as ruins*, creating a different kind of man-made beauty. Most striking of all is Mt. Amiata; nature and art are alive on the mountainside.[1]

These ideas came out of the Mediterranean past; others came from the age of discovery. Although it is not my purpose here to review the well-known consequences of that age, it might be well to say something about the intellectual resources which men could use in interpreting the findings made available to them by the travels and the voyages. One of the well-worn themes of European and world history is the expansion of the intellectual horizons made possible by the age of discovery and especially by the voyages of Columbus. We need not elaborate on this theme except to say that the broadening and deepening of the intellectual life of mankind as a result of the age of discovery came about not quickly but slowly and that our most sensitive accounts and appreciations (Giovanni Botero and Father Lafitau, for example) come long after the age of discovery. It is equally important to recognize that men did not greet with empty minds the age of discovery and the questions it raised regarding the relationships of man to nature. The ideas whose history we have been discussing could still do yeoman service.

## 2. The Age of Discovery

The idea of a designed earth, as we shall see, was a commonplace of Renaissance thought, embodying, as did the conceptions of the medieval theologians, both the classical concepts and those derived from the Old Testament. What

---

[1] Although it is an abridgment, the references here are to *Memoirs of a Renaissance Pope. The Commentaries of Pius II*, trans. by Florence A. Gragg and edited with an intro. by Leona C. Gabel, because of its far greater accessibility. The unabridged trans.

greater proof of the wisdom, the power, and the creativity of God, then, could one ask for than these unexpected tidings from the New Lands? The lushness of the vegetation, the great expanses of the wet tropics, the sight of peoples living in a manner which demanded immediate answers to questions regarding human origins and the migrations not only of man but of domestic animals (the latter in fact a more difficult problem than the former), were but a few of the observations that evoked wonderment. The tales of the voyagers far surpassed in extravagant description anything the theologians and the philosophers had written on the evidences of the existence of God as seen in the works of creation. The world was larger, more full of wonders, and much more of it was habitable than had been thought. "I kept a diary of noteworthy things," said Amerigo Vespucci, "that if sometime I am granted leisure I may bring together these singular and wonderful things and write a book of geography or cosmography, that my memory may live with posterity and that the immense work of Almighty God, partly unknown to the ancients, but known to us, may be understood."[2]

The discovery of the existence of the antipodes, of climates and environments different from the dry deserts, the Mediterranean, and northwestern Europe reinforced ideas of the God-given fullness, richness, and variety of nature. And secular ideas of climatic and environmental influence could be equally serviceable. While it is true that in the late seventeenth and early eighteenth centuries men began to realize that a reading of history and of the reports from the voyages and travels often cast doubt on climatic explanations, it is nevertheless true that they remained favorite explanations, if not for cultural differences, at least for cultural behavior. If one knew nothing of tropical diseases or their causes, if one's knowledge of the daily life and physical activities of primitive peoples was of a very superficial sort, consisting of elementary observations of physical characteristics and subjective appraisals of character, what was more logical than to interpret the spectacle of sleepy natives lying in the shade in the hot warm climates as creatures held in thralldom by their climate? The age-old ideas of environmental influence, far from being discredited, actually increased in effectiveness—not only in the voyages to the New World but in the travels through Eurasia and in the reports about Persia and China.

Even the idea of man as a modifier of his environment acquired a dramatic character in the new lands. Men could see with their own eyes the changes—some of them temporary it is true—that they could make with fire and clearing in what many considered virgin lands unchanged since the creation. They

---

by Gragg and Gabel is in *Smith College Studies in History*, Vols. 22, 25, 30, 35, and 43. The Siena country, pp. 154–155; Asia Minor, pp. 190–191; Tivoli, pp. 193–194; Subiaco, p. 213; Viterbo, p. 261; Mt. Amiata, p. 277; Appian Way, p. 317.

[2] Amerigo Vespucci, *Mundus Novus, Letter to Lorenzo Pietro di Medici*, trans. by George N. Northrup, p. 12.

could apply experiences and theories which had emerged in scattered localities in Europe regarding the effects of clearing and drainage. Later on, especially in the eighteenth century, the literature on man's changes in the New World environment began to grow, and men could realize both their power to change the earth and the value of apparently primeval landscapes as outside laboratories for the pursuit of nature's secrets. In a *Relación* of Diego de Esquivel (November 1, 1579) on the Indians of the province of Chinantla, there is a remarkable passage about health and clearing and the drying of the land in the New World. The author contrasts the present with the past conditions of the Indians, the theme being that their populations have declined and thus also their ability to control the growth of swamps and jungles and forests:

> They live less long and have more illness than formerly because the country was then more thickly populated with Indians who cultivated and tilled the land, and cleared the jungle. At the present time there are great jungles and forests which make all the region wild, swampy and unhealthy. The Indians being [now] so few, and scattered over more than fifty leagues of territory, and the region being damp and rainy since it rains eight months in the year, and they are not able to clear the ground so that the winds play over it and dry it as of old.[3]

There was a quickening of interest in things both human and divine as new questions were asked about the peoples of the world. It was realized early after the discoveries that revised interpretations of the history of the human race were now required. New chapters in the population history of mankind since the days of Noah and his sons had to be written to bring the customs and the characteristics of the newly found peoples within the protective cover of the divine design; to account for the differences (perhaps through climatic explanations) between these people and the more familiar types of Europe, western Asia and North Africa; to explain how, through the manipulation of their environment, they were able to live and clothe themselves. Inquiries would have to be made regarding their innate inventiveness. Was it the product of human intelligence and local circumstances (what was later known as the psychic unity of mankind) that enabled men everywhere independently to put nature to their own uses?

On June 4, 1537, Paul III issued the bull, *Sublimis Deus*, directed to all Christendom (*universis Christi fidelibus*), declaring that God in his love for the human race created men that they might participate in the good enjoyed by other creatures, that He had endowed them further with the capacity to

---

[3] Diego de Esquivel, "Relación de Chinantla," in Francisco Del Paso y Troncoso, ed., *Papeles de Nueva España*, 2nd. Ser., Vol. 4 (Madrid, 1905), pp. 58–68, passage on p. 63. Translated into English (from which the quotation is taken) and included as an appendix to Publication 24 of the Instituto Panamericano de Geografía y Historia, Bernard Bevan, *The Chinantec and Their Habitat*, Mexico (?), 1938, p. 139.

attain the Supreme Good, to behold it face to face. Since man was created in order to enjoy eternal life and happiness—but only through faith in Jesus Christ—he must also possess the nature and faculties enabling him to embrace that faith. "Nor is it credible that any one should possess so little understanding as to desire the faith and yet be destitute of the most necessary faculty to enable him to receive it." Quoting Christ's words, "Go ye and teach all nations," Paul further declared that Jesus had made no exceptions, "for all are capable of receiving the doctrines of the faith." (*Omnes dixit, absque omni deletu, cum omnes fidei disciplinae capaces existant.*) Basing the bull on the text, *Euntes docete gentes,* Paul said that the Indians of the West and South "and other people of whom We have recent knowledge," should not be treated as dumb brutes, created for our service and assuming them to be incapable of conversion. Enslaving them cannot be justified. The Indians are truly men, capable of understanding the faith which, according to our information, Paul continued, they wish to receive. (*Attendentes Indos ipsos, ut potè veros homines, non solum Christianae Fidei capaces existere, sed ut nobis innotuit, ad fidem ipsam promptissimè currere.*) Neither the Indians nor any other peoples later discovered by Christians are to be deprived of their liberty or their property, even though they live outside the faith; any enslavement is null and void. Twenty-five years after the *Laws of Burgos* (1512), the sustained denunciations of slavery by Bartolomé de las Casas, Bernadino de Minaya, and Julian Garcés, and their affirmations that Indians were human beings, finally secured the *Sublimis Deus* of Paul III. Even it did not put an end to the notion that the Indians, on a low scale of savagery, were worthy of nothing better than serving their Christian masters.[4]

It is difficult to generalize about the opinions held of primitive peoples by observers immediately after the age of discovery. It is true that many were dismissed as wild, naked, and ferocious barbarians or cannibals.[5] It has been said that conceptions of the native peoples progressed from the early period when they were regarded as barbarians to the time when they were studied as primitives.[6] Certainly there is a growing sophistication in observation from

[4] The Latin text and an Engl. trans. of the bull, *Sublimis Deus,* is in MacNutt, *Bartholomew de las Casas,* pp. 427–431. On Las Casas' activity, see pp. 182–199. See also Lewis Hanke, "Pope Paul III and the American Indians," *Harvard Theolog. Rev.,* Vol. 30 (1937), pp. 65–102, and esp. pp. 67–74 on Spanish attitudes toward the Indians, on De Minaya, and Bishop Garcés; pp. 94–95 on Las Casas and the bull. Hanke thinks Paul III does not deserve the praise usually given him as a friend and protector of the Indian; no pope, he argues, in view of the Catholic faith and of canon law, could have refused to issue the bull. See also the discussion in Ludwig Freiherrn von Pastor, *Geschichte der Päpste seit dem Ausgang des Mittelalters,* Vol. 5, *Geschichte Papst Pauls III,* 13th ed., pp. 719–721; Engl. trans., *History of the Popes,* ed. by Kerr, Vol. 12, pp. 518–520.

[5] Mühlmann, *Methodik der Völkerkunde,* pp. 18–19.

[6] Plischke, Hans, *Von den Barbaren zu den Primitiven. Die Naturvölker durch die Jahrhunderte.*

the sixteenth to the nineteenth century, but many of the early descriptions, Acosta's for example, do not give the impression that the authors believe they are dealing with barbarians and cannibals. Although it is not possible here to give an account of the writings about the peoples of the newly discovered lands and the attitudes toward them held by their conquerors, two common ones were (1) that they were addicted to idleness and vice, characteristics which could be corrected by conversion and acceptance of the Christian faith and by living close to the Spanish, from whom they could learn the acceptable customs, and (2) that although they were creatures of God they had been under the control of the Devil, and that it was now part of God's design, through missionary activity leading to conversion, to bring all the newly discovered peoples under the Christian faith. The *Laws of Burgos* illustrate many of these points well. They reveal the fear of idleness, the desire for conversion of the heathen, a recognition of their characteristics as peoples in their own right and of the nature of cultural contact and imitation, even an acknowledgment of the need to respect Indian customs.[7]

Father Lafitau (1670–1740), the French Jesuit missionary to the Iroquois who made the first extensive study of the ethnology of the Indians using the comparative method, makes some interesting comments on the works of his predecessors, and in doing so epitomizes the conventional attitudes toward the people of the New World. He criticized those who thought these people lacked any sentiment of religion, knowledge of the divine, laws, or government, who thought that their only human characteristic was their form. Even missionaries and other men of good will, he said, had circulated inaccurate and false opinions like these.

Even though he is writing late—the first volume of *Moeurs des Sauvages Ameriquains, Comparées aux Moeurs des Premiers Temps* appeared in 1724— he expresses the orthodox Catholic attitude to the New World and its peoples. The age of discovery, he said, was not the chance discovery it might seem; on the contrary, it had been reserved by God among the treasures of his providence in order to enlighten, with the light of the faith, the multitudes held in slavery by the Demon, multitudes shrouded in the darkness of error, in the shadow of death, plunged in all those horrors which created brutal ferocity and all the errors of idolatry. So surprising indeed was their appearance, even to the learned, Lafitau continues, that the first questions asked about them were whether they were of the race of Adam, and if they were the issue of our first parents—our faith does not permit us to doubt it—at what time, how, and whence had they come? Very early, therefore, the problem of diffusion, of migrations and migratory routes, became of importance in reconciling the new discoveries with the biblical accounts of the creation, the Deluge, of the

[7] Simpson, *The Laws of Burgos of 1512–1513*.

multiplication of the descendants of Noah, of God's grace and care for the world, even if the persistence of the Devil's hegemony to such a late date in the New World went unexplained.[8]

Many men of the time were well aware of the significance of the age of discovery both in overthrowing older opinions and in broadening men's horizons. It is a New World, said Amerigo Vespucci, because the ancients had no knowledge of it; the old ideas that there was no land to the south of the equator, or if there was, that it was uninhabitable, have been proved false— "for in those southern parts I have found a continent more densely peopled and abounding in animals than our Europe or Asia or Africa, and in addition, a climate milder and more delightful than any other region known to us. . . ."[9] Similar expressions appear in the comedy by Lope de Vega, *El Nuevo Mundo Descubierto por Cristóbal Colón* (early seventeenth century), in which Columbus, cast in the role of a self-conscious discoverer of the New World, rebuts the classical notion of the uninhabitability of the torrid zones. If people can live in cold Scythia, they can live in a burning climate as well. He is going to look for the people in the antipodes. Why should there not be people who stand opposite us on the other side of the earth? Do not people known to us live six months of the year in night and is not Norway a cold country?[10] These comments, of which Lope de Vega's are but one example, are indicative of the awareness of the corrections needed in the supposed distribution of earthly environments, concerned chiefly with the simple questions of latitude and climate, and the antipodes.

Francisco Lopez de Gómara likewise is harsh on the geographical theories of the ancients which the experience of modern voyagers had now refuted. He surveys classical ideas about the plurality of worlds and finds them unfounded. The earth is round, not flat; not only is it habitable, it is inhabited. His critical historical discussion of climatic zones reveals a wide acquaintance with classical thought. He points out the adaptability of man to climatic extremes, for man is made of the earth, and God had commanded Adam and Eve to increase, multiply, and exert their dominion over it. In the Scriptures, he finds evidence that the existence of the New World was known. Reconciling the new discoveries and observations of the widespread distribution of man with the Bible is another example of the resiliency of old ideas in the presence of new facts. Noteworthy too are his short histories of thought concerning the antipodes and the habitability of the tropics. Even more striking are the noble opening lines of his great work: the beauty and diversity of the world are now laid open to intelligent men to study and to understand its marvels. "Es el mundo tan grande y hermoso, y tiene tanta diversidad de cosas tan diferentes unas de otras, que pone admiración á quien bien lo piensa

---

[8] *Moeurs des Sauvages Ameriquains*, Vol. I, pp. 27–29.
[9] Amerigo Vespucci, *op. cit.* (see n. 1 above), p. 1.
[10] Act I, Scenes 1, 2, 7, 10. Act III, Scene 11.

y contempla. Pocos hombres hay, si ya no viven como brutos animales, que no se pongan alguna vez á considerar sus maravillas, porque natural es á cada uno el deseo de saber."[11]

### 3. SEBASTIAN MÜNSTER

Often we obtain a truer sense of prevailing ideas and their relationships to one another if we examine selected works as a whole, especially if they are published sufficiently after an era such as the age of discovery to allow for maturation of theories and observations and their fusion with the old. I have chosen three such men, Sebastian Münster, Joseph de Acosta, and Giovanni Botero. All of them were involved in the new thought which came as a response to the new discoveries; all of them wrote with an awareness of European ideas, of their importance in interpreting the new knowledge, and of the revisions they themselves now must undergo.

Sebastian Münster, born in 1489 at Nieder-Ingelheim (between Mainz and Bingen), became a Franciscan monk (a Minorite) in 1505. In 1529, he was converted to the Protestantism of the Swiss Reformed faith. He was an Hebraist, a cartographer, an editor of classical works (Pomponius Mela and Solinus), but he is remembered as a cosmographer whose fame rests on the *Cosmographey*, the most impressive of the early compendia of geography published after the voyages of discovery. This world-famous book, first published in 1544, was the culmination of eighteen years of work with the help of 120 scholars, artists, and persons of rank. The editions which followed in 1545, 1546, 1548, were changed very little, but that of 1550 contained many corrections and supplements and included many fine woodcuts of towns and cities, and maps which added luster to the work's fame. The book, with the supplements added after Münster's death from the plague in Basel in 1552, was very influential in Germany, indeed in many other parts of Europe for over a century.[12]

This exceedingly long work is divided into six books of uneven length and

[11] Francisco Lopez de Gómara, *Historia General de las Indias*, in *Biblioteca Autores Españoles*, Vol. 22 (Vol. I of 2 vols. in *Historiados Primitivos de Indias*).

[12] Viktor Hantzsch, "Sebastian Münster. Leben, Werk, Wissenschaftliche Bedeutung," in *Abhandlungen der königl. Sächsischen Gesellschaft der Wissenschaften* (Philhist. Kl. ), Vol. 18 (1898), No. 3. Hantzsch mentions the superiority of the Wallis (Valais) description and the poverty of the New World materials. Two essays by Margaret Hodgen have captured the flavor of this period: "Sebastian Muenster (1489–1552): A Sixteenth-Century Ethnographer," *Osiris*, Vol. 11 (1954), pp. 504–529; and "Johann Boemus (fl. 1500): An Early Anthropologist," *American Anthropologist*, Vol. 55 (1953), pp. 284–294. See also Miss Hodgen's masterly chapters v–vii on collections of customs; the ark of Noah and the problem of cultural diversity; diffusion, degeneration, and environmentalism, in *Early Anthropology in the Sixteenth and Seventeenth Centuries*. Also of great interest is Rowe's *Ethnography and Ethnology in the Sixteenth Century*. See also generally, Gallois, *Les Géographes Allemands de la Renaissance*; and François de Dainville, *La Géographie des Humanistes*, Paris, 1940, esp. pp. 85–87.

quality. Book I is a general outline of physical and mathematical geography concluding with an account, based on the Bible, of the dispersion of the human race after the Flood. Book II, probably the best, is on southern and western Europe; it is notable, as Hantsch says, for its sharp and lively delineations of customs and folk character, with observations about land productivity, soil fertility, and material culture.[13] Book III, on Germany, is the longest; Book IV is on northern and eastern Europe, Book V, on Asia and the New Islands (the New World), and Book VI, on Africa.

The most significant general observation to be made about this cosmography, first published over fifty years after Columbus's first voyage, is that Book V on Asia and the New World is poor. In it are cuts showing a dog-headed man, a headless man with his face in his chest, Siamese twins, a one-legged man with a giant foot, the same cut being reproduced in Book VI on Africa. Münster mentions briefly the voyages of Columbus and of Vespucci, adds a notice or two describing the bodily constitution and way of life of the Indians, even though a literature now existed in German on the voyages. Münster himself had helped his friend Grynaeus on the *Novus orbis*, which contained Columbus's first three voyages, those of Pinzon, Vespucci, the travels of Marco Polo and his successors.[14] He ignores the conquest of Mexico and Peru, which had attracted universal attention at the time, the Welsers' colonization of Venezuela (Charles V had granted the Santa Ana de Coro to the rich Augsburg banking firm in 1527 and it soon sent out colonists to the valley of the Orinoco), German fortune-hunters in the New World, the Fugger colonial undertakings in Chile and the South Seas, and flourishing settlements of German traders in Brazil. In editions published after his death, the literature on America and the collections of voyages made by the Frankfurt copper-engraver Theodor de Bry and the Nürnberg publisher Levinus Hulsius, "inexhaustible sources of knowledge of the east and west Indies," seem to have gone completely unnoticed by the editors.[15]

What was Münster's philosophy of geography, his conception of its meaning and significance? To him, knowledge of geography meant deeper learning and understanding of practical affairs and of religious matters.

Geography, he thinks, is important to the historian. Münster himself makes constant if conventional use of historical materials. Strabo was his model and he was flattered when friends referred to him as the German Strabo.[16] Cosmography, the description of the world and everything that is in it, opens up

---

[13] Hantzsch, *op. cit.*, p. 52.

[14] *Novus orbis* was issued in separate editions at Basel and Paris in 1532. Grynaeus wrote the preface, but the compilation was made by John Huttich, Grynaeus subsequently revising it. See Justin Winsor's introduction to Vol. I, of *Narrative and Critical History of America*, xxiv–xxvii, also with portraits of Grynaeus and Münster.

[15] Hantzsch, *op. cit.*, pp. 56, 68.

[16] *Ibid.*, p. 59.

the hidden secrets of Holy Writ and reveals the forces of a wise and judicious Nature. One learns of new customs, and the path of exploration leads to knowledge of new animals, trees, plants.

Münster shows a remarkable awareness of environmental change as being part of cultural history. Patriotic Germans like him, who knew German history well, were struck by the contrast between the Germany depicted by Strabo and Ptolemy and that of their own times which, he says, is as cultivated as Gaul or Italy. He contrasts the German improvement throughout time with the deterioration in the environment of the Holy Land but without further explication.

In his outline of cultural history, Münster says that as civilization advances, clearing and draining go on, towns are born, castles rise on the hills. Earthworks and dams control the water. Man finishes the creation. Gradually by cultivation, with settlements, castles, villages, fields, meadows, vineyards, and the like, the earth has been so changed from its original state that it can now be called another earth.

Even though he failed badly to give his eager readers riches from the voyages and travels to the New World, he was not unaware of their implications, for they also were part of the design. We can gaze with wonderment at the creation, for each land is given something not found in the other. The Creator has so marvelously apportioned his gifts in order that men can learn that they and their land always need one another.[17]

Aside from this conventional theology, Münster's geography is descriptive, not theoretical. He is struck by the advantage of Europe's position. Following the ancient division of the Old World into three regions separated by the Don, the Mediterranean, and the Nile, Münster comments that Europe is the smallest, but it is fertile, it has a temperate climate for fruits, grapes, and many kinds of trees. It is inferior to none and can be compared with the best. It is built up with wonderfully attractive cities, castles, markets, and villages, and the strength of its peoples is far superior to those of Africa and of Asia.[18] He speaks too of the broadening of man's geographic horizon since antiquity with the colonization of western Europe, and now with the new discoveries; this vision is suffused, however, with the melancholy air of the transitoriness of things supported by Solomon's observations about novelty.

It is generally agreed that the best description in the work is that of Wallis (Valais); it is based on the work of Johannes Kalbermatter, a provincial governor under Bishop Hadrian of Sion, and can stand comparison with a modern description. This famous canton of Switzerland is now known mainly for its resorts and skiing, the Alpine passes, the Matterhorn and Zermatt, with its two cities on the Rhone, Martigny (German *Martinach*) and Sion (German

---

[17] The above paragraphs are based on *Cosmographey*, "Vorrede."
[18] *Ibid.*, Bk. I, chap. 16; Hantzsch, *op. cit.*, p. 51.

*Sitten*). The valleys and the alps (the alpine meadows), the wild animals, including bears and boars, the summer pasturing of cows, sheep, goats, are briefly mentioned. Nothing is lacking in this enclosed land with its grain, fruit, meat, fish, and wines; there are kind words for the exceptional quality of the red wine of Sion and Sierre (German *Siders*), so black one can write with it, more words on the mountain pastures, goat cheese, butter, the cattle sold in Italy, the fish in the rivers. Medicinal herbs and roots (the prevalence of goiter and its possible causes), turpentine, ores and mining, hot baths, round out this stocktaking without statistics.[19]

In this sixteenth century description, one of the most beautiful and charming landscapes of Europe comes to life. It is longer, more complete, and more accurate than is the description of the whole New World.

## 4. JOSÉ DE ACOSTA

Since we know from the Scriptures, says Acosta, that all men descended from the first man, how then did men reach America and by what means? Acosta eliminates at once a second ark and intervention by an angel; the peopling of the New World came about through natural causes according to the rule of reason. He then considers the possibility of coming by sea and whether such a voyage might be purposeful or accidental. We must not think, he says, that the art of sailing is confined to us; these early people may, like us, have possessed navigation and pilots. Solomon had taken masters and pilots from Tyre and Sidon. Acosta, however, is not of the opinion that such a voyage was purposeful, mainly because these early people lacked the lodestone and the compass, and it would be impossible to cross the Atlantic without the latter. The ancients navigated, he says, by the sun, moon, stars, by observing landmarks and differences between lands. For these reasons, he thinks, the discovery, if it was by sea, was by chance (most likely being blown by the winds), for such accidental discoveries happen in our time. Furthermore, much invention and discovery have been accidental rather than the result of the industry of man, though Acosta adds that discovery is accidental only in relation to man, for such discoveries come about only through the Creator's will.

But Acosta rejects this possibility of accidental discovery by sea, because of the difficulty in explaining how animals reached the New World, especially the carnivores, foxes, tigers, lions, which are of no profit to man. An occasional animal might be transported, but the presence of larger predators causes Acosta to conclude that the peopling of America by both man and beast took place by land; somewhere—in the north or in the south—there is either a joining of the New World with the Old or a narrow body of water

[19] Bk. III, chap. 43, "Von Fruchtbarkeit des Lands Wallis."

separating them. The absence of beasts on islands far enough offshore to prevent them from swimming to the mainland convinces him further that a land passage was the only plausible explanation for the movement of life from one continent to another. Tigers, bears, boars, and foxes are found on the mainland but not in Cuba, Hispaniola, Jamaica, Margarita, or Dominica, the only beasts found on these islands being those introduced by the Spaniards.[20]

From the sixteenth to the middle of the nineteenth century, many believed that the native Americans were of the stock of the lost tribes of Israel. Many of the early priests, including Las Casas, believed it; Acosta did not.[21] Questions about the animals of the New World, Acosta said, had long perplexed him. Men might carry a hen with them from place to place even as they do today. It is more difficult to account for the origin of beasts found now in the Indies but not in Europe. If they were created in the New World, there was no need for Noah's ark. Neither was there any need to save birds and beasts if they were to be created a second time in the New World, and if this later creation took place, it could not then be said that the world was made and finished in six days. If Noah preserved all the beasts, it follows that even if they are not now found in the Old World, they came from there. Why should none of their kind remain in the Old World when they are found in the New as travelers and as strangers? If the alpaca, guanaco, and the sheep of Peru are found in no other place in the world, who carried them here? Why are they here when there is no trace of them elsewhere? If they have not come from elsewhere, were they created in the New World? Perhaps God has made a new creation of beasts? "¿Por ventura hizo formaron Dios nueva formacion [sic] de animales?" What applies to the alpacas and the guanaco applies also to a thousand kinds of birds and beasts of the forest known neither to us nor to the Romans or Greeks. Acosta finally concludes that all animals indeed did come from the ark, that they dispersed in environments proper to them, that they died out in other places, but survived in the New World. This is not an uncommon occurrence, he adds, there being examples from many nations in Asia, Europe, and Africa. The elephant, he

[20] Acosta, *Historia de las Indias*, Bk I, chap. 16, 19, 20.
[21] See *The Apocrypha*, trans. by Goodspeed, "The Second Book of Esdras," xiii, 39–47. In 1650 Thomas Thorowgood published the first discussion in English, *Jewes in America, or, Probabilities that the Americans are of that Race*. Leading New England divines of the seventeenth century accepted the theory. In 1768 Charles Beatty found traces of the lost tribes among the Delawares repeating the Indian story that they long ago sold "the same sacred book to the whites with which the missionaries in the end aimed to make them acquainted." In the early nineteenth century there was interest in similarities between native languages and Hebrew, and between the customs of the Indians and the ancient Hebrews. Here I wish to do no more than call attention to this diffusionist literature. These notes are based on Winsor, "Pre-Columbian Explorations," being chap. 2 of Vol. I of Winsor, ed., *Narrative and Critical History of America*, pp. 115–117, with extensive bibliographical references. See also Acosta, *op. cit.*, Bk. I, chap. 23.

says, is found only in the East Indies but he too came out of the ark as did the alpaca and the guanaco.[22]

Thus very early the problem of the diffusion of man and the beasts was closely tied up with Christian theology. The diffusion of man meant the diffusion of his customs. Acosta's observations show how theories of diffusion and independent invention and even nineteenth and twentieth century controversies about the Old World origins of New World civilizations could come into being.

### 5. GIOVANNI BOTERO

Giovanni Botero, a Jesuit-trained scholar writing during the Counter-Reformation, published three major works, *Greatness of Cities* (1588), *Reason of State* (1589), and *Relazioni Universali*, the first part of which appeared in 1591. The *Greatness of Cities*, the most interesting and charming of these works, also has some of the most stimulating ideas; the *Reason of State*, written, its author says, to counteract the influence of Machiavelli, belongs to a genre of political treatises—often addressed to a ruler—of which Plato's *Laws*, St. Thomas's *On Kingship*, Dante's *On Monarchy*, and Machiavelli's *Prince* were the outstanding examples up to that time. The *Relazioni* is a compendium of geographical facts of much less theoretical interest.

Botero says that a prince must excel in eloquence in order to properly rule his subjects, but it cannot be "subtle or convincing or impressive" without knowing the works of nature which underlie the works of man.

> Nothing awakens the intellect, illumines the judgment and rouses the mind to great things more than a knowledge of the disposition of the world, of the order of nature, the motions of the heavens, the qualities of simple and compound bodies, of the generation and corruption of matter, the essence of the spirit and its powers, the properties of herbs, plants, stones and minerals, of the behaviour and sensations of animals and the production of imperfectly blended substances: rain, mist, hail, thunder, snow, meteorites, rainbows, the origin of springs, rivers, lakes, winds, earthquakes, and the ebb and flow of the sea.[23]

If this seems much to expect of a prince, Botero has admirable shortcuts at hand, for various kinds of learned men can surround him, teaching him through edifying conversation.

In order to rule well, a prince must understand his subjects. A man's nature, characteristics, and temperament are formed by geographical situation, age, fortune, and education; many have written on education, and Aristotle has written on age and fortune. Botero therefore will confine himself to geographical situation.

---

[22] Acosta, Bk. IV, chap. 36.
[23] *Reason of State*, Bk. II, chap. 2.

What follows is a restatement of the case for the superior influences of temperate climates; in the universe as in everything the ideal lies between the two extremes. Botero makes the usual sweeping generalizations that are characteristic of these echoes of classical antiquity. The classical ideas are there, but the regions to which they are applied have changed. For example, peoples of the north (excluding those of the extreme north) are bold but lack cunning; they are physically vigorous, simple and straightforward, but frequently they are under the influence of Bacchus. The northern peoples now live in Transylvania, Poland, Denmark, Sweden. The southerners, as one would expect, have the opposite characteristics: they are cunning but lack boldness, they are thin and dry, and given to the influences of Venus. The peoples of the temperate lands combine the best qualities of each.

More interesting is Botero's analysis of religion and climate. As a Jesuit writer during the Counter-Reformation he naturally had opinions on the non-Christian religions and on the new schisms within the Christian Church created by the Reformation. The southerners, as they appear in his vague language, are largely the peoples of the non-Christian world, in which he includes India, and the "dominion of the Saracens." "Southerners are much given to speculation and are greatly influenced by religion and superstition: astrology and magic originated among them, and priests, gymnosophists, brahmins and wise men have been held in esteem by them." After some unflattering remarks about the Koran, Botero adds, "It is also remarkable that the most subtle and speculative of the heresies which have troubled the Church of God have had their origins in the south; those that are more gross and material have originated in the north." Botero illustrates the statement with specific examples and offers in effect an environmental explanation for the cause of the Reformation. The northerners

> deny the authority of the Vicar of Christ because being stout of heart they are immoderate lovers of liberty; and because their temporal rule, being either republican or monarchical, is decided by their own will and choice, they desire in the same way to choose their own form of spiritual government. The captains and soldiers of the northern countries rely upon force rather than skill in war, and in disputes with Catholics their representatives trust to strong words rather than argument.

Botero's other environmental ideas are of interest only because they illustrate the continuity of an old tradition. The correlations are applied to the northern hemisphere, but he says they could be applied equally to those in the southern. We have seen that in the classical period it was realized that latitudinal differences alone were not considered adequate explanations of differences among peoples. Longitudinal, terrain, and meteorological differences also existed. Botero continues in this tradition by making distinctions between peoples who live in the east (they are easygoing and malleable in character) and in the west (they are proud and reserved), in windswept lands (they are restless and turbulent), in quiet restful places (they are tranquil and mild too), in mountains (they are wild and proud), in valleys (they are soft and effeminate), in barren lands (they are industrious and diligent), in fertile lands (they are idle and refined), in maritime lands (they are alert, sagacious, and prosperous in business), in the interior lands (they are sincere, loyal, easily contented).[24]

Botero's use of environmental ideas illustrates their resiliency and adaptability to new historical circumstances; he is also concerned, however, with potential human achievement, with cultural contact, with population growth and its relation to cities, disease, and resources. In the nineteenth century, these topics probably would have been discussed together under a heading like the reciprocal influences of man and the environment. In Botero's work they are scattered and the expositor gives them their unity and coherence. It is wrong, however, to emphasize the environmental aspect of this thought without discussing the other and more vigorous ideas which bear the stamp of personal observation, thought, and feeling.

Botero discusses the evil influences coming from the intrusion of the "soft ways" of Asia into Greece and their subsequent catastrophic results on Rome, and the fate of the kingdom of Portugal "whose downfall was brought about not by the Moors but by the soft ways of the Indies." These are more than sermons on temperance; they assert that one people can be be influenced by direct or indirect contact with another, and give an entirely different impression than do the simple climatic correlations of heat with cunning and cold with boldness. Later Botero paraphrases inexactly Polybius's idea (without mentioning him) of the effects of music in changing a people whose original condition was caused by climate.[25]

Botero also makes interesting observations about population and environment. He advocates a large population, but stresses the advantage to a country of having a dense one as well. Italy and France have their own mines of gold and silver, but they possess more of these metals than any other European country because their dense populations attract money, through trade and commerce, from all parts of the earth. "Where there are many people, the land must be well cultivated, and the land provides the foodstuffs necessary for life, and the raw materials for industry." If Spain is a barren land, its condition is owing to the sparseness of its inhabitants; neither the nature and quality of the soil nor the air itself has changed; it is the decrease in the number of the inhabitants and the decline in the cultivation of the land, comments which are followed by an analysis of the historical reasons for the decline in the population.[26]

Botero asks whether the fertility of the soil or the industry of man is the

[24] *Ibid.*, chap. 5.
[25] *Ibid.*, chap. 17; Bk. V, chap. 4.
[26] *Ibid.*, Bk. VII, chap. 12.

more important to make a state great and populous and unhesitatingly answers that it is human industry: "Firstly, the products of the manual skill of man are more in number and of greater worth than the produce of nature, for nature provides the material and the object but the infinite variations of form are the result of the ingenuity and skill of man."[27]

Botero's description of the divine plan as manifested on earth is illustrated in his warmed-over version of the traditional contrasts between land and water. God created water not only because it was a "necessary element to the perfection of nature, but more than so, for a most ready means to conduct and bring goods from one country to another." The Creator, in his geographic plan, distributed his blessings throughout the earth in order that men would have need of one another and that "there might grow a community, and from a community love and from love an unity between us."[28]

A prince must not hesitate to change the physical nature of his country. Warmth and dampness are indispensable to success in agriculture; therefore, "the prince must also contrive to assist nature by leading rivers or lakes through his country." He praises Milanese governors for the canals drawing off the waters of the Ticino and the Adda. A prince "must keep alive and flourishing whatever serves to make his country fertile and productive of all that it can provide." Neither should he hesitate to import seeds, trees, animals, from other countries. Land should not be converted to parks, as in England, if the people must bear a shortage of grain to have them. The practical means of accomplishing these noble public works are less enchanting; Botero thought slaves, galley-slaves, criminals, beggars, strays, and vagabonds might do the labor, but soldiers and ordinary people (as in Switzerland) had engaged in it too. He speaks of the cultivation of the Pontine Marshes and land improvements made by rulers more solicitous of the future of their country than immediate advantage. The raw materials of a country are there to be used, and in Botero's mind human skills create them. "Nature gives a form to the raw materials and human industry imposes upon this natural composition an infinite variety of artificial forms; thus nature is to the craftsman what raw material is to the natural agent."[29]

To Botero, population policy is closely related to the welfare of a state, to the improvement of its lands, and to monogamy. Marriages do not insure the multiplication of the human species, for the young must be cared for. He attacks polygamy among the Turks and the Moors and praises Christian monogamy. Through envy and jealousy "the wives hinder one another's pregnancies, or injure by sorcery the children who have already been born." A father who has children by several wives dilutes his love; he lacks interest in their education or the means to rear them.

---

[27] *Ibid.*, Bk. VIII, chap. 3.
[28] *Greatness of Cities*, Bk. I, chap. 10.
[29] *Reason of State*, Bk. VIII, chaps. 2 and 3.

Plague and disease keep populations stable.

What benefit has Cairo from its multitudinous population, when thousands of them die of plague every seventh year? How does Constantinople benefit from its populousness if every third year the contagion almost deprives the city of its inhabitants? Plague and disease arise in fact from the closeness and discomfort of the dwellings, the filth and dirt of living conditions and lack of care on the part of the government to keep the cities clean and the air purified, and other similar causes. All these things make it difficult to rear children, and although great numbers are born, comparatively few survive or grow to be men of any value.[30]

Botero's discussion of city life, in contrast with the crudities of the traditional environmental correlations in which he himself indulges, shows that he believed the life and character of a people could be shaped by the manner in which they lived. Theseus could easily persuade the rural people living in dispersed villages to join in with Athens because he could show them the advantages of such a union. Like other Christian writers Botero was concerned with the propagation of the faith in the New World; he was therefore interested in the pattern of settlement and in the possibilities of the native peoples living in more densely settled places and closer to the centers of Portuguese culture:

Those people [in Brazil] dwell dispersed here and there in caves and cottages (not to call them houses) made of boughs and leaves of the palm. And forasmuch as this manner of life, to live so dispersedly, causeth these people to remain in that same savage mind of theirs, and roughness of manner and behaviour, and bringeth therewith much difficulty and hindrance to the preaching of the Gospel, to the conversion of the infidels and the instruction of those that travail painfully, to convert them and to bring them to knowledge and civility, the Portuguese and Jesuits have used extreme diligence and care to reduce and draw them into some certain place together more convenient for their purpose, where living in a civil conversation they might more easily be instructed in the Christian faith and governed by the magistrate and ministers of the King. . . .[31]

The argument here is an argument for conversion through imitation brought about by culture contact. More sophisticated, too, than the traditional environmental ideas is Botero's analysis of the reason that people live in cities. Clearly an admirer of the display and magnificence of cities as opposed to rural life, he praises places like Antioch, Damascus, Brusa, Cordova, and Seville, and the practical reasons men have for living in them:

"Men are also drawn to live together in society through the delight and pleasure that either the site of the place or of the art of man doth minister and yield unto them. The site attracts by the freshness of the air, the pleasant view of the valleys, the pleasing shade of the woods, the commodity to hunt, and the abundance of good waters. . . ." Belonging to human art are "the

[30] *Ibid.*, chap. 4.
[31] *Greatness of Cities*, Bk. I, chap. 2.

straight and fair streets of a city, the magnificent and gorgeous buildings," the theaters, races, fountains, and other "wonderful things as delight and feed the eyes of the people with an admiration and wonder at them."[32]

In *Greatness of Cities*, Botero returns to a theme he mentioned in *Reason of State*, that cities "once grown to a greatness increase not onward according to that proportion." Citing Dionysius of Halicarnassus, Botero says that Rome had 3,300 men able to do military service when it was founded by Romulus. By the end of his 37-year reign the number had increased to 47,000. About 150 years later, in the time of Servius Tullius (578–534 B.C.), there were 80,000 men. Gradually the population grew to 450,000. Botero then asks why the population of Rome stopped increasing and why the population of Milan and Venice has remained unchanged for 400 years. He dismisses the explanation that plagues, wars, and famines are the cause, because they were even more severe in former times than they are at present. "For war is now drawn out of the field to the walls, and the mattock and the spade are more used than the sword."

He is not content, without further probing, with the simple explanation that it is the will of God. God so disposes, but He acts through secondary causes in governing nature: "My question is with what means that Eternal Providence maketh little to multiply, and much to stand at a stay and go no further." The answer is that the population of a city, or of the whole earth, will increase to the number permitted by the food supply. Cities increase partly by "the virtue generative of men" and partly out of the "virtue nutritive of the cities." The virtue generative is constant through history; if there were nothing to interfere with it, "the propagation of mankind would increase without end, and the augmentation of cities would be without term. And if it do not increase in infinite I must needs say it proceedeth of the defect of nutriment and sustenance sufficient for it."[33]

These famous passages, which long have had their place in pre-Malthusian theories of population, are based on a different kind of environmental theory —not one involving distinctions among hot, cold, and temperate regions, but a theory of the total environment seen in terms of its capacity to produce food and thus directly to control the population of a single place or of the whole world. This environmental theory, the earth as a limiting factor, in contrast with the older environmental theories used mainly to explain cultural differences, is, I believe, a modern idea. It is true there are hints of it in the Middle Ages, and in antiquity overpopulation was a traditional explanation of the cause of migrations. Botero can easily advance the theory within a religious framework. The numbers of the world's people and the amount of food available to them are determined by the Creator's design, but this design can be discovered by observing regularities and secondary causes, by means

[32] *Ibid.*, chap. 6.
[33] *Ibid.*, Bk. III, chap. 2.

of which one can arrive at more satisfying answers than are forthcoming from simple replies that the balance between population and food supply is an evidence of the wisdom of God.

These three men were quite conscious of the questions concerning man and his environment raised by the age of discovery and by the changing life of Europe. Sebastian Münster is still on the edge of wonderment but he sees vaguely the excitement of old cultures in new environments. Acosta sees clearly the environmental conditions which might govern the diffusion of the human race within the guidelines imposed by Genesis. Botero discusses all the ideas whose history we have been tracing. New uses are found for old environmental theories. New and brighter raiment appears on the divinely planned earth, for the divine tailor had more cloth than anyone suspected. It was being seen too that influences more complex than the physical environment might affect a people. And in Botero the need for a ruler to change the natural order in order to advance civilization is clearly expressed, as is the essentially modern idea that there are environmental limitations upon population growth.

# Chapter 8

# Physico-Theology:
# Deeper Understandings of the Earth
# as a Habitable Planet

### 1. Introduction

Ideas of final causes have flourished with undiminished vigor in modern times, greedily soaking up new proofs from the hitherto unexplored portions of the earth, from new discoveries in astronomy, from the insights into the structure of organic and inorganic matter revealed by the microscope. Bacon's *The Advancement of Learning*, Kant's *Critique of the Teleological Judgment*, and Goethe's views on teleology caused some to pause, but "following in the footsteps of the Creator," by composing treatises on natural theology illustrating design in the plant, insect, animal, and inorganic world, continued unabated, especially among the English, to the time of Lyell and Darwin. One of the most famous of these later productions, the *Natural Theology* of Paley, was far inferior in breadth and perception, with its overburden of utilitarian argument, to the works of Ray and Derham.

For the Renaissance thinkers the chief inspiration of the themes came from Plato's *Timaeus* and Cicero's *De natura deorum*. In Petrarca's long, almost apostolic, tribute to Cicero, even in his affectionate scolding, one sees how impressive to Petrarca were the classical arguments from design so masterfully set forth by Cicero.[1]

Many different men—whether they were Jesuits or not—could exist under the protective shade of the Jesuit text that one seeks God in everything ("Ut Deum in omnibus quaerant"). In 1592 at the Jesuit college of Coimbre the question arose in a treatise on the four elements whether the earth had been created with or without mountains; the answer was that it had been created with mountains because of their usefulness and beauty. Mountains in fact later became a keystone in the teleological arch for an earth designed as a habitation for man; mountains meant rain, rivers, alluvium. Running water—from small rivulets to the great rivers of the earth—presupposed the existence of mountains, for how else could vast quantities of water flow downhill? Mountains forced moisture-laden air from the sea to rise and condense. The particles of the fertile soil of the valleys had been carried down by streams from the mountaintops now gradually growing barren in the process.[2]

## 2. FINAL CAUSES AND THEIR CRITICS

Most of the great names in early modern science did not deny design in nature nor the validity of final causes, but there were differences in the enthusiasm with which these were applied to immediate problems. The Copernican theory had not called the creation into question; the cosmic system was a product of divine design and order.[3] Galileo deftly said that to prohibit the teaching of Copernican astronomy "would be but to censure a hundred passages of holy Scripture which teach us that the glory and greatness of Almighty God are marvelously discerned in all his works and divinely read in the open book of heaven."[4] Kepler, a devoted and mystical believer in the divine harmony and the music of the spheres, pointed out the wisdom shown in the earth's inclination on its axis; it caused the seasons and hence was pertinent to an appraisal of the fitness of the earthly environment. By its daily rotation, the earth was warmed more equably, and by its inclination on its axis —from the point of view of final causes—it became a home well suited to organic

---

[1] Francesco Petrarca, "On His Own Ignorance," trans. Hans Nachod, in *The Renaissance Philosophy of Man*, ed. Cassirer, Kristeller, and Randall, pp. 80–89; on a comparison of Cicero's writings with St. Paul's, p. 85.

[2] Dainville, *op. cit.*, p. 91; on mountains, p. 28.

[3] For example, the prooemium to Bk. I of Copernicus' "De revolutionibus orbium caelestium libri sex," in *Nikolaus Kopernikus Gesamtausgabe* (Munich: Verlag R. Oldenburg, 1949), Vol. 2.

[4] "Letter to Madame Christina of Lorraine," in *Discoveries and Opinions of Galileo*, Trans. Stillman Drake (Anchor Books), p. 196.

life, favoring its wide distribution, by seasonal change, on the earth's surface.[5] Newton had strong teleological beliefs, but he was less enthusiastic about the ecliptic. In his letter of December 10, 1692, he told Bentley, ". . . I see nothing extraordinary in the inclination of the earth's axis for proving a Deity; unless you will urge it as a contrivance for Winter and Summer, and for making the earth habitable towards the poles. . . ." Newton's teleology, however, was grounded in the order, beauty, and motion of the heavens rather than in the order of nature on earth.[6] Boyle's famous treatise on final causes, published after Ray's work, pulled out all the traditional stops, and used the traditional exclamation points: design in the creation as a whole, in its individual parts, in the parts of plants and animals; and the creation in the service of human ends. Leibniz, dedicated defender of final causes, wrote that they awaken better than do efficient causes, admiration for the beauty of divine works.[7] I shall deal at length with his thought in chapter XII. His idea of the preestablished harmony of the cosmos he considered a fresh proof of the existence of God, this kind of harmony being an explanation superior to the artisan analogy. Leibniz wrote eloquently of the chain or scale of being in nature; the progress of mankind, as part of the preestablished harmony, is accompanied by changes in the earth because with the lapse of time mankind cultivates it more, refines it, cares for it.[8]

These great names in science and philosophy kept alive the spirit of teleology and design in nature despite the criticisms that were made of it. The idea of design applied to the earth is but one of the violins in a mighty orchestra, for teleology has been one of the great preoccupations of Western theology, philosophy, and science; eminent men such as Bacon, Spinoza, Descartes, Buffon, La Mettrie, Goethe, and Kant criticized ideas of final causes, but who that has read the controversies over evolution or the letters of Lyell to Darwin would say that these criticisms had found their mark? Bacon had no objection to final causes as such; they were, however, inappropriate to the study of natural history.[9] Descartes too rejected final causes as a tool of inquiry, and many of the seventeenth century natural theologians like Ray criticized him for it. It would be presumptuous to search for final causes and to think that "God could take us into his counsels." Thus he limits himself to regarding God as "the efficient cause of all things." It is not only presumptuous but self-centered of man to deal in final causes, because so many of the natural phenomena of the past and the present are irrelevant to his

---

[5] Kepler, *Epitome astronomiae copernicanae*, Bk. III, Pl. 4 = Kepler's *Gesammelte Werke*, Vol. 7, p. 209.

[6] See Newton's four letters to Bentley, in *Opera quae exstant omnia*, Vol. 4, pp. 429–442. Quotation on p. 433. On Newton's teleology, see Burtt, *The Metaphysical Foundations of Modern Science*, rev. ed. (Anchor Books), pp. 288–290.

[7] Leibniz, *Selections*, ed. Wiener, pp. 132, 318.

[8] *Ibid.*, pp. 192, 221, pp. 354–355.

[9] *De Augmentis Scient.* Bk. 3, chap. 5, *Adv. of Learning* (Everyman ed.), pp. 96–97 where he criticizes Plato, Aristotle, Galen.

experience and to his existence.[10] Spinoza wrote as if the search for final causes was an oafish impertinence, ridiculing the threadbare examples like the eye that was devised for seeing. Thus, "nature has set no end before herself, and that all final causes are nothing but human fictions."

Spinoza's basic objections to final causes are that they are figments of men's minds, that they are based on an analogy derived from the purposiveness of human activity. They are reduced to absurdity by the problem of evil, for do not natural catastrophies kill and maim the good and the bad alike? A wise man wants to understand nature, not to gape at it like a fool. Like Hume and Kant later, he does not know if the parts of nature are really interconnected. He does not attribute to nature beauty or ugliness, order or confusion; these are products of the imagination. The famous maxim that nature does nothing in vain he regards as pure anthropocentrism. "The attempt, however, to show that nature does nothing in vain (that is to say, nothing which is not profitable to man), seems to end in showing that nature, the gods, and man are alike mad."[11]

One sees in the writings of this period a conflict between two views of nature, the mechanical and the organic. In the mechanical, the actions of the individual parts of a whole are explained by known laws, the whole being the sum of the parts and their interaction. In the organic, the whole exists first, perhaps in the mind of an artisan, before the parts; the design of the whole explains the actions and reactions of the parts.[12] The mechanical view, emphasizing secondary causes, eliminated final causes as active guides in investigation, relegating them to theology or private piety. In the seventeenth century writings on natural law, matter, and motion, one frequently reads attacks on Democritus, Epicurus, Lucretius, by partisans of final causes who are, moreover, interested in appropriating to their own uses the new knowledge embodied in natural law. Classical authors are often cited as authorities against the "mechanical ideas," and Plato, Seneca, and Cicero are constantly making depositions. Was nature a system based on law, or providentially designed, or the product of design for a purpose?[13]

If one wishes to understand the earth as a habitable planet, however, it is necessary to understand it as a whole. The fundamental physical causes govern its inclination on the axis, the waves and currents of the winds, the relief. Furthermore, much of the matter on earth is living, and doctrines of final causes have always been more convincing and have lasted longer in the life sciences primarily because life cycles in the living world lend credence to the belief that the end governs the conception, birth, and life stages of an individual existence.

---

[10] *Principles of Philosophy*, Pt. 1, Prin. 28; Pt. 3, Prin. 3.

[11] Spinoza, *Ethica*, Pt. I, Appendix following Prop. 36; and *Correspondence of Spinoza*, trans. A. Wolf, Letter 32, to Henry Oldenburg.

[12] Fulton, *Nature and God*, p. 134.

[13] On this point see Greene, *Death of Adam*, pp. 12–13.

## 3. Deterioration and Senescence in Nature

It is the theme of this chapter that a group of writers, most of them living in the seventeenth century, and none in the front rank with Newton, Descartes, or Galileo, became interested in natural history, physico-theology, and scientific research, that these inquiries were identified with further discoveries of the wisdom of the Creator in his individual productions of nature and in the interrelationships he had established among them. Such studies and interpretations of living nature as a whole became the basis for modern ideas of the unity of nature advanced by such men as Count Buffon in the eighteenth century and Darwin in the nineteenth century. Darwinism in turn led to the concept of balance and harmony in nature, the web of life, and then to the recent concept of an ecosystem.

Two older ideas stood in the way of the essentially optimistic idea that the order of nature on the earth was the result of the beneficent design of the Creator. The first was that the fall of man had produced a corresponding deterioration in nature, a view common in the Middle Ages, as we have seen; interest in it was revived in the seventeenth century because the discoveries of Galileo, Kepler, and Newton stimulated men interested in theorizing about the origin of the earth and its physical appearance at crucial periods of its history: at the Creation, at the time Adam and Eve were living in the Garden of Eden, at the time of the Fall, the Deluge, and at the time when the earth was reconstituted after the waters had subsided. Knowledge of gravity, of comets, of the orbits of the planets, of the tides, created opportunities for far more colorful and dramatic commentaries on Genesis than had ever been presented by the less learned and recondite piety of the past. Some of these theories denied the fitness of the earth's environment, either because it was a wasteland with superfluous mountains, deserts, and salty oceans, or because an imperfect earth was more appropriate for sinful and wicked man than was a perfect one.

The second, possibly inspired by the doctrine of Lucretius, was the idea of senescence in nature, an application of the organic analogy to the earth itself. To achieve a philosophy of nature based on the assumption that the Creator in his wisdom had made a fit environment, it was necessary first to show that senescence did not exist in nature as a whole, even though individual life forms were mortal, and that there had been no deterioration in nature through the sin of man. Then one could proceed to prove that a benign Creator desired constancy in nature, that the natural order was dependent not on the sin of man, but on God's will, that God willed a beneficent nature.

The newer vision of the earth was best grasped by John Ray, whose *The Wisdom of God Manifested in the Works of the Creation* is probably the best natural theology ever written. This vision is not evolutionary; the earth and all its plant and animal species had been created in their present form from the beginning, but the importance of their interrelationships was seen, and the whole could change in outward aspect by natural forces or by the ever-increasing cultivation of the earth owing to the multiplication of mankind. Furthermore, this vision of the earth was allied with a hopeful view of the lot of man, sympathetic, as were its opponents, the critics of doctrines of final causes, to the influence science and technology could exert in the improvement of society. The adherents of the design argument saw in the new science the means by which man could fulfill his destiny, under God's plan and guidance, to improve the earth as his dwelling place; they saw that new principles of scientific investigation meant knowledge of natural law, that the knowledge of law meant control over nature in the widest possible sense. There remained, however, strong residues of the earlier conviction that men were sinful and wicked, that their too frequent moral lapses continually tried the patience of God. Among those who believed in the possibilities of improving human society, this thought often took the form of exhortation, that men should stamp out the evil in themselves, even as their powerful minds found ever more powerful means of controlling nature.

In order to see how the idea of the unity and constancy of nature was developed with scientific evidence available at that time, let us look more closely into these questions of senescence and deterioration.

In the nineteenth and twentieth centuries, scholars became aware of the importance of the comparisons that an age makes with those that have preceded it; every self-conscious and literate age has such a body of thought. One of the most striking figures of speech used in the seventeenth century dispute between the ancients and moderns, for example, is that of the modern knowing more than the ancient because even if he is only a dwarf he is standing on the shoulders of a giant; the figure of speech, however, has been ascribed by John of Salisbury to Bernard de Chartres in the twelfth century; perhaps it goes back even further.[14] In the seventeenth century, many such comparisons were made. It was not only a question of the literary, artistic, and technological superiority of the ancients or the moderns; also involved were the validity of the method of science, attitudes toward nature and toward natural and revealed religion, and the nature of change in human affairs.[15]

We are not directly concerned with the bearing of this much-studied quarrel on the idea of progress, but with certain other ideas which were used

[14] John of Salisbury, *The Metalogicon*, trans. McGarry, Bk. III, chap. 4, p. 167; cited by Jones, *Ancients and Moderns*, p. 293, note 12; C. S. Baldwin, *Medieval Rhetoric and Poetic*, pp. 167–168.

[15] On the quarrel, see Rigault, *Hist. de la Querelle des Anciens et des Modernes*; Gillot, *La Querelle des Anciens et des Modernes en France*; Jones, *Ancients and Moderns*; Burlingame, *The Battle of the Books in its Historical Setting*. Short but suggestive characterizations of the quarrel (part of which was satirized by Jonathan Swift in the *Battle of the Books*) in George Hildebrand's *Introduction. The Idea of Progress: an Historical Analysis* to the revised edition of Frederick J. Teggart's collection of readings, *The Idea of Progress*, p. 12; Bury, *The Idea of Progress*, chap. 4; Teggart, *Theory of*

as arguments in the quarrel itself. It involved a conflict between two conceptions of nature: a nature constant in its operations, or a nature decaying in time, like a living organism, the latter supported, as Hakewill showed, by a potpourri of miscellaneous evidence of deterioration in nature. The proponents of ancient superiority often believed in the superior potency of nature in times past, in its lesser force in the modern period because it was more aged; the moderns upheld the constancy of nature through the unchanging regularity of natural law, asserting there was no observable exhaustion, deterioration, or worsening of nature. The constancy of natural law, of course, had been one of the great teachings of René Descartes, assuming an orderliness in natural processes which were independent of and did not require divine intervention. God may have made a chaos at first among his creative acts, but if "He had established the laws of nature and sustained nature itself in acting according to custom, all purely material things would, in the course of time, have assumed the form in which we see them today, without this belief being a slight upon the miracle of creation."[16]

Several old ideas may have contributed to the revival of belief in the senescence of nature in modern times. The medieval idea that the fall of man had also affected nature may have quickened interest in it. Frequently quoted passages in Esdras and in the Psalms might hade added a bit. It may have started with the revived study of Lucretius and Columella. The earliest reference to the theory in England, according to Jones, appears in *A blazyng Starre*, by Francis Shakelton, published in 1580.[17] Shakelton believed the earth had been changed and corrupted by floods, fire, and the heat of the sun; great catastrophes such as earthquakes and inundations of the sea were evidence of the coming end; another indication, he thought, was the shortening of distance from the sun to the earth since Ptolemy's time, an indication of change in the celestial sphere. "For there is lesse vertue in Plants and hearbes than ever was before. And more feeble strength in every living creature than ever was before. It remaineth therefore (of necessitie) that shortly there shall be an ende and consummation of the Worlde, because it is (as it were) subjecte to olde age, and therefore feeble in every parte."[18] Even the widening of knowledge and the deeper understandings that came from the age of discovery were insufficient to pry Samuel Purchas away from the popular and gloomy idea: "It cannot be without some great worke of God, thus in the old and

---

*History*, chap. 8; Wodbridge, *Sir William Temple*, pp. 303–319. For the quarrel as seen by one contemporary, see William Wotton, *Reflections upon Ancient and Modern Learning* (1694), pp. 1–10.

[16] *Discourse on Method* (1637), 5, trans. by Wollaston, Penguin Classics ed., p. 71.

[17] I have been unable to consult the works of Shakelton and Goodman, and the discussion is based on Jones, *Ancients and Moderns*, pp. 24–30 (who points out that Bruno also had the idea), and on Harris, *All Coherence Gone*, pp. 8–46.

[18] Quoted in Jones, *op. cit.*, p. 25.

decrepit age of the World, to let it have more perfect knowledge of it selfe." To which Jones adds, "All this in an age which produced Shakespeare, Spenser, and Bacon!"[19]

The most famous of these works, however, was Godfrey Goodman's *The Fall of Man* (1616), which seems inspired more by the Bible than by the organic analogy from the classical writers.

> Evidence of corruption he [Goodman] finds in the evils of his times, in the sickness, suffering, vices, passions, and unhappiness of man, in the warring of the elements, in flies, worms, and monsters, in the decay of beauty and wither-ing of fruit. Nature gives man infinite desires, as if she had an infinite treasure, but in truth she is barren and defective. . . . As man through his fall brought death upon himself, so he imposed death upon all nature. In general, Goodman's idea is that the course of man and nature has been one of continual decline from a perfect state to the decay of old age.

Nature was so bountiful in the ancient age that experimentation was unneces-sary, while now the inventiveness of man is needed to satisfy his wants. "Art serves like a cobbler, or tinker, to peece up the walls and repaire the ruines of nature."[20] The decline is everywhere: there are less fish in the sea; the earth is losing its fertility; and the heavens know decline and death. (Quotes Psalm 102:26.)

### 4. GEORGE HAKEWILL'S *Apologie*

It is possible for a religious man, who believes in the beneficence and wisdom of the Creator, to argue in quite the opposite fashion. Why should an all-wise and beneficent Creator so arrange nature that with each new generation man-kind is faced with its own increasing corruption and a decline in fertility and the productiveness of nature as well? Broadly speaking, this was the prob-lem Hakewill addressed himself to.

George Hakewill's *An Apologie, or Declaration of the Power and Provi-dence of God in the Government of the World* (first edition, 1627; second, 1630; third, 1635) shows clearly, and with the easy familiarity of a learned contemporary at home in his materials, the bearing of the supposed deteriora-tion in nature on geological phenomena, on the appearance of the landscape, and on religion. It shows how urgent was the need to believe in the constancy of nature and in the regular operation of its laws if any forward-looking at-titude toward nature, science, and civilization was to be achieved. How could man and the civilizations he had created be expected to progressively improve if the nature which supported him and them was becoming weaker day by day? Hakewill met all these questions and for the most part discussed them clearly; his book bears the stamp of greatness.

[19] *Purchas his Pilgrimage* (1613), p. 43. Quoted in Jones, *op. cit.*, p. 26.
[20] Quoted in Jones, *op. cit.*, pp. 27, 28.

In my opinion, no other work enables us to see so clearly, in these formative periods of modern science, the gropings toward an understanding of the nature of the earth, using evidence from geography, geology, earth and natural history, for it is a book of interpretation and synthesis, not of original research. Unfortunately it has not achieved a cosmopolitan fame and is mentioned little in general histories of thought. In its use of the classics, of the continental writers like Du Bartas, it becomes an imaginative synthesis of Renaissance thought of high worth; far lesser figures are textbook immortals. Perhaps Hakewill has suffered because he had little that was new to offer, or perhaps as Jones has said, he did not, like Bacon, look forward in proving his points, nor did he appreciate as much as did his unashamed imitator Jonston the impressiveness of modern discovery, invention, and science in general. But how much underbrush he hacked away! how many bogs and swamps he drained! how many clearings he made for the sun to reach the ground![21]

Hakewill thinks there are better means than organic analogies to explain the stars of the heavens, the earth, and the nature of human accomplishment throughout history. Decay is not the order of the day; men have accomplished much, and they have an active role to play in their own improvement and in that of the earth—which is not decaying while they are striving.

Is it accidental that Hakewill begins his work, as did Columella (see pp. 135 f.), whom he quotes at length later, by protesting against prevailing opinions of a decay of nature, a decay inherent in things, and against which man can do nothing?[22] "The opinion of the Worlds Decay is so generally received, not onely among the Vulgar, but of the Learned, both Divines and others, that the very commonnesse of it makes it currant with many, without any further examination."

The rebuttal of this opinion, which requires almost four hundred closely written pages, is remarkable for the depth and historical range of its learning,

---

[21] For a tribute to Hakewill and a discussion of his influence and shortcomings see Jones, *op. cit.*, pp. 36–38. Hakewill's ideas were summarized (to use a charitable word) by John Jonston of Poland with far less acknowledgment of indebtedness to Hakewill than should have been made. His book, *An History of the Constancy of Nature*, is really an outline of Hakewill's work in 180 pages. In the 1635 edition of the *Apologie*, Hakewill contemptuously complains of Jonston's plagiarism. Jonston's work was originally published in Latin in Amsterdam in 1632. I have seen only the Rowland translation cited here. See Jones, p. 295, note 21. Although there is no question of Jonston's dependence on Hakewill, idea by idea, quotation by quotation, there is substance to Jones's statement that Jonston emphasized more than Hakewill had "modern discoveries, inventions, and science in general" (pp. 38–39, p. 295, note 21). See Jonston's discussion of modern inventions, *An History of the Constancy of Nature* (1657), pp. 105–115, and Harris, *All Coherence Gone*, which describes the controversy over the decay of nature (and its historical antecedents) with particular emphasis on Godfrey Goodman, the chief advocate, and George Hakewill, the cogent opponent, of the doctrine. The title is from John Donne's *An Anatomie of the World*. Godfrey Goodman's *The Fall of Man* (1616) is exceedingly rare, and I have been unable to consult it.

[22] *Apologie*, p. 1.

the force of its reasoning, and the brisk common sense of its opinions. Hakewill divides his book into several treatises, whose exhaustiveness is testimony to the currency of the ideas he is combatting and of their appearance in very different disciplines, ranging from arguments for the decay of the heavenly bodies to the decay of manners and customs. The unifying theme is the assumption by his opponents of a general decay in nature. In the revised edition of 1635, Hakewill wrote six treatises: on decay in general, on decay of the heavens and the four elements, of mankind (in length of life, strength, stature, artisanship, and intelligence), of manners and the future destruction of the earth. The fifth and sixth treatises answered objections advanced since the second impression of the book. The range of these topics, each with its full *apparatus criticus*, shows how vital was the rebuttal in resolving the question of the relative superiority of the ancients and the moderns and how crucial a role the outcome played in the emergence of the idea of progress. Diffused through the opinions of opponents is the assumption of change for the worse; sometimes it is of a physical or organic character. In human affairs it often is of an institutional or moral character.

Of even greater interest are Hakewill's reasons for undertaking a task of such monumental proportions; they reveal the philosophical, moral, and religious position of Hakewill and of others who thought like him. Despite the popularity, lay and scholarly, of ideas of decay, Hakewill could still have asked himself whether they were worth refuting. He believes they are, for the following reasons: (1) "The redeeming of a captivated truth"; the truth must be known, the argument of decay is false; it has gained too many adherents, and it must be challenged and defeated.[23] (2) "The vindicating of the Creator's honour." Even though, he thought, the earth ultimately will be consumed by fire, it is inconsistent with the honor, the wisdom, the power, and the justice of God to create a world and then allow "such a dayly, universall and irrecoverable consumption in all the parts of Nature. . . ."[24] "What do they but implicitly impeach and accuse his Power?" he asks, who complain of this decay. He answers in the language of the scholastics. God's power "indeed is nothing else but *Natura Naturans* (as the *Schooles* Phrase is), *Active Nature,* and the creature the workmanship thereof, *Natura Naturata, Nature Passive.* . . ." He quotes approvingly Scaliger's rebuttal of Cardanus: the dissolution of the world will not come from fatigue, as if nature were an ass at a mill; the power of Almighty God governs now with the same infinite command it exercised at the creation. ("Non ex fatigatione mundum solutum iri, quasi natura sit asinus ad molas, non autem Dei Opt. Max. potestas, quae eodem natu? gubernat infinito quo creavit.")[25] (3) The "contrary opinion [i.e., the idea of decay] quailes the hopes, and blunts the edge of vertuous

[23] *Ibid.,* pp. 16–18.
[24] *Ibid.,* pp. 18–19.
[25] *Ibid.,* p. 19.

endeavours."[26] This is the point Lucretius had made: the husbandman should not complain about his poor crops, for he was helpless in the general aging of mother earth. (4) Hakewill saw also the danger of moral corrosion in such beliefs: "It makes men more carelesse as in matter of repentance, so likewise both in regard of their present fortunes, and in providing for posteritie."[27] Man is exempted from responsibility, his vices becoming the diseases of a wasting nature. (5) And finally "the weake grounds which the contrary opinion is built upon."[28]

Here we are concerned with only a few of Hakewill's rebuttals, those regarding his conceptions of the earth, of living nature, and the idea of design. It will be well, however, to mention the reasons Hakewill gives for the prevalence of the ideas of decay in general. He divides his opponents' proof into three categories: proof from reason, from human authority, and from Scripture. Each one is closely examined, criticized, and rejected. The chief argument, he says, and the one on which all the rest depend is "that the Creature the nearer it approaches to the first mould, the more perfect it is, and according to the degrees of its removeall and distance from thence, it incurres the more imperfection and weaknesse, as streames of a fountaine, the farther they runne thorow uncleane passages, the more they contract corruption."[29]

Hakewill's answer in essence is that the works of art, of nature, of grace, belie this generalization, that "they all proceed by certaine steps from a more imperfect & unpolished beeing, to that which is more absolute and perfect." With the works of grace, we grow in the course of Christianity in knowledge, virtue, illumination, sanctification; we grow in virtue by adding virtue to virtue and by the increase too of individual virtue. Works of art have small beginnings, like a weaver beginning his work. An architect with his plan really begins with rubbish, reaching perfection in the furnishings and decorations of the completed building. In nature it is the same; the world came from chaos, the large trees from small seed. Hakewill seems to have in mind here the improvement to be expected by experience and the lapse of time and by the elimination of error, so that creature perfection—human, natural, or divine—is at the end, not the beginning, of things.[30]

The second argument from reason, that the whole decays because all of its parts decay, Hakewill also dismisses summarily. He denies that living nature, the earth as it is now constituted, would decline as a unit because the individual plants, animals, and men, are mortal.

Among the authorities cited by Hakewill in support of these arguments for decay are Origen, St. Ambrose, Gregory the Great, and Cyprian whom he

---

[26] *Ibid.*, p. 21.
[27] *Ibid.*, pp. 23–25.
[28] *Ibid.*, p. 25.
[29] *Ibid.*, p. 57.
[30] *Ibid.*, pp. 57–58.

quotes at length. Although he is respectful of the martyred saint of the third century who felt that the earth and all about him were declining and dying, he seriously questions his qualifications as a philosopher or as a "sound Divine." Hakewill sees Cyprian's thought in the light of the times in which he lived. Life was bitter and miserable; it was a time of famine, war, and mortality. These dreadful times were succeeded by the conversion of Constantine; Cyprian in that reign would have written as triumphantly as he wrote bitterly of the hardship and tragedy of his own time. The persecution of the Christians and the words of Scripture leading the devout to the belief that the second coming of Christ was at hand made them stand "in continuall allarums and expectation of the day of Judgment, and the end of the world . . . and their thoughts still running thereupon, all things seemed sutable thereunto, and to draw towards that end."[31] Hakewill quotes Lucretius on decay, then contrasts him with Cyprian, noting that in the 1,600 years since Lucretius, the 1,400 since St. Cyprian, there has been no such decay as would be required to prove these thinkers right.[32] Skillfully he quotes Arnobius whose *The Case Against the Pagans* (see chap. 5, sec. 1) defends Christians from accusations that they have been responsible for many of the world's disasters. St. Augustine made a like defense exhaustively in the first ten books of the *City of God*. Wars and conquests existed before Christianity; the existence of words for them proved it. In using Arnobius' defense of Christianity to rebut Cyprian and Lucretius, Hakewill says that great natural catastrophes, moral crises, all the vicissitudes of things, prove nothing about decay; they have existed in all periods of history.[33] The third human authority is II Esdras 5:51–55, one upon which Cyprian himself had relied.[34]

Esdras, however, he says, lacks the authority of scripture, and the sacred writings usually cited in support of the idea of decay. Isaiah 24:2; Romans 8:20–22; and the misunderstood but "most of all stood upon," II Peter 3:4, Hakewill says lack "explication and application." The passages as quoted are not what they seem, owing to inaccurate translation, faulty exegesis, or failure to understand the thought in context.[35]

Proceeding now to ideas more directly affecting our theme, Hakewill quickly disposes of the argument that the fall of man caused a deterioration in nature. The seeds of decay were in the world either before the fall of man or after. If the decay of nature had in truth been caused by man's sin and his punishment, the world could not have been created subject to decay "except we should make the effect before the cause, and the punishment before the

---

[31] *Ibid.*, p. 62.
[32] *Ibid.*, p. 64.
[33] *Ibid.*, pp. 65–70, of which almost five pages are quoted from Arnobius.
[34] *Ibid.*, pp. 70–73. The argument of the Esdras passage is weak and inconsequential, suggesting a decline since ancient times and that this decline is like the life cycle of a living organism.
[35] *Ibid.*, pp. 73–74.

offence, in as much as the world was built and furnished before man was made, and consequently before he had sinned. . . ."[36] Besides, when God had completed his creation, he pronounced it good.

Hakewill's argument against the decay of nature consequent upon the Fall is equally cogent. Sin cannot be a cause of such a decline. Nature's principles have been established by the Creator. Men and angels may corrupt themselves, and other creatures, but neither men nor angels "have, or possibly can alter the fundamentall lawes of nature in themselves, much lesse in the other creatures; from whence it inevitably followes, that if upon the fall of man the principles of nature be corrupted, they are undoubtedly corrupted by the Author of them, there being none other power of sufficient ability to produce such an effect."[37]

There has been no decay in the heavens, including the sun.[38] If the present habitability of the Torrid Zone is owing to the old age of the heavens, the cold zones of earth, Hakewill says, should have become more uninhabitable.[39] Neither has there been a decay of the elements; there are still four of them, they maintain the same proportions and dimensions; he quotes Du Bartas, in English translation, on the association of air, fire, water, arm in arm like "Countrey-maidens, in the moneth of May."[40] The elements are "all the linkes of th' holy chaine, which tether / The many members of the World together. . . ."[41] It reminds one of Nature speaking in the *Romance of the Rose*:

> God honors me so much that in my ward
> He leaves the lovely golden chain that binds
> The elements, which bow before my face.[42]

Hakewill's rebuttals of the arguments based on geographical and meteorological phenomena are revealing because they show the astonishingly miscellaneous array of occurrences seriously regarded as evidence of decay; almost any natural phenomenon was suitable: air pollution, storminess, weather changes, earthquakes, volcanoes, and so forth. The dominating thought is that they occur with increasing frequency and violence in modern times; Hakewill replies that they have occurred in all periods of world history, and indeed that the virulence of disease and the violence of earthquakes and volcanoes may have been more severe in ancient times.[43]

To the argument that there is a possibility the land is being gradually inundated by the sea, another indication of decay, Hakewill replies that the

---

[36] *Ibid.*, p. 55.
[37] *Ibid.*, p. 56.
[38] *Ibid.*, pp. 75–103.
[39] *Ibid.*, p. 105.
[40] *Ibid.*, p. 118.
[41] Bartas quoted, *ibid.*, p. 119.
[42] Chap. 81, 64–66. (See p. 241.)
[43] *Apologie*, pp. 124–137.

areas taken up by seas, rivers, baths, are about the same as they were in the past; what is lost in one place is recovered in another.[44]

He quotes with approval Zanchius' *De operibus creationis*, Book 4, Thesis 3, on the long-term balance in the hydrologic cycle starting with evaporation of seawater and ending with the rivers emptying into the sea. God, Zanchius said, had ordained the changing of one element into another (i.e., of water into air and water vapor) in order to preserve the earth for beasts and man. It was madness of Democritus, Zanchius said, to argue that evaporation would ultimately cause the drying up of the sea. One can be sympathetic with poor Democritus, however, if his observation was based on the Mediterranean; the runoff of rivers is a very small part of its gains, evaporation a large part of its losses.

Hakewill's discussions are based on current geological theory or that derived from antiquity, that ocean water is led back to land by secret veins to form springs and rivers.[45] The losses of land to the sea and vice versa offset one another. There may be frequent changes in small streams or fountains, but the courses or the currents of the great rivers, the Indus, the Ganges, the Danube, the Rhine, and the Nile have varied little in history. The medicinal value of fountains and baths is unchanged. The supply of fish may have declined, but Hakewill says that he can neither affirm nor deny this statement of his own knowledge; he reduces this argument to absurdity by saying that if the number of fish is declining because of the world's decay, then the store of plants, animals, and birds on earth would be less for the same reason.[46]

Hakewill considers the "pretended decay of the earth" as a whole, as he had previously considered the supposed decay of the plant and animal kingdom. The rebuttal is based on common sense, natural law, and observation. God has not everywhere ordained either fruitfulness or barrenness, or that one or the other will endure forever. Present wastelands and sandy deserts were fertile lands in former ages, or the conditions might be reversed. Lands also may be "worne and wasted with tillage" and need time and rest to recover; here too Hakewill shows his kinship with Columella.[47] In the cycle of erosion, nothing is lost, but the earth is the scene of great transports of soil from one place to another, in the wearing down of mountains, in the building up of deltaic plains. He quotes Blancanus's *De mundi fabrica* on the diminution of mountains by flowing rainwater and rivers, and the removal of earth, building up the valleys by leveling the mountains: "... in the whole Globe of the earth nothing is lost, but onely removed from one place to another, so that in processe of time the highest mountains may be humbled into valleyes, and

[44] *Ibid.*, p. 139.
[45] See Adams's discussion of origin of springs and rivers, *The Birth and Development of the Geological Sciences*, pp. 432–445.
[46] *Apologie*, pp. 140–144.
[47] *Ibid.*, p. 37.

againe the lowest valleyes exalted into mountains."[48] Blancanus predicted that if the world lasts long enough, it will again be inundated by sea as it was in the beginning through the relentless processes of leveling brought about by terrestrial erosion. This is too much for Hakewill, who remarks that Blancanus forgets the divine covenants of Genesis 9:11; Job 38:8; and Psalm 104:9.[49] The earth is the same, its dimensions are the same, its fertility is the same, at least since the Flood. The balance is always maintained, the level of the sea by the rivers of the land, the fertility of the earth by the decay of organic matter which in life it had nourished.[50]

### 5. Quarrels Over the Ancients and Moderns and the Mechanical View of Nature

Later in the seventeenth century, as the quarrel continued in the writings of Perrault and Fontenelle in France, Sir William Temple and William Wotton in England, one can see the possibilities in combining ideas of design or environmental influence in support of either position. Fontenelle dexterously uses environmental ideas with relation to plants, withholds them from mankind; Sir William Temple finds strong environmental reasons for the original creative activity of the "Eastern Regions"; William Wotton sees in the quarrel fresh sources of inspiration for the Christian believer.

Perrault considered the merits of the idea of a decline of nature in his poem *Le Siècle de Louis le Grand* (1687) which set off the debate in France between the ancients and moderns, leading to Perrault's own *Parallèle des Anciens et des Modernes*, whose volumes were published from 1688–1696. In his poem Perrault stated flatly there is no enfeeblement of nature; we can expect constancy in its powers and in its operations whether we look at the stars, the flowers, or the productions of great men.

> A former les esprits comme à former les corps,
> La Nature en tout temps fait les mesmes efforts,
> Son estre est immuable, & cette force aisée
> Dont elle produit tout, ne s'est point épuisée.[51]

Similar ideas regarding nature were again expressed by Perrault in the *Parallèle des Anciens et des Modernes*. "The lions and the tigers which rove the deserts of Africa to-day are quite as proud and as cruel as those of the time of Alexander or of Augustus, our roses are as deep a crimson as those

---

[48] *Ibid.*, p. 147. Giuseppe Blancani—Josepheus Blancanus—Professor of Mathematics at Parma, 1566–1624. NA.
[49] *Ibid.*, pp. 147–148.
[50] *Ibid.*, pp. 148–149.
[51] *Le Siècle de Louis le Grand. Poème.* Separately paged at the end of Vol. I of Perrault's *Parallèle des Anciens et des Modernes*, p. 21.

of the golden age; [repeating thoughts already expressed in *Le Siècle de Louis le Grand*] why should men be excepted from this general rule?"[52]

Although the criticism had been made long ago by Hakewill, Fontenelle dealt cleverly—almost with studied perfunctoriness—with the relationship between the supposed decline in nature and the relative superiority of the ancients and the moderns. The problem can be solved by knowing if the trees of yesterday were greater than those of today. If the ancients had superior intellects, then their brains must have been better. Nature is responsible for trees and brains. Therefore a greater vigor in ancient times would have manifested itself in greater and more beautiful trees and in brainier men. Fontenelle rejects the notion that nature exhausted herself in the mighty creations of antiquity. "Nature possesses a kind of paste which is always the same, which she ceaselessly moulds and remoulds in a thousand different ways, and of which she forms men, animals, and plants." Fontenelle now shows how the idea of nature's constancy is compatible with differences observable in nature. Trees can be equally great in any age; those of every country are not. This truth applies to men's minds. We must search for explanations of differences which can have both physical and cultural causes.[53]

William Wotton's *Reflections upon Ancient and Modern Learning* (1694), however, is the most striking of these works, because his claim to present the case impartially, even though he sympathized with the moderns, is largely justified and because he saw the relation of the quarrel to broader questions of human existence. Studying the question of the relative superiority of the ancients and moderns would be helpful to religion, throwing light on that most dangerous of beliefs to the faith, the plausible hypothesis of the eternity of the world. Wotton admits that the histories of the Egyptians, the Chaldeans, and the Chinese, going back so far into the past, lend credence to this belief, but he criticizes the proponents of this idea for the ease with which they used floods and barbarian invasions to obliterate previous records of mankind; mankind is thus really not young on the earth, but very old. Wotton replies that the world has constantly improved, that much more is now known than was known in remote time; there is no evidence either for believing that human genius was greater in ancient times or that the earth was more vigorous then. There is no proof of those deluges that supposedly obliterated the records of early humanity. Although nothing is known of conquests before the time of Moses, they could not have erased all records of civilization. Wotton bases his argument on the consequences of invasions in historical times. These invasions did not obliterate civilizations; the barbarian invaders ulti-

[52] Perrault, *Parallèle des Anciens et des Modernes*, Vol. I, p. 89. Translated by Leona M. Fassett in the selection from Perrault in Teggart and Hildebrand, *The Idea of Progress*, pp. 191–192.

[53] "Digression sur les Anciens et les Modernes," *Oeuvres* (nouv. ed.; A la Haye, 1728), Vol. 2, p. 125. Trans. by Leona M. Fassett in the selection from Fontenelle in Teggart and Hildebrand, *The Idea of Progress*, p. 176.

mately adopted much of the civilization they conquered. In essence Wotton believes that civilization has never lost anything of fundamental importance, and that with time more and more improvement is made in it. The evidence therefore points to the youth of civilization, as it does to the youth of the world, to the truth of the Bible, to the falseness of the Aristotelian idea of the eternity of the world which had no need of the Christian Creator. This study led him, he says, to other studies both useful and pleasurable. "For discoveries are most talked of in the Mechanical Philosophy, which has been but lately revived in the World. Professors had drawn in to it the whole knowledge of Nature. . . ." Paraphrasing Romans 1:20, Wotton says this knowledge of nature exists "in an Age wherein Natural Religion is denied by many, and Revealed Religion by very many more, [that it] seemed highly important to be so far known at least, as that the Invisible Things of the Godhead may be clearly proved by the Things that are seen in the World." [I could discover,] he added, what was anciently known, what is new, acquiring in the process opportunities to "furnish my Mind with new Occasions of admiring the boundless Wisdom and Bounty of that Almighty and Beneficent Essence, in and by whom alone this whole Universe, with all its Parts, live, and move, and have their Being."[54] Historical knowledge and knowledge of nature afford proofs and illustrations of the truth of the Christian conception of the nature of the earth, of history, and of the creation.

Toward the end of the seventeenth century, one influential conception of nature—against which William Wotton complained and the one which has been emphasized in histories of science—was the mechanistic view that owed its widespread acceptance to the prestige of mathematics and to the scientific and philosophical works of Galileo, Descartes, Newton, and others: the universe of which the earth is a part is like a great machine and is to be understood in geometrical terms. Nature owes its harmonies to an underlying mechanical order which is the most worthy and urgent for study, an order far removed from the bright and colorful beauties of external nature. Whitehead thought this conception was characteristic of seventeenth century thought, but his characterization applies to only one segment of it because it neglects those in the life sciences who, far from accepting the implications of the mechanical view, emphasized—with the inspiration and prestige of an idea probably as old as Western civilization itself—that the earth was a divinely designed environment, fit for the coexistence of the countless variety of beings.[55] Their form, beauty, and all those secondary qualities dismissed as unimportant were really exceedingly important in studying the concrete realities of natural history. The emphasis on anthropocentrism and teleology, which later science was to find so distasteful, should not blind one to the fact

---

[54] *Reflections*, preface, no pagination.
[55] *Science and the Modern World, Lowell Lectures, 1925* (Pelican Mentor Books), pp. 55–56.

that it called forth (what the abstract mechanical view had not) an appreciation of the beauties of nature, and stimulated study of the interrelationships (even of secondary qualities so important in natural history) existing in it. By so doing, it was argued, one not only learned more about nature but found in these discoveries further evidence of the wisdom of God. Today, with the impingement of civilization on all phases of the natural environment, we probably are more friendly toward secondary qualities, to the study of external appearances, to the scientific aspects of natural beauty, to the fundamental, not the secondary, importance of these interrelationships which formerly were the subject matter of natural history and are now covered in part by ecology, in part by aesthetic description.

### 6.  The Cambridge Platonists

The main difference between the modern physico-theologies and those of medieval and ancient times is not in the fundamental ideas and assumptions—they are virtually the same—but in the increased opportunity for illustration, which was more convincing owing to the greater scientific rigor of modern times. Xenophon had expressed himself in lines, the Stoics in scattered paragraphs, St. Basil in a few homilies, but modern writers have required volumes. These theologies gathered their evidence from a variety of sources. It may have been the observation of a country vicar on a stroll; of an amateur scientist in his garden, in his laboratory, or at his telescope; the report of an experiment in the transactions of a scientific journal. Physico-theology was contrasted with revealed theology; it was a logical expansion of the physico-theological proof of the existence of God. It also was contrasted with astro-theology whose concern was the harmony of the cosmos. Generally speaking, in modern times the favorite topics of physico-theologies have been the human body and its adaptations to its environment, similar adaptations of animals, birds, and insects, and the harmonies observable on the terraqueous sphere as a whole. William Derham, author of one of the most famous and most influential physico-theologies of the early eighteenth century, an enlargement and supplement of Ray's *The Wisdom of God Manifested in the Works of the Creation*, also wrote another book on astro-theology. The physico-theologists, even the best of them, had the annoying habit of using the same illustrations and arguments over and over again, leading often to accusations of plagiarism. The clock was one of the most famous of these (if one found a clock or a watch in an uninhabited place, he would have to conclude it was the product of design and planning, the analogy then being applied to the obvious planning of the heavens and the earth); it was in the *Theologia Naturalis* of Nieuwentijdt but it may be older. So hackneyed were many of the ideas and illustrations that Derham confessed poignantly—and more revealingly than he perhaps realized—that he had purposely avoided reading the earlier works of other physico-theologists so that he could himself write with more originality!

Many of these writers emphasized the significance of organic interrelationships on the earth, and their views are not unlike modern ideas of the balance and order of nature. There are, however, two significant differences. The destructive interferences of human cultures on the balance and harmony of nature did not enter into their works, and the harmonies, the adaptations of organisms to the environment and to each other, were works performed by God at the creation. The emphasis was therefore on form, adaptation, and arrangement, not on growth and development as in modern evolutionary theory.

Ray and Derham, whose physico-theologies were far superior to all the others in their treatment of the natural processes on earth, were sympathetic with the Cambridge Platonists, especially the doyen of the group, Ralph Cudworth, who developed in *The True Intellectual System of the Universe* the idea of plastic nature, a "subordinate ministry of God which executes his laws, like the angels which execute the works of Providence." His ideas have been compared with the later concepts of a vital principle, or the *élan vital*.[56] Cudworth's reasons for believing in this plastic nature throw light on his disagreements with those committed to the "mechanick philosophy" in scientific research.

According to him, this is not a fortuitous creation, nor is it brought into being by unguided mechanism; on the other hand, God does not do all things immediately or miraculously. Between God and the creation is "plastick nature," an inferior and subordinate instrument of God which "doth drudgingly execute that part of his providence, which consists in the regular and orderly motion of matter. . . ." Plastic nature cannot choose its own course nor act at its own discretion; a higher providence intervenes to counteract any defects and may overrule it. The difference between plastic nature and the philosophy of the "mechanic theists" (he considered Descartes to be one) was that the latter have God do only "the first impressing of a certain quantity of motion upon the matter, and the after-conserving of it, according to some general laws. . . ."[57] Plastic nature acts ἕνεκά του, for the sake of something. It is holistic, determining the form and function of the subordinate parts of nature: "There is a mixture of life or plastic nature, together with mechanism, which runs through the whole corporeal universe." Cudworth discusses at length the kinship of his idea with that of the world soul (*anima mundi*), and his indebtedness to early thinkers like Plato. The doctrine of plastic nature therefore presupposes purpose and design without representing God

---

[56] Hunter, "The Seventeenth Century Doctrine of Plastic Nature," *Harvard Theological Review*, Vol. 43 (1950), pp. 197–213.
[57] *True Intellectual System*, Vol. 1, pp. 223–224.

as a workingman at his daily tasks. If He were forced to do everything personally He would be "operose, solicitous, and distractious." Cudworth childishly takes an analogy from the pseudo-Aristotelian *De mundo* to drive home his point: Xerxes is a great ruler, but he does not do the meanest tasks himself; subordinate tasks are for subordinate officials or offices. If such mean tasks were unworthy of Xerxes, how much less decorous would it be for God to do the minor tasks as well.[58]

A God with all these duties would discourage belief and encourage the atheists, against whom the heavy cannonading of Cudworth was constantly being directed. Ray added the thought that it is not seemly that God would tend to all the minutiae of creation without making use of a subordinate ministry. For an omnipotent agent, "The slow and gradual Process that is in the Generation of Things would seem to be a vain and idle Pomp"; it would be affectation in the Divine to do that slowly (as in organic growth) which He could do instantaneously. Plastic nature accounts for sports and monstrosities, suggesting that nature is not infallible and is capable—as is human art—"of being sometimes frustrated and disappointed by the Indisposition of the Matter. . . ." No monstrosities or irregularities in nature would appear were they the direct creation of an infallible, omnipotent, and perfect Creator. Allowing for an intermediary between the Creator and the created avoided the two extremes of belief, that God was a mere overseer once he had set things in motion and that God's personal intervention was required in every creative act, no matter how trivial.[59] "The Cambridge Platonists wish to look upon nature as plastic rather than mechanical. Instead of resolving complex reactions into their simple elements, they like to proceed from the whole to the parts, and show how the one original vital force governing nature is infinitely exemplified, yet not lost, in these exemplifications."[60] Such a doctrine obviously is attractive to religious men with a knowledge of, and an intense interest in, living nature, as was the naturalist Ray, who believed that each discovery adds fresh and shining proof of the wisdom of God. Progress in science also means progress in knowledge of the intricacies of the design.

In turning to philosophers like Cudworth, whose intellectual indebtedness lay with Plato, Plotinus, and Renaissance thinkers like Marsilio Ficino, Ray thus embraced the old and traditional interpretation of nature, divorcing himself from the doctrine, stressed by Bacon, that final causes have no place in science. It represented, I think, too, an insistence on the unique qualities of life, a rejection of the idea that life processes were like those of a machine, an impatience with the crudities in Descartes' ideas of animal physiology, for to him they were nothing more than machines.

[58] *Ibid.*, pp. 221, 223.
[59] Ray, *Wisdom of God*, p. 51.
[60] Cassirer, *The Platonic Rennaissance in England*, trans. Pettegrove, p. 51. Cassirer stresses the indebtedness of the Cambridge Platonists to the Renaissance thinkers.

In *An Antidote Against Atheism* (1652) Henry More summarized the physico-theological arguments of the Cambridge Platonists that were used more effectively by Ray and Derham with their deeper knowledge of biology and natural history. Despite disclaimers that the world is not made for man, that God intended that other living things should enjoy themselves, More's recitation of the advantages of the earth is basically utilitarian and anthropocentric. The parallelism of the earth's axis, its steadiness so that it does not "carelessly tumble," is advantageous in navigation and dialing, the lodestone and the lodestar being dependent on it.[61] He discusses the possible postures of the earth with relation to the plane of the ecliptic: the perpendicular, the coincident, finally showing the one that actually exists to be the best (in a scholia, More reproduces a drawing showing the effects of the axis being coincident with the plane of the ecliptic),[62] concluding that under the present dispensation, more of the earth is habitable, there is more seasonal change, and that "an orderly *vicissitude* of things is most pleasant unto us, and doth much more gratifie the *Contemplative* Property in Man," a thought Ray repeated almost verbatim without acknowledgement. Following the alembic theory, More envisages mountains as nature's stillatories, man as the flower and chief of the globe's products whose materials are needed to exercise his faculties.[63] The clear distinction between land and sea (instead of an ooze of mire and water), and navigation with its importance to the physical and mental aspects of life, are other evidences of the usefulness of relief features. More speaks of the form and beauty of plants: in beholding them man can but acknowledge a hidden cause, like his own nature, that "is *Intellectual*, is the contriver and perfecter of these so pleasant Spectacles in the World," because of their form and because their basis is in an intellectual principle.[64] The usefulness and beauty of nature are consistent with man's duty to understand it, to learn about it, even to control for his advantage. ". . . Man seems to be brought into the World on purpose that the rest of the Creation might be improved to the utmost Usefulness and Advantage."[65] The earth and its present landscapes are unthinkable without man and the  domesticated animals about him; the wild and the feral animals chased away into retreats are indicative of his presence and his power. Even the natural—the wild—is a pleasant subject of natural history, exercising man's wit and valor. More's idea of man as a possible improver of the earth goes a step farther than the traditional idea of man dressing the earth or even completing the creation; man participates (possibly through plant and animal selection) in the actual betterment of life.

In 1692, Richard Bentley, the famous English classical scholar who had

---

[61] *An Appendix to the Foregoing Antidote against Atheism. Antidote*, p. 41.
[62] *Scholia on the Antidote Against Atheism*, p. 154.
[63] *Antidote*, pp. 41, 48–49.
[64] *Ibid.*, pp. 52–54. Quote on p. 53.
[65] *Ibid.*, p. 63.

corresponded with Newton on design, delivered eight sermons, *A Confutation of Atheism*, on the lectureship established by Boyle. Bentley was also active in the quarrel of the ancients and moderns, annihilating some of poor Sir William Temple's arguments and thereby incurring the wrath of Jonathan Swift, in whose *Battle of the Books* he is an unsympathetic figure. These sermons are among the best attempts made by seventeenth century English divines to popularize Newtonian science and, with Newton's sympathy, to marry it to the cozy piety of the argument for design. Bentley was close to Newton's discoveries and had corresponded with him on scientific and religious questions.[66] As one might expect, Bentley's three sermons (VI, VII, VIII) devoted to confuting atheism "from the origin and frame of the world" consist largely of a discussion of gravity, the earth's relation to the sun, the inclination of the earth on its axis, the earth's rotation, and its revolution, although Newton had written in a letter to Bentley that he was disinclined to give much weight to the inclination of the earth on its axis as an argument for final causes.[67]

Bentley's discussion is enriched by his classical learning. The order and the beauty of the systematic parts of the world, their discernible ends and final causes, the "$\tau\grave{o}$ $\beta\epsilon\lambda\tau\iota o\nu$" or "meliority above what was necessary to be," show, he says, an intelligent benign agent.[68] Like so many of his religious contemporaries, he feared that the revival of classical atomism would breathe new life into Aristotle's doctrine of the eternity of the world. Neither the human race nor the world is eternal. Man had a beginning; so did the present form of the earth and the system of the world.[69] Although "we need not, nor do not confine and determine the purpose of God in creating all mundane bodies merely to human ends and uses," all bodies, like the earth, are formed for the sake of intelligent minds—not for the enjoyment of the brute creation; therefore the earth "was principally designed for the being and service and contemplation of man." Consistent with this principle, other planets may well be inhabited.[70]

Bentley agrees with those who think that the present form and structure of the earth are best suited for life; clearly he has little patience for theories like Burnet's (See below, pp. 407 f.) The distance of the earth from the sun, the periods of its rotation and its revolution, are all well devised to permit life, the orderly growing of crops, and a periodization in living.[71] A uniform, calm, serene climate (as Burnet had thought; see below, pp. 408) is not necessarily conducive to health and longevity, change and variety being prob-

[66] See Newton, *Opera omnia*, Vol. 4, pp. 429–442, and Bentley's *Works*, ed. Dyce, Vol. 3, pp. 203–215.
[67] See above, p. 377. Letter of Dec. 10, 1692; Bentley's *Works*, ed. Dyce, Vol. 3, p. 207.
[68] *Confutation of Atheism*, pp. 132, 172.
[69] *Ibid.*, pp. 135–136.
[70] *Ibid.*, pp. 174–175.
[71] *Ibid.*, pp. 181–185.

ably better for both.[72] Following the usual proofs derived from the circulation of water from land to sea and from sea to land, from the area of the sea being proportionate to the size of the great rivers whose inflowing waters it must receive, Bentley meets forthrightly the problem of the physical confusion on earth, that is, the greater difficulty of applying ideas of final causes to relief, to jagged mountains, to boulder-strewn valleys, to irregular and asymmetrical coastlines than to biology. (Burnet argued that the earth is a wreck and a ruin, not a harmonious habitat.) Bentley ridicules those who see only chance and confusion in creeks, inlets, bays, and harbors, but his appraisal is based on their utility to man. It is much better that they be irregular, ununiform, for this apparent confusion makes much better harbors for navigation than would straight seacoasts. On the question of the confusion of the earth's physical geography, Bentley makes two telling replies, one theological, the other from natural law, each standing on its own feet. The theological justification is that it is clear enough that the earth is not a paradise, a variant of the idea that man cannot expect a better habitat than his sinful nature entitles him to. ". . . We reckon it only as the land of our *peregrination*, and aspire after *a better and a celestial country*." The justification in natural law is that the apparent confusion in the earth's relief is a result of the storminess of the sea and wave erosion, of rains washing down material from the mountaintops, and the great earth displacements caused by earthquakes and volcanoes. The evidence is based on water erosion on land, wave erosion, delta building, the hydrologic cycle, earthquake and volcanic action; possibly if glaciation had been understood (moraines, cirques, striations, and matterhorns are hard to explain by final causes) a satisfactory explanation of the history of the earth's landscape could have been achieved at that time.[73]

Intrenched as he is in the argument for utility, Bentley nevertheless stresses more than most the beauty of nature and the asymmetry of nature. An irregular feature—like a land form—is not necessarily less beautiful than a regular one. Possibly reacting against the notion that God is a mathematician acting geometrically, Bentley says,

> All pulchritude is relative; and all bodies are truly and physically beautiful under all possible shapes and proportions, that are good in their kind, that are fit for their proper uses and ends of their natures. We ought not then to believe that the banks of the ocean are really deformed, because they have not the form of a regular bulwark; nor that the mountains are out of shape, because they are not exact pyramids or cones; nor that the stars are unskilfully placed, because they are not all situated at uniform distance. These are not natural irregularities, but with respect to our fancies only; nor are they incommodious to the true uses of life and the designs of man's being on the earth.[74]

[72] *Ibid.*, p. 189.
[73] *Ibid.*, p. 195.
[74] *Ibid.*, pp. 196–197.

These men did not question that the earth is a divinely designed planet; but neither did they believe in the senescence of nature nor that the flood had left the earth in such a wretched and deformed condition that it was only indifferently suited to human life.

### 7. DESIGN AND THE MULTIPLICATION AND DISPERSION OF MANKIND

It has been said that John Graunt (1620–1674) made four contributions to statistical knowledge, the first two of which had been previously unrecognized: the regularity of certain social phenomena (including the incidence of disease) hitherto thought to be ascribable to chance, the excess of male over female births, the high rate of mortality in early life, and the excess of the urban over the rural death rate.[75] *Natural and Political Observations Made upon the Bills of Mortality*, first published in 1662, became, without any apparent conscious effort on the part of its author, an extremely important contribution to physico-theology because it brought population theory, now with statistical support, under the wing of natural theology much more effectively than had any previous contribution. Graunt's influence carried far, including Derham and Süssmilch. And we might add, the checks of Malthus.[76]

Graunt compared the bills of mortality of London with the rural environment of Hants, famous, he said, neither for the longevity nor the healthfulness of its inhabitants. (Modern statisticians would frown upon the generalizations Graunt made about rural populations from such a small sample as Hants.) The bills of mortality, according to Graunt, first appeared in 1592, being resumed in 1603 after the great plague; he wanted "real fruit from these ayrie Blossoms," to advance beyond their ordinary uses for curiosity, for warning the rich about the state of the sickness, and informing tradesmen what they might expect.[77] His findings regarding male and female births show, he says, that the Christian religion is more agreeable to the law of nature (that is, the law of God) than is the Muslim; it signifies nothing if Muslim law grants a man many wives if there is not a parallel proportion in nature. Graunt calculates that the births of males to females are in the ratio of 14:13 in London, and of 16:15 in Hants.[78] He shows that

---

[75] Hull's introduction to *The Economic Writings of Sir William Petty*, Vol. 1, pp. lxxv–lxxvi.

[76] Hull, *op. cit.*, p. lxxix.

[77] *Observations*, 5th enlarged ed., 1676, preface, pp. 2, 16; on Hants, p. 86.

[78] *Ibid.*, p. 86. Willcox in his introduction to a reprint of the first edition of the *Observations* says that Graunt's statement that male exceed female births by a 1/13 part does not agree with his figures for births or deaths, that Graunt's figures show the ratio of the sexes to be different at death than at birth. On the authorship of the pamphlet (whether it is by Graunt or Sir William Petty) see Hull, *op. cit.*, for the controversy up

populations grow despite the plague; according to his computations, the population can double every 64 years, and Adam and Eve in 5,610 years "by the ordinary proportion of Procreation" have produced more people than actually are now living on earth.[79] Graunt's work is a businesslike treatise on the subject with little philosophizing; nevertheless, in it were the elements of higher generalizations applicable to the idea of design: the regularities in male and female births could not be capricious; the agreement of the Christian religion with the laws of nature is shown in the moral worth and the reasonableness of monogamy; the multiplication of the human race from the time of the Flood could now be understood accurately. These ideas were used by Sir Matthew Hale who, with Süssmilch in the eighteenth century, was the most impressive contributor (if we do not include Malthus) to population theory within the design argument.

Sir William Petty is more interesting for his general views regarding population, the capacity of the earth, and the encouragement that should be given to its peopling; Petty's discussion shows how easily—and how interestingly—the question of population growth and distribution can be related to the broader implications of physico-theology. It is to the honor of God and the advantage of man, said Petty, that the earth be peopled as quickly as possible; there need be no worry about any population problem for a thousand years, or until there is more than one person for every three acres. The more people there are, the greater the value of each individual. To honor God is to acknowledge his power and wisdom; if it is true, as is commonly said, that the earth and the fixed stars are made for the use of man, it is a comfort only to atheists if three-fourths of it is uninhabited. If the earth is so underpopulated, there is uncertainty and confusion regarding the real purpose of its creation. Some might believe it a creation of chance, not of design. Peopling it to capacity would remove any doubts about the purpose of its creation. The arts and sciences are better cultivated in cities than in deserts. "If there were as many men on Earth as It could bear, the works and wonders of God's Wisdome would bee the sooner discovered and God the sooner honored really and heartily. . . . I say that God's first and greatest comand to Man and Beast was *to encrease and multiply to replenish the Earth*. Why therefore should this duty bee put off?"[80] As people increase, so will philosophers, the lands of the King of England, and the Irish holdings of Sir William Petty

to 1899, pp. li–liii; on the case for Petty, see *inter alia*, the Marquis of Lansdowne, ed.; *Petty-Southwell Correspondence 1676–1687*, pp. xxiii–xxxii; for the situation up to 1939, see Willcox, *op. cit.*, pp. iii–xiii. Hull concluded the two collaborated, "the essential and valuable part" being Graunt's, Willcox that it was a joint production but he has far more respect for Graunt who writes "statistical music" than for Petty who "is like a child playing with a new musical toy which occasionally yields a bit of harmony" (Willcox, *op. cit.*, p. x).

[79] *Observations*, p. 86.

[80] *Petty-Southwell Correspondence*, p. 154.

and Robert Southwell! Until the earth has one person for every three acres, "there is no cause for obstructing the designe," an interesting thought similar to Condorcet's remark, almost a century later, which so aroused Malthus, that if it were necessary at some future time to control world population growth, mankind would then do so.[81] Petty and many other thinkers advocated a propopulationist policy on economic and political grounds; basing it on religious grounds as well gives it broader significance because it puts the growth and distribution of the world's peoples within the framework of design, implying that man's numbers and the resources of the earth will always be a harmony and a balance.

Sir Matthew Hale's *The Primitive Origination of Mankind* (1677) is an example of a synthesis possible in the late seventeenth century, using the ideas and knowledge then current regarding the numbers and dispersion of mankind, man's relationship to other aspects of nature, considering also the implications of his growing control over nature as commanded of him in the Scripture.

Its opening lines set the tone for the book and reveal the intellectual framework within which Hale is writing. "It is an admirable evidence of the Divine Wisdom and Providence, that there is that sutable [sic] accommodation and adaptation of all things in Nature, both to their own convenience and exigence, and to the convenience, use, and exigence of one another. . . ."

There are intermediate beings in the chain between God and man, but man, despite his sins and imperfections, bears in greater measure the Divine image than does any one of the visible creatures known to us.[82] In the "admirable gradation of things," ranging from the minerals to the plants, animals, and man (a participant, though an imperfect one, in angelic nature), the lower ranks have "some rough draughts, and strokes, and shadows of those perfections which are in the superior." There is also a blending within ranks, taking on many of the characteristics of the lowest manifestations of the next highest rank. Thus, the lowly minerals "seem to have some shadow of the Vegetable Life in their growth, increase, and specifick configurations." The most advanced forms of plant life "seem to come up to the confines and borders of the lowest Form of Sensible Beings." The higher terrestrial animals, like the horse and the elephant, "are advanceable by Industry and disciplinable Acts to a great perfection, and seem to be the next rank of natures below the animal nature of Man. . . ." Man is the highest rank of visible animals, but "in his intellectual nature he seems to participate of the angelick nature." (Quotes Psalm 8:5.) Man "participates of the highest degree of Animals and the lowest degree of Intelligences [i.e., the angels];

[81] William Penn, too, apparently shares his enthusiasm for the speedy peopling of the world, for Pennsylvania would share in it too. The *Petty-Southwell Correspondence 1676–1687*, ed. the Marquis of Lansdowne, pp. 143, 148, 153–155, 165.

[82] *Prim. Orig. of Man.*, pp. 1, 15–16; other discussions on pp. 310, 349, 371.

participating of both natures, to keep as it were a continuity between the Upper World and the lower, and to maintain a communion with them and between them." This is the key thought in interpreting the relationship of man to the rest of the creation.[83] Hale, however, also looks at the human race in another way, as a species of life which has had an origin, has multiplied its numbers, has dispersed throughout the world, and in so doing has developed differences among its constituent peoples. These differences Hale ascribes to environmental causes. Color, figure, stature, humor, and disposition of peoples are caused by climate; as examples, he lists the "black, flat-nosed and crisp-haired" Ethiopian with the "tawny" Moor, the "swarthy, little, haughty, deliberate" Spaniards, "the spritely, sudden" French, and the "large, fair-complexioned, strong, sinewy, couragious [*sic*]" northern peoples. It is all very traditional and there is no attempt— except by implication in the use of the humor theory—to explain how climate could cause these differences. Within the same type of climate ("more conterminous climates") there is a great variety in people, the differences being due to other environmental causes. There are the "strong, sinewy, hardy Men" of the English uplands, the large and tall men of the marshlands, especially around Somersetshire, the "commonly sharp-visaged" Welsh living in the mountains.[84]

The account in Genesis, the presence of an aboriginal population and of native plants and animals in the New World raised questions, as did Acosta, regarding the origin of man, the domesticated plants and animals, and the diffusion or independent invention of the arts and sciences. The presence of animals in the New World was a more difficult problem than that of man, Hale thought, after reading Acosta's account of the alpacas, the guanacos, and "the Indian sheep of Peru" (los carneros de Perú). "Cierto es cuestion," Acosta had said, "que me ha tenido perplejo mucho tiempo."[85]

Hale discusses the arguments for the independent origin of man in the New World, among them, that America has long been inhabited; the lack of evidence of pre-Columbian migration because navigation was discovered too late to account for America's large aboriginal population; hence, the Americans derived neither from Adam nor Noah, but either had an "eternal succession" or had multiplied "from other common stocks than what the Mosaical History imports." Admitting that traditions of the peoples of America might favor this conclusion, Hale nevertheless sees little difficulty in the possibility of transoceanic voyaging for man, but sees serious difficulties for the animals.[86] Beasts, especially beasts of prey, could not easily be transported over the seas; nor is it easy to see how animals known in the New World

---

[83] *Ibid.*, pp. 310–311.
[84] *Ibid.*, pp. 200–201.
[85] *Ibid.*, pp. 182–183; Acosta, *Historia Natural y Moral de las Indias* (1590), Bk. IV, chap. 36.
[86] *Ibid.*, p. 89.

could be taken over seas in order to be preserved in the ark, and then transported back to the New World again.[87] Some answer that the Flood was not
universal, or that new creations of animals, known only to America, occurred
after the Flood.[88] Hale weighs all the arguments: the possibility that the antediluvian earth was flatter; that the Flood covered only part of the earth; that
the antediluvian earth, growing full of sin, of men, of beasts, needed a deluge
to make room for future inhabitants; that pre-Columbian contacts with the
New World were made by the British, the Norwegians, the Tartars or
Scythians, Phoenicians and Carthaginians, and the Chinese.[89] He concludes
that the New World had been peopled from the Old in successive waves of
migration, all of which occurred since the Deluge but at so remote a time
they could no longer be dated. If the migrations occurred 2,000 years ago,
he said, enough people had been propagated to fill the continent, and the
lapse of time, forgetfulness, degeneration, or change of new plantations
perhaps obliterated the memory of the past.

The storing of America with animals and birds, he added, after examining
the evidence, was also the result of migration. The lack of lions, tigers, and
bears in Cuba, Jamaica, Margarita, Hispaniola, remote from the Spanish settlements, showed that these animals were not native to the New World. Differences among animals as among men may be caused by mixtures of species,
by differences in climate and soils; the diversity of life in the New World
is no argument against a common origin. As primitives they may have been
the same, accidental variations occurring in time, and accidental change
coming about "in inuring themselves to a certain Continent or part thereof."[90]
Birds may have flown to the New World, but this feat might assume the
existence of Atlantis. Domestic animals may have come to the New World
in trade; Hale points to the ancient trade in peacocks and apes, and cites
II Chronicles 9:21. Admitting that the domestic animals can be accounted
for in the New World by migration either by means of or independent of
human agency, it is improbable that man has been an agent in the distribution of the feral and the wild animals. Hale admits the difficulties, and supposes that ancient land bridges, which were subsequently destroyed by water
or earthquakes, may have existed. In support of this theory he notes the possibility of a route from China to the Philippines, to Terra Australis, thence
to Tierra del Fuego, the possibility that China and the islands between New
Guinea and the New World were once one land mass, and that North Asia,
Europe, and America once were joined.[91]

Hale's intelligent and informed exposition of the difficulties reveals, as

[87] *Ibid.*, p. 184.
[88] For exhaustive discussion, see *ibid.*, pp. 197–203.
[89] *Ibid.*, pp. 195–196.
[90] *Ibid.*, p. 199. Cites Acosta, *op. cit.*, Bk. I, chap. 21. *Prim. Orig. of Man.*, p. 201.
[91] *Ibid.*, pp. 202–203.

did Acosta's (from whom he obviously derived many of his ideas), a relationship between Judeo-Christian theology and ideas of diffusion and independent invention. In many ways the design argument is not hospitable to diffusionist ideas. It is strong on the adaptation of plants to the climate, animals to the plants, and the dependence of man on both, differences among them from place to place being caused by differing environmental conditions. Nature is purposive, does nothing in vain, and man in each region invents things called forth by his needs. On the other hand, the account in Genesis of the Flood, the ark, the subsequent repeopling of the earth, unavoidably suggests the great influence of migration and diffusion in human history. The extravagant diffusionism of earlier theories, including tribes of Israel being in the New World, was one cause of a reaction, especially in the eighteenth and nineteenth centuries, in favor of the idea of independent invention owing to the psychic unity of mankind. Many of the problems discussed by Hale are still here today in another form: the question wheिher the high civilizations of the New World are autochthonous (a response to environmental causes, necessity being the mother of invention, psychic unity) or the result of pre-Columbian influences from the Old World.

Closely related to the origin and dispersal of the human race is the question of the means by which it has gradually increased, allowing the repeopling of the world from the eight people who survived the flood: Noah, his wife, their sons—Shem, Japhet, and Ham—and their wives. The natural tendency of mankind, says Hale, is to increase. If a father has a first child at age twenty-seven, a second at thirty, when he reaches sixty (which he adopts as the length of life for the male) there will be eight in the family (himself, his wife, their children, and four grandchildren). In about thirty-four years— the period from the birth of the first son until the death of the father—the unit will have quadrupled. Conditions were much more favorable in the ancient times, the long lives after the Flood and the long continuation of sexual potency allowing the procreation of great multitudes of men.[92]

In his calculations, Hale acknowledges his debt to Graunt, and includes a summary of his work. Graunt's writings "give a greater Demonstration of the Gradual Increase of Mankind upon the face of the Earth, than a hundred notional Arguments can either evince or confute. . . ."[93]

Hale's attempt to reconstruct the population history of the world, taking into account the Bible, Graunt's studies, and evidences of longevity in ancient and modern times, leads him to a position very similar to that taken later by Derham, that the growth of mankind and its present numbers give evidence of an order and regularity that can be accounted for only by design. In all life there is neither an excess of births to overcharge the earth nor an insuf-

[92] *Ibid.*, p. 205.
[93] *Ibid.*, p. 206.

ficiency of them, nor too many deaths to put a "period" to the various species and thus bring about a total dissolution in nature.

Hale, as did William Derham later, took his examples from all varieties of life; he notes the tendency of nonhuman populations to increase. They are, however, kept in bounds by certain correctives. Here, for example, are checks on the increase of animals, birds, fish, insects; they remind one of Darwin.

Animals (natural increase much greater than that of men): food; domesticated animals like cats and dogs not used for food but kept within bounds by destroying the young or by drowning; harmful wild animals; extinction by man.

Birds (natural increase apparently much greater than that of animals or men): human food; destruction of harmful birds; natural shortness of life of many that are heavy breeders; destruction of weaker birds by birds of prey; winter cold, birds dying either of the cold or of starvation.

Fish (natural increase infinitely greater than that of animals, men, or birds; their uncontrolled multiplication would lead to overstocking of fish in the sea): eggs "not sprinkled" (follows Aristotle *Hist. animalium*, Bk. VI, 13, 567b); eggs devoured by the male, by other fish, spoilage of eggs; fish eggs for human food; the prey of other fish; destruction of fish in the sea, rivers, ponds, lakes, and by birds, freezing and drought; destruction of freshwater fish by the drying up of lakes, ponds, and rivers, or "tainting the water with excessive heat."[94]

Insects (characterized by great power of multiplication and shortness of life): lacking checks to their power of reproduction, "the whole Atmosphere, Earth and Waters would be crouded with their numbers." Observation does not confirm this crowding because correctives exist: destruction by man; antipathy of certain animals to insects even though they are not used for food; food for animals; airs not conducive to putrefaction abate the "prolific power of their eggs or seeds"; rains, showers, floods, cold, frost, snow, drowning by rain, and so forth. By divine disposition, checks on "these small and inconsiderable pieces of Nature" permit the preservation of their kind, prevent an excess which would be "to the detriment and surcharge of the inferior World."[95] Hale sees among animals, birds, fish, insects, "a continued invading and prevalence of the more powerful, active and lively, over the more weak, flegmatick, and unactive creatures."[96]

Analogous correctives exist, says Hale, controlling the generation and the

[94] *Ibid.*, pp. 207–208.
[95] *Ibid.*, p. 210.
[96] *Ibid.*, p. 211.

growth of mankind; there are "prunings" to prevent a surcharge of the earth. Plagues and epidemics, local and universal, have existed in all historical periods. Famines, though not so severe in modern times because of the industry of man—"partly by those Supplies that have come by Sea to those Countries that are in Want but principally by the goodness of God"—were very serious in former times, especially the simultaneous occurrence of famines and plagues, or famine following the plague. Wars, because of their frequency at all periods of history, and their duration, have been powerful checks.[97] Casting aside apparent or surface causes, wars to Hale "seem to be in a manner a Natural Consequence of the over-plenitude and redundancy of the Number of Men in the world. . . ."[98] Inundations and conflagrations, local or universal, have also contributed to the control of human populations. The checks on population are governed by providence: they punish sins, and they keep the numbers of people in the world consistent with convenience and the capacity of the earth. Mankind has increased in numbers because of and despite the checks, maintaining the balance of individuals, thus preventing a tragic overpopulation, but they have not been severe enough to destroy mankind.[99]

The reasons Hale gives for the creation of man last are consistent with his ideas of the stewardship of man over earth (see below, pp. 481 f.), with the diffusion of mankind from a single source of origin, and with his explanation of the growth of human population from the time of the Flood. The creation is a procession from the less to the more perfect; it furnishes men with conveniences for his use: grass was created before the brutes, and fruits and food before man. The Creator intended giving man a liberal patrimony, but His subordinate ruler on earth first needed his furniture. The creation, as this stewardship would imply, was not merely for man; the inferior world was principally designed for man, but it would be folly to conclude that it was intended for his exclusive use. "Almighty God hath the Glory of his own Greatness, and the Communication of his Goodness as the great End of all his Works"; consequently, an accommodation and harmony exist befitting man as steward and tenant of God.[100] Hale (1609–1676) is remembered as a jurist; he was lord chief justice of King's Bench and his name is more closely linked with the history of English common law than it is with early anthropology; furthermore, he writes like a lawyer. The important thought is the adaptation of one being to another and to man as a "Steward and Tenant of Almighty God"; it is the harmony of the whole, not its usefulness to man, which reflects the wisdom of God, who acts like a great ruler with *jus disponendi* over the human race, whose legal rights have been bestowed upon it in the best traditions of English law![101]

---

[97] *Ibid.*, p. 213.
[98] *Ibid.*, p. 215.
[99] *Ibid.*, p. 226.
[100] *Ibid.*, p. 328.
[101] For example, *ibid.*, pp. 354–355.

### 8.  FANTASY, COSMOLOGY, AND GEOLOGY
### AND WHAT THEY LED TO

The revival of Platonism at Cambridge, the strong arguments for the constancy of nature, the discrediting of those who saw everywhere evidences of mortality and decay in nature or hopeless physical confusion of the post-diluvian world consequent upon the fall of man, made a new synthesis possible: the earth is not a mechanical creation that can be understood without considering final causes; one has to know the purpose for which the Creator intends things in order to apprehend their significance. Nor can the earth be understood through a series of deductions from abstract premises, such as Descartes had made, for natural theology was peculiarly hospitable—altogether too hospitable for its own good—to the visible, to the detailed, to the secondary qualities, to random and casual observations that could be made of plants, animals, insects, parts of the body, streams, clouds, snowflake formation. If one granted the initial assumption that every natural phenomenon was the product of design, then the justification for observation and the gathering of detail was that each bit became additional proof of the design; such research also opened up hitherto unsuspected proofs in the discovery of details in little-known fields. Physico-theology has always been much more successful and has persisted longer—to the intense displeasure of historians of science—in the life sciences because there are in them so many opportunities of finding plausible evidence of final causes in the observation of organic growth, in the relationship of plant and animal life to one another and to their habitats, in plant and animal communities, in the pattern of distribution of organic life throughout the earth. Contemplation of the earth, of its plants and animals, of man—and even of the inorganic substances—convinced the believers in natural theology that in the curiosity, enthusiasm, and intensity with which they were pursuing knowledge, they were also by uncovering fresh proofs of His existence and omniscience, contributing to the greater glory of God. The denial of a deterioration in nature was also an affirmative belief; so was the rejection of the biological analogy, applied to nature itself. One need not fear that the earth at one period was less fertile, less fruitful than at any other. The rebuttals brought the forward-looking men both in contemporary science and in contemporary theology (many times they might be represented in the same man) to the defense of the physical earth as it is. It was a defense that was not forgotten in the next century when Herder reassured his readers of the beauties and advantages of the present-day earth in much the same way as had the writers of the seventeenth century.

During the last two decades of the seventeenth century, four remarkable works were produced in England, all concerned with the origin of the earth, all attempting to make full use of the discoveries of Galileo, Kepler, Newton, and others in order to achieve a reconciliation of these discoveries with Genesis. Thomas Burnet's *Telluris Theoria Sacra* was first published in 1681, the English translation, *Sacred Theory of the Earth*, following in folio between 1684 and 1689. The first edition of John Woodward's *An Essay Towards a Natural History of the Earth, and Terrestrial Bodies, especially Minerals . . ."* appeared in 1695, the second in 1702, the third in 1723. William Whiston's *New Theory of the Earth*, published in 1696, was followed in 1698 by John Keill's *Examination of Dr. Burnet's Theory*. Keill, an astronomer, mathematician, and friend of Newton, had taken the latter's side against Leibniz in the quarrel over the priority of the discovery of the calculus. These works usually are mentioned in histories of geology or cosmology as illustrations of the fantasy period in the histories of these subjects when the earth was universally thought to be very young; Archbishop Ussher's dating of 4004 B.C. for the creation, or other estimates close to it, was widely accepted.[102] To these authors and others like them, the creation, the Fall, the Flood, and the newly constituted earth after the recession of the flood waters were the significant events in the history of the physical changes which the earth had undergone. These works were more than privately spun out combinations of piety and inventiveness; they were widely read, commented upon, and some of them, like Burnet and Woodward, were translated into foreign languages. They were sufficiently significant for Buffon to analyze the systems of Burnet, Whiston, and Woodward in his *Histoire Naturelle*.[103]

Here I am only slightly interested in the main purposes for which these books were written; more compelling are the incidental questions which these authors discuss: the habitability of the earth; the application of ideas of final causes to the features of the earth's surface, especially land and sea relationships, mountains, rivers, and valleys; comparisons of the antediluvian with the postdiluvian world because they throw light on the question of the effect on nature of the sin of man and on the broader question of correspondences between earth features and the moral stature of man.

Let us begin this story with Thomas Burnet (1635–1715), a clergyman, whose much respected *Sacred Theory of the Earth* divided the history of his benighted planet into three periods, an antediluvian, a postdiluvian, and a future one which would be physically like the first. Burnet's work is important because the rebuttals which it evoked emphasized the essential goodness of the creation, the fitness of the earthly environment, and the reasonableness of the biological and physical interrelationships existing among natural phenomena. His most famous assertion was that the face of the antediluvian world had been smooth, regular, and uniform. Although it lacked mountains and the sea, it was habitable. To critics who said there could be no rivers without

---

[102] Raven, *Ray*, p. 421, note 8.
[103] See *Preuves de la Théorie de la Terre*, art. 2 on Whiston, 3 on Burnet, 4 on Woodward, and 5 on other theorists.

mountains, Burnet replied that there were, accounting for the flow of rivers by the oval shape of the earth; but neither his contemporary nor his present critics could see how the earth's ovoid shape could cause water to run down hill. Burnet did not believe in a deluge within the accepted meaning of the word; water lay underneath the surface of the land and the smooth earth fell into the watery abyss. Evidences from observing the present configuration of the earth, with proofs from Genesis 8, satisfied him. The imperfections of the earth—he meant its relief—were the consequence of land falling into the watery abyss; earthquakes were evidences of its inner hollowness, which was also demonstrated by subterranean communication of the seas.

Burnet's antediluvian world was a paradise, contemporary with the golden age of the ancients and with a perpetual equinox. At that time, the earth did not tilt on its axis.[104] The ungenerous divine even denied rainbows to the antediluvian world. In the so-called Deluge, the earth was so broken up and so dislodged that it lost its balance and its center of gravity changed, one pole inclining to the sun and bringing about the obliquity of the earth's axis. As a consequence, the postdiluvian world was neither so pleasant, so fruitful, nor so convenient a place as was the antediluvian world; it was too broken up to be a paradise, and nature, with so much dislocation and poor land, became hard and niggardly. The soils of the postdiluvian world had none of the spontaneous fruitfulness of those of the golden age; the new earth required human art for its cultivation because of the decay of the soil and the diversity of the seasons. Changes of season lacked the advantages of a perpetual equinox; the people of the postdiluvian world were short-lived because of the seasonal changes and the absence of a stable medium like the smooth earth of the past. Although the torrid zone was uninhabitable even in antediluvian time, there was plenty of room in the other zones because there were no seas. The posture of the earth in its wretched postdiluvian period had, however, to be changed to make it habitable.

Continuing his speculations to their remorseless end, Burnet thought that after fire destroyed the present earth, it would again become a paradise like the first—even and uniform, for fire would melt everything. Burnet's speculations forced those who disagreed with them to state the case for the advantages to mankind and to other forms of life of the planet as it is at present constituted and to justify, as part of the Creator's design, the wisdom of having the earth incline twenty-three and a half degrees from the line drawn perpendicular to the plane of the ecliptic. To Burnet, sinful man lived on an earth which was a physical ruin, a wasteland; mountains, seas, deserts had neither use nor beauty; they were doleful reminders that mankind deserved no better.[105]

[104] *Sacred Theory*, p. 188.
[105] For a discussion of Burnet and mountains, see Nicolson, *Mountain Gloom and Mountain Glory*, pp. 207–224.

Woodward disagreed completely with Burnet, but his views were flattering neither to mankind nor to the globe. Physically, he thought the antediluvian earth differed little from the present earth and that the ratio of land to sea was about the same. His proof was based on fossil evidence: shells, teeth, bones of sea fish, indicated the extensive area of the sea in the antediluvian period, and shells of freshwater fish indicated rivers; rivers suggested mountains with valleys in between, proving against Burnet that the relief of the antediluvian world was similar to that of the present earth.

How did the fossils survive the Deluge? Woodward answered lamely that the Deluge dissolved stone and mineral solids, but did not dissolve shells, teeth, bones, trunks and roots of trees, and other parts of plants and animals. To a critic who asked how these survivals and those solutions were possible, he replied that they must have occurred thus because of the widespread distribution of fossils. The fossil record was used, therefore, to prove the existence of seas, rivers (and thus of mountains) in the antediluvian earth and the basic physical similarities of the two earths.[106]

Woodward said the Deluge had two purposes, to punish man, and—more important—to alter the earth so that it would have a constitution consistent with human frailty, its former state being suited to man in a state of innocence.[107] If the antediluvian world was so much like the present, what then was the difference between the two? Woodward's most interesting answer reminds one of some of Robert Wallace's and Thomas Malthus's ideas. The antediluvian world was far more fertile, and so productive that it required little care or tillage, the plow being a postdiluvian invention.[108] Man in his innocence could use the antediluvian earth to this great and edifying advantage, but with the Fall the fertility of the earth became a "continual *Decoy* and *Snare* unto him," the fertility of the earth granting him leisure which led only to cumulative opportunities for wickedness and promiscuity. The Deluge punished man, but his punishment did not require a deluge were it not necessary also "to *reclaim* and *retrieve* the *World* out of this *wretched* and *forlorn State*...."[109] Following the Fall, the lushness of plant growth and the multiplication of animals imposed a burden on the earth which could be eased only by a deluge. Again his proof was the fossil evidence:

I appeal to the *Remains* of *that Earth*: the *Animal* and *Vegetable Productions* of it still preserved; the vast and incredible *Numbers* whereof notoriously testifie the extreme *Luxuriance* and *Faecundity* of it. And I need but produce *these* as Evidences that at the time that the *Deluge* came, the *Earth* was so *loaded* with *Herbage*, and *throng'd* with *Animals*, that such an *Expedient* was even wanting to ease it of the *Burden*, and to make room for a *Succession* of its *Productions*.[110]

---

[106] *An Essay Towards a Natural History of the Earth*, pp. 107, 244, 251, 254–255.
[107] *Ibid.*, p. 83; see also pp. 90, 92.
[108] *Ibid.*, pp. 83, 84.
[109] *Ibid.*, pp. 85, 87.
[110] *Ibid.*, p. 101.

In the Deluge, the organic matter on the earth's surface responsible for its antediluvian fertility (Woodward here seems an early advocate of the humus theory of soil composition) settled, in the general mingling of all kinds of vegetable and mineral matter, to the bottom of the flood waters to rest on solid rock, "leaving only so much of it near the *Surface* as might just sufficiently *satisfie* the *Wants* of *humane Nature*, but little or no more; and even *that* not *pure*, not free from the intermixture of meer *steril* mineral *Matter*, and such as is in no wise fit for the *Nutrition* of *Vegetables*. . . ."[111] The postdiluvian earth therefore required the industry and the care of man, by cultivation and manuring; it became a hard world and nature was niggardly.

In a remarkable passage showing the interrelationships of the Deluge, humus accumulation, soil erosion, population growth, and final causes, Woodward argues that there was more to the design than to "*retrench* and abridge the *Luxury* and *Superabundance* of the Productions of the *Earth*" and to provide for a more sparing and frugal production from the soil.[112] The humus which settled on the floor of the sea at the Deluge accumulated on the lower strata of stone and other mineral matter, becoming in effect, with the disappearance of the waters, a reserve store of soil fertility for posterity. Humus (Woodward calls it "vegetative matter"), decayed shells, teeth, bones, the parts of dead plants and animals, are a "proper and natural Manure to the Earth." Had all of the antediluvian humus remained on the surface, it gradually would have been washed down from the hills. Rocks, mountains, or other elevations, "especially those whose *Surfaces* are yearly stirr'd and disturbed by digging, plowing, or the like," become gradually lower as their surface soils are washed away by running water and carried to the plains and valleys below. Even stone—bare or covered with a layer of earth—is not immune; it too "is *dissolved* by degrees, and wash'd also down, in its turn, as well as the looser Earth."[113]

If this humus had remained as topsoil in the postdiluvian earth instead of being precipitated during the Deluge, the processes of erosion—Woodward calls it "deterration"—would have caused soil transport from the higher elevations to the lower, and with the loss, "decrement," of the humus, only a sterile and infertile stratum underneath would remain. Even this would not end the matter. The infertile stratum of the higher elevations would gradually have been eroded away and would have been "likewise by degrees *borne down* successively to the *Roots* and *Bottoms* of the *Hills*, and upon the neighbouring parts of the *Valleys* and *Plains*; it would, as far as it reach'd, have *cover'd* and *buried* the *upper* and *vegetative Stratum* that was expanded over those Valleys and Plains, and render'd as much of them as it so covered also frustrate,

[111] *Ibid.*, p. 89.
[112] *Ibid.*, p. 238.
[113] *Ibid.*, p. 230.

*steril*, and *unfruitful*."[114] Meanwhile the population of the earth would have grown until it was fully peopled, with "all *Quarters* and *Corners* of it *stock'd* with *Inhabitants*" who would need every bit of fertile soil for food; there would now be much less soil, for the earth would have become barren by slow erosion. "So that they might have e'en *starved*, had it not been for this Providential *Reserve*: this *Hoord*, if I may so say, that was stowed in the *Strata* underneath, and now seasonably *disclosed* and brought forth."[115] The explanation rests on the humus theory of the soils (that it is only decayed organic matter which provides the food for plants), but it is a striking conception of the gradual leveling of the earth, each fresh denudation of the higher elevations supplying the precious humus for the valleys and plains, the leveling progressing gradually as the increasing population of the earth demands more and more fertile soil. Even among these fantastic theories, the realities of everyday life are not far away. It is clear that to Woodward tillage, manuring, soil fertility, and soil erosion are closely bound up together, and that the relation of man to the earth is very close indeed.

Woodward also takes issue with Burnet on aesthetic grounds. Burnet was so obsessed with the idea that the earth is a pile of "Ruines and Rubbish" whose mountains have not the "least foot steps of Art or Counsel," a globe which is a "rude *Lump*," a "*little dirty Planet*," that he would grant it neither order nor beauty.[116] Woodward sees in the contrasts of sea and land, of hill and dale, something which "is indeed extremely charming and agreeable." This is not only his own opinion, he continues, but the common opinion of mankind, agreed in by the ancients, the moderns, and the heathen alike. The aesthetic pleasures derived from natural beauty were considered by Woodward and later also by Ray, as another proof of the wisdom of God.

One can see the old stones gradually being moved away. If there is a constancy in the processes of nature, if there is a reasonable order in the postdiluvian world, and beauty in it as well, a new relationship between man and nature now seems possible; discoveries in theoretical science and technology dissipate some of the bleakness. Man becomes an industrious being working the none too fertile soil, and in the process improves both himself and the earth, providing as well for his future increase in numbers.

Although the author of the article on Whiston in the eleventh edition of the *Encyclopaedia Britannica* described him as "not only paradoxical to the verge of craziness, but intolerant to the verge of bigotry," how is it possible to withhold one's admiration for the ingenuity of a man who theorized that the primeval chaos was composed of the atmosphere of a comet; that the revolu-

---

[114] *Ibid.*, pp. 239–240.

[115] *Ibid.*, p. 240.

[116] On Burnet's contradictory attitudes toward mountains, see Nicolson, *op. cit.*, pp. 207–216.

tion of the earth around the sun began with the creation; that the rotation of the earth on its axis, and the obliquity of the axis were both caused by a comet striking the earth after the fall of man, the comet being the mechanical means by which the earth was reconditioned for a now far less noble creature?

To Whiston a perfect earth is incongruous as a home for imperfect man; the physical nature of the earth must be adapted to the moral stature of mankind. One can expect little of an earth whose inhabitants are unworthy of anything better than they possess. "As to the main Use of this Earth, 'tis to afford Habitation to a sinful and lapsed Race of Creatures, of small Abilities or Capacities at present, but of great Vices and Wickedness. . . ."[117] He ridicules often in eloquent language the idea that the universe has been devised for man; the creation described in Genesis applies only to the earth, a probationary place, truly not one of the noblest globes but suited to man as he is presently constituted.[118]

Although critical in detail, Whiston followed Woodward in most of his views about the physical configuration of the antediluvian earth, the main difference being that Whiston thought the antediluvian earth had less water and no real ocean.[119] It was also far more populous because it was more fertile and there was more land; in estimating its population he was guided by the calculations of Petty and Halley on the time required for the doubling of a population.[120] The postdiluvian world was inferior to the antediluvian because it was less fertile, owing to the fact that it received less heat from the sun: after the Deluge the earth's orbit became an ellipse instead of a circle, solar heat being now only 96 per cent of that of the antediluvian period. The earth is also wetter, both from the waters of the Deluge, which did not originate on earth, and from waters on or near the surface of the earth, dampness, he thought, impeding fertility. Both the quantity and the quality of fertile soil is therefore less now than in the antediluvian world. Whiston's appraisal of the fertility of the earth was somewhat like Woodward's, for both depicted an earth of struggle and of hardship; the inferior nature of the earth's productions, however, is consistent with the moral qualities of man.[121]

Fresher, more modest, and less ambitious appraisals appeared in John Keill's astringent criticism of the modern cosmogonists who are "as wild, extravagant, and presumptuous as any of the Ancients. . . ."[122] For this he blamed Descartes because "he has encouraged so very much this presumptuous pride in the Philosophers, that they think they understand all the works of Nature, and are able to give a good account of them, whereas neither he, nor any of his

---

[117] *Of the Mosaick History of the Creation*, p. 57.
[118] *Ibid.*, pp. 60–61, 70–77, 88, 90–94.
[119] *New Theory of the Earth*, pp. 233–237, 256, 264–265, 359–361.
[120] *Ibid.*, pp. 247, 254–255.
[121] *Ibid.*, pp. 358–360, 363–365.
[122] *An Examination of Dr. Burnet's Theory of the Earth*, p. 9.

followers, have given us a right explication of any one thing."[123] Keill believes in final causes; like Ray, he leaves the way open for optimism regarding man's place in nature because he cannot believe that a wise Creator would make an earth with no more order than exists in a pile of rubbish.

Keill attacks the folly of believing that the "Fabrick of the earth" from its pristine state of chaos to its present condition can ever be deduced from known mechanical principles and natural causes. To Burnet's argument for the smoothness, regularity, and uniformity of the antediluvian earth, Keill replies in the language of final causes, explaining why mountains must have existed in the antediluvian world. Mountains were as necessary in it as they are in our own. In his defense of final causes, and citing Boyle and Ray in support, Keill says it is now impossible to live or to subsist on an earth without mountains.[124]

In addition to secondary uses for plant life—for their mineral production, as a refuge for animals, as determinants of wind direction and thus of weather, in constituting international boundaries—their greatest importance is that they are responsible for rivers and freshwater currents. Keill quotes Edmund Halley on the importance of relief to rivers and thus to life.[125] There is, said Halley, an "equilibre of receipt and Expence in the whole Sea," the sea neither drying up nor flooding the land because water is evaporated from the sea, blown thence over the lowlands toward the mountains where it is forced to rise, thus producing both rain and the water for springs, the same water then, by means of springs, rivulets, brooks, and great rivers such as the Rhine, Rhone, and the Danube, being returned to the sea and completing the cycle. (More water is returned to the sea by dew and rain over its surface, from plants on land, from surplus rainwater flowing back to the sea.) Like organic growth, this kind of cycle fits in convincingly with the idea of a microcosm and a macrocosm and with the argument for design. (See Ecclesiastes 1:7.) If we may apply final causes to hills, Halley says, the design seems to be "that their Ridges being placed through the midst of the continents, might serve as it were for Alembicks to distil fresh Water for the use of Man and Beast, and their heights to give a descent to those Streams to run gently, like so many Veins of the *Macrocosm*, to be the more beneficial to the creation."[126] In another passage, Halley makes further reference to the alembic. Part of the water vapor enters caverns in the hills, the waters "gather as in an Alembick" into stone basins, whose surplus water overflows into springs that then might form into brooks, rivulets, and lastly into rivers. Halley's reference to the

[123] *Ibid.,* p. 10.
[124] *Ibid.,* pp. 37, 46.
[125] See "An Account of the Circulation of the Watry Vapours of the Sea, and of the Cause of Springs," *Royal Society of London Philosophical Transactions,* No. 191, Vol. 17 (1694), pp. 468–473.
[126] *Ibid.,* p. 473.

alembic is a reminder of the long history of the theory of internal alembics. Seawater in the depths of the earth was distilled and then condensed in cold caves and caverns in the higher portions of the mountains from which it then could emerge.[127]

In Halley's system, accepted by Keill, the evaporation of seawater, the transportation of the vapor by the winds, the production of orographic rainfall, and the river regimes produced by uneven relief of the earth's surface were best explained by final causes.

Keill also agreed with Kepler that the obliquity of the earth's axis is evidence of the Creator's beneficence.[128] Keill's argument is also traditional, that the obliquity of the axis has beneficial effects in seasonal change; moreover, people living northward of the forty-fifth parallel receive more solar heat annually with the present inclination of the earth on its axis than if the sun shone always directly over the equator.[129]

"I believe there would be few so fond of changes, as to be willing to have the present oblique position altered for the perpendicular one of the Theorist [i.e., Burnet], which would render this whole Island no better than a wilderness, and the greatest part of the Earth not habitable."[130] The argument that the obliquity of the axis provided a greater habitable area, and thus more opportunities for expansion and more intense occupancy of the earth's surface as world population grew was, despite Newton's demurrer, a more convincing proof of design and of the existence of God than was Burnet's gloomy view based on sin and the Fall.

Keill showed more common sense than had the others in explaining the reasons why the earth was habitable. To Keill, Burnet's belief that too much of the earth is taken up by sea showed ignorance of natural philosophy. If the seas' area were reduced by one-half, so would be the quantity of water vapor. Mountains had to exist in the antediluvian earth, for like the postdiluvian earth it also needed rivers and fresh water.[131]

To a modern mind, these works may seem unworthy of discussion. My own interpretation, however, is that there is here—and this will be seen more clearly in Ray and Derham—a growing awareness that one must consider an everwidening series of relationships on earth in order to understand the processes of nature, and the past, present, and future of mankind, and that, notwithstanding the ingenuousness of resorting to final causes, one must bring within one synoptic view the march of the seasons (represented by the argument over the inclination of the earth on its axis), the circulation of the

[127] See Adams, *The Birth and Development of the Geological Sciences*, pp. 434–441, and the illustrations from Kircher's *Mundus Subterraneus*. Halley's reference to the macrocosm reminds one also of Kircher. See Adams, pp. 435–436.

[128] Keill, *op. cit.* (see n. 122 above), pp. 53–55.

[129] *Ibid.*, p. 58.

[130] *Ibid.*, p. 5.

[131] *Ibid.*, p. 77. See his summary and conclusions, pp. 134–139.

atmosphere (represented by the evaporation of seawater, onshore winds, and orographic rainfall), and the importance of river systems (as distributors of fresh water and as agents of erosion) to all life on earth.

With these discussions of Burnet, Woodward, Whiston, Halley, and Keill in mind, we can now turn to the work of two men, John Ray and William Derham, who created, largely by synthesizing the ideas and the discoveries of others, a religious and philosophical view of the unity of nature that was based on physical and biological principles and supported by the argument from design. By modern standards, these ecological principles are crude, but they are an advance over the utilitarian simplicities of the classical period and the many conventional pieties of the Middle Ages in their attempt to understand what Darwin later called "the web of life."

### 9. RAY AND DERHAM ON THE WISDOM OF GOD

Ray's *The Wisdom of God Manifested in the Works of the Creation* (1691) is an excellent example of a physico-theology which examines the nature of the earth and the natural harmonies observable on it, and which attempts at the same time to find a place for man and his works—the inventions, the techniques, the changes made in the physical environment. (In addition to technical works on plants and plant classification, Ray wrote about his travels to the Lowlands, and in *The Dissolution of the World* he replied in the spirit of Hakewill to those who believed in a decline in the powers of nature.)

Ray rejected the belief in the exhaustion and dissolution of the world on philosophic, religious, and scientific grounds; his objections rested, too, on observations of the present state of nature, showing similarities with the uniformitarianism of the nineteenth century geology. There is nothing in nature, he said, that argues for or infers a future dissolution, although unlikely accidents (flooding, extinction of the sun, an eruption of a central fire enclosed in the earth, a dryness and inflammability of the earth under the Torrid Zone, which could possibly be set on fire by volcanoes, or the simultaneous eruption of all volcanoes) might overwhelm the earth.[132] Ray mentions the possibility of the ultimate destruction of the earth owing to the erosion of running water, using explanations that would seem strange neither to an adherent of uniformitarianism in nineteenth century geology nor to a disciple of William Morris Davis. The ultimate effect of running water on land is to level it, wearing down the mountains, building up deltas such as those of the Po, the Athesis (the Adige), the Nile, and the Brenta. Gradually the deltas would increase in area, rainwater would accumulate on them, the flat, level plain would extend itself inland until the sea, assisted by subterranean rivers, would cover the whole earth.[133] Any end of the world—and Ray clearly was trying

---

[132] Ray, *Dissolution*, pp. 39, 44, 148–149.
[133] *Ibid.*, pp. 44, 44–52, citing Varenius and Kircher; p. 49, on wave action on shorelines.

to put off the biblical prophecies as far into the future as possible—would
have to be sudden because there is no such present tendency toward dissolution. Ray believed the earth probably would be refined and purified in the
future, not annihilated, for he could not see the reason for the earth's existence
if mankind is destroyed in the final conflagration.[134]

To Ray a belief in the constancy of nature, in the consistent fertility and
fruitfulness of the earth, is not only a logical inference from the divine plan,
but is warranted by the evidences of contemporary observation; it is obvious
from the use men make of natural products about them. Ray is sympathetic
too with advances in technology and in the arts and sciences; he is optimistic
(with the usual reservations concerning human wickedness) about the future
of civilization and the technological advances which bring a future state about.
This optimism, self-evidently, could not rest on dismal doctrines of a decay
and dissolution of nature whatever the ancients and their modern sympathizers
might think.

The significance of Ray's work to our theme is that it is an impressive
marshaling of the known knowledge of natural history (including his own
contributions) to demonstrate the unity of nature and from this the wisdom
of God in the creation. Ray himself considered his book a work of synthesis:
". . . all the Particulars contain'd in this Book cannot be found in any one
Piece known to me, but lie scatter'd and dispers'd in many. . . ."[135]

The works of creation are those created by God: it is a creation unchanged
and continuous from the beginning. In a passage suggesting the *creatio continua* of the Middle Ages, he refers to ". . . The Works created by God at
first, and by him conserv'd to this Day in the same State and Condition in
which they were at first made; for *Conservation* (according to the *Judgment
both of Philosophers and Divines*) is a continu'd Creation."[136]

The work begins with the quotation of the twenty-fourth verse of Psalm
104, every theme in the book ultimately revolving around the unifying religious idea of this exceedingly influential verse. Following naturally the
thought of the psalm, the case is boldly stated for the legitimacy of ideas of
final causes in studying the works of the creation; Ray takes comfort in the
authority of Cicero's *De finibus bonorum et malorum* and in the *De natura
deorum*, rebutting the Aristotelian idea of the eternity of the world and the
atomic theories of the Epicureans.[137] In place of the "atheistical" atomic
theories, Ray adopts Cudworth's idea of a plastic nature, a subordinate ministry which God uses to administer the world. Cudworth considers "plastic
nature" as a vital principle, the word "vital" being used as an antonym of
"mechanical," suggesting the Stoic idea of the *logos spermatikos*.[138] Like More

---

[134] *Ibid.*, pp. 190, 198–199.
[135] *Wisdom of God*, Pref.
[136] *Ibid.*, Pref. ad fin.
[137] *Ibid.*, pp. 30–34.
[138] See Pohlenz, *Die Stoa*, Vol. I, p. 353.

and Cudworth, Ray is opposed to the "mechanick theists" (he considers Descartes to be one); he opposes the Cartesian conception of animals as machines, *automata*, as being contrary to the common observation that animals are sensitive to pain; there is no excuse for cruelty to them.[139] The atomic theists "utterly evacuate," Ray says, "that grand Argument for a God taken from the *Phaenomenon of the Artificial Frame of things....*"[140] In the analogy between art and nature, Ray adds that if human art has reason behind its conception, how much more must nature have it because nature is so much superior to art.[141] He quotes the Bishop of Chester, John Wilkins, who saw in the microscopic investigation of things strong proof of the superiority of nature over art, contrasting the perfection of nature even in the smallest details of order and symmetry in plant and animal life, as revealed by the microscope, with the bluntness and clumsiness of artifacts when seen under the unflattering magnification of the same instrument.[142]

At this time, the theory of the four elements involved no conflict with theology or science. What Ray says of them, however, shows how strong, even in a man of his scientific stature, was the legacy of the utilitarian bias in physico-theology. His discussion of the utility of fire and his list of its uses are proud summaries of the technology of his time.[143] The discussion of air more matter-of-factly mentions its role in maintaining life, including the fetus, and as the medium of flight. The dramatic role of water, aside from its humdrum uses in washing, is sketched with enthusiasm. The size and the placement of the oceans, the distribution of water on the earth's surface by springs and rivers are evidences of the greatest wisdom. Leaning on Keill's criticism of Burnet, Ray states, "Might not at least Half the Sea have been spar'd and added to the Land, for the Entertainment and the Maintenance of Men, who, by the continual Striving and Fighting to enlarge their Bounds, and encroaching upon one another, seems to be streightened for Want of Room."[144] Ray deflates this argument, saying that any large gain of land at the expense of the sea would yield more area, but the earth would be drier and less productive. Population capacity of the world thus is closely related to land-sea areas.[145] To the objection that the earth often has too much water and devastating floods in consequence, Ray answers that floods return water to the sea after the earth has had enough.[146] Speaking in modern terms, rain, streams, and floods are inseparably connected with geological erosion, the hydrological cycle, delta building, and the formation of alluvial soils, those of the Nile and

[139] *Wisdom of God*, pp. 38, 41, 43, 46, 54–55.
[140] *Ibid.*, p. 42.
[141] *Ibid.*, pp. 35–37.
[142] Wilkins, *Of the Principles and Duties of Natural Religion*, Bk I, chap. 6 = pp. 70–71; quoted in part by Ray, *Wisdom of God*, p. 58.
[143] *Wisdom of God*, p. 71.
[144] *Ibid.*, pp. 79–80.
[145] *Ibid.*, pp. 88–91.
[146] *Ibid.*, pp. 82–83.

the Ganges being especially impressive. The casual justification of floods is a reminder of the *tout est bien* philosophy that is often an unpleasantly complacent characteristic of the more hopeful and anthropocentric physicotheologies; floods were less of a blessing to those experiencing their fury. Voltaire's satire in *Candide* of the *tout est bien* philosophy could have been applied here to Ray.

Like Woodward, Ray adopted a vitalistic view toward the soil, a thin covering of the earth's mantle and the source of food, its special importance lying in the decayed vegetable matter, the humus contained in it.[147]

Moreover, there is some aesthetic appreciation of nature in Ray's work. "How variously is the Surface of this Earth distinguish'd into Hills, and Valleys, and Plains, and high Mountains, affording pleasant Prospects? How curiously cloath'd and adorn'd with the grateful Verdure of Herbs and stately Trees, either dispers'd and scatter'd singly, or as it were assembled in Woods and Groves, and all these beautified and illustrated with elegant Flowers and Fruits. . . ."[148] This is more than a conventional and sentimental description of an idealized landscape; it is, I think, a positive reaction to Burnet's description of the earth's ugliness; the appeal is to the senses and it balances somewhat the strong utilitarian bias of so much of Ray's writing.

Anticipating the nineteenth century geologists, who tried to reconcile structure and mineral distribution with the design of the Creator, Ray's discussion of the baser metals becomes a panegyric (reminiscent of Agricola) on the wisdom of God in supplying man with the means of lifting himself out of savagery, for without them we could have "nothing of Culture or Civility"; they are needed for tillage, reaping, mowing, plowing, digging, pruning, and grafting. Without them there would be no mechanical arts or trades, no household vessels or utensils, no dwelling places, no shipping or navigation. "What a kind of barbarous and sordid Life we must necessarily have liv'd," he says, in a sentence illustrating the use of contemporary ethnology in reconstructing the hypothetical origin of society, "the *Indians* in the Northern Part of *America* are a clear Demonstration."[149] Ray does not explain, however, why the Divine Wisdom had withheld from the heathen savage what had been lavishly bestowed upon the English. The usefulness of the four elements, of the natural resources created by them, the advantages of certain arrangements in nature (such as the mountains and the plains) are seen as advantages to a people who have reached the cultural and technological level of late seventeenth century England.

As a naturalist, Ray is greatly impressed with the richness and variety of plant life, even more startlingly and unexpectedly revealed after the age of discovery, "there being in the vast Continent of *America* as great a Variety

---

[147] *Ibid.*, p. 83; see Woodward, *Essay Towards a Natural History of the Earth*, p. 227.
[148] *Wisdom of God*, pp. 87–88.
[149] *Ibid.*, p. 96.

of *Species* as with us." Concluding a survey of natural history, based on personal observation in England, on the writings of European students, and on travelers' accounts from elsewhere in the world, Ray says that a wise and powerful artificer was needed to create such variety. Expressing in his own words "the principle of plenitude," Ray adds that the very richness and lushness of nature are indications of wisdom and power: " . . . The Almighty discovers more of his Wisdom in forming such a vast Multitude of different Sorts of Creatures, and all with admirable and irreproveable Art, than if he had created but a few; for this declares the Greatness and unbounded Capacity of his Understanding."[150] He is also a fertile God: the visible works of nature prove that He is, and here Ray is writing as a naturalist who believes in the strength and convincing power of the physico-theological proof of God's existence. Supernatural demonstrations, inner illuminations of the mind, a spirit of prophecy, miracles, are proofs that are subject to "Cavil and an Exception by atheistical Persons," but not the proofs "taken from Effects and Operations expos'd to every Man's View."[151] Here Ray speaks in the language of Ramon Sibiude. The way to reinforce one's belief in God is to study Nature, to see the richness and variety of things on earth—and in the heavens too—and to note the infinite adaptations of living things to their environment.

If one shifts one's attention from these simple and traditional general ideas to the materials Ray uses as evidence to prove them, it is apparent that he is interested not only in plants and animals, but in their habitats, and in the relation of man to the earth, considering also his talents and his prowess: his mind and the faithful executors of its decisions, the eye, and the hand; his use of tools, and the living agents of human power, the domestic animals. It is the organic wholeness of things that interests him; one feels his concrete interest in the pasture, the barnyard, the forest, that he is unwilling to cast aside these living individual manifestations, covering them up with abstract general laws. There is a balance, an order in nature; it need not be a mathematical order. There is a significant passage in his *Physico-Theological Observations* in which he criticizes Burnet's belief that mountains are but a confusion in nature. Like those who saw hope for man in his abilities and in his own growing masterful technology, Ray thought these hopes could be realized only in a physical environment that itself possessed order; one observes such an order in mountains—so indispensable to life—but it is an order incompatible with the dictum that the Creator always acts geometrically. It is not a geometric order, but a living order beyond the reach of mechanism and of geometry.

Naturally, Ray is at his best in discussing matters close to his own professional interest. Nature has seen to the propagation and growth of plants because they are designed to be food for animals; hence the variety of ways in which they are propagated, the vitality of their seed, their devices for survival.

[150] *Ibid.*, p. 25.
[151] *Ibid.*, Pref.

The distribution of plants is correlated with climate and differing human demands of various regions. There is some truth, he says, "that there are, by the wise Disposition of Providence, such *Species* of Plants produc'd in every Country, as are the most proper and convenient for the Meat and Medicine of the Men and Animals that are bred and inhabit there."[152] Many interesting illustrations follow, showing the close relationship between life and the environment, all of course being adduced as evidence for design. That birds lay eggs and do not bring forth their young alive is proof of divine wisdom, for this is a way of preserving them so that "neither the birds of prey, the Serpent, nor the Fowler should straiten their Generation too much."[153] In their instinctive behavior, animals are guided to ends, unknown to them, by a wise Superintendent.[154] The migrations of birds and fish, a homely illustration showing how birds keep from fouling their nests, the guile possessed by weak animals, the adaptation of swine to rooting, the different kinds of animal noises, are other instances of the harmony of form and function within the environment.[155]

In his discussion of wild and domestic animals Ray shows an interest in their adaptability to the environment, in population growth, animal fertility, the proportions of the sexes and the ratio of births to death. He finds it hard to believe that keeping the numerical proportion between the sexes is merely a result of mechanism; it must infer a superintending Providence. The association of some animals with man, however, has created a weakness in the animal; the sheep now needs the "care and Tuition of Man" as a means of survival. The hog, another homely example of design, has a long snout adapted for rooting—so adaptable in fact that the wily Italians use him to find mushrooms, a cord tied to the hind leg preventing him from eating what he finds.[156]

What is man's relationship to nature? Essentially it is a harmonious one, the verdict being based on the design argument and on Ray's optimism which often contains more than a dash of smugness. Of the uses to which man can put many phenomena of nature, Ray says, "It may be objected, that these Uses were not design'd by Nature in the Formation of the Things, but that the Things were by the Wit of Man accommodated to those Uses."[157] Ray seems to regard the objection as quibbling. Taking the lead from More's *Antidote against Atheism*, Ray replies that materials (e.g., stones, timber, metal) are scattered on the earth "to employ the Wit and Industry of an intelligent and active Being"; God has created in man such a being who can use them and by using them rule over inferior creatures. The Creator would know all the uses to which men might put them and "to them that acknowl-

---

[152] *Ibid.*, p. 114.
[153] *Ibid.*, p. 116.
[154] *Ibid.*, p. 125.
[155] *Ibid.*, p. 159.
[156] *Ibid.*, pp. 137, 139.
[157] *Ibid.*, p. 160.

edge the Being of a Deity; it is little less than a Demonstration, that they were created intentionally, I do not say only, for these Uses."[158] Although Ray disclaims belief in the idea that all nature is designed by the Creator for man, he often forgets his disclaimers in his enthusiasm for the uses of material things to man. (On Ray's ideas about man as a modifier of nature, see *infra*, pp. 483 f.)

If we can assume—and I think we can—that Ray's *Wisdom of God* is representative of a widely held and more hopeful attitude toward theology, science, and civilization, the metamorphosis in thought is striking. Ray continues, less pointedly and less impressively, the positive affirmations of Hakewill. The earth, formerly a divinely designed planet spoiled and weakened by the sin of man, emerges as a place of beauty and usefulness whose powers do not decline with age, as do the plants and animals which it supports, whose relief and climatic variation are not evidences of wreckage and ruins, of a no-man's-land of creation but of beauty and order, with man—still sinful it is true, but with abilities emerging from his social nature and his devotion to God—now given an opportunity to use the earth and to exploit it, gaining new knowledge in order to put it to new uses.

Moreover, when Ray considers the planet as a unit, he finds convincing evidence of the wisdom and power of God in the familiar examples of the sphericity of the earth, its revolution and its rotation, the parallelism and obliquity of its axis. The seasonal change caused by the obliquity affects the world of the intellect, for ". . . an orderly Vicissitude of Things, doth much more gratifie the contemplative Property in Man."[159]

This view of man in his relation to the earth is a gracious, almost idyllic, one: a friendly abode for man has been created by Ray's beneficent Creator, who is full of hints and advice (often gratuitous) about its use, and grateful man, endowed with reason and inventiveness, uses the beautiful earth, and in using it changes it, even if it was not designed especially for him.

The physico-theology of Ray's friend, the Reverend William Derham, was a worthy supplement of Ray's and became influential in its own right. In some ways, Derham's book (1713) is a more exhaustive and richer work. Like the authors of the Bridgewater treatises of the nineteenth century, Derham gave a series of lectures whose aim it was to illustrate the wisdom of God in the creation; the series had been provided for in the will of Robert Boyle to defend the Christian religion from the attacks of infidels and atheists. Derham's influential work was translated into several foreign languages. One can see its influence clearly in the famous German work on population of Johann Peter Süssmilch, *Die Göttliche Ordnung,* whose title reveals its underlying philosophy, and in Kant's discussion of the physico-theological proof for the existence of God in the *Critique of Pure Reason.*

Derham's *Physico-Theology,* like Ray's, stresses the utility and to some ex-

[158] *Ibid.,* p. 161.
[159] *Ibid.,* p. 198.

tent the beauty of the earth, but there is no need of repeating these ideas here. Concepts of the food chain, of the interdependence of all forms of organic life, the distribution of land forms, the working of physical agents like streams and winds, the providential position of the earth on its axis, however, are discussed more elaborately.

One significant advance over Ray's discussion—and the application of the design argument to population theory endeared him to Süssmilch—was his consideration of population growth with relation to the earth as a whole. To Derham, it is self-evident that there is a limit to the number of people the earth can support. Uncontrolled multiplication of animal life would lead to starvation or to one animal devouring another. This uncontrolled multiplication has not occurred because Divine Providence has kept a balance—the significant word is Derham's—of population through control of longevity and different rates of increase for different species: those with long lives increase slowly, those with a short life, with great speed. Useful creatures, he thinks, are also produced more generously than the less useful. (Cites Pliny, *NH*, Bk. VIII, chap. 55.) In this way Divine Providence achieved a balance of populations, including human, through the ages. With human populations, extraordinary longevity after the creation and after the Flood was necessary, but by the time the earth was becoming fairly well peopled, the life span had decreased to 120 years. (Cites Gen. 6:3.) From Moses' time to Derham's, the period during which the earth became fully peopled, the life span had lowered again—to about 70–80 years. Derham, however, sees in the regularity of excess of births over deaths evidence of design to insure a steadiness between the population and the earth's capacity to support it. In the same way that Malthus later (1798) wrote of the beneficent nature of the principle of population, Derham says this admirable provision takes care of emergencies, the peopling of unhealthful places "where death out-runs life," compensates for losses at sea, from war, from disease and plague, and makes it possible to colonize the uninhabited parts of the earth.[160]

The serious application of the design argument to population theory is one of the noteworthy developments of the seventeenth and early eighteenth centuries; so widely accepted was this population theory based on design that it became an important block in the way of the Malthusian theory just as the whole design argument became a block in the nineteenth century for the theory of evolution.

Like Ray, Derham thought the earth an orderly, well-planned place in which there was "nothing wanting, nothing redundant or frivolous, nothing botching or ill-made. . . ."[161] The creation is inexhaustible, so great is the munificence of the Creator. There is greater breadth, too, in his attitude to-

[160] Derham, *Physico-Theology*, Vol. I, pp. 257–261, 267; on the balance of animals, pp. 257–270.
[161] *Ibid.*, p. 51.

ward the usefulness of the creation, broader understanding of the changing values of resources, "So what hath seemed useless in one age, hath been received in another; as all the new discoveries in physic, and all the alterations in diet so sufficiently witness."[162] Plants like the cassava, minerals, and insects may be useful in one form, poisonous in another. Many forms of life, useless to man, are indispensable in the economy of nature, the insects of the air and water being food for birds, fishes, reptiles, other insects. To Derham nature is so bountiful that man can afford to ignore what seems useless to him, can judge it by standards other than its utility to him.[163]

Once the focus is taken away from man, the emphasis is no longer on utility but on the wider interrelationships characteristic of all nature. These relationships may even be unknown to man. Rudimentary ideas of the food chain are introduced. That the design affects the broadest interrelationships of nature, that these relationships may exist unknown to man, was seen also by Wollaston, a contemporary of Ray and Derham.

> If it should be objected that many things seem to be *useless*, many births are monstrous, or the like, such answers as these may be made. The *uses* of some things are known to *some* men and not to *others*: the uses of some are known *now* that were not known to any body *formerly*: the uses of many may be discovered *hereafter*: and those of some other things may *for ever* remain unknown to all men, and yet *be in nature*, as much as those discovered were before their discovery, or are now in respect of them who know them not.[164]

It is dangerous to speak confidently of times when ideas first emerge. Clearly the idea of a unity in nature is very old, but some ideas of Ray and Derham have a kinship with modern ecology, especially with autecology. I am convinced that modern ecological theory, so important in our attitudes toward nature and man's interferences with it, owes its origin to the design argument: The wisdom of the Creator is self-evident, everything in the creation is interrelated, no living thing is useless, and all are related one to the other.[165]

In this grand design of nature which Ray and Derham so exultantly and piously described, God, living nature and the earth, and human knowledge were indissolubly joined. The Creator had shown exquisite workmanship in making his creatures, but this great array is not for the careless or the incurious; it is to be admired by the rational part of nature, that is, man. Derham spoke for himself, Ray, and many others who shared their hopes for the power

[162] *Ibid.*, pp. 84, 90.
[163] *Ibid.*, pp. 91–94.
[164] Wollaston, *Religion of Nature*, sec. 5, par. 14, p. 84. Derham, *Physico-Theology*, p. 89n.
[165] The editor of the 1798 edition of Derham's *Physico-Theology* cited a Mr. Sturm who told of the attempts of the American colonists to exterminate jackdaws because they harmed the corn; with fewer jackdaws, the worms, caterpillars, and may-bugs increased; and when they stopped the war on the jackdaws they were relieved of the plague of vermin. Derham, *op. cit.*, Vol. I, p. 94n.

of knowledge, with the miraculous discoveries of Newton, when he wrote, "My text commends God's works, not only for being great, but also approves of those curious and ingenious inquirers, that *seek them out*, or *pry into them*."[166]

Physico-theology in the seventeenth and early eighteenth centuries is in a minor key compared with the new scientific methodology forged by Galileo, Descartes, and Newton; it differs from the physico-theology of the past in successfully bringing into sharp focus many old examples, adding new ones, taking advantage of new knowledge and new inspirations, and in being endowed with a more concrete sense of interrelationships among terrestrial phenomena, probably because of Ray's biological interests. Many of these points of view continued into the eighteenth and nineteenth centuries despite a widespread disenchantment with ideas of final causes.

The possibilities of explaining the nature of the habitable earth in terms of the design argument were realized with much greater clarity: its shape, its relation to the sun, seasonal change and the obliquity of the axis, the awesome processes on the earth expressed on a gigantic scale in the meeting of land and sea, erosion, and the hydrologic cycle. On its surface (and in a very thin layer of topsoil) was the vegetable mold or humus upon which all life on land was thought to depend, for the importance attached to humus was due in part to vitalism, and in part to the belief that humus was the real source of soil fertility. John Woodward expressed the idea well:

> The *upper* or outermost *Stratum* of *Earth*: that *Stratum* whereon Men and other Animals tread, and Vegetables grow, is in a *perpetual Flux*, and *Change*; this being the *common Fund* and *Promptuary* that supplies and sends forth *Matter* for the *Formation* of *Bodies* upon the *Face* of the *Earth*. That all *Animals*, and particularly *Mankind*, as well as *all Vegetables*, which have had *Being* since the *Creation* of the *World*, derived all the *Constituent Matter* of their *Bodies* successively, in *all Ages*, out of this *Fund*.[167]

One notices in these works—as well as in the works of antiquity and the Middle Ages—a strong emphasis on the utility of living nature, but they are not free of vacillation; sometimes they embrace a broader view that sees the whole of which man is a part. More common is the happy listing of the uses of nature to man with solemn reminders that nature does not exist for him alone; this attitude is characteristic of Henry More, John Ray, and William Derham; of Linnaeus in the eighteenth and of Paley in the early nineteenth century. One must be charitable toward this utilitarian bias even though one tires of its superficialities. It expresses, I think, a significant relationship between theology and economics, especially in a preindustrial age when the dependence on plant and animal life was more direct, intense, and local than it later was. One could

[166] *Ibid.*, Vol. II, p. 394.
[167] *An Essay Towards a Natural History of the Earth*, p. 227.

piously look at living nature and be exalted with such evidence of God's wisdom; a worldly, calculating, practiced eye could also see its uses.

That aspect of the design argument which saw man as the highest being of nature without granting that nature existed for man alone, saw physical beauty and physical evil, and the struggle for existence in nature as part of a design which transcended human interests, demands, and understanding. The struggle for existence in nature is often depicted with great complacency; but the descriptions are also adumbrations of an ecological point of view. With the gradual elaboration of these interrelationships the design scaffolding can be eliminated; it was in fact largely eliminated by Buffon, Von Humboldt, Lamarck, and Darwin.

Physico-theology was also concerned with man's control over nature. Although Christian thinkers have never kept silent for long about the wickedness and sinfulness of man, these seventeenth century writers, Hakewill, Ray, Derham, saw beauty and purposefulness in work. Activity was more than the consequence of sin (see chap. X).

They saw mankind as a whole in its role as a superintendent and arbiter in nature, but they could still accept, as being consistent with the design, explanations of cultural differences based on climate or a combination of environmental factors. Christian theology gave them a natural interest in cultural diffusion, stimulated perhaps by the second book of Esdras; the native Americans might well be modern representatives of the lost tribes of Israel.

These Christian thinkers, accepting the truth revealed both by the Word and by the world of nature, so eager for knowledge that they made their own the saying that the creation existed so that man by his ever-increasing knowledge of it could admire even more the wondrous works of God, naturally interested themselves in the extremely important questions which had so puzzled José de Acosta, concerning the diffusion of man and his culture traits and of domestic animals and wild beasts throughout the world. If one accepted the unity of the human race and its origin at a single place, as the Scriptures taught, then the study of the peoples and the flora and fauna of the New World unavoidably brought up the question of cultural diffusion. The question of population growth was unavoidable too, because of the need to explain, in terms acceptable to Christian theology, the growth in the earth's population from the Flood to the present. Population had held its own despite wars and plagues; plants multiplied rapidly but so did animals and men to consume them; "prunings" prevented an overabundance of individuals. (Comparisons between human and animal populations were inspired also in part by Aristotle's *Historia animalium* and by Genesis 1:22 and 1:28.) Scriptural exegesis thus posed questions concerning the length of life, the period of doubling, the mechanisms by which the population increased, the checks which had prevented it from increasing too much.

The most important generalization to emerge was that populations slowly grew despite checks through wars, plagues, and the like; some such generalization was unavoidable, given the knowledge that the population of the world had sprung from eight people, Noah and his wife, and their three sons and their wives, assuming that Noah went on the ark with his family A.M. 1657, and that Christ was born A.M. 3999, four years and six days before the commonly accepted beginning of the Christian Era, A.M. 4004.

Graunt's discovery of a regularity in the number of births of each sex with a predominance of males over females (differing slightly in city and in rural environments) introduced a concept of mathematical order, balance, and regularity into population theory that had not been there before. Such statistical regularity caused a gleam in the eye of every good physico-theologist. What was a more convincing proof of the wisdom of God than this regularity in nature discovered by Graunt? There were more male than female children, but did not men die in wars and drown at sea, and was not the life of a man a little more dangerous than the life of a female? Was not this discovery, as Graunt had said, an argument for monogamy, and did it not show the superiority of the Christian religion over the Muslim? Did not this clear capacity of the human race, despite all the checks, to increase and spread over the world, confirm the commands of Scripture? Did it not show also that the Creator was aware that the earth had the capacity for providing for the good souls whom He was commanding to increase and to multiply? Rev. William Derham eagerly grasped the physico-theological implications of Graunt's essay, and Johann Peter Süssmilch, reading Derham, grasped the relevance of the argument to a general population theory.

### 10.  CONCLUSION

Many of these men, believing in final causes, devoted to a study of nature which was likened to following in the Creator's footsteps, or in Sir Thomas Browne's words, "to suck Divinity from the flowers of Nature,"[168] were not in sympathy with the mechanical philosophy with its emphasis on efficient, secondary causes, nor with Descartes, even if his piety and theism were unquestioned, because he too proposed to investigate nature without the help of final causes. Both the "mechanick philosophers" and the physico-theologists, however, were united (after the nonsense about the lost vigor of nature had been swept away) in the goal of man's attaining control over nature which Descartes, in a famous passage of the *Discourse on Method* (1637), had set for mankind.

Both the dominant school, molding the scientific method with dexterous

[168] *Religio Medici*, sec. 16.

and impatient fingers, and the subordinate school, doggedly piling up evidence of design to resemble the showcases of an old-fashioned museum, saw the uses of knowledge and the need to replace scholastic speculations with it. In this plea for a science leading to the control of nature with knowledge as deep and expert as the artisan's, Descartes was showing—as did Sprat, the historian of the Royal Society, thirty years later—respect for the accomplishments of practical life, in navigation, in drainage (his residence in Holland must have made him aware of the power of man and his tools to change a landscape), and in agriculture. (See p. 476.)

These roads, however, led in different directions. The road so exultantly described by Descartes[169] led to an ideal of a purposive control over nature through applied science, the kind of control which in our own day has been in such large and triumphant measure achieved.

The road of the physico-theologists was more winding and there were blind alleys. It led to perennial amateurism, to further philosophizing on the role of man making his way between God and the brutes, finishing the creation so that he, and through him the earth, could become more perfect. Much later, perhaps by the middle of the nineteenth century, when it became apparent that man's stewardship of nature was no longer an accurate description of his role, there was disillusionment, and with it the realization that men could relentlessly destroy nature in ways that they did not even suspect themselves capable of, that many of their efforts were not divinely guided, nor the result of purposive control, but were casual and meretricious, that they could not be dignified by identifying them with the Creator's purpose. The real contribution of physico-theology—we shall meet up with it again—was that it saw living interrelationships in nature concretely. It documented them. It had already—before Darwin's "web of life"—prepared men for the study of ecology.

This period sifted and winnowed the chaff of centuries, and after the sifting and the winnowing was over, the ideas which remained were still recognizable to the past; new curiosity and knowledge, however, had given them a fresh gloss. Old notions of the decay of nature were brushed away. Out of fanciful contrasts of the present with the antediluvian earth, there ultimately emerged a bolder affirmation than had been made before, that in spite of man's sinning, the earth as it is presently known is fitted for the coexistence of many kinds of life, adapted for the interrelationships existing in living nature.

It developed to an exalted station the Christian interpretation of man's activities during his short stay on earth, validating the changes he made in it, underscoring the correctness of his acts in assuming supervision over animal and plant life. The earth was his to change, and to perfect in the literal sense of *perficio*—to bring to an end, to finish—to complete it, for without a sentient

[169] *Discourse on Method*, trans. Wollaston (Penguin Classics), chap. 6, p. 84.

being growing more knowledgeable with time there is little purpose in the creation.

The great figures of the seventeenth century no doubt created the concept of nature that Whitehead has described, but many of its minor figures rejected it. The answers to their questions could come only from concrete study of secondary qualities, of interrelationships, from the study of life in its habitat. God had been a geometer for so long. It was now time that be became a gardener, a farmer, a plant and animal breeder, even a wanderer over the mountain, the heath, the valley and along the riverbank, observing sheep, goats, weeds, and the trees of the forest.

# Chapter 9

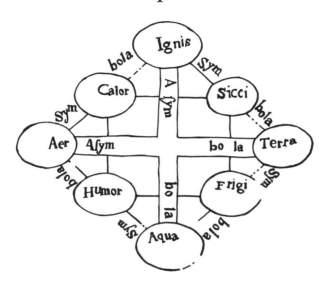

# Environmental Theories
# of Early Modern Times

## 1. Introduction

In early modern times, especially after the age of discovery, ideas of environmental influence assumed a much greater importance than they had in classical times or in the Middle Ages. The volume of ideas was far greater than in either period and it increased through the eighteenth and nineteenth centuries, criticism having little effect on their continuous production.

It is possible to cite hundreds of references in the sixteenth and seventeenth centuries, but only a handful have any theoretical interest; the others show how widely and how deeply these ideas had entered every field of thought. They were in the works of political theorists like Machiavelli, Bodin, and Botero; they were in the work of philosophers like Charron, of poets like Du Bartas and Milton, and of innumerable travelers.

## 2. ON LEON BATTISTA ALBERTI

Nothing shows more convincingly the impact of classical conceptions of environment on the thinkers of the Renaissance than Leon Battista Alberti's (1404–1472) *Ten Books on Architecture*, which was first printed in Latin in 1485. Later they do yeoman service for Bodin, Botero, Du Bartas, Burton, and many lesser writers. Bodin, in fact, became the most important single disseminator, but many derived their ideas direct from Hippocrates or Vitruvius or from contemporary works inspired by them.

Like Vitruvius, whom he had read thoroughly and critically, Alberti considers an understanding of the environment to be fundamental to the practice of architecture; this word, moreover, is not to be taken in a narrow sense, for Alberti also is much concerned with location and proper siting, whole regions, gardens, and city and town planning. A sense of public responsibility, a striving for the overall effect, a harmonizing of human creations with the natural surroundings, permeate his philosophy of craftsmanship. He cherishes the view and the prospect, the unexpected that awaits one in the turning of a street. The physical environment, healthful living conditions and environmental changes necessary to bring them about, are the broad categories within which the architect works; these interrelationships will be of continuing importance in the centuries to come. If certain environmental conditions induce certain kinds of disease, men should alter the environment. Society and its buildings and the ingenuity which creates them are all involved with the natural surroundings, for he believes it was the usefulness and necessity for roofs and walls, and not for water or fire, that first brought men together.[1]

Alberti has a profound knowledge of the classical writers; his easy familiarity is like Burton's; he values the surviving monuments of antiquity, and they have a place along with the natural beauty (memories of the past force us to think of the passage of time, of the destinies of men and things, and we are filled with wonder and admiration); he remarks on health conditions, mentioning the possibility that the environment is responsible for the misshapen and deformed people of Italy and other countries.[2]

The ancients exercised great care, he says, in avoiding harmful regions, and they were particularly sensitive to the need for wholesome air. They had limited ability in improving unhealthful conditions. They might correct through ingenuity and industry what was harmful in soil and water; but they were convinced that neither human intelligence nor the human hand could satisfactorily overcome a badness of air. He documents the importance the ancients attached to pure air, repeating with approval, possibly out of Vitruvius, the saying that the Athenians in their dry air had sharper wits than did the Thebans in their thick and moist atmosphere. Everyone knows, he

[1] *Ten Books on Arch.*, preface.
[2] *Ibid.*, Bk. VI, chap. 4; I, chap. 3.

adds, how great is the influence of climate on generation, production, and the maintenance of things. The unhealthy and disease-ridden cities of Italy and other parts of the world experience sudden changes from hot to cold and cold to hot; but also he sees the advantage of air movement. He prefers soft breezes to strong winds, but the latter are better than calm, motionless, heavy air; winds should come "broken by the Opposition of Hills and Woods, or tired with a long Journey."[3]

Alberti follows the classical writers in their concern for choosing favorable sites; besides natural advantages sites must also offer assurances of peaceful living with one's neighbors. Great edifices should not be built in remote places. The classical idea of the golden mean is very much to his liking. The best regions are neither too warm nor too moist; they will produce high-spirited, slender, and handsome men. Usefulness, healthfulness, and convenience are not enough in a building or in a city; men must be aware of beauty and aesthetics. Place no building in a valley between two hills, he says, for aside from self-evident objections, "an Edifice so placed has no Manner of Dignity, lying quite hid; and its Prospect being interrupted can have neither Pleasure nor Beauty."[4]

His ideas are reinforced by his observations. In some Italian cities, which he will not name, there is not a woman who is not at the same time the mother of a man and of a monster. So numerous are humpbacks, the squint-eyed, the crippled, and the lame people "that there is scarce a Family, but what has Somebody in it defective or distorted." We should look for signs of good or harmful climates in animals, plants, and inanimate nature. He adduces the ancients' opinions on the plague and the effects of thunder and lightning and recalls Plato's suggestion that a region might be under the influence of spirits; in certain places men have a tendency to madness. Contagion is possible in places otherwise healthful which are so situated that they are infected with plague and corruption by foreigners.[5]

In his detailed review of classical thought on the location of cities (including that of Caesar, Livy, Strabo, Varro, and Herodotus), he shares the distaste of the ancients for locating near the seashore because of the bad effects of cultural contact with foreigners.[6]

In his discussion of city planning, the concept is broadened so that the city is regarded as an environment in itself. A noble city should have a different plan from that of a modest town, and the demands of warfare must be considered, too. Health, utility, dignity, views, and prospects—all are parts of this environment created by man.[7]

---

[3] *Ibid.*, Bk. I, chap. 3.
[4] *Ibid.*, chap. 4; see also Bk. IV, chap. 2.
[5] *Ibid.*, Bk. I, chap. 5.
[6] *Ibid.*, Bk. IV, chap. 2; VII, chap. 1.
[7] *Ibid.*, Bk. IV, chap. 2.

### 3. GENERAL QUESTIONS REGARDING CLIMATE AND CULTURE

It is only with the more general discussions of climate and culture that we are concerned here, but theories of climatic influence were applied to many more specific problems, such as peculiarities within a single locality or country as contrasted with a wider region, or the effect of climate on occupations. Vegetius' remarks on the recruitment of soldiers were quoted, reviving interest in the relation of climate to war. The celebrated passage from Paul the Deacon which has already been discussed revived interest in the relation of climate to population growth, migration and in the northern regions as an *officina gentium*. These theories were also related to the idea that the northern peoples, especially the Goths, were liberty-loving.[8] Many of these works of early modern times followed the precedent set by Plato in the *Laws* and by Aristotle in the *Politics*. Although there was a continuity with the ancient world, the modern works were more than restatements of classical ideas. Too many questions had been raised by the discovery of the New World, by the deeper knowledge of the ancient world, and by the increased knowledge of the peoples and lands of contemporary Europe. Furthermore, the revival of environmental ideas in the Renaissance ultimately led to the intensely interesting and important controversies in the eighteenth century over the influence of the environment which engaged the attention of many of the leading political and social theorists like Montesquieu, Hume, Voltaire, Herder, Ferguson, Robertson, and many others.

Why did theories of environmental influence proliferate so in modern times? In the first place, there was greater opportunity to apply them. More environments were known. The oversimplifications of the ancients were discovered by the new knowledge of the equatorial regions and of cultural differences in similar latitudes. The increase in interest in manners, in the *moeurs*, encouraged the study of causes of differences. Finally, the relation of climate and geographical position to laws became important in a period when the relations of the Church to national monarchs were under close scrutiny and when the religious schisms of the Reformation posed difficult questions to political and social theorists.

Does climate, then, have a decisive effect on laws and customs? In the reading of history, with its cruelties, its senseless and continual change, its wars, intrigues, embroilments, is there anything on which to base an interpretation

---

[8] See Taylor, *Late Tudor and Early Stuart Geography 1583–1650*, esp. the various chapters on regional, economic, and human geography, and the illuminating chapter on the urbane traveler. Miss Taylor notes that the English geographers of the time lacked a philosophy of geography like Bodin's and Botero's (pp. 133–134), and that Camden in his *Britannica* follows in a general way the Hippocratic doctrine in explaining the influence of the environment on the British people (p. 9). See also Kliger's discussion of climate and liberty in *The Goths in England*, pp. 241–252. For examples from Germany, see Meuten, *Bodins Theorie von der Beeinflussung des politischen Lebens der Staaten durch ihre geographische Lage*, pp. 26–28.

of its significance? This was essentially the question raised by Bodin in the *Methodus*. Is it more rational to base one's study on the more stable physical environment and does history therefore become inextricably bound up with geography? These questions called forth more disturbing ones: Does man have only a modest superiority over the organic creation? If the distribution of plants and animals is controlled by the climate, is this control exerted also on man and does his superiority lie merely in his sensitive realization of this deterministic relationship? Questions like these raised another: Is it possible for man to resist these deterministic influences? This last question I think is the crux of the whole matter. It was asked by Bodin, by Montesquieu, and by Herder. Polybius had asked it by implication in antiquity and had answered in the affirmative.

The role assigned to environmental influences in the interpretation of history thus may be a decisive one. If they were such powerful determinants, had they reinforced the differences among men, perpetuating their rivalries and their hostilities? Had climatic theories become a divider of mankind, playing a role similar to the late nineteenth century theories of racial superiority? Theories from classical times were also revived in the contrast between the too easy environment—acting like an overly indulgent Mother Nature, making man soft by her generosity, ultimately defeating him by inducing sloth and love of luxury—and the hard environment, like a niggardly Mother Nature, spurring man's inventiveness and his industry, through necessity.

Machiavelli's *Discourses on the First Ten Books of Titus Livius* shows this classical inspiration clearly. He discusses two classical themes but with modern settings and a modern application: the theme of soil and civilization, and that of government and environment. His position is similar to Plato's in the *Laws*: In the enactment and administration of laws consideration must be given to the diverse characteristics of peoples.

A city needs a fertile soil for strength and greatness. If the fertility of the soil encourages idleness—as had been traditionally held—laws should be devised to provide the incentive equal to that which an infertile soil might give. Machiavelli praises lawgivers, like the founders of ancient Egypt and the modern pashas and their Mameluke militia, who enact laws that offset the softening effects of the climate. A ruler has power to play human against natural forces; he can select a fertile spot because laws can overcome any ill effects caused by the site.[9]

In the *Florentine History*, Machiavelli revives Paul the Deacon's idea of climate being related to the fecundity of northern regions. On the other hand, he recognized—Venice and Pisa are his examples—a certain independence of man from nature, his ability to modify it by making seemingly uninhabitable and unhealthy areas habitable. Furthermore, he rejects Vegetius' (fourth century A.D.) suggestion that soldiers should be recruited from temperate climates

---

[9] *Discourses*, Bk. I, chap. 1, Modern Library ed., pp. 108–109.

because they possess in fortunate harmony spiritual and physical courage; instead hè advocates recruiting from among the young of the country, presumably because they will love it and therefore fight for it.[10]

#### 4. ON JEAN BODIN IN GENERAL

Jean Bodin is the most important thinker of the Renaissance on the general subject of the relation between history and contemporary life and the geographic environment. He lived in one of the most disturbed periods of modern European history (the period of the great religious wars), and the problems of holding society together, of a monarchy's ability to do it, of national sovereignty, of making laws general enough yet wise enough to take account of local differences, transcended both the thinker and his country. No other thinker of the period—Machiavelli, Botero, Le Roy, Charron—can match him either in the breadth of his systematic thinking (his correlations are not mechanical ones; they have deep roots in ancient and medieval theories of physiology, body-mind relationships, physics and cosmology, astrology, and numerology) or in the industry and thoroughness with which ideas and observations, scattered hither and there through the centuries, have been gathered together and given—if not a satisfying unity to the modern mind—at least an inner coherence thanks to the medieval conception of the cosmos upon which they are based.

We would not err greatly, in fact, if we wrote the history of environmental theories around the names of Hippocrates, Aristotle, Ptolemy, Albert the Great, and St. Thomas, summarizing the results of over two thousand years of speculation in the syntheses of Bodin. From Bodin one can easily see the way to Montesquieu, for if we ignore the ponderous, scholastic style of the former and the clear fresh epigrammatic style which so effectively concealed the lack of originality of the latter, it is clear that both men were concerned with the same types of problems (their great differences were in their answers) whose general nature is implicit in this question: How is it possible to govern a people, in a small region or throughout the whole world, when they so clearly differ in customs, traditions, laws, color, physique, and mental outlook? The problem is expressed beautifully and accurately in the English of the Knolles translation (1606) of Bodin's *Republic*: "Let us now shew what may be particular to some [Commonweales], through the diversitie of peoples humors, to the end that we may accommodate the publike weale to the nature of the place. . . ."[11] This is the language of the *Republic*; in the *Methodus*, the work of earlier years, there is a broader philosophical and historical consideration of the significance of the physical environment.

The *Republic* was published in 1576, the *Methodus* in 1566. What is strik-

---

[10] *Florentine Hist.*, I, 1; *Dell'arte della guerra*, Lib. 1, (*Opere*, ed. Panella, Vol. 2, p. 492).
[11] *Rep.*, Bk. V, chap. 1.

ing about both works is their reliance on classical and medieval ideas, contemporary European travel and opinion within Europe, and the slight consideration given to the ethnology of the New World. The deep learning in the classics is manifest on every page of Bodin's discussions of environment (*Airs, Waters, Places* of Hippocrates, Plato's *Laws*, Aristotle's *Politics*, Vitruvius' *On Architecture*, and Ptolemy's *Tetrabiblos*). Strabo is referred to often but does not appear in the theoretical discussions of the environment. There is much contemporary evidence from the travelers within Europe whom he has met or read, an obvious interest in Alvarez (*Narrative of the Portuguese Embassy to Abyssinia During the Years 1520–27*), and in Leo the African (*The History and Description of Africa*) because they have something to tell him of the southern regions, but the references to the New World are few and inconsequential, such as Las Casas' talk of the large and simple Patagonians, and the cruelty of the South Americans.[12] It is revealing that an important thinker, writing almost seventy-five years after the discovery of America, still bases his arguments on classical and contemporary European evidence; no doubt part of the explanation lies in the fewness of the books and the difficulty of their dissemination, but it is a sobering reminder that the full fruits of the age of discovery—the newer ideas of humanity, human culture, the revelation of new environments—were not harvested, except for a few atypical individuals, until the seventeenth and eighteenth centuries.

Bodin is interested in national character; the nature and varying degrees of perfidy, suspiciousness, and treachery among peoples (in peace and in war); the insensate cruelty of peoples and of individuals among them; drunkenness and insanity and whether such aberrant behavior has an observable geographic distribution or if it is found everywhere or if it was dominant in certain areas.

The short sentences of Aristotle's *Politics* were continuing reminders that certain physical environments might be favorable to the existence of high civilization; Aristotle said that they were, that they were temperate in nature, and Greece was his example. The generalization—this was its beauty—did not eliminate newer choices for the temperate spot. If the favored nation was Greece in Aristotle's time, why could it not be northwestern Europe or France in the sixteenth century? One could write an illuminating essay on the relocations through the ages of the favored temperate region.

Jean Bodin's theories are the product of both the Hippocratic and the astrological traditions. The outstanding thinkers of the later Middle Ages like Albert the Great combine them and so does Bodin. However, he rejects Ptolemy's in favor of a simpler and less popular astrological theory.[13]

Recent research on the sources of Bodin's writings on climatic influences

---

[12] *Methodus*, trans. Reynolds, p. 102; Marian J. Tooley, "Bodin and the Mediaeval Theory of Climate," *Speculum* 28 (1953), p. 75.
[13] Brown, *The Methodus ad Facilem Historiarum Cognitionem of Jean Bodin. A Critical Study*, p. 14, thinks Bodin may have acquired it from the astrologer Augier Ferrier, first physician to Catherine of Medici, "philosopher, disciple of Cardan, and friend and enemy of Bodin."

has shown the continuity in his thought of conceptions already developed in the medieval period. Tooley argues, and in my opinion correctly, that the general principles of the theory of climatic influences were "too familiar to need exposition."[14] (They could scarcely be otherwise because of the flourishing condition of the classical theory of the humors [especially the refinements made by Galen], the humors of course being the real basis for the correlations between environment and health, physical and mental characteristics.) Medieval cosmologies, with discussions of the four elements, and the encyclopedias, which also discussed them and the humors, continued in popularity through the sixteenth century.

### 5. His Divisions of the Earth

Moreover, Bodin rejected the Copernican view of the universe, accepting the medieval interpretation, based on Ptolemy, that the seven spheres (Moon, Mercury, Venus, the Sun, Mars, Jupiter, and Saturn) plus an eighth, the sphere of the fixed stars, revolved around a motionless earth. If one followed the Aristotelian view that matter could be given form only by an efficient cause external to it, and the maxim that nature does nothing in vain, it further followed that the eight spheres must have a purpose. "To Bodin, as to his mediaeval predecessors, the conclusion was inescapable; it must be the stars in their courses that govern the mutations of matter. Moreover, for Bodin, since he rejected the doctrine that form is latent in matter and the stars merely elicit it, the stars are actually the source from which the multiplicity of forms immediately proceeds."[15]

Without going into technical details, it is clear that the amount and intensity of radiation from the heavens differed from place to place, and from these circumstances it was further possible to explain the continual change in time and the variety of life on earth at any one time.[16] The facility with which an expert could do this is amazingly shown in Book II, chapter 3, of Ptolemy's *Tetrabiblos*. Astrological principles likewise could explain the operation of the cosmos.

Ptolemy's system, complex in local application, is simple in its basic principles. (See also chap. II, sect. 10.) Let us repeat some of them. The inhabited world is divided into four parts, into northern and southern by an east-west line drawn roughly from the Gulf of Issus to Gibraltar, into eastern and western by a north-south line drawn from the Pontus through the Arabian Gulf. These two lines divided the world into quadrants, each governed by a triplicity: the northwest by Aries, Leo, Sagittarius, and ruled by Jupiter on account of the north wind, Mars joining in on account of the south wind; the

[14] Tooley, *op cit.*, pp. 64–83, quotation on p. 65.
[15] *Ibid.*, pp. 66–67, quotation on p. 66.
[16] *Ibid.*, p. 67.

southwest dominated by Cancer, Scorpio, Pisces, ruled by Mars and Venus in occidental aspect; the northeast, by Gemini, Libra, Aquarius, ruled by Saturn and Jupiter in oriental aspect; and the southeast, Taurus, Virgo, Capricorn, with Venus and Saturn in oriental aspects. Ptolemy then made general cultural correlations for the quadrant as a whole: the men of the northwest, for example, are independent, liberty-loving, fond of arms, industrious, very warlike, possess leadership qualities, are cleanly and magnanimous, but without passion for women, preferring men. Ptolemy made two refinements in this general scheme: The more specific characteristics of the individual peoples are described, depending upon their precise position with reference to the stars, and special attention is given the people living near the center of each quadrant. These four centers, one for each quadrant, comprised the center of the inhabited world; here there was less diversity because the peoples living in the southeast part of the northwest quadrant and the northwest part of the southeast reciprocally influenced one another as did those living in the southwest part of the northeast and the northeast part of the southwest.

Bodin was selective, however, in his use of astrological ethnology, specifically rejecting the Ptolemaic conceptions. His simpler astrological scheme is combined with environmental explanations of differences between the north, the south, and the temperate zones to account for cultural differences.

The Northern Hemisphere, with which Bodin was mostly concerned, is divided from the equator to the pole into three zones of thirty degrees each, the forty-fifth parallel being the border between the north and the south. The longitudinal divisions, much less important in Bodin's scheme, are determined by a meridian through the Canaries (Hesperides), a traditional prime meridian on the west, and another through the Moluccas on the east. Although Bodin realizes that east and west are relative positions and that the roundness of the earth precludes their meeting, he has them meeting in fact somewhere in the Americas.

Each of these three regions of thirty degrees each (representing hot, temperate, and cold zones) is subdivided into two subregions of fifteen degrees each. Bodin, however, believed that the hottest places on earth were at the two tropics, the coldest at the poles; in the Northern Hemisphere, the extremes of heat and cold would be represented by the North Pole and by the Tropic of Cancer. The reason for this belief reveals in itself a very significant attitude regarding the new knowledge of the extent and diversity of the earth's environments. If Bodin's thought is representative—and one is tempted to believe that it is—men in the sixteenth century were more impressed with the discovery that the equatorial regions were habitable than they were with the discovery of the New World. Bodin says we must eradicate the error of the ancients (Posidonius and Avicenna excepted) who believed that men could live only between the tropics and the polar circles. The equatorial regions are healthful; they possess plenteous rainfall, high mountains, and forests (proved by "frequent exploration" and by the testimony of Francisco Alvarez); in the two tropics, however, it is in fact hotter than it is at the equator. It is easy to see how Bodin made this generalization for the Old World: near or on the equator there is the lush vegetation of the tropical rain forest type of climate; the Tropic of Cancer goes through the heart of the burning heat and the virtually rainless deserts of North Africa.[17]

Bodin shifted northward the temperate region between the tropic and the pole because it is hotter on the Tropic of Cancer than on the equator; following this reasoning, he considered the most temperate region on earth to be from forty to fifty degrees north latitude; within each of the three zones he thought the eastern part to be more temperate than the west. The temperate region is the most comfortable excepting those parts of it in rugged highlands, swamps, arid or sterile lands.

Bodin says he will discuss mainly the people living between thirty and sixty degrees north latitude. His reasons are that more is known of these peoples, little of any other peoples, and, what is most indefensible to a modern mind, that "by this illustration we shall learn what must be believed about all."[18]

Bodin distinguishes between the body heat generated by peoples living from the equator to the forty-fifth parallel, and the heat of those living from the forty-fifth to the seventy-fifth, lands north of the latter parallel being virtually uninhabited. Receiving less heat from the sun, people in the northern area must generate compensatory heat within their own bodies. With this theory, Bodin explains the superiority of northern herds and flocks (the animals are more active and robust), and it is the same with humans: the greatest empires have spread from the north to the south. (These directional terms with Bodin are entirely relative, as is apparent in the following instances: the Assyrians conquered the Chaldeans; the Medes, the Assyrians; the Greeks, the Persians; the Parthians, the Greeks; the Romans, the Carthaginians, etc.)[19]

### 6. BODIN'S USE OF THE HUMORS

In the classical theory of the humors, it is assumed that habits of mind can be inferred from physical states created by the humors and that the physico-mental correlations so discovered among individuals can be applied to peoples. The body and the mind, however, may be swayed in opposite directions (a frequent theme in Aristotle's *Problems*); a strong intellect is opposed by a weak body. When applied to peoples, this generalization explains why the southern peoples, for example, have intellect but lack vigor, while the northerners possess opposite qualities. Obviously a rough balancing of qualities is thus achieved among the peoples of the earth, so that a people pre-

---

[17] *Methodus*, p. 87; see also Dainville, *La Géographie des Humanistes*, pp. 25–27.
[18] *Methodus*, chap. V, p. 97.
[19] *Ibid.*, pp. 92–93.

eminent in one aspect would compensate for this superiority by shortcomings in another. In a Christian setting, it is only natural that Bodin should ask if this arrangement is not part of Divine Wisdom.[20]

In a bold passage which shows what these ideas could lead to, Bodin says:

> This savagery [of the Southerners, meaning apparently the Carthaginians and the Egyptians, for Bodin has just been discussing them] comes partly from that despotism which a vicious system of training and undisciplined appetites have created in a man, but much more from a lack of proportion in the mixing of humors. This, in its turn, comes from elements affected unequally by external forces. The elements are disturbed by the power of the celestial bodies, while the human body is encompassed in the elements, the blood in the body, the spirit in the blood, the soul in the spirit, the mind in the soul. Although this last is free from all materiality, yet it is very much influenced by the closeness of the association. So it happens that those who are in the furthest regions are more inclined to vices.[21]

This is one of the most significant passages in the history of environmental theories because in it, in rude form to be sure, lies the reason that they have been so important in modern times. The first line of the quotation is the crucial one: a people may be helpless or partly helpless under the control of its environment, a theory of causation which could come into conflict with Christian teaching. It is true that the distribution of the humors, combinations of which are influenced by the climate, were interpreted as being part of the divine design, but it is a somewhat different matter to explain cruelty and savagery as being the result, in large part, of conditions beyond the control of a people.

It is the question of the relativity of morals, religion, and customs, based on environmental control, in my opinion, that historically has given environmental theories such a strong hold in Western thought even down to our own times. The crucial idea is the inevitable identification of climatic controls with cultural inertia: this was in essence Voltaire's criticism of Montesquieu. Of what use are attempts at institutional reform if people are doomed to possess qualities imposed on them by unchanging environmental conditions? It is true that in other parts of the *Methodus* and in the *Republic*, Bodin left the way open to retreat from this fatalism, but a close reading of his writing leads one to believe that he thought it was only with great effort that people could overcome the basic controls, and any laxness in their institutions which tended to overcome the environment would mean a return to the original control.

The theory that different environments create different combinations of the humors, thus producing different physical and mental characteristics, is used by Bodin to explain the dominant forms of madness in Europe, the incidence of diseases such as leprosy, varying degrees of fecundity in peoples,

[20] *Ibid.*, pp. 98–100.
[21] *Ibid.*, p. 102.

constancies in sexual unions. Men are more potent in winter, more lustful in summer; sexually capable people do not need to be passionate; lust therefore indicates a lack of potency. Women exhibit the opposite seasonal behavior. No evidence is given for it, but the harmonious meeting of opposites in any one season, an evidence of the wisdom of God, insures the continual reproduction of the human race. We cannot, however, analyze all these specific applications to individuals or to peoples; but one general observation can be made, that the application of the theory of humors, with all the contortions and distortions involved in applying a false theory to a body of fact, is of far less interest than the variety of questions which the helpless humor theory is called upon to answer: it must explain the fecundity of peoples, the rise of religion in one geographic area, the distribution of insanity, of leprosy, of cruelty in war.

The main idea (we will show the astrological aspect in a few moments) is based on the division into hot, cold, and temperate zones. The most interesting and revealing illustrations come in the discussion of the general mental and physical qualities of peoples.

The people of the south are a contemplative sort, adept in the secret sciences, the black bile or melancholy dominant among them, causing prolonged meditation; they have the ablest philosophers, mathematicians, prophets. "From these people letters, useful arts, virtues, training, philosophy, religion, and lastly *humanitas* itself flowed upon earth as from a fountain."[22]

The effect of climate on religion, later developed by Charron, is a touchy subject because it casts doubt on the reality of direct divine intercession in human affairs, and on the truth of a revealed religion. (The relation of environmental to religious ideas is an interesting subject in its own right; even in the twentieth century the rise of monotheism has been ascribed to the monotonous sameness and oneness of the burning sandy deserts.) The peoples of the north are skilled in activities that depend on the senses; they know well the manual crafts and the arts, and they have mechanical skills. It is noteworthy that Bodin illustrates this northern skill with the labors of the physician Georgius Agricola (George Bauer) whose *De veteribus & novis metallis lib. ii* was published in Basel in 1546; in this work he tells of his visits to mines and smelters, his reading on the history of mining and his acquaintance with men skilled in it, topics which are later exhaustively studied in *De re metallica* with its famous illustrations.[23]

Bodin revives an idea of Hippocrates (to be revived again by Montesquieu) that the three ages of man—youth, middle age, and old age (but not the state of being moribund)—are analogous to the northern, the temperate, and the southern regions respectively.

22 *Ibid.*, p. 110.
23 *Ibid.*, p. 112.

When I look more closely, the southerners, the intermediates, and the Scythians seem in a certain measure to have the customs and the humors of old men, of men, and of youths, expressed neatly in an ancient line: Prayers of the old, deeds of youth, and plans of grown men. I call them old men who are not yet decrepit. The Scythians, of course, are warm and wet in the fashion of young men. The southerners are cold and dry, as befitting old men. Those who have attained middle life have achieved the proper blending.[24]

In astrological terms, in the north, Mars, representing war, is assisted by the Moon representing the chase; in the south, Saturn represents contemplation, Venus, love; in the intermediate lands, Jupiter is equated with rulers, Mercury, with orators.

### 7. OTHER PROBLEMS

Bodin's theory of planetary influences is superimposed on the environmental distinctions existent on earth which are largely a product of moisture and temperature distribution, both controlled by the sun's heat. Bodin discards Ptolemy's astrological ethnology after a long refutation, his criticism being that the triplicities "are clearly at variance not only with previous statements but even with nature itself and history." The beginning of the error he traces to ignorance of places and of geography.[25]

The sun is common to all regions; he cites the Chaldean beliefs that "the power of Saturn controls the understanding, that of Jupiter guides action, that of Mars directs production." Saturn is said to be cold; Mars, hot; and Jupiter, moderate between the two.

Cold Saturn and Venus govern in the south. Saturn controls understanding, presides over the mind, knowledge, and contemplation (as befits black bile); this is the realm of the secret sciences. Warm Mars and the Moon are assigned to the north. Mars presides over the arts and handicrafts dependent on skill, strength, imagination. It is thus the region of the manual crafts. More moderate than Mars or Saturn, Jupiter along with Mercury guides action in the middle region: wisdom is embodied in action, embracing all the virtues and reason. The people under Jupiter and Mercury are best suited for managing affairs; they are the lawmakers, the originators of custom, governors, men of commerce.[26] Both the environmental and the astrological ideas are really based on the same zonal division that Aristotle made in his *Politics*. Ptolemy in the *Tetrabiblos*, as we have seen, considers environmental and astrological ethnology but does not fuse the two into a single theory. Bodin does because the zones of astrological influence coincide with the traditional zones based on solar radiation.

[24] *Ibid.*, p. 125.
[25] *Ibid.*, pp. 146–152, quote on p. 147.
[26] *Ibid.*, p. 112.

Bodin's system was ambitious; it was far more searching, exhaustive, and coherent than anything else produced on the subject since Albert the Great's _De natura locorum_. Although we can neglect the minute details, it is important to discuss some of the broader problems implicit in such an effort.

In addition to the cultural distinctions based on latitudinal and astrological influences, Bodin, following tradition, saw other possible environmental influences, owing to the longitude, location on rivers, swamps, or mountains and valleys. These local influences might be in conflict with the zonal correlations.

Cultural differences among people living in different longitudes had always been difficult to explain on climatic grounds. The usual contrasts were between the softness, politeness, love of finery and artistic adornment, of the eastern peoples and the rough-hewn simplicity and lack of guile characteristic of the people of northwest Europe. In hilly lands, Bodin saw the possibility of making finer distinctions—between eastern and western aspects. "Since the rising light by its moderate heat purifies the harmful thick heaviness of the air, it makes the region much more temperate. Moreover, when the sun burns with its greatest heat, that is, in the afternoon, it sets for the eastern region and rises for the western." On flat and level places the problem to Bodin is almost insuperable because there is no rising and no setting, and lands which in the morning feel the rising sun, in the evenings feel its setting; nevertheless he believes, and cites biblical and classical authorities as evidence, that the eastern quarter is more temperate and is better than the western.[27] So caught up is Bodin in the mystique of longitudinal environmental influences that it does not occur to him (as it does to him elsewhere) that differences may not be environmentally caused at all.

The people dwelling in mountains are in a category by themselves; mountain dwellers, regardless of their location, are more like one another than they are like other people of the zone in which they live. "For mountaineers are tough, uncouth, warlike, accustomed to hard work, and not at all cunning." Marshy places, as in Holland and Frisia, produce tall men, but Bodin shows the traditional fear of marshes in hot lands. People living in fertile valleys become luxury-loving in contrast with those of sterile plains. All of these ideas are abundantly illustrated with examples, mostly from classical and contemporary sources; the treatment, however, is traditional, primarily because of ignorance of the actual distribution of climatic types.[28]

In the _Republic_ Bodin applies his theories to the practical problems of government. The theoretical basis is the same; variety in peoples' humors requires a variety in their institutions; the ruler must know the humors before he changes laws and customs. The task of a ruler is likened to that of an

[27] _Ibid._, p. 130.
[28] _Ibid._, pp. 139–140, quote on p. 139.

architect who builds with the materials he can find locally. Furthermore, the theory of government is related to broader questions of philosophy, religion, and technology whose zonal distribution is part of a divine plan. For Bodin, as for Botero and Le Roy, it is easy to reconcile the theory of environment with the idea of design. In divinely ordained reciprocity, the prudent peoples of temperate lands are skilled in commerce, in the establishing of commonwealths, and in the making of laws for others; they are able to judge, persuade, command. The southern peoples, zealous in their pursuit of truth, teach the rest of mankind about the abstruse and secret sciences. The northern peoples, with their manual dexterity, have taught the world skills in the manual arts.

Indeed, Bodin's work is a masterly summary of about two thousand years of speculation regarding the influence of the environment on man. His works brought up certain broad questions in the crucial period of the great religious wars, when many men were aware of the classical heritage, some consequences of voyages and travels, and the implications of schism created by the Reformation.

The most important of these questions is the degree of environmental control over man. Bodin does not believe that climate is the only influence. "The fusion of peoples changes the customs and the nature of men not a little." Fusion and blending are common in the temperate regions because peoples from the extreme regions have moved there "as though to the region of most equable climate." Here Bodin shows his appreciation of the role of war, migration, cultural contact, in molding the life and customs of a people, but he does not apply the idea on a larger scale to show that the history of migrations and the diffusion of physical and mental traits by any means may be more fundamental explanations than climate in understanding human history.[29]

Bodin, moreover, says that divine or human training may influence human nature. "If Hippocrates truly thought that all species of plants can be domesticated, how much more is this true for human kind? Was there ever a race so huge and savage, which, when it had found leaders, was not carried forward along the path of civilization? What race once instructed in the most refined arts, but ceasing to cultivate the humanities, did not sink sometime into barbarity and savagery?"[30] Bodin answers these questions with examples of art and customs influencing the physical and mental characteristics of men.[31] To him, the most convincing evidence (he repeats the argument in the *Republic*) comes from German history from Tacitus' time to his own. It resembles Sebastian Münster's account. (See p. 365.) By their own confession, the Germans once were little better than beasts; like animals, they wandered untutored in forests and marshes. "Nevertheless, they have now so far advanced that

[29] *Ibid.*, p. 143.
[30] *Ibid.*, p. 145.
[31] *Ibid.*, pp. 145–146.

in the humanities they seem superior to the Asiatics; in military matters, to the Romans; in religion, to the Hebrews; in philosophy, to the Greeks; in geometry, to the Egyptians; in arithmetic, to the Phoenicians; in astrology, to the Chaldeans; and in various crafts they seem to be superior to all peoples." The moral of this passage seems to be that environmental theories are most appropriate in explaining an ancient past; when one is concerned with the complexities of a contemporary civilization they fail. Nothing in Bodin's previous theorizing prepares one for this flattering description of German culture of the latter part of the sixteenth century. Nevertheless, he was well acquainted with trends in German historiography, geography, technology, and with the implications of the Reformation.[32]

In the *Republic*, Bodin stresses the role of government in changing people and their dispositions. He will reject "the opinions of Polybius, and Galen, who held, That the countrey and nature of the place did rule necessarily in the manners of men"; but he fails to add that Polybius thought much like himself on this point, that it was possible for the Arcadians through institutionalized music to change their character, which originally was molded by the harsh environment of Arcadia.[33]

Bodin makes a tantalizing reference to the tendency for genius or talent to appear in clusters, examples being (1) Plato, Aristotle, Xenocrates, Timaeus, Archytas, Isocrates, and many other unnamed orators and poets; (2) Chrysippus, Carneades, Diogenes the Stoic, and Arcesilas; (3) Varro, Cicero, Livy, and Sallust; (4) Virgil, Horace, Ovid, and Vitruvius; (5) "And not long ago, Valla, Trapezuntius, Ficino, Gaza, Bessarion, and Mirandola flourished contemporaneously."[34]

The history of this idea would make an interesting study in itself. Kroeber deals with the phenomenon in his *Configurations of Culture Growth*; Teggart called attention to the importance of studying the historical circumstances surrounding the appearance of genius in clusters. In the nineteenth century Thomas De Quincey discussed the idea at length. In the ancient world Tacitus wondered why orators tended to appear in groups, and Velleius Paterculus was well aware of the phenomenon. The abbé du Bos, as we shall see, was also very interested in this question. "If anyone, then, having collected passages of memorable affairs, should compare with them these great trajections and ascertain the regions affected or the states changed, he will achieve fuller knowledge about the customs and the nature of peoples; then,

---

[32] *Ibid.*, pp. 145–146, quote on p. 145.
[33] *Rep.*, Bk. V, chap. 1.
In the cosmopolitan atmosphere of Toulouse, Bodin met and fraternized with students of all nationalities, and developed that international point of view which will find such eloquent expression in the *Methodus* in his pleas for the *Respublica mundana*. Some of his telling and accurate observations on national character (found in the fifth chapter of *Methodus*) owe much to his student associations (Brown, *op. cit.*, p. 16; see also, pp. 53–54).
[34] *Methodus*, p. 152.

also, he will make much more effective and reliable judgments about every kind of history."[35] Bodin too saw that the periodic appearance of clusters of genius and talent required historical explanation. If this line of inquiry had been pursued, it would have called into question the adequacy of environmental explanations, unless climates could conveniently be made to change with each peak or trough of cultural achievement.

Environmental theories have often posed the question: To what degree are people or peoples responsible for their good or evil qualities? Bodin now is speaking of familiar themes in history, such as a tenacious holding on to custom, failure to yield one's religion despite torture, and known shortcomings of peoples. Extreme positions are not palatable to Bodin.

> Since these vices are, as it were, innate in each race, history must be judged according to the customs and nature of each people before we can make unfavorable comments. For the moderation of the southerners is not praiseworthy, nor is the drunkenness of the Scythians, which is so much criticized, really to be scorned, because the southerners, through lack of inward heat, are at once satiated with food and drink; the Scythians, on the other hand, could not easily restrain themselves even if they wished, for they are impelled by internal warmth and lack the resources of genius.[36]

What of the case for an environmental basis of history, assuming the stability of the earthly environment amid the ever-changing human scene and uncertain fortunes of history? Bodin's answer anticipates that given by many nineteenth century geographers, and especially by Friedrich Ratzel in one of his more deterministic phases. Historians are unreliable, says Bodin; they do not write about the right things, and there is much that is changeable and capricious in human affairs.

> Since that is so, let us seek characteristics drawn, not from the institutions of men, but from nature, which are stable and are never changed unless by great force or long training, and even if they have been altered, nevertheless eventually they return to their pristine character. About this body of knowledge the ancients could write nothing, since they were ignorant of regions and places which not so long ago were opened up; instead, each man advanced as far as he could by inference of probabilities.[37]

The original stamp given by climate to a people can be changed only by effort. In this way Bodin allows for the harsh and inexorable control of climate and for the ability of a people to divorce itself by conscious effort from

[35] *Ibid.*, p. 152. On the clustering of genius, see Kroeber, *Configurations of Culture Growth*; Teggart, *Rome and China*, pp. 11–12 and the references there cited; De Quincey, "Style," in *The Collected Writings of Thomas De Quincey*, ed. Masson, Vol. 10, pp. 194–231; Tacitus, *Dialogue on Oratory*; Velleius Paterculus, *The Roman History*, Bk. I, 16–18.

[36] *Methodus*, p. 128. On similar discussions in the Middle Ages, see Tooley, *op. cit.* (see n. 12 above), p. 79.

[37] *Methodus*, p. 85.

its immediate effects, though the victory is tenuous and the ramparts must always be watched. Perhaps it is the best statement a sensitive man, learned in the classics and occupied in the theoretical and practical aspects of the law, could make in an age in which discovery, change, violence, were the order of the day. "Bodin was probably the only writer of the sixteenth century who had grasped the fact that Europe was changing rapidly. He saw that no monarchy, however stable, could last for ever, but realized that the recognition of a strong monarchy in the France of his day was the only hope of escape from political chaos."[38] Bodin's environmental theories are, in part, a consequence of the political conditions of his time; his critical attitude to ideas of church supremacy and the divine right of kings prepares the way for questions of sovereignty, the monarch, his relationships to associations of people and to individuals. He wrote during one of the most eventful periods in modern European history: Luther wrote the ninety-five theses in 1517, the Council of Trent closed in 1563 after eighteen years of irregular meetings, and the French civil wars lasted from 1562 to 1598. France had seven monarchs between 1548 and 1610 and "there was scarcely a year when these monarchs were not coping with foreign war, civil insurrection or both" (Bruun). Bodin wished to devise a political philosophy consistent with the relativity of faith in an age of schism; to him the role of the environment in human affairs showed the need for both tolerance and unity in a centralized monarchy which should be aware of the variety in local custom.

Even when this is said, the fact remains that in a wider perspective Bodin was a traditionalist. If one traces theories of environmental influence back from the present to the thinkers of the nineteenth, eighteenth, and seventeenth centuries and then to Bodin, he seems an innovator, a man who thought deeply about these questions in a recognizably modern setting—after the age of discovery, after the rediscovery of many writings of classical antiquity, after the Reformation. If, however, one approaches Bodin's writings by way of the past, from Hippocrates, Aristotle, Ptolemy, to Albert the Great and St. Thomas Aquinas, their traditional—and often painfully garbled—character is only too apparent. Modern students of Bodin have praised him, making excuses for the astrology and for the numerology (which I have not even brought up) as vices of the time; it is said that he was a precursor of Montesquieu, that his theories were not fatalistic because they left room for other influences, that they were the forerunners of a body of theory later to become a science. (This claim was made mostly by those who regarded scientific geography as the study of environmental influences.) Bodin's thought about environment could by no conceivable means lead to science. The main interest of his ideas today—aside from their historical significance—is that they reveal the complexity of historical and contemporary problems in Bodin's eyes and the inability of two millennia of accumulated lore to be of any real

[38] *EB*, art., "Bodin," 14th ed., Vol. 3, p. 771.

help in explanation. It is true that there were some advantages; the theories by their concentration on differences and similarities may have led the way to a new regional geography, they may have sharpened the eye for cultural observations. But what kind of guides could such theories be when they rested on presuppositions fantastically wide of the mark?

This long analysis of Bodin's ideas simplifies one's task because many writers either borrowed from Bodin, as did Botero, Charron, and probably Du Bartas, or borrowed, as did Bodin, from a common, widely held body of belief so admirably organized by him.

### 8. FURTHER APPLICATIONS OF ENVIRONMENTAL THEORIES

Historically, as we have seen, it has not been a difficult task to reconcile theories of environmental causation with the design argument. If they were carried too far into ethics or religion, however, they might undermine both by showing their doctrines to be the result of more local circumstances than most systems of ethics or revealed religions are willing to allow. The relation of environment to religion and religious schism was discussed frequently after the Reformation and through the eighteenth century. We have encountered such discussions in Botero and Bodin; we will meet them again in Montesquieu and Voltaire.

In *De la Vicissitude des Choses* (1579), Louis Le Roy wrote that the variety of things is in accordance with differences in places and in climates; every country possesses its own gifts and singularities, distributed by a Divine Providence careful to create universal good for the world. Divine Providence cannot persevere in its perfection without such variety "to the end that one having need of the other they might communicate together and succour each other."[39] These relationships are not a law unto themselves; it is the Christian God and not the physical environment nor the stars that is responsible for them.

Le Roy shows how climatic influences may be part of the argument for design, but Pierre Charron shows how they can assume a more independent and challenging character. This is not because of anything new in his climatic theories, for most of the discussion seems to be lifted from Bodin. Charron probes deeper than Bodin did, however, into environmental influences on morality and religion, in an inquiry which earned for Charron accusations of atheism, especially from the Jesuit François Garasse. (Charron's earlier work was more orthodox.) Charron says that the customs or manners of a

---

[39] Louis Le Roy, *Of the Interchangeable Course, or Variety of Things*, trans. Robert Ashley (London, 1594), 10r–11v. Cf., discussion of Sebastian Münster, Pt. III, Intro. essay. Le Roy follows Ptolemy in his astrological ethnology (*ibid.*, 13v–13r), adopts the familiar north, south, and intermediate correlations (14v), and refers to ideas expressed by Servius the Grammarian (about A.D. 400) in his commentary on Virgil's *Aeneid*.

people cannot be regarded as either vices or virtues; they are the works of nature and are most difficult either to change or to renounce. Virtue can mitigate, temper, and reduce the extremes in favor of the mean.[40] More pointed is his comment that it is a frightful thing to observe the great diversity in religious beliefs, but frequently also there is doctrinal agreement among them. Different doctrines might arise in the same climate. Furthermore, one religion is often based on another, the younger borrowing from the older. A man acquires his religion from the environment in which he is born and from the people living there.[41]

Another Frenchman—a Gascon, a poet, a Protestant, and a contemporary of Bodin, Guillaume de Salluste, Sieur Du Bartas (1544–1590)—shows how easily environmental theories can become involved in cosmology and sacred history. His chief works, *La Première Sepmaine* and *La Seconde Sepmaine*, belong to the hexaemeral literature; but in fact they are much more than this, being an impressive repository of long-held ideas of the four elements, the humors, environmental influences, astrology, and traditional biblical exegesis. In one poem, *Les Colonies*, first published in 1584,[42] Du Bartas explains the diffusion of the human race after Noah's time and the present differences observable among peoples. Du Bartas speaks both of the marvelous fecundity of nature and of the great physical, mental, and cultural variety among men. The sharp contrasts among the people of the north, south, and the intermediate regions are reminiscent of those made by Bodin in the *Methodus*. There are many similarities in their points of view. The peoples of the south are knowledgeable and contemplative, those of the north possess manual skill, the prudent peoples in between have abilities in government and administration.[43] "Et bref, l'un studieux admire la science, / L'autre a les arts en main, et l'autre la prudence."[44] Like Bodin, Du Bartas emphasizes the technological skill of the northern peoples ("Qui fait tout ce qu'il veut de metal et du bois"), their martial vigor and their fecundity, compared with the southerners.[45]

The dispersion of mankind over the earth is in accordance with divine will—God wishes to lead his children away from the crimes of their birthplaces—in order that His devout servants will sound His name from Scythia to Zanzibar and that foreign lands may now be put to human use ("Que les tresors produits par les champs estrangers / Ne fussent comme vains par faute d'usagers").[46]

Du Bartas paints a lively picture of the grandeur of a great city with its trades, occupations, commerce, and intellectual life; he is aware of the depen-

---

[40] *De la Sagesse*, Bk. I, chap. 38, and the table on p. 219.
[41] *De la Sagesse*, Bk. II, chap. 5, pp. 257, 351–352.
[42] Holmes, "Guillaume De Salluste Sieur Du Bartas. A Biographical and Critical Study," in *Works*, ed. Holmes, Lyons, Linker, Vol. I, p. 18.
[43] *Les Colonies*, lines 541–584.
[44] *Ibid.*, lines 585–586.
[45] *Ibid.*, lines 530–540, 566, 580.
[46] *Ibid.*, lines 623–624.

dence of one country on another through trade which he illustrates with a list including sugar from the Canaries, white ivory from India, and horses from Germany. "Bref, chaque terre apporte un tribut tout divers / Es coffres du trésor de ce grand univers."[47]

*Les Colonies* ends with fervent praise of the earth as an environment for man, of the sea as a great reservoir of life and of nourishment for man, and of France as the pearl of Europe and a paradise on earth. It is a remarkable poem, contrasting the manners and national characters of people, mostly because of differing climates, and at the same time recognizing the mobility and adaptability of man who lives by divine command on an earth well suited to him.

Historians of English Literature, especially students of Milton, have shown considerable interest in Du Bartas, whose work was translated into English by Joshua Sylvester under the title *Bartas His Devine Weekes & Workes*, the complete edition, except for minor omissions, being published in 1608.[48] It has been thought, especially since the publication in 1934 of George C. Taylor's *Milton's Use of Du Bartas*, that the French poet inspired Milton's interest in theories of climatic influence. The most striking passage in Milton (whose substance is derived ultimately from Paul the Deacon) is in *Paradise Lost*. Milton says of "those bad Angels seen / Hovering on wing under the cape of Hell":

> A multitude like which the populous North
> Poured never from her frozen loins to pass
> Rhene or the Danaw, when her barbarous sons
> Came like a deluge on the South, and spread
> Beneath Gibraltar to the Libyan sands.[49]

One reason for the interest in climatic theories in England was the traditional disparagement, according to the climatic theory, of the intellectual capacity and ability of northern peoples. Often the unhappy British appeared uncomfortably in the northern rather than in the middle group. All kinds of mischief were possible. Milton could doubt his own talents, and whole peoples might be dismissed as without significant intellectual endowment. One flattering aspect was that the Goths, a northern people, were staunch lovers of liberty, a love induced by their climate.[50]

Climatic theories, mostly variants of the types discussed by Bodin, enjoyed wide currency in the sixteenth and seventeenth centuries. Their popularity is noticeable in their frequent application to individual countries or topics.

[47] *Ibid.*, lines 647–648.
[48] For the complex publication history of the Sylvester translation, see *Works*, Vol. III, pp. 538–539.
[49] *Paradise Lost*, Bk. I, vss. 351–355.
[50] For the literature on climate relating to Milton and his times, see Z. S. Fink, "Milton and the theory of Climatic Influence," *Modern Language Quarterly*, Vol. 2 (1941), pp. 67–80. This article quotes contemporary writers, studies exhaustively the appearance of the climatic theory in Milton's works, and comes to conclusions regarding its effect

Montaigne's and Bacon's ideas, for example, are in this category. Montaigne refers to Vegetius, Plato, Cicero, and Herodotus. Men are not only influenced by the place, he adds, but like plants, they will assume new characteristics when they migrate.[51] Less traditional, however, is the cultural relativism revealed in the essay on cannibals, but here Montaigne is not concerned with environmental questions. Francis Bacon gives three possible reasons for his theory that wars originate in the martial regions of the north: the stars, the probable greater continental size of the Northern Hemisphere, and most likely "the cold of the northern parts, which is that which, without aid of discipline, doth make the bodies hardest, and the courage warmest."[52] Elsewhere, however, he is far more perceptive and far less traditional. If one considers "the immense difference between men's lives in the most polished countries of Europe, and in any wild and barbarous region of the new Indies he will think it so great, that man may be said to be a god unto man, not only on account of mutual aid and benefits, but from their comparative states—the result of the arts, and not of the soil or climate."[53]

Fresher breezes, however, were crossing the sea; they came from the personal observations of the Jesuit father José de Acosta. Like the modern altitudinal divisions of *tierra caliente*, *tierra templada*, and *tierra fría*, Acosta divided the Indies into the low, the high, and the middle lands lying between the two extremes. The coastal lowlands, very hot, humid, unhealthful, were uninhabitable in many places because of the dangerous sands and because the rivers, finding no outlet to the sea, created swamps. Their population, diminished by twenty-nine thirtieths, was almost extinct because the Indians had been forced to unendurable labor; they had altered their customs because of the Spanish contact, and had acquired the habit of excessive drinking and other vices. The lowlands possessed also the cities, points of entry for the Spanish trade. The highlands, cold, dry, infertile, healthful if not peaceable, were well populated. These were pasturelands with livestock, whose people, lacking crops from their own cultivated fields, obtained food by barter and exchange. The gold mines of the highlands accounted also for the dense population. The middle lands, areas where wheat, barley, and maize grew, also possessed many pastures, much livestock (*ganado*), and groves. It was the best of all the regions for health and contentment.[54]

---

on Milton personally and its influence on English society. See also "The Reputation of Du Bartas in England and America," in *Works of . . . Du Bartas*, Vol. 3, pp. 537–543; George Coffin Taylor, *Milton's Use of Du Bartas*, pp. 55–57; Samuel Kliger, *The Goths in England*, pp. 241–252; and Elbert N. S. Thompson, "Milton's Knowledge of Geography," *Studies in Philology*, Vol. 16 (1919), pp. 148–171.

[51] "An Apologie of Raymond Sebond," *Essays*, Bk. 2, chap. 12.
[52] *Of the Vicissitude of Things*, 1625.
[53] *Novum Organum*, Bk. I, Aph. 129.
[54] P. José de Acosta, *Historia Natural y Moral de las Indias*, Madrid, 1894 (1590), Vol. 1, Bk. III, chap. 19, pp. 249–254.

## 9. ON NATIONAL CHARACTER

Although an awareness of cultural differences apparently has not been lacking in any age, there was a conspicuous interest in the subject in the seventeenth century in England; this was quite unlike Bodin's, over whose environmental writings there hovered a heavy pall of astrological ethnology. Neither, however, was it conspicuously theoretical. It was an interest in national character, observations made by Europeans of other Europeans; and in the peoples of far-off places like Persia, India, and China. Often these characteristics were described without causal explanation, but it was also common to see them as products of the climate.[55]

These writings on national character had their attractive and their seamy sides. They provided an outlet for curious, active, and open-minded intelligence; sharp observation often resulted in valuable descriptions of the workaday world, diet, and regional differences. Their great weakness was their proneness to bias, to insufferable smugness, often to bigotry. Their crudity lay in the assumption that it was possible to label nations or peoples quickly and firmly; peoples had to submit bravely to a single label which summed them up. Earlier writings on national character had similar shortcomings, and our own age with its two world wars and many small ones has seen a proliferation of them. Bishop Hall castigated such oversimplification in his *Mundus alter et idem* (1605):

> The French are commonly called rash; the Spaniard proud; the Dutch drunken; the English the busi-bands; the Italians effeminate; the Swethen timorous; the Bohemians inhumaine; the Irish barbarous and superstitious; but is any man so sottish, as to thinke that France hath no staid man at all in it; Spaine, no meacock; or Germanie none that lives soberly? They are fooles (beleeve it) that will tie mens manners so firme unto the starres, that they will leave nothing to a mans owne power, nothing to the parents natures, nothing to nurture and education.[56]

Let us look at three examples, all from England and all from the early seventeenth century: Sir Thomas Overbury, John Barclay, and Sir William Temple. Sir Thomas Overbury's *Observations in His Travailes Upon the State of the XVII. Provinces as They Stood Anno Dom. 1609* (1623) is an example of straightforward description; he is aware of national differences among people and of differences among groups within a single nation. Holland was a natural choice because of its recent liberation and its unique geography, partly natural, partly man-made. Sir Thomas Overbury, like Sir William Temple, remarks upon the favorable geographic position of a country formed by the deltas of the Rhine, the Maas, and the Scheldt. The Dutch

[55] See Miss Taylor's chapter "The Urbane Traveller," in *Late Tudor and Early Stuart Geography.*
[56] Joseph Hall, *The Discovery of a New World* (Mundus alter et idem), trans. from the Latin by John Healey, pp. 10–11; Taylor, *op. cit.,* p. 150.

had replaced the Venetians as conveyors of the goods from the Indies to the rest of Christendom except England; they were favorably placed for the European north-south trade and for the trade in the east with Germany, Russia, and Poland. Their natural slowness is contrasted with the rashness and changeableness of the French and the Florentines; they are like the Swiss in their "equality of spirits" which "renders them so fit for a democracy," but Sir Thomas does not seem to admire democracies very much.[57]

He comments on the national strength, the shape, and the regional diversity of France. The French have adopted "into themselves the lesser adjoyning nations, without destruction, or leaving any marke of strangnesse upon them, as the *Bretons, Gascoignes, Provincalls,* and others which are not *French;* towards the which unions, their nature, which is easie and harborous to strangers, hath done more then [*sic*] any lawes could have effected, but with long time." Later he describes how France has achieved a certain cosmopolitanism by the addition to the nation of diverse but related peoples, "For *Picardie, Normandie,* and *Bretaigne* resemble *England; Languedoc, Spaine, Province, Italie,* and the rest is *France.*"[58] Cultural similarities of the old *pays* around the central French core appear to be the result of contiguity and cultural contact.

The most impressive work on national character of this time is the *Icon Animorum* of John Barclay, first published in 1614; a translation from the Latin to the English was made by Thomas May, and this work, entitled *The Mirrour of Mindes,* was published in 1631.[59]

Barclay says that every age, almost, has a particular genius different from others; that "there is a proper Spirit to every Region, which doth in a manner shape the studies, and the manners of the inhabitants, according to it selfe."[60]

He is looking from a Greenwich hill at the scenes along the Thames and he is struck by the natural and the man-made beauty he sees. The charm of a panorama, the most beautiful of England and possibly of all Europe "unawares had ravished" his spirit. It was "soe faire a variety, and the industry (as it were) of Nature, displaying her riches." Even the beauty of nature, however, cannot tolerate monotony. Any beauty would "glut and weary" the beholder unless it were "beautified with contrarieties, and change of endowments, to refresh continually the wearied beholder with unexpected novelties."[61]

---

[57] "Observations," *The Miscellaneous Works in Prose and Verse of Sir Thomas Overbury,* pp. 228, 230.

[58] *Ibid.,* pp. 236–237.

[59] For a less enthusiastic appraisal, see Taylor, *op. cit.;* pp. 134–136. For an exhaustive study of the work see Collignon, "Le Portrait des Esprits (*Icon animorum*) de Jean Barclay," *Mémoires de l'Académie de Stanislas, 1905–1906* Ser. 6, Vol. 3 (1906), pp. 67–140.

[60] *Mirrour of Mindes,* p. 36.

[61] *Ibid.,* p. 42.

Nature has created a variety of physical environments. Some countries are on mountaintops, others are in valleys, some suffer immoderate heat, others extreme cold, "the residue, shee ordained (though not equally) temperate."

The fertility of countries varies also in time; the stars do not have the same influences (there is some astrology in Barclay). Therefore, "does noe yeare altogether imitate that that [*sic*] went before, nor is the exact rule of the following yeare."[62]

This variety in space and time is typical also of man, created after the image of the Deity "and for whose sake especially, all other ornaments of world were framed," who is the greatest exemplar of this beauty of variety. No diversity is more worthy of wonder than that men born to liberty should also serve, "their owne dispositions, the fate of the times, wherein they live, forcing them as it were, into certaine affections, and rules of living." Every age of the world has a certain Genius, "which over-ruleth the mindes of men, and turneth them to same desires." Some ages breathe nothing but martial discipline; then in a few years all "are againe composed to peace, and quietnesse."[63]

Ages of accomplishment (he cites the Greeks and the Roman period from Augustus to Nero) are paralleled by another force, "that spirit which being appropriate to every region, infuseth into men, as soon as they are borne, the habit, and affections of their owne country."[64]

Barclay now begins a lengthy analysis of national character, but the exposition, following a sketch of the physical setting of each country, is descriptive. Geography, trade, production, are not linked together causally. Barclay dismisses the barbarian world of Africa and the New World as being beneath his notice; he spends most of his time on western Europe, beginning courteously with France (the book is dedicated to Louis XIII) with occasional remarks of special interest here (the extension of pasturelands caused the disappearance of wolves, who were now killed off by the hunters). After France Barclay describes England, Scotland, and Ireland, returning to the continent to Germany. Of this country he remarks that it was once full of woods and wild inhabitants and is now beautified with towns, its woods "which were once great and orespread the country, now reduced to use and ornament."[65] There now follow descriptions of the United Provinces and Flanders, loyal to the Spanish throne, and Italy, whose great cultural diversity he ascribes to social causes; despite a common tongue it has a great variety of customs, owing to the fragmentation of the country into many states, the diversity of its governments, and the surviving traces of foreign occupations. He describes the Spaniard, living on poor, arid, and sterile soil, and the Hun-

---

[62] *Ibid.*, p. 43.
[63] *Ibid.*, pp. 44–45.
[64] *Ibid.*, pp. 54–55.
[65] *Ibid.*, pp. 144–145.

garians, Poles, Muscovites, and other peoples of the north. (The vast forests of Poland, he says, produce needed wood for heating and are the havens of animals whose pelts make very precious furs; they also have numbers of swarms of wild bees.) He uses Paul the Deacon's notion of the north being a hive of nations as an example of mores changing through the ages. How is it, he asks, that this seemingly inexhaustible source of men in the Cimbrian Chersonese (Jutland) no longer exists? Today it has few towns and it is thinly populated. Barclay's explanation (common among European writers) is that the Dutch, the Germans, and the Scandinavian peoples, each playing at various times the leading roles, drink too much. In former times the people moved because there were too many of them for such a poor soil; with eating and drinking to excess the people now have so weakened their ability to reproduce that they can scarcely produce enough for their own needs. In the final section on national character, Barclay discusses the Turks and the Jews together because, he says, they are united in the hatred men hold for them.

Barclay's most interesting ideas are that there is certain clustering of human achievement at various times and that there are also spatial contrasts among peoples. Barclay fortified Abbé du Bos in his belief in this clustering of genius.[66]

Sir William Temple's *Observations Upon the United Provinces of the Netherlands* (1673) lacks the freshness and speculative boldness of Barclay, but it suggests, too, causal relationships between environment and national character. Though these ideas are conventional, there is a subtlety and discrimination in analysis, for example, in his recognition that within the United Provinces there are classes with different characteristics, but that all of them also have some characteristics in common.[67]

The discussion of the people is preceded by a clear and imaginative description of the geography of the country, its winds, speculations on the youth of the Zuider Zee, the flat soil, and the place of human industry in drainage of the land.[68]

In down-to-earth and often blunt words, Sir William Temple describes the social classes of Holland, the Clowns or Boors (the farmers); the Mariners or Schippers; the Merchants, or Traders; the *Renteeners* (those living on rent or interest); the gentlemen; and the army officers. In incisive sentences he

[66] Abbé du Bos, *Reflexions*, Vol. 2, p. 260, who refers to Barclay's *Euphormionis Lusinini* the reason being that in all the editions since the Hess Strasbourg edition of 1623, the *Icon* customarily was erroneously regarded as being Part IV of the former work. Collignon, *op. cit.* (see n. 59 above), pp. 67–68.

[67] On the esteem in which this book was held see G. N. Clark's introduction to the *Observations*, pp. v–x. "What holds the book together," says Clark, "is a method of interpreting history, a method which is summed up in the dictum: 'Most national customs are the effect of some unseen, or unobserved, natural causes or necessities.' This idea and ideas related to it were kindling much of the best thought of that time, and Temple must have been in contact with them from his youth" (p. ix).

[68] *Observations*, pp. 89–96.

quickly establishes differences among them. The common characteristic of all classes is their "great Frugality, and order in their Expences," public and private.[69] Of the people as a whole he says, "In general, All Appetites and Passions seem to run lower and cooler here, than in other Countrys where I have converst. Avarice may be expected." Part of the explanation—he considers them much less than passionate in lovemaking—may be owing to the dullness of the air which, however, may also "dispose them to that strange assiduity and constant application of their Minds, with that perpetual Study and Labour upon any thing they design and take in hand." The qualities of the air may also influence their drinking habits. There follows an entertaining discussion of drinking and abstentions from drinking in the morning.[70]

Less conventional, however, was the observation, which also attracted the attention of Abbé du Bos, that diet in time could change the character of a people. After several illustrations relating diet (mostly meat eating) to bravery, Sir William gives his explanation for the differences between the ancient warlike inhabitants of Holland and the people living there in his day:

> That not only the long disuse of Arms among the Native *Hollanders,* (especially at Land,) and making use of other Nations, chiefly in their Milice; But the Arts of Trade, as well as Peace, and their great Parsimony in Diet, and eating so very little Flesh (which the common people seldom do, above once a week,) may have helpt to debase much the ancient valour of the Nation, at least, in the occasions of Service at Land.[71]

Temple, who was on the side of the ancients in the quarrel over the ancients and the moderns, was also interested in broader questions of the nature of civilization, the geographic march of history, and environmental conditions favorable to the arts and sciences. To him, one civilization is built on its predecessors, an interpretation often more in accordance with modern findings than many nineteenth century views which, hampered by the rudimentary advances in archaeological discovery, often saw, as they did with classical Greece and the Renaissance, a sudden efflorescence based on favorable environmental conditions.

Temple was impressed, too, with the creative accomplishments of the Eastern regions, China, Ethiopia, Egypt, Chaldea, Persia, Syria, Judea, Arabia, and India. Greek learning, he said, came originally from Egypt or Phoenicia, whose flourishing civilizations may have owed much to the Ethiopians, Chaldeans, Arabians, and Indians. Behind the philosophy of Pythagoras and nourishing it were his stays in Memphis, Thebes, Heliopolis, Babylon, and his travels to Ethiopia, Arabia, India, Crete, Delphos (*sic*). Democritus' philosophy may have come from his travels in Egypt, Chaldea, India, that of Spartan Lycurgus from antecedent civilizations which in turn enjoyed favorable

[69] *Ibid.,* pp. 97–102, quote on p. 102.
[70] *Ibid.,* pp. 106–108, quotes on pp. 105, 106.
[71] *Ibid.,* pp. 111–112; Du Bos, *op. cit.,* Vol. 2, pp. 288–289.

environmental conditions that encouraged high culture unless a catastrophic conquest or invasion had taken place.

> Besides, I know no Circumstances like to contribute more to the Advancement of Knowledge and Learning among Men, than exact temperance in their races, great pureness of air, and equality of climate, long tranquillity of empire or government: and all these we may justly allow to those eastern regions, more than any others we are acquainted with, at least till the conquests made by the Tartars, upon both India and China, in the latter Centuries.

It is as pardonable, he adds, "to derive some parts of learning from thence" as it is to accept the Indian origin of chess.[72]

### 10. On Melancholy

These newer enthusiasms for views, prospects, and changes of air emerge from old theory, but they also have a freshness that comes from alertness to contemporary life; perhaps Barclay and Burton are the finest examples of the genre at this time.

In many periods certain works acquire a character transcending their own subject matter; their breadth and depth of learning make them repositories of ideas. In our own day, Toynbee's *A Study of History* is certainly such a work; so in other eras were Cicero's *On the Nature of the Gods*, Hakewill's *Apologie*, and Pope's *Essay on Man*. Robert Burton's *Anatomy of Melancholy* belongs in this class because of its massive learning and his deep knowledge of classical thought and of the continental and English writings of his own time. On environmental matters, he depends greatly on Bodin and Botero. Burton confessed to a love for cosmography, and many of his pages bear witness to it, including the introduction, and two remarkable essays, "Bad Air a Cause of Melancholy" and "Air Rectified. With a Digression of the Air."[73]

Since melancholy is widely diffused in time and space and since Burton is a very thorough man with awesome erudition (even the most casual reader soon discovers this) it is easy to see how such an anatomy could require almost a thousand pages. Questions concerning the environment arise because the book is a discourse on certain mental states especially melancholy; it therefore becomes involved with such topics as the relation of the body to the mind, the effect of airs and waters on melancholy and its dissipation, on the disposition in general, and the effect of a change in air and of views. With Alberti, Pius II, and Barclay he is one of the few early writers known to me who dwell on the beauty and stimulation of a view. The parts of the work devoted to airs

---

[72] "An Essay upon the Ancient and Modern Learning," in *The Works of Sir William Temple, Bart*, new ed. (1814), Vol. 3, pp. 446–459; quote on p. 458.

[73] Part. 1, sect. 2, memb. 2, sub. 5; Part. 2, sect. 2, memb. 3. Burton divides his work into partitions, sections, members, and subsections. See the valuable index and biographical and bibliographical dictionary in the Dell Jordan-Smith edition of the *Anatomy of Melan.*

and waters are particularly interesting because they are based on contemporary and on classical medicine, particularly Hippocrates and Galen.

Because the history of environmental theories is so closely related to the history of medicine, much attention has been given by writers on these subjects to water, running and still. Burton writes vividly about stagnant waters and their dangers.

> Standing waters, thick and ill coloured, such as come forth of pools and moats, where hemp hath been steeped, or slimy fishes live, are most unwholesome, putrefied, and full of mites, creepers, slimy, muddy, unclean, corrupt, impure, by reason of the sun's heat, and still standing. They cause foul distemperatures in the body and mind of man, are unfit to make drink of, to dress meat with, or to be used about men inwardly or outwardly. They are good for many domestical uses, to wash horses, water cattle, &c., or in time of necessity, but not otherwise.[74]

Sooner or later in any study of melancholy, food has to be considered; in his discussion of bad diet as a cause of melancholy, Burton remarks on the influence of custom on diet; he makes comparisons taken from Bodin between the diet of peoples of the north and south and their basis in climate. Lemnius, a Dutch physician and theologian of the sixteenth century and author of several books on medicine, he says, "reckons up two main things most profitable and most pernicious to our bodies; air and diet. . . ." Examples are given of the effects of madness from exposure in hot places, but he has also read Acosta's description of temperate equatorial lands under the equator.[75] He mentions the bad air of notoriously unhealthy places—Alexandretta, the port of Saint John de Ullua in New Spain, Durazzo, the Pontine Marshes, Romney Marsh —but there is no blind resignation to environmental factors, for men also "through their own nastiness and sluttishness, immund and sordid manner of life," allow their air to putrefy.[76] All this is based on the theory of the humors; Burton's exposition comes from Andreas Laurentius, a writer on anatomical subjects "out of Hippocrates."[77]

"The body is the home of the soul, her house, abode, and stay." Mental states are derived from physical; ". . . or as wine savours of the cask wherein it is kept, the soul receives a ˙ncture from the body through which it works. We see this in old men, chil. ren, Europeans, Asians, hot and cold climes. Sanguine are merry, Melancholy sad, Phlegmatick dull, by reason of abundance of those humors, and they cannot resist such passions which are inflicted by them."[78]

This deeply learned man, who had never traveled, revealed his obvious wanderlust in a love of reading travel books. There is very little determinism

[74] *Ibid.*, Part. 1, sect. 2, memb. 2, subs. 1, p. 195.
[75] *Ibid.*, subs. 5, pp. 206–207.
[76] *Ibid.*, p. 209.
[77] *Ibid.*, sect. 1, memb. 2, subs. 2, pp. 128–129. See also "Laurentius," p. 1016.
[78] *Ibid.*, sect. 2, memb. 5, subs. 1, p. 319.

despite his reliance—and that of the physicians of his age—on the medical heritage of antiquity. In his imaginary travels, he will look into many problems of physical geography himself.[79] Whence come different customs and the variety of life, the differences in distribution of plants and animals between the old world and the new? There is no better physic than a change of air.

> For peregrination charms our senses with such unspeakable and sweet variety, that some count him unhappy that never travelled, a kind of prisoner, and pity his case that from his cradle to his old age he holds the same still; still, still the same, the same: insomuch that Rhasis doeth not only commend but enjoin travel, and such variety of objects to a melancholy man, and to lie in diverse Inns, to be drawn in to several companies.

He admires views and prospects and seascapes, and every country had them: the view from "that old decayed castle in Corinth" from which one can see the Peloponnesus, Greece, and the Ionian and Aegean seas, from the square top of the great pyramid over the Nile Valley, from the sultan's palace in Cairo, from Mt. Zion in Jerusalem; he agrees with Barclay that the view from the Greenwich Tower is one of the best prospects in Europe.[80]

In the long member on love and love melancholy, he sees a relation of site or place to love. "The place itself makes much wherein we live, the clime, air, and discipline if they concur." He cites Galen's remark that there are scarcely any adulterers in Mysia, but many in Rome because of its delights, and Strabo on Corinth which with all its plenty could entertain foreigners; it had a thousand whores. "All nations resorted thither as to a school of Venus." He follows Bodin in the relation of climate to sexual desire. The fruits of the Neapolitan soil, the pleasant air, enervate the bodies and alter constitutions, Florus calling it a contest of Bacchus and Venus, Foliet admiring it.[81]

## 11.   CONCLUSION

By the latter part of the seventeenth century, a learned and critical thinker like Fontenelle could see that climate did not have the same influence on all forms of life and that human society was far more complex than many had thought. "It is certain, at least that, because of the connection and inter-dependence existing between all parts of the material world, the differences in climate which affect plants must needs influence brains also." With brains, however, the influence is more remote, for one must take into account the influence of "art and culture." Fontenelle's position is similar to that of Polybius. The differences originally determined by climate can be altered by cultural influences: "As a consequence of the ease with which minds influence

[79] *Ibid.*, Part. 2, sect. 2, memb. 3, pp. 407–415.
[80] *Ibid.*, pp. 437–438. Quotation on p. 437.
[81] *Ibid.*, Part. 3, sect. 2, memb. 2, subs. 1, p. 661.

one another it comes about that peoples do not retain the original mental characteristics which they would naturally derive from their respective climates." Fontenelle in effect ignores the influence of climate because climates apparently have advantages and disadvantages which offset one another.

In a few short paragraphs, he dismisses the notion of the force of nature being superior in ancient times, distinguishes between environmental influences affecting the plant world and man, and calls on men to study their own minds and customs, not climate, in order to explain similarities and differences among peoples. "The reading of Greek books produces in us much the same effect as if we intermarried solely with Greeks."[82]

The design argument, as we have seen and will see in many other connections, is hospitable to a wide variety of ideas, for it is human beings who are discovering the design, who thereafter are following in the footsteps of the Creator, and any subordinate pattern corresponding with the real or supposed facts can be included. If it is true that Providence had predetermined a place for everyone under the sun, establishing the racial, physical, and cultural differences among people living in different parts of the world, it is also true that the Creator had so designed man that he could endure extremes of temperature, accommodate himself to miscellaneous discomforts, move continually from one place to another, as Du Bartas had said. This type of thinking emphasizing man's adaptive qualities presupposed that the whole earth is intended for his habitat; hence human migration. It presupposes also a plasticity and a malleability in human nature. An eloquent and colorful expression of this thought was written by P. Jean François in his *La Science des eaux* (1655), but it expressed a point of view held even earlier than his time. Of man, François wrote:

> He lives with the lions in the extreme heat of the Torrid Zone and with bears in the frozen wastes of the Cold Zone; he roams in the forests of America with the moose, and hides underground and in caves in the province of Paraguay, and lives on the water in many parts of China. In Martinique, he feeds on lizards, in upper Egypt on the locusts which he has collected and salted, in the island of Java on snakes and rats. . . . In short, the varieties of air, water, and earth, and of the products growing on them is so great on the terrestrial sphere that animals and plants are unable to tolerate them and to live. Only man lives and adapts himself everywhere.[83]

How is one to interpret the mélange of ideas—simple in conception and uncertainly applied—which appears in this period? There are different possi-

---

[82] Bernard Le Bovier de Fontenelle, "Digression sur les Anciens et les Modernes," (1688) *Oeuvres*; quotations are from the translation of Leona M. Fassett in the selection from Fontenelle's "On the Ancients and Moderns," in Teggart and Hildebrand, *The Idea of Progress*, pp. 176–178.

[83] I have been unable to consult François' rare and little-known work. I am indebted for this discussion to Dainville, *La Géographie des Humanistes*, pp. 276–303, my translation being from François' preface quoted on p. 316.

bilities: they could be blended in with astrological ethnology, they could be used simply by themselves, they could be subordinated to the idea of design, and finally they could embody the idea of adaptation imposed upon mankind as a consequence of its worldwide dispersion.

With the passage of time, astrological ethnology begins to slip away in the night, but the environmental correlations and generalizations live a hardy life all through the eighteenth century.

Respect for Hippocrates and Galen continues, but they seem now more and more like consultants than like fountainheads of knowledge because there is a great deal of contemporary observation and study of climate, health, mental and physical states, as one can see so well in *The Anatomy of Melancholy*. Opposed to them is the increasing awareness of other influences and an awareness that the distribution of mankind is evidence of creativity and adaptability of a high order, as François had hinted.

Fontenelle balks at applying the same environmental criteria to men as he applies to plants and animals. A clustering of ability or talent at certain periods is noticed, an observation which challenges by implication the uniformity of climatic influences through time. Abbé du Bos in the eighteenth century, as we shall see, considered this problem at length. There is an increasing interest in national character. Temple's ideas of the importance of borrowing, whether by individuals or by civilizations, suggest the role of imitation and copying, of the cultural milieu. Environmental theories become more secular, they are less tied to the design argument, and they are used as explanations of religious schism. Finally, with Alberti, Barclay, and Burton, the appreciation of the air of a place, of a change of air, of the effects of views, prospects, seascapes, hint at the study of the aspects of nature that is to come.

Ideas of environmental influence which appeared in our period were significant largely because of their volume and because of the variety of uses to which they were put; it is useless to claim that they contributed anything to understanding the relation of human cultures and their natural environment. It is very well to say that the climatic correlations, capricious and foolish as they were, stimulated study of regions and led to a realization of cultural differences. These differences had been understood, however, for a long time. The way to creative understanding did not lie through Bodin; a more open way was through the ideas of Acosta and François. The study of the classics, the reading of travels in the New World and in the Old failed to achieve a new departure which would make the most of the implications of the new discoveries: that traces of living men could be found almost everywhere in the world, that movement, migration, war, invasion, had been a large part of human history, that men lived and survived in a bewildering variety of conditions in widely different physical environments, and that they used their land, too, in widely different ways.

# Chapter 10

# Growing Consciousness
# of the Control of Nature

### 1. INTRODUCTION

Men have long been aware of their ability to change their physical environment, but only a few have regarded these changes as part of a broader philosophical, religious, or scientific attitude concerning man's place in nature. I am not referring to the theme of man's control over nature through the application of theoretical science to applied science and technology, nor to technical improvements and inventions made by artisans which lead to new and purposeful uses of and demands on natural resources. However, these general themes cannot be neglected, because of the newer philosophic outlook of the modern period toward the improvement of life and the importance of practical activity, especially in the philosophy of Francis Bacon. The theme of man's control over nature, flattering to man and his works, has, however, been concerned only casually with the theme of man as a geographic agent, in which changes have been apprehended from the point of view of their effects on the earth and not as evidences of purposeful mastery over environmental obstacles.

The idea of man as a geologic or geographic agent is a modern one even though its sources lie in observations which differed little from those made frequently in the Middle Ages, of changes which could easily be made in a preindustrial age: the clearing of trees; the burning of forests or using them for grazing or for charcoal making; drainage of bogs and swamps; the heating of cities whose chimneys made the urban atmosphere warmer than that of the countryside; agriculture; and occupations in which the ax, the plow, or fire might be used. These activities had been going on from time immemorial, but one must look to the late seventeenth and eighteenth centuries for the beginnings of bolder syntheses. The stimulus for this came in part from successes in agriculture, drainage, engineering, and other occupations often directly concerned with the land, whose activities resulted either in change in the land itself or in its geographical relationship to another piece of land.[1] Scattered here and there in this period are isolated notices of subjects which today have become organized bodies of knowledge: air pollution, soil erosion, fertilizers, forestry, climatic change, ecology. It is possible that these observations, and many like them unrecorded, were so commonplace that they were common knowledge from which more philosophic generalizations could later emerge. In the eighteenth century, this was a significant achievement of Count Buffon.

## 2. RENAISSANCE PHILOSOPHIES OF TECHNOLOGY

In the Renaissance and in writings of the seventeenth and eighteenth centuries there is a continuation of two different outlooks: one which comes out of theoretical science, theology, or philosophy and emphasizes man's role in changing or controlling nature as the expected function of his position in the scale of being and of his unique ability through his intelligence to interpret the significance of the creation. Examples of this type are in the writings of Ficino, Paracelsus, and Francis Bacon. The other outlook has a much less exalted origin, often being derived from everyday observations without philosophizing or moralizing. These often have been made almost as asides in discussions of techniques in mining, forestry, irrigation, or engineering; they may appear in law or legislative history, or from the practical needs of statecraft.

Let us examine some of these points of view in the Renaissance; they are indicative more of the possibility of making such observations than they are of any purposive scientific or philosophic inquiry into the relationship of human society to environmental change.

[1] See especially *A History of Technology*, Vol. 3, ed. Singer, *et al.*, pp. 12–13, chapters 2, 3, 12, 17, 25.

The third sign of immortality, says Marsilio Ficino in the *Platonic Theology*, is taken from the activities of the arts and of government. In this work the hymn to man may be too fervid, the belief in final causes too unyielding, but it also is a refreshing affirmation of the creativity of man after the baleful castigation that mars so much of Christian theology—that man is unworthy, cursed, full of sin.

Man, Ficino says, is much freer than are the animals which either lack art entirely or have only one and do what they do fatalistically. Men not only invent—they improve on their inventions. Man "imitates all the works of the divine nature, and perfects, corrects and improves the works of lower nature. Therefore the power of man is almost similar to that of the divine nature, for man acts in this way through himself."[2] Man is not only creative; he also binds the parts of nature together by his art. He is a transformer of materials, a user of all the elements. "Man not only makes use of the elements, but also adorns them, a thing which no animal ever does. How wonderful is the cultivation of the soil all over the earth, how marvelous the construction of buildings and cities, how skillful the control of the waterways!" It reminds one of Cicero and the lyrical passages of St. Augustine. "Man is really the vicar of God, since he inhabits and cultivates all elements and is present on earth without being absent from the ether." He uses and rules the animals, which despite their natural gifts of self-protection fight a losing battle with him. In a passage strongly reminiscent of Philo's remarks (*On the Creation*, 84–85) which already have been quoted, Ficino asks,

> Who has ever seen any human beings kept under the control of animals, in such a way as we see everywhere herds of both wild and domesticated animals obeying men throughout their lives? Man not only rules the animals by force, he also governs, keeps and teaches them. Universal providence belongs to God, who is the universal cause. Hence man who provides generally for all things, both living and lifeless, is a *kind* of god.[3]

The more one studies the early history of the idea of man as a controller of nature, the more one is struck with the depth of this awareness of power, particularly over the larger animals. Historically, these broader conclusions based on successes in plant and animal domestication have been of the utmost importance in shaping attitudes toward other forms of life. Ficino's interpretation of man's part in modifying the earth differs also from the religious interpretation which came from the monastic orders, especially in the Middle Ages. With the monks, clearing, the establishment of monasteries, and conversions are but different aspects of one activity, the founding of the kingdom of Christ on earth. Ficino's emphasis is different: those qualities which enable

[2] Marsilio Ficino, *Platonic Theology*, Bk. XIII, chap. 3, selections trans. Josephine L. Burroughs, *JHI*, Vol. 5 (1944), pp. 227–239.
[3] *Ibid.*, p. 234.

man to do what he does, to make the changes of the earth he is capable of making, and to force the lower orders of life to do his bidding are those qualities which bring him closest to the divine and which mark him off most decisively from all other kinds of life. The conclusion is irresistible that it is the uniqueness of man that enables him to perform the wonders he does perform.

Although it is difficult to see any marked change in the ideas being discussed from the Middle Ages to the Renaissance, nevertheless in the latter period, if one is to judge from the writings of men like Leonardo, Paracelsus, Agricola, and Palissy, there is a more self-conscious and self-confident attitude toward artisanship, invention, and technology. Basically this awareness is an enlargement of the observation that through human agency things existing in one form in nature are transformed into another form inconceivable without the intervention of man. Man is not a creator of raw materials—God is; but man is a powerful transformer; this, as we shall see, is a leading idea of Paracelsus.

There is little doubt of this growing self-consciousness in the Renaissance regarding the power of man to transform not only the elements but the landscape. The interest in the things of this world was greater than in the Middle Ages; the rediscovery of the literature of classical antiquity included the technical literature such as Vitruvius' work as well, and the technology of the Middle Ages could be improved and built upon. "Technical achievement received special stimulus during the Renaissance period from greater general preoccupation with active life and from the increased desire of many a farseeing craftsman for intellectual enlightenment and a scientific foundation for his customary rule-of-thumb manual work."[4]

In technical writings on architecture, mining, canal building, and metallurgy one often finds comments concerned with the broader implications of transformations being made or of the planning that brings them about. Thus Leon Battista Alberti's broad conception of the nature of an architect's duties was based not only on science as he knew it, but on a philosophy of man, human aspirations stimulating activities which lead to planning and to changing the landscape. Alberti is quite conscious of human ability—it shows itself in the long history of artisanship and invention. He observes that one can beautify nature, including in the adornment the surviving relics of the Italian past. He is well aware too of the role of plant introductions in the aesthetic and economic life of a country.[5]

> Why should I insist on the great plenty of Waters brought from the most remote and hidden Places, and employed to so many different and useful Purposes? Upon Trophies, Tabernacles, sacred Edifices, Churches and the like, adapted to divine Worship and the Service of Posterity? Or lastly, why should I mention the Rocks cut, Mountains bored through, Vallies filled up, Lakes confined, Marshes discharged into the Sea, Ships built, Rivers turned, their

---

[4] Klemm, *A History of Western Technology*, p. 111.
[5] *Ten Books on Architecture*, trans. Leoni, Bk. VI, chap. 4.

Mouths cleared, Bridges laid over them, Harbours formed, not only serving to Men's immediate Conveniences, but also opening them a way to all Parts of the World.[6]

Leonardo da Vinci was also interested in technology and planning and their relation to the physical environment. A man who could say, "Every large river may be led up the highest mountains on the principle of the siphon," showed that he understood the relationship of physical theory to applied technology through a middle term of resolute human activity.[7] In a country with a long tradition of land reclamation, river control, and canal construction, it is not surprising that Leonardo, a canal builder, would often see that the ability of man to change his environment was related to water and its control. Rivers, he said, deposit more soil when they are near populated districts. Because the mountains and hills are cultivated, the rains can wash away the loose soil much more easily than they can a hard ground covered with weeds. Leonardo observed the erosive power of water and its role as a leveling agent. "The water wears away the mountains and fills up the valleys, and if it had the power it would reduce the earth to a perfect sphere." Later, applying this principle, he proposes the purposeful use of running water to fill up the marshes with the soil of mountains, thus purifying the air as well.[8]

One finds in Leonardo what one finds also in Paracelsus, Palissy, Agricola, and Bacon, an admiration for the inventor and experimenter, the skilled of hand, and a contempt for the pretensions of authority: "If indeed I have no power to quote from authors as they have, it is a far bigger and more worthy thing to read by the light of experience, which is the instructress of their masters. They strut about puffed up and pompous, decked out and adorned not with their own labours but by those of others, and they will not even allow me my own."[9]

Another attempt, broad and philosophic in scope like Ficino's and Francis Bacon's, to interpret intelligent and creative man—in his ordinary daily activities, in health and illness, in the work with tools which changed his surroundings—as a vital part of the cosmos, was made by the celebrated physician and student of alchemy and natural history, Theophrastus Bombastus von Hohenheim (Paracelsus). Paracelsus considers a problem which Bacon, steeped in star lore and in the teaching of Romans 1:20, will also consider, of a unified conception of man, coming from three different strands of thought: The creation of man as an event in God's six days' work, the effects of the curse on man, and the relation of these two events to human creativity.

Paracelsus solves the first problem by using the ancient idea of the macrocosm, the whole universe, and the microcosm, man, who has the same elements

[6] *Ibid.*, p. x. Quoted in Klemm, *op. cit.*, pp. 112–113.
[7] *The Notebooks of Leonardo da Vinci*, ed. MacCurdy, p. 775.
[8] *Ibid.*, p. 310, quote on p. 317, and p. 322.
[9] *Ibid.*, p. 57.

within him but in different forms and who reflects, in a small way, the processes characteristic of the whole. In creating man, the microcosm, God plans that he shall collaborate in the creation, and alchemy becomes a technique, a method, a philosophy of change and transformation all in one, whose purpose it is to put the finishing touches on a nature uncompleted at the creation.

The solution to the second problem is breathtaking and bold, and quite out of keeping with the traditionally gloomy and pessimistic interpretations of the Fall. During the six days' work all matter was created, but art, that is, artisanship and craft and the "light of nature," was not. This celebrated phrase of Paracelsus, when applied to man, meant his creative faculty. Man did not possess this light of nature at the creation; it was bestowed upon him when Adam was driven from Paradise, man being commanded to work with his hands, woman to bring forth children in sorrow. Adam and Eve, who in Paradise resembled heavenly creatures, now become earthly. Since Paracelsus obviously believes that necessity is the mother of invention, "Eve was taught to bring up her children, and thus cradles and nursing came into being." As a creature of earth, man required a reason and an understanding of which he had no need as a heavenly creature living in Paradise. When man was expelled from Eden, he received from the angels their knowledge but not all knowledge. Henceforth man also had to ferret out the secrets of nature by craft. "For he and his children must learn one thing after another in the light of Nature, in order to bring to light that which lies hidden in all things. For although man was created whole as regards his body, he was not so created as regards his 'art.' All the arts have been given him, but not in an immediately recognizable form; he must discover them."[10]

Furthermore, it is God's will that we do more than accept nature as we find it. We must "investigate and learn why it has been created. Then we can explore and fathom the use of wool on the sheep and of the bristles on the sow's back; so we can place each thing where it belongeth, and can cook raw food so that it tasteth good in the mouth, and can build for ourselves winter apartments and roofs against the rain. . . ."[11]

All things on earth have been given into the hands of man "in order that he may bring them to the highest development, just as the earth does with all that it brings forth." This task means striving, exploration, and inquiry; man has the obligation to improve upon what has been given him. Consistent with his belief that necessity is the mother of invention and that created things exist to entice man into activity, Paracelsus says that because created things are made for man, he needs them and must explore everything in the creation. In Para-

---

[10] *Paracelsus, Selected Writings*, pp. 176–177. From "Das Buch Paragranum," in *Paracelsus Sämtliche Werke*, ed. Sudhoff and Matthiessen, Pt. I, Vol. 8, pp. 290–292. Quoted in Klemm, *op. cit.*, p. 144; I am indebted to this work for the references to P.

[11] "Die Bücher von den unsichtbaren Krankheiten," 1531–1532, Sudhoff, Vol. 9; Klemm, p. 144.

celsus' philosophy, man is restless, curious, active, his status in the world being determined by a God whose secrets are not visible but must be discovered. "It is not God's will that His secrets should be visible; it is His will that they become manifest and knowable through the works of man who has been created in order to make them visible." God is revealed in his works; so is man; hence, the need for man to work continually to discover God's gifts to him.[12]

This introduces the third point and leads to an examination of the nature of human art and creativity, especially as they bear on technology and toolmaking, the means by which man can transform nature. Paracelsus' answers are reminiscent of the fire and the smoke of the foundry, the clank and the bustle of the mines, and redolent with the wood and the shavings of the carpenter's shop, with which he, in his journeys, was quite familiar. Paracelsus believed what was written in the Bible, that everything was created from nothing; but the creation, even if entirely accomplished, was not entirely completed. He believed that the earth was created for man, that it surrounded him as the flesh of the apple surrounds its core with its seeds. The completion of the creation is therefore envisaged anthropocentrically: everything was created *ex nihilo* but not in the form in which it is used by man. The necessary completion of the creation is accomplished by fire and its master, Vulcan. "God hath created iron, but not that which can be made from it, not rust or iron bars or sickles; only iron ore, and as ore he giveth it to us. The rest he commandeth to Fire, and to Vulcan, the master of Fire. It followeth that iron itself is subject to Vulcan, and so is the craft thereof." Fire is the powerful agent of change whether one is smelting ore or baking bread. Neither does God create medicines in completed form: it is fire which separates the medicine from the dross.

Thus alchemy, most frequently through the use of fire, is a human creation, an art, a means of completing the creation. The alchemist is identical with the artisan. "Thus there are alchemists of wood, such as carpenters who prepare the wood that it may become a house; also the woodcarvers who make of the wood something quite alien to it, and thus is a picture formed from it." God creates nothing to perfection, but he commands Vulcan to complete the process: "Bread is created and bestowed on us by God; but not as it cometh from the baker; but the three vulcans, the cultivator, the miller and the baker make of it bread."[13] He has in mind the Greek conception of Hephaestus as a craftsman's god, as a divine craftsman. In these lines Paracelsus not only expresses his philosophy of alchemy but shows his affinity with the age-old no-

[12] *Paracelsus*, pp. 182–184; *Lebendiges Erbe*, pp. 113–116; Sudhoff, Pt. I, Vol. 7, pp. 264–265; Vol. 14, pp. 116–117; Vol. 12, pp. 59–60.
[13] "Labyrinthus Medicorum errantium," 1537–38, in *The Hermetical and Alchemical Writings of Paracelsus*, trans. Waite; *Paracelsus. Selected Writings*, p. 185; Klemm, p. 145. See Jacobi, ed., Theophrastus Paracelsus *Lebendiges Erbe* (Zürich a..d Leipzig,

tions of man as a doer, maker, finisher, expressed, as we have seen, in the Stoic and Hermetical writings.

Like Paracelsus, Georgius Agricola (George Bauer) thought that manual work was more than ordinary daily activity, that it was embodied in a philosophy as well; he "was another of those truly versatile men of the Renaissance who combined with humanist learning a mind directed to the contemplation of Nature and also to practical technological activity."[14] Of special interest to our theme is Agricola's defense of mining, which, he insists, requires great skill not only in the craft itself but in prospecting for ores. It is an error to emphasize its temporary nature, he says, citing examples of mines whose ores are unexhausted after hundreds of years, in contrast with the permanence of agriculture. The real problems of health and safety in mines cannot be met by advocating the abolition of mining because it is dangerous. He is particularly severe on the opinion that mining is useless because metals perform no fundamental service either to the soul or to the body of man.

Agricola scarcely dignifies with a reply a teleological argument that if it had been nature's design to make the products of mines available to man, the ores would have been close to the surface. He scorns the notion that the earth hides nothing, keeps nothing, conceals nothing that is useful or necessary to man, but "like a beneficent and kindly mother she yields in large abundance from her bounty and brings into the light of day the herbs, vegetables, grains, and fruits, and the trees."[15] Because minerals, on the other hand, lie deeply buried it cannot be argued that they should not be sought after.

In another important passage Agricola denounces the belief—apparently widely held in his time—that mining is a destroyer of nature. The strongest argument

> of the detractors [of mining] is that the fields are devastated by mining operations, for which reason formerly Italians were warned by law that no one should dig the earth for metals and so injure their very fertile fields, their vineyards, and their olive groves. Also they argue that the woods and groves are cut down, for there is need of an endless amount of wood for timbers, machines, and the smelting of metals. And when the woods and groves are felled, then are exterminated the beasts and birds, very many of which furnish a pleasant and agreeable food for man. Further, when the ores are washed, the water which has been used poisons the brooks and streams, and either destroys the fish or drives them away. Therefore the inhabitants of these regions, on account of the devastation of their fields, woods, groves, brooks and rivers, find great difficulty in procuring the necessaries of life, and by reason of the destruction

---

1942), and *Paracelsus. Selected Writings*, Eng. trans. Guterman, for many selections from Paracelsus on a wide variety of topics; both have a valuable glossary of terms used by P.

[14] Klemm, *op. cit.*, p. 145.
[15] *De re metallica*, Bk. I, Hoover trans. p. 7.

of the timber they are forced to greater expense in erecting buildings. Thus it is said, it is clear to all that there is greater detriment from mining than the value of the metals which the mining produces.[16]

To these arguments Agricola made two replies, one touching upon the specific abuses mentioned, the other raising the broader philosophical issue of the usefulness of metals to man.

Miners do slight damage if any to the fields, Agricola said, because they dig in otherwise unproductive mountains or in gloomy valleys. Cleared areas, with the roots of shrubs and trees removed, may be planted in grain, the bountiful crops of the new fields compensating for losses suffered because of higher timber prices. Birds, edible beasts, and fish furthermore can be purchased and stocked in these mountainous regions with the profits from the metal industry.

To all the more general objections to mining (including the one that metals, especially the nobler and the more valuable, are corrupters of mankind) Agricola replies simply that civilization cannot exist without metals. None of the arts is older than agriculture, but the metal arts "are at least equal or coeval, for no mortal man ever tilled a field without implements."[17] Even though he respects the honesty, innocence, and goodness of men who despise metals for the corruption and calamities they have brought upon the human race, to him they are putting the blame in the wrong place. War cannot be blamed on the metals; lacking iron or bronze, men would fight with their hands. Agricola insists on blaming human nature, not advances in metallurgy, for slaughter, robbery, and war. To speak ill of metals is to accuse and condemn as wicked the Creator himself, for by the condemnation of these, men assume that the Creator fashioned something in vain and without good cause. Pious and sensible men cannot conceive of the Creator being the author of evils.[18]

Metals are not concealed in the earth to prevent man from getting at them, "but because provident and sagacious Nature has appointed for each thing its place." He ridicules the argument that the metals were concealed because they were not intended for use by pointing out that man, a terrestrial animal, goes into the depths of the sea to fish and it is stranger for man to search the sea than to search the bowels of the earth. Moreover, birds live in the air, fish, in water, other creatures have the earth, particularly man, so that "he might cultivate it and draw out of its caverns metals and other mineral products." Agricola gives a lengthy list of the uses of metals in various occupations where they are needed directly, or indirectly through metal-made tools to perform the required tasks. "If we remove metals from the service of man, all methods of protecting and sustaining health and more carefully preserving the course of life are done away with." Without them Agricola thinks men could only

16 *Ibid.*, p. 8.
17 *Ibid.*, Pref., p. xxv.
18 *Ibid.*, Bk. I, pp. 11–12.

live lives like those of wild beasts. Men should not try to degrade the metals; as a creation of nature they supply human needs of man, both adorning man and being useful to him.[19]

In *The Admirable Discourses* (1580), Bernard Palissy expressed a similar philosophy, that once the truth about nature has been discovered men should do what is necessary to profit from the discovery. Contemptuously disclaiming any knowledge of the classical languages, Palissy scorned also those who were more interested in written authority than in observation. His attitude toward authority was similar to Leonardo's.

> Once I knew without any doubt that the waters of natural fountains were caused and produced by rains, I have thought that it was stupid for those who possess lands barren of water not to learn ways of making fountains, seeing that God sends waters on sandy lands as well as on others, and that it takes very little science to know how to catch it. If the ancients had not otherwise studied the works of God, they would have lived on the pasturage of animals, they would only have taken the fruits of the fields as they came, without work: but they wisely decided to plant, sow and cultivate, to aid nature. That is why the first inventors of some good thing, to help nature, have been so honored by our predecessors, that they have thought them to be participants in the spirit of God. [God] wishes us to work to help nature. . . .[20]

Knowledge of the care of nature comes also through observation of its processes. In the *Dialogue on Waters and Fountains*, Theory asks if the trees along the mountain that he wishes to use for a park should be cut down.

> Good Lord, no! don't do that: for these trees will be very useful to you in this matter. There are in many parts of France, and particularly at Nantes, wooden bridges, where, to break the violence of water and ice against the pillars of these bridges, great quantities of upright posts have been placed in front of the pillars, for otherwise they would not last long. In the same way, trees planted along the mountain, where you wish to make your park, will serve much to reduce the violence of the waters, and far from advising you to cut them down, I would advise you to plant some if there were none: for they would serve to prevent the waters from excavating the ground, and by such means grass will be preserved, and along this grass the waters will flow quietly straight down to your reservoir.[21]

Alberti, Leonardo, Paracelsus, Agricola, and Palissy all lived during the fifteenth and sixteenth centuries, and they lived in widely scattered places. They were all unusual men; one of them, Leonardo, was a genius; the others

[19] *Ibid.*, pp. 12, 14, 18.

[20] *The Admirable Discourses*, pp. 58–59. Palissy here expounds his theory of the origin of springs and fountains in rainwater, but see p. 13 on the question of Palissy's originality. On his attitude toward authority see La Rocque's introduction to his trans. of the discourses.

[21] *Ibid.*, p. 63. See also his discussion of the multiple uses of land made possible by careful planning, p. 67, and of the importance of wood, pp. 71–72. "If I wanted to put in writing how great is the necessity of wood, and how impossible it is to do without it, I should never be finished" (p. 72).

were men of great talent. They all had in common an interest in technology, in artisanship, and in environmental change. They have, moreover, a kinship with the political theorist Giovanni Botero, who advised princes to concern themselves with improving their kingdoms through drainage or clearing; they also have a kinship with Albrecht Dürer, who, like Leonardo an artist, engineer, and artisan, was interested in improving artisanship by more exacting scientific and mathematical methods.[22]

## 3. FRANCIS BACON

Broadly speaking, there was a growing optimism throughout the seventeenth and eighteenth centuries that man's accumulating knowledge was increasing his control over nature. There were dissenters who still saw in classical antiquity an early apogee of human accomplishment, or who believed in a senescence in nature or that the curse on man was accompanied by a curse on nature as well. The optimistic trend, however, can be observed in Agricola, in Paracelsus, and in Francis Bacon whose name is associated with the early history of the scientific method, with speculation on the application of theoretical science to applied science and technology, and with the broad question of man's control over nature. Bacon has much of interest to say on this last theme, some that is reminiscent of medieval thought, some that resembles the thought of the eighteenth and nineteenth centuries.[23]

In his plea for an understanding of nature (he uses this word synonymously with the creation), Bacon warns that men should realize they are dealing with a creation of God, not a construct of the human mind.

> For we copy the sin of our first parents while we suffer for it. They wished to be like God, but their posterity wish to be even greater. For we create worlds, we direct and domineer over nature, we will have it that all things *are* as in our folly we think they should be, not as seems fittest to the Divine wisdom, or as they are found to be in fact; and I know not whether we more distort the facts of nature or our own wits; but we clearly impress the stamp of our own image on the creatures and works of God, instead of carefully examining and recognising in them the stamp of the Creator himself. Wherefore our dominion over creatures is a second time forfeited, not undeservedly; and whereas after the fall of man some power over the resistance of creatures was still left to him—the power of subduing and managing them by true and solid arts—yet this too through our insolence, and because we desire to be like God and to follow the dictates of our own reason, we in great part lose. If therefore there be any humility towards the Creator, any reverence for or disposition to magnify His works, any charity for man and anxiety to relieve his sorrows and necessities, any love of truth in nature, any hatred of darkness, any desire for the purification of the understanding, we must entreat men again and again to discard, or at least set

[22] See Klemm, *op. cit.*, p. 131.
[23] Francis Bacon, 1561–1626. *Advancement of Learning*, 1605; *Novum Organum*, 1620; *New Atlantis*, 1629.

apart for a while, these volatile and preposterous philosophies, which have pre-ferred theses to hypotheses, led experience captive, and triumphed over the works of God; and to approach with humility and veneration to unroll the volume of the Creation, to linger and meditate therein, and with minds washed clean from opinions to study it in purity and integrity.[24]

Human ignorance is like a second fall of man; it is, like the Fall, also a form of failure if the old philosophy can triumph even over the words of God. In the exhortation to "unroll the volume of the creation," Bacon makes good use of the old idea of learning in the book of nature.

Bacon's philosophy of man's attaining control over nature by cultivating the arts and sciences and encouraging invention is not divorced from religion; it is a vital part of religion, being closely related to the history of the creation and to the fall of man. Repeatedly he invokes the lesson of Genesis that the creation of light took place on the first day; when he says that experiments should imitate the creation of light, human science is exalted by the com-parison with divine creation. ". . . We look for experiments that shall afford light rather than profit, imitating the divine creation, which, as we have often observed, only produced light on the first day, and assigned that whole day to its creation, without adding any material work."[25]

To Bacon, the fall of man, "the sin of our first parents," was of decisive importance in the subsequent history of both man and nature, as is apparent in the eloquent closing lines of the *Novum Organum*:

> For man, by the fall, lost at once his state of innocence, and his empire over creation, both of which can be partially recovered even in this life, the first by religion and faith, the second by the arts and sciences. For creation did not become entirely and utterly rebellious by the curse, but in consequence of the Divine decree, "in the sweat of thy brow shalt thou eat bread," she is compelled by our labors (not assuredly by our disputes or magical ceremonies), at length, to afford mankind in some degree his bread, that is to say, to supply man's daily wants.

Not only are separate roles assigned to religion and faith and to the arts and sciences, but the latter mitigate the physical consequences of the first fall and of the second fall (that is, the adoption of philosophies that prevent an investi-gation and understanding of nature.)

How does Bacon envisage human control over nature? For one thing, it is a lofty and objective position for man, as one would expect from the com-parisons with the creation of light. This position is revealed in the famous passage on the three ambitions: men may want to enlarge their own power in

[24] "The Natural and Experimental History for the Foundation of Philosophy: or Phenomena of the Universe: Which is the Third part of the Instauratio Magna," *The Works of Francis Bacon*, ed. Spedding, Ellis, and Heath, Vol. 5 (Vol. 2 of the transla-tions of *The Philosophical Works*), pp. 131–134. Quotation on p. 132.

[25] *Novum Organum*, Bk. I, Aph. 121.

their own country, an ambition which Bacon thinks vulgar and degenerate; men may strive to enlarge the power and empire of their native country over mankind, a more dignified ambition than the first, but still covetous; or they may strive for an enlargement of the power of man over the whole universe, a sounder and a nobler ambition. Bacon follows the passage on the three ambitions with one of the most quoted of his sentences: "Now the empire of man over things is founded on the arts and sciences alone, for nature is only to be commanded by obeying her."[26]

In the goal for the knowledge that will lead to mastery over nature, Bacon has little patience with those who think the ancient world superior. The present is a true antiquity. One expects more from an old than from a young man; similarly, since the world now is older, its stock has increased, and so have experiments and observations. Bacon is struck by the recent expansion of man's geographic vision; it must be matched by a comparable growth in his intellectual vision. The contrast between the fresh air of the voyages and discoveries and the stale adherence to authority and to classical knowledge is a fundamental observation in his philosophy. Men must rise to the opportunities afforded them by the age of discovery.

"It would, indeed, be dishonorable to mankind, if the regions of the material globe, the earth, the sea, and stars, should be so prodigiously developed and illustrated in our age, and yet the boundaries of the intellectual globe should be confined to the narrow discoveries of the ancients."[27]

The importance of voyages and travels to discovery and invention, in the interchange of ideas which lead to further mastery over nature, is clear when the governor of the *New Atlantis* describes the mission of the three fellows of Saloman's House, who set out in two ships "to give us knowledge of the affairs and state of those countries to which they were designed; and especially of the sciences, arts, manufactures, and inventions of all the world; and withal to bring unto us books, instruments, and patterns in every kind. . . ." The governor, remembering the creation of light on the first day, continues, "But thus you see we maintain a trade, not for gold, silver, or jewels, nor for silks, nor for spices, nor any other commodity of matter; but only for God's first creature, which was light; to have light, I say, of the growth of all parts of the world."[28]

In Bacon's thought the voyages of discovery, especially those of scientific travelers, become a standing rebuke to those who uncritically accept authority and precedent in an age conscious of the stimulus that comes from the broadening of its horizons. In fact there seems to be a parallel between the voyages of discovery and invention, for philosophies and sciences founded

---

[26] *Ibid.*, Aph. 129.
[27] *Ibid.*, Aph. 84.
[28] "New Atlantis," in *Ideal Commonwealths*, World's Greatest Literature ed., pp. 119–120.

on nature grow; those on opinion, neither change nor increase. Comparing the stationary sciences unfavorably with the mechanical arts, Bacon says that the latter "are founded on nature and the light of experience, for they (as long as they are popular) seem full of life, and uninterruptedly thrive and grow, being at first rude, then convenient, lastly polished, and perpetually improved."[29] Bacon hints here at an ideal series of stages in the development of technology.

Saloman's House, known also as Solomon's House and as the College of the Six Days' Works (the latter name showing Bacon's attraction to the symbolism of the hexaemeral creation, beginning with the creation of light), was named, says the governor, after the king of the Hebrews "famous with you, and no strangers to us"; here some of his works, lost elsewhere, have been preserved, including Solomon's "natural history which he wrote of all plants, from the cedar of Libanus to the moss that groweth out of the wall; and of all things that have life and motion." Saloman's House, as described by the governor, represents that active aspect of Christian thought which worships the workmanship of God in the creation, sees at the same time the usefulness of created things to man. Our king [he said] learned from the Hebrews that God created the world within six days, "and therefore he instituted that house, for the finding out of the true nature of all things, whereby God might have the more glory in the workmanship of them, and men the more fruit in their use of them, did give it also that second name."[30]

Since Saloman's House is such an important institution in New Atlantis, where the arts, science, ethics, and religion are intertwined to the strength and the glory of all, one would expect, in addition to more invention, more research in medicine, more inquiry in the fields of theoretical science, an active interest in transforming the environment in the service of mankind; in these proposals, moreover, there is no hint that environmental change by man might ever be undesirable. "The end of our foundation is the knowledge of causes, and secret motions of things; and the enlarging of the bounds of human empire, to the effecting of all things possible."[31]

In New Atlantis, a great variety of composts and soils make the earth fruitful. Salt- and fresh-water lakes are exploited for their fish and fowl; natural bodies are buried in them, too. Salt water is made into fresh, fresh water into salt. Streams, cataracts, and "engines for multiplying and enforcing of winds" are sources of power. In the orchards and gardens "we do not so much respect beauty as variety of ground and soil, proper for divers trees and herbs, and some very spacious, where trees and berries are set, whereof we make divers kinds of drinks, beside the vineyards." Grafting is

[29] *Novum Organum*, Bk. I, Aph. 74.
[30] *New Atlantis*, p. 119.
[31] *Ibid.*, p. 129.

much practiced. Gardens, trees, flowers, are made by art to ripen earlier or later than they would naturally. By art also they are larger, their fruit sweeter, their taste, smell, color, and figure different. Many are discovered to have medicinal value. "We have also means to make divers plants rise by mixtures of earths without seeds, and likewise to make divers new plants, differing from the vulgar, and to make one tree or plant turn into another."

Parks and enclosures for beasts and birds are used not only for view or rareness but likewise for dissections and trials, to discover through them "what may be wrought upon the body of man." Experiments of like kind are made on fish, and breeding places are set aside for worms and flies.[32]

In New Atlantis the human activities which affect the natural environment are primarily those concerned with agriculture and horticulture (soil fertilization, plant breeding and selection) and the use of the waters and the winds as energy to drive the machines of an industrial society in the service of God and man. "We have certain hymns and services, which we say daily, of laud and thanks to God for His marvellous works. And forms of prayers, imploring His aid and blessing for the illumination of our labors; and turning them into good and holy uses."[33]

## 4. Optimism of Seventeenth Century Writings

In the spirit of Bacon and Romans 1:20, Sir Thomas Browne says he will find evidences of Him in nature, "that universal and publick Manuscript," the servant of God. The world "was made to be inhabited by Beasts, but studied and contemplated by Man; 'tis the Debt of our Reason we owe unto God, and the homage we pay for not being Beasts; without this, the World is still as though it had not been, or as it was before the sixth day, when as yet there was not a Creature that could conceive, or say there was a World." Again we meet the thought that it is God-given reason possessed alone by man that gives meaning to the creation. And the higher man's endowment the better is this meaning understood. It is not "those vulgar Heads that rudely stare about, and with a gross rusticity admire his works" who honor the wisdom of God, but those "whose judicious inquiry into His Acts, and deliberate research into His Creatures, return the duty of a devout and learned admiration."[34]

Man is an "amphibious piece between a corporal and spiritual Essence"; indeed he is a microcosm, for he embodies in his own life all five kinds of existence. First he is a rude mass of dull being "not yet privileged with life,"

[32] *Ibid.*, pp. 129–132.
[33] *Ibid.*, p. 137.
[34] *Religio Medici*, Gateway ed., Pt. I, sect. 16, p. 27; sect. 13, p. 24. Browne wrote the *RM* in 1635 and it was first published in 1643.

then successively he lives the lives of plants, animals, man, and finally spirits. In "one mysterious nature" man with these five kinds of existences comprehends the creatures of the world and of the universe; "thus is man that great and true Amphibium," a spanner of worlds. The embodiment of all five existences in his life uniquely qualifies him for his role on earth. God made the creation for His own glory and then made man as the only being able to do him homage.[35] His creation on the sixth day changes completely the meaning of the creative acts which preceded him. If we add (which Browne did not) the injunctions of Genesis 1:28, man becomes God's workman and governor of nature. The most highly gifted men through inquiry and research will accomplish these tasks the best. Sir Matthew Hale will expand eloquently on this theme. (See pp. 481–482.)

Like Bacon, Descartes had confidence in the power of knowledge to control the environment; in fact, the relevant passage in the *Discourse on Method* has become almost as famous as Bacon's statement that we can command nature only by obeying her. Perhaps his enthusiasm for technology as an ally in the struggle to better the lot of the human race may have been intensified by his studies and observations during his residence in the Netherlands, where dramatic transformations of the land by drainage and polder making were then taking place.

To digress for a moment, one could write an illuminating essay on the influence of Dutch hydraulic engineering on optimistic interpretations of modifications of the land by human agency. The first half of the seventeenth century was a golden age of accomplishment; even before this, the expert outside the dikes, Andries Vierlingh, wrote in old age his work on making dams, dikes, and sluices and "creating new land from sandbanks or sandy foreshores." Of the work Vierlingh wrote, "It is not really such a great art, a shepherd might be able to imitate it. But making new land belongs to God alone. For He gives to some people the intelligence and power to do it. It takes love and very much labour, and it is not everybody who can play that game." After the year 1600, windmills became active pumpers on a large scale. Jan Leeghwater (1575–1650), the expert inside the dikes, also writing in old age, had seen the face of the country change in his own lifetime. In the peninsula north of Amsterdam he had by 1640 counted twenty-seven lakes which had been pumped dry, and he himself proposed draining the Haarlemmermeer with the help of a hundred and sixty windmills. Finally Cornelius Vermuyden, commissioned by James I in 1621 to repair the Thames wall at Dagenham, remained to supervise the draining of the fens.[36]

When, Descartes says, he had acquired knowledge of "certain general

[35] *Ibid.*, Pt. 1, sect. 34–35, pp. 52–54.
[36] Van Veen, *Dredge, Drain, Reclaim*, pp. 34–47. The quotes are on pp. 34, 39. On Dutch activity abroad, pp. 47–59 with maps. See also L. E. Harris, "Land Drainage and Reclamation," in *A History of Technology*, ed. Singer *et al.*, Vol. 3, pp. 306–308, 319.

notions in physics," when he realized how much these principles differed from those of the past which were still being honored, he could not withhold his knowledge "without greatly sinning against the law which enjoins upon us the duty of procuring, as well as we can, the general good of mankind." It is now possible to attain knowledge of "the utmost use" to men, a practical knowledge which can gain ascendancy over the speculative philosophy taught in the schools. By means of this practical knowledge, "by ascertaining the force and action of fire, water, the air, the heavenly bodies, and the skies, of all the physical things that surround us, as distinctly as we know the various trades of our artisans, we can apply them in the same way to all the uses for which they are fit, and thus make ourselves, as it were, the lords and masters of nature."[37]

Leibniz, also, saw the possibilities of the arts and sciences contributing to the advancement of mankind. He repeatedly made proposals for their promotion, including elaborate plans for exhibitions, museums, and academies. He was impressed with the vastness of human knowledge; it was difficult to ascertain how much was known because so much valuable knowledge was unrecorded. He believed in learning from the occupations of daily life, from men—and children too—at play, whether at games of skill or of chance. "Concerning unwritten knowledge scattered among men of different callings, I am convinced that it surpasses in quantity and in importance anything we find in books, and that the greater part of our wealth is not yet recorded."[38]

With his ideas of a divinely preestablished harmony, his enthusiasm for the doctrine of final causes, his conviction that the arts and sciences were on the march, that, encouraged, they would prevent a return to barbarism, with his belief that progress was characteristic of the cosmos, Leibniz saw no reason why the inevitable progress of mankind could not be balanced by a similar process with relation to the earth, its ultimate perfection being a witness of the cumulative talents of man:

> And in addition to the general beauty and perfection of the works of God, we must recognize a certain perpetual and very free progress of the whole universe, such that it advances always to still greater improvement (*cultum*). It is thus that even now a great part of our earth has received cultivation and will receive more and more. And although it is true that sometimes certain parts of it grow up wild again or again suffer destruction and deterioration, this nevertheless must be understood as we interpreted affliction above, that is to say, this very destruction and deterioration leads to some greater result, so that we profit in some way by the loss itself.[39]

[37] Descartes, "Discourse on Method," 6, in *Discourse on Method and Other Writings*. Trans. with an intro. by Arthur Wollaston. Penguin Books (1960), p. 84.
[38] "Discourse Touching the Method of Certitude, and the Art of Discovery in Order to End Disputes and to Make Progress Quickly," *Leibniz Selections*, ed. Wiener, pp. 46–47.
[39] "On the Ultimate Origin of Things" (1697), *Leibniz Selections*, ed. Wiener, p. 354.

This is an important passage because it reveals the optimism possible in the doctrine of final causes and in the idea of a preestablished harmony which includes the earth as a physical body within this harmony. All changes on the whole can be for the best; the entire earth will ultimately be cultivated like a garden. The slow gathering of isolated fragments of information showing that man could cumulatively make undesirable changes in nature, that these could not be overcome by mere belief in an inevitable progress, unfortunately have proved this assumption, this bold vision of Leibniz, wrong.

The spirit of Francis Bacon and Descartes and their precursors, Leonardo, Paracelsus, Agricola, and Palissy, continued among many prominent thinkers of the seventeenth century to whom the industry of man, lifted to a higher plane of human experience, illustrated a widening control over nature through the arts and sciences. Philosophically this industry might be considered as an exercise of the mind and the skillful hand toward desirable ends, theologically as the activity of a being who was both a steward of God on earth and a worshipper of the divine workmanship he could see everywhere in nature, and practically as useful activity which used the earth's resources and brought order to an otherwise chaotic nature. This vision of man's controlling nature and changing his environment was to Descartes evidence of a remarkable achievement, a divorcement from the past, and to Leibniz evidence of a progress characteristic of the cosmos.

We have already seen the role that Hakewill (and John Jonston of Poland, a popularizer of his work) played in combatting the notion of a decay of nature sponsored so vigorously by Godfrey Goodman. Hakewill believed that the earth would come to an end, as predicted in the Bible; how this end would come about he thought was unascertainable by reason; it would be brought about by a miracle. Since he did not believe that any processes now observable on earth were bringing about its decay in the sense that an organism decays, he became a Columella against Lucretius and discovered more immediate and plausible reasons for changes taking place in the environment.[40]

The quality of Hakewill's mind and his discernment are revealed in his discussion of the physical decline of the Holy Land. Hakewill says it has undoubtedly decayed; possibly its early fruitfulness may have been a special favor of God. (Quotes Deut. 11:3, Levit. 26, "If you walk in mine ordinances and keep . . ." etc.) The decline there, he concludes after considering Scripture and the reports of Brocardus' *De Terra Sancta* (Pt. 2, chap. 1), may be owing to the curse of God or to "their ill manuring of the earth, (from which the proverbe seems to have growne, that where the Grand Signiors

---

[40] For a comparison between the views of Hakewill and Goodman on the decay of the world, the earth being designed for man, teleology, and final state of the earth, see Victor Harris, *All Coherence Gone*, pp. 82–85.

horse once treades, the grasse never growes afterward), than to any *Naturall decay* in the goodness of the soyle." Labor and industry have a dignity in Hakewill's conception of man's relation to the earth, for human industry makes things better than unassisted nature could. "And it is certaine that God so ordained it, that the *industry of man* should in all things concurre with the *workes of Nature*, both for the bringing of them to their perfection, and for the keeping of them therein being brought unto it."[41]

The conflict between the older pessimistic ideas regarding the effects of the curse on nature and modern aspirations for improvement in the natural surroundings by purposeful and planned industry is well brought out in Robert Burton's *The Anatomy of Melancholy.*

Burton accepts this older pessimistic view of a decay in nature owing to the Fall, man's sins being reflected in the barrenness of the earth.[42] Among the secondary causes bringing these conditions about are unfriendly influences of the stars, though he grants that astrology inclines but does not compel, the air (meteors, bad weather inducing plague, referring to Giovanni Botero's observations of the unhealthiness of Cairo and Constantinople), earthquakes, floods, fires, and the animals at war with man. However, he does not take too serious a view of these calamities visited on man by the elements and by other forms of life; the knavery of man to man is far worse and cannot, like the others, be avoided.[43]

This conventional pessimism, however, does not mix well with other prescriptions of this authority on melancholy.[44] Burton in fact is very much interested in human creativity, in the increase of man's power to control nature. Citing Botero's observation with approval (quoted above, p. 371), Burton says that kingdoms, like men, are subject to melancholy. Rulers should improve the physical environment of their kingdoms to overcome this morbid state. He admires the Dutch and the improvements they have made in their country and contrasts the progress achieved by them with the inertia of his own countrymen.

> Yea, and if some travellers should see (to come nearer home) those rich United Provinces of Holland, Zealand, &c., over against us; those neat cities and populous towns, full of industrious artificers, so much land recovered from the sea, and so painfully preserved by those artificial inventions, so wonderfully approved, as that of Bemster in Holland, so that you would find nothing equal to it or like it in the whole world, saith Bertius the Geographer, all the world cannot match it, so many navigable channels from place to place, made by men's hands, &c., and on the other side so many thousand acres of our fens lie drowned, our cities thin, and those vile, poor, and ugly to behold in respect to theirs, our

---

[41] *Apologie*, pp. 151, 156. Quotes Columella, and Pliny, xviii, 3. Quotes Calvin, p. 157.
[42] *Anat. of Melancholy*, Part 1, sect. 1, memb. 1, subs. 1, pp. 113–114.
[43] *Ibid.*, pp. 113–117. On astrology, Part 1, sect. 2, memb. 1, subs. 4, p. 179.
[44] See also Victor Harris, *All Coherence Gone*, pp. 138–139.

trades decayed, our still running rivers stopped, and that beneficial use of transportation wholly neglected, so many havens void of ships and towns, so many parks and forests for pleasure, barren heaths, so many villages depopulated, &c., I think sure he would find some fault.[45]

Burton agrees with Botero that fertility of soil is not enough; art and industry must be added to it. Of Holland he says, "their chiefest loadstone which draws all manner of commerce and merchandize, which maintains their present estate, is not fertility of soil, but industry that enricheth them, the gold mines of Peru or New Spain may not compare with them."[46] He also agrees with Columella that there is no tiredness or exhaustion in the soil; it becomes barren through laziness; he is interested in the correct management of water, in irrigation, in the drainage of fens, bogs, and moors, in stream pollution, in the relation of water to disease, in running water, in the settling of water as it flows, and in the history of cisterns and aqueducts.[47]

In *The Primitive Origination of Mankind*, Sir Matthew Hale considered the broad questions posed by the multiplication and dispersion of mankind over the earth, man's place in the scale of being, and the implications of his growing control over nature. (See *supra* pp. 400–405.) To Hale man acts as the steward of God on earth, man is a being who creates order in what without him would be chaos; he implies that man's works, stimulated by self-conscious intelligence, and the control man has achieved over the lower forms of life confer a dignity and value on all life that it would not otherwise have. This is broader and more defensible than is the view that the earth is made for man.

In an exciting and imaginative discussion, Hale says that man's place in nature can be known from observation without revelation. The creation of man seems to have an end or a purpose with relation to the order of nature on earth. The wild untamable animals need man's coercive power to prevent their destroying the more profitable and weaker animals. Man can preserve from extinction the useful but easily destroyed domesticated animals; he can protect the useful birds; he can war on the beasts and birds of prey. He can play a similar role in the care of tender and delicate plants lest they become extinct or degenerate; fruit trees, herbs, choice flowers, are examples of his loving care. Man has a duty to protect the world from the ponding of water in marsh and bog, and from too luxurious a plant growth; his is a "superintendent industry" correcting their excesses lest the spontaneous plant production make of the earth a wilderness of trees, weeds, thorns, briars. Without a "superintendent Cultivation" the earth's surface would grow marshy, boggy, weedy, "overgrown with excessive excrescences." It is a frame of mind quite similar to Count Buffon's in the eighteenth century.

[45] *Anat. of Melancholy*, Intro., Democritus to the Reader, p. 72.
[46] *Ibid.*, p. 74.
[47] Part 2, sect. 2, memb. 1, subs. 1, pp. 397–398.

It does not take Hale long to dispose of the question of the curse. This infertility and unprofitable excrescence might be the result of man's sin; God foreseeing sin, also provided a remedy. Man had to work harder after the Fall, but his employment did not differ from the times in Eden where God put man in the garden to dress it and keep it.

To my knowledge, there is no more masterly exposition of Christian belief in the reality of man's dominion over nature as set forth in Genesis than the following words of Hale:

> In relation therefore to this inferior World of Brutes and Vegetables, the End of Man's Creation was, that he should be the Vice-Roy of the great God of Heaven and Earth in this inferior World; his Steward, *Villicus*, Bayliff or Farmer of this goodly Farm of the lower World, and reserved to himself the supreme Dominion, and the Tribute of Fidelity, Obedience, and Gratitude, as the greatest recognition or Rent for the same, making his Usufructuary of this inferior World to husband and order it, and enjoy the Fruits thereof with sobriety, moderation, and thankfulness.
>
> And hereby Man was invested with power, authority, right, dominion, trust, and care, to correct and abridge the excesses and cruelties of the fiercer Animals, to give protection and defence to the mansuete and useful, to preserve the *Species* of divers Vegetables, to improve them and others, to correct the redundance of unprofitable Vegetables, to preserve the face of the Earth in beauty, usefulness, and fruitfulness. And surely, as it was not below the Wisdom and Goodness of God to create the very Vegetable Nature, and render the Earth more beautiful and useful by it, so neither was it unbecoming the same Wisdom to ordain and constitute such a subordinate Superintendent over it, that might take an immediate care of it.
>
> And certainly if we observe the special and peculiar accommodation and adaptation of Man, to the regiment and ordering of this lower World, we shall have reason, even without Revelation, to conclude that this was one End of the Creation of Man, namely, To be the Vice-gerent [*sic*] of Almighty God, in the subordinate Regiment especially of the Animal and Vegetable Provinces.[48]

Sir Matthew Hale was a famous lawyer, far more famous as a chief justice and for his work on the English common law than for *The Primitive Origination of Mankind*. But the lawyer's touch is there, too. Man assumes tasks that a lawyer thinks should be done, the tasks of the steward, the bailiff. Hale outlines the legal obligations of a lord on earth to administer it justly, fairly, sternly, and without cruelty. The earth is in need of a superior creature to keep it in competent order, otherwise the balance in nature would be lost, forests and wilderness would engulf both the earth and man; the useful animals, the prey of savage beasts, would be on the road to extinction. Man is capable of this role because of his intellectual endowments, because of the *organum organorum*, the hand. He controls nature for the earth's sake and for his own. The hierarchy of life, the balance in nature on earth, is main-

---

[48] *Prim. Orig. of Man.*, p. 370; previous discussion is based on pp. 369–370.

tained and kept in order by the agency of man. "Thus the infinite Wisdom of Almighty God chains things together, and fits and accommodates all things suitable to their uses and ends."[49]

To Hale (and many seventeenth and eighteenth century thinkers agreed) man's control over nature is based on his position in the scale of being; he enjoys the topmost rung of the ladder, but he is a master whose rights are circumscribed by obligations, by a *noblesse oblige*. Man's position is a legal one; he is also an overseer of nature, like a husbandman with the earth as his farm, whose activities Hale describes in the language of law and commerce.

Man's "intellectual sagacity and contrivance" qualify him for his superintendency; he can domesticate the larger and more powerful animals—the horse, the elephant, and the camel—and make the weaker animals subservient to him. Man's ability to change nature by domesticating plants and animals seems to have impressed thinkers of this period as it did those of the past; Buffon also, as we shall see, is much impressed by it. Men's hands, manipulators of swords, pikes, arrows, darts, nets, traps, tools, give them an overwhelming advantage in struggles against the brutes. Man must continually exert his mastery over plants and animals; if he does not, he will be overwhelmed by them, an argument which anticipates the famous Romanes lecture of Thomas Henry Huxley in 1894.[50]

Men must actively interfere with brute nature, to use a characteristic expression of his time, in order to maintain civilization. Nature untouched by man is a lesser nature and the economy of nature is best where man actively superintends it. The role of man as a caretaker of nature, a viceroy, a steward of God in his relation with other forms of life, justifies both his place in the chain of being and the accomplishments of his technology—in clearing, mining, canal building, and many other activities which are perhaps not revolutionary nor radically divorced from the past, but which produce cumulative change.

In his *History of the Royal Society*—one might call it a history of Solomon's House—Sprat shows an equal enthusiasm for man as a changer of nature. Its dedication extols the value of the vulgar arts, its later pages, the wisdom of the creator as shown in his works. Sprat praises the practical things, the homely inventions and discoveries. The idea that man can improve upon nature by art is a source of pride and of self-congratulation.[51] Man can make these environmental improvements by plant introductions, by using animals, by comparative husbandry. There was no romantic primitivism in men like Sprat, in John Ray, nor later in Count Buffon. Civilization through

[49] *Ibid.*, p. 371; discussion is based on pp. 369–371.
[50] See "Evolution and Ethics. Prolegomena" (1894), in *Evolution and Ethics and Other Essays*. New York, 1896.
[51] Sprat, *History of the Royal Society*, pp. 119–121, 386.

the arts created an environment having little resemblance to the crude conditions of earlier periods in human history.

John Ray speaks for many devout Christians who are also self-confident admirers of and advocates of improvements in their natural surroundings.

> If a country thus planted and adorn'd, thus polished and civilized, thus improved to the Height by all Manner of Culture for the Support and Sustenance, and convenient Entertainment of innumerable Multitudes of People, be not to be preferred before a barbarous and inhospitable *Scythia*, without Houses, without Plantations, without Corn-fields or Vineyards . . . ; or a rude and unpolished *America* peopled with slothful and naked *Indians*, instead of well-built houses, living in pitiful Huts and Cabbins, made of Poles set endways; then surely the brute Beasts Condition, and Manner of Living, to which, what we have mention'd doth nearly approach, is to be esteem'd better than Man's, and Wit and Reason was in vain bestowed on him.[52]

Moreover, Ray made a cogent synthesis, including environmental changes by man within his physico-theology. This synthesis included the following elements: heavy reliance on teleological explanations of processes in nature, emphasis on the beauty and usefulness of nature, a vision of man as actively changing nature under the guidance of God, and the conviction that changes made by man become part of a harmony thus newly created.

To Ray, mankind clearly plays an active role in nature, and man advances by increasing his knowledge of the ways he can use the earth's resources. God designed the earth, providing an abundance for the use of man who, He knows beforehand, has the necessary reason and understanding to adapt its offering (while he is adapting himself to it) by means of discovery and invention to his own uses.[53]

In the following passage notable for its elegant smugness, Ray composes a speech for the Deity who tells man precisely what He has done for him.

> I have now placed thee in a spacious and well-furnish'd World; I have endued thee with an Ability of understanding what is beautiful and proportionable, and have made that which is so, agreeable and delightful to thee; I have provided thee with Materials whereon to exercise and employ thy Art and Strength; I have given thee an excellent Instrument, the Hand, accommodated to make use of them all; I have distinguished the Earth into Hills and Vallies, and Plains, and Meadows, and Woods; all these Parts, capable of Culture and Improvement by thy Industry; I have committed to thee for thy Assistance in thy Labours of Plowing, and Carrying, and Drawing, and Travel, the laborious Ox, the patient Ass, and the strong and serviceable Horse; I have created a Multitude of Seeds for thee to make a Choice out of them, of what is most pleasant to thy Taste, and of most wholesome and plentiful Nourishement. . . .[54]

[52] Ray, *Wisdom of God*, p. 165.
[53] *Ibid.*, p. 161.
[54] *Ibid.*, pp. 161–162.

There is no suspicion here of the Malthusian "niggardliness of nature," or of the Darwinian struggle for existence. "I have made thee a sociable Creature, [Ζῷον πολιτικόν] for the Improvement of thy Understanding by Conference, and Communication of Observations and Experiments." Furthermore, God has given man the curiosity to see strange and foreign countries, to improve his knowledge of geography, politics, and natural history.

> I persuade myself [Ray adds after the Deity has had his say] that the bountiful and gracious Author of Man's Being and Faculties, and all Things else, delights in the Beauty of his Creation, and is well pleased with the Industry of Man, in adorning the Earth with beautiful Cities and Castles; with pleasant Villages and Country-Houses; with regular Gardens and Orchards, and Plantations of all Sorts of Shrubs and Herbs, and Fruits, for Meat, Medicine, or Moderate Delight; with Shady Woods and Groves, and walks set with Rows of elegant Trees; *with Pastures cloathed with Flocks, and Valleys cover'd with Corn*, and Meadows burthened with Grass, and whatever differenceth a civil and well-cultivated Region, from a barren and desolate Wilderness.[55]

Many of these thinkers from Paracelsus and Agricola to Bacon and Ray were optimistic because the long-sought-for application of theoretical knowledge to the control of nature was being realized; to them, the difficulties were in achieving this application of knowledge, not in the consequences of control once success had been achieved. These thinkers regarded the applications as beneficent because they were purposive; men knew what they wanted and what they were about. And many of the dramatic man-made improvements in the landscape of Europe during this general period were purposive, especially the widespread drainage activities and canal building, of which the construction of the Canal du Midi (Canal de Languedoc), under the ministry of Colbert and the supervision of Pierre-Paul Riquet de Bonrepos, was the proudest example.

### 5. SILVA AND FUMIFUGIUM

These optimistic conclusions were based on the assumption that human modifications of the land were planned and beneficent, but some men also saw that certain traditional practices in resource use were wasteful or incompatible with other types of use which were emerging out of new economic conditions. In general, complaints in the early modern period are found in areas whose economic base is in mining, forestry, or agriculture. Forests especially were threatened with destruction by demands for wood in mining and metallurgy, shipbuilding and agriculture, and by the demands for more cleared land for agricultural purposes.

---

[55] *Ibid.*, pp. 163–164, 165.

It is possible to cite hundreds of illustrations of these conflicts, to show the existence of similar problems in Germany, Norway, and Sweden, but I prefer to mention and to discuss at some length two famous documents, John Evelyn's *Silva: or, A Discourse of Forest-Trees* (1664), and the *French Forest Ordinance of 1669*, which mark, it seems to me, the beginning of a more reserved attitude toward the modification of nature by man in the history of Western thought. They are by no means the first, but they are among the earliest attempts to understand—what is so often emphasized in modern literature—the unsought for, unplanned, often unnoticed consequences of modifications in the environment undertaken for rational economic reasons. Both recognize the influence of the past in the continued vigor of customary rights of use; both recognize the claims of posterity. Both are important divides: Colbert's ordinance not only exposed the nature of centuries-long abuse, but it codified French law and superseded all previous legislation on the subject, while it has been said of Evelyn's *Silva* that it looks back on the old era of forest exploitation, forward to a new era recognizing the need for conservation.

In a broad sense, Evelyn's work is an appeal for proper understanding of the relationship of forestry to agriculture, grazing, and industry. In forceful, often earthy, language ("And the reader is to know, that if these dry sticks afford him any sap, it is one of the least and meanest of those pieces which are every day produced by that illustrious assembly [the Royal Society]"), frequently testy and haughty ("It is not therefore to gratify these magnificent fops, whose talents reach but to the adjusting of their perukes, courting a Miss, or, at the farthest, writing a smutty or scurrilous libel, which they would have to pass for genuine wit, that I concern myself in these papers . . ."), he states the case for forest conservation and for considering forestry as a science, deploring the snobbery of those who consider it unworthy of their talents. His discourse, he says, is not for rustics who cannot understand such matters, but for gentlemen who can. It is therefore no horticultural manual written for the barely literate, but a work appealing to councillors, knowledgeable horticulturalists, and men of science. (Evelyn was one of the founders of the Royal Society, becoming its secretary in 1662.) His plea for dignifying forestry as a science and field of learning reminds one of Agricola's earlier plea for mining: it is no discipline for the ignorant, it requires knowledge of the sciences and of techniques, respect for artisanship. There is an occasional quotation from others with a similar respect for artisanship like Palissy and Francis Bacon. Evelyn defends the Royal Society against the criticisms of well-placed or well-born but hopelessly uninformed triflers; he sees, through its agency, applications of science to the amelioration of the human condition and to the improvement of the land. But he is no doctrinaire. If, in his opinion, the ancients have anything useful to say, he quotes them at length. The *Silva* has many quotations from Virgil's Georgics, from Theophrastus, Pliny, and Columella. He makes no distinction between an ancient and a modern authority, the test to him being their correctness and pertinence to the discussion.

Although the book recommends forest conservation and afforestation, a large proportion of the text is concerned with technical details, descriptions of individual trees, methods of planting or grafting, their uses, and so forth. In discussing the following themes in Evelyn's *Silva*, I should add that they do not occupy a prominent place in the work as a whole.

The first is the theme of competing uses of land, including the encroachment of one use on another and multiple use of land. The illustrations, like those in the *French Forest Ordinance*, come from agriculture, grazing, and industry (especially iron- and glass-making).

To Evelyn, the state of the forests is vital to national policy, pertinent to the interests of the Royal Society. The biggest threat to the country is the possible decay of her wooden walls (a favorite expression of his for the navy) which are in turn related to the production of timber. The Royal Society can therefore study the question of timber and national power.[56]

There are many causes, Evelyn says, for the drain on the country's forests: the increase in shipping, the multiplication of glassworks and iron-furnaces, the "disproportionate spreading of tillage," and the selfish desire of men "utterly to extirpate, demolish, and raze, as it were, all those many goodly woods and forests, which our more prudent ancestors left standing for the ornament and service of their country." Evelyn describes this devastation as "epidemical," in need of immediate arresting lest "one of the bulwarks of this nation" be totally ruined.[57]

To correct this devastation by letting nature take its course "would cost (besides the inclosure) some entire ages repose of the plow. . . ." Since a country must feed itself, an alternative method would be to sow and plant selected species of the most useful trees. "Truly, the waste and destruction of our woods has been so universal, that I conceive nothing less than an universal plantation of all the sorts of trees will supply, and well encounter the defect. . . ."[58]

In addition to the indiscriminate felling of the agriculturalist there is grazing. Evelyn is not opposed to grazing which since time immemorial had been associated with the forests of Europe, but he advocates more rigor in understanding its effects. "It were to be wished that our tender and improvable woods should not admit of cattle by any means, till they were quite grown out of reach; the statutes which connive at it, in favour of custom, and for

---

[56] *Silva*, To the Reader, no pagination.
[57] *Ibid.*, pp. 1–2.
[58] *Ibid.*, p. 3.

the satisfying of a few clamourous and rude *Commoners*, are too indulgent. . . ."[59]

The "exhorbitance and increase of devouring iron-mills" could ruin England; he suggests they be removed into a new world, "the *Holy Land* of New-England. . . . It were better to purchase all our iron out of America, than thus to exhaust our woods at home although (I doubt not) they might be so ordered as to be rather a means of preserving them. . . . One Simon Sturtivant had a patent from King James I. 1612, pretending to save 300,000 l. a year, by melting iron oar, and other metals, with pit-coal, sea-coal, and brush-fuel; it is pity it did not succeed." Evelyn admits that if iron-masters were enlightened it would be possible by care and replanting to smelt iron and maintain forests; his own father had told him this would be possible. But without this care, "I am no advocate for iron-works, but a declared Denouncer. But nature has thought fit to produce this wasting oar more plentifully in woodland than any other ground, and to enrich our forests to their own destruction." He quotes from his friend, the poet Abraham Cowley, on the Forest of Dean: "Woods tall and reverend, from all time appear / Inviolable, where no Mine is near."[60]

Evelyn is aware of the effect of fencing on natural vegetation; in fact, the following passage can be compared with Darwin's illustration from the heaths of Farnham in Surrey. One of his relatives has "a wood of more than sixty years standing; it was, before he purchased it, exposed and abandoned to the cattle for divers years: some of the outward skirts were nothing, save shrubs and miserable starvelings; yet still the place was disposed to grow woody; but by this neglect continually suppressed." His kin fenced in some acres, cut all plant growth close to the ground, and in eight or nine years it has become better than the sixty-year-old wood; ". . . and will, in time, prove most incomparable timber; whilst the other part, so many years advanced, shall never recover; and all this from no other cause than preserving it fenced. Judge then by this, how our woods come to be so decried."[61]

He is familiar with theories of climatic change owing to clearing and would like to see them applied to local conditions. Dense trees and woods "which hinder the necessary evolition [that is, the action of flying out or away] of this superfluous moisture and intercourse of the air" make the countries in which they are found more subject to rain and mist, unwholesome, as in the American plantations, and as Ireland formerly was, "both since so much im-

[59] *Ibid.*, p. 565. See p. 399, which passage is discussed below.
[60] *Ibid.*, pp. 567–568; the theme of removing iron mills, using New England, and of preserving the wooden walls is continued on pp. 577–578. Evelyn translated the quotation from *Plantarum*, the Latin poem by Cowley. See *The Works of Mr. Abraham Cowley*, 3 vols. (London, 1721), *Of Plants*, Book VI (*Silva*), where the English translation differs from Evelyn's, Vol. 3, p. 430.
[61] *Ibid.*, p. 399.

proved by felling and clearing these spacious shades, and letting in the air and sun, and making the earth fit for tillage and pasture, that those gloomy tracts are now become healthy and habitable." In his opinion, many "noble seats and dwellings" in England may still be suffering from similar conditions because of "some groves, or hedge-rows of antiquated dotard trees . . . filling the air with musty and noxious exhalations, which being ventilated by glades cut through them, for passage of the stagnant vapours, have been cured of this evil, and recovered their reputation."[62]

Finally, Evelyn realizes that a landscape changes through time very often because of the continuous felling of its trees. Great Britain, he said, like Germany, was once a vast forest, and now the Caledonian forest of old has scarcely a single tree. Deforestation must be supplanted by more self-conscious conservation methods. Evelyn's acquaintance with the forest history of other countries (particularly Spain, Germany, and France), and his knowledge of the history of forest law in England give him historical perspective which becomes a powerful ally in the argument for arresting long-term destructive trends. He quotes Thomas Tusser (?1524–1580), the author of *Five Hundreth Good Pointes of Husbandry* (1573), in the original Gothic script in support of his claim that enclosure is the way of preserving the land and getting the most out of it.[63]

Evelyn's *Silva* is usually thought a classic in the history of conservation, but his vision is even broader. This breadth is owing to his interpretation of deforestation as one aspect of continual landscape change through history, of afforestation as active intervention in fashioning something new, not in returning to an impossible past. His philosophy is one of rational land use, not only of forests but of all types of lands, a philosophy friendly to the creation of useful and pleasing landscapes. If His Majesty's forests and chases were stored with the oak

> at handsome intervals, by which grazing might be improved for the feeding of deer and cattle under them (for such was the old Saltus) benignly visited with the gleams of the sun, and adorned with the distant landscapes appearing through the glades and frequent valleys, nothing could be more ravishing. We might also sprinkle fruit-trees amongst them for cyder, and many singular uses, and should find such goodly plantations the boast of our rangers, and forests infinitely preferable to any thing we have yet beheld, rude and neglected as they are.[64]

There is a similar eagerness to intervene actively in the improvement of the land by transforming its physical character. If lands are so wet that woods cannot thrive in them, convert them to pasture, "or bestow the same industry on them which good husbands do in meadows by *draining*; which instead of

---

[62] *Ibid.*, pp. 30–34. On "evolition," see *Oxford English Dictionary* under "evolation."
[63] *Ibid.*, pp. 572, 586–587.
[64] *Ibid.*, pp. 85–87.

those narrow rills (gutters rather) might be reduced to a proportionable canal, cut even and straight, the earth taken out and spread upon the weeping and uliginous places; nor would the charge be so much as that of the yearly and perpetual renewing and cleansing of those numerous and irregular sluices; besides, there is a profit in storing the canal with fish." Such drainage would make good grass or timber land. "Where poor hungry woods grow, rich corn, and good cattle would be more plentifully bred; and it were beneficial to convert some woodland (where the proper virtue is exhausted) to pasture and tillage, provided that fresh land were improved also to wood in recompence, and to balance the other."[65]

Evelyn recalls the words of Melanchton spoken over a century earlier, "That the time was coming, when the want of *three* things would be the ruin of Europe, *Lignum, probam Monetam, probos Amicos*; *Timber, good Money, sincere Friends*."[66] On this note of urgency "this rustick Discourse, using the freedom of a plain Forester" comes to an end. Evelyn had made his plea for the same conscious purposive use and maintenance of the land as others had made for purposiveness in discovery and invention in general. This is Evelyn's significance in the broader trends of these ideas; what at first seems a horticultural manual is in reality a philosophy of land use.

John Evelyn wished to save the trees of England; he also wished to save the air of London. His *Fumifugium*, crisp and blunt like the *Silva*, is a protest against air pollution; published in 1661, it describes the results of industrial concentration in a city.

He knows Hippocrates' *Airs, Waters, Places*, he accepts the influence of the airs on rebellion, island peoples, religion, and secular affairs, but he does not wish to pursue these matters; he is more interested in pure airs, citing the importance attached to them by Hippocrates and Vitruvius.

London is built "upon a sweet and most agreeable Eminency of Ground" and the natural fumes from the waters and lower grounds to the southward are readily dissipated by the sun. It is the sea-coal, not the culinary fires, whose smoky clouds lie "perpetually imminent over her head."[67] It is the smoke from the "Tunnells and Issues" of the brewers, dyers, limeburners, salt and soap boilers and other private trades, "One of whose *Spiracles* alone, does manifestly infect the *Aer*, more than all the Chimneys of London put together besides." With such belching forth from "sooty jaws," London "resembles the face rather of *Mount Aetna*, the *Court of Vulcan*, *Stromboli*, or the Suburbs of *Hell*, than an Assembly of Rational Creatures, and the Imperial Seat of our incomparable *Monarch*."[68] "For is there under Heaven such *Coughing* and *Snuffing* to be heard, as in the *London* Churches and Assem-

[65] *Ibid.*, pp. 587–588.
[66] *Ibid.*, p. 599.
[67] *Fumifugium*, pp. 13, 17, 18.
[68] *Ibid.*, p. 19.

blies of People, where the Barking and the Spitting is uncessant and most importunate." "It is this horrid Smoake which obscures our Churches, and makes our Palaces look old, which fouls our Clothes and corrupts the Waters, so as the very Rain, and refreshing Dews which fall in the several Seasons, precipitate this impure vapour, which, with its black and tenacious quality, spots and contaminates whatever is exposed to it."[69] Remove these nuisances, he says, which poison birds, kill bees and flowers, prevent the ripening of fruit. Churchyards and charnel houses contaminate the air and the pumps and waters near them, to say nothing of the chandlers and butchers responsible for "those horrid stinks, *nidorous* and unwholesome smells which proceed from the Tallow and corrupted Blood . . ."[70] to say nothing of cattle slaughtering, the fishmongers, the nasty prisons and the common jails within the city.

When the smoke is gone one can see again the glories of a clear day, the beneficent effects of a fair sky, of air in good temper. For we are composed of the elements, we participate in their qualities. The humors have their source in the elements, our passions come from the humors, and the *"Soul* which is united to this *Body* of ours, cannot but be affected with its Inclinations."[71]

He quotes an act of parliament which prohibited heath- and moor-burning from April through September in several English counties to prevent the destruction of wild fowl and moor game, the smoke-laden air from harming crops, and the spread of fire to crop and meadow land. If such solicitude is shown for fowl, game, crops, and grasses, "how much greater ought there to be for the City, where are such Multitudes of Inhabitants concern'd?"[72]

Evelyn has a detailed plan for improvement: square plots planted with aromatic plants and fragrant flowers and vegetables can replace the smoky areas, and the ugly tenements can be cleared away. In his dedicatory epistle to the king he adroitly reminds the monarch of the harm being done to his buildings, gardens, and pictures, adding that the king's sister, the Duchess of Orleans, in a recent visit to London "did in my hearing, complain of the Effects of this Smoake both in her Breast and Lungs, whilst She was in Your Majesties Palace."[73] Evelyn is like Alberti; the plan is more than technique. It is based on a philosophy of man's relation to his surroundings. It is not only a question of health; aesthetics is involved, and so is the being of man, since the humors of the body, affected by the air, have their influence on the soul.

This is the earliest account known to me of air pollution owing to industrialization; it certainly is one of the most vivid. Like Graunt, whom he quotes, Evelyn thinks London more unhealthful than the rural countryside ("almost one half of them who perish in *London,* dye of *Phthisical* and *Pul-*

[69] *Ibid.,* pp. 20, 26, and also 22–27.
[70] *Ibid.,* p. 42.
[71] *Ibid.,* p. 44.
[72] *Ibid.,* p. 42; text of the act, pp. 39–41.
[73] *Ibid.,* pp. 2–3.

*monic* distempers") but these conditions need not be, for other great cities of Europe, like Paris, do not have this smoky stench; they are still healthful. No other great city would tolerate it.[74]

### 6. The French Forest Ordinance of 1669

The *French Forest Ordinance of 1669*, like Evelyn's work in England, is regarded as a landmark in the history of European forestry; this pioneering codification of forest law, influential throughout Europe as well as in the subsequent history of French forest legislation, was the response to a fear expressed by Colbert and by Sully earlier that France would die for lack of wood; such fears had been expressed from time to time since the fourteenth century. Colbert, particularly concerned for marine timber, easily communicated his fears to Louis XIV. The ordinance was not a bolt out of the blue but an example of climax legislation, resting on law, custom, and regulation, reaching far back into French history. Its revolutionary character lay less in its departures from the past than in its collating, sifting, rationalizing, and synthesizing the confused and miscellaneous body of custom, ordinance, and rights of use of the past.[75]

The ordinance, from the hands of a distinguished council, was long in preparation; miraculously, during the eight-year period from 1661 to 1669, by royal ordinance, no cutting was done in the forests of the king, no one with rights of use took wood from them, no livestock went into them. "Le roi savait se faire obeir et il fut obei."[76] The purpose of the ordinance, said Louis XIV in his proclamation of August, 1669, putting it into effect, was to bring

---

[74] *Ibid.*, Preface, pp. 18–20, 25–26, 30, 34.

[75] The text of the law with commentary and texts of laws and ordinances which preceded it even to classical times is in *Jurisprudence Générale. Répertoire Methodique et Alphabetique de Legislation de Doctrine et de Jurisprudence*, etc., new edition edited by D. Dalloz with the collaboration of Armand Dalloz (Paris, 1849), Vol. 25, this volume being devoted to Forests. The text of the 1669 ordinance begins on p. 15. An English translation of it was made by John Croumbie Brown. *French Forest Ordinance of 1669 with Historical Sketch of Previous Treatment of Forests in France*. Edinburgh, 1883. As in many of his works which are mostly compilations, but well selected and often drawing on obscure sources difficult to come by in this country, Brown translates several works describing earlier conditions of the forests and the events leading up to the ordinance. There is valuable background material in Pierre Clément, *Histoire de Colbert et de Son Administration*, 3d ed. (Paris, 1892), Vol. 2, pp. 64–84. As one might expect, the history of the forest of any country is bound up with the history of trade, warfare, attitudes toward commerce and agriculture, etc. For example, Clément says, "A partir de 1572, les temps avaient été mauvais pour la propriété forestière. Les guerres civiles renaissantes, l'augmentation de la valeur des terres, la préférénce de plus en plus donnée aux prairies, l'ouverture de nombreux chemins au travers des terrains boisés, le développement de l'industrie métallurgique, firent craindre la destruction des forêts" (p. 65). See also Huffel, *Économie Forestière*, Vol. 1:2, pp. 267–291. The quotations which follow are taken from Brown's translation.

[76] Huffel, *op cit.*, Vol. 1:2, p. 291.

order into what had become a chaos. A disorder "had slipped (s'était glissé) into the waters and forests of our kingdom and become so universal and rooted that a remedy seemed impossible." Order had now been restored with the work of Colbert and the twenty-one commissioners who assisted him over a period of eight years (1661–1669).[77]

Even in the formal language of Louis XIV's proclamation it is clear that the ancient abuses stood in the way of modern aspirations, in war, in peace, in commerce stimulated by lengthened voyages throughout the world. In an early appeal to the needs of posterity the proclamation sounded a note heard with increasing frequency in the centuries to come, for "it is not enough to have re-established order and discipline, if we do not by good and wise regulations see to it that the fruit of this shall be secured to posterity. . . ."[78] By the nineteenth and twentieth centuries, the appeal to posterity had become indispensable to conservation literature.

The ordinance was noteworthy too because it sought to guide the future management of a whole resource. Although its main provisions affected the royal forests, they also applied to the holdings of ecclesiastical bodies, civil corporations and communities for which the government had the right to prescribe rules, and to individuals with certain legal rights. Within limits it had a right to prescribe regulations for the exploitation of forests by private persons.[79]

The ordinance regulated the cutting or pulling up of wood and the pasturing of animals in the forest (Title II, 6). There was an absolute prohibition against sheep, goats, ewes, lambs in the forest or even in "lands and heaths, or void and bare places on the borders of the woods and forests . . ." (Title XIX, 13). Restrictions were imposed on kilns, furnaces, charcoal making, grubbing and uprooting, lifting or removal of beacons, acorns, and other produce (Title III, 18). Access to the keys of the chest in the council chamber in which was deposited the *marteau*, the hammer-stamp "for marking corner trees, divisions, border trees, balliveaux or seed-bearing reserved trees, and others to be reserved" was subject to rigid regulations (Title II, 3). Procedures were set up for the sale of acorns and beechnuts when they were in sufficient supply and the sale could be held without injury to the forest.

Estimating the pannage the forest could provide was a group responsibility. The Forest-Master, the Lieutenant, or the king's Attorney "shall visit the spot, and in presence of the Garde-Marteau, and of the Sergeant of the Guard, they shall prepare a minute of the number of hogs which may be put on pannage in the forests of the Maitrise . . ." (Title XVIII, 1). In order to guard the

---

[77] Dalloz, *op. cit.*, pp. 15, 21.

[78] Preamble, Brown trans, p. 61.

[79] Dalloz, *op. cit.*, pp. 25–27. On opposition to the law, pp. 29–32, and Huffel, *op. cit.*, Vol. 1:2, pp. 293–294.

young shoots of timber trees or coppice woods along roads or routes over which animals travel to forest pastures, ditches broad and deep enough to preserve the trees are to be dug and old ditches are to be cleaned out, the expense being borne by "the communities of usagers proportionally to the number of beasts which they send on pasturage" (Title XIX, 12).

The twenty-seventh title brings out clearly the delicate weighing and balancing of rights of use, the needs of conservation, and the requirements of industry.

Reserved trees and the balliveaux ("the stallions," the seedlings left for regenerating the forest) "shall, in time coming be reckoned as part of the capital of our woods and forests, without the dowagers, donees, contractors, usufructiers, and their receivers, or farmers, being able to make any pretensions to them, or to any fines which proceed from them" (Title XXVII, 2).

On his inspection visits, the Grand-Master must make a note of "all void places not alienated or given under title of quit-rent or of lease," and so forth, for resowing, reafforestation, or other suitable use. Owners of woods adjacent to the royal forest must separate theirs from the royal properties by a trench four feet wide and five feet deep, maintenance being their responsibility (Title XXVII, 3–4).

The uprooting of young oaks, yoke elms, or other trees is controlled by strict regulations, including the king's permission countersigned by the Grand-Master. Equally severe restrictions prohibit removal of sand, earth, marl, or clay from the forests and the making of lime within a hundred *perches* distant of the forests. Delivery of copsewood and small wood, green or dry, to powder manufacturers or makers of saltpeter is also prohibited under heavy penalties (Title XXVII, 11–13).

Huts built of stakes within the circuit or border or within half a league of the forest are prohibited; those in present violation will be demolished, and in the future none can be built within two leagues of "our woods and forests" (Title XXVII, 17).

Merchant-buyers, usagers, and all other persons are prohibited from making ashes in the royal forests and in those of the ecclesiastics and communities as well (Title XXVII, 19).

Charring and burning trees are also prohibited; so is removing the bark. Charcoal pits "shall be put in the most void places, and the most remote from trees and young new growths," provisions being made for the restoration of these empty places if so judged expedient by the Grand-Master of the forest. "Coopers, tanners, turners, sabot makers, and others of like occupations, cannot keep workshops within a distance of half a league from our forests, under pain of confiscation of their stock-in-trade, and a fine of a hundred livres" (Title XXVII, 22–23).

Plucking, knocking down pannage, mast, other fruits, are forbidden. There are absolute prohibitions against conveying or kindling fires (Title XXVII, 27, 32).[80]

Historical evidence of gradual destruction had created the forest ordinance of 1669.[81] On the death of Mazarin, it was realized that strict measures were needed to give France a renewed forest. A memoire of 1665 explains the reasons for the king's action. The royal forests had been wasted for a long time; there were no provisions for a reserve for great projects and occasions; in the majority of provinces they had produced no revenue in forty years. They had almost been entirely alienated in Normandy, and revenue from them, formerly approaching a million livres, now scarcely reached fifty thousand.[82]

The ordinance symbolizes an awareness of a broader relationship between men organized in societies and the physical environment; it epitomizes Bagehot's "cake of custom" which intervenes between the exploiter and the resource being used. It calls attention to the philosophic attitudes toward the earth engendered by the *moeurs*. Were the ancient usages and rights dissipating or even destroying resources, making them progressively inaccessible to newer and more modern uses, which were now demanding their share, too?

## 7.  CONCLUSION

In the period roughly from the end of the fifteenth until the end of the seventeenth century one sees ideas of man as a controller of nature beginning to crystallize, along more modern lines. It is in the thought of this period (not the commands of God in Genesis to have dominion over nature, as the Japanese authority on Zen Buddhism, Daisetz Suzuki,[83] thinks) that there begins a unique formulation of Western thought, marking itself off from the other great traditions, such as the Indian and the Chinese, which also are concerned with the relationship of man to nature. This awareness of man's power increases greatly in the eighteenth century, as will be apparent in the works of Buffon and others. It increases even more dramatically in the nineteenth century with the host of new ideas and interpretations, while in the twentieth, Western man has attained a breathtaking anthropocentrism, based on his power over nature, unmatched by anything in the past.

[80] Discussion of the law's enforcement and its efficacy is beyond the scope of this essay. In the early eighteenth century complaints like those which preceded its enactment were still common. It is believed, however, that without it things would have been much worse, at least until 1789. The law remained almost intact until 1827. Two frequent criticisms made of it are the severity of the punishments and its subordination of the interest of the individual to that of the state. On these points, see Clément, *Histoire de Colbert*, Vol. 2, pp. 75–76.

[81] *Ibid.*, Vol. 2, p. 65.

[82] *Ibid.*, Vol. 2, pp. 71–72.

[83] "The Role of Nature in Zen Buddhism," *Eranos-Jahrbuch 1953*, Vol. 22 (1954), pp. 291–321; see esp. pp 291–296.

Several trends may be discerned at the end of this period. They keep their own identities; they are like the Brenta, the Adige, and the Po, streams whose sources are far removed from one another, but whose courses roughly parallel one another as they flow to a common delta.

The religious idea that man has dominion over the earth, that he completes the creation, becomes sharper and more explicit by the seventeenth century. Hale's ideas are the clearest; man by his existence is a balancing force in the existence of other forms of life. He becomes an arbiter, checking the spread of the wild plants and the wild animals, encouraging the dispersion of the domesticated plants and animals. The encroachments of the wild are soon apparent in areas from which man has withdrawn his superintendence. Through eliminating natural vegetation, by draining, in frightening wild animals into retreats by his presence, through his protection of the domestic plants and animals, he exercises almost a juridical role over living nature. Men like Hale had an eye on their own times; they realized that cultural landscapes—drained bogs, cleared lands, lands in grains—and wild lands of forest, scrub, and brush were explainable only as the result of human activity; hunting, a foray into a land not held by man directly, showed too that wild animals lived under the threat of extinction.

These ideas were associated with a belief that man with tools and knowledge was improving the earth as surely as he was improving himself; the two improvements could go hand in hand. How could mankind progress on an earth dying of decay, or unimproved by tillage, drainage, and clearing?

Then there are the ideas which one distinguishes only with difficulty from the first: those from which religion is not excluded but in which religion is not the dominant motif. If the idea of man as a finisher of nature, a completer of the creation, leads both to piety and to practical-mindedness, the latter attitude alone can encourage a predominantly secular emphasis on achievement by mind, manual skill, knowledge. Agricola, Palissy, Bacon, and Descartes represent this point of view.

Finally there is the antiphonal idea that men make undesirable changes in nature, changes which are reckless and devoid of conscious purpose as far as long-term trends are concerned, purposive for narrower ends. If trees are felled so that the iron-master can smelt the iron, using conscious techniques based on science and his trade secrets to manufacture a tool, the whole process is purposive as far as the iron-master is concerned even if the long-term change —perhaps deterioration—of the natural environment brought about by him and others is not. From time to time in the past, evidences of these conflicting trends in land use appear, but in Evelyn's *Silva* and in Colbert's *Forest Ordinance* they are dramatized and become harbingers of more complex and more widely distributed conflicts.

The idea of a purposive human control of nature, so forcefully expressed by Bacon, Descartes, and others, has led historically to an emphasis on human society and its accomplishments, to the possibility of improving society by the purposive application of scientific law to the needs of food, housing, transportation, and the like.

The idea that men can and do make undesirable changes in nature (often without realizing they do, because these ill effects may not be understood or may be too slow in showing themselves) has, on the other hand, led historically to the study of environments disturbed by man, the emphasis being placed on physical changes on the earth, not on changes in human society. It is this point of view which has produced much of the literature on environmental change by human. agency, and has stimulated historical geography, ecological studies of vegetation change, and investigations in many other fields today.

What lay behind this more self-conscious awareness of man as not only a part of nature but as an extremely active form of life with ambitions for control and change? A proper answer would require volumes, drawing liberally from economic and religious history, philosophy, and the history of technology; here there are three or four points I wish to make. First, the observation that there were few contacts between science and technology in the Middle Ages compared with those in the seventeenth century is correct, in my opinion. "Only in the seventeenth century (though the idea had been adumbrated in the Middle Ages) was it realized—and even then by few—that science and the crafts were alike concerned with natural phenomena and could aid each other. Gradually it was seen that knowledge of nature conferred power to control its forces."[84]

If there was no great revolution in existing technologies in this period, if there was no new invention of a prime mover, there was nevertheless a certain majestic sweep in the geographical expansion of known activities. An important one was the spread of metallurgy and the concomitant extension of forest use and forest destruction. A second was the popularity of drainage and land reclamation, polder building in the Netherlands, draining the fens in England, controlling the river courses and draining the swamps of Italy, and draining marshes, ponds, and lakes in France. (In 1891, the Comte de Dienne published a history, of over five hundred pages, of the drainage of lakes and swamps of France alone before 1789.)[85] Finally there were the canals and bridges, conspicuous and dramatic evidence of an elementary victory over physical handicaps, crowned for this period by the completion under the ministry of Colbert and the supervision of Pierre-Paul Riquet de Bonrepos (1604–1680) of the Canal du Midi (the canal of Languedoc, the canal of the two seas). Few canals have fired the imagination of men more (at least prior to Suez and Panama) than this one joining the Atlantic and the Mediterranean.

[84] Preface by the editors to Vol. 3 of *A History of Technology*, pp. v–vi.
[85] Le Comte de Dienne, *Histoire du Desséchement des Lacs et Marais en France avant 1789* (Paris, 1891).

Even in the next century, Voltaire, in his *Siècle de Louis XIV*, said that the most glorious monument of the reign, because of its utility, grandeur and difficulties, was "ce canal de Languedoc qui joint les deux mers," and not the Louvre, nor Versailles, the Trianon, Marli, nor any other construction of the time.[86]

With hindsight, one can now see that the prevailing optimism was based on ignorance of the extent of both old custom and new technique as potential forces in changing the environment. Hidden also were the realization that a great upsurge of world population was beginning, and a real awareness of the awesome and frightening complexities of man himself.

[86] "Siècle de Louis XIV," in *Oeuvres de Voltaire*, Beuchot ed., Vol. 20, p. 252. On the history of the canal, see also Clément, *op. cit.*, Vol. 2, pp. 97–126.

# PART FOUR

# Culture and Environment in the Eighteenth Century

# Introductory Essay

In no other preceding age had thinkers discussed questions of culture and environment with such thoroughness and penetration as did those of the eighteenth century. These men were acquiring a better understanding of human society than had those of the past; they were moving away from the study of the individual and of man in the abstract; they were moving away, too, from the older religious idea, still popular in the seventeenth century, of man the "amphibious piece," as Sir Thomas Brown had called him. It is true that these ideas lasted into the eighteenth century, but they could no longer satisfy those eager for more knowledge about societal bonds, tradition, national character, the environmental influences affecting the lives of individuals and of nations, and for deeper understanding of the complexities of human life, society, and history. More was constantly being learned about natural history, too; the eighteenth is the century of the greatest natural historians: Linnaeus, Buffon, Bonnet, Bernardin de St. Pierre, Peter Simon Pallas, and Sir Joseph Banks.

Furthermore, men avidly made use of the accumulating voyages and travels which had been and were being published. What is the state of nature, the primitive stage in mankind's development? What are primitive peoples like? What influences, according to the travelers, determine the character of far-off peoples? These questions were asked in the seventeenth century also, but its thinkers still leaned heavily on the classical writers. From the middle of the eighteenth to the early part of the nineteenth century, in the writings of Buffon, Montesquieu, Herder, and Malthus (in the second and following editions of his work) one sees what a refreshing and inexhaustible well these voyages and travels had become. The closing decades of the century mark the fresh stimulus to natural history and ethnography coming from Cook and the Forsters. After Joseph Banks withdrew as botanist on the *Resolution* in Cook's second voyage (1772–1775), John Reinhold Forster and his son George were chosen in Banks' place. The son's book, *A Voyage Around the World* (1777), not only charmed and inspired Alexander von Humboldt, but was the harbinger of the coming era of scientific travel undertaken by Humboldt, Darwin, Livingstone, Stanley, Bates, Wallace, and many others.

Interest in the design argument as it was applied to the constitution of the earth continued but there was more penetrating criticism of final causes. Many agreed that the design argument still had a useful place in the study of the earth, of plant and animal life, and of man's place in nature. The eighteenth century was a prosperous time for physico-theologies, propitious for finding the traces of the Creator's wisdom—even in the study of stones and insects. Many of the great names still were not inhospitable to doctrines of final causes. Others, rejecting them, retained a strong belief in a balance and harmony of nature. The writings of Buffon, Hume, Goethe, Kant, and the conclusions drawn from the Lisbon earthquake, however, cast doubt both on optimistic implications of doctrines of final causes and on their efficacy as tools for advancing scientific knowledge. The most important works were Hume's *Dialogues Concerning Natural Religion* and Kant's *Critique of Judgement* (1790), especially the critique of the teleological judgment. Both men explored carefully and profoundly the question of teleology both in nature and in man's relation to it.

Montesquieu's dramatic revival of environmental theories, expressed so epigrammatically and often so wittily that their traditional character was concealed, raised questions, as had Bodin and Botero, of the nature of law and of lawmaking, and of human society and social institutions in general. What physical and moral causes were influencing them?

Furthermore, Malthus's first essay on population (1798) propounded an environmental theory of population growth. It was not the environment of the geographers or the cosmographers, delineating cultural differences by climatic type or relief; the physical environment, conceived abstractly as a limiting whole, affected men and their numbers. Moreover, it was considered narrowly as arable land available for producing food. Many of the important thinkers of the eighteenth and nineteenth centuries, Montesquieu, Buffon, Malthus, Humboldt, had something to say about climatic influences and population theory. Malthus's bold, forceful, and unrelenting style, however, attracted wider and more general interest in population theory than had the hundreds of speculations of those who preceded him. A subordinate quarrel over the relative populousness of ancient and modern nations within the broader quarrel over the relative superiority of the ancients and moderns became in fact a great divide; a population theory favoring the sympathizers with antiquity and assuming senescence in nature was supplanted by one assuming a constancy in nature's operations. Two syntheses emerged by the end of the century, the physico-theological synthesis of Süssmilch, and the more secular doctrine of Malthus.

Lastly, in the work of Count Buffon, especially in the last epoch of *Des Époques de la Nature*, the idea of man as an agent of environmental change comparable in power to other agents of geographic and geological change like the wind and the water, becomes an important concept in understanding the relation of mankind to the rest of life and to inanimate nature. Although there were often environmentalistic overtones in Buffon's thinking, his ideas of man as a modifier of his environment underscored the weakness of theories of environmental influence because they emphasized the power and the force of human creativity.

The great names which illustrate, and whose thoughts are representative of, these complex themes are Buffon, Herder, Hume, Kant, Malthus, and Montesquieu. They built on the past, but the world became a richer place for their departures. Even today their questions suggest our questions, but it would be a miracle if they did more than that. For they lived in a world which resembled the past more than what was to come, at least as far as problems of human culture and the natural environment are concerned.

# Chapter 11

# Final Strengths and Weaknesses
# of Physico-Theology

### 1. INTRODUCTION

Natural- or physico-theology had its emissaries in religion, science, and philosophy because it was concerned with fundamental questions such as the proofs of God's existence, final causes, and orderliness in nature. Physico-theology was not, as is so often said, primarily concerned with demonstrating that everything in nature had been designed for man; often its sights were much higher, for there is a vast difference between regarding man as the highest being in the hierarchy of creation while assuming that each being lower on the scale exists for a purpose which may or may not have any relevance to man's existence, and regarding the creation as serving man, like a middle-aged housekeeper in Victorian novels who cares for her bachelor employer. St. Augustine, as we have seen, made a distinction between gradations of existence according to nature (the living being ranked above the nonliving, the sentient above those lacking sensation, the intelligent above the unintelligent) and gradations based on utility to man, for men may prefer for their uses the nonliving to the living even though the latter is higher on the scale of nature.[1] There was no question of conflict between religion and science. In natural theology, religion and science were included; often it played a synthesizing role in an attempt to achieve a grand interpretation of nature which was not inconsistent with science or religion.

In this chapter, however, we are concerned with a narrower field than the history of physico-theology with all of its works on insects, rocks, the human body, and so forth. Our concern is with the specific applications of its leading ideas to the study of living nature and to the earth as a habitable planet. Although many important thinkers had opinions on the subjects, in my opinion the striking contributions were made by Leibniz, Linnaeus, Süssmilch, Büsching, and Herder as supporters of physico-theology, and by Buffon, Maupertuis, Hume, Goethe, and Kant as the critics, special places being reserved for Hume and Kant. The application of design arguments and of teleology to nature and to the earth had strong defenders and attackers, and the discussions of the eighteenth century were often far more cogent than those of the nineteenth century.

Galileo did not cause teleology to fade away from science while he admired the handiwork of God in the creation.[2] It is true that his scientific method could do without teleological explanation; the basic forces controlling the creation could be stated in mathematical terms, and teleology could be put to one side, or survive in the form of conventional piety. It was not so easy, however, to ignore its hold on the earth and life sciences from the seventeenth to the nineteenth centuries. The so-called triumph of "the mechanical philosophy" of secondary or efficient causes is hard to reconcile with the volume of teleological thought unless one dismisses the latter as the product of second-class minds of no consequence and of no influence.

The influence of the doctrine of final causes was, as one would expect, more lasting and vivid in those disciplines concerned with life, with the relationships of one kind of life to another and of life to inanimate matter, with problems of the preservation of life, and of death and decay, and with the interrelationships among plants, animals, and man. These are also some of the reasons that physico-theology was so important in the history of geographical thought and lasted so long in it.

## 2.  On Leibniz

The philosophic and scientific interest in final causes and the liveliness with which these doctrines were advocated may be illustrated from the writings of Leibniz, which span the two centuries. How Leibniz wished to keep what was useful in the old, how critical he was of the new that he thought had

---

[1] *City of God*, Bk. XI, chap. 16; Bk. XII, chap. 4.
[2] See Galileo's "Letter to Madame Christina of Lorraine, Grand Duchess of Tuscany" (1615), in *Discoveries and Opinions of Galileo*, trans. Stillman Drake (Anchor Books),

failed, how he embraced the new that held promise for the improvement of the human condition! The old he passionately wished to keep was the union of science and theology and the doctrine of final causes. In the *Discourse on Metaphysics* (1686), Leibniz criticized not final causes but partial views subject to human error derived from them. "I am quite willing to grant that we are liable to err when we wish to determine the purposes or councils [*sic*] of God, but this is the case only when we try to limit them to some particular design, thinking that he has had in view only a single thing, while in fact he regards everything at once."[3] Leibniz argues also for the value of final causes in scientific work. It is better to consider "God's decree always to carry out his plan by the easiest and most determined way" than it is to consider secondary or efficient causes alone.[4] Leibniz cites as an illustration Willebrord Snellius' discovery of the law of refraction. Accepting the doctrine of final causes purges "from mechanical philosophy the impiety that is imputed to it" and leads to "nobler lines of thought" as well.[5]

What was his criticism of the new? To him neither Descartes' nor Newton's view of nature provided an adequate explanation for the order of the world. Furthermore, Cartesianism had failed to provide the needed stimulus to invention and to the control of nature. Perhaps he was thinking of important discoveries made by Galileo, Newton, Huygens, of himself, none being Cartesians. "Car la plus part des Cartesiens [*sic*] ne sont que des commentateurs," he wrote to Malebranche, adding that he wished any one of them could have contributed as much to physics as he, Malebranche, had to metaphysics.[6] Leibniz criticized the Cartesians for being sterile, for espousing a philosophy that did not lead to scientific advance.

Man lives in a nature controlled by final causes, but he can improve himself and his surroundings; his thought here is akin to the Christian idea of man being a finisher of nature, using his brains and his hands, imitating on a small scale the acts of God in the universe. In 1697 Leibniz, as we have seen, (see p. 377), applied the concept of order to the earth, regarding this order as progressively increasing, with the help of man. He boldly applied the idea of progress to the earth as a unit, assuming both an orderliness on earth and an orderliness in the changes it had undergone by man.

Leibniz is greatly impressed with the advances in knowledge of his own age and the age immediately preceding it. Inventions and discoveries show the cogency of the design argument. The microscope and the telescope reveal the intricacy and magnitude of the design; they also reveal order and purpose.

---

p. 196. See also Herschel Baker, *The Wars of Truth*, pp. 316–317, and chap. 8, "The Conquest of Nature."

[3] Wiener, *Leibniz Selections*, p. 318.

[4] *Ibid.*, p. 321.

[5] *Ibid.*, p. 323.

[6] Leibniz to Malebranche, 22 June (2 July), 1679, Preuss. Akademie ed. Vol II, I, 472. Quoted in Barber, *Leibniz in France*, p. 34.

"Through the grace of God we now possess excellent instruments for examining the secrets of nature, and in these enquiries we can achieve more in a single year than our ancestors achieved in ten or a hundred years."[7] In lines which suggest Whitehead's famous statement that the "greatest invention of the nineteenth century was the invention of the method of invention," Leibniz writes, "The *'organum organorum,'* the *'vraye logique'* or *'ars inveniendi'* seems now at last to be discovered; and by means of it our intellect has been no less improved than our eyes have been by means of the telescope." We acquire a correct conception of the great edifice of the world and the grandeur of God's works. Men in our age can illumine His wisdom much more than could the ancients, whose poor notions did little honor to the Creator. Technology and invention are closely linked not only with the informed, the inquisitive, the intelligent, the dissipators of ignorance, but also with piety and love of God. Microscopes allow us to see the great world in the small, millions of things whose aggregate size is equal to a grain of sand.[8] "Yet this 'vraye logique' is also a 'psychologique,' designed not only to increase man's understanding of himself, but also to help him to assert his Self and to find his bearings 'in the turmoil of the age.'" It is a means for the dissemination of knowledge, the elimination of prejudice and ignorance.[9]

Leibniz also sees the new opportunities for an infinitely expanded vision of the scope of life. The researches on spermatozoa of Leeuwenhoek and Swammerdam promised new insights into reproduction and biological growth. Leeuwenhoek denied spontaneous generation, asserting that even the smallest animals have reproductive powers. Swammerdam's monographs on insects, the preformation theory, his study of the anatomy of the bee and many other insects, had heightened the sense of the wonder of life.[10] The theme of the organic and the living suffuses much of Leibniz' thought; here he is close to the Cambridge Platonists, to Ray and Derham, sharing their enthusiasm for final causes.

His windowless monads are "substantial centers of living energy" (Wiener), their relationship to each other being in accordance with a preestablished harmony of God's devising. Some modern students of Leibniz, however, have pointed to less idyllic implications in his philosophy than has formerly been thought. While this may be the best of all possible worlds, it may not necessarily be best for human beings.[11]

Mechanistic explanations are unsatisfactory because they themselves require

[7] "Vorschläge für eine Teutschliebende Genossenschafft," *Werke*, ed. Klopp, Vol. 6, p. 214. See also Wiener, *op. cit.*, p. xxx.

[8] *Ibid.*, pp. 214–215; Whitehead, *Science and the Modern World* (Pelican Mentor Books), p. 98.

[9] R. W. Meyer, *Leibnitz (sic) and the Seventeenth-Century Revolution*, pp. 123, 208–209; I am indebted to this work for these references.

[10] See Nordenskiöld, *The History of Biology*, pp. 165–171. Barber, *Leibniz in France*, p. 108.

[11] Barber, *op. cit.*, p. 88.

explanation. In the "Histoire des Ouvrages des Savans" (1705), he insists on the need for both secondary and final causes. "There are as it were, two king-doms, the one of efficient causes, the other of final; each of which separately suffices in detail for explaining all as if the other did not exist. But the one does not suffice without the other in the general nature of their origin, for they both emanate from one source in which the power which constitutes efficient causes and the wisdom which regulates final causes are found united."[12] These words might well have been spoken—albeit with less skill—by all believers in final causes. The law of sufficient reason, assuming God's thought follows principles familiar to human thinking, is defined by Leibniz in the following words: "no fact can be real or existing and no proposition can be true unless there is sufficient reason, why it should be thus and not otherwise, even though in most cases these reasons cannot be known to us."[13] The principle is derived from the assumed order and harmony of the creation, all of whose component parts have a purpose and a reason for existence. By assuming a preestablished harmony and the law of sufficient reason, Leibniz concludes that rationality and morality are uniformly characteristic of the universe.[14]

In his letter to Bourguet (1714), Leibniz dealt with the familiar question of chaos and disharmony in nature, admitting that these might appear at first sight to exist on earth. The chaos produced by the mass of volcanic materials thrown up by Vesuvius is only apparent; ". . . whoever would have sensitive organs penetrating enough to perceive the small parts of things would find everything organized, and if he could continually augment his penetration to the degree needed, he would always see new organs which were imperceptible pre-viously."[15]

The world that opened up to Leibniz was not the dreary mechanical uni-verse of the closing years of the seventeenth century which Whitehead has described.[16] There is too much sympathy in him for the organic and the teleo-logical. To him the world of the senses is alive. The plenitude of nature entrances him. He desires to do more than to contemplate God's works; he wishes to use them, to transform them for human welfare.[17]

## 3. NATURAL HISTORY

The teleological view of nature became the philosophical—and theological—support for the conventional natural histories of the eighteenth century. The influence of Derham's Physico-Theology, which went through several Eng-

---

[12] Wiener, *Leibniz Selections*, pp. 193–194.

[13] *Monadology*, p. 32 (Everyman's Library ed., p. 8). See also the passages in Wiener, *Selections*, pp. 93–96.

[14] On these points, see also Barber, *Leibniz in France*, pp. 35, 55; Wiener's introduction to the *Selections*, p. xxxviii; and Ruth Lydia Saw, *Leibniz* (Pelican Books), p. 72.

[15] Wiener, *Leibniz Selections*, p. 200.

[16] *Science and the Modern World* (Pelican Mentor Books), pp. 55–56.

[17] See Meyer, *Leibnitz*, p. 43–44.

lish editions and was translated into German and French, extended far beyond English borders. De Pluche used it as a source in his natural history which rivaled Buffon's in popularity; Linnaeus refers to it in his discourse on the *Oeconomy of Nature*; Süssmilch's celebrated *Die Göttliche Ordnung*, a study of population and population theory based on the design argument, praised and criticized him, and Kant, in his discussion of the cosmological and physico-theological proofs for the existence of God, referred to the works both of Derham and of the Dutch physico-theologist, Nieuwentijdt, the latter writer emphasizing evidences of design in many fields but adding nothing of particular interest to the ideas concerning the earth and animate nature.[18]

The problems posed by natural history encouraged both those who worked within the traditional molds and those who departed impatiently from them to the study of the secondary rather than the final causes underlying the order and unity of nature. There was room for De Pluche; there was also room for Buffon. Men had become interested too in the concrete, in the living, an interest derived in great measure from the successful accumulation of enormous amounts of material about plants, animals, and man from all parts of the world, from the zeal for collecting plants and animals and putting them in gardens and museums such as Kew Gardens and the Jardin du Roy.

The popular interest in natural history is clearly evident in the works of the abbé de Pluche. His *Spectacle de la Nature* has been ridiculed for its simple-minded and naïve arguments from design, and it is true that it ignores the fundamental problems that Buffon concerned himself with in the *Histoire Naturelle* even though the latter work was almost contemporary with De Pluche. Even with all these shortcomings, De Pluche turned attention to the regularities of nature, its wholeness, its unity. The work, as Mornet has shown, rivaled Buffon's in popularity in France in the eighteenth century. There was also a greater interest in the ordinary and the usual in nature, in contrast with earlier fascinations with its oddities and marvels.[19] The geometrical view of nature failed also to satisfy basic curiosities about details of living nature, which could only come about by discoveries, concrete descriptions, that might emphasize rather than despise the secondary qualities of color, scent, and so forth.

Geometry lost its former supremacy

> because people came to the very definite conclusion that it added nothing to the stock of knowledge. All it did was to develop, to add, by deduction on deduction, to principles already securely established. Thus it had no contact with reality. Seeing that in real life there is no such thing as surface without depth,

---

[18] Nieuwentijdt, *The Religious Philosopher: Or, The Right Use of Contemplating the Works of the Creator.* Trans. from the Dutch by John Chamberlayne, 2 vols. See his citations from the Scriptures, the watch analogy, and the wide variety of "contemplations," esp. Contemplation 2, sect. 3, based on Romans 1:20, and Vol. 2. Nieuwentijdt's work is one of the vastest compilations of natural theology ever made.

[19] Mornet, *Les Sciences de la Nature en France, au XVIIIᵉ Siècle*, pp. 9, 13–14, 33–34.

length without breadth, nor anything answering to the definition of position without magnitude, nor anything exhibiting the theoretic regularity which geometry assigns to things, what we learn from geometry would appear to be no more than a dream expressed in a number of equations. The idea of explaining creation in terms of motion and extension was the purest moonshine. It was M. Descartes who started it, and M. Descartes had had his day.[20]

It is true that De Pluche was a popular writer, but the design argument also continued as a tool in the study of living nature among serious scientists, such as Linnaeus. Piety and the praise of the Creator's works are the hymns on Sunday; the practicality and sober appraisal of the earth's resources are the tasks for the rest of the week. It is the Christian's duty to praise God; it is also proper to inquire into the usefulness of the plants and the animals. Linnaeus' interest in natural theology had been inspired by Johann Arndt's *True Christianity*.[21] In his celebrated lecture on the economy of nature delivered before the University Academy at Stockholm in 1749, Linnaeus, however, departs from the traditional standbys of natural theology to a more secular position which, admitting design, stresses environmental influences in the distribution of plants, animals, and men and their activities.[22] Linnaeus as a philosopher of natural history resembles Carl Ritter as a philosopher of geography: neither was an innovator, but they were epitomizers of the natural theology of their times.

Even in the eighteenth century it was occasionally necessary to meet the criticism that the planet is only a passably fit environment for life. To Linnaeus the present relief and position of the earth are evidences of planned order. He points out the wisdom of the hydrological cycle; he is interested in plant succession (how an area through natural processes can be transformed from marsh to meadow); he justifies the relief of the earth both on aesthetic and on utilitarian grounds, for it is pleasing to the eye and it increases the surface area of the earth.[23] This veering away, as did Ray and Derham, from naïve simplicities to a blending of natural theology with theories of environmental causation is illustrated in Linnaeus' analysis of life existing on earth. The Creator decreed that the earth should be covered with plants. Since both seasonal change and the nature of soils preclude uniformity in the vegetable

[20] Hazard, *European Thought in the Eighteenth Century from Montesquieu to Lessing*, p. 130. For a contemporary view, see Buffon's criticism of Descartes, *Histoire Naturelle, Générale et Particulière* (1749-1767), Vol. 2, pp. 50-53. See also Ernst Cassirer, *The Philosophy of the Enlightenment*, chap. 2.

[21] Arndt, a Lutheran theologian, published *Vom Wahren Christentum* in 1609. This is a veritable handbook containing accumulations of the ages on physico-theology. See esp. Bk. 4, "Liber Naturae."

[22] On Linnaeus and the natural theology of Arndt, see Hagberg, *Linnaeus*, p. 34; see p. 44 for the influence of Aristotle's *History of Animals*, and pp. 48-49 for other influences.

[23] "The Oeconomy of Nature," in *Stillingfleet's Pamphlets* (1791), pp. 44-45.

cover, plants differ because each is adapted to its own climate. Utilitarian and anthropocentric conceptions, however, support Linnaeus' discussion of grasses and humus. Grasses are widely distributed, for of all plants they are most necessary for cattle; humus (black mold) is a key substance in maintaining the uninterrupted fertility of the earth through the cyclical process of birth, growth, death, decay, and the reabsorption of the organic residues into the earth.[24]

Linnaeus also shares in the contemporary speculations about animals and animal populations: those with the greatest reproductive power are the smallest. Others are useful or serve as food for other animals. Because each animal species eats certain kinds of food and because nature sets limits to the appetite, the earth can support all kinds and varieties of life, and because of this variety it produces nothing useless or superfluous. Although Linnaeus does not use these terms, a harmony in nature and a balance in population are assumed. The limitation in numbers of any one species is evidence of divine intent to prevent any one species becoming so numerous that it threatens the existence of man and the other animals. It is a wise provision of nature that there is variety, not uniformity, in life forms. Following Derham, Linnaeus warns of the dangers of "overstocking."[25]

His cart wheels deep in the track of the tradition which constantly reminded man that nature was not created solely for his benefit, Linnaeus says that the economy of nature was not planned according to individual principles of economy. He makes the interesting point that cultural differences are evidences of this truth. There are among men great variations in the ways of life, as evidenced in the contrasts between the Laplander, the European husbandman, and the Hottentot. These human economies, differing among themselves, are contrasted with "the stupendous oeconomy of the Deity [which] is one throughout the globe. . . ."[26] Later Linnaeus lapses into more anthropocentric reflections. It seems, he says, that the three kingdoms, fossil (that is, things which are dug up), animal, vegetable, are intended by the Creator for man. Man's ability to make use of nature and to modify it is evidence that he possesses this divinely endowed creativity. Man has hunted or tamed the wild animals, he has increased the number of plants, and he has mined the earth.

Finally, Linnaeus sees the earth as a self-renewing and self-cleansing natural system. The luxuriance of life and the vigor of growth have their counterparts in decay and putrefaction which are taken care of by animals and insects who

---

[24] *Ibid.*, p. 78.

[25] For a modern statement of a similar idea, of "a general principle [which] is gradually emerging from ecological study to the effect that the more complex the biological community, the more stable," see Bates, *The Forest and the Sea*, p. 261, and Elton, *The Ecology of Invasions by Animals and Plants*, pp. 143–153, 155. "Oeconomy of Nature," p. 119; Derham, *Physico-Theology*, p. 237.

[26] "The Oeconomy of Nature," p. 121.

live off the dead, whose remains are reabsorbed to become the materials of new life. These cyclic processes which keep the earth alive and fresh also make possible a permanency in nature as a whole, permitting the continuing existence of these harmonious interrelationships.

### 4.  Population and Geography in the Divine Order

In modern times, population theories have often been based on religion and on theories of environmental influence. They have relied also on several kinds of evidence: observations, for example, that food supply offers an effective check to increases in population, or that wars, disease, plague, death at birth or in early childhood, certain customs, might be effective checks to the growth in numbers. These observations could be—and often were—related to historical problems posed by events mentioned in the Bible and to the design argument. Analyses of bills of mortality, which called attention to contrasts in health between city and country life, the ratios of the sexes and of births to deaths, were evidences of statistical regularities easily reconciled with the design argument.

Many of these threads were gathered together by Johann Süssmilch, the Prussian army chaplain whom many Germans regard as the founder of demography. Although overshadowed by Malthus, Süssmilch's work is an intensely interesting synthesis of population theory, geography, and theology. He will save the Christian religion against "die neuen und gefährlichen Anschuldigungen" of a Montesquieu. Should not, he adds, a theology be aware of what is happening in the world about it? The title of the three-volume work, *Die Göttliche Ordnung*, aptly prepares one for its argument and the traditional character of its constituent ideas. Süssmilch stresses the importance of those chapters of Genesis (9: 1–2, 6) that command men to multiply and to assure dominion over all life on earth, distinguishing between man and the animals, the latter obeying the less all-encompassing injunction to multiply themselves, while man—fulfilling God's command—spreads himself everywhere on an earth which is already quite filled up. (Gen. 9: 1–2, 6; 8: 17; 1: 21–22.) Each animal requires and is confined to its own climate, but man can go where he pleases. The Creator, anticipating the worldwide distribution of man, provided special kinds of plants and animals for every climate in which he lives. Theology is thus reconciled with the truths made known during the age of discovery, whose expanded horizons cast new light on man's place in nature: his adaptability to many different environmental conditions, the variety of peoples despite the unity of the human race, and the striking distributions of plants and animals, dramatized by the differences in the flora and fauna of the Old and the New Worlds.[27]

It is the blessed command of God, says Süssmilch, that the earth be filled—

[27] *Die Göttliche Ordnung*, Vol. 1, p. xii, 9–16.

but not to overflowing. The German example shows God's care for the world. The country, whose population increases by a million souls every five years, is without doubt the most cultivated and most populous land in Europe; despite wars, disease, and emigration, its losses are made up because of a 10:13 proportion of deaths to births.[28] Increase in the world population brings about cultural diversity, for the earth cannot be filled up everywhere in the same way. Perhaps the Creator had intentionally joined physical and moral causes in his plan for the multiplication and dispersal of the human race. The uninhabitable deserts might prevent the world from being too greatly filled up, providing at the same time physical barriers to check an easy diffusion of moral poison, to prevent the destruction of national customs from reaching harmful proportions, to discourage war and misery. Süssmilch's figures of speech are often taken from the language of the professional soldier, and he likens the gradual and orderly growth of population to the march of a regiment.[29]

Süssmilch insists that it is possible to reconcile population growth with sacred and profane history. Indeed, his reconstruction is ingenious, the key notion being that the period required for a population to double has varied throughout time. The people living before the Flood had more food, and the earth's population was therefore greater. Also, the seas of the antediluvian world were more narrowly confined and smaller than now; consequently, there was less sand, and the soils were more fertile, for floods cause disorder and devastation.[30] After the Flood, the Creator cut down the life span, lowering it in Noah's time, shortening it still more to its present period; He gradually lowers life expectancy as the earth's population increases. The postdiluvian world, however, posed problems even for the Creator who had made his covenant that no more floods would destroy the earth (Gen. 9:11); He could not treat postdiluvian as he had treated antediluvian man. The poorer environment, the large areas of sea and sand, the lesser fertility, reduced the capacity of the postdiluvian world. In shortening life and lengthening the time for doubling the population, He avoided the evil consequences of a too rapid population increase. Süssmilch therefore concludes that the biblical account is well in accord with experience and reason.[31]

Süssmilch discusses at length the checks to population growth; often social and religious factors decisively influence their operation. The Muslim religion, for example, helps in spreading the plague, for to the true believer death is not an evil and he need not put obstacles in its path. For this reason, the plague has a permanent abode in Turkish lands, scarcely a year passing without an outbreak.[32]

[28] *Ibid.*, pp. 20–21, 271–272.
[29] *Ibid.*, pp. 29–32, 33–34, 52–53.
[30] *Ibid.*, p. 298; Vol. 3, pp. 160–161.
[31] *Ibid.*, Vol. 1, p. 299.
[32] *Ibid.*, p. 315.

Christian theology inevitably calls attention to population questions because of the increase and multiply injunctions and because of its commitment to monogamy. Botero was also interested, as we have seen, in comparing the influence of the Muslim and the Christian religions on population growth. (See the introductory essay to Part III.) Does polygamy with its constant competition of wives and their children for a husband's or a father's attention act as a check on population?

Clerical celibacy and various kinds of emasculation naturally would concern a writer basing his population theory on the divine order. Süssmilch severely criticizes these practices in the history of Christianity, singling out Origen's self-emasculation for special condemnation, acknowledging at the same time that he was a learned man worthy of respect. Such practices are evil readings of Matthew 19:12, and Epithanius rightly called Origen and his followers heretics; they deserve the epithet because they act contrary to God's purpose, they harm themselves, and are arch foes of the state. He is equally firm in disapproving of castration and mutilation in the East, adding that castration is the oriental counterpart of occidental celibacy, especially in lands under the laws of the Roman Church. His attitude toward celibacy reminds one of Jean De Meun's lines in *The Romance of the Rose*. If God wanted to remove desire from some men, why not from all? In trying to achieve such celibacy, Süssmilch says, men forget they are men, forget their mission (*Bestimmung*) in life, ignore the Creator's wish; they want to be more than men, to be angels, but man's nature is not yet compatible with angelic being. He asks whether mutilation (*Verstümmelung*) is not better than celibacy in which men have their full vigor, for in emasculation the spiritual being is protected against the dreadful temptations which cause so much anxiety, cruelty, and scandal. Clerical celibacy to him becomes a spiritual castration; it and actual physical emasculation alike are in conflict with the divine order.[33]

In his extensive analysis of war as a check to population growth, Süssmilch, condemning its destructiveness and inhumanity, remarks upon the recuperative powers of populations, apparent after the Thirty Years' War, and on the lesser violence of modern war.[34] Similar analyses are made of famines, including the effects of insects and pests, floods and earthquakes. Are these and other checks to population growth necessary in order to carry out the divine order? Are war, plague, hunger, earthquakes necessary to maintain the balance in population and avoid world overpopulation? Are they in effect secondary agents acting in accordance with the wisdom of the Creator? There are two views of this matter, he replies, one that they are indeed, and the other that they are punishments for man's sin. Most people would agree with the first.[35]

[33] *Ibid.*, pp. 371–373; on Origen, pp. 370–371. For another side of Origen, see pp. 184–186. *The Romance of the Rose*, chap. 91, p. 244, lines 90–94.
[34] *Ibid.*, pp. 331–335, 336, 339–340.
[35] *Ibid.*, pp. 390–391.

But Süssmilch allies himself with the second view—with the *Gottesstraf* for Lisbon theology. In that event of November 1, 1755, he writes, we have "einen Beweis, wie leicht der gerechte Schöpfer den Erdboden umkehren könne." The Creator does not need terrible plagues and famines in order to prevent world overpopulation because far milder means are available to him.[36] No, they are punishments. If the Creator governing the divine order wished to control population growth, he could slowly increase the death rate by increasing the power of fever or by invoking other gentle (*gelinde*) ways of assuring higher mortality.

In his later assertions that rulers have an obligation to see that the population of their countries is consistent with food supply, Süssmilch links population policy in the secular world with population theory and history based on theology. How different this is from Malthus! To Süssmilch the goodness of God is revealed in his concern for the multiplication of life, the wickedness of man by dreadful visitations which restrict his numbers. To Malthus the principle of population is also divinely ordained, and the checks are part of the principle which is beneficent because it insures that no check or combination of checks will lead to the extinction of the human race.

A similar natural theology, transcending either religiosity or simple piety, appeared in the writings of two other Germans, D. Anton Friederich Büsching and Johann Gottfried von Herder, both important names in the history of modern geography. (On Herder, see below, pp. 537–543.)

Büsching is among the first to write a modern compendium of geography; the Schaffhausen edition of 1767 was in eleven volumes. He has often been cast aside as an unimaginative fact-gatherer, but recently a German geographer summarizing the commonly held unflattering views of him defended him from this harsh verdict.[37]

Büsching's introductory essay, *Von dem Nutzen der Erdbeschreibung*, is unexcelled as a short statement of the role of geography in natural theology and in Christian theology in particular, the chief usefulness of geography being its ability to further a knowledge of God as a creator and as a preserver of all things.[38]

With elegant compression, Büsching presents, in less than seven pages, arguments for the usefulness of geography ranging from the opportunities for the sublime contemplation of the Creator's works it affords to the commercial

---

[36] *Ibid.*, pp. 362, 392.

[37] Plewe, "Studien über D. Anton Friederich Büsching," in *Geographische Forschungen, Festschrift zum 60. Geburtstag von Hans Kinzl*, pp. 203–223. Büsching's work was translated into several languages, among them English, Dutch, French, Italian, and Russian; it apparently was very influential throughout Europe (pp. 203–204).

[38] If one fails to understand this function of geography, Plewe remarks correctly, "bleibt uns nicht nur Büsching fremd, sondern auch die Geographie bis hin zu Carl Ritter" (*ibid.*, p. 209). See also his remarks on pietism, and Protestant thought, pp. 209–211.

transactions of everyday life. Its main use, in effect, is that it furnishes evidence of the physico-theological proof; the earth on which we live may be a very small part of the universe, but it is full of sublimity, of beauty, and what exists on it constitutes a proof of God's existence.

Using the ancient distinction between nature and art, Büsching says we find remarkable works of nature, of art, or of both simultaneously. God is the creator of the beauty, the loveliness and the splendor of the kingdom of nature, and he is the creator of landscapes, cities, buildings, arising from the activity of man. Nature untouched by man and nature modified by man are equally God's creations. Man thus is merely an agent of God, his skills, a gift of God and not his own creation.[39]

The great natural variety in the earth's climates, vegetables, fruits, animals, is all available to man. It was a wise provision, too, that there was but one man originally, his descendants in time spreading over the face of the earth, acquiring differences in outer form, language, customs, and ways of living; God saw fit to set territorial limits for various peoples and nations.[40] Through His wisdom, the peoples of the known world have been brought closer together; they help one another, food shortages and surpluses being distributed by means of world trade and commerce. (This thought anticipates the statement commonly heard in the latter part of the nineteenth century that not only had the new marvels in transportation—steamships, railroads, canals—brought the lands of the world closer together but the earth's resources, now available to all peoples, could free men from their age-old dependence on local resources.) God has been responsible too for the migrations of peoples; through them they have become better known to one another and have grown more alike.

If we behold cities, fortresses, buildings, and gardens, we are astounded that God has bestowed upon man so much understanding, so much power, so many blessings. A city, a castle, a fortress, is situated on what was, perhaps a very short time ago, an empty, deserted place, a forest, a rough and forlorn cliff, an inaccessible bog or swamp. Nature, triumphantly changed by art and forced by man into these new molds, becomes a wonder in their eyes. But should they regard this work as theirs? In Büsching's comforting philosophy—man seems to have little responsibility for good or evil—the answer is "no" because these are works of God; they could not have been made against His will.[41]

A good geography is among the most necessary and most useful of books; only a detailed knowledge of it can enable us to understand the works of creation. Then, following customary usage, the religious is succeeded by the utilitarian argument. Geographical knowledge is pleasant, useful, and necessary in our striving to learn about the earth. How can we understand newspapers and histories, read about wars and journeys on land and sea if we do

---

[39] *Neue Erdbeschreibung*, Vol. 1, pp. 17–20.
[40] *Ibid.*, p. 18.
[41] *Ibid.*, pp. 19–20.

not know where places are? Geography belongs in the education of the young. Away with the ghost and witch stories, the fairy tales and other trifles! Geography becomes the mentor of the ruler, the statesman, the natural historian, the merchant, and the traveler. And Büsching will not put up with ignorance among the clerics; the theologian cannot properly understand and interpret holy writ if he knows nothing of the earth's wonders revealed by geography.[42]

Once again, in Büsching, one sees the force and vigor left in eighteenth century natural theology. There is room for environmentalistic explanations, there is room for the creativity of man. God has made the habitats of man, and the two natures—untouched nature and the landscapes of man—are really but a single manifestation of His providence and creativity. Geography, the study of the works of the creation, is for vastly different reasons indispensable to the theologian and to the merchant alike.[43]

## 5. ON FINAL CAUSES IN NATURE

The nineteenth century controversies—over the fixity of species, special creation, the nature of geological change, doctrines of final causes—associated with the publication of Darwin's *Origin of Species* have, except in the more specialized literature, overshadowed discussions of fundamental questions regarding final causes and the order of nature on earth which went on in the eighteenth. I need mention only Hume and Kant.

Of the eighteenth century thinkers critical of the design argument and the teleological view of living nature, the general opinion was that they often drifted into triviality; they were too centered on human problems, they too readily identified human needs with natural law. Maupertuis—sympathetic to doctrines of final causes, impatient with the excesses of its zealots—said, "A host of natural scientists since Newton have found God in stars, in insects, in plants, and in water. Some find him in the wrinkles of the rhinoceros' hide because this animal covered with a very thick hide would be unable to shake himself without his wrinkles. . . . Leave these bagatelles to those who do not realize their own folly." He saw disaster awaiting those who applied the design argument to the minutest manifestations of nature. In passages showing a close reading of Derham, he criticizes "those who see intelligence everywhere; those nowhere." "The organization of animals, the multiplicity and minuteness of the parts of insects, the immensity of celestial bodies, their distances and their revolutions are better suited to astonish the mind than to

[42] *Ibid.*, pp. 22–23.
[43] Büsching (1724–1793) published the first volume of *Neue Erdbeschreibung* in Hamburg in 1754; ten more followed. This discussion is based on the "newest edition," the Schaffhausen of 1767, Vol. 1, pp. 17–24. Plewe's article analyzes the contents of the work and discusses many other interesting ideas in it.

enlighten it. . . . Let us search for Him in the fundamental laws of the cosmos, in those universal principles of order which underlie the whole, rather than in the complicated results of those laws." He saw that in every age men who sought for proofs of this kind would find them; he saw also a fundamental truth about the absorbing capacity of physico-theology: The greater the advances made in the study of natural phenomena, the greater was the number of these proofs.[44] Maupertuis, who headed the expedition sent by Louis XV to Lapland (1736–1737) in order to measure a degree of longitude, was pleading for more industry and more rigor in scientific inquiry. Stop the wonderment, away with the apostrophes, to work on basic discoveries!

Voltaire, who had often made fun of Maupertuis because of his vanity about the discovery that the earth was an oblate spheroid, was, as we shall see, even more sympathetic than he with final causes. But it was the minute tracing of God's handiwork in the details of nature coupled with complacent optimism (which infatuation with final causes could quickly induce) that also provoked Voltaire's scorn. When Candide sees the Anabaptist drowning after bravely saving a sailor, he wants to rescue him, but Dr. Pangloss stops him, saying that "the Tagus approach to Lisbon had been created on purpose for this Anabaptist to be drowned in it."[45]

One sees in the serious writers on nature, like Buffon and Goethe, an even greater impatience with final causes in studying nature and with the glaring failure to distinguish between the laws of nature and the conveniences of man.

Count Buffon rejected final causes as tools in the study of nature, even though some passages in his work do have a teleological flavor. In *Des Époques de la Nature*, for example, man does not appear on earth until the violent transformations it has undergone are over and it has quieted down to a point at which it has become a suitable home for man.[46]

More characteristic of Buffon, however, is the remark that the swine does not seem to have been formed according to an original, particular, and perfect plan but seems to be composed of the parts of other animals. It has useless parts or apparently useful parts which it is unable to use. The bones of the toes are perfectly formed, but they do not assist the animal. He concludes that nature does not subject itself to the guidance of final causes in the composition of beings. If it did, why would there be superfluous parts, or why would essential parts so often be lacking? To be continually seeking ideas of purpose means deserting the point of view that asks the *how* of things (le *comment* des choses), the manner in which nature acts, and substituting for this inquiry the vain idea of searching for the *why* (encherchant à deviner le *pourquoi*), for the end which nature has in mind when it acts.[47]

---

[44] *Essai de Cosmologie*, pp. 13–14, 28–30, 55, 60–62.
[45] *Candide*, chap. 5.
[46] *Des Époques de la Nature*, esp. 5th epoch, *ad fin*, HNS, Vol. 5 (1778), pp. 189–190.
[47] "Le cochon, le cochon de Siam, et le sanglier," *HN*, Vol. 5 (1755), pp. 102–104.

So niggardly are the endowments of the sloths, says Buffon, that the wretched creatures ("ces ébauches imparfaites mille fois projetées exéctutées par la Natur") have survived only because no one interfered with them. If they had not inhabited deserted lands, if man and the powerful animals had pre-empted their habitat, they would not have survived; indeed, some day they will be destroyed. That they exist is proof that all potentialities of life have been realized in actuality, that all that which can be is. The Creator has not confined himself to a set number of species; there are infinite combinations—harmonious and inharmonious. But this plenitude in nature does not prove the validity of final causes. To admit ideas of final causes for such incongruous creatures as the sloths, to claim that nature sparkles in them as brilliantly as it does in its beautiful works, is to see through a narrow tube, and to confound nature's ends with our own.[48]

What happens to the concept of the harmony of nature when the idea of final causes is abandoned? Buffon's answer is that nature should be envisaged and studied for itself. In such a conception, environmental factors immediately assume greater significance. In his *De la Nature, Première Vue* (1764), Buffon defined nature as a system of laws established by the Creator for the existence of things and for the succession of beings. It is not a thing, for then it would be everything; neither is it a being, for then it would be God. One can con-sider it as a living power (*puissance vive*), immense, embracing and animating everything, subordinate to a supreme being; it began functioning only at His command, it continues on its course only with His consent. The power in nature is that part of divine power that is manifest to us. "La Nature est le trône extérieur de la magnificence Divine." It is at the same time cause and effect, means and substance, design and the finished work. Unlike human art whose productions are composed of dead things, nature herself is a perpetually living worker unceasingly active, who knows how to use everything, who works always on the same foundations, whose store is inexhaustible. Time, space, matter, are the means, the universe its object, the movement of life its end.[49]

Such precepts, no matter how grandiloquently stated and how seemingly devout, relieve the Creator of the task of taking care of the minutiae, of plan-ning the detailed and intricate interrelationships of life and matter on earth. As a result Buffon stresses the adaptability of life to environmental conditions, notwithstanding his interest in the power of man to modify the environment.

Historically, as we have seen, environmental ideas have been important subordinate elements in the design argument; harmonious adaptations, with or without divine care, meant a harmony among all forms in life and a harmony also between the organic and the inorganic world. In Buffon one sees a shift

---

[48] "L'unau et l'aï," *HN*, Vol. 13 (1765), pp. 38–40; see also "De la manière d'étudier et de traiter l'Histoire Naturelle," *HN*, Vol. 1 (1749), 11–13.

[49] "De la Nature, Première Vue," *HN*, Vol. 12 (1764), pp. iii, xi.

taking place; despite the pious protestations, adaptations of life to the environment are not being brought about by the specific intention of the Creator; they take place because of conditions and interractions (like the struggle of life in a limited environment) observable in nature itself without invoking final causes at all.

The Baron d'Holbach, who had similar views, wrote with enthusiastic awareness of the triumphs of mechanistic over teleological explanation in physics; it is Newton's method in science, not his pious faith in final causes, that the Baron d'Holbach admires. To him, the idea of order is a human creation derived from observing the necessary, regular, and periodical motion in the universe. What man calls confusion is really that which does not conform to his ideas of order. "It is therefore, in his imagination alone man finds the model of that which he terms order, or confusion, which, like all his abstract, metaphysical ideas, supposes nothing beyond his reach. Order, however, is never more than the faculty of conforming himself with the beings by whom he is environed, or with the whole of which he forms a part."[50]

When D'Holbach applies these general ideas in the elucidation of the nature of life, he sees it to be the result of several phenomena, among them the rotation of the earth and the effects of seasonal change on the life of plants, animals, and man. Whatever theories one adopts regarding the early history of the earth and man's occupance of it, "plants, animals, men, can only be regarded as productions inherent in and natural to our globe, in the position or in the circumstances in which it is actually found."[51] If some accident should occur to the globe, the productions peculiar to it would change with the new circumstance, and the human race might even be eradicated. The distribution of plant, animal, and human life clearly reveals differences; all vary with the climates. "Man, in different climates, varies in his colour, in his size, in his conformation, in his power, in his industry, in his courage, in the faculties of his mind. But, what is it that constitutes climate? It is the different position of parts of the same globe relatively to the sun; positions that suffice to make a sensible variety in its productions." This passage illustrates better than any other known to me in the writings of natural historians the fact that once the design argument is eliminated as a fundamental explanation of the distribution of various kinds of life, what often remains is some form of environmental theory. In an interesting passage discussing man's ability to adjust himself to nature—his position is like Voltaire's against Pope—D'Holbach says that if the peculiar physical conditions existing on earth were altered, man would have to change or disappear. "It is this aptitude in man to co-order himself with the whole, that not only furnishes him with the idea of order, but also makes him exclaim, *Whatever is, is right*, whilst everything is only that which it can be, and the whole is necessarily what it is, and whilst it is positively neither

---

[50] *The System of Nature*, Vol. I, chap. 5, pp. 33–34.
[51] *Ibid.*, chap. 6, pp. 44–45.

good nor bad. It is only requisite to displace a man to make him accuse the universe of confusion."[52] The environment not only brings about differences among men, but accounts for their thinking in analogies.

D'Holbach had no patience with the artisan analogy.

> Let us not be told that we cannot have the idea of a work without having also that of a workman distinguished from his work. *Nature is not a work* [La nature n'est point un ouvrage]; she has always been self-existent; it is in her bosom that everything is operated; she is an immense elaboratory [*sic*], provided with materials, and who makes the instruments of which she avails herself to act: all her works are the effect of her own energy, and of those agents or causes which she makes, which she contains, which she puts in action.[53]

In rejecting the traditional view that nature is a work whose constituent parts have purposive and interlocking existences—plants for the antelope that is the lion's dinner—a harmony coming from wise planning, D'Holbach suggests a view shorn of final causes in which relationships in nature are based on natural laws whose operation can be ascertained if men know enough. The environment of the earth, its relationship to the sun, the variations in the distribution of solar heat, permit plants, antelopes, and lions to exist. That the antelope eats plants, and the lion the antelope, is no more mysterious than is their existence in the first place.

### 6. Tout est bien

Complacent attitudes toward the earth as a habitable planet were seriously undermined by the Lisbon earthquake of 1755. This frightful catastrophe and the accompanying tsunami dramatized the problem of evil and the role of physical catastrophe affecting living things indiscriminately; it also raised questions about the order and harmony on earth and the fitness of the environment, and the validity of final causes in nature.

Natural catastrophes and the interpretations to be put upon them in an age that knew little of the processes at work were as baffling as was the problem of moral evil. The traditional answer of Christian apologetics to the problem of physical evil had been that catastrophes causing great suffering served as lessons and warnings, and in aggravated cases as punishments. If a natural catastrophe of the character of an earthquake induced doubts in the minds of men regarding the competence of the Creator in devising such a faulty structure, the traditional answer—it was Bishop Butler's in the *Analogy of Religion*—was that human beings could not be expected to comprehend a creation planned on such a colossal scale.

The two small London earthquakes of February and March, 1750, pro-

---

[52] *Ibid.*, p. 45.
[53] *Ibid.*, Vol. II, chap. 3, p. 232. See also chap. 5, on theism or deism, optimism, and final causes, pp. 246–274.

voked much speculation regarding the physical, moral, and religious causes of earthquakes. The Lisbon earthquake, however, which began at 9:30 A.M. on November 1, 1755, was probably the most terrifying natural catastrophe and the most widely known in Western history since the eruption of Vesuvius in A.D. 79.

The earthquake became important in the history of ideas not only because of the religious interpretation put upon it but also because of Voltaire's *Poème sur le Désastre de Lisbonne* and *Candide*. The poem was immediately directed at the *tout est bien* philosophy of Alexander Pope; both it and *Candide* were bitter expressions of contempt for the optimism Voltaire thought he saw in the philosophy of Leibniz. In the general gloom of the survivors on the day following the earthquake, Dr. Pangloss explains that everything had to turn out the way it did. "For," he said, "all this is necessarily for the best; because if there is a volcano under Lisbon, it could not be anywhere else, since it is impossible that things should not be exactly as they are. For *tout est bien*!" The *tout est bien* had come from Pope's *An Essay on Man* in the passage beginning, "Cease then, nor ORDER imperfection name":

> All nature is but art, unknown to thee;
> All chance, direction, which thou canst not see;
> All discord, harmony not understood;
> A partial evil, universal good:
> And, spite of pride, in erring reason's spite,
> One truth is clear, WHATEVER IS, IS RIGHT.[54]

Although Voltaire was untiring in his criticism of Leibniz, Wolff, and their followers, the philosophy to which he objected owed more to Pope, whose belief that this is the best of all possible worlds is based on respect for science and on empirical, not *a priori*, grounds as was that of Leibniz. To Pope science revealed the all-embracing unity of the world. Here he speaks the language of the Cambridge Platonists ("See plastic nature working . . .") and of Ray and Derham.[55] The English poet, however, was not acquainted with Leibniz' works, and Bolingbroke, who had inspired many of Pope's ideas, was contemptuous of the German philosopher. What Voltaire ridiculed in *Candide* were extreme believers in final causes and uncritical followers of Pope. Later Voltaire's pessimism seems to have deepened mainly by the events of the Seven Years' War.[56] The earthquake and the fame of

---

[54] *Candide*, chap. 5. *Essay on Man*, Ep. I, x. This epistle also contains the famous passages on the chain of being (viii) and the passage beginning, "All are but parts of one stupendous whole, / Whose body Nature is, and God the soul," etc. (ix).

[55] *Essay on Man*, Ep. I, lines 281–294, quotation is of lines 289–294; Ep. III, 1, lines 1–26. Barber, *Leibniz in France*, pp. 110, 174–177, 194.

[56] Barber, *op. cit.*, pp. 118, 230, 232; on "tout est bien," pp. 238–241. According to him, Catholic orthodoxy often associated optimism with deism (pp. 114–115); Pope, however, aroused interest in Leibniz (p. 122); Wolff's popularity in Germany and the

Voltaire shoved aside the more fatuous extravagances about harmony in nature, smug optimism in human affairs, and uncritical assumptions of an inevitable improvement in the course of time without, however, giving a mortal blow to final causes and to the idea of design as the key to an understanding of nature.[57]

Voltaire himself was no enemy of final causes. The first draft of his poem on the Lisbon earthquake was written by December 7, 1755, and it was in final form (after several revisions) by March, 1756.[58] His pronouncements on final causes were published much later. His essay on final causes which appeared in the *Dictionnaire Philosophique* was published originally in *Des Singularités de la Nature* (1768). It begins with a long quotation from the Baron d'Holbach's *Système de la Nature*, attacking them. Voltaire remarks on the usefulness of the great mountain chains—they strengthen the earth, they help irrigate it, they confine all the metals and the minerals at their bases. But he also disapproves of abuses and of carrying matters to absurd extremes: noses were not made for spectacles, the tides were not, as some had claimed, attached to the oceans so that ships could go in and out of ports more easily. Final causes, to be considered valid, require a uniform effect and invariability in time and in space. Thus the argument that the sea is created for trade and navigation is erroneous because ships have not existed at all times nor on all seas. In disagreeing with the Baron d'Holbach, Voltaire emphasizes that the world of nature is indeed like a work of art, for they both reveal a sense of purpose. Voltaire is impressed, too, with the argument that beauty in nature suggests final causes, as do the usefulness and beauty of the mountain-river-plains triad.[59]

In other articles of the *Dictionnaire Philosophique*, Voltaire expresses similar ideas. He disagrees with Spinoza, and Lucretius; he thinks it is folly to deny that the eye is made to see, the ear to hear, the stomach to digest. Nature is like the arts; there are final causes in both. An apple tree is made to bear apples, a watch to tell time.[60] It is the geometers (e.g., Descartes), not the

---

attempts of enthusiastic followers to spread his philosophy to France acquainted the public with Leibniz' doctrines (p. 141); some of Voltaire's early ideas were similar to Pope's (pp. 215–216); Voltaire often failed to distinguish between Pope and Leibniz, he was unfamiliar with the *Theodicy*, and did not have a profound understanding of Leibniz (p. 232).

[57] For the London earthquakes, see Kendrick, *The Lisbon Earthquake*, pp. 11–44; the description of the Lisbon earthquake, pp. 45–70; the "wrath of God theme," pp. 113–169; the importance of Voltaire, p. 183 ff.; Rousseau and Voltaire on the earthquake, pp. 194–197; Kant's interpretations—he was then under the influence of the philosophy of Leibniz, pp. 198–200. The part of the book most pertinent to our theme is chap. 7, "Optimism Attacked," pp. 180–212.

[58] On the history of the poem, *ibid.*, p. 180, note 2; pp. 184–191.

[59] "Des Singularités de la Nature," *Oeuvres Complètes de Voltaire*, ed. Beuchot, Vol. 44, p. 236; and "Causes Finales," *ibid.*, Vol. 27, pp. 520–533.

[60] "Dieu, Dieux," *Oeuvres*, Vol. 28, pp. 374–375.

philosophers, who reject final causes; a true philosopher will admit them. The catechist proclaims God to the children, Newton proves Him to the wise.[61] In his popularization of Newton's philosophy, he criticizes Descartes and Spinoza, citing in rebuttal Newton's faith in final causes as expressed in the *Opticks*; what was good enough for Newton was good enough for Voltaire.[62]

Voltaire and the Baron d'Holbach's writings are examples of the debate over final causes among literary men; both of them are popular defenders of philosophies that also engage the attention of serious students of nature. Voltaire's defense of final causes is pitiful; it is the simple argument of Xenophon; he adds nothing to enrich it as did Ray, Derham, and even Linnaeus. The best contemporary criticism of Voltaire and comment on the pitfalls in interpreting the cosmic and human meaning of natural catastrophes known to me came from Herder.

> Very unlike the conduct of a philosopher was the complaint made by Voltaire at the catastrophe of Lisbon, on account of which he almost blasphemously arraigned the Deity himself. Are not we ourselves, and all that belong to us, including even our habitation the Earth, indebted to the elements? And when these, agreeably to the ever-acting laws of nature, periodically rouse and claim their own; when fire and water, air and wind, which have rendered our Earth habitable and fruitful, proceed on their course and destroy it; when the Sun, after having long warmed us with paternal care, fostered all living beings, and linked them to his cheering visage with golden bands, ultimately attracts into his fiery bosom the superannuated powers of the Earth, which she can no longer renovate and uphold; what more happens, than the eternal laws of wisdom and order require? In a system of changeable things, if there be progress, there must be destruction: apparent destruction, that is; or a change of figures and forms. But this never affects the interiour of nature, which, exalted above all destruction, continually rises as a phenix [*sic*] from it's [*sic*] ashes, and blooms with youthful vigour. The formation of this our abode, and all the substances it can produce, must have already prepared us for the frailty and mutability of the history of man; and the more closely we inspect it, the more clearly do these unfold themselves to our perception.[63]

## 7. HUME

Considering the long period over which ideas of design and doctrines of final causes have been applied to conceptions of living nature and of the habitable earth, considering too the countless repetitions of threadbare examples and

[61] "Athéisme," *Oeuvres*, Vol. 27, p. 189.

[62] "Éléments de la Philosophie de Newton," *Oeuvres*, Vol. 38, pp. 13–14. In the *Histoire de Jennie, ou l'athée et le Sage* (1775), chap. 8, Voltaire presents arguments like those in his article on God (*Oeuvres*, Vol. 34, p. 390).

[63] Herder, *Outlines of a Philosophy of the History of Man*, Bk. I, chap. 3 *ad fin*, trans. Churchill, p. 9.

analogies and the dreary copying of ideas too sterile to justify the effort of copying, it is impossible to withhold one's admiration from the critiques of Hume and Kant, both surpassing by far any that had appeared to date, and probably remaining unsurpassed to our day for their cogency. Kant's examples are especially striking because he was very interested in geography and anthropology, and these interests show up in his critique of teleology.

The artisan analogy was based on the assumption that God thought like man. But Hume saw with great clarity men's limitations in understanding the creation, the difficulties in interpreting nature that were opened up by the invention of the telescope and the microscope, and the problem of physical evil in the light of natural law.

In this discussion I am not concerned with the vexing question of Hume's own opinions (see note 75) but with the ideas which the interlocutors in the dialogues express. Philo, the most interesting, provocative, and cogent of them, says that in everyday speculations one has the advantage of an appeal to common sense and reason, but this is of little use in theology, whose questions are too overpowering for human apprehension. Our ideas reach no farther than our experience; obviously we have none with divine attributes.

Cleanthes' case for the design argument is dignified, well defined, and conventional. The world is a machine whose intricately adjusted and accurately fitted parts work well together. Adaptation of means to ends is characteristic of all life; thus nature is like the works of the human artificer, but its results are far more impressive and on a grander scale. If there is an analogy between the effects observable in nature and the creations of human purpose, then there can be an analogy between the causes, human and divine respectively, which bring them about. If these statements are true, we may then say that the Author of Nature acts with a mind like that of man, with the usual reservation that the divine is infinitely greater. Philo replies that the analogy will not bear analysis. It is stretching things too far, for example, to suggest that a house is like the universe.[64] Furthermore, existence of order and arrangement and proper functioning is in itself no proof of design. An animal whose body does not function properly would pass away; so would the universe. Order might simply be inherent in matter; one might say that such a constitution allows it to function as it does, and without reference to design.

Men and animals possess thought, design, and intelligence, but these attributes are no more than one of "the springs and principles of the universe" and are totally inadequate to explain its principles. "What peculiar privilege has this little agitation of the brain which we call *thought*, that we must thus make it the model of the whole universe?" Nature has an infinite number of springs and principles. Witnessing the origins of ships or of cities and

[64] *Dialogues Concerning Natural Religion*, Pt. I, pp. 9–10; Pt. II, p. 18.

their later developments are experiences too trivial to serve as a guide in speculation on the origin of the universe.[65]

The unrelenting Philo now dissects an argument which many previous writers had assumed to be the clincher, that is, that the telescope and the microscope immeasurably widened and deepened men's understanding of the order of nature and the wisdom of God because they could now behold the whole spectrum of being from the infinitely vast to the infinitesimally small. The conventional conclusion—Leibniz himself exultantly agreed with it— was that these newly revealed worlds confirmed the design a thousandfold; they showed an order and patterning in wholly unsuspected realms. Philo says that this enlargement of the bounds of nature hitherto known to man makes the problem more difficult rather than easier, the analogy becoming even more remote.

The arguments of Lucretius and Cicero in the ancient world are now being brought up to date with the help of modern knowledge. "The further we push our researches of this kind [microscopy] we are still led to infer the universal cause of all to be vastly different from mankind, or from any object of human experience and observation." Kant came to a similar conclusion.[66]

And what in the everyday world is artisanship? Behind the contemporary human artisan lie ages of trial and error, the accumulation of skills, invention, craft traditions; the human artisan is the carrier of long-accumulated skills and he is their contemporary embodiment, not an inventive genius himself. Furthermore, ambitious undertakings are cooperative enterprises; they are the work of many men. Can the excellences of the work, Philo asks, be ascribed to the workman even granting the world to be a perfect production? "If we survey a ship, what an exalted idea must we form of the ingenuity of the carpenter who framed so complicated, useful, and beautiful a machine? And what surprise must we feel when we find him a stupid mechanic who imitated others, and copied an art which, through a long succession of ages, after multiplied trials, mistakes, corrections, deliberations, and controversies, had been gradually improving?" The cooperative nature of human productivity thus is not helpful evidence in support of the single-handed artisanship of the Deity. Such an argument invites the possibility that many worlds "might have been botched and bungled, throughout an eternity," by groping trial and error with gradual improvement "in the art of world-making."[67]

The rebuttal based on the complex, historical, and cooperative character of human artisanship and invention presses home again the hopelessness of explaining the apparent order of nature by comparing it with human capaci-

[65] *Ibid.*, Pt. II, p. 23.
[66] *Ibid.*, Pt. V, p. 38. See Lucretius, *De rerum natura*, Bk. XI, 2, and Cicero, *De natura deorum*, Bk. I, chap. 8.
[67] *Ibid.*, p. 39.

ties for creating order. Actually, says Philo, if analogies must be made, the world resembles a vegetable or an animal more than it does a watch or a loom, and it more probably arose through a process similar to or analogous with generation than from causes producing the watch or the loom. Neither is this idea pressed for its own sake, but it shows that "we have no *data* to establish any system of cosmogony."[68]

Cleanthes complains that Philo places too much emphasis on the inability of a form to exist unless it possesses powers and organs necessary for its existence. But how in fact have conveniences and advantages possessed by man and animals originated? "Two eyes, two ears are not absolutely necessary for the subsistence of the species. [The] human race might have been propagated and preserved without horses, dogs, cows, sheep, and those innumerable fruits and products which serve to our satisfaction and enjoyment. If no camels had been created for the use of man in the sandy deserts of Africa and Arabia, would the world have been dissolved?" Cleanthes here and with other illustrations objects to the stress on the niggardliness in nature; other facts point to beneficence and generosity.[69] To this, Philo counters, "you have run into anthropomorphism." As we have seen, one of the earliest interpretations of domestication was that animals were purposefully designed by a beneficent and generous Creator to function within an economy dominated by man; this view too assumed a generosity in nature solicitous for the welfare of man.

And what, says Demea, of the general human consensus that human misery is commonplace in the world? When he says no one has denied its existence, Philo corrects him, saying that Leibniz had (on the falseness of this see pp. 507, 522–523). "The whole earth, believe me, Philo, is cursed and polluted. A perpetual war is kindled amongst all living creatures. Necessity, hunger, want stimulate the strong and courageous; fear, anxiety, terror agitate the weak and infirm." Observe, Philo says, "the curious artifices of nature in order to embitter the life of every living being." The strong are predatory, the weak are also—and vexatious like the insects; "every animal is surrounded with enemies which incessantly seek his misery and destruction." Man, Demea replies, seems in part to be an exception to this rule; by joining together in society, he can save himself from, indeed master, the large predators. Philo replies that man's mastery of the creation does not solve this problem, because he creates his own problems; a few of them are superstition, man's inhumanity to man, mental and physical illness, labor and poverty. The effect is to bring out without anger or pathos the precariousness of human life; man's endowment is enough for survival, but with struggle.[70]

These outspoken passages on human misery lead to the problem of the

[68] *Ibid.*, Pt. VII, pp. 47–48.
[69] *Ibid.*, Pt. VIII, p. 55.
[70] *Ibid.*, Pt. X, pp. 62–63.

observer. Again, one is reminded of similar discussions in Cicero and Lucretius. How would the order of nature be seen (a) by one antecedently convinced of its reality, and (b) by one not so convinced?

The first of these alternatives is imaginary, the second represents the actual experience of man. Of the first, he says that if a person of very limited intelligence, unacquainted with the universe, were assured beforehand that it had been created by "a very good, wise, and powerful Being," his notion of what it would be like before he saw it would be quite different from what we know it by experience to be like. Knowing the attributes of the Divine, he would never suspect "that the effect could be so full of vice and misery and disorder, as it appears in this life." When this person, however, is brought into the world, he might be disappointed in what he saw but he would blame this on his own inadequacies, retaining his preconception because he "must allow that there may be many solutions of those phenomena which will forever escape his comprehension." Of the second alternative, representing the true human situation, there is no antecedent conviction of a benevolent and powerful divine intelligence nor is any prior instruction provided; man "is left to gather such a belief from the appearances of things—this entirely alters the case, nor will he ever find any reason for such a conclusion." Even if he recognizes the narrowness of his understanding, this inadequacy will not help him to form an inference regarding the Divine Being from what he beholds "since he must form that inference from what he knows, not from what he is ignorant of."[71]

Then in the manner of Lucretius, even of Burnet, Philo ridicules the disarray of nature; if it must have an artisan-creator, it is indeed the work of a bumbling and incompetent architect, who cannot excuse his poor work by saying it could be worse. The architect could with proper skill have made a good plan to start with.[72]

Philo concludes that the world might be consistent with the idea of a powerful, wise, and benevolent Deity, but "it can never afford us an inference concerning his existence." Considering the earth and life as it really is, why is it that everyone cannot be happy, why is physical anguish and hardship necessary? The answers are like the ingredients which later are to fashion the Malthusian and Darwinian theories. Philo says there are four main causes of human misery and evil: (1) It is part of the economy of creation that pains and pleasures "excite all creatures to action, and make them vigilant in the great work of self-preservation." But why not pleasure alone? Is there any reason why pain should be necessary? (2) The capacity for pain would not in itself produce pain if the world were not governed by general laws; but this governance "seems nowise necessary to a very perfect Being." Might

[71] *Ibid.*, Pt. XI, p. 72.
[72] *Ibid.*, pp. 72–73.

not the Deity "exterminate all ill, wherever it were to be found, and produce all good, without any preparation or long progress of causes and effects?"[73] (3) The economy of nature is characterized by "the great frugality with which all powers and faculties are distributed to every particular being." The adjustment of the living parts of the animal mechanism is so fine that it is doubtful that any have ever become extinct, but endowments are bestowed upon them by so frugal a hand that any considerable diminution of them would destroy the life. Nature is a hard, not an indulgent, parent, a *"rigid master"* who has given her creatures "little more powers or endowments than what are strictly sufficient to supply those necessities." An indulgent parent would have given generously to avoid accidents, and to insure the creature's happiness and welfare. Why should an all powerful Creator possessing, possibly, inexhaustible force act so rigidly and parsimoniously? If his power is in fact extremely limited, it would have been better "to have created fewer animals, and to have endowed these with more faculties for their happiness and preservation."[74] (4) Lastly, there is "the inaccurate workmanship of all the springs and principles of the great machine of nature." Granting that the universe holds together, that it seemingly functions fairly well, that few parts of it seem not to serve some purpose, nevertheless carelessness and sloppiness are evident in execution. "One would imagine that this grand production had not received the last hand of the maker—so little finished is every part, and so coarse are the strokes with which it is executed." Here Philo departs from the traditional view that the divinely ordered creation is unfinished in order to permit man to finish it through cultivation, making cities, and other activities.

Winds and rains may be benign, but why have hurricanes and excessive heat? But this physical evil is a consequence of natural law. Hurricanes, volcanoes, excessive heat, earthquakes, are explained by causes acting independently of human life. This is Herder's point in criticizing Voltaire for his poem on the Lisbon disaster. But why are such operations of nature's laws, conflicting in their effects on man, necessary at all?

Since natural evil comes about, for the most part, from these four circumstances, the interlocutor comes to a conclusion opposed to that of Romans 1:20. What we see cannot lead us to safe inferences regarding either the artisan or the artisanship of nature.

> Look round this universe. What an immense profusion of beings, animated and organized, sensible and active! You admire this prodigious variety and fecundity. But inspect a little more narrowly these living existences, the only beings worth regarding. How hostile and destructive to each other! How insufficient all of them for their own happiness! How contemptible or odious to the spectator!

[73] *Ibid.*, p. 74.
[74] *Ibid.*, p. 76.

The whole presents nothing but the idea of a blind nature, impregnated by a great vivifying principle, and pouring forth from her lap, without discernment or parental care, her maimed and abortive children![75]

## 8. KANT AND GOETHE

Hume's *Dialogues* prepare us for Kant who had already discussed the physico-theological proof and teleology in the *Critique of Pure Reason* (1781), in which one can already sense Kant's regret that the cosmological and physico-theological proofs must be rejected.[76] His most penetrating discussions of design, order, and man's place in nature, however, are in the *Critique of Teleological Judgement*.[77]

Let us look at some of Kant's illustrations which apply to geography. Alluvial deposition is a kind of physical process which might evoke teleological explanations. Rivers, carrying soil in suspension, create good agricultural land near their banks or in their deltas. High tide, carrying this alluvial material inland or depositing it along the shore, may rescue it from the sea, while arable land may be augmented if man can prevent ebb tide from carrying it off again, and the land increased at the expense of the sea. Nature is continually building up new lands this way, and the question arises whether "this result is to be considered an end on the part of nature, since it is fraught with benefit to man. I say 'to man,' for the benefit to the vegetable kingdom cannot be taken into account, inasmuch as against the gain to the land there is, as a set off, as much loss to sea-life."[78] Or we may consider the agency of certain natural phenomena in enabling other phenomena to achieve their ends. Take as an example, Kant says, pine trees growing on sandy soil. There is none healthier for them than that left behind when the primeval seas withdrew; on this soil, unfavorable for agriculture, many pine forests could grow —"forests which we frequently blame our ancestors for having wantonly destroyed." Was the sand then the end nature had in view for the possible benefit of pine forests? If the forests are presumed to be the end, then so must the sand, and behind it the primeval sea, and so forth, as subordinate ends. In a third example, Kant says that if one grants that cattle, sheep, horses, and the like were for some reason to be in the world, then there had to be grass to feed them and there had to be special alkaline plants in the

---

[75] *Ibid.*, pp. 78–79. The *Dialogues* (published after his death) have long puzzled the students of Hume. To what degree does Philo express Hume's ideas, considering the apparent "recantation" of Part XII? Then Pamphilus says in the concluding paragraph that "Philo's principles are more probable than Demea's, but that those of Cleanthes approach still nearer to the truth." See Henry D. Aiken's introduction to this edition.

[76] *Critique of Pure Reason*, Bk. 2, chap. 3, sec. 7. See Kant's discussion of environmental theory, his criticism of Leibniz, Burnet, and the chain of being; on the earth and its figure.

[77] On Kant's teleology, see S. Körner, *Kant* (Pelican Books), pp. 196–217.

[78] *Critique of the Teleological Judgement*, p. 13 (367).

deserts if camels were to survive. These and other herbivora had to exist if the carnivora—the wolves, tigers, and lions—were to exist. "Consequently objective finality based on adaptability is not an immanent objective finality of things: as though the sand, as simple sand, could not be conceived as the effect of its cause, the sea, unless we made this cause look to an end, and treated the effect, namely the sand, as an art-product."[79] Herbs or plants may be considered in their own right as organized products of nature, and may be regarded at the same time as mere raw material if attention is directed to the animals that feed on them.

The intervention of man in nature, through his use of plants and animals, casts even more doubt on teleological explanations of nature. The "freedom of man's causality enables him to adapt physical things to the purposes he has in view." Man may foolishly decorate himself with birds' plumes, wisely use domestic animals for transport or for plowing, but these interventions do not prove that these uses were inherent in their natures. "All we can say is that *if* we assume that it is intended that men should live on the earth, then at least, those means without which they could not exist as animals, and even, on however low a plane, as rational animals, must also not be absent. But in that case, those natural things that are indispensable for such existence must equally be regarded as ends of nature."[80]

Kant extends his analysis to the distribution of life on the earth's surface and the relationship of living forms to the environment, starting out innocently enough by remarking that snow makes intercourse easier among peoples in cold countries because they can use sleighs. The Laplander can enjoy his sleigh because he has a reindeer to pull it and thus bring about the desired social intercourse. The reindeer, subsisting on the dry moss they scrape out from under the snow, submit to taming, readily allowing themselves to be deprived of their freedom. Similar complex interrelationships between man, animals, and the inorganic environment are found among other Arctic peoples who depend on sea animals for food, clothing, and fuel, and on driftwood for their fires.

> Now here we have a truly marvellous assemblage of many relations of nature to an end—the end being the Greenlanders, Laplanders, Samoyeds, Jakutes, and the like. But we do not see why men should live in these places at all. To say, therefore, that the *facts* that vapour falls from the atmosphere in the form of snow, that the ocean has its currents that wash into these regions the wood grown in warmer lands, and that sea-monsters containing quantities of oil are to be found there, *are due* to the idea of some benefit to certain poor creatures underlying the cause that brings together all these natural products, would be a very hazardous and arbitrary assertion. For supposing that all this utility on the part of nature were absent, then the capacity of the natural causes to serve this order of existence would not be missed. On the contrary it would seem audacious

[79] *Ibid.*, p. 14 (368).
[80] *Ibid.*, pp. 14–15 (368).

and inconsiderate on our part even to ask for such a capacity, or demand such an end from nature—for nothing but the greatest want of social unity in mankind could have dispersed men into such inhospitable regions.[81]

Kant then points out the inadequacies of analogies which liken nature to a machine or to an artisan. Organized nature cannot be considered to be a machine. The cause responsible for producing the watch lies outside it; one wheel of a watch cannot produce another, one watch cannot produce others by using or organizing foreign material, it cannot replace parts, correct deficiencies, nor can it repair itself. No doubt Kant purposefully uses the watch example because it had been a perennial favorite in illustrating the artisan analogy: it is inconceivable to think of a watch without a maker, and of nature . . . and so forth.

> But these are all things which we are justified in expecting from organized nature. An organized being is, therefore not a mere machine. For a machine has solely *motive power*, whereas an organized being possesses inherent *formative* power, and such, moreover, as it can impart to material devoid of it—material which it organizes. This, therefore, is a self-propagating formative power, which cannot be explained by the capacity of movement alone, that is to say, by mechanism.[82]

Then he disposes of the artisan analogy. It is not enough to speak of the capacity of nature "in organized products" as being an analogue of art, for in the idea of art there is an artist—a rational being—working from without. "But nature, on the contrary, organizes itself, and does so in each species of its organized products—following a single pattern, certainly, as to general features, but nevertheless admitting deviations calculated to secure self-preservation under particular circumstances. . . . Strictly speaking, therefore, the organization of nature has nothing analogous to any causality known to us."[83]

Kant, however, repeatedly asserts that teleology is useful in the study of nature, if we look upon it as a guide, as perhaps furnishing a clue, by acting, so to speak, as if the eye were made to see.

> The concept of a thing as intrinsically a physical end is, therefore, not a constitutive conception either of understanding or of reason, but yet it may be used by reflective judgement as a regulative conception for guiding our investigation of objects of this kind by a remote analogy with our own causality according to ends generally, and as a basis of reflection upon their supreme source. But in the latter connexion it cannot be used to promote our knowledge either of nature or of such original source of those objects, but must on the contrary be confined to the service of just the same practical faculty of reason in analogy with which we considered the cause of the finality in question.[84]

81 *Ibid.*, p. 16 (369).
82 *Ibid.*, p. 22 (374).
83 *Ibid.*, p. 23 (374-375).
84 *Ibid.*, p. 24 (375).

With his interest in geography and anthropology, it is not surprising that Kant considers ends in nature with relation to man, to cultural differences among men, to other forms of life, and to the configuration of the earth's surface. We are not entitled, he says, to consider rivers as physical ends because they facilitate international intercourse in inland countries, or mountains as physical ends because they make rivers possible or store snow so rivers can flow in the dry season. "For, although this configuration of the earth's surface is very necessary for the origination and sustenance of the vegetable and animal kingdoms, yet intrinsically it contains nothing the possibility of which should make us feel obliged to invoke a causality according to ends." Kant applies the same analysis to the question of the usefulness of domesticated animals and plants. Cattle may need grass and men may need cattle to survive. "But we do not see why after all it should be necessary that men should in fact exist (a question that might not be so easy to answer if the specimens of humanity that we had in mind were, say, the New Hollanders or Fuegians). We do not then arrive in this way at any categorical end. On the contrary all this adaptation is made to rest on a condition that has to be removed to an ever-retreating horizon."[85]

It is a pity that Kant did not expand on his remarks about the New Hollanders and the Fuegians. For he implies that the questions he is discussing are meaningful only if high cultures exist, that civilization is a prerequisite to the study of meaning in nature. Does this mean that the advances of man dignify a study which, had man remained in a primitive condition, would not and could not have been carried on and that nature therefore would be meaningless?

Pursuing the theme that final causes may be regarded as a guide without interfering with the principle that nature is to be studied through the investigation of secondary causes, Kant discusses the unpleasant and the annoying in nature—a favorite theme, as we have seen, of the older teleology—and their relation to man. Vermin, he says, may be nature's way of inciting man to cleanliness; this idea comes close to that of necessity being the mother of invention. "Or the mosquitoes and other stinging insects that make the wilds of America so trying for the savages, may be so many goads to urge these primitive men to drain the marshes and bring light into the dense forests that shut out the air, and, by so doing, as well as by the tillage of the soil, to render their abodes more sanitary." The principle can be applied also to the appreciation of beauty in nature. "We may regard it as a favour that nature has extended to us, that besides giving us what is useful it has dispensed beauty and charms in such abundance, and for this we may love it, just as we view it with respect because of its immensity, and feel ourselves ennobled

[85] *Ibid.*, pp. 27–28 (378) .

by such contemplation—just as if nature had erected and decorated its splendid stage with this precise purpose in its mind."[86]

Kant says we cannot find in nature "any being capable of laying claim to the distinction of being the final end of creation." At first we might look upon the vegetable kingdom "as a mere product of the mechanism which nature displays in its formations in the mineral kingdom. But a more intimate knowledge of its indescribably wise organization precludes us from entertaining this view, and drives us to ask: For what purpose do these forms of life exist?" If we reply that they exist for the herbivora, then we must ask why the herbivora exist, and the answer would be that they exist for the carnivora. If we pursue the inquiry further to ascertain the ultimate purpose of the creation, we answer that it is for man and for "the multifarious uses to which his intelligence teaches him to put all these forms of life. He is the ultimate end of creation here upon earth, because he is the one and only being upon it that is able to form a conception of ends, and from an aggregate of things purposively fashioned to construct by the aid of his reason a system of ends." Following a suggestion of Linnaeus, Kant considers the consequences of taking "the seemingly opposite course." Herbivorous animals might exist in order to keep the profuse growth of the vegetable kingdom in check, the carnivora, in order to set "bounds to the voracity of the herbivora; and finally man exists so that by pursuing the latter and reducing their numbers a certain equilibrium between the productive and destructive forces of nature may be established. So, on this view, however much man might in a certain relation be esteemed as end, in a different relation he would in turn only rank as a means." In this last illustration man's role in nature reminds one of Hale's idea of man as a steward or regulator of nature, except that Hale believes man assumes the role because he is at the apex of creation.[87]

If we adopt the principle of final causes for individual forms, we must then take the next rational step and say that the system of the whole kingdom of nature is also organized in accordance with the same principle. If there is such an end in the whole system of nature, it can only be placed in man, but there is no evidence that this is true. "For, so far from making man, regarded as one of the many animal species, an ultimate end, nature has no more exempted him from its destructive than from its productive forces, nor has it made the smallest exception to its subjection of everything to a mechanism of forces devoid of an end."[88]

Again Kant reveals his intense interest in geography and in natural science. If nature as a whole is a system governed by final causes, the habitats of living things would have to illustrate the principle. The habitat, the soil or other

---

[86] *Ibid.*, pp. 29–30 (379–380).
[87] *Ibid.*, pp. 88–89 (426–427).
[88] *Ibid.*, p. 89 (427).

elements intended to support life, show "no trace of any causes but those acting altogether without design, and in fact tending towards destruction rather than calculated to promote genesis of forms, order, and ends." This passage brings up the old question of the fitness of the earthly environment for life, a question which, as we have seen, stimulated many thinkers of the seventeenth and eighteenth centuries following the criticisms of the earth made by Burnet. Kant takes the position that the present configuration of the earth's surface, regardless of the convenience and wise contrivance of slope, springs, subterranean waters, and other desirable attributes, is a result not of design but of geological history; a closer investigation of them "shows that they have resulted simply as the effect partly of volcanic eruptions, partly of floods, or even of invasions of the ocean." The important point here is not the geological theory adopted by Kant but the statement that the configuration of the earth is the result of historical events, not of final causes. Human history unfolds itself on a planet with its own history.[89]

Kant's analysis of final causes in nature and of the idea of the earth as a product of design is really a harvesting of thoughts spanning more than two thousand years; to take a shorter view, it is also the culmination of speculation and study inspired by Burnet in the *Sacred Theory of the Earth* because Burnet forced men, at a time when Newtonian science had given them many new ideas to work on, to think of the form, shape, and position of the earth and of its fitness for life, a task undertaken with such interesting results by Ray, Derham, and others. From their attempts to find the wisdom of God in the creation emerged ideas of interrelationships that were ultimately to supersede the doctrine of final causes.

Goethe also was very critical of the effects of a teleological interpretation of nature on scientific inquiry; fundamentally, he too objected to the design argument because it was based on an analogy. When a science, he says, seems to be slowing down or coming to a halt, the fault often lies in "a certain basic concept that treats the subject too conventionally" or in the unthinking and continued use of an accepted terminology. Although Goethe thought the "idea that living organisms are created and shaped to certain ends by a teleological life force," pleasing to some, indispensable to certain modes of thought ("I myself find it neither possible nor desirable to oppose it as a whole"), it is a weak reed in serious scientific work. The difficulties are that men, through experience of life, have respect for purposeful activity; their temperaments and situations predispose them to think they exist as an end of the creation. A word like *weeds* reveals the nature of their misconceptions.

> Why should he [i.e., man] not call a plant a weed, when from his point of view it really ought not to exist? He will much more readily attribute the existence of thistles hampering his work in the field to the curse of an enraged benevolent

[89] *Ibid.*, pp. 89–90 (428).

spirit, or to the malice of a sinister one, than simply regard them as children of universal Nature, cherished as much by her as the wheat he carefully cultivates and values so highly.

Goethe makes the same point as did Buffon, that human ends are poor guides to an understanding of nature's ends. "And since man values highest, in himself and others, those processes which are intentional and purposeful, he will ascribe intentions and purposes to Nature also, for his concept of Nature cannot possibly transcend the concept he has formed of himself."

Such a conception of nature, with so much emphasis on purpose and usefulness, makes nature seem like a gigantic toolshed. If everything in nature exists for man, then he assumes Nature is making tools for him, just as he does for himself. "Thus the hunter who procures a gun for killing game cannot extol sufficiently the maternal solicitude of Nature in having created the dog at the very beginning of things, to enable him to retrieve the game."

More original is Goethe's objection that, "Man, in considering all things with reference to himself, is obliged to assume that external forms are determined from within, and this assumption is all the easier for him in that no single living thing is conceivable without complete organization." Its internal organization is clearly defined, but its external existence is possible only under environmental conditions favorable to it. In Goethe's hands, the environment is metamorphosed from a passive medium of life to an active creative role in conditioning and maintaining it.

> . . . We see moving about on the earth, in the water, and in the air the most varied forms of animals; these elements, according to popular interpretation, have been furnished to these creatures expressly in order that they may produce their various movements and preserve their various existences. But does not the original life force, or the wisdom of a reasoning creator customarily attributed to it, gain greater stature when we accept even its power as limited, and grant that it creates just as well *from* the outside as well as *toward* the outside. To say that the fish exists for the water, seems to me to say less than that the fish exists *in* water and *by means* of water; for this latter statement expresses much more clearly what is only darkly suggested in the first, namely, that the existence of creatures called fish is possible only if there exists an element called water, and that these fish not only exist but also develop there. The same thing holds true for all other creatures.

Here too is an adumbration of an ecological viewpoint, including the study of environmental conditions as they affect life—which give it form or set limits to it. The oak cannot be explained by the acorn alone; its secrets are found too in the wind, the hill slopes, the sun, the soil.[90] Neither Hume, Kant, nor Goethe had the final word; as we all know, the controversies over Genesis

---

[90] Goethe, "An Attempt to Evolve a General Comparative Theory," in *Goethe's Botanical Writings*, trans. Bertha Mueller, pp. 81–84. The emphasis is in the original. On the circumstances of the composition—the piece belongs to the early 1790's—see footnote 32, p. 81. See also, "Preliminary Notes for a Physiology of Plants," pp. 91–93; "The In-

and Geology (to use Andrew D. White's expression), over the relation of natural theology and revealed religion to evolutionary theory, lasted, especially in England, for the greater part of the nineteenth century. The most influential and the most embarrassingly shoddy of these works, the *Natural Theology* of William Paley, published in 1802, twelve years after the publication of Kant's critique, was remote indeed from the intellectual distinction of these men. The protagonists of the design argument in the scientific world acted like ministers infatuated with their sermons, while their opponents, including Darwin, Lyell, and Huxley, seemed to have little understanding of the historical significance of the design argument and the questions it had raised in many fields concerning the relationship of man to nature.

## 9. HERDER

Two men, Herder and Humboldt, it seems to me, are representatives of ideas held toward the earth as a whole in the late eighteenth and early nineteenth centuries. Herder represents, in his synthesis of the three ideas we have been discussing, the best in the old that was now to vanish, with hints of the new. Humboldt represents an approach to nature study which leads into nineteenth century thought.

Herder's *Ideen zur Philosophie der Geschichte der Menschheit* (1784–1791) has long been recognized as a masterful work of synthesis. Ideas concerning the fitness of the earth's environment, widely discussed by the physico-theologists of the late seventeenth and early eighteenth centuries; speculations regarding the influence of climate, given new status by Montesquieu (see below, pp. 565–581); ideas concerning the influence of man on the physical environment—these were brought to bear on two problems: the relation of mankind, considered as a whole, to the earth as a whole, and the relation of individual peoples to the different parts of the earth in which they happened to be living. As far as the second problem is concerned, Herder belongs in the company of Buffon, Montesquieu, and Voltaire: all of them were interested in man and his physical environment, all were interested in voyages and travels, all revealed by references or citations the intellectual heritage from which they derived their inspiration.[91]

Although it is a great temptation to embark on a long analysis of Herder's work because his absorbing discussions touch upon so many aspects of man,

---

fluence of the New Philosophy" (1817), in which Goethe expresses his appreciation to Kant for his analysis of final causes in the *Critique of Judgement*, pp. 230–231, and his famous "Nature (A Fragment)," and his "Commentary on Nature," pp. 242–245.

[91] Because there are many editions of Herder's *Ideen*, it is cited by book and chapter. The standard edition of Herder's works is that of Bernard Suphan, the *Ideen* comprising Vols. 13 and 14 of this edition. In the quotations, I have used with minor changes or

human culture, history, and the physical environment, epitomizing the awarenesses of the learned of his time, I will confine myself to pointing out two significant achievements of Herder: (1) the three ideas that have been discussed are brought together in a meaningful synthesis, and (2) he distinguishes between humanity and its relation to the earth as a whole and individual peoples and their relation to individual parts of the earth, the latter relationships requiring consideration of the differences among peoples and the physical and cultural conditions which might explain these differences.

Herder argues that the earth, despite the physical changes it has undergone, is a fit environment for life; he believes that, at least, the most salient characteristics of the earth are a product of design. In his exposition of geological history, he follows Buffon (presumably *Des Époques de la Nature*), accepting the latter's thesis that man appears after the catastrophic revolutions—fires, floods, earthquakes—which had characterized the earlier eras of earth history had taken place. The present earth, says Herder, is perfected—it has grown old—but it will never be entirely free (Buffon believed this, too) of the catastrophes that had characterized its past. Consistent with this position, Herder, as we have seen, criticized Voltaire for taking a philosophically indefensible position about the Lisbon earthquake because such disasters have their own individual causes in natural law. The earth is the scene of constant change—destruction of the old, creation of the new. Man lives uncertainly on a physically precarious earth for the simple reason that these catastrophes, with their own laws of causation, unavoidably make it so. Voltaire's criticisms of God for the Lisbon earthquake therefore are irrelevancies. "The formation of this our abode [die Bildung unsres Wohnhauses], and all the substances it can produce, must have already prepared us for the frailty and mutability of the history of man; and the more closely we inspect it, the more clearly do these unfold themselves to our perception."[92]

Despite the catastrophic revolutions—Herder again follows Buffon here—the fitness of the earth's environment has been preserved. Order and unity have survived on earth, whose history has been characterized by so many catastrophic events. "The multifarious variety, that actually exists on our Earth, is astonishing; but still more astonishing is the unity, that pervades this inconceivable variety. It is a mark of the profound northern barbarity [ein Zeichen der tiefen nordischen Barbarei], in which we educate our children, that we give them not from their infancy a deep impression of this beauty, this uniformity and variety of our Earth."[93]

---

corrections (e.g., the possessive pronoun *its* has been written instead of *it's*) the graceful translation of T. Churchill, *Outlines of a Philosophy of the History of Man.* See Clark, *Herder*, esp. chap. x, and Grundmann, *Die geographischen und völkerkundlichen Quellen und Anschauungen in Herders "Ideen zur Geschichte der Menschheit."*

[92] *Ideen*, Bk. I, chap. 3 *ad fin*, Churchill trans., p. 9.

[93] *Ibid.*, chap. 4, Churchill trans., pp. 9–10.

The old polemics about the inclination of the earth on its axis being a proof of design seem forgotten; the advantages of the present inclination are self-evident. Herder shows how the design, the inclination, and environmental differences are related to one another:

> The Earth must have a regular inclination, that regions, which would otherwise lie in cimmerian cold and darkness, may behold the beams of the Sun, and be fitted for organization. As the history of the Earth from the remotest times informs us, that the difference of the zones has had considerable influence on all the revolutions of the human mind and its operations; for neither from the torrid nor the frigid zones have those effects ever been produced, to which the temperate zones have given birth: we see with what fine traits the finger of omnipotence has described and encircled all the changes and shades on the Globe.[94]

This strong environmentalistic explanation, however, is not consistently maintained by Herder.

The earth therefore must be regarded as the theater of the history of man ("Da wir hier die Erde als einen Schauplatz der Menschengeschichte betrachten.") In a striking metaphor, Herder says that "Nature stretched the rough but firm outline of the history of man and its revolutions, with the lines of mountains she drew, and the streams she let flow from them. [So hat also die Natur mit den Bergreihen, die sie zog, wie mit den Strömen die sie herunterrinnen liess, gleichsam den rohen, aber festen Grundriss aller Menschengeschichte und ihrer Revolutionen entworfen.]"[95] Herder correlates the configuration with settlements (e.g., riverbanks and the seashore; typical habitats of the hunter, shepherd, farmer, and fisherman.) The earth's relief can explain also the persistence of age-old customs and habits, and changes which peoples have undergone as well.[96] There is divine planning in the place of origin of the human race, in the location of the mountains, and in the irregularity of the earth's surface. The Creator placed the main trunk (*Hauptstamm*) of the mountain ranges of the old world in the temperate zone, the most civilized nations living at their base.

> There the primitive races could at first live in peace, then gradually draw off along the mountains and rivers, and become inured to ruder climates. Each cultivated its little circle, and enjoyed it, as if it had been the universe. . . . Thus the Creator of the World has ever ordained things better than we could have directed; and the irregular form of our Earth has effected an end, that greater regularity could never have accomplished.[97]

Man appears on earth—again Herder seems to be influenced by Buffon's *Des Époques de la Nature*—as an intruder. "All the elements, rivers and

---

[94] *Ibid.*, chap. 4 *ad fin*, Churchill trans., p. 12.

[95] *Ibid.*, chap. 6, Churchill trans., pp. 18, 22.

[96] Herder applies these general observations on the relation of relief to human affairs in interesting discussions of each of the continents. *Ibid.*, pp. 19–22.

[97] *Ibid.*, p. 22.

morasses, earth and air, were filled or filling, with living creatures: and he had to make room for his dominion by his godlike qualities, skill and power."[98] His skills, originally acquired by observing the animals, allowed him to assume his place on earth, through time gaining the ascendancy which he now enjoys.

Herder assumes the unity of the human race. Man is linked with all nature, he is no independent being; he breathes air, he obtains his food and drink from the products of nature, he uses fire, absorbs the light, contaminates the air; "awake or asleep, in motion or at rest, contributing to the change of the universe; shall he not also be changed by it? It is far too little to compare him to the absorbing sponge, the sparkling tinder: he is a multitudinous harmony, a living self, on whom the harmony of all the powers that surround him operates."[99]

Having considered mankind as a whole in its relation to the earth as a whole, there remains the second question: since many different peoples compose the human race, do the environmental conditions under which they live influence them and do they in turn influence the environment?

Despite an occasionally expressed sympathy with ideas of climatic influences, in his more critical moments Herder is dissatisfied with them. Although he admires Hippocrates and Montesquieu, his own views on the causes of cultural differences are more eclectic; "while some build so much upon it [climate], in the philosophy of the history of man, and others almost deny its influence altogether, I shall venture on nothing more than problems."[100] The old idea that man cannot live in a climate whose temperature exceeds that of his own blood has to be abandoned, he says, but on the other hand we do not know enough about body temperature to possess a climatology applicable either to the body or to the mind. Herder also saw the fallacies of the climatic theories refurbished by Montesquieu (see pp. 565–581).

There is always room for an environmentalistic concept in the design argument because both lean so heavily on the idea of adaptation. Herder sees perspicacity in the distribution of the earth's habitable land: the Southern Hemisphere was created to be the large reservoir of the earth's water in order that the Northern could enjoy a better climate. "Thus, whether we consider the World geographically, or climatically, we find Nature intended mankind to be neighbourly beings, dwelling together, and imparting to each other climatic warmth, and other benefits, as well as the plague, diseases, and climatic vices."[101]

Herder is well aware, however, that if men are adapted to differing en-

---

[98] *Ibid.*, Bk. II, chap. 3, Churchill trans., p. 36.
[99] *Ibid.*, Bk. VII, chap. 1, Churchill trans., p. 164.
[100] *Ibid.*, chap. 2 *ad fin*, Churchill trans., p. 172.
[101] *Ibid.*, chap. 3, Churchill trans., p. 175.

vironments, whether they be physical or cultural, they are also able to change them. Man's use of fire, steel, plants and animals and his fellow men has had profound geographical consequences. "Once Europe was a dank forest; and other regions, at present well cultivated, were the same. They are now exposed to the rays of the Sun; and the inhabitants themselves have changed with the climate." Anticipating a popular theme of the nineteenth century of reciprocal influences of nature on man and man on nature, Herder observes that an environment changed by man in turn influences him.

The face of Egypt would have been nothing more than the slime of the Nile, but for the art and policy of man. He has gained it from the flood; and both there, and in farther Asia, the living creation has adapted itself to the artificial climate. We may consider mankind, therefore, as a band of bold though diminutive giants [das Menschengeschlecht als eine Schaar kühner, obwol kleiner Riesen], gradually descending from the mountains, to subjugate the earth, and change climates with their feeble arms. How far they are are capable of going in this respect futurity will show.[102]

More admonitory, more critical of human activity than was Buffon (see p. 665), Herder says man should avoid reckless and abrupt changes in the physical environment. "One should not suppose that human art can with despotic power at once transform a foreign region into a Europe by cutting down its forests and cultivating its soil. For the whole living creation is closely interrelated; one should act prudently in altering this interdependence."

Herder was impressed by Peter Kalm's observations on the effects of the European settlement of North America. The Swedish naturalist was struck by the newness of cultivation, the differences between the European and the Indian uses of the woods, the Indians scarcely interfering with them except for small local firings. Kalm agreed with a common belief that the Europeans had been the first since the creation to put the land under the plow, thus heightening the contrast between environments changed by man and the stability of the pristine natural order. The birds have diminished because Europeans cut down their forest habitats, frightened them away, or exterminated them; the multiplication of mills, the variety of gear, had similarly reduced the numbers of fish. Clearing and drainage of swamps had changed the climate. Kalm was most critical of agricultural methods, particularly the prolonged use of newly cleared land and deforestation. "We can hardly be more hostile towards our woods in Sweden and Finland than they are here: their eyes are fixed upon the present gain, and they are blind to the future." Everywhere Kalm saw evidences of the wisdom and goodness of God in creating nature in its original state; it was man who was failing to use it with understanding. Herder was sympathetic to such religious ideas;

---

[102] *Ibid.*, p. 176. "Arms" is Churchill's trans. of "die Erde zu unterjochen und das Klima mit ihrem schwachen Faust zu verändern."

no wonder he thought prudence was required in interfering with natural processes.[103]

Like Buffon, Herder was struck with Hugh Williamson's essay concerning the warming effects of clearing on the climate of the middle colonies of North America, and the healthful effects of drainage.[104] "Nature," says Herder, "is everywhere a living whole [ein lebendiges Ganze], and will be gently followed and improved, not mastered by force."[105]

To Herder nature is a kind parent, a teacher of mankind.

> What man of understanding, who contemplates the structure of our Earth, and the relation man bears to it, would not incline to think, that the father of our race, who has determined how far and how wide nations should spread, has also determined this, as the general teacher of us all? Will he who views a ship deny the purpose of its builder? and who, that compares the artificial frame of our nature with every climate of the habitable Earth, will reject the notion, that the climatic diversity of various man was an end of the creation for the purpose of educating his mind?[106]

Herder adds, however, that the place of abode does not affect everything, for we as living human beings instruct and influence one another.

Man must consider his own history, his traditions, his customs. In his interpretation of the historical experience of man, Herder concludes that the principal law is this, *"that every where on our Earth whatever could be has been, according to the situation and wants of the place, the circumstances and occasions of the times, and the native or generated character of the people."*[107]

Herder's work is the flowering of a philosophy of man and nature which

---

[103] Herder's *Ideen*, Bk. VII, chap. 5, par. 3. This passage trans. by Glacken. Peter Kalm, *Travels in North America*, Vol. I, pp. 51, 60, 97, 152–154, 275, 307–309, covering entries from Sept. 22, 1748, to May 18, 1749. See also Chinard, "Eighteenth Century Theories on America as a Human Habitat," *Proceedings of the American Philosophical Society*, Vol. 91 (1947), pp. 27–57, and Glacken, "Count Buffon on Cultural Changes of the Physical Environment," *AAAG*, Vol. 50 (1960), pp. 1–21; reference on pp. 19–20. "This is the account given by Kalm," Herder adds, "and however local we may consider it, still it shows, that Nature loves not too speedy, too violent a change, even in the best work, that men can perform, the cultivation of a country" (*Ideen*, Bk. VII, chap. 5, Churchill trans., p. 186).

[104] See below, pp. 659–661 and Hugh Williamson, M.D., "An Attempt to Account for the CHANGE OF CLIMATE, Which Has Been Observed in the Middle Colonies in North-America," *Transactions of the American Philosophical Society*, Vol. 1 (second edition corrected, 1789), pp. 336–345. Herder refers to a German translation in the *Berliner Sammlung*, Theil VII. On the French translation of Williamson see Glacken, *op. cit.*, p. 11, footnote 39.

[105] *Ideen*, Bk. VII, chap. 5, Churchill trans., p. 187.

[106] *Ibid.*, Bk. IX, chap. 1, Churchill trans., p. 227.

[107] "Dass allenthalben auf unsrer Erde werde, was auf ihr werden kann, theils nach Lage und Bedürfniss des Orts, theils nach Umständen und Gelegenheiten der Zeit, theils nach dem angebornen oder sich erzeugenden Charakter der Völker" (*ibid.*, Bk. XII, chap. 6, Churchill trans., p. 348).

in his time had reached its zenith and was beginning to decline, even granting the superiority of his eclecticism over some of the more dogmatic ideas of men like Montesquieu. The design—the fitness of the earth as an environment, the fitness of humanity to live on it, the influence of humanity on the earth and of the earth on humanity—admirably as it was worked out by Herder, still was formed in an old mold. When Friedrich Ratzel criticized Herder, whom he greatly admired, for fantasies about the earth being the nursery and the cradle of mankind, as if the whole earth—and not just a few favored parts of it—was like a pleasant estate, Ratzel should have added, to place his criticism in proper perspective, that Herder was speaking not for himself but for a tradition which he had enriched and which had glorified this view of nature for centuries.[108] Herder's work was a glorious sunset; the sunrises belong to Hume, Kant, Goethe, and Alexander von Humboldt.

## 10. HUMBOLDT

If indeed there was such a sunset, what other view of nature was possible at the end of the eighteenth century, considering the exploration that had taken place, the interest in natural history, the discussions of final causes? One can see, I think, such possibilities emerging in the *Essai sur la Géographie des Plantes* and the *Tableau Physique des Régions Équinoxiales* first published in French in 1805 by Humboldt and Bonpland. (A full-scale analysis of Humboldt's ideas on these subjects is beyond the scope of this work; many of the ideas however developed in Humboldt's later work are mentioned in these short essays.) The titles of these essays do not suggest the broad philosophy of nature which they express. The *Essai sur la Géographie des Plantes* is more than a landmark in the history of plant geography (as it is usually considered); Humboldt himself obviously considered it a fundamental program for the study of nature.[109] His view òf nature is more specific and detailed than earlier ones mainly because he had traveled so widely and had made many observations personally; it is free of teleological explanations and takes into account both modifications of nature by man and environmental influences on him.

Humboldt dedicated the *Essai* to Goethe, saying he had conceived the idea of the work in early youth, expressing also his gratitude to George Forster, who had accompanied his father, the botanist, on Cook's second voyage (1772–1775). Humboldt had traveled to England with George Forster in 1790 and had submitted an early draft of a geography of plants to him. Study of several of the physical-mathematical sciences, he added, had given him the opportunity to broaden his views, but above all it was the materials

---

[108] *Anthropogeographie*, Part II, pp. 3–4.
[109] *Tableau Physique*, pp. 42–43; *Naturgemälde*, p. 39.

he gathered in the tropics which contributed to "l'histoire physique du globe."[110] It is with the Forsters' and Humboldt's work that the great world of the tropics, seen from the point of view of contemporary science, begins to exert its influence on conceptions of nature. Later we see this continuing in Darwin and Wallace.

Although Humboldt did not disparage botanical activity—the search for new species, descriptions of the external form of plants, taxonomy—it was necessary, he said, to recognize that the equally important study of plant geography was an essential segment of general science still existing in name only.[111] It is not enough, he says, to study the geography of plants according to zones or altitude or even in relation to air pressure, temperature, humidity, electric tension, but to consider them also according to their manner of living: those which grow singly and are dispersed, and those—like the bees and the ants among the insects—that are the social plants.[112]

It would be interesting, he continues, to map these areas of plant assemblages of the same species; they would appear like long bands whose irresistible extension lessens the population of states, separates neighboring nations, and offers greater obstacles than do the mountains and the seas to communication and commerce. In the German edition, he speaks of these bands as being "now heath, now grassy plains—the steppes and the savannas." In showing the relation of these social plants (the assemblages of plants of one species) to human society, he cites as an example the associations *Erica vulgaris, Erica tetralix, Lichen icmadophila* and *haematomma* spreading out from the northernmost extremity of Jutland through Holstein and Lüneberg to the fifty-second parallel, turning then west through the granitic sands of Münster and Breda, and on to the Channel.[113] Human modifications of the heath landscape are described as little enclaves of a substituted plant life whose fresh greenness—a man-created oasis—is contrasted with the surrounding areas of barren heath. Here man's task (in which he has been only partly successful) is envisaged as a struggle with nature in order to substitute a new kind of plant life for that which had dominated these regions for centuries.[114] Contrasting the original cover with man's substitutions, Humboldt says that a moss, *Sphagnum palustre*, a social plant, once covered a large part of Ger-

---

[110] *Essai*, pp. vi–vii. *Ideen*, German ed. 1807, pp. iii–iv. The latter is not an exact translation of the former, and contains ideas and illustrations not found in the French ed.

[111] "Science dont il n'existe encore que le nom, et qui cependant fait un partie essentielle de la physique générale" (*Essai*, p. 1).

[112] *Essai*, pp. 14–15.

[113] *Ibid.*, p. 17.

[114] "Ces végétaux, depuis une longue suite de siècles, répandent la stérilité sur le sol et exercent un empire absolu sur ces régions: l'homme, malgré ses efforts, luttant contre une nature presque indomptable, ne leur a enlevé que peu de terrain pour la culture" (*Essai*, p. 18).

many; the clearing of the forest by agricultural peoples lowered the humidity, the bogs gradually disappeared, and useful plants have replaced the moss.

Humboldt contrasts these dreary areas with the vast species variety of the tropical lands, although even they have the social plants in the higher mountains. Single and scattered species form the dense stands of the tropical rain forest, whose density, compared with that of Europe, leads Humboldt to interesting speculations on the origin of agriculture in the Old and in the New World. The first traces of agriculture begin when the nomad gives up his way of life and begins gathering the useful plants and animals about him. This transition from nomadism to agriculture was late among the northern peoples. In the tropical regions between the Orinoco and the Amazon—the German edition uses the old name, Marañon—the density of the forest prevents the primitive people from getting food from the hunt. Fishing, the fruits of the palm, small cultivated patches, are the subsistence bases of the Indians of South America.[115] In the German edition, however, Humboldt says that the depth and the swiftness of the streams, floods, bloodthirsty crocodiles and boa constrictors, make fishing profitless and laborious, and Nature here forces man to cultivate plants. Everywhere the condition (*état*) of the savage is altered by the nature of the climate and soil which he inhabits. These modifications alone distinguish the first inhabitants of Greece from the nomadic Bedouins, and the latter from the Indians of Canada.[116] Humboldt thus attempts to explain by environmental causation a problem which had puzzled Lord Kames in 1775: that the assumed universal sequence in the cultural development of mankind from a hunting and fishing stage to pastoralism and then agriculture was not true of the New World.

Pursuing the themes both of environmental change by man and of environmental influences on him, Humboldt points to the efficiency—and caprice—of human influence in the dissemination of plants throughout the world; man gathers about him the products of the most remote climates, and his agriculture establishes the dominion of foreign-plant invaders, sheltered by him over the indigenous ones which are pressed into an ever-narrowing space. The general result of such activity is a monotony of the scenery of highly civilized countries with large populations.[117]

Humboldt emphasizes the overwhelming luxuriance of plant life in the tropical world, but it does lack the tender greens, grassy plains and meadows of the temperate lands. In one remark with a teleological flavor, he says that

[115] *Essai*, pp. 24–25. See also *Ideen*, pp. 16–17.
[116] But in the German edition the statement is different though the thought is the same. "So modificiren Klima und Boden, mehr noch als Abstammung, die Lage und die Sitten des Wilden. Sie bestimmen den Unterschied zwischen den beduinischen Hirtenvölkern und den Pelasgern der altgriechischen Eichenwälder, zwischen diesen und den jagdliebenden Nomaden am Mississipi" (*Ideen*, p. 17).
[117] *Essai*, pp. 25–28.

a careful Nature has given each zone its own advantages. Anticipating themes he later developed at length in his history of ideas concerning nature in the *Kosmos*, Humboldt asks what influence plant distribution—and the sight of plants—have on the imagination (*Phantasie*) and artistic sensitivity (*Kunstsinn*). In what does the character of the vegetation of this land or that consist? Does the character of the vegetation conjure up sensations in the soul of him who contemplates it?[118] Inquiries of this type are all the more interesting because they are directly related to the mysterious means by which landscape painting and even descriptive poetry in part exert their influence. Of all the geographers nourished in the Western civilization, Humboldt in this passage and in his voluminous writings on the same subject in later life clearly sees a common ground shared by geography and aesthetics. Subjective, suggesting aesthetic and psychological theory as well, this field of study has never been pursued with the ardor shown for other kinds of systematic geography whether cultural or physical. It is true that many geographers have often written on themes of nature appreciation and beauty of natural scenery, but this writing was then as it is today a literary rather than a professional genre. It is only since the creation of so much ugliness in the landscape since the latter half of the nineteenth century that one sees the great loss to a discipline like geography which lacks a strong historical base in aesthetics and art history.

Viewing nature as a whole, the sight of meadows and forests engenders an enjoyment different from that which the study of an organic body and its wonderful structure arouses. The detail of the latter excites the desire for knowledge; the ensemble, the great mass of the former, works on the imagination. How different are the feelings aroused by the fresh green of the meadow and the dark shadows of the fir! Does the difference in feelings thus aroused lie in the very greatness of the mass, in absolute beauty, or in the contrast, in the grouping of plant forms? In what does the pictorial advantage of tropical vegetation lie?[119]

The inhabitant of the tropical lands can enjoy the sight of all plant forms, an enjoyment in which the European peoples to whom many plant forms are unknown cannot participate. The Europeans, however, have their own substitutes in the richness and perfection of their languages, in the imagination of their poets and painters. With the enchantment of an art imitating nature, the European without leaving his home can rise to magnificent conceptions of nature, appropriating for his own the discoveries of the bravest explorers. It is through this ability to make use of the far-off, the exotic, what is unknown at home, that we acquire the insights which exert the most influence on our individual happiness: we can see the present and the past, the varying pro-

---

[118] *Essai*, p. 30, *Ideen*, pp. 24, 30.
[119] *Essai*, p. 30; *Ideen*, pp. 24–25.

ductions of nature in different climates, and we are in communication with all the peoples of the earth. Sustained by past discoveries, we continue into the future, advancing in the discovery of laws of nature. It is in the environment of such inquiries that we have intellectual pleasure, a moral freedom fortifying us against the blows of fate, and which cannot be destroyed by any exterior force.

The same philosophy permeates the more detailed essay, *Tableau Physique des Régions Équatoriales*; it is a program for nature as a whole. "Dans ce grand enchaînement de causes et d'effets, aucun fait ne peut être considéré isolément," for Humboldt sees a general equilibrium of nature transcending the play of opposing forces.[120]

In this essay (following the principle of unity underlying diversity and of equilibrium and balance in nature) Humboldt shows the altitudinal distribution of plants, animals, even of rocks, on the famous map of Chimborazo, adding a plea for similar maps for the polar, temperate, and equatorial zones and for others showing the contrasts between the Northern and Southern Hemispheres and the Old and the New Worlds. It was Humboldt's ambition to put flesh on the bones of the principle of unity in diversity through worldwide botanical exploration followed by the publication of the results on suitable maps.

Here too he is sympathetic to an old environmental theory (which reappears in various forms in his later writings), the stimulus of hard environments—first mentioned by Herodotus and advanced in modern dress, more elaborately and with greater sophistication, by Arnold Toynbee. The degree of civilization attained by peoples bears an inverse relationship to the fertility of their soil and the beneficence and luxuriance of the nature which surrounds them: the more nature opposes obstacles to surmount, the more rapidly are the social factors developed. In essence the theory is a variant of the idea of necessity being the mother of invention.[121]

Assuming the greater richness and fertility of the wet tropics (a conception of tropical soils which has lasted in some quarters to the present), Humboldt asks why civilization developed not there but in the temperate lands. Why did New World civilization prosper in the high plains of the Andes and not on the shores of great rivers; why do the Indians prefer to live at an altitude of 3,300 meters under an unfriendly sky, cultivating their stony ground, when fertile plains at the base of the mountains lie hardly a day's journey from their huts? Humboldt thinks they remain in these inhospitable lands because of love of their native land and the force of custom; he compares settlements at high altitudes here with similar places in Europe, remarking that in Peru there are cities at altitudes at which in Europe there are only

---

[120] *Tableau Physique*, pp. 42–43.
[121] *Ibid.*, pp. 139–140; *Naturgemälde*, pp. 168–169.

transhumant huts. This is all casual and sketchy but it hints too at a human geography that cannot be explained by environment alone, that encompasses customs and cultural inertia, that can profit by comparison of environments.[122]

Humboldt's views of nature were noble as were those of the Forsters and Buffon, breathing the air of freedom and free inquiry.[123] He showed what a gifted, sensitive, well-traveled student of man and nature could achieve in the late eighteenth and early nineteenth centuries; the inspiration of his example can be traced readily in the writings of many famous naturalists of the nineteenth century from Skouw in Denmark to the paragraphs of a grateful Darwin. It was probably the best conception of living nature that could be achieved with existing knowledge before the Darwinian theory of evolution. It would be a great mistake, however, to think of an easy path in the history of natural history from Humboldt to Darwin, for we would fail to take into account the spectacular vigor—if not the intellectual depth—of believers in the design argument, in final causes within the framework of Christian theology. Lyell recognized the opposition of the physico-theologists. In June, 1830, he wrote to Poulette Scrope, "If you don't triumph over them, but compliment the liberality and candour of the present age, the bishops and enlightened saints will join us in despising both the ancient and modern physico-theologians."[124] The vitality of the design argument of the teleological view of nature in geography was clear in the works of Humboldt's friend, Carl Ritter. A voluminous "following in the footsteps of the Creator" literature accumulated in the nineteenth century as if Spinoza, Buffon, Kant, Goethe, Humboldt had never criticized design arguments.

## 11. Conclusion

Eighteenth century nature study stood on the shoulders of that of the seventeenth, but to vary an old figure of speech, it was not a dwarf on the shoulders of a giant; the two were comparable in strength. The march of thought from Burnet to Ray created its own *grand spectacle de la nature*. In the eighteenth century, within a teleological framework or outside of it, many students were moved and inspired by the new opportunities for nature study; they ignored the spirit of Pope's schoolmasterish instructions about not scanning God and about the proper study of mankind. The exclamation points of Buffon and Bernardin de St. Pierre and others were not mere rhetoric. Neither were the ecstatic remarks of Leibniz. The infinitely small and the near, the infinitely large and the far, brought into view by the microscope and the

---

[122] *Tableau*, pp. 139–141.

[123] For more extensive development of these ideas see Humboldt's introduction to the *Cosmos*.

[124] K. M. Lyell, *Life of Charles Lyell*, Vol. I, 271. See also Gillispie, *Genesis and Geology*, p. 133, to whom I am indebted for this reference.

telescope, now old friends, gave substance and depth to the grand array. In the hands of the naturalists, organic themes flourished, fed on speculation, travel, engravings, and plant collecting. *Le grand spectacle de la nature* underlay the philosophy of De Pluche, St. Pierre, Linnaeus, Pallas, Buffon, Goethe, and the Forsters.

Involved in this nature study was also the problem of physical evil. The *tout est bien* philosophy of Pope and Dr. Pangloss is frequently discussed with reference to optimism in the social world, but it is pertinent also in interpreting the processes of nature. The doctrine of final causes obscured the distinction between the earth and the physical processes which account for its beauties and convenience, its earthquakes, violent storms, volcanic eruptions, slides, and the human world manifested concretely in the geography of human settlement. The physical evil visited upon mankind as a result of such catastrophes depends upon the numbers and distribution of people. People living in a metropolis that lies on a fault or in a village at the foot of a live volcano cannot expect their presence to alter conditions that bring about earthquakes and eruptions.

Furthermore, the relationship of final causes to mental processes was seen with greater perspicuity by Hume and Kant than by any of their predecessors. Hume's analysis of the meaning of artisanship and Kant's saying that the organization of nature has nothing analogous to causality known to us called attention to the participation of the human mind in constructing a concept of nature. This truth is quite apparent today in the idea of an ecosystem. In implying that human intelligence gives a meaning to nature which animals, lacking higher understanding, and plants cannot, Kant suggests that men may strive for an enlightened and satisfying understanding of the creation within their own set of values; it seems akin to an existentialist idea.

One can see in Hume's dialogues what the struggle for existence in nature means when the web of design is shorn off. Conflict and competition become meaningless; a niggardly nature is quite in contrast with the bountiful mother of design. In the nineteenth century, men will often hear this phrase from Malthus and others struck by the contrast between the fecundity of life and the availability of food. When the protective cover of design is removed, lesser ideas escape and assert themselves like children rebelling from their parents. The idea of progress has similarly concealed supposedly minor failures in the millennial march of civilization. Remove it, and these failures stand on their own feet. Many trends in civilization no longer appear to be in necessary harmony with one another. The growth of knowledge and the progress of technology might not accompany progress in ethics and the decline of warfare; these in turn may not inevitably bring about the better use of the soils and the preservation of the forests.

By the nineteenth century, the decline of the older physico-theology had already begun; with Lamarck and Darwin attention is focused on adaptation to environment. They begin the task, building on this older thought, of creating a new concept of interrelationships in nature, the web of life; their successors followed with biotic communities, and finally the ecosystem.

Teleology did not vanish in the mechanistic monisms of the nineteenth century. A secular version and critiques of it superseded the older theologically oriented teleology and its critics. The idea of progress, Marxism, the Darwinian theory, have their own teleologies. Later studies of biotic communities, especially those with holistic overtones, have strong if submerged links with teleology. For teleological explanation and analysis of apparent "goal-directed activity" (Braithwaite) are still forces in thought. They can concern any field.[125] Does not a linguist ask if a language is evolving toward greater simplicity of grammar or greater precision in meaning, or if there is simply a rearrangement superseding the old? Do not such questions constantly recur in attempts to see emergent patterns and evolution in human society? In the man-earth relationship, Kant was correct, in my opinion, in saying that teleological explanation breaks down. The caprice of human acts and a wide variety of motives lead to environmental change. What man creates on the surface of the earth, the lines, the squares, the contours, the leveled areas and the entrenched are not consequences of societal evolution as a whole but of different cultural histories. The matching of earth changes with societal aspiration could be brought about only by dictatorship of land use by a world government. But then this would be not teleology but planning. Some may believe in the teleological development of a culture or of a society, but it is hard to believe, as did Leibniz, that there is a concomitant and coordinate change of the earth with the progress of civilization.

Teleology will be with us for a long time because it is an expression in ever-recurring form of the quest for meaning in man, in nature, and in the relationship between the two. For as much as we rightly insist that mankind is part of nature, we must still isolate human activities as a unique force requiring special techniques for study and its own philosophy. It is wrong to say that the Western tradition has emphasized the contrast between man and nature without adding that it has also emphasized the union of the two. The contrasting viewpoints arise both because man is unique and because he shares life and mortality with the rest of the living creation.

---

[125] See Braithwaite, *Scientific Explanation*, pp. 319–341.

# Chapter 12

# Climate, the Moeurs, Religion, and Government

### 1. Introduction

The sharp, often witty, apothegms of Montesquieu surprised his age, his bold climatic correlations convincing many of his freshness and originality, but a lightness of touch did not conceal his knowledge of the classical world, western Europe, and the post-Columbian literature of travel. So great was Montesquieu's influence on his contemporaries, and on those who subsequently read him, that he seemed to appear with fresh tidings—commanding and unannounced—a hundred and fifty years after Bodin. Voltaire saw this error; other Frenchmen of modern times—Bodin, Fontenelle, Chardin, and the abbé du Bos—had written about climate, and Voltaire saw also their kinship with the thinkers of antiquity. Critical of Montesquieu but disdainful of his critics, Voltaire said, "The author of the 'Spirit of Laws,' without quoting authorities, carried this idea [of climatic influence] farther than du Bos, Chardin and Bodin. Certain classes believe him to have first suggested it, and imputed it to him as a crime. This was quite in character with the classes referred to. There are men everywhere who possess more zeal than understanding."[1]

Voltaire's point was well taken, for continuities in thought had not been broken. Ideas of environmental influence, as we have seen, had begun to perform important functions. Pierre Charron, for example, showed his disbelief in revelation, in the truth of Judaism, Christianity, and Mohammedanism by making the climate of Arabia responsible for all of them.[2]

Furthermore, there had been no lagging of interest in health and medicine. If Hippocrates—and Galen—had been regarded in the Middle Ages as if he were a Christian doctor, he had become in the Renaissance, and in the seventeenth and eighteenth centuries as well, less a symbol of Christian medicine, more the archetype of the empirical observer whose observations began with nature and with nature alone, and he was even believed by some to espouse atheism.[3] Throughout the eighteenth century the extravagant admiration for Hippocrates continued among the doctors; it was scarcely less among students of man for the *Airs, Waters, Places*.

### 2. FONTENELLE, CHARDIN, AND DU BOS

If environmental causation was related to religion and health, it was also concerned with historical change, with travel and exploration, with the geographical distribution of human achievement. Let us first look at these men whom Voltaire mentioned—Fontenelle, Chardin, and the abbé du Bos—to see what they had to say in the days before Montesquieu tried, in his famous experiment with the sheep's tongue (see p. 569) to put the investigation of climatic influences on a scientific basis.

In his essay *On the Ancients and Moderns*, Fontenelle had tried to bring some sense into the discussion of the relative merits of both; this had involved Fontenelle and many others in the more fundamental inquiry into the validity of applying the organic analogy to nature as a whole (see above, p. 390). Taking a position reminiscent of that of Polybius, Fontenelle assumes that the original mental characteristics of peoples are derived from their climates; these however are lost later because men influence one another's minds. Showing an awareness of the force of imitation and culture contact (which Hume possessed in greater measure in the next century), Fontenelle added:

> The reading of Greek books produces in us much the same effect as if we intermarried solely with Greeks. It is certain, that as a result of such frequent alliances, the blood of Greece and that of France would alter, and that the facial

---

[1] "Climat," in *Dictionnaire philosophique*, Morley trans. Text in *Oeuvres*, ed. Beuchot, Vol. 28, p. 115.

[2] Charron, *Of Wisdom* (1601), p. 258. See chap. IX, sec. 8.

[3] Deichgräber, "Goethe und Hippokrates," *Sudhoffs Archiv für Geschichte der Medizin und der Naturwissenschaften*, Vol. 29 (1936), pp. 27–56, ref. on p. 27.

characteristics peculiar to the two nations would undergo some change. . . . [Since the effects of climate are inconclusive and one influence might offset another,] it follows that differences in climate may be discounted, provided the minds in question are otherwise equally cultivated. At the most it might be credited that the Torrid Zone and the two Polar Regions are not particularly well suited to the development of the sciences. Up to the present these have not extended their influence farther than Egypt and Mauritania on the one hand and Sweden on the other; perhaps it is not wholly a matter of chance that they have been restricted to the territory between Mt. Atlas and the Baltic Sea; we do not know that these are not boundaries which nature has imposed upon them, and whether we can ever hope to see great scientists among the Lapps or Negroes.

Fontenelle leaves open the question whether there are geographic areas of conspicuous achievement but he rejects environmental explanations for differences between the peoples of the ancient and the modern world. Anticipating Hume again, he continues:

> The centuries produce no natural difference between men. The climate of Greece or of Italy and that of France are too nearly alike to cause any sensible difference between the Greeks or the Latins and ourselves. Even if they should produce a difference of some sort, it would be very easy to efface, and finally, it would be no more to their advantage than to ours. We are all, then, perfectly equal, ancients and moderns, Greeks, Latins, and French.[4]

Voltaire, critical of Chardin and the abbé du Bos, quoted the "ingenious Fontenelle" approvingly.

The *Journal du Voyage du Chevalier Chardin*, especially the *Voyage en la Perse*, was a famous and influential travel book of the seventeenth century. Sir John Chardin (1643–1713) was a jeweler and a trader in jewels, occupations which enticed him not only to Persia but to India as well. His book is an interesting but matter-of-fact account which stresses business and trade, often, however, describing with zest the customs of the people. Chardin's observations furnished apparent proof of the ancient belief in the effeteness of the East as a whole, of the backwardness of the Persians, and in particular the unchanging nature of their society. Chardin ascribed these conditions to climate:

> . . . The hot Climates enervate the Mind as well as the Body, lay the quickness of the Fancy, necessary for the invention and improvement of Arts. In those Climates the Men are not capable of Night Watchings, and of a close Application, which brings forth the valuable Works of the Liberal, and of the Mechanick Arts. 'Tis by the same Reason likewise, that the Knowledge of the *Asiaticks* is

---

[4] Bernard Le Bovier de Fontenelle, "Digression sur les Anciens et les Modernes," *Oeuvres* (nouvelle édition, A la Haye, 1728), Vol. 2. The passages here quoted in translation are on p. 127. I am indebted to the translation of Leona Fasset, made for the selection from Fontenelle, in Teggart (revised by Hildebrand), *The Idea of Progress, A Collection of Readings*, pp. 177–178.

so restrained that it consists only in learning and repeating what is contain'd in the books of the Ancients; and that their Industry lies Fallow and Untill'd, if I may so express my self. 'Tis in the North only we must look for the highest improvement and the greatest perfection of the Arts and sciences.[5]

Of this passage, Voltaire wrote, "But Chardin did not recollect that Sadi and Lokman were Persians, nor that Archimedes belonged to Sicily, where the heat is greater than in three-fourths of Persia. He forgot that Pythagoras once taught geometry to the Brahmins."[6]

Modern travel, the observation and the description of non-European peoples, could thus give verisimilitude to the judgments of antiquity, even though the places involved were different. Chardin's may not be the first modern work—it certainly was one of the earliest—to offer an environmental explanation for the "unchanging East" (so popular among European and American writers even up to World War II), the contrast between China, Persia, and India on the one hand and western Europe on the other being one between cultural persistence and cultural change.

The third work mentioned by Voltaire—also important and influential—was the abbé du Bos' study of genius. The connection with Chardin is direct, for the abbé cited Homer's eulogy of Ulysses as appropriate to honor Sir John's accomplishments.[7]

Du Bos was interested in a question which, as we have seen, had also interested both ancient and modern thinkers: the clustering of human genius, or of certain kinds of talent at certain periods of history. Or in Du Bos's words, "Tous les siècles ne sont pas également fertiles en grands Artisans."[8]

Du Bos dismisses moral, that is, social, causes, as adequate explanations of the distribution of gifted artists in place and time. Moral causes—a happy state of affairs in a country, the interest of the ruler and the citizen in literature and the arts, the presence of qualified teachers—create a favorable environment for the arts but do not really add any more *esprit* to the artists; they make no change whatsoever in nature. They provide opportunities for artists to perfect their genius, moral causes making their work easier, stimulating them through emulation and by rewards for study and application. Four centuries, he says, have been admired by all subsequent ones: the first, beginning ten years before the reign of Philip of Macedon; the second, of Julius Caesar and

[5] *The Travels of Sir John Chardin in Persia*, Vol. 2, p. 257.

[6] "Climat," *Dict. philos., op. cit.*

[7] *Reflexions Critiques sur la Poesie et sur la Peinture*, Quatriéme édition revue, corrigée & augmentée par l'auteur. The work first appeared in 1719. See also Koller, *The Abbé du Bos—His Advocacy of the Theory of Climate. A Precursor of Johann Gottfried Herder.* This work has an interesting introductory essay on the place of Du Bos's work in the history of aesthetics; it also contains translations of many key passages and in essence is a précis of the environmental portions of the book. I have emphasized, as Koller did not, the significance of Fontenelle's discussions of climate and of Barclay's *Icon Animorum.*

[8] *Reflex.*, Vol. 2, p. 128. See chap. IX, sec. 7.

of Augustus; the third, of Julius II and of Leo X; and the fourth, of Louis XIV.[9] Remarking that men often attribute to moral causes effects which really are the result of physical ones, Du Bos questions whether the former can explain periods of artistic efflorescence; often the arts do not flourish with moral causes favorable to them, and an Achilles does not always have his Homer. Arts and letters do not reach their perfection by a slow progress, proportional to the time spent in cultivating them—progress is sudden. Furthermore, moral causes have failed to hold achievement at its peak level, have been unable to prevent its subsequent decline.[10]

Du Bos discusses each of these points at length. In the first place, poetry and painting have a well-defined geographical distribution: the genuine arts are confined to Europe, the poleward march of poetry and painting stops at Holland. (The arts he confines between the twenty-fifth and the fifty-second degrees of north latitude.)[11] Du Bos now combines the ideas of Velleius Paterculus with those of Fontenelle. Paterculus had observed this clustering effect in the ancient world. Du Bos, however, is more selective in his borrowings from Fontenelle, from whom he quotes the following passage:

> Different ideas are like plants or flowers which do not thrive equally well in all sorts of climates. Perhaps our French soil is not suited to the Egyptian manner of thinking any more than to their palm trees; and, without going so far afield, perhaps the orange trees, which do not thrive so well here as in Italy, are an indication that in Italy there is a certain turn of thought which is not exactly duplicated in France. It is certain, at least, that, because of the connection and inter-dependence existing between all parts of the material world, the differences in climate which affect plants must needs influence brains also.

Fontenelle, however, added—and Du Bos did not quote this—"In the latter case, however, the effect is less pronounced and less obvious, for art and culture can exercise a much greater influence upon brains than upon the soil, which is of a harder and more intractable nature. Hence the thoughts of one country are more readily conveyed to another than are plants, and we should experience less difficulty in adopting the Italian genius in our works than in raising orange trees."[12]

Fontenelle continues with his criticism of environmental explanations, coming to the conclusions I have already quoted. And so while Du Bos is lamenting that a talented writer like Fontenelle has not pursued this matter further, he parts company, either intentionally or carelessly, with Fontenelle at the point where the latter becomes critical of environmental theories, friendly to moral causes! Du Bos concludes that arts arise by themselves in climates fa-

[9] *Ibid.*, pp. 130, 134–135.
[10] *Ibid.*, pp. 146–148.
[11] *Ibid.*, pp. 148, 150–151.
[12] "On the Ancients and Moderns," in Teggart and Hildebrand, *op. cit.* (see n. 4 above), pp. 176–177, translating "Digression sur les Anciens et les Modernes," *op. cit.*, Vol. 2, p. 126; quoted in Du Bos, Vol. 2, pp. 149–150.

vorable to them. "Les arts naissent d'euxmêmes sous les climats qui leur sont propres.") He believes sculpture and painting originated in Egypt because its climate favored their development. Arts will arise in countries suited to them if they are not introduced; they might appear a little late, but appear they will. The arts do not flourish in climates unsuited to them.

Du Bos thought the seat of genuine art was Europe, that it suffered in quality as it became removed from that continent. He granted that other peoples were inventive; but although the Chinese discovered gunpowder and printing, this was merely chance! and Europe had so perfected both inventions that it could now give lessons to their Chinese inventors. The abbé discusses sculpture and painting in Egypt, their further development by the Greeks and Italians, dismisses as mediocre the art revealed by Chardin's drawings of Persepolis; he is condescending to "d'étoffes, de porcelaine, & des autres curiositez de la Chine & de l'Asie Orientale," concluding that the artists of Mexico and Peru were without genius, that if the Brahmans and ancient Persians had produced a poet of Homer's stature the voyaging Greeks would have had him in their libraries.[13]

This argument is supported by an elaborate theory concerning the power of air over the body and of the body over the mind and the soul, for during life the soul remains united with the body. The character of the human spirit and our inclinations depend a great deal on the qualities of the blood which nourishes our organs and furnishes the material which permits their growth during infancy and adolescence. The qualities of the blood, in turn, depend a great deal on the air which is breathed; they depend even more on the quality of the air in the place where a person has been reared, because it has determined the qualities of the blood during infancy. These qualities of the air thus have contributed to the conformation of the organs, which in turn through necessary linkages contribute in maturity to the qualities of our blood. It is for these reasons peoples living under different climates differ so greatly in spirit and inclinations.[14]

The qualities of the air are dependent on the qualities of emanations from the earth which the air envelops. Since earth emanations are different, the air is different. Earth is a mixed body, subject to varying fermentations; the emanations therefore vary, changing the air and influencing the nature of peoples.

Du Bos observes that in France certain generations are more spiritually inclined (*plus spirituelles*) than others. These differences among generations living in the same climate, he says, have the same cause as do the differences among peoples living in different climates. Physical causes determine the climatic variations, and these determine the quality of the harvest from one year to another. There is an organic linkage, cyclical in nature, involving the air,

[13] *Reflex.*, Vol. 2, pp. 151, 156–157, 159–162.
[14] *Ibid.*, pp. 238–239.

the earth's surface, man, and the other forms of organic life. The air we breathe brings to the blood in the lungs the qualities infused in it; the air also deposits on the surface of the earth matter which contributes the most to its fertility. Men in working the soil—digging it up and manuring it—really are recognizing that the soil is much more fertile when a large number of particles have absorbed the matter from the air. Men eat some of the earth's products, leaving the rest to animals, whose flesh they subsequently convert to their own substance by eating it. The qualities of the air are also brought to the waters of springs and rivers by snow and rain, which are always infused with part of the corpuscles suspended in the air.[15]

This explanation assumes a complexity in the composition of the air permitting a large number of combinations with varying influences. Since the atmosphere is composed of air, emanations absorbed from the earth, animalcules and their seed, differences in the amounts of these constituents cause variations in the nature of the air, and these, of the products of nature dependent upon it.

The abbé du Bos is interested in two general kinds of human behavior: the different characteristics noticeable among people from one place to another, and the differences in mood and temperament of people living in the same place.

In order to explain both kinds of differences, he distinguishes between air having temporary qualities and that with permanent qualities owing to external causes like the sun and the wind. The changes which the permanent types of qualities produce in humans are called alterations, those which the temporary or transient qualities produce are vicissitudes. The differing effects of the sun because of its altitude, its proximity, the exposure, the nature of the terrain upon which its rays fall, are examples of vicissitudes; so are the winds which make air subject to change through cold and heat, aridity and humidity. Vicissitudes resulting from the air, reflected in our daily moods, are reminders that the influences of the permanent qualities on men—and especially on children—are much greater.

People's humors—even the esprit of adults—depend a great deal on the vicissitudes of the air. We change mechanically from gay to sad as the air is dry or humid, cold, hot, or temperate; we are content or peevish without motive (*sans sujet*), and we find it difficult to apply our minds to the tasks at hand. The "fermentation" in preparation for the storm so acts on our spirit that it becomes heavy, preventing us from thinking with our usual freedom of imagination; it even spoils our foods. Spells of excessive heat cause unusually high seasonal crime rates in Rome (if there are twenty crimes a year, fifteen are committed in the two hottest summer months); they can affect the suicide rate of France (in Paris, for every sixty suicides in the year, fifty occur at the

[15] *Ibid.*, p. 241.

beginning or at the end of winter, times when the northeast wind is blowing, blackening the sky and visibly afflicting the most robust). Annual differences in crimes rates cannot be ascribed, according to French magistrates, to scarcity of food, discharge of soldiers from the army, or to other "sensible" reasons. To Du Bos the causes are climatic.[16] He also discusses the effects of excessive cold. If vicissitudes can affect man's thinking and his imagination and temperament so much, if they can cause violence, crime, and suicide, how much greater, he says, must be the effects of the permanent qualities of the air. One notices their force in traveling from one climate to another. When permanent qualities are changed, they may cause epidemics. The air of one's birthplace is like a medicine; homesickness (*Hemvé*) to Du Bos is literally a bodily pain caused by the climate.[17]

In turning his attention to the more fundamental alterations—as distinguished from the vicissitudes—Du Bos asks: Why do men differ despite their descent from common parents? The divergence began with migration—it was a gradual process toward both the pole and the equator—and ten centuries were sufficient to make the descendants of the same parents as different as are the Negroes and the Swedes today. Further, Du Bos makes the traditional assumption that if climate produces differences in color, trunk, and voice, it also affects the subtler and less apparent characteristics of mankind. Its effects on the genius, inclinations, and customs of a country are even greater than on the physical because of the greater sensitivity both of the brain and of those parts of the body which determine, physically speaking, the esprit and inclinations of men; differences in air may be capable of causing mental differences (a convenient and resilient mixture is this air of Du Bos) even if they are not powerful enough to produce the grosser, visible physical differences.

The Portuguese experience in Africa, he says, supports his belief in the correctness of climatic explanations. It has been only three centuries since they established colonies on the west coast of Africa. No longer do the descendants of the first colonists resemble the Portuguese of Portugal. They have acquired the frizzed and curled hair, the flat nose and the thick lips of the Negro, although they continue to consider themselves white men. (If a colony of Negroes, however, were to establish itself in England, Du Bos says, the same influences would be at work and their skins would grow whitish.) Even considering the crude theories of heredity of the time, it is astonishing that it did not occur to Du Bos that the sexual unions between the races might have something to do with the changed hair, lips, and noses.[18]

Du Bos's example of the Roman Catholic religion, whose liturgy and dogma

---

[16] *Ibid.*, pp. 242–246. As Koller remarks, these observations on crime anticipate Lombroso's work, *op. cit.* (see n. 7 above), p. 72.

[17] *Ibid.*, pp. 249–250. On the word *Hemvé* see Koller, *op. cit.*, pp. 74–75. Du Bos adopts the word into French, borrowing from the German *Heimweh* and similar forms in the Scandinavian languages.

[18] *Ibid.*, pp. 251, 253–256.

(*le culte comme pour les dogmes*) are essentially the same in all countries with the Catholic communion, is more subtle and perceptive. Despite the common religion, each country reveals much of its unique character in its manner of worship (*dans la pratique de ce culte*). Depending on the genius of each nation, services are conducted with more or less pomp and dignity, with more or less outward manifestations of penitence or of gaiety.

Through these pages of Du Bos—and this observation is true of Bodin and Montesquieu as well—there is an awareness of national character (hardly avoidable in Europe!) and of the observations about it made in antiquity; furthermore, the characteristics of the peoples described by the classical writers are recognizable in their descendants. Do the peasants of North Holland and Andalusia think in the same way? Have they the same passions? Do they even experience in the same way the passions they, as human beings, have in common? Do they want to be governed in the same way? For Du Bos to ask these questions is to answer them. When outward differences are so distinct, the inner difference, the difference in minds, must be enormous. Du Bos clinches the point with Fontenelle's remark about the contrast between the face of nature in China and in Europe. "Voïez [a] combien la face de la nature est changée d'ici à la Chine. D'autres visages, d'autres figures, d'autres moeurs, & presque d'autres principes de raisonnements."[19]

Du Bos respects John Barclay as an authority on national character and refers his readers to him.[20] He remarks upon the similarities between the original inhabitants of a country and their descendants: Livy's description of the Goths is compared with the present Catalans; Caesar's comment on the Gauls' talent for imitating foreign inventions is true, he says, of the modern French. Even changing the environment by forest clearance, draining of swamps, building of towns instead of the old villages, had not succeeded in obliterating the German character, an observation which may well have been inspired by Barclay.[21]

Throughout its history the climatic theory has played a significant role as an explanation of cultural inertia; it had this role with Du Bos and later with Montesquieu (*Spirit of Laws* XIV, 4). Du Bos writes as if it were a matter of common knowledge that climate is more powerful than blood or origin. The Gallo-Greeks, descendants of the Gauls who had settled in Asia, he says, in five or six generations became as soft and effeminate as the Asiatics, although they were descendants of warlike ancestors. All peoples famed for their skill

[19] *Ibid.*, p. 259. See Fontenelle's *Entretiens sur la Pluralité des Mondes* (1686) Second Jour.

[20] *Ibid.*, pp. 259–260. On Barclay see chap. IX, sec. 9, and chap. 9, note 69.

[21] *Ibid.*, p. 266. See above, chap. IX, sec. 9, and Barclay, *The Mirrour of Mindes*, pp. 144–145. According to Albert Collignon, "Le Portrait des Esprits (Icon Animorum) de Jean Barclay," *Mémoires de l'Académie de Stanislas*, 6th Series, Vol. 3 (1905–1906), pp. 67–140, one French translation of the *Icon Animorum* appeared in 1623, and two in 1625. See pp. 129–135 for the editions of this work in the original Latin and in German, English, and French translations.

at arms became soft and pusillanimous (*mous et pusillanimes*) when they moved into places whose climate softens also the character of the indigenous peoples. Colonists assume the characteristics of the place; climate makes different people alike and keeps them alike.[22]

What about the apparent exceptions to the theory? Du Bos discusses two, the Romans and the Dutch. His highly interesting explanations, essentially invalidations of his theory, indicate that in the early eighteenth century the results of travel and commerce and of human activities were already breaking down the simpler determinisms of the past—even though the abbé du Bos did not seem to realize it. Let us consider these two exceptions.

The ancient Romans, he says, were famous for their military virtues and discipline; the modern Romans, in an age seeking a cure for the sickness of ceremony, have by no means been the last to rid themselves of it. To them ceremony is *à la mode*; they try to be as superior in this respect to other peoples as the ancient Romans tried to be superior to others in military discipline.[23]

Du Bos answers that the modern Romans have failed to understand and to properly control environmental conditions within the city and in its environs, whose atmosphere is quite different from that prevailing in the times of the Caesars. With the exception of the Trinità di Monte and the Quirinal quarters, Du Bos says, the air of the city of Rome is so unhealthful during the hot summer months that it could be endured only by those who accustomed themselves to it gradually, as Mithridates accustomed himself to poison. Long neglect caused the deterioration of the aqueducts and the cloaca; new environments have created new conditions. Here Du Bos assumes that the active participation of man is indispensable to the proper maintenance of life.

In his discussion of the related problem of the Pontine Marshes, Du Bos says the plain of Rome has poisonous air; since the poison comes from the soil, the latter must have changed either because it is no longer cultivated as it was in the times of Caesars, or because the swamps of Ostia and those of Ofanto are no longer drained. He wonders whether the mining of alum, sulphur, and arsenic, and the long columns of burning exhalations (swamp gas) may not also have had something to do with the unhealthy air.

Finally, he believes the climate was warmer in the eighteenth century than it was in ancient times even though the country then was more densely inhabited and more cultivated.[24] Noah Webster has shown in a remarkably perceptive and critical essay how prevalent was this belief in climatic change and how flimsy was the evidence to support it; it came mostly from ancient writings which described climatic conditions of certain places which were strikingly different from contemporary conditions. "This opinion [that the winter seasons have become warmer in the northern latitudes in modern times] has

---

[22] *Ibid.*, pp. 267–268.
[23] *Ibid.*, pp. 277–278.
[24] *Ibid.*, pp. 283–284. The only evidence cited is Juvenal, Sat. VI.

been adopted and maintained by many writers of reputation, as the Abbé du Bos, Buffon, Hume, Gibbon, Jefferson, Holyoke, Williams; indeed I know not whether any person, in this age, has ever questioned the fact."[25]

The example of the Dutch is even more interesting; they too, like the Romans, had changed. The warlike Batavians and Frisians of ancient times were unlike their modern representatives so adept in commerce and the arts. Du Bos's explanation for the change is that the Hollanders literally no longer possess the same soil although they inhabit the same country. This change of soil, he thinks, came about through natural processes. The isle of the Batavians, a low country, was covered with woods in ancient times, but that part of the country inhabited by the ancient Frisians (making up the greater portion of Holland today), he says, was then covered with hollow hills. The sea, flooding these hollows, caused the land to sink, but it was subsequently reclaimed from the sea by natural causes. The waves washed up the sands on the coast, the rivers in flood deposited their alluvium. (Du Bos seems to be arguing that the sea completely inundated the land, then retreated, that sand dunes which were subsequently formed cut off the remaining water from the sea, while at the same time alluvium deposited by the Rhine and the Maas filled in and replaced the isolated water which now would evaporate.) When the land dried out, it could then be settled again; in fact, it now has become a level plain crisscrossed with canals and dotted with lakes and ponds. The complete exchange of soil brought about changes in agriculture and livestock raising, and thus in diet and different ways of living. The bulls and cows are larger, the population—which has increased more than that of any other part of Europe—can eat legumes, dairy products, fish, instead of the flesh of the herds and of feral animals, which their ancestors ate.[26] Du Bos refers at this point to Sir William Temple's work on the United Provinces; Sir William thought the airs influenced the national character of the Dutch and that the striking differences between the Batavians and the Hollanders was owing to a change of diet. Unlike Du Bos, Temple thought the modern diet parsimonious, deficient in meat.[27] Du Bos's ingenious argument may be summed up by saying that through the operation of natural causes the original soil is replaced by new soil and that, consequently, the qualities of the air are changed; this air in turn influences the character, the soil, and the diet; such a change in diet alters also the character of the country. Du Bos supports the argument with a quotation from Chardin on the influences of the climate on the people of Persia.[28] In the Dutch example, Du Bos, however, apparently

[25] Webster, "Dissertation on the Supposed Change of Temperature in Modern Winters" (read before the Connecticut Academy of Arts and Sciences, 1799), in *A Collection of Papers on Political, Literary and Moral Subjects*, pp. 119–162; quote on p. 119.

[26] *Reflex.*, Vol. 2, pp. 277, 285–287.

[27] See above, chap. IX, sec. 9, and Sir William Temple, *Observations upon the United Provinces of the Netherlands*, pp. 105–107, 109–112.

[28] *Reflex.*, Vol. 2, pp. 288–289.

under the influence of Sir William Temple's account, shifts the argument to less deterministic ground. Environmental conditions and human industry are in a reciprocal relationship although climate is still a fundamental influence.

An even more remarkable illustration showing how in the early eighteenth century climatic determinism could be broken down and replaced with a less dogmatic solution is Du Bos's honest attempt to account for the distribution of the arts and sciences over a wide range of climates; this forces him to acknowledge that it is only the environmental extremes that fail to encourage conspicuous human achievement. Even here the determinism breaks down.

Another illustration is his assertion that trade has replaced dependence on local agriculture and that mankind can now draw its sustenance from all quarters of the earth for necessities and luxuries alike. Commerce gives to people of the north the foods and wines denied them by their own soils. The hot countries have made their sugar, spices, brandies, tobacco, coffee, and chocolate available to the peoples of the cold countries. The salts and the spiritous juices of these products add an ethereal oil which is not present in their own foods. Commerce and trade accomplish what the soils and airs cannot. Spanish spirits fill the blood of the men of the north; the sap and the air of the Canaries come to England with their wines. Frequent and habitual use of the products of the hot countries, he says in a striking figure of speech, brings, so to speak, the sun to the northern countries, and it puts into the blood and the imagination of the inhabitants of these countries a vigor and a delicacy which their ancestors, contented in their simplicity with the products of the earth which they had watched germinating, never had. Du Bos continues, however, with unfavorable reports of diseases apparently caused by the introduction of these new foods.[29]

The abbé du Bos combined several ideas in putting his own system together. The idea that genius, talent, artisanship, clustered in space and time came from a classical writer; stimulating thoughts came also from Fontenelle who, like Sir William Temple, was engrossed in the argument over the ancients and the moderns and in the possible validity of a climatic explanation; the discussions of national character, in the work of Barclay, Chardin, and Sir William Temple, were grist for his mill. Classical thought, contemporary European travel and wider voyaging, curiosity about the nature of human achievement, thus were the building blocks of this stimulating work published twenty-seven years before *L'Esprit des Lois.*

### 3.   Arbuthnot on the Effects of Air

In 1731, John Arbuthnot, a celebrated English doctor, published *An Essay Concerning the Effects of Air on Human Bodies*; he was interested in the relationship of the atmosphere to disease and especially to diseases recurring

[29] *Ibid.*, pp. 290–292.

seasonally. The *Essay* shows a deep respect for, and a thorough knowledge of, the Hippocratic corpus, particularly the *Airs, Waters, Places* and the *Epidemics*; he sympathized with the Hippocratic conceptions of the etiology of disease, that it had natural not supernatural causes. In this lucid and rigorous work, ideas of design are passed over quickly to consider the baffling problem of diseases and their control. The wise author of nature, he says, has created a salubrious air near the surface, charged with heterogeneous particles which, except for a few accidental cases, is well suited to animals. Nature tries to preserve a healthful air by not having too many particles in it and by circulating it mostly by the wind; but unhealthy air, still air, air full of putrefactions, often defeat the purpose of nature. In an age whose physicians knew nothing of the germ theory of disease but suspected that epidemics spread at unequal pace, sometimes slowly, sometimes jumping quickly from one place to another (and thus might be related to congestion), Arbuthnot echoed the advice of Hippocrates that when men build cities they should make them "open, airy, and well perflated."[30]

Arbuthnot's fine book probably would have been noticed only by historians of medicine had it not been for Joseph Dedieu's assertion that Montesquieu's climatic theories were "une adaptation vigoureuse, mais une adaptation" of the English physician's work.[31] Dedieu's case is even more convincing because he apparently has used the French translation of Arbuthnot's work; he casually mentions Arbuthnot's debt to Hippocrates without making it crystal clear that Arbuthnot's discussion on the influence of climate on peoples is a carefully condensed précis of the Hippocratic *Airs, Waters, Places*. The parallel passages on this subject therefore are more between Montesquieu and Hippocrates than between Montesquieu and Arbuthnot.[32]

Arbuthnot accepts the Hippocratic philosophy of medicine, but he is very much alive to the results of contemporary investigation; the Hippocratic generalizations on the influence of climate, however, are accepted uncritically. The physiological theory is of course contemporary, including discussions of the effects of the air on the human body, the body's heat balance, atmospheric conditions influencing sickness, and epidemics.

Following traditional methodology, Arbuthnot shows the effect of airs on the human body by pointing to the role of heat, cold, humidity, and the circulation of the blood.[33]

Heat, but not extreme heat, "lengthens and relaxes the Fibres; from whence proceed the Sensation of Faintishness and Debility in a hot Day. . . ." Cold induces the opposite reactions: "It contracts animal Fibres and Fluids, which are denser as far as the Cold reacheth. In cold Weather Animals are really of

---

[30] *Essay*, 1751 ed., p. vii, 13–17.

[31] Dedieu, *Montesquieu et la Tradition Politique Anglaise en France*, p. 212. See pp. 214–223 where parallel passages are compared.

[32] Arbuthnot, pp. 122–124; Dedieu, p. 221, note 2.

[33] See Dedieu, *op. cit.*, pp. 214–216, for parallel passages in Montesquieu.

less Dimensions. Cold braceth the Fibres not only by its condensing Quality but likewise by congealing the Moisture of the Air, which relaxeth." Humidity also causes a relaxation of the fibers of animals and vegetables; given as evidence are the effects of soaking, of a relaxing cold bath after initial contraction, of a relaxing hot bath, and so forth.[34] Of the effects of cold and hot on the blood circulation, Arbuthnot writes, "Obstructions by Cold in the outward Parts of the Body, drive the Blood pressing with a greater Force upon the inward Parts, and increase Heat."[35]

Without going into further detail about Arbuthnot's physiological theory, we can see from the following the kind of generalization to which his researches led:

> But as there is still a great Penury of such Observations [about constitution, diet, disease, climate], all we can do is to reason from the Laws of Mechanicks, and the known Properties and Qualities of Air, what must be their natural Effects. It seems agreeable to Reason and Experience, that the Air operates sensibly in forming the Constitutions of Mankind, the Specialities of Features, Complexion, Temper, and consequently the manners of Mankind which are found to vary much in different Countries and Climates.[36]

Arbuthnot notes the ease with which "People of delicate nerves and moveable Spirits" can be affected by the daily weather changes, that on some days the memory, imagination, and judgment are more vigorous, that it therefore seems probable that the "Genius of Nations depends upon that of their Air: Arts and Sciences have hardly ever appeared in very great or very small latitudes." Inhabitants of colder countries succeed in the arts requiring industry and application because it is easier to work in them, and the hot countries, hospitable to a liveliness of imagination, produce arts requiring the latter.[37]

Arbuthnot also observed, as had others before him, the persistent traits of national character, as illustrated by the Gauls and the French. It is the country that is responsible "even tho' the Race has been changed." "Governments stamp the manners but cannot change the Genius and Temper of the Inhabitants; and as far as they are unrestrain'd by Laws, their Passions, and consequently their National Virtues and Vices will bear some Conformity with the Temperature of the Air . . . Nations, as well as Individuals, have their constitutional Vices. . . ."[38]

Thus Arbuthnot has modern explanations for anciently observed cultural differences. He agrees with Hippocrates that there are indeed differences between northern and southern peoples but his explanation is derived from the science of his day. In northern countries, where there are frequent and great

[34] *Essay*, 1751 ed., pp. 48, 56, 61–62.
[35] *Ibid.*, p. 161.
[36] *Ibid.*, p. 146.
[37] *Ibid.*, pp. 148–149.
[38] *Ibid.*, pp. 149–150.

changes in atmospheric pressure (no source is given), the human fibers (nerves and blood vessels?) are alternately expanding and contracting. Because of this difference in the tension of the fibers "the whole nervous System, and the animal Spirits, are in some measure affected." Extremes of heat and cold cause similar effects, the fibers relaxing and contracting or "constringing" in turn. The extreme cold, acting also as a stimulus, brings about an "Activity and Tolerance of Motion and Labour, in dry frosty Weather, more than in hot; whereas the People living within the Tropicks are constantly in the State of our hottest Weather." The greater variety of oscillatory motion of the fibers of the northern peoples produces the same oscillation in their spirits, "and therefore a proportional Inequality in their Passions, and consequently greater Activity and Courage." The hot climates, with small differences in atmospheric pressure and air temperature, feel only a tension of fibers coming from drought and moisture (that is, the dry and rainy seasons), and "the Motions of their Fibres and Spirits being more uniform, they may be for that Reason, and from excessive Heats, lazy and indolent: From Inactivity and Indolence there will follow naturally a slavish Disposition, or an Aversion to contend with such as have got the Mastery of them."[39]

Arbuthnot has now "ventur'd to explain the Philosophy of this sagacious old Man [Hippocrates], by mechanical Causes arising from the Properties and Qualities of the Air. . . ." Despotic governments "tho' destructive of Mankind in general are most improper in cold Climates, for where great Labour is required the Workman ought to have a certain Title to the Fruits of it. There are Degrees of Slavery, and generally speaking, it is most extreme in some hot and fruitful Countryies." Arbuthnot speculates also upon the influence of climate on language and remarks on earlier sexual maturity of human beings in the hot countries, a theme discussed also by Montesquieu.[40]

### 4. On Montesquieu in General

Enough has been said here and in chapter IX to show that the period between Bodin and Montesquieu was one in which theories of environmental influence were exceptionally influential; they were involved in arguments over the relative merits of the ancients and moderns, in legal and legislative theory, in conceptions of disease and public health, and in explaining the *moeurs* and national character. Interest in Montesquieu thus is due less to his originality than to his influence. It is of less importance in the history of thought that Montesquieu's witty and epigrammatic sentences are restatements of long-known ideas even if he made use of advances in knowledge—here the contrast with Bodin, oriented to the Middle Ages, is so striking—than that Montesquieu turned the thoughts of intellectuals writing in the second

[39] *Ibid.*, pp. 151–152.
[40] *Ibid.*, pp. 151–153, 153–155.

half of the eighteenth century away from a moral philosophy that hitherto had been content to consider social causes to one which now must consider the relation of moral to physical causes. Even if one convicts Montesquieu of a dogmatic determinism—an easy matter, if one considers Books XIV through XVIII of *L'Esprit des Lois*, harder if one considers the work as a whole—his book nevertheless marks a turning point in the prehistory of the social sciences, laying out a route that ultimately leads to human geography. For the most part, the writers between Bodin and Montesquieu, Du Bos excepted, employed the climatic argument, more or less casually and incidentally; in Montesquieu and in works showing his influence, physical causes are well entrenched in the general body of theory.

Furthermore, the sources of Montesquieu's ideas are of unusual interest because, like those of Du Bos, they reveal many of the building blocks of moral philosophy, the matrix of the future social sciences. The works of Montesquieu, Buffon, and Herder are of such outstanding interest because they are more than the thoughts of an individual and are also more individual and personal than the *Encyclopédie*; they become repositories of the ideas of an age.

Later in the century Montesquieu was the authority cited on the relationship of physical to moral causes, just as Buffon was the authority cited on natural history, but this position was not achieved at once; the work was received with hostility by many contemporary representatives of respectable intellectual traditions who were not interested in discovering the relation between the physical milieu and the social milieu in which men lived, formed nations, and enacted laws. And even if the work as a whole did not bind men as closely to the physical milieu as did the individual books on climate, Montesquieu still had said that "the empire of the climate is the first, the most powerful, of all empires."[41] Students of jurisprudence did not like to see the law being traced back to temperature; philosophers objected to what they thought a noisy revival of fatalistic materialism. And there was general ridicule as well, surprise at its novelty, and puzzlement.[42]

Among the many religious attacks on the book, the most acute came from the pen (it is believed) of the abbé Fontaine de la Roche in a Jansenist periodical *Nouvelles Ecclésiastiques*. This critic perceived the dangers to the church in a preoccupation both with natural (versus revealed) religion and with cli-

---

[41] *De l'Esprit des Loix. Texte Établi et Présenté par Jean Brethe de la Bressaye.* Hereafter referred to as *EL*. Book XIX, chap. 14.

[42] Dedieu, *op. cit.* (see n. 31 above), pp. 192–193.

Aucun livre ne provoqua autant d'étonnement, [says Dedieu,] n'excita autant d'invectives que ceux-là. Théologiens, philosophes, jurisconsultes, ou même simples curieux de littérature, tous, avec une unanimité touchant, accablèrent Montesquieu et son "infâme" doctrine. Les curieux étaient déroutés. Les jurisconsultes ne pouvaient se résoudre à laisser en détresse leurs calculs politiques, immolés à l'empire du climat, "le premier de tous les empires." Les philosophes et les théologiens connurent à nouveau leurs terreurs d'autrefois: la "nécessité" de Spinoza, le materialisme fataliste, sortant de leur obscurité, réapparaissaient avec fracas (p. 193).

matic theory; he concluded that the book tended to show that religion must accommodate itself to the manners (*moeurs*), usages, customs of different peoples, whatever they may be, and that it depends more on climate and the political system (*l'état politique*). The book is therefore fundamentally opposed to revealed religion.[43]

What were the sources of Montesquieu's general and leading ideas? In the first place, it seems obvious that Montesquieu was aware of the passage in the *Politics* of Aristotle regarding climate, that his work, like that of Thomas Aquinas and Bodin, belongs to a genre that can be traced to Plato's *Laws*: a legislator or lawgiver should know the nature of his people and the conditions under which they live before he makes laws for them.

Joseph Dedieu argued (1909) that Montesquieu had derived the main theses of his climatic books from John Arbuthnot's *An Essay Concerning the Effects of Air on Human Bodies*. Dedieu's evidence is the striking similarity between Arbuthnot's physiological theory and that of Montesquieu in Book XIV of *De l'Esprit des Lois*, chapter 2, which is the scientific basis of Montesquieu's ideas.[44] And, in 1929, Muriel Dodds, in a work of extraordinary interest because it demonstrates so clearly how the voyages and travels were used by the philosophic stay-at-homes, said that Chardin had fundamentally influenced Montesquieu in the formulation of his climatic theories.[45]

And what about Montesquieu's two most famous precursors, Hippocrates and Bodin? These questions also can now be answered with some assurance. There was a marked revival of interest in Hippocrates from 1721 to 1748, an interest associated with general medicine but in particular with the etiology of communicable diseases and their relation to quick changes in temperature and the influence of the air on them.[46]

It is now known that Montesquieu had a short précis of the *Airs, Waters,*

[43] On this see *De l'Esprit des Loix*. Vol. 1, pp. lxx–lxxi. The attack appeared in the issues of October 9 and 16, 1749, of *Nouvelles Ecclésiastiques*.

[44] Arbuthnot's work was translated into French by Boyer de Pébrandié and published in 1742 (Dedieu, *op. cit.*, p. 204, note 1). An obstacle to accepting Dedieu's argument was that the date of composition of an earlier work of Montesquieu, *Essai sur les causes qui peuvent affecter les esprits et les caractères*, from which he borrowed many of the ideas for Book XIV, was not then known; it is now believed that this earlier essay was written between 1736 and 1741. It now seems likely that Montesquieu, as Dedieu had argued, indeed owed much to Arbuthnot. Dedieu's list of parallel passages from both works is very convincing (Dedieu, *op. cit.*, pp. 213–225). For a resumé of the evidence based on findings, subsequent to Dedieu's work, at the chateau of La Brède, see *EL*, Vol. 2, pp. 176–178.

[45] Dodds, *Les Récits de Voyages. Sources de l'Esprit des Lois de Montesquieu*, pp. 55–56. Chardin was not the only influence; she also included *Les Six Voyages de Jean-Baptiste Tavernier qu'il a fait en Turquie, en Perse, et aux Indes*. 2 vols. Paris, 1676; and François Bernier, *Voyages, Contenant la Description des États du Grand Mogol, de l'Hindoustan, du Royaume de Kachemire*, etc. 2 vols. Amsterdam, 1699. See her "Tableau des Sources de l'Esprit des Lois," under Livre XIV, pp. 201–213.

[46] On the details of the revival of Hippocrates, see Dedieu, pp. 205–207, whose source is Emile Littrés edition, *Oeuvres complètes d'Hippocrate*, Vol. 2.

*Places* in his library, and that his copy of Bodin's *Methodus* was "couvert d'annotations autographes en marge du chapitre V."[47]

Montesquieu's theories of climate also grew out of important preoccupations of the time. Reconciliation of the different sources of French law (Roman law, canon law, customs with the force of law, royal ordinances, etc.) called attention to the importance of history, custom, and tradition. How is one to interpret the colorful descriptions of strange peoples living under various climates, to understand disease and optimum conditions of health?[48] The travels Montesquieu read and relied upon were in general written by informed and talented men like Jean Chardin, Father du Halde, and Engelbert Kaempfer. Nevertheless, Montesquieu retained the basic assumption which had been made by all writers since the classical period: that (1) climate (to him it is little more than temperature varying with latitude) influences the physical state of the human body (in the form of contractions or expansions of nerves and blood vessels, circulation of the blood); that (2) this physical influence in turn influences mental states (ardent passion, love, bravery, cowardice); and that (3) these supposed individual mental effects apply also to peoples collectively.

### 5.   Climatic Theory in the *Esprit des Lois*

Montesquieu wishes to contribute to human well-being by showing the purpose of laws and the considerations framing them. "If it be true that the temper of the mind and the passions of the heart are extremely different in different climates, the laws ought to be in relation both to the variety of those passions and to the variety of those tempers."[49] The theory is derived from Arbuthnot:

> Cold air constringes the extremities of the external fibres of the body; this increases their elasticity, and favors the return of the blood from the extreme parts to the heart. It contracts those very fibres [a vague usage, apparently meaning both the blood vessels and the nerves]; consequently it increases also their force. On the contrary, warm air relaxes and lengthens the extremes of the fibres; of course it diminishes their force and elasticity.

From this, it would seem a human being scarcely needed a heart.[50] Montesquieu concludes that people are more vigorous in cold climates. "Here

---

[47] *EL*, Vol. 2, p. 174. De la Gressaye thus makes a strong case for the inspiration of Bodin in opposition to Dedieu who did not give this much weight. (Dedieu, *op. cit.*, pp. 211–212); *EL*, pp. 174–175.

[48] See also Dedieu, *op. cit.*, p. 207.

[49] Bk. XIV, chap. 1. Quotations in English are from the Nugent trans. except where another is specifically mentioned.

[50] On the source of this passage in Montesquieu's early work, see *EL*, Vol. 2, pp. 396–397, notes 1–3.

the action of the heart and the reaction of the extremities of the fibres are better performed, the temperature of the humors is greater, the blood moves more freely towards the heart, and reciprocally the heart has more power."[51] Superiority in strength produces various mental states, such as the feeling of being courageous. Using a hackneyed metaphor, Montesquieu likens the people of cold countries to young and brave men, those of hot, to old and timorous men; individuals going from one climate will be subject to the influences of the new climate, as had happened, he says, to northern soldiers who fought in the War of the Spanish Succession.

It is the experiment on the sheep's tongue, however, and the conclusions drawn from it that show how little Montesquieu understood reasoning in science:

> I have observed the outermost part of a sheep's tongue, where, to the naked eye, it seems covered with papillae. On these papillae I have discerned through a microscope small hairs, or a kind of down; between the papillae were pyramids shaped towards the ends like pincers. Very likely these pyramids are the principal organ of taste.
>
> I caused the half of this tongue to be frozen, and observing it with the naked eye I found the papillae considerably diminished: even some rows of them were sunk into their sheath. The outermost part I examined with the microscope, and perceived no pyramids. In proportion as the frost went off, the papillae seemed to the naked eye to rise, and with the microscope the miliary glands began to appear.
>
> This observation confirms what I have been saying, that in cold countries the nervous glands are less expanded: they sink deeper into their sheaths, or they are sheltered from the action of external objects; consequently they have not such lively sensations.
>
> In cold countries they have very little sensibility for pleasure; in temperate countries, they have more; in warm countries, their sensibility is exquisite. As climates are distinguished by degrees of latitude, we might distinguish them also in some measure by those of sensibility. I have been at the opera in England and in Italy, where I have seen the same pieces and the same performers; and yet the same music produces such different effects on the two nations: one is so cold and phlegmatic, and the other so lively and enraptured, that it seems almost inconceivable.

The opening sentences call to mind a picture, common in the late seventeenth and the eighteenth century, of the experimenting amateur philosopher-scientist who writes notices or observations to the Royal Society. The experimenter comes to certain conclusions regarding the physical effects of heat and cold. On them are based generalizations regarding psychological differences. Finally the horizon broadens by way of the opera house to show differences in national character.

Herder saw the pitfalls in such reasoning and the danger of basing cultural generalizations on physiological experimentation.

[51] Bk. XIV, chap. 2.

Every one indeed knows [Herder says] that heat extends and relaxes the fibres, attenuates the fluids, and promotes perspiration; and that thus it is capable in time of rendering the solids light and spongy, &c. [From the effects of heat and] its antagonist, cold, many physical phenomena have been already explained: but general inferences from this principle, or from a part of it, as relaxation or perspiration for instance, to whole nations and countries, nay to the most delicate functions of the human mind, and the most accidental ordinances of society, are all in some measure hypothetical; and this the more, in proportion as the head that considers and arranges them is acute and systematic. They are contradicted almost step by step by examples from history, or even by physiological principles; because too many powers, partly opposite to each other, act in conjunction. It has even been objected to the great Montesquieu, that he has erected his climatic spirit of laws on the fallacious experiment of a sheep's tongue. It is true, we are ductile clay [*einbildsamer Thon*] in the hand of Climate; but her fingers mould so variously, and the laws, that counteract them, are so numerous, that perhaps the genius of mankind alone is capable of combining the relations of all these powers in one whole.

This cogent criticism can be applied to virtually all theories of climatic influence fashionable during and before Herder's time. Even if environmental factors can be shown to influence the physical and mental characteristics of the individual, it does not follow that they have similar effects on whole peoples. Hot weather may cause debility in an individual, but one cannot conclude from this observation that peoples of hot countries lack the energies to create a civilization. The reasoning against which Herder complained has also, and with less justification, characterized much of the thinking on climatic influences in the nineteenth and twentieth centuries.[52]

There now follow more correlations between climate and other human, all-too-human, experiences like pain and lovemaking. At this point, Montesquieu makes a significant departure from the traditional view that temperate climates bring about a harmonious blending of the best qualities of the extremes.

If we travel towards the North, we meet with people who have few vices, many virtues, and a great share of frankness and sincerity. If we draw near the South, we fancy ourselves entirely removed from the verge of morality; here the strongest passions are productive of all manner of crimes, each man endeavoring, let the means be what they will, to indulge his inordinate desires. In temperate climates we find the inhabitants inconstant in their manners, as well as in their vices and virtues: the climate has not a quality determinate enough to fix them.[53]

Montesquieu may have Europe in mind here, England, Germany, the Baltic and Scandinavian countries being the North; Spain and Italy, the South; and

---

[52] Herder, *Ideen*, Bk. VII, chap. 3, Churchill trans., p. 173. *EL*, Bk. XIV, chap. 2. On the experiment see *EL*, Vol. 2, p. 397, note 6, and Dominique Gautier, *Biologie et Médecine dans l'Oeuvre de Montesquieu*, thèse médecine, Bordeaux, 1949, which I have been unable to consult.

[53] Bk. XIV, chap. 2; *EL*, Vol. 2, p. 398, note 10.

France, between the two. The climatic explanation for the mid position is so enfeebled that it practically breaks down. It apparently did not occur to Montesquieu, even with his extensive knowledge of Roman history, the period of the migrations, the subsequent invasions and cultural mixings in Europe, that these blurred effects and inconstancies possibly were the result of culture contact and borrowings; indeed, the body of French law of his own time in which he was so interested was largely a result of these events.

If climate can explain cultural differences, it can also explain persistence in culture. Montesquieu sees climatic causes in the "unchanging East," a phrase popular in many works of the nineteenth century. The idea was known to Du Bos, but the original source is probably Chardin.

> If to that delicacy of organs which renders the eastern nations so susceptible of every impression you add likewise a sort of indolence of mind, naturally connected with that of the body, by means of which they grow incapable of any exertion or effort, it is easy to comprehend that when once the soul has received an impression it cannot change it. This is the reason that the laws, manners, and customs, even those which seem quite indifferent, such as their mode of dress, are the same to this very day in eastern countries as they were a thousand years ago.

Granting for purposes of argument that the East is unchanging, it is still strange that Montesquieu could not see that the cultural persistence of the Eastern nations contrasted sharply with change in the European countries and that the former might be caused by isolation or lack of culture contact. This passage is the full text of a chapter entitled "Cause of the Immutability of Religion, Manners, Customs, and Laws in the Eastern Countries," and although it did not mention Europe, it brought up the touchy question of the relation of climate to religion. The author of the articles in *Les Nouvelles Ecclésiastiques* had in fact complained about the close bond which Montesquieu found between an unchanging religion and the hot climates of the East.[54] He complained with reason, for what was to prevent physical causes from playing an equally important role in the history of Christianity?

Montesquieu pursues the religious question in a key chapter of the work (Book XIV, chapter 5) in which he says that Buddhism is a product of India's climate. "Foe [Buddha], the legislator of the Indies, was directed by his own sensations when he placed mankind in a state extremely passive; but his doctrine arising from the laziness of the climate favored it also in its turn; which has been the source of an infinite deal of mischief." In swiftly killing two birds with one stone, Montesquieu accounts for the origin of a religion and teaches that a lawgiver should not reinforce but should counteract undesirable effects of the climate.[55]

[54] Bk. XIV, chap. 4; *EL*, Vol. 2, p. 399, note 18.
[55] Many writers of the period use *Fo* (*Foë*) or some variant spelling for Buddha; here it is taken from Du Halde, *Description Géographique, Historique, Chronologique, Poli-*

"The legislators of China were more rational when, considering men not in the peaceful state which they are to enjoy hereafter, but in the situation proper for discharging the several duties of life, they made their religion, philosophy, and laws all practical. The more the physical causes incline mankind to inaction, the more the moral causes should estrange them from it." The Chinese had been successful, the Buddha had not. There is a place for a wise choice. A good ruler will not by his acts increase the influences of a bad climate; neither will he limit the benefits of a good one. Thus a moral philosophy is possible with due consideration to physical causes.

Then Montesquieu's attack on monachism poured salt on the wounds.

> In Asia the number of dervishes or monks seems to increase together with the warmth of the climate. The Indies, where the heat is excessive, are full of them; and the same difference is found in Europe.
> In order to surmount the laziness of the climate, the laws ought to endeavor to remove all means of subsisting without labor: but in the southern parts of Europe they act quite the reverse. To those who want to live in a state of indolence, they afford retreats the most proper for a speculative life, and endow them with immense revenues.

The lesson to be learned was similar to that of the Buddhist example. Montesquieu ignored prayer, meditation, and other forms of physical inactivity, and even the geographical distribution of monasteries in various climates of Europe.[56]

What was Montesquieu's reply to the criticism that he was finding physical causes for the origin and persistence of religions? Christianity, he said, being a revealed religion, is not grounded in physical causes as are the other religions, which are purely human inventions that grew out of earthly conditions and the circumstances of life! False religions could be explained by physical causes; Christianity, a revealed religion, could not.[57]

The relationship of climate to law and custom inevitably raises the question of freedom of choice or determinism. In this respect, there are parallels in the history of environmental and astrological theory. The early Church Fathers were bitterly opposed to astrology, as we know from the writings of St. Augustine and others, but in the high Middle Ages astrology was more acceptable. The stars, those awesome creations, influenced all earthly things.

---

*tique, et Physique de l'Empire de la Chine et de la Tartarie Chinoise.* Vol. III, pp. 22–34. Quoted in Muriel Dodds, *op. cit.*, (see note 45 above), pp. 203–204; see also *EL*, Vol. 2, p. 400, note 22.

[56] Book XIV, chap. 7. On the reaction to this passage, which figures prominently in the report of Mgr. Bottari to the Congregation of the Index–the *Esprit des Lois* was placed on the *Index Librorum Prohibitorum* of the Roman Catholic Church on November 29, 1751–see *EL*, Vol. 1, p. lxxix; Vol. 2, pp. 400–402, note 25.

[57] Montesquieu, *Défense de l'Esprit des Lois*, Part 2; *EL*, Vol. 1, pp. lxxi–lxxiv, gives the history of the publication of the *Défense* (anonymously in Paris in 1750) and summarizes Montesquieu's rejoinders.

On the other hand, man need not be a slave to their influences; one could nullify bad influences with intelligence and will, and encourage the good.

Astrology represented the cosmic environment which men could study for guidance; the climate was an earthly influence which men should study for the same reasons. It is in this human choice available through knowledge of physical causes that Montesquieu avoids fatalism and relieves himself of the charge of reviving Spinoza.

Environmental determinism in Montesquieu's hands could justify cultural and moral relativism; it could also explain certain differences in religious belief and the origin of laws and of customs with the force of law. The effects of drinking alcohol vary in different climates, and laws prohibiting wine drinking in hot climates are reasonable prohibitions. A law forbidding wine drinking in a northern or colder climate would not be proper, nor would it be just to inflict the same punishments for excessive drinking in the climatic extremes. "Drunkenness predominates throughout the world in proportion to the coldness and humidity of the climate." Different needs exist in different climates and bring about different ways of life (*manières de vivre*) and these in turn different kinds of laws.[58]

The theory of climatic influence could also point the way to active human interventions, for example, in public health matters, for climates friendly to leprosy, venereal diseases, or the plague may be isolated by cutting off physical communication with them. On the other hand, suicide may have moral or physical causes. Montesquieu contrasts Roman suicide, a product of education, with that of the British, a product of distempers ultimately owing to the climate.[59] More direct are the climatic influences on the imagination and sexual desires.[60]

Although Montesquieu was opposed to slavery, he saw how it could arise in countries whose climate induced so lazy and slothful a condition among the people that their masters could force them to work only by the fear of punishment; even the masters had a position with relation to the sovereign like that of their slaves to them.[61] In his discussion of domestic slavery, Montesquieu argues that in hot climates women mature sexually and attain the ripeness of their beauty while young and at an earlier age than they attain maturity in reason; they therefore become dependent, and conditions are favorable—if no direct laws oppose it—to male dominance and for the widespread practice of polygamy. In the temperate climates, women's beauty, reason, and knowledge tend to keep pace with one another and to mature together; women are on a more nearly equal footing with their men, since there is more chance

[58] Bk. XIV, chap. 10.
[59] Bk. XIV, chaps. 12–13.
[60] Bk. XIV, chap. 14; note the amusing contrast between the law of the Alemanni on crimes against women compared with those of the Visigoths.
[61] Bk. XV, chap. 7.

for equality between the sexes, and conditions are favorable to monogamy. In cold countries, men's intemperate drinking gives their more abstemious women the advantage of reason over their husbands. Thus a law which permits one wife to a man is more suited to the climate of Europe than it is to Asia. This is one of the reasons, he says, that it has been so easy for the Muslim religion to establish itself in Asia, so difficult in Europe; that Christianity has maintained itself in Europe but has been destroyed in Asia; that the Muslims have made so much progress in China, the Christians so little.[62] Human considerations (*raisons*), he adds, in an apparent intent to allay the fears of those who thought he was assigning climate too powerful a role in determining the geographical distribution of religion, are always subordinated to that Supreme Cause which does what it wishes and makes use of whatever it wishes. Montesquieu pays his respects to a creator-deity who acts only through the intermediary of secondary causes in the governance of human affairs. Since man also is subject to law, the influences of climate, like other secondary causes, are understandable.[63]

Later, Montesquieu attempts a bolder geographic generalization than he has hitherto attempted in explaining the differences between the peoples of Asia and Europe and their histories. Asia, he says, has no temperate zone; it is a land mass of extremes. Its cold part, swept by freezing winds on its sterile soils, extending eastward from Muscovy to the Pacific and northward from the fortieth parallel (including Siberia and Great Tartary, generally, present-day Siberia, Mongolia, and Manchuria) is contrasted with warm and fertile Turkey, Persia, India, China, Korea, and Japan.[64]

Applying the correlations between cold countries and courage, already developed in Book XIV, Montesquieu concludes that Asia is the continent of despotic government; it is also a continent of extremes. It follows that in Asia the north dominates the south. Europe, however, has a temperate zone—

[62] Bk. XVI, chap. 2. See *EL*, Vol. 2, p. 424, notes 6 and 7, for the less dogmatic assertions in this than in the original 1748 ed. On the position of women in M.'s thought, see also Roger B. Oake, "Montesquieu and Hume," *Modern Language Quarterly*, Vol. 2 (1941), pp. 238–246.

[63] Bk. XVI, chap. 2; *EL*, Vol. 2, p. 425, note 8. Neither the Sorbonne nor the Congregation of the Index censured this chapter.

[64] The main sources, as given in Dodds, *op. cit.* (see note 45 above), pp. 226–232, are *Recueil de Voyages au Nord, contenant divers mémoires très utiles au Commerce et à la Navigation* (Amsterdam, 1715), Vol. VIII, pp. 389–392, pp. 45–47; *Histoire des Tatars*, Part. II, pp. 127–129, where *La Grande Tartarie* is described as having the finest climate in the world, as of extraordinary excellence and fertility but high and in many places lacking water; and Du Halde, *op. cit.* (see n. 55 above), Vol. IV, esp. pp. 82, 54, 147, 149, 7, 36–37. See also *EL*, Vol. 3, following p. 74, for maps of Europe and Asia in the original ed. of *EL*. Montesquieu said (Bk. XVII, chap. 2) that his contrasts among nations on a climatic basis applied also to regions within a single country; using materials from Father du Halde (*op. cit.*, Vol. I, pp. 111–112; IV, p. 448, as in Dodds, *op. cit.*, p. 226), he distinguishes between the courage of the peoples of North China and of North Korea and their respective countrymen in the south.

and here the mean assumes a more positive importance than in other parts of Montesquieu's work—that permits blendings, gradual transitions from the extremes, thus avoiding the juxtaposition of extremes characteristic of Asia. The contrasts are vivid and there is a suggestion with reference to Europe that geographical or perhaps political conditions may not be permanent but may vary with time and circumstance. (Montesquieu, like virtually all his contemporaries and precursors, did not consider that as historical circumstances changed with time they would also enforce changes in the influence of relief features in history.)

Hence it comes that in Asia the strong nations are opposed to the weak; the warlike, brave, and active people touch immediately upon those who are indolent, effeminate, and timorous; the one must, therefore, conquer, and the other be conquered. In Europe, on the contrary, strong nations are opposed to the strong; and those who join each other have nearly the same courage. This is the grand reason of the weakness of Asia, and of the strength of Europe; of the liberty of Europe, and of the slavery of Asia: a cause that I do not recollect ever to have seen remarked. Hence it proceeds that liberty in Asia never increases; whilst in Europe it is enlarged or diminished, according to particular circumstances.[65]

What ignorance this passage reveals! It assumes uniformities within the extreme regions of Asia, disregards contrasting ways of life known since Marco Polo, fails to acknowledge that whatever liberty existed in Europe might, as Montesquieu well knew, have some relation to the diffusion of knowledge.[66] It has often been said that Montesquieu wrote like a Cartesian; in this passage the deductions from the supposedly simple contrasts are breathtaking. In criticizing this passage, Voltaire said that Roman power lasted more than five hundred years in a Europe which could not breed empires, and that Montesquieu ignored the mountains which crisscrossed Persia, the Caucasus, Taurus, and so forth.[67] The passage still sets off Asia and Europe; the idea that Europe is a peninsula of Eurasia, that its history is part of Eurasian history, comes later.

These discussions of political geography are enlivened with remarks on the capital city; it is of the greatest importance for a prince to choose the seat of his empire carefully. If he places it to the south, he will be in danger of losing the north, but if he places it in the north, he may easily hold on to the south. "I do not speak of particular cases. In mechanics there are frictions by which the effects of the theory are frequently changed or retarded; and policy has also its frictions."[68]

[65] Bk. XVII, chap. 3.
[66] Note the tone of Bk. XV, chap. 3.
[67] "L'A, B, C," *Oeuvres*, ed. Beuchot, Vol. 45, p. 8, and "Lois (Esprit des)" in the "Dict. philos.," *Oeuvres*, Vol. 31, p. 103.
[68] *EL*, Bk. XVII, chap. 8. On this passage, which did not appear in the 1748 ed., see *EL*, Vol. 2, p. 441, note 39.

6.   ANOTHER SIDE OF MONTESQUIEU

Books XIV–XVII of the *Esprit des Lois* elaborate in various ways upon the climatic theory explained in the opening chapters of Book XIV. In Book XVIII, Montesquieu considers the influence of other physical factors. This ancient body of thought grew in part out of the recognition that latitude or temperature does not tell the whole story because we do not live on an earth with a level and homogeneous surface; hence, the contrasts between fertile and infertile lands, mountains and plains, areas of cultural contact and of isolation, inland and coastal situations. On the whole, this literature has been less dogmatic than the climatic-physiological-psychological lore, I think, because it could easily be shown that such influences are modified or even overcome by invention, especially in transportation, in tool making, and in improved techniques of farming, draining, and clearing.

Montesquieu's dishes are from old and well-tested recipes. The fertile lands are associated with subjugation; men, preoccupied with their own affairs, are not so interested in liberty; fertile countries, inviting pillage and attack, seem more suited to monarchy. His example is that the barrenness of the soil of Attica leads to a democracy, the fertility of the soil of Lacedaemon, to an aristocratic constitution.[69] Voltaire also ridiculed this generalization; he rebutted the idea that soil fertility has had anything to do with government. Of Montesquieu's claim that the soils of Sparta were fertile, Voltaire asks, "Óu a-t-il pris cette chimère?"[70]

The theme of the attractiveness of fertile soils and hence their undesirability ("Countries are not cultivated in proportion to their fertility, but to their liberty; and if we make an imaginary division of the earth, we shall be astonished to see in most ages deserts in the most fruitful parts, and great nations in those where nature seems to refuse everything") is related to the classical idea of the stimulus of a harsh environment. "The barrenness of the earth renders men industrious, sober, inured to hardship, courageous, and fit for war; they are obliged to procure by labor what the earth refuses to bestow spontaneously."[71] Fertile lands are level and hence defenseless; their people, having once lost their liberty, lose it forever. Mountaineers can preserve what little they have, their liberty being "the only blessing worthy of their defence. It reigns, therefore, more in mountainous and rugged countries than in those

---

[69] *EL*, Bk. XVIII, chap. 1. Montesquieu refers to the passage in Plutarch's *Life of Solon* in which it is said that after the Cilonian sedition the city again fell into its old quarrels dividing itself into as many parties as there were varieties of regions in the country; the men of the hill quarter preferred democracy; those of the plain, oligarchy; and those who lived near the sea, a mixed form of government. According to Gressaye, "Cette citation de Plutarque montre d'où M. a tiré l'idée d'un rapport entre la forme de gouvernement et la fertilité plus ou moins grande du sol." *EL*, Vol. 2, p. 442, note 4. See also Thuc. I, 1.

[70] "Lois (Esprit des)" in "Dict. Philos.," *Oeuvres*, ed. Beuchot, Vol. 31, p. 101.

[71] Bk. XVIII, chaps. 3–4.

which nature seems to have most favored."[72] It is the argument of isolation and inaccessibility; it reads like a generalization taken from the history of Switzerland, or from that of the French and Spanish Pyrenees.

In his discussion of the changes made by man in the soil, the tone changes, resembling the presentation of population questions in Book XXIII. Countries which the industry of man has made habitable and which need his continuing care in order to exist require a moderate government. His examples are the provinces of Kiang-nan (made up of modern Anhwei and Kiangsu) and Chekiang in China; Egypt, and Holland.[73] Montesquieu touches but does not expand upon the relation of environmentalistic ideas to the idea of man as a modifier of the environment. The wise ancient emperors of China, he says, raised "from beneath the waters two of the finest provinces of the empire; these owe their existence to the labor of man." To preserve these creations, wisdom and the exercise of lawful, not tyrannical, authority were required. Power was moderated in China as it was in Egypt and Holland "which nature has made to attend to herself, and not to be abandoned to negligence or caprice."[74] It is noteworthy that all examples are concerned with water: Chinese drainage and canal building, Egyptian irrigation using the Nile's waters, and the Dutch polders. From the Chinese example, Montesquieu concludes that despite climate and size of the empire, the first Chinese lawgivers were obliged to make very good laws, and the government was often obliged to follow them.

Montesquieu generalizes further on the significance of man's efforts to change the physical environment; it is a theme which Buffon is to enlarge upon greatly. "Mankind by their industry, and by the influence of good laws, have rendered the earth more proper for their abode. We see rivers flow where there have been lakes and marshes: this is a benefit which nature has not bestowed; but it is a benefit maintained and supplied by nature." Montesquieu's examples of water control as a beneficial kind of environmental change being made by man is not surprising in view of the long history of such work in France.[75]

---

[72] *Ibid.*, chap. 2.

[73] The sources for China are Du Halde, *op. cit.* (see n. 55 above), Vol. I, p. 128 for "Kiang-nan," and p. 273 for "Tche Kiang." See Dodds, *op. cit.* (see n. 45 above), p. 233, who says (p. 232) that a passage from Le P. le Comte, *Nouveaux Mémoires sur l'État Présent de la Chine, 1696,* Vol. I, pp. 227–228, describing the previous flooding of the Southern provinces of China and the water control through a network of canals, may have suggested an idea to Montesquieu. "Si cela est, je ne sçaurois assez admirer la hardiesse & l'industrie de leurs ingénieurs, qui ont creusé des provinces entières & fait naistre d'une espèce de mer, les plus belles & les plus fertiles plaines du monde."

[74] Bk. XVIII, chap. 6. "Il est bien vrai que la terre cultivée en Hollande a été conquise sur la mer, mais M. ne démontre pas que c'est la raison de l'établissement de la république dans ce pays au xviie siècle." *EL*, Vol. 2, p. 442, note 12. Eighteenth century hydraulic civilization à la Wittfogel!

[75] Bk. XIX, chap. 7; see Le Comte de Dienne, *Histoire du Desséchement des Lacs et Marais en France avant 1789.* Paris, 1891. 541 pp.

In these passages, the tone is not deterministic but permissive; social causation is more complex, involving the state of the arts and sciences, the degree and kind of land cultivation, law in relation to the type of economy, and environmental change by human agency.[76] In outlook they are like one of the least deterministic passages of the *Esprit des Lois*:

> Mankind are influenced by various causes: by the climate, by the religion, by the laws, by the maxims of government, by precedents, morals, and customs; whence is formed a general spirit of nations.
>
> In proportion as, in every country, any one of these causes acts with more force, the others in the same degree are weakened. Nature and the climate rule almost alone over the savages; customs govern the Chinese; the laws tyrannize in Japan; morals had formerly all their influence at Sparta; maxims of government, and the ancient simplicity of manners, once prevailed at Rome.[77]

Moreover, Book XXIII, "Of Laws in the Relation They Bear to the Number of Inhabitants," is not dogmatic; one of the most impressive in the *Esprit des Lois*, it is concerned mainly with population theory, food, and land use. Here Montesquieu points out the influences of society on human reproduction.[78] (See chap. XIII, sec. 2.) These influences are illustrated also in the laws of succession, pride in family names and family tradition.[79] "Principles of religion have had an extraordinary influence on the propagation of the human species. Sometimes they have promoted it, as among the Jews, the Mahommedans, the Gaurs [Guèbres, i.e., Ghebers] and the Chinese; at others they have put a damp to it, as was the case of the Romans upon their conversion to Christianity."[80]

Population growth is considered in relation both to kinds of food and to types of land use. Seaport towns have fewer men than women (the men are exposed to a thousand dangers), but there are more children there than in other places, because of the greater ease of obtaining subsistence; he speculates that the oily parts of fish influence human reproduction. "This may be one of the causes of the infinite number of people in Japan and China, where they live almost wholly on fish."[81]

---

[76] Bk. XVIII, chaps. 8–10.

[77] Bk. XIX, chap. 4.

[78] Bk. XXIII, chap. 1.

[79] *Ibid.*, chap. 4.

[80] *Ibid.*, chap. 2. Cf. *Lettres Persanes*, 114–117. In the *EL*, Montesquieu does not mention social influences on birth and death rates, such as religion (prohibition of divorce, monachism), mass movements of peoples after conquest, wars, famines, epidemics, which he had dwelled upon in the *LP*, 112–132. The *EL* is less critical than is *LP* of Christian influences on population policy, less pessimistic about world depopulation since classical antiquity. On these points, see *EL*, Vol. 3, p. 402, note 2.

[81] Bk. XXIII, chap. 13, a generalization based on Du Halde, who mentioned the large number of fish in rivers, lakes, ponds, canals, and ditches. Du Halde, *op. cit.* (see n. 55 above), Vol. II, p. 139, quoted in part in Dodds, *op. cit.* (see n. 45 above), p. 257.

Of greater interest is Montesquieu's correlation of population density with types of land use. "Pasture-lands are but little peopled, because they find employment only for a few. Corn-lands (*les terres à bled*) employ a great many men, and vineyards infinitely more."[82]

The increase in pastureland in England is related to a decline in its population, the large number of vineyards in France, to the large population. Since coalfields furnish fuel formerly supplied by forests, all the land can now be cultivated. Impressed by Father du Halde's description of rice cultivation, Montesquieu notes that a unit of rice land feeds more people than does land sown with other grains. In rice culture men are closer to the soil; they perform the duties of animals, consume the rice directly, and "the culture of the soil becomes to man an immense manufacture."[83]

How does Montesquieu link climate to population theory? He applies the general ideas of the whole work: the lawgiver must know what predispositions to expect of the climate, how one physical cause might reinforce or offset another, and how these are related to the matter in hand.

"Regulations on the number of citizens depend greatly on circumstances. There are countries in which nature does all; the legislator then has nothing to do. What need is there of inducing men by laws to propagation when a fruitful climate yields a sufficient number of inhabitants? Sometimes the climate is more favorable than the soil; the people multiply, and are destroyed by famine: this is the case of China."[84] In assuming that famine is related to soil fertility, Montesquieu reveals how ill-advised it was to generalize from travel accounts. There is no suggestion that Chinese famines may also be caused by drought or floods.

In Montesquieu's time it was widely believed that population growth should be encouraged.[85] To this Montesquieu agreed heartily. In the *Esprit des Lois*, he repeated ideas which he had already more forcibly expressed in the *Persian Letters*.[86] He belonged to a small but very articulate group (to be discussed later) that thought the population of the world was greater in ancient times than in modern, that there had been a general depopulation of the globe since antiquity; hence it was urgent to encourage population growth.

In the twenty-fourth book, Montesquieu gives his views of laws in relation to religion. "I am not a divine but a political writer." The Christian religion has succeeded, he says, in overcoming the influence of the climate by hinder-

[82] Bk. XXIII, chap. 14. This thought apparently was copied by Hume. See also Oake, *op. cit.* (see n. 62 above), p. 36.

[83] See Du Halde, *op. cit.*, Vol. I, p. 71, quoted in Dodds, *op. cit.*, p. 257. Bk. XXIII, chap. 14.

[84] Bk. XXIII, chap. 16.

[85] See Spengler, *French Predecessors of Malthus*, pp. 20–43; 48–76; 77–109, on Montesquieu and the repopulationists who followed him.

[86] *LP*, esp. letter 113.

ing "despotic power from being established in Ethiopia," and by carrying "into the heart of Africa the manners and laws of Europe."[87] On the other hand, physical causes were at work in bringing about the Reformation. The people of the northern countries who embraced Protestantism "have, and will forever have, a spirit of liberty and independence, which the people of the south have not; and, therefore, a religion which has no visible head is more agreeable to the independence of the climate than that which has one." (Denominations within Protestantism, however, are ascribed to political causes.)[88] In speculating on the origins of religion, Montesquieu is sympathetic to utilitarian explanations. Belief in metempsychosis is consistent with the climate of India. A country whose cattle are difficult to breed and are subject to disease will find a law of religion preserving them "more suitable to the policy of the country."[89] Despite his assertion that the Christian religion is the only true one and is, as a revealed religion, not subject to laws of physical causation, he finds climatic causes for the geographical distribution of Christian and Muslim believers.

"When a religion adapted to the climate of one country clashes too much with the climate of another it cannot be there established; and whenever it has been introduced it has been afterwards discarded. It seems to all human appearance as if the climate had prescribed the bounds of the Christian and the Mahommedan religions."[90]

What general conclusions can one make about Montesquieu's wide-ranging and occasionally contradictory ideas about culture and the environment? If one points to Books XIV-XVII, as many of Montesquieu's critics have done, the thought is deductive, unscientific, dogmatic, and deterministic, and there is every justification for this harsh judgment. If, however, in order to avoid too narrow a judgment, one compares these four books with the rest of the work, what is the result? The impression is less clear. Defenders of Montesquieu against the charge of determinism have pointed to passages in the *Esprit des Lois* that prove he was not a determinist (typically, Book XIV, chapter 1, and especially Book XIX, chapter 4.) But, the nondeterministic passages cannot be used to rebut the deterministic ones; it is more to the point to say that each rebuts the other.

If one reads Montesquieu's work without trying to decide if he was or was not a determinist, it becomes clear that many interesting ideas with differ-

---

[87] Bk. XXIV, chap. 3. *EL*, Vol. 3, p. 420, note 12.

[88] *Ibid.*, chap. 5.

[89] *Ibid.*, chap. 24.

[90] *Ibid.*, chap. 26, providing another opportunity for Voltaire's criticism, largely on the basis of inaccuracy. See "L'A, B, C," *Oeuvres*, Vol. 45, pp. 8–9; on some religious objections, see *EL*, Vol. 3, p. 432, note 66. The Sorbonne objected because the Christian religion originated in Palestine, a country with the same climate that Arabia had. One wonders how Montesquieu could ignore the obvious changing distribution of both the Christian and Muslim faiths throughout history and over a wide variety of climates.

ent histories are presented, and that it is not easy to reconcile one with another. Montesquieu's defenders and critics have labored to find a dominant thought; they become impatient if a logical summation of his thought is difficult. But the presence in a single work of many ideas, poorly thought out and poorly reconciled with one another, is common in the history of thought. There is no doubt that the classical tradition is strong in his work; that he is aware of the influence of the moeurs, of human institutions, of different kinds of economies; that he is aware of men's power to change the environment and create new opportunities for human life. These are subsumed in his belief that man, like the other phenomena of nature, is subject to laws, that the Deity governs him through the operation of secondary sources. In his defense, Montesquieu said that climate and other physical causes produce an infinite number of effects; if, he added, he had said the contrary, he would have been regarded as a stupid man—"Il semble que j'aie inventé le climat & que je vienne apprendre aux hommes." The author of the *Esprit des Lois*, he said, should be the last to be accused of ignoring the power of moral causes; he spoke of climate where the subject was climate and of moral causes through almost the whole work.[91]

Montesquieu's work in fact is eloquent in its failure to create a consistent synthesis out of the theories of physical and social causation he inherited from the past. The unscientific arguments found sly but unreliable allies in a travel literature that was itself often too impressionistic, too inexact for a rigorous philosophy about man's relation to the environment. There is no uncertainty about what Montesquieu thought if one quotes individual passages; the uncertainties arise with increase in quotation.

Montesquieu, Buffon, and Malthus had one characteristic in common: they made their thought cosmopolitan. Montesquieu had hundreds of precursors, but it was his reformulation of climatic influence that made these ideas so powerful in the second half of the eighteenth and the early part of the nineteenth centuries. Many had studied natural history before Buffon, but he was the authority on natural history in the same general period. And Malthus, probably with as many precursors as Montesquieu, was responsible for bringing population theory into the mainstream of Western thought.

## 7. Critics of Climatic Theory

The implications of Montesquieu's climatic theories were not lost on Voltaire, who was much too concerned with the hold on men of government, religion, and the moeurs to allow Montesquieu's climates to explain cultural phenomena which could be explained better by other causes. The innocent beginning to the article on climate, that the sun and the atmosphere impress themselves on

[91] "Défense de l'Esprit des Lois," *Oeuvres de Montesquieu*, 1950, pp. 643, 650–652.

all nature's productions from man to mushrooms, led on to critical remarks about Chardin and Du Bos to his real belief that "climate has some influence, government a hundred times more; religion and government combined, more still."[92]

Voltaire's most telling criticism of the climatic theory was that it could not adequately explain cultural change: How is one to account for the sad state of modern Greece compared with the Athens of the Periclean Age? Since the climate had not changed, other causes must have been at work. He asked several such rhetorical questions without bothering to answer them because to him it was obvious that moral causes explained these changes. Voltaire was right; it was a clear weakness of the climatic theory, indeed of all environmental theories which, in assuming an unchanging influence through time, made no allowance for changing historical conditions. Obviously the insular character of Britain meant one thing in the eleventh century, another in the seventeenth. If the Greeks, the Romans, or the Egyptians had changed in historical time, and if the climate were as powerful a determinant as its defenders thought, the climate also should have altered to bring about the historical changes. Abbé du Bos had considered this possibility (p. 560 f.). There was, however, more to this than Voltaire's dislike of the *Esprit des Lois*; he feared that climatic determinism weakened the attack on the moeurs, on bad government and bad laws, for how could these be changed if they were firmly in the grip of climate? To him, there was too broad a jump from the world of experimental science to the world of social causation: It was all very well, he remarked sarcastically, to experiment on sheep's tongue, but

> une langue de mouton n'expliquera jamais pourquoi la querelle de l'empire et du sacerdoce scandulisa et ensanglanta l'Europe pendant plus de six cents ans. Elle ne rendra point raison des horreurs de la rose rouge et de la rose blanche, et de cette foule de têtes couronnées qui sont tombées en Angleterre sur les échafauds. Le gouvernement, la religion, l'éducation, produisent tout chez les malheureux mortels qui rampent, qui souffrent, et qui raisonnent sur ce globe.[93]

Voltaire was willing, however, to recognize the secondary influences of climate. In distinguishing between religious belief and the rites and ceremonies attendant upon it, he thought the latter might well be influenced by climate. Of Montesquieu's ideas of religion, he said, "Je pense avec lui que les rites en dépendent entièrement. Mahomet n'aurait défendue le vin et les jambons

---

[92] Voltaire's chief statements on this subject are: "Climat," *Dict. philos.*, in *Oeuvres*, ed. by Beuchot, Vol. 28; "Lois (Esprit des)," *Dict. philos.*, *Oeuvres*, Vol. 31; "L'A, B, C," *Oeuvres*, Vol. 45; and "Commentaire sur Quelques Principales Maximes de l'Esprit des Lois," *Oeuvres*, Vol. 50. The quotations in English are taken from the Morley English ed. of Voltaire's works.

[93] "Commentaire sur Quelques Principales Maximes de l'Esprit des Lois," *Oeuvres*, ed. Beuchot, Vol. 50, pp. 132–133.

ni à Bayonne ni à Mayence." One wonders at the dispatch with which Voltaire could make such distinctions and under what heading he would classify holy communion.[94] Belief, however, is of an entirely different nature; it depends on education. Opinion, education, the appeal to doctrine, and not climate, are the foundation stones of religion. Men have believed, he says, in polytheism in all climates. "The doctrine of the unity of God passed rapidly from Medina to Mount Caucasus."[95] In this interesting distinction, belief is associated with tradition, diffusion, and the power of ideas; ceremonies and rites are shrugged off with utilitarian and economic explanations. A country dependent on vineyards does not prohibit wine drinking, and indeed, it will become part of religious ritual. Voltaire, however, was willing to let religious movements be judged on less universal principles. Poverty was the cause of the Reformation; indulgences and deliverances from purgatory were too expensive. "The prelates and monks absorbed the whole revenue of a province. People adopted a cheaper religion." Beneath the hostility to Christianity lay a more general belief that many superficial—and even colorful—aspects of a religion are influenced by climate, by the local natural resources, by the physical uniqueness of a country or a region, but that fundamental doctrine is to be explained by moral causes. Voltaire's ideas, like Hume's, had a strong kinship with John Locke's remark about the Hottentots and King Apochancana.

> Had you or I been born at the bay of Soldania [Saldanha Bay, Union of South Africa, about sixty miles northwest of Capetown] possibly our thoughts and notions had not exceeded those brutish ones of the Hottentots that inhabit there; and had the Virginia king Apochancana been educated in England, he had been perhaps as knowning [*sic*] a divine, and as good a mathematician, as any in it. The difference between him and a more improved Englishman lying barely in this, that the exercise of his faculties was bounded within the ways, modes, and notions of his own country, and never directed to any other, or farther inquiries: and if he had not any idea of a God, it was only because he pursued not those thoughts that would have led him to it.[96]

Like many eighteenth century thinkers, Helvétius was interested in the problem of inequality—in individual endowment, among different peoples at the same time, among the same peoples at different periods of their history. Hélvetius argues that the causes of inequalities among individuals are moral ones, that the scarcity or abundance of great men in certain ages is not owing to the influence of air and of different climates. Like Voltaire, he appeals to history, comparing the ancient Greeks, Romans, and Asiatic peoples, presumably living in a climate which has not changed, with their modern counterparts. The arts and sciences, too, have successfully flourished in all climates.

[94] *Ibid.*, p. 112. Similar statements are in "L'A, B, C," and the article "Climat."
[95] "Climat," *Oeuvres*, Vol. 28, pp. 118–119.
[96] *An Essay Concerning Human Understanding* (1690), I, 4, § 12.

Flattering as it might be to the vanity of the peoples of northwestern Europe, he dismisses the belief in a climatically induced northern courage as being groundless. Are there physical causes, he asks, for the conquests made by these peoples? He answers in the negative after examining the nature of courage, concluding that it is not an effect of climate "but of the passions and wants common to all men."

Western nations proud of their liberty (comparing themselves with Eastern despotisms) have often ascribed it to physical causes, but such conjectures are contradicted by history and experience, for freedom is not related to climate but to the state of civilization.

Neither can a case be made for the lasting superiority of certain nations in the different sciences. The natural situation of Greece has remained the same, but the people have not; their form of government has changed. He is critical too of blithe attempts to sum up national character in a phrase. Have those who call all Frenchmen gay observed the grim life of the French peasant? Superficial judgments about national character, many of which, as we have seen, were based on climate, concealed broad differences of behavior and individual characteristics within a people.

Helvétius' position is thus like Voltaire's; he assumes that the geographical influences on a country are constant throughout time; the effect of government on national character he compares with a vessel which forces the water contained in it to assume its own shape. Moral causes account for the superiority of one nation over another, for "Nature, in this respect, has not made a partial distribution of her favours. Indeed, if the greater or less strength of mind depended on the different climate of countries, it would be impossible, considering the age of the world, but that what was in this respect most favoured, should by its progress have acquired a great superiority over all others."[97]

Diderot, on the other hand, criticized Helvétius for a too sweeping dismissal of climatic influences. ("*Il dit*: L'influence du climat est nulle sur les esprits. *Dites*: On lui accorde trop.") Helvétius, he says, claims that impure water, rough foods, depraved appetites, do not affect the spirit. Diderot asks in reply whether they do not in fact ultimately brutalize men. Is not the climate—whatever it may be—a cause with continuous effects? And as to situation, is not the mountaineer lively and vigorous, the plainsman heavy and lethargic?[98]

The article on climate in Diderot's *Encyclopédie*, however, does not take the subject of influences too seriously; it has full coverage of the seven *klimata* and modern meanings of the word. Montesquieu is discussed, and praised, and

---

[97] Helvétius, *De l'Esprit*; or *Essays on the Mind, and its Several Faculties*, pp. 340, 341–342, 350, quote on p. 358. See the entire discussion, Essay III, chaps. 27–30.

[98] "Réfutation Suivie de l'Ouvrage d'Helvétius Intitulé l'Homme (Extraits)," in Diderot, *Oeuvres Philosophiques*, ed. Paul Vernière, pp. 601, 607.

dropped. Traditionally, according to the climatic theory, sexual precocity and passion are characteristic of the hot climates of the south; but, says the author, the girls of Paris are more precocious than those of the warmer southern climates; they are also more advanced than are country girls and even more than girls living in the environs of Paris which have the same climate. Paris is a kind of focus both of knowledge and of vices ("une espèce de foyer de connoissances & de vices) and this girlish physical precocity perhaps is but a natural result of the early exercise of the mental faculties.

The most penetrating criticism of environmental determinism that had yet appeared, however, was made by David Hume in his essay, "Of National Characters" (1748).[99] Hume had followed Montesquieu's work closely and with considerable admiration, although in his essay, "Of the Populousness of Ancient Nations," he showed little patience with the beliefs of Montesquieu and Robert Wallace in the superior populousness of the ancient world.

The theme of this short masterpiece on national character is that a determinism based on physical causes can lead neither to an understanding of the nature of society nor to explanations of the differences among peoples. Moral causes ("all circumstances, which are fitted to work on the mind as motives or reasons, and which render a peculiar set of manners habitual to us") are much more adequate explanations. Physical causes are "those qualities of the air and climate, *which are supposed* to work insensibly on the temper, by altering the tone and habit of the body, and giving a particular complexion, which, though reflection and reason may sometimes overcome it, will yet prevail among the generality of mankind, and have an influence on their manners."[100] Hume's essay is not a new kind of criticism; it is a traditional analysis of national character, assuming that it is the product of political and social conditions and that similarities among peoples are often the result of cultural contact; this and imitation bring about likenesses, while isolation, owing to physical conditions or different governing traditions, brings about differences.

Hume listed nine "signs of a sympathy or contagion of manners, none of the influence of air or climate" which could be found existing in contemporary life or in the past: (1) the influence of a durable government ruling over a wide area for a long time, the Chinese being the best example; (2) differences among neighboring peoples divided up into several governments like the Athenians and Thebans; (3) boundary lines revealing marked differences among peoples, like those of Spain and those of Languedoc and Gascony in France; (4) similarities of groups with international or cosmopolitan interests, like the Jews and the Jesuits; (5) differences in languages or religion among

---

[99] In *Essays Moral, Political, and Literary*, ed. T. H. Green and T. H. Grose. 2 vols., London, 1898. Vol. 1, pp. 244–258. Montesquieu is not mentioned in this essay, but for evidence that Hume may have had the *Esprit des Lois* in mind, see Roger B. Oake, "Montesquieu and Hume," *Modern Language Quarterly*, Vol. 2 (1941), pp. 234–237.
[100] *Essays*, Vol. 1, p. 244.

two peoples (like the Greeks and the Turks) in the same nation; (6) the retention of national character in colonies—"The Spanish, English, French, and Dutch colonies are all distinguishable even between the tropics"; (7) changes in national character through time, owing to changes of government, cultural contact, or "that inconstancy to which all human affairs are subject"; (8) similarities coming among peoples owing to close communication with one another; and (9) the variety of manners and characters existing in one nation (England being the example par excellence) with the same language and government, owing to a variety of religious belief, class structure, liberty and independence, the English government being "a mixture of monarchy, aristocracy, and democracy."[101]

Hume was examining the causes of differences in national character, but his discussion called attention also to broader questions of imitation, diffusion, and isolation as factors in the formation of nations and peoples. Observations which might occur to anyone replaced the hoary theories of causation based on physiology and psychology:

> The human mind is of a very imitative nature; nor is it possible for any set of men to converse often together, without acquiring a similitude of manners, and communicating to each other their vices as well as virtues. The propensity to company and society is strong in all rational creatures; and the same disposition, which gives us this propensity, makes us enter deeply into each other's sentiments, and causes like passions and inclinations to run, as it were, by contagion, through the whole club or knot of companions.[102]

Hume was aware of predecessors who were interested in similar matters, citing Strabo, Lord Bacon, and Bishop Berkeley; he was also skeptical of environmental differences within restricted areas. Plutarch had discussed the effects of air on the mind, observing that the people of Piraeus, four miles from Athens, had different temperaments from those of Athens. "But I believe no one attributes the difference of manners, in Wapping and St. James's, to a difference of air or climate."[103]

What Hume had to say about culture (for this is really what he is talking about) is similar to the observations, already quoted, of his fellow empiricist, John Locke, almost sixty years earlier about the education of Hottentots and King Apochancana. Hume, however, does not completely disown climatic explanations. Is the commonly accepted notion correct—that northern people have a greater inclination to strong liquor, and southern people to love and women? Maybe wine and distilled liquor warm the frozen blood in the cold climates, while the sun's heat in the south inflames the blood and exalts the passion. On the other hand, there may be moral causes: liquors in the north

---

[101] *Ibid.*, pp. 249–252. In quotation, printing of proper names in capitals has not been retained.
[102] *Ibid.*, p. 248.
[103] *Ibid.*, p. 249.

are scarce and coveted; going naked or partly dressed in the south might excite the passions. "Nothing so much encourages the passion of love as ease and leisure, or is more destructive to it than industry and hard labour; and as the necessities of men are evidently fewer in the warm climates than in the cold ones, this circumstance alone may make a considerable difference between them." Like Malthus and Humboldt later, Hume combines the idea of necessity being the mother of invention with the notion that hot countries provide insufficient stimulus to industry to explain differences in the geographical distribution of civilization. Hume asks whether there is any such distribution of these inclinations; several illustrations seem to indicate there is not. But even if there is, he cannot accept the influence on more subtle human characteristics: "We can only infer, that the climate may affect the grosser and more bodily organs of our frame; not that it can work upon those finer organs, on which the operations of the mind and understanding depend."[104]

Again, in the essay on commerce, Hume is much taken with the relationship between climate and invention. Why is it that no people living between the tropics has yet achieved "any art of civility," "any police in their government, and any military discipline; while few nations in the temperate climates have been altogether deprived of these advantages?" One reason may be that with the "warmth and the equality" of the tropical climate less clothing and housing are needed, and the people in order to live there do not experience that "necessity which is the great spur to industry and invention."[105]

## 8.   CLIMATE AND NATURAL HISTORY

It was possible to consider environmental influences from the point of view of natural history as well as from that of law or political theory, as Count Buffon did in the *Histoire Naturelle*. Montesquieu employed such materials as an aid in understanding custom, law, and government; his work was utopian in the sense that it was a plan for an ideal government. In Buffon's encyclopedic *Histoire Naturelle* the coverage is broader, encompassing environmental influences on all life including racial and cultural differences in mankind. This view of all nature enabled Buffon to ask more profound questions—about differences in degree of environmental influence on man and on other forms of life, and about differences within the human race—and to answer them more

---

[104] *Ibid.*, pp. 256–257, 257–258.
[105] *Ibid.*, pp. 298–299. In his essay on taxes, Hume examines a possible relationship between commercial nations and fertile land. Tyre, Athens, Carthage, Rhodes, Genoa, Venice, and Holland have labored under many disadvantages; only the Netherlands, England, and France have possessed trade and fertile lands, the first two owing it to a maritime situation, France to the perspicacity of its people. Hume quotes Sir William Temple's observations approvingly about the Dutch success being due to a necessity arising out of disadvantages. *Ibid.*, pp. 356–357. See above, chap. IX, sec. 9, on Sir William Temple.

imaginatively and in a less traditional manner than had Montesquieu and his followers.

A consideration of the influence of climate on life is unavoidable in a work on natural history, basically because of the striking geographic distribution of life on earth. In his vast but unfinished work, Count Buffon considered it many times, the most systematic expositions being in two essays: "Variétés dans L'Espèce Humaine," a remarkable survey of the world's peoples which appeared in *De L'Homme* (published in the third volume of the *Histoire Naturelle* in 1749), and "De la Dégénération des Animaux," published in the fourteenth volume of the *Histoire Naturelle* in 1766.[106]

After surveying the different peoples of Europe and Asia, Buffon, impressed by their variety compared with those of the New World and of Africa, concluded that differences in racial color were owing to the climate, and that cultural differences were owing to the climate, to food, and to customs or manner of living (*moeurs ou la manière de vivre*).[107]

His comparison of the New World peoples with those of Europe, Asia, and Africa brought up two fundamental lines of inquiry: why primitive life was so prominent in the New World and in such contrast with the highly organized society of Europe, and the reasons for the conspicuous absence of Negro peoples in the New World in the pre-Columbian times. Their absence in the New World tropics had to be accounted for if Buffon's theory that climate caused racial differences was correct.[108]

Buffon admired neither primitive peoples nor the environments in which they lived and which they apparently changed so little. To him, a modern society of the European type could, through government, guard its peoples from many of life's dangers and provide a well-regulated existence; its peoples would therefore be stronger, more handsome, and better formed than those of an independent and savage nation who, receiving no help from others, depend on one another.

In his close, intimate, and often dangerous contact with nature the savage must live more like an animal than like a man. To Buffon, civil society is a humanly created sheltering enclosure for man, giving him a security unknown to primitive peoples. So great is this security that there are fundamental structural differences in the two types of social organization. In civil societies, the hunchbacks, the lame, the deaf, the squint-eyed—in fact all human beings who are defective or deformed in some way—not only can live but can multiply in a cooperative endeavor in which one helps the other, in which the strong cannot harm the weak and where the qualities of the body are valued much

---

[106] See also, however, *Histoire Naturelle*, Vol. 4, "Le Cheval," 1753, and Vol. 6, "Les Animaux Sauvages," 1756.

[107] *HN*, Vol. 3, pp. 446–448, 529–530.

[108] *Ibid.*, pp. 484, 510–514.

less than those of the spirit. Among the savage peoples, there is no such protection, each individual continuing to live by his own prowess; those born feeble or defective or those who have become a burden do not take part in the group. One may take exception to this rather idyllic picture of advanced society, questioning also the baleful description of the American Indian, and to the naïve contrast between a well-knit, cooperative modern society and primitive groups with no societal coherence. But it must be granted that Buffon was aware that the composition of a modern society is owing to social factors, and that the people who compose it, and its social structure, are cumulative expressions of values and attitudes toward people which have arisen in society and stand, so to speak, between man on the one hand and nature on the other.[109]

The peoples of the New World, Buffon thought, belonged to one race, all more or less tawny (*basanés*) except a few in the north resembling the Old World Lapps and some who were like the blond-haired Europeans (albinos?). In a generalization which tells us more about the state of knowledge of American ethnology than it tells the truth, Buffon wrote that, with the above exceptions, "tout le reste de cette vaste partie du monde ne contient que des hommes parmi lesquels il n'y a presqu' aucune diversité; au lieu que dans l'ancien continent nous avons trouvé une prodigieuse variété dans les différents peuples." He then attempts to explain the cultural uniformities of one continent by contrasting them with the diversities of the others. The peoples of the New World, he says, live in the same way as savages or near savages, and even the civilizations of Mexico and Peru emerged so recently that they ought not to be considered an exception. The peoples of the New World are of the same stock, they have preserved their way of living through historical time without great change because they have not advanced beyond savagery, their climate lacks the Old World contrasts of heat and cold. Since settlement is but recently established, there has not yet been time for the causes which produce a variety to bring about any noticeable changes. Buffon was convinced of the recency of human settlement in the New World, the short life of the advanced civilizations existing there at the conquest, and the relatively small population. From these convictions he drew the important conclusion that the New World peoples lacked the force and vigor to change the physical environment, as other peoples, especially in the Old World, had done.[110]

In his essay, "De la Dégénération des Animaux," Buffon pursues similar subjects, and in addition considers at length the distinction between man and other forms of life in their relation to the physical environment. (Buffon does not use "degeneration" in a modern sense; basically he means the variability of a species under the influence of climate and food.)

[109] *Ibid.*, pp. 446–447.
[110] *Ibid.*, pp. 510–512, quote on p. 510.

From the time when man first began to change the climate (*ciel*)—probably by clearing—and then to spread out from one climate to another, his nature has undergone many changes, only slight in temperate countries because they presumably are adjacent to his place of origin, but increasing in proportion as the distance of his present habitat from it grows. In the course of centuries, after generations have changed under the influence of different environments, man has so adapted himself to extreme conditions, the changes which he has undergone have become so great and so obvious that one might believe that the Negro, the Lapp, the white, are separate species if one did not have good reason for believing in the unity of the human race and knowledge of its ability to interbreed. These racial differences, though real, are not important to Buffon compared with the profound similarities which unite all members of the human race.

Man thus has greater force, flexibility, and range (*étendue*) than other forms of life. The range and expansiveness come less from the qualities of the body than from those of the mind (*âme*), by whose means man has discovered how to cope with the delicacy and fragility of his body, to withstand inclement weather, to triumph over poor soils, to discover fire, to make clothing and shelter, and, most important, to achieve dominance over the animals, even taking possession of places that, it would seem, Nature has exclusively set aside for them. Environmental themes are interwoven with themes of the power of human agency in changing the environment; the latter is only mentioned here, Buffon's broad interpretations regarding the changes of the environment by man being reserved for later discussion (see pp. 663–681).[111]

The effect of climate is strongest in producing skin, hair, and eye color; other attributes like figure (*taille*), features (*traits*), hair quality, have more complex causes. What is noteworthy in this analysis is that Buffon confines the role of climate to physical anthropology; he does not carry climatic influences over into the psychological or social spheres.

Food influences the internal form, and its quality depends on that of the soil. Unlike the superficial effects of the climate, the food influences form and quality by properties which are constantly being derived from the soil producing them.

These influences of climate and soil require a long time to make themselves felt—especially the influence of the soil through the food. It might require centuries, during which the same diet is continually eaten, to influence the features, body size, the hair, and internal changes which, perpetuated by reproduction, become general and constant characteristics, thus distinguishing the races and even the different nations of mankind.

Buffon makes sharp distinctions between environmental influences on man

[111] *HN*, Vol. 14, pp. 311–312.

and on the animals. The effects of climate and soil are more quickly felt, stronger, much more direct on the animals: they lack clothing, houses, and fire; because their exposure to the elements is much more direct, each animal has not only chosen its habitat but has kept to it. Here, but without elaboration, Buffon suggests a plant and animal geography based on physical factors, particularly climate; if, however, animals are forced from their natural habitats by natural catastrophes or by man, they undergo so many changes in time that proof of their origin can be given only after painstaking investigation. Wild animals are therefore subject to the influences of climate and food, the domestic animals, in addition, to the "yoke of [human] slavery."[112]

The influences on man are more indirect. Climate (mainly temperature) influences skin, hair type, eye color; food production depends on climate—even more on soil; the moeurs depend on both climate and food. Climate is thus the basic factor in the sense that without solar heat, life is impossible. Old traditions die hard, and Buffon, like many of his contemporaries, is convinced of the advantages of temperate climates; that climate prevailing from the fortieth to the fiftieth degree of latitude is the most temperate and it is the zone where one finds the handsomest and the best made people. Accepting his theory that man originated in a temperate climate, one can derive from the peoples now living there an idea of the true original color of man, and also the model by which all the other shades (*nuances*) of color or of beauty may be judged.[113]

In pointing out the selective effects of climate, Buffon showed by implication why plant or animal and human geography differed. His stress on the unity of mankind rather than on the significance of racial differences maintained a broad humanitarian base for the study of man. Buffon's theories of causation were more permissive than those of the political and social theorists, which were derived from the medical tradition. He grasped the importance of considering human power and skill and its role in the geography of man, the agency of man in disturbing natural arrangements and harmonies among the animals and their habitats. If he had lived to complete the natural history of plants, Buffon, if one can judge by scattered remarks in the *Histoire Naturelle*, would have studied human interventions in the plant kingdom also. Buffon's scope was broader than Montesquieu's; in studying all life, it was possible to achieve a bolder and more imaginative synthesis than could be achieved by a humanistic thinker alone. And Buffon included within the scope of his natural history man's skills and his power to change nature at a time when almost all thinkers thought exclusively in terms of the molding power of nature over man, or of the influences on him of moral causes.

---

112 *Ibid.*, pp. 314–317.
113 *HN*, Vol. 3, p. 528.

## 9.  BUILDING ON THE FOUNDATIONS OF
## MONTESQUIEU, BUFFON, AND HUME

The interest in society and environment so characteristic of thinkers in the eighteenth century shows itself in Rousseau's writings, primarily because he too thought that custom stood in the path of change, and that law should recognize local cultural and environmental conditions. Thus a small state is stronger proportionately than a large one; administrative difficulties of large empires arise in part because the same laws cannot be applied to many different provinces with different customs situated in the most various climates.[114] Rousseau follows Montesquieu's lead in these matters; if, he says, we ask what the greatest good for all consists in, we would limit it to liberty and equality, but these desirable ends of a political system "need modifying in every country in accordance with the local situation and the temper of the inhabitants."[115]

In agreement again with Montesquieu, Rousseau says, "Liberty not being a fruit of all climates, is not within the reach of all peoples."[116] "We find then, in every climate natural causes according to which the form of government which it requires can be assigned, and we can even say what sort of inhabitants it should have." Unfriendly and barren lands might remain so or be inhabited only by savages; barbarous peoples might live on lands that yield only the barest minimums. Lands with moderate surplus production would be suitable for free peoples, while those whose soil is abundant and fertile could afford the luxury of monarchial government. Rousseau believed that democracies, aristocracies, and monarchies are expensive in that ascending order. Despotism is suited to hot climates, barbarism, to cold, and good government, to temperate regions. On the whole, he argues, hot countries are more fertile than cold; men consume less per capita in the hot countries, whose climate requires sobriety in the interest of health. Rousseau quotes with approval Chardin's remark that "we are carnivorous animals, wolves, in comparison with the Asiatics." "The nearer you get to the equator," he adds, "the less people live on. Meat they hardly touch; rice, maize, curcur, millet and cassava are their ordinary food." Differences can be noted between north and south Europe. A Spaniard will live for a week on a German dinner." "Hot countries need inhabitants less than cold ones and can support more of them." Since hot countries can produce more and consume less, they have a greater surplus to support despotic rule.[117]

---

[114] *The Social Contract*, Bk. I, chap. 9, Everyman's Library ed. p. 41; cf. the remarks on custom in Bk. I, chap. 8.
[115] *Ibid.*, chap. 11, p. 46. In Bk. I, chaps. 8–10 and Bk. II, chap. 8, Rousseau shows his interest in land use, population, and agricultural geography.
[116] *Ibid.*. Bk. II, chap. 8, p. 68.
[117] *Ibid.*, pp. 70–72.

Climate also plays a role in Rousseau's theory of education. Man comes to full growth in temperate climates, where he lives between the extremes. Because of his situation, he can accommodate himself to either extreme (hot or cold) much better than can an inhabitant of one extreme adapt himself to the other. "A Frenchman can live in New Guinea or in Lapland, but a negro cannot live in Tornea nor a Samoyed in Benin. It seems also as if the brain were less well organized in the two extremes. Neither the negroes nor the Lapps are as wise as the Europeans. So if I want my pupil to be a citizen of the world I will choose him in the temperate zone, in France for example, rather than elsewhere."[118]

Rousseau had pronounced views on the need of instruction in geography at an early age, and on national character, travel, and travel books. He wrote one of the best essays ever written on travel, but he had little confidence in travel books: "In no country of Europe are so many histories and books of travel printed as in France, and nowhere is there less knowledge of the mind and manners of other nations." He is contemptuous of the provincialism of a cosmopolitan city. "A Parisian thinks he has a knowledge of men and he knows only Frenchmen; his town is always full of foreigners, but he considers every foreigner as a strange phenomenon which has no equal in the universe."[119] To know other peoples we must see them, not read about them. Books "are able to set fifteen-year-old Platos discussing philosophy in the clubs, and teaching people the customs of Egypt and the Indies on the word of Paul Lucus or Tavernier." To know mankind one must compare peoples, one with the other, but one need not study every people living on the globe; selections can be made. "When you have seen a dozen Frenchmen you have seen them all." And when one has studied and compared a dozen nations one knows mankind as a whole. But even travel can be unrewarding for those who neither think nor know how to see for themselves. "The French travel more than any other nation, but they are so taken up with their own customs, that everything else is confused together. There are Frenchmen in every corner of the globe. In no country of the world do you find more people who have travelled than in France. And yet of all the nations of Europe, that which has seen most, knows least."[120] Even if the ancients, like Homer, Herodotus, and Tacitus, traveled little, read little, and wrote few books, they were better observers than modern contemporaries. Many do not even realize that national character changes during the course of history, "As races blend and nations intermingle, those national differences which formerly struck the observer at first sight gradually disappear." Before our time, he says, nations were more isolated, there were fewer means of communication, there was less traveling and intercourse,

---

[118] *Emile*, Everyman's Library ed., pp. 19–20.
[119] *Ibid.*, pp. 134, quotes on p. 414.
[120] *Ibid.*, p. 415.

"those intricate schemes of royalty, miscalled diplomacy, were less frequent," long voyages were rare, and there was little foreign trade.

> The relations between Europe and Asia in the present century are a hundredfold more numerous than those between Gaul and Spain in the past; Europe alone was less accessible than the whole world is now.
>
> Moreover, the peoples of antiquity usually considered themselves as the original inhabitants of their country; they had dwelt there so long that . . . the place had made a lasting impression on them; but in modern Europe the invasions of the barbarians, following upon the Roman conquests, have caused an extraordinary confusion.

Blendings have obliterated the old differences among the Gauls, Germans, Iberians, and Allobrogians. Europeans "are all Scythians, more or less degenerate in countenance, and still more so in conduct." Those who have not considered these historical events are too quick "to ridicule Herodotus, Ctesias, Pliny for having described the inhabitants of different countries each with its own peculiarities and with striking differences which we no longer see."[121]

In the following remarkable passage, Rousseau shows how the obliteration of these former sharp distinctions in national character are related to social changes and to modifications which men make in the physical environment.

> This is why the ancient distinctions of race, the effect of soil and climate, made a greater difference between nation and nation in respect of temperament, looks, manners, and character than can be distinguished in our own time, when the fickleness of Europe leaves no time for natural causes to work, when the forests are cut down and the marshes drained, when the earth is more generally, though less thoroughly, tilled, so that the same differences between country and country can no longer be detected even in purely physical features.[122]

In Condorcet's eloquent and moving work (moving today because the hopes of this humanitarian have fallen so wide of the mark), climate and custom are seen in different perspective; they are factors producing cultural differentiation, the study of which leads to knowledge of the primitive state of society and the stages in its progressive development. Some peoples, Condorcet says, have remained in the tribal or pastoral stages for great lengths of time, having made no progress either by their own efforts or through trade or intercourse with civilized peoples. This apathy, this cultural persistence, is owing to climate and custom, but Condorcet by his emphasis clearly thinks custom is the more important. Independence, attachment to customs held in childhood, to customs of their own country; an aversion to what is new and strange, the discouraging effect on curiosity of physical and mental indolence, the power of superstition, keep them from advancing into higher stages of cultural development. Among contemporary primitive peoples the tyrannical

[121] *Ibid.*, pp. 416–417.
[122] *Ibid.*, p. 417.

hold of custom is reinforced by fear of civilized societies. Here, judging from subsequent remarks, he may be referring to Spanish and Portuguese treatment of the native peoples of the New World. "The bones of five million men covered those unfortunate lands where the Portuguese and the Spaniards brought their greed, their superstitions and their wrath."[123]

> But we must also take into account the greed, cruelty, corruption and preju-
> dice of civilized nations. For these may well seem to primitive races to be richer,
> more powerful, more educated and more active than they, but also more de-
> praved, and above all, unhappier; and so savages, instead of being impressed by
> the superiority of civilized nations, must often have been terrified by the extent
> and multiplicity of their needs, by the torments they suffer through avarice, and
> by the eternal agitation of their always active and never satisfied desires.[124]

The reasons given for lack of scientific progress in China despite the great endowments of the people and for the "shameful stagnation in those vast empires whose uninterrupted existence has dishonoured Asia for so long" are institutional, not environmental.[125] With great understanding and great bitterness toward the Portuguese and the Spanish, Condorcet writes of the consequences of the age of discovery when "for the first time man knew the globe that he inhabited, was able to study in all countries the human race as modified by the long influence of natural causes or social institutions, and could observe the products of the earth or of the sea, in all temperatures and all climates."[126]

Lord Kames, an erratic but often arresting thinker who had studied Buffon carefully, often disagreeing with him, illustrates how ingeniously environmental ideas can be intertwined with theology and interpretations of history and theories of cultural development. Different climates produce the varied plant life of the earth; its consumption by animals and man is part of the Creator's plan. Men are like the plants and animals in this respect, that specific types of men are peculiarly suited to specific kinds of climate. Men have degenerated (in Buffon's sense of a change from an assumed prototype or model because of the influence through time of food and climate) in various climates; but he disagrees with Count Buffon that climate explains color and racial differences. These differences were present, says Kames, at the beginning, and were such a theory not against Scripture, it would be reasonable to assume that God had created several pairs, each suited to the climate in which they would live. Abandoning this reasoning as being contrary to Scripture, Kames suggests that a convulsion caused the degeneration of man from his original state. With the building of the Tower of Babel, the confounding of tongues, and the dispersion of the human race, men became savages, hardened in their

---

[123] *Sketch for a Historical Picture of the Progress of the Human Mind*, p. 104.
[124] *Ibid.*, pp. 23–24.
[125] *Ibid.*, pp. 38–39.
[126] *Ibid.*, p. 104.

new habitats and divided into different types fitted for the climates in which they found themselves. In this way the unity of the human race was destroyed.

The differences among men are primordial despite those who are biased in favor of the new and unusual and those who ascribe everything to soil and climate. (Quotes Vitruvius.) In a passage quoted by many of his contemporaries, Kames said that the people of Malacca contradicted the idea that a hot climate was an enemy of courage; other instances were also given.[127]

It was the Creator's intention that the whole earth be peopled; he criticized Montesquieu for implying that the Torrid Zone is unfit for habitation; although he had probably intended no imputation on Providence, it was one.[128]

Kames is one of the early modern thinkers who grants a significant role to race in his theory of society, although many had considered the races to be of unequal endowment; Hume, for example, considered the white race superior to the others.[129] What Kames had to say about climate and its relation to culture was ordinary enough despite the ingenuity of dating the origin of the races from the confusion of Babel. More stimulating were his speculations about cultural development in the New World.

Kames assumes an independent development of man in America. Influenced by Buffon's geological theories, he assumed that America and Terra Australis were local creations. American culture, now still in the fishing and hunting stage, had not known a pastoral stage. This omission was not owing to want of cattle; the inhabitants, having enough food, persisted in their old ways and were not forced, as were the peoples of the Old World, to advance to a higher stage. The peoples of the New World had passed from the hunting and fishing stage directly to agriculture. Less daring than he was in his Tower of Babel theory of race, Kames confesses his inability to explain either the omission of this stage in the presumed cultural development of man or the efflorescence of high civilization in the New World tropics. Kames touches on a question that also interested Humboldt, whose solution was chiefly environmental. The question was interesting because it had been long believed that mankind went through hunting and fishing, pastoral, and agricultural stages, as Varro citing Dicaearchus had said.[130]

Many of the ideas discussed by Montesquieu, Buffon, and Hume were brought together in a synthesis by James Dunbar which was as remarkable as Herder's. Dunbar, Professor of Philosophy in King's College and the University of Aberdeen, first published *Essays on the History of Mankind in Rude*

---

[127] *Sketches of the History of Man*, Vol. I, p. 22.
[128] *Ibid.*, pp. 26–31.
[129] "Of National Characters," *Essays*, Vol. I, p. 252, note 1. This note, according to the editors, was added in Edition K, 1753–1754, p. 85. On Kames's racial doctrines, see Bryson, *Man and Society*, pp. 64–66.
[130] *Sketches*, Bk. II, Sketch 12, Vol. II, pp. 76, 77–79, cites Buffon, p. 84.

*and Cultivated Ages* in 1780.[131] Few of Dunbar's ideas, considered individually, are of interest; they had been expressed many times before. It is his
combining of them that attracts one's attention.

Frugal environments goad men to industry—necessity is the mother of invention—but a middle situation between extremes "of munificence and rigour"
is best. The series of events which lead men on to civilization may be started
by physical causes which will, however, be superseded by moral causes, the
direct influence of "the outward elements" receding; the evolution of civilization is a process by which man progressively frees himself from the control of
his physical environment.[132]

Superstition, fanaticism, sublime theology, have existed in the same climates
at different periods; to "account for so striking an effect in any latitude or
climate, there is no need to recur to the positive and direct influence of the
outward elements on the human mind. The series of events, once begun, is
governed more perhaps by moral than by physical causes: and this propensity
of genius and temper may owe its original to the primary direction of the
sciences, and their early alliance with theology and civil government."[133]

Dunbar sees a geographical march of civilization (the result, for the most
part, of a preoccupation with the history of western Europe) from tropical
climates, good for beginnings, to the temperate, which are suitable for maturity. Civilization came from the south to Europe and flowered there. He
assumes a tropical origin of the civilizations of the Old and the New Worlds
and that they arose independently. If the New World civilization had not
been interfered with, a similar march to more favorable environments would
also have taken place.[134] The design of Providence, however, brings order and
reasonableness into the physical arrangements existing on earth. Geography
sets bounds to conquest, war, and tyranny; it prevents the establishment of a
universal empire which is such an undesirable eventuality "that we can scarce
resist supposing it to have been one design of Providence," in making the
natural divisions of the earth.[135] Diversity in nature and the cultural variety
coming from a world of nations—rather than the uniformity of a world empire
—encourage human achievement. Men, in primitive and advanced societies
alike, need variety and diversity to nurture their endowments. Although the
optimum limits to government cannot be mathematically determined, a country with an imperfect government could improve it by decreasing its area, for
the arts can be encouraged and reform, control, and innovation can be accom-

---

[131] See Fletcher, *Montesquieu and English Politics (1750–1800)*, pp. 98–99, whose discussion made me realize Dunbar's importance in this history.

[132] *Essays*, pp. 221–222, 225.

[133] *Ibid.*, p. 225.

[134] *Ibid.*, pp. 231–234.

[135] *Ibid.*, p. 252.

plished in small states. "But the reformation of a wide domain is an immense and laborious work, that needs a long preparation of time, and presupposes an intercourse of regions and enlightened by philosophy and learning."[136]

Two apparent exceptions to the generalization that small geographical areas are favorable to human progress, the Russia of Peter I and of Catherine, and China, are examined by Dunbar, who recognizes the far-reaching nature of Peter's reforms—the introduction of foreign artisans, commercial and governmental planning, the establishment of an army, and the tranquillity following the treaty of Nystadt. "Yet so glorious a reign could animate a few parts only, without infusing life or vigour into so vast a body." Catherine and Peter had executed their plans on too large a scale. "And the late accession of territory [i.e., in the Treaty of Nystadt between Sweden and Russia in 1721], how greatly soever it may augment the revenue, or the splendor of the sovereign, tends in reality to encumber, in those regions, the efforts of the human species.[137]

The Chinese, Dunbar grants, achieved a high state of civilization for a long historical period. But if there is no decline in the sciences there, they also seem to have been stationary or "slowly progressive"; they have not reached a level of achievement one might expect from so long a history. The reasons for the failure are authority, respect for ancient opinion, and the lack of a spirit of philosophical inquiry.[138] Adopting the principle of Montesquieu that physical conditions in Asia are favorable for extended governments, Dunbar questions whether the stability of the Chinese government is owing to the wisdom with which it was organized. So large is the country, however, that its people outnumber even their conquerors, who "have no fixed usages, manners, or institutions of their own"; helpless before such an established system, they are absorbed. Thus an immutability is possible through size, population, and continuity of tradition "without regard to the degree of its perfection." China need fear change only from within and not from an invader—so great is the power of its manners, laws, and religion. "Thus China forms an illustrious example of the connexion of human affairs with geographical limits. Secure on the east and south by the ocean, and on the west by inaccessible deserts, she is vulnerable on the side of Tartary alone."[139]

After this excursion into political geography, Dunbar tries to find a middle ground between the views of Montesquieu and Hume; to him, neither type of causation is necessarily permanent in its effects.

> But it deserves to be remembered, that causes *physical* in their nature, are often *moral* only in their operations; that these operations are limited and pre-

[136] *Ibid.*, pp. 253–254, quote on p. 254.
[137] *Ibid.*, pp. 256–257.
[138] *Ibid.*, p. 258.
[139] *Ibid.*, pp. 262–263.

carious, and relative to the conjuncture; that a people may be long incapable to avail themselves of external advantages, that circumstances ultimately beneficial, may have proved for a long while incommodious or destructive; and, consequently, that the importance of local station, far from being permanent, varies not only with the contingencies of the natural world, but with the course of political events, and the general state of human improvement.

A fundamental change in the nature of insularity occurred, he said, with the era of navigation; before, it meant isolation and divorcement from the rest of the world; after, as British experience showed, an insular situation became a fertile source of national security, opulence, and grandeur.[140]

Living in an age in which men were becoming aware of travel and exploration for economic reasons, Dunbar thinks that trade and commerce mean mobile resources, and independence from the limitations of local environment; all nature becomes available to man everywhere. "Riches or poverty must no longer be estimated by the position of a people on the globe. Art, if I may say so, alters the dispensation of nature, and maintains a sort of distributive justice in the division of opulence among mankind."[141] Dunbar realized, however, that this millennial sentiment was only the statement of a possibility; trade restrictions, commercial regulations, and national monopolies were still very much alive.

The effects of cultural contact vary, however, with distance or contiguity. Commerce with far-off nations seldom can form the intimate connections that are possible with closer neighbors.

Geographical relation therefore will always be, in some degree, instrumental in retarding or accelerating, in every country, the progress of civil life. Communities, as well as private persons, are formed by example. And the character of a people must bear a resemblance in manners, in genius, and in arts, to that which predominates in the system with which they are more immediately connected. Civility and rudeness being distributed like light and darkness in the natural world, contiguous nations are often contemporary in their progress and decline: and the more enlightened regions, tho' always shifting, form at any one time a complete and undivided whole situated around a common centre.[142]

In agreement with Count Buffon, he notes the ubiquity and the adaptability of man: "Man erects for himself a mansion in every country." There is general agreement that no one country is "the fittest residence for man. That influence of the heavens seems to be relatively the best, which habit has rendered the most familiar."[143] Adopting the idea of a chain of being and Count Buffon's distinction between man and the animals ("L'homme est en tout l'ouvrage du ciel; les animaux ne sont à beaucoup d'egards que des productions de la terre"),

[140] *Ibid.*, pp. 280–282, quote on pp. 280–281.
[141] *Ibid.*, pp. 294–295.
[142] *Ibid.*, pp. 300–301.
[143] *Ibid.*, pp. 304–306, 330, quote on p. 306.

Dunbar says that because of his high rank in the creation, man has a different relationship with the physical world. "Soil and climate seem to act with a gradation of influence on vegetable, animal, and intellectual nature. . . . Man, therefore, by his rank in the creation, is more exempted from mechanical dominion than the classes below him." Anticipating an idea that Alexander von Humboldt expanded into an elaborate history of ideas, Dunbar says the superior status of man makes him more vulnerable to impressions coming from nature, unlike an animal which "feels only what disturbs the animal oeconomy. The scenery of creation it regards with total indifference; but that scenery acts on a human being in a peculiar manner, and without annoying his person, affects the sensibility and delicacy of his moral frame."[144] This theme of the subjective influences of nature on man, here lightly touched upon by Dunbar, became in the writings of Humboldt, Ritter, and Buckle a powerful and subtle reinforcement of the environmental argument.[145]

Dunbar carries the argument that man and the rest of life differ fundamentally in their dependence on nature a step further (possibly under the influence of Buffon), claiming that man is the arbiter of his own future. Recognition of man's power to change nature follows from the doctrine of the freedom of the will. Natural and moral ills are part of man's lot on earth; "it is in vain to enquire into their origin." There is a reciprocal relation between man and the elements. "He has a range allowed him in the creation peculiar to himself alone; and he seems to have had delegated to him a certain portion of the government of the natural world." Although unavoidable natural revolutions occur and physical limitations do exist, still "soil and climate are subject to his dominion; and the natural history of the terraqueous globe varies with the civil history of nations."[146]

Dunbar repeats ideas which Count Buffon had made familiar: men have altered the climates, and their activity has modified the environments of the Old and New Worlds. (See chapter XIV.) In a plea for the transformation of America by cultivating the soil, clearing, and drainage, Dunbar says, "Let us learn then to wage war with the elements, not with our own kind; to recover, if one may say so, our patrimony from Chaos, and not to add to his empire." This interesting statement suggests that nature left to itself is unordered and unorganized, that it has no significance except when converted into an order by man.[147] This order-making involves the elimination of disease or a lessening of its severity with environmental change, especially by drainage. Thus there is little determinism left; soil and climate, like the human mind, are variable and

[144] *Ibid.*, pp. 325–326, 330.
[145] See *ibid.*, pp. 326–328, for an elaboration of these views; Humboldt's *Cosmos*, trans. by Otté, Vol. 2, Pt. 1, "Incitements to the Study of Nature," and Buckle's *History of Civilization in England*, chap. 2.
[146] *Ibid.*, pp. 335, 336–337.
[147] *Ibid.*, p. 338; see also pp. 336–339.

susceptible of change and improvement "with the progress of civil arts."[148]
In employing ideas of design, of the influence of location, and of environmental change by man in his interpretation of the nature and history of civilization, Dunbar achieves an impressive and thoughtful synthesis.

## 10. ON WILLIAM FALCONER

The 552 pages of text of William Falconer's *Remarks on the Influence of Climate, Situation, Nature of Country, Population, Nature of Food, and Way of Life, on The Disposition and Temper, Manners and Behavior, Intellects, Laws and Customs, Form of Government, and Religion, of Mankind* (London, 1781) is, of all the works produced on this subject during the eighteenth century, the most remarkable in its scope and tone, and the most convincing evidence of the importance attached at that time to climate, religion, customs, and ways of life.

A large part of the book is devoted to familiar themes. Book I, "On the Effect of Climate," comprising over one-third of the work, is suffused with the spirit of Montesquieu, though he is not accepted uncritically. The second book, twelve pages long, "Of the Influence of Situation and Extent of a Country," also pursues a traditional interest, including the position of Europe, the effects of island and continental environments. The third, "On the Influence of the Nature of the Country itself," somewhat longer, corresponds roughly to Montesquieu's discussion of the influence of soils in the eighteenth book of the *Esprit des Lois*. The fourth book, "On the Influence of Population," is concerned mainly with the advantages of a large or a small population; and the fifth, "On the Influence of the Nature of Food and Diet," cultivated a field already tilled by Temple, Montesquieu, Buffon, Kaempfer, Arbuthnot, and others. The last and by far the longest book, "On the Influence of Way of Life," is organized around a conjectural history of mankind, that is, the influence of the savage, the barbarous, and the agricultural states, of commercial life, literature and science, and of luxury and refinement. Broadly speaking, therefore, the work attempts to understand society through the study of physical causes, causes transitional between the physical and moral, and the moral causes in various stages of cultural development and in various types of social institutions.

Falconer had read widely in classical literature; often the classical writers are cited as authorities along with modern writers on the humors. No better proof is needed of the continuing influence of Hippocrates' *Airs, Waters, Places*, for Falconer discusses it, as had Arbuthnot, as if it were a scientific document of first rank. Falconer was like the distinguished English physicians, Thomas Sydenham (1624–1689), often called the English Hippocrates, and

[148] *Ibid.*, p. 342.

John Arbuthnot (1667–1735), in his interest in the wider aspects of medicine.

Despite a first impression that the work is an English recasting of Montesquieu, Falconer is too eclectic a thinker to accept unreservedly any author or any single-element theory of causation. Writers propounding the effects of climate have made them too universal; they are general, not particular, and there may be exceptions to these general influences among nations or individuals living in a certain climate. Following the conventional view, Falconer says that one cause may counteract another. "Thus a hot climate naturally renders men timid and slothful; but the necessity induced by a barren country, number of inhabitants, animal diet, and a savage way of life, may any of them correct this tendency of the climate, and dispose the manners to a different turn."

Less conventional is Falconer's conception of the nature of these causes. The various climatic effects are discrete and separate but capable of combining with one another; in combination they may overpower, temper, or modify one another, "but have each of them a separate existence and action, however they may concur with one another in the general effect." They are likened to "the mechanic powers" which in combination "frequently produce an effect different from what any of them would have caused separately; but still their specific action remains, though its inferior force renders it imperceptible to our examination."[149]

The book is an authoritative summary of ideas concerning man's relation to the environment which were widely held in the eighteenth century. First, the adaptability of man to all climates is seen as a mark of his rationality; the range and ubiquity of man are explained teleologically, for it may be assumed "that he was intended by nature to inhabit every part of the world." This adaptability and ubiquity are owing to an excellent mental rather than physical endowment. "But notwithstanding this assistance afforded by nature, it may be justly doubted if this universality of the human species be not owing more to his rational faculties, which enable him to supply the defects, and correct the exuberances of particular climates and situations, than merely to his animal formation."[150]

By this time, moreover, it was a commonplace that the effects of climate could be counteracted; the more that was known about climates and their effects, the easier would it be through scientific methods to encourage or thwart these influences. Thus a kind of possibilism already flourished in the eighteenth century, but it lacked the background possessed by nineteenth century thinkers in ecological studies, in knowledge of man's influence on the environment, of Darwinian evolution, and of sociological and ethnological theory.

---

[149] *Remarks on the Influence of Climate*, p. vi.
[150] *Ibid.*, p. 2.

Falconer, however, like many of his contemporaries, cannot conceal his admiration for the temperate climates as seats of civilization, and there is a great deal to be said for this correlation if one identifies the history of civilization with that of Western civilization.[151]

Like Montesquieu, Falconer thinks hot climates encourage cultural inertia.[152] Peter the Great's success in part is owing to the climate; people living in cold climates are far less attached to their countries than are those of hot climates. "The Czar Peter the First, accomplished an almost entire change in the manners and customs throughout the vast empire of Russia, and this without any great opposition, or the being obliged to have recourse to arms. An attempt of the like kind in China, though far less extensive, produced a revolution in the state."[153] The latter statement is based on a remark by Du Halde that one of the Chinese emperors provoked a revolution by ordering his subjects to pare their nails and cut their hair. A uniformity in the Chinese climate is assumed.

Falconer, an anti-Catholic thinker, is also interested in the bearing of climate on religion. Historically, there are good reasons for this association of climate with religion in Western thought. The Christian religion originated in the arid margins of a Mediterranean type of climate. It achieved great successes in the entirely different environment of northwestern Europe. The success of the Reformation in the Scandinavian countries, in the North European plain, and in England, Scotland, Wales, and Ulster suggested that geography might have an influence on the distribution of faiths. Schisms and the emergence of denominations within Protestantism were problems of a different kind. The enemies of revealed religion, deists and those sympathetic with deism, were inclined, like Voltaire, to ascribe to environment at least some kinds of religious observance.

According to Falconer, the hot countries are notable for worshiping sensible objects (the sun, the moon, the earth, fire, winds, water, images) and for deifying men; he criticizes the Catholic worship of images of saints, extravagant veneration of sacred relics, or remains of religious persons, the severest criticism being reserved for worship of the Virgin Mary and the doctrine of transubstantiation. With the people of the cold climates, on the other hand, religion "is rather a subject of internal contemplation; and its influence is directed more to the reason than to the passions." The peoples of the north at first received "the absurdities of the Romish church" but with the diffusion of learning and the spirit of inquiry, they "broke their chains, and established a mode of worship consonant to the ideas suggested by the climate."[154] Even Christianity, a revealed religion, is here subject to the influence of climate.

---

[151] *Ibid.*, pp. 10, 18–24.
[152] *Ibid.*, pp. 47, 112–114.
[153] *Ibid.*, p. 116.
[154] *Ibid.*, pp. 133–134.

Temperate climates are best suited for religion. "Greece and Italy, formerly, furnished the justest notions concerning the being and nature of the Deity [cites Epictetus, Bk. II, chap. 14, § 2, and Marcus Aurelius, Bk. II, § 3] and although it pleased the Almighty to make a warm climate the scene of his particular revelation, it has been in temperate latitudes that Christianity has been best understood and practised."[155]

Nothing can illustrate the resilience of the idea of climatic influence and its application to all phases of cultural life well as Falconer's approach, as a doctor, to the influence of the environment on man in the tradition of Hippocrates and Galen, and of Sydenham, Arbuthnot, Haller, and Hoffman in modern times. Although the relation of environmental theory to concepts of public health is beyond the scope of this essay, it is necessary to say that a more active philosophy of man as a being capable of changing his environment emerged from a purely medical interest in climate and in the human body. Interests in sweating, in the circulation of the blood under different climatic conditions, in bodily reactions under extremes of heat and cold, were related not only to health but to the etiology of disease, and here a blending with cultural phenomena is possible. Falconer cites Haller's statement that excessive sweating in burning hot climates (Barbados, Carthagena, Surinam) suddenly saps the strength of Europeans; such sweatings "are not less weakening than violent purgings by stool."[156]

A sound mental state and physical health, said Falconer, are closely related to freedom and regularity of perspiration; "the obstruction of this discharge is generally attended with low spirits. The obstruction, therefore, which a moist air gives to perspiration, is a presumption that it is unfavourable to the powers of the mind and understanding." The ill effects are greater when the moist air is in combination with "marsh effluvia."[157] Falconer is also interested in the relation of the qualities of the air to putrefaction. Although these interests are ancient ones, with him there is a strong disposition to explore an ever-widening relationship of airs to physical and mental health. Environments which are by nature unhealthful, like a marsh in a hot and humid climate, become challenges to human ingenuity; men need not passively accept environmentally induced disease. Hopes of making localities more healthful were thus strong inducements to environmental change. The history of drainage would tell us much, not only about the history of public health but of man's attitude toward the physical environment, of his empirical understanding, before the germ theory of disease, of the value of dryness and openness in his natural surroundings.

---

[155] *Ibid.*, p. 134, followed by long discussions of the influence of climate on forms, ceremonies, institutions, food habits, and tabus.

[156] *Ibid.*, p. 12, citing Albrecht von Haller, *Elementa Physiologiae Corporis Humani*, Vol. 6, pp. 66–67.

[157] *Ibid.*, pp. 163–165, quote on p. 163. Falconer gives as an example the people living on the banks of the Phasis, mentioned in Hippocrates' *Airs, Waters, Places*, p. 164.

In Falconer's work we can see how broad interests had been intensified over the century: the relation of environmental ideas to social institutions (climate and religion), to public health and medicine, to diet (with comparisons of diets as materials gradually accumulated from the voyages and travels), to moral causes (overcoming environmental disadvantages by social measures), and to technology and engineering (purposeful planning to change environments unfavorable to man).

## 11. New Cultivations: Robertson and America

The climatic theories of Montesquieu floated ashore in Scotland, whose moral philosophers were most interested in the development of culture and in a science of man. Adam Ferguson, for example, traced the stages in the development of human society, considering the influences of climate and situation. Man as an animal can exist in any climate, but "this animal has always attained to the principal honours of his species within the temperate zone."[158] Although differences among polished nations may be owing to climate, government is the strongest influence; there is a tendency to ascribe the backwardness of primitive peoples to climatic causes, and the differences among modern societies to moral ones. But there is nothing new here and we need not go into details except to say that Montesquieu's racy discussion of love becomes heavy and soggy in Scottish translation.

More interesting is William Robertson's use of geographical ideas current in the century; he belonged to a cosmopolitan world of European learning and letters whose membership, ignoring national boundaries, included many of the great names of the time—Buffon, Montesquieu, Hume, Voltaire—who were familiar with the advanced societies of Europe, the impressive cultures of non-European peoples, and the primitive peoples so far discovered. The Scottish group, of which Robertson was a member, included David Hume, Adam Ferguson, Lord Kames, Lord Montboddo, Adam Smith, and Dugald Stewart, who wrote biographies of both Smith and Robertson.[159] He corresponded with Gibbon, and his historiography betrayed the inspiration of Voltaire at least as much as one could expect from a Presbyterian minister. His taste for the broad surveys of history, his interest in eras of striking and abrupt historical change, such as the fall of Rome, the Crusades, the age of discovery and the diffusion of knowledge following it, marked him as a widely read man of vigorous intellect, whose graceful and simple, if somewhat monotonous, English can still be read with pleasure.

In "A View of the Progress of Society in Europe, from the Subversion of the Roman Empire to the Beginning of the Sixteenth Century," which served

[158] *An Essay on the History of Civil Society*, p. 180. See Pt. II, sec. I, "Of the Influences of Climate and Situation."
[159] On this group, see Gladys Bryson, *Man and Society: The Scottish Inquiry of the Eighteenth Century*. Princeton University Press, 1945.

as the introduction to *The History of the Reign of the Emperor Charles V*, Robertson had shown his interest in migrations, in the relative populousness of ancient and modern nations, and in climatic influences. His *History of America* (first published in 1777) is a valuable work because it is based on knowledge and lore about the New World and its peoples collected since the age of discovery which raised questions of major importance in the interpretation of New World history, especially of its earlier phases. These are: floral and faunal differences between the Old World and the New, the origin of the peoples of the New World, particularly of its high civilizations in Mexico and Peru, racial and cultural differences, and contrasts between the Old World and the New in the environmental changes by human agency. These questions might readily occur to an historian of America, especially of the period from the original settlement to the conquest. In answering them, Robertson used many of the original sources relating to the conquest, and the theories of Montesquieu and Buffon.

Like many writers of the second half of the eighteenth century, Robertson is impressed with the new knowledge of the world that trade and communication have brought, and he distinguishes sharply between these new intellectual resources and the limitations of the classical thinkers. He is keenly aware of the interchange of ideas that comes about through migrations and crusades, trade and travel.[160] The design argument is very subdued; with the age of discovery, he said, "the period arrived when Providence decreed that men were to pass the limits within which they had been so long confined, and open to themselves a more ample field wherein to display their talents, their enterprise, and courage."[161] This statement is not mere rhetoric; it combines religious feeling with admiration for intellectual and physical venturesomeness and activity. This admiration of activity in new environments is related also to the zeal men must show in changing the environment, often by draining, in order to improve the health of mankind.[162]

To Robertson, the New World, America, is a magnificent region, its physical attributes being created large in the scale of nature. The shape of the mountains, rivers, lakes, newly discovered continents, is favorable to commercial intercourse. Mentioning themes developed at length later in the nineteenth century, Robertson compares the embayments of the New World and their influence on human settlement favorably with those of Europe and Asia, commenting on their relative absence in Africa.[163]

His conceptions of natural history are borrowed from Buffon; he accepts Acosta's climatology with Buffon's daring elaborations (see p. 680).[164] Fol-

---

[160] *Hist. Amer.*, Vol. I, pp. 31–33.

[161] *Ibid.*, p. 40, cf. pp. 65–66.

[162] *Ibid.*, p. 125.

[163] *Ibid.*, pp. 254–255.

[164] *Ibid.*, pp. 257, 361–363. José de Acosta, *Historia Natural y Moral de las Indias* (1590), esp. Bk. II.

lowing Buffon, he distinguishes between countries which have long been occupied by man and those of recent settlement, agreeing with the French natural historian that "no small part of that fertility and beauty which we ascribe to the hand of nature, is the work of man."[165]

With the aid of Buffon, Acosta, and others Robertson satisfied himself regarding the nature of the New World environment. It was hostile to higher forms of life, encouraged the less noble forms; it could produce only peoples of a low and rude culture who could do little to embellish and improve upon nature as Buffon had prescribed.

Robertson now turned to the question of the peopling of the New World, the answers to which were dependent upon different but still related matters: the unity of the human race, contrasts between the Old World and the New in inventions and domesticated animals, the absence of pastoral nomadism in the New World. Theories of the peopling of the New World were also directly related to opposing theories of social change, independent invention, and diffusion. Although it will take us too far afield to study the history of these ideas, it may be said that the opposing ideas themselves are natural outgrowths of more general ideas in Western culture. The idea of independent invention, one of the oldest in Western civilization, is based on the belief that necessity is the mother of invention, or in environmentalistic terms, that a people (assuming that, on the whole, mental and physical endowments are distributed uniformly) under similar environmental conditions will arrive at similar solutions of problems. This idea of independent invention had a rival, however, in the diffusionism implicit in the Bible and in the body of Christian theology based on it. Historically, in fact, the idea of independent invention as it was expressed by many thinkers of the eighteenth and nineteenth centuries, was a reaction to early diffusionists who, long before Elliot Smith and W. J. Perry, were prone to find everything originating in Egypt or Palestine. Robertson is scornful of the older diffusionists. After disposing of those who believed in the multiple origin of the human race, and of those who thought the Americans to be descendants of "some remnant of the antediluvian inhabitants of the earth, who survived the deluge," he continues, "There is hardly any nation from the north to the south pole, to which some antiquary, in the extravagance of conjecture, has not ascribed the honour of peopling America." In ancient times, the Jews, the Canaanites, the Phoenicians, the Carthaginians, the Greeks, the Scythians, supposedly settled in the New World; in later times, the Chinese, the Swedes, the Norwegians, the Welsh, the Spaniards, are said to have established colonies there. "Zealous advocates stand forth to support the respective claims of those people; and though they rest upon no better foundation than the casual resemblance of some customs, or the supposed affinity between a few words in their different languages, much erudition and more

---

[165] *Hist. Amer.*, Vol. I, p. 261. See below, chap. XIV, sec. 7.

zeal have been employed, to little purpose, in defence of the opposite systems."[166]

Robertson's solution, since become commonplace, was that the human race had originated in a single place, and that the peopling of the New World occurred at so early a period that the migrants came without the arts necessary to establish a civilization; whatever civilization flourished in the New World was therefore autochthonous. On religious authority, he accepts the original unity of the human race, but throws up his hands at any attempt to account for the precise means by which the earth was peopled. From an examination of the state of the New World at the time of its discovery and from the analysis of what was known of the pre-Columbian civilizations in his time, Robertson reasons that the progenitors of the people of the New World came originally from northeast Asia, not from Europe; they had neither domesticated animals nor had they made any progress toward civilization.[167] The historical sequence had therefore been the origin of mankind in a single homeland in the Old World, the dispersion of the human race throughout the world in prehistoric times, the gradual development of differences among peoples as a result of the dispersion and because they were stationary or progressing at varying speeds through assumed stages of development. The case can now be made for autochthonous development based on environmental conditions.

> If we suppose two tribes, though placed in the most remote regions of the globe, to live in a climate nearly of the same temperature, to be in the same state of society, and to resemble each other in the degree of their improvement, they must feel the same wants and exert the same endeavours to supply them. The same objects will allure, the same passions will animate them, and the same ideas and sentiments will arise in their minds.

Similarities among peoples living in widely separated parts of the earth therefore do not mean connections between them, and he takes Fathers Garcia and Lafitau and others to task for assuming that similarities meant cultural contact or diffusion.

> A tribe of savages on the banks of the Danube must nearly resemble one upon the plains washed by the Mississippi. Instead then of presuming from this similarity that there is any affinity between them, we should only conclude that the disposition of manners of men are formed by their situation, and arise from the state of society in which they live. The moment that begins to vary, the character of a people must change. In proportion as it advances in improvement, their manners refine, their powers and talents are called forth.

Only specific similarities among peoples living in different parts of the world, such as giving over the seventh day to religious worship and rest, should lead one to suspect a relationship; similarities in customs are to be expected in similar environments and in similar states of society.[168]

Robertson is aware of the leading contemporary thought regarding the New

[166] *Ibid.*, pp. 271–272.
[167] *Ibid.*, pp. 269–270, 275–278, 286.
[168] *Ibid.*, pp. 273–274.

World peoples; he himself is cautious, critical of system builders. There is Buffon's theory of the weakness of nature in the New World, that its peoples, owing to the recency of its settlement, could not be compared with the peoples of the Old World and their improved environments.[169] There is De Pauw's theory that an unkindly and enervating climate had prevented man in the New World from attaining the perfection proper to him, remaining an animal, defective in body and mind. Robertson, however, apparently did not realize that these excesses of De Pauw—and of Peter Kalm—were inspired by Buffon, who later in life repudiated the exaggerations of writers who had accepted his theory (see below, p. 685).[170] Finally there is Rousseau's theory which supposes, says Robertson, that "man arrives at his highest dignity and excellence long before he reaches a state of refinement; and, in the rude simplicity of savage life, displays an elevation of sentiment, and independence of mind, and a warmth of attachment, for which it is vain to search among the members of polished societies."[171]

Caution is the moral which Robertson squeezes from these opinions. He follows the thought of his time in comparing the superiority of man over the animals in his adaptability to all kinds of climates, except extremes of heat and cold. Robertson forgets his caution, however, when he reads travelers' accounts; agreeing with Buffon, he comments on the lack of sexual ardor among the North Americans. How did a Scottish Presbyterian minister know that "The negro glows with all the warmth of desire natural to his climate; and the most uncultivated Asiatics discover that sensibility, which from their situation on the globe, we should expect them to have felt. But the Americans are, in an amazing degree, strangers to the force of this first instinct of nature. In every part of the New World the natives treat their women with coldness and indifference"? This coldness exists in the New World even in climates where one might expect sexual vigor and ardor, for their lack is not owing to any respect for chastity, "an idea too refined," he adds smugly, "for a savage, and suggested by a delicacy of sentiment and affection to which he is a stranger."[172]

[169] *Ibid.*, p. 293. See Buffon, *HN*, Vol. 3, pp. 484, 103, 114.

[170] *Hist. Amer.*, Vol. I, p. 293. See De Pauw's *Recherches Philosophiques sur les Américains*, Vol. 1, "Discours Preliminaire," esp. pp. iii-iv, xiii; 35-36, 42, 60-61, 105-108, 112-114; these passages frequently show unacknowledged borrowing from Buffon. See also Vol. 3, chaps. 1-9, and *passim*. The history of ideas concerning America and its peoples is a vast subject in itself, beyond the scope of this work. See Church, "Corneille de Pauw, and the Controversy over His Recherches Philosophiques sur les Américains," *PMLA*, Vol. 51 (1936), pp. 178-206. See pp. 185-191 for a summary of De Pauw's opinions, and Gilbert Chinard, "Eighteenth Century Theories on America as a Human Habitat," *PAPS*, Vol. 91 (1947), pp. 27-57. The subject is treated exhaustively by Gerbi, *La Disputa del Nuovo Mondo. Storia di Una Polemica 1750-1900*, esp. chaps. 1-4.

[171] *Ibid.*, pp. 293-294. See Lovejoy, "The Supposed Primitivism of Rousseau's Discourse on Inequality," *Modern Philology*, Vol. 21 (1923), pp. 165-186. Reprinted in *Essays in the History of Ideas* (Capricorn Books), New York, 1960, pp. 14-37.

[172] *Hist. Amer.*, Vol. I, p. 299; in footnote 38, listing the sources, Buffon is not mentioned, but I think much of this came from him.

Robertson emerges as a friend of eclectic views: it is too one-sided to consider physical, political, or moral causes alone. Polished societies, for example, modify "the degree of attachment between the sexes"; they also allow, as Buffon had stressed, for the survival of individuals who, in primitive societies, would have perished.[173] The greater uniformity of the human beings in the New World than in the Old is explained, as Buffon had explained it, by the lesser heat of the New World tropics.[174]

The eclecticism includes traditional points of view as well, for in America, as in other parts of the world, the cold or temperate countries are friendly to freedom and independence. In America the power of those vested with authority gradually increases, and the spirit of the people becomes more tame and passive as one journeys from north to south.[175]

Borrowing from Adam Ferguson (who echoes Montesquieu), Robertson concludes that one must be aware of the diversity of climates in which people live. "In every part of the earth where man exists, the power of climate operates, with decisive influence, upon his condition and character." After mentioning again the superiority of the temperate climates and the more powerful effects of climate on rude nations than on polished societies, he ends with a theory of multiple causation, not unlike Herder's, with the warning "Even the law of climate, more universal, perhaps, in its operation than any that affects the human species, cannot be applied, in judging of their conduct, without many exceptions."[176]

## 12. New Cultivations: The Forsters and the South Seas

Contemporaries, including the learned men who participated in the voyages, were well aware of the scientific and philosophical significance of Cook's discoveries. In his essay on the American fur trade, George Forster speaks of recent advances in the study of nature and of man, the progress of discovery, and of geographical knowledge. The voyages of Cook had torn away the veil from an unknown half the world ("von einer unbekannten Hälfte des Erdbodens den Schleier hinweggerissen").[177] Forster makes generous reference to the accomplishments of Cook and his men. The principal purposes of the voyages had been fulfilled. There was no southern continent in the temperate zone nor indeed was there a vast tract of land within the Antarctic Circle; the great ice masses floating in the sea were composed of fresh water;

[173] *Ibid.*, pp. 301, 305.

[174] *Ibid.*, pp. 305–307.

[175] *Ibid.*, Vol. 2, pp. 21–22. His view of climactic influences on drunkenness, p. 79, is also conventional.

[176] *Ibid.*, pp. 97, 98–99, 100–101.

[177] "Die Nordwestküste von Amerika und der dortige Pelzhandel," *SS*, Vol. 4, pp. 5–7, 116–119, quote on p. 117. Note the following abbreviations: *Obs.*, Johann Reinhold Forster, *Observations Made During a Voyage Round the World*; *VRW*, George Forster, *A Voyage Round the World*; *SS*, George Forster's *Sämmtliche Schriften*.

geographers had been given new islands, naturalists new plants and birds, the friends of mankind "with the various modifications of human nature."[178] There was no Terra Australis with millions of people, but these losses were made up by the rich ethnological findings of Cook and his companions.

Although Cook's descriptions are full and vivid, they lack the theoretical interest of the writings of Johann Reinhold Forster and his son, George, who were on the "Resolution" with Cook on his second voyage (1772–1775). It is difficult to separate the thoughts of the son from those of the father, because the boy was not yet eighteen when he left; he wrote *A Voyage Round the World* in order to present his father's findings before the public, because the Admiralty forbade the older Forster to publish a separate account of the voyage. George Forster expresses bitterness about their treatment by high government officials and the malevolence of the sailors on the sloop.[179]

Johann Reinhold Forster's *Observations Made During a Voyage Round the World* (1778) appeared the year following the publication of his son's *A Voyage Round the World*. The elder Forester acknowledges his indebtedness to Bergman and Buffon for the physical geography and to Isaac Iselin for the "Philosophical History of the Human Species." The botanical principles come from Linnaeus, and the grand views of nature are inspired by Buffon. "My object was nature in its greatest extent; the Earth, the Sea, the Air, the Organic and Animated Creation, and more particularly that class of Beings to which we belong." Respectful of authorities but aware of their limitations—many of their philosophies were composed in the closet or in the bosom of a highly civilized nation—Forster adds that none of them had contemplated the scale of primitive life from abject animality "to the more polished and civilized inhabitants of the Friendly and Society Isles."[180] Both men are sympathetic to the design argument, but it does not lean heavily on them; they are closer to Buffon's rhetoric than to conventional natural theology.

Alexander von Humboldt acknowledged being inspired by the writings of George Forster, and it is easy to see how he would be struck with the beauty of tropical landscapes whose New World exemplars were to absorb him as well.[181] In the thinking of both men, the tropical environment plays a key role in natural history and in their philosophy of civilization. Johann Reinhold Forster wrote of environments without vegetation as bleak, barren, desolate. It is the land clad with plants and diversified with birds and animals that gives us "an idea of the vivifying powers of nature and its Great Lord."[182] In the tropics a constant succession of vegetation infuses all places with life;

---

[178] *VRW*, Vol. 2, pp. 605–606; see also Cook's *Voyages*, Vol. 2, p. 49.

[179] See the preface to *VRW*; and "A Letter to the Right Honorable The Earl of Sandwich," and accompanying appendices at end of *Obs.*; on sailors' behavior, *VRW*, Vol. 2, p. 420, note. See the articles on Johann and George Forster by Alfred Dove in *Allgemeine Deutsche Biographie*, Vol. 7, pp. 168–171, 173–174.

[180] *Obs.*, p. ii.

[181] *Cosmos*, Vol. 2, p. 20.

[182] *Obs.*, p. 37.

the temperate zone vegetation enlivens the scene, but in frozen climates like Tierra del Fuego and Staten Island, the Creation seems lifeless and torpid. The nearer places lie to the course of the sun, the more are soil and mold, promoters of vegetation, increased; "in the same proportion all organic bodies animate the lifeless, chaotic part of the strata of our globe."[183]

In the past, thinkers frequently assumed a cultural uniformity over areas in which a certain climate was believed to be dominant. Forster is not guilty of such naïveté. His writings on the ethnology of the South Seas describe the complexity of social organization; historical and linguistic evidence plays an important part in his reconstructions, and comparative ethnology is a keystone in his arch. He recognizes classes within Tahitian society (the "aree, manahoùna, and towtow") and differences among the islanders of the South Seas; he compares the inhabitants of Tierra del Fuego with those of New Zealand, Greenland, and northern North America.[184]

Forster divides the peoples of the South Seas into two main groups: (1) those living in Tahiti (O-Tahéitee) and the Society Islands, the Marquesas, the Friendly Islands, Easter Island and New Zealand—these peoples are fair, well limbed, athletic, fine sized, and have a kind, benevolent temper; (2) the peoples of New Caledonia, of Tana ("Tanna"), and especially Malekula ("Mallicollo") in the New Hebrides. They are blacker in color, their hair is just beginning to become woolly and crisp, their bodies are more slender and low, their temper, "if possible more brisk, though somewhat mistrustful."[185] These two groups correspond of course to the modern division between Polynesia and Melanesia. The peoples of Tahiti and the Society Islands are the most beautiful examples of the first race, "but even here Nature seems to follow that richness, luxuriance, and variety, which we have observed in its vegetation; it is not confined to a single type of model."[186] The Forsters see variety, richness, and abundance in human life in those places whose natural surroundings also possess these characteristics.

The existence of the two types of peoples in the South Seas had been known long before Cook's voyages. On his first voyage (1567–1569), Alvaro de Mandaña reached the Melanesian Solomons, missing the Polynesian islands on the way, but on his second (1595) he discovered the Marquesas, thus providing the first ethnology of a Polynesian people. What are the reasons, Forster asks, for the differences between them? It would be easy simply to rely on Holy Writ, and assume that mankind had descended from one couple and that the present varieties on earth are accidental. But this explanation does not satisfy him, although he is convinced that the Bible expresses a historical truth in asserting what men hostile to religion also assert on philosoph-

---

[183] *Ibid.*, p. 134.
[184] *Ibid.*, pp. 212–213; on the names of the Tahiti classes, *VRW*, Vol. 1, p. 365.
[185] *Ibid.*, p. 228.
[186] *Ibid.*, pp. 228–229, quote on p. 229.

ical grounds, that all men are descended from one couple.[187] (Later, as we shall see, George considered the unity of the human race to be an open question.) Johann Reinhold Forster examines the possible physical causes for these differences, but his explanations are neither satisfactory nor clear because they are based for the most part on a crude theory of the inheritance of acquired characteristics. Skin color, for example, he believes to be the result of exposure to air, the sun's influence, and differences in the ways of living. The Tahitians, dressed and covered, expose themselves less than the people of Tana, New Caledonia, Malekula, who are always naked and therefore infinitely darker than they.[188] Negroes are of dark hue because they are living closer to the equator. The theory runs into difficulties in the South Seas, even if the sea mitigates the effects of the tropical sun. "This cause cannot be applied to the difference of colour in the Taheiteans and the Mallicolese [i.e., the people from Malekula], as both nations enjoy the same advantage."[189]

Forster thinks "peculiar modes of living" cooperate with these other causes "in producing the many changes in colour in the human species."[190] The explanation is naïve indeed. The Tahitians are very clean and bathe frequently, but the more tawny New Zealanders are unclean, abhor bathing, and are exposed to the smoke and nastiness of their cottages, practices which may account for differences in color. Climate, food, and exercise may influence bodily size, but here too there are difficulties, notably differences in size in Tahiti between the common people and their chiefs.

Climate therefore is an insufficient explanation for the observed differences. The Dutch at the Cape of Good Hope, living near the Hottentots, have remained fair for 120 years. Even all the causes mentioned cannot explain differences, for some remote Dutch farmers live almost like the Hottentots; they have wretched huts, they lead a nomadic life, yet they retain their identity. He concludes that if climate can make any material alteration, it would require an immense period of time to produce it.

The inadequacy and difficulty of climatic explanations cause him to consider cultural and historical evidence. The peoples of the South Seas, descended from two different races, live in the same climate, preserve differences in character, color, size, form, and habit of body.[191] Forster examines the linguistic evidence, putting aside simple environmental explanations. All the Polynesians have fundamentally the same language, but migrations of constituent peoples have brought about changes. They move to a new country and find there new birds, fishes, and plants, the names for which could not have existed in any other "co-generic dialects." Names for the qualities of the

---

[187] *Ibid.*, pp. 252–253, 257.
[188] *Ibid.*, pp. 257–260.
[189] *Ibid.*, p. 261.
[190] *Ibid.*, p. 261.
[191] *Ibid.*, p. 276. On the Dutch, pp. 271–272.

new animals and plants, the new foods and garments derived from them, gradually lead to a distinction between this new language and the original.[192] In this way he accounts for varieties in cultures which are basically similar.

An explorer noting the population distribution of the South Seas would naturally ask how they had been peopled. Forster believes migrations took place from the Asiatic mainland; for him there was no "Kon-Tiki" expedition from the New World. The easterly winds might make it possible, but he has a low opinion of pre-Columbian New World technology. The New World was peopled only a few centuries before the Spanish Conquest, and he finds no similarity between the American and the South Sea island languages. The distances are too great, the boats poor. He rejects Australia (New Holland) for similar reasons; the crudeness of aborigine culture, its poverty in domesticated plants and animals, the language differences, tell against it as a hearth of original dispersal.[193] Let us go north, he says, where the South Sea islands are connected to the East Indian islands, many of which are inhabited by two different races. The older live in the interior, hilly country, the newcomers on the shores and coasts; he finds examples in the Moluccas, the Philippines, and Formosa. Here again there are no climatic simplicities; one culture is superimposed over the other. The peoples of New Guinea, New Britain, and New Ireland (New Hibernia) are like the Melanesians in New Caledonia, Tana, and Malekula, and the blacks of New Guinea are probably related to those in the Moluccas and the Philippines. The peoples of the Ladrones and Carolines suggest the Polynesians. With linguistic evidence from Malaya, he concludes that the eastern South Sea islands were probably peopled from the Indian or Asiatic northern islands, those lying to the westward, possibly from the neighborhood of New Guinea.[194] The differences in the two races are traced to two different migrations into the South Seas. The first race descended from the Malays of the north who dispersed via the Carolines, the Ladrones, "the Manila," and Borneo. The blacks, the second group, probably came from stocks originally inhabiting the Moluccas, withdrawing into the interior parts when the Malay tribes came.[195]

Generally speaking, anyone concerned with the history of civilization, with a philosophy of history, or with comparisons between primitive societies and civilization, has been forced to consider such factors as environment, isolation, and culture contact. Johann Reinhold Forster is involved with such questions; he, his son, and Captain Cook were conscious of the tremendous contrast between European culture and the manners of the peoples they visited in the Pacific and on the Pacific shore. Sometimes these comparisons were favorable to one, sometimes to another, but never to the peoples

---

[192] *Ibid.*, pp. 276, 277–278. See Forster's comparative table of languages, *Obs.*, facing p. 284.
[193] *Ibid.*, pp. 280–281.
[194] *Ibid.*, pp. 281–283.
[195] *Ibid.*, p. 575.

of Tierra del Fuego. Even though both Forsters and Cook had a lively appreciation of scenery, natural and cultural, and of the physical beauty of native peoples, none of them sentimentalized about primitive life or environments unchanged by the native peoples living in them. They had little patience with the idea of the noble savage. Those sympathetic with such ideas have never seen that most abject of peoples, the Tierra del Fuegians, whom Johann Reinhold called the "Pecherias."[196] An example of the great adaptability of the human race to climatic extremes they certainly were, but until it can be proved "that man in continual pain from the rigour of climate is happy," one cannot take these philosophers seriously who themselves have not had the opportunity to contemplate the modifications of human nature "or who have not felt what they have seen." Those on the voyage had suffered much and had seen much suffering; false stoicism had little appeal, George tracing it back to Seneca, "who made light of the distresses of others, being himself in affluence."[197] (Since Cook's time, the Tierra del Fuegians have been favorite examples of peoples low in the cultural scale. Interest in those still surviving has not lagged to this day because their adaptability to cold makes them ideal subjects for studies in physiological climatology.)[198]

The Forsters constantly refer to European influences on the South Sea islands. Both are conscious of the misery which European cruelty brought in its train, and they recognize the selective nature of the influences. Johann Reinhold praises the introduction of plants (Cook himself had planted introductions), animals, and iron tools, but the Europeans did not bring about intellectual, moral, or social improvement. Such ends could not be expected from the crew of a man-of-war, and those capable of such tasks had little time or leisure, or lacked knowledge of the language, and each had duties ashore assigned by superiors. These latter remarks may allude to the difficulties experienced by the Forsters on board and to their distaste for the behavior of the common sailors toward the native peoples and themselves.[199]

Both men use the word *happiness* frequently, and it seems to mean well-being, contentment, satisfactory adjustment by a people to its natural surroundings, including "physical, moral, and social felicity." When men live in a genial climate, nature does everything to vigorously promote their happiness; in less favorable environments, nature must be assisted by art, while in the most unfavorable climates, happiness requires physical power and creative genius.[200]

---

[196] *Ibid.*, pp. 201–202.

[197] *VRW*, Vol. 2, pp. 502–503.

[198] On the history of their study, see Gusinde, *Die Yamana*, pp. 45–192; on their contemporary interest, Wulsin, "Adaptations to Climate Among Non-European Peoples," in Newburgh, ed., *Physiology of Heat Regulation and the Science of Clothing*, pp. 27–31, and Coon, *The Origin of Races*, pp. 64, 69.

[199] *Obs.*, pp. 305–307. See also *VRW*, Vol. 1, p. 213, 303, 370, 464; Vol. 2, p. 12.

[200] *Ibid.*, pp. 337–343.

Forster believes that islands tend to promote and to accelerate civilization more than do continents, because their circumscribed size discourages dispersal, encourages association; but they cannot be too small, for there would be insufficient room for a populous country or for the necessary cultivation.[201]

Do islands influence the occupations of mankind? Forster only touches upon this question. The small size of the South Sea islands and the lack of wild quadrupeds prevented the first settlers from living by the chase. Neither did the confined space permit the breeding of numerous herds of domestic animals; the peoples therefore had to cultivate the soil, "especially when they could not support themselves by fishing."[202] It will be remembered that Lord Kames and Humboldt mentioned the absence of pastoralism in the New World; Forster here hints at environmental explanation for its absence in the Pacific.

To Johann Reinhold Forster, the Pacific was not necessarily an isolated area before the Europeans came. Noting the contrast between the high tropical civilizations of Mexico and Peru and the other indigenous cultures of the New World, he thinks the former are of a recent date, probably brought there by a few families by chance or necessity. "The ancient Mexicans and Peruvians seem to be descended from those nations, whom *Kublaikhan* sent to conquer Japan, and who were dispersed by a dreadful storm, and it is probable that some of them were thrown on the coast of America, and there formed these two great empires."[203] Could this speculation have awakened the interest of Humboldt in the subject from the New World side? Like Cook, both Forsters occasionally imply that accidental rather than planned voyaging may have brought about settlement.[204]

Johann Reinhold Forster was greatly impressed by tropical island environments; his knowledge of them was of course far greater than his knowledge of the continental wet tropics of the Old and New Worlds. The tropics are the birthplace of man: the climate promotes rapid plant, and therefore animal, growth, with consequent ease in obtaining food, dress, and shelter. A tropical origin would also account for the fact that men originally went around naked; here he is influenced by the near-nakedness of the Pecherias in a forbiddingly cold climate. The inhabitants of the South Sea islands are the more advanced as they dwell more distantly from the poles, and the inhabitants of the frozen extremes toward the poles are "degenerated and debased from that original happiness which the tropical nations more or less enjoy."[205] The outstanding example are the Pecherias whom he saw on Waterman Island. No more

---

[201] *Ibid.*, p. 345.
[202] *VRW*, Vol. 2, p. 360.
[203] *Obs.*, p. 314; quote on p. 316.
[204] On accidental voyaging and Cook, see Sharp, *Ancient Voyagers in the Pacific*, *passim*, and the opposing views of Suggs, *The Island Civilizations of Polynesia*, pp. 82–84, and Sharp's replies in *Ancient Voyagers in Polynesia*, *passim*.
[205] *Obs.*, p. 287.

wretched people, he thinks, can be found anywhere. They are so miserable and forlorn that they are not even conscious of their misery; they probably originated in more civilized regions, but when they were forced into their new environment they carried little or nothing of their culture with them. These people are his prize exhibit showing the foolishness of romanticizing indiscriminately about the native peoples.

Men are much more dispersed as one approaches the poles. Primitive peoples, therefore, who have no contact with civilization become debased as the distance from the tropics increases. The causes of this debasement are environmental and cultural—the effect of the cold climate, and isolation from the original center of cultural diversity and abundance.[206]

Forster regards Tahiti as "the queen of tropical isles." The climate certainly contributes to the happy state of its inhabitants and it may be the main source of it, but inferior peoples living on islands to the west in the same climate point to "some other cause of this remarkable circumstance." In essence, this cause is the body of tradition, the cumulative experience of mankind. "All the ideas, all the improvements of mankind relative to sciences, arts, manufactures, social life, and even morality, ought to be considered as *the sum total of the efforts of mankind ever since its existence.*"[207]

These ideas are elaborated upon in an interesting conjectural history of mankind, assuming again a tropical homeland. The original tribes of mankind, hoarding up and propagating knowledge, no doubt kept in contact with one another. In time "two remarkable systems" branched out from Chaldea and Egypt, one to India, China, "and the extremities of the East," the other over the west and north; "but in the interior of Southern parts of Africa, and over the whole continent of America, few, if any, traces of those ancient systems have been discovered." The successful tribes or nations preserved their ancient system, modifying it and adapting it to their "particular situation, climate and other circumstances, or raised new ideas and principles upon the first base or foundation. . . ." Thus preservation and modification of tradition and the addition of new ideas not inconsistent with it are the keys to the progress of a people. The tribes or nations that have failed have forgotten or lost their tradition, "their situation, climate, and other circumstances, having obliged them to neglect or to depart from them without making up the defect by new principles and ideas, founded on the same plan. . . ."[208]

In this way contrasts can develop between tropical and poleward-lying peoples: internecine struggles may force part of a tropical nation to migrate to a colder climate; the migrants must now cultivate the earth for their necessities "because vegetation is not so luxuriant, so rapid, and powerful in climates remote from the sun." They succeed nevertheless in forming a new nation,

---

[206] *Ibid.*, pp. 293, 295–300.
[207] *Ibid.*, p. 295; italics in original.
[208] *Ibid.*, p. 296.

but the process then repeats itself, a further splintering taking place, driving part of the new nation farther poleward. New occupations and hardships alter their mode of living, their habits and language, "and I might almost say their nature; their ideas are quite changed, the improvements, which they had in their former situation, are neglected and lost. . . ."[209] They have now become a debased people of lost arts, unrecognizable descendants of the mother culture. Forced by the chase or fishing to live in small tribes distant from one another, they lose the social contact so characteristic of life in the tropical homeland. They are at the mercy of the elements, and the contrast between their low state and that of the original model is at its sharpest.

A mild climate "contributes greatly to soften the manners of mankind," the poleward extremes render "the fibres and the whole frame of our bodies more harsh, rigid, and insensible"; these effects, undoubtedly operating on the mind and the heart, almost completely destroy all social feelings. But there is a second great cause, "the want of education, by which means the most useful notions, tending to improve our physical, mental, moral, and social faculties, are propagated, perpetuated, and lastly increased by new additional ideas."[210] Is it too much to say that this philosophy of civilization—which makes so much of climate, of cultural tradition and lost arts, of splintering and migration to less hospitable lands, of new ideas arising from social intercourse, or lack of them and stagnation through isolation—is inspired by the contrast between the peoples of Tahiti and those of Tierra del Fuego?

Many of the themes discussed by Johann Reinhold had previously been discussed by George in *A Voyage Round the World* (1777). Because of George's youth there seems little doubt that the language is his but that the scientific and philosophical ideas are those of his father. For this work he paid a price in the scorn heaped upon him for putting his name to a work which in substance was not his own.[211]

Like Montesquieu, George Forster believes climate and government to be interrelated; in his colorful description of Madeira he says the warm climate of that island must tend to encourage indolence among the people if laws do not counteract it. The Portuguese government fails in this. He is critical also of the Portuguese administration of St. Jago in the Cape Verde Islands, which confirms the people in vices already encouraged by the climate. Progress through free and equal government is related to knowledge of cultural traits which climate is likely to encourage or discourage. A government more enlightened than the Portuguese could achieve much in these islands.[212]

George Forster is sensitive to cultural differences, to the widespread distribution of apparent similarities among peoples, and to the "arbitrary whims"

---

[209] *Ibid.*, pp. 297–298.
[210] *Ibid.*, pp. 300–301.
[211] See article on George Forster by Alfred Dove in *Allgemeine Deutsche Biographie*, Vol. 7, pp. 173–174.
[212] *VRW*, Vol. 1, pp. 34–38.

of mankind, especially in sexual customs.[213] Both men are interested in comparisons either among contemporary, or between contemporary and historical, cultures, but when George compares the Tahitians with the Greeks, the heroes of Homer with the chiefs of Tahiti,[214] he is conscious that ideas of diffusion and contact may be accepted too uncritically. Men "in a similar state of civilization resemble each other more than we are aware of, even in the most opposite extremes of the world. I should be sorry to have made these slight remarks [about Greeks and Tahitians], if they should unfortunately lead some learned schemer on a wrong scent. The itch of tracing the pedigree of nations has lately made such havock in history, by endeavouring to combine the Egyptians and Chinese, that the learned must sincerely wish, it may never become a contagious distemper."[215]

Another facet of his interest in culture shows itself in the comparison—suggested by the escape of a seaman (later captured and put in irons for a fortnight) as the boat departed from Tahiti—between life for the common man on Tahiti and in England. This passage, too long for quotation here, realistically describes the miseries and hardships of the common people of England and shows how more comfortable life in Tahiti could be for the sailor, for on his return to England he might ship out again, be forced to war or live a life of drudgery. He concludes unconvincingly, and in sharp contrast with the preceding realism in *tout est bien* fashion, that different nations have different conceptions of happiness. "As the productions and apparent good qualities of our globe, are either profusely or sparingly distributed, on its different parts, the diversity of human opinions is a convincing proof of that paternal love, and unerring wisdom, which, in the plan of this world, has provided for the good of mankind, alike in the torrid and the frigid zone."[216]

We have seen that the elder Forster believed in the unity of the human race; his son was not so sure of this nor of Buffon's theory that climate causes racial differences. In his essay on the races of mankind (1786), Forster, now a mature scholar in his own right, takes issue with Kant's racial theories, including his belief in the unity of the human race. The difficulty, as Forster saw it, still was the contrast between Polynesians and Melanesians living in very similar environments. It would be better for many hypotheses if the Melanesians let themselves be explained away—out of the South Seas entirely—but there they are.[217] Forster did not claim the multiple origin of the human race to be established; he merely said that the question was beset with difficulties, that the theory of multiple origin was no more difficult to comprehend than the theory that mankind descended from a single pair. The celebrated zoologist, Zimmerman, for example, thought it highly unlikely that

[213] *Ibid.*, pp. 457–458.
[214] *Ibid.*, Vol. 2, pp. 104–107.
[215] *Ibid.*, pp. 106–107.
[216] *Ibid.*, pp. 112–113.
[217] "Etwas über die Menschenracen," *SS*, Vol. 4, p. 285.

plants and animals had originated in one place and had then diffused throughout the world. Could not every region, therefore, bring forth its own creatures adapted to its environment, and could not there be, for this reason, a multiple origin of mankind?[218]

The Forsters were remarkable men who had remarkable opportunities. They were conscious of them, sensitive as well to history and the philosophy of civilization. They had the advantage of new departures. They were on a voyage which, like all of Cook's voyages, was a scientific undertaking, a harbinger of the nineteenth century scientific traveling of Humboldt, Darwin, and the "Challenger." They were their own sources. Their theories about civilization and primitive life were derived, in part at least, from personal observation. They enjoyed a great advantage over the philosophical thinkers—Montesquieu, Buffon, Herder, and Robertson, all of whom depended on the observations and judgments of others. Like Captain Cook's journals, their writings still convey an impression of freshness, beauty, reliability in detail, and authenticity.

## 13. CONCLUSION

Climatic causality had flourished, as we have seen, in previous centuries, but never so independently as it did in the eighteenth; moreover in those earlier times, it was used less comprehensively, often being ancillary to religion and astrology or to both. In the nineteenth century, on the other hand, new knowledge, like a swollen stream, flowed around it, and there were other geographical fields to till more carefully than in the eighteenth; the configuration of continents, and the influence of place and position, of altitude, of routes, passes, migration corridors. The idea of adaptation, expressed in the evolutionary theories of Lamarck and Darwin, meant adaptation not to climate but to the whole physical environment. Then in the latter part of that century a racial, not an environmental, determinism ominously asserted itself with ugly and dogmatic vigor.

We can speak correctly therefore of the secularization of climatic theories in the eighteenth century. Paradoxically, one of the reasons they flourished so luxuriantly was that so little was known about climate, about the general circulation of the atmosphere, climatic classification, and climatic contrasts in far-off countries. Ignorance permitted wider generalization. How it simplified matters to assume that the Chinese or Persians lived in a uniform climate! Generalization would have melted away in the warmth of more detail. And most travelers exhibited little rigor in observation.

These developments are not disembodied; they are enmeshed in others. The

[218] *Ibid.*, pp. 301–303.

comparative ethnology of primitive peoples—weak, uncertain, often trivial in the latter part of the seventeenth century and the early part of the eightenth—grows in strength with Cook and the Forsters as the century draws to a close. There is a parallel interest in national character within the advanced cultures, conspicuous, it is true, in the seventeenth century, but attaining sophisticated expression in Hume. The profound interest in natural history, a study concerned with all life and its milieu, leads to grand and holistic views of nature which encompass all environments, human and non-human alike. Finally, some thinkers are beginning to see that the world is drawing closer together through the inventions, the commerce, the avarice, and the desire for knowledge of the Europeans, and a fluidity is seen in geographical relationships which might change from one era to another in response to advances in the arts and sciences and in discovery. Cook's voyages are dramatic examples, but there are many others of a different kind like Father du Halde's work on the history, geography, and culture of the Chinese.

In the eighteenth century, climate is deeply involved in fundamental questions. The historic association of climate with health and medicine deepened in that century, as one can see clearly in the works of Arbuthnot and Falconer. The triad of climate, health, and medicine evoked speculation into the physical and moral effects of climate, and such interrelationships suggested that human initiative could improve environmental conditions. Common areas of interest today between cultural anthropology and geography and public health can be traced to these historic associations which indeed go far back into time. Observed empirical correlations between environment and disease call forth activity in drainage and land reclamation. Such proposals are often expressed by the European doctors; they are characteristic, as we shall see, of early American physicians. The Hippocratic inspiration remains, but knowledge has also grown and insight has deepened.

The relation of climate to religion becomes very important with the Reformation. The divisions within Protestantism and the criticism of all religion which follows in the wake of controversy, schism and religious war, left openings for climatic causation which led to relativism; even revealed religions, to say nothing of schisms, might then have earthly and human explanations.

The old association of climate with political and social theory continues, faithful to the model example set by Plato in the *Laws*, but horizons expand as men become interested in cultural inertia, diffusion, and independent invention.

Not the least of the effects of climatic theories was the stimulus their simplicity and tantalizing dogmatism gave to a more searching study of social causation and history. In the *Esprit des Lois*, Montesquieu wanted to give physical causes their due in an age which he thought had neglected them. Those who disagreed—men like Hume, Voltaire, and Helvétius—replied that moral causes were decisive. Achilles heels in climatic theory now opened up exciting possibilities. Why not compare a people at one period of its history with another period? When such comparisons were made, peoples living in similar environments turned out to be brave and weak, creative and indolent. Climatic theories also stimulated inquiry, as had the abbé du Bos, into the unequal distribution of talent and the clustering of genius in different eras, a fact already noticed in the ancient world. Historical study became a direct challenge to generalizations derived from physical causes.

# Chapter 13

# Environment, Population, and the
# Perfectibility of Man

## 1.  INTRODUCTION

In the eighteenth century another idea, distinct from older orthodox theories
of environmental influence, commanded attention: the earth itself sets limits
to population growth and to human well-being and hence to human aspirations and achievement. One might call it the idea of closed space, a much-
discussed subject since the end of World War II. The best of the vast new
tracts that opened up after the age of discovery, it is so argued, have now
been taken up, and mankind once again is faced with the limiting factors
of the physical environment regardless of ameliorations possible through
social institutions, applied science, and the like.

What are the roots of this idea? It is hard to say. In my opinion it can be
traced to the principle of plenitude.[1] The principle emphasized, as we have

---

[1] See above, pp. 5–6, and Lovejoy, *The Great Chain of Being*, p. 52.

seen, the richness, fullness, and variety of being, and thus indirectly the fecundity of nature. Basically this principle may have originated in nothing more complicated than observations that a piece of ground which has been cleared will soon, unless closely attended, have fresh and vigorous plant life, that some animals like the rabbits, and insects have great reproductive power, that there are few vacant places in nature, and if there are some, they are soon filled up. Linnaeus remarked that three flies will consume the carcass of a horse as quickly as a lion can.[2] Life has the capacity to swell out to its limits, and the multiplication of individual organisms will be arrested only by the competition of other organisms or by the limitations on life imposed by the physical environment; these general ideas too could have originated in common observation such as the consumption of plants by animals, the preying and the preyed upon in the animal world, the destruction of both by violent storms or other forms of natural catastrophe.

In Western civilization one of the distinctive characteristics of the history of thought regarding animate nature is its emphasis on fecundity, the potentiality of life for expansion and multiplication both of individuals and in bulk. Buffon often mentioned this characteristic of life: nature had a greater bias toward life than toward death. Such was life's power of procreation that the whole earth could easily be covered with a single species, and nature would know no limits to the production of organized bodies if her progress were not obstructed by matter not susceptible of organization.[3] Franklin had said that such was the reproductive power of plants and animals that had the face of the earth no plants, it could easily be "overspread" with one kind only, like fennel, or had it no inhabitants, it could easily in a few ages be replenished from one nation only, the English.[4] And Malthus, in a dramatic illustration which drew the anger and ridicule of his critics, said that the human race, if its growth were unimpeded by checks, could fill not only the earth "so that four should stand in every square yard" but all the planets of the solar system and the planets revolving around the visible stars.[5] Darwin, following Malthus in an enthusiastic tribute to fecundity, said that even the elephant, "the slowest breeder of all known animals," could, if unchecked, stock the world in a few thousand years.[6] These patently absurd extravagances (how could one species alone fill up the earth, existing to the exclusion of

---

[2] Cited by J. Arthur Thomson, *The System of Animate Nature*, Vol. 1, pp. 53–54. I have been unable to find this statement in Linnaeus' writings.

[3] See Count Buffon, "De la reproduction en général," being chap. 2 of the "Histoire Générale des Animaux," in *HN*, Vol. 2 (1749), pp. 37–41.

[4] "Observations concerning the Increase of Mankind and the Peopling of Countries," [1751], in *The Writings of Benjamin Franklin*, ed. Smyth, Vol. 3, pp. 63–73, par. 22, p. 71.

[5] *Principles of Political Economy*, pp. 227–228.

[6] See *The Descent of Man*, Modern Library ed., chap. 2, p. 430; the discussion of "Rate of Increase" is based almost entirely on Malthus, as is chap. 2 of the *Origin of Species*, "Geometrical Ratio of Increase," *ibid.*, pp. 53–54.

all others? how could elephants feed except on other elephants?) were clearly meant to dramatize two general observations: the prodigious capacity of populations to increase their numbers, and the fact that they do not. Barriers, perhaps physical, perhaps of other forms of life, prevent any single species from realizing its potential.

The idea that the environment sets limits to the expansion of life seems to appear after the age of discovery.[7] As we have seen, Botero compared the virtue generative of men to virtue nutritive of cities (see p. 373). Sir Walter Raleigh, whose account of the increase and dispersion of the human race was inspired by Old Testament history, who saw the "sun's travaille" from tropic to tropic as an evidence of design, observed,

> For let us now reckon the date of our lives in the Age of the World [in contrast with the first age when lives lasted 800 or 900 years]: wherein if one exceed 50. yeeres, tenne for one are cut off in that passage, and yet wee find no want of people; nay, wee know the multitude such, as if by warres or pestilence they were not sometimes taken off by many thousands, the earth with all the industrie of man could not give them food. What strange heapes then of soules had the first Ages, who enjoyed 800. or 900. yeeres, as aforesaid?[8]

Sir Matthew Hale also made exhaustive lists of the checks to the multiplication of many kinds of life (pp. 403–405). The checks mentioned in these and similar statements attain the dignity of being necessary parts of the Creator's design.

It was clear, therefore, that the fecundity of life had overcome the decimations of war, plague, and unhealthful environments. Otherwise mankind would be extinct. Nature could not produce enough food for all the life it was capable of creating, and checks to growth were part of the natural order. Hunger, misery, predation, among all forms of life, were proof of this insufficiency.

## 2. ON THE POPULOUSNESS OF ANCIENT AND MODERN NATIONS

Furthermore, the controversy over the populousness of the ancient and modern worlds, part of the broader controversies over senescence in nature and the relative superiority of the ancients and the moderns, showed the necessity of critically examining the evidence in order to unravel the history of population. If there were in fact a senescence of nature, one would expect smaller populations with the aging of the earth, and if classical civilization

---

[7] What follows is in no sense even a summary of population theories. On these see Bonar, *Theories of Population from Raleigh to Arthur Young*; Fage, "La Révolution Française et la Population," *Population*, 8 (1953), pp. 311–338; Mombert, *Bevölkerungslehre*; Spengler, *French Predecessors of Malthus*; and Stangeland, "Pre-Malthusian Doctrines of Population: a Study in the History of Economic Theory," in *Columbia University Studies in History, Economics, and Public Law*, Vol. 21, No. 3, 1904.

[8] *The History of the World*, Bk. I, chap. 8, sec. 11, 5, pp. 158–159.

were superior to modern, one might also expect to find in it better conditions of life, higher ethical standards, and more people to perform the tasks of a more advanced culture.[9]

The controversy dates back to 1685 when Isaac Vossius (1618–1689), in a discussion of the large cities of China, estimated the world's population to be about five hundred million—three hundred in Asia and thirty in Europe, with no attempt to distribute the remaining one hundred seventy million. Vossius, within living memory of the devastation and hideous loss of life of the Thirty Years' War brought to a close by the treaties of Westphalia in 1648, was in opposition to an earlier view of Giovanni Battista Riccioli (1598–1671), the Jesuit astronomer, who in about 1672 had estimated the world's population to be one billion: in millions, one hundred in Europe, five hundred in Asia, one hundred in Africa, two hundred in the New World and one hundred in the Southern Continent (Terra Australis), which did not vanish from estimates of world population until Captain Cook on his second voyage disproved its existence.[10] The value of these examples is that they show the extremes to which estimates could go and that they were based entirely on supposed European experience. Who knows, Vossius asks, but that in former times there were more people in Sicily alone than are now in Sicily and Italy combined, more people formerly in Athens alone than are now in Greece and the Peloponnesus combined? Vossius' total of thirty million in Europe was indeed gloomy, for he estimated that imperial Rome alone had had fourteen million people; his low figure for contemporary Europe may therefore well reflect the overwhelming impression caused by death and destruction in the Thirty Years' War.[11]

Montesquieu unearthed the old estimates (especially those of Vossius) and communicated them to Rhedi, a hero of the *Persian Letters*, who writes to Usbek in Paris in 1718 inquiring, "How can the world be so sparsely populated in comparison with what it once was? How can nature have lost that prodigious fertility of primitive times. Could she be already in her old age, and will she fall into her dotage?" In Italy Rhedi saw more ruins than people, whose numbers were so few they did not even occupy the area of the ancient town site; they seemed "to go on existing only to mark the spot where those cities so talked of by history once existed." Rhedi found evidences of depopulation in Rome, Sicily, Greece, Spain, the northern countries, Poland, European Turkey, France, even America, and the African and Asian shore

[9] On the controversy, see Bonar, *op. cit.*, chap. 6.
[10] For a convenient table of estimates of the world's population with sources from the seventeenth to the nineteenth centuries, see Behm and Wagner, "Die Bevölkerung der Erde, II," *Petermanns Mitteilungen Ergänzungsband* 8, No. 35 (1873–74), pp. 4–5. I am indebted to this work for the references. Riccioli, *Geographiae et hydrographiae reformatae libri XII* (Venetiis, 1672), pp. 677–681. This work was not available to me, the discussion being based on Behm and Wagner, who think the estimate might date from 1660 (p. 4).
[11] *Isaaci Vossii Variarum Observationum Liber*, pp. 64–68.

of the Mediterranean. "In fine, I survey the whole earth, and I find only remains. I have an idea that I can trace it to the ravages of pestilence and famine." He thinks the ancient world probably had ten times as many people as the modern. The sight-seeing Persian mournfully wrote from Venice a general castigation of mankind.[12]

Indeed, Montesquieu's *Persian Letters* are sensitive indicators of eighteenth century humanitarianism and interest in moral causes and their effects on population; the letters are notable for their emphasis on influences coming from religion, marriage customs, disease, cultural attitudes. He is also interested in the history of plagues and the effects of venereal disease, which he believes to be a modern phenomenon.[13] The division of the Roman world into Christian and Muslim parts had great social consequences, both religions being far less favorable to propagation than was the religion of the Romans, who forbade polygamy and permitted divorce. Both, he thought, encouraged population growth. Muslim polygamy leads to exhaustion of the male, like an athlete who overtaxes himself; it enforces an artificial continence on the several wives, to say nothing of the protective eunuchs and the slave girls who grow old "in sad virginity." Polygamy puts too much sexual strain on the man, prevents many women from childbearing, demands sexless or abstinent servants, and thus leads to depopulation.[14] Ancient slavery did not bring about through its cruelties the great loss of life characteristic of the modern institution.[15] In pitilessly candid sentences Montesquieu condemns enforced continuance, in Christian countries, of marriages long since destroyed by bitterness and loss of affection. "Repulsion, whim, and the anti-sociability of temperament were counted for nothing. They tried to stabilize the heart—which is to say, the thing in human nature that is most variable and inconstant." When couples have only an eternity of indissoluble marriage ahead of them, compulsion, discord, and contempt arise. "After scarcely three years of marriage, the essential function is neglected. Thereafter the couple passes together thirty years of indifference," and the man, repelled by an eternal wife, will turn to prostitutes.[16] There are harsh words for clerical celibacy in the Christian world, and the Catholic are contrasted unfavorably with Protestant countries in the encouragement the latter give to economic development and hence to propagation; there are harsh words, too, for the slave trade, the depopulation of Africa, the barbarous treatment of aborigines in the New World.[17] The fertility of a people is related to the belief and attitudes held by them. The Jews, continually persecuted and exterminated, have survived because they hope to see the birth of a powerful king-ruler of the earth. The high popula-

[12] *LP* 112, trans. Loy.
[13] *LP* 113.
[14] *LP* 114.
[15] *LP* 115.
[16] *LP* 116, pp. 212–213.
[17] *LP* 118, 121.

tions of ancient Persia, Usbek says, were the result of the teaching of the Magi religion, that men can please the divinity most by producing a child, tilling the soil, and planting a tree. In an atmosphere of respect for one's elders and for the dead, and for the family system, the Chinese is encouraged to increase his family, while the people of Muslim countries, Usbek continues, live "in a general state of unfeelingness, and we leave everything up to providence."[18] In advanced countries unjust rights of primogeniture discourage propagation, as the distaste for cultivating the land does in primitive societies.[19] Of colonies, he complains that the "normal effect is to weaken the countries from which they are drawn, without populating those to which they are sent."[20] A mild government like that of Switzerland or Holland is the key to population growth. "Men are like plants; they never grow well unless they are well cultivated. Among people living in poverty, the human race loses and even degenerates."[21]

Even if these Persian letters fall short of their mark in proving the superior populousness of the ancient world, they reveal how sensitive Montesquieu was to the uniqueness of human populations. "The females of brutes," he wrote later in *Esprit des Lois*, "have an almost constant fecundity. But in the human species, the manner of thinking, the character, the passions, the humor, the caprice, the idea of preserving beauty, the pain of child-bearing, and the fatigue of a too numerous family, obstruct propagation in a thousand different ways."[22]

In the *Esprit des Lois* Montesquieu continues his interest in population questions, including the relation of population growth to land use, progress in the arts, and the type of government. It is a mistake to believe that the industrious poor, living under a strict government, would have large families. Differences in population among various countries might be owing to differences in the fertility of women, to location, or to diet.[23]

The larger nations and empires of modern times had caused depopulation. "All these little republics [Italy, Sicily, Asia Minor, Gaul, and Germany] were swallowed up in a large one, and the globe insensibly became depopulated." It was a fortunate circumstance that Charlemagne's empire had been "divided into an infinite number of petty sovereignties." Montesquieu concludes that "Europe is at present in a condition to require laws to be made in favor of the propagation of the human species."[24] But he never made it clear whether the whole earth or only Europe was suffering from depopulation.

In his *Pensées*, Montesquieu contrasted the relatively unpeopled earth with

---

[18] *LP* 119.
[19] *LP* 120.
[20] *LP* 121.
[21] *LP* 122.
[22] *EL*, Bk. 23, chap. 1.
[23] *Ibid.*, chaps. 10–13. See above, pp. 578–579.
[24] *Ibid.*, chaps. 16, 19, 24, 26. Quotes in chaps. 19, 24, 26.

the bounty of its resources: the earth yields to human industry. Fifty million people could live in France, which now has only fourteen. The fertility of places in the vicinity of towns can give us an idea of what we can expect from others. The more workers there are in France, the more tillers of the soil will there be in Barbary, and one tiller will feed ten workers.[25]

Montesquieu's opinions on depopulation, like those on climate, were harshly criticized and with justice, because the moral and physical causes could not without more evidence be assumed to be of sufficient force to effect the claimed results.[26]

The best criticism came from Hume, who brushed aside the "extravagances of Vossius" to consider the arguments of "an author of much greater genius and discernment," Montesquieu. The physical and mental endowment of human beings has been about the same in all ages. Hume will have none of the biological analogy nor will he grant that even if the ancient world had more people, this superiority is due to "the imaginary youth and vigour of the world. . . ." "These *general physical* causes ought entirely to be excluded from this question." It was an important point, for if nature, like an individual organism, had been more fruitful in its youth, the largest populations would have lived in the remotest period. Hume's essay is a reminder that influential ideas of supposed universal applicability can prosper without facts to support them. We do not know, he said, the exact population of any European kingdom or even of any city; how then can we pretend to know the population of ancient cities and states?[27] The case for the superior populousness of the modern world is largely made on the basis of its new inventions, a broader geographic base, and service industries.

> All our later improvements and refinements, have they done nothing towards the easy subsistence of men, and consequently toward their propagation and encrease? Our superior skill in mechanics; the discovery of new worlds, by which commerce has been so much enlarged; the establishment of posts; and the use of bills of exchange: These seem all extremely useful to the encouragement of art, industry, and populousness. Were we to strike off these, what a check should we give to every kind of business and labour, and what multitudes of families would immediately perish from want and hunger?[28]

Quoting Diodorus Siculus (first century B.C.), who bewailed the depopulation and emptiness of the world of his own time compared with that of past

[25] *Pensées et Fragments Inédits de Montesquieu*, Vol. I, p. 180.

[26] See for example D'Amilaville's article on population in the *Encyclopédie*, which has an excellent summary of the dispute, and Voltaire's on the same subject in his *Philosophical Dictionary*. See also "Nouvelles Considérations sur l'Histoire," *Oeuvres*, ed. by Beuchot, Vol. 24, p. 27; "Population" (*Dict. Philos.*), Vol. 21, p. 474; "Des Singularités de la Nature," chap. 37, Vol. 44, pp. 310–312.

[27] "Of the Populousness of Ancient Nations," in *Essays Moral, Political, and Literary*, Vol. 1, pp. 381–383, quote on p. 382.

[28] *Ibid.*, pp. 412–413.

times, Hume says, "Thus an author, who lived at that very period of antiquity which is represented as most populous, complains of the desolation which then prevailed, gives the preference to former times, and has recourse to ancient fables as a foundation for his opinion."[29] Any living Diodorus Siculus could feel this sting, but one of them, Robert Wallace, a tireless supporter of the ancients, did his best to shore up the boats of the ancients. Wallace's first work, *A Dissertation on the Numbers of Mankind, in Ancient and Modern Times* (1753), was written before but published after Hume's essay; Hume was instrumental in having the work published. In a long appendix, Wallace ransacked the classical writings in order to rebut Hume; he admitted it was impossible to determine the population of the present or of any preceding age, but by using several crude estimates—which need not be explained here—Wallace concluded that the population of the ancient world was greater than one billion, his maximum estimate of the world's population of his time. The estimates for the ancient world were in reality based on his moral and philosophical biases: that morality, government, and education in ancient times were superior to those of modern times, these conditions being favorable to a larger population. Anticipating an argument in *The Various Prospects of Mankind, Nature, and Providence* (1761), Wallace wrote that "had it not been for the errors and vices of mankind, and for the defects of government and of education, the earth must have been much better peopled, perhaps might have been overstocked, many ages ago." Wallace derived his population estimates from Thomas Templeman's *New Survey of the Globe* (*ca.* 1729), which included population figures for some countries and for the most noted cities of Europe. "A Calculation of this Nature, I am sensible, is liable to Censure and Objection, as being too much Conjecture, and the Dictates of Imagination." So he took a middle course; he could not agree that London had two million people "nor assent to the ridiculous and romantick Accounts that represent some Cities in China to contain 6 or 8 Millions of people." "Notwithstanding the absurdity of such extravagant Conjectures, the learned Vossius fell into an equal, if not greater Weakness and Credulity when he attempted to demonstrate that there were 14 millions of Souls in Ancient Rome." Templeman's *Survey* is worth notice mainly because it reveals the foggy uncertainty in which these men worked.[30]

Unlike Malthus, Wallace believed that the causes of population growth had not operated uniformly throughout history. Small shares in land, only slight trade and commerce, simplicity in living, were more characteristic of ancient than of modern times; these too encouraged a large population, for modern cities drew many away from the countryside, lowering the numbers employed in agriculture. In order to have a fully peopled world, all mankind

---

[29] *Ibid.*, p. 443. See Diodorus, II, 5.
[30] *A Dissertation on the Numbers of Mankind*, p. 13; Templeman, *New Survey of the Globe*, p. iii.

must be employed directly in food production; this situation was truer of ancient than of modern times. Wallace thought the absence of syphilis (*lues venerea*) and smallpox were other good reasons for the superior populousness of antiquity.

All was not well, however, even in the ancient world, for wicked tendencies characteristic of the modern period were making themselves felt after the simple luster of ancient life had been tarnished by the conquests of Alexander, the policies of the Ptolemies and of the Romans, who mistakenly introduced into the West the effete, luxury-loving, and debilitating manners and customs of the East. The loss of simplicity in taste, the introduction of luxury, had helped to gradually diminish the population of mankind. "The world was overwhelmed with a corrupted taste, and has never been able to repair its desolation."[31]

Admirers of the ancients, like Wallace, were friendly to the idea of senescence in nature, and exulted in the moral, artistic, and literary inferiority of modern times. Those favoring the moderns believed in the constancy of nature's operations; they had faith in the invention, technology, and communications of modern man and thought the changes men were bringing about through cultivation, clearing, and drainage were improving the earth.

After Montesquieu and Wallace, no important converts made up for the attrition on the side of the ancients. In the *Encyclopédie*, D'Amilaville discussed Wallace—the dissertation had been translated into French under the supervision of Montesquieu—but for him he had no sympathy. Vossius, he said, had estimated the population of France to be five million at the revocation of the Edict of Nantes (1685) when the accepted estimate was thirty million; Montesquieu had chosen a few depopulated lands, but depopulation was not proceeding throughout the whole world. Moral shortcomings were not the cause of modern depopulation, as Wallace claimed, for all people on earth had them. D'Amilaville saw that the argument has been too provincial, too centered on Europe. But he could be bland and wry: "Le Christianisme n'a pas proprement pour objet de peupler la terre; son vrai but est de peupler le ciel. . . ." Modern times has smallpox and syphilis, but antiquity had leprosy. To prove their case, these men had to show that worldwide depopulation was owing to physical causes universal in operation. D'Amilaville thought that population remains relatively constant, of course with local variations and differences, being part of a general balance and equilibrium in the system of nature; assuming such a balance, he then concluded that the total number of people living on earth had been, is, and always will be about the same.

---

[31] *A Dissertation*, Appendix, p. 355. Later writers have been more generous to Alexander the Great and have done less moralizing about him. Humboldt regarded his campaigns as scientific expeditions (*Cosmos*, Vol. II, pp. 516–525). In addition to his full-length work on Alexander, see also W. W. Tarn, "Alexander the Great and the Unity of Mankind," *Proc. of the Br. Academy*, XI (1933), pp. 123–166.

By 1798, however, Malthus writes as if there is no longer any occasion for debate: the world, and especially Europe, is more populous simply because industrious people have produced a greater amount of food. This controversy took place, as we now know, when the population of western Europe was beginning its spectacular increase, which dates from about the time Wallace was diligently proving the case for the ancients.[32]

### 3. PROGRESS AND THE LIMITATIONS OF THE ENVIRONMENT

This dispute and the quarrel over the relative merits of the ancients and moderns led to three different interpretations of the relation of man to the earth: (1) the environment sets up limits to the numbers and well-being of man, clearly stated by Wallace in his second work; (2) the earth, as a physical environment, places no obstacles in the way of the perfectibility of mankind, a viewpoint associated particularly with Condorcet but also with Godwin; and (3) environmental conditions are insurmountable barriers to utopian hopes, based on either individual or institutional reform, a doctrine which Malthus made famous. Let us examine these three points of view.

In the first part of *The Various Prospects of Mankind, Nature, and Providence* (1761), Robert Wallace painstakingly analyzes the possibilities of attaining a Utopia on earth, and in the second he turns on his own argument, demolishing it with the objection that physical conditions on earth would not permit such a millennial society.

Wallace maintains that the world could have been fully peopled long ago; it could easily have produced food for ten times the number that have in fact been propagated. "The earth has never been cultivated to the full extent of what it was able to bear." Bad taste, war, and mutual destruction, ignorance of the earth despite extensive travels and voyages, had contributed to this failure.[33]

Under a perfect government founded on equality, men could multiply faster than in the happiest of previous governments. Such a perfect future government, intricate in its harmony, is possible; if it comes into being, it will do so slowly and imperceptibly, by divine intention. It could even be reconciled with passion and frailty. But we discover later that a government of this kind is inconsistent with the human condition. Under perfect government, the difficulties of having a family would be removed; despite plagues, there would be many encouragements to population growth, mankind "would encrease so prodigiously, that the earth would at last be overstocked, and be-

[32] D'Amilaville, "Population," *Encyclopédie*, Vol. 13, p. 73. Vossius, *op. cit.* (see n. 11 above), p. 66. Malthus, 1798 *Essay*, pp. 53–56. For Malthus's criticism of Wallace and Hume, see the 7th ed., Vol. 1, pp. 151–153.

[33] *Various Prospects*, pp. 3, 6, 8, 10. Quote on p. 8.

[34] *Ibid.*, pp. 46, 47, 70–71, 107, 114–115, 116.

come unable to support its inhabitants."[34] What then should happen? Should women be shut up in cloisters and men be debarred from marriage? Should eunuchry and infant exposure be allowed? Should life be shortened by decree? On these questions there would be no agreement; a decision would be made by force, and deaths in battle would provide the needed room for the survivors. A perfect government would bring about horrors more unnatural than present vices. "But there are certain primary determinations in nature, to which all other things of a subordinate kind must be adjusted. A limited earth, a limited degree of fertility, and the continual increase of mankind are three of these original determinations. To these determinations, human affairs, and the circumstances of all other animals must be adapted."[35] The vices and the shortcomings of mankind prevent the establishment of such utopian government even if the earth's surface is "especially fitted to be an agreeable and convenient habitation for men." It is physico-theology with a pronounced pessimistic turn. It is a good earth, but not good enough to exempt its inhabitants from life's miseries. Man with his vices and depravities is unworthy of a perfect earth. The existing imperfect earth is but the physical reflection of his sinful nature, its frame being adjusted "to chastise and punish the vices of rational creatures and give check to their follies." Wallace's defense of nature, however, is more spirited than is his defense of man, for he is not in agreement with Burnet's *Sacred Theory of the Earth*. One cannot blame nature too much, for one cannot say with certainty that it would be a better earth were there less water, no thunder, wind, or fog, more moderate rainfall, fewer earthquakes or inundations, or a different angle of inclination of the earth on its axis. Burnet had forgotten these truths; his ideal earth would have been barren.[36]

With such a limiting environment on earth, death can aspire to a more exalted role than that of being the debt paid for sin. It is a necessity. Death permits earth's fullness; it makes room for more animal life, particularly for small animals which can find their niches; since death and birth take place in a limited environment, nature can in this way fill up her "vacant interstices." Wallace in fact suggests in rude form the community concept in ecology: the close interdependence of all forms of organic life, the indispensability to life of dead organic matter, the food chain, and the niche. Great variety in the bulk of individual organisms is required to fill up the world of nature.

Death is consistent with the limited fertility of soils, with the regular and abundant production of life. "If this once be admitted, it will help us to account for that neglect and prodigious havock of animal life, which are so visible through every part of nature." Wallace may well be the first thinker who saw in the earth's basic structure and constitution elements of a natural

---

[35] *Ibid.*, p. 122. The discussion is based on pp. 118–121.
[36] *Ibid.*, pp. 227, 278–282, 286.

law which limited man's numbers and which transcended the efforts of individuals, government, or society to improve the human conditions.[37]

Wallace was walking down increasingly lonely corridors, for many eighteenth century thinkers were interested not in the sin of man nor in cataloging the imperfections of an earth consistent with his sin but in man's inhumanity to man, in the reform of individuals and human institutions; their confidence in the idea of progress and the perfectibility of man made the limitations of the earth too remote to think about, unworthy of the time of men intent on more urgent problems.

The Marquis de Condorcet was such a man. In the *Sketch for a Historical Picture of the Progress of the Human Mind* (1793), published posthumously in 1795, he expressed the philosophy of progress so eloquently and so triumphantly, extending it to all phases of human effort, that it became an inspiration for all who followed and thought like him. Neither Condorcet nor Godwin sought in the limitations of the earthly environment the obstacles to human progress; neither did they believe the perfectibility of human society to be impossible, that the earth would fail as an environment for these millennial prospects. These men had their eyes on reform in human affairs, Condorcet primarily in the reform of law and institutions, Godwin of the individual to the point that government would become unnecessary. Since population questions took a back seat to the idea of progress, both men came under Malthus's fire because he believed the principle of population deserved the closest scrutiny in such discussions of perfectibility and indefinite progress, although Malthus did not deny the possibility of advances in certain fields.

The views of Condorcet and Godwin and Malthus are not without interest in the controversies of our own day, especially in the optimistic and pessimistic literature on population growth, soil erosion, and technological advance published since the end of World War II. Faith in science, technology, and invention have now replaced the naïvetés of the eighteenth and nineteenth centuries, but the conflict remains a familiar one: the idea of a limited environment now hard pressed by increased population whose poverty and distress only accelerates soil erosion and other man-induced disasters, versus faith that science and technology can, despite population growth, create new food, new frontiers, new sources of energy, and rehabilitate old environments.

The kind and humane Condorcet, a revolutionary of Girondist persuasion and a member of the "Société des Amis des Noirs," will show

> by appeal to reason and fact that nature has set no term to the perfection of human faculties; that the perfectibility of man is truly indefinite; and that the progress of this perfectibility, from now onwards independent of any power that might wish to halt it, has no other limit than the duration of the globe upon which nature has cast us. This progress will doubtless vary in speed, but it will

[37] *Ibid.*, pp. 294–295, 297. Mombert, *Bevölkerungslehre*, comes to a similar conclusion regarding Wallace (p. 158).

never be reversed as long as the earth occupies its present place in the system of the universe, and as long as the general laws of this system produce neither a general cataclysm nor such changes as will deprive the human race of its present faculties and its present resources.[38]

This was a consistent position for Condorcet to take, for it would be hard to argue for the indefinite progress of mankind without envisaging an earth whose resources would still be sufficient were demands made upon it by larger populations and more ravenous technologies increased a thousandfold or a millionfold.

Condorcet in fact anticipated the objection that progress would bring such improvement in human well-being and therefore more healthy and more numerous populations that the time might come in the distant future when increased prosperity, industry, and general improvement might be incompatible with a vastly increased world population. To this question Condorcet, unlike Wallace, replied in essence that the future will take care of itself. If a large population is the consequence of the continuing progress of man on his march to perfection, and if the large numbers of men then become a difficulty, men with the theoretical knowledge and applied power which at that future time will be at their disposal because of advances in every realm of human activity, can meet the difficulty; arts and sciences will continue their advance, superstitions will decline in effectiveness. Men at that time

will know that, if they have a duty towards those who are not yet born, that duty is not to give them existence but to give them happiness; their aim should be to promote the general welfare of the human race or of the society in which they live or of the family to which they belong, rather than foolishly to encumber the world with useless and wretched beings. It is, then, possible that there should be a limit to the amount of food that can be produced, and, consequently, to the size of the population of the world, without this involving that untimely destruction of some of those creatures who have been given life, which is so contrary to nature and to social prosperity.[39]

This passage is not so remote from his own point of view as Malthus thought. It is true that, unlike Malthus, Condorcet sees the problem as a possible future one, and even then active steps can achieve adjustments as problems of living on finite resources become apparent. The significant distinction between the two men is that Condorcet sees population as a possible future concern while Malthus sees the principle of population as a natural law operating uniformly in time and space, with strong reservations about human interferences with it.

In his *Political Justice* (1793) Godwin had also considered the perfectibility of man and the idea of progress. It was "Mr. Godwin's Essay on avarice and profusion, in his *Enquirer*," however, and Malthus's ensuing conversation with

[38] *Sketch for a Historical Picture of the Progress of the Human Mind*, intro., pp. 4–5.
[39] *Ibid.*, pp. 188–189. See also Fage, "La Révolution Française et la Population," *Population*, 8 (1953), pp. 322–326.

a friend about it that stimulated him to write his 1798 *Essay*.[40] Indignant with Wallace for abruptly abandoning belief in the perfectibility of man in favor of a pessimism which saw in continued progress in government and in civilization only misery for the human race, Godwin reached, from different premises, conclusions similar to Condorcet's regarding progress and environmental limitations which might impede or prevent it. With deep faith in the existence of a natural harmony and equilibrium in all nature, Godwin abhorred governmental interference; he also was suspicious of social institutions.[41]

To Godwin the earth's resources offered no obstacles to the perfectibility of man; the idea of progress could be believed in with confidence.

> Three-fourths of the habitable globe, are now uncultivated. The improvements to be made in cultivation, and the augmentations the earth is capable of receiving in the article of productiveness, cannot, as yet, be reduced to any limits of calculation. Myriads of centuries of still increasing population may pass away, and the earth be yet found sufficient for the support of its inhabitants. It were idle therefore to conceive discouragement from so distant a contingency. The rational anticipations of human improvement, are unlimited, not eternal. The very globe that we inhabit, and the solar system, may, for anything we know, be subject to decay. Physical casualties of different denominations, may interfere with the progressive nature of intellect. But, putting these out of the question, it is certainly most reasonable, to commit so remote a danger to the chance of such remedies, (remedies, of which perhaps we may, at this time, not have the smallest idea) as shall suggest themselves, at a period sufficiently early for their practical application.[42]

On the other hand, the Malthusian theory, considered as a theory of resource use, denied that solutions to economic and social well-being can be found in the social world alone, ignoring the limitations of an environment which can and does set limits to human achievement.

The idea of progress had opened up new perspectives in interpreting the nature of the physical environment. These perspectives had been seen by Leibniz, who found progress in the cultivation of the earth accompanying progress in human affairs as well (see p. 377). Even to the lukewarmly religious it must have seemed that it was the Creator's purpose that men and their institutions improve in time; that a deity with such a purpose would be niggardly neither with the food nor with the pleasures He set before the human race. Man's progress was clear in the many beneficial changes already made on the earth's surface, in his control of nature, in his adaptation of the entire planet to his needs and desires, and in his thirst for knowledge and wisdom. Such ideas were held also by men hostile to organized religion. This humane spirit, this faith

---

[40] See Malthus's preface to the 1798 *Essay*.

[41] *Enquiry Concerning Political Justice*, Bk. 8, chap. 9, Priestly ed., Vol. 2, pp. 515–516.

[42] *Ibid.*, pp. 518–519.

in man and his ability to achieve goals and improve himself, suffuse the work of Condorcet, whose "Sketch" make poignant reading today because the technical mastery that Condorcet had hoped for has been achieved to a degree undreamed of by him, indeed, undreamed of by hundreds of millions less than twenty-five years ago, without that parallel progress in other phases of human existence he also assumed would occur. The idea of progress implied concomitant improvement in agriculture, soil fertility, drainage, and health measures. It did not envisage permanent deterioration of soil and forest; it supplied the all-enveloping optimism regarding the capacity of the earth to support its peoples. In its emphasis on human amelioration, the environment often seemed to become more and more abstract. It is a situation not unknown in the social sciences today.

4. On the Malthusian Principle of
Population in General

Seventeenth and eighteenth century writers on population had shown the historical relationship of population theory to the Christian religion, to the idea of progress, and to the physical environment; in Malthus these threads were woven into a cohesive whole which neither defenders nor detractors forgot. Malthus easily excelled his predecessors in this fresh attempt to show the environmental limitations which men must understand and accept. He was not interested in showing how environments mold culture (ideas of this kind gleaned perhaps from Humboldt and others do occasionally appear in his writings) nor to any extent in how human cultures have modified the environment. Few men in the history of Western thought have exerted an influence comparable to his; this was based on his own ideas and the researches he undertook for editions following the first essay, and on the skill with which, in his forceful writings, he combined ideas which individually by now had become quite familiar. His ideas, brought into biology by Darwin and Wallace, reentered the world of men through the social Darwinism of the late nineteenth century. Towering figures of nineteenth century thought, like August Comte and Herbert Spencer, have become indistinct in the twentieth century; they lack the freshness and interest of Malthus, although it must be acknowledged that the revival of interest in his writings is due to widespread alarm over population growth, even if what Malthus had to say on these subjects is of little relevance to the present.

Malthus's doctrine is based on two general ideas: the fecundity and plenitude of life, and the forces in nature (in life and in the inanimate world) which constantly are at work controlling this relentless expansiveness. All living things have a tendency to increase geometrically if their multiplication is uninterfered with and if there is sufficient food for them. They do not increase in this manner either under natural conditions or under man's control because other forms of life or environmental controls prevent it. Living things under man's control are subject to the hazards of man's neglect or his inability to provide good soils or pasture. The same principles apply to man, but owing to long settlement in populated areas, their operation is not clearly apparent. A relatively unoccupied country like the United States provides the example of what can be expected of a small population in a large area of plentiful food, despite the fact that it is not an ideal example because of disease and hardships common there. In no country, in no state of society known, "has the power of population been left to exert itself with perfect freedom."[43] The amount of food for human populations is subject to unavoidable limitations; good lands are not available in abundance, and when all are occupied, providing the world's food will become increasingly difficult. Furthermore, machinery and invention are less likely to produce spectacular improvements in agriculture than in industry and manufacturing. With the exception of famine conditions, food is never an immediate check to population; customs, which Malthus apparently thinks are fears transformed into folk tradition, disease, and all causes "of a moral or physical nature, which tend prematurely to weaken and destroy the human frame" are the immediate checks.[44] Since the principle of population is a law of nature, it is constant in its operation; it is wrong to think it a theory of overpopulation, to represent the difficulties as arising "at a great and almost immeasurable distance," to think that it operates geographically, with more intensity, for example, in India or China than in Europe.[45]

Human institutions, customs, ideals, may alleviate conditions somewhat but they too must bow to natural law. This insistence on the principle being a natural law earned Malthus the enmity of men who saw in human institutions, economic systems, fossilized custom, sufficient causes of the miseries of mankind. Human institutions, Malthus wrote in answer to Godwin, "appear to be, and indeed often are, the obvious and obtrusive causes of much mischief to society, they are, in reality, light and superficial in comparison with those deeper-seated causes of evil which result from the laws of nature and the passions of mankind."[46] Permanent improvement is possible only from a lowered birthrate. Malthus opposed artificial birth control as an unwarranted and perhaps dangerous interference in natural processes. In Condorcet's allusions "either to a promiscuous concubinage, which would prevent breeding, or to something else as unnatural," Malthus saw destruction of "that virtue and

[43] Vol. 1, p. 7.

[44] Vol. 1, p. 12.

[45] Vol. 2, p. 1. Many variants—among them, that the principle of population acted in the past; that it applies only to certain geographical areas; that it will operate only in the future—are foreign to Malthus's thought. On this point, see Mombert, *Bevölkerungslehre*, pp. 199–200, 204.

[46] Vol. 2, p. 12.

purity of manners which the advocates of equality and of the perfectibility of man profess to be the end and object of their views."[47]

National or even local conditions might show the principle erroneous, but Malthus thought such a conclusion to be based on a partial view. The whole earth is the proper unit for study: It could not have been peopled nor could its population have been replenished when decimated by war, natural catastrophe, disease, without that spur of necessity caused by the constant tendency of a population to increase up to the limits of the food available to it. The principle of population is responsible for the geographic distribution of mankind on earth. The spur of necessity had prevented a concentration of population on the world's best lands, while the rest remained deserted.[48]

Malthus likened the earth variously to a closed room, to an island, and to a reservoir. The closed-room metaphor was intended to show the irrelevancy to the principle of population of the argument that there was no population problem as long as large areas of the world were still uninhabited and great tracts of land in the inhabited areas were still available for use: "A man who is locked up in a room may be fairly said to be confined by the walls of it, though he may never touch them; and with regard to the principle of population, it is never the question whether a country will produce *any more*, but whether it may be made to produce a sufficiency to keep pace with a nearly unchecked increase of people."[49] The moral of the reservoir comparison is that human beings are more skilled in the utilization than in the creation of resources.

> Where there are few people, and a great quantity of fertile land, the power of the earth to afford a yearly increase of food may be compared to a great reservoir of water supplied by a moderate stream. The faster population increases, the more help will be got to draw off the water, and consequently an increasing quantity will be taken every year. But the sooner, undoubtedly, will the reservoir be exhausted, and the streams only remain.[50]

This revealing comparison shows how narrowly Malthus regarded land as merely the container of agriculture; land was abstract, static, with no hint of destructive land use; a modern student of natural resources would say that

---

[47] Vol. 2, p. 5. This does not pretend to be a general exposition of the Malthusian theory. My purpose here is to discuss his ideas as a form of environmental theory. See Penrose, *Population Theories and Their Application*; Keynes's essay on Malthus in his *Essays in Biography*; Spengler, "Malthus's Total Population Theory: a Restatement and Reappraisal," *Canadian Journal of Economics*, Vol. XI (1945), pp. 83–110, 234–264; Mombert, *Bevölkerungslehre*, pp. 159–170; Bonar's discussion of Malthus's theses, *Malthus and His Work*, pp. 60–84; Smith, *The Malthusian Controversy*; and Boulding's foreword to *Population: The First Essay*. Peterson, *Population*, pp. 507–535. The already large literature on Malthus has increased considerably in the last fifteen years or so, coinciding with the revival of interest in him.

[48] 1798 *Essay*, pp. 363–365; 7th ed., Vol. 1, p. 59.

[49] Vol. 2, p. 149.

[50] 1798 *Essay*, pp. 106–107, footnote.

when the reservoir was exhausted, the help would go to the stream and continue upward. Comparing the world to an island disposed of those who saw in emigration a permanent cure for distress caused by local or temporary overcrowding. "There is probably no island yet known, the produce of which could not be further increased. This is all that can be said of the whole earth. Both are peopled up to their actual produce. And the whole earth is in this respect like an island."[51]

Malthus's insistence that the whole earth should be regarded as a unit presents difficulties which are realized more poignantly today than in his time. Despite the obvious barriers to the free movement of peoples, such as national boundaries, customs, law, and regulation, population is often considered with relation to the whole earth because it is the ultimate finite limit to the support of human life. There is a polarity of views, those who say that it is unrealistic to think of population and food in relation to the world as a whole because of the existence of national states, and those who say that it is meaningful to calculate the potential population of the earth by some formula that indicates the carrying capacity of the earth, because the condition of the total population ultimately will affect its national component parts. Malthus realized that the earth, in his time, was only partially populated, that many areas were still open to settlement, but it is an error, he said in reply to Godwin, to suppose "that no distress or difficulty would arise from a redundant population before the earth absolutely refused to produce any more."[52] Certainly the world could be more densely populated than it is; but there are difficulties in colonization and emigration: Indigenous peoples could not be starved out; if they were taught and their minds improved, their population would increase and "it would rarely happen that a great degree of knowledge and industry would have to operate at once upon rich unappropriated soil."[53] These interesting arguments, including Malthus's sensitivity to the treatment of native peoples, are really cultural arguments that modify the principle of population. Since indigenous peoples, with education and new techniques, would quickly fill up their sparsely settled lands, these no longer are open to others. When all fertile lands are occupied, further increases must come from improvements in land already being cultivated. "When acre has been added to acre till all the fertile land is occupied, the yearly increase of food must depend upon the melioration of the land already in possession. This is a fund, which, from the nature of all soils, instead of increasing must be gradually diminishing."[54]

In the following passage that aroused the contemptuous anger of Godwin, Malthus reveals how impressed he is with the fecundity of nature, how he tries, as a Christian, to make his principle conform to his belief in a benevolent Creator, how at the same time he turns aside objections from defenders of the

[51] 7th ed., Vol. 1, p. 44.
[52] *Ibid.*, Vol. 2, p. 13.
[53] *Ibid.*, Vol. 1, p. 9.
[54] *Ibid.*, p. 3.

design argument who saw in his principle a contradiction to the commands of Genesis to increase and multiply:

> But, if any person will take the trouble to make the calculation, he will see that if the necessaries of life could be obtained and distributed without limit, and the number of people could be doubled every twenty-five years, the population which might have been produced from a single pair since the Christian aera, would have been sufficient, not only to fill the earth quite full of people, so that four should stand in every square yard, but to fill all the planets of our solar system in the same way, and not only them, but all the planets revolving around the stars which are visible to the naked eye, supposing each of them to be a sun, and to have as many planets belonging to it as our sun has. Under the law of population, which, excessive as it may appear when stated in this way, is, I firmly believe, best suited to the nature and situation of man, it is quite obvious that some limit to the production of food, or some other of the necessaries of life, must exist. . . . It is not easy to conceive a more disastrous present—one more likely to plunge the human race in irrecoverable misery, than an unlimited facility of producing food in a limited space. A benevolent Creator then, knowing the wants and necessities of his creatures, under the laws to which he had subjected them, could not, in mercy, have furnished the whole of the necessaries of life in the same plenty as air and water. This shews at once the reason why the former are limited in quantity, and the latter poured out in profusion.[55]

How will the earth become fully peopled? Assuming in the beginning a small population in a large area, the population would increase and would press upon food supply until poverty and misery intervened; these would cause a cheapness of labor and provide the incentive for increased industry. (Malthus's use of contemporary English situations is jarring in this description of an historical process seemingly of great antiquity.) Cultivators would employ more men by whose efforts lands already in use would be improved and the area of cultivation simultaneously extended, thus increasing the means of subsistence and permitting the population to increase. The cycle could then begin anew until the whole earth would fill up and become the final limiting factor; the amplitude of the oscillations would progressively decrease until there would be only minor ones in a state approaching but not reaching equilibrium. Ironically, one byproduct of this theory was Malthus's insistence on the importance of cultural history. The oscillations will not be noticed by superficial observers and even the most penetrating may find it difficult to calculate its periods. Why has it been so little noticed? One reason is that histories are largely those of the upper classes. "We have but few accounts that can be depended upon of the manners and customs of that part of mankind, where these retrograde and progressive movements chiefly take place."[56]

Although Malthus does not discuss the possible destructive effects of increasing population pressure on the land (he should not be chided for this, because few in his day did), he thought that population increase would

[55] Godwin, *Of Population*, pp. 500–501; Malthus, *Principles of Political Economy* (London, 1820), pp. 227–228.
[56] 1798 *Essay*, p. 32, substantially repeated in 7th ed., Vol. 1, pp. 16–17.

"force" good lands and require the cultivation of poor ones; the costs, however, apparently are seen only in terms of capital and labor required. He does, however, mention accusations of ill-considered deforestation by the Swedes and Norwegians. The deeply pessimistic implications of Malthus's doctrine do not come, as many seem to believe, from the ratios but from the doctrine—advanced by Malthus in his *Political Economy* and other writings, as well as by James West and David Ricardo—that in the history of civilization, the best lands are taken up first; thus as civilization advances and mankind increases in numbers, it expands onto poorer and poorer lands. The question of the historical sequence in the occupation of land received considerable attention in the nineteenth century (to Mill, for example, it is crucial) because of its effect on the idea of progress. If civilization has within it the seeds of inevitable progress, heavy blocks are in its path if it is forced to rely on poorer and poorer lands. Malthus, West, and Ricardo all had their eyes on England and they were generalizing from it.[57] In 1848 the American social scientist, H. C. Carey, complained that "Mr. Ricardo places his settler on the best lands, and the children of that settler on those which are inferior. He makes man the victim of a sad *necessity*, increasing with his numbers," whereas he is "exercising constantly increasing *power*, derived from combined exertion by those numbers." Carey, whose eye was on American history, applies the idea of progress to agriculture as well. The historical progression, in his view, has been from the poor to the best soils because he assumes the best soils to be the most inaccessible to a primitive technology, the most luxuriantly covered with vegetation, and the most unhealthful. Poor soils of uplands are used first because man's control of nature is feeble; the progression to the best soils is related to the history of technology, to the increasing control over nature.[58]

The illuminating comparisons which Malthus made between the soils and the machines of factories and manufacturing plants show the source of his pessimism to be partly in his appraisal of soils: "The earth has sometimes been compared to a vast machine, presented by nature to man for the production of food and raw materials," but the soil is really a great number of machines, "of very different original qualities and powers." Unlike the machinery employed in manufacturing—where constant improvements are made and production can increase after patents have expired—soils as the machines of food production vary from very poor to the very good.[59]

[57] Malthus, *An Inquiry into the Nature and Progress of Rent* [1815], pp. 15–17, 20–21, 33–34; West, *The Application of Capital to Land*, pp. 9–16; Ricardo, *The Principles of Political Economy and Taxation* (Everyman's Library ed.), p. 35. On the history of this idea, see Cannan, *A History of the Theories of Production and Distribution in English Political Economy from 1776 to 1848*, 3rd ed., pp. 155–182. On the Scandinavian deforestation, 7th ed., Vol. 1, pp. 169–170.
[58] H. C. Carey, *The Past, The Present, and the Future*, pp. 17–24; quote on p. 24; *Principles of Social Science*, Vol. I, pp. 94–146, on the occupation of the earth.
[59] Malthus, *Principles of Political Economy*, pp. 184–186.

Since the best soils cannot alone provide for an increased population, the poorer ones must be cultivated, with more and more labor being applied less and less efficiently. Agriculture and manufacturing thus are at opposite extremes. The conclusion is inescapable that, with advancing civilization and population increase, it becomes more and more costly in money and human effort to obtain a subsistence.

Soils alone, however, do not determine agricultural progress; one must also take into account the moral and physical qualities of those who till them. If soil fertility alone were an adequate stimulus to wealth, the human race would not have the stimulus to work which is the secret of progress. Malthus quotes Humboldt in support of this argument.

He was impressed with Humboldt's account of the various foods of New Spain, among them the banana, manioc, and maize, and the manner of their cultivation. Humboldt singled out the banana for special praise ("Je doute qu'il existe une autre plante sur le globe qui, sur un si petit espace de terrain, puisse produire une masse de substance nourrissante aussi considérable"), a wonderful food grown with ridiculous ease on fertile soils. It is repeatedly said in the Spanish Colonies that the inhabitants of the *tierra caliente* will only emerge from their centuries-long apathy when a royal decree orders the destruction of the banana trees, adding that those who so zealously propose this violent remedy display generally no more activity than the lower classes they wish to force to serve their growing needs. He hopes the Mexicans will become more industrious without the necessity of destroying the trees. In considering, however, the ease with which man can sustain himself in such a climate, it is not surprising that, in the equinoctial region of the New World, civilization arose in the mountains on a less fertile soil and in an environment less favorable for the development of organic life and in which need is the spur to industry. Malthus concluded that tropical luxuriance induced lethargy among people; nature is generous, not niggardly, and this generosity is favorable to continual poverty, thinly peopled lands, and to unprogressive civilizations. Malthus quoted Humboldt with approval; he was not going to let anyone progress without hard work.[60]

It is land that is suited for agriculture, especially cereal farming, that seems to interest Malthus most. Moreover, when he discusses Chinese agriculture, he is interested in the cultural milieu; it is not depicted solely as a function of environment. Agriculture there can produce a large population because social tradition is behind it. China's deep and excellent soils and the way in which they are manured, cultivated, and watered; its situation in favored areas of the temperate zone; the industry of its inhabitants; its lakes, rivers, brooks, and canals; and its long tradition of respect for agriculture and governmental encouragement of it—these are responsible for supporting the Chinese popula-

[60] *Ibid.*, pp. 382–384; Humboldt, *Essai Politique sur le Royaume de la Nouvelle-Espagne*, Vol. 3, pp. 37–39; quote on p. 28.

tion. Here, as in so many eighteenth century discussions of China, is the fine hand of Father du Halde.[61]

Elsewhere he clearly sees that ways of life ask cultural questions, not simply environmental ones. The prolific power of nature seems ready to exert its full force in every country, he says; but can governments suppose they could induce their peoples to produce the maximum amount the earth was capable of? Such action would violate the law of property,

> from which everything that is valuable to man has hitherto arisen. . . . But what statesman or rational government could propose that all animal food should be prohibited, that no horses should be used for business or pleasure, that all the people should live upon potatoes, and that the whole industry of the nation should be exerted in the production of them, except what was required for the mere necessaries of clothing and houses? Could such a revolution be effected, would it be desirable? particularly as in a few years, notwithstanding all these exertions, want, with less resource than ever, would inevitably recur.[62]

Although he thought agriculture the basic factor in population growth, he saw in the combination of agriculture, commerce, and industry the key to economic progress, and his ideas here are closer to those of twentieth century economists than to the physiocrats writing a generation before him.

Malthus wrote before the beginning of modern soil science. Theories of soils were not scientific; they could only be judged empirically. When Malthus was comparing soils with machines, the agricultural chemists of the period were for the most part committed to the humus theory.[63]

With his soil theory and his belief that historically the best lands were taken up first, the pessimism regarding the food-producing capacities of the earth for future populations becomes deeper, environmental limitations more unyielding and less subject to human intervention.

### 5. Conceptions of Progress, Theology, and the Nature of Man in the Malthusian Doctrine

Malthus did not believe that any improvement in human nature could be expected, or that reform in government and institutions could—or should—alter the operations of the principle of population. That they helped could not be denied, but the hopes of those who relied on institutional reform would be dissolved in sterner and deeper realities of nature.

Moreover, he had views of his own on progress. In the second and fol-

---

[61] 7th ed., Vol. 1, p. 126; Du Halde, *Description Géographique, Historique, Chronologique, Politique, et Physique de l'Empire de la Chine et de la Tartarie Chinoise*, Vol. 2, esp. pp. 163–186, "De l'abondance qui régne à la Chine." This volume also has discussions of Chinese agriculture, artisans, climate, canals and lakes, etc., which M. read.

[62] 7th ed., Vol. 2, p. 52.

[63] Charles A. Browne, *A Source Book of Agricultural Chemistry*. See excerpts from Wallerius, Lavoisier, Thaer, and Einhoff.

lowing editions of his work, Malthus does not begin with a discussion of population at all but with the method of inquiring into the improvement of society; the way "which naturally presents itself, is, 1. To investigate the causes that have hitherto impeded the progress of mankind towards happiness; and, 2. To examine the probability of the total or partial removal of these causes in future."[64]

This is not the program of a man biased in favor of inevitable social change. Quite the contrary, it is the statement of one who assumes a resistance to change among men and in society, of a believer in progress through human effort. In several places in his works Malthus mentions the slothful nature of man. This conception of man's nature is fundamental in his philosophy because it is the constant spur of necessity that goads him on. Niggardly nature and slothful man are the ingredients of the principle of population.[65]

The principle of population is the motive force of progress; because of it, the earth was peopled and its habitability maintained by cultivation. He had no plan, he said, to improve society; he was content with understanding the obstacles in the way of improvement.[66] In place of a law of progress which applied to every aspect of human life, he offered a conception much less comprehensive. "I have endeavoured to expose the fallacy of that argument which infers an unlimited progress from a partial improvement, the limits of which cannot be exactly ascertained."[67]

He disagreed with Ricardo on unilinear progress, expressing his opinion that "the progress of society consists of irregular movements," that "we see in all the countries around us, and in our own particularly, periods of greater or less prosperity and sometimes adversity, but *never* the uniform progress which you seem alone to contemplate."[68] This he wrote in 1817, but it expressed sentiments similar to those of 1798:

> The present rage for wide and unrestrained speculation seems to be a kind of mental intoxication, arising perhaps, from the great and unexpected discoveries which have been made of late years, in various branches of science. To men elate, and giddy with such successes, everything appeared to be within the grasp of human powers; and, under this illusion, they confounded subjects where no real progress could be proved, with those, where the progress had been marked, certain, and acknowledged.[69]

Malthus was more optimistic, however, than many of his interpreters have represented him to be:

> From a review of the state of society in former periods compared with the present, I should certainly say that the evils resulting from the principle of population

[64] 7th ed., Vol. 1, p. 5.
[65] For a typical statement regarding slothful man, see *ibid.*, p. 59.
[66] *Ibid.*, Vol. 2, p. 258.
[67] 1798 *Essay*, p. 216.
[68] Quoted in John Maynard Keynes, *Essays in Biography*, pp. 139–140.
[69] 1798 *Essay*, p. 31; 7th ed., Vol. 2, p. 26.

have rather diminished than increased, even under the disadvantage of almost total ignorance of the real cause. And if we can indulge the hope that this ignorance will be gradually dissipated, it does not seem unreasonable to expect that they will be still further diminished. The increase of absolute population, which will of course take place, will evidently tend but little to weaken this expectation, as everything depends upon the relative proportion between population and food, and not on the absolute number of people.[70]

The 1798 essay appeared at a time when little was known either about the population of the world or the details of its distribution. In Europe, the estimate of a world population of about a billion had become somewhat of a convention, Süssmilch's estimate of 1761 being accepted throughout the latter part of the eighteenth century. From 1781 to 1815 the *Almanach de Gotha* had repeated the 1761 Süssmilch estimate of one billion.[71]

Because the great mass of criticism directed at Malthus has come from those who have opposed the social and political implications of his principle—utopian and Marxist socialists, and reformists within the capitalistic system among them—it is necessary to add that Malthus, like Lyell and Darwin later, had to meet the criticism from religion and physico-theology, typically inherent in the thought of Süssmilch and in Luther's famous saying, "Gott macht die Kinder und will sie ernähren." The biblical injunction to increase and multiply, Malthus realizes, might seem to oppose the principle. One of the principal reasons, he says, preventing agreement with his principle "is a great unwillingness to believe that the Deity would by the laws of nature bring beings into existence, which by the laws of nature could not be supported in that existence."[72] In reply Malthus appeals to natural laws to which human beings are subject, rejecting by implication any anthropocentrism which would involve the personal and active concern of the Deity. The Deity operates through these laws, and the incidental evils arising from them constantly direct attention to the need for moral restraint as the "proper check to population." It is natural law that must be understood. Our duties are pointed out to us by the light of nature and reason; they are confirmed and sanctioned by revelation.[73]

Taking his cue from St. Paul, he thinks marriage is right if it does not interfere with one's higher duties, wrong if it does. We learn the will of God from the light of nature, he says, quoting Paley approvingly, by inquiring into the tendency of an action to promote or diminish general happiness. Malthus argues for restraint, maintaining that one of the worst acts diminishing happiness is to marry without the means to support children. Such acts are against the will of God, a burden on society, and they make it difficult to

---

[70] 7th ed., Vol. 2, p. 26.
[71] Behm and Wagner, "Die Bevölkerung der Erde, II," *Petermanns Mitteilungen Ergänzungsband* 8, No. 35, p. 5 (1873–74).
[72] Vol. 2, p. 160.
[73] *Ibid.*

preserve virtuous habits in the family. Moral restraint exercised by individuals therefore has a key position in the doctrine, because Malthus believes the problem of population is closely related to "internal tyranny and internal tumult" and to war.[74] Virtue in observance of natural law avoids evil consequences to the individual and to society, and there is therefore no reason to impeach divine justice. "It is the apparent object of the Creator to deter us from vice by the pains which accompany it, and to lead us to virtue by the happiness that it produces. This object appears to our conceptions to be worthy of a benevolent Creator."[75]

Malthus's discussion of disease is also consistent with this concept of a Deity acting through the laws of nature. If they are intermediate between God and nature including man, natural and moral evil become instruments of admonishment—not direct and personal, of course, but through the lessons they teach, the knowledge they impart, the experience they give. Diseases should be regarded not as inevitable inflictions of Providence but more "as indications that we have offended against some of the laws of nature." Plagues are such admonitions; properly heeded, they enable man to improve his condition. The lessons of the plague prevalent in London until 1666 were not lost on our ancestors. They removed nuisances, constructed drains, widened streets, permitted more room and air in their houses, measures which had "the effect of eradicating completely this dreadful disorder, and of adding greatly to the health and happiness of the inhabitants."[76] Thus to Malthus, mankind is subject to the general laws of nature, not to specific intercessions of the Deity; these laws are benevolent if men know their operations and abide by their teachings. There is therefore, in his opinion, no conflict between the biblical injunction to increase and multiply and the principle of population. "A common man, who has read his Bible, must be convinced that a command given to a rational being by a merciful God cannot be intended so to be interpreted as to produce only disease and death instead of multiplication. . . ."[77]

Thus in a period when there was still much conjecture about the true state of population, of war and economic uncertainty, of migration to cities, of the beginning of a new kind of industrialization, one of the most influential ideas of modern times was formulated and disseminated, its simplicity permitting quick popularization, easy quotation, and both accurate and inaccurate paraphrasing. Western thought has never been the same since Malthus; over 150 years of controversy is sufficient proof of his place in Western thought. He created a new view of the world out of old materials, a synthesis coming from notions of fecundity, from theology, from known or suspected statistical regularities, from the social conditions of Europe, from travelers' accounts of widely scattered regions, from reports of great population growth

[74] *Ibid.*, pp. 165–166.
[75] *Ibid.*, p. 167.
[76] *Ibid.*, pp. 152–153.
[77] *Ibid.*, p. 67.

in the newly settled regions of America. In Malthus's forceful prose, the environment had become a perpetual challenge to mankind. If however we probe deeper, beyond the principle of population and the ratios, what is the philosophy of God, man, and nature that is expounded? I do not think it is an error to base the reply mainly on the first essay, for the fundamental philosophical ideas of Malthus did not change, although there are great differences between the first essay and the thoroughly documented treatises that followed it.

In Malthus's writings there is a strong emphasis on emotion and passion, no doubt in part stimulated by the irrationality and brutality of the Reign of Terror. But there is no denigration of sensual pleasure.[78] Men have deep and violent passions, but they are also indolent and averse to labor, constantly needing something or someone to prod them along. Malthus is no ranter about sin. "Life is, generally speaking, a blessing independent of a future state."[79] In the book of nature we alone can read God as he is. The world and this life are a "mighty process of God, not for the trial but for the creation and formation of mind."[80]

Neither does he deny the force and vigor of the sexual drives. In fact, any diminution of them might make it difficult to attain the great end of the creation, the peopling of the earth. The emphasis therefore is on control. Commenting on Godwin's remark, "Strip the commerce of the sexes of all its attendant circumstances, and it would be generally despised," Malthus says, "He might as well say to a man who admires trees, strip them of their spreading branches and lovely foliage, and what beauty can you see in a bare pole? But it was the tree with the branches and foliage and not without them, that excited admiration."[81]

He was dazzled by the fullness and luxuriance of nature, with an awe so characteristic of Western thought, and by the profligate extravagance of life despite all checks. Like Humboldt, he saw the infinite variety of form and operations of nature, awakening and improving the mind "by the variety of impressions that it creates," opening also new avenues for investigation and research.[82] The middle regions of society between riches and poverty seem most favorable to intellectual improvement, but one cannot expect all society to be a middle region. Similarly, "The temperate zones of the earth, seem to be the most favourable to the mental, and corporeal energies of man; but all cannot be temperate zones."[83]

Malthus's contribution to the ideas we are discussing was that he related population theory to philosophy, history, and ethnology; on the whole, the

---

[78] 1798 *Essay*, pp. 210–212.
[79] *Ibid.*, p. 391.
[80] *Ibid.*, p. 353.
[81] Vol. 2, p. 155, citing *Political Justice*, Vol. 1, Bk. 1, chap. 5.
[82] 1798 *Essay*, p. 378.
[83] *Ibid.*, p. 367.

principle is not yoked up enthusiastically with a philosophy of design and final causes. Malthus did not accept, as Süssmilch did, a close connection between Genesis and population theory; he ignored the cheerful optimism of writers steeped in physico-theology. His emphasis is on natural law, on the study of mankind in human terms, in history, ethnology, and statistics. If he was an innovator in none of these, his writings gave them new significance and new incentives for study. Malthus's essay also is one of the early challenges to the assumption of inevitable progress; he advises men to study social and cultural history with a look to backslidings as well; in essence he called for a more profound kind of historiography than then existed.

Man modifies the earth, and it is by the design of Providence that he does so because only by the principle of population would the earth be fully cultivated. The principle of population thus accounts for the peopling of the world, the distribution of mankind and its settlement in less desirable places and repopulation after catastrophe, and indirectly for modifications of the earth by man. "The processes of ploughing and clearing the ground, of collecting and sowing seeds, are not surely for the assistance of God in his creation; but are made previously necessary to the enjoyment of the blessings of life, in order to rouse man into action, and form his mind to reason."[84]

Thus there are in Malthus's writings evidences of the ideas whose history we have been discussing. The physico-theology is restrained and in the English tradition of Ray and Derham. The religion of nature is inspired by Romans 1:20. Environmental influences, however, are subordinated to the more fundamental and abstract influence of a limited total environment. And man modifies his environment in order to live, to act, to use his mind.

Finally, Malthus put in forceful, strikingly metaphorical language, and particularly in the first essay, the choice between environmental and social causation. Much of the subsequent history of population theory can be written in terms of the choices posed by Malthus; the Marxian hostility in the U.S.S.R. (which later extended even to Darwin) to Malthusian theory is a well-known example because to Marxists population questions are meshed with a teleology of economic and social development, and are not matters of natural law against which human beings strive in vain. Malthus had stated the case for the limitations of the environment; he had also shown that the assumptions of those who believed in the inevitability of progress in all phases of human activity were in need of reexamination.

## 6.  A FINAL ANSWER TO MALTHUS

Twenty-two years after the appearance of Malthus's essay, William Godwin published *Of Population*, a book over six hundred pages long; it is largely concerned with Malthus. One of the men responsible for Malthus's first essay

---

[84] *Ibid.*, p. 361.

now returned to combat in the hope of finishing off the Malthusian theory
once and for all.[85]

*Of Population* is a neglected work; no one, not even Godwin's admirers,
seems to have taken it seriously. It is poorly organized and it lacks intellectual
distinction. Though he repeatedly says he bears Malthus no personal resent-
ment, the frequently declamatory and intolerant tone is inconsistent with
Godwin's claim of objective and dispassionate refutation. Nevertheless Godwin, who looks forward to the dawn of a brighter age, made some telling
objections to the Malthus doctrine. It was a fallacy to base a doctrine (a
"system that has gained a success in the world wholly unprecedented") on
one example. Malthus had discovered the principle of population in the northeastern part of the United States. "If America had never been discovered, the
geometrical ratio, as applied to the multiplication of mankind, would never
have been known. If the British colonies had never been planted, Mr. Malthus
would never have written."[86] There was no proof, Godwin said, that the increased population of the United States had come from procreation only.
The United States, a free government with liberal institutions, wished "greater
multitudes to partake [of] these blessings." The entire lower classes of Europe
would migrate in a body were it not for the love men have for their birthplace and for their poverty. It was emigration from the Old World, and
emigrants in the "flower of their lives," that caused the American increase.
Godwin denied there was a greater number of children and that there were
fewer premature deaths from disease and other causes in America than in
Europe. America, like all newly settled countries, is unhealthful and North
America abounds in swamps. Relying largely on Count Volney's *View of
the Climate and Soil of the United States*, Godwin stressed the toll taken in
America by tuberculosis, dysentery, and yellow fever. The widespread pre-
mature tooth decay, observed by Volney, was also evidence of unhealthful
American conditions.[87]

(One could write an interesting essay concerning the influence of American settlement history on social and political thought in the nineteenth and
twentieth centuries. Its early population growth in a thinly populated region
proved, so Malthus thought, the truth of the geometrical ratio. Its further
settlement, cultivation, and exploitation, and the wheat surpluses, especially
those of the seventies and eighties of the nineteenth century, revealed the
fallacy of the principle. Henry George said as much in *Progress and Poverty*
in denouncing the Malthusian theory, and many others agreed with him.
Finally, interpretations of the frontier by Turner and others opened up a new
phase in the history of ideas of closed space.)

Since Malthus's discovery is based on the American increase, once "this

---

[85] *Of Population*, pp. iv–vii.
[86] *Ibid.*, pp. 142, 139–140.
[87] *Ibid.*, pp. 374–380, 403–404, 418, 430–443. See Volney, *View of the Climate and Soil
of the United States*, pp. 278–332.

idle and extravagant hypothesis" is removed, "the whole science stands just as it did before Mr. Malthus wrote. . . ."[88] Godwin repeatedly says we live in an "unpeopled world."[89] Would it not have been fairer to have deduced a principle of population by surveying the entire globe? Any such survey would reveal the thinness and scattering of the world's population, how to make better use of the uninhabited regions, and how they might be "replenished with a numerous and happy race."[90]

Godwin would not allow Malthus to enact laws of nature. His principle "is not *the Law of Nature*. It is *the Law of very artificial life*."[91] If Malthus is right, why is not the globe fully peopled? If such strenuous measures are necessary to restrain the tendency of population to increase, how is it that "the world is a wilderness, a wide and desolate place, where men crawl about in little herds, comfortless, unable from the dangers of freebooters, and the dangers of wild beasts to wander from climate to climate, and without that mutual support and cheerfulness which a populous earth would most naturally afford?"[92]

Godwin's rebuttal of the natural law is based on the evidence from the history of human settlement and on the actual distribution of mankind on earth. Godwin was right! Why should population theory be considered independently of the history of human settlement? To Godwin, problems of population growth are basically historical ones. What of depopulation? Why are European and Asiatic Turkey, Persia, Egypt, and a multitude of other countries so thinly inhabited now compared "to what they were in the renowned periods of their ancient history?" Godwin answers that soil exhaustion is not the cause. "Certainly it is not because another blade of corn refuses to grow on their surface." The cause is to be found "in the government and political administration of these countries."[93] He is sympathetic with the complaints of depopulation which Montesquieu voiced in the *Persian Letters*; and he felt that Hume's essay had done little more than "to throw some portion of uncertainty on the subject."[94]

Why had not the geometrical ratio been tested by the experience of an Old World country like China?[95] It would be an ideal example, since marriage is encouraged, celibacy discouraged; it has no manufacturing cities to produce waste; and the quiet life of women makes them more prolific, safeguarding them from untimely births. Neither he nor Malthus, he says, knows anything about the population of China, but on the basis of statements made

[88] *Ibid.*, p. 141.
[89] *Ibid.*, pp. 485–486.
[90] *Ibid.*, pp. 15–16.
[91] *Ibid.*, p. 20.
[92] *Ibid.*, pp. 20–21.
[93] *Ibid.*, pp. 309–310.
[94] *Ibid.*, p. 40. Godwin is referring to *Persian Letters*, No. 108, and to Hume's essay, "Of the Populousness of Ancient Nations."
[95] *Ibid.*, chap. 6.

by Malthus himself, Godwin thinks that "the statesmen and legislators of China, who have proceeded with a steady, and perhaps I may add an enlightened, attention to the subject for centuries, not only have no suspicion of the main principles taught in the Essay on Population, but are deeply impressed with the persuasion that, without encouragement and care to prevent it, the numbers of the human species have a perpetual tendency to decline."[96]

Racial and cultural intermingling and migrations seem to affect population growth. Could not population increase be ascribed to such mixing, decline to isolation and inbreeding? Crossing seems to improve the breed in both men and animals. "May not the qualities of the present race of Europeans ... be materially owing to the invasions of the Celts and the Cimbri, the Goths and Vandals, the Danes, the Saxons, and the Normans?"[97]

In denying that the principle of population is a law of nature, Goodwin in effect said that the numbers and distribution of the world's peoples are basically problems of history and geography.

"Population, if we consider it historically, appears to be a fitful principle, operating intermittently [*sic*] and by starts. This is the great mystery of the subject; and patiently to investigate the causes of its irregular progress seems to be a business highly worthy of the philosopher."[98]

Furthermore Godwin, like Malthus, viewed the earth and its resources as a whole, making one of the earliest estimates known to me of its carrying capacity—which he computed to be nine billion people.[99]

The productivity of the earth can be endlessly improved, substituting the plough for the pasture, and then the spade for the plough. "The productiveness of garden-cultivation over field-cultivation, for the purposes of human subsistence, is astonishingly great."[100] The only objection is that less manual labor is desirable in an improved society but there must be a "probation of extensive labor," for the greater part of mankind is as yet unprepared for leisure. Use the resources of the sea, see how many more people can be fed on a vegetable rather than an animal diet, become a world of gardeners! "Nature has presented to us the earth, the *alma magna parens*, whose bosom, to all but the wild and incongruous ratios of Mr. Malthus, may be said to be inexhaustible. Human science and ingenuity have presented to us the means of turning this resource to the utmost account."[101]

[96] *Ibid.*, p. 52.

[97] *Ibid.*, pp. 365–366.

[98] *Ibid.*, pp. 327–328.

[99] He estimates that 39 million square miles of the earth are habitable, of which 1.3 million are in China with an estimated population of 300 million. Using the cultivation of China as the standard for possible cultivation and its population as the standard of possible population density, the result is 9 billion: 39 million divided by 1.3 and multiplied by 300 million. *Ibid.*, pp. 448–449.

[100] *Ibid.*, p. 495.

[101] *Ibid.*, p. 498.

In Godwin's writings as in those of Malthus there is the conviction that man bestows dignity on the order of nature, that in the continual peopling of the world the changes that man effects will be beautiful and useful. The earth is a better place because of man:

> Man is an admirable creature, the beauty of the world, which, if he did not exist in it, would be a "habitation of dragons, and a court for owls; the wild beast of the desert would cry to the wild beast of the islands; baboons would dance there; and its pleasant places be filled with all doleful creatures." How delightful a speculation then is it, that man is endowed by all-bountiful nature with an unlimited power of multiplying his species? I would look out upon the cheerless and melancholy world which has just been described, and imagine it all cultivated, all improved, all variegated with a multitude of human beings, in a state of illumination, of innocence, and of active benevolence, to which the progress of thought, and the enlargement of mind seem naturally to lead, beyond any thing that has yet any where been realised.[102]

Both Godwin's idea of progress and Malthus's principle of population apparently led to a future world of gardeners.

Malthus neither ignored this work nor replied to it, contenting himself with a few unflattering sentences about it.[103] Behind Godwin's appraisal of the earth is the idea of progress. The physical environment will not be a limiting factor in human advance in the foreseeable future, and there are new hopes in the dawning technological and chemical age.

Godwin does not suggest—and neither does Malthus—that these advances will create problems nor that man's relationship to the world of nature by the growth of his numbers and the persistence of his settlement in favored places, might change rapidly. On the contrary, he is full of hope and cheer as he envisions the forward march of mankind to a complete and permanent occupation of all the earth's lands.

### 7.  Conclusion

By his advocacy of climatic influences, Montesquieu in the *Esprit des Lois* had provoked some of the most searching thought on social and environmental questions that had yet appeared in Western civilization; he did this by his learning, wit, humanity, dogmatism. In the *Lettres Persanes* he had a similar effect on population questions and here he had given great weight to moral causes as reasons for modern depopulation. When he pursued these inquiries in the *Esprit des Lois*, again cultural not environmental causation interested him and he saw clearly the uniqueness of human populations, and he had his own causal population theory; it might even be Malthus without fanfare.

[102] *Ibid.*, pp. 450–451.
[103] See the last paragraph of the appendix to the 6th ed. of *A Principle of Population*.

"Wherever a place is found in which two persons can live commodiously, there they enter into marriage. Nature has a sufficient propensity to it, when unrestrained by the difficulty of subsistence."[104]

If Montesquieu's data were poor, if his conclusions about modern depopulation were misguided and provincial, the matters he and his Persians discussed with such earthiness and practicality were indeed important. The dispute over the populousness of ancient nations, fatuous as were some of the arguments, had its rewards; like the more important quarrel over the ancients and moderns of which it was a part, it induced comparisons with the ancient world, it gave prominence to the moral and social consequences of modern slavery, European colonial expansion after the age of discovery, of religion, disease, and morality.

It is thus no exaggeration to say that this comparison between the ancients and the moderns, whether in the form of culture, arts, population, morality, and the idea of progress which emerged as a higher generalization from the quarrel set the stage for the debates on social and environmental causation culminating in Malthus and in Godwin's final reply to him. Upon what does one base his thought, on the force of human institutions or the omnipotence of natural law? Godwin's belligerent words, already quoted, state the alternatives clearly and fairly. Malthus's principle "is not *the Law of Nature. It is the Law of very artificial life.*"

One sees repeatedly the powerful influence of the idea of progress—as one now sees its modern substitute, faith in science—on population questions. Condorcet and Godwin accept it as a basic principle which gives meaning to civilization, and Malthus denies its inevitability and the perfectibility of man, arguing that progress is uneven and uncertan.

Most important was the association of the idea of progress with the environmental limitations of the earth. Malthus and Godwin had extended the argument to include the whole earth, and it was a welcome development despite the obvious pitfalls in considering as a unit an earth so politically, culturally, and religiously divided.

Neither thinker was concerned to any degree with environmental change by man. They recognized it but gave little thought to its implications. For Malthus, to be sure, the environment was limiting, but to Godwin it posed few problems crucial to the human race. For their purposes they assumed a stable physical environment. Both men saw that ultimately the earth might be cultivated like a garden, but neither thought that an environment, deteriorating as a result of long human settlement, might offer hard choices in the future. Nor did Count Buffon, but he did see the great influence of man on the land and on all life, and it is to this subject—and to him—that we now in the last chapter turn.

---

[104] *EL*, Bk. 23, chap. 10.

# Chapter 14

EPOQUES DE LA NATURE.  237

font devenues fon domaine; enfin la face entière de la
Terre porte aujourd'hui l'empreinte de la puiſſance de
l'homme, laquelle, quoique ſubordonnée à celle de la
Nature, ſouvent a fait plus qu'elle, ou du moins l'a ſi
merveilleuſement fecondée, que c'eſt à l'aide de nos
mains qu'elle s'eſt développée dans toute ſon étendue,
& qu'elle eſt arrivée par degrés au point de perfeſtion &
de magnificence où nous la voyons aujourd'hui.

# The Epoch of Man in the History of Nature

## 1. INTRODUCTION

In *Des Époques de la Nature*, Count Buffon had named the seventh and last as the age when man assumes an active role, "seconding," to use his phrase, the operations of nature. From a secular point of view man was in control of nature; from a religious, he was completing the creation with unexpected speed. Most of those who held such views were optimistic and believers in the idea of progress, the growth of knowledge enabling man to enlarge his horizons and to refashion his surroundings more to his taste. What pessimism there was, was not organized around a general principle, but there were observations that man must interfere with caution in the economy or equilibrium of nature. Isolated works, however, like Jean Antoine Fabre's *Essai sur la Théorie des Torrents*, foreshadow new and delicate sensitivities to cultural geography and history, to the longevity of customs and usages which continually—and cumulatively—affect the land.

2. Opportunities for Comparison

More than ever, our problem now is one of selection; it is easy to justify the inclusion of any one work, difficult to explain its inclusion to the exclusion of another. The volume of pertinent material increases enormously and the increase will accelerate in the nineteenth and twentieth centuries. First, there is the literature—often of broad theoretical interest—which each nation accumulates about its natural resources; by the end of the eighteenth century many of the nations of western Europe, such as England, France, the Germanies, and Sweden, already had impressive collections. Secondly, there are the works of synthesis, particularly the natural histories like Buffon's, which embraced cosmology, geology and historical geology, geography, botany and zoology, ethnology, and mineral resources and their distribution. Natural histories like Buffon's—factual, often compendium-like, composed inductively, concrete in detail but with supporting theory—inevitably considered man's place in nature, the environmental influences on man, and increasingly the man-made changes in nature, visible proof of which lay in the contrasts between environments long settled by man and those remote from his influence. Thirdly, there is the ever-increasing volume of literature about the New World, especially about the United States, some of it clustering around men like Franklin and Jefferson, statesmen and political theorists who are also deeply concerned with pure and applied science and with plans for altering the American landscape. Franklin is well received in Europe, Count Buffon belongs to the American Philosophical Society, Alexander von Humboldt visits Monticello. This literature on the United States, written by Europeans and Americans alike, is distinct from the literature on political and social institutions and the frontier, represented by the works of a De Tocqueville or a De Crèvecoeur. Men wrote technical works on the forests, travelers like Count Volney published widely quoted works which carefully described the geography of the country, including the forests, soils, climate, the effects of clearing. Similar in treatment and even more technical is Jefferson's "Notes on the State of Virginia." There are the Bartrams on natural history, Franklin's short essays on population and the equilibrium of nature. The early volumes of the *Transactions of the American Philosophical Society* reveal clearly the scope of learned and scientific interest in the new country. By the late eighteenth century a respectable literature on soils, crops, and farming methods was already in being. One sees in this literature the influence of the English theorists from Tull to Townshend and the Norfolk four-course rotation, but the English methods and theories are not accepted uncritically, for men were learning from observations, without waiting for nods of approval from European theorists, about the effects of maize or tobacco on their land, the dangers of soil exhaustion or of soil erosion, and the nature of manures. A new body of knowledge about the American environment begins to take shape, drawn perhaps from Lavoisier or Sir Humphry Davy but also from far less eminent practical observers like John Lorain, whose comparative study of the methods of clearing used by the Pennsylvania and the Yankee farmers we will be looking into.

The essential point is that by the latter part of the eighteenth century opportunities for comparison had increased vastly. The most dramatic comparison was that between long-settled Europe (many of whose lands had been under the plow for centuries, whose forests had been cut to make way for grain fields, vines, orchards, or villages, towns, and cities, many of whose rivers had now become tractable—their courses deepened and straightened—and were attended, as by bridesmaids, by many small canals) and the relatively virgin areas of the colonies of North America. It was also, I think, even more dramatic than the more familiar contrast which Count Volney made, in the *Ruins of Empire*, between Europe and the Near East with its evidences of present decay and former glory. The European travelers to the New World saw the contrasts; it would be amazing if they did not. They all seemed to agree that here too nature must submit to changes imposed upon it by its new inhabitants. The thoughts of men charged with governing the new land were often on a higher philosophic plane than practical concern with farm policy or the development of the country. They could reach, as they did with Jefferson and his friend the Marquis de Chastellux, a general in Rochambeau's army, a point at which they envisaged the planned creation of a new environment—clearings alternating with woodlands—that would be economically useful, aesthetically pleasing, healthful, and biologically sound.

It is obviously out of the question to survey this vast national and systematic literature in this work, but I do wish to select several themes which illustrate this growing awareness of the depth and breadth of human power. They include the influence of research in natural history, especially that of Count Buffon, the greatest of the eighteenth century natural historians, in awakening interest in the effect of man on other forms of life and on the physical environment as a whole. They include themes that since have become of world importance, such as the idea of a primordial balance in nature which civilized man interferes with at his own risk; the contrasting idea of purposeful change to create a better environment, the effects of clearing on climate, of clearing and drainage on health; the cultural aspects of forest protection and torrent control.

Great names in the eighteenth century science, Buffon in France, Linnaeus in Sweden, Banks in England, were committed to the advancement of natural history, which in many ways brought the activity of man into bold relief. Collecting for museums, interest in introducing economically useful plants and animals, made men more aware of their role as worldwide distributors of plant and animal life. The voyages of the last part of the century, like Cook's, brought new word of the various ways peoples, rude or polished and of all hues, exploited their natural resources.

### 3. CLIMATIC CHANGE AND THE INDUSTRY OF MAN

Although this chapter stresses Count Buffon's contributions, it is necessary to add that others had touched on the subject of man as an active modifier of nature and that Buffon's expositions owed much to a widespread if diffuse interest in it.

Montesquieu, for example, whose name is so closely identified with ideas of environmental influence (see above, pp. 568–575), observed that countries had been brought to their present condition by the industry of man, which, indeed, had transformed the physical environment of Europe and that of the Chinese empire. The indigenous peoples of the New World had achieved no such successes. Eighteenth century students were impressed by the fact that its population could not be compared with the large numbers of people living in Asia, Africa, and Europe.[1] This failure, it would seem, explained the contrasts between the landscapes of the New World and those of Europe and China whose industrious populations had lived there long enough and were sufficiently numerous to achieve these great historical transformations. This sensible observation, buttressed by his erroneous belief in the decline of world population in modern times, led him to emphasize the importance of population increase and the active intervention of man in the natural environment.[2]

Correlations are made between population densities and land use practices, the pasturelands supporting only a few, grain lands more, vineyards even more. Human industry becomes more intense with the grains and the vines. Rice culture is the best example of all; men substitute their labor for that of cattle, and this "culture of the soil becomes to man an immense manufacture." Apparently unconcerned with the problems of forest use since the ordinance of 1669, Montesquieu says that countries with coalpits for fuel "have this advantage over others, that not having the same occasion for forests, the lands may be cultivated." The statement does show, however, the dynamic quality of his thought, the coal relieving the economy of its dependence on the forests, which can now be sacrificed for agricultural clearing; it shows, however, little appreciation of the forest as a vital element in the landscape.[3]

Although Montesquieu's fears—that the population of the modern world

---

[1] Chinard, "Eighteenth Century Theories on America as a Human Habitat," *PAPS*, Vol. 91 (1947), p. 28.

[2] See above, p. 579, and *The Persian Letters*, tr. Loy (Meridian Books), letters 113–123, and *EL*, Bk. 23, chaps. 1–4, 10–19, 24–26.

[3] *EL*, Bk. 23, chap. 14.

was becoming so dangerously low that its few inhabitants could not exploit it and could not keep nature at bay—were unfounded, he shows an awareness of the relationship between population and the exploitation of the earth's resources which is out of keeping with the assumption of the passivity of man in his environmental theories. The world's population must increase. In his *Pensées* he makes a vigorous appeal for the active intervention of man in nature: The earth always yields in proportion to the exactions made of it. The fish of the seas are inexhaustible; only fishermen, boats, and merchants are lacking. Flocks increase with the people to care for them. If the forests are exhausted, open up the earth, and you will find fuel. Why do you go to the New World to kill bulls solely for their hides? Why do you allow so much water that could irrigate your fields to go to the sea? Why do you leave in your fields waters which should go to the sea?[4]

Climatic change was discussed even by literary men. Hume speculated about it in Europe in historical times, concluding that such a change had occurred, and that the warmer climates of his time were owing to human agency alone, because woods which formerly kept the rays of the sun from the surface of the earth have now been cleared off. The northern colonies of America became more temperate with clearing, the southern more healthful.[5]

Furthermore, Kant had recognized human activity as being among those agencies, past and present, which, like earthquakes, rivers, rain, the sea, wind, and the frost, cause physical changes through historical time. Men build works to keep out the sea, to create land at the mouths of the Po, the Rhine, and other streams. They drain marshes and clear the forests, and by so doing they visibly change the climate of countries.[6] The chief interest of these otherwise conventional remarks is that Kant thinks it necessary in the study of physical geography to include man as one of the natural phenomena that bring about environmental change.

Interest in the changes made by man in the landscape was stimulated by the theory that the climate changed following forest clearance; reports from the New World claimed that the climate then became warmer. Hugh Williamson, an American doctor, read a paper on the subject before the American Philosophical Society in 1760; its French translation influenced Count Buffon. The people living in Pennsylvania and the neighboring colonies, Williamson said, remarked that the climate has changed within the last forty to fifty years, the winters being less harsh, the summers cooler. Williamson accepts these claims at face value, explaining that man can make local modifications in the general climatic pattern.

The coasts of the middle colonies, he says, trend from the northeast to the

[4] *Pensées et Fragments Inédits de Montesquieu*, Vol. 1, pp. 180–181.
[5] "Of the Populousness of Ancient Nations," *Essays Moral, Political, and Literary*, Vol. 1, p. 434.
[6] "Physische Geographie," in *Immanuel Kant's Sämmtliche Werke*, ed. Hartenstein (Leipzig, 1868), Vol. 8, p. 300.

southwest. The Atlantic, retaining some of the heat gained in summer and warmed by the Gulf Stream, is warmer than the land in winter, hence the violent northwestern winter winds blowing toward the ocean: "The colder the air is over the continent, the more violent will those North-Westers be." What, Williamson asks, would reduce the violence of this wind? Hard smooth surfaces reflect heat better than do rough and irregular ones—a clear smooth field reflects more heat than one covered with bushes and trees. "If the surface of this continent were so clear and smooth, that it would reflect so much heat as might warm the incumbent atmosphere, equal to the degree of heat produced by the neighbouring Atlantic, an equilibrium would be restored, and we should have no stated north-west winds."[7]

Several observers, including seamen at sea, have reported a declining severity of the northwesters; less severe frosts, snowfall less in quantity and more irregular, have also been remarked upon since the settlement of the province. A cleared field is warmed up in winter more than one covered with bushes or trees. Since the temperature difference between the clearings and the sea is reduced, the frequency, violence, and duration of the winter storms are also reduced.

In seeking corroborating evidence from Europe, Williamson comments on a claim made that Italy was better cultivated in the age of Augustus than it is now, but that the climate is more temperate now than it was then, thus contradicting "the opinion, *that the cultivation of a country will render the air more temperate.*"[8] He replies that even if the winters of Italy in the Augustan age were colder, it is not enough to consider the evidence from Italy alone, for the explanation is not in Italy but in "those vast regions to the northward of Rome"—Hungary, Poland, Germany. The Germans have increased in number, progressed in agriculture since Caesar's time; all these kingdoms were once covered with forests, but only a few remain today. In ancient times, the north winds blowing from the cold and forested north countries chilled Italy; today these northern countries—cleared and cultivated—do not provide the same opportunity for such violent winds; and if the cold is less in Germany and in the adjacent states, it follows that it is also less in Italy. One wonders, as did Noah Webster about a similar argument, how it was possible to ignore the Alps.[9]

What of the objection that if clearing makes the winters milder, it will also

---

[7] "An Attempt to Account for the CHANGE OF CLIMATE, Which Has Been Observed in the Middle Colonies in North-America," *TAPS*, Vol. I (2d ed., corrected, 1789), p. 339.

[8] Williamson, *op. cit.*, p. 340. The source is Barrington Daines, "An Investigation of the Difference Between the Present Temperature of the Air in Italy and Some Other Countries, and What it was Seventeen Centuries Ago," *Philosophical Transactions of the Royal Society of London*, Vol. 58 (1768), pp. 58–67. Williamson refers to a passage on p. 64.

[9] Williamson, *op. cit.*, pp. 340–342.

make the summers hotter? Williamson suggests a planned diversification of the landscape with "vast tracts of cleared land, intersected here and there by great ridges of uncultivated mountains. . . ." The warmed air can rise more easily from the cleared tracts than it can from timbered country; its rising permits inflow of colder air from the uncultivated mountains, resulting in both cold and warm breezes. The land winds, and those which might come from the sea or the lakes, will bring a moderate summer.[10]

Williamson's interests are even broader than this plan to control climate through rational and planned clearing: such artifically induced climatic changes will permit different crops and new plant introductions. As a physician, he sees the importance of studying the effects of clearing on health and of recording the history of disease.

While the face of this country was clad with woods, and every valley afforded a swamp or stagnant marsh, by a copious perspiration through the leaves of trees or plants, and a general exhalation from the surface of ponds and marshes, the air was constantly charged with a gross putrescent fluid. Hence a series of irregular, nervous, bilious, remitting and intermitting fevers, which for many years have maintained a fatal reign through many parts of this country, but are now evidently on the decline. Pleuritic and other inflammatory fevers, with the several diseases, of cold seasons, are also observed to remit their violence, as our winters grow more temperate.[11]

Relationships between the spread of disease and the existence of open spaces, and between certain kinds of diseases and marshes, have been observed since the times of the Hippocratic school, but the idea that man should actively intervene in the environment to prevent disease was most eloquently expressed, it seems to me, by Hugh Williamson and Benjamin Rush, both American physicians. These men saw the relationships of a people to the environment in which it first settles, to the environment which it then alters, and finally to the succeeding alterations resulting from agriculture and plant introductions, drainage, and public health measures.

Many eighteenth century writers were interested in climatic change. Their theories, as Williamson's essay demonstrates, often consider the role of human agency in modifying the landscape. Noah Webster made a remarkable appraisal of this literature in 1799.[12] (See chap. 12, sec. 2, pp. 560–561.) After a crisp analysis of the capricious and casual use of classical sources by modern authors (in which poor Samuel Williams, the historian of Vermont, comes off badly), Webster observes that the distribution of plants characteristic of the

[10] *Ibid.*, p. 343.
[11] *Ibid.*, pp. 344–345.
[12] "Dissertation on the Supposed Change of Temperature in Modern Winters," in *A Collection of Papers on Political, Literary and Moral Subjects*, pp. 119–161. The essay, originally read before the Connecticut Academy of Arts and Sciences in 1799, includes supplementary remarks read to the same academy in 1806, pp. 148–162; quote on p. 119.

Mediterranean—the fig, pomegranate, olive—has apparently not changed since ancient times, and that probably the winters then were no colder than they are today. From the classical sources, he outlines the probable geographical limits of the olive in ancient times, concluding that its ancient limits are about the same as those marked by Arthur Young for modern times, beginning at the foot of the Pyrenees in Roussillon, then northeast through Languedoc, to the south of the Cévennes, crossing the Rhône at Montélimar, and continuing via the vicinity of Grenoble to its terminus in Savoy.[13]

Rejecting popular belief in large-scale climatic change in historical times, Webster then examines the possibility that such changes might occur in a restricted area owing to human agency. He takes Buffon to task (and Gibbon and Williams for accepting Buffon's authority) for saying that the reindeer retreated northward to colder regions where it could subsist because the regions in south Europe and France formerly cold enough for the animal have now become too warm for it.

> I consider this argument as very fallacious. The rane seeks the forest, and flies before the ax of the cultivator, like the bear, the common deer, and the Indian of America. How can the deer subsist in open fields? We might as well expect a fish to live in air, as the rane in a country destitute of woods, and frequented by man. The Hyracanian forest no longer exists; the husbandman has deprived that animal of his shelter, his food, his element. He does not like the company of man, and has abandoned the cultivated parts of Europe. . . . How could the rane subsist in an open, cultivated country, when it is well known that his favorite food is a species of lichen [rangiferinus] which grows only or chiefly on heaths and uncultivated hilly grounds? Instead of proving a change of climate, the retirement of the rane seems to have been the natural consequence of cultivation.[14]

These arguments are similar to many that Buffon himself had expressed, both men pointing out the power of civilized men to alter, by changing their habitat or threatening them, the distribution not only of wild animals but even of primitive peoples. Webster, moreover, is less than fair to Buffon. Buffon does say that the reindeer now is found only in the most northerly countries, that the climate of France because of its woods and marshes was formerly much colder than it is today. There is evidence, Buffon says, that the moose and the reindeer lived in the forests of the Gauls and of Germany. As the forests were cleared and the waters of the marshes were dried up, the climate became milder and the cold-loving animals migrated. Among many factors causing a change in the habitat of the animals were the diminution of waters, the multiplication of men and their works. Buffon is in closer agreement with Webster than the famous lexicographer makes it appear. Both recognize the effect of man's increasing numbers, of his installations, of clearing and drainage, on the distribution of animals.[15]

[13] *Ibid.*, pp. 133–134.
[14] *Ibid.*, p. 135.
[15] See Buffon, "L'Élan et le Renne," *HN*, Vol. 12 (1764), pp. 85–86, 95–96.

Webster concluded that for all practical purposes the climate had been uniform since the creation and that there had been no variation of consequence in the inclination of the earth's axis to the plane of the ecliptic. Men, however, could make significant local changes. The contrasts, so typical of men of this period to whom forest clearance is closely connected with the march of civilization, are between the forest and open land; in the former the "vibrations" in air temperature and in the temperature of the earth near the surface are less numerous and less considerable than in the latter. When the earth is covered by trees, it is not swept by violent winds, and the temperature is more uniform. The earth of the forest floor is not frozen in the winter; neither is it scorched in summer. Such extremes are found in open or cleared land, a fact which Webster says disproves the common theory (held by Williamson) that clearing brings a moderation of cold in the winter; in fact, "the cold of our winters, though less steady, has been most sensibly increased." He denies that forces affecting the entire globe have anything to do with climatic change. "It appears that all the alterations in a country, in consequence of clearing and cultivation, result only in making a different distribution of heat and cold, moisture and dry weather, among the several seasons. The clearing of lands opens them to the sun, their moisture is exhaled, they are more heated in summer, but more cold in winter near the surface; the temperature becomes unsteady, and the seasons irregular."[16]

### 4. Count Buffon: On Nature, Man, and the History of Nature

Count Buffon repeatedly expressed interest in the changes which men had made in their natural environment, particularly the transformations which had accompanied the growth and expansion of civilization and the migration and dispersion of human beings and their domesticated plants and animals throughout the habitable parts of the earth. He considered this question of the physical changes in the earth brought about by human agency in more detail than had any of his contemporaries, indeed more than any man in Western science or philosophy until George P. Marsh's *Man and Nature* was published in 1864. His interest in the physical changes in the earth peculiarly associated with the activities of man were philosophical, scientific, and practical. These changes, he thought, had been necessary to create civilization and to permit its growth and diffusion. "Wild nature is hideous and dying; it is I, I alone, who can make it agreeable and living." Dry out the marshes, he said, make their stagnant waters flow in brooks and canals, clear out the thickets and the old forests with fire and iron. In their place make pastures and arable fields for the ox to plow so that a "new nature can come forth from our hands."[17]

[16] Webster, *op. cit.*, pp. 147, 184; see also p. 162.
[17] "De la Nature. Première Vue," *HN*, Vol. 12, p. xiii.

Buffon's ideas are also pertinent to contemporary theory regarding the origin and growth of civilization. Many of the most famous thinkers of the century—Condorcet, Montesquieu, Voltaire, Rousseau, Turgot, and Herder—had written on such themes as the progress of mankind, the significance of cultural inertia, and environmental influences which caused some peoples to progress and others to lag behind. These studies included theories of the origin of human society and of the arts and sciences. They involved also speculation regarding physical environments hospitable to early civilization. Were they harsh, unhealthful, and forbidding compared with the comfortable landscapes of civilized life? On this question Buffon took an unequivocal stand. He had little patience with romanticizing about the state of nature, of primitive society, or of primeval environments.

To Buffon, the power of nature is immense, living, and inexhaustible. Its divine origin is manifest in the creation. On earth, man whose power is also of divine origin, is destined to further the plans and intentions of nature. In this teleological conception, nature is virtually personified. Man is a "vassal of heaven," a "king on earth," and his position on earth is central and crucial. Man can bring order to it, improve it. By increasing his own numbers he increases nature's most precious productions.[18]

A great source of men's power lay in their ability to live in and adapt themselves to many climates, but he thought men were more efficient in adapting themselves to the extremes of cold than to those of heat. The history of man's migrations and dispersions showed how ancient this adaptability was; in his migrations, taking with him his arts, his techniques of agriculture and knowledge of plant and animal domestication, he could transform nature in each new area in which he settled in accordance with the tastes he had acquired. With time, with new discovery and exploration, he would be living throughout the whole habitable world, creating a nature in great contrast to the world of primeval nature.

Man is not only adaptable; he is intelligent, inventive, and able to profit from the accumulated knowledge of the past. These qualities enable him to exercise an immense power in changing nature. Man is a creative being whose accomplishments not only accumulate with time but expand through space. Buffon repeatedly distinguishes between man and the animals in this respect: their life, their manner of living, their habitats, and their geographic distribution are governed much more by the environment than is the human wanderer who intrudes upon them, changing their lives and habitats, if indeed he condescends to spare them.

The theme of migrating and adaptable man thus is set in sharp contrast with the theme of the less mobile plants and animals whose distribution, if uninterfered with by man, is controlled by climate. It is part of a primordial

[18] *Ibid.*, p. xi.

harmony characteristic of the creation. "It would seem that nature had made the climate for the species or the species for the climate in order to obtain more *rapport*, more harmony in its productions," a truth applying even more forcefully to vegetation, for each region (*pays*) and each degree of temperature has its own kind of plant life.[19]

Regions which had never been inhabited by man, however, had little attraction for Buffon. On their heights were the dark, thick forests, their debris covering the forest floor and choking out all life. There were the stagnant waters, the fetid marshes of their lowlands, useless alike to inhabitants of land or water. And between them was a wasteland of thickets and useless brambles having nothing in common with the meadows of inhabited lands.

No doubt Buffon shared a widespread eighteenth century attitude toward nature, a nature in the words of Roger Heim, well cared for, ordered, a little too well raked, embellished with decorations.[20] It is, however, the same feeling which one observes in the English writers of an earlier date, like Ray and Sprat. They desired to win new land from the moors, the fens, the old forests. They gloried in the ideal of a beautiful village resting in well-tilled fields. They had faith in technology and in the possibility of improving the individual and society. They admired science and its methods and applauded the advances of knowledge; they saw that nature also could be improved with this new knowledge, itself the product of an awakened curiosity.

In his essay on nature, Buffon, a lover of exclamation points, writes "Qu'elle est belle, cette Nature cultivée! que par les soins de l'homme elle est brillante et pompeuscment parée!" Man is nature's most noble product; and nature, cherished by man, multiplies itself in desirable ways under his care. Flowers, fruits, grains, useful species of animals, have been transported, propagated, and increased without number; useless species have been eliminated. Mining has advanced. Torrents have been restrained and the rivers directed and controlled. The sea has been conquered. Land has been restored and made fertile. The laughing meadows, the pastures, the vines and the orchards of the hills whose summits are crowned with useful trees and young forests, the great cities arising on deserted places, roads and communications, are but a few reminders "of power and of glory, showing sufficiently that man, master of the domain of the Earth, has changed it and renewed its entire surface and that he will always share the empire with Nature."[21] If the style of this quotation seems pompous to the modern taste, the ideas which it contains are worth expressing: the activity of man in artificially multiplying domesticated plants and animals

---

[19] "Les Animaux Sauvages," *HN*, Vol. 6, pp. 55–59. The translated quotation is from p. 57. The whole statement is important in the history of ideas of the geographic distribution of animals. See also "De la Dégénération des Animaux," *HN*, Vol. 14, pp. 311–317.

[20] Heim, "Préface à Buffon," in Bertin, *et al.*, *Buffon*, p. 7.

[21] "De la Nature. Première Vue," *HN*, Vol. 12, pp. xiii–xv. The quotation in French is on p. xiii, the translated quotation on p. xiv.

and in replacing one kind of vegetation with another, and the importance of cultural diffusion in distributing them throughout the world.

Buffon's descriptions of primeval nature are as grim as many which followed the publication of the *Origin of Species*. They lack the sense of the unceasing and unrelenting struggle for existence emphasized by Huxley, but they carry a warning similar to his, that man reigns over nature by right of conquest, and nature will reclaim her rights and efface the works of man if he becomes lazy or falters through war, poverty, or depopulation.[22]

To Buffon the history of the earth is like human history: both can be reconstructed by examining the inscriptions, monuments, and relics of the past. In addition, physical phenomena, like the social, are subject to continual change; the earth and life upon it therefore assume different forms in different periods. "The state in which we see nature today," he says in the introduction to *Des Époques de la Nature*, "is as much our work as it is hers. We have learned to temper her, to modify her, to fit her to our needs and our desires. We have made, cultivated, fertilized the earth; its appearance, as we see it today, is thus quite different than it was in the times prior to the invention of the arts." And again, "One must seek out, see nature in the newly discovered regions, in the countries which have never been inhabited, to form an idea of its former state, and the latter is still quite modern compared with the ages in which the continents were covered with water, fish swam on our plains, or the mountains formed reefs in the seas."[23]

This earth history is the subject matter both of the *Histoire et Théorie de la Terre* with its added notes, proofs, and revisions, and of Buffon's masterpiece, *Des Époques de la Nature*, which divides earth history into seven epochs. These are the formation of the earth and the planets, the consolidation of the rock in the interior of the earth, the invasion of the continents by the seas, the retreat of the seas and the beginning of volcanic activity, the north as the habitat of elephants and other animals of the south, the separation of the continents, and the power of man aiding that of nature. In the seventh epoch, there begins that "seconding of nature" which leads to the transformation of the earth. Buffon's reconstruction of this early period of human history may be summarized as follows: man had appeared when the worldwide catastrophic convulsions of the preceding epochs in earth history had not yet quite subsided. Even the first men, living under the terror of earthquakes, volcanoes, and wild animals and without the blessings of civil society, were forced to adapt nature to their needs, to unite for self-defense and mutual help in making houses and such weapons as hard flints shaped like an ax. Early men may have

[22] *Ibid.*, pp. xiv–xv. Thomas H. Huxley, "Evolution and Ethics. Prolegomena," in *Evolution and Ethics and Other Essays*, pp. 9–11.
[23] "Des Époques de la Nature," intro., hereinafter "EN," *HNS*, Vol. 5, pp. 1–5; the quotations are translated from pp. 3 and 4, respectively.

obtained fire from flints or from volcanoes and burning lavas to communicate with one another and to make open clearings in the thickets and the forests. With the help of fire, the land was made habitable, while with their stone axes, they cut trees, working the wood into weapons and other tools which pressing need suggested to them. In their inventiveness, they could devise weapons to strike at a distance. Gradually family groups consolidated into small nations, and those whose territories were limited by the waters or hemmed in by the mountains became so populous that they were forced to divide up their lands among themselves. "It is at this moment [i.e., with the land division] that the Earth became the domain of man; he took possession of it by the labor of cultivation, and from this one can trace the subsequent appearance of attachment to one's native land and to civil order, administration, and lawmaking."[24]

This description of the activities of early man strongly resembles—in outline if not in actual details—Lucretius' famous account of the early development of human culture.[25] In his writings, Buffon clearly appreciated the role of fire in human history. Firing and clearings are mentioned often in the literature relating to the New World, and they were commonplace practices in the Europe of his day. Buffon's description suggests also the conclusions of modern research in demonstrating the ease with which early man, with simple tools and the use of fire, can make important, lasting, and widespread changes in the environment. To Buffon, early man is something else than a frightened animal adapting himself to a terrifying environment.

These efforts of early man, however, were slight compared with the accomplishments of a civilization which Buffon believed to have existed about three thousand years before his time in an area from the fortieth to the fifty-fifth degree of north latitude in Central Asia. Buffon was impressed with the report of Peter Simon Pallas, the German natural historian, of evidences of cultivation, arts, and towns scattered in this part of Asia, which Pallas thought were survivals of an ancient and flourishing empire; perhaps Buffon is also anticipating one of the major interests in the nineteenth century study of man, the search for the Aryan homeland. According to Buffon's theories of historical geology, this region (southern Siberia and Tartary of his day) was best suited to the development of civilization because it was in a relatively tranquil part of the earth, sheltered from inundations, distant from terrifying volcanoes and earthquakes, more elevated and consequently more temperate than the other; in "this region in the center of the continent of Asia" with its pleasant climate, clear skies for observing the stars, and fertile earth to cultivate, men attained knowledge, science, and then power. This ancient civilization was destroyed by a people driven out of the north by overpopulation; here Buffon uses the old idea of the northlands as an *officina gentium* advanced

[24] *Ibid.*, pp. 225-227 (intro. to the 7th Epoch).
[25] Lucretius, *De rerum natura*, V. 1245-1457.

as early as the sixth century by Jordanes. Many of the achievements of this civilization were lost, but agriculture and building techniques survived intact and were diffused and improved, their progress following the great centers of population: first, the ancient Chinese Empire and then Atlantis, Egypt, Rome, and Europe. "It is thus only about thirty centuries ago that the power of man was combined with that of nature and spread over the greatest part of the Earth." Among these great and purposeful changes were the domestication of animals, the drying up of marshes, the control of river courses and elimination of cataracts, forest clearance, and land cultivation. With art, science, and exploration, even isolated parts of the world have become his domain: "Finally the entire face of the Earth bears today the stamp of the power of man, which although subordinate to that of Nature, often has done more than she, or at least has so marvellously aided her, that it is with the help of our hands that she has developed to her full extent and that she has gradually arrived at the point of perfection and of magnificence in which we see her today."[26] These strong words represent Buffon's true belief in the creative power of man; if he often faltered in his faith in human nature and despaired of man's destructiveness and his propensity to war, it nevertheless was the nature "si merveilleusement secondée" by man that had meaning for him, a transformed nature that was living proof of man's place in the natural order and of his power in molding it to his desires.

### 5. Count Buffon: On Forests and Soils

That Buffon, himself a farmer, nurseryman and plant breeder, an experimenter in forest plantings, should have something to say about forests is to be expected; what he has to say, however, at first appears contradictory, for he advocates both the destruction and conservation of the forests. This seeming inconsistency can be explained by analyzing the role of the forest in Buffon's theory of the earth.

Buffon advanced as one of the five basic facts about the earth the proposition that the heat emitted by the sun and received by the earth is quite small in comparison with the earth's own heat and that solar heat alone would be insufficient to maintain living nature.[27] The internal heat of the earth is being dissipated and it therefore is imperceptibly but relentlessly growing colder, the sun's heat alone being insufficient to arrest this tendency. Buffon underestimated the amount of solar radiation and he knew nothing of the greenhouse effect. Since he knew of the heat of the earth's interior, as experienced in deep mine shafts, he concluded that the heat loss from the earth exceeds the

[26] "EN," 7th Epoch, *HNS*, Vol. 5, pp. 228–237. The quotations are translated from pp. 236, 237.
[27] *Ibid.*, p. 6.

heat gain from the sun. Man can therefore increase the effectiveness of solar heat by deforestation, permitting the sun's heat to reach and warm up the surface of the earth, thus compensating, at least in part, for the heat lost because of the cooling of the earth.

Buffon here relied on reports from the New World that the climate became warmer after forest clearance, being particularly impressed with the paper, already discussed, which Hugh Williamson had read before the American Philosophical Society on August 17, 1770, and which was later translated into French.[28] Combining his theory with the reports on climatic change, Buffon concluded that it was possible for man to regulate or to change the climate radically.[29] In proof he chose an unfortunate example. Paris and Quebec, he said, have about the same latitude and elevation. (Buffon knew that latitude and elevation alone do not determine the climate as he here assumed they do.) Paris would be cold, like Quebec, were France and the countries bordering upon it deprived of their population, covered with forests, and surrounded by waters. By making a country healthful, that is, by clearing away the accumulated dead organic matter, draining swamps, cutting down trees, and settling people on its lands, it will be provided with sufficient heat for several thousand years. According to his reasoning, Buffon said, France in his day should be colder than were Gaul and Germania two thousand years ago, but it is not colder because the forests have been cut, the marshes drained, the rivers controlled and directed, lands covered by the dead remains of organic life cleared; if these changes had not been accomplished, modern France would be even colder than Gaul or Germania had been.[30] In further proof, he cites the deforestation, scarcely a century earlier, of a district around Cayenne (there are many references to French Guiana throughout the *Histoire Naturelle*), which caused considerable differences in air temperature, even at night, between the cold, wet, dense forest, into which the sun seldom penetrated, and the clearings; rains even began later and stopped earlier in them than in the forest. Man's power, however, is limited. He can make warm air ascend but he cannot make cold air descend. His power of lowering the temperature of the hot deserts is thus largely confined to creating shade; it is easier to warm up the humid earth of a dense forest by clearing than it is to plant trees in Arabia to cool the hot dry sands. For such environments, he suggested that a forest in the midst of scorching desert might bring rain, fertility,

---

[28] Hugues Williamson, "Dans Lequel on Tâche de Rendre Raison du Changement de Climat qu'on a Observé dans les Colonies Situées dans l'Intérieur des Terres le l'Amérique Septentrionale," *Journal de Physique (Observations sur la Physique, sur l'Histoire Naturelle et sur les Arts)*, Vol. 1 (1773), pp. 430–436. The quotation from Williamson given at the end of *Des Époques de la Nature* is an inexact quotation from the French translation (*HNS*, Vol. 5, pp. 597–599).

[29] This discussion is based on "EN," 7th Epoch, *HNS*, Vol. 5, p. 240.

[30] *Ibid.*, pp. 240–241.

and a temperate climate; this idea was based on the very old belief that trees attracted clouds and moisture.[31]

With the exception of the hot deserts, Buffon thought it important to increase temperature at the surface of the earth because all life is dependent upon heat. In making solar heat more readily available at the earth's surface, man can modify what is harmful to him by opening up useful clearings. "Happy are the countries where all the elements of temperature are balanced and sufficiently well combined to bring about only good effects! But is there any one of them which from its beginnings has had this privilege, any place where the power of man has not aided that of nature?"[32] Thus by systematic deforestation, or planting where called for, man could convert lands of unequal endowment to lands of temperate qualities. Men's bodies—tiny furnaces they were—even heated up the earth, and man's use of fire increased the temperature of every place he inhabited in numbers. "In Paris, during severe cold spells, the thermometers in the Faubourg Saint-Honoré [in the northwestern part of Paris] register two or three degrees colder than in the Faubourg Saint-Marceau [in the southeast] because the northwind is modified in passing over the chimneys of this great city."[33]

Buffon saw no good in thickets, dense forests, accumulated organic debris, poisonous swamps—fundamentally, I think, because (in an era long before the microbiology of the soils was understood) he believed they safeguarded moisture at the expense of heat. Forests kept away heat necessary to the maintenance and multiplication of life; they were inimical to nature and to civilization. The role of man, in the past as in the present, has been one of creating harmonious balances in nature in places where they were needed.

Buffon, however, would not have advocated the deforestation of a modern country. His interest in forests began early in life; he had studied and experimented and he had read well-known English books on forestry like John Evelyn's *Silva: or, a Discourse of Forest-Trees*. Like many French writers before him, he warned of the perils in deforesting his country. His essay on the conservation of forests (1739), combining exhortation with practical advice, was a plea for conservation, for better administration and better regulation, for satisfying the needs of the present while not forgetting the welfare of posterity. All forest projects could be reduced to two tasks: "to conserve those which remain, to renew a part of those we have destroyed."[34] French forests in the old *pays* of Brittany, Poitou, La Guyenne, Burgundy, and Champagne had been destroyed to be replaced by wasteland and thickets; these lands should be restored.[35] In 1742, he complained that men had learned

---

[31] *Ibid.*, pp. 241–243.

[32] *Ibid.* The translation is from p. 246.

[33] *Ibid.*, p. 243.

[34] *HNS*, Vol. 2, pp. 249–271. The quotation is on p. 241. This work, "Sur la Conservation & le Rétablissement des Forêts," is reprinted from *Histoire de l'Académie Royale des Sciences, Mémoires*, 1739, pp. 140–156.

[35] *Ibid.*, p. 259.

through observation and experiment much about the practical arts like agriculture but they knew little of forestry: "Nothing is less known; nothing more neglected. The forest is a gift of nature which it is sufficient to accept just as it comes from her hands." Even the simplest ways of conserving forests and of increasing their yield were ignored.[36] He showed continuing interest in the effects of local deforestation when he took part, around 1778, in the *Compagnie pour l'Exploitation et l'Épuration du Charbon de Terre*, an organization interested in coal as an industrial resource, in coke making, and in relieving the drain on the forests of the kingdom.[37]

His attitudes toward the forests can be reconciled in this way: large areas inimical to man had to be cleared to make the earth habitable, but once societies were established on them, the forests were resources which had to be treated with care and foresight.

Buffon classifies soils into three groups: clays, calcareous earths, and vegetable earths (*terre végétale*) composed mostly of the detritus of plants and terrestrial animals. There are two kinds of this vegetable earth: leaf mold (*terreau*) and *limon*, the residue representing the final stages in the decomposition of the leaf mold. These soil types are seldom found in pure form in nature. Soils are mixtures of them, a soil concept neglected by chemists and mineralogists who, he says, study the clays and the calcareous earths, slighting the vegetable earth.[38]

This vegetable earth is always thicker in uninhabited virgin lands than in inhabited countries, for it naturally increases in places from which man and fire (his agent of destruction) are absent. The thick, centuries-long accumulations of vegetable earth are confined to virgin lands. Vegetable earth is thinner on mountains than in valleys or plains because the limon is washed down from the highlands by streams and deposited on plains. This soil would remain fertile if it were not overworked; where it has been destroyed, only dry sands or bare rocks remain, unlike the rich leaf mold and limon of the virgin lands.[39] In inhabited regions, the vegetable earth is more thoroughly mixed with the vitreous sands and the calcareous gravels because the plowshare turns up the lower layers of the inorganic soils. This thin layer of vegetable earth which covers the earth's surface is "le trésor des richesses de la Nature vivante," the "magasin universel des élémens [*sic*] qui entrent dans la composition de plupart des minéraux."[40] These organic soils contain minerals which, like iron, give the yellow stain to limon. They are vital to mankind

[36] *Ibid.*, pp. 271-290. This work, "Sur la Culture & Exploitation des Forêts," is reprinted from *Histoire de l'Académie Royale des Sciences, Mémoires*, 1742, pp. 233-246.

[37] Bertin, in *Buffon*, quotes a passage from the Mémoires de Bachaumont (1780) in which he mentions government interest in treating coal as a means of arresting the degradation of the forests of the kingdom caused by forced cutting owing to the excessive use of wood in domestic hearths and in the industrial arts (pp. 212-213).

[38] "De la Terre Végétale," *HNM*, Vol. 1, pp. 384, 388.

[39] *Ibid.*, pp. 389-390.

[40] *Ibid.*, p. 416.

because they contain in abundance all the four elements (air, water, earth, fire—the classical doctrine of the four elements still dominated the chemistry and soil theory of the day) as well as organic molecules. For this reason the soil has become "la mère de tous les êtres organisés, et la matrice de tous les corps figurés." These matters are often better understood, says Buffon, by the farmer in the fields than by the naturalists.[41]

In inhabited countries, especially where the population is numerous and all lands are cultivated, the quantity of vegetable earth diminishes century by century because fertilizers do not restore as much to the soil as is taken from it and because the greedy farmer or the short-term owner, more interested in reaping benefits than in conserving soils, exhausts and starves them and makes them carry more than they can.[42]

One obtains higher yields by working the soil over and over again until it becomes comminuted, but then both the fine and heavy particles are more easily washed away by streams. "Each summer thunderstorm, each heavy rain of winter loads all the waters with yellow *limon*"; so often and so great are the losses that they cannot be remedied by soil fertilizers, and one cannot help but be surprised that sterility has not come sooner, especially on hillside slopes. Rich soils which have become poor through cultivation will gradually be abandoned; such land must be left fallow to allow the beneficent forces of nature to repair the damage and "work to reestablish what man never ceases to destroy."[43] Buffon was also interested in fertilizers; he saw a close relationship between soil improvement and the manure of the sheepfolds.[44]

It is remarkable that Buffon makes the sharp distinction between soils formed by natural processes and those which have been altered through cultivation. This genetic approach to soil study resembles the investigations of Dokuchaiev and his school in Russia, and of Hilgard in America in the nineteenth century more than it resembles soil investigations in western Europe, which at least to the time of Liebig were primarily concerned with the practical problems of soils under cultivation.

### 6. Count Buffon: On Domestications

Buffon was convinced that plant and animal domestications were the most important means by which man had changed virgin nature into environments suitable for high civilization. His ideas on their importance remind one of the first chapter of the *Origin of Species*, in which Darwin shows how great the power of natural selection must be if one reflects on the enormous

[41] *Ibid.*, pp. 424–425; quote on p. 424.
[42] *Ibid.*, p. 425.
[43] *Ibid.*, p. 426.
[44] "La Brebis," *HN*, Vol. 5, pp. 3–6, 19–20. One hundred sheep in one summer could improve 8 arpents of land for six years. An arpent is about 1.5 acres.

changes which infinitely less powerful man brings about in nature through his successes in plant and animal breeding.

Buffon accepts the utilitarian theory of domestication which originated in classical times; man purposefully and self-consciously domesticates animals because they have qualities of use in the human economy—the ox is suitable as a draft animal, the dog, as a shepherd, the sheep, as a supplier of wool. Man has chosen only a few; he has used but a fraction of what nature is capable of giving him. Awaiting him in reserve are other possible domestications, for man does not know sufficiently well what nature is capable of nor how much he can get from her. Instead of embarking on new researches, he prefers to misuse the knowledge he has acquired.[45] The utilitarian theory of domestication persisted far beyond Buffon's time until it was effectively challenged by Hahn's theories of domestications of animals for ceremonial reasons.

Domestic animals provided man with the necessary help in transforming and controlling all nature. They had another enormously important effect: man had increased and multiplied, almost at will, the populations of domestic plants and animals, whose lives and reproduction took place under carefully controlled conditions; in undisturbed nature, on the other hand, reproduction was subject to the hazards of predation and of climatic and other environmental conditions.[46]

In Buffon's language, the domesticated animals were almost like feudal serfs; they owed much to man, returning their labor, their flesh, and their products for shelter and food. As they multiplied and were diffused throughout the earth, they took over the habitats of the wild animals. Buffon even credits man with the extinction of the gigantic animals whose bones were still being found; voracious and injurious species have also been destroyed or reduced in number. Man has set the animals against one another, controlling some by skill, others by force, and still others by dispersing them. Man's empire is now bounded only by inaccessible places, remote wildernesses, burning deserts, icy-cold mountains, and obscure caverns which become retreats for a small number of indomitable animal species that cannot be subjugated.[47] The artificial distribution of the domesticated animals is different from the natural distribution of the wild animals, who live in well-defined and climatically controlled habitats.[48]

Another living nature has been created, that of man and his domesticated

[45] "L'Élan et le Renne," *HN*, Vol. 12, p. 96.
[46] "Les animaux domestiques," intro., *HN*, Vol. 4, pp. 169–171; "De la dégénération des animaux," *HN*, Vol. 14, pp. 326–328; "Le Mouflon," *HN*, Vol. 11, pp. 352–354.
[47] "Les Animaux Domestiques," intro., *HN*, Vol. 4, pp. 171, 173. See also "EN," 7th Epoch, *HNS*, Vol. 5, pp. 246–248.
[48] "De la Dégénération des Animaux," *HN*, vol. 14, pp. 311, 316–317. The first paragraph distinguishes between the climatic influences on man and on the plants and animals. In the fourth paragraph there is an important statement regarding the differences in distribution between the wild and the domestic animals.

plants and animals, propagated by him, accompanying him on his migrations throughout the world, helping to create new environments for civilization at the expense of pristine nature and so escaping in part its inexorable laws of birth, or postponing reproduction, and death. Man with his plants and animals displaces natural plant and animal habitats, often disturbing or destroying the societies of the bees, the ants, the beavers, and the elephants. Through his own reproduction and the reproduction of useful domestic species, man multiplies the quantity of certain kinds of life and the amount of activity and movement, ennobling all life, including his own, in the process, because under his intelligent leadership a higher form of organized existence has been created. The domestications, permitting the multiplication and expansion of the human race, brought on further conquests of nature to enable man to produce abundance everywhere. Millions of men, he said, now exist in the same space which in former times was occupied by two or three hundred savages.[49] Similar increases in densities occurred with the replacement of a few wild animals by thousands of domesticated animals.

Through the agency of man, the kind and quality of life on earth have been radically altered, a pregnant idea when one considers that many modern evolutionists with a knowledge of genetics denied to Buffon have emphasized the directive influences of man on his own evolution and on the evolution of the plants and animals.[50]

Buffon attached great importance to the "degeneration" of animals; by this term he meant the variability of a species under the influence of climate and food; in the case of the domestic animals, there was the added influence of the "yoke of slavery."[51] Degeneration was even more marked among the domestic animals reduced to slavery (a favorite word of Buffon's), whose history was much more complicated than that of wild animals because their lives and the perpetuation of the species were so artificially controlled. He saw the advantages of deliberate crossing of animals. The inevitable promiscuity in mixed grazing should be avoided and enclosures encouraged in the interests of careful animal breeding. He remarked that the color of domesticated animals is often more vivid than that of wild animals.[52] There is so much variety in the horns of domestic cattle that it is now impossible to discover the "model of nature" from which they were derived. The amours of domesticated animals are in marked contrast with those in nature. Castration, the selection of a single male for breeding purposes, the transportation of domestic animals from one climate to another, are other important causes of the degeneration of animals under domestication.[53]

[49] "EN," 7th Epoch, *HNS*, Vol. 5, p. 248.

[50] *Ibid*. See George G. Simpson, *The Meaning of Evolution*, Mentor Books (New York, 1951), p. 110.

[51] "De la Dégénération des Animaux," *HN*, Vol. 14, p. 317.

[52] *Ibid*., p. 324. "L'état de domesticité a beaucoup contribué à faire varier la couleur des animaux, elle est en général originairement fauve ou noire. . . ."

[53] "Le Buffle, etc.," *HN*, Vol. 11, pp. 293–296.

Buffon thought the weakest of the useful animals were domesticated first, the sheep and goat coming before the horse, ox, or camel. The priorities, however, are confused, for elsewhere he describes the camel as man's oldest, most laborious, and most useful slave. The camel has no wild counterparts because its natural habitat is in a climate where human societies have first developed, and apparently only the domesticated ones have survived. Its good qualities have come from nature, its bad from its sufferings at human hands.[54]

In its northward migration, the reindeer was domesticated by the Laplanders, who had no opportunities for the other domestications because of the rudeness of their society and the cold climate. If the people of France had also lacked domestic animals, the reindeer would have been domesticated there. Buffon used this example to moralize about the shortcomings of man in making use of the opportunities offered to him by nature.[55]

To Buffon the noblest animal domesticated by man was the horse, but even this courageous and intrepid being was obedient and docile; one could see these marks of servitude well by observing horses feeding in the pastures. He compared the freedom of movement of the feral horses of Spanish America with the lesser qualities of dexterity and agreeableness of the animal under the constant surveillance of man.[56] Sometimes domestications had gone so far as to render the animal virtually helpless in its dependence on man. Buffon questioned whether the sheep with its many useful attributes had ever existed independently of man. The fat-tailed sheep was an even more exaggerated example of this dependence. He had such a low opinion of the ovine intelligence that his English translator, Smellie, found it necessary to come to its defense. According to Buffon, the mouflon, a nobler and more self-reliant animal found in the mountains of Greece, in Cyprus, Sardinia, Corsica, and the deserts of Tartary, was probably the primitive stock from which all the different varieties of sheep had degenerated.[57] The goat, more wild and robust than the sheep, was also more independent of man. Goats could eat a wide variety of plants and were little affected by harsh climates. Under domestication, these friendly animals multiplied until they became nuisances. Although he mentioned the harm done by goats to the fields and woods, he did not castigate the goat as a destroyer of vegetation as have so many writers of the nineteenth and twentieth centuries.[58]

To Buffon the domestication of the dog was an event of the highest historical importance. In order to realize its significance, one should try to

[54] "Le Mouflon," *HN*, Vol. 11, p. 352; "Le Chameau et la Dromadaire," *ibid.*, pp. 228–229.

[55] "Le Élan et le Renne," *HN*, Vol. 12, pp. 85–86, 95–96.

[56] "Le Cheval," *HN*, Vol. 4, pp. 174–176. In this article, Buffon returns to the theme of the lesser influences of climate and food upon the human species than upon the animals, repeating the theme of migrating, adaptable man, pp. 215–223.

[57] "Le Mouflon," *HN*, Vol. 11, pp. 363–365. On Smellie's comments, see his translation of Buffon, "Natural History, General and Particular," Vol. 4, pp. 268–272.

[58] "La Chèvre," *HN*, Vol. 5, p. 60, 66, 68.

imagine what mankind would have done if the dog, this docile friend of man that was more adaptable than any other animal, had never existed. How would man have conquered and domesticated the other animals? And even now how could he discover, pursue, and destroy wild and useless beasts? To make himself master of living nature and to provide for his own security, man had to intervene in the animal world, winning over those animals capable of attaching themselves to him, obeying him, and thus becoming his agents in controlling the others: "The first art of man thus has been the education of the dog and the fruit of this art [has been] the conquest and peaceful possession of the Earth."[59] With the help of the dog, which was both a shepherd and an intelligent companion on the hunt, man domesticated other animals, gradually attaining greater dominance through more domestication. Since the original stamp of nature never preserved its purity in beings long under the management of man, the dog exhibited this degeneration to a high degree. Buffon compared the varieties of the dog to those of wheat;[60] both species bore the marks of long human experimentation. The most conspicuous refinements in the art of dog breeding were found in the most advanced societies; the dog also owed many of its most endearing and brilliant qualities to its association with man.[61] Buffon thought that the shepherd (*chien de berger*) was the domestic variety closest to the wild prototype; in the essay on the dog, he included a diagram showing the degeneration of the domestic dogs from the chien de berger. Similarly, the varieties of the domesticated cat, like those of the dog, were most numerous in the temperate climates and in the advanced societies.[62]

It has been the same with plants: the bread grains were not a gift of nature; they were a product of experiment and the application of intelligence to agriculture. Wild wheat was found in no part of the world. The grain with its marvelous characteristics, its climatic adaptability, its keeping qualities, has been perfected by man.

The changes which men have made in plant and animal life do not belong to the past alone; they are continuing. One need only compare, he says, the vegetables, flowers, fruits of today with those of the same species 150 years ago; one can make this comparison by looking at the great collection of colored drawings beginning in the times of Gaston d'Orléans (1608–1660) and continuing until Buffon's own day. Some of the most beautiful flowers of that time would be rejected at the later day, not by the florists but by the home gardeners. One can assign a very late date to our better seed and stony fruits; they are actually new fruits with old names.

[59] "Le Chien," *HN*, Vol. 5, pp. 186–188.

[60] *Ibid.*, pp. 193–196.

[61] "L'Éléphant," *HN*, Vol. 11, pp. 2–3.

[62] *HN*, Vol. 5, p. 201. See also diagram, facing p. 228, on the derivation of the domestic breeds from the shepherd. Vol. 6, pp. 16–17 ("Le Chat"). This passage also summarizes man's influence on the nature, habits, even the form of animals.

Buffon marveled at the persistence and patience of man in selecting and developing new plant varieties and his ability to recognize "certain individual plants having sweeter and better fruits than others." This selection, presupposing so much experience and skill, would have been an empty accomplishment without the discovery of grafting, which requires as much genius as the other requires patience.[63]

The most arresting idea of Buffon concerning domesticated plants and animals is his interpretation of them as secondary creations replacing virgin nature under carefully planned artificial conditions, and paralleling this interpretation, his idea that these domesticated plants and animals, diffused by man, become new centers from which further changes in virgin nature take place.

Buffon's theory of earth history and his philosophy of man assumed the superiority of a nature which had been improved by human endeavor. He was not, however, insensitive to wildlife; even if his harsh denunciations of the vegetation of virgin nature showed his strong preferences for the ordered nature of human workmanship, Buffon saw "naïve beauties in the wild" and was not indifferent to the harm which civilized man had done, even in those parts of the earth in which he was only beginning to make his influence felt.

His praises of the wild animals are in fact transparent criticisms of human society. Have those animals, which we call wild because they have not been subdued, need of anything more than they have, to be happy? They are neither the slaves nor the tyrants of their fellow creatures; the individual, unlike man, does not fear the rest of his species. They are peaceful among themselves, and war comes to them only from strangers or from men. They have good reason to avoid man and to establish themselves as far as possible from him.[64] Themes like these occur frequently in Buffon's writings: despite his faith in improvement and his respect for human achievement, he constantly reverts to man's warlike and destructive nature.

Within living nature, in regions remote from human influence, elephant, beaver, monkey, ant, and bee societies flourished. If they were not the product of a reasoning mind, they seemed based on a sense of what was reasonable. As man migrated and settled throughout the earth, the result was to destroy, or at least to partially break up these societies, which, if uninterfered with, led a fairly peaceable existence among themselves. Even if his settlements were remote from their habitats, man's presence caused them to retreat farther and farther, pressed by fear and necessity, not only making them wilder but diminishing their faculties and talents. In their natural state, they had means of self-protection. "But what can they do against beings who know how to

---

[63] "Le Chien," *HN*, Vol. 5, pp. 195–196. This essay has some interesting comments on wheat. See also "EN," concluding paragraphs of 7th Epoch, *HNS*, Vol. 5, pp. 249–250. Since the *HN* is an unfinished work, Buffon's remarks about the domestications of plants are very scanty.

[64] "Les Animaux Sauvages," intro., *HN*, Vol. 6, pp. 55–56. This volume was published in 1756.

find them without seeing them, to cut them down without approaching them?" The freely migrating, expanding, and deadly human race changed the primeval distributions of plants and, with them, of the animals. Although he recognized that this triumphant process was indistinguishable from the growth, development, and maintenance of civilization, one often feels in Buffon's writings a sense of sorrow at the indiscriminate destruction of wildlife, so remote from sportsmanlike hunting and the chase. The carnivores, he said, are harmful only because they are rivals of man, and he repeatedly mentions the relationship between human populations and their expansion and the diminution of the larger predators. If in a few centuries the expanding human race settles uniformly throughout the habitable earth, the story of the beaver will seem a fable.[65] In the introductory chapter on the carnivores, Buffon discussed sympathetically the wild animal in nature;[66] and in the essay on the lion, he said that species of animals that, like the lion, are of no use to man, appear to have been reduced in number because man everywhere is more numerous and because he has become more clever and has learned how to make weapons which nothing can resist. Buffon pointed to the diminution in the numbers of the lion as evidence of the falseness of a notion (which Montesquieu had revived in the *Persian Letters*) that the population of the earth was greater in ancient than in modern times. How could one maintain, Buffon asked, that the population of the earth had declined since Roman times if the numbers of lions had been reduced to a fiftieth, or even only to a tenth part of what they were before? The human race had not declined but had increased in numbers; reductions in animal populations could scarcely be compatible with diminution of human populations. With declining human populations their numbers would have increased.[67]

The sloths had been saved from extinction because they avoided places frequented by man and the more powerful animals. Buffon drew two other important conclusions from the existence of sloths: they illustrated the doctrine that in nature everything that can exist does exist, and they showed the absurdity of the doctrine of final causes because of their many crippling physical defects. Buffon thought their extinction at the hands of man inevitable. Man had been largely responsible for the disappearance of the Libyan elephant; the animal had retired in proportion to the interference it had met with from the human species.[68] He also remarked upon the role of man in the

[65] *Ibid.*, pp. 55–62. The quotation translated is on p. 61; on the beaver, p. 62.
[66] "Les Animaux Carnassiers," *HN*, Vol. 7, p. 3. In the introduction, Buffon writes: "Si nuire est détruire des êtres animés, l'homme, considéré comme faisant partie du système général de ces êtres, n'est-il pas l'espèce la plus nuisible de toutes?"
[67] "Le Lion," *HN*, Vol. 9, pp. 4–5.
[68] On the sloths, "L'Unau et L'Aï," *HN*, Vol. 13, p. 40. "L'Eléphant," *HN*, Vol. 11, p. 41. As in his discussion of the lion, Buffon in this essay uses the example of the elephant to argue that the present-day population of North Africa is greater than in Carthaginian times.

worldwide diffusion of the rat.[69] There was less direct influence on birds, but he noticed the effect of man on the songs of birds and their mimicry of him,[70] and the threatened extinction of the ostrich because of the "prodigious consumption" in Europe of its plumes for hats, helmets, theatrical costumes, furniture, canopies, funeral ceremonies, and feminine finery.[71] Nor was the life of the sea undisturbed. The widespread killing of the common seal[72] and of the walrus[73] illustrated trends already observed concerning animal societies on land. The deserted coasts of the newly discovered lands and the extremities of the two continents have become the last haven of the seal, "ces peuplades marines," for they have fled the inhabited coasts and appear only as scattered individuals in our seas, which no longer offer them the peace and security which their "grandes sociétés" need. They have gone in search of that liberty— again the allusion to human society is unmistakable—which is necessary for all social intercourse and have found it only in the seas little frequented by man.[74] The volume in which this passage appeared was published in 1782.

### 7. COUNT BUFFON: ON NATURAL AND CULTURAL LANDSCAPES

Even if one dismisses the physical theories upon which Buffon's ideas of the necessity of human intervention in the natural order are based, one is impressed with the shrewd, if short and scattered, contrasts which he makes between environments scarcely touched by man and those which had long been the scene of human settlement and activity. In these, he anticipates the ideas of Lyell, Humboldt, Marsh, Ratzel, and Vidal de la Blache.

Rude and uninhabited lands have rivers with many cataracts; the land might be flooded with water or burned by drought. Every spot capable of growing a tree has one. Among countries inhabited for a long time, there are few woods, lakes, or marshes, but they have many heaths and shrubs (meaning no doubt that heaths and shrub take over deforested and barren mountaintops). Men destroy, drain, and in time give a totally different appearance to the face of the earth. In general Europe is a new continent; its traditions of migrations and the recency of its arts and sciences indicate that this is so, for not so long ago it was covered by marshes and forests.[75]

[69] "Le Rat," *HN*, Vol. 7, p. 283.
[70] "Discours sur la Nature des Oiseaux," *HNO*, Vol. 1, pp. 21–22.
[71] "L'Autruche," *ibid.*, p. 444. Buffon has an interesting discussion of the uses of the ostrich by various peoples in historical times (pp. 440–448). See also his remarks on pp. 455–456 ("Le Touyou").
[72] "Le Phoque Commun," *HNS*, Vol. 6, p. 335.
[73] "Le Morse ou la Vache Marine," *HN*, Vol. 13, pp. 367–370. Buffon mentions also the "cruel war" on the manatee whose numbers have been much diminished in places well populated by man. "Les Lamantins," *HNS*, Vol. 6, pp. 382–383.
[74] "Le Phoque Commun," *HNS*, Vol. 6, p. 335.
[75] "Histoire et Théorie de la Terre," Proofs, Art. 6, "Géographie," *HN*, Vol. 1, pp. 210–211.

In a passage suggesting Lyell's remark that man tends to become a leveling agent, Buffon says that in countries whose population is too small to form and to support advanced societies, the surface of the earth is more rugged and unequal. Riverbeds are wider, more interrupted by cataracts. The Rhône and the Loire are tamed rivers, which under natural conditions would require a very long time to be made navigable. Rivers acquire a fixed determinate course when their waters are confined and directed and their bottoms are cleared out.[76] He mentions Tournefort's statement that the famous labyrinth of Crete is not a work of nature alone; old mines and quarries had been dug there, and with the lapse of time it is no longer easy to distinguish between a work of nature and a work of man. The Maastricht quarries, the Polish salt mines, the hollows near large cities, are other instances of man as an earth mover, although these operations he thought—and how wrongly—would always be minor in the history of nature.[77] In a discussion of the large marshes remaining in the world, he said that the plains of America are one continuous marsh, proof of the newness of the country, of the small number of inhabitants, and still more, of their lack of industry.[78]

Buffon's physical theories, his comparative studies of the quadrupeds, his notions concerning primitive society in the New World, and his self-satisfaction with the improvement of nature by man in Europe led him to the curious notion that nature in the New World was weaker and on a lower scale of magnitude than that of the Old World.

The physical explanation of this weakness was based on the same theory as was his explanation of racial differences: the main reason was that the New World tropics were more humid and cooler, owing to the trades and to the Andes, than the Old World tropics. Even though he admitted that the New World produced its share of species of the large reptiles, insects, and plant life, he persisted in his belief that New World nature was weaker because he had proved to his own satisfaction that the animals of the New World were smaller, that wild and domestic animals of the Old World became smaller when they lived in the New, and that there were, on the whole, fewer species in the New World.

Primitive man of the New World had, moreover, few talents. He was cruel and indifferent to life and had little ardor for his women. His societies were therefore small, and their increase in population was insufficient to develop the arts. Primitive man in the New World had been unable to play the role of aiding nature and of developing it from its rude state. The reason for the few domesticated animals of the New World was not any lack of docility among the animals, but the weakness of man.[79]

---

[76] *Ibid.*, Proofs, Art. 10, "Des Fleuves," p. 368.

[77] *Ibid.*, Proofs, Art 17, "Des Isles Nouvelles, etc.," p. 549.

[78] *Ibid.*, Proofs, Art. 18, "De l'Effet des Pluies, des Marécages, etc.," p. 575.

[79] This general theme of the weakness of man in the New World is repeated many times in the *HN*, but the whole argument is in three articles: *HN*, Vol. 9, "Animaux de

The environmental theory and Buffon's harsh judging of primitive man in the New World explained the contrast between its primeval landscapes and the well-ordered landscapes of the Old World. In his failure to clear the forests and to drain the marshes, the American Indian revealed his incapacity to change nature to the degree necessary for a high civilization.

To Buffon the changes which man had made on the earth were inextricably woven into the history of civilization. It is true that in the eighteenth century there was nothing novel in the idea that civilization was the result of man's control over nature through theoretical and applied science, but the emphasis of most expositors of this idea was on invention, social change, the purposive applications of scientific truth to practical matters. It was a totally different matter to see, as Buffon had seen, man-made changes of the earth in their historical perspective. The one idea concerned society; the other, earth history.

## 8. THE AMERICAN PANDORA'S BOX

Buffon's claim that nature was weaker in the New World than in the Old was a disastrous error which affected his reputation in America and strongly influenced contemporary interpretations of the New World environment and its cultures. Many of them cannot be understood without reference to his thesis. Such ex cathedra pronouncements from the *Jardin des Plantes*, however, were not received with equanimity in the New World. Some of the ablest men in America—Franklin, Adams, and Jefferson among them—were becoming impatient with facile generalizations from the study-rooms of European philosophers. These men resented the implications of Buffon's thesis and denied its truth. Probably the aging and humane Buffon did not realize what really was in this Pandora's box.

Jefferson wrote a superb rebuttal, but it was kindly and respectful, condemning the false European notions of the Indian and dismissing accounts of the South American Indians as being too full of fable to be worthy of credence. Too little was known of climate to support Buffon's theories. Who were the travelers who had furnished Buffon information about the quadrupeds? Were they natural historians, did they actually measure the animals they spoke of, were they acquainted with the animals of their own country, did they know enough to distinguish one species from another? "How unripe we yet are, for an accurate comparison of the animals of the two countries, will appear from the work of Monsieur Buffon." Jefferson dismissed as ridiculous the question of the degeneration of European domesticated animals in

---

l'Ancien Continent," pp. 56–83; "Animaux du Nouveau Monde," pp. 84–96, and "Animaux Communs aux Deaux Continents," pp. 97–128. The passages upon which this discussion is based are in the introduction to the essay on animals of the New World, pp. 84–88, and in the essay on animals common to both continents, pp. 102–111.

the New World. If they were smaller, weaker, less hardy, the reasons for their poor condition would be the same in the New as in the Old World: neglect, poor food, poverty of the soil, and poverty of man. Jefferson asked "whether nature has enlisted herself as a Cis- or Trans-Atlantic partisan?" The answer was an emphatic "No."

On his visit to France, Jefferson protested to Buffon personally. "I told him also that the reindeer [of the Old World] could walk under the belly of our moose; but he entirely scouted the idea." Jefferson then wrote to General Sullivan of New Hampshire for the bones, skin, and antlers of the moose. Six months later, after much work by General Sullivan and his party and at an expense of forty guineas to Jefferson, the evidence was presented to Buffon, who was convinced. "He promised in his next volume to set these things right also, but he died directly afterwards." Had Buffon lived, one wonders if he would have changed his mind about the weakness of nature and of primitive man in the New World; as Jefferson generously grants, and as the *Histoire Naturelle* repeatedly shows, he did not stubbornly stand on his errors.[80]

The continuing interest in Jefferson as a scientist, farmer, geographer, agriculturalist, and planner has probably kept alive a dispute which, with less celebrated protagonists, would have quietly died of absurdity. Since the controversy over Buffon's New World thesis has been exhaustively studied by others, I will comment briefly on a few ideas. Their expositors were better copyists than observers; there was much noise, but it was a clanking of dull swords.[81]

Count Buffon, who had repeatedly stressed the role of man in changing the environment, paradoxically encouraged those observers of the New World who were partial to environmental ideas. Certain of the weak sexual endowment of the American Indians, Buffon believed them, like other animals, to be a somewhat passive element in nature, victims of its lesser powers in the New World, whose humid coolness they had been unable to overcome by

[80] "Notes on the State of Virginia, Query VI," in Padover, ed., *The Complete Jefferson*, pp. 495–611. On Jefferson's visit with Buffon, p. 891. See also Boorstin, *The Lost World of Thomas Jefferson*, pp. 100–104.

[81] The controversy, much of which is difficult to read with patience, cannot be summarized both accurately and briefly, in part because the European thinkers shifted their ground frequently. It is best to start with Count Buffon's original statement (see note 79 above), following with Jefferson's "Notes on the State of Virginia," Query 6, and then Count Buffon's reconsideration, "Addition à l'Article des Variétés de l'Espèce Humaine. Des Américains," *HNS*, Vol. 4, pp. 525–532. The best study in English is Gilbert Chinard's "Eighteenth Century Theories on America as a Human Habitat," *PAPS*, Vol. 91 (1947), pp. 27–57, which is more meaningful if read with his "The American Philosophical Society and the Early History of Forestry in America," *PAPS*, Vol. 89 (1945), pp. 444–488. The most exhaustive study is the impressive work of Antonello Gerbi, *La Disputa del Nuovo Mondo. Storia di Una Polemica 1750–1900*. Also translated into Spanish. I am indebted to Chinard and Gerbi for many of the references, and especially to Chinard for the American materials.

draining and clearing away thickets and forests. How impressive must the swamps and tales of them have been to the thinkers of this age, how frequently their existence was related to theology, geological theory, and medicine!

Other writers, less cautious even than Buffon, now rode off to combat. Peter Kalm, the Swedish naturalist, remarked that European cattle "degenerate by degrees" in the New World, attributing this degeneracy largely to climate, soil, and food. European colonists mature younger and die sooner than do the people of Europe. Even the trees have the same qualities as the inhabitants. If cattle and colonists are both affected, it would seem that the prospects of changing pristine nature in the New World become more and more uncertain.[82] The abbé Arnaud reviewed Kalm's work favorably in the *Journal Etranger* (1761), emphasizing its more sensational aspects; he was instrumental in further disseminating these views about America. So was Rousselot de Surgy.[83] Cornelius de Pauw adopted Buffon's ideas with latter-day improvements of his own; his work *Recherches Philosophiques sur les Américains ou Mémoires intéressants pour servir à l'Histoire de l'Espèce Humaine* (Berlin, 1768) quickly superseded the others, becoming the ranking text in the field. De Pauw cannily selected all the unfavorable evidence on America, maintained the Europeans born there show the same weaknesses as the indigenous peoples, thought the New World to be depopulated, and in a radical departure from Buffon argued that the American is neither an immature animal nor a child, but a degenerate. The Western Hemisphere is not imperfect, it is actually decayed and decaying.[84]

The argument was continued by the authors, chiefly Raynal, of *Histoire Philosophique et Politique des Établissemens et du Commerce des Européens dans les deux Indes*. They accept Buffon's opinion on the comparatively recent origin of the New World and the lack of erotic vigor of its people; hence, its miserable and deserted condition. Raynal, however, admired the ability of European colonists to change their environment, thus distinguishing their capacities from those of the Indians. European man "immediately changed the face of North America. He introduced symmetry by the assistance of all the instruments of the arts." His notable achievements included clearing, replacement of wild by domesticated animals, plantings for thorns and briars,

---

[82] *Travels into North America*, Vol. 1, pp. 80–82. See Chinard's comments on Kalm's credulity and his aptitude for scientific investigation, "America as a Human Habitat," *PAPS*, Vol. 91, pp. 32–34.

[83] Chinard, *op. cit.*, pp. 34–35.

[84] De Pauw, *Recherches Philosophiques*, Vol. 1, p. 307. On De Pauw, see Chinard, *op. cit.*, pp. 35–36 and p. 55, note 1. Chinard says Frederick the Great, who had good reasons for discouraging German emigration to America, was delighted by the "anti-promotional literature of his protégé." See also Gerbi, *op. cit.*, pp. 59–89, 719–720 (on Spanish-American reactions). Church, "Corneille de Pauw, and the Controversy over his *Recherches Philosophiques sur les Américains*," *PMLA*, Vol. 51 (1936), pp. 178–206. Despite the criticism, De Pauw wrote the article on America for the supplement (1776) to the *Encyclopédie*, and all the basic theses remain. Chinard, *op. cit.*, p. 36.

drainage. "The wastes were covered with towns, and the bays with ships; and thus the new world, like the old became subject to man." The spirit of liberty and religious toleration were responsible for these achievements.[85]

Buffon argued for nature's (including man's) weakness in the New World in order to support his belief that pristine nature requires the ordering hand and intelligent mind of civilized man to make it fruitful. Neither hand nor mind had been skilled enough in the pre-Columbian New World. Indeed, Count Buffon's literary excursions into the New World had mired him in swamps of his own creating, but his conception of man's place in nature was a noble one, inspiring new insights into both earth and human history. Buffon concludes *Des Époques de la Nature* with a plea for the abolition of war and for moral reform in order to make man's tenure of the earth a benefit to him, affording him with the abandonment of these destructive activities, an opportunity for an even greater realization of his imaginative and inventive powers.

In his *History of America*, William Robertson disseminated Buffon's views to the English-speaking world, but he made no attempt to improve on the exaggerations. With the exception of the two "monarchies" of the New World, Robertson said, the small independent tribes who inhabited the continent possessed neither the talent, the skill, nor the desire to improve the lands they lived on. "Countries occupied by such people were almost in the same state as if they had been without inhabitants." Immense forests and the luxuriant vegetation of the rainy tropics swallowed up men even more.

Environmental change thus is characteristic of civilized man. Again in the Spirit of Buffon he says, "The labour and operations of man not only improve and embellish the earth, but render it more wholesome and friendly to life."[86] The pregnant thought that man has a creative role in the order of nature shows Robertson's sympathy with the idea that the life principle is dignified by its association with human life: Since America "is on the whole less cultivated and less peopled than the other quarters of the earth, the active principle of life wastes its force in productions of this inferior form [i.e., the lower forms of life like reptiles and insects]." This should not be dismissed as naïve anthropocentrism; it suggests a more profound question, that is, whether nature is only a meaningless chaos without civilized man, for primitive man without skill or the desire to improve himself is enveloped in the luxurance of other kinds of life; civilized man, as Buffon had also thought, has some control over the kind and quality, if not the amount, of plant and animal life.[87]

Again following Buffon, Robertson attaches great importance to domestication ("this command over the inferior creatures") as a means of controlling nature. "Without this his dominion is incomplete. He is a monarch who has no

[85] Chinard, *op. cit.*, pp. 36–37; pp. 36–38 with accompanying notes provide guides along tortuous paths.

[86] *Hist. Amer.*, Vol. I, p. 263; Robertson also combines the themes of man as a modifier of the environment and man as an eradicator of disease, pp. 263–265.

[87] *Hist. Amer.*, Vol. I, p. 266.

subjects; a master without servants, and must perform every operation by the strength of his own arm." The use of domestic animals has also been a primary force in the ordering of nature. "It is a doubtful point whether the dominion of man over the animal creation, or his acquiring the use of metals, has contributed most to extend his power."[88] Robertson thus follows Buffon's lead in making the superior ability of the peoples of the Old World to change the face of nature a fundamental difference between them and the primitive peoples of the New World.

Let us prolong this discussion a bit further. When Count Buffon ruefully protested against Kalm's and De Pauw's excesses, little was left of either Count Buffon's original theses or those of his more careless followers.[89] What other interpretations were possible? Moral rather than physical causes might account for the activities of the Americans in changing their new lands. "The world has been too long abused with notions," said John Adams," that climate and soil decide the characters and political institutions of nations. The laws of Solon and the despotism of Mahomet have, at different times, prevailed at Athens; consuls, emperors, and pontiffs have ruled at Rome. Can there be desired a stronger proof, that policy and education are able to triumph over every disadvantage of climate?"[90] The Florentine, Filipo Mazzei, agreed with his friend Jefferson in criticizing Buffon for assuming that nature did not operate uniformly throughout the earth and for his ignorance of primitive peoples; moral, not environmental, causes were at work in shaping the culture of the American people.[91] Many American thinkers also were more impressed with their power than with their plasticity and docility. There was too much to be observed, too much that had been done and could be done to allow the Americans to obediently memorize catechisms prepared by Europeans thousands of miles away. Men such as Thomas Jefferson, Jared Eliot, Hugh Williamson, John Lorain, were witnesses of changes going on in the New World which made the opinions of many Europeans laughable.

### 9. "IN A SORT, THEY BEGAN THE WORLD A NEW"

The physical environment of the New World often was regarded as a great outdoor laboratory for scientific study.[92] Old questions could now be answered as one observed the effects of clearing on climate, of drainage on

---

[88] *Hist. Amer.*, Vol. 2, pp. 9–10, 11.

[89] *HNS*, Vol. 4, pp. 525–532. "Addition à l'Article des Variétés de l'Espèce Humaine. Des Américains."

[90] "A Defence of the Constitutions of Government of the United States of America," in *The Works of John Adams*, Vol. 6, p. 219. Quoted in Chinard, "America as Habitat," *op. cit.*, p. 45.

[91] Mazzei, *Recherches Historiques et Politiques sur les États-Unis de l'Amérique Septentrionale*, Vol. 2, p. 32. See Gerbi, *op. cit.*, pp. 290–298; Chinard, "America as Habitat," *op. cit.*, p. 44. I have not been able to consult Mazzei's work.

[92] Chinard, "Early History of Forestry," *op. cit.*, p. 452.

health. It was a great laboratory of nature because most men regarded it as being a natural harmony which, until the changes made by the European colonists, had been undisturbed since the creation. Before the Europeans came, Peter Kalm said, the woods had "never been meddled with, except that sometimes a small part was destroyed by fire." And of the depth of American soil, he wrote, "We can almost be sure, that in some places it never was stirred since the deluge."[93] The Vicomte de Chateaubriand was struck by the massive, still, strong forests he saw in America. Of one unidentified forest he exclaimed, "Who can describe the feelings that are experienced on entering these forests, coeval with the world (*aussi vieilles que le monde*), and which alone afford an idea of the creation, such as it issued from the hands of the Almighty."[94]

While the Marquis de Chastellux meditated "on the great process of Nature," requiring fifty thousand years to make the earth habitable, a new spectacle by contrast aroused his attention and curiosity: a single man in one year had cut down several arpents of wood and had built his house on land he had cleared himself. He saw the process of settlement going on before his eyes, the man with a modest capital buying land in the woods, moving there with his animals and his provisions of flour and cider. The smaller trees, felled first, and branches of the larger ones provide the fence for his clearing. He "boldly attacks those immense oaks, or pines, which one would take for the ancient lords of the territory he is usurping," strips off their bark, lays them open with his ax. Fire in the spring completes the work of his ax, the spring sun on the humus of the clearing encouraging the grasses, the grazing of the animals. The clearings expand; a handsome wooden house replaces the log cabin. Tools and neighborliness are the keys to creating the settlement. The French general saw processes of environmental change at work, which within a hundred years, he said, had peopled a vast forest with three million inhabitants.[95] Even in the nineteenth century John Lorain could say that "the value of animal and vegetable matter is best seen in our lonely forests, where neither art nor ignorance has materially interfered, with the simple but wise economy of nature."[96]

Themes long familiar to European science could be pursued further in this new laboratory where one could observe soil erosion, soil exhaustion, the effects of deforestation and of draining, and many other topics. The notices were based on local observation; they do not constitute a coherent body of inquiry. Warnings about deforestation and the need for conserving trees could be heard in one place, grandiose plans for clearing in another; some thought man should interfere carefully in the equilibrium of nature, others that he should set about boldly fashioning a new world.

[93] *Travels into North America*, Vol. 1, pp. 86–87, 118.
[94] *Travels in America and Italy*, Vol. 1, p. 148.
[95] *Travels in North-America in the Years 1780, 1781, and 1782*, Vol. 1, pp. 44–48.
[96] *Nature and Reason Harmonized in the Practice of Husbandry* (Philadelphia, 1825), p. 24.

In the course of time the accumulation of such scattered observations led to a deeper understanding of natural processes and of human interferences with them. The intense interest in climate in the eighteenth and nineteenth centuries was a broader and deeper continuation of seventeenth century interest. John Woodward (whose work was discussed in chap. VIII sec. 8) typically said that countries having many trees were damper, more humid, and had more rainfall. As the first settlers in America overcame these disadvantages by burning and destroying woods and groves "to make way for Habitation and Culture of the Earth, the Air mended and clear'd up space, changing into a Temper much more dry and serene than before."[97]

The broad philosophic lesson of these works was that men created distinctive environments of their own which possessed a unique kind of order—or disorder—lacking in nature. Men were aware of a unity in nature but also that they had the opportunity to create new kinds of order, substituting one kind of environment for another. On his visit with Jefferson, Chastellux describes the possibilities of creating a planned equilibrium between the wooded and the farmed land. Nothing "is more essential than the manner in which we proceed in the clearing of a country, for the salubrity of the air, nay even the order of the seasons, may depend on the access which we allow the winds, and the direction we may give them." The air of Rome, Chastellux continues, was less healthful after the trees between Rome and Ostia which protected it from the Sirocco and the Libico had been cut down, and the droughts of Castile probably owed their origin to deforestation. Applying these lessons to Virginia, he said that since the greatest part of the state is very swampy, it can be dried out only by cutting down the woods. It can never be so completely drained that it will no longer have noxious exhalations. Whatever their nature may be, vegetation absorbs them, trees being well suited to this purpose. "It appears equally dangerous either to cut down or to preserve a great quantity of wood; so that the best manner of proceeding to clear the country, would be to disperse the settlements as much as possible, and to leave some groves of trees standing between them." The settled land would be healthful, the woods would be a brake on the winds, which would also carry off the exhalations.[98]

Chastellux's remarks suggest a continuing interest in the relationship between clearing and health, as happened in the Old World. Benjamin Rush, for example, argued that there had been a higher incidence of disease in Philadelphia in the past few years, and that this was caused by the establishment—and the increase—of millponds and the cutting of trees. "It has been remarked that intermittents [fevers] on the shores of the Susquehannah have kept an exact pace with the passages which have been opened for the propagation of

[97] *Miscellanea Curiosa*, Vol. 1, p. 220. Quoted in Chinard, "The Early History of Forestry," p. 452.
[98] Chastellux, *Travels in North-America in the Years 1780, 1781, and 1782*, Vol. 2, pp. 53–54.

marsh effluvia, by cutting down the wood which formerly grew in the neighborhood." In explaining this correlation, Rush made a sharp distinction between clearing and cultivation. Clearing is merely a rough and ready way of getting rid of trees; it actually may encourage the spread of fever. With cultivation, intervention in the environment is more complete, and natural processes now under human guidance are substituted for the old. Cultivating a country, which means "draining swamps, destroying weeds, burning brush, and exhaling the unwholesome or superfluous moisture of the earth, by means of frequent crops of grain, grasses, and vegetables of all kinds, renders it healthy." His conclusions are based on comparative data which he does not publish, but he envisages an interesting stage-like development in the changes which occur: "The first settlers received these countries [in the U.S.] from the hands of nature pure and healthy. Fevers soon followed their improvements, nor were they finally banished until the higher degrees of cultivation that have been named took place." Rush's proposal was based on a planned equilibrium between what remained in the natural state and what had been substituted by man: plant trees around the millponds, for they absorb the unhealthy air "and discharge it in a highly purified state in the form of what is now called 'deflogisticated' air" (Priestley's term for oxygen).[99]

In a paper read before the American Philosophical Society in November, 1794, Thomas Wright, a licentiate of the Irish College of Surgeons, proposed artificial wind corridors to resist the spread of disease. If drainage on a large scale was impracticable, evaporation of water from marshes and swamps could be encouraged. Despite rainy Irish winters and short summers, and air which is "chemically dry" and lacking in heat, temporary pools (*turloughs*) are quickly dried up; the continental wind, dry but lacking heat, in one month's blowing "rids the whole island of its superfluous water," leaving parched fields and almost impassable dusty roads. If a few weeks will "exsiccate" Ireland, why cannot the Americans make use of their dry and hot winds? Clear the woods! But by conscious effort. A line one or two hundred miles long and running in the direction of the prevailing winds (northwest to southeast) could be cleared of trees: "Then every blast from these two opposite points will ventilate 200 miles of country, bearing along the fumes of all the marshes, while the great *visto* [*sic*] or avenue skirted with wood at both sides would furnish the most salubrious and consequently valuable situation for settlers."[100]

And William Curry, another man with a theory and a remedy, in 1795 described agriculture as "a great engine" which could counteract forces depriving the atmosphere "of its salutary and vivifying principle [oxygen],"

[99] "An Enquiry into the Cause of the Increase of Bilious and Intermitting Fevers in Pennsylvania, with Hints for Preventing Them," *TAPS*, Vol. 2, No. 25 (1786), pp. 206–212; quotes on pp. 206, 207, 209.
[100] Thomas Wright, "On the Mode Most Easily and Effectually Practicable of Drying up the Marshes of the Maritime Parts of North America," *TAPS*, Vol. 4 (1799), pp. 243–246; quote on p. 246.

and a "great magazine" which could provide a sufficient source of it. Drain off stagnant waters, burn the dead wood and grass, fill up flats, hollows, and sinks with clay, sand, or lime. Well-chosen cultivated grasses and plants will now supply profuse oxygen. If marshes are too large to drain, flood them with dams and sluices, for dead organic matter immersed in water and without contact with the air can only putrefy slowly and imperfectly. Naturally marshy countries should be cultivated, "preserved dry and clean by means of the spade, the plow, and the rake."[101]

As has happened frequently in the past, conservative believers in the design argument opposed such changes. There should be no interferences with the processes of nature because if the Creator had wished what is now desired by art He would have created it in the first place. Dr. Adam Seybert, for example, reversing his own and a widely accepted view that marshes and their airs are unhealthful, concluded they are a necessary part of nature. Animals can die of air that is too pure as well as from impure air; they live too fast in air "overcharged with oxygen gas." Marshes "appear to me to have been instituted by the Author of Nature in order to operate against the powers which vegetables and other causes possess of purifying the atmosphere, so that the oxygen may exist in a proper proportion, fit to support animal life and combustion." Marshes might well be blessings; perhaps the Creator had intended they should be uninhabited "that their only use should be that of correcting the too pure atmospheres. Although their immediate inhabitants suffer disease from them, still but a small portion of the human race choose marshy situations as their residence." Using the design argument, Seybert seems to be justifying the reasonableness of the observed *tempo* of growth and decay in nature, and marshes seem to play in the biological world a role like that of evil in the moral world.[102]

Observations regarding the effects of settlement on climate were, like the cloves of Zanzibar, pleasant smells for believers in climatic change. Samuel Williams, the historian of Vermont, claimed the state's climate was becoming more moderate and less predictable. It is changing so rapidly and constantly "that it is the subject of common observation and experience." Such changes are most "sensible and apparent in a new country, which is suddenly changing from a state of vast uncultivated wilderness, to that of numerous settlements, and extensive improvements." When the earth's surface is cleared, it is open to the influence of the sun and winds, becoming warm and dry. The area of the clearings increases with the progress of settlement, and the climate then becomes more uniform and moderate. Observations of older authors (Noah Webster scolded him for accepting them), the mills which are no longer useful

---

[101] William Currie, "An Enquiry into the Causes of the Insalubrity of flat and Marshy Situations; and directions for preventing or correcting the Effects thereof," *TAPS*, Vol. 4 (1799), pp. 127–142; quotes on pp. 140–142.
[102] Adam Seybert, "Experiments and observations, on the atmosphere of marshes," *TAPS*, Vol. 4 (1799), pp. 415–430; quote on p. 429.

for lack of water, and the arable lands which were formerly in swamps convince him that it was colder in the days when settlements were fewer. Clearing entices the sea breezes inland because the earth and the atmosphere above it are now warmer than the water. The contrast thus is between a stable country unaltered by man—with regular seasonal changes, the course and appearance of nature varying little from one age to another—and an altered land whose seasons fluctuate, become more irregular, inconstant, and uncertain.[103]

Similar ideas reappear in the writings of Count Volney whose travels in many parts of the long-settled and well-used Old World made him sensitive to the appearance of apparently virgin lands.[104] It is, in fact, a great temptation to embark upon a digression about Volney, for his writings on geographic subjects well deserve study. He was acquainted with current theory that forests attracted rainfall and that clearing promoted aridity; he had also studied the writings on this subject of earlier foreign travelers and of American residents. A belief is widespread in the United States, he says, "that very perceptible partial changes in the climate took place which displayed themselves in proportion as the land was cleared." Citing earlier observers, including Peter Kalm, Samuel Williams, Benjamin Rush, and Thomas Jefferson, he adds that he has collected similar testimony on the course of his journey and that a sensible alteration in the climate of the United States is an "incontestable fact."

> On the Ohio, at Gallipolis, at Washington in Kentucky, at Frankfort, at Lexington, at Cincinnati, at Louisville, at Niagara, at Albany, everywhere the same circumstances have been repeated to me: "longer summers, later autumns, and also later harvests; shorter winters, snows less deep, and of shorter duration, but cold not less intense." And in all the new settlements these changes have been represented to me not as gradual and progressive, but as rapid and almost sudden, in proportion to the extent to which the land is cleared.

Volney sees what is happening in America as a historical process with no surprises, for climatic change followed settlement in Europe and no doubt in Asia and in the entire inhabited world.[105] In Kentucky he sees changes occurring in even less altered country; again, his observations are supported by the testimony of those who had experienced their consequences. Drought seems to keep pace with clearing. Nevertheless, many Kentucky streams have had more abundant waters since the woods were cut down; with the removal of the thick leaf-bed of the forest, rainwater was no longer retained. With clearing and plowing, it sank in the ground, forming "more durable and abundant

---

[103] *The Natural and Civil History of Vermont*, pp. 57–65. Williams gives experimental evidence for ground temperature change; he is not certain, however, if clearing is the only cause of a change in climate.

[104] *View of the Climate and Soil of the United States of America*, pp. 7–8.

[105] *Ibid.*, pp. 266–278; quotes on pp. 266, 268–269. Volney discusses Samuel Williams at some length; also see his very realistic description of prevailing diseases in the U.S. and their probable social and environmental causes, pp. 278–332.

reservoirs." He is so committed, however, to the forest-rainfall theory that he fails to see a real problem here. One might add that the relation of forests to stream flow is still a much studied and controversial problem.[106] In such writings, one sees clearly the pros and cons of clearing as they were then understood. Forest clearance was required for the extension of civilization, for public health, and for the promotion of agriculture necessary for this extension, but it threatened also to defeat these purposes by diminishing the water supply in springs and brooks and thus perhaps even bringing about permanent aridity.

Volney's remarks call attention again to the question which to me is the most interesting of all, that of man's place in nature as it was then understood. The activities of European man, in an environment which up to this time had existed in an apparently unchanged form since the creation, set him off sharply from his natural surroundings, even though he was part of them, while the Indians seemed fused with theirs. Early travelers, it is true, occasionally were aware that indigenous peoples altered their environment to a noticeable degree; they saw—and some quite early—their fires and the effects on plant and animal life. William Wood, for example, in the early seventeenth century describes the underwood growing in swamps and wet low places. The Indians, he says, customarily burn this wood in November when, owing to the dryness of the grass and of the leaves, it is possible to burn the underbrush and debris easily. If there were no burning, the area would become impassable, thus spoiling the Indian hunting. The burned areas therefore are evidence of Indian settlement, for "in those places where the Indians inhabit, there is scarce a bush or bramble, or any combersome underwood to bee seene in the more champion ground. ... In some places where the Indians dyed of the Plague some fourteene yeares agoe, is much underwood, as in the mid way betwixt Wessaguscus and Plimouth, because it hath not been coorect, beene burned. ..."[107]

To the travelers of advanced civilizations, however, the contrasts between the apparently virgin land and the land settled, cleared, and under cultivation are vivid; and the processes of nature going on from the creation until the Europeans came obviously had been interfered with after their arrival. If one wished to know about soil fertility, John Bartram wrote, he could inspect the riverbanks of lowlands which are annually enriched by floodwaters carrying their mud and debris. Before clearing, many hazels, weeds, and vines grew in these lowlands, entangling the debris brought down by the streams in flood; its subsequent decay kept the soil rich. After clearing the lowlands and planting them, an opposite effect was noticed: the floods no longer deposited the debris but passed over the land, carrying off in addition soil from the cleared land. A stream with a pronounced gradient would deposit coarse sand on the

---

[106] *Ibid.*, pp. 25–26.
[107] William Wood, *New Englands Prospect* (1634). Reprinted with an intro. by Eben Moody Boynton, pp. 16–17.

lowlands. Further, when the higher grounds are trod and pastured, the rain creates gullies, bringing down more coarse sand or clay than before. "As I have observed when I was in yᵉ back parts of yᵉ Country above 20 years past when yᵉ woods was not pastured & full of high weeds & yᵉ ground light then yᵉ rain sunk much more into yᵉ earth and did not wash & tear up yᵉ surface (as now)."

In a narrow sense this is one of many interesting early warnings of soil erosion in the United States; in a broader sense it is a recognition that human activity, directly, or indirectly through domestic animals, in upland areas or on lowland clearings alters the natural processes of erosion and sedimentation. We have already seen that the physico-theologists of the seventeenth century were much impressed with the role of soil deposition in the design, the carrying of soil particles from uplands to plains and deltas being a physical process fundamental to the life of the human race.[108]

Jared Eliot himself marveled at the physical changes that had taken place since the first settlement of New England, whose colonists, small in number, had come from a cultivated to a thickly forested and unimproved country, with little in their former experience to guide them, with no beasts of burden or carriage; "unskill'd in every Part of Service to be done: It may be said, That in a Sort, *they began the World a New.*"[109] He also understood the process by which a valley was enriched through sedimentation at the expense of denuding the hillsides and depriving them of their fertility. Implicit in the ideas of careful observers like Bartram and Eliot, I think, is the realization that the new processes under human control should be acceptable biological substitutions for those processes going on before human interference.

> When our fore-Fathers settled here, they entered a Land which probably never had been Ploughed since the Creation; the Land being new they depended upon the natural Fertility of the Ground, which served their purpose very well, and when they had worn out one piece, they cleard another, without any concern to amend their land, except a little helped by the Fold and Cart-dung, whereas in *England* they would think a Man a bad Husband, if he should pretend to sow Wheat on Land without any Dressing.[110]

The comparison of the work of man in the new land with an act of creation, which is frequently made by early writers on America, recurs in Eliot's enthusiastic praise of drainage.

> Take a View of a Swamp in its original Estate, full of Bogs, overgrown with Flags, Brakes, poisonous Weeds and Vines, with other useful Product, the gen-

---

[108] See the undated letter from John Bartram to Jared Eliot published in Jared Eliot, *Essays upon Field Husbandry in New England and Other Papers, 1748–1762.* Ed. by Harry J. Carman and Rexford G. Tugwell (New York, 1934), pp. 203–204. I am indebted to Angus McDonald's *Early American Soil Conservationists,* USDA Misc. Public. No. 449 (Washington, 1941), for the references to Bartram, Eliot, and Lorain.

[109] Jared Eliot, *op. cit.,* p. 7.

[110] *Ibid.,* p. 29.

uine Offspring of stagnant Waters. Its miry Bottom, and Harbour to Turtles, Toads, Efts, Snakes, and other creeping Verm'n. The baleful Thickets of Brambles, and the dreary Shades of larger Growth; the Dwelling-Place of the Owl and the Bittern; a Portion of Foxes, and a Cage of every unclean and hateful bird.

Then see it after clearing, ditching, draining, burning, "and other needful Culture" have transformed it.

Behold it now cloathed with sweet verdant Grass, adorned with the lofty wide spreading well-set Indian-Corn; the yellow Barley; the Silver coloured Flax; the ramping Hemp, beautified with fine Ranges of Cabbage; the delicious Melon, and the best of Turnips, all pleasing to the Eye, and, many, agreeable to the Taste; a wonderful Change this! and all brought about in a short Time; a Resemblance of Creation, as much as we, impotent Beings, can attain to, the happy Product of Skill and Industry.[111]

Human activities, however, might interfere with the harmony of nature, and man must proceed with awareness and caution. Benjamin Franklin's example of the blackbirds and the corn illustrates, as did Darwin's cats-to-clover chain in 1859, the workings of the web of life.

Whenever we attempt to amend the scheme of Providence, and to interfere with the government of the world, we had need be very circumspect, lest we do more harm than good. In New England they once thought *blackbirds* useless, and mischievous to the corn. They made efforts to destroy them. The consequence was, the blackbirds were diminished; but a kind of worm, which devoured their grass, and which the blackbirds used to feed on, increased prodigiously; then finding their loss in grass much greater than their saving in corn, they wished again for their blackbirds.[112]

## 10. Nature and Reason Harmonized

The most thoughtful and sustained contemporary discussion of the effects of the American settlement known to me is by John Lorain (*ca.* 1764–1819) whose *Nature and Reason Harmonized in the Practice of Husbandry* was published posthumously in 1825. Lorain is a practical man, aware, however, that land use practices of the late eighteenth and early nineteenth centuries are not mere techniques but belong to a philosophy of nature. Such an attitude has not been unusual in Western civilization among writers on agriculture, forestry, and animal husbandry, partly, I think, because of the strength of the design argument, partly also because these men felt close to the field, the clearing, and the barnyard and saw them as part of the economy of nature.

Wild and untamed nature did not horrify Lorain as it did Count Buffon; it

[111] *Ibid.*, pp. 96–97.
[112] *The Origin of Species.* Modern Library Giant ed., p. 59 = Chap. 3; Franklin, "To Richard Jackson," *Writings,* ed. Smyth, Vol. 3, p. 135. Curiously similar to the example cited by Derham's editor. See chap. VIII, note 165. Quoted in Chinard, "America as Human Habitat," *PAPS,* Vol. 91 (1947), p. 40.

is described dispassionately as an interdependent natural system. In the lonely forests every piece of ground is covered with vegetation, the smaller trees, shrubs, and annuals growing at proper though not regular distances between the large trees. "The whole gradually [descends] in size from the largest trees to the mosses." Nature carefully spreads vegetation wherever it can, even on fallen tree trunks, the plants sinking with them and taking root in the earth as they decay.[113] Large living trees often stand on the durable wood of fallen timber. Each year new fallen leaves cover the vegetation of yesteryear, preventing grasses from growing and injuring nature's design. This covering is screened in winter by stems and branches, in the summer more effectively by the foliage. Fermentation and decomposition provide food for plants, enrich the soil, "and also minutely divide and keep the soil more open and mellow for the ready admission of their roots, than could be effected by the general mode of cultivation pursued in fields." Foliage, branches, dead trees, and other plants produce a "prodigious mass of decaying vegetation." It is full of life; the larger animals, reptiles, birds, find shelter here. "Every leaf and every crevice in the bark or elsewhere, is thickly peopled." Animalcula live off the decaying vegetation, other animalcula and worms find similar food in the soil. "It is also probable that incalculable tribes of animalcula . . . live plentifully on the dead carcasses and on the scraps and crumbs left by the large ones: added to this, the quantity of animal matter is prodigiously increased, by the creation of animals of every size, whose existence either in part or altogether depends on preying on others." The smaller animals of a limited life-span multiply fast; alive, their excreta return to the soil and manure it; dead, their remains greatly increase it. The cumulative mass of manure from all forms of animal life is adequate for the purposes for which nature intended it.

> It was certainly a very wise provision of nature, to cause the greater part of this matter to exist in small bodies. This has vastly increased the quantity, and promoted the ready and effectual application of it. If the whole or the greater part of this prodigious bulk of animal matter, had been made to exist in the larger animals, they could not have been supported; neither, could the manure furnished by them have been so intimately blended with the soil, as is the vegetable matter, which we all see has been made to exist in plants, that spread over and cover the surface of the habitable parts of the earth.

There is something wonderful in the blending of animal and vegetable matter. "The fertilizing effects of this perfect system of economy, is equally as clearly seen in our glades and prairies, as in our forests, where nature is suffered to pursue her own course."

Lorain has described here a system of nature without man; in the hierarchy of plant and animal life, individual species have varying rates of population growth. Life and death are closely interrelated, and in the life cycle the small individual bulk of vast numbers of organisms and the manufacture of fertil-

---

[113] *Nature and Reason Harmonized in the Practice of Husbandry*, p. 24.

izers by decomposition are vital in maintaining the stability of the environment.[114]

To Lorain the creations of civilized man—the term is his—bring about a new order in this primordial cycle of the natural world. "The living as well as the dead vegetation found in his way is destroyed and the grounds are cultivated. By these means, by far the greater part of the animalcula within, as well as upon the soil are destroyed." If the agriculturist keeps his lands in grass, keeps livestock to graze on it, and spreads their manure over the soil, then "nature is assisted by art, and the fertility of the soil is considerably increased."[115] By these methods man creates acceptable artificial substitutes for that portion of the process he has eliminated; but if a backwoods farmer plows and crops, paying no attention to grass or to stock, the cycle is broken and the soil is exhausted.

Lorain is impressed with the role of animalcula in the economy of nature untouched by man. After clearing, the quality of their excreta will be inferior to that produced under natural conditions, but even in artificial processes, the grasses will provide them with much food. Farmers have too casual an attitude toward them, he says, paying too much attention to the annoyances they endure. "Although it would appear at least probable, that neither man, nor the domesticated animals in which he seems to be more immediately interested, could have existed in any thing like the same numbers, or have been supplied with an abundance of nutriment, if animalcula had not been created. [*sic*] The same may be said of weeds, notwithstanding slovenly farmers complain still more loudly of the injury done by them."[116]

Lorain's conception of the biology of the soil—the importance of the animalcula and of the accumulation and subsequent decomposition of organic matter in the cycle of life and death which insures the continuity of nature—explains his fear of soil exhaustion (caused by continual plowing and cropping) and erosion when the soil is exposed to the injurious action of the sun, wind, rain, and melting snow.[117]

In an interesting passage notable for the posterity argument and for the ease with which the biblical curse on man and the land is dispatched, Lorain says such ruinous practices bring about poverty of soil and of purse. Posterity, "heirs of the wretchedness introduced by their inconsiderate forefathers," has the Herculean task of counteracting this curse of poverty. "Whether Satan is also the instigator of this evil, I do not presume to determine, but certain I am, that it is much greater (so far as farming be concerned), than the curse entailed on the soil by the fall of Adam. That seems to consist simply in brambles and thorns, including in these, such other vegetation as would compel man to earn his bread by the sweat of his brow." The curse is irrevocable, but it is

[114] *Ibid.*, pp. 25–26.
[115] *Ibid.*, pp. 26–27.
[116] *Ibid.*, p. 27.
[117] *Ibid.*, p. 517.

also a mild decree from Heaven, for man need only remove these obstacles to plant growth for a flourishing agriculture and the satisfaction of rational wants. "But when the hand of folly introduces the additional curse of poverty on the soil, this insatiable monster, like Aaron's serpent, swallows all the rest." This "hand of folly" is the perpetual plowing and cropping which destroy nature with little or no attention to the priceless decaying living matter or to livestock.[118]

Lorain's graphic comparisons between the clearing methods of the Pennsylvania and the Yankee farmers reveal their efficacy and their rudeness. He is critical of both, but more severely critical of the Pennsylvania farmer primarily because he breaks the organic cycle in nature. These descriptions have a universality that transcends their value as descriptions of early farming practices in the United States, for with few changes they could well apply to the clearings of Neolithic man, surprising results coming from simple tools and perseverance.

The Pennsylvania farmer begins his clearing by girdling the timber. The land is then logged off and the grubs are taken out by the roots. The smaller trees are also cut down and logged off. This logging continues with no thought of possible exhaustion even if stone coal could be used for fuel. In the war against the trees, the Pennsylvania backwoods farmer believes his crops are multiplied in proportion to the area of land he clears, and as a perpetual plower and cropper he invites soil exhaustion.[119]

In criticizing the backwoods farmer, Lorain grants that soils formed and remaining free of human interference for ages may not be stable. Torrents and winds may sweep organic matter away. Hillsides and hillocks are susceptible of denudation even under natural conditions; hence, in cultivating them great care is needed to form water furrows to prevent washing away the soil on hillsides and declivities. The steeper parts can be put in grass, for "it is useless and very injurious to cultivate grounds, from which the soil must be soon washed away."[120]

Man thus can interfere in two fundamental processes of nature: the cycle of growth and decay when he fails to return humus to the soil, and the normal relation between highland erosion and lowland stream deposition by failing to provide an adequate vegetative cover to control the natural tendency toward the gradual removal of upland soils to the lowlands.

With his perpetual plowing and cropping, his inadequate attention to grass, and his failure even to use the barnyard manure accumulating in his yard, the Pennsylvania farmer is far more destructive than is the Yankee, who does all in his power to increase his livestock, and who clears his woods by burning (waiting, however, until everything is so dry that the fire burns the soil; enough

[118] *Ibid.*, p. 518.
[119] *Ibid.*, p. 333.
[120] *Ibid.*, p. 339.

moisture should be retained in order to keep the fire from penetrating deeply in the soil and destroying too much organic matter).

The Yankee farmer finishes chopping down the already fallen timber and scalps off the grubs level with the ground; he then cuts down all the trees so that they fall regularly side by side. Some log off the timber before, some after, the fire. In any event, the farmer awaits an opportune dry period for the firing. The cleared ground is then worked with a heavy harrow, and the texture thus created favors the processes of vegetation. The salts in the ash and the organic matter that has escaped the flames can also produce very large crops. The Pennsylvania farmer is careless of the humus and manuring; the Yankee, of fire. Like others witnessing the extension of settlement and cultivation, Lorain saw the contrast between the patient accumulations of slowly acting nature and the dramatic changes which man could make in days or even in hours. "Perhaps a better method could not be devised for clearing woodlands, or a more profitable first course of crops be introduced, if it were not that by far the greater part of the animal and vegetable matter which nature had been accumulating for a great length of time, is destroyed in a day or two, by the destructive and truly inconsiderate and savage practice of burning." The ruin is compounded when the two methods are joined: Yankee burning with Pennsylvania continual cropping.[121] The humus theory of the soils may have been responsible for part of this emphasis, but in the main, the concept of the economy and unity of nature was the matrix from which the warnings came.

In the preceding discussion, I have made no attempt to explore these attitudes as a chapter in American history. A practical and utilitarian attitude toward change, most dramatically by deforestation, seems to have had an early and powerful hold, as in Richard Frame's poem, "A Short Description of Pennsilvania" [1692]:

> Although I have a good intent,
> Yet hardly can express,
> How we, through Mercy, were content
> In such a Wilderness.
> When we began to clear the Land
> For room to sow our Seed
> And that our Corn might grow and stand,
> For Food in time of Need,
> Then with the Ax, with Might and Strength,
> The trees so thick and strong
> Yet on each side such strokes at length,
> We laid them all along.
> So when the Trees, that grew so high
> Were fallen to the ground,
> Which we with Fire, most furiously
> To ashes did Confound.

[121] *Ibid.*, pp. 335–336.

The American examples also illustrate the impact of clearing, the dramatic contrasts between supposedly pristine and altered lands, and between the long time processes of nature and the short ones of man. Jared Eliot, John Bartram, John Lorain, and others saw evidences of destructive interferences in biological processes apparent in soil erosion and exhaustion, overcropping, burning, and deforestation. What they feared, I think, was that European man in the New World was failing to understand the organic cycle in nature, from life to death and from decay to life, and its importance to human welfare.[122]


11. THE TORRENTS OF THE VAR


Let us return to the Old World to examine a question that interested an eighteenth century French engineer, Jean Antoine Fabre. It is an upland-lowland problem, and man is in the center of it. Fabre's work begins a new chapter in Western natural science and engineering whose nineteenth and twentieth century practitioners will study torrents carefully and publish on them voluminously.[123] Fabre was chief engineer of bridges and highways in

[122] The following works are valuable guides into the complex history of American attitudes toward nature: Arthur A. Ekirch, *Man and Nature in America*; Hans Huth, *Nature and the American*; Leo Marx, *The Machine in the Garden; Technology and the Pastoral Ideal in America*; and John K. Wright, *Human Nature in Geography*, especially chap. 14, "Notes on Early American Geopiety." See the works of Gerbi, Chinard, and McDonald already cited for early American attitudes to nature in general, and to the forests, the soil, to humus, etc. Frame's poem (quoted in part by Huth, p. 5) is in Albert Cook Myers, ed., *Narratives of Early Pennsylvania, West New Jersey and Delaware 1603–1707*, pp. 301–305. See also the papers of Ralph Brown, published posthumously in *AAAG*, Vol. 41 (1951), pp. 188–236: "A Letter to the Reverend Jedidiah Morse Author of the American Universal Geography," pp. 188–198; "The Land and the Sea: Their Larger Traits," pp. 199–216; "The Seaboard Climate in the View of 1800," pp. 217–232; and "A Plea for Geography, 1813 Style," pp. 233–236. In the third essay, Brown discusses several writers that I have mentioned and gives more examples; see esp. the discussion of climatic change, pp. 227–230. I do not agree, however, with his statement that "Volney evaded the question [that the climate was changing] altogether" (p. 227). See note 105 above.

Josephine Herbst, *New Green World* (New York, 1954), on John Bartram and the early naturalists, shows the importance of scientific traveling, plant collecting and introductions, and attitudes toward nature of the early American naturalists; Jefferson's writings also illustrate this contemporary interest in environmental change. See Saul K. Padover, ed., *The Complete Jefferson*: "To the Miamis, Powtewatamies, and Weeauks," on the advantages of cultivation, raising animals, and of the civilized arts, p. 459; "To Brother Handsome Lake," on a similar theme, p. 461; "To the Choctaw Nation," on the advantages of cultivation over hunting, p. 465; "To the Chiefs of the Cherokee Nation," on a similar subject, pp. 478–479; "To Little Turtle, Chief of the Miamis," pp. 497–498; "To Captain Hendrick, the Delawares, Mohiccons, and Munries," pp. 502–503. See also his comments in "Notes on the State of Virginia," Query 7, on winds and clearing, pp. 619–620. In his intro. to the Carman and Tugwell ed. of Jared Eliot's *Essays upon Field Husbandry in New England and Other Papers, 1748–1762*, Rodney True discusses Eliot and the modifications which Americans made of English soil and agricultural theory of Tull, Townshend, and others.

[123] Surell, *A Study of the Torrents in the Department of the Upper Alps*, 2nd ed., Vol. 1, trans. Augustine Gibney. To my knowledge this trans. has not been published; a carbon

the Département du Var; his studies of torrents and their control, published in 1797, were based on areas of France, the departments of the Var, Basses-Alpes, and Bouches-du-Rhone, in which he had worked and which he knew well. He had also studied the courses of the Rhône and the Durance.

Alexander Surell, one of the most remarkable nineteenth century students of the High Alpine torrents of France, was critical of his work, but it was a kindly criticism that understood the pioneer nature of Fabre's contribution. Surell thought Fabre's observations, stated virtually as aphorisms, detracted from their scientific value, and he chided him with giving too much space to reasoning without giving evidence in support of his deductions, so that it became difficult to distinguish between his observations and surmises, the certain and the doubtful. Curiously, Fabre had criticized his predecessors for the same faults.

Fabre's short studies are symbolic of new inquiries into old practices, into the relation between mountain and plain, and into the effect of stream flow on settlement. Such researches were greatly expanded in the nineteenth century, as studies of man's modifications of the environment, divorced from idealism, meliorism, philosophy, and religious considerations were made with reference to cultural and economic policy, but on a far higher plane than a purely engineering outlook. Fabre was certainly an imaginative pioneer in this new trend. His pages are notable for a sense of time and history (earth history and human history), and a skepticism which makes him critical of theory.

Environmental change owing to natural causes, Fabre says, is characteristic of the earth's history since the creation. Rain, storms, avalanches, freezing and thawing, clearly make such changes, their cumulative effects being greatest at the present, decreasing as one goes backward in time to the creation. Then mountain slopes were stable, appearing quite different than they do at present, for they were not degraded nor were massifs separated from one another by valleys. The causes producing the effects now observable on the landscape have been operative since the creation, and in a great number of places existing slopes are so steep that the mountains are no longer stable.[124]

Although the waters of the earth and of streams have reduced and dissected these primitive massifs, they are neither the sole nor the principle cause of tearing down the mountains. Fabre thinks that alternating freezing and thawing cause these steep precipices on the flanks of mountains (perhaps he is referring to the Matterhorn type of glacial landforms) as well as the avalanches which follow in their wake. Degradation results usually from gullies, the

---

copy of it is in the Forestry Library of the University of California at Berkeley. The fact that earlier technical French works are hard to come by in this country makes John Croumbie Brown's studies especially important; in his *Reboisement in France* are generous excerpts from many eighteenth and nineteenth century French students of torrents including Fabre and Surell.

[124] *Essai*, pp. 5–6.

frightful ravines so often torn out of the sides of mountains. Powerful avalanches can take rocks and boulders with them down the slope, but snow is
not necessary to reduce the mountains; freezing and thawing are sufficient to
accomplish their wearing away. Avalanches make soils extremely friable,
and they even crack and weaken stones. To Fabre, who wrote before glaciation was understood, the history of the earth is marked by constant change—
by dissection, heating and cooling of rock, avalanches from melting snow,
and deposition of alluvium at the mouths of rivers.[125] A man with such a vivid
conception of the operation of natural processes in transforming the earth's
surface throughout time would also be sensitive, I think, to the acts of man
or other geologic agents which might accelerate the processes, or which
might keep them at their present rate, taking measures to control them if
they are harmful.

It is the study of the torrent which unifies Fabre's work. The best lands in
the mountains, he observes, lie along streams; they are exposed to floods which
become more severe with deforestation because rainwater collects in a much
shorter time and the water of rivers rises much more rapidly. The fertile banks
are thus eroded away, the bed is enlarged and elevated as a result of the deposition of its load. The damage is not confined to mountains; the disharmony is
apparent in the building up of the banks of rivers, in deposition along the
Mediterranean, the shallow river mouths inhibiting navigation. Torrent control at the source will bring about better agriculture, preserve the fine stream-
deposited soil particles (limon), enhance the opportunities for irrigation.[126]

Fabre's explanation for the slight progress made so far in torrent control is
of considerable interest. Many authors have tried to express mathematically
the laws governing stream flow, but this general theory cannot be applied
to these rivers because of the infinite variety of conditions. One must study
the actual course of the river. Furthermore, students of the subject have
lacked a point of view; observations have been desultory and often have
been made out of pure curiosity.

The fundamental cause of torrents, according to Fabre, is the destruction
of the mountain woods. Foliage and branches intercept a considerable part
of the rain, while the rest of the water, falling drop by drop and at sufficiently
long intervals, filters into the soil. Vegetable earth, gradually accumulating in
undisturbed conditions, absorbs a considerable quantity, and shrubbery may
bar the way, controlling at their source torrents which may have formed
despite all these other obstacles. When the woods are destroyed, water from
gentle rain or from storms cannot be absorbed into the earth as fast as it
accumulates, and no shrubbery breaks up and divides the torrent's course.

Clearings on the mountains loosen the soil, diminish the cohesiveness of
the earth materials of which the mountain is formed, thus encouraging the
formation of torrents. The law of the *ancien régime*, which permitted clear-

[125] *Ibid.*, pp. 9–10.
[126] *Ibid.*, p. vii.

ing on slopes if sustaining walls were constructed at intervals on the slopes, was futile in a great number of areas because people planted two or three crops and then abandoned the land; they could not make enough from their crops to pay for the walls.

Fabre lists (unfortunately without elaboration) seven kinds of disasters that ensue from these two causes: (1) The forest is ruined. (2) Vegetable earth in many mountainous areas, earths which formerly provided abundant sheep pasture, are washed away, leaving denuded and dry rocks. (3) Properties along river banks are ruined. The character of holdings at the foot of mountains has also been changed by deposits of the torrents. (4) Damage to downstream and river-mouth navigation, formerly an infrequent occurrence, results from the division of watercourses owing to torrents. (5) Strife and quarreling occur on both banks of a stream; when it had only one bed it formed a permanent boundary. (6) A much more rapid deposition of alluvium than formerly at river mouths such as the Rhone impedes navigation. (7) The waters of the springs which feed the rivers are diminished in volume. Water no longer infiltrates the soil, and there is only surface flow off the mountains despoiled of their vegetable earth. If the springs diminish, the streams too will lose volume. Fabre seems to be comparing stream flow under natural conditions with a less stable regime characterized by torrential flow during heavy rains, followed by diminished volume, the instability being consequent upon deforestation and clearing.

Fabre's remedies are technical ones, and we need not discuss them here, but we should mention the assumption upon which the proposals are based. In essence, Fabre advocates the restoration of natural conditions in the mountains, allowing trees to grow where enough vegetable earth still remains. Restoration can be promoted by protecting young trees and with strict enforcement of goat laws. These measures may be supplemented by the conservation of existing woods.

Equally strict measures should be adopted regarding clearings; none should ever be permitted, for any reason, on a slope of one in three. The old law was too tolerant of such excesses. Clearings on lands of less declivity should also be strictly controlled. If they are allowed, they should be made in transverse horizontal strips, with intervening uncultivated strips (about five toises —about thirty-two feet—wide) for woods to grow in. These belts should be used in lieu of the sustaining walls; they would permit the destruction of torrents which may have been forming above. Fabre advocates strict legal supervision by the communes of all clearings. Since nature is more active when aided by human industry, acorns, beechnuts, or the seeds of other trees could be sown on the steep slopes, areas lacking sufficient soil for trees could be put in grass, and the turf would resist the formation of torrents and create useful pasture as well.[127]

---

[127] *Ibid.*, pp. 131–134.

This far-sighted French engineer saw the widespread effects of age-old practices in the mountains on social and economic conditions in southern Provence. He saw that man must understand his power to create conditions favorable to the movement of things, whether they are soil particles or rocks. By simulating through restoration the natural conditions which formerly prevailed, he can control the speed of water, its volume, its absorption into the earth, its runoff. Man can imitate natural processes by the mass planting of trees on hillsides, but in permitting the washing away of the vegetable earths, he can make these processes irreversible.[128] Social conditions including ancient custom are thus directly related to physical processes: anticipating a theme stressed by Marsh in 1864, the notion of the irreversibility of certain kinds of environmental change is introduced, a far more pessimistic idea than a simple warning about damage to a single holder or to a commune.

## 12.　The Society Islands: A Union of Nature and Art

Areas that are different, both culturally and physically, naturally offer different examples. County Volney in Kentucky sees different effects than does Fabre in the Alpine lands of Provence. Let us find a last illustration from another New World, Oceania, which Cook and the Forsters described. Both Forsters notice changes which man makes in the natural environment, for they are interested in science, in society, and in nature. Neither of the Forsters admires environments, whether inhabited by Tahitians or Europeans, which are unchanged by human culture. In both cases the influence of Buffon is clear and acknowledged.[129] Johann Reinhold Forster says that the changes made by man are not the least of those which the earth has undergone. Where man has not attempted any change, nature seems to thrive; but this impression is only an appearance, for it languishes and "is deformed by being left to itself." Such observations are inspired by Buffon: Decaying and rotting trees accumulate, the ground cover is thick, mosses, lichens, and mushrooms suffocate and bury all that vegetates and thrives. Stagnant waters and swamps make the surroundings unhealthful. But man eradicates plants which are useless to him and to the useful animals; he opens up passages "for himself and his assistants" through the woods and luxuriant vegetation; he preserves and cultivates the useful plants; he keeps noxious effluvia from the air and channels the swampy waters. By drying out the earth he promotes husbandry and then, where needed, he can irrigate. The emphasis thus is on the role of man in increasing the beauty of the earth and its usefulness to him. The significant acts are the opening up of nature, so to speak, by making passageways, by increasing air circulation, by encouraging the evaporation of surplus

[128] Selections from Fabre's work are published in trans. in Brown, *Reboisement in France*, pp. 55–59.
[129] *Obs.*, pp. 135–137; G.F., "Ein Blick in das Ganze der Natur," *Sämmtliche Schriften*, Vol. 4, pp. 316–325.

water. New Zealand and Tahiti illustrate the contrasts Forster is making. In Tahiti the breadfruit, the apple, the mulberry, and beautiful gardens have in part replaced the native vegetation. The beauty of the Society Islands is an expression of the union of nature and art. The plains are inhabited and cultivated like gardens, with planted beds of grass, with fruit trees and dwellings, while the sides of some hills are wooded and the highest summits are covered with forests. This is the kind of primitive life and environment which both Forsters admire—a life based on cultivation of plants and on improvement of the beauty of natural surroundings. The reason for this praise of cultivation and plant growing is that the Forsters consider them to be pathways to civilization, encouraging it more than do pastoralism and a dependence on animals.[130]

In their general and all-encompassing views of nature, both Forsters follow Buffon. In his essay, "Ein Blick in das Ganze der Natur," Forster says, "An Büffons Hand sei uns denn heute ein Blick ins Heiligthum vergönnt! Dann erst empfinden wir die Würde unserer Wissenschaft, wenn der ganze Reichthum der Natur und ihres grössern Schöpfers sich unserm innern Sinne majestätisch entfaltet!"[131] He paraphrases and even directly translates several passages from Buffon.[132] As it is with Buffon, too, appreciation for the beauty of nature is combined with a realization of its usefulness. And the sea, like the land, is not dead or infertile; it is a new kingdom (*ein neues Reich*) as productive and as populous as the land. Man, the highest being in the creation, should come to the help of nature, for beauty and perfection of the whole are its general end. Since, unassisted, the earth is burdened with the ruins of its own production, Forster, like Buffon, sees man opening and clearing it, drying up its stagnant waters and swamps.

In his essay on the breadfruit tree, one of the most interesting of George Forster's writings, he says that man is probably responsible for the distribution of this plant, that it is not found in uncultivated places. In his migrations, man seems to have carried it with him and spread it throughout the South Seas from the Asian mainland. In a striking paragraph, Forster speaks of the incomparable richness of life in the island groups, particularly Java and Sumatra, of the western Pacific near the Asian shore where the breadfruit is also found. The general area, he thinks, is a kind of hearth of plants, listing many valuable products which have come from it. He notes improvements made in the plant by artificial selection, and there are interesting paragraphs on its manifold uses; until the work of Rumpf, he says, the virtues of this tree, a "modest beauty" (*eine sittsame Schöne*), were unsuspected in the outside world long after the discoveries in the Pacific.[133]

George Forster also showed considerable interest in the contrast between

---

[130] *Obs.*, pp. 135–137, 161–163, 177–178.
[131] "Ein Blick in das Ganze der Natur," *SS*, Vol. 4, p. 310.
[132] See for example "De la Nature. Première Vue," *HN*, Vol. 12, p. xiii, and "Ein Blick in das Ganze der Natur," *SS*, Vol. 4, pp. 324–326.
[133] "Der Brothbaum," *SS*, Vol. 4, pp. 329, 332–341.

inhabited and uninhabited lands. In a charming passage describing activities at Dusky Bay, on the southwest coast of South Island, New Zealand, he describes an apparently primeval forest, its climbing plants, shrubs, and rotten trees being perpetually succeeded by new generations of trees, by parasitic plants, ferns, and mosses from the rich mold derived from the rotten timber. The animal creation afforded further proof of a primeval environment untouched by man, and numbers of unsuspecting birds "familiarly hopped upon the nearest branches, nay on the ends of our fowling pieces." (Soon they were more cautious, made so by a sly cat on board.)[134] At Dusky Bay within a few days the superiority of civilization over barbarism was quickly demonstrated. "In the course of a few days, a small part of us had cleared away the woods from a surface of more than an acre, which fifty New Zealanders, with their tools of stone, could not have performed in three months." A confused, in-animated heap of living plants and decayed residues was converted "into an active scene." Trees were felled, a better passage was made for the rivulet to wind to the sea, the men prepared casks, brewed a drink from the indigenous plants, and they fished. Caulkers and riggers worked on the sides of the boat and the masts. The noise of the anvil and hammer resounded on the hills. An artist, in his sketches, imitated the animal and the vegetable creation. A small observatory with the most accurate instruments was set up, while the plants and animals attracted the notice of philosophers. "In a word, all around us we perceived the rise of arts, and the dawn of science, in a country which had hitherto lain plunged in one long night of ignorance and barbarism!" Then, as quickly as it was created, it vanished like a meteor as the men reimbarked and left the bay.[135]

But in this passage Forster is not talking about the peoples of the Society Islands but about the primitive New Zealanders. He sees no cleavage between civilized societies and the more simple ones, as Buffon did, in seconding the hand of nature. The Tahitians, too, are capable of creating new beauty in the landscape, in joining art with nature.


13.  CONCLUSION

By the end of the eighteenth century, the cumulative observations and insights of many generations had placed the idea of man as a modifier of nature in new perspective; it was still, however, too diffuse, too casually handled, except by Buffon, to attain the philosophic importance it deserved. Such recognition was not achieved until later in the nineteenth century in the writings of Marsh, Shaler, Reclus, Woeikof, and many others. The conviction that earth history had been more complex than the creation, the deluge, and the retirement of the waters, that the changes the earth has undergone

---

[134] *VRW*, Vol. 1, pp. 127–128.
[135] *VRW*, Vol. 1, pp. 177–178, 179.

since the creation are the results of natural processes (notably in Fabre), that its history may be divided into epochs, suggested that man had also contributed to earth history. This conception of man as a geographical agent in a historical continuum along with other historical agents of change was the message of Buffon, who also saw the great historic significance of domestication. The idea that man creates in the domesticated animals secondary agents of change subservient to him, that he makes massive substitutions of life forms (also well developed by Buffon), transforms conceptions concerning the nature of landscapes dominated by man.

The study and observations of uninhabited environments, or those sparsely inhabited by primitive peoples thought to be existing in ageless harmony and equilibrium owing to the interplay of natural forces, dramatized the role of man as an outsider intervening in a primordial balance of nature. The contrasts between the New World and the Old did not engender this idea, but they were powerful schoolmasters. John Lorain is an excellent example, but there are many others who see man as an accelerator of natural processes, as an interloper substituting his choices in a world which already has been well and judiciously furnished by the Creator. The apparent timelessness and permanence of nature is illusory as time-conscious man destroys or makes changes in nature in a matter of hours or days.

Buffon's ideas were not lost on George Forster, and Forster's were not lost on Humboldt. Fabre's torrents led to other and more searching Alpine adventures. Their works and those of many others whom I have mentioned or neglected to mention became building blocks for Marsh's great synthesis *Man and Nature* in 1864, whose pages on the significance of human changes of the environment were nourished on activities with which men had long been familiar: drainage, clearing, irrigation, canal building, firing, plant introductions, domestications. The great transformations of the earth's surface which were now to come through the Industrial Revolution, as we can divine in the pages of Buffon and Malthus, can now barely be seen on the horizon.

But the Industrial Revolution—how unfortunate this term is—does not displace these older forms of environmental change; it supplements them. The shepherd and goatherd are still in Cyprus, the charcoal burner is in the Ardennes, the tree girdler in New England, but it will not be long before men will look on the vistas of the new Lièges, the Manchesters, the Düsseldorfs.

With the eighteenth century there ends in Western civilization an epoch in the history of man's relationship to nature. What follows is of an entirely different order, influenced by the theory of evolution, specialization in the attainment of knowledge, acceleration in the transformations of nature.

# Conclusion

A historian of ideas throws his own pebbles into the water, and the concentric ripples he creates naturally are different from those of another. If the pebbles are thrown close enough together, the ripples visibly interfere with one another; if far enough apart, the interferences may not be discernible. So one person's pebble might be another's ripple, the choice of what is to be discussed deciding what is central and what is peripheral. If instead of the idea of a designed earth, I had chosen the idea of an artisan-deity; instead of environmental influence, the idea of culture; instead of environmental change, the idea of technology, what now are the stones would have become the ripples.

And so I thought in summary it might be worthwhile to say a few words about each of these ideas, the wider fields of which they are a part, and how they often confronted or interfered with one another despite divergent historical backgrounds, and to follow the discussions with some observations about certain periods of unusual significance in the history of these ideas. In their development, in the changes and accretions coming about through time and circumstance, in their application at different times and places to different situations, they neither completely lost their original identity nor did they retain it. This process is typical of the history of an idea; it is like the history of a culture, which changes and innovates, accepting this, rejecting that, abandoning something as useless or obsolescent, retaining something held dear, each new synthesis preparing its own opportunities for further change, retention, or innovation.

The idea of a designed earth, the doctrine of final causes applied to the natural processes on earth, is an important segment—but only that—of a much broader and deeper body of thought suffused throughout all types of writings: science, philosophy, theology, literature. This is the idea of teleology in general. One cannot deny, however, its immense historical force in the field of nature and earth study, nor the reinforcements to the broader area of teleological explanation coming from its use here. The idea of a designed earth, whether created for man or for all life with man at the apex of a chain of being, has been one of the great attempts in Western civilization, before the theory of evolution and modern ecological theories emerging from it, to create a holistic concept of nature, to bring within its scope as many phenomena as possible in order to demonstrate a unity which was the achievement of an artisan-creator. It is a doctrine at home with the religious interpretation of nature, with pre-evolutionary thought which was congenial to the belief in special creation and the fixity of species. (Evolution, admittedly, could be and has been interpreted as part of a design.) The combination of special creation and fixity of species meant the existence of harmonies in nature from the beginning. It is a mistake, however, to speak of the design argument without including the criticism it evoked, in the ancient world centering mainly around the Epicurean philosophy, in the seventeenth and eighteenth centuries by such thinkers as Spinoza, Buffon, Hume, and Kant. Protagonists of both sides contributed to the idea of a unity in nature because it was not the order that was in dispute but the nature of it, the validity of the artisan analogy, and the relation of this order to the creative activity of a deity. As this idea developed through the centuries, it drew sustenance from many different sources; obviously it has affinities with the literature on nature. With exaltation at the beauty of nature comes wonderment as well, and the belief that man comes closer to the heartbeats of the creation when he is alone in primordial harmonies, away from other men and their artifacts, because unlike the haunts of men these are sacred precincts. It is self-evident that these need not be religious ideas but many of them are. In natural history the design argument was favorable to the study of associations of things and their interrelationships rather than to taxonomies. Of necessity there was the conception of an interlocking in nature—much of it was crude, unnecessarily anthropocentric, too full of the spirit of wonderment rather than inquiry—and yet the effect was to see man and nature as a whole, to see life on earth in all its manifestations as a great living mosaic sustained by inanimate nature. Much has been learned since the end of the eighteenth century in the study of nature based on evolutionary theory, genetics, ecological theory; but it is no accident that ecological theory —which is the basis of so much research in the study of plant and animal populations, conservation, preservation of nature, wildlife and land use management, and which has become the basic concept for a holistic view of nature —has behind it the long preoccupation in Western civilization with interpreting the nature of earthly environments, trying to see them as wholes, as manifestations of order.

It is easy to see also why the phrase "man's place in nature" has in recurrent forms been one of the great themes of our period—indeed it has continued to the present, as so much of the literature on modifications of the environment and nature protection proves. Man is of nature, a part of it, yet there is good reason for the age-old dichotomy. Why is there? It is too simple to put it down to a narrow preoccupation with man. Few of the men whose writings we have reviewed could be accused of this. It is, I think, because early in this period (it is already relatively late in the history of thought if we bear in mind that the "Theology of Memphis" dates from about 2500 B.C.) the fundamental cleavage of human from other forms of life was recognized. It was recognized by Sophocles, in the Genesis verses, by Panaetius, by Philo the Jew as he marveled at the ability of unimpressive men to force beasts far larger and stronger than they to obey them. Skill, combining the powers of hand and brain, was an obvious human attribute. The countless examples in the ancient world alone of the long tradition of artisanry, of the accumulation from generation to generation of skills, of lore, of knowledge, influenced the men who were trying to see the human world existing in the natural one. Furthermore, the dichotomy was tied up with the question of purpose and meaning in the creation. I know of no more dramatic contrast illustrating this fact than that cited in the first chapter, the contrast between Balbus the Stoic and Lucretius the Epicurean. The Stoic sees the beauties of the earth about him and concludes that such an astonishingly wonderful creation could not be for the sake of plants that lack intelligence or for the dumb animals; it could only be for the sake of a being like man who partakes of the divine and the gods themselves. The Lucretian-Epicurean position on this was unflattering to both the nature of man and the nature of the earth: how is it possible to conceive of a world made for man when so many are wicked and stupid, so few good and wise, when the physical constitution of the earth is so obviously imperfect? In such a philosophy, lacking a benevolent Mother Nature, man achieves his place in nature, not by sharing the attributes of a divine artisan, but by imitation of natural processes and learning from them or by working hard to supply his needs on the principle that necessity is the mother of invention. Christian thought is saturated with the idea, too, because so much Judeo-

Christian theology has been concerned with the creator and the creature and because man, sinful and wicked as he is, is a special creature of God. In no other body of thought have the ramifications and implications of man's place in nature been discussed with more thoroughness than in the literature on design and teleology in nature.

Since the design argument applied to the earth was an all-encompassing attempt to bring a unity into the observed phenomena—nonliving matter, plants, animals, and man—it is only natural that it involved the other two ideas, but they, as we have seen, also enjoyed an independent existence and history of their own.

The idea of environmental influences on culture is as important historically for the questions it suggested as for its own intellectual and philosophical content. It is part of that broad and ancient contrast between *physis* and *nomos*, between nature and law or custom. It is an idea deeply involved with interpreting the endlessly fascinating array of human differences, rich new materials for which were furnished in the ancient world during the Hellenistic period, in the modern by the age of discovery. It probably grew out of medicine; travel and voyaging have both helped it along, for men apparently lived everywhere—in deserts, on hot sandy coasts, near swamps, in mountains—and brought it into disfavor as examples appeared which contradicted it. If one is inclined to emphasize its monistic nature, the attempt to explain all culture as a product of environment, one should also remember that it had a relativist side which came out clearly after the Reformation when climatic factors were thought to be active in determining religious observances if not fundamental doctrine. The important point in its impingement on ethical and religious theory was the implication that people living under a certain environment could be expected to act as they did, the environment rather than human frailty being responsible for shortcomings. Thus climate was a favorite explanation for inebriety or sobriety of whole peoples. Nomos, however, was never completely forgotten. Men's customs, their governments, their religions, were great cultural molding forces. These truths were seen in the Hippocratic writings; they were seen with greatest clarity, during our period, in the eighteenth century. Theories of environmental influence are compatible with design arguments because adaptation of life to environment is assumed in both cases; both provided answers to the question why men were living where they were, how they prospered, why and how they lived in inhospitable and bleak environments. In the modern period, continuing a trend noticeable in the ancient world and culminating in Hume's essay, theories of environmental influence have had strong affiliations with writings on national character; more often than not they have encouraged monolithic summation: the Germans, the French, the Arabs, could be characterized in a few sentences. On the other hand, they were safeguards—albeit negative ones—against a purely cultural determinism. Surely it is a mistake to think the history of civilization can be written purely as cultural, social, or economic history; it is significant that during the period discussed the most impressive works in this field were written in the eighteenth century and that the outstanding example, Herder's *Outlines of a Philosophy of the History of Man*, makes full use of the historical, ethnographic, and geographic knowledge then available.

In the eighteenth century, the writings of Montesquieu, Wallace, Hume, and particularly Malthus bring to maturity and influence a different kind of environmental theory, emphasizing not the elements of climate or the physical differences in environment but the limitations which the environment as a whole imposes on all life. This idea in varying forms has produced some of the most polemical writing of the last century and a half.

The idea of design in nature really focused attention on God as artisan, man and nature being in the subordinate position as the created. The idea of environmental influence centered on nature; if it were expressed within a religious context, God was there as creator and man was largely plastic in the molds of nature. The idea of man as a modifier of nature, however, centered on man; if the idea is expressed in a religious context, God often becomes an artisan purposefully leaving the creation unfinished; nature is there to be improved by human skill. In many ways it is the most interesting of the three ideas because it assumes choices; different results come from different skills. Its sources lie, I think, in ideas of artisanry and order-bringing, and when man's activity is seen within a religious framework, he becomes a finisher of nature, set on earth as its guardian and custodian. One of the most distinctive aspects of this idea is the fundamental distinction, often implicit, between the nature of human and animal art. It was not that animals or lowly insects lacked skills—we need only read the homilies on the ants and bees and the eager moralizing in them. In the ancient world, the distinction was implied in the combined power of hand and mind. In the modern, the quarrel between the ancients and the moderns, and the development of the idea of progress throw light on the nature of the human endowment: it is greater because what is known in one generation may be communicated to the next, and an accumulation of skills, knowledge, artisanry, may take place, and over a period of time broaden the gulf between human and animal skill. In secular thought, the idea in general has optimistic overtones, especially with men like Ray and Buffon (despite some sour notes). The pessimism comes later in the nineteenth century with more frequent communication of ideas, knowledge of the historical depth of the changes, and observation of the unprecedented pace of the changes consequent upon the increase in technological ability and the growth in world population. The historical march of this idea has been from local to more general observation and generalization. At the present day it is all-pervasive, a natural and expected outcome of the tremendous force of human agency.

In the long time-span covered by this work, certain periods stand out when intensifications of thought clustered about one or more of these ideas. In the ancient world I would single out the Hellenistic period for special emphasis.

It is true that the sources of these ideas go far back in time, but they begin to take on life and shape in the Hellenistic age and the Hellenized Roman period that followed. So, for example, there are Chrysippus, Panaetius, and Posidonius; Epicurus and Lucretius; Polybius and Strabo; Eratosthenes, Theophrastus, and Theocritus, to say nothing of the writers of a later period, such as Virgil, Horace, Tibullus, Varro, and even Columella and Plutarch. A philosophy of resource development seems to go hand in hand with the economic and political aspirations of the Hellenistic monarchs. It is hard to forget those Greeks in foreign lands, impatient for their olives, their wine, their wool, their fruits and vegetables, and the kind of experimentation this impatience in part brought about and the changes in the appearance of the land it caused. The confrontation of Epicureanism with Stoicism, especially in Cicero's *De natura deorum* and Lucretius' poems, broadened the idea of design and deepened the criticisms of it. Both had the idea of a unity in nature, to both came more evidence from the world of nature and of man. Communication over the Hellenistic world by a common language—New Testament Greek is written in it—and encouragement by the Seleucids and the Ptolemies, especially, to maintain the customs of native cultures engendered, I believe (one cannot prove this), a more self-conscious awareness of cultural differences than had existed before. If the geographical and ethnological writings of Posidonius had survived in whole rather than in garbled fragments in the works of others, one might see this.

The second is the early Christian period centering on the writings of such men as Basil the Great and St. Ambrose and reaching a climax in St. Augustine, although one can see the preparations in Tertullian and Origen. Part of these are homiletics, part are polemics, part are apologetics. From Origen's *Contra Celsum* to St. Augustine's *City of God* what stands out is the need for the new religion to defend itself. In its early beginnings, the literature reaches back into still essentially Hellenistic Alexandria which in Gilson's words had been "for a long time a sort of clearing house for the religions of the Roman Empire." There was a meeting of ideas from different sources in the writings of Basil, Ambrose, and St. Augustine, and ideas of nature, nature appreciation (not always but in the vast majority of cases for religious reasons), conceptions of the creator and the created, came from the various matrixes of religious feeling and belief, natural history, ancient philosophy and science. Viewed in this light St. Augustine's writings are most important syntheses and collations as well, bringing together not only Christian ideas but Hellenic, Hellenistic, and Roman ideas of nature and religious interpretations of it, granting, as we must, the contradictions and the difficulties in exploring that intractable subject, the Christian view of nature, once one has advanced beyond the first easy assertions. The design argument in Christian form and applied to nature observable on earth is filled out in this period; and one can recognize the continuity from the homilies of Basil the Great to Ray's *Wisdom of God*, both exceptional works in their genre. This period was strong in exegesis, preeminent in examining the idea of creation. The theme of the creator and the created dominated the design argument from this period to the natural theology of the eighteenth century, which could make use of recent scientific discovery.

Both the Hellenistic and the early Christian periods, therefore, were notable for an interest in nature and natural history. In the former period, it was manifest in both Stoic religious belief and in the antireligious philosophy of Epicurus as expressed by Lucretius. In the latter, it is strong in St. Basil and in St. Augustine; St. Ambrose, his teacher, is inspired by the nature imagery of Virgil even though it is transformed into religious symbolism.

In the twelfth and thirteenth centuries there was another such period, and the most important contributions to the three ideas made during the Middle Ages come from it. It is the period of Albert the Great, of Thomas Aquinas, of *The Romance of the Rose*, of naturalistic motifs in religious art. Like the Hellenistic, it was a period of great activity, resource development, building of cathedrals and cities, with opportunities for contrasts and interpretation.

It is not improper for our purposes to think of the Renaissance and the age of discovery, insofar as our ideas are concerned, as compatible partners; one brought news and criticism of the past, the other news from abroad. Both enforced revisions of a fundamental kind. They widened the scope of ideas and knowledge of ancient thought—as witness Alberti's history of architecture—and the age of discovery revealed that both men and the environments in which they live were far more varied than had been realized. Indeed their variety seemed to be inexhaustible. With time the marvelous adaptability of the human race to all kinds of environments was plain for all men to see. This realization, however, does not come to full fruition until the eighteenth century, but it was an important insight in the history of Western thought relating to nature and culture.

The penultimate period is the golden age of natural theology in the late seventeenth and early eighteenth centuries. The religious underpinnings and assumptions are the same as they had always been, but the earth is now seen in ways which suggest more scientific knowledge, leaving behind forever the fantastic, grim, and stark cosmogonies of the past. Profiting from the scientific successes of the age of Newton, the argument as expressed by Ray, Derham, and others becomes a late seventeenth century statement of the case for the fitness of the earthly environment: the earth is suited for life and well organized for it; the conception was achieved partly in the course of rebutting atheism, sometimes vaguely and anoymously identified with modern sympa-thizers of Lucretius—even Descartes did not escape censure here as an abettor of ungodly thoughts—mainly in rebutting the cosmologists beginning with Burnet who saw too clearly for their own good—and other people's, too—man's sins enshrined and ossified, impressed for all to see and for all time in the constitution of the earth's surface.

The last period spans the eighteenth century; here the publication of Montesquieu's *Esprit des Lois* in 1748 and the first volumes of Buffon's *Histoire Naturelle*, beginning in 1749, are the landmarks. Only a few sentences need be added to what has already been said of it. The thinkers of this period garnered much from the past; they added much of their own. Their contribu-tions were only possible because of the increased knowledge of the world's peoples and the earth's environments—Buffon's *Variétés de l'Espèce Humaine* and *Théorie de la Terre* are examples—that had been accumulating since the age of discovery. It was not only increased knowledge of primitive peoples, of the Indian, Muslim, or Chinese and the places in which they lived. Euro-peans knew more about their own history, customs, and lands, too; one can see this truth already in Bodin.

The ideas of the eighteenth century with which this work is brought to a close were generated in a preindustrial world; it may even be permissible to call it also a traditional society if we do not imply that such a society does not change. One might regard them as an introductory chapter to a work which continues the history to the present, but I prefer not to think of them as pre-ludes (the term to me implies that their worth lies in their introducing some-thing better that follows) but as a closing, once and for all, of a period in the history of Western civilization. The ideas generated by growing indus-trialization of the Western world, the theories about the origin and evolution of life and of human culture, the growing specialization of knowledge that come with the nineteenth century and continue on to the present, are more appropriately cast in the role of preludes.

The design argument explaining the nature of earthly environment really looked upward to the creativity and activity of God; the idea of environmental influence, to the force and strength of natural conditions; the idea of man as a modifier of nature, to the creativity and activity of man. In exploring the history of these ideas from the fifth century B.C. to the end of the eighteenth century, it is a striking fact that virtually every great thinker who lived within this 2300-year period had something to say about one of the ideas, and many had something to say about all of them.

# Bibliography

Ackerknecht, Erwin H. "George Forster, Alexander von Humboldt, and Ethnology," *Isis*, Vol. 46 (1955), pp. 83–95.

Acosta, José de. *Historia Natural y Moral de las Indias* (Sevilla: Casa de Juan de León, 1590; reprinted Madrid: Ramón Anglés, 1894). 2 vols.

Acosta, José de. *The Natural and Moral History of the Indies*. Trans. from the Spanish by Edward Grimston, ed., with notes and intro. by Clements R. Markham (London: Printed for the Hakluyt Society, 1880).

Adam of Bremen. *History of the Archbishops of Hamburg-Bremen*. Trans. from the Latin with intro. and notes by Francis J. Tschan (New York: Columbia University Press, 1959).

Adams, Frank D. *The Birth and Development of the Geological Sciences* (New York: Dover Publications, 1954 [1938]).

Adams, John. *The Works of John Adams* (Boston: Little, Brown, and Co., 1852–1865). 6 vols.

Adelard of Bath. "Die Quaestiones naturales des Adelardus von Bath," ed. Martin Miller, *Beiträge zur Geschichte der Philosophie und Theologie des Mittelalters*, Bd. 31, Heft 2, 1934.

Aeschylus. *The Choephori*. Text, intro., comm., trans. into English by A. W. Verrall (London and New York: Macmillan & Co., 1893).

Agricola, Georgius. *De re metallica*. Trans. from the first Latin ed. of 1556 by Herbert C. Hoover and Lou H. Hoover (New York: Dover Publications, 1950 [1912]).

Alan of Lille (Alanus de Insulis). "Opera omnia," *PL*, Vol. 210.

——. *The Complaint of Nature*. Trans. from the Latin by Douglas M. Moffat, Yale Studies in English, No. 36 (New York: Henry Holt and Co., 1908).

Albert the Great (Albertus Magnus). Beati Alberti Magni, Ratisbonensis Episcopi, Ordinis Praedicatorum, opera quae hactenus haberi potuerunt. . . . Studio et labore R. A. P. F. Petri Jammy. . . . (Lugduni: Sumptibus Claudii Prost, Petri et Claudii Rigaud, Frat., Hieronymi de la Garde, Joan. Ant. Huguetan. Filii. . . . 1651). 21 vols. Cited as *Works*, ed. Jammy.

——. "De animalibus," *Beiträge zur Geschichte der Philosophie des Mittelalters*, ed. Hermann Stadler, Vols. 15–16 (1916).

——. "De causis proprietatum elementorum liber primus," *Works*, ed. Jammy, Vol. 5, pp. 292–329.

——. "De natura locorum," *Works*, ed. Jammy, Vol. 5, pp. 262–292.

——. "De vegetabilibus," *Works*, ed. Jammy, Vol. 5, pp. 342–507.

Alberti, Leon Battista. *Ten Books on Architecture*. Trans. from the Latin into Italian by Cosimo Bartoli and into English by James Leoni. Ed. Joseph Rykwert (London: A Tiranti, 1955; repr. of 1755 ed.).

Alexander Neckam. *Alexandri Neckham de naturis rerum libri duo*. Ed. Thomas Wright (London: Longman, Green, Longman, Roberts, and Green, 1863), being Vol. 34 of *Rerum Britannicarum Medii Aevi Scriptores* = Rolls Series.

Allbutt, T. Clifford. *Greek Medicine in Rome* (London: Macmillan and Co., 1921).

Ambrose, St. "Hexaemeron." Edited with a German trans. by Johann Niederhuber, *BDK*, Vol. 17.

——. "Hexaemeron libri sex," *PL*, Vol. 14, cols. 131–288.

——. *Letters*. Trans. from the Latin by Sister Mary Melchior Beyenka (New York: Fathers of the Church, 1954).

Amilaville, d'. "Population," *Encyclopédie ou Dictionnaire Raisonée des Sciences, des*

*Arts, et des Métiers* (2nd. ed., Lucca: Vincenzo Giuntini, 1758–1771), Vol. 13, pp. 70–84.

Anon. "The So-Called Letter to Diognetus," edited and translated by Eugene R. Fairweather, *The Library of Christian Classics*, Vol. 1, *Early Christian Fathers* (London: SCM Press, 1953), pp. 205–224.

The Ante-Nicene Fathers. *Translations of the Writings of the Fathers Down to A. D. 325.* Eds. the Rev. Alexander Roberts and James Donaldson. American reprint of the Edinburgh ed. rev. by A. Cleaveland Coxe (Buffalo: Christian Literature Publishing Co., 1885–1907). 10 vols.

Anthes, Rudolf. "Mythology in Ancient Egypt," in Samuel Noah Kramer, ed., *Mythologies of the Ancient World*. Anchor Books (Garden City, N. Y.: Doubleday & Company, 1961), pp. 15–92.

Anton, Karl Gottlob. *Geschichte der teutschen Landwirthschaft von den ältesten Zeiten bis zu Ende des fünfzehnten Jahrhunderts.* (Görliz: Christian Gotthelf Anton, 1802). 3 vols.

Apelt, Otto. *Die Ansichten der griechischen Philosophen über den Anfang der Cultur* (Elsenach: Hofbuchdruckerei, 1901).

*The Apocrypha of the Old Testament.* Revised Standard Version (New York, Toronto, Edinburgh: Thomas Nelson & Sons, 1957).

*The Apocrypha. An American Translation by Edgar J. Goodspeed.* Modern Library Paperbacks (New York: Random House, 1959).

Apochrypha. See also *Enoch.*

Apollonius Rhodius. *The Argonautica.* Trans. from the Greek by R. C. Seaton. Loeb Classical Library (Cambridge, Mass.: Harvard University Press; London: Wm. Heinemann, 1955 [1912]).

Arbuthnot, John. *An Essay Concerning the Effects of Air on Human Bodies* (London: Printed for J. and R. Tonson and S. Draper, 1751 [1733]).

Aristotle. *Metaphysics.* Trans. from the Greek by Richard Hope. Ann Arbor Paperbacks (Ann Arbor: University of Michigan Press, 1960 [1952]).

——. "On Length and Shortness of Life." Trans. from the Greek by W. S. Hett, *Aristotle. On the Soul, Parva Naturalia, on Breath.* Loeb Classical Library (London: Wm. Heinemann; Cambridge, Mass.: Harvard University Press, 1935).

——. *Parts of Animals.* Trans. from the Greek by A. L. Peck. Loeb Classical Library (London: Wm. Heinemann; Cambridge, Mass.: Harvard University Press, 1937).

——. *Politica.* Trans. from the Greek by Benjamin Jowett (Rev. ed., Oxford: Clarendon Press, 1946), being Vol. 10 of W. D. Ross, ed., *The Works of Aristotle Translated into English.*

——. *Problems.* Trans. from the Greek by W. S. Hett. Loeb Classical Library (London: Wm. Heinemann; Cambridge, Mass.: Harvard University Press, 1936–1937). 2 vols.

Armstrong, A. H. *Plotinus* (London: George Allen & Unwin, 1953).

Arnaud, François. "Notice historique sur les Torrents de la Vallée de l'Ubaye," in Demontzey, Prosper, *L'Extinction des Torrents en France par le Reboisement* (Paris: Imprimerie Nationale, 1894), Vol. 1, pp. 408–425.

Arndt, Johann. *Vom Wahren Christenthum* (Leipzig: J. S. Heinsius, 1743).

Arnim, Ioannes ab, ed. *Stoicorum veterum fragmenta* (Lipsiae: in aedibus B. G. Teubneri, 1905–1913). 3 vols.

Arnobius of Sicca. *The Case Against the Pagans.* Trans. and annotated by George E. McCracken (Westminster, Maryland: Newman Press, 1949). 2 vols.

Athanasius. "Oratio contra Gentes," *PG*, Vol. 25, cols. 1–95.

Athenaeus. *The Deipnosophists.* Trans. from the Greek by Charles B. Gulick. Loeb Classical Library (London: Wm. Heinemann; New York: G. P. Putnam's Sons, 1927–1957). 7 vols.

Athenagoras. "A Plea Regarding Christians." Edited and translated by Cyril C. Richardson. *The Library of Christian Classics*, Vol. 1, *Early Christian Fathers* (London: SCM Press, 1953), pp. 290–340.

Augustine, St. *The City of God*. Trans. from the Latin by Marcus Dods, George Wilson, Glenluce; and J. J. Smith. Modern Library (New York: Random House, 1950).

——. *Confessions*. Trans. from the Latin by R. S. Pine-Coffin. Penguin Classics (Baltimore: Penguin Books, 1961).

——. "Contra Epistolam Manichaei quam vocant Fundamenti liber unus," *OCSA*, Vol. 25, pp. 431–477.

——. "Contra Faustum Manichaeum libri triginta tres," *OCSA*, Vol. 25–26; *NPN*, Vol. 4.

——. "Contra Julianum," *OCSA*, Vol. 31.

——. "De Genesi ad litteram libri duodecim," *OCSA*, Vol. 7, pp. 40–381.

——. "Epistola 137," *OCSA*, Vol. 5, pp. 160–174.

——. "Epistola 205," *OCSA*, Vol. 6, pp. 108–119.

——. "In Joannis Evangelium," Tractatus 23, *OCSA*, Vol. 9.

——. "In Psalmum 39," *OCSA*, Vol. 12, pp. 261–293.

——. "In Psalmum 44," *OCSA*, Vol. 13, pp. 91–111.

——. "In Psalmum 45," *OCSA*, Vol. 12, pp. 383–398.

——. "In Psalmum 108," 16th Disc. on Psalm 118, *OCSA*, Vol. 14, pp. 585–588.

——. "In Psalmum 136," *OCSA*, Vol. 15, pp. 243–262.

——. *Oeuvres Complètes de Saint Augustin*. French and Latin text. Trans. into French and annotated by Péronne, Vincent, Écalle, Charpentier, and Barreau (Paris: Librairie de Louis Vivès, 1872–1878). 34 vols.

——. "Of the Work of Monks (De opere monachorum), *NPN*, Vol. 3, pp. 503–524.

——. *On Christian Doctrine*. Trans. from the Latin by D. W. Robertson, Jr. (New York: Liberal Arts Press, 1958).

——. "On the Holy Trinity," *NPN*, 1st Ser., Vol. 3, pp. 1–228.

——. "Sermones ad populum," 1st Ser., 46, *OCSA*, Vol. 16, pp. 251–285.

——. "Sermones ad populum," 1st Ser., 80, *OCSA*, Vol. 16, pp. 566–573.

——. "Sermones ad populum," 1st Ser., 158, *OCSA*, Vol. 17, pp. 485–492.

——. "Sermones ad populum," 2nd Ser., 241, *OCSA*, Vol. 18, pp. 237–245.

Ausonius, Decimus Magnus. *The Mosella*. Trans. from the Latin into English verse by E. H. Blakeney (London: Eyre & Spottswood, 1933).

Averroès (Ibn Rochd). *Traité Décisif sur l'Accord de la Religion et de la Philosophie Suivi de l'Appendice*. Arab text with French trans., notes, and intro. by Léon Gauthier (3rd ed.; Alger: Éditions Carbonel, 1948).

Avicenna. "Das Lehrgedicht über die Heilkunde (Canticum de Medicina)." Trans. from the Arabic into German by Karl Opitz, *Quellen und Studien zur Geschichte der Naturwissenschaften und der Medizin*, Vol. 7, Heft 2/3 (1939), pp. 150–220.

Bacon, Francis. *The Advancement of Learning*. Everyman's Library (London: J. M. Dent & Sons; New York: E. P. Dutton & Co., 1954 [1915]).

——. "The Natural and Experimental History for the Foundation of Philosophy: or Phenomena of the Universe: Which is the Third Part of the Instauratio Magna," *The Works of Francis Bacon*, eds. James Spedding, Robert L. Ellis, and Douglas D. Heath, Vol. 5 (being Vol. 2 of the translations of *The Philosophical Works*. . . . London: Longman & Co., etc., etc., 1861), pp. 131–134.

——. "New Atlantis," *Ideal Commonwealths*. Rev. ed. by Henry Morley (New York: P. F. Collier & Son, 1901).

——. *Novum Organum* (New York: P. F. Collier & Son, 1901).

——. "Of the Vicissitude of Things," [1625], Bacon's *Essays and Wisdom of the Ancients* (New York: Thomas Nelson & Sons, n.d.), pp. 292–300.

Bacon, Roger. *The Opus Majus of Roger Bacon*. Trans. from the Latin by Robert B. Burke (Philadelphia: University of Pennsylvania Press; London: H. Milford, Oxford University Press, 1928). 2 vols.

Bailey, Cyril. *Epicurus, The Extant Remains. With Short Critical Apparatus Translation and Notes* (Oxford: Clarendon Press, 1926).

——. *The Greek Atomists and Epicurus* (Oxford: Clarendon Press, 1928).

——. See also Lucretius.

Baker, Herschel. *The Wars of Truth* (Cambridge, Mass.: Harvard University Press, 1952).

Baldwin, Charles S. *Medieval Rhetoric and Poetic (to 1400) Interpreted From Representative Works* (New York: Macmillan Co., 1928).

Barber, W. H. *Leibniz in France From Arnauld to Voltaire. A Study in French Reactions to Leibnizianism, 1670–1760* (Oxford: Clarendon Press, 1955).

Barclay, John. *Mirrour of Mindes, or Barclay's Icon Animorum*. Trans. from the Latin by Thomas May (London: T. Walkley, 1631).

Bark, William Carroll, *Origins of the Medieval World*. Anchor Books (Garden City, N. Y.: Doubleday & Co., 1960).

Baron, Hans. "Towards a More Positive Evaluation of the Fifteenth-Century Renaissance," *JHI*, Vol. 4 (1943), pp. 21–49.

Bartholomew of England (Bartholomaeus Anglicus). *De proprietatibus rerum* (Nuremberg: Anton Koberger, 1492).

——. See also Humphries, William J.

Basil of Caesarea (Basil the Great). "The Hexaemeron," *NPN*, 2nd Ser., Vol. 8, pp. 51–107.

Bates, Marston. *The Forest and the Sea* (New York: Random House, 1960).

Bauer, George. See Agricola.

Beazley, Sir Charles R. *The Dawn of Modern Geography* (London: J. Murray, 1897–1906, Vol. 3; Oxford: Clarendon Press). 3 vols.

Bede [the Venerable]. *A History of the English Church and People*. Trans. from the Latin by Leo Sherley-Price. Penguin Classics (Harmondsworth: Penguin Books, 1955).

——. "Hexaemeron," *PL*, Vol. 91.

Behm, E., and Wagner, H. "Die Bevölkerung der Erde, II," *Petermanns Mitteilungen Ergänzungsband* 8, No. 35 (1873–1874).

Benedict, St. *The Rule of St. Benedict*. Trans. from the Latin by Sir David Oswald Hunter-Blair (2nd ed., London and Edinburgh: Sands & Co.; St. Louis, Mo.: B. Herder, 1907). Latin and English.

Bentley, Richard. *A Confutation of Atheism*. See *Eight Sermons Preached at the Hon. Robert Boyle's Lecture*, etc.

——. "Eight Sermons Preached at the Hon. Robert Boyle's Lecture in the Year MDCXCII," *The Works of Richard Bentley, D. D.* Collected and edited by Alexander Dyce, Vol. 3 (London: Francis Macpherson, 1838), pp. 1–200.

Berger, Hugo. *Geschichte der wissenschaftlichen Erdkunde der Griechen* (Zweite verbesserte und ergänzte Auflage, Leipzig: Veit & Co., 1903).

Bernard, St. (Bernard of Clairvaux.) *Life and Works of St. Bernard, Abbot of Clairvaux*. Trans. by Samuel J. Eales (2nd ed.; London: Burns and Oates; New York: Benziger Bros., 1912). 2 vols.

Bertin, Léon, *et al. Buffon* (Paris: Muséum Nationale d'Histoire Naturelle, 1952).

Bevan, Bernard. "The Chinantec and Their Habitat," *Instituto Panamericano de Geografía y Historia*, Publication 24 (Mexico? 1938). Appendix has an English translation of Diego de Esquivel's *Relación de Chinantla*.

*Bibliothek der Kirchenväter*, hrsg. by O. Bardenhewer, Th. Scherman, and K. Weyman (Kempten & München: 1st Ser., J. Kösel, 1911–1928, 61 vols.; 2nd Ser., J. Kösel and F. Pustet, 1932–1938, 20 vols.).

"Das Bibra-Büchlein," ed. Alfred Kirchoff, *Die ältesten Weisthümer der Stadt Erfurt über ihre Stellung zum Erzstift Mainz* (Halle: Verlag der Buchhandlung des Waisenhauses, 1870).

Biese, Alfred. *The Development of the Feeling for Nature in the Middle Ages and Modern Times*. Trans. from the German (London: G. Routledge and Sons; New York: E. P. Dutton & Co., 1905).

——. *Entwicklung des Naturgefühls im Mittelalter und in der Neuzeit* (2nd ed.; Leipzig: Veit & Co., 1892).

——. *Die Entwicklung des Naturgefühls bei den Griechen und Römern* (Kiel: Lipsius & Tischer, 1882–1884). 2 vols.

Billeter, Gustav. *Griechische Anschauungen über die Ursprünge der Kultur* (Zurich: Zürcher & Furrer, 1901).

Bion. See Greek Bucolic Poets.

Bloch, Marc. "Avènement et Conquêtes du Moulin à Eau," *Annales d' Histoire Économique et Sociale*, Vol. 7 (1935), pp. 538–563.

——. *Les Caractères Originaux de l'Histoire Rurale Française*. New ed. with supp. by R. Dauvergne (Paris: Librairie Armand Colin, Vol. 1, 1960; Vol. 2, 1961).

Bluck, R. S. *Plato's Life and Thought with a Translation of The Seventh Letter* (Boston: Beacon Press, 1951).

Boas, George. *Essays on Primitivism and Related Ideas in the Middle Ages* (Baltimore: Johns Hopkins Press, 1948).

Bock, Kenneth E. *The Acceptance of Histories. Toward a Perspective for Social Science.* University of California Publications in Sociology and Social Institutions, Vol. 3, No. 1 (Berkeley and Los Angeles: University of California Press, 1956).

Bodin, Jean. *Method for the Easy Comprehension of History*. Trans. from the Latin by Beatrice Reynolds (New York: Columbia University Press, 1945).

——. *The Six Books of a Commonweale*. (The Republic). Trans. from French and Latin copies by Richard Knolles (London: G. Bishop, 1606).

Boethius. *The Consolation of Philosophy*. Trans. from the Latin by Richard Green. The Library of Liberal Arts (Indianapolis and New York: Bobbs-Merrill Co., 1962).

Boissonnade, Prosper M. *Life and Work in Medieval Europe (Fifth to Fifteenth Centuries)*. Trans. from the French by Eileen Power (New York: Alfred A. Knopf, 1927).

Boll, Franz. "On Astrological Ethnology," being a Footnote to Gisinger, F., "Geographie," *PW*, Supp. Vol. 4, col. 656.

—— (Unter Mitwirkung von Carl Bezold). *Sternglaube und Sterndeutung. Die Geschichte und Das Wesen der Astrologie*. 4th ed. rev. by W. Gundel (Leipzig: B. G. Teubner, 1931).

Bonar, James. *Malthus and His Work* (New York: Macmillan Co., 1924).

——. *Theories of Population from Raleigh to Arthur Young* (London: G. Allen & Unwin, 1931).

Bonaventura, St. "In quatuor libros sententiarum expositio," *Opera omnia*. Ed. A. C. Peltier (Parisiis: Ludovicus Vivès, 1864–1866), Vols. 1–6.

——. *The Mind's Road to God*. Trans. from the Latin by George Boas (New York: Liberal Arts Press, 1953).

Boorstin, Daniel. *The Lost World of Thomas Jefferson* (New York: H. Holt, [1948]).

Botero, Giovanni. *The Reason of State*. Trans. from the Italian by P. J. and D. P. Waley, and *The Greatness of Cities*, trans. by Robert Peterson (New Haven: Yale University Press, 1956).

Boulding, Kenneth E. See Malthus, *Population: the First Essay*.

Boyle, Robert. *A Disquisition about the Final Causes of Natural Things* (London: Printed by H. C. for John Taylor, 1688).

Braithwaite, Richard B. *Scientific Explanation* (Cambridge: at the Univ. Press, 1955).

Bretzl, Hugo. *Botanische Forschungen des Alexanderzuges* (Leipzig: B. G. Teubner, 1903).

Brown, Charles A. *A Source Book of Agricultural Chemistry. Chronica Botanica*, Vol. 8, No. 1 (Waltham, Mass.: Chronica Botanica Publishing Co., etc., 1944).

Brown, John Croumbie, ed. *French Forest Ordinance of 1669*. Trans. from the French by John C. Brown (Edinburgh: Oliver and Boyd; London: Simpkin, Marshall & Co., 1883).

——. *Reboisement in France* (London: C. Kegan Paul & Co., 1880).

Brown, John L. *The Methodus ad Facilem Historiarum Cognitionem of Jean Bodin. A Critical Study* (Washington, D. C.: Catholic University of America Press, 1939).

Brown, Ralph. "A Letter to the Reverend Jedidiah Morse Author of the American Universal Geography," "The Land and the Sea: Their Larger Traits," "The Seaboard Climate in the View of 1800," "A Plea for Geography, 1813 Style," *AAAG*, Vol. 41 (1951), pp. 187–236.

Browne, Sir Thomas. *Religio Medici and Other Works*. Gateway Editions (Los Angeles, Chicago, New York: Henry Regney Co., 1956).

Brutails, Jean Auguste. *Étude sur la Condition des Populations Rurales du Roussillon au Moyen Âge*. (Paris: Imprimerie Nationale, 1891).

Bryson, Gladys. *Man and Society: The Scottish Inquiry of the Eighteenth Century* (Princeton: Princeton University Press, 1945).

Buckle, Henry Thomas. *History of Civilization in England* (from the 2nd London ed., New York: D. Appleton and Co., 1873), Vol. 1.

Bühler, Johannes. *Klosterleben im deutschen Mittelalter nach zeitgenössischen Quellen* (Leipzig: Insel-Verlag, 1923).

——. *Ordensritter und Kirchenfürsten nach zeitgenössischen Quellen* (Leipzig: Insel-Verlag, 1927).

Büsching, D. Anton Friderich [*sic*]. *Neue Erdbeschreibung* (Schaffhausen: Benedict Hurter, 1767–1769). 11 vols.

Buffon, Comte de (Georges-Louis Leclerc). *Histoire Naturelle, Générale et Particulière* (Paris: Imprimerie Royale, puis Plassan, 1749–1804). 44 vols. This is the general entry; the specific citations which follow will enable the reader to locate articles in other editions of the *HN*.

——. "Addition à l'Article des Variétés de l'Espèce Humaine. Des Américains," *HNS*, Vol. 4.

——. "Les Animaux Carnassiers," *HN*, Vol. 7.

——. "Animaux de l'Ancien Continent. Animaux du Nouveau Monde. Animaux Communs aux Deux Continents," *HN*, Vol. 9.

——. "Les Animaux Domestiques," *HN*, Vol. 4.

——. "Les Animaux Sauvages," *HN*, Vol. 6.

——. "L'Autruche," *HNO*, Vol. 1.

——. "La Brebis," *HN*, Vol. 5.

——. "Le Buffle, le Bonasus, l'Auroch, le Bison et le Zébu," *HN*, Vol. 11.

——. "Le Chameau et la Dromadaire," *HN*, Vol. 11.

——. "Le Chat," *HN*, Vol. 6.

——. "Le Cheval," *HN*, Vol. 4.

——. "La Chèvre et la Chèvre d'Angora," *HN*, Vol. 5.

——. "Le Chien avec ses Variétés," *HN*, Vol. 5.

——. "De la Dégénération des Animaux," *HN*, Vol. 14.

——. "Des Époques de la Nature," *HNS*, Vol. 5.

——. "De la Nature. Première Vue," *HN*, Vol. 12.

——. "De la Terre Végétale," *HNM*, Vol. 1.

——. "Discours sur la Nature des Oiseaux," *HNO*, Vol. 1.

——. "L'Élan et le Renne," *HN*, Vol. 12.

——. "L'Éléphant," *HN*, Vol. 11.

——. "Histoire et Théorie de la Terre. Preuves de la Théorie de la Terre," *HN*, Vol. 1.

——. "Les Lamantins," *HNS*, Vol. 6.

——. "Le Lion," *HN*, Vol. 9.

——. "Le Morse ou la Vache Marine," *HN*, Vol. 13.

——. "Le Mouflon et les Autres Brebis," *HN*, Vol. 11.

——. "Le Phoque Commun," *HNS*, Vol. 6.

——. "Le Rat," *HN*, Vol. 7.

——. "Sur la Conservation & le Rétablissement des Forêts," *HNS*, Vol. 2. (Repr. from *Histoire de l'Académie Royale des Sciences, Mémoires*, 1739, pp. 140–156.)

——. "Sur la Culture & Exploitation des Forêts," *HNS*, Vol. 2. (Repr. from *Histoire de l'Académie Royale des Sciences, Mémoires*, 1742, pp. 233–246.)

—. "Le Touyou," *HNO*, Vol. 1.

—. "L'Unau et L'Aï," *HN*, Vol. 13.

—. *Natural History, General and Particular*. . . . Trans. from the French by William Smellie. New ed., corr., enl. (London: T. Cadell and W. Davies, 1812). 20 vols.

Bugge, Alexander. *Den norske Traelasthandels Historie* . . . (Skien: Fremskridts Boktrykkeri, 1925). Vol. 1.

Bultmann, Rudolf. *Primitive Christianity in its Contemporary Setting*. Trans. from the German by R. H. Fuller (New York: Meridian Books, 1956).

Bunbury, E. H. *A History of Ancient Geography* (2nd ed.; New York: Dover Publications, 1959 [1883]). 2 vols.

Burch, George B. *Early Medieval Philosophy* (New York: King's Crown Press, 1951).

Burlingame, Anne. *The Battle of the Books in its Historical Setting* (New York: B. W. Huebsch, 1920).

Burnet, Thomas. *The Sacred Theory of the Earth* (Glasgow: R. Urie, 1753). 2 vols.

Burton, Robert. *The Anatomy of Melancholy*. Eds. Floyd Dell and Paul Jordan-Smith (New York: Tudor Publishing Co., 1955).

Burtt, Edwin A. *The Metaphysical Foundations of Modern Science*. Rev. ed., Anchor Books (Garden City, N. Y.: Doubleday & Co., 1954).

Bury, J. B. *The Idea of Progress* (New York: Dover Publications, 1955 [repub. of 1932 ed.]).

Butler, Joseph. *The Analogy of Religion, Natural and Revealed, to the Constitution and Course of Nature*. . . . (London and New York: George Bell & Sons, 1893).

Caesar, Julius. *Caesar's War Commentaries (The Gallic Wars and The Civil War)*. Trans. from the Latin by John Warrington. Everyman Paperback (New York: E. P. Dutton & Co., 1958).

*The Cambridge Economic History of Europe from the Decline of the Roman Empire*; Vol. 1, *The Agrarian Life of the Middle Ages*, eds. J. H. Clapham and Eileen Power (Cambridge: at the University Press, 1941); Vol. 2, *Trade and Industry in the Middle Ages*, eds. M. Postan and E. E. Rich (Cambridge: at the University Press, 1952).

Campenhausen, Hans von. *The Fathers of the Greek Church*. Trans. from the German by Stanley Godman (New York: Pantheon Books, 1959).

Cannan, Edwin. *A History of the Theories of Production and Distribution in English Political Economy from 1776 to 1848* (3rd ed.; London: P. S. King and Son, 1917).

Capelle, W. "Meteorologie," *PW*, Supp. Vol. 6, cols. 315–358.

Cappuyns, Maïeul. *Jean Scot Érigène, sa Vie, son Oeuvre, sa Pensée* (Louvain: Abbaye du Mont César, 1933).

Carcopino, Jérôme. *Daily Life in Ancient Rome*. Trans. from the French by E. O. Lorimer (New Haven: Yale University Press, 1960 [1940]).

Carey, Henry C. *The Past, the Present, and the Future* (Philadelphia: H. C. Baird, 1869).

—. *Principles of Social Science* (Philadelphia: J. P. Lippincott & Co.; London: Trüben & Co., etc., 1858–1859). 3 vols.

Carré, Meyrick H. *Realists and Nominalists* (Oxford: Oxford University Press, 1946).

Cary, Max. *The Geographic Background of Greek and Roman History* (Oxford: Clarendon Press, 1949).

Cassiodorus Senator. *An Introduction to Divine and Human Readings*. Trans. with an intro. and notes by Leslie Webber Jones. Records of Civilization—Sources and Studies, No. 40 (New York: Columbia University Press, 1946).

—.*The Letters of Cassiodorus. Being a Condensed Translation of the Variae Epistolae of Magnus Aurelius Cassiodorus Senator*. Intro. by Thomas Hodgkin (London: Henry Frowde, 1886).

—. *Variae*. Ed. Theodor Mommsen (Berlin: apud Weidmannos, 1894).

Cassirer, Ernst. *The Individual and the Cosmos in Renaissance Philosophy*. Trans. from the German by Mario Domandi. Harper Torchbooks/Academy Library (New York: Harper & Row, 1964).

—. *The Philosophy of the Enlightenment*. Trans. from the German by Fritz C. A.

Koelln and James P. Pettegrove. Beacon Paperback ed. (Boston: Beacon Press, 1955).

——. *The Platonic Renaissance in England.* Trans. from the German by James Pettegrove (Austin: University of Texas Press, 1953).

——. "Some Remarks on the Question of the Originality of the Renaissance," *JHI*, Vol. 4 (1943), pp. 49–56.

——; Kristeller, Paul Oskar; Randall, John Herman, Jr., eds. *The Renaissance Philosophy of Man.* Phoenix Books (Chicago: University of Chicago Press, 1948).

Cato, Marcus Porcius. *On Agriculture.* Trans. from the Latin by William D. Hooper; rev. by Harrison B. Ash. Loeb Classical Library (London: Wm. Heinemann; Cambridge, Mass.: Harvard University Press, 1934). (Published with Marcus Terrentius Varro. *On Agriculture.*)

Chardin, Sir John. *The Travels of Sir John Chardin in Persia* (London: Printed for the Author, Sold by J. Smith, 1720). 2 vols.

——. *Voyages de Monsieur Le Chevalier Chardin en Perse et autres lieux de l'Orient* (Amsterdam: chez Jean Louis de Lorme, 1711). 3 vols.

Charlemagne (Karoli Magni capitularia). "Admonitio generalis," [789], *Mon. Ger. Hist. Capit. Reg. Franc.,* Vol. 1, pp. 52–62.

——. "Capitulare de villis," *Mon. Ger. Hist. Capit. Reg. Franc.,* Vol. 1, pp. 82–91.

Charlesworth, M. P. *Trade-Routes and Commerce of the Roman Empire* (Cambridge [Eng.]: Cambridge University Press, 1924).

Charron, Pierre. *De la Sagesse, Livres Trois.* . . . (A Bovredeavs: Simon Millanges, 1601).

——. *Of wisdome* . . . Trans. from the French by Samuel Lennard (London: E. Blount and W. Aspley, 1620?).

*Chartularium Universitatis Parisiensis.* Eds. Henricus Denifle and Aemilio Chatelain. Vol. 1, A. D. 1200–1286 (Paris: ex typis Fratrum Delalain, 1889).

Chastellux, François Jean de. *Travels in North-America in the Years 1780, 1781, and 1782* (London: Printed for G. G. J. and J. Robinson, 1787). 2 vols.

Chateaubriand, Le Vicomte de. *Travels in America and Italy* (London: Henry Colburn, 1828). 2 vols.

Chenu, R. P. "Découverte de la Nature et Philosophie de l'Homme à l'École de Chartres au XIIe Siècle," *JWH*, Vol. 2 (1954), pp. 313–325.

Chinard, Gilbert. "The American Philosophical Society and the Early History of Forestry in America," *PAPS*, Vol. 89 (1945), pp. 444–488.

——. "Eighteenth Century Theories on America as a Human Habitat," *PAPS*, Vol. 91 (1947), pp. 27–57.

Church, Henry W. "Corneille de Pauw, and the Controversy over His Recherches Philosophiques sur les Américains," *PMLA*, Vol. 51 (1936), pp. 178–206.

Cicero, Marcus Tullius. *Cicero's "Offices," Essays on Friendship, & Old Age, and Select Letters.* Everyman's Library (London: J. M. Dent & Co.; New York: E. P. Dutton &. Co., 1930).

——. *De finibus bonorum et malorum.* Trans. from the Latin by H. Rackham. Loeb Classical Library (Cambridge, Mass.: Harvard University Press; London: Wm. Heinemann, 1951 [1931]).

——. *De natura deorum. Academica.* Trans. from the Latin by H. Rackham. Loeb Classical Library (Cambridge, Mass.: Harvard University Press, 1951).

——. *De officiis.* Trans. from the Latin by Walter Miller. Loeb Classical Library (London, Wm. Heinemann; New York: Macmillan Co., 1913).

——. *De oratore.* Trans. from the Latin by E. W. Sutton and H. Rackham, *De fato* trans. by H. Rackham. Loeb Classical Library (Cambridge, Mass.: Harvard University Press, 1948). 2 vols.

——. *De republica. De legibus.* Trans. from the Latin by Clinton Walker Keyes. Loeb Classical Library (London, Wm. Heinemann; New York: G. P. Putnam's Sons, 1928).

——. *De senectute, de amicitia, de divinatione.* Trans. from the Latin by William A. Falconer. Loeb Classical Library (Cambridge, Mass.: Harvard University Press; London: Wm. Heinemann, 1959 [1923]).

—. *Letters to Atticus.* Trans. from the Latin by E. O. Winstedt. Loeb Classical Library (London: Wm. Heinemann; New York: Macmillan Co., 1912). 3 vols.

—. *M. Tulli Ciceronis de natura deorum.* Ed. by Arthur S. Pease (Cambridge, Mass.: Harvard University Press, 1955–1958). 2 vols.

Clark, Robert T., Jr. *Herder. His Life and Thought* (Berkeley and Los Angeles: University of California Press, 1955).

Clarke, W. K. Lowther. *Concise Bible Commentary* (New York: Macmillan Company, 1953).

Clément, Pierre. *Histoire de Colbert et de Son Administration* (3rd ed.; Paris: Perrin & Cie., 1892). 2 vols.

Clement, St. "The Letter of St. Clement to the Corinthians." Trans. from the Greek by Francis X. Glimm, *The Fathers of the Church. The Apostolic Fathers* (New York: Cima Publishing House, 1947).

Clifford, Derek. *A History of Garden Design* (London: Faber & Faber, 1962).

Collignon, Albert. "Le Portrait des Esprits (*Icon animorum*) de Jean Barclay," *Mémoires de l'Académie de Stanislas*, Ser. 6, Vol. 3 (1905–1906), pp. 67–140.

Columella, Lucius Junius Moderatus. *De re rustica (On Agriculture).* Trans. from the Latin by Harrison Boyd Ash, I–IV; E. S. Forster and E. Heffner, V–XII. Loeb Classical Library (London: Wm. Heinemann; Cambridge, Mass.: Harvard University Press, 1941–1955). 3 vols.

Condorcet, Antoine-Nicolas de. *Sketch for a Historical Picture of the Progress of the Human Mind.* Trans. from the French by June Barraclough (New York: Noonday Press, 1955 [1795]).

Cook, James. *A Voyage to the Pacific Ocean* (3rd ed.; London: Printed by H. Hughs for C. Nicol and T. Cadell, 1785). 3 vols.: Vols. 1–2 by Cook, Vol. 3 by James King.

Cook, Stanley. *An Introduction to the Bible.* Pelican Books (Harmondsworth: Pelican Books, 1954 [1945]).

Coon, Carleton S. *The Origin of Races* (New York: Alfred A. Knopf, 1962).

Copernicus. "De revolutionibus orbium caelestium libri sex," Vol. 2 of *Nikolaus Kopernikus Gesamtausgabe* (Munich: Verlag R. Oldenburg, 1949).

Cornford, Francis M. *Principium sapientiae; the Origins of Greek Philosophical Thought* (Cambridge: Cambridge University Press, 1952).

Cosmas [Cosmas Indicopleustes]. *The Christian Topography.* Trans. from the Greek, with notes and intro. by J. W. McCrindle (London: Printed for the Hakluyt Society [Publication #98], 1897).

Coulton, George G. *Five Centuries of Religion* (Cambridge: Cambridge University Press, 1923–1950). 4 vols.

—. *Medieval Village, Manor, and Monastery.* Harper Torchbooks/Academy Library (New York: Harper & Brothers, 1960). First published as *The Medieval Village* (Cambridge: Cambridge University Press, 1925).

Crombie, Alistair C. *Medieval and Early Modern Science*, Vol. 1. *Science in the Middle Ages. V–XIII Centuries.* Anchor Books (rev. 2d. ed.; Garden City, N. Y.: Doubleday & Co., 1959).

—. *Medieval and Early Modern Science*, Vol. 2. *Science in the Later Middle Ages and Early Modern Times. XIII–XVII Centuries.* Anchor Books (rev. 2d. ed.; Garden City, N. Y.: Doubleday & Co., 1959).

—. *Robert Grosseteste and the Origins of Experimental Science, 1100–1700* (Oxford: Clarendon Press, 1953).

Cudworth, Ralph. *The True Intellectual System of the Universe.* Trans. from the Latin by John Harrison (London: Printed for Thomas Tegg, 1845). 3 vols.

Cumont, Franz. *Astrology and Religion Among the Greeks and Romans* (New York: Dover Publications, 1960).

Currie, William. "An Enquiry into the Causes of the Insalubrity of flat and Marshy Situations; and directions for preventing or correcting the Effects thereof," *TAPS*, Vol. 4 (1799), pp. 127–142.

Curtius, Ernst Robert. *European Literature and the Latin Middle Ages.* Trans. from the German by Willard R. Trask. Bollingen Series, 36 (New York: Pantheon Books, 1953).

Daines, Barrington. "An Investigation of the Difference Between the Present Temperature of the Air in Italy and Some Other Countries, and What it was Seventeen Centuries Ago," *Philosophical Transactions of the Royal Society of London,* Vol. 58 (1768), pp. 58–67.

Dainville, François de, S. J. *La Géographie des Humanistes. Les Jésuites et l'Éducation de la Société Française* (Paris: Beauchesne et Ses Fils, Éditeurs, 1940).

Dalloz, M. D., and Dalloz, Armand, eds., with the collaboration of Édouard Meaume. *Jurisprudence Forestière.* Being Vol. 25, "Forêts," of *Repértoire Méthodique et Alphabétique de Législation, de Doctrine et de Jurisprudence* (Nouv. ed., Paris: Bureau de la Jurisprudence Générale, 1849).

Darby, H. C. "The Clearing of the Woodland in Europe," *MR,* pp. 183–216.

——. "The Face of Europe on the Eve of the Discoveries," *The New Cambridge Modern History,* Vol. 1 (Cambridge: Cambridge University Press, 1961), pp. 20–49.

——. "The Geographical Ideas of the Venerable Bede," *The Scottish Geographical Magazine,* Vol. 51 (1935), pp. 84–89.

——. "Geography in a Medieval Text-Book," *The Scottish Geographical Magazine,* Vol. 49 (1933), pp. 323–331. (Bartholomew of England).

Darwin, Charles. *The Origin of Species* [1859] and *The Descent of Man* [1871]. Modern Library (New York: Random House, n.d.).

Dawson, Christopher. *The Making of Europe. An Introduction to the History of European Unity* (New York: Meridian Books, 1958 [1932]).

——. *Medieval Essays.* Image Books (Garden City, N. Y.: Doubleday & Co., 1959).

Dedieu, Joseph. *Montesquieu et la Tradition Politique Anglaise en France; les Sources Anglaises de l'"Esprit des Lois"* (Paris: J. Gabalda & Cie, 1909).

Deichgräber, Karl. "Goethe und Hippokrates," *Sudhoffs Archiv für Geschichte der Medizin und der Naturwissenschaften,* Vol. 29 (1936), pp. 27–56.

De Lacy, P. H. "Lucretius and the History of Epicureanism," *Trans. and Proc. of the Amer. Philological Assn.,* Vol. 79 (1948), pp. 12–23.

Delisle, Léopold. *Études sur la Condition de la Classe Agricole et l'État de l'Agriculture en Normandie en Moyen-Âge* (Paris: H. Champion, 1903).

——. "Traités Divers sur les Propriétés des Choses," *Histoire Littéraire de la France,* Vol. 30 (Paris: Imprimerie Nationale, 1888), pp. 334–388.

De Quincey, Thomas. "Style," *The Collected Writings of Thomas De Quincey,* ed. David Masson. Vol. 10 (London: A. and C. Black, 1897), pp. 134–245.

Derham, William. *Physico-Theology: or, A Demonstration of the Being and Attributes of God, from His Works of Creation* (New ed., London: Printed for A. Strahan, et al., 1798). 2 vols.

Descartes, René. *Discourse on Method.* Trans. from the French by Arthur Wollaston. Penguin Classics (Baltimore: Penguin Books, 1960).

——. "The Principles of Philosophy," *The Philosophical Works of Descartes.* Trans. from the French by Elizabeth S. Haldane and G. R. T. Ross. Vol. 1 (Cambridge: Cambridge University Press, 1911), pp. 201–302.

Dicaearchus. *Vita Graecia.* (Βίος Ἑλλάδος) See Lovejoy and Boas, *Primitivism and Related Ideas in Antiquity;* Porphyry, *De abstinentia.*

Diderot, Denis. "Réfutation Suivie de l'Ouvrage d'Helvétius Intitulé l'Homme (Extraits)," *Diderot, Oeuvres Philosophiques.* Ed. Paul Vernière (Paris: Éditions Garnier Frères, 1959), pp. 555–620.

Diederich, Sister Mary Dorothea. *Vergil in the Works of St. Ambrose.* . . . Catholic University of America Patristic Studies, Vol. 29 (Washington: Catholic University of America, 1931).

Diels, Hermann. *Die Fragmente der Vorsokratiker.* 6 verb. Aufl. Ed. Walter Cranz. Greek and German (Berlin: Weidmann, 1951–1952). 3 vols.

Dienne, Louis E. M. H., Comte de. *Histoire du Desséchement des Lacs et Marais en France avant 1789* (Paris: H. Champion and Guillaumin et Cie., 1891).

Dimier, M. A., and Dumontier, P. "Encore les Emplacements Malsains," *Revue du Moyen Âge Latin*, Vol. 4 (1948), pp. 60–65.

Diodorus Siculus. *Diodorus of Sicily*. Various trans. from the Greek. Loeb Classical Library (London: Wm. Heinemann; New York: G. P. Putnam's Sons, 1933–1963, etc., etc.).

Diogenes Laertius. *Lives of Eminent Philosophers*. Trans. from the Greek by R. D. Hicks. Loeb Classical Library (London: Wm. Heinemann; New York: G. P. Putnam's Sons, 1925). 2 vols.

Diognetus. See Anon. *Letter to Diognetus*.

Dirscherl, Josef F. "Das ostbayerische Grenzgebirge als Standraum der Glasindustrie," *Mitteilungen der Geographischen Gesellschaft in München*, Vol. 31 (1938), pp. 1–120.

Dodds, Muriel. *Les Récits de Voyages. Sources de l'Esprit des Lois de Montesquieu* (Paris: H. Champion, 1929).

Dove, Alfred. "Forster, Johann Reinhold"; "Forster, Johann Georg Adam," *Allgemeine Deutsche Biographie*, Vol. 7 pp. 166–181.

Drew, Katherin Fischer, and Lear, Floyd Seyward, eds. *Perspectives in Medieval History*. Rice University Semicentennial Series (Chicago: University of Chicago Press, 1963). Contains articles by A. C. Crombie, Gaines Post, E. Dwight Salmon, S. Harrison Thomson, and Lynn White, Jr.

Du Bartas. *The Works of Guillaume de Salluste, Sieur du Bartas*. Eds. Urban T. Holmes, Jr., John C. Lyons, Robert W. Linker, and others (Chapel Hill: University of North Carolina Press, 1935–1940). 3 vols.

Du Bos, Jean Baptiste. *Reflexions Critiques sur la Poesie et sur la Peinture* (4th ed. rev., corr., et aug. par l'auteur, Paris: J. Mariette, 1740). 3 vols.

Du Cange, Charles Du Fresne. *Glossarium mediae et infimae latinitatis*. (New ed; ed. Léopold Favre, Niort: L. Favre, 1883–1887). 10 vols.

Du Halde, J. B. *Description Géographique, Historique, Chronologique, Politique, et Physique de l'Empire de la Chine et de la Tartarie Chinoise* (A la Haye: Henri Scheurleer, 1736). 4 vols.

Duhem, Pierre. *Études sur Léonard de Vinci* (Paris: A. Hermann, 1906–1913). 3 vols.

——. *Le Système du Monde* (Paris: A. Hermann et fils, 1913–1959). 10 vols.

Dunbar, James. *Essays on the History of Mankind in Rude and Cultivated Ages* (London: Printed for W. Strahan, etc., 1780).

Durand, Dana B. "Tradition and Innovation in Fifteenth Century Italy," *JHI*, Vol. 4 (1943), pp. 1–20.

Edelstein, Ludwig. *Peri aerōn und die Sammlung der Hippokratischen Schriften* (Berlin: Weidmannsche Buchhandlung, 1931).

Edgar, C. C. *Zenon Papyri* (Le Caire: Impr. de l'Institut Française d'Archéologie Orientale, 1925–1931). 5 vols.

Ehrenberg, Victor. *The People of Aristophanes* (New York: Schocken Books, pub. by arr. with Harvard University Press, 1962).

Eisler, Robert. *Weltenmantel und Himmelszelt* (München: C. H. Beck, 1910). 2 vols.

Ekirch, Arthur A. *Man and Nature in America* (New York: Columbia University Press, 1963).

Eliade, Mircea. *Cosmos and History. The Myth of the Eternal Return*. Trans. from the French by Willard R. Trask. Harper Torchbooks (New York: Harper & Brothers, 1959 [1954]).

——. *Patterns in Comparative Religion*. Trans. from the French by Rosemary Sheed. Meridian Books (Cleveland and New York: World Publishing Co., 1963 [1958]).

Eliot, Jared. *Essays upon Field Husbandry in New England and Other Papers, 1748–1762*. Eds. Harry J. Carman and Rexford G. Tugwell (New York: Columbia University Press, 1934).

Elton, Charles S. *The Ecology of Invasions by Animals and Plants* (London: Methuen & Co. Ltd.; New York: John Wiley & Sons, Inc., 1958).

Enoch. *The Book of Enoch*. Trans. from Dillman's Ethiopic text by R. H. Charles (Oxford: Clarendon Press, 1893).

Esquivel, Diego de. "Relación de Chinantla," *Papeles de Nueva España*, ed. Francisco Del Paso y Troncoso. 2nd Ser., Vol. 4 (Madrid: Est. Tipográfico "Sucesores de Rivadeneyra," 1905), pp. 58–68.

Evelyn, John. *Fumifugium* [1661] repr. of 1772 ed. (Oxford: The Old Ashmolean Reprints, 1930).

——. *Silva: or, A Discourse of Forest-Trees, and the Propagation of Timber in his Majesty's Dominions*. . . . (York: Printed by A. Ward. . . . 1776).

Fabre, Jean Antoine. *Essai sur la Théorie des Torrens [sic]et des Rivières*. . . . (Paris: chez Bidault, An VI, 1797).

Fage, Anita. "La Révolution Française et la Population," *Population*, Vol. 8 (1953), pp. 311–338.

Falconer, William. *Remarks on the Influence of Climate, Situation, Nature of Country, Population, Nature of Food, and Way of Life, on The Disposition and Temper, Manners and Behaviour, Intellects, Laws and Customs, Form of Government, and Religion, of Mankind* (London: Printed for C. Dilly, 1781).

Ferguson, Adam. *An Essay on the History of Civil Society* (5th ed.; London: Printed for T. Cadell, etc., etc., 1782).

Ferguson, Walter K. *The Renaissance in Historical Thought, Five Centuries of Interpretation* (Boston: Houghton Mifflin Co., 1948).

Ficino, Marsilio. *Platonic Theology*. Selections trans. from the Latin by Josephine L. Burroughs, *JHI*, Vol. 5 (1944), pp. 227–239.

Fink, Z. S. "Milton and the Theory of Climatic Influence," *Modern Language Quarterly*, Vol. 2 (1941), pp. 67–80.

Florus, Lucius Annaeus. *Epitome of Roman History*. Trans. from the Latin by E. S. Forster. Loeb Classical Library (London: Wm. Heinemann; New York: G. P. Putnam's Sons, 1929).

Fontenelle, Bernard Le Bovier de. "Digression sur les Anciens et les Modernes," *Oeuvres Diverses de M. de Fontenelle*. Nouv. ed. (A la Haye, Chez Gosse & Neaulme, 1728), Vol. 2, pp. 125–138.

——. "Entretiens sur la Pluralité des Mondes," *Oeuvres Diverses de M. de Fontenelle*. Nouv. ed. (A la Haye: Chez Gosse & Neaulme, 1728), Vol. 1, pp. 149–221.

Forbes, R. J. "Metallurgy." Singer, Charles, *et al.*, eds., *A History of Technology*, Vol. 2, pp. 41–80.

Forster, George and Johann. See also Dove, Alfred.

Forster, George. "Ein Blick in das Ganze der Natur," *SS*, Vol. 4, pp. 307–327.

——. "Der Brothbaum," *SS*, Vol. 4, pp. 328–359.

——. "Die Nordwestküste von Amerika und der dortige Pelzhandel," *SS*, Vol. 4, pp. 3–109.

——. *A Voyage Round the World* (London: Printed for B. White, J. Robson, P. Elmsly, and G. Robinson, 1777).

Forster, John Reinhold [Johann Reinhold]. *Observations Made During a Voyage Round the World, on Physical Geography, Natural History, and Ethic Philosophy* (London: Printed for G. Robinson, 1778).

Fosberg, F. R. "The Island Ecosystem." F. R. Fosberg, ed., *Man's Place in the Island Ecosystem* (Honolulu: Bishop Museum Press, 1963), pp. 1–6.

Frame, Richard, "A Short Description of Pennsilvania," [1692]. Myers, Albert C., ed., *Narratives of Early Pennsylvania, West New Jersey and Delaware 1603–1707* (New York: Charles Scribner's Sons, 1912), pp. 301–305.

Francesco d'Assisi, St. (Legend.) *The Little Flowers of St. Francis* (of Ugolino di Monte Santa Maria). *Also The Considerations of the Holy Stigmata, The Life and Sayings of Brother Giles, The Life of Brother Juniper*. Trans. from the Latin and Italian by

Raphael Brown. Image Books (Garden City, New York: Doubleday & Co., 1958). Contains St. Francis' "The Canticle of Brother Sun," pp. 317–318.

Frankfort, Henri; Frankfort, Mrs. Henri; Wilson, John A; Jacobsen, Thorkild. *Before Philosophy. The Intellectual Adventure of Ancient Man.* A Pelican Book (Harmondsworth: Penguin Books, 1949).

Franklin, Benjamin. "Observations Concerning the Increase of Mankind, Peopling of Countries, etc." [1751]. *The Writings of Benjamin Franklin.* Collected and edited by Albert H. Smyth, Vol. 3 (1750–1759) (New York: Macmillan Co., 1907), pp. 63–73.

——. "To Richard Jackson" [1753]. *The Writings of Benjamin Franklin.* Collected and edited by Albert H. Smyth, Vol. 3 (1750–1759) (New York: Macmillan Co., 1907), pp. 133–141.

Frazer, Sir James G. *Folk-lore in the Old Testament; Studies in Comparative Religion, Legend, and Law* (London: Macmillan and Co., 1919). 3 vols.

Frederick II of Hohenstaufen, Emperor. *The Art of Falconry, Being the De Arte Venandi cum Avibus of Frederick II of Hohenstaufen.* Trans. and edited by Casey A. Wood and F. Marjorie Fyfe (Stanford: Stanford University Press, 1943).

*French Forest Ordinance of 1669.* See Brown, John Croumbie.

Fulton, William. *Nature and God* (Edinburgh: T. & T. Clark, 1927).

Gaertringen, Hiller v. "Busiris, 5," *PW*, Vol. 3, cols. 1074–1077.

Galenus. Γαληνοῦ περὶ χρείας μορίων ἰζ *De usu partium libri xvii*, ed. Georgius Helmreich (Leipzig, B. G. Teubner, 1907–1909). 2 vols.

Galen [Galenus]. *On the Natural Faculties.* Trans. from the Greek by Arthur J. Brock. Loeb Classical Library (London: Wm. Heinemann; New York: G. P. Putnam's Sons, 1916).

Galileo. "Letter to Madame Christina of Lorraine, Grand Duchess of Tuscany" [1615], *Discoveries and Opinions of Galileo.* Trans. by Stillman Drake. Anchor Books (Garden City, N. Y.: Doubleday & Co., 1957), pp. 173–216.

Gallois, Lucien. *Les Géographes Allemands de la Renaissance* (Paris: Ernest Leroux, 1890).

Ganshof, François, *et al.* "Medieval Agrarian Society in its Prime," *CEHE*, Vol. 1, pp. 278–492.

Ganzenmüller, Wilhelm. "Das Naturgefühl im Mittelalter," *Beiträge zur Kulturgeschichte des Mittelalters*, Vol. 18 (1914), pp. 1–304.

Gautier, Dominique. *Biologie et Médecine dans l'Oeuvre de Montesquieu* (Bordeaux, 1949). NA.

Gerbi, Antonello. *La Disputa del Nuovo Mondo. Storia di Una Polemica 1750–1900* (Milano, Napoli: Riccardo Ricciardi, 1955).

Gilbert, Otto. *Die meteorologischen Theorien des griechischen Altertums.* Allgemeiner Theil (Leipzig: B. G. Teubner, 1907).

Giles of Rome. *Errores Philosophorum.* Ed. Josef Koch, trans. from the Latin by John O. Riedl (Milwaukee: Marquette University Press, 1944).

Gille, Bertrand. "Les Développements Technologiques en Europe de 1100 à 1400," *JWH*, Vol. 3 (1956), pp. 63–108.

——. "Machines," *HT*, Vol. 2, pp. 629–658.

——. "Le Moulin à Eau," *Techniques et Civilisations*, Vol. 3 (1954), pp. 1–15.

——. "Notes d'Histoire de la Technique Métallurgique. I. Les Progrès du Moyen-Âge. Le Moulin à Fer et le Haut-Fourneau," *Métaux et Civilisations*, Vol. 1 (1946), pp. 89–94.

Gillispie, Charles C. *Genesis and Geology* (Cambridge, Mass.: Harvard University Press, 1951).

Gillot, Hubert. *La Querelle des Anciens et des Modernes en France* (Paris: E. Champion, 1914).

Gilson, Etienne. *History of Christian Philosophy in the Middle Ages* (New York: Random House, 1955).

——. *La Philosophie au Moyen Âge, des Origines Patristiques à la Fin du XIVᵉ Siècle* (2ᵉ éd. rev. et augm., Paris: Payot, 1952 [c. 1944]).

——. "Sub umbris arborum," *Medieval Studies*, Vol. 14 (1952), pp. 149–151.

Gimpel, Jean. *The Cathedral Builders* (New York: Grove Press, 1961).

Giraldus Cambrensis. *The Historical Works of Giraldus Cambrensis Containing the Topography of Ireland, and the History of the Conquest of Ireland.* Trans. by Thomas Forester. *The Itinerary Through Wales.* Trans. by Sir Richard C. Hoare. Revised and edited by Thomas Wright (London: George Bell & Sons, 1905).

Gisinger, F. "Geographie," *PW*, Supp. Vol. 4, cols. 521–685.

——. "Oikumene," *PW*, Vol. 17:2, cols. 2123–2174.

Glacken, Clarence J. "Changing Ideas of the Habitable World," *MR*, pp. 70–92.

——. "Count Buffon on Cultural Changes of the Physical Environment," *AAAG*, Vol. 50 (1960), pp. 1–21.

Glover, Terrot R. *Herodotus* (Berkeley: University of California Press, 1924).

Godwin, William. *Enquiry concerning Political Justice and its Influence on Morals and Happiness.* Photographic facsimile of 3rd ed. corrected and edited . . . by F. E. L. Priestley (Toronto: University of Toronto Press, 1946). 3 vols.

——. *Of Population* (London: Printed for Longman, Hurst, Rees, Orme, and Brown, 1820).

Goethe, Johann Wolfgang von. *Goethe's Botanical Writings.* Trans. from the German by Bertha Mueller (Honolulu: University of Hawaii Press, 1952).

Gómara, Francisco López de. "Historia General de las Indias," *Biblioteca Autores Españoles*, Vol. 22, being Vol. 1 of *Historiadores Primitivos de Indias* (Madrid: Ediciones Atlas, 1946).

Goodman, Godfrey. *The Fall of Man, or the Corruption of Nature, Proved by the Light of Our Naturall Reason* (London: Felix Kyngston, 1616). NA.

Goyau, Georges. "La Normandie Bénédictine et Guillaume le Conquérant," *Revue des Deux-Mondes*, 15 Nov. 1938, pp. 337–355.

Grand, Roger, and Delatouche, Raymond. *L'Agriculture au Moyen Âge de la Fin de l'Empire Romain au XVIᵉ Siècle* (Paris: E. De Boccard, 1950). (Vol. 3 of *L'Agriculture à Travers les Âges. Collection Fondée par Emile Savoy.*)

Grant, Robert M. *Miracle and Natural Law in Graeco-Roman and Early Christian Thought* (Amsterdam: North-Holland Publishing Co., 1952).

Graunt, John. *Natural and Political Observations Made upon the Bills of Mortality.* Ed. with an intro. by Walter F. Willcox (Baltimore: Johns Hopkins University Press, 1939).

*The Greek Bucolic Poets.* Trans. from the Greek by J. M. Edmonds. Loeb Classical Library (Cambridge, Mass.: Harvard University Press; London: Wm. Heinemann, 1960).

Greene, John C. *The Death of Adam* (Ames: Iowa State University Press, 1959).

Gregory of Nyssa. "The Great Catechism," *NPN*, Ser. 2, Vol. 5, pp. 471–5c9.

——. "On the Making of Man," trans. by H. A. Wilson, *NPN*, Ser. 2, Vol. 5, pp. 386–427.

Grimm, Jacob. *Weisthümer* (Göttingen: in der Dieterichschen Buchhandlung, 1840–1878). 7 vols.

Gronau, Karl. *Poseidonios und die Jüdisch-Christliche Genesisexegese* (Leipzig and Berlin: B. G. Teubner, 1914).

Grundmann, Johannes. *Die geographischen und völkerkundlichen Quellen und Anschauungen in Herders "Ideen zur Geschichte der Menschheit"* (Berlin: Weidmann, 1900).

Grunebaum, Gustave E. von. *Medieval Islam.* Phoenix Books (2nd ed.; Chicago: University of Chicago Press, 1961).

——. "The Problem: Unity in Diversity," Gustave E. von Grunebaum, ed., *Unity and Variety in Muslim Civilization* (Chicago: University of Chicago Press, 1955).

Guillaume de Lorris and Jean de Meun. *The Romance of the Rose.* Trans. from the French by Harry W. Robbins; edited with an intro. by Charles W. Dunn. A Dutton Paperback (New York: E. P. Dutton & Co., 1962).

Gunkel, Hermann. *Genesis. Übersetzt und Erklärt*. Göttinger Handkommentar zum Alten Testament (Dritte neugearbeitete Aufl., Göttingen: Vandenhoeck & Ruprecht, 1910).

Gunther of Pairis. *Der Ligurinus Gunthers von Pairis im Elsass*. Trans. into German by Theodor Vulpinus (Strassburg: J. H. E. Heitz, 1889).

Gusinde, Martin. *Die Yamana. Vom Leben und Denken der Wassernomaden am Kap Hoorn* (Wien: Mödling, Verlag der International Zeitschrift "Anthropos," 1937).

Guthrie, W. K. C. *The Greeks and Their Gods* (London: Methuen & Co. 1950).

Guyan, Walter U. *Bild und Wesen einer mittelalterlichen Eisenindustrielandschaft in Kanton Schaffhausen* (Basel: Buchdruckerei Gasser & Cie., 1946).

——. "Die mittelalterlichen Wüstlegungen als archäologisches und geographisches Problem dargelegt an einigen Beispielen aus dem Kanton Schaffhausen," *Zeitschrift für Schweizerische Geschichte*, Vol. 26 (1946), pp. 433–478.

Guyot, Arnold. *The Earth and Man: Lectures on Comparative Physical Geography, in Its Relation to the History of Mankind*. Trans. from the French by C. C. Felton (Boston: Gould and Lincoln, 1859).

Hagberg, Knut H. *Carl Linnaeus*. Trans. from the Swedish by Alan Blair (London: Cape, [1952]).

Hakewill, George. *An Apologie, or Declaration of the Power and Providence of God in the Government of the World* (Oxford: Printed by W. Turner, 1635).

Hale, Sir Matthew. *The Primitive Origination of Mankind* (London: Printed by W. Godbid for W. Shrowsbery, 1677).

Hall, Joseph. *The Discovery of a New World (Mundus alter et idem)*. Orig. in Latin by Joseph Hall, *ca.* 1605; trans. into English by John Healey, *ca.* 1609. Ed. Huntington Brown (Cambridge, Mass.: Harvard University Press, 1937).

Halley, Edmund. "An Account of the Circulation of the Watry Vapours of the Sea, and of the Cause of Springs," *Royal Society of London Philosophical Transactions*, No. 192, Vol. 17 (1694), pp. 468–473.

Halphen, Louis. *Études Critiques sur l'Histoire de Charlemagne* (Paris: F. Alcan, 1921).

Hanke, Lewis. "Pope Paul III and the American Indians," *Harvard Theological Review*, Vol. 30 (1937), pp. 65–102.

Hansiz, Marcus. *Germaniae Sacrae* (Augustae Vindelicorum: Sumptibus Georgii Schlüter & Martini Happach, 1727–1755). 3 vols. in 2. NA.

Hantzsch, Viktor. "Sebastian Münster. Leben, Werk, Wissenschaftliche Bedeutung," *Abhandlungen der königl. Sächsischen Gesellschaft der Wissenschaften (Phil.-hist. Kl.)*, Vol. 18 (1898), No. 3.

Harris, L. E. "Land Drainage and Reclamation," *HT*, Vol. 3, pp. 300–323.

Harris, Victor. *All Coherence Gone* (Chicago: University of Chicago Press, 1949).

Haskins, Charles H. "The 'De Arte Venandi cum Avibus' of the Emperor Frederick II," *English Historical Review*, Vol. 36 (1921), pp. 334–355.

——. "The Latin Literature of Sport," *Speculum*, Vol. 2 (1927), pp. 235–252.

——. *Studies in the History of Mediaeval Science* (Cambridge, Mass.: Harvard University Press, 1924).

Hazard, Paul. *European Thought in the Eighteenth Century, from Montesquieu to Lessing*. Trans. from the French by J. Lewis May (London: Hollis & Carter, 1954).

Hehn, Victor. *Kulturpflanzen und Hausthiere in ihrem Übergang aus Asien nach Griechenland und Italien sowie in das Übrige Europa* (7th ed., Berlin: Gebrüder Bornträger, 1902).

Heichelheim, Fritz. "Effects of Classical Antiquity on the Land," *MR*, pp. 165–182.

——. "Monopole," *PW*, Vol. 16:1, cols. 147–199.

Heinimann, Felix von. *Nomos und Physis. Herkunft und Bedeutung einer Antithese im Griechischen Denken des 5. Jahrhunderts* (Basel: Verlag Friedrich Reinhardt, 1945).

Helbig, Wolfgang. "Beiträge zur Erklärung der campanischen Wandbilder," *Rheinisches Museum*, N. F. Vol. 24 (1869), pp. 251–270, 497–523.

——. *Untersuchungen über die Campanische Wandmalerei* (Leipzig: Breitkopf und Härtel, 1873).

Helvétius, Claude Adrien. *De l'Esprit; or Essays on the Mind, and its Several Faculties.* Trans. from the French (London: Printed for James Cundee, and Vernor, Hood, and Sharpe, 1810).

Herbst, Josephine. *New Green World* (New York: Hastings House, 1954).

Herder, Johann Gottfried von. "Ideen zur Philosophie der Geschichte der Menschheit." *Herder's Sämmtliche Werke,* ed. Bernhard Suphan (Berlin: Weidmann, 1877–1913), Vols. 13–14.

——. *Outlines of a Philosophy of the History of Man.* Trans. from the German by T. Churchill (London: Printed for J. Johnson by L. Hansard, 1800).

Hermes Trismegistus. *Hermetica. The Ancient Greek and Latin Writings Which Contain Religious or Philosophic Teachings Ascribed to Hermes Trismegistus.* Edited and trans. from the Greek by Walter Scott. Vol. 1: Intro., texts, and trans. (Oxford: Clarendon Press, 1924). 4 vols.

Herodotus. *The History of Herodotus.* Trans. from the Greek by George Rawlinson. Everyman's Library (London: J. M. Dent & Sons, 1910). 2 vols.

Herwegen, Ildefons. *Sinn und Geist der Benediktinerregel* (Einsiedeln/Köln: Benziger and Co., 1944).

Hesiod. *The Homeric Hymns and Homerica.* Trans. from the Greek by Hugh G. Evelyn-White. Loeb Classical Library (Cambridge, Mass.: Harvard University Press; London: Wm. Heinemann, 1959).

Heyne, Moriz. *Das deutsche Nahrungswesen von den ältesten Geschichtlichen Zeiten bis zum 16. Jahrhundert* (Leipzig: Verlag von S. Hirzel, 1901).

Hicks, L. E. *A Critique of Design-Arguments* (New York: Charles Scribner's Sons, 1883).

Hildebrand, George H. See Teggart, Frederick J.

Hippocrates. *Airs, Waters, Places.* Trans. from the Greek by W. H. S. Jones. Loeb Classical Library (Cambridge, Mass.: Harvard University Press, 1948 [1923]). Being Vol. I of *Works of Hippocrates.*

——. *Ancient Medicine.* Trans. from the Greek by W. H. S. Jones. Loeb Classical Library (Cambridge, Mass.: Harvard University Press, 1948 [1923]). Being Vol. I of *Works of Hippocrates.*

——. *Nature of Man.* Trans. from the Greek by W. H. S. Jones. Loeb Classical Library (New York: G. P. Putnam's Sons, 1931). Being Vol. IV of *Works of Hippocrates.*

Hitti, Philip K. *The Arabs. A Short History.* A Gateway Edition (Chicago: Henry Regnery Co., n.d.).

Hodgen, Margaret T. *Early Anthropology in the Sixteenth and Seventeenth Centuries* (Philadelphia: University of Pennsylvania Press, 1964).

——. "Johann Boemus (fl. 1500): An Early Anthropologist," *American Anthropologist,* Vol. 55 (1953), pp. 284–294.

——. "Sebastian Muenster (1489–1552): A Sixteenth-Century Ethnographer," *Osiris,* Vol. 11 (1954), pp. 504–529.

Holbach, Paul Henri T., Baron d'. *The System of Nature.* Trans. from the French by H. D. Robinson (Boston: J. P. Mendum, 1868).

*Holy Bible.* Revised Standard Version (New York, Toronto, Edinburgh: Thomas Nelson & Sons, 1952).

Honigmann, Ernst. *Die Sieben Klimata und die* ΠΟΛΕΙΣ ΕΠΙΣΗΜΟΙ (Heidelberg: Carl Winter's Universitätsbuchhandlung, 1929).

Hooykaas, R. "Science and Theology in the Middle Ages," *Free University Quarterly,* Vol. 3, No. 2 (1954), pp. 77–163.

Horace. *The Odes and Epodes.* Trans. from the Latin by C. E. Bennett. Loeb Classical Library (Cambridge, Mass.: Harvard University Press; London, Wm. Heinemann, 1960 [1927]).

——. *Satires, Epistles, and Ars Poetica.* Trans. from the Latin by H. Rushton Fairclough. Loeb Classical Library (Cambridge, Mass.: Harvard University Press; London: Wm. Heinemann, 1961 [1929]).

——. *The Works of Horace*. Trans. by C. Smart, rev. by Theodore A. Buckley (London: George Bell & Sons, 1888).

How, W. W. and J. Wells. *A Commentary on Herodotus* (Oxford: Clarendon Press, 1912). 2 vols.

Huffel, G. *Economie Forestière* (Vol. 1:1, Paris: Lucien Laveur, 1910; Vol. 1:2, Paris: Librairie Agricole de la Maison Rustique, Librairie de l'Académie d'Agriculture, 1920).

——. "Les Méthodes de l'Aménagement Forestier en France," *Annales de l'École Nationale des Eaux et Fôrets*, Vol. 1, Fasc. 2 (1927).

Humboldt, Alexander von. *Cosmos: A Sketch of a Physical Description of the Universe*. Trans. from the German by E. C. Otté (New York: Harper and Brothers, 1844). 4 vols. in 2.

——. *Essai Politique sur le Royaume de la Nouvelle-Espagne* (Paris: Chez F. Schoell, 1811). 3 vols.

——. *Ideen zu einer Geographie der Pflanzen nebst einem Naturgemälde der Tropenländer.* . . . (Tübingen: F. G. Cotta, etc., 1807).

—— and Bonpland, Aimé. *Essai sur la Géographie des Plantes; Accompagné d'un Tableau Physique des Régions Équinoxiales* (Ed. facsimilaire, México: Institut Panaméricain de Géographie et d'Histoire, 1955).

Hume, David. *Dialogues Concerning Natural Religion*. Edited with intro. by Henry D. Aiken (New York: Hafner Publishing Co., 1962 [1948]).

——. "Of Commerce," *Essays Moral, Political, and Literary*. Eds. T. H. Green and T. H. Grose (London: Longmans, Green and Co., 1882), Vol. 1, pp. 287–299.

——. "Of National Characters" [1748], *Essays Moral, Political, and Literary*. Eds. T. H. Green and T. H. Grose (London: Longmans, Green and Co., 1882), Vol. 1, pp. 244–258.

——. "Of the Populousness of Ancient Nations," *Essays Moral, Political, and Literary*. Eds. T. H. Green and T. H. Grose (London: Longmans, Green and Co., 1882), Vol. 1, pp. 381–443.

——. "Of Taxes," *Essays Moral, Political, and Literary*. Eds. T. H. Green and T. H. Grose (London: Longmans, Green and Co., 1882), Vol. 1, pp. 356–360.

Humphries, William J. *An Edition and Study, Linguistic and Historical, of the French Translation of 1372 by Jean Corbechon of Book XV (Geography) of Bartholomaeus Anglicus' De proprietatibus rerum*. Ph.D. thesis (Berkeley: University of California, 1955).

Hunt, Arthur S. and J. Gilbart Smyly. *The Tebtunis Papyri* (London: Humphrey Milford, 1933). 3 vols.

Hunter, William B., Jr. "The Seventeenth Century Doctrine of Plastic Nature," *Harvard Theological Review*, Vol. 43 (1950), pp. 197–213.

Hunter-Blair, David Oswald. *The Rule of St. Benedict*. Latin and English with notes (2nd ed.; London and Edinburgh: Sands & Co.; St. Louis, etc.: B. Herder, 1907).

Hussey, J. M. *The Byzantine World*. Harper Torchbooks/Academy Library (New York: Harper & Brothers, 1961).

Huth, Hans. *Nature and the American* (Berkeley and Los Angeles: University of Calif. Press, 1957).

Huxley, Thomas Henry. "Evolution and Ethics. Prolegomena," *Evolution and Ethics and Other Essays* (New York: D. Appleton and Co., 1896), pp. 1–45.

Ibn Khaldūn. *The Muqaddimah; an Introduction to History*. Trans. from the Arabic by Franz Rosenthal (New York: Pantheon Books, 1958). 3 vols.

——. *Les Prolégomènes de Ibn Khaldoun*. Trans. from Arabic to French by M. Mac Guckin de Slane (Paris: Impr. Impériale, 1863–1865).

Irenaeus. "Against Heresies," *ANF*, Vol. 1, pp. 309–567.

Isidore of Seville. "De natura rerum ad Sisebutum regem Liber," *PL*, Vol. 83, cols. 963–1018.

——. "Etymologiarum libri xx," *PL*, Vol. 82, cols. 73–728.

——. "Sententiarum libri tres," *PL*, Vol. 83, cols. 537–738.

Isocrates. "Busiris," in *Isocrates*. Trans. from the Greek by Larue van Hook. Loeb Classical Library (London: Wm. Heinemann; Cambridge, Mass.: Harvard University Press, 1954), Vol. 3, pp. 100–131.

Jacks, Leo V. *St. Basil and Greek Literature*. Catholic University of America Patristic Studies, Vol. 1 (Washington: Catholic University of America, 1922).

Jacoby, Felix. *Die Fragmente der Griechischen Historiker* (Berlin: Weidmannsche Buchhandlung, 1926).

Jean de Meun. See Guillaume de Lorris and Jean de Meun.

Jefferson, Thomas. *The Complete Jefferson*. . . . Ed. by Saul K. Padover (New York: Distr. by Duell, Sloan & Pearce, 1943).

——. "Notes on the State of Virginia," Saul Padover, ed., *The Complete Jefferson* (q.v.).

Jessen, Karl F. W. *Botanik der Gegenwart und Vorzeit in culturhistorischer Entwickelung. Ein Beitrag zur Geschichte der abendländischen Völker* (Waltham, Mass.: The Chronica Botanica Co., 1948 [1864]).

John Chrysostomus. "The Homilies of S. John Chrysostom on the Epistle of St. Paul the Apostle to the Romans." Trans. by J. B. Morris. *A Library of the Fathers of the Holy Catholic Church Anterior to the Division of the East and West*, Vol. 7 (Oxford: John Henry Parker; London; J. G. F. and J. Rivington, 1842).

——. "The Homilies on the Statues, or to the People of Antioch," *A Library of the Fathers of the Holy Catholic Church Anterior to the Division of the East and West*, Vol. 9 (Oxford: J. H. Parker, etc., etc., 1842).

John Damascene. "Expositio accurata fidei orthodoxae" (Greek and Latin), *PG*, Vol. 94, cols. 790–1228.

——. "Genaue Darlegung des Orthodoxen Glaubens." Trans. from the Greek into German by Dionys Stiefenhofer. *BDK*, Vol. 44 (Munich: Joseph Kösel & Friedrich Pustet, 1923).

John of Salisbury. *The Metalogicon. A Twelfth-Century Defense of the Verbal and Logical Arts of the Trivium*. Trans. from the Latin by Daniel D. McGarry (Berkeley and Los Angeles: University of Calif. Press, 1962).

John the Scot (Joannes Scotus Erigena). "De divisione naturae," *PL*, Vol. 122, cols. 439–1022.

——. *Uber die Eintheilung der Natur*. Trans. from the Latin into German by Ludwig Noack (Berlin: L. Heimann, 1870–1874). 2 vols. in 1.

Johnson, Francis R. "Preparation and Innovation in the Progress of Science," *JHI*, Vol. 4 (1943), pp. 56–59.

Jones, Gwilym P. "Building in Stone in Medieval Western Europe," *CEHE*, Vol. 2, pp. 493–518.

Jones, Richard F. *Ancients and Moderns. A Study of the Background of the "Battle of the Books"* (St. Louis: Washington University Studies—New Series Language and Literature—No. 6, 1936).

Jonston, John of Poland. *An History of the Constancy of Nature* (London: Printed for John Streater, 1657).

Jordanes (Iordanis). *De origine actibusque Getarum*. Ed. Theodor Mommsen, *Mon. Ger. Hist., Auctores Antiquissimi*, Vol. 5: 1 (Berlin: apud Weidmannos, 1882).

——. *The Gothic History*. Trans., intro., comm., by Charles C. Mierow (Princeton: Princeton University Press; London: Oxford University Press, 1915).

Josephus. *Against Apion*. Trans. from the Greek by H. St. J. Thackeray. Loeb Classical Library (London: Wm. Heinemann; New York: G. P. Putnam's Sons, 1926). Being Vol. I of *Josephus*, pp. 161–411.

Jurisprudence forestière. See Dalloz, M. D., and Dalloz, Armand, eds., *Répertoire méthodique*, etc.

Kaerst, J. *Die antike Idee der Oikumene in ihrer politischen und kulturellen Bedeutung* (Leipzig: B. G. Teubner, 1903).

——. *Geschichte des Hellenismus. Bd. 2. Das Wesen des Hellenismus* (2d ed., Leipzig and Berlin: B. G. Teubner, 1926).

Kahn, Charles H. *Anaximander and the Origins of Greek Cosmology* (New York: Columbia University Press, 1960).

Kalm, Peter. *Peter Kalm's Travels in North America*. Rev. from the original Swedish and edited by Adolph B. Benson (New York: Wilson-Erickson, Inc., 1937). 2 vols.

——. *Travels into North America*. Trans. by John Reinhold Forster (2nd ed.; London: T. Lowndes, 1772). 2 vols.

Kames, Henry Home, Lord. *Sketches of the History of Man* (Edinburgh: Printed for W. Creech, Edinburgh; and for W. Strahan, and T. Caddel, London, 1774). 2 vols.

Kant, Immanuel. *Critique of Pure Reason*. Trans. from the German by F. Max Müller 2nd ed., rev.; New York: Macmillan Co., 1902).

——. *Critique of Teleological Judgement*, Being Part II of *The Critique of Judgement*. Trans. from the German by James Creed Meredith (Oxford: Clarendon Press, 1952).

——. "Physische Geographie," *Immanuel Kant's Sämmtliche Werke*. Ed. G. Hartenstein, Vol. 8 (Leipzig: L. Voss, 1868), pp. 145–452.

Kantorowicz, Ernst. *Kaiser Friedrich der Zweite* (Berlin: George Bondi, 1927), *Ergänzungsband* (Berlin: George Bondi, 1931).

Kees. "Sesostris," *PW*, Vol. 2A:2, cols. 1861–1876.

Keill, John. *An Examination of Dr. Burnet's Theory of the Earth with Some Remarks on Mr. Whiston's New Theory of the Earth. Also an Examination of the Reflections on the Theory of the Earth. . . .* (2nd ed., corr.; London: Printed for H. Clements and S. Harding, 1734).

Kendrick, T. D. *The Lisbon Earthquake* (Philadelphia and New York: J. B. Lippincott Co., 1957?).

Kepler, Johannes. "Epitome astronomiae copernicanae," *Johannes Kepler Gesammelte Werke*, Vol. 7 (München: C. H. Beck'sche Verlagsbuchhandlung, 1953).

Keynes, John Maynard. "Robert Malthus: The First of the Cambridge Economists," *Essays in Biography* (New York: Harcourt, Brace and Co., 1933), pp. 95–149.

Kimble, George H. T. *Geography in the Middle Ages* (London: Methuen and Co., 1938).

Kirk, G. S., and Raven, J. E. *The Presocratic Philosophers* (Cambridge: Cambridge University Press, 1960).

Kitto, H. D. F. *Greek Tragedy: A Literary Study*. Anchor Books (Garden City, N. Y.: Doubleday & Co., 1955).

Klauck, Karl. "Albertus Magnus und die Erdkunde," *Studia Albertina*, ed. by Heinrich Ostlender (Münster: Aschendorffsche Verlagsbuchhandlung, 1952), pp. 234–248. (Supplementband 4 of *Beiträge zur Geschichte der Philosophie und Theologie des Mittelalters*).

Klemm, Friedrich. *A History of Western Technology*. Trans. from the German by Dorothea Waley Singer (New York: Charles Scribner's Sons, 1959).

Kliger, Samuel. *The Goths in England. A Study in Seventeenth and Eighteenth Century Thought* (Cambridge, Mass.: Harvard University Press, 1952).

Kock, Theodorus, ed. *Comicorum Atticorum Fragmenta*, Vol. 3:2 (Lipsiae: in aedibus B. G. Teubneri, 1888).

Koebner, Richard. "The Settlement and Colonisation of Europe," *CEHE*, Vol. 1, pp. 1–88.

Körner, S. *Kant*. A Pelican Book (Harmondsworth: Penguin Books, 1955).

Koller, Armin Hajman. *The Abbé du Bos—His Advocacy of the Theory of Climate. A Precursor of Johann Gottfried Herder* (Champaign, Ill.: The Garrard Press, 1937).

Koyré, Alexander. "The Origins of Modern Science: A New Interpretation," *Diogenes*, No. 16, Winter 1956, pp. 1–22.

——. "Le Vide et l'Espace Infini au XIVᵉ Siècle," *Archives d'Histoire Doctrinale et Littéraire du Moyen Âge*, Vol. 24 (1949), pp. 45–91.

Kramer, Samuel Noah. *History Begins at Sumer* (New York: Doubleday & Co., 1959).

——. "Sumerian Historiography," *Israel Exploration Journal Vol. 3* (1953), pp. 217–232.

——. *Sumerian Mythology* (New York: Harper & Brothers, 1944).

Kretschmer, Konrad. *Die physische Erdkunde im christlichen Mittelalter* (Wien und Olmütz: Eduard Hölzel, 1889). (*Geographische Abhandlungen herausgegeben von Albrecht Penck*, Vol. 4:1).

Kristeller, Paul O. *Renaissance Thought. The Classic, Scholastic, and Humanist Strains.* Harper Torchbooks/Academy Library (New York: Harper & Brothers, 1961).

Kroeber, Alfred L. *Configurations of Culture Growth* (Berkeley and Los Angeles: University of California Press, 1944).

—— and Kluckhohn, Clyde. *Culture. A Critical Review of Concepts and Definitions.* Vintage Books (New York: Alfred A. Knopf, Inc. and Random House, 1963). Originally published in the *Papers of the Peabody Museum of American Archeology and Ethnology*, Harvard University, Vol. 47 (1952), No. 1.

Lactantius. "The Divine Institutes," *ANF*, Vol. 7, pp. 9–223.

——. "The Epitome of the Divine Institutes," *ANF*, Vol. 7, pp. 224–255.

——. "A Treatise on the Anger of God," *ANF*, Vol. 7, pp. 259–280.

Lafitau, Joseph François. *Moeurs des Sauvages Ameriquains, Comparées aux Moeurs des Premiers Temps* (Paris: Saugrain l'Aîné [etc.], 1724). 2 vols.

Lage, G. Raynaud de. *Alain de Lille. Poète du XIIᵉ Siècle* (Montreal: Institut d'Études Médiévales, 1951).

Lamprecht, Karl. *Deutsches Wirtschaftsleben im Mittelalter* (Leipzig: Alphons Dürr, 1885–1886). 3 vols.

Langlois, C. V. *La Connaissance de la Nature et du Monde au Moyen Âge d'après quelques Écrits Français à l'Usage des Laïcs* (Paris: Hachette et Cie., 1911).

*Lavoisne's Complete Genealogical, Historical, Chronological, and Geographical Atlas, etc., etc.* (3rd ed.; London: J. Barfield, 1822).

*The Laws of Burgos of 1512–1513. Royal Ordinances for the Good Government and Treatment of the Indians.* Trans. from the Spanish by Lesley Byrd Simpson (San Francisco: John Howell, 1960).

Leclercq, H. "Chasse," *Dictionnaire d'Archéologie Chrétienne et de Liturgie* (Paris: Letouzy et Ané, 1907– ). Vol. 3:1, cols. 1079–1144.

Leclercq, Jean. *The Love of Learning and the Desire for God. A Study of Monastic Culture.* Trans. from the French by Catharine Misrahi, Mentor-Omega (New York: New American Library Books, 1962).

Lefebvre des Noëttes, Richard. *L'Attelage, le Cheval de Selle à Travers les Âges. Contribution à l'Histoire de l'Esclavage* (Paris: A. Picard, 1931). 2 vols.

Leff, Gordon. *Medieval Thought, St. Augustine to Ockham* (Baltimore: Penguin Books, 1962 [1958]).

Leibniz, Gottfried Wilhelm. *Leibniz: Philosophical Writings.* Trans. by Mary Morris. Everyman's Library (London: J. M. Dent & Sons; New York: E. P. Dutton & Co., 1956 [1934]). Includes *The Monadology* 1714.

——. *Leibniz. Selections.* Ed. Philip P. Wiener (New York: Charles Scribner's Sons, 1951).

——. *Sämtliche Schriften und Briefe*, herausgegeben von der Preussischen Akademie der Wissenschaften (Darmstadt: Otto Reichl, 1923–1962). 11 vols.

——. "Vorschläge für eine Teutschliebende Genossenschafft," *Die Werke von Leibniz*, ed. Onno Klopp (Hannover: Klindworth's Verlag, 1864–1884), Vol. 6, pp. 214–219.

Leonardo da Vinci. *The Notebooks of Leonardo da Vinci.* Arr. and trans. from the Italian with intro. by Edward MacCurdy (New York: George Braziller, 1956).

Le Roy (Leroy), Louis. *Of the Interchangeable Course, or Variety of Things in the Whole World. . . .* Trans. from the French by Robert S. Ashley (London: C. Yetsweirt, 1594).

Levy, Reuben. *The Social Structure of Islam.* Being the 2nd ed. of *The Sociology of Islam* (Cambridge: Cambridge University Press, 1962).

*Lexicon Manuale.* See Maigne d'Arnis, W. H.

Lietzmann, Hans. *The Founding of the Church Universal. A History of the Early*

*Church*, Vol. 2. Trans. from the German by Bertram Lee Woolf (3rd ed. rev.; New York: Meridian Books, 1958 [1953]).

Linné, Carl von [Linnaeus]. "Oeconomia naturae." Trans. from the Latin into Swedish by Isac [*sic*] I. Biberg, *Valda Smärre Skrifter af Allmänt Naturvetenskapligt Innehåll* (Upsala: Almquist & Wiksells, 1906), pp. 1–64. With notes.

——. "The Oeconomy of Nature." Benjamin Stillingfleet, ed., *Miscellaneous Tracts Relating to Natural History, Husbandry, and Physick* (4th ed.; London: Printed for J. Dodsley, etc., etc., 1791), pp. 37–129. (Isaac [*sic*] Biberg, really trans. of L. from Latin to Swedish, is shown here as author.)

Locke, John. *An Essay Concerning Human Understanding* [1690], *The Works of John Locke* (12th ed.; London: Printed for C. and J. Rivington, etc., 1824). 9 vols. Vols. 1–2.

Lockwood, Dean P. "It is Time to Recognize a New Modern Age," *JHI*, Vol. 4 (1943), pp. 63–65.

Lope de Vega. *El Nuevo Mundo Descubierto por Cristóbal Colón*. Ed. Ed. Barry (Paris: Garnier Frères, c. 1897).

Lorain, John. *Nature and Reason Harmonized in the Practice of Husbandry* (Philadelphia: H. C. Carey & I. Lea, 1825).

Louis, Conrad. *The Theology of Psalm VIII. A Study of the Traditions of the Text and the Theological Import*. Catholic University of America, Studies in Sacred Theology No. 99 (Washington, D. C.: Catholic University of America Press, 1946).

Lovejoy, Arthur O. *The Great Chain of Being: A Study of the History of an Idea*. The William James Lectures Delivered at Harvard University, 1933 (Cambridge, Mass.: Harvard University Press, 1948).

——. "The Supposed Primitivism of Rousseau's Discourse on Inequality," *Modern Philology*, Vol. 21 (1923), pp. 165–186; repr. in *Essays in the History of Ideas*. Capricorn Books (New York: G. P. Putnam's Sons, 1960 [1948]), pp. 14–37.

—— and Boas, George. *Primitivism and Related Ideas in Antiquity. A Documentary History of Primitivism and Related Ideas*. Vol. I (Baltimore: Johns Hopkins Press, 1935).

Lucretius. *The Nature of the Universe*. Trans. from the Latin by R. E. Latham. Penguin Classics (Harmondsworth: Penguin Books, 1951).

——. *Titi Lucreti Cari De Rerum Natura Libri Sex*. Ed. *with Prolegomena, Critical Apparatus, Translation, and Commentary by Cyril Bailey* (Oxford: Clarendon Press, 1947). 3 vols.

Lukermann, F. "The Concept of Location in Classical Geography," *AAAG*, Vol. 51 (1961), pp. 194–210.

Lyell, Katharine M. *Life, Letters and Journals of Sir Charles Lyell, Bart . . .* (London: J. Murray, 1881). 2 vols.

Mabillon, Iohannes, ed. *Acta sanctorum Ordinis s. Benedicti in saeculorum classes distributa . . .* (Lutetiae Parisiorum: apud Ludovicum Billaine, 1668–1671). 6 vols. in 9 (NA).

McCann, Justin. *Saint Benedict*. Image Books (rev. ed., Garden City, N. Y.: Doubleday & Co., 1958).

McDonald, Angus. *Early American Soil Conservationists*. U. S. Dept. of Agric., Misc. Pub. No. 449 (Washington, 1941).

Machiavelli, Niccolò. "Dell'arte della guerra," *Opere*, ed. by Antonio Panella, Vol. 2 (Milano-Roma: Rizzoli & Co., 1939).

——. *Florentine History*. Trans. from the Italian by W. K. Marriott. Everyman's Library (London: J. M. Dent and Co.; New York: E. P. Dutton and Co., [1909]).

——. *The Prince and the Discourses*. Modern Library (New York: Random House, 1940).

MacNutt, Francis A. *Bartholomew de las Casas. His Life, His Apostolate, and His Writings* (New York and London: G. P. Putnam's Sons, 1909).

Maigne D'Arnis, W. H. *Lexicon Manuale ad Scriptores Mediae et Infimae Latinitatis. . . .* (Paris: apud Garnier Fratres, 1890).

Maimonides, Moses. *The Guide for the Perplexed*. Trans. from the Arabic by M. Friedländer. (2nd ed. rev.; New York: Dover Publications, 1956).

Mâle, Émile. *The Gothic Image. Religious Art in France of the Thirteenth Century*. Trans. from the French by Dora Nussey. Harper Torchbooks/Cathedral Library (New York: Harper & Brothers, 1958).

Malthus, Thomas R. *An Essay on Population*. Everyman's Library (7th ed. London: J. M. Dent & Sons; New York: E. P. Dutton & Co., 1952 [1914]). 2 vols.

———. *First Essay on Population 1798; with notes by James Bonar*. Repr. for the Royal Economic Society (London: Macmillan & Co., 1926).

———. *An Inquiry into the Nature and Progress of Rent, and the Principles by Which it is Regulated* [1815]. A Reprint of Economic Tracts edited by Jacob H. Hollander (Baltimore: Johns Hopkins Press, 1903).

———. *Population: The First Essay; with a foreword by Kenneth E. Boulding*. Ann Arbor Paperbacks (Ann Arbor: University of Michigan Press, 1959).

———. *Principles of Political Economy Considered with a View to Their Practical Application* (London: John Murray, 1820).

Marsh, George P. *Man and Nature; or Physical Geography as Modified by Human Action* (New York: Charles Scribner & Co., 1871 [1864]).

Martini, "Dikaiarchos, 3," *PW*, Vol. 5, cols. 546–563.

Marx, Leo. *The Machine in the Garden; Technology and the Pastoral Ideal in America* (New York: Oxford University Press, 1964).

Maulde, René de. *Étude sur la Condition Forestière de l'Orléanais au Moyen Âge et à la Renaissance* (Orléans: Herluison, 1871).

Maupertuis, Pierre Louis Moreau de. *Essai de Cosmologie* (Leide?, 1751).

Maury, Alfred. *Les Forêts de la Gaule et de l'Ancienne France* (Paris: Librairie Philosophique de Ladrange, 1867).

Mazzei, Filippo. *Recherches Historiques et Politiques sur les États-Unis de l'Amérique Septentrionale.* . . . (A Colle, et se trouve a Paris, chez Froullé, 1788). 4 vols. NA.

Meaume, Édouard. See *Jurisprudence forestière*.

Meuten, Anton. *Bodins Theorie von der Beeinflussung des politischen Lebens der Staaten durch ihre geographische Lage* (Bonn: Carl Georgi, Universitäts-Buchdruckerei und Verlag, 1904).

Meyer, Ernst. "Albertus Magnus. Ein Beitrag zur Geschichte der Botanik im dreizehnten Jahrhundert," *Linnaea*, Vol. 10 (1836), pp. 641–741; Vol. 11 (1837), pp. 545–595.

———. *Geschichte der Botanik* (Gebrüder Bornträger, 1854–1857). 4 vols.

Meyer, R. W. *Leibnitz and the Seventeenth-Century Revolution*. Trans. from the German by J. P. Stern (Cambridge: Bowes and Bowes, 1952).

Migne, Jacques Paul. *Patrologiae cursus completus.* . . . *Series graeca* (Parisiis: excudebatur et venit apud J. P. Migne, 1857–1899).

———, ed. *Patrologiae cursus completus.* . . . *Series latina* (Parisiis excudebat Migne, 1844–1902).

Milton, John. *The Poetical Works of John Milton*. Everyman's Library (London & Toronto: J. M. Dent & Sons; New York: E. P. Dutton & Co., 1929 [1909]).

Minucius Felix. "The Octavius of Minucius Felix." Trans. by Robert E. Wallis. *ANF*, Vol. 4, pp. 169–198.

Mombert, Paul. *Bevölkerungslehre* (Jena: G. Fischer, 1929).

Montaigne. "An Apologie of Raymond Sebond," *The Essayes of Michael Lord of Montaigne*. Trans. from the French by John Florio. Everyman's Library (London & Toronto: J. M. Dent & Sons; New York: E. P. Dutton & Co., 1921 [1910]), Vol. 2, pp. 125–326.

Montalembert, Count de. *The Monks of the West, from St. Benedict to St. Bernard*. Trans. from the French (London: John C. Nimmo, 1896). 6 vols.

Montesquieu. Charles de Secondat Baron de la Brède et de Montesquieu. "Défense de l'Esprit des Lois," *Oeuvres Complètes de Montesquieu*. Ed. Edouard Laboulaye (Paris: Garnier Frères, 1875–1879). Vol. 6.

——. *De l'Esprit des Loix.* Texte Établi et Présenté par Jean Brethe de la Gressaye (Paris: Société Les Belles Lettres, 1950–1961). 4 vols.

——. *Pensées et Fragments Inédits de Montesquieu.* Ed. Le Baron Gaston de Montesquieu (Bordeaux: G. Gounouilhou, 1899–1901). 2 vols.

——. *The Persian Letters.* Trans. from the French by J. Robert Loy. Meridian Books (New York: World Publishing Co., 1961).

——. *The Spirit of Laws.* Trans. from the French by Thomas Nugent (rev. ed.; New York: The Colonial Press, 1899). 2 vols.

*Monumenta Germaniae Historica Diplomatum Imperii,* ed. by Pertz. Vol. 1 (Hannoverae: Impensis Bibliopolii Avlici Hahniani, 1872).

More, Henry. *A Collection of Several Philosophical Writings of Henry More* (4th ed. corr. and much enl. London: Printed by Joseph Downing, 1712). Includes "An Antidote against Atheism," "Scholia on the Antidote against Atheism."

Mornet, Daniel. *Les Sciences de la Nature en France, au XVIIIᵉ Siècle* (Paris: A. Colin, 1911).

Moscati, Sabatino. *The Face of the Ancient Orient.* Trans. from the Italian. Anchor Books (Garden City, N. Y.: Doubleday & Co., 1962).

Moschus. See *Greek Bucolic Poets.*

Mühlmann, Wilhelm. *Methodik der Völkerkunde* (Stuttgart: Ferdinand Enke Verlag, 1938).

Münster, Sebastian. *Cosmographey. . . .* (Basel: durch Sebastianum Henricpetri, 1598).

Muggenthaler, Hans. *Kolonisatorische und wirtschaftliche Tätigkeit eines deutschen Zisterzienserklosters im XII. und XIII. Jahrhundert* (München: Hugo Schmidt Verlag, 1924).

Mullach, Friedrich W. A. *Fragmenta philosophorum graecorum* (Parisiis: A Firmin Didot, 1875–1881). 3 vols.

Mummenhoff, Ernst. *Altnürnberg* (Bamberg: Buchnersche Verlagsbuchhandlung, 1890).

Myres, Sir John Linton. "Herodotus and Anthropology." R. R. Marett, ed., *Anthropology and the Classics* (Oxford: Clarendon Press, 1908), pp. 121–168.

Neckam, Alexander. *See* Alexander Neckam.

Nef, John U. *Cultural Foundations of Industrial Civilization.* Harper Torchbooks/Academy Library (New York: Harper & Bros., 1960 [1958]).

——. "Mining and Metallurgy in Medieval Civilisation," *CEHE,* Vol. 2, pp. 429–492.

Nestle, W. *Herodots Verhältnis zur Philosophie und Sophistik* (Stuttgart: Stuttgarter Vereinsbuchdruckerei [1908]).

Newton, Isaac. "Four Letters from Sir Isaac Newton to Doctor Bentley: Containing Some Arguments in Proof of a Deity," *The Works of Richard Bentley, D. D.,* collected and edited by Alexander Dyce, Vol. 3 (London: Francis Macpherson, 1838), pp. 203–215.

——. *Opera quae exstant omnia* (London: J. Nichols, 1779–1785). 5 vols.

Nicolson, Marjorie H. *Mountain Gloom and Mountain Glory: The Development of the Aesthetics of the Infinite* (Ithaca: Cornell University Press, 1959).

Niederhuber, Johann. See Ambrose, St.

Nieuwentijdt, Bernard. *The Religious Philosopher: Or, the Right Use of Contemplating the Works of the Creator.* Trans. from the Dutch by John Chamberlayne (London: Printed for J. Senexi, etc., etc., 1718–1720). 2 vols.

Ninck, Martin. *Die Entdeckung von Europa durch die Griechen* (Basel: Benno Schwabe & Co. Verlag [1945]).

Nordenskiöld, Erik. *The History of Biology.* Trans. from the Swedish by Leonard B. Eyre (New York: Tudor Publishing Co., 1928).

Nougier, Louis-René; Beaujeu, Jean; and Mollat, Michel. "De la Préhistoire à la fin du Moyen Âge," being Vol. 1 of *Histoire Universelle des Explorations* (Paris: F. Sant' Andrea, 1955–1956).

Oake, Roger B. "Montesquieu and Hume," *Modern Language Quarterly,* Vol. 2 (1941), pp. 25–41, 225–248.

*Oesterreichische Weisthümer* (Wien: Oesterreichische Akademie der Wissenschaften, Kaiserliche Akademie der Wissenschaften Vols. 1-11, 1870-1958).

Olschki, Leonardo. *Die Literatur der Technik und der angewandten Wissenschaften vom Mittelalter bis zur Renaissance*. Vol. 1 of *Gesch. der neusprachlichen wissenschaftlichen Literatur* (Leipzig, Firenze, Roma, Genève: Leo S. Olschki, 1919).

——. *Marco Polo's Asia*. Trans. from the Italian by John A. Scott (Berkeley and Los Angeles: University of California Press, 1960).

——. *Marco Polo's Precursors* (Baltimore: Johns Hopkins Press, 1943).

Opstelten, J. C. *Sophocles and Greek Pessimism*. Trans. from the Dutch by J. A. Ross (Amsterdam: North-Holland Publishing Co., 1952).

Orderic Vital. "Histoire de Normandie." Ed. Guizot, *Collection des Mémoires Relatifs à l'Histoire de France*. Vols. 25-26 (Paris: J. L. J. Brière, 1825).

Origen. *Contra Celsum*. Trans. with intro. and notes by Henry Chadwick (Cambridge: Cambridge University Press, 1953).

——. "De Principiis (Peri Archon)." Trans. by Frederick Crombie, *ANF*, Vol. 4, pp. 239-382.

Orosius, Paulus. *Seven Books of History Against the Pagans*. Trans. with intro. and notes by Irving W. Raymond (New York: Columbia University Press, 1936).

Ostrogorsky, Georg. "Agrarian Conditions in the Byzantine Empire in the Middle Ages," *CEHE*, Vol. 1, pp. 194-223.

Otto, Bishop of Freising, and his continuator Rahewin. *The Deeds of Frederick Barbarossa*. Trans. from the Latin by Charles C. Mierow (New York: Columbia University Press, 1953).

Otto, Bishop of Freising. *The Two Cities, A Chronicle of Universal History to the Year 1146 A.D.* Trans. by Charles Christopher Mierow (New York: Columbia University Press, 1928).

Overbury, Sir Thomas. "Observations in His Travailes Upon the State of the XVII. Provinces as They Stood Anno Dom., 1609," *The Miscellaneous Works in Prose and Verse of Sir Thomas Overbury, Knt.*, ed. Edward F. Rimbault (London: John Russell Smith, 1856), pp. 221-251.

Ovid. *Metamorphoses*. Trans. from the Latin by Frank J. Miller. Loeb Classical Library (London: Wm. Heinemann; New York: G. P. Putnam's Sons. Vol. 1, 1916, 2d ed. 1921; Vol. 2, 1916).

Palissy, Bernard. *The Admirable Discourses*. Trans. from the French by Aurèle la Rocque (Urbana: University of Illinois Press, 1957).

Paracelsus, Theophrastus. *The Hermetic and Alchemical Writings of Aureolus Philippus Theophrastus Bombast of Hohenheim called Paracelsus the Great*. Trans. from the German by Arthur E. Waite (London: J. Elliott and Col Co., 1894). 2 vols.

——. *Lebendiges Erbe. Eine Auslese aus seinen sämtlichen Schriften mit 150 zeitgenössischen Illustrationen*. Edited with intro. by Jolan Jacobi (Zürich und Leipzig: Rascher Verlag, 1942).

——. *Sämtliche Werke*. Eds. Karl Sudhoff and Wilhelm Matthiessen. *Abt. 1, Medizinische naturwissenschaftliche und philosophische Schriften; Abt. 2, Die theologischen und religionsphilosophische Schriften* (München: Barth, 1922-   ).

——. *Selected Writings*. Ed. by Jolande [*sic*] Jacobi, trans. from the German (*Lebendiges Erbe*) by Norbert Guterman (New York: Pantheon Books, 1951).

Parain, Charles. "The Evolution of Agricultural Technique," *CEHE*, Vol. 1, pp. 118-168.

Partsch, J. "Die Grenzen der Menschheit. I Teil: Die antike Oikumene," *Berichte über die Verhandlungen der Königl. Sächsischen Gesellschaft der Wissenschaften zu Leipzig. Phil.-hist. klasse*, Vol. 68 (1916).

Pastor, Ludwig Freiherrn von. *Geschichte der Päpste seit dem Ausgang des Mittelalters*, Vol. 5 being *Geschichte Papst Pauls III* (13th ed., Freiburg im Breisgau: Herder and Co., 1956). Earlier ed. trans. by Kerr under the title, *History of the Popes*, Vol. 12 being on Paul III.

Patin, M. *Études sur la poésie latine* (3d ed., Paris: Librairie Hachette et Cie., 1883). 2 vols.

Paul the Deacon. *History of the Langobards*. Trans. from the Latin by William D. Foulke (New York: Sold by Longmans Green & Co., 1907).

———. "Pauli Warnefridi Diaconi Foroiuliensis De Gestis Langobardorum," *PL*, Vol. 95.

Paul III, Pope. The Bull, "Sublimis Deus," of Pope Paul III, MacNutt, Francis A., *Bartholomew de las Casas* (New York and London: G. P. Putnam's Sons, 1909), pp. 427–431. Latin text and English trans.

*Paulys Real-Encyclopädie der classischen Altertumswissenschaft*, hrsg. von Wissowa, Kroll, Witte, Mittelhaus and others (Stuttgart: J. B. Metzler and later publishers, 1894– ).

Pauw, Corneille de. *Recherches Philosophiques sur les Américains* (London, 1770). 3 vols.

Pease, A. S. "Caeli enarrant," *Harvard Theological Review*, 34 (1941), pp. 103–200.

———. See also Cicero, *De natura deorum*.

Penrose, Ernest F. *Population Theories and Their Application with Special Reference to Japan* (Stanford University: Food Research Inst., 1934).

Perrault, Charles. *Parallèle des Anciens et des Modernes en ce qui Regarde les Arts et les Sciences. Dialogues. Avec le Poème du Siècle de Louis le Grand, et une Epistre en Vers sur le Genie* (2nd ed.; Paris: La Veuve de Jean Bapt. Coignard and Jean Baptiste Coignard fils, 1692), Vol. 1.

Petersen, William. *Population* (New York: Macmillan Co., 1961).

Petrarca, Francesco. "On His Own Ignorance and That of Many Others." Trans. by Hans Nachod. Cassirer, Ernst; Kristeller, Paul O.; and Randall, John H., Jr., eds., *The Renaissance Philosophy of Man* (Chicago: University of Chicago Press, 1948), pp. 47–133.

Petty, Sir William. *The Economic Writings of Sir William Petty*. Ed. Charles H. Hull, Vol. 1 (Cambridge: Cambridge University Press, 1899).

———. *The Petty-Southwell Correspondence 1676–1687*, edited . . . by the Marquis of Lansdowne (London: Constable and Co., 1928).

Pfeifer, Gottfried. "The Quality of Peasant Living in Central Europe," *MR*, pp. 240–277.

Philipp, Hans. "Die historisch-geographischen Quellen in den etymologiae des Isidorus v. Sevilla," *Quellen und Forschungen zur alten Geschichte und Geographie*, Heft 25, Pt. 1, 1912; Pt. 2, 1913.

Philo (Philo Judaeus). "On the Account of the World's Creation Given by Moses," *Philo*, Vol. 1. Trans. from the Greek by The Rev. G. H. Whitaker. Loeb Classical Library (London: Wm. Heinemann; New York: G. P. Putnam's Sons, 1929).

———. "On Joseph," (De Josepho), *Philo*. Trans. from the Greek by F. H. Colson. Loeb Classical Library (London: Wm. Heinemann; Cambridge, Mass.: Harvard University Press), Vol. 6 (1935), pp. 140–271.

Plato. *Laws*. Trans. from the Greek by R. G. Bury. Loeb Classical Library (London: Wm. Heinemann; New York: G. P. Putnam's Sons, 1926). 2 vols.

———. *Phaedo*. Trans. from the Greek by R. S. Bluck (London: Routledge & Kegan Paul, 1955).

———. "Protagoras," *The Dialogues of Plato*, Vol. 1. Trans. from the Greek by Benjamin Jowett (2nd ed. rev.; Oxford: Clarendon Press, 1875). 5 vols.

———. *Timaeus, Critias, Cleitophon, Menexenus, Epistles*. Trans. from the Greek by R. G. Bury. Loeb Classical Library (Revised and reprinted, Cambridge, Mass.: Harvard University Press, 1952).

Plewe, Ernst. "Studien über D. Anton Friederich Büsching," *Geographische Forschungen (Schlern-Schriften No. 190), Festschrift zum 60. Geburtstag von Hans Kinzl* (Innsbruck: Universitätsverlag, 1958), pp. 203–223.

Pliny. *Natural History*. Trans. from the Latin by H. Rackham. Loeb Classical Library (Cambridge, Mass.: Harvard University Press, 1938). 10 vols.

Plischke, Hans. *Von den Barbaren zu den Primitiven. Die Naturvölker durch die Jahrhunderte* (Leipzig: F. A. Brockhaus, 1926).

Plotinus. *The Enneads*. Trans. from the Greek by Stephen Mackenna (2nd ed. rev. by B. S. Page, London: Faber & Faber, 1956).

Plutarch. "Of Those Sentiments Concerning Nature With Which Philosophers were Delighted [De placitis philosophorum naturalibus, libri V]." Trans. from the Greek by several hands, *Plutarch's Morals*, corr. and rev. by William Goodwin, Vol. 2 (New York: The Athenaeum Society, n.d.), pp. 104–193.

——. *Moralia*. Loeb Classical Library. Trans. from the Greek by several hands (London: Wm. Heinemann; New York: G. P. Putnam's Sons, etc., etc.). Vols. 1–7, 9–10, 12 published.

——. "Concerning the Face Which Appears in the Orb of the Moon," *Moralia*. Loeb Classical Library, Vol. 12.

——. "De placitis philosophorum libri V," *Moralia*, ed. Gregorius N. Bernardakis, Vol. 5 (Lipsiae: in aedibus B. G. Teubneri, 1893).

——. "Isis and Osiris," *Moralia*. Trans. from the Greek by F. C. Babbitt. Loeb Classical Library, Vol. 5.

——. "On Exile," *Moralia*. Trans. from the Greek by P. H. De Lacy and Benedict Einarson. Loeb Classical Library, Vol. 7.

——. "On the Fortune or the Virtue of Alexander," *Moralia*. Loeb Classical Library, Vol. 4.

——. "Whether Fire or Water is More Useful," *Moralia*. Loeb Classical Library, Vol. 12.

Pohlenz, Max. *Der Hellenische Mensch* (Göttingen: Vandenhoeck & Ruprecht, 1947).

——. "Panaitios. 5," *PW*, 18:3, cols. 418–440.

——. *Die Stoa. Geschichte einer geistigen Bewegung* (Göttingen: Vandenhoeck & Ruprecht, Vol. 1, 1948; Vol. 2 [Erläuterungen], 1949).

Polybius. *The Histories*. Trans. from the Greek by W. R. Paton. Loeb Classical Library London: Wm. Heinemann; New York: G. P. Putnam's Sons, 1922–1927). 6 vols.

Pope, Alexander. "Essay on Man," *The Complete Poetical Works of Alexander Pope*. Cambridge ed. (Boston and New York: Houghton, Mifflin and Co., 1903).

Pope, Hugh. *Saint Augustine of Hippo*. Image Books (Garden City, N. Y.: Doubleday & Co., 1961).

Porphyry. "De abstinentia," *Porphyrii philosophi platonici Opuscula tria*. Greek text edited by Augustus Nauck (Leipzig: Teubner, 1860).

Postan, Michael. "The Trade of Medieval Europe: the North," *CEHE*, Vol. 2, pp. 119–256.

Power, Eileen. *Medieval English Nunneries c. 1275 to 1535* (Cambridge: Cambridge University Press, 1922).

Préaux, Claire. *Les Grecs en Égypte d'après les Archives de Zénon*. Collection Lebègue (Bruxelles: Office de Publicité, 1947).

Pritchard, James B., ed. *Ancient Near Eastern Texts Relating to the Old Testament* (Princeton: Princeton University Press, 1950).

Probst, Jean-Henri. *Le Lullisme de Raymond de Sebonde (Ramon de Sibiude)* (Toulouse: E. Privat, 1912).

Przywara, Erich. *An Augustine Synthesis*. Harper Torchbooks/Cathedral Library (New York: Harper & Brothers, 1958).

Pseudo-Xenophon. See Xenophon.

Ptolemy, Claudius. *Tetrabiblos*. Trans. from the Greek by F. E. Robbins. Loeb Classical Library (London: Wm. Heinemann; Cambridge, Mass.: Harvard University Press, 1940). Published with *Manetho*, trans. by W. G. Waddell.

Purchas, Samuel. *Purchas his Pilgrimage* . . . (2nd ed.; London: Printed by W. Stansby for Henrie Fetherstone, 1614).

Raftis, J. A. "Western Monasticism and Economic Organization," *Comparative Studies in Society and History*, Vol. 3 (1961), pp. 452–469.

Raleigh, Sir Walter. *The History of the World* (London: Printed for Walter Burre, 1617).

Rankin, O. S. *Israel's Wisdom Literature* (Edinburgh: T. & T. Clark, 1936).

Ratzel, Friedrich. *Anthropogeographie* (4 unveränderte Aufl. Stuttgart: J. Englehorns Nachf., 1921–22). 2 vols.

Raven, Charles E. *John Ray, Naturalist: His Life and Works* (Cambridge: Cambridge University Press, 1942).
——. *Natural Religion and Christian Theology. The Gifford Lectures 1951, First Series: Science and Religion* (Cambridge: Cambridge University Press, 1953).
Ray, John. *Miscellaneous Discourses Concerning the Dissolution and Changes of the World*. . . . (London: Printed for S. Smith, 1692).
——. *The Wisdom of God Manifested in the Works of the Creation* (12th ed., corr., London: John Rivington, John Ward, Joseph Richardson, 1759).
Raymundus de Sabunde (Ramon Sibiude, Raymond Sebond). *La Théologie Naturelle de Raymond Sebon*. Trans. from Latin into French by Michel, Seigneur de Montaigne (Paris: L. Conard, 1932–1935). 2 vols.
Raynal, Guillaume Thomas François. *Histoire Philosophique et Politique des Établissemens et du Commerce des Européens dans les deux Indes* (Neuchatel & Geneve: chez les Libraires Associés, 1783–1784). 10 vols.
Reinhardt, Karl. *Kosmos und Sympathie* (München: C. H. Beck, 1926).
——. *Poseidonios* (Munich: C. H. Beck'sche Verlagsbuchhandlung, Oskar Beck, 1921).
——. "Poseidonios von Apameia," *PW*, 22:1, cols. 558–826.
Ricardo, David. *The Principles of Political Economy and Taxation*. Everyman's Library (London: J. M. Dent & Sons; New York: E. P. Dutton & Co., 1957 [1912]).
Riccioli, Giovanni Battista. *Geographiae et hydrographiae reformatae libri XII* (Venetiis, 1672). NA.
Richardson, Cyril C., ed. and trans., *et al. Early Christian Fathers*. Vol. 1 of *The Library of Christian Classics* (London: SCM Press, 1953).
Rigault, Hippolyte. *Histoire de la Querelle des Anciens et des Modernes* (Paris: L. Hachette et Cie., 1856).
Robbins, Frank E. *The Hexaemeral Literature. A Study of the Greek and Latin Commentaries on Genesis* (Chicago: University of Chicago Press, 1912).
Robertson, William. "The History of America," being Vols. 8–10 of *The Works of William Robertson, D. D.* (London: Printed for Thomas Tegg, etc., 1826). 3 vols.
——. "A View of the Progress of Society in Europe, from the Subversion of the Roman Empire to the Beginning of the Sixteenth Century," being the intro. to *The History of the Reign of the Emperor Charles V. The Works of William Robertson, D. D.* (London: Printed for Thomas Tegg, etc., 1826), Vol. 4.
Robinson, H. Wheeler. *Inspiration and Revelation in the Old Testament* (Oxford: Clarendon Press, 1946).
*The Romance of the Rose*. See Guillaume de Lorris and Jean de Meun.
Ross, James Bruce, and McLaughlin, Mary Martin, eds. *The Portable Medieval Reader* (New York: The Viking Press, 1949).
Ross, W. D. *Aristotle* (New York: Meridian Books, 1959).
——. "Diogenes (3)," *OCD*, p. 285.
Rostovtzeff, Michael. *A Large Estate in Egypt in the Third Century B. C., a Study in Economic History*. University of Wisconsin Studies in the Social Sciences and History, No. 6 (Madison, 1922).
——. *The Social and Economic History of the Hellenistic World* (Oxford: Clarendon Press, 1941). 3 vols.
Rousseau, Jean Jacques. *Émile; or, Education*. Trans. from the French by Barbara Foxley. Everyman's Library (London and Toronto: J. M. Dent & Sons; New York: E. P. Dutton & Co., 1930 [1911]).
——. *The Social Contract and Discourses*. Everyman's Library (London and Toronto: J. M. Dent & Sons; New York: E. P. Dutton & Co., 1930 [1913]).
Rowe, John H. *Ethnography and Ethnology in the Sixteenth Century* (Berkeley: The Kroeber Anthropological Society Papers, No. 30, Spring 1964).
Rush, Benjamin. "An Enquiry into the Cause of the Increase of Bilious and Intermitting Fevers in Pennsylvania, with Hints for Preventing Them," *TAPS*, Vol. 2, No. 25 (1786), pp. 206–212.

Salin, Édouard, and France-Lanord, Albert. *Le Fer à l'Époque Mérovingienne*, being Vol. 2 of *Rhin et Orient* (Paris: P. Geuthner, 1939–1943).

Sambursky, S. *The Physical World of the Greeks*. Trans. from the Hebrew by Merton Dagut (New York: Collier Books, 1952).

Sandmo, J. K. *Skogbrukshistorie* (Oslo: Aschehoug and Co., 1951).

Sarton, George. *Appreciation of Ancient and Medieval Science During the Renaissance* A Perpetua Book (New York: A. S. Barnes and Co., 1961; University of Pennsylvania Press, 1955).

——. *A History of Science. Ancient Science Through the Golden Age of Greece* (Cambridge, Mass.: Harvard University Press, 1952).

——. *A History of Science. Hellenistic Science and Culture in the Last Three Centuries B. C.* (Cambridge, Mass.: Harvard University Press, 1959).

——. "Remarks on the Theory of Temperaments," *Isis*, Vol. 34 (1943), pp. 205–208.

Sauvage, R. N. *L'Abbaye de Saint-Martin de Troarn au Diocèse de Bayeux des Origines au Seizième Siècle* (Caen: Henri Delesques, Imprimeur-Éditeur, 1911).

Saw, Ruth Lydia. *Leibniz*. A Pelican Book (Harmondsworth: Penguin Books, 1954).

Schmidt, Christel. *Die Darstellungen des Sechstagewerkes von Ihren Anfängen bis zum Ende des 15 Jahrhunderts* (Hildesheim: Buchdruckerei August Lax, 1938).

Schönbach, Anton E. "Des Bartholomaeus Anglicus Beschreibung Deutschlands gegen 1240," *Mitteilungen des Instituts für österreichische Geschichtsforschung*, Vol. 27 (1906), pp. 54–90.

Schoepflin, J. D. *Alsatia diplomatica* (Mannhemii, 1772–1775). 2 vols. NA.

Schwappach, Adam. *Handbuch der Forst- und Jagdgeschichte Deutschlands* (Berlin: Verlag von Julius Springer, 1886–1888).

——. "Zur Bedeutung und Etymologie des Wortes, 'Forst,' " *Forstwissenschaftliches Centralblatt*, Vol. 6 (1884), pp. 515–522.

Sclafert, Thérèse. "A Propos de Déboisement des Alpes du Sud," *Annales de Géographie*, Vol. 42 (1933), pp. 266–277, 350–360.

——. *Cultures en Haute-Provence. Déboisements et Pâturages au Moyen Âge. Les Hommes et La Terre*, IV. (Paris: S. E. V. P. E. N., 1959).

Scully, Vincent. *The Earth, The Temple, and the Gods. Greek Sacred Architecture* (New Haven and London: Yale University Press, 1962).

Seeliger, K. "Weltalter," Vol. VI, cols. 375–430; "Weltschöpfung," cols. 430–505. Wilhelm H. Roscher, ed., *Ausführliches Lexikon der griechischen und römischen Mythologie* (Leipzig and Berlin: B. G. Teubner, 1924–1937).

*A Select Library of Nicene and Post-Nicene Fathers of the Christian Church*. Ed. by Philip Schaff, *et al.* (New York: Christian Literature Co., 1886–1890). 14 vols.

Sellar, W. Y. *The Roman Poets of the Republic* (3d ed., Oxford: Clarendon Press, 1895).

Seltman, Charles. *Approach to Greek Art* (New York: E. P. Dutton & Co., 1960).

Semple, Ellen Churchill. *Influences of Geographic Environment on the Basis of Ratzel's System of Anthropo-geography* (New York: H. Holt and Co., etc., 1911).

Seneca, L. Annaeus. "De ira." Trans. from the Latin by John W. Basore, *Moral Essays*, Vol. 2; "De consolatione ad Helviam," Vol. 3. Loeb Classical Library (London: Wm. Heinemann; New York: G. P. Putnam's Sons, 1928–1932).

——. *Epistolae Morales*. Trans. from the Latin by Richard M. Gummere. Loeb Classical Library (London: Wm. Heinemann; New York: G. P. Putnam's Sons, 1917–1925). 3 vols.

——. *On Benefits*. Trans. from the Latin by Aubrey Stewart (London: Bell & Sons, 1912).

Servius the Grammarian. *Servii Grammatici Qui Feruntur in Vergilii Carmina Commentarii*. Vol. 2, *Aeneidos Librorum VI–XII Commentarii*, ed. Georg Thilo (Leipzig: B. G. Teubner, 1884).

Seybert, Adam. "Experiments and observations, on the atmosphere of marshes," *TAPS*, Vol. 4 (1799), pp. 415–430.

Sharp, Andrew. *Ancient Voyagers in the Pacific* (Harmondsworth: Penguin Books, 1957).

——. *Ancient Voyagers in Polynesia* (Berkeley: University of California Press, 1964).

Sikes, Edward E. *The Anthropology of the Greeks* (London: D. Nutl, 1914).

Simpson, George G. *The Meaning of Evolution.* Mentor Books (New York: New American Library, 1951).

Simson, Otto von. *The Gothic Cathedral. Origins of Gothic Architecture and the Medieval Concept of Order* (2nd rev. ed.; Harper Torchbooks, New York: Harper and Row, The Bollingen Library, 1964; Bollingen Foundation, 1962).

Singer, Charles; Holmyard, E. J.; Hall, A. R., and Williams, Trevor I. *A History of Technology* (New York and London: Oxford University Press, 1954–1958). 5 vols.

Sinz, P. "Die Naturbetrachtung des hl. Bernard," *Anima* I (1953), pp. 30–51. NA.

Smalley, Beryl. *The Study of the Bible in the Middle Ages* (Oxford: Clarendon Press, 1941).

Smith, Kenneth. *The Malthusian Controversy* (London: Routledge & Paul, 1951).

Soutar, George. *Nature in Greek Poetry* (London: Oxford University Press, 1939).

Spengler, Joseph J. *French Predecessors of Malthus* (Durham: Duke University Press, 1942).

——. "Malthus's Total Population Theory: a Restatement and Reappraisal," *Canadian Journal of Economics*, Vol. 11 (1945), pp. 83–110, 234–264.

Spinoza, Benedictus de. *The Correspondence of Spinoza.* Trans. by A. Wolf (London: G. Allen & Unwin, 1928).

——. *Ethica.* Trans. from the Latin by W. H. White, rev. by Amelia H. Stirling (3rd ed. rev. and corr.; London: Duckworth & Co., 1899).

Spitzer, Leo. "Classical and Christian Ideas of World Harmony," *Traditio*, Vol. 2 (1944), pp. 414–421.

Springer, Sister Mary Theresa of the Cross. *Nature-Imagery in the Works of St. Ambrose.* Catholic University of America Patristic Studies, Vol. 30 (Washington: Catholic University of America, 1931).

Stangeland, Charles E. "Pre-Malthusian Doctrines of Population: a Study in the History of Economic Theory," *Columbia University Studies in History, Economics, and Public Law*, Vol. 21, No. 3 (1904).

Steinen, Wolfram von den. *Der Kosmos des Mittelalters von Karl dem Grossen zu Bernard von Clairvaux* (Bern und München: Francke Verlag, 1959).

Stenton, Doris M. *English Society in the Early Middle Ages* (Harmondsworth: Penguin Books, 1951).

Strabo. *The Geography of Strabo.* Trans. from the Greek by H. C. Hamilton and W. Falconer. Bohn's Classical Library (London: Bohn, 1854–1856). 3 vols.

Süssmilch, Johann Peter. *Die Göttliche Ordnung* (Berlin: Im Verlag der Buchhandlung der Realschule, 1775–1776). 3 vols.

Suggs, Robert C. *The Island Civilizations of Polynesia.* A Mentor Book (New York: New American Library, 1960).

Surell, Alexander. *A Study of the Torrents in the Department of the Upper Alps* [1870]. Trans. of Vol. 1 of 2nd ed. from the French by Augustine Gibney (carbon typescript copy in Forestry Library, University of California, Berkeley).

Suzuki, Daisetz: "The Role of Nature in Zen Buddhism," *Eranos-Jahrbuch 1953*, Vol. 22 (1954), pp. 291–321.

Tacitus. *The Annals.* Rev. Oxf. trans. from the Latin (London: George Bell & Sons, 1906).

——. *Dialogus* (Dialogue on Oratory), with the *Agricola* and *Germania. Dial.* trans. from the Latin by William Peterson. Loeb Classical Library (London: Wm. Heinemann; New York: Macmillan Co., 1914).

Talbot, C. H., trans. and ed. *The Anglo-Saxon Missionaries in Germany. Being the Lives of SS. Willibrord, Boniface, Sturm, Leoba and Lebuin, together with the Hodoeporicon of St. Willibald and a selection from the correspondence of St. Boniface* (New York: Sheed and Ward, 1954).

Tarn, W. W. "Alexander the Great and the Unity of Mankind," *Proceedings of the British Academy*, Vol. 11 (1933), pp. 123–166.

——. "The Date of Iambulus: a Note," *Class. Quarterly*, Vol. 33 (1939), p. 193.

——. *Hellenistic Civilization* (3d ed., rev. by Tarn and Griffith, London: Edward Arnold, 1952).

Tatian. "Address of Tatian to the Greeks," *ANF*, Vol. 2, pp. 65–83.

Taylor, E. G. R. *Late Tudor and Early Stuart Geography 1583–1650* (London: Methuen & Co., 1934).

Taylor, George C. *Milton's Use of Du Bartas* (Cambridge, Mass.: Harvard University Press, 1934).

Taylor, Henry Osborn. *The Medieval Mind* (London: Macmillan and Co., 1911).

*The Tebtunis Papyri.* See Hunt, Arthur S.

Teggart, Frederick J., ed. *The Idea of Progress. A Collection of Readings.* Rev. ed., with intro. by George H. Hildebrand (Berkeley and Los Angeles: University of California Press, 1949).

Teggart, Frederick J. *Rome and China* (Berkeley: University of California Press, 1939).

——. *Theory of History* (New Haven: Yale University Press, 1925).

Temple, Sir William. "An Essay Upon the Ancient and Modern Learning," *The Works of Sir William Temple, Bart.* (new ed.; London: F. C. and J. Rivington, etc., 1814), Vol. 3, pp. 446–459.

——. *Observations upon the United Provinces of the Netherlands* (Cambridge: Cambridge University Press, 1932).

Templeman, Thomas. *A New Survey of the Globe: or, an Accurate Mensuration of all the Empires, Kingdoms, Countries, States, Principal Provinces, Counties, & Islands in the World* (London: Engr. by T. Cole, [1729]).

Tertullian. "Apology." Trans. from the Latin by S. Thelwall, *ANF*, Vol. 3, pp. 17–55.

——. "On the Pallium" (De pallio). Trans. from the Latin by S. Thelwall, *ANF*, Vol. 4, pp. 5–12.

——. *Quinti Septimi Florentis Tertulliani De Anima.* Ed. with intro. and commentary, by J. H. Waszink (Amsterdam: North-Holland Publishing Co., 1947).

——. "A Treatise on the Soul." Trans. from the Latin by Peter Holmes, *ANF*, Vol. 3, pp. 181–235.

Theiler, Willy. *Zur Geschichte der teleologischen Naturbetrachtung bis auf Aristoteles* (Zürich: Verlag Dr. Karl Hoenn, 1924).

Theocritus. See Greek Bucolic Poets.

Theodoret of Cyrrhus. *Théodoret de Cyr. Discours sur la Providence.* Trad. avec. intro. et notes par Yvan Azéma (Paris: Société d'Edition "Les Belles Lettres," 1954).

Theophrastus. *Enquiry into Plants.* Trans. from the Greek by Sir Arthur Hort. Loeb Classical Library (New York: G. P. Putnam's Sons, 1916). 2 vols.

——. *Metaphysics.* Trans., comm., and intro. by W. D. Ross and F. H. Fobes (Oxford: Clarendon Press, 1929).

——. *Theophrasti Eresii opera, quae supersunt, omnia.* Graeca recensuit, latine interpretatus est. Fridericus Wimmer, ed. (Parisiis: Firmin-Didot, 1866).

Thomas, Franklin. *The Environmental Basis of Society; a Study in the History of Sociological Theory* (New York and London: Century Co., 1925).

Thomas Aquinas, St. *On Kingship. To the King of Cyprus.* Trans. by Gerald B. Phelan, rev. by I. Th. Eschmann (Toronto: Pontifical Institute of Mediaeval Studies, 1949).

——. *On the Truth of the Catholic Faith. Summa Contra Gentiles. Book One: God.* Trans. by Anton C. Pegis. *Book Two: Creation.* Trans. by James F. Anderson. *Book Three: Providence, Part I.* Trans. by Vernon J. Bourke. Image Books (Garden City, N. Y.: Doubleday & Co., 1955–1956).

——. *Philosophical Texts.* Selected and trans. by Thomas Gilby. A Galaxy Book (New York: Oxford University Press, 1960).

——. *Summa Theologica.* Literally trans. by Fathers of the English Dominican Province, 3 vols., Vol. 1 (London: Burns & Oates, 1947).

Thomas, D. Winton, ed. *Documents from Old Testament Times.* Harper Torchbooks/Cloister Library (New York: Harper & Brothers, 1961).

**Thomas of Celano.** "The First Life of S. Francis of Assisi." Trans. by A. G. Ferrers

Howell. Repr. in Mary L. Cameron, *The Inquiring Pilgrim's Guide to Assisi* (London: Methuen & Co., 1926), pp. 163–270.

Thomas, William L., ed. *Man's Role in Changing the Face of the Earth* (Chicago: University of Chicago Press, 1956).

Thompson, Elbert N. S. "Milton's Knowledge of Geography," *Studies in Philology,* Vol. 16 (1919), pp. 148–171.

Thompson, James Westfall. *An Economic and Social History of the Middle Ages (300–1300)* (New York, London: The Century Co., c. 1928).

Thomson, James Oliver. *History of Ancient Geography* (New York: Biblo and Tannen, 1965; Cambridge University Press, 1948).

Thomson, John Arthur. *The System of Animate Nature.* The Gifford Lectures for 1915–1916 (London: Williams & Norgate, 1920). 2 vols.

Thomson, R. H. G. "The Medieval Artisan," *HT*, Vol. 2, pp. 383–396.

Thorndike, Lynn. *A History of Magic and Experimental Science During the First Thirteen Centuries of Our Era* (New York: Macmillan Co., 1923-1958). 8 vols.

——. "Renaissance or Prenaissance," *JHI*, Vol. 4 (1943), pp. 65–74.

——. "The True Place of Astrology in the History of Science," *Isis*, Vol. 46 (1955), pp. 273–278.

Thorp, James. *Geography of the Soils of China* (Nanking: National Geological Survey of China, 1936).

Thucydides. *History of the Peloponnesian War.* Trans. from the Greek by Richard Crawley. Everyman's Library (London & Toronto: J. M. Dent & Sons, 1926 [1910]).

Tibullus. In: *Catullus, Tibullus, and Pervigilium Veneris.* Tibullus trans. from the Latin by J. P. Postgate. Loeb Classical Library (London: Wm. Heinemann; New York: Macmillan Co., 1914).

Tittel, C. "Geminos, 1," *PW*, Vol. 7:1, cols. 1026–1050.

Tod, Marcus N. *A Selection of Greek Historical Inscriptions to the End of the Fifth Century B. C.* (2nd ed., Oxford: Clarendon Press, 1951 [1946]).

Tooley, Marian J. "Bodin and the Mediaeval Theory of Climate," *Speculum*, Vol. 28 (1953), pp. 64–83.

Toynbee, Arnold J. *Greek Historical Thought from Homer to the Age of Heraclius.* Mentor Books (New York: New American Library, 1952).

——. *A Study of History* (London, New York, Toronto: Oxford University Press, Vol. 1, 1955 [1934]).

——. *A Study of History.* Abridgement of Volumes I–VI by D. G. Somervell (New York and London: Oxford University Press, 1947).

Treves, Piero. "Historiography, Greek," *OCD*, pp. 432–433.

——. "Posidonius (2)," *OCD*, p. 722.

Trüdinger, Karl. *Studien zur Geschichte der griechisch-römischen Ethnographie* (Basel: E. Birkhauser, 1918).

Tscherikower, V. "Die hellenistischen Städtegründungen von Alexander dem Grossen bis auf die Römerzeit," *Philologus*, Supp. Bd. 19, Heft I (1927), vii+ 216 pp.

Untersteiner, Mario. *The Sophists.* Trans. from the Italian by Kathleen Freeman (Oxford: Basil Blackwell, 1954).

Varro, Marcus T. *On Farming.* Trans. from the Latin by Lloyd Storr-Best (London: George Bell & Sons, 1912).

Veen, Johan van. *Dredge, Drain, Reclaim. The Art of a Nation* (5th ed.; The Hague: Martinus Nijhoff, 1962).

Velleius Paterculus. *Compendium of Roman History.* Trans. from the Latin by Frederick W. Shipley. Loeb Classical Library (London: Wm. Heinemann; New York: G. P. Putnam's Sons, 1924).

Vespucci, Amerigo. *Mundus novus, Letter to Lorenzo Pietro di Medici.* Trans. from the Italian by George T. Northrup (Princeton: Princeton University Press, 1916).

Villard de Honnecourt. *The Sketchbook of Villard de Honnecourt.* Ed. by Theodore Bowie (2nd ed. rev.; Bloomington: Indiana University, 1962).

Virgil. *The Aeneid*. Prose trans. from the Latin by W. F. Jackson Knight. Penguin Classics (Baltimore: Penguin Books, 1962 [1958]).

——. *The Eclogues, Georgics, Aeneid*. Trans. from the Latin by John Jackson (Oxford: Clarendon Press, 1930 [1908]).

Vitruvius. *The Ten Books on Architecture*. Trans. from the Latin by Morris Hicky Morgan (Cambridge, Mass.: Harvard University Press, 1914).

Volney, Constantine François Chasseboeuf. *View of the Climate and Soil of the United States of America*. Trans. from the French (London: Printed for J. Johnson, 1804).

Voltaire. *Oeuvres Complètes de Voltaire*. Edited by Adrien Jean Quentin Beuchot (Paris: Garnier Frères, 1877–1885). 52 vols.

——. "L'A, B, C," Beuchot, Vol. 45, pp. 1–135.

——. "Athéisme" (Dict. Philosophique), Beuchot, Vol. 27, pp. 166–190.

——. "Candide," Beuchot, Vol. 33.

——. "Causes finales" (Dict. Philosophique), Beuchot, Vol. 27, pp. 520–533.

——. "Climat," Beuchot, Vol. 28, pp. 113–120.

——. "Commentaire sur Quelques Principales Maximes de l'Esprit des Lois," Beuchot, Vol. 50, pp. 55–145.

——. "Des Singularités de la Nature," Beuchot, Vol. 44, pp. 216–317.

——. "Dieu, Dieux" (Dict. Philosophique), Beuchot, Vol. 28, pp. 357–398.

——. "Elements de la Philosophie de Newton," Beuchot, Vol. 38.

——. "Histoire de Jennie, ou l'Athée et le Sage," Beuchot, Vol. 34.

——. "Lois (Esprit des)," Beuchot, Vol. 31, pp. 86–109.

——. "Nouvelles Considérations sur l'Histoire," Beuchot, Vol. 24, pp. 24–29.

——. "Poème sur le Désastre de Lisbonne," Beuchot, Vol. 12, pp. 183–204.

——. "Siècle de Louis XIV," Beuchot, Vols. 19–20.

Vossius, Isaac. *Isaaci Vossii Variarum Observationum Liber* (London: apud Robertum Scott Bibliopolam, 1685).

Waddell, Helen. *Mediaeval Latin Lyrics*. Trans. by Helen Waddell. Penguin Classics (Harmondsworth: Penguin Books, 1962 [1952]).

Wagner, Thomas, ed. *Corpus Iuris Metallici Recentissimi et Antiquioris. Sammlung der neuesten und älterer Berggesetze* (Leipzig: J. S. Heinsius, 1791).

Wallace, Robert. *A Dissertation on the Numbers of Mankind, in Ancient and Modern Times* (2nd ed. rev. and corr.; Edinburgh: A. Constable and Co., etc., etc., 1809).

——. *Various Prospects of Mankind, Nature, and Providence* (London: A. Millar, 1761).

Warmington, E. H. "Dicaearchus," *OCD*, p. 275.

Webb, Clement C. J. *Studies in the History of Natural Theology* (Oxford: Clarendon Press, 1915).

Webster, Noah. "Dissertation on the Supposed Change of Temperature in Modern Winters [1799]," *A Collection of Papers on Political, Literary and Moral Subjects* (New York: Webster & Clark; Boston: Tappan and Dennett, etc., 1843), pp. 119–162.

Wehrli, Fritz. *Die Schule des Aristoteles. Texte und Kommentar. Heft I Dikaiarchos* (Basel: Benno Schwabe & Co., Verlag, 1944).

Werner, Karl. *Beda der Ehrwürdige und Seine Zeit* (Neue Ausgabe, Wien: Wilhelm Braumüller, 1881).

West, Sir Edward. *The Application of Capital to Land* [1815] (Baltimore: Lord Baltimore Press, 1903).

Whiston, William. *A New Theory of the Earth . . . With a large Introductory Discourse concerning the Genuine Nature, Stile, and Extent of the Mosaick History of the Creation* (4th ed. rev. and corr.; London: Printed for Sam. Tooke and Benj. Motte, 1725).

White, Lynn T., Jr. *Medieval Technology and Social Change* (Oxford: Clarendon Press, 1962).

——. "Natural Science and Naturalistic Art in the Middle Ages," *AHR*, Vol. 52 (1947), pp. 421–435.

——. "Technology and Invention in the Middle Ages," *Speculum*, Vol. 15 (1940), pp. 141–159.

Whitehead, Alfred N. *Science and the Modern World. Lowell Lectures, 1925* (New York: Pelican Mentor Books, 1948).

Wiener, Philip P., and Noland, Aaron, eds. *Roots of Scientific Thought* (New York: Basic Books, 1957).

Wilkins, John. *Of the Principles and Duties of Natural Religion.* . . . (9th ed.; London: J. Waltos, 1734).

William (Gulielmus), Archbishop of Tyre. *A History of Deeds Done Beyond the Sea.* Trans. from the Latin by Emily A. Babcock and A. C. Crey (New York: Columbia University Press, 1943). 2 vols.

William of Conches. "De philosophia mundi," *PL*, Vol. 90, cols. 1127–1178; also in Vol. 172, pp. 39–102.

William of Malmesbury. *Willelmi Malmesbiriensis monachi de gestis pontificum anglorum libri quinque.* Ed. N. E. S. A. Hamilton (London: Longman & Co. and Trübner & Co., etc., etc., 1870), being Vol. 52 of *Rerum Britannicarum Medii Aevi Scriptores* = Rolls Series.

Williams, George H. *Wilderness and Paradise in Christian Thought* (New York: Harper & Brothers, 1962).

Williams, R. J. "The Hymn to Aten," Thomas, D. Winton, ed., *Documents from Old Testament Times.* Harper Torchbooks/Cloister Library (New York: Harper & Brothers, 1961 [1958]), pp. 142–150.

Williams, Samuel. *The Natural and Civil History of Vermont* (Walpole, Newhampshire: Isaiah Thomas and David Carlisle, Jun., 1794).

Williamson, Hugh. "An Attempt to Account for the CHANGE OF CLIMATE, Which Has Been Observed in the Middle Colonies in North-America," *TAPS*, Vol. 1 (2nd ed. corr., 1789), pp. 337–345. (Read before the Society in 1770).

Williamson, Hugues. "Dans Lequel on Tâche de Rendre Raison du Changement de Climat qu'on a Observé dans les Colonies Situées dans l'Intérieur des Terres de l'Amérique Septentrionale," *Journal de Physique* (*Observations sur la Physique, sur l'Histoire Naturelle et sur les Arts*), Vol. 1 (1773), pp. 430–436.

Wilson, John A., *The Culture of Ancient Egypt.* Phoenix Books (Chicago: University of Chicago Press, 1951).

Wimmer, Josef. *Deutsches Pflanzenleben nach Albertus Magnus 1193–1280* (Halle: Verlag der Buchhandlung des Waisenhauses, 1908).

——. *Geschichte des deutschen Bodens mit seinem Pflanzen- und Tierleben von der keltisch-römischen Urzeit bis zur Gegenwart. Historisch-geographische Darstellungen* (Halle: Verlag der Buchhandlung des Waisenhauses, 1905).

——. *Historische Landschaftskunde* (Innsbruck: Wagner, 1885).

Winsor, Justin, ed. *Narrative and Critical History of America*, Vol. 1 (Boston and New York: Houghton, Mifflin and Co., 1889).

Winter, Franz. *Die Cistercienser des nordöstlichen Deutschlands* (Gotha: Friedrich Andreas Perthes, 1868–1871). 3 vols.

Woermann, Karl. *Die Landschaft in der Kunst der alten Völker* (München: Ackermann, 1876).

——. *Ueber den landschaftlichen Natursinn der Griechen und Römer* (München: Ackermann, 1871).

Wölkern, L. C. von. *Historia diplomatic Norimbergensis* (Nürnberg, 1738). NA.

Wollaston, William. *The Religion of Nature Delineated* (6th ed.; London: Printed for John & Paul Knapton, 1738).

Wood, William. *New Englands Prospect* [1634]. (Repr. for E. M. Boynton, Boston?, 1898?)

Woodbridge, Homer E. *Sir William Temple, the Man and His Work* (New York: Modern Lang. Assoc. of America; London: Oxford University Press, 1940).

Woodward, John. *An Essay Towards a Natural History of the Earth, and Terrestrial Bodies, especially Minerals.* . . . (2nd ed.; London: Printed by T. W. for Richard Wilkin, 1702).

Workman, Herbert B. *The Evolution of the Monastic Ideal*. A Beacon Paperback (Boston: Beacon Press, 1962. First publ. in 1913 by Epworth Press, London).

Wotton, William. *Reflections upon Ancient and Modern Learning* (London: Printed by J. Leake for Peter Buck, 1694).

Wright, G. Ernest, and Fuller, Reginald H. *The Book of the Acts of God*. Anchor Books (New York: Doubleday & Company, 1960).

Wright, John K. *The Geographical Lore of the Time of the Crusades* (New York: Amer. Geographical Society, 1925).

——. *Human Nature in Geography* (Cambridge, Mass.: Harvard University Press, 1966).

Wright, Thomas. "On the Mode Most Easily and Effectually Practicable for Drying up the Marshes of the Maritime Parts of North America," *TAPS*, Vol. 4, No. 29 (1799), pp. 243–246.

Wulsin, Frederick R. "Adaptations to Climate Among Non-European Peoples." L. H. Newburgh, ed., *Physiology of Heat Regulation and The Science of Clothing* (Philadelphia and London: W. B. Saunders Co., 1949), pp. 3–69.

Xenophon. *Die pseudoxenophontische* ΑΘΗΝΑΙΩΝ ΠΟΛΙΤΕΙΑ. *Einleitung, Übersetzung, Erklärung von Ernst Kalinka* (Leipzig and Berlin: B. G. Teubner, 1913).

——. *Memorabilia and Oeconomicus*. Trans. from the Greek by E. C. Marchant. Loeb Classical Library (Cambridge, Mass.: Harvard University Press, 1953).

Zeller, Eduard. *Outlines of the History of Greek Philosophy*. Trans. from the German by L. R. Palmer (13th ed., rev. by Wilhelm Nestle, New York: Noonday Press, A Meridian Book, 1955).

——. *Die Philosophie der Griechen in ihrer geschichtlichen Entwicklung*. II Tl., II Abt., *Aristoteles und die alten Peripatetiker*. 4th Aufl. (Leipzig: O. R. Reisland, 1921).

Zöckler, D. O. *Geschichte der Beziehungen zwischen Theologie und Naturwissenschaft mit besondrer Rücksicht auf Schöpfungsgeschichte. Erste Abtheilung: Von den Anfängen der christlichen Kirche bis auf Newton und Leibnitz. Zweite Abtheilung: Von Newton und Leibnitz bis zur Gegenwart* (Gütersloh: C. Bertelsmann, 1877–1879). 2 vols.

# Index

Acosta, Jose de: on migration of man and animals to New World, 366–367; and Hale, 401; on the Indies, 450; m. 361, 401, 425, 606–607

Acts 14 and Romans 1:20: on evidences of God in creation, 161

Adam, 153, 159

Adelard of Bath: on human science in nature, 219

*Aedificare*: meanings of, 331

Aesculapius: cult of, 5

Aesthetics: and geography in Humboldt, 546–547

*Afforestatio*: meaning of, 326–327. *See also* Forest conservation

Agatharchides: on ethnology of Red Sea shore, 20–21; custom and climate, 96–97

Age of Discovery: and the Renaissance, 355; and ideas of environmental influence, 358, 374; and design, 358; and population theory, 359; and Vespucci on New World, 362; Munster on, 364; F. Bacon on, 473–474; Condorcet on, 595

Agricola, Georgius: Bodin on, 440; in defense of mining, 468–469; m. 495

Air. *See* Atmosphere

Akh-en-Aton: Hymn to sun, 37–38

*Alaise*: meaning of, 345. *See also* Forest conservation

Albert the Great (Albertus Magnus): natural theology of, 227–229; on astrology, 266; on environmental influence, 268–270; on rational use of natural environment, 314–315; on environmental change by man, 316, 351; on soil fertility, 346; m. 174, 256, 264

Alberti, Leon Battista: environmental ideas of, 125, 430–431, 464–465; m. 355, 490

Albert I: ordinance of 1304 on forest care, 337–338

Albertus Magnus. *See* Albert the Great

Alan of Lille: on nature as a book, 204, 216–218, 241–242

Alchemy: as human creation in Paracelsus, 467

Alcmaeon of Croton: theory of health of, 11

Alembics: theory of, 395, 413–414

Alexander the Great: and diffusion of civilization, 23; and brotherhood of man, 24; m. 101, 631 n. 31

Alexander Neckam: on man's dominion of nature, 206

Ambrose. *See* St. Ambrose

Amun: hymn to, 37–38

Anaxagoras, 39–40

Anaximander, 8–9

Animals, 47; and design argument, 43; extinction of, 139, 677–678; destructiveness of domestic, 143, 342–343; feral, 290, 311, 675; in Christian lore, 309–311; degeneration of, 589. *See also* Buffon

Anthropocentrism: 44, 391–392, 684; in Ecclesiasticus, 160; and man's rationality, 185; and St. Augustine, 198; and insects, 205; in John the Scot, 212; in Paracelsus, 467; in Linnaeus, 511; Goethe on, 535–536

Anthropomorphism, 527

Antiteleological ideas: and Theophrastus, 50; and atomic theory, 62–64; in Democritus, 65; in Epicurus, 66; in Lucretius, 68; in Hellenistic Age, 73; in 17th cent., 377–378; in 18th cent., 517; in Buffon, 518, 678; and Hume, 525. *See also* Final causes; Design argument; Artisan analogy; Artisan diety; Teleology

Apollonius of Egypt: and religion, 21–22; on planting, 122–123

Apollonius Rhodius: descriptions of nature by, 26–27

Arbuthnot, John: on effects of air on health, 562–565; and Montesquieu, 567; m. 601, 602

Arab thought. *See* Muslim thought

Arcadia: Polybius on, 95–96

Architects: in Hellenistic Age, 125. *See also* Alberti

Aristotle: on the divine, 4; and principle of plenitude, 6; and the four elements, 9–10; on animals, 47; teleology of, 47–49; and Christian theology, 49; climatic theory of, 93; *Problems* of, 93–94; revival of interest in, in 12th and 13th cents., 219; and Frederick II, 225; in Thomas Aquinas, 233–234, 274; in *The Romance of the Rose*, 242; and condemnations of 1277, 248–249

Arnaud, Francois: on Ubaye Valley, 341–342

Arndt, Johann: and physcio-theology, 510

Arnobius: on Christianity and natural calamities, 179–180; m. 386

Artificial selection: Darwin on, 56, 672–673; Buffon on, 674

Artisan: Seltman on Greek, 46; Seneca on, 118–119; Hume on, 526

Artisan analogy: and a creator-deity, 14; St. Augustine on, 177; Thomas Aquinas on, 230–231; Ramon Sibiude on, 239–240; and the clock, 392; Ray on, 394; Cudworth on, 394; D'Holbach on, 521; Hume on, 525; Kant on, 532

Artisan deity, 44–46, 528

Astrology: and astrological ethnology, 15, 111, 265–266, 280, 282, 437, 460; Cumont on, 15; as unifying principle, 15–16; Thorndike on, 16, 53; Diodorus on Chaldean training in, 22–23; and Posidonius, 53, 100; and Cicero, 102–103; and St. Augustine, 201; in *The Romance of the Rose*, 242; condemned in 1277, 249; and Christian thought in Middle Ages, 254–255; and theories of environmental influence, 265–266, 572–573; and Albert the Great, 266; and R. Bacon, 282

Astro-theology, 392

Aten: hymn to, 36, 37–38

Athenaeus: on effect of climate, 98 n. 46; m. 101

Athenagoras: on God as artist, 182–183

Atmosphere: related to mind or temperament, 56, 81–82, 101–102, 258, 457; pollution of London's, 488–491; Seybert on, 689

Atomic theory: in ancient philosophy, 64–65

Attica: deforestation and erosion of, 121; farming in 133–134

Augustine. *See* St. Augustine

Averroes: on design and teleology, 220–222

Avicenna: on climate and health, 264–265

Bacon, Francis: against final causes in natural history, 377; on relation of climate to activity, 450; on man's control of nature, 471–474; m. 383, 495

Bacon, Roger: on geography and astrological ethnology, 282–285

Bailey, Cyril: atomic theory and antiteleological ideas of, 62–64 *passim*

*baliveau*: meaning of, 328–329. *See also* Forest conservation

Baltic: peoples of, 285–286

*bannovium*: meaning of, 342–343. *See also* Forest conservation

Barclay, John: on national character, 451–454, 559

Bartholomew of England (Bartholomaeus Anglicus): his *De proprietatibus rerum*, 262–263; on climate and ethnology, 272–273; m. 115, 209, 256

Bartram, J.: on erosion, 691–692

Basil of Caesarea: homilies of, 189–190, 189–195 *passim*, 240, 298

Bede the Venerable: on effect of man's Fall on nature, 205–206; on founding of monasteries, 306

Beekeeping: custom and consequences of, 322

Benedict. *See* St. Benedict

Benedictbeuern: nature poetry of, 247–248

Benedictine order: and transformation of Monte Cassino, 304; and use of land at Troarn, 331

Benedictine Rule, 214, 289 n. 1, 294, 304–306, 350 n. 210

Bentley, Richard: and Newton, 395–397

Bernard. *See* St. Bernard

Bion: *The Lament* of, 28–29

Birds: Buffon on, 679

Birth control: Malthus on, 638–639

Bloch, Marc: on hydraulic saw, 320; m. 317

Bodin, Jean: importance of, 434–435; his theories in relation to the times, 435, 445–446; on national character, 435; on the universe, 436; on astrological ethnology, 437, 441; on humors and design, 438–439; on strength of environmental control, 439; on sexual activity, 439–440; on effect of climate on religion, 440; and Agricola, 440; on cultural diversity, 442; on theories applied to government, 442–443; and Hippocrates, 443; on theories of environment and design argument, 443; on German culture, 443, 441; on non-environmental influences, 443–444; on life in Toulouse, 444; on clustering of genius, 444; on environmental basis of history, 445; on morals, 445; and Montesquieu, 567–568

Boethius, 208

Bonaventura. *See* St. Bonaventura

Botero, Giovanni: on duties of a prince, 368; on environmental influences, 369; on evils of culture contact, 370; and Polybius, 370; and design argument, 371; on urban life, 372; on population, 370–374 *passim*; m. 471, 625

"Boundless": concept of, in Anaximander, 8

Boyle, Robert: on final causes, 377

Breasted, James H.: on origins of Psalm 104, 38 n. 6

Browne, Sir Thomas: *Religio Medici*, 426, 475–476, 501

Buffon, Comte Georges Louis Leclerc: on domestication, 139, 672–677 *passim*; on earth and earth history, 407, 503, 655, 666, 668; antiteleological ideas of, 518, 678; on conceptions of nature, 519, 624, 663–664, 680–681; and Herder, 538, 539–540; on climate and natural history, 587–588; on cultural differences, 588, 591; on primitive peoples, 588–589, 681; on degeneration of animals, 589; on causes of racial differences, 590–591; on man's place in nature, 590, 664, 668, 684; and Montesquieu, 591; and Lord Kames, 595; and Dunbar, 599–600; influence on the Forsters, 611, 702–703; on man as disturber and exterminator of life, 662, 677–679; anti-primitivism of, 665; on natural and cultural landscapes, 665–666; 668, 679–680; on human history, 666–667; on deforestation and forest conservation, 669–671; and Williamson, 669; on soils, 671; on fertilizers, 672; on animal and insect societies, 677; and praise of wildlife, 677; and Jefferson, 681–682; and De Pauw, 683, 685; and Kalm, 683, 685; and W. Robertson, 684; m. 6, 509, 536, 537, 581. *See also* Chap. 14, Secs. 4–8

Building: during Hellenistic Ages, 125; during Middle Ages, 350. *See also* Alberti

Bull: *Sublimis Deus* of Paul III, 359–360

Burgos, Laws of, 360–361

Burnet, Thomas, 396–397, 407–408, 633

Burton, Richard, 456–458, 479–480

Busching, D.: on geography and natural theology, 515–517

Busiris. *See* Isocrates

Caesar, Julius: and ethnology, 103

Caesarius of Prum: on environmental change by man, 292

Cambridge Platonists, 78–79, 393–394, 522; m. 252, 406, 507

Canals: in ancient Egypt, 127; du Midi, 496–497

Canticle of Brother Sun: of St. Francis, 214

*Capitulare de Villis* of Charlemagne, 333–335

Carre, Meyrick: on Aquinas, 233, 251 nn. 259 and 260

Cassiodorus: effect of nature on man, 257–258; m. 254

Catastrophes, natural: as punishment for sin, in Christian thought, 160, 521–522; Hume on, 529. *See also* Evil

Cathedral building: in Middle Ages, 350

Causes, final. *See* Final causes

Celibacy, clerical, 243–244, 514, 627

Centuriation, Roman; system of described, 146–147; m. 117

Chain of being, 481–482, 599–600

Characteristics, acquired: inheritance of, 85, 613

Charcoal: use of in Middle Ages, 322; restrictions on making of, 493

Chardin, Sir John: climate and cultural persistence, 553–554, 567, 592

Charlemagne: and *Capitulare de Villis*, 333–334

Charron, Pierre: on environmental influence on morality and religion, 447–448, 552

Chartres, Bernard de, 380

Chartres, Cathedral of, 245

Chastellux, 657, 686–687

Chimborazo: Humboldt's map of, 547

China, 572, 577, 595, 598, 643–644, 651–652

Christian thought: conceptions of nature in, 150–153, 165–166; and feeling for nature, 151, 196–197; and God's care for the world, 151, 153; and man as steward of God, 152–153, 155; and Psalm 8 on man's place in creation, 155; and Syncretism of New Testament, 161; and rejection of the world and of nature, 162, 181; and environmental theories, 167; and diffusionism, 167, 368, 403, 425, 607; and independent invention, 167; and preoccupation with creation, 168, 253, 708–709; and importance of patristic period, 172; and ties with classical thought, 178; and St. Augustine, 201–202; Muslim challenge to, 218–219, 222; reflected in 13th cent. iconography, 247; and astrology, 254–255; and man

as a modifier of nature, 151, 293; and dignity of labor, 302; and population theory, 425, 512, 514, 637; place of natural catastrophes in, 160, 521–522

Christianity: Thomas Aquinas' defense of, 232; and condemnations of 1277, 249; and human origin and dispersal, 261

Chrysippus: on purpose in cosmos, 56–58; m. 51

Cicero: on Strato, 51; and Posidonius, 54; *De natura deorum*, 54–55, 376; on Stoic view of world, 55; and Renaissance thinkers, 62 n. 71; on sites of cities, 101–102; on effects of moist air, 102; on environmental and astrological determinism, 102; on man's power to change earth, 145; Ray on, 416; m. 144, 252

Cistercian order: Otto of Freising joins, 278; and rule of work, 308–309; and cultivation, 349–350

Cities: in Hellenistic Age, 126–127; Theocritus on Ptolemy's, 128; contrast to country in Middle Ages, 246; on sites of, 101–102, 276; R. Bacon on influence of, 285; and the sacred, 303; Botero on, 372–373

Civilization: Hippocrates on age of, 119; Virgil on development of, 143; idea of geographic march of, 276–277, 455, 597; of wood, 318; autochthonous in New World, 608; J. R. Forster on development of, 617–618; and historical sequence in land occupation, 643. *See also* entries under Cultural and Culture

Clearing. *See* Deforestation

Clearings: prohibition of, 338; as earthly paradises, 349

Climate: and custom, 96–97; changes of, due to human agency, 129–130, 137, 316, 487–488, 542, 560, 659, 669, 689–691; and cultural relativism, 255 n. 3, 256; and race, 258; and pregnancy, 269; and religion, in Botero, 369; and relation to laws, 432; and love of liberty, 449; and cultural persistence, 553–554, 567, 592; and crime, 558; and homesickness, 558; and cultural inertia, 559–560; Montesquieu on relation of, to population, 579; Helvetius' dismissal of influence of, 583–584; and natural history, in Buffon, 587–588; and degeneration in Kames, 595–596; de Pauw on degeneration of in New World, 609, 683, 685; Hume on, 659; Webster on, 661–662; Adams' rejection of influence of, 685; Woodward on, 687. *See also* entries under Environmental influence; Nature, modifications by human agency

Columella: on rural-urban contrasts, 32–33; on senescence in nature, 72, 135–136; on care of the land, 136–137; on plant introductions, 137; and Hakewill, 383; Burton on, 480; m. 125, 381, 388

Comparative method, 6–7, 141

Condemnations of 1277, 248–250

Condorcet, Antoine-Nicolas de: on population control, 400; on climate and custom, 594–595; on progress and population, 634–635, 637

Cook, Captain James: stimulus of his voyages on natural history and ethnology, 502, 610, 620; and population theories, 626

Cooking: Hippocrates on, 88

Copernican theory: and final causes, 376

Cosmas Indicopleustes: on man's stewardship of nature, 300–301

Cosmos: history of the word, 16–17; as organic whole in Plotinus, 77; in Greek thought, 174; in Old Testament, 174

*creatio continua*, 153, 416

Creation: Hermes Trismegistus, 75; Plotinus on, 76, 78; man's control over, 151; in Genesis, 151, 153, 159; regret of God for, 154; evidence of God in, 161; Christian preoccupation with, 168, 253, 708–709; unfinished by God, 181; in Athenagoras, 181–182; a work of love, 183; rational creatures give meaning to, 186; and the hexaemeral literature, 187; St. Augustine on, 196, 199; as a divine revelation, 211; R. Bacon on, 282; and cosmicizing lands, 303; Browne on, 475; resemblance of New World to, 685–686, 692

Creator: deity, 14; goodness of in Plato, 45; his relation to created in Augustine, 196

Crime: climatic causes of, 558

Cudworth, Ralph, on plastic nature, 393–394

Cultural determinism, 709

Cultural development, 140–142

Cultural differences: after the Fall, 262; concern with in 17th cent. England, 451; Herder on, 540, 542; Fontenelle on, 559; Buffon on, 588, 591; G. Forster on, 612–620 *passim*; and fertility, Montesquieu on, 627–628

Cultural milieu: and Bacon, 285; in Fontenelle, 458–459, 552–553; in Hume, 585–586; and Malthusian theory, 638; in Montesquieu, 653–654

Cultural persistence, 439, 553–554, 559–560, 567, 571, 592, 594–595

Cultural relativism: and climate in Muslim thought, 255 n. 3; in Montesquieu, 573

Culture: development of, 6–7, 107–109, 281–282, 545, 595–596; Strabo on, 104–105; 18th cent. interest in, 501. *See also* Comparative method

Culture contact: in classical writings, 92, 102; Vitruvius on, 108; Bartholomew of England on, 273; Thomas Aquinas on, 275–276; Giraldus Cambrensis on, 281; Otto of Freising on, 287 n. 81; Botero on, 370; Hale on pre-Columbian, between Old and New World, 402–403; Alberti on, 431; Hume on, 585–586; Rousseau on, 593–594; Dunbar on, 599; Forster on, 619

Custom: role of, among Longheads, 85; in Herodotus, 89; in Polybius, 95; in Agathar-chides, 96; in Posidonius, 97; counteracts environment, 95–96; and environmental change in Middle Ages, 316, 322–330; and rational use of forest in Middle Ages, 323–325

Cyprian, 385–386

D'Amilaville: on constancy of population, 631

Darius, 131

Darwin, Charles: and Lucretius, 139; and web of life, 427; on effects of fencing, 487; and Malthus, 624–625; on artificial selection, 56, 672–673; m. 119, 404, 517, 548, 549, 550, 620, 693

Dawson, Christopher: on Thomas Aquinas, 219–220 and n. 146; on condemnations of 1277, 250 n. 257; on Christian religion and peasant life, 293; on forest clearance, 294; on acts of synod of Troslé, 355 n. 161

Deforestation, 121; effects on climate, 130, 270, 659–661, 687, 691; in Middle Ages, 290–292, 294, 318–320, 333–335, 340–341, 345; and torrents, 341–342, 700–701; Buffon on, 669–671; Richard Frame on, 697

Degeneration: Buffon's concept of, 589, 674

Democritus: and atomic theory, 64–65

*De natura locorum* literature, 174–175; 263–264

Depopulation. *See* Population

*De proprietatibus rerum* literature, 263–264

Derham, William: physico-theology of, 421–423; on food chain, 423

Descartes, René: on final causes, 377; on constancy of natural law, 381; on control over nature, 426–427, 476–477; Cudworth on, 393; Ray on, 394, 417; Keill on, 412–413; Hazard on, 509–510; Voltaire on, 523–524; Leibniz on Cartesians, 506; m. 406, 495

Design argument: in antiquity, 42–44; and eye and hand, 42; and domestication, 58; in Seneca, 61; and ideas of environmental influence, 255; and Botero, 371; in Copernicus, 376; in Galileo, 376; in Newton, 377; in Boyle, 377; in Spinoza, 378; and optimism, 380; and Bentley, 395–396; and population theory, 398, 403–404, 625; and microscope, 417, 526; in 18th cent. natural history, 510; and telescope, 526; in Herder, 539; vitality of, in 19th cent., 548; in G. Forster, 619

Dicaearchus: on cultural development, 7; on Golden Age, 133, 140; on domestication of animals, 141; m. 281, 596

Diderot, Denis: on climatic influences, 584–585

Diffusionism: and Genesis, 167; and Christian theology, 368, 403, 425; Robertson on, 607–608; G. Forster on, 619

Diodorus: on Chaldean training in astrology, 22; on Chaldean concept of the world, 36; on African ethnology, 96; Hume on, 629–630

Diogenes of Apollonia: and teleology, 39–40

Diognetus: letter to, on the Christians, 182
Discoveries, accidental: Acosta on, 366
Discovery. *See* Age of Discovery
Disease: among the Greeks, 11; Lucretius, 101; Wallace, on venereal, 631
Division: and the four elements, 64
Domestication; utilitarian theory of, 57, 139; and design argument, 58; Chrysippus on, 58; Hippon on, 129; Theophrastus on, 129; Pliny on, 137; Lucretius on animal, 138; Buffon on, 139, 672–678 *passim*; Dicaearchus on, 141; Varro on, 141; and Fall of man, 206, 236, 471; and *Romance of the Rose*, 242; Gregory of Nyssa on, 298; and legends of animals as servants, 311; late recognition of implications, 344; Ray on, 420; Ficino on, 463; Hale on, 480–482; Hume on, 527; Kant on, 533; Robertson on, 684–685
Drainage: and health, 348; Dienne's history of, 496; Evelyn's advocacy of, 488–489
Drunkenness: J. Barclay on, 454; and climate, 573, 586–587
Du Bartas, Guillaume de Salluste, Sieur: environmental theories of, 448–449; and Milton, 449
Du Bos, Jean Baptiste: on climatic influences, 444, 554–562 *passim*; on progress, 555; on European art, 556; on homesickness, 558; on the Romans, 560; on the Dutch, 561; on trade, 562; and Fontenelle, 555; and Barclay, 559; and Temple, 561–562
Du Halde, J. B.: on China, 621, 644
Dunbar, James; environmental ideas of, 596–600 *passim*
Dutch: Du Bos on, 561; of Cape of Good Hope, 613

Earth: as orderly, harmonious whole, 36, 54, 392, 396–397, 422–423; a product of design, 42–43, 59, 60–61, 178, 202, 357, 379–380, 406, 505, 707, 710; utilitarian and aesthetic attitudes toward, 52; Clemente of Rome on, 178; a school and training place for man, 191; F. de Gómara on its beauty and diversity, 362–363; its resources as limiting factor in population growth, 373, 623, 633, 636, 639; inclination of its axis an evidence of design, 408, 414; Woodward on, 409–411; antediluvian, 412; Leibniz on progress of its cultivation, 477–478; as fit environment for life, 510; as theater of human history, 539; history of, 666, 668, 669–700
Earth as a mother: myth of, 13–14; Philo on, 14; Plutarch on, 36; Columella on, 136; St. Augustine on, 197
East, the unchanging: Chardin on, 554, 571, 595
East-West contrasts, 279–280
Ecology: succession in, 194; and physico-theology, 423, 425, 427, 633; and Goethe, 536; antecedents of, 707–708
Ecosystem, 6, 379, 511 n. 25, 549–550

Eden, Garden of, 153, 164, 235, 273, 347–348
Education: relation of, to climate, 593
Egypt: civilization of, 21, 36–38, 89, 90, 128
Element: concept of, 63–64
Elements: four, 9–10, 12, 64, 263–265 *passim*; and observation, 10, 154, 241
Emasculation and self-mutilation, 514
Empedocles: and four elements, 9–10; and Parmenides, 63; on existence of life before sun's creation, 193 n. 52
Encyclopedists: of Middle Ages, 209, 256, 262–264, 271
Engineers: in Hellenistic Age, 125
Environment: hard and soft, 87, 547; cosmicized, 117, 303; Plato on relict, 121; sacred of Prussians, 330; fitness of, 408, 427, 535, 543; adaptation to, 549–550
Environmental change by human agency. *See* Nature, modifications by human agency
Environmental influence, theories of: sources, 80; types, 80–81; in Hippocrates, 87; in Herodotus, 89; in Thucydides, 91; Pseudo-Xenophon, 91–92; Plato, 92; Aristotle, 93–95; Polybius, 95–96; Agatharchides, 96–97; Posidonius, 98; Athenaeus, 101; Florus, 101; Seneca, 101; Horace, 101; Tacitus, 103; Cicero, 103; Strabo, 103–105; Vitruvius, 105; static quality of, 109; and theories of cultural development, 109; temperate climates and civilization, 110; Philo on, 110; Josephus, 110–111; Ptolemy, 113–114; Servius, 114–115; and Christian theology, 254; as theories of adaptation, 255; and design argument, 255, 519–520; and political theory, 256; and classical continuities in Middle Ages, 256; Orosius, 257; Cassiodorus, 257–258; Paul the Deacon, 259–261; and Goth's love of liberty, 260–261; John the Scot, 261–262; and religion, 263, 447; and astrology, 265–266; Albert the Great, 268–270; Bartholomew of England, 271–273; Thomas Aquinas, 274, 276; Giraldus Cambrensis, 279; Gunther of Pairis, 286; Botero, 369; Alberti, 430–431; relation to history in early modern times, 432–433; Machiavelli, 433; Bodin, 434–447; and cultural relativity, 439, 440; Louis Le Roy, 447; Du Bartas, 448–449; Charron, 447–448, 552; Burton, 456–457; critique of early modern ideas of, 460; Herder, 539, 570; Humboldt, 545; from Bodin to Montesquieu, 551; Fontenelle, 552–553; Chardin, 554; Du Bos, 556–562 *passim*; Arbuthnot, 562–565; Montesquieu, 577, 580–581; Voltaire, 582–583; Helvetius, 583–584; Diderot, 584–585; Hume, 585–587; Buffon, 587, 591; Rousseau, 592–593; Condorcet, 594; Dunbar, 596, 601; Falconer, 601–605; Ferguson, 605; Robertson, 605; Forster, J. R., and George, 610–620 *passim*; Malthus, 636; John Adams, 685; summary, 709–710
Environmentalism, cosmic, 15

Epicurean philosophy, 51, 55, 62–65, 66, 67, 73
Epidemics: Lucretius on, 101
Epimetheus: myth of, 41–42
Equatorial regions: habitability of, 235, 437–438
Erosion, 389, 415, 465, 691–692
Eternal recurrence. *See* Recurrence, eternal
Ethiopia, 96, 259; people of, 21, 112
Ethnology: Greek, 8; in Hellenistic Age, 20–21; in Hippocrates, 85; in Herodotus, 89; classical, 100–101, 103; Caesar on, 103; Tacitus on, 103; astrological, 15, 111, 265–266, 280, 282, 437, 460; and Genesis 2, 164; and religion, 167; of the South Seas, 612; comparative, in 18th cent., 621
Evelyn, John: on environmental change by man, 485–491; on forest conservation, 485–486; and Darwin, 487; and historical perspective of, 488; and advocacy of draining, 488–489; on London's air pollution, 489–491; m. 134, 670
Evil: St. Augustine on, 197–201; and secondary causes, 234; Hume on natural, 529; Lisbon earthquake as physical, 521; physical, and *tout est bien*, 549
Exegesis: biblical, 176; and number, 188; and Averroes, 222; as a sociology of knowledge, 222; in Maimonides, 222; and Ramon Sibiude, 239; importance of, 253; allegorical, 283; m. 379, 712. *See also* Hexaemeron literature
Exemplarism, 237–238. *See also* Nature, as a book
Extinctions, 480, 677–678

Falconry: and nature study, 224–225; Frederick II on, 224
Fallow land, 132
Farmers: in Attica, 133–134; Yankee and Pennsylvanian, 696–697
Fencing: effects of, 487
Fertilizers, 345, 672, 694–695
Final causes, 64, 375–378, 502, 517–521, 523
Fire: Lucretius on discovery of, 139; and origin of metallurgy, 139; and the forest, 294; 322, 344–345, 492, 667, 696–697
Florus: effects of hard climate, 101
Fontenelle, Bernard: on constancy of nature and observable differences, 390; on influences of climate and culture, 458–459, 552–553, 555, 559
Food: Greek interest in, 21; and national character, 455; and melancholy, 457
Forest: retreats as paradise, 294; uses of, in Middle Ages, 294, 320–321, 324–326, 336–337, 341, 493; history of word, 325 n. 122, 327; conservation, 326–327, 329–330, 336–339, 342, 345, 347, 669–671; as habitat of living things, 344; fires, 344; Chastellux and Chateaubriand on, 686. *See also* Deforestation
Forster, George: and scientific voyages, 502;

and Humboldt, 543–544; and South Seas, 616, 618–619, 703–704
Forster, John R., 502; and South Seas, 611–618, 703
Fossils, 409
Four elements. *See* Elements, four
Francis. *See* St. Francis
Franciscans: and observation of nature, 237
Franklin, Benjamin: on reproductive power of life, 624, 693
Frederick II: his *Art of Falconry*, 224–225
French, national character of, 452, 556, 593
Frontier in Middle Ages: and United States of 19th cent., 289–290

Galen: on humors, 11, 111; Bodin opposes, 444; m. 83, 460
Galileo: on final causes, 376, 505
Garden: in Middle Ages, 347–348
Genesis: and population questions, 166–167, 512
Genesis 1, 151–153, 159, 163–164, 193, 198, 202, 646
Genesis 2, and ethnological thought, 164
Genesis 3, curse on nature, 153, 162, 164
Genesis 6, 154
Genesis 8, 408
Genius: clustering of, 444–445, 454, 554–555 ·
Geographic march of civilization. *See* Civilization
Geography: cultural, 18, 365, 547–548; relation to religion, 35, 167, 173–174, 283–284, 364; late Tudor and early Stuart, 432 n. 8; physico-theology in history of, 505, 515–517, 597–598; need for, 516–517; Kant's interest in, 534–535; defects of education in, 538; and aesthetics, 546; and art history, 546; Rousseau's sympathy for, 593
German culture, 443–444
Giles of Rome: his *Errores Philosophorum*, 224 n. 160
Gilson, Etienne: on Minucius Felix, 176–177; on Tertullian, 177 n. 1; on Arnobius, 180 n. 6; on Irenaeus, 183 n. 11; on Origen, 184 n. 14; on Alan of Lile, 217 n. 136; on Muslim threats to Christian theology, 220 n. 148; on exemplarism, 238; on condemnations of 1277, 250 n. 257
Giraldus Cambrensis, 279; m. 256
Glassmaking: in forests, 340
Goats: destructiveness of, 142–143, 342–343; Buffon on, 675; Fabre on, 701
God: his care for the world, 5, 36–39, 151–153, 162, 179, 213, 513; as creator, 153–154; his covenant with Noah, 154; wisdom of, in Psalm 8, 157; creativeness of, in Corinthians I, 161–162; as artisan, 202–203; in control of nature, 208; revealed in his works, 376, 396, 467; wrath of, 523 n. 57
Gods: proofs of existence of, 55–56, 59, 229, 239–240, 419, 528, 530

Godwin, William: on progress and environmental limitations, 634–636; on population, 649–652

Goethe, Johann Wolfgang von: coolness to teleology of, 535–536; m. 543

Golden Age, 7, 118, 131–134, 139, 140, 143, 408

Goodman, Godfrey, 381

Goths: love of liberty and climate, 260–261, 432, 449

Graunt, John: his work on bills of mortality, 398–399, 403, 426, 490–491

Grazing, 321–322, 323–324, 328–329, 334–335, 342, 492

Gregory of Nyssa, 298

Groves: sacred, 135, 310

*Gruerie*: meaning of, 326–327

Grunebaum, Gustave E. von: on Thomas Aquinas and Muslim scholasticism, 220 and n. 147; on Muslim ideas of geographical influence, 255 n. 3; on geographic march of civilization, 277

Gunther of Pairis, 285–286

Habitats, animal: in Job, 155–156; destruction of, by man, 662, 674

Hahn, Edward, m. 58, 673

Hakewill, George: refutes idea of senescence in nature, 383–389; on man perfecting nature, 478; m. 70, 134

Hale, Matthew: man and nature, 400–403; design argument and population theory, 403–404; man as steward of God, 405, 480–482; m. 495, 534, 625

Harmonic analogy, 17

Harmony, preestablished: of Leibniz, 477, 507

Harpalus: and plant acclimatization, 124

Health: concepts of, in antiquity, 11; and drainage, 348; Arbuthnot's conception of, 563–564; public, 573, 604; and climate, 18th cent. summary, 621; and disease, 647, 661; and clearing, 687–689

Hehn, Victor, 137

Hellenistic Age: characteristics of, 18–25; and urbanization, 33; teleological and antiteleological ideas during, 62, 73–74; and environmental change during, 122–127; architecture and engineering in, 125

Helvétius, Claude A.: his dismissal of climatic influences, 583–584

Herder, Johann G. von: 537–543; on Voltaire and Lisbon earthquake, 524, 538; Buffon's use of, 538, 539–540; criticism of Montesquieu, 569–570; m. 12, 406, 612

Heresy, 218, 222, 232, 233

Hermetical writings: on order and purpose in the cosmos, 75–76, 146, 266

Herodotus: teleology of, 40–41; general ideas, 88–89; on the Nile, 89–90, 127; on influence of hard environments, 90–91, 104; m. 8, 18, 38, 262

Hesiod: on cultural history of man, 131–133

Hexaemeral literature: nature of, 163–164, 174; links with Genesis 1, 177, 189–190; relation to creation, 187; in Philo, 187; in Basil of Caesarea, 189–190; in St. Augustine, 196; and iconographical representation, 247

Hippocrates: his medical corpus, 5; on humors, 11, 80; *Airs, Waters, Places*, Edelstein on textual problems of, 82–83; on culture and environment, 82–88; and *Problems* of Aristotle, 94; on present ways of living, 119; his influence in Middle Ages, 256; and Bodin, 443; and Burton, 457; respect for, in early modern times, 460; and Herder, 540; attitude toward, in 18th cent., 552; and Arbuthnot, 562–563; and Montesquieu, 567–568; and Falconer, 601

History: typical chronology of sacred, 167; and environmental change by human agency, 289–292

Hodgen, Margaret, 363 n. 12

Holbach, Paul Henri d': critic of final causes, 520; nature not a work, 521; and Voltaire, 523

Holy Land: Hakewill on physical decline of, 478

Homosexuality, 217

Horace: on rural life, 31–32; on atmosphere of Boeotia, 101

Hottentots: Locke on, 583; J. R. Forster on, 613

House: Vitruvius on development of, 108

Humboldt, A. von: on Basil's hexaemeron, 177; on pastoral stage unobserved in New World, 142; on vegetation, 543–548; and G. Forster, 543–544, 611; on environmental stimuli and map of Chimborazo, 547; on settlement, 547–548; and Dunbar, 600; and Malthus, 643; m. 12, 119, 596, 616

Hume, David: 525–529; and climatic theories, 585–587; and senescence in nature, 629; on population history, 629, 630, 651; on climatic change by man, 659; m. 552, 621

Humors: theory of, 10–12, 80–82; Avicenna on, 264; Bodin on, 438–439; Evelyn on, 490; Du Bos on, 557

Humus, 410, 424

Hunting: reservation of forests for, 326, 338; passion for, in Middle Ages, 346–347; prohibition of, 347

Huxley, Thomas H., 482, 666

Hydrologic cycle, 193, 388, 413, 510

Hymn to Sun, 36–38

Iconography, 247

Ideas: stemming from daily life and observation, 49, 71–72, 272, 295–296, 392, 624

Indians: of Chinantla, D. de Esquivel on, 359; Garcés against enslavement of, 360; *Sublimus Deus* of Pope Paul III on humanity of, 360; Acosta on origin of, 366–368

Industrial Revolution, 705

Insects: and design, 76, 205, 533, 677
Institutions: effects of, on culture, 7–8
Invention: independent, 108, 167, 607–608; and climate, 587
Irenaeus: shortcomings of knowledge of nature, 183
Iron mills: Evelyn on, 487
Isaiah: curse on earth, 162 n. 32; and Cedd's founding of a monastery, 306
Isidore of Seville: as transmitter of classical knowledge, 115, 208–209, 227; and environmental influences, 257–258, 264; geography of, 260, 264, 272
Islands: encourage rise of civilizations, 616
Isocrates, 127–128
Isolation: effects on culture of, 7, 282, 593–594
Israel, lost tribes of, and America, 367

Jefferson, Thomas: and Buffon, 681–682; m. 685
Jerome. *See* St. Jerome
Jerusalem, 303
Job, Book of, on God as creator of an ordered world, 155–156
John, Chrysostom: on nature as a book, 203, 205
John the Scot: his theophany, 209–212; Gilson on his theophany, 238; environmental causes of human differences, 261–262
Josephus: on Greek historians, 110–111

Kahn, Charles H., 8–9, 10, 17
Kalm, Peter: on North America, 541, 609, 683, 685–686
Kames, Lord: on pastoralism, 142; on climate and degeneration, 595–596; m. 545, 616
Kant, Immanuel: on teleology in nature, 529–535; and George Forster on race, 619; on environmental change by man, 659; m. 50, 509
Keill, John: defense of final causes, 412–414; m. 74
Kepler, Johannes: on final causes, 376
Kliger, Samuel: on climate and Gothic love of liberty, 261 n. 17
Klimata, the seven: in Posidonius, 98; in *Art of Falconry*, 226; in Ibn Khaldūn, 255 n. 3; mixtures in, 265; traditional classification of, 267; in Albert the Great, 267; in Diderot's Encyclopédie, 584
Koran, Latin translation of, 218

Labor: dignity of, in Christian thought, 302–306, 350 n. 210
Lactantius: on utility of earth to man, 180–181
Lafitau, Joseph Francois: on Indians, 361; Robinson's objections to, 608
Land: late study of nonagricultural, 137; multiple uses of, 470 n. 21; historical sequence in occupation of, 642
Landscapes: ancient, J. Bradford on, 146–147; Buffon's distinction between natural and cultural, 679–680

Lamarck, Chevalier de: on adaptive evolution, 549, 620
Las Casas, Bartolome de, 360, 367
Law: and environmental change in Middle Ages, 316; and climate, 432
Lefebvre des Nöettes, Richard: inventions and environmental changes, 318–319
Leff, Gordon: on John the Scot's view of nature, 212 n. 125; on condemnations of 1277, 250, n. 257; on Duns Scotus, 251; on Thomas Aquinas, 251
Leibniz, Gottfried W.: defender of final causes, 377, 506–508; on preestablished harmony, 477; on human knowledge, 477; optimism of, 477–478; on progress in earth's cultivation, 477, 478, 636; on partial views, 505–506; on the Cartesians, 506; and advances in the study of life, 507; on invention, 507; on monads, 507; on law of sufficient reason, 508; on principle of plenitude, 508; on rationality and morality in the universe, 508
Le Roy, Louis, 447
Leucippus: and classical atomist theory, 64
Liberty: and the Goths, 261; reigns in mountains, 576–577
Life: Origen on, 184; existence of before sun's creation, 193 and n. 52; fecundity of, 624
Linnaeus: and design argument with reference to plants and animals, 510–512; m. 624
Lisbon earthquake, 515, 521–522, 524
Locke, John: on moral causes, 583
Logos: creativity of, in Posidonius, 54
London: Evelyn's plan for, 489–490
Lope de Vega: on the New World, 362
Lorain, John: on land uses in 18th cent. America, 693–697; m. 685
Lorris, Guillaume de. *See Romance of the Rose*
Love: and the four elements, 63
Lovejoy, Arthur O.: principle of plenitude, 5–6; in Plotinus, 77 and nn. 122, 123
Lucretius: his organic analogy, 7; his feeling for nature, 29–30; and Theophrastus's teleology, 50–51; and Democritus, 65; Epicureanism of, 67; on design argument, 68–69; on senescence in nature, 70–72, 135; teleology in, 70; on niggardliness of nature, 72–73; environmental biology on, 101; on wisdom of gods, 134; on animal domestication, 138–139; on forest fires and origin of metallurgy, 139; summary, 140; on environment changed by man, 140; and Arnobius, 179; and Celsus, 185; and Hakewill, 386; m. 17, 357, 381, 667
Ludwig of Bavaria: forest regulations of, 339
Lull, Ramon. *See* Ramon Lull
Lyell, Charles: versus physico-theologists, 548; anticipation of his ideas in Buffon, 679–680; m. 646

Machiavelli, Nicolò: on soil and civilization, 433–434

Macrocosm: in Greek thought, 17; Stoic idea of sympathy and, 57; Maimonides on, 223; Paracelsus on, 465–466; m. 413

Maimonides, Moses: on creation and design, 222–224

Mâle, Émile: on love of nature in Middle Ages, 173; on medieval religious art and nature, 245–246; m. 253

Malthus, Thomas R.: general ideas, 502, 637–638; and Süssmilch, 515, 649; on fecundity of life, 624, 640–641, 648; on populousness of ancient nations, 632; and Condorcet and Godwin, 634, 635; and Godwin, 640, 649–650, 653; and birth control, 638–639; on earth as a limiting factor, 639; and distribution of world population, 639–641; on concept of land, 639–640, 643; and modifications of nature by man, 641–642, 649; pessimism of, 642; his concepts of soil, 642; and Humboldt, 643; and institutional reform, 644; and progress, 644–645; on nature of man, 645; optimism of, 645–647; and religion, 646–647; and disease, 647; philosophy of, 647–648; human passions in, 648; m. 6, 399, 422, 581

Man: significance of his erect carriage, 42, 52, 117, 187; as apex of creation, 52, 57, 60; on origin of, 96, 261, 401–402; as creator of novelty in nature, 116; as steward of God, 152, 155, 168, 236, 311–312, 405, 463, 480–482; and rationality, 185–186; evaluations of human nature, 198; St. Augustine on his nature, 201; as finisher of the Creation, 293, 427–428, 466, 506, 529; reasons for his creation, 405; adaptability of, 459–460, 590; uniqueness of, 463–464; an amphibious piece, 475–476; as exterminator of life, in Buffon, 677–678. *See also* entries under Man's; and Nature, modification by human agency

Man's dominion over nature: and Genesis, 151, 159, 293; and daily observation, 166; in Psalm 8, 166; and relation of, to God, 168; Bede on, 205–206; Neckam on, 206; Thomas Aquinas on, 236; Philo on, 295; Origen on, 297; Gregory of Nyssa on, 298; ideas of monks on, 310; after the Fall, 311. *See also* Nature, control of

Man's Fall: Raven on, 163 n. 34; symbolism of, 163 n. 35; St. Augustine on, 200; Neckam on, 206; John the Scot on, 212; Albert the Great on, 228–229; Thomas Aquinas on, 236; and cultural diversity, 262; and his dominion over nature, 311, 349; and curse on nature, 379; Woodward on, 409; Whiston on, 411; F. Bacon on, 471–472; Lorain on, 695

Man's place in nature: Stoic and Epicurean views, 67; in Stoicism, 145; in Psalm 8, 155; in Job 38, 156; Lactantius on, 181; Philo on, 189; St. Augustine on, 198; Maimonides on, 222–223; Ramon Sibiude on, 240; in *The Romance of the Rose*, 243; Albert the Great on, 270–271; Cosmas Indicopleustes on, 300–

301; H. More on, 395; Hale on, 400–401, 405, 480; Ray on, 420–421; in physico-theology, 425, 504; F. Bacon on, 471–472; T. Browne on, 475; Linnaeus on, 511; Büsching on, 515–516; Kant on, 533–534; in Malthus and Godwin, 653; Buffon on, 590, 664, 668, 684; Wm. Robertson on, 684; summary, 708–709

Manuring, 136–137, 316 n. 95

Maritime location: effects of, on culture, 7, 102, 431

Marsh, George P.: on human changes of environment, 149, 663, 679, 702, 704, 705

Marshes, 680, 689

Marxism, 550, 646, 649

Maulde, René de: on use of forests in Middle Ages and Renaissance, 323–324, 326–327; m. 336

Maury, Alfred: on Salic law on forest protection, 344

Mediterranean environment, 10, 39, 85, 148, 155

Memphite theology: J. A. Wilson on, 36–38

Metallurgy: origin of, 139

Metals: agricola on civilizations' need of, 469

Metempsychosis, 296, 580

Meun, Jean de. See *The Romance of the Rose*

Microcosm: in Greek thought, 17; Stoic idea of sympathy and, 57; Paracelsus on, 465–466

Microscope, 375, 417, 506–507, 526

Middle Ages: modern study of, 172–173, 288–289, 319

Migration: causes of, 259–261

Milton, John: and theories of climatic influence, 449

Minerals: Seneca on distribution of, 61

Mining, 290, 340; Agricola's defense of, 468–469

Minucius Felix: on the earth as a planned abode, 176–179

Moisture: and thinking, 81–82, 102, 258

Monads: Leibniz on, 507

Monasteries, 303–309; selection of sites for, 306–307, 312; Thomey abbey, 313; land use by Troarn abbey, 331

Monastic siting: Orderic Vital on, 312

Monks: labor of, G. Coulton on, 289 n. 1, 314 n. 87; friendship with animals, 346

Monogamy: Botero on, 371; Graunt on, 398; and Christian religion, 514; Montesquieu on, 573–574, 627

Montaigne, M.: and Ramon Sibiude, 238; influence of place, 450

Monte Cassino: poet Mark's description of, 303–304

Montesquieu: senescence in nature, 134; revival of environmental theories, 502, 551; Süssmilch on, 512; Herder on, 540; reception of his *L'ésprit des Lois*, 566–567; influences on, 567–568; sources of his ideas, 567–568, 574 n. 64; and sheep's tongue experiment, 569; on climate and religion, 571–572, 579–580; on China, 572, 577; cultural relativism in,

573; on drunkenness, 573; on public health, 573; on slavery, 573; on peoples of Asia and Europe, 574–575; and Plutarch, 576 n. 69; on liberty in mountains, 576–577; population theory of, 578–579, 627–629, 653; and A. Ferguson, 605; on clerical celibacy, 627; Godwin on, 651; and cultural milieu, 653–654; on environmental change by man, 658; m. 12, 537

Moon: Plutarch on life on, 74–75

More, Henry: physico-theology of, 395

Moschus: feeling for nature in, 28–29

Mountains: necessary in the design, 376, 413, 419; attitude to, 411; as alembics, 413; and liberty, 576–577

Münster, Sebastian: cosmography of, 363–366

Music: of spheres, 17; Polybius on, 95–96

Muslim theology. *See* Theology, Muslim

Muslim thought: and ideas of environmental influence, 255 n. 3

Myth: concepts of order and purpose in, 3; personification of natural forces, 5; celestial archetypes, 117; man as orderer of nature, 117

National character: Greek interest in, 8; Servius on, 115, 209; Medieval interest in, 263; Bodin on, 435; 17th cent. interest in, 451; Bishop Hall on, 451; Overbury on, 451–452; Barclay on, 452–454; Temple on, 454–455; changed by diet, 455; Du Bos on, 559; Arbuthnot on, 564; Helvétius on, 584; Hume on, 586; 18th cent. interest in, 621; and environmental theories, 709.

Natural history, 416, 419–420, 423–424, 508–509, 587–588, 621, 657–658, 707

Nature: constancy of, 7, 165, 380–382, 384, 387, 389–390, 416; as proof of God's existence, 36, 175, 392; niggardliness of, 72–73, 165, 433, 527, 529, 549, 636, 645; struggle in, 77; curse on, 153–154, 162–165, 212, 232, 236, 481; rejection of, in Christian thought, 162, 181; beauties of, 392, 395, 397; asymmetry in, 397; light of, 466; chaos of disharmony in, 508; blindness of, 529–530

Nature as a book: in Athanasius, 203; in St. Augustine, 203–204; in Alan of Lille, 204; in E. Curtius, 204–205; in Thomas Aquinas, 232; in St. Bonaventura, 237; in Ramon Sibiude, 238

Nature, conceptions of: 3; ecosystem, 6; principle of plenitude, 6; balance, harmony, and unity of, 6, 14–15, 17, 380, 391, 393, 502, 508, 519, 527–528, 547, 693–698 *passim*; and astrology, 16; and terrestrial unity, 17; in Stoicism, 51–52; utilitarian view of, 57–58, 198–199, 395, 397, 423–424; Yahweh, God of an ordered universe, 155; in Book of Job, 155–156; in Psalm 104, 157; in Romans 1:20, 161; in Psalms, 165; creator and the created,

165–166; Judeo-Christian idea of habitable world, 168; providence creates for rational nature, 185; St. Augustine on, 175, 198–199; as movement powered by the love of God, 212; in Alan of Lille, 216–217; in Thomas Aquinas, 230, 232–233; in *The Romance of the Rose*, 241, 245; in 12th and 13th cents., 245; in Duns Scotus, 251; in 17th cent., 378–379, 391, 406, 414–415; in 17th and 18th cents., 424; in Wotton, 391; in Ray, 394, 419; in Leibniz, 505–506; teleological view of, 508–509; geometrical view of, 509–510; in Linnaeus, 511; in D'Holbach, 521; in Hume, 524–526; in Kant, 532; in Goethe, 536; as parent and teacher, 542, 549; in Humboldt, 543; in Malthusian theory, 647; dignity of, bestowed by man, 653; in Buffon, 664, 680–682; weakness of, in New World, 681–685; in the Forsters, 703

Nature, feeling for: Scully on sacred landscapes, 12–13; in Hellenistic Age, 13, 24–25, 32–25, 32–33; in Homer, 13, 25, 32; in Apollonius Rhodius, 26–27; in Theocritus, 27–28; in Bion, 29–30; in Lucretius, 30; in Virgil, 30; in Tibullus, 31–32; in Horace, 31–32; in Columella, 32–33; in Varro, 32–33; contrasts between natural and cultural landscapes, 32–33; in Panaetius, 51–52; in Plotinus, 77–78; in Christian thought, 151, 196–197; in Psalms, 157–158, 165; in Proverbs 8, 158; in the Wisdom literature, 158; in Ecclesiasticus, 160; in Middle Ages, 173, 207, 245–246; in St. Augustine, 199; and cloister foundings, 207; in St. Bernard, 213–214; in St. Francis, 214–215; in Villard de Honnecourt, 246–247; in manuscript of Benedictbeuern, 247–248; in Gunther of Pairis, 285–286; in Pope Pius II, 355–357; in Ray, 418; in Barclay, 452–453; in Kant, 533–534; in Humboldt, 546–547; in Dunbar, 600; in G. Forster, 703

Nature, man's control of: in ancient world, 116–117; and human memory, 146; Philo on, 295–296; modern ideas on, contrasted with earlier ones, 349; modern interest in, 425–427, 494; and idea of man as a geographic agent, 461–462; and domestication, 463; optimism of in 17th–18th cent., 471, 478; F. Bacon on, 472–473; Descartes on, 476; Hale on, 480–485; purposive nature of, 495–496; and technology, 496. *See also* Man's dominion over nature

Nature, man's place in. *See* Man's place in nature

Nature, modifications by human agency: in myth, 117; in antiquity, 119; in Sophocles' *Antigone*, 119–120; in Plato's *Critias*, 119–120; in Hellenistic Age, 122–123; Isocrates on, 127; Herodotus on, 127; Strabo on, 128; Eratosthenes on, 128–129; and significance of domestication (*see also* domestication),

129, 236, 463; Theophrastus on, 129–130; and soil fertility, 131; and the natural order, 135; and arable land, 137; in Stoic philosophy, 138, 144; Lucretius on, 138; Varro on, 141; Virgil on, 143; Cicero on, 145; in Hermetical writings, 146; ancient and modern contrasts, 149; in Christian thought, 151, 293; in Psalm 8, 157; in Middle Ages, 175, 206, 288 n. 1, 290, 292–293, 318–320, 323–324, 331, 350; Lactantius on, 181; Origen on, 185, 297; Philo on, 187–188, 295; St. Bernard on, 214; in *The Romance of the Rose*, 242; Albert the Great on, 270, 314–316, 351; as history, 289–292; and theology, 294; by monastic settlements, 294, 302, 308–309, 312, 313; and attitude of early Church Fathers, 295, 301; Tertullian on, 296; Gregory of Nyssa on, 298; St. Ambrose on, 298–299; St. Augustine on, 299–300; Theodoret on, 300; in Cosmas Indicopleustes, 300–301; and creations in the wilderness, 312–313; and undesirable changes, 316, 495; and law and custom, 316–317, 322–330, 333; and destructiveness of domestic animals, 342–343; and deforestation, 345; and Age of Discovery, 358–359; Sebastian Münster on, 365; Botero on, 371; Henry More on, 395; in early modern period, 427–428, 462, 471, 484–485, 494–497; in 17th cent. thought, 425, 471, 478; Ficino on, 463–464; Alberti on, 464–465; Leonardo da Vinci on, 465; Paracelsus on, 466–467; in F. Bacon's *New Atlantis*, 474–475; Hakewill on, 478; Burton on, 479–480; Hale on, 480–482; Ray on, 483–484; and optimism of modern interpretations, 484–485, 494–497, 704–705; Evelyn on, 485–491; in French Forest Ordinance of 1669, 494; Büsching on, 516; Kant on, 531, 659; Herder on, 541–542; Kalm on, 541–542, 686; Du Bos on, 559; Montesquieu on, 577, 658; Rousseau on, 594; Malthus on, 641–642, 649; modern literature on, 656–657; and climatic change, 659; Hume on, 659; and destruction of animal habitats, 662; Noah Webster on, 663; in Buffon (*see also* chap. 14), 663, 676; Chateaubriand on, 686; in New World, 686–698; Chastellux on, 686–687; B. Rush on, 687–688; T. Wright on, 688; Seybert on, 689; Volney on, 690–691; Bartram on, 691–692; uniqueness of by European man, 691–693; Jared Eliot on, 691–693; and harmony of nature, 693; Lorain on, 695–697; and pristine and altered nature, 698; and study of torrents, 698–699; Fabre on, 699–702; J. Forster on, 702; in 18th cent. thought, 704–705; summary, 710

Nature, senescence in. *See* Senescence in nature

Necessity: idea of, in Democritus, 65; the mother of invention, 68, 73, 88, 180, 185, 297, 466, 547, 587, 597, 607, 708

*New Atlantis* of F. Bacon, 473–475

New World: Acosta and Lafitau on, 361; Lope de Vega and Vespucci on, 362; migrations to, 366–367; pre-Columbian contacts with, 616; weakness of nature in, 681–684; like the creation, 685–686

Newton, Isaac: teleological beliefs of, 377

Nieuwentijdt, Bernard: and clock analogy, 392, 509

Nile, 38, 89, 127–128

Nominalism, 251

Number in the Creation: Philo and St. Augustine on, 188–189

Nürnberg: protection of its forest, 338–339

Oak, destruction of, for bees, 322

*Officina gentium*: the Northlands as a hive of nations, 260, 277, 432, 449, 667–668

Oikoumenē: meanings of, 17–18; of Eratosthenes, 20; cultural connotations of, in Hellenistic Age, 23–24

Opposites: order characterized by struggle of, 9–10

Optimism: about control of nature in 17th and 18th cents., 471, 476–478, 549

Organic analogy: in Greek philosophy, 17; in Lucretius, 134

Origen: on designed earth and man as modifier of environment, 183–185; and Augustine, 198; and Thomas Aquinas, 233; on role of necessity, 297; in Hakewill, 385

Otto of Freising, 263; and Church influence, 277–278

Ovid, 133

Paley, W., 375, 537, 646

Palissy, Bernard: on profiting from knowledge of nature, 470, 495

Panaetius: and feeling for nature, 12, 51–52; m. 100, 144

Pangloss, Dr., in Voltaire's *Candide*, 518, 522, 549

Paracelsus, 465–468

Paradises: monastery sites as, 303, 306–307, 313, 349

Parmenides, 63

Pathetic Fallacy, 28–30 *passim*

Paul III: his *Sublimis Deus*, 359–360

Paul the Deacon: on climate, overpopulation, and migration, 259–261 *passim*; influence of his ideas, 432–433, 454

Paul. *See* St. Paul

Perrault, Charles: on constancy in nature, 389

Petty, William: on population, 399

Philo: on nature as mother, 14; on Greek civilization, 110; on artisan deity, 187–188; on man's control over nature, 295–296; m. 174, 463

Physico-theology, 177, 392, 406, 421–422, 424–425, 504, 548, 603

760 *Index*

Pigs: destructiveness of, 342–343
Pius II, Pope: his feeling for nature, 355–357
Plants: Hippon on form of, 129; Linnaeus on design and, 510–512; domestication of, 676–677; man as a distributor of, 703
Plastic nature: idea of, 393–394, 416
Plato: principle of plenitude, 5; Plutarch on *The Laws*, 23; and myths of Epimetheus and Prometheus, 41; on goodness of creator, 45; on influence of natural environment, 92; on erosion of Attica, 121; and *Timaeus*, 198, 208, 376; and Machiavelli, 433; m. 7, 38, 621
Plenitude, principle of: in antiquity, 5–6; in Plato, 46; in Lucretius, 69–70; in Plotinus, 77; optimistic and pessimistic implications of, 79; in Alan of Lille, 217 n. 136; in Thomas Aquinas, 230; in *The Romance of the Rose*, 241, 243; in Ray, 419; in Leibniz, 508; in Buffon, 519; and theories of population, 623–624; and the Malthusian theory, 637–638, 640–641
Pliny: on climate and race, 109–110, 258; and Posidonius, 110 n. 71; on climatic change, 130, 137; on care of the land, 131; on domestication, 137; soils not mortal, 137; hillside plowing, 137; cited by Bartholomew, 272
Plotinus, 76–79, 113–114
Pluche, abbé de: his natural history, 509
Plutarch: on Alexander's civilizing Asia, 23–24; on knowledge of gods, 36; and teleological explanations, 74–75; in Montesquieu, 576 n. 69
Political theory: and theories of environmental influence, 256, 273–274
Pollution: air of London, 489–491; air of Rome, 560
Polynesians, 619
Polybius: and Posidonius, 53; on climate and music, 95; on Arcadia, 96; and Botero, 370; Bodin on, 444; and Fontenelle, 458; m. 433, 552
Polygamy, 371, 398, 514, 573, 627
Ponds: artificial, 348
Pope, Alexander, and *tout est bien*, 522
Population: Acosta on peopling of New World, 366; checks to growth of, 297, 372, 513, 624–625, 633–634, 638; Petty on, 399; Linnaeus on animal, 511; depopulation of modern world, 579; J. R. Forster on peopling of South Seas, 614; world estimates of 17th–19th cents., 626 n. 10, 630
Population, theories of: St. Augustine on man's ability to propagate after the Fall, 200; Age of Discovery, 359; and the Bible, 359; of Botero, 370–371, 373; and design argument, 398, 401, 403–404, 422; of Graunt, 399; and physico-theology, 399; of Hale, 403–405; of Woodward, 410; Ray on statistical regularities, 420; influence of Christian theology on, 425, 512, 514, 637; of Süssmilch, 512–515; modern, 512; of Montesquieu, 578–579, 626–

627, 653; of Lord Kames on, 596; of William Robertson, 607–608; earth as limiting factor in, 623; and principle of plenitude, 623–624; of Hume, 629; of Robert Wallace, 630, 632; of d'Amilaville, 631; of Condorcet, 634–635; of Godwin, 636, 649–653; of Malthus, 637, 649; and settlement of United States, 650–651
Populousness: of ancient and modern nations, 625–632 *passim*
Posidonius: emphasis on biology, ethnology, geography, and history in, 52–54, 97–101 *passim*; as influence on Vitruvius, 107; Seneca's criticism of, 118; on man's powers, 144–145; m. 12
Possibilism: of 18th cent., 602
Primitive peoples, 20–21, 282, 359–361, 418, 502, 545, 588–589, 594–595, 611, 615–617, 680–681, 691, 704
Primitivism: cultural, 164, 482–483, 665
Progress, idea of: and Leibniz, 506; Du Bos on, 555; and faith in science, 634; Condorcet on, 634, 654; and environment, 634, 636; Ricardo on, 645; Malthus on, 644–645, 649, 654; Godwin on, 635–636, 654; and environmental change, 655
Prometheus: interpretations of myth of, 41–42
Proverbs 8, 158, 159 n. 22
Psalm 8, 155, 157, 166
Psalm 19, 157
Psalm 39, 197
Psalm 65, 157–158
Psalm 104, 5, 37–38, 156–157, 162, 416
Psalm 115, 155
Psalms, feeling for nature in, 165
Psychic unity, 108
Ptolemies: cultural policy of, 19, 21–22, 122–127; and natural resources, 124–125
Ptolemy, Claudius: environmental and astrological theories of, 111–113; m. 280, 441
Purchas, S.: on senescence in nature, 381–382

Quarrying, 290
Quarrel over ancients and moderns: significance of, 380 n. 15, 654

Race: and climate, Pliny on, 258; Buffon on, 590–591; Lord Kames on importance of, 596; origins of, G. Forster on, 619
Ramon Lull: and Ramon Sibiude, 238; m. 203, 205, 231
Ramon Sibiude: on God revealed in nature, 238–240; m. 203, 205, 231, 419
Ratzel, Friedrich, 445, 543, 679
Raven, Charles E., 163 n. 33 and 34, 202 n. 94, 227 n. 170
Ray, John: on Cambridge Platonists, 79; on Plotinus, 79; on *creatio continua*, 153, 416; on Psalm 104, 157, 416; his *Wisdom of God*, 379–380; on Descartes, 394, 417; and Henry More, 395; and conceptions of nature, 415–

421; on man's active role in nature, 483–484; m. 74, 392, 665

Recurrence, eternal, 6–7, 184–185

Reindeer: retreat of, 662, 675

Religion: and ethnology, 167; and geography, 167; and theories of environmental influence, 447; Montesquieu on relation of to population, 578; and climate, 369, 558–559, 571–572, 603–604, 621

Renaissance: and Age of Discovery, 355

Resources, natural: interest of ancient world in, 118, 124

Ricardo, David: on sequence of land occupation, 642

Ritter, C.: teleological view of geography of, 191, 277, 510, 548

Rivers: Buffon on, 680

Robertson, William: on the New World, 605–610, 684–685

*Romance of the Rose, The,* 217, 240–244, 249, 514

Romans 1:20: 161–162, 183, 202, 204, 215, 231, 237, 391, 475

Romans 5: 162, 163

Rome: Cicero on site of, 102; Du Bos on site of, 560

Rostovtzeff, Michael: on cultural policy of the Ptolemies, 19, 21, 22, 122–127 *passim*

Rousseau, Jean Jacques: on effect of climate and environment, 592–594

Rural-urban contrasts, 32–33

Ruskin, John: feeling for nature in antiquity, 13; on the pathetic fallacy, 28

St. Ambrose: and nature, 194–196; on man as cultivator, 298–299; m. 385

St. Augustine: and Romans 1:20, 162; on order in nature, 175; and artisan analogy, 177; and Origen, 184, 198; on exegesis, 188; hexaemeron of, 196; on creation, 196, 199; on Psalm 39, 197; on pagan ideas, 197; on evil, 197, 201; and Plato's *Timaeus,* 198; on values in nature, 198–199; on the Fall, 200; on divine governance of arts, 200; and astrology, 201, 266; on relation of God to man, 201; thought of as creator of Christian synthesis, 201–202; on his father, 202; on nature as a book, 203–204; on human genius in the arts, 299–300; on manual work, 304–306

St. Benedict: on work, 306; contribution of, 350 n. 120

St. Bernard: and nature, 213–214; and monasticism, 303; and activity, 349–350

St. Bonaventura: on God's traces in sensible world, 162, 237–238

St. Francis: feeling for nature, 214–216; m. 10

St. Paul: on relationships between God, man, and nature, 161–162; St. Augustine and, 305; m. 646

St. Sturm: and founding of Fulda, 306–307, 310

St. Thomas Aquinas: and Romans 1:20, 162;

231; on Origen, 184, 233; on combating error, 222, 232; on proofs for existence of God, 229; on nature of the creation, 230; on hierarchy in nature, 230; on artisan analogy, 230–231, 234; and nature passages in Bible and Apocrypha, 231; on natural and revealed theology, 231–232; Carre on, 233, 251 n. 259, 260; on goodness of nature, 233; on otherworldliness, 233; and Aristotle, 233–234, 274; and evil, 234; on phases in the creation, 234; on goodness of the Creator, 235; on man's role in paradise, 235; on Garden of Eden, 235; on habitability of equatorial regions, 235; on animal domestication, 236; on the Fall, 236; on man's dominion over nature, 236; on philosophy of man and nature, 236; and condemnations of 1277, 249; on divine and created, 251; on environment and government, 273–274; and Aristotle and Vegetius, 274; and Vitruvius, 275; and trade, 275–276; on divine and kingly planning, 287; on dressing and keeping paradise, 302; m. 174, 256

Sand dune: fixation of, 348

Savage, noble, 615

Saw, hydraulic, 247, 319–320

Sawmills, 340

Science: origin of modern, 173, 250, 252 n. 263; faith in, 634, 654

Scythians: Hippocrates on, 84, 86, 89, 112

Sea: in teleological arguments, 74, 75 n. 115, 181, 192–193, 195–196

Sebond, Raymond. *See* Ramon Sibiude

Selection, artificial. *See* Artificial selection

Seleucids: cultural policy of, 23

Seneca: and design argument, 61–62; primitivism of, 118–119; on soil fertility, 133; m. 101, 145 n. 76

Senescence in nature: 294, 379, 503; Democritus on, 65; Epicurus on, 70; Lucretius on, 70; Columella on, 72, 134, 136; Pliny on, 73, 137; Montesquieu on, 134, 626; in II Esdras, 165; Giraldus Cambrensis on, 279; and modern belief in, 381; Hakewıl on, 383–389; Perrault on, 389; Fontenelle on, 390, 459; Ray on, 415–416; Burton on, 479; and populousness of ancient and modern nations, 625–626; Hume on, 629

Servius: on environmental influences, 114–115, 259

Settlement: as act of creation, 117; Humboldt on Old and New World, 547–548

Seven klimata. *See* Klimata

Sex: deviations, 217, 244; abstinence from, 243–244; and divine intent, 244; in condemnations of 1277, 249; and environment, 268, 458–585; and humors, 439–440; Montesquieu on, 573; Robertson on, 609; Malthus on, 648; and New World primitive peoples, 680

Shepherds: Varro on antiquity of, 141; and forest fires, 344

Sibiude, Ramon. *See* Ramon Sibiude

Sidon, 126

Sin, original: in Romans 5, 162

Slavery: of Indians, 360; Montesquieu on, 573, 627

Societies, animal and insect: Buffon on, 677

Socrates: on Anaxagoras, 39; as interlocutor in Xenophon, 42–43

Soil: concepts of, 642, 644, 671, 695; Albert the Great on erosion of, 315, 691–692

Soil, fertility of: and golden age, 7, 132–133, 143; Cato on, 131; Lucretius on, 135; Columella on, 136–137; Albert the Great on, 346; Woodward on, 424

Soil, theory of: in Middle Ages, 345; Sclafert on, 345–346; and humus, 410; Ray on, 418

Sophocles: on man's control of nature, 119–120

South Seas: peoples of, 614–615; and Captain Cook, 502, 610, 620, 626; and G. and J. Forster, 610–619

Spinoza: on final causes, 378; Voltaire on, 524

Sprat, Thomas: on man's improvement of nature, 482, 665

Sterility: Hippocrates on, 86

Stewardship, idea of, 152, 155, 168, 405, 427, 463, 480

Stoicism, 23–24, 51, 54–59 *passim*, 73, 144, 297 n. 20

Strabo: Rostovtzeff on, 19; on design, 61, 104–105; and Posidonius, 97–99, 104; on ideas of environment, 103–105; on the Nile, 128

Strato, 51

Struggle for existence, 139, 425, 527, 549

Sturm. *See* St. Sturm

Sumerian: concept of civilization, 4, theology, 3, 16

Sun: hymn to, 5, 37–39

Süssmilch, Johann: and Derham, 421–422; population theory of, 512–515; and Malthus, 515, 649; on Lisbon earthquake, 515; on world population estimate, 646; m. 399, 509

Suzuki, Daisetz, 494

Swineherds: edict on, 343


Tacitus: ethnology of, 103; on religion and preservation of natural order, 134–135; m. 444

Tahiti: J. R. Forster on, 617; G. Forster compares with England, 619

Tatian, 183

*Tebtunis Papyri*: and agriculture, horticulture, and reclamation, 122–123

Technology: in ancient world, 118; in early modern period, 464; and control over nature, 496

Teggart, Frederick J., 260 n. 12, 444

Teleology: 375, 707; in Diogenes of Apollonia, 39; in Herodotus, 40–41; and sense of wonderment in, 43–44; utilitarian bias of, 44; in Aristotle, 47–49; in Theophrastus, 49–51; in Stoicism, 51–52; and man's changes of the

earth, 59; in Lucretius, 70; in Hellenistic Age, 73; in Plutarch, 74; in earth and life sciences, 233, 505; in Newton, 377; in Kant, 529–535; Goethe on, 535; persistence of, and Braithwaite, 550. *See also* Antiteleological ideas; Design argument; Final causes.

Telescope: and the design argument, 506–507, 526

Tempier, Étienne, Bishop of Paris: and condemnations of 1277, 248, 250; and origins of modern science, 250

Temple, Sir William: on peoples of the Netherlands, 454–455, 561; on philosophy of civilization, 455–456; on Du Bos, 561

Terra Australis, 611, 626

Tertullian, 296–297, 301

Theocritus: feeling for nature in, 27–28; on human skill and the Nile, 128

Theodoret, 300

Theology: Sumerian, 3, 16; relation to geography, 35, 173–174, 515–517; Memphite, 36–38; Muslim, 218–222; supported by Reason, 251; Christian, and ideas of environmental influence, 254–255; and environmental change, 294

Theophany: John the Scot on, 209–212; Gilson on, 238–239; R. Bacon on, 282

Theophrastus: and botany in Hellenistic Age, 19; on teleology, 49–51; as source for Plutarch, 75; on plant acclimatization, 124; on domestication, 129; on climatic change due to human agency, 129–130; and Hippon, 129; and Pliny, 130, 137

Thomas Aquinas. *See* St. Thomas Aquinas

Thorndike, Lynn: on astrology as unifying principle, 16, 53; on feeling for nature in Middle Ages, 173; on Adelard of Bath, 219 n. 143; on William of Conches, 219 n. 144; on condemnations of 1277, 250 n. 257; m. 175

Thucydides: and historical method, 6; and geographical explanations, 91

Tibullus, 31–32

Tierra del Fuego, 615, 618

*Timaeus* of Plato: artisan deity in, 44–46; and St. Augustine, 198

Tongue of sheep: Montesquieu's experiment on, 569, 570, 582

Torrents: Arnaud on Ubaye, 341; and deforestation, 342; modern study of, 698; Fabre, 698–702

*Tout est bien*, 418, 507, 522 n. 56, 549, 619

Transhumance: Seneca on, 61–62; Varro on, 142; regulation of, 342

Travels and voyages: 18th cent. as stimulus to natural history and ethnography, 502; in Montesquieu, 568

Trees: planting of in Hellenistic Age, 122, 125; classified as to grazing value, 321; Palissy on cutting of, 470

Trinity: symbolism of, and cloister sites, 207 n. 104

Tropics: habitability of, 267, 362; Humboldt on, 545–546, 611; J. R. and G. Forster on, 611; J. R. Forster on islands of, 616
Turf: removal of, 341
Tyre, 126

United States: and history of ideas, 609 n. 170; settlement history and population theories, 650–651; literature on environmental change by human agency in, 656. *See also* New World
Unity in the Universe: and God's care for the world, 39
Ussher, Archbishop: dating the creation, 407

*vagina gentium*, 261 n. 18. See also *officina gentium*
Varro: on rural-urban contrasts, 32–33; on stages of cultural development, 140; on domesticated animals, 141–143; and St. Augustine on pagan ideas, 197; and Tertullian, 296; m. 7, 133, 137, 293–294
Vegetation: Humboldt on distribution of, 545–547
Vegetius, 274; m. 432
Velleius Paterculus, 444
Vespucci, Amerigo: and discovery of the New World, 358, 362
Villard de Honnecourt; his descriptions of nature, 246–247; m. 320
Vinci, Leonardo da: interest in environmental change by man, 465
Virgil: and nature, 30; on civilization and control of nature, 143–144; m. 293–294
Viticulture: and deforestation in Middle Ages, 340–341
Vitruvius: on environmental influences, 105–108 *passim*; and acculturation, 108; and Alberti, 125, 430; and Hellenistic conception of architect, 125; used by Thomas Aquinas, 275; m. 7, 355
Volney, C.: on geography of United States, 650, 656, 690
Voltaire: and Montesquieu, 439, 551, 575, 581–583; on Canal du Midi, 497; on final causes, 518, 523–524; on *tout est bien*, 522–523; on Lisbon earthquake, 522–523; and Herder, 524; on Fontenelle, 553; on Chardin, 554; on climatic influence on religion, 582–583; and interest in environment, 537
Voyaging, accidental, 616

Wallace, Robert: and population estimates, 630–633 *passim*, 636
Water mills: Ansonius on, 319
Webster, Noah: on climatic change, 560–561, 660, 661, 689
Weisthümer: as sources on medieval customs, 336–337, 341, 343
Whiston, William: and theory of earth, 411–412
White, Lynn: on view of nature in St. Francis, 216; on art in Middle Ages, 247 n. 247; on 13th and 14th cent. science, 252 n. 263
Whitehead, Alfred N.: on 17th cent. conception of nature, 391, 428, 507 n. 8
William of Ockham: on nominalism, 251
William of Tyre: his descriptions of places, 263, 286–287
Williams, Samuel: on clearing and climate, 661, 689–690
Williamson, Hugues: on clearing and climate, 542, 659–669; and Buffon, 669
Windmills: for draining, 476
Wisdom literature, 158
Wollaston, William, 423
Woman: and the plowed earth, 244
Wood: use of in Middle Ages, 318, 320–321, 323–324; Palissy on importance of, 470
Woodward, John: and theory of earth, 409–411, 687
Workman, Herbert, 302–303, 350 n. 210
World: Chaldean concept of, 36; eternity of, 248–249, 396
Worlds, best of all possible: in Plato, 46, in Stoicism, 59, in Plotinus, 78, in Leibniz, 507. See also *Tout est bien*.
Worlds: plurality of, 64, 362
Wotton, William, 390–391
Wright, John K.: on equatorial regions, 235 n. 202; *Geographical Lore*, 255 n. 3; on geographic march of civilization, 276–277
Wright, Thomas, 688

Xenophon: design argument in, 42–43; influence of *Memorabilia*, 43; on hard environments, 91; on care of the land, 131
Xenophon-Pseudo: on distribution of resources and control of sea, 91–92

Zeno: Plutarch on, 23–24; Balbus on, 58
Zenon: and Apollonius, 122

**DATE DUE**

GAYLORD                                    PRINTED IN U.S.A.